Beginning Java 2
JDK 1.3 Edition

Ivor Horton

ALSO HAS A C++ BOOK
THAT USES THE SAME
EXAMPLES AS THIS
BOOK

Wrox Press Ltd. ®

Beginning Java 2 – JDK 1.3 Edition

Printing History

First Published   March 2000
Latest Reprint   November 2000

Published by Wrox Press Ltd
Arden House, 1102 Warwick Road, Acock's Green, Birmingham B27 6BH, UK
Printed in Canada
5 6 TRI 02 01 00
ISBN 1-861003-66-8

Trademark Acknowledgements

Wrox has endeavored to provide trademark information about all the companies and products mentioned in this book by the appropriate use of capitals. However, Wrox cannot guarantee the accuracy of this information.

Credits

Author
Ivor Horton

Additional Material
Ron Phillips (JDBC)

Editors
Robert FE Shaw
Andrew Tracey

Managing Editor
Paul Cooper

Development Editor
Tim Briggs

Project Manager
Chandima Nethisinghe

Index
Andrew Criddle

Technical Reviewers
Robert Chang
David Hudson
Jim MacIntosh
Gavin Smyth
John Timney
David Whitney

Design/Layout
Tom Bartlett
Mark Burdett
Jonathan Jones
Laurent Lafon

Illustrations
William Fallon

Cover Design
Chris Morris

Cover photograph by John Wright Photography, Warwick

A Note from the Author

In all my *Beginning…* books, my objective is to minimize what, in my judgment, are the three main hurdles the aspiring programmer must face: getting to grips with the jargon that pervades every programming language and environment, understanding the *use* of the language elements (as opposed to what they are), and appreciating how the language is applied in a practical context.

Jargon is an invaluable and virtually indispensable means of communication for the competent amateur as well as the expert professional, so it can't be avoided. My approach is to ensure that the beginner understands what the jargon means and gets comfortable with using it in context. In that way, they can use the documentation that comes along with most programming products more effectively, and can also feel competent to read and learn from the literature that surrounds most programming languages.

Comprehending the syntax and effects of the language elements are obviously essential to learning a language, but I believe illustrating *how* the language features work and *how* they are used are equally important. Rather than just use code fragments, I always try to provide the reader with practical working examples that show the relationship of each language feature to specific problems. These can then be a basis for experimentation, to see at first hand the effects of changing the code in various ways.

The practical context needs to go beyond the mechanics of applying individual language elements. To help the beginner gain the competence and confidence to develop their own applications, I aim to provide them with an insight into how things work in combination and on a larger scale than a simple example with a few lines of code. That's why I like to have at least one working example that builds over several chapters. In that way it's possible to show something of the approach to managing code as well as how language features can be applied together.

Finally, I know the prospect of working through a book of doorstop proportions can be quite daunting. For that reason it's important for the beginner to realize three things that are true for most programming languages. First, there *is* a lot to it, but this means there will be a greater sense of satisfaction when you've succeeded. Second, it's great fun, so you really will enjoy it. Third, it's a lot easier than you think, so you positively *will* make it.

Ivor Horton

Table of Contents

Chapter 2: Programs, Data, Variables and Calculation 33

Chapter 5: Defining Classes   159

Chapter 6: Extending Classes and Inheritance 221

Chapter 7: Exceptions 279

Chapter 8: Streams, Files and Stream Output   313

Chapter 9: Stream Input, and Object Streams   359

Chapter 10: Utility Classes   399

Chapter 11: Threads   467

Chapter 12: Creating Windows   **513**

Chapter 13: Handling Events   587

Chapter 14: Drawing in a Window   647

Chapter 15: Extending the GUI   713

Chapter 16: Filing and Printing Documents 791

Chapter 18: Adding Sound to your Programs 921

Chapter 19: Talking to Databases   997

Chapter 20: The JDBC in Action   **1057**

Appendix A: Java Archives – JAR files   1125

Appendix B: Creating Java Documentation   1133

Appendix C: Keywords   1157

Appendix D: ASCII Codes   1161

Introduction

Welcome

Welcome to the second edition of *Beginning Java 2*, a comprehensive and easy-to-use tutorial guide to learning the Java language and the Java 2 platform API. This book provides you with the essential know-how for developing programs using the JDK 1.3 or later.

In this book, as well as teaching you Java, we introduce you to the wide variety of topics that will be relevant to you as a Java programmer. We've structured the book so that you learn Java programming in a carefully designed and logical way, and at each stage you will be building on what you have learnt at the previous stage.

Who is this Book For?

Java programming is a huge and rapidly expanding area. Since its release, the growth of Java as *the* object-oriented language of choice for Internet programming and teaching has been phenomenal. The Java 2 platform is a significant maturing in the level of support offered to you, especially for application development. It is now a very serious contender for major application development, offering advantages in ease of development and maintenance compared to other languages, as well as built-in capability to run on a variety of computers and operating systems without code changes. Java has not become any more complicated, just a lot bigger. With it you can do a lot more, more quickly, and more easily.

In this book we aim to provide you with a comprehensive understanding of the language, plus suitable experience of Java application contexts to give you a solid base in each of these core areas. Every aspect of Java that is covered in the book is illustrated by fully working program examples that you can and should create and run for yourself. With an understanding of the topics in this book, you can start to write fully featured and effective Java programs.

The word *Beginning* in the title refers more to the style of the book's teaching than to your skill level. It could equally well be called *Straight into Java,* because the tutorial structure is designed so that, whether you're a seasoned programmer from another language or a newcomer to programming in general, this book takes you straight to your floor.

We assume, as a minimum, that you know something about programming, in that you understand at least the fundamental concepts of how programs work. However, you don't need to have significant prior programming experience to use the book successfully. The pace of the book is fairly rapid, but without stinting on any of the necessary explanations of how Java works.

What's Covered in this Book

The book aims to teach you Java programming following a logical format:

❑   First, it covers some of the main terms and concepts that underpin programming in Java. Without these we'll get nowhere fast.

❑   Second, it provides you with a clear explanation of the features of the Java language – the basic data types, the control structures which manipulate data, the object-oriented features of the language, the way runtime errors are handled and how threads are used. The book doesn't just explain what the language elements do, but also how you can apply them in practice.

❑   Third, it gives you an extensive introduction to the key packages in the Java class library – amongst others, the `io`, `util`, `awt`, `awt.event`, `applet`, `sql` and `javax.swing` packages are all covered and illustrated with full working examples.

❑   Fourth, it guides you through the process of building a substantial application, `Sketcher`, in which you apply the Java language capabilities and the Java class library in a realistic context. Our sketching application will have menus, toolbars, a status panel, the ability to draw and manipulate a number of elements, handle text, print, and save sketches. This will give you a much better understanding of how you apply Java in practical projects of your own, something that's hard to appreciate from any number of more trivial examples.

❑   Lastly, it shows how you can use the various tools that come with the JDK 1.3.

As we progress through these topics, we introduce you to the theory, and then illustrate it with an appropriate example and a clear explanation. You can learn quickly on a first read, and look back over things to brush up on all the essential elements when you need to. The small examples in each chapter are designed mainly to illustrate a class and its methods, or some new piece of theory in action. They focus specifically on showing you how the particular language feature or method works.

To get the most from the chapters, we strongly recommend that you try out the examples as you read. Type them in yourself, even if you have downloaded the example source code. It really does make a difference. The examples also provide a good base for experimentation and will hopefully inspire you to create programs of your own. It's important to try things out – you will learn as much (if not more) from your mistakes as you will from the things that work first time.

The source code for all of the example programs in the book is available at http://www.wrox.com.

What You Need to Use this Book

This book has been tested against the JDK 1.3 release code so you should ideally be using JDK1.3 or later. Other requirements for most of the chapters are fairly minimal: a copy of a text editor and a command line window from which to run the Java tools. Details of the requirements for the book and how to acquire and install them are provided in Chapter 1.

Conventions

To help you get the most from the text and keep track of what's happening, we've used a number of conventions throughout the book.

For instance, when discussing code, we have two conventions,

> *Background, which is used to hold asides on programming code.*

while,

> **These boxes hold important, not-to-be-forgotten information which is directly relevant to the surrounding text.**

When we introduce important words, we **highlight** them. We show keyboard strokes as: *Ctrl-A*.

The command line and terminal output is shown as,

```
C:\> java ShowStyle
When the command line is shown, it's in the above style, whereas terminal output
is
in this style.
```

while text for windowed applications, such as on buttons, is shown as OK and Cancel. Filenames are shown as MyFile.java.

We present code in four different ways. Firstly, variables, Java keywords, methods and classes are referenced in the text using a code style.

Definitions of Java methods and structures are shown in definition boxes. For example:

```
if(life==aimless)
{
  DoSomething;             // Italics show that words should be replaced
  DoSomethingElse;         // with something more meaningful
}
```

```
Lastly in our code examples, the code foreground style shows new, important,
   pertinent code;
while code background shows code that's less important in the present context,
   or has been seen before.
```

We'll presage example code with a Try It Out, which is used to split the code up where that's helpful, to highlight the component parts and to show the progression of the application. When it's important, we also follow the code with a How It Works to explain any salient points of the code in relation to previous theory. We find these two conventions help break up the more formidable code listings into more palatable morsels.

Tell Us What You Think

We've worked hard to make this book as useful to you as possible, so we'd like to get a feel for what it is you want and need to know, and what you think about how we've presented things to you. The positive feedback we received about the first edition of this book has helped make this new and revised edition an even better book.

Return the reply card in the back of the book, and you'll register this copy of Beginning Java 2 with Wrox Press, and be put on our mailing list for information on the latest Wrox products.

If you've anything to say, let us know on:

feedback@wrox.com

or at

http://www.wrox.com

Errata & Updates

We've made every effort to make sure there are no errors in the text or the code. However, to err is human and as such we recognize the need to keep you informed of any mistakes as they're spotted and amended.

While you're visiting our web site, please make use of our *Errata* page that's dedicated to fixing any small errors in the book or, offering new ways around a problem and its solution. Errata sheets are available for all our books – please download them, or take part in the continuous improvement of our tutorials and upload a 'fix'.

p2p.wrox.com

This book introduces a totally comprehensive and unique support system. Wrox now has a commitment to supporting you not just while you read the book, but once you start developing applications as well. We provide you with a forum where you can put your questions to the authors, reviewers and fellow industry professionals. You have the choice of how to receive this information; you can either enroll onto one of several mailing lists, or you can just browse the online forums and newsgroups for an answer.

Go to `http://p2p.wrox.com`. Here you'll find a link to the **Beg_Java** forum. If you find something wrong with this book, or you just think something has been badly explained or is misleading in some way then leave your message here. You'll still receive our customary quick reply, but you'll also have the advantage that the author will be able to see your problem at once and help deal with it.

Enroll now; it's all part of our free support system. For more instructions on how to enroll, please see Appendix F at the back of this book.

Introducing Java

This chapter will give you an appreciation of what the Java language is all about. Understanding the details that we'll introduce in this chapter is not important at this stage; you will see all of them again in greater depth in later chapters of the book. The intent of this chapter is to introduce you to the general ideas that underpin what we'll be covering through the rest of the book, as well as the contexts in which Java programs can be used and the kind of program that is applicable in each context.

In this chapter you will learn:

❏ The basic characteristics of the Java language.

❏ How Java programs work on your computer.

❏ Why Java programs are portable between different computers.

❏ The basic ideas behind object-oriented programming.

❏ How a simple Java program looks and how you can run it using the Java Development Kit.

❏ What HTML is and how it is used to include a Java program in a Web page.

What is Java All About?

Java is an innovative programming language that is becoming the language of choice for programs that need to run on a variety of different computer systems. First of all Java enables you to write small programs called **applets.** These are programs that you can embed in Internet Web pages to provide some intelligence. They might simply display an animated logo, or support data entry of some kind. Java also allows you to write large-scale application programs that you can run normally on any computer that supports the language. You can even write programs that will work both as ordinary applications and as applets. Java has matured immensely over the past couple of years, particularly with the introduction of Java 2. The breadth of capability provided by the standard core Java has grown incredibly, with the latest release extending into sampled sound and MIDI data processing.

Being able to embed executable code in a Web page introduces a vast range of exciting possibilities. Instead of being a passive presentation of text and graphics, a Web page can be interactive in any way that you want. You can include animations, games, interactive transaction processing – the possibilities are almost unlimited.

Of course, embedding program code in a Web page creates special security requirements. As an Internet user accessing a page with embedded Java code, you need to be confident that it will not do anything that might interfere with the operation of your computer, or damage the data you have on your system. This implies that execution of the embedded code must be controlled in such a way that it will prevent accidental damage to your computer environment, as well as ensure that any Java code that was created with malicious intent is effectively inhibited. Java implicitly incorporates measures to minimize the possibility of such occurrences arising with a Java applet.

Aside from its ability to create programs that can be embedded in a Web page, perhaps the most important characteristic of Java is that it was designed from the outset to be machine independent. Java programs can run unchanged on any computer that supports Java. Of course there is still the slim possibility of the odd glitch as you are ultimately dependent on the implementation of Java on any particular machine, but Java programs are intrinsically more portable than programs written in other languages. An interactive application written in Java will only require a single set of source code, regardless of the number of different computer platforms on which it is run. In any other programming language, the application will frequently require the source code to be tailored to accommodate different computer environments, particularly if there is an extensive graphical user interface involved.

Possibly the next most important characteristic of Java is that it is **object oriented**. The object-oriented approach to programming is also an implicit feature of all Java programs, so we will be looking at what this implies later in this chapter. Not only is Java object oriented, but it also manages to avoid many of the difficulties and complications that are inherent in some other object-oriented languages, making it very straightforward and easy to learn.

Learning Java

Java is not difficult, but there is a great deal to it. The language itself is fairly compact, but very powerful. To be able to program effectively in Java, however, you also need to understand the libraries that go with the language, and these are very extensive. In this book, the sequence in which you learn how the language works, and how you apply it, has been carefully structured so that you can gain expertise and confidence with programming in Java through a relatively easy and painless process. As far as possible, each chapter avoids the use of things you haven't learnt about already. A consequence, though, is that you won't be writing Java to be embedded in Web pages right away. While it may be an appealing idea, this would be a bit like learning to swim by jumping in the pool at the deep end. Generally speaking, there is good evidence that by starting in the shallow end of the pool and learning how to float before you try to swim, the chance of drowning is minimized, and there is a high expectation that you will end up a competent swimmer.

Java Programs

As we have already noted, there are two kinds of programs you can write in Java. Programs that are to be embedded in a Web page are called Java **applets**, and normal standalone programs are called Java **applications**. You can further subdivide Java applications into **console applications,** which only support character output to your computer screen (in a DOS window on a PC under Windows, for example), and **windowed Java applications** that can create and manage multiple windows. The latter use the typical graphical user interaction (GUI) mechanisms of window-based programs – menus, toolbars, dialogs and so on.

While we are learning the Java language basics, we will be using console applications as examples to illustrate how things work. This is because we can then focus on the specifics of the language, without worrying about any of the complexity involved in creating and managing windows. Once we are comfortable with using all the features of the Java language, we'll move on to windowed applications and applet examples.

Learning Java – the Road Ahead

Before starting out, it is always helpful to have an idea of where you are heading and what route you should take, so let's take a look at a brief road map of where you will be going with Java. There are five broad stages you will progress through in learning Java using this book:

1. The first stage is this chapter. It sets out some fundamental ideas about the structure of Java programs and how they work. This includes such things as what object-oriented programming is all about, and how an executable program is created from a Java source file. Getting these concepts straight at the outset will make learning to write Java programs that much easier for you.

2. Next you will learn how statements are put together, what facilities you have for storing basic data in a program, how you perform calculations and how you make decisions based on the results of them. These are the nuts and bolts you need for the next stages.

3. In the third stage you will learn about classes – how you define them and how you can use them. This is where you learn the object-oriented characteristics of the language. By the time you are through this stage you will have learnt all the basics of how the Java language works so you will be ready to progress further into how you can use it.

4. In the fourth stage, you will learn how you can segment the activities that your programs carry out into separate tasks that can execute concurrently. This is particularly important for when you want to include several applets in a Web page, and you don't want one applet to have to wait for another to finish executing before it can start. You may want a fancy animation to continue running while you play a game, for example, with both programs sitting in the same Web page.

5. In the fifth stage you will learn in detail how you implement an application or an applet with a graphical user interface, and how you handle interactions with the user in this context. This amounts to applying the capabilities provided by the Java class libraries. As well as learning about GUI implementation, you will also learn about handling images in various ways, as well as using the database access facilities in Java. You will also learn a bit about how you can handle sound in your programs, and how you can access relational databases. When you finish this stage you will be equipped to write your own fully-fledged applications and applets in Java. At the end of the book, you should be a knowledgeable Java programmer. The rest is down to experience.

Throughout this book we will be using complete examples to explore how Java works. You should create and run all of the examples, even the simplest, preferably by typing them in yourself. Don't be afraid to experiment with them. If there is anything you are not quite clear on, try changing an example around to see what happens, or better still, write example of your own. If you are uncertain how some aspect of Java that you have already covered works, don't look it up right away – try it out. Making mistakes is a great way to learn.

The Java Environment

You can run Java programs on a wide variety of computers using a range of operating systems. Your Java programs will run just as well on a PC running Windows 95/98/NT/2000 as it will on Linux or a Sun Solaris workstation. This is possible because a Java program does not execute directly on your computer. It runs on a standardized hypothetical computer that is called the **Java virtual machine** or **JVM**, which is emulated inside your computer by a program.

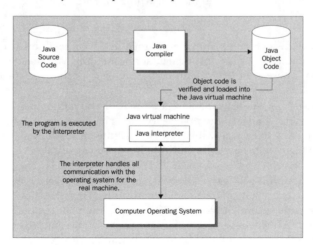

A **Java compiler** converts the Java source code that you write into a binary program consisting of **byte codes**. Byte codes are machine instructions for the Java virtual machine. When you execute a Java program, a program called the **Java interpreter** inspects and deciphers the byte codes for it, checks it out to ensure that it has not been tampered with and is safe to execute, and then executes the actions that the byte codes specify within the Java virtual machine. A Java interpreter can run stand-alone, or it can be part of a Web browser such as Netscape Navigator or Microsoft Internet Explorer where it can be invoked automatically to run applets in a Web page.

Because your Java program consists of byte codes rather than native machine instructions, it is completely insulated from the particular hardware on which it is run. Any computer that has the Java environment implemented will handle your program as well as any other, and because the Java interpreter sits between your program and the physical machine, it can prevent unauthorized actions in the program from being executed.

In the past there has been a penalty for all this flexibility and protection in the speed of execution of your Java programs. An interpreted Java program would typically run at only one tenth of the speed of an equivalent program using native machine instructions. With present Java machine implementations, much of the performance penalty has been eliminated, and in programs that are not computation intensive – which is usually the case with the sort of program you would want to include in a Web page, for example – you really wouldn't notice this anyway. With the JVM that is supplied with the current Java Development Kit (JDK) available from the Sun web site, there are very few circumstances where you will notice any appreciable degradation in performance compared to a program compiled to native machine code. If you happen to have a Java environment that supports **'Just-In-Time' compilation** of your programs, you will not suffer the penalty in any event. On-the-fly compilers can convert your Java programs to native machine instructions as they are loaded. Your programs will take a little longer to load, but once loaded they execute at maximum speed.

Java Program Development

There are a number of excellent Java program development environments available, including products from Sun, Borland and Symantec. These all provide very friendly environments for creating and editing your source code, and compiling and debugging your programs. These are powerful tools for the experienced programmer, but for learning Java using this book, I recommend that you use the Java Development Kit from Sun. While it is not the easiest to use, the lowest cost development package with the most up-to-date libraries for Java programs is undoubtedly the Java Development Kit (JDK) from Sun, because it is free. You can download this for a variety of hardware platforms and operating systems, either directly from the Sun Java Web site at http://java.sun.com (for Windows, Solaris, and Linux operating systems), or from sites that you can link to from there. For instance a version of the JDK for Mac OS is available from http://devworld.apple.com/java/.

I would urge you to install the JDK even if you are using one or other of the interactive development environments that are available. The JDK provides an excellent reference environment that you can use to check out problems that may arise. Not only that but your programs will only consist of the code that you write plus the classes from the Java libraries that you use. Virtually all commercial Java development systems provide pre-built facilities of their own to speed development. While this is very helpful for production program development, it really does get in the way when you are trying to learn Java. A further consideration is that the version of Java supported by a commercial Java product is not always the most recent. This means that some features of the latest version of Java just won't work. If you really do prefer to work with a commercial Java development system for whatever reason, and you have problems with running a particular example from the book, try it out with the JDK. The chances are it will work OK.

To make use of the JDK you will need a plain text editor. Any editor will do as long as it does not introduce formatting codes into the contents of a file. There are quite a number of shareware and freeware editors around that are suitable, and you should have no trouble locating one. A good place to start looking if you don't have one is http://www.download.com.

Installing the JDK

You can obtain detailed instructions on how to install the JDK for your particular operating system from the Sun web site, so I won't go into all the variations for different systems here. However, there are a few things to watch out for that may not leap out from the pages of the installation documentation.

First of all, the JDK and the documentation are separate and you install them separately. You will find it easier to install the JDK first, followed by the documentation. It is important to install the documentation into the same directory as the JDK. By doing this the documentation files will be in the correct directories in relation to the directory hierarchy for the JDK. If you install the JDK to drive C: under Windows, the directory structure shown in the diagram will be created.

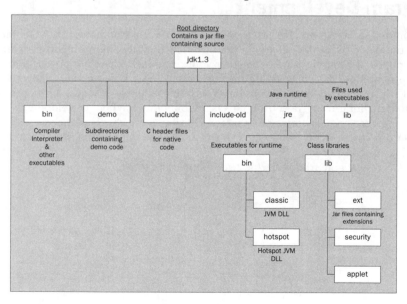

You should now install the documentation to the same directory that you chose for the JDK. This corresponds to C: as we have described here. This will create a new subdirectory, docs, to the jdk1.3 root directory, and install the documentation files to that. You should not install the documentation into C:\jdk1.3 as you might imagine, otherwise you will get an extra sub-directory jdk1.3, so the documentation will end up in C:\jdk1.3\jdk1.3\docs. To look at the documentation you just open the index.html file that is in the docs subdirectory.

You don't need to worry about the contents of most of these directories, at least not to get started, but the jdk1.3\bin directory should be in your PATH for convenience. That way you can run the compiler and the interpreter from anywhere without supplying the full path to it. A word of warning if you have previously installed a commercial Java development product. Check that it has not modified your PATH in autoexec.bat to include the path to its own executables. If it has, when you try to run the Java compiler or interpreter, you are likely to get the versions supplied with the commercial product rather that those that came with the JDK. If you don't want to remove the paths that were inserted for the commercial product, you will have to use the full path specification when you want to run the compiler or interpreter from the JDK. The jre directory contains the Java Runtime facilities that are used when you execute a Java program. The classes in the Java libraries are stored in the jre\lib directory. They don't appear individually though. They are all packaged up in the archive, rt.jar. Leave this alone. The Java Runtime takes care of retrieving what it needs from the archive when your program executes.

Extracting the Source Code for the Class Libraries

The source code for the class libraries is included in the archive src.jar that you will find in the jdk1.3 root directory. Browsing this source can be very educational, and it can also be helpful when you are more experienced with Java in giving a better understanding of how things works – or when they don't, why they don't. You can extract the source files from the archive using the jar utility, jar.exe, that is in the jdk1.3\bin directory – but be warned – there's a lot of it and it takes a while! To extract the source, change to the directory jdk1.3 and execute the command (in a DOS window):

```
jar xvf src.jar
```

This will create a new subdirectory, src, to the current directory, jdk1.3, and install the source code in subdirectories to this. To look at the source code, just open the .java file that you are interested in, using any plain text editor.

Running a Java Application

Java source code is always stored in files with the extension .java. Once you have created the source code for a program and saved it in a .java file, you need to process the source using a Java compiler. Using the compiler that comes with the JDK, you would do this with the following command:

```
javac MyProgram.java
```

Here, javac is the name of the Java compiler, and MyProgram.java is the name of the program source file. Assuming your program contains no errors, the compiler generates a byte code program that is the equivalent of your source code. The compiler stores the byte code program in a file with the same name as the source file, but with the extension .class. Java executable modules are always stored in a file with the extension .class.

If you are using some other product to develop your Java programs, you will probably be using a much more user-friendly, graphical interface for compiling your programs that won't involve entering commands such as that shown above. The file name extensions for your source file and the object file that results from it will be just the same however.

To execute the byte code program in the `.class` file with the Java interpreter in the JDK, you enter the command:

```
java MyProgram
```

Note the absence of any file extension here. This is because the name `MyProgram` in this instance is not the name of a file, it is the name of a Java class (we will further explain the meaning of this term shortly). If you put a file extension on `MyProgram`, your program won't execute. To execute your program, the Java interpreter analyzes and then executes the byte code instructions. The Java virtual machine is identical in all computer environments supporting Java, so you can be sure your program is completely portable. As we already said, your program will run just as well on a Unix Java implementation as it will on that for Windows 95/98/NT/2000, for OS/2, or any other operating system that supports Java. (Beware of variations in the level of Java supported though. Some environments, such as the Macintosh, tend to lag a little, so implementations for Java 2 will typically be available later than under Windows or Solaris.)

Note that the Java compiler in the JDK will compile both applications and applets. However, an applet is not executed in the same way as an application. You must embed an applet in a Web page before it can be run. You can then execute it either within a Java-enabled Web browser, or by using the `appletviewer`, a bare-bones browser provided as part of the JDK. It is a good idea to use the `appletviewer` to run applets while you are learning. This ensures that if your applet doesn't work, it is almost certainly your code that is the problem, rather than some problem in integration with the browser.

If you have compiled an applet and you have included it in a Web page stored as `MyApplet.html` in the current directory on your computer, you can execute it by entering the command:

```
appletviewer MyApplet.html
```

So how do you put an applet in a Web page?

The Hypertext Markup Language

The HyperText Mark-up Language, or **HTML** as it is commonly known, is used to define a Web page. If you want a good, compact, reference guide to HTML, I recommend the book *Instant HTML Programmer's Reference* (Wrox Press, ISBN 1-861001-56-8). Here we will gather just enough on HTML so that you can run a Java applet.

When you define a Web page as an HTML document, it is stored in a file with the extension `.html`. An HTML document consists of a number of elements, and each element is identified by **tags**. The document will begin with `<HTML>` and end with `</HTML>`. These delimiters, `<HTML>` and `</HTML>`, are tags, and each element in an HTML document will be enclosed between a similar pair of tags between angle brackets. All element tags are case insensitive, so you can use upper or lower case, or even a mixture of the two, but by convention they are capitalized so they stand out from the text. Here is an example of an HTML document consisting of a title and some other text:

```
<HTML>
<HEAD>
<TITLE>This is the title of the document</TITLE>
</HEAD>
<BODY>
You can put whatever text you like here. The body of a document can contain all
kinds of other HTML elements, including <B>Java applets</B>. Note how each element
always begins with a start tag identifying the element, and ends with an end tag
that is the same as the start tag but with a slash added. The pair of tags around
'Java applets' in the previous sentence will display the text as bold.
</BODY>
</HTML>
```

There are two elements that can appear directly within the <HTML> element, a <HEAD> element and a <BODY> element, as in the example above. The <HEAD> element provides information about the document, and is not strictly part of it. The text enclosed by the <TITLE> element tags that appears here within the <HEAD> element, will be displayed as the window title when the page is viewed.

Other element tags can appear within the <BODY> element, and they include tags for headings, lists, tables, links to other pages and Java applets. There are some elements that do not require an end tag because they are considered to be empty. An example of this kind of element tag is <HR>, which specifies a horizontal rule, a line across the full width of the page. You can use the <HR> tag to divide up a page and separate one type of element from another. You will find a comprehensive list of available HTML tags in the book I mentioned earlier.

Adding an Applet to an HTML Document

For many element tag pairs, you can specify an **element attribute** in the starting tag that defines additional or qualifying data about the element. This is how a Java applet is identified in an <APPLET> tag. Here is an example of how you include a Java applet in an HTML document:

```
<HTML>
<HEAD>
<TITLE> A Simple Program </TITLE>
</HEAD>
<BODY>
<HR>
<APPLET code = "MyFirstApplet.class"  width = 300  height = 200 >
</APPLET>
<HR>
</BODY>
</HTML>
```

The two shaded lines between tags for horizontal lines specify that the byte codes for the applet are contained in the file MyFirstApplet.class. The name of the file containing the byte codes for the applet is specified as the value for the code attribute in the <APPLET> tag. The other two attributes, width and height, define the width and height of the region on the screen that will be used by the applet when it executes. These always have to be specified to run an applet. There are lots of other things you can optionally specify, as we will see. Here is the Java source code for a simple applet:

```
import javax.swing.JApplet;
import java.awt.Graphics;

public class MyFirstApplet extends JApplet
{
  public void paint(Graphics g)
  {
    g.drawString("To climb a ladder, start at the bottom rung", 20, 90);
  }
}
```

Note that Java is case sensitive. You can't enter `public` with a capital P – if you do the program won't compile. This applet will just display a message when you run it. The mechanics of how the message gets displayed are irrelevant here – the example is just to illustrate how an applet goes into an HTML page. If you compile this code and save the previous HTML page specification in the file `MyFirstApplet.html` in the same directory as the Java applet code, you can run the applet using `appletviewer` from the JDK with the command:

```
appletviewer MyFirstApplet.html
```

This will display a window something like that shown below:

In this particular case, the window is produced under Windows 95/98/NT/2000. Under other operating systems it is likely to look a little different since Java 'takes on' the style of the platform on which it is running. Since the height and width of the window for the applet is specified in pixels, the physical dimensions of the window will depend on the resolution and size of your monitor.

This example won't work with Internet Explorer or Netscape Navigator as neither of these supports Java 2 directly. Let's see what can be done about that.

Making Applets Run in any Browser

The `APPLET` tag, introduced in HTML 3.2, was deprecated in HTML 4.0 in favor of the `OBJECT` tag. However, to date, Internet Explorer supports this tag, while on Netscape Navigator you use the `EMBED` tag. To make matters more complicated, you can't depend upon a client browser having the latest virtual machine.

The equivalent to the previous HTML code but using the <OBJECT> tag instead of the <APPLET> tag, is:

```
<OBJECT WIDTH = 300 HEIGHT = 200>
<PARAM NAME = CODE VALUE = MyFirstApplet.class >
<PARAM NAME = TYPE VALUE = "application/x-java-applet;version=1.3">
</OBJECT>
```

Unfortunately, this will still not work on Internet Explorer unless it has a virtual machine that can find a JApplet class, and this depends on support for Java 2 being available.

JavaSoft distributes a Java Plug-in product that can plug the latest virtual machine into the browser reading the Web page. Using this, you can make sure that clients of your applets can run the code, even on older browsers that don't support the latest version of Java.

> **The details of making Java applets that use Java 2 classes run on all browsers is the subject of some very good pages at http://java.sun.com/products/plugin/**

You will also be able to download a utility from this web site called the **HTML Converter**. This program will process an HTML file to automatically convert <APPLET> tags to a form that combines <OBJECT> and <EMBED> tags. The resultant HTML will automatically make use of the Java plug-in if it is installed. It can also download the plug-in to the local machine automatically if the machine is connected to the Internet when the page is viewed.

Applying the HTML Converter utility (version 1.2, the results may be slightly different for later versions) to the HTML file that we used with the MyFirstApplet example will produce a file containing the following:

```
<OBJECT CLASSID = "clsid:8AD9C840-044E-11D1-B3E9-00805F499D93"
WIDTH = 300
HEIGHT = 200
CODEBASE = "http://java.sun.com/products/plugin/1.2/jinstall-12-
win32.cab#Version=1,2,0,0">
<PARAM NAME = CODE VALUE = MyFirstApplet.class >
<PARAM NAME = TYPE VALUE = "application/x-java-applet;version=1.2">

<COMMENT>
<EMBED TYPE = "application/x-java-applet;version=1.2"
CODE = MyFirstApplet.class
WIDTH = 300
HEIGHT = 200
PLUGINSPACE = "http://java.sun.com/products/plugin/1.2/plugin-install.html">
<NOEMBED></COMMENT>
ALT = "Your browser understands the &lt;APPLET&gt; tag but isn't running the
applet, for some reason."
Your browser is completely ignoring the &lt;APPLET&gt; tag!
</NOEMBED></EMBED>
</OBJECT>
```

The OBJECT tag now has CLASSID and CODEBASE attributes to locate the Java Plug-in for Windows platforms. If the plug-in is not installed when this file is displayed in Internet Explorer, and your PC is connected to the Internet, the browser will download the plug-in from the location specified by the CODEBASE attribute. The COMMENT tag hides the EMBED tag so far as Internet Explorer is concerned, but it will still be seen by Netscape Navigator. Netscape Navigator will read it, and will download a Java plug-in suitable for itself from the page specified by the PLUGINSPACE attribute if it is not already installed.

appletviewer copes with all three tags. We'll use the APPLET tag for the rest of the book as it suits our needs and is much less verbose. If you want to generate the tags suitable for the general browser environment, just use the HTML Converter.

Object-Oriented Programming in Java

As we said at the beginning of this chapter, Java is an object-oriented language. When you use a programming language that is not object oriented, you must express the solution to every problem essentially in terms of numbers and characters – the basic kinds of data that you can manipulate in the language. In an object-oriented language like Java, things are different. Of course, you still have numbers and characters to work with – these are referred to as the **basic data types** – but you can define other kinds of entities that are relevant to your particular problem. You solve your problem in terms of the entities or objects that occur in the context of the problem. This not only affects how a program is structured, but also the terms in which the solution to your problem is expressed. If your problem concerns baseball players, your Java program is likely to have BaseballPlayer objects in it; if you are producing a program dealing with fruit production in California, it may well have objects that are Oranges in it. Apart from seeming to be inherently sensible, object-oriented programs are usually easier to understand.

In Java almost everything is an object. If you haven't delved into object-oriented programming before, or maybe because you have, you may feel this is a bit daunting. But fear not. Objects in Java are particularly easy. So easy, in fact, that we are going to start out by understanding some of the ideas behind Java objects right now. In that way you will be on the right track from the outset.

This doesn't mean we are going to jump in with all the precise nitty-gritty of Java that you need for describing and using objects. We are just going to get the concepts straight at this point. We will do this by taking a stroll through the basics using the odd bit of Java code where it helps the ideas along. All the code that we use here will be fully explained in later chapters. Concentrate on understanding the notion of objects first. Then we can ease into the specific practical details as we go along.

So What Are Objects?

Anything can be thought of as an object. Objects are all around you. You can consider Tree to be a particular class of objects: trees in general; although it is a rather abstract class as you would be hard pushed to find an actual occurrence of a totally generic tree. Hence the Oak tree in my yard which I call myOak, the Ash tree in your yard which you call thatDarnedTree, and a generalSherman, the well known redwood, are actual instances of specific types of tree, subclasses of Tree: Oak, Ash and Redwood. Note how we drop into the jargon here – **class** is a term that describes a specification for a collection of objects with common properties. A class is a specification, or template – expressed as a piece of program code – which defines what goes to make up a particular sort of object. A subclass is a class that inherits all the properties of the parent class, but that includes extra specialization. Of course, you will define a class specification to fit what you want to do. There are no absolutes here. For my trivial problem, the specification of a Tree class might just consist of its species and its height. If you are an arboriculturalist, then your problem with trees may require a much more complex class, or more likely a set of classes, that involve a mass of arboreal characteristics.

Every object that your program will use will have a corresponding class definition somewhere for objects of that type. This is true in Java as well as in other object-oriented languages. The basic idea of a class in programming parallels that of classifying things in the real world. It is a convenient and well-defined way to group things together.

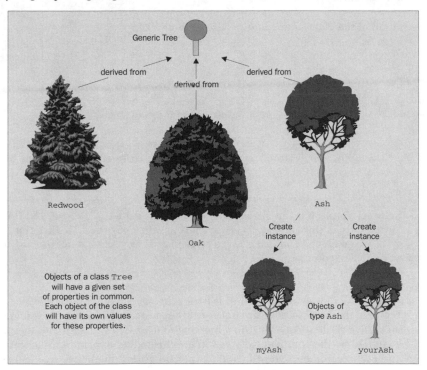

An **instance** of a class is a technical term for an existing object of that class. Ash is a specification for a type of object and yourAsh is an object constructed to that specification, so yourAsh would be an instance of the class Ash. Once you have a class defined, then you can come up with objects, or instances of that class. This raises the question of what differentiates an object of a given class, an Ash class object say, from a Redwood object. In other words, what sort of information defines a class?

What Defines a Class of Objects?

You may already have guessed the answer. A class definition lists all the parameters that you need to define an object of that particular class, at least, so far as your needs go. Someone else might choose a larger or smaller set of parameters to define the same sort of object – it all depends on what you want to do with the class. You will decide what aspects of the objects you need to include to define that particular class of object, and you will choose them depending on the kinds of problems that you want to address using the objects of the class. Let's think about a specific class of objects. For a class `Hat` for example, you might use just two parameters in the definition. You could include the type of hat as a string of characters such as `"Fedora"` or `"Baseball cap"`, and its size as a numeric value. These parameters that define an object of a class are referred to as **instance variables** or **attributes** of a class. The instance variables can be basic types of data such as numbers, but they could also be other class objects. For example, the name of a `Hat` object could be of type `String` – the class `String` defines objects that are strings of characters.

Of course there are lots of other things you could include to define a `Hat` if you wanted to, `color` for instance, which might be another string of characters such as `"Blue"`. To specify a class you just decide what set of attributes suit your needs, and those are what you use. This is called **data abstraction** in the parlance of the object-oriented aficionado, because you just abstract the attributes you want to use from the myriad possibilities for a typical object.

In Java the definition of the class `Hat` would look something like:

```
class Hat
{
  // Stuff defining the class in detail goes here.
  // This could specify the name of the hat, the size,
  // maybe the color, and whatever else you felt was necessary.
}
```

The name of the class follows the word `class`, and the details of the definition appear between the curly braces.

> Because the word **class** has this special role in Java it is called a **keyword**, and it is reserved for use only in this context. There are lots of other keywords in Java that you will pick up as we go along. You just need to remember that you must not use any of them for any other purposes.

We won't go into the detail of how the class `Hat` is defined, since we don't need it at this point. The lines appearing between the braces above are not code, they are actually **program comments**, since they begin with two successive slashes. Anything on a line that follows two successive slashes in your Java programs will be ignored by the compiler, so you will use this to add explanations to your programs. Generally the more useful comments you can add to your programs, the better. We will see in Chapter 2 that there are other ways you can write comments in Java.

Each object of your class will have a particular set of values defined that characterize that particular object. You could have an object of type `CowboyHat` which might be defined by values such as `"Stetson"` for the name of the hat, `"White"` for the color, and the size as 7.

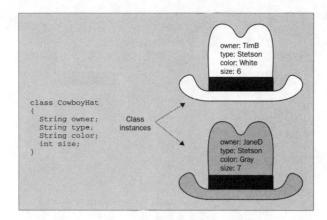

The parameters defining an object are not necessarily fixed values though. You would expect the name and size attributes for a CowboyHat object to stay fixed, but you could have other attributes. You might have state for example, which could indicate whether the hat was on or off the owner's head, or even owner, which would record the owner's name, so the value stored as the attribute owner could be changed when the hat was sold.

Operating on Objects

The fundamental difference between a class and the complex data types that you find in some other languages is that a class includes more than just data. A class specifies what you can do with an object of the class – that is, it defines the operations that are possible on objects of the class. Clearly for objects to be of any use in a program, you need to decide what you can do with them. This will depend on what sort of objects you are talking about, the attributes they contain, and how you intend to use them.

To take a very simple example, if your objects were numbers, of type Integer for example, it would be reasonable to plan for the usual arithmetic operations; add, subtract, multiply and divide, and probably a few others you can come up with. On the other hand it would not make sense to have operations for calculating the area of an Integer, boiling an Integer or for putting an Integer object on. There are lots of classes where these operations would make sense, but not those dealing with integers.

Coming back to our CowboyHat class, you might want to have operations that you could refer to as putHatOn and takeHatOff, which would have meanings that are fairly obvious from their names, and do make sense for CowboyHat objects. However, these operations would only be effective if a CowboyHat object also had another defining value that recorded whether it was on or off. Then these operations on a particular CowboyHat object could set this value for the object. To determine whether your CowboyHat was on or off, you would just need to look at this value. Conceivably you might also have an operation changeOwner by which you could set the instance variable recording the current owner's name to a new value. The illustration shows two operations applied in succession to a CowboyHat object.

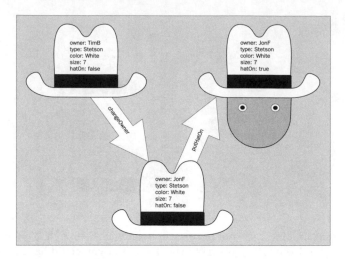

You may be wondering at this point how an operation for a class is defined. As we shall see in detail a bit later, it boils down to a self-contained block of program code called a **method** that is identified by the name you give to it. You can pass data items – which can be integers, floating point numbers, character strings or class objects – to a method, and a method can return a data item as a result. Performing an operation on an object amounts to 'executing' the method that defines the operation for the object.

> **Of course, the only operations you can perform on an instance of a particular class are those defined within the class, so the usefulness and flexibility of a class is going to depend on the thought that you give to its definition. We will be looking into these considerations more in Chapter 5.**

Let's take a look at an example of a complete class definition. The code for the class CowboyHat we have been talking about might look like the following:

```
class CowboyHat
{
  private String owner;          //Name of the current  owner
  private String type;           //The type of hat
  private int size;              //Stores the hat size
  private boolean hatOn=false;   //Records whether a hat is on or off

  // Constructor to cretae a CowboyHat object
  public CowboyHat (Sting anOwner, StringaType, int aSize)
  {
    size =aSize;             //  Set the hat size
    type = aType;           //Set the hat type
    owner = anOwner;        //Set the owner name
  }

  // Method to put the hat on
  public voidputHatOn()
  {
    hatOn = true;           // Record hat status as on
  }

  // Method to take the hat off
  public void takeHatOff()
  {
    hatOn = false;          // Record hat status as off
  }

  // Method to change the owner name
  public void changeOwner(String newOwner)
  {
    owner = newOwner;
  }

  // Method to get the hat size
  public int getSize()
  {
    return size;            // Return the size of the hat
  }
}
```

These specify the attributes of the class

This is a special metod that creates CowboyHat objects

These braces enclose the class definition

These braces enclose the code for the method putHatOn()

These are the other class methods

This code would be saved in a file with the name CowboyHat.java – the file name is always the same as the class name, and the extension will be .java because the file contains source code.

The code for the class definition appears between the braces following the identification for the class, as shown in the illustration. The code for each of the methods in the class also appears between braces. The class has four instance variables, owner, type, size and hatOn, and this last variable is always initialized as false. Each object created according to this class specification holds its own independent copy of these variables, so each object's variables can have unique values.

The keyword private, which has been applied to each instance variable, ensures that only code within the methods of the class can access or change the values of these directly. Methods of a class can also be specified as private. Being able to prevent access to some members of a class from outside is an important facility. It protects the internals of the class from being changed or used incorrectly. Someone using your class in another program can only get access to the bits to which you want them to have access. This means that you can change how the class works internally – the private methods that is – without affecting other programs that may use it.

Our CowboyHat class also has five methods, so you can do five different things with a CowboyHat object. One of these is a special method called a **constructor**, which creates a CowboyHat object – this is the method with the name, CowboyHat, that is the same as the class name. The items between the parentheses that follow the name of the constructor specify data that is to be passed to the method when it is executed – that is, when a CowboyHat object is created.

> In practice you might need to define a few other methods for the class to be useful; you might want to compare **CowboyHat** objects for example, to see if one was larger than another. However, at the moment you just need to get an idea of how the code looks. The details are of no importance here, as we will return to all this in Chapter 5.

Java Program Statements

As you saw in the CowboyHat class example, the code for each method in the class appears between braces, and it consists of **program statements**. Each program statement is terminated by a semicolon. A statement in Java can spread over several lines if necessary, since the end of each statement is defined by the semicolon, not the end of the line. Here is a Java program statement:

```
hatOn = false;
```

If you wanted to, you could also write this as:

```
hatOn =
        false;
```

You can generally include spaces and tabs, and spread your statements over multiple lines to enhance readability if it is a particularly long statement, but sensible constraints apply. You can't put a space in the middle of a name for instance. If you write hat On, for example, the compiler will read this as two words.

Encapsulation

At this point we can introduce another bit of jargon you can use to impress or bore your friends – **encapsulation**. Encapsulation refers to the hiding items of data and methods within an object. This is achieved by specifying them as `private` in the definition of the class. In the `CowboyHat` class, the instance variables, `owner`, `type`, `size` and `hatOn` were encapsulated. They were only accessible through the methods defined for the class. Being able to encapsulate members of a class in this way is important for the security and integrity of class objects. You may have a class with data members that can only take on particular values. By hiding the data members and forcing the use of a method to set or change the values, you can ensure that only legal values are set.

We mentioned earlier another major advantage of encapsulation – the ability to hide the implementation of a class. By only allowing limited access to the members of a class, you have the freedom to change the internals of the class without necessitating changes to programs that use the class. As long as the external characteristics of the methods that can be called from outside the class remain unchanged, the internal code can be changed in any way that you, the programmer, want.

A particular object, an instance of `CowboyHat`, will incorporate, or encapsulate, the `owner`, the hat `type`, the `size` of the object and the status of the hat in the instance variable `hatOn`. Only the constructor, and the `putHatOn()`, `takeHatOff()` and `getSize()` methods can be accessed externally.

> **Whenever we are referring to a method in the text, we will add a pair of parentheses after the method name to distinguish it from other things that have names. Some examples of this appear in the paragraph above. A method always has parentheses in its definition and in its use in a program, as we shall see, so it makes sense to represent it in this way in the text.**

Classes and Data Types

Programming is concerned with specifying how data of various kinds is to be processed, massaged, manipulated or transformed. Since classes define the types of objects that a program will work with, you can consider defining a class to be the same as defining a data type. Thus `Hat` is a type of data, as is `Tree`, and any other class you care to define. Java also contains a library of standard classes which provide you with a whole range of programming tools and facilities. For the most part then, your Java program will process, massage, manipulate or transform class objects.

There are some basic types of data in Java that are not classes. We will go into these in the next chapter, but they are essentially data types for numeric values such as 99 or 3.75, for single characters such as 'A' or '?', and for logical values that can be `true` or `false`. Java also has classes that correspond to the basic types for reasons that we will see later on. Every other entity in your Java program will be an object of a class – either a class that you define yourself, a class supplied as part of the Java environment, or a class that you obtain from somewhere else, such as from a specialized support package.

Classes and Subclasses

Many sets of objects that you might define in a class can be subdivided into more specialized subsets that can also be represented by classes, and Java provides you with the ability to define one class as a more specialized version of another. This reflects the nature of reality. There are always lots of ways of dividing a cake – or a forest. Conifer for example could be a subclass of the class Tree. The Conifer class would have all the instance variables and methods of the Tree class, plus some additional instance variables and/or methods that make it a Conifer in particular. You refer to the Conifer class as a **subclass** of the class Tree, and the class Tree as a **superclass** of the class Conifer.

When you define a class such as Conifer using another class such as Tree as a starting point, the class Conifer is said to be **derived** from the class Tree, and the class Conifer **inherits** all the attributes of the class Tree.

Advantages of Using Objects

As we said at the outset, object-oriented programs are written using objects that are specific to the problem being solved. Your pinball machine simulator may well define and use objects of type Table, Ball, Flipper and Bumper. This has tremendous advantages, not only in terms of easing the development process, but also in any future expansion of such a program. Java provides a whole range of standard classes to help you in the development of your program, and you can develop your own generic classes to provide a basis for developing programs that are of particular interest to you.

Because an object includes the methods that can operate on it as well as the data that defines it, programming using objects is much less prone to error. Your object-oriented Java programs should be more robust than the equivalent in a procedural programming language. Object-oriented programs take a little longer to design than programs that do not use objects since you must take care in the design of the classes that you will need, but the time required to write and test the code is sometimes substantially less than that for procedural programs. Object-oriented programs are also much easier to maintain and extend.

Java Program Structure

To summarize the necessary elements of a program structure:

❏   A Java program always consists of a number of classes.

❏   There is at least one class in every program, and there can be many.

❏   You typically put the program code for each class in a separate file, and you must give each file the same name as that of the class that is defined within it.

❏   A Java source file must also have the extension .java.

Thus your file containing the class Hat will be called Hat.java and your file containing the class BaseballPlayer must have the file name BaseballPlayer.java.

A typical program will consist of several files as illustrated in the following diagram.

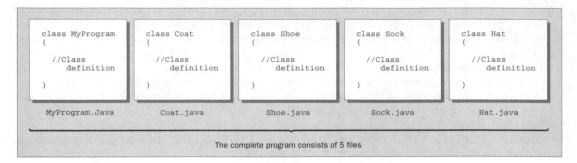

This program clearly majors on apparel with four of the five classes representing clothing. Each source file will contain a class definition and all of the files that go to make up the program will be stored in the same directory. The source files for your program will contain all the code that you wrote, but this is not everything that is ultimately included in the program. There will also be code from the **Java standard class library** that we mentioned earlier, so let's take a peek at what that can do.

Java's Class Library

A library in Java is a collection of classes – usually providing related facilities – that you can use in your programs. The Java class library provides you with a whole range of goodies, some of which are essential for your programs to work at all, and some of which make writing your Java programs easier. The standard class library covers a lot of ground so we won't be going into it in detail here, but we will be looking into how to apply many of the facilities it provides throughout the book.

Since the class library is a set of classes, it is stored in sets of files where each file contains a class definition. The classes are grouped together into related sets that are called **packages**, and each package is stored in a separate directory. A class in a package can access any of the other classes in the package. A class in another package may or may not be accessible. We will learn more about this in Chapter 5.

The package name is based on the path to the directory in which the classes belonging to the package are stored. Classes in the package java.lang for example are stored in the directory path java\lang (or java/lang under Unix). This path is relative to a particular directory that is automatically known by the Java runtime environment that executes your code. You can also create your own packages that will contain classes of your own that you want to reuse in different contexts, and that are related in some way.

The JDK includes a growing number of standard packages – over 70 the last time I counted. Some of the packages you will meet most frequently are:

Package Name	Description
java.lang	These classes support the basic language features and the handling of arrays and strings. Classes in this package are always available directly in your programs by default because this package is always automatically loaded with your program.

Package Name	Description
java.io	Classes for data input and output operations.
java.util	This package contains utility classes of various kinds, including classes for managing data within collections or groups of data items.
javax.swing	These classes provide easy-to-use and flexible components for building graphical user interfaces (GUIs). The components in this package are referred to as Swing components.

Package Name	Description
java.awt	Classes in this package provide the original GUI components (JDK1.1) as well as some basic support necessary for Swing components.
java.awt.image	These classes support image handling.
java.awt.event	The classes in this package are used in the implementation of windowed application to handle events in your program. Events are things like moving the mouse, pressing the left mouse button, or clicking on a menu item.

As noted above, you can use any of the classes from the java.lang package in your programs by default. To use classes from the other packages, you will typically use an import statement for each package that you need. This will allow you to reference the classes by the simple class name. Without an import statement you would need to specify the full path to each class each time you refer to it. This would make your program code rather cumbersome, and certainly less readable. You can also use an import statement to import a single class from a package into your program. The two import statements at the beginning of the code for the applet you saw earlier in this chapter are examples of this. The first was:

```
import javax.swing.JApplet;
```

This statement imports the JApplet class that is defined in the javax.swing package. You can import all the classes in the javax.swing package with the statement:

```
import javax.swing.*;
```

Importing classes one at a time makes compilation more efficient, but when you are using a lot of classes from a package you will find it much more convenient to import the whole package. This saves typing reams of import statements for one thing.

Formally, the class name is not really JApplet – it is javax.swing.JApplet. You can only use the unqualified name when you import the class or the complete package containing it into your program. You can still reference a class from a package even if you don't import it though – you just need to use the full class name, javax.swing.JApplet. You could try this out with the applet you saw earlier if you like. Just delete the two import statements from the file and use the full class names in the program. Then recompile it. It should work the same as before.

> You will see more on how to use **import** statements in Chapter 5, as well as more about how packages are created and used, and you will be exploring the use of classes from the standard packages in considerable depth throughout the book.

As we indicated earlier, the standard classes do not appear as files or directories on your hard disk. They are packaged up in a single compressed file, rt.jar, that is stored in the jre/lib directory. This directory is created when you install the JDK on your computer. A .jar file is a **Java archive** – a compressed archive of Java classes. The standard classes that your executable program requires are loaded automatically from rt.jar, so you don't have to be concerned with it directly at all. You will find more on .jar archives in Appendix A.

Java Applications

Every Java application contains a class that defines a method called main(). You can call the class whatever you want, but the method which is executed first in an application is always called main(). When you run your Java application the method main() will typically cause methods belonging to other classes to be executed, but the simplest possible Java application program consists of one class containing just the method main(). As we shall see below, the main() method has a particular fixed form, and if it is not of the required form, it will not be recognized by the Java interpreter as the method where execution starts.

We'll see how this works by taking a look at just such a Java program. You need to enter the program code using your favorite plain text editor, or if you have a Java development system with an editor, you can enter the code for the example using that. When you have entered the code, save the file with the same name as that used for the class and the extension .java. For this example the file name will be OurFirstProgram.java. The code for the program is:

This is the definition of the class OurFirstProgram. The class definition only contains the method main().

```
public class OurFirstProgram
{
    public static void main(String[] args)
    {
        System.out.println("Krakatoa, EAST of Java??");
    }

}
```

This is the definition of the method main().
The keyword public indicates it is globally accessible.
The keyword static ensures it is accessible even though no objects of the class exist.
The keyword void indicates it does not return a value.

The program consists of a definition for a class we have called `OurFirstProgram`. The class definition only contains one method, the method `main()`. The first line of the definition for the method `main()` is always of the form:

```
public static void main(String[] args)
```

The code for the method appears between the pair of curly braces. Our version of the method has only one executable statement:

```
System.out.println("Krakatoa, EAST of Java??");
```

So what does this statement do? Let's work through it from left to right:

- ❏ `System` is the name of a standard class that contains variables and methods for supporting simple keyboard input and character output to the display. It is contained in the package `java.lang` so it is always accessible just by using the simple class name, `System`.

- ❏ The object `out` represents the standard output stream – your display screen, and is a data member of the class `System`. The member, `out`, is a special kind of member of the `System` class. Like the method `main()` in our `OurFirstProgram` class, it is `static`. This means that `out` exists even though there are no objects of type `System` (more on this in forthcoming chapters). The `out` member is referenced by using the class name, `System`, separated from the member name `out` by a period – `System.out`.

- ❏ The bit at the rightmost end of the statement, `println("Krakatoa, EAST of Java??")`, calls the `println()` method that belongs to the object `out`, and that outputs the text string that appears between the parentheses to your display. This demonstrates one way in which you can call a class method – by using the object name followed by the method name, with a period separating them. The stuff between the parentheses following the name of a method is information that is passed to the method when it is executed. As we said, for `println()` it is the text we want to output to the screen.

For completeness, the keywords `public`, `static` and `void`, that appear in the method definition are explained briefly in the annotations to the program code, but you need not be concerned if these still seem a bit obscure at this point. We will be coming back to them in much more detail later on.

You can compile this program using the JDK compiler with the command,

```
javac OurFirstProgram.java
```

Once you have compiled the program successfully, you can execute it with the command:

```
java OurFirstProgram
```

When you run the program, it will display the text:

```
Krakatoa, EAST of Java??
```

Java and Unicode

Programming to support languages that use anything other than the Latin character set has always been a major problem. There are a variety of 8-bit character sets defined for many national languages, but if you want to combine the Latin character set and Cyrillic, for example, in the same context, things can get difficult. If you want to handle Japanese as well it becomes impossible with an 8-bit character set as there just aren't enough character codes to accommodate Japanese. Unicode is a standard character set that was developed to allow the characters necessary for almost all languages to be encoded. It uses a 16-bit code to represent a character (so each character occupies two bytes), and up to 65,535 non-zero character codes can be distinguished. With so many character codes available, there is enough to allocate each national character set its own set of codes, including character sets such as Kanji which is used for Japanese, and which requires thousands of character codes.

As we shall see in Chapter 2, Java source code is in Unicode characters. Comments, identifiers (names – see Chapter 2), and character and string literals can all use characters outside of the first 128 in the Unicode set. Java also supports Unicode internally to represent characters and strings, so the framework is there for a comprehensive international language capability in a program. The normal ASCII set that you are probably familiar with corresponds to the first 128 characters of the Unicode set. Apart from each character occupying two bytes, you can ignore the fact that you are handling Unicode characters in the main, unless of course you are building an application that supports multiple languages from the outset.

Summary

In this chapter we have looked at the basic characteristics of Java, and how portability between different computers is achieved. We have also introduced the elements of object-oriented programming.

The essential points we have covered in this chapter are:

❑　Java applets are programs that are designed to be embedded in an HTML document. Java applications are stand-alone programs. Java applications can be console programs that only support text output to the screen, or they can be windowed applications with a graphical user interface.

❑　Java programs are intrinsically object-oriented.

❑　Java source code is stored in files with the extension `.java`.

❑　Java programs are compiled to byte codes, which are instructions for the Java Virtual Machine. The Java Virtual Machine is the same on all the computers on which it is implemented, thus ensuring the portability of Java programs.

❑　Java object code is stored in files with the extension `.class`.

❑　Java programs are executed by the Java interpreter, which analyses the byte codes and carries out the operations they specify.

❑　The Java Development Kit supports the compilation and execution of Java applications and applets.

Resources

You can download the source code for the examples in the book from any of:

❑   http://www.wrox.com

❑   ftp://www.wrox.com

❑   ftp://www.wrox.co.uk

The source code download also includes sample databases that are used in Chapters 19 and 20. In addition, the download includes a utility program called `build_tables` that uses a text file of SQL statements to create a database for Microsoft Access or for mSQL.

If you have any questions on the fine formal detail of Java, the reference works we've used are:

❑   *The Java Language Specification*, James Gosling et al., Addison-Wesley, ISBN 0-201-63451-1, http://java.sun.com/docs/books/jls/html/index.html

❑   *The Java Virtual Machine Specification*, Tim Lindholm and Frank Yellin, Addison-Wesley, ISBN 0-201-43294-3, http://java.sun.com/docs/books/vmspec/2nd-edition/html/VMSpecTOC.doc.html

❑   *Concurrent Programming in Java, 2nd Edition: Design Principles and Patterns*, Doug Lea, Addison-Wesley, ISBN 0-201-31009-0

❑   *JDBC Database Access with Java*, Graham Hamilton et al., Addison-Wesley, ISBN 0-201-30995-5

Other sites of interest are:

❑   http://www.wrox.com for support for this book and information on forthcoming Java books.

❑   http://java.sun.com/docs/books/tutorial/index.html for the JavaSoft tutorials. Follow that Java trail.

And for online magazine reading and opinion, check out:

❑   http://www.javalobby.org/

❑   http://www.javaworld.com/javasoft.index.html

❑   http://www.javareport.com/

❑   http://www.sys-con.com/java/index2.html

We also like the Java Developer Connection, subscribe to it at http://java.sun.com/jdc

Programs, Data, Variables and Calculation

In this chapter we will look at the entities in Java that are not objects – numbers and characters. This will give you all the elements of the language you need to perform numerical calculations, and we will apply these in a few working examples.

By the end of this chapter you will have learnt:

❑ How to declare and define variables of the basic integer and floating point types

❑ How to write an assignment statement

❑ How integer and floating point expressions are evaluated

❑ How to output data from a console program

❑ How mixed integer and floating point expressions are evaluated

❑ What casting is and when you must use it

❑ What `boolean` variables are

❑ What determines the sequence in which operators in an expression are executed

❑ How to include comments in your programs

Data and Variables

A **variable** is a named piece of memory that you use to store information in your Java program – a piece of data of some description. Each named piece of memory that you define in your program will only be able to store data of one particular type. If you define a variable to store integers, for example, you cannot use it to store a value that is a decimal fraction, such as 0.75. If you have defined a variable that you will use to refer to a `Hat` object, you can only use it to reference an object of type `Hat` (or any of its subclasses, as we saw in Chapter 1). Since the type of data that each variable can store is fixed, whenever you use a variable in your program the compiler is able to check that it is not being used in a manner or a context that is inappropriate to its type. If a method in your program is supposed to process integers, the compiler will be able to detect when you inadvertently try to use the method with some other kind of data, for example, a string or a numerical value that is not integral.

Explicit data values that appear in your program are called **literals**. Each literal will also be of a particular type: 25, for instance, is an integer value of type int. We will go into the characteristics of the various types of literals that you can use as we discuss each variable type.

Before you can use a variable you must specify its name and type in a **declaration** statement. Before we look at how you write a declaration for a variable, we should consider what flexibility you have in choosing a name.

Variable Names

The name that you choose for a variable, or indeed the name that you choose for anything in Java, is called an **identifier**. An identifier can be any length, but it must start with a letter, an underscore (_) or a dollar sign ($). The rest of an identifier can include any characters except those used as operators in Java (such as +, - or *), but you will be generally better off if you stick to letters, digits and the underscore character.

Java is case sensitive so the names republican and Republican are not the same. You must not include blanks or tabs in the middle of a name, so Betty May is out, but you could have BettyMay or even Betty_May. Note that you can't have 10Up as a name since you cannot start a name with a numeric digit. Of course, you could use tenUp as an alternative.

Subject to the restrictions we have mentioned, you can name a variable almost anything you like, except for two additional restraints – you can't use **keywords** in Java as a name for something, and a name can't be anything that is a constant value. Keywords are words that are an essential part of the Java language. We saw some keywords in the previous chapter and we will learn a few more in this chapter. If you want to know what they all are, a complete list appears in Appendix C. The restriction on constant values is there because, although it is obvious why a name can't be 1234 or 37.5, constants can also be alphabetic, such as true and false for example. We will see how we specify constant values later in this chapter. Of course, the basic reason for these rules is that the compiler has to be able to distinguish between your variables, and other things that can appear in a program. If you try to use a name for a variable that makes this impossible, then it's not a legal name.

Clearly, it makes sense to choose names for your variables that give a good indication of the sort of data they hold. If you want to record the size of a hat for example, hatSize is not a bad choice for a variable name whereas qqq would be a bad choice. It is a common convention in Java to start variable names with a lower case letter and, where you have a name that combines several words, to capitalize the first letter of each word, as in hatSize, or moneyWellSpent. You are in no way obliged to follow this convention but since almost all the Java world does, it helps to do so.

> *If you feel you need more guidance in naming conventions (and coding conventions in general) take a look at* http://www.javasoft.com/docs/codeconv/

Variable Names and Unicode

Even though you are likely to be entering your Java programs in an environment that stores ASCII, all Java source code is in Unicode (subject to the reservations we noted in Chapter 1). Although the original source that you create is ASCII, it is converted to Unicode characters internally, before it is compiled. While you only ever need ASCII to write any Java language statement, the fact that Java supports Unicode provides you with immense flexibility. It means that the identifiers that you use in your source program can use any national language character set that is defined within the Unicode character set, so your programs can use French, Greek or Cyrillic variable names for example, or even names in several different languages, as long as you have the means to enter them in the first place. The same applies to character data that your program defines.

Variables and Types

As we mentioned earlier, each variable that you declare can store values of a type determined by the **data type** of that variable. You specify the type of a particular variable by using a **type name** in the variable declaration. For instance, here's a statement that declares a variable that can store integers:

```
int numberOfCats;
```

The data type in this case is `int`, the variable name is `numberOfCats`, and the semi-colon marks the end of the statement. The variable, `numberOfCats`, can only store values of type `int`.

Many of your variables will be used to reference objects, but let's leave those on one side for the moment as they have some special properties. The only things in Java that are not objects are variables that correspond to one of eight basic data types, defined within the language. These fundamental types, also called **primitives**, allow you to define variables for storing data that falls into one of three categories:

❑   Numeric values, which can be either integer or floating point

❑   Variables which store a single Unicode character

❑   Logical variables that can assume the values `true` or `false`

All of the type names for the basic variable types are keywords in Java so you must not use them for other purposes. Let's take a closer look at each of the basic data types and get a feel for how we can use them.

Integer Data Types

There are four types of variables that you can use to store integer data. All of these are signed, that is they can store both negative and positive values. The four integer types differ in the range of values they can store, so the choice of type for a variable depends on the range of data values you are likely to need.

The four integer types in Java are:

Data Type	Description
byte	Variables of this type can have values from -128 to +127 and occupy 1 byte (8 bits) in memory
short	Variables of this type can have values from -32768 to 32767 and occupy 2 bytes (16 bits) in memory
int	Variables of this type can have values from -2147483648 to 2147483647 and occupy 4 bytes (32 bits) in memory
long	Variables of this type can have values from -9223372036854775808 to 9223372036854775807 and occupy 8 bytes (64 bits) in memory

Let's take a look at declarations of variables of each of these types:

```
byte smallerValue;
short pageCount;
int wordCount;
long bigValue;
```

Each of these statements declares a variable of the type specified,

The range of values that can be stored by each integer type in Java, as shown in the table above, is always the same, regardless of what kind of computer you are using. This is also true of the other basic types that we will see later in this chapter, and has the rather useful effect that your program will execute in the same way on computers that may be quite different. This is not necessarily the case with other programming languages.

Of course, although we have expressed the range of possible values for each type by decimal values, integers are stored internally as binary numbers and it is the number of bits available to store each type that determines the maximum and minimum values, as shown on the next page.

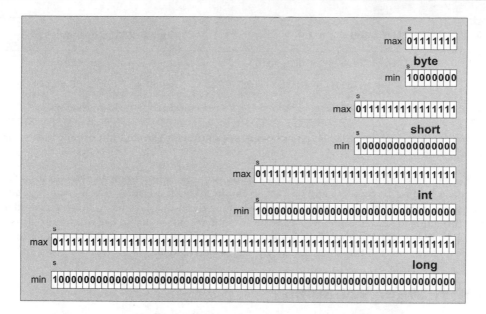

For each of the binary numbers shown here, the leftmost bit is the sign bit, marked with an 's'. When the sign bit is 0 the number is positive, and when it is 1 the number is negative. Binary negative numbers are represented in what is called 2's complement form. If you are not familiar with this, you will find an explanation of how it works in Appendix E.

Integer Values

An integer variable stores an integer value, so before we get to use integer variables we need to investigate how we write various integer values. As we said earlier, a value of any kind in Java is referred to as a **literal**. So 1, 10.5 and "This is text" are all examples of literals.

Any **integer literal** that you specify is of type int by default. Thus 1, -9999, 123456789 are all literals of type int. If you want to define an integer of type long, and the value that you assign to the variable is bigger than an int, you need to append an L to the value. The values 1L, -9999L and 123456789L are all of type long. You can also use a lower case letter 1, but don't – it is too easily confused with the digit 1.

You are perhaps wondering how you specify literals of type byte or short. It's simple really – explicitly you can't. But as we shall see a bit later, there's a good reason. Because of the way integer arithmetic works in Java, they just aren't necessary in the main. We will see a couple of instances where an integer literal may be interpreted by the compiler as type byte or short later in this chapter, but these situations are the exception.

Integer literals can also be specified to base 16, in other words as hexadecimal numbers. Hexadecimal literals in Java have 0x or 0X in front of them and follow the usual convention of using the letters A to F (or a to f) to represent digits with values 10 to 15 respectively. In case you are a little rusty on hexadecimal values, here are some examples:

0x100	**$1*16^2 + 0*16^1 + 0*16^0$**	**which is 256 in decimal**
0x1234	$1*16^3 + 2*16^2 + 3*16^1 + 4*16^0$	which is 4660 in decimal
0xDEAF	$13*16^3 + 14*16^2 + 10*16^1 + 15*16^0$	which is 57007 in decimal
0xCAB	$12*16^2 + 10*16^1 + 11*16^0$	which is 3243 in decimal

If you are not familiar with hexadecimal numbers, you can find an explanation of how these work in Appendix E.

There is a further possibility for integer constants – you can also define them as octal, to base 8. Octal numbers have a leading zero so 035 and 067 are examples of octal numbers. Each octal digit defines three bits, so this number base was used a lot more frequently in the days when machines used a multiple of three bits to store a number. You will rarely find it necessary to use octal these days, and you should take care not to use them by accident. If you put a leading zero at the start of an integer literal, the Java compiler will think you are specifying an octal value.

Declaring Integer Variables

As you saw earlier, we can declare a variable of type `long` with the statement:

```
long bigOne;
```

This statement is a **declaration** for the variable `bigOne`. This specifies that the variable `bigOne` will store a value of type `long`. When this statement is compiled, 8 bytes of memory will be allocated for the variable `bigOne`. Java does not automatically initialize a variable such as this. If you want your variables to have an initial value rather than a junk value left over from when the memory was last used, you must specify your own value in the declaration. To declare and initialize the variable `bigOne` to 2999999999, you just write:

```
long bigOne = 2999999999L;
```

The variable will be set to the value following the equals sign. It is good practice to always initialize your variables when you declare them. Note that if you try to use a variable in a calculation that has not had a value assigned to it, your program will not compile.

You can declare a variable just about anywhere in your program, but you must declare a variable before you use it in a calculation. The placement of the declaration therefore has an effect on whether a particular variable is accessible at a given point in a program, and we will look deeper into the significance of this in the next chapter. Broadly, you should group related variable declarations together, before the block of code that uses them.

You can declare and define multiple variables in a single statement. For example:

```
long bigOne = 999999999L, largeOne = 100000000L;
```

Here we have declared two variables of type `long`. A comma separates each variable from the next. You can declare as many variables as you like in a single statement, although it is usually better to stick to declaring one variable in each statement as it helps to make your programs easier to read. A possible exception occurs with variables that are closely related – an (x,y) coordinate pair representing a point for example, which you might reasonably declare as:

```
int xCoord = 0, yCoord = 0;        // Point coordinates
```

On the same line as the declaration of these two variables, we have a **comment** following the double slash, explaining what they are about. Everything from the double slash until the end of the line is ignored by the compiler. Explaining in comments what your variables are for is a good habit to get into, as it can be quite surprising how something that was as clear as crystal when you wrote it transmogrifies into something as clear as mud a few weeks later. There are other ways in which you can add comments to your programs which we will see a little later in this chapter.

You can also spread a single declaration over several lines if you want. This also can help to make your program more readable. For example:

```
int miles    = 0,      // One mile is 8 furlongs
    furlongs = 0,      // One furlong is 22 yards
    yards    = 0,      // One yard is 3 feet
    feet     = 0;
```

Naturally, you must be sure that an initializing value for a variable is within the range of the type concerned, otherwise the compiler will complain. Your compiler is intelligent enough to recognize that you can't get a quart into a pint pot, or, alternatively, a `long` constant into a variable of type `int`, `short` or `byte`.

To complete the set we can declare and initialize a variable of type `byte` and one of type `short` with the following two statements:

```
byte luckyNumber = 7;
short smallNumber = 1234;
```

Here the compiler can deduce that the integer literals are of type `byte` and `short` respectively. Most of the time you will find that variables of type `int` will cover your needs for dealing with integers, with `long` ones being necessary now and again when you have some really big integer values to deal with. Variables of type `byte` and `short` do save a little memory, but unless you have a lot of values of these types to store, that is values with a very limited range, they won't save enough to be worth worrying about. Of course, when you are reading data from some external source, a disk file for instance, you will need to make the type of variable for each data value correspond to what you expect to read.

Floating Point Data Types

Numeric values which are not integral are stored as **floating point** numbers. A floating point number has a fixed number of digits of accuracy but with a very wide range of values. You get a wide range of values, even though the number of digits is fixed, because the decimal point can "float". For example the values 0.000005, 500.0 and 5000000000000.0 can be written as 5×10^{-6}, 5×10^2 and 5×10^{12} respectively – we have just one digit '5' but we move the decimal point around.

There are two basic floating point types in Java, `float` and `double`. These give you a choice in the number of digits precision available to represent your data values, and thus, in the range of values that can be accommodated:

Data Type	Description
float	Variables of this type can have values from -3.4E38 (-3.4x10^{38}) to +3.4E38 (+3.4x10^{38}) and occupy 4 bytes in memory. Values are represented with approximately 7 digits accuracy.
double	Variables of this type can have values from -1.7E308 (-1.7x10^{308}) to +1.7E308 (+1.7x10^{308}) and occupy 8 bytes in memory. Values are represented with approximately 17 digits accuracy. The smallest non-zero value that you can have is roughly ±4.9x10^{-324}.

> **All floating point operations and the definition for values of type `float` and type `double` in Java conform to the IEEE 754 standard.**

As with integer calculations, floating point calculations in Java will produce the same results on any computer.

Floating Point Values

When you are specifying floating point literals they are of type `double` by default, so 1.0 and 345.678 are both of type `double`. When you want to specify a value of type `float`, you just append an `f`, or an `F`, to the value, so `1.0f` and `345.678F` are both constants of type `float`.

When you need to write very large or very small floating point values, you will usually want to write them with an exponent – that is, as a decimal value multiplied by a power of 10. You can do this in Java by writing the number as a decimal value followed by an `E`, or an `e`, preceding the power of 10 that you require. For example, the distance of the earth to the sun is approximately 149 600 000 kilometers, more conveniently written as 1.496E8. Since the `E` (or `e`) indicates what follows is the exponent, this is equivalent to 1.496x10^8. At the opposite end of the scale, the mass of an electron is around 0.00000000000000000000000000009 grams. This is much more convenient, not to say more readable, when it is written as 9.0E-28 grams.

Declaring Floating Point Variables

You declare floating point variables in a similar way to that we've already used for integers. We can declare and initialize a variable of type `double` with the statement:

```
double sunDistance = 1.496E8;
```

Declaring a variable of type `float` is much the same. For example:

```
float electronMass = 9E-28F;
```

You can of course declare more than one variable of a given type in a single statement:

```
float hisWeight = 185.2F, herWeight = 108.5F;
```

Note that you must put the `F` or `f` for literals of type `float`. If you leave it out, the literal will be of type `double`, and the compiler won't convert it automatically to type `float`.

Now that we know how to declare and initialize variables of the basic types, we are nearly ready to write a program. We just need to look at how to calculate and store the results of a calculation.

Arithmetic Calculations

You store the result of a calculation in a variable by using an **assignment statement**. An assignment statement consists of a variable name followed by an **assignment operator**, followed by an arithmetic expression, followed by a semicolon. Here is a simple example of an assignment statement:

```
numFruit = numApples + numOranges;        // Calculate the total fruit
```

Here, the assignment operator is the = sign. The value of the expression to the right of the = sign is calculated, and stored in the variable that appears to the left of the = sign. In this case, the values in the variables numApples and numOranges are added together and the result is stored in the variable numFruit. Of course, we would have to declare all three variables before this statement.

Incrementing a variable by a given amount is a common requirement in programming. Look at the following assignment statement:

```
numApples = numApples + 1;
```

The result of evaluating the expression on the right of the = is one more than the value of numApples. This result is stored back in the variable numApples, so the overall effect of executing the statement is to increment the value in numApples by 1. We will see an alternative, more concise, way of producing the same effect shortly.

You can write multiple assignments in a single statement. Suppose you have three variables a, b and c, of type int, and you want to set all three to 777. You can do this with the statement:

```
a = b = c = 777;
```

Note that an assignment is different from initialization in a declaration. Initialization causes a variable to have the value of the constant that you specify when it is created. An assignment involves copying data from one place in memory to another. For the assignment statement above, the compiler will have allocated some memory (4 bytes) to store the constant 777 as type int. This value will then be copied to the variable c. The value in c will be extracted and copied to b. Finally the value in b will be copied to a. (However, strictly speaking, the compiler optimizes these assignments when it compiles the code to reduce the inefficiency of successive assignment of the same value.)

With simple assignments of a constant value to a variable of type short or byte, the constant will be stored as the type of the variable on the left of the =, rather than type int. For example:

```
short value = 0;
value = 10;
```

This declaration, when compiled and run, will allocate space for the variable value, and arrange for its initial value to be 0. The assignment operation needs to have 10 available as an integer literal of type short, occupying 2 bytes, because value is of type short. The value 10 will then be copied to the variable value.

Now let's look in more detail at how we can perform calculations with integers.

Integer Calculations

The basic operators you can use on integers are +, -, * and /, which have the usual meanings – add, subtract, multiply and divide, respectively. Each of these is a **binary operator**; that is they combine two operands to produce a result, 2 + 3 for example. An **operand** is a value to which an operator is applied. The priority or precedence that applies when an expression using these operators is evaluated is the same as you learnt at school. Multiplication and division are executed before any addition or subtraction operations, so the expression:

```
20 - 3*3 - 9/3
```

will produce the value 8, since it is equivalent to 20 - 9 - 3.

As you will also have learnt in school, you can use parentheses in arithmetic calculations to change the sequence of operations. Expressions within parentheses are always evaluated first, starting with the innermost when they are nested. Therefore the expression:

```
(20 - 3)*(3 - 9)/3
```

is equivalent to 17*(-6)/3 which results in -34.

Of course, you use these operators with variables that store integer values as well as integer literals. You could calculate area from values stored in the variables length and breadth, by writing:

```
area = length * breadth;
```

The arithmetic operators we have described so far are **binary operators**, so called because they require two operands. There are also **unary** versions of the + and – operators that apply to a single operand to the right of the operator. Note that the unary – operator is not just a sign, as in a literal such as –345, it is an operator that has an effect. When applied to a variable it results in a value that has the opposite sign to that of the value stored in the variable. For example, if the variable count has the value -10, the expression –count has the value +10. Of course, applying the unary + operator to the value of a variable results in the same value.

Let's try out some simple arithmetic in a working console application:

Try It Out – Apples and Oranges (or Console Yourself)

Key in this example and save it in a file Fruit.java. You will remember from the last chapter that each file will contain a class, and that the name of the file will be the same as that of the class with the extension .java.

```
public class Fruit
{
  public static void main(String[] args)
  {
    // Declare and initialize three variables
    int numOranges = 5;                    // Count of oranges
    int numApples = 10;                    // Count of apples
    int numFruit = 0;                      // Count of fruit

    numFruit = numOranges + numApples;     // Calculate the total fruit count
```

```
      // Display the result
      System.out.println("A totally fruity program");
      System.out.println("Total fruit is " + numFruit);
   }
}
```

Just to remind you, to compile this program using the JDK, first make sure that the current directory is the one containing your source file, and execute the command:

```
javac Fruit.java
```

If there are no errors, this will generate a file, `Fruit.class`, in the same directory, and this file contains the byte codes for the program. To execute the program you then invoke the Java interpreter with the class name for your application program:

```
java Fruit
```

In some Java development environments, the output may not be displayed long enough for you to see it. If this is the case, you can add a few lines of code to get the program to wait until you press *Enter* before it ends. The additional lines to do this are shown shaded in the following listing:

```
import java.io.IOException;   // For code that delays ending the program

public class Fruit
{
  public static void main(String[] args)
  {
    // Declare and initialize three variables
    int numOranges = 5;                   // Count of oranges
    int numApples = 10;                   // Count of apples
    int numFruit = 0;                     // Count of fruit

    numFruit = numOranges + numApples;   // Calculate the total fruit count

    // Display the result
    System.out.println("A totally fruity program");
    System.out.println("Total fruit is " + numFruit);
      // Code to delay ending the program
      System.out.println("(press Enter to exit)");
      try
      {
        System.in.read();                  // Read some input from the keyboard
      }
      catch (IOException e)                // Catch the input exception
      {
        return;                            // and just return
      }
  }
}
```

We won't go into this extra code here. If you need to, just put it in for the moment. You will understand exactly how it works later in the book.

The stuff between parentheses following `main` – that is `String[] args` – provides a means of accessing data that is passed to the program from the command line when you run it. We will be going into this in detail later on so you can just ignore it for now, though you must always include it in the first line of `main()`.

All that additional code in the body of the main() method just waits until you press *Enter* before ending the program. If necessary, you can include this in all of your console programs to make sure they don't disappear before you can read the output. It won't make any difference to how the rest of the program works. We will defer discussing in detail what is happening in the bit of code that we have added until we get to exceptions in Chapter 7.

If you run this program with the additional code, the output will be similar to the following window:

The basic elements in the original version of the program are shown below:

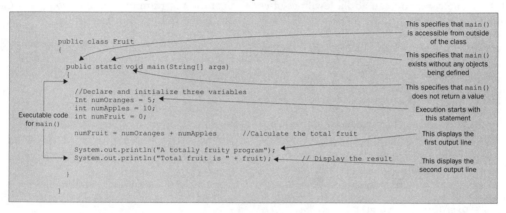

Our program consists of just one class, Fruit, and just one method, main(). Execution of an application always starts at the first executable statement in the method main(). There are no objects of our class Fruit defined, but the method main() can still be executed because we have specified it as static. The method main() is always specified as public and static and with the return type void. We can summarize the effects of these on the method as:

public	Specifies that the method is accessible from outside the Fruit class
static	Specifies that the method is a class method that is to be executable, even though no class objects have been created. (Methods that are not static can only be executed for a particular object of the class, as we will see in Chapter 5.)
void	Specifies that the method does not return a value

Don't worry if these are not completely clear to you at this point – you will meet them all again later.

The first three statements in main() declare the variables numOranges, numApples and numFruit to be of type int and initialize them to the values 5, 10 and 0 respectively. The next statement adds the values stored in numOranges and numApples, and stores the result, 15, in the variable numFruit. We then generate some output from the program.

Producing Output

The next two statements use the method `println()` which displays text output. The statement looks a bit complicated but it breaks down quite simply:

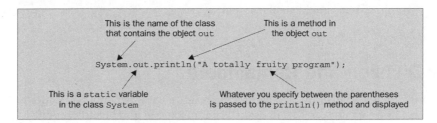

The text between double quotes, `"A totally fruity program"`, is a character string. Whenever you need a string constant, you just put the sequence of characters between double quotes.

You can see from the annotations above how you execute methods that belong to an object. Here we execute the method `println()` which belongs to the object `out`, which, in turn, is a `static` variable of the class `System`. Because the object `out` is `static`, it will exist even if there are no objects of type `System` in existence. This is analogous to the use of the keyword `static` for the method `main()`.

Most objects in a program are not static members of a class though, so calling a method for an object typically just involves the object name and the method name. For instance, if you guessed from the last example that to call the `putHatOn()` method for an object `cowboyHat` of type `Hat` introduced in Chapter 1, you would write,

```
cowboyHat.putHatOn();
```

you would be right. Don't worry if you didn't though. We will be going into this again when we get to look at classes in detail. For the moment, any time we want to output something as text to the console, we will just write,

```
System.out.println( whateverWeWantToDisplay );
```

with whatever data we want to display plugged in between the parentheses.

Thus the second statement in our example,

```
System.out.println("Total fruit is " + numFruit);
```

outputs the character string `"Total fruit is "` followed by the value of `numFruit` converted to characters, that is 15. So what's the + doing here – it's obviously not arithmetic we are doing, is it? No, but the plus has a special effect when used with character strings – it joins them together. But `numFruit` is not a string, is it? No, but `"Total fruit is "` is, and this causes the compiler to decide that the whole thing is an expression working on character strings. It therefore converts `numFruit` to a character string to be compatible with the string `"Total fruit is "` and tacks it on the end. The composite string is then passed to the `println()` method. Dashed clever, these compilers.

If you wanted to output the value of numOranges as well, you could write:

```
System.out.println("Total fruit is " + numFruit
                    + " and oranges = " + numOranges);
```

Try it out if you like. You should get the output:

```
Total fruit is 15 and oranges = 5
```

Integer Division and Remainders

When you divide one integer by another and the result is not exact, any remainder is discarded, so the final result is always an integer. The division 3/2, for example, produces the result 1, and 11/3 produces the result 3. This makes it easy to divide a given quantity equally amongst a given number of recipients. To divide numFruit equally between four children, you could write:

```
int numFruitEach = 0;                    // Number of fruit for each child
numFruitEach = numFruit/4;
```

Of course, there are circumstances where you may want the remainder and on these occasions you can calculate the remainder using the **modulus operator**, %. If you wanted to know how many fruit were left after dividing the total by 4, you could write:

```
int remainder = 0;
remainder = numFruit % 4;    // Calculate the remainder after division by 4
```

You could add this to the program too if you want to see the modulus operator in action. The modulus operator has the same precedence as multiply and divide, and is therefore executed in a more complex expression before any add or subtract operations.

The Increment and Decrement Operators

If you want to increment an integer variable by one, instead of using an assignment you can use the **increment operator**, which is written as two successive plus signs, ++. For example, if you have an integer variable count declared as:

```
int count = 10;
```

you can then write the statement:

```
++count;       // Add 1 to count
```

which will increase the value of count to 11. If you want to decrease the value of count by 1 you can use the **decrement operator**, --:

```
--count;       // Subtract 1 from count
```

At first sight, apart from reducing the typing a little, this does not seem to have much of an advantage over writing:

```
count = count - 1;      // Subtract 1 from count
```

One big advantage of the increment and decrement operators is that you can use them in an expression. Try changing the arithmetic statement calculating the sum of numApples and numOranges in the previous example:

```
public class Fruit
{
  public static void main(String[] args)
  {
    // Declare and initialize three variables
    int numOranges = 5;
    int numApples = 10;
    int numFruit = 0;

      // Increment oranges and calculate the total fruit
      numFruit = ++numOranges + numApples;

    System.out.println("A totally fruity program");
    // Display the result
      System.out.println("Value of oranges is " + numOranges);
    System.out.println("Total fruit is " + numFruit);
  }
}
```

The lines that have been altered or added have been highlighted. In addition to the change to the numFruit calculation, an extra statement has been added to output the final value of numOranges. The value of numOranges will be increased to 6 before the value of numApples is added, so the value of fruit will be 16. You could try the decrement operation in the example as well.

A further property of the increment and decrement operators is that they work differently in an expression depending on whether you put the operator in front of the variable, or following it. When you put the operator in front of a variable, as in the example we have just seen, it's called the **prefix form**. The converse case, with the operator following the variable, is called the **postfix form**. If you change the statement in the example to,

```
numFruit = numOranges++ + numApples;
```

and run it again, you will find that numOranges still ends up with the value 6, but the total stored in numFruit has remained 15. This is because the effect of the postfix increment operator is to change the value of numOranges to 6 *after* the original value, 5, has been used in the expression to supply the value of numFruit. The postfix decrement operator works similarly, and both operators can be applied to any type of integer variable.

As you see, no parentheses in the expression numOranges++ + numApples are necessary. You could even write it as numOranges+++numApples and it will still mean the same thing but it is certainly a lot less obvious what *you* mean. You could write is as (numOranges++) + numApples if you want to make it absolutely clear where the ++ operator belongs. It is a good idea to add parentheses to clarify things when there is some possibility of confusion.

Computation with Shorter Integer Types

With arithmetic expressions using variables of type `byte` or `short`, the calculation is carried out in the same way as with type `int` – using 32-bit arithmetic, and the result will be a 32-bit integer. As a consequence, if you change the types of the variables `numOranges`, `numApples` and `numFruit` in the original version of the program to `short` for example,

```
short numOranges = 5;
short numApples = 10;
short numFruit = 0;
```

then the program will no longer compile. The problem is with the statement:

```
numFruit = numOranges + numApples;
```

Since the expression `numOranges + numApples` produces a 32-bit result, the compiler cannot store this value in `numFruit`, as the variable `numFruit` is only 16-bits long. You must modify the code to convert the result of the addition back to a 16-bit number. You do this by changing the statement to:

```
numFruit = (short)(numOranges + numApples);
```

The statement now calculates the sum of `numOranges` and `numApples` and then converts or **casts** it to the type `short` before storing it in `numFruit`. This is called an **explicit cast**, and the conversion process is referred to as **casting**. The cast applies to whatever is to the right of `(short)` so the parentheses around the expression `numOranges + numApples` are necessary. Without them the cast would only apply to the variable `numOranges` which is a `short` anyway, and the code would still not compile. Similarly, if the variables here were of type `byte`, you would need to cast the result of the addition to the type `byte`.

The effect of the cast to `short` is just to take the least significant 16 bits of the result, discarding the most significant 16 bits. For the cast to type `byte` only the least significant 8 bits are kept. This means that if the magnitude of the result is such that more than 16 bits are necessary to represent it (or 8 bits in the case of a cast to `byte`), your answer will be wrong. You will get no indication from the compiler that this has occurred so you should avoid explicit casts unless they are absolutely essential.

An integer arithmetic operation involving a value of type `long` will always be carried using 64-bit values. If the other number in such an operation is not of type `long`, it will be cast to `long` before the operation is executed. For example:

```
long result = 0;
long factor = 10L;
int number = 5;
result = factor*number;
```

To execute the last statement, because the variable, `factor`, is of type `long`, the multiplication will be carried out using `long` values. The value stored in the variable, `number`, will be converted to type `long`, and that will be multiplied by the value of `factor`.

All other integer arithmetic operations involving types other than `long` are carried out with 32-bit values. Thus, you only really need to consider two kinds of integer literals:

❑ The type `long` for operations with 64-bit values where the value has an `L` appended

❑ The type `int` for operations with 32-bit values for all other cases where there is no `L` at the end of the number

Errors in Integer Arithmetic

If you divide an integer value by zero, no sensible result can be produced so an **exception** will be thrown. An exception is the way of signaling errors in Java that we will discuss in detail in Chapter 7. Using the `%` operator with a variable or expression for the right hand operand that has a zero value will also cause an exception to be thrown.

Note that if an integer expression results in a value that is outside the range of the type of the result, the result will be truncated to the number of bits for the type you are using and therefore incorrect, but this will not be indicated in any way. It is up to you to make sure that the integer types that you are using in your program are always able to accommodate any value that might be produced by your calculations. Problems can arise with intermediate results in some situations. Even when the ultimate result of an expression is within the legal range, if any intermediate calculation is outside the range it will be truncated causing an incorrect result to be produced. To take a trivial example – if you multiply 1000000 by 2000000 and divide by 500000 using type `int`, you will not obtain the correct result if the multiplication is executed first, because the result of the multiplication exceeds the maximum that can be stored as type `int`. Obviously where you know this sort of problem can occur, you may be able to circumvent it by using parentheses to make sure the division takes place first – but you need to remember that integer division produces an integer result, so a different sequence of execution can produce a different answer.

Floating Point Calculations

The four basic arithmetic operators, +, -, *, /, are also available for use in floating point expressions. We can try some of these out in another version of the `Fruit` program we'll call `AverageFruit`:

Try It Out – Average Fruit

Make the following changes to the `Fruit.java` file, and save this as `AverageFruit.java`. If necessary, you can add in the code we used earlier to make the program wait for the *Enter* key to be pressed before finishing.

```java
public class AverageFruit
{
  public static void main(String[] args)
  {
    // Declare and initialize three variables
    double numOranges = 50.0E-1;
    double numApples = 1.0E1;
    double averageFruit = 0.0;

    averageFruit = (numOranges + numApples) / 2.0;

  System.out.println("A totally fruity program");
    System.out.println("Average fruit is " + averageFruit);
  }
}
```

This will produce the output:

```
A totally fruity program
Average fruit is 7.5
```

The program just computes the average number of fruits by dividing the total by 2.0.

> **As you can see, we have used various representations for the initializing values for the variables in the program, which are now of type `double`. It's not the ideal way to write 5.0 but at least it demonstrates that you can write a negative exponent value.**

Other Floating Point Operators

You can use ++ and -- with floating point variables, and they have the same effect as with integer variables, incrementing or decrementing the floating point variable to which they are applied by 1.0. You can use them in prefix or postfix form, and their operation in each case is the same as with integer variables.

You can apply modulus operator, %, to floating point values too. For the operation,

```
floatOperand1 % floatOperand2
```

the result will be the floating point remainder after dividing `floatOperand2` into `floatOperand1` an integral number of times. For example, the expression `12.6 % 5.1` will give the result `2.4`.

Error Conditions in Floating Point Arithmetic

There are two error conditions that are signaled by a special result value being generated. One occurs when a calculation produces a value which is outside the range that can be represented, and the other arises when the result is mathematically indeterminate, such as when your calculation is effectively dividing zero by zero.

To illustrate the first kind of error we could use a variable to specify the number of types of fruit. We could define the variable:

```
double fruitTypes = 2.0;
```

and then rewrite the calculation as:

```
averageFruit = (numOranges + numApples) / fruitTypes;
```

This in itself is not particularly interesting, but if we happened to set `fruitTypes` to 0.0, the output from the program would be:

```
A totally fruity program
Average fruit is Infinity
```

The value `Infinity` indicates a positive but effectively infinite result, in that it is greater than the largest number that can be represented as type `double`. A negative infinite result would be output as `-Infinity`. You don't actually need to divide by zero to produce this effect; any calculation which generates a value that exceeds the maximum value that can be represented as type `double` will have the same effect. For example, repeatedly dividing by a very small number, such as `1.0E-300`, will yield an out-of-range result.

If you want to see what an indeterminate result looks like, you can replace the statement to calculate `averageFruit` with:

```
averageFruit = (numOranges - 5.0)/(numApples - 10.0);
```

This statement doesn't make much sense but it will produce an indeterminate result. The value of `averageFruit` will be output as NaN. This value is referred to as **Not-a-Number**, indicating an indeterminate value. A variable with an indeterminate value will contaminate any subsequent expression in which it is used, producing the same result of NaN.

A value that is `Infinity` or `-Infinity` will be unchanged when you add, subtract, or multiply by finite values, but if you divide any finite value by `Infinity` or `-Infinity` the result will be zero.

Mixed Arithmetic Expressions

You can mix values of the basic types together in a single expression. The way mixed expressions are treated is governed by some simple rules that apply to each operator in such an expression. The rules, in the sequence in which they are checked, are:

❑ If either operand is of type `double`, the other is converted to `double` before the operation is carried out.

❑ If either operand is of type `float`, the other is converted to `float` before the operation is carried out.

❑ If either operand is of type `long` the other is converted to `long` before the operation is carried out.

The first rule in the sequence that applies to a given operation is the one that is carried out. If neither operand is `double`, `float` or `long`, they must be `int`, `short` or `byte`, so they use 32-bit arithmetic as we saw earlier.

Explicit Casting

It may well be that the default treatment of mixed expressions listed above is not what you want. For example, if you have a `double` variable `result`, and you compute its value using two `int` variables `three` and `two` with the values 3 and 2 respectively, with the statement:

```
result = 1.5 + three/two;
```

the value stored will be 2.5, since `three/two` will be executed as an integer operation and produce the result 1. You may have wanted the term `three/two` to produce the value 1.5 so the overall result would be 3.0. You could do this using an explicit cast:

```
result = 1.5 + (double)three/two;
```

This causes the value stored in `three` to be converted to `double` before the divide operation takes place. Then rule 1 applies for the divide operation, and the operand `two` is also converted to `double` before the divide is executed. Hence the value of `result` will be 3.0.

> You can cast any of the basic types to any other, but you need to take care that you don't lose information when you do so. Obviously casting from a larger integer type to a smaller has the potential for losing information, as does casting any floating point value to an integer. Casting from **double** to float can also produce effective infinity when the original value is greater than the maximum value for a float.

Casting in Assignments

When the type of the result of an expression on the right of an assignment statement differs from the type of the variable on the left, an automatic cast will be applied as long as there is no possibility of losing information. If you think of the basic types that we have seen so far as being in the sequence:

byte → short → int → long → float → double

then an automatic conversion will be made as long as it is upwards through the sequence, that is, from left to right. If you want to go in the opposite direction, from double to float or long for example, then you must use an explicit cast.

The *op=* Operators

The *op=* operators are used in statements of the form:

```
lhs op= rhs;
```

where *op* can be any of the operators +, -, *, /, %, plus some others you haven't seen yet. The above is a shorthand representation of the statement:

```
lhs = lhs op (rhs);
```

The right hand side is in brackets because it is worked out first – then the result is combined with the left hand side using the operation, *op*. Let's look at a few examples of this to make sure it's clear. To increment an int variable count by 5 you can write:

```
count += 5;
```

This has the same effect as the statement:

```
count = count + 5;
```

Of course the expression to the right of the *op=* operator can be anything that is legal in the context, so the statement,

```
result /= a % b/(a + b);
```

is equivalent to:

```
result = result/(a % b/(a + b));
```

> You should note that if the type of the result of the *rhs* expression is different from the type of *lhs*, the compiler will automatically insert a cast. In the last example, the statement would work with `result` being of type `int` and `a` and `b` being of type `double`, for instance. This is quite different from the way the normal assignment operation is treated.

The complete set of *op=* operators appears in the precedence table later in this chapter.

Mathematical Functions and Constants

Sooner or later you are likely to need mathematical functions in your programs, even if it's only obtaining an absolute value or calculating a square root. Java provides a range of methods that support such functions as part of the standard library stored in the package `java.lang`, and all these are available in your program automatically.

The methods that support various additional mathematical functions are implemented in the class `Math` as `static` methods, so to reference a particular function you can just write `Math` and a period in front of the name of the method you wish to use. For example, to use `sqrt()` which calculates the square root of whatever you place between the parentheses, you would write `Math.sqrt(aNumber)` to produce the square root of the floating point value in the variable `aNumber`.

The class `Math` includes a range of methods for standard trigonometric functions. These are:

Method	Function	Argument type	Result type
`sin(arg)`	sine of the argument	`double` in radians	`double`
`cos(arg)`	cosine of the argument	`double` in radians	`double`
`tan(arg)`	tangent of the argument	`double` in radians	`double`
`asin(arg)`	$\sin^{-1}$ (arc sine) of the argument	`double`	`double` in radians with values from $-\pi/2$ to $\pi/2$.
`acos(arg)`	$\cos^{-1}$ (arc cosine) of the argument	`double`	`double` in radians, with values from 0.0 to π.
`atan(arg)`	$\tan^{-1}$ (arc tangent) of the argument	`double`	`double` in radians with values from $-\pi/2$ to $\pi/2$.
`atan2(arg1,arg2)`	$\tan^{-1}$ (arc tangent) of `arg1`/`arg2`	Both `double`	`double` in radians with values from $-\pi$ to π.

As with all methods, the arguments that you put between the parentheses following the method name can be any expression that produces a value of the required type. If you are not familiar with these trigonometric operations you can safely ignore them.

You also have a range of numerical functions that are implemented in the class `Math`. These are:

Method	Function	Argument type	Result type
`abs(arg)`	Calculates the absolute value of the argument	`int`, `long`, `float` or `double`	The same type as the argument
`max (arg1,arg2)`	Returns the larger of the two arguments, both of the same type	`int`, `long`, `float` or `double`	The same type as the argument
`min (arg1,arg2)`	Returns the smaller of the two arguments, both of the same type.	`int`, `long`, `float` or `double`	The same type as the argument
`ceil(arg)`	Returns the smallest integer that is greater than or equal to the argument	`double`	`double`
`floor(arg)`	Returns the largest integer that is less than or equal to the argument	`double`	`double`
`round(arg)`	Calculates the nearest integer to the argument value	`float` or `double`	Of type `int` for a `float` argument, of type `long` for a `double` argument
`rint(arg)`	Calculates the nearest integer to the argument value	`double`	`double`
`IEEEremainder (arg1,arg2)`	Calculates the remainder when `arg1` is divided by `arg2`	Both of type `double`	Of type `double`

The `IEEEremainder()` method produces the remainder from `arg1` after dividing `arg2` into `arg1` the integral number of times that is closest to the exact value of `arg1/arg2`. This is somewhat different from the remainder operator. The operation `arg1 % arg2` operator produces the remainder after dividing `arg2` into `arg1` the integral number of times that does not exceed the absolute value of `arg1`. In some situations this can result in markedly different results. For example, executing the expression `9.0%5.0` results in `4.0`, whereas the expression `Math.IEEEremainder(9.0,5.0)` results in `-1.0`. You can pick one approach to calculating the remainder or the other, to suit your requirements.

Where more than one type of argument is noted in the table, there are actually several methods, one for each type of argument, but all having the same name. We will see how this is possible in Java when we look at implementing class methods in Chapter 5.

The mathematical functions available in the class `Math` are:

Method	Function	Argument type	Result type
sqrt(arg)	Calculates the square root of the argument	double	double
pow (arg1,arg2)	Calculates the first argument raised to the power of the second argument $arg1^{arg2}$	Both double	double
exp(arg)	Calculates **e** raised to the power of the argument e^{arg}	double	double
log(arg)	Calculates the natural logarithm (base **e**) of the argument	double	double
random()	Returns a pseudo random number greater than or equal to 0.0 and less than 1.0.	None	double

The `toRadians()` method in the class `Math` will convert a `double` argument that is an angular measurement in degrees to radians. There is a complementary method, `toDegrees()` to convert in the opposite direction. The `Math` class also defines `double` values for **e** and π, which you can access as `Math.E` and `Math.PI` respectively.

Let's try out a sample of the contents of the class `Math` in an example to make sure we know how they are used.

Try It Out – The `Math` Class

Type in the following program, which will calculate the radius of a circle in feet and inches, given that it has an area of 100 square feet.

```
public class MathCalc
{
  public static void main(String[] args)
  {
    // Calculate the radius of a circle
    // which has an area of 100 square feet
    double radius = 0.0;
    double circleArea = 100.0;
    int feet = 0;
    int inches = 0;
    radius = Math.sqrt(circleArea/Math.PI);
    feet = (int)Math.floor(radius);  // Get the whole feet and nothing but the
feet
    inches = (int)Math.round(12.0*(radius - feet));
    System.out.println("The radius of a circle with area " + circleArea +
                   " square feet is\n " + feet + " feet " + inches + "
inches");
  }
}
```

Save the program as `MathCalc.java`. When you compile and run it, you should get:

```
The radius of a circle with area 100.0 square feet is
 5 feet 8 inches
```

How It Works

The first calculation, after defining the variables we need, uses the `sqrt()` method to calculate the radius. Since the area of a circle, with radius r, is given by the formula πr^2, the radius must be $\sqrt{(area/\pi)}$, and we specify the argument to the `sqrt()` method as the expression `circleArea/Math.PI`, where `Math.PI` references the value of π. The result is in feet as a `double` value. To get the number of whole feet we use the `floor()` method. Note that the cast to `int` is essential in this statement, otherwise you will get an error message from the compiler. The value returned from the `floor()` method is type `double`, and the compiler will not cast this to `int` for you automatically because the process potentially loses information.

Finally, we get the number of inches by subtracting the value for whole feet from the original radius, multiplying the fraction of a foot by 12 to get the equivalent inches, and then rounding the result to the nearest integer using the `round()` method.

Note how we output the result. We specify the combination (or concatenation) of strings and variables as an argument to the `println()` method. The statement is spread over two lines for convenience here. The `\n` in the output specifies a newline character, so the output will be on two lines. Any time you want the next bit of output to begin a new line, just add `\n` to the output string. You can't enter a newline character just by typing it because when you do that the cursor just moves to the next line. That's why it's specified as `\n`. There are other characters like this that we'll look into now.

Storing Characters

Variables of the type `char` store a single character. They each occupy 16 bits, two bytes, in memory because all characters in Java are stored as Unicode. To declare and initialize a character variable `myCharacter` you would use the statement:

```
char myCharacter = 'X';
```

This initializes the variable with the Unicode character representation of the letter 'X'. You must put the single quotes around a character in a statement – `'X'`. This is necessary to enable the compiler to distinguish between the character `'X'` and a variable with the name `X`.

Character Escape Sequences

If you are using an ASCII text editor you will only be able to enter characters directly that are defined within ASCII. You can define Unicode characters by specifying the hexadecimal representation of the character codes in an **escape sequence**. An escape sequence is simply an alternative means of specifying a character, often by its code. A backslash indicates the start of an escape sequence, and you create an escape sequence for a Unicode character by preceding the four hexadecimal digits of the character by `\u`. Since the Unicode coding for the letter X is 0x0058 (the low order byte is the same as the ASCII code), you could also declare and define `myCharacter` with the statement:

```
char myCharacter = '\u0058';
```

You can enter any Unicode character in this way, although it is not exactly user-friendly for entering a lot of characters.

> You can get more information on the full Unicode character set on the Internet by visiting http://www.unicode.org/.

As you have seen, we can write a character string (a `String` literal as we will see in Chapter 4) enclosed between double quotes. Because the backslash indicates the beginning of an escape sequence in a character string, you must use an escape sequence to specify a backslash character itself in text strings, \\. Since a single quote is used to delimit characters, and we use a double quote to delimit a text string, we also need escape sequences for these. You can define a single quote with the escape sequence \', and a double quote with \". For example, to produce the output:

```
"It's freezing in here", he said coldly.
```

You could write:

```
System.out.println("\"It\'s freezing in here\", he said coldly.");
```

In fact, it's not strictly necessary to use an escape sequence to specify a single quote within a string, but obviously it will be when you want to specify it as a single character. Of course, it is always necessary to specify a double quote within a string using an escape sequence, otherwise it would be interpreted as the end of the string.

There are other escape characters you can use to define control characters:

\b	Backspace
\f	Form feed
\n	New line
\r	Carriage return
\t	Tab

Character Arithmetic

You can perform arithmetic on `char` variables. With `myCharacter` containing the character 'X', the statement,

```
myCharacter += 1;      // Increment to next character
```

will result in the value of `myCharacter` being changed to 'Y'. You could use the increment operator ++ to increase the code stored in `myCharacter` by just writing:

```
++myCharacter;         // Increment to next character
```

You can use variables of type `char` in an arithmetic expression, and their values will be converted to type `int` to carry out the calculation. It doesn't necessarily make a whole lot of sense, but you could write,

```
char aChar = 0;
char bChar = '\u0028';
aChar = (char)(2*bChar + 8);
```

which will leave `aChar` holding the code for X – which is 0x0058.

Bitwise Operations

As you probably already know, all these integer variables we have been talking about are represented internally as binary numbers. A value of type `int` consists of 32 **binary digits**, known to computer fans as **bits**. You can operate on the bit values of integers using the **bitwise operators**, of which there are four available:

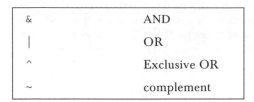

&	AND
|	OR
^	Exclusive OR
~	complement

Each of these operators works with individual bits as follows:

❑ The **complement** operator, ~ , takes a single operand in which it inverts all the bits, so that each 1 bit becomes 0, and each 0 bit becomes 1.

❑ The **bitwise AND** operator, & , combines corresponding bits in its two operands such that if the first bit *AND* the second bit are 1, the result is 1 – otherwise the result is 0.

❑ The **bitwise OR** operator, | , combines corresponding bits such that if either one bit *OR* the other is 1, then the result is 1. Only if both bits are 0 is the result 0.

❑ The **bitwise exclusive OR** (XOR) operator, ^, combines corresponding bits such that if both bits are the same the result is 0, otherwise the result is 1.

You can see the effect of these operators in the following examples.

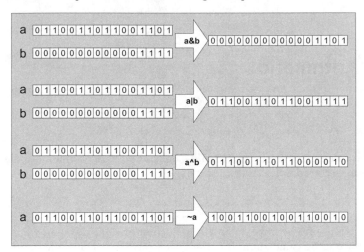

The illustration shows the binary digits that make up the operands and the results. Each of the three binary operations apply to corresponding individual pairs of bits from the operands separately. The complement operator flips the state of each bit in the operand.

Since you are concerned with individual bits with bitwise operations, writing a constant as a normal decimal value is not going to be particularly convenient. A much better way of writing binary values in this case is to express them as hexadecimal numbers, because you can convert from binary to hexadecimal, and vice versa, very quickly. There's more on this in Appendix E.

Converting from binary to hexadecimal is easy. Each group of four binary digits from the right corresponds to one hexadecimal digit. You just work out what the value of each four bits is and write the appropriate hexadecimal digit. For example, the value of a from the illustration is:

Binary	0110	0110	1100	1101
Decimal value	6	6	12	13
Hexadecimal	6	6	C	D

So the value of the variable a in hexadecimal is 0x66CD, where the 0x prefix indicates that this is a hexadecimal value. The variable b in the illustration has the hexadecimal value 0x000F. If you think of the variable b as a **mask** applied to a, you can view the & operator as keeping bits unchanged where the mask is 1 and setting the rest to 0. **Mask** is a term used to refer to a particular configuration of bits designed to select out specific bits when it is combined with a variable using a bitwise operator. So if you want to select a particular bit out of an integer variable, just AND it with a mask with that bit set to 1 and all the others as 0.

You can also look at what the & operator does from another perspective – it forces a bit to 0, if the corresponding mask bit is 0. Similarly, the | operator forces a bit to be 1 when the mask bit is 1.

The & and | operators are the most frequently used, mainly for dealing with variables where the individual bits are used as state indicators of some kind for things that can be either true or false, or on or off. You could use a single bit as a state indicator determining whether something should be displayed, with the bit as 1, or not displayed, with the bit as 0. A single bit can be selected using the & operator – for example to select the third bit in the variable indicators, you can write:

```
thirdBit = indicators & 0x4;      // Select the 3rd bit
```

We can illustrate how this works if we assume the variable indicators contains the hexadecimal value 0xFF07:

	Hexadecimal	Binary			
indicators	0xFF07	1111	1111	0000	0111
mask value	0x4	0000	0000	0000	0100
indicators & 0x4	0x4	0000	0000	0000	0100

All these values should have 32 bits and we are only showing 16 bits here, but you see all you need to know how it works. The mask value sets all the bits in indicators to zero except for the third bit. Here, the result of the expression is non-zero because the third bit in indicators is 1.

On the other hand, if the variable `indicators` contained the value `0xFF09` the result would be different:

	Hexadecimal	Binary			
indicators	0xFF09	1111	1111	0000	1001
mask value	0x4	0000	0000	0000	0100
indicators & 0x4	0x0004	0000	0000	0000	0000

The result of the expression is now zero because the third bit of indicators is zero.

To set a particular bit on, you can use the | operator, so to set the third bit in `indicators` on, you can write:

```
indicators = indicators | 0x4;    // Set the 3rd bit on
```

We can see how this applies to the last value we had for indicators:

	Hexadecimal	Binary			
indicators	0xFF09	1111	1111	0000	1001
mask value	0x4	0000	0000	0000	0100
indicators & 0x4	0xFF0D	1111	1111	0000	1101

As you can see, the effect is just to switch the third bit of indicators on. All the others are unchanged. Of course, if the bit were already on, it would stay on.

The bitwise operators can also be used in the *op=* form. Setting the third bit in the variable `indicators` is usually written as:

```
indicators |= 0x4;
```

Although there is nothing wrong with the original statement we wrote the one above is just a bit more concise.

To set a bit off you need to use the & operator again, with a mask that has 0 for the bit you want as 0, and 1 for all the others. To set the third bit of `indicators` off you could write:

```
indicators &= ~0x4;                      // Set the 3rd bit off
```

With `indicators` having the value `0xFF07`, this would work as follows:

	Hexadecimal	Binary			
indicators	0xFF07	1111	1111	0000	0111
mask value	0x4	0000	0000	0000	0100
~0x4	0xFFFB	1111	1111	1111	1011
indicators & ~0x4	0xFF03	1111	1111	0000	0011

The ^ operator has the slightly surprising ability to interchange two values without moving either value somewhere else. If you execute three statements,

```
a ^= b;
b ^= a;
a ^= b;
```

this will interchange the values of a and b, but remember this only works for integers of course.We can try this out with a couple of arbitrary values for a and b, 0xD00F and 0xABAD respectively – again we will just look at 16 bits for each variable. The first statement will change a to a new value:

a ^= b	Hexadecimal	Binary			
a	0xD00F	1101	0000	0000	1111
b	0xABAD	1010	1011	1010	1101
a from a^b	0x'/BA2	0111	1011	1010	0010

Now the next statement which calculates a new value of b using the new value of a:

b ^= a	Hexadecimal	Binary			
a	0x7BA2	0111	1011	1010	0010
b	0xABAD	1010	1011	1010	1101
b from b^a	0xD00F	1101	0000	0000	1111

So b now has a value that looks remarkably like the value that a started out with. Let's look at the last step, which calculates a new value for a using the new value of b:

a ^= b	Hexadecimal	Binary			
a	0x7BA2	0111	1011	1010	0010
b	0xD00F	1101	0000	0000	1111
a from a^b	0xABAD	1010	1011	1010	1101

61

Lo and behold, the value of a is now the original value of b. In the old days when all programmers wore lab coats, when computers were driven by steam, and when memory was measured in bytes rather than megabytes, this mechanism could be quite useful since you could interchange two values in memory without having to have extra memory locations available. So if antique computers are your thing this may turn out to be a valuable technique. In fact it's more useful than that. When we get to do some graphics programming you will see that it is very relevant.

Don't forget – all of these bitwise operators can only be applied to integers. They don't work with any other type of value. As with the arithmetic expressions, the bitwise operations are carried out with 32 bits for integers of type short and of type byte, so a cast to the appropriate type is necessary for the result of the expression on the right of the assignment operator.

Shift Operations

Another mechanism that you have for working with integer variables at the bit level is shifting. You can shift the bits in an integer to the right or the left. Shifting binary digits right or left can be envisaged as dividing or multiplying by powers of two. Shifting the binary value of 3, which is 0011, to the left one bit multiplies it by two. It becomes binary 0110 which is 6. Shifting it to the right by one bit divides it by 2. It becomes binary 0001 which is 1.

Java has three shift operators:

<<	Shift left, filling with zeros from the right
>>	Shift right, propagating the sign bit from the left
>>>	Shift right, filling with zeros from the left

The effect of the operators is shown in the following illustration:

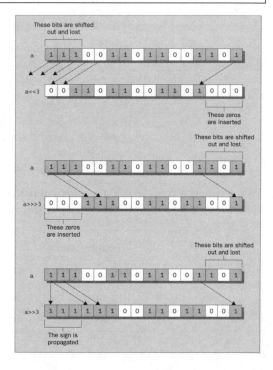

Of course, if the high order bit in the >> operation in the illustration was zero, there would be three zeros at the leftmost end of the result.

Shift operations are often used in combination with the other bitwise operators we have discussed to extract parts of an integer value. In many operating systems a single 32-bit value is sometimes used store multiple values – two 16-bit values for instance that might be screen coordinates. This is illustrated opposite.

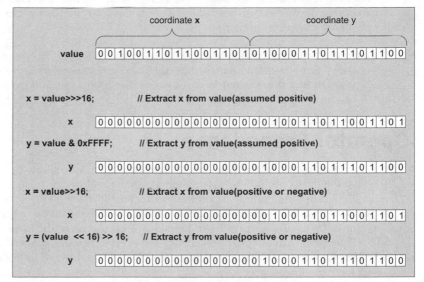

This shows how the shift operations can be used to extract either the left or right 16 bits from the variable value. You can see here why you have an extra shift right operation that propagates the leftmost bit. It is related to the notion of a shift as multiplying or dividing by a power of 2, and the implications of that in the context of negative integers represented in 2's complement form (see Appendix E).

Boolean Variables

Variables that can only have one of two values, true or false, are of type boolean, and the values true and false are Boolean literals. You can define a boolean variable, called state, with the statement:

```
boolean state = true;
```

This statement also initializes the variable state with the value true. You can also set a boolean variable in an assignment statement. For example, the statement,

```
state = false;
```

sets the value of the variable state to false.

At this point we can't do much with a boolean variable, other than to set its value to true or false, but, as you will see in the next chapter, Boolean variables become much more useful in the context of decision making in a program, particularly when we can use expressions that produce a boolean result.

There are several operators that combine Boolean values including operators for Boolean AND, Boolean OR, and Boolean negation (these are `&&`, `||` and `!`, respectively), as well as comparison operators that produce a Boolean result. Rather than go into these here in the abstract, we will defer discussion until the next chapter where we will also look at how we can apply them in practice to alter the sequence of execution in a program.

> **One point you should note is that `boolean` variables differ from the other basic data types in that they cannot be cast to any other basic type, and the other basic types cannot be cast to `boolean`.**

Operator Precedence

We have already introduced the idea of a pecking order for operators, which determines the sequence in which they are executed in a statement. A simple arithmetic expression such as 3+4*5 results in the value 23 because the multiply operation is executed first – it takes precedence over the addition operation. We can now formalize the position by classifying all the operators present in Java. Each operator in Java has a set priority or precedence in relation to the others, as shown in the following table. Operators with a higher precedence are executed before those of a lower precedence. Precedence is highest for operators in the top line in the table, down through to the operators in the bottom line, which have the lowest precedence:

Operator Precedence Group	Associativity
(), [], . postfix ++, postfix --	left
unary +, unary -, prefix ++, prefix --, ~, !	right
(type), new	left
*, /, %	left
+, -	left
<<, >>, >>>	left
< ,<= , >, >=, instanceof	left
==, !=	left
&	left
^	left
|	left
&&	left
||	left
?:	left
=, +=, -=, *=, /=, %=, <<=, >>=, >>>=, &=, |=, ^=	right

Most of the operators that appear in the table you have not seen yet, but you will meet them all in this book eventually, and it is handy to have them all gathered together in a single precedence table that you can refer to when necessary.

By definition, the postfix ++ operator is executed after the other operators in the expression in which it appears, despite its high precedence. In this case, precedence determines what it applies to, in other words the postfix ++ only acts on the variable that appears immediately before it. For this reason the expression oranges+++apples that we saw earlier is evaluated as (oranges++) + apples rather than oranges + (++apples).

The sequence of execution of operators with equal precedence in a statement is determined by a property called **associativity**. Each group of operators appearing on the same line in the table above are either **left associative** or **right associative**. A left associative operator attaches to its immediate left operand. This results in an expression involving several left associative operators with the same precedence in the same expression being executed in sequence starting with the leftmost and ending with the rightmost. Right associative operators of equal precedence in an expression bind to their right operand and consequently are executed from right to left. For example, if you write the statement:

```
a = b + c + 10;
```

The left associativity of the group to which the + operator belongs implies that this is effectively:

```
a = (b + c) + 10;
```

On the other hand = and *op=* are right associative, so if you have int variables a, b, c and d each initialized to 1, the statement,

```
a += b = c += d = 10;
```

sets a to 12, b and c to 11 and d to 10. The statement is equivalent to:

```
a += (b = (c += (d = 10)));
```

Note that these statements are intended to illustrate how associativity works, and are not a recommended approach to coding.

You will probably find that you will learn the precedence and associativity of the operators in Java by just using them in your programs. You may need to refer back to the table from time to time, but as you gain experience you will gain a feel for where the operators sit and eventually you will automatically know when you need parentheses and when not.

Program Comments

We have been adding comments in all our examples so far so you already know that // plus everything following in a line is ignored by the compiler (except when the // appears in a character string between double quotes of course). Another use for // is to comment out lines of code. If you want to remove some code from a program temporarily, you just need to add // at the beginning of each line you want to eliminate.

It is often convenient to include multiple lines of comment in a program, for example at the beginning of a method to explain what it does. An alternative to using // at the beginning of each line in a block of comments is to put /* at the beginning of the first comment line and */ at the end of the last comment line. Everything between the /* and the next */ will be ignored. By this means you can annotate your programs, like this for example:

```
/******************************************
 *    This is a long explanation of        *
 *    some particularly important          *
 *    aspect of program operation.         *
 ******************************************/
```

Of course, you can frame blocks like this in any way that you like, or even not at all, just so long as there is /* at the beginning and */ at the end.

Documentation Comments

You can also include comments in a program that are intended to produce separate documentation for the program. These are called **documentation comments**. All the documentation that you get with the JDK is produced in this way. The documentation is produced by processing a program that contains documentation comments with a program called javadoc. The documentation that is generated is in the form of Hypertext web pages that can be viewed using a browser such as Netscape Navigator or Internet Explorer. A full discussion of documentation comments is outside the scope of this book – not because they are difficult, they aren't, but it would need a lot of pages to cover it properly. We will just describe it sufficiently so that you will recognize documentation comments when you see them.

A documentation comment begins with /** and ends with */. An example of a simple documentation comment is:

```
/**
 * This is a documentation comment.
 */
```

Any asterisks at the beginning of each line in a documentation comment are ignored, as are any spaces preceding the first *.

A documentation comment can also include HTML tags, as well as special tags beginning with @ that are used to document methods and classes in a standard form. The @ is followed by a keyword that defines the purpose of the tag. Here are some of the keywords that you can use:

@author	Used to define the author of the code.
@deprecated	Used in the documentation of library classes and methods to indicate that they have been superseded and generally should not be used in new applications.
@exception	Used to document exceptions that the code can throw and the circumstance which can cause this to occur.
{@link}	Generates a link to another part of the documentation within the documentation that is produced. The curly brackets are used to separate it from the rest of the in-line text.
@param	Used to describe the parameters for a method.
@return	Used to document the value returned from a method.
@see	Used to specify cross references to some other part of the code such as another class or a method. It can also reference a URL.
@throws	A synonym for @exception
@version	Used to describe the current version of the code.

You can use any HTML tags within a documentation comment except for header tags. The HTML tags you insert are used to structure and format the documentation appropriately when it is viewed, and javadoc will add HTML tags to format the comments that include the special @ tags that we mentioned above.

The few comments I have made here really don't do justice to the power and scope of javadoc. For that you need to look into it in detail. The JDK comes with the javadoc program and documentation. Javadoc also has its own home page on the Javasoft web site at:

http://java.sun.com/products/jdk/javadoc/.

Summary

In this chapter you have seen all of the basic types of variables available in Java. The discussion of boolean variables will be more meaningful in the context of the next chapter since their primary use is in decision making and modifying the execution sequence in a program.

The important points you have learned in this chapter are:

❑ The integer types are byte, short, int and long, occupying 1, 2, 4 and 8 bytes respectively.

❑ Variables of type char occupy 2 bytes and can store a single Unicode character code.

❑ Integer expressions are evaluated using 64-bit operations for variables of type long, and using 32-bit operations for all other integer types. You must therefore add a cast for all assignment operations storing a result of type byte, short or char.

❑ A cast will be automatically supplied where necessary for *op=* assignment operations.

❑ The floating point types are float and double, occupying 4 and 8 bytes respectively.

❑ Values that are outside the range of a floating point type are represented by a special value that is displayed as either Infinity or -Infinity.

❑ Where the result of a floating point calculation is indeterminate, the value is displayed as NaN. Such values are referred to as **not-a-number**.

❑ Variables of type boolean can only have either the value true, or the value false.

❑ The order of execution of operators in an expression is determined by their precedence. Where operators are of equal precedence, the order of execution is determined by their associativity.

Exercises

1. Write a console program to define and initialize a variable of type `byte` to 1, and then successively multiply it by 2 and display its value 8 times. Explain the reason for the last result.

2. Write a console program to declare and initialize a `double` variable with some value such as 1234.5678. Then retrieve the integral part of the value and store it in a variable of type `long`, and the first four digits of the fractional part and store it in an integer of type `short`. Display the value of the `double` variable by outputting the two values stored as integers.

3. The diameter of the Sun is approximately 865,000 miles. The diameter of the Earth is approximately 7600 miles. Use the methods in the class `Math` to calculate,

❑   the volume of the Earth in cubic miles

❑   the volume of the Sun in cubic miles

❑   the ratio of the volume of the Sun to the volume of the Earth

and then output the three values. Treat both the earth and the sun as spheres. The volume of a sphere is given by the formula $4\pi r^3/3$ where r is the radius.

Loops and Logic

In this chapter we'll look at how you make decisions and choices in your Java programs. You will also learn how to make your programs repeat a set of actions until a specific condition is met. We'll cover:

- ❏ How you compare data values.

- ❏ How you can define logical expressions.

- ❏ How you can use logical expressions to alter the sequence in which program statements are executed.

- ❏ How you can select different expressions depending on the value of a logical expression.

- ❏ How to choose between options in a fixed set of alternatives.

- ❏ How long your variables last.

- ❏ How you can repeat a block of code a given number of times.

- ❏ How you can repeat a block of code as long as a given logical expression is true.

- ❏ How you can break out of loops and statement blocks.

All your programs of any consequence will use at least some, and often most, of the language capabilities and programming techniques we will cover in this chapter, so make sure you have a good grasp of them.

But first, how do we make decisions in code, and so affect the way the program runs?

Making Decisions

Making choices will be a fundamental element in all your programs. You need to be able to make decisions like, "If the bank balance is fat, buy the car with the go-faster stripes, else renew the monthly bus ticket". In programming terms this requires the ability to make comparisons between variables, constants and the values of expressions, and then to execute one group of statements or another, depending on the result of a given comparison. The first step to making decisions in a program is to look at how we make comparisons.

Making Comparisons

Java provides you with six relational operators for comparing two data values. Either of the data values you are comparing can be variables, constants or expressions drawn from Java's primitive data types – byte, short, int, long, char, float or double.

Relational Operators	Description
>	Produces the value true if the left operand is greater than the right operand, and false otherwise.
>=	Produces the value true if the left operand is greater than or equal to the right operand, and false otherwise.
==	Produces the value true if the left operand is equal to the right operand, and false otherwise.
!=	Produces the value true if the left operand is not equal to the right operand, and false otherwise.
<=	Produces the value true if the left operand is less than or equal to the right operand, and false otherwise.
<	Produces the value true if the left operand is less than the right operand, and false otherwise.

As you see, each operator produces either the value true, or the value false, and so is eminently suited to the business of making decisions.

If you wish to store the result of a comparison, you use a boolean variable. We saw how to declare these in the previous chapter. For example you can define a boolean variable state and you can set its value in an assignment as follows:

```
boolean state = false;
state = x - y < a + b;
```

The value of the variable state will be set to true in the assignment if x-y is less than a+b, and to false otherwise.

To understand how the expression above is evaluated, take a look back at the precedence table for operators that we introduced in the last chapter. You will see that the comparison operators are all of lower precedence than the arithmetic operators, so arithmetic operations will always be completed before any comparisons are made, unless of course there are parentheses saying otherwise. The expression,

```
x - y == a + b
```

will produce the result true if x-y is equal to a+b, since these arithmetic sub-expressions will be evaluated first, and the values that result will be the operands for the == operator. Of course, it is helpful to put the parentheses in, even though they are not strictly necessary. It leaves no doubt as to what is happening if you write:

```
(x - y) == (a + b)
```

Note that if the left and right operands of a relational operator are of differing types, values will be promoted in the same way as we saw in the last chapter for mixed arithmetic expressions. So if aDouble is of type double, and number is of type int, in the following expression,

```
aDouble < number + 1
```

then the value produced by number + 1 will be calculated as type int, and this value will be promoted to type double before comparing it with the value of aDouble.

The if Statement

The first statement we will look at that can make use of the result of a comparison is the if statement. The if statement, in its simplest configuration, is of the form:

```
if(expression)
  statement;
```

where *expression* can be any expression that produces a value true or false. You can see a graphical representation of this logic in the following diagram:

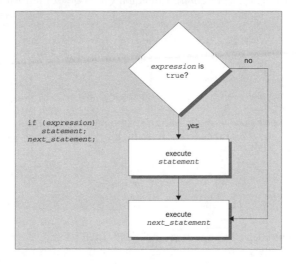

If the value of *expression* is true, the *statement* that follows the if is executed, otherwise it isn't. A practical example of this is as follows:

```
if(number%2 != 0)              // Test if number is odd
   ++number;                   // If so make it even
```

The if tests whether the value of number is odd by comparing the remainder, after dividing by 2, with 0. If the remainder isn't equal to 0, the value of number is odd, so we add 1 to make it even. If the value of number is even, the statement incrementing number will not be executed.

> Note how the statement is indented. This is to show that it is subject to the `if` condition. You should always indent statements in your Java programs as cues to the program structure. We will gather more guidelines on the use of statement indenting as we work with more complicated examples.

You may sometimes see a simple `if` written on a single line. The previous example could have been written:

```
if(number%2 != 0) ++number;  // If number is odd, make it even
```

This is perfectly legal. The compiler ignores excess spaces and newline characters – the semi-colon acts as the delimiter for a statement. Writing an `if` in this way saves a little space, and occasionally it can be an aid to clarity, when you have a succession of such comparisons for instance, but generally it is better to write the action statement on a separate line to the condition being tested.

Statement Blocks

In general, wherever you can have one executable statement in Java, you can replace it with a block of statements enclosed between braces instead. So a statement block between braces can also be nested in another statement block to any depth. This means that we can use a statement block within the basic `if` statement that we just saw. The `if` statement can equally well be of the form:

```
if(expression)
{
  statement 1;
  statement 2;
  ...
  statement n;
}
```

Now if the value of *expression* is `true`, all the statements enclosed in the following block will be executed. Of course, without the braces to enclose the block, the code no longer has a statement block:

```
if(expression)
  statement 1;
  statement 2;
  ...
  statement n;
```

Here, only the first statement, `statement 1`, will be omitted when the `if` expression is `false`; the remaining statements will always be executed regardless of the value of `expression`. You can see from this that indenting is just a visual cue to the logic. It has no effect on how the program code executes. This looks as though the sequence of statements belong to the `if`, but only the first one does because there are no braces. The indenting is just plain wrong here.

> In this book, we will adopt the convention of aligning the bounding braces for a block and indenting all the statements within the block from the braces so that they are easily identified as belonging to the block. There are other conventions that you can use if you prefer, the most important consideration being that you are consistent.

As a practical example of an `if` statement that includes a statement block, we could write:

```
if(number%2 != 0)            // Test if number is odd
{
   // If so make it even and output a message
   ++number;
   System.out.println("Number was forced to be even and is now " + number);
}
```

Now both statements between the braces are executed if the `if` expression is `true`, and neither of them is executed if the `if` expression is `false`.

Statement blocks are more than just a convenient way of grouping statements together – they affect the life and accessibility of variables. We will learn more about statement blocks when we discuss variable scope later in this chapter. In the meantime let's look a little deeper into what we can do with the `if` statement.

The else Clause

We can extend the basic `if` statement by adding an `else` clause. This provides a second choice of statement, or statement block, that is executed when the *expression* in the `if` statement is `false`. You can see the syntax of this clause, and how the program's control flow works, in this diagram:

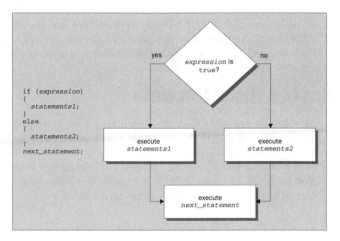

This provides an explicit choice between two courses of action – one for when the `if` expression is `true` and another for when it is `false`.

We can apply this in a console program and try out the `random()` method from the `Math` class at the same time.

Try It Out – if-else

When you have entered the program text, save it in a file called `NumberCheck.java`. Compile it and then run it a few times to see what results you get.

```
public class NumberCheck
{
  public static void main(String[] args)
  {
    int number = 0;
    number = 1+(int)(100*Math.random());   // Get a random integer between 1 & 100
```

```
        if(number%2 == 0)                        // Test if it is even
            System.out.println("You have got an even number, " + number); // It is even
        else
            System.out.println("You have got an odd number, " + number);  // It is odd
    }
}
```

How It Works

We saw the method `random()` in the standard class `Math` in the previous chapter. It returns a random value of type `double` between 0.0 and 1.0, but the result is always less than 1.0, so the largest number you will get is 0.9999... (with the number of recurring digits being limited to the maximum number that the type `double` will allow, of course). Consequently, when we multiply the value returned by 100.0 and convert this value to type `int` with the explicit cast, we discard any fractional part of the number and produce a random integer between 0 and 99. Adding 1 to this will result in a random integer between 1 and 100, which we store in the variable `number`. We then generate the program output in the `if` statement. If the value of `number` is even, the first `println()` call is executed, otherwise the second `println()` call in the `else` clause is executed.

Note the use of indentation here. It is evident that `main()` is within the class definition, and the code for `main()` is clearly distinguished. You can also see immediately which statement is executed when the `if` expression is `true`, and which applies when it is `false`.

Nested if Statements

The statement that is executed when an `if` expression is `true` can be another `if`, as can the statement in an `else` clause. This will enable you to express such convoluted logic as "if my bank balance is healthy then I will buy the car if I have my check book with me, else I will buy the car if I can get a loan from the bank". An `if` statement that is nested inside another can also itself contain a nested `if`. You can continue nesting `if`s one inside the other like this for as long as you still know what you are doing – or even beyond if you enjoy confusion.

To illustrate the nested `if` statement, we can modify the `if` from the previous example:

```
if(number%2 == 0)                 // Test if it is even
{
    if(number < 50)               // Output a message if number is < 50
        System.out.println("You have got an even number < 50, " + number);
}
else
    System.out.println("You have got an odd number, " + number); // It is odd
```

Now the message for an even value is only displayed if the value of `number` is also less than 50.

The braces around the nested `if` are necessary here because of the `else` clause. The braces constrain the nested `if` in the sense that if it had an `else` clause, it would have to appear between the braces enclosing the nested `if`. If the braces were not there, the program would still compile and run but the logic would be different. Let's see how.

With nested `if`s, the question of to which `if` statement a particular `else` clause belongs often arises. If we remove the braces from the code above, we have:

```
if(number%2 == 0)                     // Test if it is even
  if(number < 50 )                    // Output a message if number is < 50
    System.out.println("You have got an even number < 50, " + number);
else
    System.out.println("You have got an odd number, " + number); // It is odd
```

This has substantially changed the logic from what we had before. The `else` clause now belongs to the nested `if` that tests whether `number` is less than 50, so the second `println()` call is only executed for **even** numbers that are greater than or equal to 50. This is clearly not what we wanted since it makes nonsense of the output in this case, but it does illustrate the rule for connecting `else`s to `if`s, which is:

> An `else` **always belongs to the nearest preceding** `if` **that is not in a separate block, and is not already spoken for by another** `else`.

You need to take care that the indenting of statements with nested `if`s is correct. It is easy to convince yourself that the logic is as indicated by the indentation, even when this is completely wrong.

Let's try the `if-else` combination in another program:

Try It Out – Deciphering Characters the Hard Way

Create the class `LetterCheck`, and code its `main()` method as follows.

```java
public class LetterCheck
{
   public static void main(String[] args)
   {
     char symbol = 'A';
     symbol = (char)(128.0*Math.random());        // Generate a random character

     if(symbol >= 'A')                             // Is it A or greater?
     {
        if(symbol <= 'Z')                          // yes, and is it Z or less?
           // Then it is a capital letter
           System.out.println("You have the capital letter " + symbol);
        else                                       // It is not Z or less
           if(symbol >= 'a')                       // So is it a or greater?
              if(symbol <= 'z')                    // Yes, so is it z or less?
                 // Then it is a small letter
                 System.out.println("You have the small letter " + symbol);
              else                                 // It is not less than z
                 System.out.println(
                          "The code is greater than a but it's not a letter");
           else
              System.out.println(
                          "The code is less than a and it's not a letter");
     }
     else
        System.out.println("The code is less than A so it's not a letter");
   }
}
```

How It Works

This program figures out whether the character stored in the variable `symbol` is an uppercase letter, a lower case letter or some other character. The program first generates a random character with a numeric code between 0 and 127, which corresponds to the characters in the basic 7-bit ASCII (ISO 646) character set. You will find the ASCII character codes in Appendix D. The Unicode coding for the ASCII characters is numerically the same as the ASCII code values. Within this character set, the letters 'A' to 'Z' are represented by a contiguous group of ASCII codes with decimal values from 65 to 90. The lowercase letters are represented by another contiguous group with ASCII code values that have decimal values from 97 to 122. So to convert any capital letter to a lowercase letter, you just need to add 32 to the character code.

The `if` statements are a bit convoluted so let's look at a diagram of the logic.

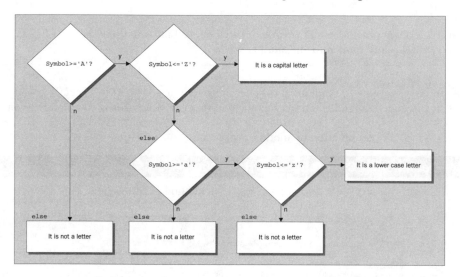

We have four `if` statements altogether. The first `if` tests whether `symbol` is 'A' or greater. If it is, it could be a capital letter, a small letter, or possibly something else. But if it isn't, it is not a letter at all, so the `else` for this `if` statement (towards the end of the program) produces a message to that effect.

The nested `if` statement, which is executed if `symbol` is 'A' or greater, tests whether it is 'Z' or less. If it is, then `symbol` definitely contains a capital letter and the appropriate message is displayed. If it isn't then it may be a small letter, so another `if` statement is nested within the `else` clause of the first nested `if`, to test for this possibility.

The `if` statement in the `else` clause tests for `symbol` being greater than 'a'. If it isn't, we know that `symbol` is not a letter and a message is displayed. If it is, another `if` checks whether `symbol` is 'z' or less. If it is we have a small letter, and if not we don't have a letter at all.

You will have to run the example a few times to get all the possible messages to come up. They all will – eventually.

Having carefully crafted our convoluted and cumbersome condition checking, now's the time to reveal that there is a much easier way to achieve the same result.

Logical Operators

The tests we have put in the if expressions have been relatively simple so far, except perhaps for the last one. Real life is typically more complicated. You will often want to combine a number of conditions so that you execute a particular course, for example, if they are all true simultaneously. You can ride the roller coaster if you are over 12 years old, over four feet tall *and* less than six feet six. Failure on any count and it's no go. Sometimes, though, you may need to test for any one of a number of conditions being true, for example, you get a lower price entry ticket if you are under 16, or over 65.

You can deal with both of these cases, and more, using **logical operators** to combine several expressions that have a value true or false. Because they operate on boolean values they are also referred to as **boolean operators**. There are five logical operators that operate on boolean values:

Symbol	Long name
&	logical AND
&&	conditional AND
|	logical OR
||	conditional OR
!	logical negation (NOT)

These are very simple, the only point of potential confusion being the fact that we have the choice of two operators for each of AND and OR. The extra operators are the bitwise & and | from the previous chapter that you can also apply to boolean values where they have an effect that is subtly different from && and ||. We'll first consider what each of these are used for in general terms, then we'll look at how we can use them in an example.

Boolean AND Operations

You can use either AND operator, && or &, where you have two logical expressions that must both be true for the result to be true – that is, you want to be rich *and* healthy. Either operator will produce the same result from the logical expression. We will come back to how they are different in a moment. First, let's explore how they are used. All of the following discussion applies equally well to & as well as &&.

Let's see how logical operators can simplify the last example. You could use the && operator if you were testing a variable of type char to determine whether it contained an upper case letter or not. The value being tested must be both greater than or equal to 'A' AND less than or equal to 'Z'. Both conditions must be true for the value to be a capital letter. Taking the example from our previous program, with a value stored in a char variable symbol, we could implement the test for an upper case letter in a single if by using the && operator:

```
if(symbol >= 'A' && symbol <= 'Z')
    System.out.println("You have the capital letter " + symbol);
```

If you take a look at the precedence table back in Chapter 2, you will see that the relational operators will be executed before the && operator, so no parentheses are necessary. Here, the output statement will be executed only if both of the conditions combined by the operator && are true. However, as we have said before, it is a good idea to add parentheses if they make the code easier to read. It also helps to avoid mistakes.

In fact, the result of an && operation is very simple. It is true only if both operands are true, otherwise the result is false.

We can now rewrite the set of ifs from the last example.

Try It Out – Deciphering Characters the Easy Way

Replace the outer if-else loop and its contents in LetterCheck.java with the following:

```
if(symbol >= 'A' && symbol <= 'Z')          // Is it a capital letter
   System.out.println("You have the capital letter " + symbol);
else
   if(symbol >= 'a' && symbol <= 'z')       // or is it a small letter?
      System.out.println("You have the small letter " + symbol);
   else                                     // It is not less than z
      System.out.println("The code is not a letter");
```

How It Works

Using the && operator has condensed the example down quite a bit. We now can do the job with two ifs, and it's certainly easier to follow what's happening.

You might want to note that when the statement in an else clause is another if, the if is sometimes written on the same line as the else, as in:

```
if(symbol >= 'A' && symbol <= 'Z')          // Is it a capital letter
   System.out.println("You have the capital letter " + symbol);
else if(symbol >= 'a' && symbol <= 'z')     // or is it a small letter?
   System.out.println("You have the small letter " + symbol);
else                                        // It is not less than z
   System.out.println("The code is not a letter");
```

I think the original is clearer, so I prefer not to do this.

&& versus &

So what distinguishes && from & ? The difference between them is that the conditional && will not bother to evaluate the right hand operand if the left hand operand is false, since the result is already determined in this case to be false. This can make the code a bit faster when the left hand operand is false.

For example, consider the following statements:

```
int number = 50;
if(number<40 && (3*number - 27)>100)
   System.out.println("number = " + number);
```

Here the expression `(3*number - 27)>100` will never be executed since the expression `number<40` is always `false`. On the other hand, if you write the statements as,

```
int number = 50;
if(number<40 & (3*number - 27)>100)
    System.out.println("number = " + number);
```

the effect is different. The whole logical expression is always evaluated, so even though the left hand operand of the & operator is `false` and the result is a forgone conclusion once that is known, the right hand operand (`(3*number - 27)>100`) will still be evaluated. So, we can just use && all the time to make our programs a bit faster and forget about &, right? Wrong – it all depends on what you are doing. Most of the time you can use &&, but there are occasions when you will want to be sure that the right hand operand is evaluated – and equally, there are instances where you want to be certain the right hand operand won't be evaluated if the left operand is `false`.

The first situation can arise for instance when the right hand expression involves modifying a variable – and you want the variable to be modified in any event. An example of a statement like this is:

```
if(++value%2 == 0 & ++count < limit)
    // Do something
```

Here, the variable `count` will be incremented in any event. If you use && instead of &, `count` will only be incremented if the left operand of the AND operator is `true`. You get a different result depending on which operator is used.

We can illustrate the second situation with the following statement:

```
if(count > 0 && total/count > 5)
    // Do something...
```

In this case the right operand for the && operation will only be executed if the left operand is true – that is, when count is positive. Clearly, if we were to use & here, and `count` happened to be zero, we will be attempting to divide the value of `total` by 0, which in the absence of code to prevent it, will terminate the program.

Boolean OR Operations

The OR operators, | and ||, apply when you want a `true` result if either or both of the operands are `true`. The conditional OR, ||, has a similar effect to the conditional AND, in that it omits the evaluation of the right hand operand when the left hand operand is `true`. Obviously if the left operand is `true`, the result will be true regardless of whether the right operand is `true` or `false`.

Let's take an example. A reduced entry ticket price is issued to under 16 year olds and to those aged 65 or over; this could be tested using the following `if`:

```
if(age < 16 || age>= 65)
    ticketPrice *= 0.9;        // Reduce ticket price by 10%
```

The effect here is to reduce `ticketPrice` by ten percent if either condition is `true`. Clearly in this case both conditions cannot be `true`.

With an | or an || operation, you only get a `false` result if both operands are `false`. If either or both operands are `true`, the result is `true`.

Boolean NOT Operations

The third type of logical operator, !, takes one Boolean operand and inverts its value. So if the value of a `boolean` variable, `state`, is `true`, then the expression `!state` has the value `false`, and if it is `false` then `!state` becomes `true`. To see how the operator is used with an expression, we could rewrite the code fragment we used to provide discounted ticket price as:

```
if(!(age >= 16 && age < 65) )
   ticketPrice *= 0.9;          // Reduce ticket price by 10%
```

The expression `(age >= 16 && age < 65)` is `true` if age is from 16 to 64. People of this age do not qualify for the discount, so the discount should only be applied when this expression is `false`. Applying the ! operator to the result of the expression does what we want.

We could also apply the ! operator in an expression that was a favorite of Charles Dickens:

```
!(Income>Expenditure)
```

If this expression is `true`, the result is misery, at least as soon as the bank starts bouncing your checks.

Of course, you can use any of the logical operators in combination if necessary. If the theme park decides to give a discount on the price of entry to anyone who is under 12 years old and under 48 inches tall, or someone who is over 65 and over 72 inches tall, you could apply the discount with the test:

```
if((age < 12 && height < 48) || (age > 65 && height > 72))
   ticketPrice *= 0.8;              // 20% discount on the ticket price
```

The parentheses are not strictly necessary here, as && has a higher precedence than ||, but adding the parentheses makes it clearer how the comparisons combine and makes it a little more readable.

> Don't confuse the bitwise operators &, | and !, with the logical operators that look the same. Which type of operator you are using in any particular instance is determined by the type of the operands with which you use it. The bitwise operators apply to integer types and produce an integer result. The logical operators apply to operands that have `boolean` values and produce a result of type `boolean` – `true` or `false`. You can use both bitwise and logical operators in an expression if it is convenient to do so.

Character Testing Using Standard Library Methods

While testing characters using logical operators is a useful way of demonstrating how these operators work, in practice there is an easier way. The standard Java packages provide a range of standard methods to do the sort of testing for particular sets of characters such as letters or digits that we have been doing with `if` statements. They are all available within the class `Character` which is automatically available in your programs. For example, we could have written the `if` statement in our `LetterCheck` program as shown in the following example.

Try It Out – Deciphering Characters Trivially

Replace the code body of the `LetterCheck` class with the following code:

```
if(Character.isUpperCase(symbol))
    System.out.println("You have the capital letter " + symbol);
else
    if(Character.isLowerCase(symbol))
        System.out.println("You have the small letter " + symbol);
    else
        System.out.println("The code is not a letter");
```

How It Works

The `isUpperCase()` method returns `true` if the `char` value passed to it is upper case, and `false` if it is not. Similarly, the `isLowerCase()` method returns `true` if the `char` value passed to it is lower case.

The following table shows some of the other methods included in the class `Character` which you may find useful for testing characters. In each case the argument to be tested is of type `char`, and is placed between the parentheses following the method name:

Method	Description
isDigit()	Returns the value `true` if the argument is a digit (0 to 9) and `false` otherwise.
isLetter()	Returns the value `true` if the argument is a letter, and `false` otherwise.
isLetterOrDigit()	Returns the value `true` if the argument is a letter or a digit, and `false` otherwise.
isWhitespace()	Returns the value `true` if the argument is whitespace, which is any one of the characters: space (' '), tab ('\t'), newline ('\n'), carriage return ('\r'), form feed ('\f') The method returns `false` otherwise.

You will find information on other methods in the class `Character` in the documentation for the class that is part of the Java Development Kit.

The Conditional Operator

The **conditional operator** is sometimes called a **ternary operator** because it involves three operands. It is best understood by looking at an example. Suppose we have two variables of type int, yourAge and myAge, and we want to assign the greater of the values stored in yourAge and myAge to a third variable also of type int, older. We can do this with the statement:

```
older = yourAge > myAge ? yourAge : myAge;
```

The conditional operator has a logical expression as its first argument, in this case yourAge>myAge. If this expression is true, the operand which follows the ? symbol – in this case yourAge – is selected as the value resulting from the operation. If the expression yourAge>myAge is false, the operand which comes after the colon – in this case myAge – is selected as the value. Thus, the result of this conditional expression is yourAge, if yourAge is greater than myAge, and myAge otherwise. This value is then stored in the variable, older. The use of the conditional operator in this assignment statement is equivalent to the if statement:

```
if(yourAge > myAge)
   older = yourAge;
else
   older = myAge;
```

Remember, though, the conditional operator is an operator and not a statement, so it can be used in a more complex expression involving other operators.

The conditional operator can be written generally as:

```
logical_expression ? expression1 : expression2
```

If the *logical_expression* evaluates as true, the result of the operation is the value of *expression1*, and if *logical_expression* evaluates to false, the result is the value of *expression2*. Note that if expression1 is evaluated because *logical_expression* is true, then *expression2* will not be, and vice versa.

There are lots of circumstances where the conditional operator can be used, and one common application of it is to control output, depending on the result of an expression or the value of a variable. You can vary a message by selecting one text string or another depending on the condition specified.

Try It Out – Conditional Plurals

Type in the following code which will add the correct ending to 'hat' depending on how many hats you have:

```
public class ConditionalOp
{
   public static void main(String[] args)
   {
      int nHats = 1;        // Number of hats
      System.out.println("I have " + nHats + " hat" + (nHats == 1 ? "." : "s."));

      nHats++;               // Increment number of hats
      System.out.println("I have " + nHats + " hat" + (nHats == 1 ? "." : "s."));
   }
}
```

The output from this program will be:

```
I have 1 hat.
I have 2 hats.
```

How It Works

The result of the conditional operator is a string containing just a period when the value of nHats is 1, and a string containing an s followed by a period in all other cases. The effect of this is to cause the output statement to automatically adjust the output between singular and plural. You can use the same technique in other situations such as where you need to choose "he" or "she" for example, as long as you are able to specify a logical expression to differentiate the situation where you should use one rather than the other.

The switch Statement

The switch statement enables you to select from multiple choices based on a set of fixed values for a given expression. The expression must produce a result of type char, byte, short or int, but not long, otherwise the statement will not compile. In normal use it operates rather like a rotary switch in that you can select one of a fixed number of choices. For example, on some makes of washing machine you choose between the various possible machine settings in this way, with positions for cotton, wool, synthetic fiber and so on, which you select by turning the knob to point to the option that you want.

A switch statement reflecting this logic would be:

```
switch(wash)
{
  case 1:                       // wash is 1 for Cotton
    System.out.println("Cotton selected");
    break;
  case 2:                       // wash is 2 for Linen
    System.out.println("Linen selected");
    break;
  case 3:                       // wash is 3 for Wool
    System.out.println("Wool selected");
    break;
  default:                      // Not a valid value for wash
    System.out.println("Selection error");
    break;
}
```

In the switch statement, the selection is determined by the value of an expression that you specify, which is enclosed between the parentheses after the keyword switch. In this case it's the variable wash which would need to be previously declared as of type char, byte, short or int. You define the possible switch positions by one or more **case values**, also called **case labels**, that are defined using the keyword case. All the case labels for a switch are enclosed between the braces for the switch statement and they can appear in any order. We have used three case values in the example above. A particular case value is selected if the value of the switch expression is the same as that of the particular case value.

When a particular case is selected, the statements which follow that case label are executed. So if `wash` has the value 2, the statements that follow:

```
case 2:                               // wash is 2 for Linen
```

are executed. In this case, these are:

```
System.out.println("Linen selected");
break;
```

When a `break` statement is executed here, it causes execution to continue with the statement following the closing brace for the `switch`. The break is not mandatory, but if you don't put a `break` statement at the end of the statements for a case, the statements for the next case in sequence will be executed as well, through to whenever another `break` is found or the end of the switch block is reached. This is not usually what you want. The `break` after the `default` statements in our example is not strictly necessary, but it does protect against the situation when you might add another case label at the end of the `switch` statement block, and overlook the need for the `break` at the end of the last case.

There is a case label for each handled choice in the `switch`, and they must all be unique. The `default` case we have in the example above is, in general, optional. It is selected when the value of the expression for the `switch` does not correspond with any of the case values that have been defined. If you don't specify a `default` case and the value of the `switch` expression does not match any of the case labels, execution continues at the statement following the closing brace of the `switch` statement.

We can illustrate the logic of the general `switch` statement in a flow chart.

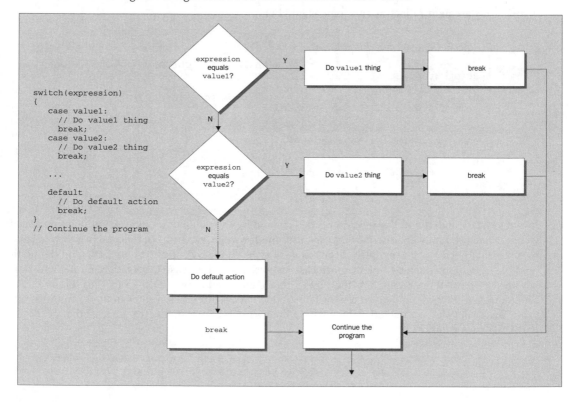

Each `case` value is notionally compared with the value of an expression. If one matches then the code for that case is executed and the `break` branches to the first statement after the switch. As we said earlier, if you don't include the `break` statements, the logic is quite different, as shown below.

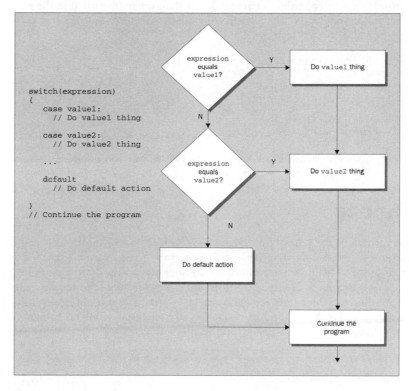

```
switch(expression)
{
    case value1:
        // Do value1 thing

    case value2:
        // Do value2 thing

    ...

    default
        // Do default action

}
// Continue the program
```

Now when a case label value is equal to the `switch` expression, the code for that case is executed, and we fall through to execute all the other cases that follow, including that for the default case, if that follows. This is not usually what you want, so make sure you don't forget the `break` statements.

You can arrange to execute the same statements for several different case labels, as in the following `switch` statement:

```
char yesNo = 'N';
// more program logic…

switch(yesNo)
{
  case 'n':
  case 'N':
      System.out.println("No selected");
      break;
  case 'y':
  case 'Y':
      System.out.println("Yes selected");
      break;
}
```

Here the variable `yesNo` receives a character from the keyboard somehow. You want a different action depending on whether the user enters `'Y'` or `'N'` but you want to be able to accept either upper or lower case entries. This `switch` does just this by putting the case labels together. Note that there is no default case here. If `yesNo` contains a character other than those identified in the case statements, the switch statement has no effect. You might add a default case in this kind of situation to output a message to indicate that the value in `yesNo` is not valid.

Of course, you could also implement this logic using `if` statements:

```
if(yesNo=='n' || yesNo=='N')
   System.out.println("No selected");
else
   if(yesNo=='y' || yesNo=='Y')
     System.out.println("Yes selected");
```

I prefer the `switch` statement as I think it's easier to follow, but you decide for yourself.

Variable Scope

The **scope** of a variable is the part of the program over which the variable name can be referenced – in other words, where you can use the variable in the program. Every variable that we have declared so far in program examples has been defined within the context of a method, the method `main()`. Variables that are declared within a method are called **local variables**, as they are only accessible within the confines of the method in which they are declared. However, they are not necessarily accessible everywhere in the code for the method in which they are declared. Look at the example in the illustration below that shows nested blocks inside a method.

```
{
    int a = 1;                          // Declare and define a

    // Reference to a is OK here
    // Reference to b here is an error
    {

        // Reference to a here is OK
        // Reference to b here is still an error

        int b = 2;                      // Declare and define b

        // References to a and b are OK here - b exists now

    }
    // Reference to b is an error here - it doesn't exist
    // Reference to a is still OK though
}
```

A variable does not exist before its declaration, you can only refer to it after it has been declared. It continues to exist until the end of the block in which it is defined, and that includes any blocks nested within the block containing its declaration. The variable b only exists within the inner block. After the brace at the end of the inner block, b no longer exists so you can't refer to it. The variable a is still around though since it survives until the last brace.

So, the rule for accessibility of local variables is simple. They are only accessible from the point in the program where they are declared to the end of the block that contains the declaration. At the end of the block in which they are declared they cease to exist. We can demonstrate this with an example:

Try It Out – Scoping

We will define our method `main()` to illustrate how variable scope works. First we declare and initialize the variable `outer`, then start an inner block. Within that block, we will define another variable `inner`. When the block closes we have to redeclare `inner` to use it once more.

```
public class Scope
{
  public static void main(String[] args)
  {
    int outer = 1;                              // Exists throughout the method

    {
      // You cannot refer to a variable before its declaration
      // System.out.println("inner = " + inner);  // Uncomment this for an error

      int inner = 2;
      System.out.println("inner = " + inner);      // Now it is OK
      System.out.println("outer = " + outer);      // and outer is still here

      // All variables defined in the enclosing outer block still exist,
      // so you cannot redefine them here
      // int outer = 5;                             // Uncomment this for an error
    }

    // Any variables declared in the previous inner block no longer exist
    // so you cannot refer to them
    // System.out.println("inner = " + inner);      // Uncomment this for an error

    // The previous variable, inner, does not exist so you can define a new one
    int inner = 3;
    System.out.println("inner = " + inner);          // ... and output its value
    System.out.println("outer = " + outer);          // outer is still around
  }
}
```

As it stands, this program will produce the output:

```
inner = 2
outer = 1
inner = 3
outer = 1
```

If you uncomment any or all of the three statements as suggested, it won't compile:

```
C:\>javac Scope.java
Scope.java:11: Undefined variable: inner
        System.out.println("inner = " + inner);   // Uncomment this for an error
                                        ^
1 error
```

```
C:\>javac Scope.java
Scope.java:19: Variable 'outer' is already defined in this method.
        int outer = 5;                          // Uncomment this for an error
            ^
1 error

C:\>javac Scope.java
Scope.java:23: Undefined variable: inner
      System.out.println("inner = " + inner);    // Uncomment this for an error
                                      ^
1 error
```

How It Works

The method `main()` in this program has one block nested inside the block containing the code for the method. The variable `outer` is defined right at the start, so you can refer to this anywhere within the method `main()`, including inside any nested blocks. You are not allowed to re-declare a variable, so the commented statement that re-declares `outer` within the inner block will cause a compiler error, if you remove the double slash at the beginning of the line.

The variable `inner` is defined inside the nested block with the initial value 2, and you can refer to it anywhere from its declaration to the end of the inner block. After the closing brace of the inner block, the variable `inner` no longer exists, so the commented output statement that refers to `inner` is illegal. However, since the variable `inner` has expired, we can declare another one with the same name and with the initial value 3.

Note that all this is just to demonstrate the lifetime of local variables. It is not good practice to redefine variables that have expired, because of the potential for confusion. Also, although we have just used variables of type `int` in the example above, scoping rules apply to variables of any type.

> There are other variables called class variables which have much longer lifetimes when they are declared in a particular way. The variables `PI` and `E` in the standard library class `Math` are examples of these. They hang around as long as your program is executing. There are also variables that form part of a class object called instance variables. We will learn more about these in Chapter 5.

Loops

A loop allows you to execute a statement or block of statements repeatedly. The need to repeat a block of code arises in almost every program. If you did the first exercise at the end of the last chapter, based on what you had learned up to that point you would have come up with a program along the lines of:

```
public class TryExample1_1
{
  public static void main(String[] args)
  {
    byte value = 1;
    value *= 2;
    System.out.println("Value is now "+value);
    value *= 2;
    System.out.println("Value is now "+value);
    value *= 2;
```

```
      System.out.println("Value is now "+value);
      value *= 2;
      System.out.println("Value is now "+value);
      value *= 2;
      System.out.println("Value is now "+value);
      value *= 2;
      System.out.println("Value is now "+value);
      value *= 2;
      System.out.println("Value is now "+value);
      value *= 2;
      System.out.println("Value is now "+value);
      value *= 2;
      System.out.println("Value is now "+value);
    }
  }
```

The same pair of statements has been entered eight times. This is a rather tedious way of doing things. If the program for the company payroll had to include separate statements for each employee, it would never get written. A loop removes this sort of the difficulty. We could write the method `main()` to do the same as the code above as:

```
  public static void main(String[] args)
  {
    byte value = 1;
    for (int i=0;  i<8 ;  i++)
    {
      value *= 2;
      System.out.println("Value is now " + value);
    }
  }
```

The `for` loop statement causes the statements in the following block to be repeated eight times. The number of times it is to be repeated is determined by the stuff between parentheses following the keyword `for` – we will see how in a moment. The point is you could, in theory, repeat the same block of statements as many times as you want – a thousand or a million – it is just as easy and it doesn't require any more lines of code. The primary purpose of the `for` loop is to execute a block of statements a given number of times.

There are three kinds of loop statements you can use, so let's look at these in general terms first:

1. The `for` loop:

```
for(initialization_expression ; loop_condition ; increment_expression)
{
  // statements
}
```

The control of the `for` loop appears in parentheses following the keyword `for`. It has three parts separated by semi-colons.

The first part, the `initialization_expression`, is executed before execution of the loop starts. This is typically used to initialize a counter for the number of loop iterations – for example i=0. With a loop controlled by a counter, you can count up or down using an integer or a floating point variable.

Execution of the loop continues as long as the condition you have specified in the second part, the `loop_condition`, is `true`. This expression is checked at the beginning of each loop iteration, and when it is `false`, execution continues with the statement following the loop block. A simple example of what the `loop_condition` expression might be is i<10, so the loop would continue in this case as long as the variable i has a value less than 10.

The third part of the control information between the parentheses, the *increment_expression*, is usually used to increment the loop counter. This is executed at the end of each loop iteration. This could be i++, which would increment the loop counter, i, by one. Of course, you might want to increment the loop counter in steps other than 1. For instance, you might write i += 2 as the increment_expression to go in steps of 2, or even something more complicated such as i = 2*i+1.

2. The while loop:

```
while(expression)
{
   // statements
}
```

This loop executes as long as the given logical expression between parentheses is true. When expression is false, execution continues with the statement following the loop block. The expression is tested at the beginning of the loop, so if it is initially false, the loop statement block will not be executed at all. An example of a while loop condition might be, yesNo=='Y' || yesNo=='y'. This expression would be true if the variable yesNo contained 'y' or 'Y', so yesNo might hold a character entered from the keyboard in this instance.

3. The do while loop

```
do
{
   // statements
} while (expression);
```

This loop is similar to the while loop, except that the expression controlling the loop is tested at the end of the loop block. This means that the loop block is executed at least once, even if the expression is always false.

We can contrast the basic logic of the three kinds of loop in a diagram.

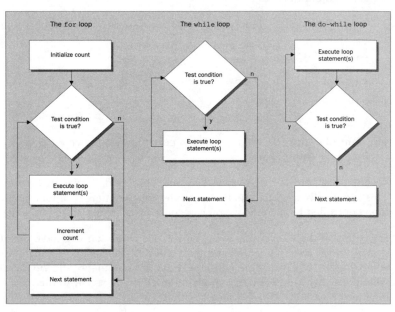

This shows quite clearly that the only difference between the `while` loop and the `do while` loop is where the test is carried out.

Let's explore each of these in turn and see how they work in a practical context.

Try It Out – The for Loop

Let's start with a very simple example. Suppose you want to calculate the sum of the integers from 1 to a given value. You can do this using the `for` loop as in the following example:

```
public class ForLoop
{
   public static void main(String[] args)
   {
      int limit = 20;                        // Sum from 1 to this value
      int sum = 0;                           // Accumulate sum in this variable

      // Loop from 1 to the value of limit, adding 1 each cycle
      for(int i = 1; i <= limit; i++)
         sum += i;                           // Add the current value of i to sum
      System.out.println("sum = " + sum);
   }
}
```

This program will produce the output,

```
sum = 210
```

but you can try it out with different values for `limit`.

How It Works

All the work is done in the `for` loop. The loop counter is `i`, and this is declared and initialized within the `for` loop statement. The syntax of the `for` loop is shown in the following diagram:

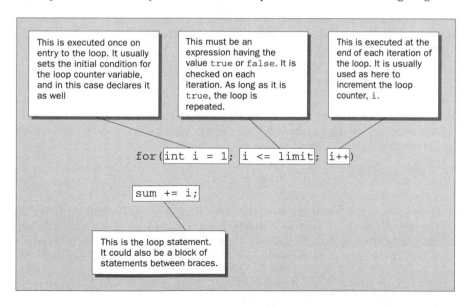

This is executed once on entry to the loop. It usually sets the initial condition for the loop counter variable, and in this case declares it as well

This must be an expression having the value `true` or `false`. It is checked on each iteration. As long as it is `true`, the loop is repeated.

This is executed at the end of each iteration of the loop. It is usually used as here to increment the loop counter, `i`.

`for(int i = 1; i <= limit; i++)`

`sum += i;`

This is the loop statement. It could also be a block of statements between braces.

As you see, there are three elements that control the operation of a `for` loop, and they appear between the parentheses that follow the keyword `for`. In sequence their purpose is to:

- ❑ Set the initial conditions for the loop, particularly the loop counter
- ❑ Specify the condition for the loop to continue
- ❑ Increment the loop counter

They are always separated by semi-colons.

The first control element is executed when the loop is first entered. Here we declare and initialize the loop counter `i`. Because it is declared within the loop, it will not exist outside it. If you try to output the value of `i` after the loop with a statement such as,

```
System.out.println("Final value of i = " + i);  // Will not work outside the loop
```

you will find that the program will not compile. If you need to initialize and/or declare other variables for the loop, you can do it here by separating the declarations by commas. For example, we could write:

```
for(int i = 1, j = 0; i <= limit; i++)
    sum += i * j++;                        // Add the current value of i*j to sum
```

We initialize an additional variable `j`, and, to make the loop vaguely sensible, we have modified the value to add the sum to `i*j++` which is the equivalent of `i*(i-1)` in this case. Note that `j` will be incremented after the product `i*j` has been calculated. You could declare other variables here, but note that it would not make sense to declare `sum` at this point. If you can't figure out why, delete the original declaration of `sum` and, put it in the `for` loop instead to see what happens. The program won't compile – right? After the loop ends the variable `sum` no longer exists, so you can't reference it.

The second control element in a `for` loop is a logical expression which is checked at the beginning of each iteration through the loop. If the expression is `true`, the loop continues, and as soon as it is `false` the loop is finished. In our program the loop ends when `i` is greater than the value of `limit`.

The third control element in a `for` loop typically increments the loop variable, as we have in our example. You can also put multiple expressions here too, so we could rewrite the above code fragment, which added `j` to the loop, as:

```
for(int i = 1, j = 0; i <= limit; i++, j++)
    sum+=i*j;                     // Add the current value of i*j to sum
```

Again, there can be several expressions here, and they do not need to relate directly to the control of the loop. We could even rewrite the original loop for summing integers so that the summation occurs in the loop control element:

```
for(int i = 1; i <= limit; sum += i, i++)
    ;
```

Now the loop statement is empty – you still need the semi-colon to terminate it though. It doesn't really improve things though and there are hazards in writing the loop this way. If you forget the semicolon the next statement will be used as the loop statement, which is likely to cause chaos. Another potential problem arises if you happen to reverse the sequence of adding to `sum` and incrementing `i`, as follows:

```
for(int i = 1; i <= limit; i++, sum += i)   // Wrong!!!
    ;
```

Now you will generate the wrong answer. This is because the expression i++ will be executed before sum += i, so the wrong value of i is used.

You can omit any or all of the elements that control the for loop, but you must include the semi-colons. It is up to you to make sure that the loop does what you want. We could write the loop in our program as:

```
for(int i = 1; i <= limit; )
   sum += i++;                          // Add the current value of i to sum
```

We have simply transferred the incrementing of i from the for loop control to the loop statement. The for loop works just as before. However, this is not a good way to write the loop, as it makes it much less obvious how the loop counter is incremented.

Counting Using Floating Point Values

You can use a floating point variable as the loop counter if you need to. This may be needed when you are calculating the value of a function for a range of fractional values. Suppose you wanted to calculate the area of a circle with values for the radius from 1 to 2 in steps of 0.2. You could write this as:

```
for(double radius = 1.0; radius <= 2.0; radius += 0.2)
{
   System.out.println("radius = " + radius + " area = " + Math.PI*radius*radius);
}
```

This will produce the output:

```
radius = 1.0 area = 3.141592653589793
radius = 1.2 area = 4.523893421169302
radius = 1.4 area = 6.157521601035994
radius = 1.5999999999999999 area = 8.04247719318987
radius = 1.7999999999999998 area = 10.178760197630927
radius = 1.9999999999999998 area = 12.566370614359169
```

The area has been calculated using the formula πr^2 with the standard value PI defined in the Math class, which is 3.14159265358979323846. Although we intended the values of radius to increment from 1.0 to 2.0 in steps of 0.2, they don't quite make it. The value of radius is never exactly 2.0 or any of the other intermediate values because 0.2 cannot be represented exactly as a binary floating point value. If you doubt this, and you are prepared to deal with an infinite loop, change the loop to:

```
// BE WARNED - THIS LOOP DOES NOT END
for(double radius = 1.0; radius != 2.0; radius += 0.2)
{
   System.out.println("radius = " + radius + " area = " + Math.PI*radius*radius);
}
```

If the value of radius reaches 2.0, the condition radius ! =2.0 will be false and the loop will end, but unfortunately it doesn't. Its last value before 2 will be approximately 1.999… and the next value will be something like 2.1999… and so it will never be 2.0. From this we can deduce a golden rule:

Never use tests that depend on an exact value for a floating point variable to control a loop.

Try It Out – The while loop

We can write the program for summing integers again using the `while` loop, so you can see how the loop mechanism differs from the `for` loop.

```
public class WhileLoop
{
  public static void main(String[] args)
  {
    int limit = 20;                      // Sum from 1 to this value
    int sum = 0;                         // Accumulate sum in this variable
    int i = 1;                           // Loop counter

    // Loop from 1 to the value of limit, adding 1 each cycle
    while(i <= limit)
      sum += i++;                        // Add the current value of i to sum
    System.out.println("sum = " + sum);
  }
}
```

You should get the result:

```
sum = 210
```

How It Works

The `while` loop is controlled wholly by the logical expression that appears between the parentheses that follow the keyword `while`. The loop continues as long as this expression has the value `true`, and how it ever manages to arrive at the value `false` to end the loop is up to you. You need to be sure that the statements within the loop will eventually result in this expression being `false`. Otherwise you have an infinite loop.

How the loop ends in our example is clear. We have a simple count as before, and we increment `i` in the loop statement that accumulates the sum of the integers. Sooner or later `i` will exceed the value of `limit` and the `while` loop will end.

You don't always need to use the testing of a count limit as the loop condition. You can use any logical condition you want.

And last, but not least, we have the `do while` loop.

Try It Out – The do while Loop

As we said at the beginning of this topic, the `do while` loop is much the same as the `while` loop, except for the fact that the continuation condition is checked at the end of the loop. We can write an integer summing program with this kind of loop too:

```
public class DoWhileLoop
{
  public static void main(String[] args)
  {
    int limit = 20;                      // Sum from 1 to this value
    int sum = 0;                         // Accumulate sum in this variable
    int i = 1;                           // Loop counter
```

```
   // Loop from 1 to the value of limit, adding 1 each cycle
   do
   {
     sum += i;                       // Add the current value of i to sum
     i++;
   }
   while(i <= limit);

   System.out.println("sum = " + sum);
 }
}
```

How It Works

The statements within the loop are always executed at least once because the condition determining whether the loop should continue is tested at the end of each iteration. Within the loop we add the value of i to sum, and then increment it. When i exceeds the value of limit, the loop ends, at which point sum will contain the sum of all the integers from 1 to limit.

The loop statement here has braces around the block of code that is within the loop. We could rewrite the loop so that only one statement was within the loop, in which case the braces are not required. For instance:

```
   do
     sum += i;                       // Add the current value of i to sum
   while(++i <= limit);
```

Of course, you could still put the braces in if you want. There are often several ways of writing the code to produce a given result, and this is true here – we could also move the incrementing of the variable i back inside the loop and write it as:

```
   do
     sum += i++;                     // Add the current value of i to sum
   while(i <= limit);
```

Note the semi-colon after the while condition is present in each version of the loop. This is part of the loop statement so you must not forget to put it in. The primary reason for using this loop over the while loop would be if you want to be sure that the loop code always executes at least once.

Nested Loops

You can nest loops of any kind one inside another to any depth. Let's look at an example where we can use nested loops.

A **factorial** of an integer, *n*, is the product of all the integers from 1 to *n*. It is written as *n*!. It may seem a little strange if you haven't come across it before, but it can be a very useful value. For instance, *n*! is the number of ways you can arrange *n* different things in sequence, so a deck of cards can be arranged in 52! different sequences. Let's try calculating some factorial values.

Try It Out – Calculating Factorials

Our example will calculate the factorial of every integer from 1 up to a given limit. Enter the following code with the two `for` loops:

```
public class Factorial
{
  public static void main(String[] args)
  {
    long limit = 20;          // to calculate factorial of integers up to this value
    long factorial = 1;       // factorial will be calculated in this variable

    // Loop from 1 to the value of limit
    for(int i = 1; i <= limit; i++)
    {
      factorial = 1;          // Initialize factorial
      for(int factor = 2; factor <= i; factor++)
        factorial *= factor;
      System.out.println(i + "!" + " is " + factorial);
    }
  }
}
```

This program will produce the output:

```
1! is 1
2! is 2
3! is 6
4! is 24
5! is 120
6! is 720
7! is 5040
8! is 40320
9! is 362880
10! is 3628800
11! is 39916800
12! is 479001600
13! is 6227020800
14! is 87178291200
15! is 1307674368000
16! is 20922789888000
17! is 355687428096000
18! is 6402373705728000
19! is 121645100408832000
20! is 2432902008176640000
```

How It Works

The outer loop, controlled by i, walks through all the integers from 1 to the value of limit. In each iteration of the outer loop, the variable `factorial` is initialized to 1 and the nested loop calculates the factorial of the current value of i using `factor` as the control counter which runs from 2 to the current value of i. The resulting value of `factorial` is then displayed, before going to the next iteration of the outer loop.

Although we have nested a `for` loop inside another `for` loop here, as we said at the outset, you can nest any kind of loop inside any other. We could have written the nested loop as:

```
for(int i = 1; i <= limit; i++)
{
  factorial = 1;          // Initialize factorial
  int factor =2;
  while(factor <= i)
    factorial *= factor++;
  System.out.println(i + "!" + " is " + factorial);
}
```

Now we have a `while` loop nested in a `for` loop. It works just as well, but it is rather more natural coded as two nested `for` loops because they are both controlled by a counter.

> If you have been concentrating, you may well have noticed that you don't really need nested loops to display the factorial of successive integers. You can do it with a single loop that multiplies the current factorial value by the loop counter. However, this would be a very poor demonstration of a nested loop.

The continue Statement

There are situations where you may want to skip all or part of a loop iteration. Suppose we want to sum the values of the integers from 1 to some limit, except that we don't want to include integers that are multiples of three. We can do this using an `if` and a `continue` statement:

```
for(int i = 1; i <= limit; i++)
{
  if(i % 3 == 0)
    continue;                      // Skip the rest of this iteration
  sum += i;                        // Add the current value of i to sum
}
```

The `continue` statement is executed in this example when `i` is an exact multiple of 3, causing the rest of the current loop iteration to be skipped. Program execution continues with the next iteration if there is one, and if not, with the statement following the end of the loop block. The `continue` statement can appear anywhere within a block of loop statements. You may even have more than one `continue` in a loop.

The Labeled continue Statement

Where you have nested loops, there is a special form of the `continue` statement that enables you to stop executing the inner loop – not just the current iteration of the inner loop – and continue at the beginning of the next iteration of the outer loop that immediately encloses the current loop. This is called the **labeled continue statement**.

To use the labeled continue statement, you need to identify the loop statement for the enclosing outer loop with a **statement label**. A statement label is simply an identifier that is used to reference a particular statement. When you need to reference a particular statement, you write the statement label at the beginning of the statement in question, and separated from the statement by a colon. Let's look at an example:

Try It Out – Labeled continue

We could add a labeled `continue` statement to omit the calculation of factorials of odd numbers greater than 10. This is not the best way to do this, but it does demonstrate how the labeled `continue` statement works:

```java
public class Factorial
{
  public static void main(String[] args)
  {
     long limit = 20;        // to calculate factorial of integers up to this value
     long factorial = 1;    // factorial will be calculated in this variable

     // Loop from 1 to the value of limit
     OuterLoop:
     for(int i = 1; i <= limit; i++)
     {
        factorial = 1;                // Initialize factorial
        for(int j = 2; j <= i; j++)
        {
           if(i > 10 && i % 2 == 1)
              continue OuterLoop;      // Transfer to the outer loop
           factorial *= j;
        }
        System.out.println(i + "!" + " is " + factorial);
     }
  }
}
```

If you run this it will produce the output:

```
1! is 1
2! is 2
3! is 6
4! is 24
5! is 120
6! is 720
7! is 5040
8! is 40320
9! is 362880
10! is 3628800
12! is 479001600
14! is 87178291200
16! is 20922789888000
18! is 6402373705728000
20! is 2432902008176640000
```

How It Works

The outer loop has the label `OuterLoop`. In the inner loop, when the condition in the `if` statement is `true`, the labeled `continue` is executed causing an immediate transfer to the beginning of the next iteration of the outer loop.

In general, you can use the labeled `continue` to exit from an inner loop to any enclosing outer loop, not just the one immediately enclosing the loop containing the labeled `continue` statement.

Using the break Statement in a Loop

We have seen how to use the break statement in a switch block. Its effect is to exit the switch block and continue execution with the first statement after the switch. You can also use the break statement to break out from a loop when you need. When break is executed within a loop, the loop ends immediately and execution continues with the first statement following the loop. To demonstrate this we will write a program to find prime numbers. In case you have forgotten, a prime number is an integer that is not exactly divisible by any number less than itself, other than 1 of course.

Try It Out – Calculating Primes I

Start with the main() method in the class Primes, and declare nValues and isPrime. Then start a for loop that will loop through all integers from 2 to nValues.

```
public class Primes
{
  public static void main(String[] args)
  {
    int nValues = 50;                    // The maximum value to be checked
    boolean isPrime = true;              // Is true if we find a prime

    // Check all values from 2 to nValues
    for(int i = 2; i <= nValues; i++)
      {
```

Then we try dividing i by all integers less than its value.

```
        isPrime=true;                          // Assume the current i is prime

        // Try dividing by all integers from 2 to i-1
        for(int j = 2; j < i; j++)
        {
          if(i % j == 0)           // This is true if j divides exactly
          {
            isPrime = false;       // If we got here, it was an exact division
            break;                 // so exit the loop
          }
        }
```

The final section prints out any primes.

```
        // We can get here through the break, or through completing the loop
        if(isPrime)                    // So is it prime?
          System.out.println(i);       // Yes, so output the value
      }
  }
}
```

You should get the output:

```
2
3
5
7
11
13
17
19
23
29
31
37
41
43
47
```

How It Works

There are much more efficient ways to calculate primes, but this does demonstrate the break statement in action. The basic idea of the program is to go through the integers from 2 to the value of nValues, and check each one to see if it has an integer divisor less than the number being checked. The outer loop is indexed by i stepping through the possible values that need to be checked. The inner loop is indexed by j, the value of j being a trial divisor. This determines whether any integer less than the value being tested for primality is an exact divisor.

The checking is done in the if statement in the inner loop. If j divides i exactly i%j will be 0, so isPrime will be set to false. In this case the break will be executed to exit the inner loop – there is no point in continuing as we now know that the value being tested is not prime. The next statement to be executed will be the if statement after the closing brace of the inner loop block. You can also reach this point by a normal exit from the loop which occurs when the value is prime, so it is necessary to check the value of isPrime to see whether we do have a prime or not.

This example could be simplified if we used the labeled continue instead of the break statement:

Try It Out – Calculating Primes II

Try the following changes to the code in the Primes class.

```
public class Primes
{
  public static void main(String[] args)
  {
    int nValues = 50;                    // The maximum value to be checked
// Check all values from 2 to nValues
    OuterLoop:
    for(int i = 2; i <= nValues; i++)
    {
      // Try dividing by all integers from 2 to i-1
      for(int j = 2; j < i; j++)
      {
        if(i%j == 0)                     // This is true if j divides exactly
          continue OuterLoop;            // so exit the loop
      }
```

```
                // We only get here if we have a prime
            System.out.println(i);                  // so output the value
      }
   }
}
```

How It Works

We no longer need the `isPrime` variable to indicate whether we have a prime or not, as we can only reach the output statement through a normal exit from the inner loop. When this occurs it means we have a prime. If we get an exact divisor, implying the current value of `i` is not prime, the labeled `continue` transfers immediately to the next iteration of the outer loop. The output from this version of the program is the same as before.

Breaking Indefinite Loops

You will find that sometimes you will need to use a loop where you don't know in advance how many iterations are required. This can arise when you are processing external data items that you might be reading in from the keyboard for example, and you do not know in advance how many there are. You can often use a `while` loop in these circumstances with the loop condition determining when the loop should end, but sometimes it can be convenient to use an indefinite loop instead, with a `break` statement to end the loop.

Try It Out – Calculating Primes III

Suppose we want our `Primes` program to generate a given number of primes, rather than check up to a given integer value. In this case we don't know how many numbers we need to check to generate the required number of primes. This is a case where an indefinite loop is useful. We can code this as follows:

```
   public class FindPrimes
   {
     public static void main(String[] args)
     {
       int nPrimes = 50;                        // The maximum number of primes required

       OuterLoop:
       for(int i = 2; ; i++)                    // This loop runs forever
       {
         // Try dividing by all integers from 2 to i-1
         for(int j = 2; j < i; j++)
         {
           if(i % j == 0)                       // This is true if j divides exactly
             continue OuterLoop;                // so exit the loop
         }
         // We only get here if we have a prime
         System.out.println(i);                 // so output the value
         if(--nPrimes == 0)                     // Decrement the prime count
           break;                               // It is zero so we have them all
       }
     }
   }
```

How It Works

This program is very similar to the previous version. The principal differences are that `nPrimes` contains the number of primes required so the program will produce the first 50 primes instead of finding the primes between 2 and 50. The outer loop, controlled by `i`, has the loop condition omitted, so the loop has no direct mechanism for ending it. The loop must be terminated by the code within the loop, otherwise it will continue to execute indefinitely.

Here the termination of the outer loop is controlled by the `if` statement following the output statement. As we find each prime, the value is displayed, after which the value of `nPrimes` is decremented in the `if` statement:

```
if(--nPrimes == 0)        // Decrement the prime count
    break;                // It is zero so we have them all
```

The `break` statement will be executed when `nPrimes` has been decremented to zero, and this will exit the outer loop.

The Labeled break Statement

Java also makes a labeled `break` statement available to you. This enables you to jump immediately to the statement following the end of any enclosing statement block or loop that is identified by the label in the labeled `break` statement. This mechanism is illustrated in the following diagram:

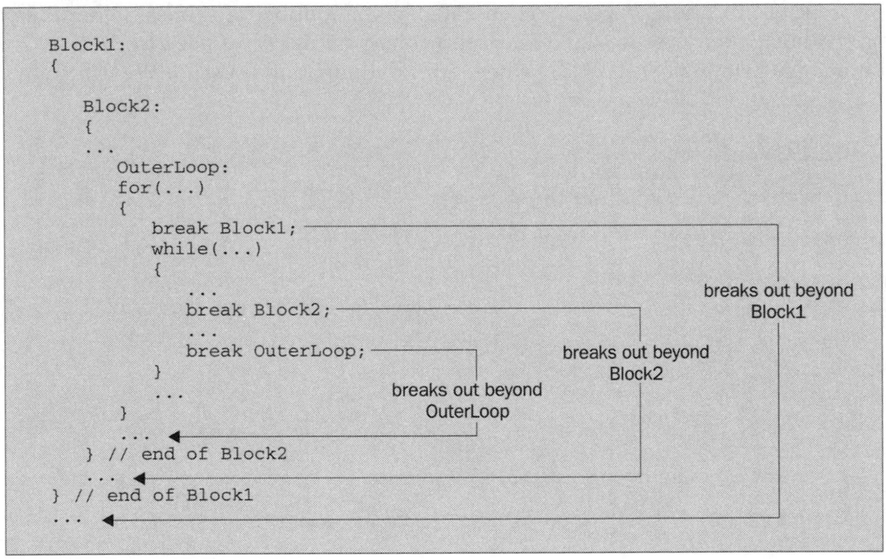

The labeled `break` enables you to break out to the statement following an enclosing block or loop that has a label regardless of how many levels there are. You might have several loops nested one within the other, and using the labeled break you could exit from the innermost loop (or indeed any of them) to the statement following the outermost loop. You just need to add a label to the beginning of the relevant block or loop that you want to break out of, and use that label in the `break` statement.

Just to see it working we can alter the previous example to use a labeled break statement:

```java
public class FindPrimes
{
  public static void main(String[] args)
  {
    int nPrimes = 50;                    // The maximum number of primes required

    // Check all values from 2 to nValues
    OuterLoop:
    for(int i = 2; ; i++)                // This loop runs forever
    {
      // Try dividing by all integers from 2 to i-1
      for(int j = 2; j < i; j++)
      {
        if(i % j == 0)                   // This is true if j divides exactly
          continue OuterLoop;            // so exit the loop
      }
      // We only get here if we have a prime
      System.out.println(i);             // so output the value
      if(--nPrimes == 0)                 // Decrement the prime count
        break OuterLoop;                 // It is zero so we have them all
    }
    // break OuterLoop goes to here
  }
}
```

The program works in exactly the same way as before. The labeled break ends the loop operation beginning with the label OuterLoop, and so effectively branches to the point indicated by the comment.

Of course, in this instance its effect is no different from that of an unlabeled break. However, in general this would work wherever the labeled break statement was within OuterLoop. For instance, it could be nested inside another inner loop, and its effect would be just the same – control would be transferred to the statement following the end of OuterLoop. The following code fragment illustrates this sort of situation. Our label this time is Outside:

```java
Outside:
for(int i = 0 ; i< count1 ; i++)
{
  ...
  for(int j = 0 ; j< count2 ; j++)
  {
    ...
    for(int k = 0 ; k< count3 ; k++)
    {
      ...
      break Outside;
      ...
    }
  }
}
  // The labeled break transfers to here...
```

The labeled break is not needed very often, but when you need to break out of a deeply nested set of loops it can be invaluable since it makes it a simple operation.

Summary

In this chapter you have learnt about all of the essential mechanisms for making decisions in Java. You have also learnt all of the looping facilities that you have available when programming. The essential points we have covered are:

- ❑ You can use **relational operators** to compare values, and such comparisons result in values of either `true` or `false`.

- ❑ You can combine basic comparisons and logical variables in more complex logical expressions by using **logical operators**.

- ❑ The `if` statement is a basic decision making tool in Java. It enables you to choose to execute a block of statements if a given logical expression has the value `true`. You can optionally execute another block of statements if the logical expression is `false` by using the `else` keyword.

- ❑ You can use the **conditional operator** to choose between two expressions depending on the value of a logical expression.

- ❑ You can use the `switch` statement to choose from a fixed number of alternatives.

- ❑ The variables in a method come into existence at the point at which you declare them, and cease to exist after the end of the block that immediately encloses their declaration. The program extent where the variable is accessible is the **scope** of the variable.

- ❑ You have three options for repeating a block of statements, a `for` loop, a `while` loop or a `do while` loop.

- ❑ The `continue` statement enables you to skip to the next iteration in the loop containing the `continue` statement.

- ❑ The labeled `continue` statement enables you to skip to the next iteration in a loop enclosing the labeled `continue` that is identified by the label. The labeled loop need not be that immediately enclosing the labeled `continue`.

- ❑ The `break` statement enables you to break out of a loop or block of statements in which it appears.

- ❑ The labeled `break` statement enables you to break out of a loop or block of statements that encloses it that is identified by the label. This is not necessarily the block that encloses it directly.

Exercises

1. Write a program to display a random choice from a set of six choices for breakfast (you could use any set, for example, scrambled eggs, waffles, fruit, cereal, toast or yogurt).

2. When testing whether an integer is a prime, it is sufficient to try to divide by integers up to the square root of the number being tested. Rewrite the program example from this chapter to use this approach.

3. A lottery requires that you select six different numbers from the integers 1 to 49. Write a program to do this for you and generate five sets of entries.

4. Write a program to generate a random sequence of capital letters that does not include vowels.

Arrays and Strings

In this chapter you will start to use Java objects. You will first be introduced to arrays which enable you to deal with a number of variables of the same type through a single variable name, and then you will look at how to handle character strings. By the end of this chapter you will have learnt:

- ❑ What arrays are and how you declare and initialize them.
- ❑ How you access individual elements of an array.
- ❑ How you can use individual elements of an array.
- ❑ How to declare arrays of arrays.
- ❑ How you can create arrays of arrays with different lengths.
- ❑ How to create `String` objects.
- ❑ How to create and use arrays of `String` objects.
- ❑ What operations are available for `String` objects.
- ❑ What `StringBuffer` objects are and how they relate to operations on `String` objects.
- ❑ What operations are available for `StringBuffer` objects.

Some of what we discuss in this chapter relates to objects, and as we have not yet covered in detail how a class (or object definition) is defined we will have to skate over some points, but all will be revealed in Chapter 5.

Arrays

With the basic built-in Java data-types we have seen in the previous chapters, each identifier corresponds to a single variable. But when you want to handle sets of values of the same type – the first 1000 primes for example – you really don't want to have to name them individually. What you need is an **array**.

An array is a named set of variables of the same type. Each variable in the array is called an **array element**. To reference a particular element in an array you use the array name combined with an integer value of type int, called an **index**. The index for an array element is the offset of that particular element from the beginning of the array. The first element will have an index of 0, the second will have an index of 1, the third an index of 2, and so on. The index value does not need to be an integer literal. It can be any expression that results in a value of type int greater than zero. Obviously a for loop control variable is going to be very useful for processing array elements – which is why you had to wait until now to hear about arrays.

Array Variables

You are not obliged to create the array itself when you declare the array variable. The array variable is distinct from the array itself. You could declare the integer array variable, primes, with the statement:

```
int[] primes;            // Declare an integer array variable
```

The variable primes is now a place holder for an integer array that you have yet to define. No memory is allocated to hold the array itself at this point. We will see in a moment that to create the array itself we must specify its type and how many elements it is to contain. The square brackets following the type in the previous statement indicates that the variable is for referencing an array of int values, and not for storing a single value of type int.

You may come across an alternative notation for declaring an array variable:

```
int primes[];            // Declare an integer array variable
```

Here the square brackets appear after the variable name, rather than after the type name. This is exactly equivalent to the previous statement so you can use either notation. Many programmers prefer the original notation, as int[] tends to indicate more clearly that the type is an int array.

Defining an Array

Once you have declared an array variable, you can define an array that it will reference:

```
primes = new int[10];    // Define an array of 10 integers
```

This statement creates an array that will store 10 values of type int, and records a **reference** to the array in the variable primes. The reference is simply where the array is in memory. You could also declare the array variable, and define the array of type int to hold 10 prime numbers with a single statement, as shown in the following illustration:

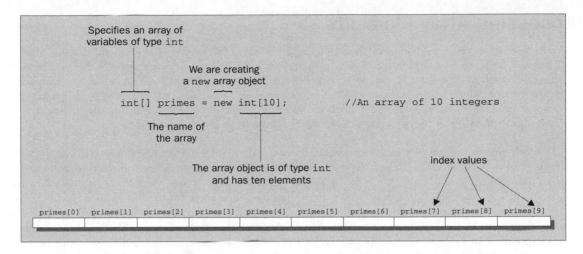

The first part of the definition specifies the type of the array. The type name, int in this case, is followed by an empty pair of square brackets to indicate you are declaring an array rather than a single variable of type int. The part following the equals sign defines the array. The keyword new indicates that you are allocating new memory for the array, and int[10] specifies you want capacity for 10 variables of type int in the array. Since each element in the primes array is an int variable requiring 4 bytes, the whole array will occupy 40 bytes, plus 4 bytes to store the reference to the array. When an array is created like this, all the array elements are initialized to a default value automatically. The initial value is zero in the case of an array of numerical values, false for boolean arrays, '\u0000' for arrays storing type char, and null for an array of a class type.

Before we go any further, let's clarify a bit of terminology we have been using in this discussion – a **declaration** for an array just defines the variable name. So the statement,

```
double[] myArray;
```

is a declaration for the array name, myArray. No memory has been allocated to store the array itself and the number of elements has not been defined.

The statement,

```
double[] myArray = new double[100];
```

is a declaration of the array variable myArray, and a **definition** of the array, since the array size is specified. The variable myArray will refer to an array of 100 values of type double and each element will have the value 0.0 assigned by default.

111

Accessing Array Elements

You refer to an element of an array by using the array name followed by the element's index value enclosed between square brackets. You can specify an index value by any expression that produces a positive result of type int. If you use a value of type long as an index, you will get an error message from the compiler; if your calculation of an index uses long variables you will need to cast it to type int. You will no doubt recall from Chapter 2 that expressions involving values of type short and type byte produce a result of type int, so you can use those in an index expression.

The first element of the primes array declared previously is referred to as primes[0], and you reference the fifth element in the array as primes[4]. The maximum index value for an array is one less than the number of elements in the array. Java checks that the index values you use are valid. If you use an index value that is less than 0, or greater than the index value for the last element in the array, an **exception** will be thrown – throwing an exception is just the way errors at execution time are signaled and there are different types of exceptions for signaling various kinds of errors. The exception in this case is called an IndexOutOfBoundsException. When such an exception is thrown, your program will normally be terminated. We will be looking in detail at exceptions in Chapter 7, including how you can deal with exceptions and prevent termination of your program.

The array, primes, is sometimes referred to as a **one-dimensional array**, since each of its elements is referenced using one index – running from 0 to 9 in this case. We will see later that arrays can have two or more dimensions, the number of dimensions being the same as the number of indexes required to access an element of the array.

Reusing Array Variables

The array variable is separate from the array itself. Rather like the way an ordinary variable can refer to different values at different times, you can use an array variable to reference different arrays at different points in your program. Suppose you have declared and defined the variable primes as before:

```
int[] primes = new int[10];    // Allocate an array of 10 integer elements
```

This produces an array of 10 elements of type int. Perhaps a bit later in your program you want the array variable primes to refer to a larger array, with 50 elements say. You would simply write:

```
primes = new int[50];          // Allocate an array of 50 integer elements
```

Now the variable primes refers to a new array of values of type int that is entirely separate from the original. When this statement is executed, the previous array of 10 elements is discarded, along with all the data values you may have stored in it. The variable primes can now only be used to reference elements of the new array. This is illustrated in the next diagram.

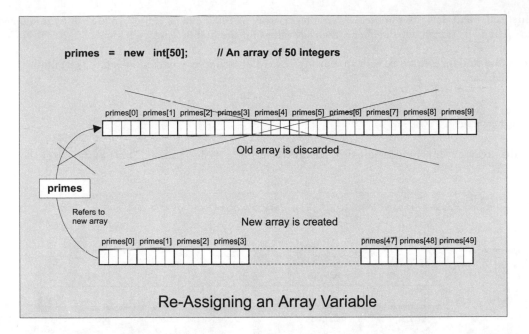

Re-Assigning an Array Variable

After executing the statement shown in the diagram, the array variable `primes` now points to a new integer array of 50 elements, with index values running from 0 to 49. Although you can change the array that an array variable references, you can't alter the type of value that an element stores. All the arrays referenced by a given variable must correspond to the original type specified when the array variable was declared. The variable `primes`, for example, can only reference arrays of type `int`. We have used an `int` array in the illustration, but everything applies equally well to `long` or `double` or to any of the basic types. More than that, you can create arrays of any other type of object, including the classes that you will be defining yourself in Chapter 5.

Initializing Arrays

You can initialize an array with your own values when you declare it, and at the same time determine how many elements it will have. Following the declaration of the array variable, simply add an equals sign followed by the list of element values enclosed between braces. For example, if you write:

```
int[] primes = {2, 3, 5, 7, 11, 13, 17};    // An array of 7 elements
```

The array is created with sufficient elements to store all of the initializing values that appear between the braces, seven in this case. The array size is determined by the number of initial values so no other information is necessary to define the array. If you specify initializing values for an array, you must include values for all the elements. If you only want to set some of the array elements to values explicitly, you should use an assignment statement for each element. For example:

```
int[] primes = new int[100];
primes[0] = 2;
primes[1] = 3;
```

The first statement declares and defines an integer array of 100 elements, all of which will be initialized to zero. The two assignment statements then set values for the first two array elements.

You can also initialize an array with an existing array. For example, you could declare the following array variables:

```
long[] even = {2L, 4L, 6L, 8L, 10L};
long[] value = even;
```

where the array even is used to initialize the array value in its declaration. This has the effect shown below.

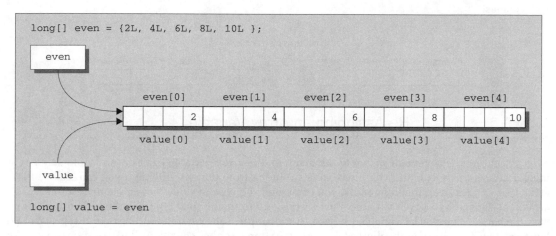

You have created two array variables, but you only have one array. Both arrays refer to the same set of elements and you can access the elements of the array through either variable name – for example, even[2] refers to the same variable as value[2]. One use for this is when you want to switch the arrays referenced by two variables. If you were sorting an array by repeatedly transferring elements from one array to another, by flipping the array you were copying from with the array you were copying to, you could use the same code. For example, if we declared array variables as,

```
double[] inputArray = new double[100];     // Array to be sorted
double[] outputArray = new double[100];    // Re-ordered array
double[] temp;                             // Temporary array reference
```

when we want to switch the array referenced by outputArray to be the new input array, we could write:

```
temp = inputArray;              // Save reference to inputArray in temp
inputArray = outputArray;       // Set inputArray to refer to outputArray
outputArray = temp;             // Set outputArray to refer to what was inputArray
```

None of the array elements are moved here. Just the addresses of where the arrays are located in memory are swapped, so this is a very fast process. Of course, if you want to replicate an array, you have to define a new array of the same size and type, and then copy each element of the array individually to your new array.

Using Arrays

You can use array elements in expressions in exactly the same way as you might use a single variable of the same data type. For example, if you declare an array `samples`, you can fill it with random values between 0.0 and 100.0 with the following code:

```
double[] samples = new double[50];     // An array of 50 double values
for(int i = 0; i < 50; i++)
samples[i] = 100.0*Math.random();   // Generate random values
```

To show that array elements can be used in exactly the same way as ordinary variables, you could write:

```
double result = (samples[10]*samples[0] -
                              Math.sqrt(samples[49]))/samples[29];
```

This is a totally arbitrary calculation of course. More sensibly, to compute the average of the values stored in the `samples` array, you could write:

```
double average = 0.0;          // Variable to hold the average

for(int i = 0; i < 50; i++)
  average += samples[i];       // Sum all the elements

average /= 50;                 // Divide by the total number of elements
```

Within the loop we accumulate the sum of all the elements of the array `samples` in the variable `average`. We then divide this sum by the number of elements.

Notice how we use the length of the array, 50, all over the place. It appears in the `for` loop, and in floating point form as a divisor to calculate the average. When you use arrays you will often find that references to the length of the array are strewn all through your code. And if you later want to change the program, to handle 100 elements for instance, you need to be able to decide whether any particular value of 50 in the code is actually the number of elements, and therefore should be changed to 100, or if it is a value that just happens to be the same and should be left alone. Java helps you avoid this problem, as we will now see.

Array Length

You can refer to the length of the array using `length`, a data member of the `array` object. For our array `samples`, we can refer to its length as `samples.length`. We could use this to write the calculation of the average as:

```
double average = 0.0;          // Variable to hold the average
for(int i = 0; i < samples.length; i++)
average += samples[i];       // Sum all the elements
average /= samples.length;     // Divide by the total number of elements
```

Now the code is independent of the number of array elements. If you change the number of elements in the array, the code will automatically deal with that. You will also see in Chapter 6 that being able to obtain the length of an array in this way is very convenient in the context of coding your own class methods that process arrays. You should always use this approach when you need to refer to the length of an array – never use explicit values.

Let's try out an array in an improved program to calculate prime numbers:

Try It Out – Even More Primes

Try out the following code derived, in part, from the code we used in Chapter 2.

```
public class MorePrimes
{
  public static void main(String[] args)
  {
    long[] primes = new long[20];        // Array to store primes
    primes[0] = 2;                       // Seed the first prime
    primes[1] = 3;                       // and the second
    int count = 2;                       // Count of primes found - up to now,
                                         // which is also the array index
    long number = 5;                     // Next integer to be tested

    outer:
    for( ; count < primes.length; number += 2)
    {
      // The maximum divisor we need to try is square root of number
      long limit = (long)Math.ceil(Math.sqrt((double)number));

      // Divide by all the primes we have up to limit
      for(int i = 1; i < count && primes[i] <= limit; i++)
        if(number%primes[i] == 0)                    // Is it an exact divisor?
          continue outer;                   // yes, try the next number

      primes[count++] = number;                      // We got one!
    }

    for(int i=0; i < primes.length; i++)
      System.out.println(primes[i]);               // Output all the primes
  }
}
```

This program computes as many prime numbers as the capacity of the array `primes` will allow.

How It Works

Any number that is not a prime must be a product of prime factors, so we only need to divide a prime number candidate by prime numbers that are less than, or equal to the square root of the candidate to test for whether it is prime. This is fairly obvious if you think about it. For every factor a number has that is greater than the square root of the number, the result of division by this factor is another factor that is less than the square root. You perhaps can see this more easily with a specific example. The number 24 has a square root that is a bit less than 5. You can factorize it as 2x12, 3x8, 4x6, then we come to cases where the first factor is greater than the square root so the second is less, 6x4, 8x3 etc., and so we are repeating the pairs of factors we already have.

We first declare the array `primes` to be of type `long`, and define it as having 20 elements. We set the first two elements of the `primes` array to 2 and 3 respectively to start the process off, as we will use the primes we have in the array as divisors when testing a new candidate. The variable, `count`, is the total number of primes we have found, so this starts out as 2. Note that we use `count` as the `for` loop counter, so we omit the first expression between parentheses in the loop statement as `count` has already been set.

The candidate to be tested is stored in `number`, with the first value set as 5. The `for` loop statement, labeled `outer`, counts in steps of two, since we don't want to check even numbers. The `for` loop ends when `count` is equal to the length of the array. We test the value in `number` in the inner `for` loop by dividing `number` by all of the prime numbers we have in the `primes` array that are less than, or equal to, the square root of the candidate. If we get an exact division the value in `number` is not prime, so we go immediately to the next iteration of the `outer` loop via the `continue` statement.

We calculate the limit for divisors we need to try with the statement:

```
long limit = (long)Math.ceil(Math.sqrt((double)number));
```

The `Math.sqrt()` method produces the square root of `number` as a `double` value, so if number has the value 7 for instance, a value of about 2.64575 will be returned. This is passed to the `ceil()` method that is also a member of the `Math` class. The `ceil()` method returns a value of type `double` that is the minimum whole number that is not less than the value passed to it. With number as 7, this will return 3.0, the smallest integral value not less than the square root of 7. We want to use this number as the limit for our integer divisors, so we cast it to type `long` and store the result in `limit`.

If we get no exact division, we exit normally from the inner loop and execute the statement:

```
primes[count++] = number;     // We got one!
```

Because `count` is the number of values we have stored, it also corresponds to the index for the next free element in the `primes` array. Thus we use `count` as the index to the array element in which we want to store the value of `number`, and then increment `count`.

When we have filled the `primes` array, the `outer` loop will end and we will output all the values in the array. Note that, because we have used the `length` member of the `primes` object whenever we need the number of elements in the array, changing the number of elements in the definition of the array to generate a larger or smaller number of primes is simple.

We can express the logical process of the program with an algorithm as follows:

1. Take the **number** in question and determine its square root.

2. Set the **limit** for divisors to be the smallest integer which is greater than this square root value.

3. Test to see if the **number** can be divided exactly (without remainder) by any of the **primes** already in the `primes` **array** that are less than the **limit** for divisors.

4. If it can, discard the existing **number** and start a new iteration of the loop with the next candidate **number**. If it can't, it is a prime, so enter the existing **number** in the first available empty slot in the array and then move to the next iteration for a new candidate **number**.

5. If the **array** of primes is full, do no more iterations, and print out all the prime number values in the array.

Arrays of Arrays

We have only worked with one-dimensional arrays up to now, that is arrays that use a single index. Why would you ever need the complications of using more indexes to access the elements of an array?

Suppose that you have a fanatical interest in the weather, and you are intent on recording the temperature each day at 10 separate geographical locations throughout the year 1999. Once you have sorted out the logistics of actually collecting this information, you can use an array of 10 elements corresponding to the number of locations, where each of these elements is an array of 365 elements to store the temperature values. You would declare this array with the statement:

```
float[][] temperature = new float[10][365];
```

This is called a **two-dimensional array**, since it has two dimensions – one with index values running from 0 to 9, and the other with index values from 0 to 364. The first index will relate to a geographical location, and the second index corresponds to the day of the year. That's much handier than a one dimensional array with 3650 elements, isn't it?

The organization of the two-dimensional array is shown in the following diagram.

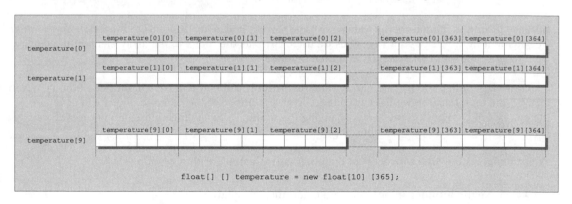

```
float[] [] temperature = new float[10] [365];
```

There are 10 arrays, each having 365 elements. In referring to an element, the first square brackets enclose the index for a particular array, and the second pair of square brackets enclose the index value for an element within that array. So to refer to the temperature for day 100 for the sixth location, you would use `temperature[5][99]`. Since each `float` variable occupies 4 bytes, the total space required to store the elements in this two dimensional array is 10x365x4 bytes, which is a total of 14,600 bytes.

For a fixed second index value in a two dimensional array, varying the first index direction is often referred to as accessing a **column** of the array. Similarly, fixing the first index value and varying the second, you access a **row** of the array. The reason for this terminology is apparent from the last diagram.

You could just as well have used two statements to create the last array, one to declare the array variable, and the other to define the array:

```
float [][] temperature;              // Declare the array variable
temperature = new float[10][365];    // Create the array
```

The first statement declares the array variable `temperature` for two dimensional arrays of type `float`. The second statement creates the array with ten elements, each of which is an array of 365 elements.

Let's exercise this two dimensional array in a program to calculate the average annual temperature for each location.

Try It Out – The Weather Fanatic

In the absence of real samples, we will generate the temperatures as random values between -10° and 35°. This assumes we are recording temperatures in degrees Celsius. If you prefer Fahrenheit you could use 14° to 95° to cover the same range of temperatures.

```java
public class WeatherFan
{
    public static void main(String[] args)
    {
        float[][] temperature = new float[10][365]; // Temperature array

        // Generate temperatures
        for(int i = 0; i < temperature.length; i++)
            for(int j = 0; j < temperature[i].length; j++)
                temperature[i][j] = (float)(45.0*Math.random() - 10.0);

        // Calculate the average per location
        for(int i = 0; i < temperature.length; i++)
        {
            float average = 0.0f;       // Place to store the average

            for(int j = 0; j < temperature[0].length; j++)
                average += temperature[i][j];

            // Output the average temperature for the current location
            System.out.println("Average temperature at location "
                    + (i+1) + " = " + average/(float)temperature[i].length);
        }
    }
}
```

How It Works

After declaring the array, `temperature`, we fill it with random values using nested `for` loops. Note how `temperature.length` used in the outer loop refers to the length of the first dimension, 10 in this case. In the inner loop we use `temperature[i].length` to refer to the length of the second dimension, 365. We could use any index value here; `temperature[0].length` would have been just as good for all the elements, since the lengths of the rows of the array are all the same in this case.

The `Math.random()` method generates a value of type `double` between 0.0 and 1.0. This value is multiplied by 45.0 in the expression for the temperature, which results in values between 0.0 and 45.0. Subtracting 10.0 from this value gives us the range we require, -10.0 to 35.0.

We then use another pair of nested `for` loops, controlled in the same way as the first, to calculate the averages of the stored temperatures. The outer loop iterates over the locations and the inner loop sums all the temperature values for a given location. Before the execution of the inner loop, the variable `average` is declared and initialized, and this is used to accumulate the sum of the temperatures for a location in the inner loop. After the inner loop has been executed, we output the average temperature for each location, identifying the locations by numbers 1 to 10, one more than the index value for each location. Note that the parentheses around `(i+1)` here are essential. To get the average we divide the variable `average` by the number of samples which is `temperature[i].length`, the length of the array holding temperatures for the current location. Again, we could use any index value here since, as we have seen, they all return the same value, 365.

Arrays of Arrays of Varying Length

When you create an array of arrays, the arrays do not need to be all the same length. You could declare an array variable `samples` with the statement:

```
float[][] samples;          // Declare an array of arrays
```

which declares the array object `sample` of type `float`. You can then define the number of elements in the first dimension with the statement:

```
samples = new float[6][];      // Define 6 elements, each is an array
```

We now have six elements allocated, each of which can hold a one-dimensional array. You can define these arrays individually if you want:

```
samples[2] = new float[6];    // The 3rd array has 6 elements
samples[5] = new float[101];  // The 6th array has 101 elements
```

This defines two of the arrays. Obviously you cannot use an array until it has been defined, but you could conceivably use these two and define the others later – not a likely approach though!

If you wanted the array, `samples`, to have a triangular shape, with one element in the first row, two elements in the second row, three in the third row, and so on, you could define the arrays in a loop:

```
for(int i = 0; i < samples.length; i++)
   samples[i] = new float[i+1];      // Allocate each array
```

The effect of this is to produce an array layout that is shown in the diagram below.

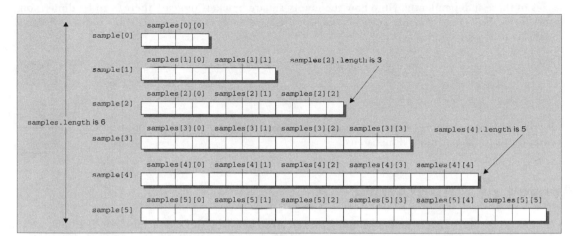

The total of 21 elements in the array will occupy 84 bytes. When you need a two dimensional array with rows of varying length, allocating them to fit the requirement can save a considerable amount of memory compared to just using rectangular arrays where the row lengths are all the same.

To check out that the array is as shown, you could implement this in a program, and display the length member for each of these arrays.

Multi-Dimensional Arrays

You are not limited to two-dimensional arrays either. If you are an international Java Bean grower with multiple farms across several countries, you could arrange to store the results of your bean counting in the array declared and defined in the statement:

```
long[][][] beans = new long[5][10][30];
```

The array beans has three dimensions. It provides for holding bean counts for each of up to 30 fields per farm, with 10 farms per country in each of 5 countries.

You can envisage this as just a three dimensional array, but remember that beans is an array of five elements, each of which holds a two dimensional array, and each of these two dimensional arrays can be different. For example if you really want to go to town, you can declare the array beans with the statement;

```
long[][][] beans = new long[3][][];   // Three two dimensional arrays
```

Each of the three elements in the first dimension of beans can hold a different two dimensional array, so you could specify the first dimension of each explicitly with the statements:

```
beans[0] = new long[4][];
beans[1] = new long[2][];
beans[2] = new long[5][];
```

These three arrays have elements which hold a one dimensional array, and you can also specify the sizes of these independently. Note how the empty square brackets indicate there is still a dimension undefined. You could give the arrays in each of these elements random dimensions between 1 and 7 with the following code:

```
for(int i = 0; i < beans.length; i++)          // Vary over 1st dimension
   for(int j = 0; j < beans[i].length; j++)    // Vary over 2nd dimension
      beans[i][j] = new long[(int)(1.0 + 6.0*Math.random())];
```

If you can find a sensible reason for doing so, or if you are just a glutton for punishment, you can extend this to four or more dimensions.

Arrays of Characters

All our arrays have been numeric so far. You can also have arrays of characters. For example, we can declare an array variable of type `char[]` to hold 50 characters with the statement:

```
char[] message = new char[50];
```

We could also define an array of type `char[]` by the characters it holds:

```
char[] vowels = { 'a', 'e', 'i', 'o', 'u'};
```

This defines an array of five elements, initialized with the characters appearing between the braces. This is fine for things like vowels, but what about proper messages?

Using an array of type `char`, you can write statements such as:

```
char[] sign = {'F', 'l', 'u', 'e', 'n', 't', ' ',
               'G', 'i', 'b', 'b', 'e', 'r', 'i', 's', 'h', ' ',
               's', 'p', 'o', 'k', 'e', 'n', ' ',
               'h', 'e', 'r', 'e'};
```

Well, you get the message – just, but it's not a very friendly way to deal with it. It looks like a collection of characters, which is what it is. What we really need is something which is a bit more integrated – something that looks like a message, but still gives us the ability to get at the individual characters if we want. What we need is a `String`.

Using Strings

You will need to use character strings in most of your programs – headings, names, addresses, product descriptions... – the list is endless. In Java, strings are objects of the class `String`. The `String` class is a standard class that comes with Java, and it is specifically designed for creating and processing strings.

String Literals

You have already made extensive use of string literals for output. Just about every time the `println()` method was used in an example, we used a string literal as the argument. A **string literal** is a sequence of characters between double quotes:

```
"This is a string literal!"
```

This is actually a `String` literal with a capital `S` – in other words, a constant object of the class `String` that the compiler creates for use in your program.

Some characters can't be entered explicitly from the keyboard for inclusion in a string literal. You can't include a double quote character as it is, for example, as this is used to indicate where a string literal begins and ends. You can't include a new line character by pressing the *Enter* key since this will move the cursor to a new line. As we saw in Chapter 2, all of these characters are provided in the same way as `char` constants – you use an escape sequence. All the escape sequences you saw when we looked at `char` constants apply to strings. Refer to Appendix D for a list of escape characters. The statement:

```
System.out.println("This is \na string constant!");
```

will produce the output:

```
This is
a string constant!
```

since `\n` is used for a new line character. Like values of type `char`, strings are stored internally as Unicode characters so you can also include Unicode character codes as escape sequences of the form `\Unnnn` where nnnn are the four hexadecimal digits of the Unicode coding for a particular character. The `U` can be upper or lower case. The Greek letter, π, for example, is `\U03C0`.

You will recall from our preliminary discussion of classes and objects in Chapter 1 that a class usually contains data and methods and this is also true of the class `String`. The sequence of characters included in the string is the class data, and the methods in the class `String` enable you to process the data in a variety of ways. We will go into the detail of how the class is defined in Chapter 5, but in this chapter we will concentrate on how we can create and use objects of the class `String`. You know how to define a `String` literal. The next step is to learn how a `String` variable is declared and how `String` objects are created.

Creating String Objects

Just to make sure there is no confusion in your mind, a `String` variable is simply an object of the class `String`. You declare a `String` variable in much the same way as you define a variable of one of the basic types. You can also initialize it in the declaration, which is generally a good idea:

```
String myString = "My inaugural string";
```

This declares the variable myString as type String, and initializes it with the value "My inaugural string". You can store a reference to another string in a String variable, once you have declared it, by using an assignment. For example, we can change the value of our String variable myString with the statement:

```
myString = "Strings can be knotty";
```

The effect of this is illustrated below:

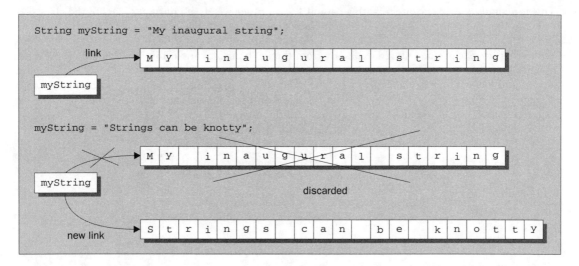

The string itself is distinct from the variable you use to refer to it. In the same way as we saw with array objects, the variable myString stores a reference to a String object, in other words it keeps track of where the string object is in memory. When we declare and initialize myString, it links to the initializing string value. When we execute the assignment statement, the original link is severed, the old string is discarded, and the variable myString stores a reference to the new string value. This means that you cannot extend the string that is referred to in a variable of type String. String objects are said to be **immutable** – which just means that they cannot be changed. To change the string referenced by a String variable you throw away the reference to the old string and replace it with a reference to a new one. The distinction between a String variable and the string it references is not apparent most of the time, but we will see situations later in this chapter where it is important to understand this, so keep it in mind.

You should also keep in mind that characters in a string are Unicode characters, so each one occupies two bytes. This is also not something you need worry about most of the time, but there are occasions where you need to be conscious of the fact.

Of course, if you declare a variable of type String in a method without initializing it:

```
String anyString;              // Uninitialized String variable
```

then it does not refer to anything. However, if you try to compile a program containing this statement you will get an error. If you don't want it to refer to anything at the outset, for instance, if you may or may not assign a `String` object to it before you use the variable, then you must initialize it to a special null value:

```
String anyString = null;       // String variable that doesn't reference a string
```

The actual value it stores in this situation is referred to as `null`, so you can test whether a `String` variable refers to anything or not by a statement such as:

```
if(anyString == null)
   System.out.println("anyString does not refer to anything!");
```

The variable `anyString` will continue to be `null` until you use an assignment to make it reference a particular string. Attempting to use a variable that has not been initialized is an error. When you declare a `String` variable, or any other variable that is not an array, in a block of code without initializing it, the compiler can detect any attempts to use the variable before it has a value assigned, and will flag it as an error. As a rule, you should initialize variables as you declare them.

Arrays of Strings

Since string variables are objects, you can create arrays of strings. You declare an array of `String` objects with the same mechanism that we used to declare arrays of elements for the basic types. You just use the type `String` in the declaration. For example, to declare an array of five `String` objects, you could use the statement:

```
String[] names = new String[5];
```

It should now be apparent that the argument to the method `main()` is an array of `String` objects.

We can try out arrays of strings with a small example:

Try It Out – Twinkle, Twinkle, Lucky Star

Let's create a console program to generate your lucky star for the day.

```
public class LuckyStars
{
  public static void main(String[] args)
  {
    String[] stars = {
                       "Robert Redford"   , "Marilyn Monroe",
                       "Boris Karloff"    , "Lassie",
                       "Hopalong Cassidy", "Trigger"
                     };
    System.out.println("Your lucky star for today is "
                       + stars[(int)(stars.length*Math.random())]);
  }
}
```

How It Works

This program creates the array `stars`, of type `String`. The array length will be set to however many initializing values appear between the braces in the declaration statement, six in this case.

We select a random element from the array by creating a random index value within the output statement with the expression `(int)(stars.length*Math.random())`. Multiplying the random number produced using the method `Math.random()` by the length of the array, we will get a value between 0.0 and 6.0 since the value returned by `random()` will be between 0.0 and 1.0. The result won't ever be 6.0 because the value returned by the `random()` method is strictly less than 1.0, which is just as well as this would be an illegal index value. The result is then cast to an `int`, making it a valid array index value.

Thus the program selects a random string from the array and displays it.

Operations on Strings

There are many kinds of operations that can be performed on strings, but we can start with one you have used already, joining strings together, often called **string concatenation**.

Joining Strings

To join two `String` objects to form a single string you use the + operator, just as you have been doing with the argument to the `println()` method in the program examples thus far. The simplest use of this is to join two strings together:

```
myString = "The quick brown fox" + " jumps over the lazy dog";
```

This will join the two strings on the right of the assignment, and store the result in the `String` variable `myString`. The + operation generates a completely new `String` object that is separate from the original `String` objects that are the operands, and this new object is stored in `myString`.

Note that you can also use the += operator to concatenate strings. For example:

```
String phrase = "Too many";
phrase += " cooks spoil the broth.";
```

After executing these statements the variable `phrase` will refer to the string `"Too many cooks spoil the broth."`. Note that this does not modify the string `"Too many"`. The string that is referenced by `phrase` after this statement has been executed is a completely new `String` object. This is illustrated on the following page.

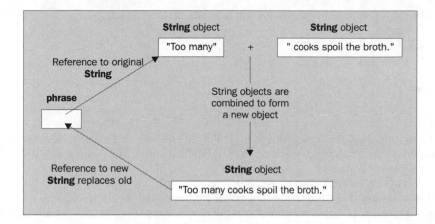

Let's see how some variations on the use of the + operator with String objects work in an example.

Try It Out – String Concatenation

Enter the following code for the class JoinStrings:

```
public class JoinStrings
{
    public static void main(String[] args)
    {
        String firstString = "Many ";
        String secondString = "hands ";
        String thirdString = "make light work";

        String myString;              // Variable to store results

        // Join three strings and store the result
        myString = firstString + secondString + thirdString;
        System.out.println(myString);

        // Convert an integer to String and join with two other strings
        int numHands = 99;
        myString = numHands + " " + secondString + thirdString;
        System.out.println(myString);

        // Combining a string and integers
        myString = "fifty five is " + 5 + 5;
        System.out.println(myString);

        // Combining integers and a string
        myString = 5 + 5 + " is ten";
        System.out.println(myString);
    }
}
```

If you run this example, it will produce some interesting results:

```
Many hands make light work
99 hands make light work
fifty five is 55
10 is ten
```

How It Works

The first line of output is quite straightforward. It simply joins the three string values stored in the String variables firstString, secondString and thirdString into a single string, and stores this in the variable myString.

The second line of output is a use of the + operator we have used regularly with the println() method, but clearly something a little more complicated is happening here. This is illustrated below:

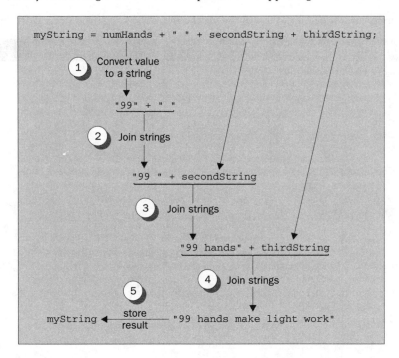

Behind the scenes, the value of the variable numHands is being converted to a string that represents this value as a decimal number. This is prompted by the fact that it is combined with the string literal, " ". Dissimilar types in a binary operation cannot be operated on, so one operand must be converted to the type of the other if the operation is to be possible. Here the compiler arranges that the numerical value stored in numHands is converted to type String to match the type of the right operand of the + operator. If you look back at the table of operator precedences, you will see that the associativity of the operator + is from left to right, so the strings are combined in pairs starting from the left, as shown in the diagram.

The left-to-right associativity of the + operator is important in understanding the next two lines of output. The two statements involved in creating these strings look very similar. Why does "5 + 5" result in "55" in one statement, and "10" in the other? The reason is illustrated below.

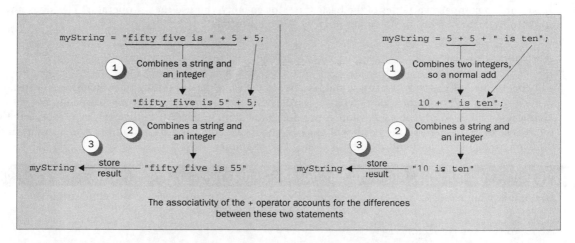

The associativity of the + operator accounts for the differences
between these two statements

The essential difference between the two is that the first statement always has at least one operand of type String, so the operation is one of string concatenation, whereas in the second statement the first operation is an arithmetic add, as both operands are integers. In the first statement each of the integers is converted to type String individually. In the second, the numerical values are added, and the result, 10, is converted to a string representation to allow the literal " is ten" to be concatenated.

You don't need to know about this at this point, but in case you were wondering, the conversion of values of the basic types to type String is actually accomplished by using a static method toString() of a standard class that corresponds to the basic type. Each of the basic types has an equivalent class defined, so for the types we have discussed earlier there are the following classes:

Basic Type	Wrapper Class
byte	Byte
short	Short
int	Integer
long	Long
float	Float
double	Double
boolean	Boolean
character	Character

A value of one of the basic types is passed to the toString() method of the corresponding class as an argument, and that returns the String equivalent. All of this happens automatically when you are concatenating strings using the + operator.We won't go into the further significance of these classes now, as we'll be covering these in more detail in Chapter 5.

Comparing Strings

Here is where the difference between the `String` variable and the string it references will become apparent. To compare variables of the basic types for equality you use the `==` operator. This does **not** apply to `String` objects (or any other objects). The expression:

```
string1 == string2
```

will check whether the two `String` variables refer to the same string. If they reference separate strings, this expression will have the value `false`, regardless of whether or not the strings happen to be identical. In other words the expression above does not compare the strings themselves, it compares the references to the strings, so the result will be only true if `string1` and `string2` both refer to one and the same string. We can demonstrate this with a little example:

Try It Out – Two Strings, Identical but not the Same

In the following code, we test to see whether `string1` and `string3` refer to the same string.

```java
public class MatchStrings
{
  public static void main(String[] args)
  {
    String string1 = "Too many ";
    String string2 = "cooks";
    String string3 = "Too many cooks";

    // Make string1 and string3 refer to separate strings that are identical
    string1 += string2;

    // Display the contents of the strings
    System.out.println("Test 1");
    System.out.println("string3 is now: " + string3);
    System.out.println("string1 is now: " + string1);

    if(string1 == string3)                    // Now test for identity
      System.out.println("string1 == string3 is true." +
                      " string1 and string3 point to the same string");
    else
      System.out.println("string1 == string3 is false." +
                " string1 and string3 do not point to the same string");

    // Now make string1 and string3 refer to the same string
    string3 = string1;

    // Display the contents of the strings
    System.out.println("\n\nTest 2");
    System.out.println("string3 is now: " + string3);
    System.out.println("string1 is now: " + string1);

    if(string1 == string3)     // Now test for identity
      System.out.println("string1 == string3 is true." +
```

```
                                   " string1 and string3 point to the same string");
        else
          System.out.println("string1 == string3 is false." +
                     " string1 and string3 do not point to the same string");
    }
}
```

We have created two scenarios. In the first, the variables `string1` and `string3` refer to separate strings that happen to be identical. In the second, they both reference the same string. This will produce the output:

```
Test 1
string3 is now: Too many cooks
string1 is now: Too many cooks
string1==string3 is false. string1 and string3 do not point to the same string

Test 2
string3 is now: Too many cooks
string1 is now: Too many cooks
string1==string3 is true. string1 and string3 point to the same string
```

How It Works

The three variables `string1`, `string2`, and `string3` are initialized with the string literals you see. After executing the assignment statement, the string referenced by `string1` will be identical to that referenced by `string3`, but as you see from the output, the comparison for equality in the `if` statement returns `false` because the variables refer to two separate strings.

Next we change the values of `string3` so that it refers to the same string as `string1`. The output demonstrates that the `if` expression has the value `true`, and that the `string1` and `string3` objects do indeed refer to the same string. This clearly shows that the comparison is not between the strings themselves, but between the references to the strings. So how do we compare the strings?

Comparing Strings for Equality

To compare two `String` variables, that is to decide whether the strings they reference are equal or not, you must use the method, `equals()`,which is defined in the `String` class. This method does a case sensitive comparison. Two strings are equal if they are the same length, that is have the same number of characters, and each character in one string is identical to the corresponding character in the other.

To check for equality between two strings ignoring the case of the string characters, you use the method `equalsIgnoreCase()`. Let's put these in the context of an example to see how they work.

Try It Out – String Identity

Make the following changes to the `MatchStrings.java` file of the previous example:

```java
public class MatchStrings
{
  public static void main(String[] args)
  {
```

```
        String string1 = "Too many ";
        String string2 = "cooks";
        String string3 = "Too many cooks";

    // Make string1 and string3 refer to separate strings that are identical
        string1 += string2;

        // Display the contents of the strings
        System.out.println("Test 1");
        System.out.println("string3 is now: " + string3);
        System.out.println("string1 is now: " + string1);

        if(string1.equals(string3))                    // Now test for equality
          System.out.println("string1.equals(string3) is true." +
                                      " so strings are equal.");
        else
          System.out.println("string1.equals(string3) is false." +
                              " so strings are not equal.");

        // Now make string1 and string3 refer to strings differing in case.
        string3 = "TOO many cooks";
        // Display the contents of the strings
        System.out.println("\n\nTest 2");
        System.out.println("string3 is now: " + string3);
        System.out.println("string1 is now: " + string1);

        if(string1.equals(string3))                    // Compare for equality
          System.out.println("string1.equals(string3) is true " +
                                      " so strings are equal.");
        else
          System.out.println("string1.equals(string3) is false" +
                              " so strings are not equal.");

        if(string1.equalsIgnoreCase(string3))          // Compare, ignoring case
          System.out.println("string1.equalsIgnoreCase(string3) is true" +
                                      " so strings are equal ignoring case.");
        else
          System.out.println("string1.equalsIgnoreCase(string3) is false" +
                              " so strings are different.");
    }
}
```

If you run this example, you should get the output:

```
Test 1
string3 is now: Too many cooks
string1 is now: Too many cooks
string1.equals(string3) is true. so strings are equal.


Test 2
string3 is now: TOO many cooks
string1 is now: Too many cooks
```

```
string1.equals(string3) is false so strings are not equal.
string1.equalsIgnoreCase(string3) is true so strings are equal ignoring case.
```

How It Works

Before we look in detail at how the program works, let's first take some time to look at how the method calls that pepper the code are put together.

In the `if` expression, we've called the method `equals()` of the object `string1` to test for equality with `string3`. This is the syntax we have been using to call the method `println()` in the object `out`. In general, to call a method belonging to an object you write the object name, then a period, then the name of the method. The parentheses following the method name enclose the information to be passed to the method – `string3` in this case. The general form for calling a method for an object is shown below.

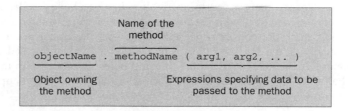

> We will learn more about this in Chapter 5, when we look at how to define our own classes. For the moment, just note that you don't necessarily need to pass any arguments to a method. On the other hand there can be several. It all depends on how the method was defined in the class.

The `equals()` method requires one argument that you put between the parentheses. This must be the `String` object that is to be compared with the original object. The method returns `true` if the value passed to it (`string3` in our example) is identical to the string pointed to by the `String` object that owns the method, in this case `string1`. As you may have already guessed, we could just as well call the `equals()` method for the object `string3`, and pass `string1` as the argument to compare the two strings. In this case, the expression to call the method would be:

```
string3.equals(string1)
```

and we would get exactly the same result.

Looking at the program code, after outputting the values of `string3` and `string1`, the next line shows that calling the `equals()` method for `string1` with `string3` as the argument returns `true`. After the `if`, we make `string3` reference a new string. We then compare the values of `string1` and `string3` once more, and of course, the result of the comparison is now `false`.

Finally we compare `string1` with `string3` using the `equalsIgnoreCase()` method. Here the result is `true` since the strings only differ in the case of the first three characters.

Checking the Start and End of a String

It can be useful to be able to check just part of a string. You can test whether a string starts with a particular character sequence by using the method `startsWith()`. If `string1` has been defined as `"Too many cooks"`, the expression `string1.startsWith("Too")` will have the value `true`. So would the expression `string1.startsWith("Too man")`. The comparison is case sensitive so the expression `string1.startsWith("tOO")` will be `false`.

A complementary method `endsWith()` checks for what appears at the end of a string, so the expression `string1.endsWith("cooks")` will have the value `true`. The test is case sensitive here, too.

Sequencing Strings

You will often need to place strings in order, for example, when you have a collection of names. Testing for equality doesn't help – what you need is the method `compareTo()` in the class `String`. This method compares the `String` object from which it is called with the argument passed to it, and returns an integer which is negative if the `String` object is less than the argument passed, zero if the `String` object is equal to the argument, and positive if the `String` object is greater than the argument. It is not that obvious what the terms 'less than', 'equal to', and 'greater than' mean when applied to strings, so let's define that a bit more precisely.

Two strings are compared in the `compareTo()` method by comparing successive corresponding characters, starting with the first character in each string. The process continues until a pair of corresponding characters are found to be different, or the last character in the shortest string is reached. Individual characters are compared by comparing their Unicode representations – so two characters are equal if the numeric values of their Unicode representations are equal. One character is greater than another if the numerical value of its Unicode representation is greater than that of the other.

One string is greater than another if it has a character greater than the corresponding character in the other string, and all the previous characters were equal. So if `string1` has the value `"mad dog"`, and `string2` has the value `"mad cat"`, then the expression

```
string1.compareTo(string2)
```

will return a positive value as a result of comparing the fifth characters in the strings; the `'d'` in `string1` with the `'c'` in `string2`.

What if the corresponding characters in both strings are equal up to the end of the shorter string, but the other string has more characters? In this case the longer string is greater than the shorter string, so `"catamaran"` is greater than `"cat"`.

One string is less than another string if it has a character less than the corresponding character in the other string, and all the preceding characters are equal. Thus the expression:

```
string2.compareTo(string1)
```

will return a negative value.

Two strings are equal if they contain the same number of characters and corresponding characters are identical. In this case the `compareTo()` method returns 0.

We can exercise the `compareTo()` method in a simple example:

Try It Out – Ordering Strings

We will just create three strings that we can compare using the `compareTo()` method. Enter the following code:

```java
public class SequenceStrings
{
  public static void main(String[] args)
  {
    // Strings to be compared
    String string1 = "A";
    String string2 = "To";
    String string3 = "Z";

    // Strings for use in output
    String string1Out = "\"" + string1 + "\"";     // string1 with quotes
    String string2Out = "\"" + string2 + "\"";     // string2 with quotes
    String string3Out = "\"" + string3 + "\"";     // string3 with quotes

    // Compare string1 with string3
    if(string1.compareTo(string3) < 0)
      System.out.println(string1Out + " is less than " + string3Out);
    else
    {
      if(string1.compareTo(string3) > 0)
        System.out.println(string1Out + " is greater than " + string3Out);
      else
        System.out.println(string1Out + " is equal to " + string3Out);
    }

    // Compare string2 with string1
    if(string2.compareTo(string1) < 0)
      System.out.println(string2Out + " is less than " + string1Out);
    else
    {
      if(string2.compareTo(string1) > 0)
        System.out.println(string2Out + " is greater than " + string1Out);
      else
        System.out.println(string2Out + " is equal to " + string1Out);
    }
  }
}
```

The example will produce the output:

```
"A" is less than "Z"
"To" is greater than "A"
```

How It Works

You should have no trouble with this example. It declares and initializes three `String` variables, `string1`, `string2`, and `string3`. We then create three further `String` variables that correspond to the first three strings with double quote characters at the beginning and the end. This is just to simplify the output statements. We then have an `if` with a nested `if` to compare `string1` with `string3`. We compare `string2` with `string1` in the same way.

As with the `equals()` method, the argument to the method `compareTo()` can be any expression that results in a `String` object.

Accessing String Characters

When you are processing strings, sooner or later you will need to access individual characters in a `String` object. To refer to a particular character in a string you use an index of type `int` that is the offset of the character position from the beginning of the string. This is exactly the same principle as we used for referencing an array element. The first character in a string is at position 0, the second is at position 1, the third is at position 2, and so on. However, although the principle is the same, the practice is not. You can't use square brackets to access characters in a string – you must use a method.

Extracting String Characters

You can extract a character from a `String` object by using the method `charAt()`. This accepts an argument that is the offset of the character position from the beginning of the string – in other words an index. If you attempt to use an index that is less than 0 or greater than the index for the last position in the string, you will cause an **exception** to be thrown, which will cause your program to be terminated. We will discuss exactly what exceptions are, and how you should deal with them in Chapter 7. For the moment just note that the specific exception thrown in this case is called `StringIndexOutOfBoundsException`.

To avoid unnecessary errors of this kind, you obviously need to be able to determine the length of a `String` object. To obtain the length of a string, you just need to call its `length()` method. Note that this is different from the way you got the length of an array. Here you are calling a method, `length()` in the class `String`, whereas with an array you were accessing a data member, `length`. We can explore the use of the `charAt()` and `length()` methods in the `String` class with an example.

Try It Out – Getting at Characters in a String

In the following code the soliloquy is analyzed character by character to determine the vowels, spaces and letters used.

```
public class StringCharacters
{
  public static void main(String[] args)
  {
    // Text string to be analyzed
    String text = "To be or not to be, that is the question;"
               +"Whether 'tis nobler in the mind to suffer"
               +" the slings and arrows of outrageous fortune,"
               +" or to take arms against a sea of troubles,"
               +" and by opposing end them?";
```

```
    int spaces  = 0,                        // Count of spaces
        vowels  = 0,                        // Count of vowels
        letters = 0;                        // Count of letters

    // Analyze all the characters in the string
    int textLength = text.length();         // Get string length
    for(int i = 0; i < textLength; i++)
    {
      // Check for vowels
      char ch = Character.toLowerCase(text.charAt(i));
      if(ch == 'a' || ch == 'e' || ch == 'i' || ch == 'o' || ch == 'u')
        vowels++;

      //Check for letters
      if(Character.isLetter(ch))
        letters++;

      // Check for spaces
      if(Character.isWhitespace(ch))
        spaces++;
    }

    System.out.println
            ("The text contained vowels:      " + vowels + "\n" +
             "                     consonants: " + (letters-vowels) + "\n"+
             "                     spaces:     " + spaces);
  }
}
```

Running the example, you'll see:

```
The text contained vowels:      60
                   consonants: 93
                   spaces:     37
```

How It Works

The `String` variable, `text`, is initialized with the quotation you see. All the counting of letter characters is done in the `for` loop, which is controlled by the index `i`. The loop continues as long as `i` is less than the length of the string, which is returned by the method `text.length()` and that we saved in the variable `textLength`.

Starting with the first character, which has the index value 0, each character is retrieved from the string by calling its `charAt()` method. The loop index `i` is used as the index to the character position string. The method returns the character at index position `i`, as a value of type `char`, and we convert this to lower case, where necessary, by calling the `static` method `toLowerCase()` in the class `Character`. The character to be converted is passed as an argument and the method returns either the original character, or if it is upper case, the lower case equivalent. This enables us to deal with the string in just one case.

There is an alternative to using the `toLowerCase()` method in the class `Character`. The class `String` also contains a method `toLowerCase()` that will convert a whole string and return the converted string. You could convert the string text to lower case with the statement:

```
text = text.toLowerCase();     // Convert string to lower case
```

This statement replaces the original string with the lower case equivalent. If you wanted to retain the original, you could store the lower case string in another variable of type `String`. For converting strings to upper case, the class `String` also has a method `toUpperCase()` which is used in the same way.

The `if` expression checks for any of the vowels by ORing the comparisons for the five vowels together. If the expression is `true` we increment the `vowels` count. To check for a letter of any kind we use the `isLetter()` method in the class `Character`, and accumulate the total letter count in the variable `letters`. This will enable us to calculate the number of consonants by subtracting the number of vowels from the total number of letters. Finally, the loop code checks for a space by using the `isWhitespace()` method in the class `Character`. This method returns `true` if the character passed as an argument is a Unicode whitespace character. As well as spaces, whitespace in Unicode also includes horizontal and vertical tab characters, new line, carriage return, and form feed characters. If you just wanted to count the blanks in the text, you could compare for a blank character. After the `for` loop ends, we just output the results.

Searching Strings for Characters

There are two methods, available to you in the class `String`, that will search a string, `indexOf()` and `lastIndexOf()`. Both of these come in four different flavors to provide a range of search possibilities. The basic choice is whether you want to search for a single character, or for a substring; so let's look first at the options for searching a string for a given character.

To search a string, `text`, for a single character, 'a' for example, you could write:

```
int index = 0;               // Position of character in the string
index = text.indexOf('a'); // Find first index position containing 'a'
```

The method `indexOf()` will search the contents of the string, `text`, forwards from the beginning, and return the index position of the first occurrence of 'a'. If 'a' is not found, the method will return the value -1.

> This is characteristic of both the search methods in the class `String`. They always return either the index position of what is sought, or -1 if the search objective is not found. It is important that you check the index value returned for -1 before you use it to index a string, otherwise you will get an error when you don't find what you are looking for.

If you wanted to find the last occurrence of 'a' in the `String` variable, `text`, you just use the method `lastIndexOf()`:

```
index = text.lastIndexOf('a');   // Find last index position containing 'a'
```

The method searches the string backwards, starting with the last character in the string. The variable `index` will therefore contain the index position of the last occurrence of 'a', or -1 if it is not found.

We can find the first and last occurrences of a character, but what about the ones in the middle? Well, there's a variation of both the above methods that has a second argument to specify a 'from position', from which to start the search. To search forwards from a given position, `startIndex`, you would write:

```
index = text.indexOf('a', startIndex);
```

This version of the method, `indexOf()` searches the string for the character specified by the first argument starting with the position specified by the second argument. You could use this to find the first 'b' that comes after the first 'a' in a string with the statements:

```
int aIndex = -1;                        // Position of 1st 'a'
int bIndex = -1;                        // Position of 1st 'b' after 'a'
aIndex = text.indexOf('a');             // Find first 'a'
if(aIndex >= 0)
   bIndex = text.indexOf('b', ++aIndex); // Find 1st 'b' after 1st 'a'
```

Once we have the index value from the initial search for 'a', we need to check that 'a' was really found by verifying that `aIndex` is not negative. We can then search for 'b' from the position following 'a'. As you can see, the second argument of this version of the method `indexOf()` is separated from the first argument by a comma. Since the second argument is the index position from which the search is to start, and `aIndex` is the position at which 'a' was found, we should increment `aIndex` to the position following 'a' before using it in the search for 'b' to avoid checking for 'b' in the position we already know contains 'a'.

If 'a' happened to be the last character in the string, it wouldn't matter, since the `indexOf()` method just returns −1 if the index value is beyond the last character in the string. If you somehow supplied a negative index value to the method, it would simply search the whole string from the beginning.

Searching for Substrings

The methods `indexOf()` and `lastIndexOf()` also come in versions that accept a string as the first argument, and will search for this string rather than a single character. In all other respects they work in the same way as the character searching methods we have just seen. The complete set of `indexOf()` methods is:

Method	Description
`indexOf(int ch)`	Returns the index position of the first occurrence of the character ch in the `String` for which the method is called. If the character ch does not occur, -1 is returned.
`indexOf(int ch, int index)`	Same as the method above, but with the search starting at position index. If the value of index is outside the legal limits for the `String` object, -1 is returned.

Table Continued on Following Page

139

Method	Description
indexOf(String str)	Returns the index position of the first occurrence of the substring, str, in the String object for which the method is called. If the substring str does not occur, -1 is returned.
indexOf(String str, int index)	Same as the method above, but with the search starting at position index. If the value of index is outside the legal limits for the String object, -1 is returned.

The four flavors of the lastIndexOf() method have the same parameters as the four versions of the indexOf() method. The difference is that the last occurrence of the character or substring that is sought is returned by the lastIndexOf() method.

The method startsWith() that we mentioned earlier also comes in a version that accepts an additional argument that is an offset from the beginning of the string being checked. The check for the matching character sequence then begins at that offset position. If you have defined a string as:

```
String string1 = "The Ides of March";
```

then the expression String1.startsWith("Ides", 4) will have the value true.
We can show the indexOf() and lastIndexOf() methods at work with substrings in an example:

Try It Out – Exciting Concordance Entries

We'll use the indexOf() method to search the quotation we used in the last example for "and" and the lastIndexOf() method for "the".

```
public class FindCharacters
{
  public static void main(String[] args)
  {
    // Text string to be analyzed
    String text = "To be or not to be, that is the question;"
              + " Whether 'tis nobler in the mind to suffer"
              + " the slings and arrows of outrageous fortune,"
              + " or to take arms against a sea of troubles,"
              + " and by opposing end them?";

    int andCount = 0;              // Number of ands
    int theCount = 0;              // Number of thes

    int index = -1;                // Current index position

    String andStr = "and";         // Search substring
    String theStr = "the";         // Search substring

    // Search forwards for "and"
    index = text.indexOf(andStr);  // Find first 'and'
    while(index >= 0)
```

```
      {
        ++andCount;
        index += andStr.length();      // Step to position after last 'and'
        index = text.indexOf(andStr, index);
      }

      // Search backwards for "the"
      index = text.lastIndexOf(theStr);    // Find last 'the'
      while(index >= 0)
      {
        ++theCount;
        index -= theStr.length();        // Step to position before last 'the'
        index = text.lastIndexOf(theStr, index);
      }

      System.out.println("The text contains " + andCount + " ands\n"
                      + "The text contains " + theCount + " thes");
    }
}
```

The program will produce the output:

```
The text contains 2 ands
The text contains 5 thes
```

If you were expecting the `"the"` count to be 3, note that there is one instance in `"whether"` and another in `"them"`. If you want to find three, you need to refine your program to eliminate such pseudo-occurrences by checking the characters either side of the `"the"` substring.

How It Works

We define the `String` variable, `text`, as before, and set up two counters, `andCount` and `theCount`, for the two words. The variable `index` will keep track of the current position in the string. We then have `String` variables `andStr` and `theStr` holding the substrings we will be searching for.

To find the instances of "and", we first find the index position of the first occurrence of "and" in the string `text`. If this index is negative, `text` does not contain "and", and the `while` loop will not execute as the condition is false on the first iteration. Assuming there is at least one "and", the `while` loop block is executed and `andCount` is incremented for the instance of "and" we have just found. The method `indexOf()` returns the index position of the first character of the substring, so we have to move the index forward to the character following the last character of the substring we have just found. This is done by adding the length of the substring, as shown on the following page:

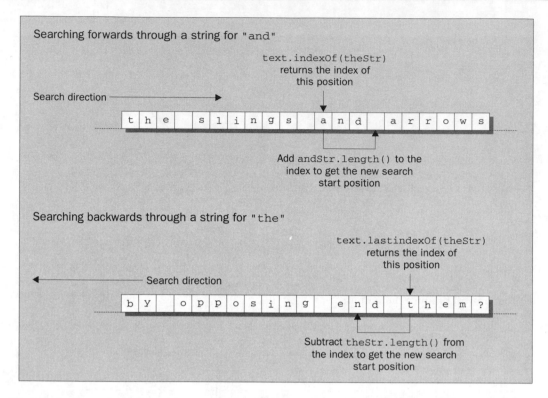

We can then search for the next occurrence of the substring by passing the new value of `index` to the method `indexOf()`. The loop continues as long as the index value returned is not -1.

To count the occurrences of the substring `"the"` the program searches the string, `text`, backwards, by using the method `lastIndexOf()` instead of `indexOf()`. This works in much the same way, the only significant difference being in the decrementing of the value of `index`, instead of incrementing it. This is because the next occurrence of the substring has to be at least that many characters back from the first character of the substring we have just found. If the string, `"the"`, happened to occur at the beginning of the string we are searching, the `lastIndexOf()` method would be called with a negative value for `index`. This would not cause any problem – it would just result in -1 being returned in any event.

Extracting Substrings

The `String` class includes a method, `substring()`, that will extract a substring from a string. There are two versions of this method. The first version will extract a substring consisting of all the characters from a given index position to the end of the string. This works as illustrated in the following code fragment:

```
String place = "Palm Springs";
String lastWord = place.substring(5);
```

After executing these statements, `lastWord` will contain the string `"Springs"`. The substring is copied from the original to form a new string. This is useful when a string has basically two constituent substrings, but a more common requirement is to extract several substrings from a string where each substring is separated from the next by a special character such as a comma, a slash, or even just a space. The second version of `substring()` will help with this.

You can extract a substring from a string by specifying the index positions of the first character in the substring, and one beyond the last character of the substring, as arguments to the method `substring()`. With the variable `place` being defined as before, the statement:

```
String segment = place.substring(7, 11);
```

will result in the variable `segment` being set to the string `"ring"`.

> The `substring()` method is not like the `indexOf()` method when it comes to illegal index values. With either version of the method `substring()`, if you specify an index that is outside the bounds of the string, you will get an error. As with the `charAt()` method, `substring()` will throw a `StringIndexOutOfBoundsException` exception.

We can see how `substring()` works with a more substantial example:

Try It Out – Word for Word

We can use the `indexOf()` method in combination with the `substring()` method to extract a sequence of substrings that are separated by spaces from a single string:

```java
public class ExtractSubstring
{
  public static void main(String[] args)
  {
    String text = "To be or not to be";      // String to be segmented
    int count = 0;                            // Number of substrings
    char separator = ' ';                     // Substring separator

    // Determine the number of substrings
    int index = 0;
    do
    {
      ++count;                                // Increment count of substrings
      ++index;                                // Move past last position
      index = text.indexOf(separator, index);
    }
    while (index != -1);

    // Extract the substring into an array
    String[] subStr = new String[count];      // Allocate for substrings
    index = 0;                                // Substring start index
    int endIndex = 0;                         // Substring end index
    for(int i = 0; i < count; i++)
    {
```

```
        endIndex = text.indexOf(separator,index);   // Find next separator

      if(endIndex == -1)                      // If it is not found
        subStr[i] = text.substring(index);      // extract to the end
      else                                            // otherwise
        subStr[i] = text.substring(index, endIndex);   // to end index

      index = endIndex + 1;                    // Set start for next cycle
    }

    // Display the substrings
    for(int i = 0; i < subStr.length; i++)
      System.out.println(subStr[i]);
  }
}
```

We will see another way to handle this sort of thing in Chapter 8 when we look into the `StringTokenizer` class. When you run this example, you should get the output:

```
To
be
or
not
to
be
```

How It Works

After setting up the string `text` to be segmented into substrings, a `count` variable to hold the number of substrings, and the separator character, `separator`, the program has three distinct phases.

The first phase counts the number of substrings by using the `indexOf()` method to find separators. The number of separators is always one less than the number of substrings. By using the `do-while` loop, we ensure that the value of `count` will be one more than the number of separators.

The second phase extracts the substrings in sequence from the beginning of the string, and stores them in an array of `String` variables that has `count` elements. Following each substring from the first to the penultimate is a separator, so we use the version of the `substring()` method that accepts two index arguments for these. The last substring is signaled by a failure to find the separator character when `index` will be -1. In this case we use the `substring()` method with a single argument to extract the substring through to the end of the string, `text`.

The third phase simply outputs the contents of the array by displaying each element in turn, using a `for` loop.

Modifying String Objects

There are a couple of methods that you can use to create a new `String` object that is a modified version of an existing `String` object. They don't change the original string, of course – as we said, `String` objects are immutable. To replace one specific character with another throughout a string, you can use the `replace()` method. For example, to replace each space in our string, `text`, with a slash, you could write:

```
String newText = text.replace(' ', '/');        // Modify the string text
```

The first argument of the `replace()` method specifies the character to be replaced, and the second argument specifies the character that is to be substituted in its place. We have stored the result in a new variable `newText` here, but you could save it back in the original `String` variable, `text`, if you wanted.

To remove whitespace from the beginning and end of a string (but not the interior) you can use the `trim()` method. You could apply this to a string as follows:

```
String sample = "   This is a string   ";
String result = sample.trim();
```

after which the `String` variable `result` will contain the string "`This is a string`". This can be useful when you are segmenting a string into substrings and the substrings may contain leading or trailing blanks. For example, this might arise if you were analyzing an input string that contained values separated by one or more spaces.

Creating Character Arrays from String Objects

You can create an array of variables of type `char` from a `String` variable by using the `toCharArray()` method in the class `String`. Because this method returns an array of type `char`, you only need to declare the array variable of type `char[]` – you don't need to allocate the array. For example:

```
String text = "To be or not to be";
char[] textArray = text.toCharArray();     // Create the array from the string
```

The `toCharArray()` method will return an array containing the characters of the `String` variable `text`, one per element, so `textArray[0]` will contain 'T', `textArray[1]` will contain 'o', `textArray[2]` will contain ' ', and so on.

You can also extract a substring as an array of characters using the method `getChars()`, but in this case you do need to create an array that is large enough to hold the characters. This enables you to reuse a single array to store characters when you want to extract a succession of substrings, and thus saves the need to repeatedly create new arrays. Of course, the array must be large enough to accommodate the longest substring.

The method `getChars()` has four parameters. In sequence, these are:

- ❏ Index position of the first character to be extracted (type `int`)
- ❏ Index position following the last character to be extracted (type `int`)
- ❏ The name of the array to hold the characters extracted (type `char[]`)
- ❏ The index of the array element to hold the first character (type `int`)

You could copy a substring from `text` into an array with the statements:

```
String text = "To be or not to be";
char[] textArray = new char[3];
text.getChars(9, 12, textArray, 0);
```

This will copy characters from `text` at index positions 9 to 11 inclusive, so `textArray[0]` will be 'n', `textArray[1]` will be 'o', and `textArray[2]` will be 't'.

You can also extract characters into a `byte` array using the `getBytes()` method in the class `String`. This converts the original string characters into the character encoding used by the underlying operating system – which is usually ASCII. For example:

```
String text = "To be or not to be";      // Define a string
byte[] textArray = text.getBytes();      // Get equivalent byte array
```

The `byte` array `textArray` will contain the same characters as in the `String` object, but stored as 8-bit characters. The conversion of characters from Unicode to 8 bit bytes will be in accordance with the default encoding for your system. This will typically mean that the upper byte of the Unicode character is discarded resulting in the ASCII equivalent.

Creating String Objects from Character Arrays

The `String` class also has a static method, `copyValueOf()`, to create a `String` object from an array of type `char[]`. You will recall that a static method of a class can be used even if no objects of the class exist:

Suppose you have an array defined as:

```
char[] textArray = {'T', 'o', ' ', 'b', 'e', ' ', 'o', 'r', ' ',
                    'n', 'o', 't', ' ', 't', 'o', ' ', 'b', 'e' };
```

You can then create a `String` object with the statement:

```
String text = String.copyValueOf(textArray);
```

This will result in the object, `text`, referencing the string `"To be or not to be"`.

Another version of the `copyValueOf()` method can create a string from a subset of the array elements. It requires two additional arguments to specify the index of the first character in the array to be extracted and the count of the number of characters to be extracted. With the array defined as previously, the statement:

```
String text = String.copyValueOf(textArray, 9, 3);
```

extracts 3 characters starting with `textArray[9]`, so `text` will contain the string `"not"` after this operation.

StringBuffer Objects

`String` objects cannot be changed, but we have been creating strings that are combinations and modifications of existing `String` objects, so how is this done? Java has another standard class for defining strings, `StringBuffer`, and a `StringBuffer` object can be altered directly. Strings that can be changed are often referred to as **mutable strings** whereas a `String` object is an **immutable string**. Java uses objects of the class `StringBuffer` internally to perform many of the operations on `String` objects. You can use a `StringBuffer` object whenever you need a string that you can change directly.

So when do you use `StringBuffer` objects rather than `String` objects? `StringBuffer` objects come into their own when you are transforming strings – adding, deleting, or replacing substrings in a string. Operations will be faster and easier using `StringBuffer` objects. If you have static strings, which you occasionally need to concatenate then `String` objects will be the best choice. Of course, if you want to you can mix the use of both in the same program.

Creating StringBuffer Objects

You can create a `StringBuffer` object that contains a given string with the statement:

```
StringBuffer aString = new StringBuffer("A stitch in time");
```

This declares a `StringBuffer` object, `aString`, and initializes it with the string `"A stitch in time"`. When you are initializing a `StringBuffer` object, you must use this syntax, with the keyword `new`, the `StringBuffer` class name, and the initializing value between parentheses. You cannot just use the string as the initializing value as we did with `String` objects. This is because there is rather more to a `StringBuffer` object than just the string that it contains initially, and of course, a string literal is a `String` object by definition.

You can just create the `StringBuffer` variable, in much the same way as you created a `String` variable:

```
StringBuffer myString = null;
```

This variable does not refer to anything until you initialize it with a defined `StringBuffer` object. For example, you could write:

```
myString = new StringBuffer("Many a mickle makes a muckle");
```

which will initialize it with the string specified. You can also initialize a `StringBuffer` variable with an existing `StringBuffer` object:

```
myString = aString;
```

Both `myString` and `aString` will now refer to a single `StringBuffer` object.

The Capacity of a StringBuffer Object

The `String` objects that we have been using each contain a fixed string, and memory is allocated to accommodate however many Unicode characters are in the string. Everything is fixed so memory usage is not a problem. A `StringBuffer` object is a little different. It contains a block of memory called a **buffer** which may or may not contain a string, and if it does, the string need not occupy all of the buffer. Thus the length of a string in a string object can be different from the length of the buffer. The length of the buffer is referred to as the **capacity** of the `StringBuffer` object.

Once you have created a `StringBuffer` object, you can find the length of the string it contains, by using the `length()` method for the object:

```
StringBuffer aString = new StringBuffer("A stitch in time");
int theLength = aString.length();
```

If the object, `aString`, was defined as in the declaration above, the variable `theLength` will have the value 16. However, the capacity of the object is larger, as illustrated in the diagram.

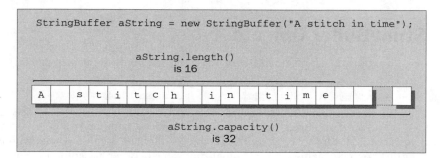

When you create a `StringBuffer` object from an existing string, the capacity will be the length of the string plus 16. Both the capacity and the length are in units of Unicode characters, so twice as many bytes will be occupied in memory.

The capacity of a `StringBuffer` object is not fixed though. For instance, you can create a `StringBuffer` object with a given capacity by specifying the capacity when you declare it:

```
StringBuffer newString = new StringBuffer(50);
```

This will create an object, `newString`, with the capacity to store 50 characters. If you omitted the capacity value in this declaration, the object would have a default capacity of 16 characters.

A `String` object is always a fixed string, so capacity is irrelevant – it is always just enough to hold the characters in the string. A `StringBuffer` object is a container in which you can store any string and therefore has a capacity – a potential for storing strings up to a given size. Although you can set it, the capacity is unimportant in the sense that it is just a measure of how much memory is available to store Unicode characters at this particular point in time. You can get by without worrying about the capacity of a `StringBuffer` object since the capacity required to cope with what your program is doing will always be provided automatically. It just gets increased as necessary.

On the other hand the capacity of a `StringBuffer` object is important in the sense that it affects the amount of overhead involved in storing and modifying a string. If the initial capacity is small, and you store a string that is long, or you add to an existing string significantly, extra memory will need to be allocated, which will take time. It is more efficient to make the capacity of a `StringBuffer` sufficient for the needs of your program.

To find out what the capacity of a `StringBuffer` object is at any given time, you use the `capacity()` method for the object:

```
int theCapacity = aString.capacity();
```

This method will return the number of Unicode characters the object can currently hold. For `aString` defined as shown, this will be 32. When you create a `StringBuffer` object containing a string, its capacity will be 16 characters greater than the minimum necessary to hold the string.

The `ensureCapacity()` method enables you to change the default capacity of a `StringBuffer` object. You specify the minimum capacity you need as the argument to the method, for example:

```
aString.ensureCapacity(40);
```

If the current capacity of the `aString` object is less than 40, this will increase the capacity of `aString` by allocating a new larger buffer, but not necessarily with a capacity of 40. The capacity will be the larger of either the value you specify, 40 in this case, or twice the current capacity plus 2, which is 66, given that `aString` is defined as before.

Changing the Length for a StringBuffer Object

You can change the length of the string contained in a `StringBuffer` object with the method `setLength()`. Note that the length is a property of the string the object holds, as opposed to the capacity, which is a property of the string buffer. When you increase the length for a `StringBuffer` object, the extra characters will contain '\u0000'. A more common use of this method would be to decrease the length, in which case the string will be truncated. If `aString` contains "A stitch in time", the statement:

```
aString.setLength(8);
```

will result in `aString` containing the string "A stitch", and the value returned by the `length()` method will be 8. The characters that were cut from the end of the string by this operation are lost.

To increase the length to what it was before, you could write:

```
aString.setLength(16);
```

Now aString will contain
"A stitch\u0000\u0000\u0000\u0000\u0000\u0000\u0000\u0000"

The setLength() method does not affect the capacity of the object unless you set the length to be greater than the capacity. In this case the capacity will be increased to accommodate the new string length to a value that is twice the original capacity plus two if the length you set is less than this value. If you specify a length that is greater than twice the original capacity plus two, the new capacity will be the same as the length you set. If the capacity of aString is 66, executing the statement

```
aString.setLength(100);
```

will set the capacity of the object, aString, to 134. If you supplied a value for the length of 150, then the new capacity would be 150. You must not specify a negative length here. If you do a StringIndexOutOfBoundsException exception will be thrown.

Adding to a StringBuffer Object

The append() method enables you to add a string to the end of the existing string stored in a StringBuffer object. This method comes in quite a few flavors, but perhaps the simplest adds a String constant to a StringBuffer object.

If we have defined a StringBuffer object with the statement:

```
StringBuffer aString = new StringBuffer("A stitch in time");
```

we can add to it with the statement:

```
aString.append(" saves nine");
```
after which aString will contain "A stitch in time saves nine". The length of the string contained in the StringBuffer object will be increased by the length of the string that you add. You don't need to worry about running out of space though. If necessary, the capacity will be increased automatically to accommodate the longer string.

The append() method returns the extended StringBuffer object, so you could also assign it to another StringBuffer object. Instead of the previous statement, you could have written:

```
StringBuffer bString = aString.append(" saves nine");
```

Now both aString and bString point to the same StringBuffer object.

If you take a look at the operator precedence table back in Chapter 2, you will see that the . operator (sometimes called the member selection operator) that we use to execute a particular method for an object has left-to-right associativity. You could therefore write:

```
StringBuffer proverb = new StringBuffer();                    // Capacity is 16
proverb.append("Many").append(" hands").append(" make").
                     append(" light").append(" work.");
```

The second statement is executed from left to right, so that the string contained in the object `proverb` is progressively extended until it contains the complete string.

Appending a Substring

Another version of the `append()` method will add part of a `String` object to a `StringBuffer` object. This version of `append()` requires you to specify two additional arguments, the index position of the first character to be appended, and the total number of characters to be appended. This operation is shown in the diagram.

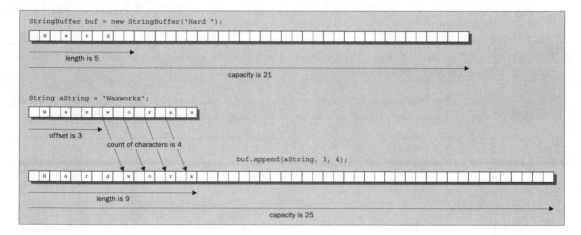

This operation appends a substring of `aString` consisting of four characters starting at index position 3 to the `StringBuffer` object, `buf`. The capacity of `buf` is automatically increased by the length of the appended substring, if necessary.

Appending Basic Types

You have a set of versions of the `append()` method that will enable you to `append()` any of the basic types to a `StringBuffer` object. These will accept arguments of any of the following types; `boolean`, `char`, `byte`, `short`, `int`, `long`, `float` or `double`. In each case, the value is converted to a string equivalent of the value which is appended to the object, so a `boolean` variable will be appended as either "`true`" or "`false`", and for numeric types the string will be a decimal representation of the value. For example:

```
StringBuffer buf = new StringBuffer("The number is ");
long number = 999;
buf.append(number);
```

will result in `buf` containing the string "`The number is 999`".

151

There is nothing to prevent you from appending constants to a `StringBuffer` object. For example, if you now execute the statement:

```
buf.append(12.34);
```

the object `buf` will contain `"The number is 99912.34"`.

There is also a version of the `append()` method which accepts an array of type `char` as an argument. The contents of the array are appended to the `StringBuffer` object as a string. A further variation on this enables you to append a subset of the elements from an array of type `char` by using two additional arguments, one to specify the index of the first element to be appended, and another to specify the total number of elements to be appended. An example of how you might use this is as follows;

```
char[] text = { 'i', 's', ' ', 'e', 'x', 'a', 'c', 't', 'l', 'y'};
buf.append(text, 2, 8);
```

This will append the string `" exactly"` to `buf`, so after executing this statement `buf` will contain `"The number is 99912.34 exactly"`.

You may be somewhat bemused by the plethora of `append()` method options, so let's collect all the possibilities together. You can append any of the following types to a `StringBuffer` object:

boolean	char	String	Object
int	long	float	double
byte	short		

You can also append an array of type `char[]`, and a subset of the elements of an array of type `char[]`. In each case the `String` equivalent of the argument is appended to the string in the `StringBuffer` object.

We haven't discussed type `Object` – it is here for the sake of completeness. You will learn about this type of object in Chapter 6.

Inserting Strings

To insert a string into a `StringBuffer` object, you use the `insert()` method of the object. The first argument specifies the index of the position in the object where the first character is to be inserted. For example, if `buf` contains the string `"Many hands make light work"`, the statement:

```
buf.insert(4, " old");
```

will insert the string `" old"` starting at index position 4, so `buf` will contain the string `"Many old hands make light work"` after executing this statement.

There are many versions of the `insert()` method that will accept a second argument of any of the same range of types that apply to the `append()` method, so you can use any of the following with the `insert()` method:

boolean	char	String	Object
int	long	float	double
byte	short		

In each case the string equivalent of the second argument is inserted starting at the index position specified by the first argument. You can also insert an array of type char[], and if you need to insert a subset of an array of type char[] into a StringBuffer object, you can call the version of insert() that accepts four arguments:

Method	Description
insert(int index, char[] str, int offset, int length)	Inserts a substring into the StringBuffer object starting at position index. The substring is the String representation of length characters from the str[] array, starting at position offset.

If the value of index is outside the range of the string in the StringBuffer object, or the offset or length values result in illegal indexes for the array, str, then an exception of type StringIndexOutOfBoundsException will be thrown.

Extracting Characters from a StringBuffer Object

The StringBuffer includes the charAt() and getChars() methods, both of which work in the same way as the methods of the same name in the class String which we've already seen. The charAt() method extracts the character at a given index position, and the getChars() method extracts a range of characters and stores them in an array of type char starting at a specified index position. You should note that there is no equivalent to the getBytes() method for StringBuffer objects.

Other StringBuffer Operations

You can change a single character in a StringBuffer object by using the setCharAt() method. The first argument indicates the index position of the character to be changed, and the second argument specifies the replacement character. For example, the statement:

```
buf.setCharAt(3, 'Z');
```

will set the fourth character in the string to 'Z'.

You can completely reverse the sequence of characters in a StringBuffer object with the reverse() method. For example, if you define the object with the declaration:

```
StringBuffer palindrome = new StringBuffer("so many dynamos");
```

You can then transform it with the statement:

```
palindrome.reverse();
```

which will result in `palindrome` containing the useful phrase "`somanyd ynam os`".

Creating a String Object from a StringBuffer Object

You can produce a `String` object from a `StringBuffer` object by using the `toString()` method of the `StringBuffer` class. This method creates a new `String` object and initializes it with the string contained in the `StringBuffer` object. For example, to produce a `String` object containing the proverb that we created in the previous section, you could write:

```
String saying = proverb.toString();
```

The object, `saying`, will contain "`Many hands make light work`".

The `toString()` method is used extensively by the compiler together with the `append()` method to implement the concatenation of `String` objects. When you write a statement such as:

```
String saying = "Many" + " hands" + " make" + " light" + " work";
```

the compiler will implement this as:

```
String saying = new StringBuffer().append("Many").append(" hands").
                                   append(" make").append(" light").
                                   append(" work").toString();
```

The expression to the right of the = sign is executed from left to right, so the segments of the string are appended to the `StringBuffer` object that is created until finally the `toString()` method is invoked to convert it to a `String` object. `String` objects can't be modified, so any alteration or extension of a `String` object will involve the use of a `StringBuffer` object which can be changed.

Summary

You should now be thoroughly familiar with how to create and use arrays. Most people have little trouble dealing with one dimensional arrays, but arrays of arrays are a bit more tricky so try to practice using these.

You have also acquired a good knowledge of what you can do with `String` and `StringBuffer` objects. Most operations with these objects are very straightforward and easy to understand. Being able to decide which methods you should apply to the solution of specific problems is a skill that will come with a bit of practice.

The essential points that we have discussed in this chapter are:

- ❑ You use an array to hold multiple values of the same type, identified through a single variable name.

- ❑ You reference an individual element of an array by using an index value of type int. The index value for an array element is the offset of that element from the first element in the array.

- ❑ An array element can be used in the same way as a single variable of the same type.

- ❑ You can obtain the number of elements in an array by using the length member of the array object.

- ❑ An array element can also contain an array, so you can define arrays of arrays, or arrays of arrays of arrays…

- ❑ A String object stores a fixed character string that cannot be changed. However, you can assign a given String variable to a different String object.

- ❑ You can obtain the number of characters stored in a String object by using the length() method for the object.

- ❑ The String class provides methods for joining, searching, and modifying strings – the modifications being achieved by creating a new String object.

- ❑ A StringBuffer object can store a string of characters that can be modified.

- ❑ You can get the number of characters stored in a StringBuffer object by calling its length() method, and you can find out what the current maximum number of characters it can store is by using its capacity() method.

- ❑ You can change both the length and the capacity for a StringBuffer object.

- ❑ The StringBuffer class contains a variety of methods for modifying StringBuffer objects.

- ❑ You can create a String object from a StringBuffer object by using the toString() method of the StringBuffer object.

Exercises

1. Create an array of String variables and initialize the array with the names of the months from January to December. Create an array containing 12 random decimal values between 0.0 and 100.0. Display the names of each month along with the corresponding decimal value. Calculate and display the average of the 12 decimal values.

2. Write a program to create a rectangular array containing a multiplication table from 1x1 up to 12x12. Output the table as 13 columns with the numeric values right aligned in columns. (The first line of output will be the column headings, the first column with no heading, then the numbers 1 to 12 for the remaining columns. The first item in each of the succeeding lines is the row heading which ranges from 1 to 12).

3. Write a program that sets up a `String` variable containing a paragraph of text of your choice. Extract the words from the text and sort them into alphabetical order. Display the sorted list of words. You could use a simple sorting method called the bubble sort. To sort an array into ascending order the process is as follows:

Starting with the first element in the array compare successive elements (0 and 1, 1 and 2, 2 and 3, and so on).

If the first element of any pair is greater that the second, interchange the two elements.

Repeat the process for the whole array until no interchanges are necessary. The array elements will now be in ascending order.

4. Set up an array of ten `String` variables each containing an arbitrary string of the form month/day /year, for example 10/29/99. Analyze each element in the array and output the date represented in the form 29th October 1999.

Defining Classes

In this chapter we will explore the heart of the Java language – **classes**. Classes specify the objects you use in object-oriented programming. These form the basic building blocks of any Java program, as we saw in Chapter 1. Every program in Java involves classes, since the code for a program can only appear within a class definition.

We will now explore the details of how a class definition is put together, how to create your own classes and how to use classes to solve your own computing problems. And in the next chapter we'll extend this to look at how object-oriented programming helps us work with related classes.

By the end of this chapter you will have learned:

❑   What a class is, and how you define one.

❑   How to implement class constructors.

❑   How to define class methods.

❑   What method overloading is.

❑   What a recursive method is and how it works.

❑   How to create objects of a class.

❑   What packages are and how you can create and use them.

❑   What access attributes are and how you should use them in your class definitions.

❑   When you should add the finalize() method to a class.

❑   What native methods are.

What is a Class?

As you saw in Chapter 1, a class is a prescription for a particular kind of object. We can use the class definition to create objects of that class type, that is, to create objects that incorporate all the components specified as belonging to that class.

In case that's too abstract, look back to the last chapter, where we used the String class. This is a comprehensive definition for a string object, with all the operations you are likely to need built in. This makes String objects indispensable and string handling within a program easy.

The `String` class lies towards one end of a spectrum in terms of complexity in a class. The `String` class is intended to be usable in any program. It includes facilities and capabilities for operating on `String` objects to cover virtually all circumstances in which you are likely to using strings. In most cases your own classes won't need to be this elaborate. You will typically be defining a class to suit your particular application. Objects that can potentially be very complicated, a `Plane` or a `Person` for instance, may well be represented by a very simple class if that fulfils your needs. A `Person` object might just contain a name, address, and phone number for example if you are just implementing an address book. In another context, in a payroll program perhaps, you might need to represent a `Person` with a whole host of properties, such as age, marital status, length of service, job code, pay rate, and so on. It all depends on what you intend to do with objects of your class.

In essence a class definition is very simple. There are just two kinds of things that you can include in a class definition:

❑ **Fields** These are variables that store data items that typically differentiate one object of the class from another. They are also referred to as **data members** of a class. Thus the terms 'class variables', 'fields', and 'data members', all refer to the same thing.

❑ **Methods** These define the operations you can perform for the class – so they determine what you can do to, or with, objects of the class. Methods typically operate on the fields – the variables of the class.

The fields in a class definition can be of any of the basic types, or they can be references to objects of any class type, including the one that you are defining.

The methods in a class definition are named, self-contained blocks of code, that typically operate on the variables that appear in the class definition. Note though, that this doesn't necessarily have to be the case, as you might have guessed from the `main()` methods we have written in all our examples up to now.

Variables in a Class Definition

An object of a class is also referred to as an **instance** of that class. When you create an object, the object will contain all the variables that were included in the class definition. However, the variables in a class definition are not all the same – there are two kinds.

One kind of variable in a class is associated with each object uniquely – each instance of the class will have its own copy of each of these variables, with its own value assigned. These differentiate one object from another, giving an object its individuality – the particular name, address, and telephone number in a given `Person` object for instance. These are referred to as **instance variables**.

The other kind of class variable is associated with the class, and is shared by all objects of the class. There is only one copy of each of these kinds of variables no matter how many class objects are created, and they exist even if no objects of the class have been created. This kind of variable is referred to as a **class variable** because the variable belongs to the class, not to any particular object, although as we have said, it will be shared by all objects of the class. These variables are also referred to as **static fields** because, as we will see, you use the keyword `static` when you declare them.

Because this is extremely important to understand, let's summarize the two kinds of variables that you can include in your classes:

Instance variables	Each object of the class will have its own copy of each of the instance variables that appear in the class definition. Each object will have its own values for each instance variable. The name 'instance variable' originates from the fact that an object is an 'instance' of a class and the values stored in the instance variables for the object differentiate the object from others of the same class type. An instance variable is declared within the class definition in the usual way, with a type name and a variable name, and can have an initial value specified.
Class variables	A given class will only have one copy of each of its class variables, and these will be shared between all the objects of the class. The class variables exist even if no objects of the class have been created. They belong to the class, and they can be referenced by any object or class, not just instances of that class. If the value of a class variable is changed, the new value is available in all the objects of the class. This is quite different from instance variables where changing a value for one object does not affect the values in other objects. A class variable must be declared using the keyword `static` preceding the type name.

For an illustration of the difference between the two, look at the following diagram.

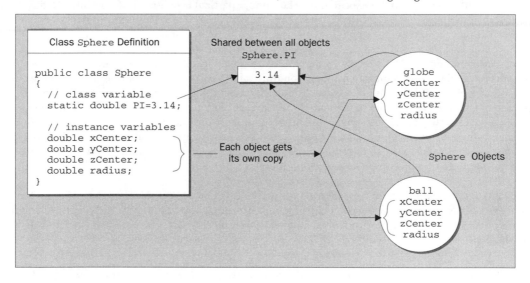

This shows a schematic of a class `Sphere` with one class variable `PI`, and four instance variables, `radius`, `xCenter`, `yCenter` and `zCenter`. Each of the objects, `globe` and `ball`, will have their own variables, `radius`, `xCenter`, `yCenter` and `zCenter`, but both will share a single copy of the class variable `PI`.

Why would you need two kinds of variables in a class definition? The instance variables are clearly necessary since they are the parameters that distinguish a particular object. The radius and the coordinates of the center of the sphere are fundamental to determining how big a particular `Sphere` object is, and where it is in space. However, although the variable `PI` is a fundamental parameter for a sphere – to calculate the volume for example – it would be wasteful to store a value for `PI` in every object, since it is always the same. Incidentally, it is also available from the standard class `Math` so it is somewhat superfluous in this case, but you get the general idea. So one use for class variables is to hold constant values such as π that are common to all objects of the class.

Another use for class variables is to track data values that are common to all objects of a class, and that need to be available even when no objects have been defined. For example, if you wanted to keep a count of how many objects of a class have been created in your program, you would define the variable storing the count as a class variable. It would be essential to use a class variable, because you would still want to be able to use your `count` variable even when no objects have been declared.

Methods in a Class Definition

The methods that you define for a class provide the actions that can be carried out using the variables specified in the class definition.

Analogous to the variables in a class definition, there are two varieties of methods – **instance methods** and **class methods**. You can execute class methods even when no objects of a class exist, whereas instance methods can only be executed in relation to a particular object, so if no objects exist, there are no instance methods to be executed. Again, like class variables, class methods are declared using the keyword `static` so they are sometimes referred to as **static methods**.

Since class methods can be executed when there are no objects in existence, they cannot refer to instance variables. This is quite sensible if you think about it – trying to operate with variables that might not exist would be bound to cause trouble. In fact the Java compiler won't let you try. If you reference an instance variable in the code for a class method, it won't compile – you'll just get an error message. The method `main()`, where execution of a Java application starts, must always be declared as static, as you have seen. The reason for this should be apparent by now. Before an application starts execution, no objects exist, so in order to start execution, you need a method that is executable even though there are no objects – a static method therefore.

The class `Sphere` might well have an instance method `volume()` to calculate the volume of a particular object. It might also have a class method `objectCount()` to return the current count of how many objects of type `Sphere` have been created. If no objects exist, you could still call this method and get the count 0.

Note that, although instance methods are specific to objects of a class, there is only ever one copy of an instance method in memory that is shared by all objects of the class, as it would be extremely expensive to replicate all the instance methods for each object. There is a special mechanism that ensures that, each time you call a method the codes executes in a manner that is specific to an object, but we will defer exploring this until a little later in this chapter.

Apart from making the method `main()` possible, perhaps the most common use for class methods is when a class is just used to contain a bunch of utility methods, rather than as a specification for objects. All executable code in Java has to be within a class, but there are lots of general purpose functions that you need that don't necessarily have an object association – calculating a square root, for instance, or generating a random number. For example, the mathematical functions that are implemented as class methods in the standard class `Math`, don't relate to class objects at all – they operate on values of the basic types. You don't need objects of type `Math`, you just want to use the methods from time to time, and you can do this as we saw in Chapter 2. The class `Math` also contains some class variables containing useful mathematical constants such as e and π.

Accessing Variables and Methods

You will often want to access variables and methods, defined within a class, from outside it. We will see later that it is possible to declare class members with restrictions on accessing them from outside, but let's cover the principles that apply where the members are accessible. We need to consider accessing static members and instance members separately.

You can access a static member of a class using the class name, followed by a period, followed by the member name. With a class method you will also need to supply the parentheses enclosing any arguments to the method after the method name. The period here is called the dot operator. So, if you wanted to calculate the square root of π you could access the class method `sqrt()` and the class variable `PI` that are defined in the `Math` class as follows:

```
double rootPi - Math.sqrt(Math.PI);
```

This shows how you call a static method – you just prefix it with the class name and put the dot operator between them. We also reference the static data member, `PI`, in the same way.

If you have a reference to an object of a class type available, then you can also use that to access a static member of a class method. You just use the variable name, followed by the dot operator, followed by the member name.

Instance variables and methods can only be called using an object reference, as by definition they relate to a particular object. The syntax is exactly the same as we have outlined for static members. You put the name of the variable referencing the object followed by a period, followed by the member name. To use a method `volume()` that has been declared as an instance method in the `Sphere` class, you might write:

```
double ballVolume = ball.volume();
```

Here the variable `ball` is of type `Sphere` and it contains a reference to an object of this type. We call its `volume()` method that calculates the volume of the `ball` object, and the result that is returned is stored in the variable, `ballVolume`.

Defining Classes

To define a class you use the keyword `class` followed by the name of the class, followed by a pair of braces enclosing the details of the definition. Let's consider a concrete example to see how this works in practice. The definition of the `Sphere` class we mentioned earlier could be:

```
class Sphere
{
   static final double PI = 3.14;   // Class variable that has a fixed value
   static int count = 0;            // Class variable to count objects

   // Instance variables
   double radius;                   // Radius of a sphere

   double xCenter;                  // 3D coordinates
   double yCenter;                  // of the center
   double zCenter;                  // of a sphere

   // Plus the rest of the class definition...
}
```

You name a class using an identifier of the same sort you've been using for variables. By convention though, class names in Java begin with a capital letter so our class name is `Sphere` with a capital `S`. If you adopt this approach, you will be consistent with most of the code you will come across. You could enter this source code and save it as the file `Sphere.java`. Remember the file containing a Java class definition must have the same name as the class, and must have the extension `.java`. We will be building on this class, and using it in a working example, a little later in this chapter.

The keyword `static` in the first line of the definition specifies the variable `PI` as a class variable rather than an instance variable. The variable `PI` is also initialized with the value 3.14. The keyword `final` tells the compiler that you do not want the value of this variable to be changed, so the compiler will check that this variable is not modified anywhere in your program. Obviously this is a very poor value for π – You would normally use `Math.PI` which is defined to twenty decimal places, close enough for most purposes.

> Whenever you want to fix the value stored in a variable, that is, make it a constant, you just need to declare the variable with the keyword `final` and specify its initial value. By convention, constants have names in capital letters.

The next variable, `count`, is also declared with the keyword `static`. All objects of the `Sphere` class will share one copy of `count`, and one of `PI`. We have initialized the variable `count` to 0, but since it is not declared with the keyword `final`, we can change its value.

The next four variables in the class definition are instance variables, as they don't have the keyword `static` applied to them. Each object of the class will have its own separate set of these variables storing the radius and the coordinates of the center of the sphere. Although we haven't put initial values for these variables here, we could do so if we wanted. If you don't specify an initial value, a default value will be assigned automatically when the object is created. Fields that are of numeric types will be initialized with zero, fields of type `char` will be initialized with `'\u000'`, and fields that store class references or references to arrays will be initialized with `null`.

There has to be something missing from the definition of the Sphere class – there is no way to set the value of radius and the other instance variables once a particular Sphere object is created. There is nothing to update the value of count either. Adding these things to the class definition involves using methods, so we now need to look at how a method is put together.

Defining Methods

We have been producing versions of the method main() since Chapter 1, so you already have an idea of how a method is constructed. Nonetheless, we will go through from the beginning to make sure everything is clear.

We'll start with the fundamental concepts. A method is a self contained block of code that has a name, and has the property that it is reusable – the same method can be executed from as many different points in a program as you require. Methods also serve to break up large and complex calculations that might involve many lines of code into more manageable chunks. A method is executed by calling the method using its name, as we will see, and a method may or may not return a value. Methods that do not return a value are called in a statement that does just that. Methods that return a value are usually called from within an expression, and the value that is returned by such a method is used in the evaluation of the expression.

The basic structure of a method is shown below.

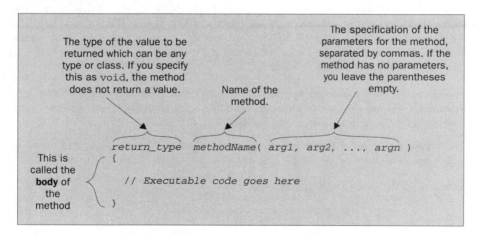

When you specify the return type for a method, you are defining the type for the value that will be returned by the method when you execute it. The method must always return a value of this type. To define a method that does not return a value, you specify the return type as void. Something called an **access attribute** can optionally precede the return type in a method definition, but we will defer looking into this until later in this chapter.

The parameters to a method appear in its definition between parentheses following the method name. These specify what information is to be passed to the method when you execute it. The parameters are optional, and a method that does not require any such information to be passed to it has an empty pair of parentheses after the name.

Returning from a Method

To return a value from a method when its execution is complete you use a `return` statement, for example:

```
return return_value;    // Return a value from a method
```

After executing the `return` statement, the program continues from the point where the method was called. The value, `return_value`, returned by the method can be any expression that produces a value of the type specified for the return value in the declaration of the method. Methods that return a value – that is methods declared with a return type other than `void` – must always finish by executing a `return` statement that returns a value of the appropriate type. Note, though, that you can put several `return` statements within a method if the logic requires this. If a method does not return a value, you can just use the keyword `return` by itself to end execution of the method:

```
return;    // Return from a method
```

Note that, for methods that do not return a value, falling through the closing brace enclosing the body of the method is equivalent to executing a `return` statement.

The Parameter List

The **parameter list**, which appears between the parentheses following the method name, specifies the type of each value that can be passed as an argument to a method, and the variable name that is to be used in the body of the method to refer to the value passed. The difference between a **parameter** and an **argument** is sometimes confusing because people often, incorrectly, use them interchangeably. We will try to differentiate them consistently, as follows:

❑ A parameter has a name and appears in the parameter list in the definition of a method. A parameter defines the type of value that can be passed to the method, and the name that is used to reference it within the code for the method.

❑ An argument is a value that is passed to a method when it is executed, and the value of the argument is referenced by the parameter name during execution of the method.

This is illustrated in the following diagram.

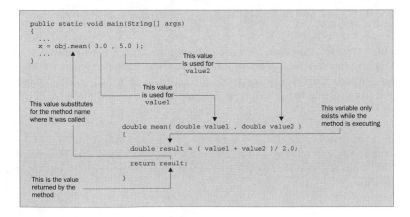

Here we have the definition of a method mean(). This can only appear within the definition of a class, but the rest of the class definition has been omitted so as not to clutter up the diagram. You can see that the method has two parameters, value1, and value2, both of which are of type double, that are used to refer to the arguments 3.0 and 5.0 respectively within the body of the method. Since this method has not been defined as static, you can only call it for an object of the class. We call mean() in our example for the object, obj.

When you call the method from another method (from main() in this case, but it could be from some other method), the values of the arguments passed are the initial values assigned to the corresponding parameters. You can use any expression you like for an argument when you call a method, as long as the value it produces is of the same type as the corresponding parameter in the definition of the method. With our method mean(), both parameters are of type double, so both argument values must always be of type double.

The method mean() declares the variable result, which only exists within the body of the method. The variable is created each time you execute the method and it is destroyed when execution of the method ends. All the variables that you declare within the body of a method are local to the method, and are only around while the method is being executed. Variables declared within a method are called **local variables** because they are local to the method. The scope of a local variable is as we discussed in Chapter 2, and local variables are not initialized automatically. If you want your local variables to have initial values you must supply the initial value when you declare them.

How Argument Values are Passed

You need to be clear about how your argument values are passed to a method, otherwise you may run into problems. In Java, all argument values that belong to one of the basic types are transferred to a method using what is called the **pass-by-value** mechanism. How this works is illustrated below.

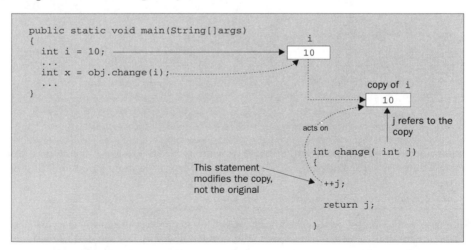

All this means is that for each argument value that you pass to a method, a copy is made, and it is the copy that is passed and referenced through the parameter name, not the original value. This implies that if you use a variable of any of the basic types as an argument, the method cannot modify the value of this variable in the calling program. In the example shown, the method change() will modify the copy of i that is created automatically, so the value of j that is returned will be 11 and this will be stored in x. However, the original value of i will remain at 10.

> While the pass-by-value mechanism applies to all basic types of arguments, the effect for objects is different from that for variables of the basic types. You can change an object, as we shall see a little later in this chapter, because a copy of a reference to the object is passed to the method, not a copy of the object itself.

Final Parameters

You can specify any method parameter as `final`. This has the effect of preventing modification of any argument that is substituted for the parameter when you call the method. The compiler will check that your code in the body of the method does not attempt to change any final parameters. Since the pass-by-value mechanism makes copies of values of the basic types, `final` really only makes sense when it is applied to parameters that are references to class objects, as we will see later on.

Specifying parameters as `final` can be useful in two ways. First, it prevents accidental modification of things that you do not expect to be changed. Second, it can enable the compiler to make your code more efficient in some situations. Declaring a parameter as `final` has no implications for the argument used when the method is called. It may be `final` or not in the calling method. It does ensure though that the method called does not alter the argument that is passed, so it is good practice to specify parameters that are class objects as `final` if you do not intend to alter them in a method.

Defining Class Methods

You define a class method by adding the keyword `static` to its definition. For example, the class `Sphere` could have a class method to return the value stored in the static variable, `count`:

```
class Sphere
{
  // Class definition as before...

  // Static method to report the number of objects created
  static int getCount()
  {
    return count;                          // Return current object count
  }
}
```

This method needs to be a class method because we want to be able to get at the count of the number of objects even when it is zero. You can amend the `Sphere.java` file to include the definition of `getCount()`.

> Note that you cannot directly refer to any of the instance variables in the class within a `static` method. This is because your `static` method may be executed when no objects of the class have been created, and therefore no instance variables exist.

Accessing Class Data Members in a Method

An instance method can access any of the data members of the class, just by using the appropriate name. Let's extend the class `Sphere` a little further by adding a method to calculate the volume of a `Sphere` object:

```
class Sphere
{
  static final double PI = 3.14;  // Class variable that has a fixed value
  static int count = 0;           // Class variable to count objects

  // Instance variables
  double radius;                  // Radius of a sphere

  double xCenter;                 // 3D coordinates
  double yCenter;                 // of the center
  double zCenter;                 // of a sphere

  // Static method to report the number of objects created
  static int getCount()
  {
    return count;                 // Return current object count
  }

  // Instance method to calculate volume
  double volume()
  {
    return 4.0/3.0*PI*radius*radius*radius;
  }

  // Plus the rest of the class definition...
}
```

You can see that the method volume() is an instance method because it is not declared as static. It has no parameters but it does return a value of type double – the required volume. The method uses the class variable PI and the instance variable radius in the volume calculation – this is the expression 4.0/3.0*PI*radius*radius*radius $(4/3)\pi r^3$ in the return statement. The value that results from this expression will be returned to the point where the method is called for a Sphere object.

We know that each object of the class will have its own separate set of instance variables, so how is an instance variable for a particular object selected in a method? How does our volume() method pick up the radius for a particular Sphere object?

The Variable this

Every instance method has a variable with the name, this, which refers to the current object for which the method is being called. This is used implicitly by the compiler when your method refers to an instance variable of the class. For example, when the method volume() refers to the instance variable radius, the compiler will insert the this object reference, so that the reference will be equivalent to this.radius. The return statement in the definition of the volume() method is actually:

```
return 4.0/3.0*PI*this.radius*this.radius*this.radius;
```

In general, every reference to an instance variable is in reality prefixed with this. – you could put it in yourself, but there's no need, the compiler does it for you. In fact, it is not good practice to clutter up your code with this unnecessarily.

When you execute a statement such as:

```
double ballVolume = ball.volume();
```

where `ball` is an object of the class `Sphere`, the variable `this` in the method `volume()` will refer to the object `ball`, so the instance variable `radius` for this particular object will be used in the calculation.

> We mentioned earlier that only one copy of each instance method for a class exists in memory, even though there may be many different objects. You can see that the variable `this` allows the same instance method to work for different class objects. Each time an instance method is called, the `this` variable is set to reference the particular class object to which it is being applied. The code in the method will then relate to the specific data members of the object referred to by `this`.

We have seen that there are four different potential sources of data available to you when you write the code for a method:

❑ Arguments passed to the method, which you refer to by using the parameter names.

❑ Data members, both instance variables and class variables, which you refer to by their variable names.

❑ Local variables declared in the body of the method.

❑ Values that are returned by other methods that are called from within the method.

The names of variables that are declared within a method are local to the method. You can use a name for a local variable or a parameter in a method that is the same as that of a class data member. If you find it necessary to do this then you must use the name `this` when you refer to the data member of the class from within the method. The variable name by itself will always refer to the variable that is local to the method, not the instance variable.

For example, let us suppose we wanted to add a method to change the radius of a `Sphere` object to a new radius value which is passed as an argument. We could code this as:

```
void changeRadius(double radius)
{
  // Change the instance variable to the argument value
  this.radius = radius;
}
```

In the body of the `changeRadius()` method, `this.radius` refers to the instance variable, and `radius` by itself refers to the parameter. There is no confusion in the duplication of names here. It is clear that we are receiving a radius value as a parameter and storing it in the `radius` variable for the class object.

Initializing Data Members

We have seen how we were able to supply an initial value for the static members `PI` and `count` in the `Sphere` class with the declaration:

```
class Sphere
{
  static final double PI = 3.14;      // Class variable that has a fixed value
  static int count = 0;               // Class variable to count objects
```

```
      // Rest of the class...
    }
```

We can also initialize ordinary non-static data members in the same way. For example:

```
class Sphere
{
  static final double PI = 3.14;          // Class variable that has a fixed value
  static int count = 0;                   // Class variable to count objects

  // Instance variables
  double radius = 5.0;                    // Radius of a sphere

  double xCenter = 10.0;                  // 3D coordinates
  double yCenter = 10.0;                  // of the center
  double zCenter = 10.0;                  // of a sphere

  // Rest of the class...
}
```

Now every object of type `Sphere` will start out with a radius of 5.0 and have the center at the point 10.0, 10.0 ,10.0.

There are some things that can't be initialized with a single expression. If you had a large array as a data member for example, that you wanted to initialize, with a range of values that required some kind of calculation, this would be a job for an **initialization block**.

Using Initialization Blocks

An initialization block is a block of code between braces that is executed before an object of the class is created. There are two kinds of initialization blocks. A static initialization block is a block defined using the keyword, `static`, and that is executed once when the class is loaded and can only initialize static data members of the class. A non-static initialization block is executed for each object that is created and thus can initialize instance variables in a class. This is easiest to understand by considering specific code.

Try It Out – Using an initialization block

Let's define a simple class with a static initialization block first of all:

```
class TryInitialization
{
  static int[] values = new int[10];                  // Static array  member

  // Initialization block
  static
  {
    System.out.println("Running initialization block.");
    for(int i=0; i<values.length; i++)
      values[i] = (int)(100.0*Math.random());
  }

  // List values in the array for an object
```

```
     void listValues()
     {
       System.out.println();                          // Start a new line
       for(int i=0; i<values.length; i++)
         System.out.print(" " + values[i]);           // Display values

       System.out.println();                          // Start a new line
     }

     public static void main(String[] args)
     {
       TryInitialization example = new TryInitialization();
       System.out.println("\nFirst object:");
       example.listValues();

       example = new TryInitialization();
       System.out.println("\nSecond object:");
       example.listValues();
     }
   }
```

When you compile and run this you will get identical sets of values for the two objects – as might be expected since the values array is static:

```
Running initialization block.

First object:

 40 97 88 63 58 48 84 5 32 67
Second object:

 40 97 88 63 58 48 84 5 32 67
```

How It Works

The `TryInitialization` class has a static member, values, that is an array of 10 integers. The static initialization block is the code:

```
   static
   {
     System.out.println("Running initialization block.");
     for(int i=0; i<values.length; i++)
       values[i] = (int)(100.0*Math.random());
   }
```

This initializes the values array with `random()` integer values generated in the `for` loop. The output statement in the block is there just to record when the initialization block executes. Because this initialization block is static, it is only ever executed once during program execution, when the class is loaded.

The `listValues()` method provides us with a means of outputting the values in the array. The `print()` method we are using in the `listValues()` method works just like `println()`, but without starting a new line before displaying the output, so we get all the values on the same line.

In `main()`, we generate an object of type `TryInitialization`, and then call its `listValues()` method. We then create a second object and call the `listValues()` method for that. The output demonstrates that the initialization block only executes once, and that the values reported for both objects are the same.

If you delete the modifier `static` from before the initialization block, and recompile and run the program again, you will get the output along the lines of:

```
Running initialization block.

First object:

 66 17 98 59 99 18 40 96 40 21

Running initialization block.

Second object:

 57 86 79 31 75 99 51 5 31 44
```

Now we have a non-static initialization block. You can see from the output that the values are different for the second object because the non-static initialization block is executed each time an object is created. In fact, the `values` array is static, so the array is shared between all objects of the class. You could demonstrate this by amending `main()` to store each object separately, and calling `listValues()` for the first object after the second object has been created. Amend the `main()` method in the program to read as follows:

```
public static void main(String[] args)
{
  TryInitialization example = new TryInitialization();
  System.out.println("\nFirst object:");
  example.listValues();

  TryInitialization nextexample = new TryInitialization();
  System.out.println("\nSecond object:");
  nextexample.listValues();

  example.listValues();
}
```

While we have demonstrated that this is possible, you will not normally want to initialize static variables with a non-static initialization block.

As we said at the outset, a non-static initialization block can initialize instance variables too. If you want to demonstrate this too, you just need to remove the `static` modifier from the declaration of `values` and compile and run the program once more.

You can have multiple initialization blocks in a class, in which case they execute in the sequence in which they appear. The static blocks execute when the class is loaded and the non-static blocks execute when each object is created. Initialization blocks are useful, but you need more than that to create objects properly.

Constructors

When you create an object of a class, a special kind of method called a **constructor** is always invoked. If you don't define a constructor for a class, the compiler will supply a default constructor in the class that does nothing. The primary purpose of a constructor is to provide you with the means of initializing the instance variables uniquely for the object that is being created. If you are creating a `Person` object with the name John Doe, then you want to be able to initialize the member holding the person's name to "John Doe". This is precisely what a constructor can do. Any initialization blocks that you have defined in a class are always executed before the constructor.

173

A constructor has two special characteristics which differentiate it from other class methods:

❑ A constructor never returns a value and you must not specify a return type – not even of type `void`.

❑ A constructor always has the same name as the class.

To see a practical example we could add a constructor to our `Sphere` class definition:

```
class Sphere
{
  static final double PI = 3.14;  // Class variable that has a fixed value
  static int count = 0;           // Class variable to count objects

  // Instance variables
  double radius;                  // Radius of a sphere

  double xCenter;                 // 3D coordinates
  double yCenter;                 // of the center
  double zCenter;                 // of a sphere

  // Class constructor
  Sphere(double theRadius, double x, double y, double z)
  {
    radius = theRadius;           // Set the radius

    // Set the coordinates of the center
    xCenter = x;
    yCenter = y;
    zCenter = z;
    ++count;                      // Update object count
  }

  // Static method to report the number of objects created
  static int getCount()
  {
    return count;                 // Return current object count
  }

  // Instance method to calculate volume
  double volume()
  {
    return 4.0/3.0*PI*radius*radius*radius;
  }
}
```

The definition of the constructor is shaded above. We are accumulating quite a lot of code to define the `Sphere` class, but as it's just an assembly of the pieces we have been adding you should find it all quite straightforward.

As you can see, the constructor has the same name as the class and has no return type specified. A constructor can have any number of parameters, including none. In our case we have four parameters, and each of the instance variables is initialized with the value of the appropriate parameter. Here is a situation where we might have used the name `radius` for the parameter, in which case we would need to use the keyword `this` to refer to the instance variable of the same name. The last action of our constructor is to increment the class variable, `count`, by 1, so that `count` accumulates the total number of objects created.

Creating Objects of a Class

When you declare a variable of type `Sphere` with the statement:

```
Sphere ball;      // Declare a variable
```

no constructor is called and no object is created. All you have created at this point is the variable `ball` which can store a reference to an object of type `Sphere`, if and when you create one.

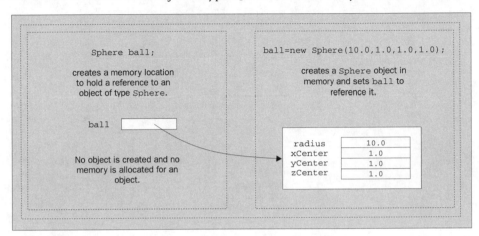

You will recall from our discussion of `String` objects and arrays that the variable and the object it references are distinct entities. To create an object of a class you must use the keyword `new` followed by a call to a constructor. To initialize `ball` with an object, you could write:

```
ball = new Sphere(10.0, 1.0, 1.0, 1.0);    // Create a sphere
```

Now we have a `Sphere` object with a radius of 10.0 located at the coordinates (1.0, 1.0, 1.0). The object is created in memory and will occupy a sufficient number of bytes to accommodate all the data necessary to define the object. The variable `ball` will record where in memory the object is – it acts as a reference to the object.

Of course, you can do the whole thing in one step, with the statement:

```
Sphere ball = new Sphere(10.0, 1.0, 1.0, 1.0);    // Create a sphere
```

which declares the variable `ball` and defines the `Sphere` object to which it refers.

You can create another variable that refers to the same object as `ball`:

```
Sphere myBall = ball;
```

Now the variable `myBall` refers to the same object as `ball`. We have only one object still, but we have two different variables that reference it. You could have as many variables as you like referring to the same object.

The separation of the variable and the object has an important effect on how objects are passed to a method, so we need to look at that.

Passing Objects to a Method

When you pass an object as an argument to a method, the mechanism that applies is called **pass-by-reference**, because a copy of the reference contained in the variable is transferred to the method, not the object itself. The effect of this is shown in the following diagram.

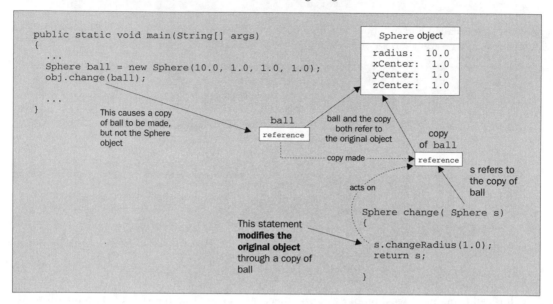

This illustration presumes we have defined a method, changeRadius(), in the class Sphere that will alter the radius value for an object, and that we have a method change() in some other class that calls changeRadius(). When the variable ball is used as an argument to the method change(), the pass-by-reference mechanism causes a copy of ball to be made and stored in s. The variable ball just stores a reference to the Sphere object, and the copy contains that same reference and therefore refers to the same object. No copying of the actual object occurs. This is a major plus in terms of efficiency when passing arguments to a method. Objects can be very complex involving a lot of instance variables. If objects themselves were always copied when passed as arguments, it could be very time consuming and make the code very slow.

Since the copy of ball refers to the same object as the original, when the changeRadius() method is called the original object will be changed. You need to keep this in mind when writing methods that have objects as parameters because this is not always what you want.

In the example shown, the method change() returns the modified object. In practice you would probably want this to be a distinct object, in which case you would need to create a new object from s. You will see how you can write a constructor to do this a little later in this chapter.

> **Remember that this only applies to objects. If you pass a variable of type int or double to a method for example, a copy of the value is passed. You can modify the value passed as much as you want in the method, but it won't affect the original value.**

The Lifetime of an Object

The lifetime of an object is determined by the variable that references it. If we have the declaration:

```
Sphere ball = new Sphere(10.0, 1.0, 1.0, 1.0);   // Create a sphere
```

then the `Sphere` object that the variable `ball` refers to will die when the variable `ball` goes out of scope. This will be at the end of the block containing this declaration. Where an instance variable refers to an object, the object survives as long as the instance variable owning the object survives.

> **A slight complication can arise with objects though. As you have seen, several variables can reference a single object. In this case the object survives as long as there is still a variable in existence that references the object.**

You can reset a variable to refer to nothing by setting its value to `null`. If you write the statement:

```
ball = null;
```

the variable `ball` no longer refers to an object, and assuming there is no other object referencing it, the `Sphere` object it originally referenced will be destroyed. Note that while the object has been discarded, the variable `ball` still continues to exist. The lifetime of the object is determined by whether any variable anywhere in the program still references it.

The process of disposing of objects is called **garbage collection**. Garbage collection is automatic in Java, but this doesn't necessarily mean that objects disappear from memory straight away. It can be some time after the object becomes inaccessible to your program. This won't affect your program directly in any way. It just means you can't rely on memory occupied by an object that is done with being available immediately. For the most part it doesn't matter; the only circumstances where it might would be if your objects were very large, millions of bytes say, or you were creating and getting rid of very large numbers of objects.

Defining and Using a Class

To put what we know about classes to use, we can use our `Sphere` class in an example.

You will be creating two source files. The first is the file `CreateSpheres.java`, which will contain the definition of the `CreateSpheres` class that will have the method `main()` defined as a static method. As usual, this is where execution of the program starts. The second file will be the file `Sphere.java` that contains the definition of the class `Sphere` that we have been assembling.

Both files will need to be in the same directory or folder – I suggest you name the directory `CreateSpheres`. Then copy or move the last version of `Sphere.java` to this directory.

Try It Out – Using the Sphere Class

Enter the following code for the file `CreateSpheres.java`:

```java
class CreateSpheres
{
  public static void main(String[] args)
  {
    System.out.println("Number of objects = " + Sphere.getCount());

    Sphere ball = new Sphere(4.0, 0.0, 0.0, 0.0);        // Create a sphere
    System.out.println("Number of objects = " + ball.getCount());

    Sphere globe = new Sphere(12.0, 1.0, 1.0, 1.0);      // Create a sphere
    System.out.println("Number of objects = " + Sphere.getCount());

    // Output the volume of each sphere
    System.out.println("ball volume = " + ball.volume());
    System.out.println("globe volume = " + globe.volume());
  }
}
```

Compile the source files and then run `CreateSpheres`, and you should get the output:

```
Number of objects = 0
Number of objects = 1
Number of objects = 2
ball volume = 267.94666666666666
globe volume = 7234.559999999999
```

This is the first time we have run a program involving two source files. If you are using the JDK compiler, then compile `CreateSpheres.java` with the current directory as `CreateSpheres` using the command:

javac CreateSpheres.java

The compiler will find and compile the `Sphere.java` source file automatically. If all the source files for a program are in the current directory, then compiling the file containing a definition of `main()` will compile all the source files for the program.

Note that by default, the `.class` files generated by the compiler will be stored in the current directory, that is, the directory containing your source code. If you want the `.class` files stored in a different directory, then you can use the −d option with the Java compiler to specify where they should go.

How It Works

The `Sphere` class definition includes a constructor and the method `volume()` to calculate the volume of a particular sphere. It also contains the `static` method, `getCount()`, we saw earlier, which returns the current value of the class variable `count`. We need to define this method as `static` since we want to able to call it regardless of how many objects have been created, including the situation when there are none.

The method `main()` in the `CreateSpheres` class puts the class `Sphere` through its paces. When the program is compiled, the compiler will look for a file `Sphere.java` to provide the definition of the class `Sphere`. As long as this file is in the current directory the compiler will be able to find it.

The first thing the program does is to call the `static` method `getCount()`. Because no objects exist, you must use the class name to call it at this point. We then create the object `ball`, which is a `Sphere` object, with a radius of 4.0 and its center at the origin point, (0.0, 0.0, 0.0). The method `getCount()` is called again, this time using the object name to demonstrate that you can call a `static` method through an object. Another `Sphere` object, `globe`, is created with a radius of 12.0. The `getCount()` method is called again, this time using the class name. Static methods are usually called using the class name because in most situations, where you would use such a method, you cannot be sure that any objects exist. After all, the reason for calling this particular method would be to find out how many objects exist. A further reason to use the class name when calling a static method is that it makes it quite clear in the source code that it *is* a static method that is being called. You can't call a non-static method using the class name.

Our program finally outputs the volume of both objects by calling the `volume()` method for each, from within the expressions, specifying the arguments to the `println()` method calls.

Method Overloading

Java allows you to define several methods in a class with the same name, as long as each method has a set of parameters that is unique. This is called **method overloading**.

The name of a method together with the type and sequence of the parameters form the **signature** of the method – the signature of each method in a class must be distinct to allow the compiler to determine exactly which method you are calling at any particular point.

Note that the return type has no effect on the signature of a method. You cannot differentiate between two methods just by the return type. This is because the return type is not necessarily apparent when you call a method. For example, suppose you write a statement such as:

```
Math.round(value);
```

Although the statement above is pointless since we discard the value that the `round()` method produces, it does illustrate why the return type cannot be part of the signature for a method. There is no way for the compiler to know from this statement what the return type of the method `round()` is supposed to be. Thus, if there were several different versions of the method `round()`, and the return type was the only distinguishing aspect of the method signature, the compiler would be unable to determine which version of `round()` you wanted to use.

There are many circumstances where it is convenient to use method overloading. You have already seen that the standard class `Math` contains two versions of the method `round()`, one that accepts an argument of type `float`, and the other that accepts an argument of type `double`. You can see now that method overloading makes this possible. It would be rather tedious to have to use a different name for each version of `round()` when they both do essentially the same thing. One context in which you will regularly need to use overloading is when you write constructors for your classes, which we'll look at now.

Multiple Constructors

Constructors are methods that can be overloaded, just like any other method in a class. In most situations, you will need to generate objects of a class from different sets of initial defining data. If we just consider our class Sphere, we could conceive of a need to define a Sphere object in a variety of ways. You might well want a constructor that accepted just the (x, y, z) coordinates of a point, and have a Sphere object created with a default radius of 1.0. Another possibility is that you may want to create a default Sphere with a radius of 1.0 positioned at the origin, so no arguments would be specified at all. This requires two constructors in addition to the one we have already written.

Try It Out – Multiple Constructors for the Sphere Class

The code for the extra constructors is:

```
class Sphere
{
  // First Constructor and variable declarations
  ...
  // Construct a unit sphere at a point
  Sphere(double x, double y, double z)
  {
    xCenter = x;
    yCenter = y;
    zCenter = z;
    radius = 1.0;
    ++count;                        // Update object count
  }

  // Construct a unit sphere at the origin
  Sphere()
  {
    xCenter = 0.0;
    yCenter = 0.0;
    zCenter = 0.0;
    radius = 1.0;
    ++count;                        // Update object count
  }

  // The rest of the class as before...
}
```

The statements in the default constructor that set three data members to zero are not really necessary, as the data members would be set to zero by default. They are there just to emphasize that the primary purpose of a constructor is to enable you to set initial values for the data members.

If you add the following statements to the CreateSpheres class, you can test out the new constructors:

```
public class CreateSpheres
{
  public static void main(String[] args)
  {
    System.out.println("Number of objects = " + Sphere.getCount());

    Sphere ball = new Sphere(4.0, 0.0, 0.0, 0.0);               // Create a sphere
    System.out.println("Number of objects = " + ball.getCount());
```

```
        Sphere globe = new Sphere(12., 1.0, 1.0, 1.0);              // Create a sphere
        System.out.println("Number of objects = " + Sphere.getCount());

        Sphere eightBall = new Sphere(10.0, 10.0, 0.0);
        Sphere oddBall = new Sphere();
        System.out.println("Number of objects = " + Sphere.getCount());

        // Output the volume of each sphere
        System.out.println("ball volume = " + ball.volume());
        System.out.println("globe volume = " + globe.volume());
        System.out.println("eightBall volume = " + eightBall.volume());
        System.out.println("oddBall volume = " + oddBall.volume());
    }
}
```

Now the program should produce the output:

```
Number of objects = 0
Number of objects = 1
Number of objects = 2
Number of objects = 4
ball volume = 267.94666666666666
globe volume = 7234.559999999999
eightBall volume = 4.1866666666666665
oddBall volume = 4.1866666666666665
```

How It Works

When you create a `Sphere` object, the compiler will select the constructor to use based on the types of the arguments you have specified. So, the first of the new constructors is applied in the first statement that we added to `main()`, as its signature fits with the argument types used. The second statement that we added clearly selects the last constructor as no arguments are specified. The other additional statements are there just to generate some output corresponding to the new objects. You can see from the volumes of `eightBall` and `oddBall` that they both are of radius 1.

It is the number and types of the parameters which affect the signature of a method, not the parameter names. If you wanted a constructor which defined a `Sphere` object at a point, by specifying the diameter rather than the radius, you have a problem. You might try to write it as:

```
// Illegal constructor!!!
// This WON'T WORK because it has the same signature as the original!!!
Sphere(double diameter, double x, double y, double z)
{
    xCenter = x;
    yCenter = y;
    zCenter = z;
    radius = diameter/2.0;
}
```

If you try adding this to the `Sphere` class and recompiling, you'll get a compile-time error. This constructor has four arguments of type `double`, so its signature is identical to the first constructor that we wrote for the class. This is not permitted – hence the compile-time error. When the number of parameters is the same in two overloaded methods, at least one pair of corresponding parameters must be of different types.

181

Calling a Constructor from a Constructor

One class constructor can call another constructor in the same class in its first executable statement. This can often save duplicating a lot of code. To refer to another constructor in the same class, you use this as the name, followed by the appropriate arguments between parentheses. In our Sphere class, we could have defined the constructors as:

```
class Sphere
{
  // Construct a unit sphere at the origin
  Sphere()
  {
    radius = 1.0;
    // Other data members will be zero by default
    ++count;                        // Update object count
  }

  // Construct a unit sphere at a point
  Sphere(double x, double y, double z)
  {
    this();                      // Call the constructor with no arguments
    xCenter = x;
    yCenter = y;
    zCenter = z;
  }

    Sphere(double theRadius, double x, double y, double z)
    {
      this(x, y, z);              // Call the 3 argument constructor
      radius = theRadius;         // Set the radius
    }

    // The rest of the class as before...
  }
```

In the constructor that accepts the point coordinates as argument, we call the default constructor to set the radius and increment the count of the number of objects. In the constructor that sets the radius, as well as the coordinates, the constructor with three arguments is called to set the coordinates, which in turn will call the constructor that requires no arguments.

Duplicating Objects Using a Constructor

When we were looking at how objects were passed to a method, we came up with a requirement for duplicating an object. The need to produce an identical copy of an object occurs surprisingly often.

> Java provides a clone() method, but the details of using it must wait for the next chapter.

Suppose you declare a Sphere object with the following statement:

```
Sphere eightBall = new Sphere(10.0, 10.0, 0.0);
```

Later in your program you want to create a new object `newBall`, which is identical to the object `eightBall`. If you write:

```
Sphere newBall = eightBall;
```

this will compile OK but it won't do what you want. You will remember from our earlier discussion that the variable `newBall` will reference the same object as `eightBall`. You will not have a distinct object. The variable `newBall`, of type `Sphere`, is created but no constructor is called, so no new object is created.

Of course, you could create `newBall` by specifying the same arguments to the constructor as you used to create `eightBall`. In general, however, it may be that `eightBall` has been modified in some way during execution of the program, so you don't know that its instance variables have the same values – for example, the position might have changed. This presumes that we have some other class methods which alter the instance variables. You could fix this by adding a constructor to the class that will accept an existing `Sphere` object as an argument:

```
// Create a sphere from an existing object
Sphere(final Sphere oldSphere)
{
  radius = oldSphere.radius;
  xCenter = oldSphere.xCenter;
  yCenter = oldSphere.yCenter;
  zCenter = oldSphere.yCenter;
}
```

This works by copying the values of the instance variables of the `Sphere` object, passed as an argument, to the corresponding instance variables of the new object.

Now you can create `newBall` as a distinct object by writing:

```
Sphere newBall = new Sphere(eightBall);  // Create a copy of eightBall
```

Let's recap what we have learned about methods and constructors with another example.

Using Objects

Let's create an example to do some simple 2D geometry which will give us an opportunity to use more than one class. We will define two classes, a class of point objects and a class of line objects – we then use these to find the point at which the lines intersect. We will call the example `TryGeometry`, so this will be the name of the directory or folder in which you should save the program files. Quite a few lines of code are involved so we will put it together piecemeal, and try to understand how each piece works as we go.

Try It Out – The Point Class

We first define a basic class for point objects:

```
class Point
{
  // Coordinates of the point
  double x;
  double y;
```

```
// Create a point from coordinates
Point(double xVal, double yVal)
{
  x = xVal;
  y = yVal;
}

// Create a point from another Point object
Point(final Point oldPoint)
{
  x = oldPoint.x;      // Copy x coordinate
  y = oldPoint.y;      // Copy y coordinate
}

// Move a point
void move(double xDelta, double yDelta)
{
  // Parameter values are increments to the current coordinates
  x += xDelta;
  y += yDelta;
}

// Calculate the distance to another point
double distance(final Point aPoint)
{
  return Math.sqrt(
     (x - aPoint.x)*(x - aPoint.x) + (y - aPoint.y)*(y - aPoint.y) );
}

// Convert a point to a string
public String toString()
{
  return Double.toString(x) + ", " + y;      // As "x, y"
}
}
```

You should save this as `Point.java` in the directory `TryGeometry`.

How It Works

This is a simple class that has just two instance variables, x and y, which are the coordinates of the Point object. At the moment we have two constructors, one which will create a point from a coordinate pair passed as arguments, and the other which will create a new Point object from an existing one.

There are three methods included in the class. First we have the move() method that moves a Point to another position by adding an increment to each of the coordinates. We also have the distance() method that calculates the distance from the current Point object to the Point object passed as an argument. This uses the Pythagorean theorem to compute the distance as shown below.

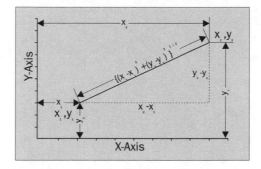

Finally we have a method `toString()` that returns a string representation of the coordinates of the current point. If a class defines the `toString()` method, an object of a class can be used as an operand of the string concatenation operator +, so you can implement this in any of your classes to allow objects to be used in this way. The compiler will automatically insert a call to `toString()` when necessary. For example, suppose `thePoint` is an object of type `Point`, and we write the statement:

```
System.out.println("The point is at " + thePoint);
```

The `toString()` method will be automatically invoked to convert `thePoint` to a `String`, and the result will be appended to the `String` literal. We have specified the `toString()` method as `public`, as this is essential here for the class to compile. We will defer explanations as to why this is so until later in this chapter.

Note how we use the static `toString()` method defined in the class `Double` to convert the x value to a `String`. The compiler will insert a call to the same method automatically for the y value as the left operand of the + operation is a `String` object.

Try It Out – The Line Class

We can use `Point` objects in the definition of the class `Line`:

```
class Line
{
  Point start;    // Start point of line
  Point end;      // End point of line

  // Create a line from two points
  Line(final Point start, final Point end)
  {
    this.start = new Point(start);
    this.end = new Point(end);
  }

  // Create a line from two coordinate pairs
  Line(double xStart, double yStart, double xEnd, double yEnd)
  {
    start = new Point(xStart, yStart);    // Create the start point
    end = new Point(xEnd, yEnd);          // Create the end point
  }
```

```
    // Calculate the length of a line
    double length()
    {
      return start.distance(end);   // Use the method from the Point class
    }

    // Convert a line to a string
    public String toString()
    {
      return "(" + start+ "):(" + end + ")";     // As "(start):(end)"
    }                                             // that is, "(x1, y1):(x2, y2)"
  }
```

You should save this as Line.java in the directory TryGeometry.

How It Works

You shouldn't have any difficulty with this class definition as it is very straightforward. The class Line stores two Point objects as instance variables. There are two constructors for Line objects, one accepting two Point objects as arguments, the other accepting the (x, y) coordinates of the start and end points. You can see how we use the variable this to differentiate the class instance variables, start and end, from the parameter names in the constructor.

Note how the constructor that accepts Point objects works:

```
    // Create a line from two points
    Line(final Point start, final Point end)
    {
      this.start = new Point(start);
      this.end = new Point(end);
    }
```

With this implementation of the constructor, two new Point objects are created which will be identical to, but independent of, the objects passed to the constructor. If you don't think about what happens you might be tempted to write it as:

```
    // Create a line from two points
    Line(final Point start, final Point end)
    {
      this.start = start;            // Dependent on external object!!!
      this.end = end;                // Dependent on external object!!!
    }
```

The important thing you should notice here, is that the way the constructor is implemented could cause problems that might be hard to track down. It's the same problem of an object variable being separate from the object to which it refers. In this version no new points are created. The start and end members of the object refer to the Point objects passed as arguments. The Line object will be implicitly dependent on the Point objects that are used to define it. If these were changed outside the Line class, by using the move() method for example, this would 'silently' modify the Line object. You might consciously decide that this is what you want, so the Line object continues to be dependent on its associated Point objects, for instance in a drawing package. But, in general, you should avoid implicit dependencies between objects.

186

In the `toString()` method for the `Line` class, we are able to use the `Point` objects directly in the formation of the `String` representation of a `Line` object. This works because the `Point` class also defines a `toString()` method.

We've now defined two classes. In these class definitions, we've included the basic data that defines an object of each class. We've also defined some methods which we think will be useful, and added constructors for a variety of input parameters. Note how the `Point` class is used in the definition of the `Line` class. It is quite natural to define a line in terms of two `Point` objects, and the `Line` class is much simpler and more understandable than if it was defined entirely in terms of the individual x and y coordinates. To further demonstrate how classes can interact, and how you can solve problems directly, in terms of the objects involved, let's devise a method to calculate the intersection of two `Line` objects.

Creating a Point from Two Lines

We could add this method to the `Line` class. The diagram below illustrates how the mathematics works out.

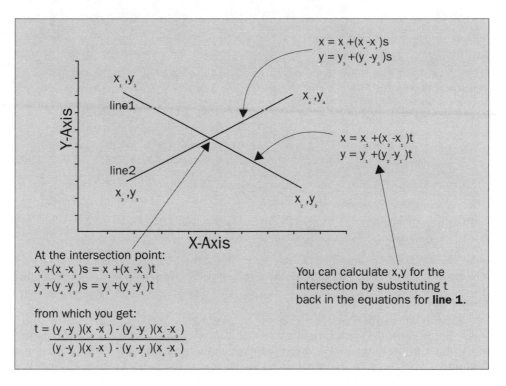

You can ignore the mathematics if you want to, as it is not the most important aspect of the example. If you are willing to take the code in the new constructor on trust, then skip to the *Try It Out* section below. On the other hand you shouldn't find it too difficult if you can still remember what you did in high school.

One way to get the intersection of two lines is to use equations like those shown. These are called parametric equations because they use a parameter value (s or t) as the variable for determining points on each line. The parameters s and t vary between 0 and 1 to give points on the lines between the defined start and end points. When a parameter s or t is 0 the equations give the coordinates of the start point of each line, and when the parameter value is 1 you get the end point of the line.

Where the lines intersect, the equations for the lines must produce the same (x, y) values, so, at this point, the right hand sides of the equations for x for the two lines must be equal, and the same goes for the equations for y. This will give you two equations in s and t, and with a bit of algebraic juggling you can eliminate s to get the equation shown for t. You can then replace t in the equations defining line 1 to get x and y for the intersection point.

Try It Out – Calculating the Intersection of Two Lines

We can use these results to write the additional method we need for the `Line` class. Add the following code to the definition in `Line.java`:

```
// Return a point as the intersection of two lines -- called from a Line object
Point intersects(final Line line1)
{
  Point localPoint = new Point(0, 0);

  double num =
    (this.end.y - this.start.y)*(this.start.x - line1.start.x) -
    (this.end.x - this.start.x)*(this.start.y - line1.start.y);

  double denom =
    (this.end.y - this.start.y)*(line1.end.x - line1.start.x) -
    (this.end.x - this.start.x)*(line1.end.y - line1.start.y);

  localPoint.x = line1.start.x + (line1.end.x - line1.start.x)*num/denom;
  localPoint.y = line1.start.y + (line1.end.y - line1.start.y)*num/denom;

  return localPoint;
}
```

Since the `Line` class definition refers to the `Point` class, the `Line` class can't be compiled without the other being available. When you compile the `Line` class the compiler will compile the other class too.

How It Works

The `intersects()` method is called from one `Line` object, and takes another `Line` object as an argument. In the code, the local variables `num` and `denom` are the numerator and denominator in the expression for t in the diagram. We then use these values to calculate the x and y coordinates for the intersection.

> **If the lines are parallel, the denominator in the equation for t will be zero, something you should really check for in the code. For the moment, we will ignore it and end up with coordinates that are `Infinity` if it occurs.**

Note how we get at the values of the coordinates for the `Point` objects defining the lines. The dot notation for referring to a member of an object is just repeated when you want to reference a member of a member. For example, for the object `line1`, the expression `line1.start` refers to the `Point` object at the beginning of the line. Therefore `line1.start.x` refers to its x coordinate, and `line1.start.y` accesses its y coordinates.

Now we have a `Line` class which we can use to calculate the intersection point of two `Line` objects. We need a program to test the code out.

Try It Out – The TryGeometry Class

We can demonstrate the two classes we have defined, with the following code in the method `main()`:

```
public class TryGeometry
{
  public static void main(String[] args)
  {
    // Create two points and display them
    Point start = new Point(0.0, 1.0);
    Point end = new Point(5.0, 6.0);
    System.out.println("Points created are " + start + " and " + end);


    // Create two lines and display them
    Line line1 = new Line(start, end);
    Line line2 = new Line(0.0, 3.0, 3.0, 0.0);
    System.out.println("Lines created are " + line1 + " and " + line2);

    // Display the intersection
    System.out.println("Intersection is " + line2.intersects(line1));

    // Now move the end point of line1 and show the new intersection
    end.move(1.0, -5.0);
    System.out.println("Intersection is " + line1.intersects(line2));
  }
}
```

The program will produce the output:

```
Points created are 0.0, 1.0 and 5.0, 6.0
Lines created are (0.0, 1.0):(5.0, 6.0) and (0.0, 3.0):(3.0, 0.0)
Intersection is 1.0, 2.0
Intersection is 1.0, 2.0
```

How It Works

We first create two `Point` objects, which we will use later in the creation of the object `line1`. We then display the points using the `println()` method. The `toString()` method that we defined in the `Point` class is used automatically to generate the `String` representation for each `Point` object.

After creating `line1` from our two points, we use the other constructor in the `Line` class to create `line2` from two pairs of coordinates. We then display the two lines. The `toString()` member of the `Line` class is invoked here to create the `String` representation of each `Line` object, and this in turn uses the `toString()` method in the `Point` class.

The next statement calls the intersects() method from the line2 object and returns the Point object at the intersection of the two lines, line1 and line2, as part of the argument to the println() method that outputs the point. As you see, we are not obliged to save an object when we create it. Here we just use it to create the string to be displayed.

We use the move()method in the class Point to modify the coordinates of the object, end, that we used to create line1. We then get the intersection of the two lines again, this time calling the intersects() method from line1. The output result demonstrates that line1 is independent of the object end, as moving the point has made no difference to the intersection.

If you change the constructor in the Line class, to the version we saw earlier that does not create new Point objects to define the line, you can run the example again to see the effect. The output will be:

```
Points created are 0.0, 1.0 and 5.0, 6.0
Lines created are (0.0, 1.0):(5.0, 6.0) and (0.0, 3.0):(3.0, 0.0)
Intersection is 1.0, 2.0
Intersection is 1.0, 2.0
```

Changing the end object now alters the line, so we get a different intersection point for the two lines after we move the point end. This is because the Line object, line1, contains references to the Point objects defined in main(), not independent Point objects.

Recursion

The methods you have seen so far have been called from within other methods, but a method can also call itself – something referred to as **recursion**. Clearly you must include some logic in a recursive method so that it will eventually stop calling itself. We can see how this might be done with a simple example.

We can write a method that will calculate integer powers of a variable, in other words, evaluate x^n, or $x*x...*x$ where x is multiplied by itself n times. We can use the fact that we can obtain x^n by multiplying x^{n-1} by x.

Try It Out – Calculating Powers

Here is the complete program including the recursive method, power():

```
public class PowerCalc
{
  public static void main(String[] args)
  {
    double x = 5.0;
    System.out.println(x + " to the power 4 is " + power(x,4));
    System.out.println("7.5 to the power 5 is " + power(7.5,5));
    System.out.println("7.5 to the power 0 is " + power(7.5,0));
    System.out.println("10 to the power -2 is " + power(10,-2));
  }

  // Raise x to the power n
  static double power(double x, int n)
```

```
  {
    if(n > 1)
      return x*power(x, n-1);      // Recursive call
    else if(n < 0)
      return 1.0/power(x, -n);     // Negative power of x
    else
      return n == 0 ? 1.0 : x;     // When n is 0 return 1, otherwise x
  }
}
```

This program will produce the output:

```
5.0 to the power 4 is 625.0
7.5 to the power 5 is 23730.46875
7.5 to the power 0 is 1.0
10 to the power -2 is 0.01
```

How It Works

The method power() has two parameters, the value x and the power n. The method performs four different actions, depending on the value of n:

$n>1$	A recursive call to power() is made with n reduced by 1, and the value returned is multiplied by x.
$n<0$	x^{-n} is equivalent to $1/x^n$ so this is the expression for the return value. This involves a recursive call to power() with the sign of n reversed.
$n=0$	x0 is defined as 1, so this is the value returned.
$n=1$	x1 is x, so x is returned.

Just to make sure the process is clear we can work through the sequence of events as they occur in the calculation of 5^4.

Level	Description	Relevant Code

1	The first call of the power() method passes 5.0 and 4 as arguments. Since the second argument, n, is greater than 1, the power() method is called again in the return statement, with the second argument reduced by 1.	```Power(5.0, 4)
		{
		  if(n > 1)
		    return 5.0*power(5.0, 4-1);
		  ...
		}```

2	The second call of the power() method passes 5.0 and 3 as arguments. Since the second argument, n, is still greater than 1, the power() method is called again in the return statement with the second argument reduced by 1.	```Power(5.0, 3)
		{
		  if(n > 1)
		    return 5.0*power(5.0, 3-1);
		  ...
		}```

Table continued on following page

Level	Description	Relevant Code
3	The third call of the power() method passes 5.0 and 2 as arguments. Since the second argument, n, is still greater than 1, the power() method is called again, with the second argument again reduced by 1.	```\nPower(5.0, 2)\n{\n if(n > 1)\n return 5.0*power(5.0, 2-1);\n ...\n}\n```
4	The fourth call of the power() method passes 5.0 and 1 as arguments. Since the second argument, n, is not greater than 1, the value of the first argument, 5.0, is returned to level 3.	```\nPower(5.0, 1)\n{\n if(n > 1)\n ...\n else\n return 5.0;\n}\n```
3	Back at level 3, the value returned, 5.0, is multiplied by the first argument, 5.0, and returned to level 2.	```\nPower(5.0, 2)\n{\n if(n>1)\n ...\n else\n return 5.0*5.0;\n}\n```
2	Back at level 2, the value returned, 25.0, is multiplied by the first argument, 5.0, and returned to level 1.	```\nPower(5.0, 3)\n{\n if(n > 1)\n ...\n else\n return 5.0*25.0;\n}\n```
1	Back at level 1, the value returned, 125.0, is multiplied by the first argument, 5.0, and 625.0 is returned as the result of calling the method in the first instance.	```\nPower(5.0, 4)\n{\n if(n > 1)\n ...\n else\n return 5.0*125.0;\n}\n```

You can see from this that the method power() is called four times in all. The calls cascade down through four levels until the value of n is such that it allows a value to be returned. The return values ripple up through the levels until we are eventually back at the top, and 625.0 is returned to the original calling point.

As a rule, you should only use recursion where there are evident advantages in the approach, as there is quite of lot of overhead in recursive method calls. This particular example could be more easily programmed as a loop and it would execute much more efficiently. One example of where recursion can be applied very effectively is in the handling of data structures such as trees. Unfortunately these don't make convenient illustrations of how recursion works at this stage of the learning curve, because of their complexity.

Before we can dig deeper into classes, we need to take an apparent detour to understand what a package is in Java.

Understanding Packages

> **Packages are fundamental to Java programs so make sure you understand this section.**

Packages are implicit in the organization of the standard classes as well as your own programs, and they influence the names you can use for classes and the variables and methods they contain. Essentially, a **package** is a named collection of classes. The purpose of grouping classes in a package is to make it easy to add the classes in a package into your program code. One aspect of this is that the names used for classes in one package will not interfere with the names of classes in another package, or your program, because the class names in a package are qualified by the package name.

Every class in Java is contained in a package, including all those we have defined in our examples. You haven't seen any references to package names so far because we have been implicitly using the **default package** to hold our classes, and this doesn't have a name.

All of the standard classes in Java are contained within packages. The package that contains the standard classes that we have used so far is called `java.lang`. You haven't seen any explicit reference to this in your code either, because this package is automatically available to your programs. Things are arranged this way because some of the classes in `java.lang`, such as `String`, are used in every program. There are other packages containing standard classes that you will need to include explicitly when you use them, as you will see.

Packaging up Your Classes

Putting one of your classes in a package is very simple. You just add a package statement as the first statement in the source file containing the class definition. Note that it must always be the first statement. Only comments or blank lines are allowed to precede the package statement. A **package statement** consists of the keyword, `package`, followed by the package name, and is terminated by a semi-colon. If you want the classes in a package to be accessible outside the package, you must declare the class using the keyword `public` in the first line of your class definition. Class definitions that aren't preceded by the keyword `public` are only accessible from methods in classes that belong to the same package.

For example, to include the class `Sphere` in a package called `Geometry`, the contents of the file `Sphere.java` would need to be:

```
package Geometry;

public class Sphere
{
   // Details of the class definition
}
```

Each class that you want to include in the package `Geometry` must contain the same package statement at the beginning, and you should save all the files for the classes in the package in a directory with the same name as the package, that is, `Geometry`. Any class that has not been declared as `public` will not be accessible from outside the package.

Packages and the Directory Structure

Packages are actually a little more complicated than they appear at first sight, because a package is intimately related to the directory structure in which it is stored. You already know that the definition of a class with the name ClassName must be stored in a file with the name ClassName.java, and that all the files for classes within a package, PackageName, must be included in a directory with the name PackageName. You can compile the source for a class within a package and have the .class file that is generated stored in a different directory, but the directory name must still be the same as the package name.

A package need not have a single name. You can specify a package name as a sequence of names separated by periods. For example, you might have developed several collections of classes dealing with geometry, one dealing with 2D shapes and another with 3D shapes. In this case you might include the class Sphere in a package with the statement:

```
package Geometry.Shapes3D;
```

and the class for circles in a package using the statement:

```
package Geometry.Shapes2D;
```

In this situation, the packages are expected to be in the directories Shapes3D and Shapes2D, and both of these must be sub-directories of Geometry. In general, you can have as many names as you like separated by periods to identify a package, but the name must reflect the directory structure where the package is stored.

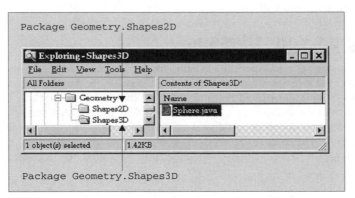

Compiling a Package

Compiling the classes in a package can be a bit tricky unless you are clear on how you go about it. We will illustrate what you need to do assuming you are using the JDK under Microsoft Windows. The path to the package directory has to be known to the compiler, even when the current directory, when you compile a source file of a class in the package, is the directory containing the package. If we have stored the Geometry package source files in the directory with the path C:\JavaStuff\Geometry, then the path to the Geometry directory is C:\JavaStuff. You can tell the compiler about this path using the -classpath option on the command line. Assuming that the current directory is the Geometry directory, we could compile the Line.java source file with the command:

```
C:\JavaStuff\Geometry>javac -classpath C:\JavaStuff Line.java
```

This will result in both the `Line.java` and `Point.java` files being compiled, since `Line.java` refers to the other. If the directories in the path contains spaces, you will need to enclose the path between double quotes.

Accessing a Package

How you access a package, when you are compiling a program that uses the package, depends on where you have put it. There are a couple of options here. The first, but not the best, is to leave the `.class` files for the classes in the package in the directory with the package name. Let's look at that before we go on to the second possibility.

With the `.class` files in the original package directory, either the path to your package must appear in the string set for the `CLASSPATH` environment variable, or you must use the `classpath` option on the command line when you invoke the compiler or the interpreter. This overrides the `CLASSPATH` environment variable if it happens to be set. Note that it is up to you to make sure the classes in your package are in the right directory. Java will not prevent you from saving a file in a directory that is quite different from that appearing in the package statement. Of the two options here, using the `-classpath` option on the command line is preferable, because it sets the classpaths transiently each time, and can't interfere with anything you do subsequently. In any event we will look at both possibilities.

If you elect to use the `CLASSPATH` environment variable, it only needs to contain the paths to your packages. The standard packages supplied with Java do not need to be considered as the compiler and the interpreter can always find them. For example, you might set it under Windows 95 or 98 by adding the command,

```
set CLASSPATH=C:\MySource;C:\MyPackages
```

to your `autoexec.bat` file. Now the compiler and the interpreter will look for the directories containing your packages in the current directory and the directories `C:\MySource` and `C:\MyPackages`. Of course, you may have as many paths as you want defined, separated by semi-colons.

Under Unix, the equivalent to this might be:

```
CLASSPATH=.:/usr/local/mysource:/usr/local/mypackages
```

If you are using the Sun Java Development Kit, you also specify where your packages can be found by using the `-classpath` option when you execute the Java compiler or the interpreter. This has the advantage that it only applies for the current compilation or execution so you can easily set it to suit each run. The command to compile `MyProgram.java` defining the classpath as in the environment variable above would be:

```
javac -classpath .;C:\MySource;C:\MyPackages MyProgram.java
```

If you don't set the classpath in one of these ways, or you set it incorrectly, Java will not be able to find the classes in any new packages you might create.

A new feature introduced with Java 2 provides you with a second way to handle packages. This provides a way of adding **extensions** to the set of standard packages.

Using Extensions

Extensions are .jar files stored within the ext directory that is created when you install the JDK. For more information on the use of the JAR tool to create .jar archives, see Appendix A. The default directory structure that is created is shown below.

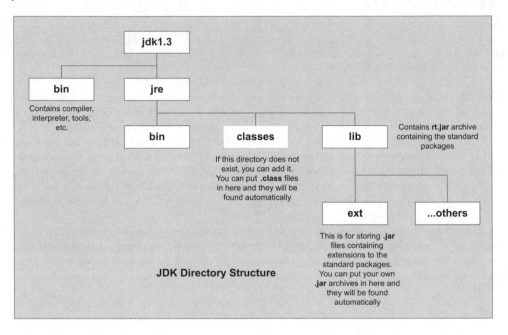

The classes and packages in the .jar archives that you place in the ext directory will automatically be accessible when you compile or run your Java programs, without the need to set the CLASSPATH environment variable, or to use the -classpath command line option. When you create a .jar file for a package, you need to make sure that you add the .class files with the directory structure corresponding to the package name – you can't just add the .class files to the archive. For example, suppose we want to store our Geometry package in an archive. Assuming we have already compiled the package and the current directory contains the package directory, the following command can be used to create the archive:

```
C:\JavaStuff\Geometry>jar cvf Geometry.jar Geometry\*.class
```

This will create the archive Geometry.jar, and add all the .class files that are in the Geometry directory to it. All you now need to do, to make the package available to any program that needs it is to copy it, to the ext directory in the JDK directory hierarchy.

The diagram above also shows the classes directory, which may not be created by default. You can put .class files in this directory and they will be found automatically when a program uses the classes they contain.

Adding Classes from a Package to your Program

Assuming they have been defined with the `public` keyword, you can add all or any of the classes in a package to the code in your program by using an **import statement**. You can reference the classes that you make available to your program using the import statement just by using the class names. For example, to make available all the classes in the package `Geometry.Shapes3D` to a source file, you just need to add the following import statement to the beginning of the file:

```
import Geometry.Shapes3D.*;    // Include all classes from this package
```

The keyword `import` is followed by the specification of what you want to import. The wildcard `*`, following the period after the package name, selects all the classes in the package, rather like selecting all the files in a directory. Now you can refer to any public class in the package just by using the class name. Again, the names of other classes in your program must be different from the names of the classes in the package.

If you want to add a particular class rather than an entire package, you specify its name explicitly in the `import` statement:

```
import Geometry.Shapes3D.Sphere;  // Include the class Sphere
```

This includes only the `Sphere` class into the source file. By using a separate import statement for each individual class from the package, you can ensure that your source file only includes the classes that you need. This reduces the likelihood of name conflicts with your own classes, particularly if you are not fully familiar with the contents of the package and it contains a large number of classes.

> Note that the `*` can only be used to select all the classes in a package. You can't use `Geometry.*` to select all the packages in the directory `Geometry`.

Packages and Names in your Programs

A package creates a self-contained environment for naming your classes. This is the primary reason for having packages in Java. You can specify the names for classes in one package without worrying about whether the same names have been used elsewhere. Java makes this possible by treating the package name as part of the class name – actually as a prefix. This means that the class `Sphere` in the package `Geometry.Shapes3D` has the full name `Geometry.Shapes3D.Sphere`. If you don't use an import statement to incorporate the class in your program, you can still make use of the class by calling it with its full class name. If you needed to do this with the class `Sphere`, you might declare a variable with the statement:

```
Geometry.Shapes3D.Sphere ball =
                 new Geometry.Shapes3D.Sphere(10.0, 1.0, 1.0, 1.0);
```

While this is rather verbose, and certainly doesn't help the readability of the program, it does ensure there will be no conflict between this class and any other `Sphere` class that might be part of your program. You can usually contrive that your class names do not conflict with those in the commonly used standard Java packages, but in cases where you can't manage this, you can always fall back on using fully qualified class names.

197

Standard Packages

All of the standard classes that are provided with Java are stored in standard packages. There is a growing list of standard packages but some of the ones you may hear about quite frequently are:

`java.lang`	Contains classes that are fundamental to Java (e.g. the Math class) and all of these are available in your programs automatically. You do not need an import statement to include them.
`java.io`	Contains classes supporting input/output operations.
`java.awt`	Contains classes that support Java's graphical user interface (GUI). While you can use these classes for GUI programming, it is almost always easier and better to use the alternative Swing classes.
`javax.swing`	Provides classes supporting the 'Swing' GUI components. These are not only more flexible and easier to use than the `java.awt` equivalents, but they are also implemented largely in Java with minimal dependency on native code.
`javax.swing.border`	Classes to support generating borders around Swing components.
`javax.swing.event`	Classes supporting event handling for Swing components.
`java.awt.event`	Contains classes that support event handling.
`java.awt.geom`	Contains classes for drawing and operating with 2D geometric entities.
`java.awt.image`	Contains classes to support image processing.
`java.applet`	This contains classes that enable you to write applets – programs that are embedded in a Web page.
`java.util`	This contains classes that support a range of standard operations for managing collections of data, accessing date and time information, and analyzing strings.
`java.util.zip`	Contains classes to support the creating of `.jar` (**Java ARc**hive) files.
`java.sql`	Contains classes that support database access using standard SQL.

The standard packages and the classes they contain cover an enormous amount of ground, so it is impossible in a book with as few pages as this to cover them all exhaustively. However, we will be applying some classes from all of these packages, plus one or two others besides, in later chapters of the book.

Standard Classes Encapsulating the Basic Data Types

You saw in the previous chapter that we have classes available that allow you to define objects that encapsulate each of the basic data types in Java. These classes are:

Boolean	Character	Byte
Short	Integer	Long
Float	Double	

These are all contained in the package `java.lang` along with quite a few other classes such as the `String` and `StringBuffer` classes that we saw in Chapter 4, and the `Math` class. Each of these classes encapsulates the corresponding basic type, and includes methods for manipulating and interrogating objects of the class, as well as a number of static methods that provide utility functions for the underlying basic types. Each of the classes corresponding to a numeric type provides a static `toString()` method to convert to a `String` object, as we saw in the last chapter. There is also a non-static `toString()` method in all of these classes that returns a `String` representation of a class object.

The classes encapsulating the numeric basic types each contain the `static final` constants `MAX_VALUE` and `MIN_VALUE` that define the maximum and minimum values that can be represented. The floating point classes also define constants `POSITIVE_INFINITY`, `NEGATIVE_INFINITY`, and NaN (stands for **N**ot **a** **N**umber as it is the result of 0/0), so you can use these in comparisons. Alternatively, you can test floating point values with the static methods `isInfinite()` and `isNaN()` – you pass your variable as an argument, and the methods return `true` for an infinite value or the NaN value respectively. Remember that an infinite value can arise without necessarily dividing by zero. Any computation that results in an exponent that is too large to be represented will produce either `POSITIVE_INFINITY` or `NEGATIVE_INFINITY`.

Conversely there are methods to convert from a `String` to a basic type. For example, the static `parseInt()` member of the class `Integer` accepts a `String` representation of an integer as an argument, and returns the equivalent value as type `int`. An alternative version of this method accepts a second argument of type `int` that specifies the radix to be used. If the `String` object cannot be parsed for any reason, if it contains invalid characters for instance, the method will throw an exception of type `NumberFormatException`. All the standard classes define methods to parse strings – `parseShort()`, `parseByte()`, and `parseLong()`.

There are many other operations supported by these classes so it is well worth browsing the JDK documentation for them.

Controlling Access to Class Members

We have not yet discussed how accessible class members are outside a class. You know that from inside a static class method you can refer to any of the static members of the class, and a non-static method can refer to any member of the class. The degree to which variables and methods within a class are accessible from other classes is more complicated. It depends on what **access attributes** you have specified for the members of a class, and whether the classes are in the same package. This is why we had to understand packages first.

Using Access Attributes

Let's start by considering classes in the same package. Within a given package, any class has direct access to any other class name – for declaring variables or specifying method parameter types, for example – but the variables and methods that are members of that other class are not necessarily accessible. The accessibility of these are controlled by **access attributes**. You have four possibilities when specifying an access attribute for a class member, including what we have used in our examples so far – that is, not to specify anything at all – and each possibility has a different effect overall. The options you have for specifying the accessibility of a variable or a method in a class are:

Attribute	Permitted access
No access attribute	From any class in the same package.
public	From any class anywhere.
private	No access from outside the class at all.
protected	From any class in the same package and from any sub-class anywhere.

The table shows you how the access attributes you set for a class member determine the parts of the Java environment from which you can access it. We will discuss sub-classes in the next chapter, so don't worry about these for the moment. We will be coming back to how and when you use the protected attribute then. Note that public, private, and protected are all keywords. Specifying a member as public makes it completely accessible, and at the other extreme, making it private restricts access to members of the same class.

This may sound more complicated than it actually is. Look at the next diagram, which shows the access allowed between classes within the same package.

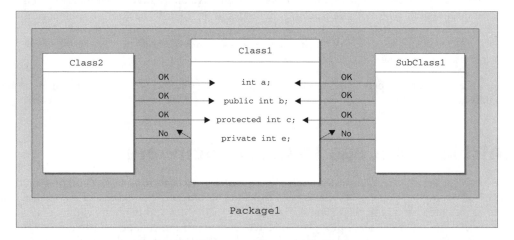

Within a package such as package1, only the private members of the class Class1 can't be directly accessed by a method in another class in the same package. Declaring a class member to be private limits its availability solely to methods in the same class.

We saw earlier that a class definition must have an access attribute of public if it is to be accessible from outside the package. The next diagram shows the situation where the classes, seeking access to the members of a public class, are in different packages.

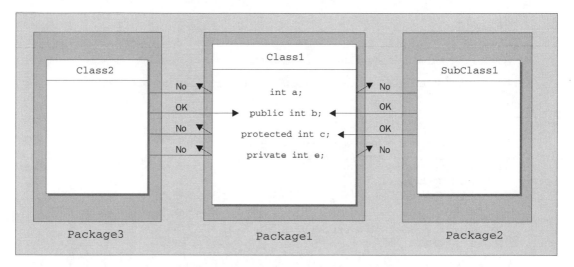

Here access is more restricted. The only members of Class1 that can be accessed from an ordinary class, Class2, in another package are those specified as public. Keep in mind that the class, Class1, must also have been defined with the attribute public. From a sub-class of Class1 that is in another package, the members of Class1, without an access attribute, cannot be reached, and neither can the private members – these can never be accessed externally under any circumstances.

Specifying Access Attributes

As you probably gathered from the diagrams that we just looked at, to specify an access attribute for a class member, you just add the keyword to the beginning of the declaration. Here is the Point class you saw earlier, but now with access attributes defined for its members:

Try It Out – Accessing the Point Class

Make the following changes to your Point class. If you save it in a new directory, do make sure Line.java is copied there as well. It will be useful later if they are in a directory with the name Geometry.

```
public class Point
{
  // Create a point from its coordinates
  public Point(double xVal, double yVal)
  {
    x = xVal;
    y = yVal;
  }
```

```
   // Create a Point from an existing Point object
   public Point(final Point aPoint)
   {
     x = aPoint.x;
     y = aPoint.y;
   }

     // Move a point
   public void move(double xDelta, double yDelta)
   {
     // Parameter values are increments to the current coordinates
     x += xDelta;
     y += yDelta;
   }

   // Calculate the distance to another point
   public double distance(final Point aPoint)
   {
     return Math.sqrt(
           (x - aPoint.x)*(x - aPoint.x) + (y - aPoint.y)*(y - aPoint.y) );
   }

   // Convert a point to a string
   public String toString()
   {
     return Double.toString(x) + ", " + y;     // As "x, y"
   }

   // Coordinates of the point
   private double x;
   private double y;
 }
```

The members have been re-sequenced within the class with the `private` members appearing last. You should maintain a consistent ordering of class members according to their access attributes, as it makes the code easier to follow. The ordering adopted most frequently is for the most accessible members to appear first, and the least accessible last, but a consistent order is more important than the particular order you choose.

How It Works

Now the instance variables x and y cannot be accessed or modified from outside the class as they are private. The only way these can be set or modified is through methods within the class, either with constructors, or the `move()` method. If it is necessary to obtain the values of x and y from outside the class, as it might well be in this case, a simple function would do the trick. For example:

```
public double getX()
{ return x;  }
```

Couldn't be easier really, could it? This makes x freely available, but prevents modification of its value from outside the class. In general, such methods are referred to as **accessor** methods, and usually have the form `getXXX()`. Methods that allow a private data member to be changed are called **mutator** methods, and are typically of the form `setXXX()` where a new value is passed as an argument. For example:

```
public void setX(double inputX)
{  x = inputX;  }
```

It may seem odd to use a method to alter the value of a `private` data member when you could just make it `public`. The main advantage of using a method in this way is that you can apply validity checks on the new value that is to be set.

Choosing Access Attributes

As you can see from the table of access attributes, all the classes we have defined so far have had members that are freely accessible within the same package. This applies both to the methods and the variables that were defined in the classes. This is not good object oriented programming practice. As we said in Chapter 1, one of the ideas behind objects is to keep the data members encapsulated so they cannot be modified by all and sundry, even from other classes within the same package. On the other hand, the methods in your classes generally need to be accessible. They provide the outside interface to the class and define the set of operations that are possible with objects of the class. Therefore in the majority of situations with simple classes (i.e. no sub-classes), you should be explicitly specifying your class members as either `public` or `private`, rather than omitting the access attributes.

Broadly, unless you have good reasons for declaring them otherwise, the variables in a public class should be `private` and the methods that will be called from outside the class should be `public`. Even where access to the values of the variables from outside a class is necessary, you don't need to make them `public` or leave them without an access attribute. As we've just seen, you can provide access quite easily by adding a simple `public` method to return the value of a data member.

Of course, there are always exceptions:

- ❏ For classes in a package that are not public, and therefore not accessible outside the package, it may sometimes be convenient to allow other classes in the package direct access to the data members.

- ❏ If you have data members that have been specified as `final` so that their values are fixed, and they are likely to be useful outside the class, you might as well declare them to be `public`.

- ❏ You may well have methods in a class that are only intended to be used internally by other methods in the class. In this case you should specify these as `private`.

- ❏ In a class like the standard class, `Math`, which is just a convenient container for utility functions and standard data values, you will want to make everything `public`.

All of this applies to simple classes. We will see in the next chapter, when we will be looking at sub-classes, that there are some further aspects of class structure that you must take into account.

Using a Package and Access Attributes

Let's put together an example that uses a package that we will create. We could put the `Point` and `Line` classes that we defined earlier in a package we could call `Geometry`. We can then write a program that will import these classes and test them.

Try It Out – Packaging up the Line and Point Classes

The source and `.class` files for each class in the package must be in a directory with the name `Geometry`. Remember that you need to ensure the path to the directory (or directories if you are storing `.class` files separately) `Geometry` appears in the `CLASSPATH` environment variable setting before you try compile or use either of these two classes. You can do this by specifying the `-classpath` option when you run the compiler or the interpreter.

To include the class `Point` in the package, the code in `Point.java` will be:

```
package Geometry;

public class Point
{
// Create a point from its coordinates
  public Point(double xVal, double yVal)
  {
    x = xVal;
    y = yVal;
  }

  // Create a Point from an existing Point object
  public Point(final Point aPoint)
  {
    x = aPoint.x;
    y = aPoint.y;
  }

    // Move a point
  public void move(double xDelta, double yDelta)
  {
    // Parameter values are increments to the current coordinates
    x += xDelta;
    y += yDelta;
  }

  // Calculate the distance to another point
  public double distance(final Point aPoint)
  {
    return Math.sqrt(
        (x - aPoint.x)*(x - aPoint.x) + (y - aPoint.y)*(y - aPoint.y) );
  }

  // Convert a point to a string
  public String toString()
  {
    return Double.toString(x) + ", " + y;     // As "x, y"
  }

  // Retrieve the x coordinate
  public double getX()
  {  return x;   }

  // Retrieve the y coordinate
  public double getY()
  {  return y;   }
```

```
   // Set the x coordinate
   public void setX(double inputX)
   {   x = inputX;   }

   // Set the y coordinate
   public void setY(double inputY)
   {   y = inputY;   }

   // Coordinates of the point
   private double x;
   private double y;
}
```

Note that we have added the getX(), getY(), setX() and setY() methods to the class to make the private data members accessible.

The Line class also needs to be amended to make the methods public and to declare the class as public. We also need to change its intersects() method so that it can access the private data members of Point objects using the set...() and get...() methods in the Point class. The code in Line.java, with changes highlighted, will be:

```
package Geometry;

public class Line
{
   // Create a line from two points
   public Line(final Point start, final Point end)

   {
      this.start = new Point(start);
      this.end = new Point(end);
   }

   // Create a line from two coordinate pairs
   public Line(double xStart, double yStart, double xEnd, double yEnd)
   {
      start = new Point(xStart, yStart);        // Create the start point
      end = new Point(xEnd, yEnd);              // Create the end point
   }

   // Calculate the length of a line
   public double length()
   {
      return start.distance(end);               // Use the method from the Point
class
   }

   // Return a point as the intersection of two lines -- called from a Line object
   public Point intersects(final Line line1)
   {

      Point localPoint = new Point(0, 0);

      double num =
          (this.end.getY() - this.start.getY())*(this.start.getX() -
line1.start.getX())-
          (this.end.getX() - this.start.getX())*(this.start.getY() -
line1.start.getY());

      double denom =
```

```
        (this.end.getY() - this.start.getY())*(line1.end.getX() -
   line1.start.getX()) -
        (this.end.getX() - this.start.getX())*(line1.end.getY() -
   line1.start.getY());
     localPoint.setX(line1.start.getX() + (line1.end.getX() -
                                        line1.start.getX())*num/denom);
     localPoint.setY(line1.start.getY() + (line1.end.getY() -
                                        line1.start.getY())*num/denom);

     return localPoint;
   }

   // Convert a line to a string
   public String toString()
   {
     return "(" + start+ "):(" + end + ")";     // As "(start):(end)"
   }                                             // that is, "(x1, y1):(x2, y2)"

   // Data members
   Point start;                                  // Start point of line
   Point end;                                    // End point of line
}
```

Here we have left the data members without an access attribute, so they are accessible from the Point class, but not from classes outside the Geometry package.

How It Works

The package statement at the beginning of each source file defines the package to which the class belongs. Remember, you still have to save it in the correct directory, Geometry. Without the public attribute, the classes would not be available to classes outside the Geometry package.

Since we have declared the data members in the class Point as private, they will not be accessible directly. We have added the methods getX(), getY(), setX() and setY() to the Point class to make the values accessible to any class that needs them.

The Line class hasn't been updated since our first example, so we first have to sort out the access attributes. The two instance variables are declared as before, without any access attribute, so they can be accessed from within the package but not from classes outside the package. This is an instance where exposing the data members within the package is very convenient, and we can do it without exposing the data members to any classes using the package. And we have updated the intersects() method to reflect the changes in accessibility made to the members of the Point class.

We can now write the program that is going to import and use the package that we have just created.

Try It Out – Testing the Geometry Package

We can create a succession of points, and a line joining each pair of successive points in the sequence, and then calculate the total line length.

```
import Geometry.*;    // Import the Point and Line classes

public class TryPackage
{
  public static void main(String[] args)
```

```
{
  double[][] coords = { {1.0, 0.0}, {6.0, 0.0}, {6.0, 10.0},
                        {10.0,10.0}, {10.0, -14.0}, {8.0, -14.0}};
  // Create an array of points and fill it with Point objects
  Point[] points = new Point[coords.length];
  for(int i = 0; i < coords.length; i++)
    points[i] = new Point(coords[i][0],coords[i][1]);

  // Create an array of lines and fill it using Point pairs
  Line[] lines = new Line[points.length - 1];
  double totalLength = 0.0;            // Store total line length here
  for(int i = 0; i < points.length - 1; i++)
  {
    lines[i] = new Line(points[i], points[i+1]); // Create a Line
    totalLength += lines[i].length();            // Add its length
    System.out.println("Line "+(i+1)+' ' +lines[i] +
                       " Length is " + lines[i].length());
  }

  // Output the total length
  System.out.println("\nTotal line length = " + totalLength);
  }
}
```

You should save this as `TryPackage.java` in the directory `TryPackage`. If the path to your `Geometry` directory on a PC running Windows is `C:\Packages\Geometry`, you can compile this with the command:

```
javac -classpath "C:\Packages" TryPackage.java
```

This assumes the current directory contains the `TryPackage.java` file. You can then execute the program with the command:

```
java -classpath "C:\Packages" TryPackage
```

When the program executes, you should see the following output:

```
Line 1 (1.0, 0.0):(6.0, 0.0)    Length is 5.0
Line 2 (6.0, 0.0):(6.0, 10.0)    Length is 10.0
Line 3 (6.0, 10.0):(10.0, 10.0)    Length is 4.0
Line 4 (10.0, 10.0):(10.0, -14.0)    Length is 24.0
Line 5 (10.0, -14.0):(8.0, -14.0)    Length is 2.0

Total line length = 45.0
```

How It Works

This example is a handy review of how you can define arrays, and also shows that you can declare an array of objects in the same way as you declare an array of one of the basic types. The dimensions of the array of arrays, `coords`, are determined by the initial values that are specified between the braces. The first dimension is determined by the number of values within the outer braces. Each of the elements in the array is itself an array of length two, with each pair of element values being enclosed within their own braces.

207

Since there are six sets of these, we have an array of six elements, each of which is itself an array of two elements. Each of these elements correspond to the (x, y) coordinates of a point.

You can see from this that, if necessary, you can create an array of arrays with each row having a different number of elements. The length of each row is determined by the number of initializing values that appear, so they could all be different in the most general case.

We declare an array of `Point` objects with the same length as the number of (x, y) pairs in the `coords` array. This array is filled with `Point` objects in the `for` loop, which we created using the pairs of coordinate values from the `coords` array.

Since each pair of `Point` objects will define a `Line` object, we need one less element in the array `lines` than we have in the `points` array. We create the elements of the lines array in the second `for` loop using successive `Point` objects, and accumulate the total length of all the line segments by adding the length of each `Line` object to `totalLength` as it is created. On each iteration of the `for` loop, we output the details of the current line. Finally, we output the value of `totalLength`, which in this case is 45.

Note that the import statement adds the classes from the package `Geometry` to our program. These classes can be added to any application using the same import statement. You might like to try putting the classes in the Geometry package in a JAR file and try it out as an extension.

Nested Classes

All the classes we have defined so far have been separate from each other – each stored away in its own file. Not all classes have to be defined like this. You can put the definition of one class inside the definition of another class. The inside class is called a **nested class**. A nested class can itself have another class nested inside it, if need be.

When you define a nested class, it is a member of the enclosing class in much the same way as other members. A nested class can have an access attribute just like other class members, and the accessibility from outside the enclosing class is determined by the attributes in the same way.

```
public class Outside
{
  // Nested class
  public class Inside
  {
    // Details of Inside class...
  }
  // More members of Outside class...
}
```

Here the class `Inside` is nested inside the class `Outside`. The `Inside` class is declared as a public member of `Outside`, so it is accessible from outside `Outside`. Obviously a nested class should have some specific association with the enclosing class. Arbitrarily nesting one class inside another would not be sensible. The enclosing class here is referred to as a **top-level class**. A top level class is a class that contains a nested class but is not itself a nested class.

Our nested class here only has meaning in the context of an object of type `Outside`. This is because `Inside` is not declared as a static member of the class `Outside`. Until an object of type `Outside` has been created, you can't create any `Inside` objects. However, when you declare an object of a class containing a nested class, no objects of the nested class are necessarily created – unless of course they are created by the enclosing class's constructor. For example, suppose we create an object with the following statement:

```
Outside outer = new Outside();
```

No objects of the nested class, `Inside`, are created. If you now wish to create an object of the type of the nested class you must refer to the nested class type using the name of the enclosing class as a qualifier. For instance, having declared an object of type `Outside`, we can create an object of type `Inside` as follows:

```
Outside.Inside inner = outer.new Inside();     // Define a nested class object
```

Here we have created an object of the nested class type that is associated with the object, `outer`, created earlier. We are creating an object of type `Inside` in the context of the object `outer`.

Within non-static methods that are members of `Outside`, you can use the class name `Inside` without any qualification as it will be automatically qualified by the compiler with the `this` variable. So we could create new `Inside` object from within the method of the object `Outside`:

```
Inside inner = new Inside();     // Define a nested class object
```

Which is equivalent to:

```
this.Inside inner = this.new Inside();     // Define a nested class object
```

All this implies that a static method cannot create objects of a non-static nested class type. Because the `Inside` class is not a static member of the `Outside` class such a member could, if there are no `Inside` objects extant in the context of an `Outside` object, refer to an object which does not exist – an error. And as `Inside` is not a static data member of the `Outside` class, if a static method in the `Outside` class tried to create an object of type `Inside` directly, without first invoking an object of type `Outside`, it would be trying to create an object outside of that object's legitimate scope – an illegal maneuver.

Also, because the class `Inside` is not a static member of the `Outside` class, it cannot in turn contain any static data members itself. Since `Inside` is not static itself it cannot act as a free standing class with static members – this would be a logical contradiction.

Nested classes are typically used to define objects that at least have a strong association with objects of the enclosing class type, and often there is a tight coupling between the two.

Static Nested Classes

To make objects of a nested class type independent of objects of the enclosing class, you can declare the nested class as `static`. For example,

```
public class Outside
{
  public static class Skinside
  {
    // Details of Skinside
  }

  // Nested class
  public class Inside
  {
    // Details of Inside class...
  }
  // More members of Outside class...
}
```

Now with `Skinside` inside `Outside` declared as `static`, we can declare objects of this nested class, independent from objects of `Outside`, and regardless of whether we have created any `Outside` objects or not. For example:

```
Outside.Skinside example = new Outside.Skinside();
```

This is significantly different from what we needed to do for a non-static nested class. Now we must use the nested class name qualified by the enclosing class name as the type for creating the object. Note that a static nested class can have static members, whereas a non-static nested class cannot.

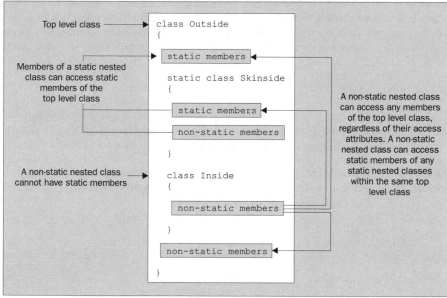

Let's see how a nested class works in practice with a simple example. We will create a class `MagicHat` that will define an object containing a variable number of rabbits. We will put the definition for the class `Rabbit` inside the definition of the class `MagicHat`. The basic structure of `MagicHat.java` will be:

```
public class MagicHat
{
  // Definition of the MagicHat class...

  // Nested class to define a rabbit
  static class Rabbit
  {
    // Definition of the Rabbit class...
  }
}
```

Here the nested class is defined as `static` because we want to be able to have static members of this class. We will see a little later how it might work with a non-static nested class.

Try It Out – Rabbits Out of Hats

Let's add the detail of the `MagicHat` class definition:

```
import java.util.Random;                       // Import Random class

public class MagicHat
{
  static int maxRabbits = 5;                   // Maximum rabbits in a hat
  static Random select = new Random();         // Random number generator

  // Constructor for a hat
  public MagicHat(final String hatName)
  {
    this.hatName = hatName;                     // Store the hat name
    rabbits = new Rabbit[1+select.nextInt(maxRabbits)]; // Random rabbits

    for(int i = 0; i < rabbits.length; i++)
      rabbits[i] = new Rabbit();               // Create the rabbits
  }

  // String representation of a hat
  public String toString()
  {
    // Hat name first...
    String hatString = "\n" + hatName + " contains:\n";

    for(int i = 0; i < rabbits.length; i++)
      hatString += "\t" + rabbits[i] + " ";    // Add the rabbits strings
    return hatString;
  }

  private String hatName;                       // Name of the hat
  private Rabbit rabbits[];                      // Rabbits in the hat

  // Nested class to define a rabbit
  static class Rabbit
```

```
    {
        // Definition of the Rabbit class...
    }
}
```

Instead of the old `Math.random()` method that we have been using up to now to generate pseudo-random values, we are using an object of the class `Random` that is defined in the package `java.util`. An object of type `Random` has a variety of methods to generate pseudo-random values of different types, and with different ranges. The method `nextInt()` that we are using here returns an integer that is zero or greater, but less than the integer value you pass as an argument. Thus if you pass the length of an array to it, it will generate a random index value that will always be legal for the array size. Note that the `MagicHat` constructor parameter has been declared as `final` as it is not altered within the constructor.

We can now add the definition of the `Rabbit` class. When we create a `Rabbit` object, we want it to have a unique name so we can distinguish one `Rabbit` from another. We can generate unique names by selecting one from a limited set of fixed names, and then appending an integer that is different each time the base name is used. Here's what we need to add for the `Rabbit` class definition:

```java
public class MagicHat
{

    // Definition of the MagicHat class - as before...

    // Nested class to define a rabbit
    static class Rabbit
    {
        // A name is a rabbit name from rabbitNames followed by an integer
        static private String[] rabbitNames = {"Floppsy", "Moppsy",
                                               "Gnasher", "Thumper"};
        static private int[] rabbitNamesCount = new int[rabbitNames.length];
        private String name;                          // Name of the rabbit

        // Constructor for a rabbit
        public Rabbit()
        {
            int index = select.nextInt(rabbitNames.length);  // Get random name
                                                             // index
            name = rabbitNames[index] + (++rabbitNamesCount[index]);
        }

        // String representation of a rabbit
        public String toString()
        {
            return name;
        }
    }
}
```

Note that the constructor in the `Rabbit` class can access the `select` member of the enclosing class `MagicHat`, without qualification. This is only possible with static members of the enclosing class – you can't refer to non-static members of the enclosing class here because there is no object of type `MagicHat` associated with it.

We can use the following application class to try out our nested class:

```
public class TryNestedClass
{
  static public void main(String[] args)
  {
    // Create three magic hats and output them
    System.out.println(new MagicHat("Gray Topper"));
    System.out.println(new MagicHat("Black Topper"));
    System.out.println(new MagicHat("Baseball Cap"));
  }
}
```

When I ran the program, I got the output:

```
Gray Topper contains:
      Moppsy1      Moppsy2      Floppsy1

Black Topper contains:
      Thumper1     Moppsy3      Thumper2     Gnasher1

Baseball Cap contains:
      Moppsy4      Moppsy5      Thumper3
```

You are likely to get something different.

How It Works

Each `MagicHat` object will contain a random number of `Rabbit` objects. The constructor for a `MagicHat` object stores the name of the hat in its private member `hatName`, and generates a `Rabbit` array with at least one, and up to `maxRabbits` elements. This is done with the expression `1+select.nextInt(maxRabbits)`. Calling `nextInt()` with the argument `maxRabbits` will return a value that is from 0 to `maxRabbits-1` inclusive. Adding 1 to this will result in a value from 1 to `maxRabbits` inclusive. The array so created is then filled with `Rabbit` objects.

The `MagicHat` class also has a method `toString()` method which returns a `String` object containing the name of the hat and the names of all the rabbits in the hat. This assumes the `Rabbit` class also has a `toString()` method defined. We will be able to use the `toString()` implicitly in an output statement when we come to create and display `MagicHat` class objects.

The base names that we use to generate rabbit names are defined in the `static` array `rabbitNames[]` in the `Rabbit` class. The count for each base name which we will append to the base name to produce a unique name is stored in the `static` array `rabbitNamesCount[]`, which has the same number of elements as the `rabbitNames` array. The `Rabbit` class has the data member, `name`, to store a name that is initialized in the constructor. A random base name is selected from the `rabbitNames[]` array using an index value from 0 up one less than the length. We then append the current count for the name incremented by 1, so successive uses of any base name `Gnasher`, for example, will produce names `Gnasher1`, `Gnasher2` and so on. The `toString()` method for the class returns the name for the `Rabbit` object.

The method `main()` in `TryNestedClass` creates three `MagicHat` objects and outputs the string representation of each of them. Putting the object as an argument to the `println()` method will call the `toString()` method for the object automatically, and the `String` object that is returned will be output to the screen.

Using a Non-Static Nested Class

In our previous example, we could define the `Rabbit` class as non-static by deleting the keyword `static`. However, if you try that, the program will no longer compile and run. The problem is the static data members `rabbitNames` and `rabbitNamesCount` in the `Rabbit` class. A non-static nested class cannot have static members, so we must seek an alternative way of dealing with names.

We could consider making these arrays non-static. This has several disadvantages. First, each `Rabbit` object would have its own copy of these arrays – an unnecessary duplication of data. A more serious problem is that our naming process would not work. Because each object has its own copy of the `rabbitNamesCount` array, the names generated are not going to be unique.

The answer is to keep `rabbitNames` and `rabbitNamesCount` as static, but put them in the `MagicHat` class instead. Let's see that working.

Try It Out – Accessing the Top Level Class Members

We need to modify the class definition to:

```
public class MagicHat
{
  static int maxRabbits = 5;                    // Maximuum rabbits in a hat
  static Random select = new Random();          // Random number generator
  static private String[] rabbitNames = {"Floppsy", "Moppsy",
                                          "Gnasher", "Thumper"};
  static private int[] rabbitNamesCount = new int[rabbitNames.length];

  // Constructor for a hat
  public MagicHat(final String hatName)
  {
    this.hatName = hatName;                          // Store the hat name
    rabbits = new Rabbit[1+select.nextInt(maxRabbits)]; // Random rabbits

    for(int i = 0; i < rabbits.length; i++)
      rabbits[i] = new Rabbit();                     // Create the rabbits
  }

  // String representation of a hat
  public String toString()
  {
    // Hat name first...
    String hatString = "\n" + hatName + " contains:\n";

    for(int i = 0; i < rabbits.length; i++)
      hatString += "\t" + rabbits[i] + " ";  // Add the rabbits strings
    return hatString;
  }
```

```
    private String hatName;        // Name of the hat
    private Rabbit rabbits[];       // Rabbits in the hat

  // Nested class to define a rabbit
    class Rabbit
  {
    private String name;                        // Name of the rabbit

    // Constructor for a rabbit
    public Rabbit()
    {
      int index = select.nextInt(rabbitNames.length);  // Get random name
                                                // index
      name = rabbitNames[index] + (++rabbitNamesCount[index]);
    }

    // String representation of a rabbit
    public String toString()
    {
      return name;
    }
  }
}
```

The only changes are the deletion of the static keyword in the definition of the Rabbit class – the data members relating to rabbit names have been moved to the MagicHat class. You can run this with the same version of TryNestedClass and it should produce output much the same as before.

How It Works

Although the output is much the same, what is happening is distinctly different. The Rabbit objects that are created in the MagicHat constructor are now associated with the current MagicHat object that is being constructed. The Rabbit() constructor call is actually this.Rabbit().

Using a Nested Class outside the Top-Level Class

You can create objects of an inner class outside the top-level class containing the inner class. As we discussed, how you do this depends on whether the nested class is a static member of the enclosing class. With the first version of our MagicHat class, with a static Rabbit class, you could create an independent rabbit by adding the following statement to the end of main():

```
    System.out.println("An independent rabbit: " + new MagicHat.Rabbit());
```

This Rabbit object is completely free – there is no MagicHat object to restrain it. In the case of a non-static Rabbit class, things are different. Let's try this using a modified version of the previous program.

Try It Out – Free Range Rabbits (Almost)

We can see how this works by modifying the method `main()` in `TryNestedClass` to create another `MagicHat` object, and then create a `Rabbit` object for it:

```
static public void main(String[] args)
{
  // Create three magic hats and output them
  System.out.println(new MagicHat("Gray Topper"));
  System.out.println(new MagicHat("Black Topper"));
  System.out.println(new MagicHat("Baseball Cap"));

    MagicHat oldHat = new MagicHat("Old hat");        // New hat object
    MagicHat.Rabbit rabbit = oldHat.new Rabbit();     // Create rabbit object
    System.out.println(oldHat);                       // Show the hat
    System.out.println("\nNew rabbit is: " + rabbit); // Display the rabbit
}
```

The output produced is:

```
Gray Topper contains:
     Thumper1

Black Topper contains:
     Moppsy1      Thumper2     Thumper3

Baseball Cap contains:
     Floppsy1     Floppsy2     Thumper4

Old hat contains:
     Floppsy3     Thumper5     Thumper6  Thumper7        Thumper8

New rabbit is: Thumper9
```

How It Works

The new code first creates a `MagicHat` object, `oldHat`. This will have its own rabbits. We then use this object to create an object of the class `MagicHat.Rabbit`. This is how a nested class type is referenced – with the top-level class name as a qualifier. You can only call the constructor for the nested class in this case by qualifying it with a `MagicHat` object name. This is because a non-static nested class can refer to members of the top-level class – including instance members. Therefore, an instance of the top-level class must exist for this to be possible.

Note how the top-level object is used in the constructor call. The object name qualifier goes before the keyword `new` which precedes the constructor call for the inner class. This creates an object, `rabbit`, in the context of the object `oldHat`. This doesn't mean `oldHat` has `rabbit` as a member. It means that, if top-level members are used in the inner class, they will be the members for `oldHat`. You can see from the example that the name of the new rabbit is not part of the `oldHat` object, although it is associated with `oldHat`. You could demonstrate this by modifying the `toString()` method in the `Rabbit` class to:

```
public String toString()
{
   return name + " parent: "+hatName;
}
```

If you run the program again, when each `Rabbit` object is displayed it will also show its parent hat.

Local Nested Classes

You can define a class inside a method – where it is called a **local nested class**. It is also referred to as a **local inner class**, since a non-static nested class is often referred to as an **inner class**. You can only create objects of a local inner class locally – that is, within the method in which the class definition appears. This is useful when the computation in a method requires the use of a specialized class that is not required or used elsewhere.

A local inner class can refer to variables declared in the method in which the definition appears, but only if they are `final`.

The finalize() Method

You have the option of including a method `finalize()` in a class definition. This method is called automatically by Java before an object is finally destroyed and the space it occupies in memory is released. Please note that this may be some time after the object is inaccessible in your program. When an object goes out of scope, it is dead as far as your program is concerned, but the Java virtual machine may not get around to disposing of the remains until later. When it does, it calls the `finalize()` method for the object. The form of the `finalize()` method is:

```
protected void finalize()
{
   // Your clean-up code...
}
```

This method is useful if your class objects use resources that require some special action when they are destroyed. Typically these are resources that are not within the Java environment and are not guaranteed to be released by the object itself. This means such things as graphics resources – fonts or other drawing related resources that are supplied by the host operating system, or external files on the hard disk. Leaving these around after an object is destroyed wastes system resources and, in some circumstances (with graphics resources under Windows 95 for instance) if you waste enough of them, your program, and possibly other programs the system is supporting, may stop working. For most classes this is not necessary, but if an object opened a disk file for example, but did not guarantee its closure, you would want to make sure that the file was closed when the object was destroyed. You can implement the `finalize()` method to take care of this.

Another use for the `finalize()` method is to record the fact that the object has been destroyed. We could implement the `finalize()` method for the `Sphere` class to decrement the value of the static member, `count`, for instance. This would make `count` a measure of how many `Sphere` objects were around, rather than how many had been created. It would, however, not be an accurate measure for reasons that we will come to in a moment.

You cannot rely on an object being destroyed when it is no longer available to your program code. The Java virtual machine will only get rid of unwanted objects and free the memory they occupy if it runs out of memory, or if there is no activity within your program – for example when waiting for input. As a result objects may not get destroyed until execution of your program ends. You also have no guarantee as to when a `finalize()` method will be called. All you are assured is that it will be called before the memory that the object occupied is freed. Nothing time-sensitive should be left to the `finalize()` method.

One consequence of this is that there are circumstances where this can cause problems – when you don't allow for the possibility of your objects hanging around. For example, suppose you create an object in a method that opens a file, and rely on the `finalize()` method to close it. If you then call this method in a loop, you may end up with a large number of files open at one time, since the object that is created in each call of the method will not necessarily be destroyed immediately on return from the method. This introduces the possibility of your program attempting to have more files open simultaneously than the host operating system allows. In this situation, you should make sure a file is closed when you have finished with it, by including an object method to close it explicitly – for example `close()`.

Native Methods

It is possible to include a method in a class that is implemented in some other programming language, such as C or C++, external to the Java Virtual Machine. To specify such a method within a class definition you use the keyword `native` in the declaration of the method. For example:

```
public native long getData();      // Declare a method that is not in Java
```

Of course the method will have no body in Java since it is defined elsewhere, where all the work is done, so the declaration ends with a semi-colon. The implementation of a native method will need to use an interface to the Java environment. The standard API for implementing native methods in C for example, is called JNI – the Java Native Interface.

The major drawback to using native methods in Java is that your program will no longer be portable. Security requirements for applets embedded in Web pages require that the code must all be written in Java – using native methods in an applet is simply not possible. Since the primary reasons for using Java are the portability of the code and the ability to produce applets, the need for you to add native methods to your Java programs will be minimal. We will, therefore, not delve any deeper into this topic.

Summary

In this chapter you have learned all the essentials of defining your own classes. You can now create your own class types to fit the context of the problems you are dealing with. We will build on this in the next chapter to enable you to add more flexibility to the operations on your class objects by showing you how to realize polymorphism.

The important points covered in this chapter are:

❑   A class definition specifies the variables and methods that are members of the class.

❑   Each class must be saved in a file with the same name as the class, and with the extension `.java`.

❑ Class variables are declared using the keyword `static`, and one instance of each class variable is shared amongst all objects of a class.

❑ Each object of a class will have its own instance variables – these are variables declared without using the keyword `static`.

❑ Methods that are specified as `static` can be called even if no class objects exist, but a `static` method cannot refer to instance variables.

❑ Methods that are not specified as `static` can access any of the variables in the class directly.

❑ Recursive methods are methods that call themselves.

❑ Access to members of a class is determined by the access attributes that are specified for each of them. These can be `public`, `private`, `protected`, `private protected`, or nothing at all.

❑ Classes can be grouped into a package. If a class in a package is to be accessible from outside the package the class must be declared using the keyword `public`.

❑ To designate that a class is a member of a package you use a `package` statement at the beginning of the file containing the class definition.

❑ To add classes from a package to a file you use an `import` statement immediately following any package statement in the file.

❑ A native method is a method implemented in a language other than Java. Java programs containing native methods cannot be applets and are no longer portable.

Exercises

1. Define a class for rectangle objects defined by two points, the top-left and bottom-right corners of the rectangle. Include a constructor to copy a rectangle, a method to return a rectangle object, that encloses the current object and the rectangle passed as an argument, and a method to display the defining points of a rectangle. Test the class by creating four rectangles, and combining these cumulatively, to end up with a rectangle enclosing them all. Output the defining points of all the rectangles you create.

2. Define a class, `mcmLength`, to represent a length measured in meters, centimeters, and millimeters, each stored as integers. Include methods to add and subtract objects, to multiply and divide an object by an integer value, to calculate an area resulting from the product of two objects, and to compare objects. Include constructors that accept: three arguments – meters, centimeters, and millimeters; one integer argument in millimeters; one double argument in centimeters and no arguments, which creates an object with the length set to zero. Check the class by creating some objects and testing the class operations.

3. Define a class, `tkgWeight`, to represent a weight in tons, kilograms, and grams, and include a similar range of methods and constructors as the previous example. Demonstrate this class by creating and combining some class objects.

4. Put both the previous classes in a package called `Measures`. Import this package into a program that will calculate and display the total weight of the following: 200 carpets – size: 4 meters by 2 meters 9 centimeters, that weigh 1.25 kilograms per square meter, and 60 carpets – size: 3 meters 57 centimeters by 5 meters, that weigh 1.05 kilograms per square meter.

Extending Classes and Inheritance

A very important part of object oriented programming allows you to create a new class based on a class that has already been defined. The class that you use as the base for your new class can be either one you have defined, a standard class in Java, or a class defined by someone else – perhaps from a package supporting a specialized application area.

This chapter focuses on how you can reuse existing classes by creating new classes based on the ones you have, and explores the ramifications of using this facility, and the additional capabilities it provides. We will also delve into an important related topic – **interfaces** – and how you can use them.

In this chapter you will learn:

- ❑ How to reuse classes by defining a new class based on an existing class.
- ❑ What polymorphism is and how to define your classes to take advantage of it.
- ❑ What an abstract method is.
- ❑ What an abstract class is.
- ❑ What an interface is and how you can define your own interfaces.
- ❑ How to use interfaces in your classes.
- ❑ How interfaces can help you implement polymorphic classes.

Using Existing Classes

Let's start by understanding the jargon. Defining a new class based on an existing class is called **derivation**. The new class, or **derived class**, is referred to as a **direct subclass** of the class from which it is derived. The original class is called a **base class** because it forms the base for the definition of the derived class. The original class is also referred to as a **superclass** of the derived class. You can also have classes derived from derived classes, which in turn were derived from some other derived class, and so on. This is illustrated in the following diagram:

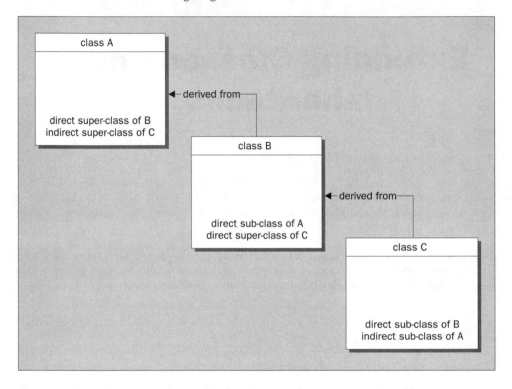

This shows just three classes in a hierarchy, but there can be as many as you like.

Let's consider a more concrete example. We could define a class Dog that could represent a dog of any kind.

```
class Dog
{
   // Members of the Dog class...
}
```

This might contain a data member identifying the name of a particular dog such as "Lassie" or "Poochy" and another data member to identify the breed, such as "Border Collie" or "Pyrenean Mountain Dog". From the Dog class, we could derive a Spaniel class that represented a dog which was a spaniel:

```
class Spaniel extends Dog
{
  // Members of the Spaniel class...
}
```

The extends keyword that we use here identifies that Dog is a base class for Spaniel, so an object of type Spaniel will have members that are inherited from the Dog class, in addition to the members of the Spaniel class that appear in its definition. The breed would be "spaniel" for all instances of the class Spaniel although in general the name for each spaniel would be different. The Spaniel class might have some additional data members that characterize the specifics of what it means to be a spaniel. We will see in a moment how we can arrange for the base class data members to be set appropriately.

A Spaniel object is a specialized instance of a Dog object. This reflects real life. A spaniel is obviously a dog and will have all the properties of a basic dog, but it has some unique characteristics of its own which distinguish it from all the dogs that are not spaniels. The inheritance mechanism which adds all the properties of the base class – Dog in this instance – to those in the derived class, is a good model for the real world. The members of the derived class define the properties that differentiate it from the base type, so when you derive one class from another, you can think of your derived class as a specification for objects that are specializations of the base class object.

Class Inheritance

In summary, when you derive a new class from a base class, the process is additive in terms of what makes up a class definition. The additional members establish what makes the derived class object different from the base. Any members declared in the new class are in addition to those that are already members of the base class. For our Spaniel class, derived from Dog, the data members to hold the name and the breed, that are defined for the class Dog, would automatically be in the class Spaniel. A Spaniel object will always have a complete Dog object inside it – with all its data members and methods. This does not mean that all the members defined in the Dog class are available to methods that are specific to the Spaniel class. Some are and some aren't. The inclusion of members of a base class in a derived class so that they are accessible in that derived class is called **class inheritance**. An **inherited member** of a base class is one that is *accessible* within the derived class. If a base class member is not accessible in a derived class, then it is not an inherited member of the derived class, but base class members that are not inherited still form part of a derived class object.

An inherited member of a derived class is a full member of that class and is freely accessible to any method in the class. Objects of the derived class type will contain all the inherited members of the base class – both fields and methods, as well as the members that are specific to the derived class. Note that a derived class object always contains a complete base class object within it, including all the fields and methods that are not inherited. We need to take a closer look at how inheritance works, and how the access attribute of a base class member affects its visibility in a derived class.

We need to consider several aspects of defining and using a derived class. First of all we need to know which members of the base class are inherited in the derived class. We will look at what this implies for data members and methods separately - there are some subtleties here we should be quite clear on. We will also look at what happens when you create an object of the derived class. There are some wrinkles in this context that require closer consideration. Let's start by looking at the data members that are inherited from a base class.

223

Inheriting Data Members

The next diagram shows which access attributes permit a class member to be inherited in a subclass. It shows what happens when the subclass is defined in either the same package or a different package from that containing the base class. Remember that inheritance implies accessibility of the member in a derived class, not just presence.

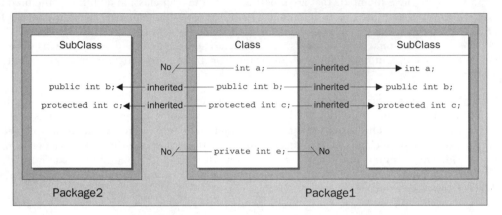

> Note that to derive a class from outside the package containing the base class, the base class must be declared as `public`. If a class is not declared as `public` it cannot be reached directly from outside the package.

As you can see, a subclass that you define in the same package as its base inherits everything except for `private` data members of the base. If you define a subclass outside the package containing the base class, the `private` data members are not inherited, and neither are any data members in the base class that you have declared without access attributes. Members defined as `private` in the base class are never inherited under any circumstances.

You should also be able to see where the access specifiers now sit in relation to one another. The `public` specifier is the least restrictive, and `protected` comes next. `protected` limits access from classes outside of a package, but does not limit inheritance. Putting no access specifier limits access to within the package, and prevents inheritance in subclasses outside. The most restrictive is `private` since access is constrained to the same class.

The inheritance rules apply to class variables as well as instance variables – class variables are variables that you have declared as `static`. You will recall that only one occurrence of each `static` variable exists, and is shared by all objects of the class, whereas each object has its own set of instance variables. So for example, a variable that you declare as `private` and `static` in the base class is not inherited in a derived class, whereas a variable that you declare as `protected` and `static` will be inherited, and will be shared between all objects of a derived class type, as well as objects of the base class type.

Hiding Data Members

You can define a data member in a derived class with the same name as a data member in the base class. This is not a recommended approach to class design generally, but it is possible that it can arise unintentionally. When it occurs, the base class data member may still be inherited, but will be hidden by the derived class member with the same name. The hiding mechanism applies regardless whether the respective types or access attributes are the same or not – the base class member will be hidden in the derived class if the names are the same.

Any use of the derived class member name will always refer to the member defined as part of the derived class. To refer to the inherited base class member, you must qualify it with the keyword `super`. Suppose you have a data member, `value`, as a member of the base class, and a data member with the same name in the derived class. In the derived class, the name `value` references the derived class member, and the name `super.value` refers to the member inherited from the base class. Note that you cannot use `super.super.something` to refer to a member name hidden in the base class of a base class.

In most situations you won't need to refer to inherited data members in this way as you would not deliberately set out to use duplicate names. The situation can commonly arise if you are using a class as a base that is subsequently modified by adding data members – it could be a Java library class for instance, or some other class in a package designed and maintained by someone else. Since your code did not presume the existence of the base class member, with the same name as your derived class data member, hiding the inherited member is precisely what you want. It allows the base class to be altered without breaking your code.

Inherited Methods

Ordinary methods in a base class, by which I mean methods that are not constructors, are inherited in a derived class in the same way as the data members of the base class. Those methods declared as `private` in a base class are not inherited, and those that you declare without an access attribute are only inherited if you define the derived class in the same package as the base class. The rest are all inherited.

Constructors are different from ordinary methods. Constructors in the base class are never inherited, regardless of their attributes. We can look into the intricacies of constructors in a class hierarchy by considering how derived class objects are created.

Objects of a Derived Class

We said at the beginning of this chapter that a derived class extends a base class. This is not just jargon – it really does do this. As we have said several times, inheritance is about what members of the base class are *accessible* in a derived class, not what members of the base class *exist* in a derived class object. An object of a subclass will contain **all** the members of the original base class, plus any new members defined in the derived class (see following diagram).

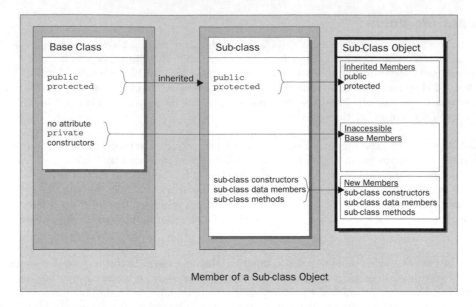

Member of a Sub-class Object

The base members are all there in a derived class object – you just can't access some of them in the methods that you have defined for the derived class. The fact that you can't access some of the base class members does not mean that they are just excess baggage – they are essential members of your derived class objects. A `Spaniel` object needs all the `Dog` attributes that make it a `Dog` object, even though some of these may not be accessible to the `Spaniel` methods. Of course, the base class methods that are inherited in a derived class can access all the base class members, including those that are not inherited.

Though the base class constructors are not inherited in your derived class, you can still call them to initialize the base class members. More than that, if you don't call a base class constructor from your derived class constructor, the compiler will try to arrange to do it for you. The reasoning behind this is that since a derived class object has a base class object inside it, a good way to initialize the base part of a derived class object is using a base class constructor.

To understand this a bit better, let's take a look at how it works in practice.

Deriving a Class

Let's take a simple example. Suppose we have defined a class to represent an animal as follows:

```
public class Animal
{
  public Animal(String aType)
  {
    type = new String(aType);
  }

  public String toString()
  {
```

```
      return "This is a " + type;
   }

   private String type;
}
```

This has a member, `type`, to identify the type of animal, and this is set by the constructor. We also have a `toString()` method for the class to generate a string representation of an object of the class.

We can now define another class, based on the class `Animal`, to define dogs. We can do this immediately, without affecting the definition of the class `Animal`. We could write the basic definition of the class `Dog` as:

```
public class Dog extends Animal
{
   // constructors for a Dog object

   private String name;                       // Name of a Dog
   private String breed;                      // Dog breed
}
```

We use the keyword `extends` in the definition of a subclass to identify the name of the superclass. The class `Dog` will only inherit the method `toString()` from the class `Animal`, since the `private` data member and the constructor cannot be inherited. Of course, a `Dog` object will have a `type` data member that needs to be set to `"Dog"`, it just can't be accessed by methods that we define in the `Dog` class. We have added two new instance variables in the derived class. The `name` member holds the name of the particular dog, and the `breed` member records the kind of dog it is. All we need to add is the means of creating `Dog` class objects.

Derived Class Constructors

We can define two constructors for the subclass `Dog`, one that just accepts an argument for the name of a dog, and the other accepts both a name and the breed of the `Dog` object. For any derived class object, we need to make sure that the `private` base class member, `type`, is properly initialized. We do this by calling a base class constructor from the derived class constructor:

```
public class Dog extends Animal
{
   public Dog(String aName)
   {
      super("Dog");                           // Call the base constructor
      name = aName;                           // Supplied name
      breed = "Unknown";                      // Default breed value
   }

   public Dog(String aName, String aBreed)
   {
      super("Dog");                           // Call the base constructor
      name = aName;                           // Supplied name
      breed = aBreed;                         // Supplied breed
   }
```

```
    private String name;                    // Name of a Dog
    private String breed;                   // Dog breed
}
```

The statement in the derived class constructors that calls the base class constructor is:

```
super("Dog");                              // Call the base constructor
```

The use of the super keyword here as the method name calls the constructor in the direct base class of the class Dog, which is the class Animal. This will initialize the private member type to "Dog" since this is the argument passed to the base constructor. The superclass constructor is always called in this way, in the subclass, using the name super rather than the constructor name Animal. The keyword super has other uses in a derived class, as you will see later in this chapter.

Calling the Base Class Constructor

You should always call an appropriate base class constructor from the constructors in your derived class. The base class constructor call must be the first statement in the body of the derived class constructor. If the first statement in a derived class constructor is not a call to a base class constructor, the compiler will insert a call to the default base class constructor for you:

```
super();                         // Call the default base constructor
```

Unfortunately, this can result in a compiler error, even though the offending statement was inserted automatically. How does this come about?

When you define your own constructor in a class, as is the case for our class Animal, no default constructor is created by the compiler. It assumes you are taking care of all the details of object construction, including any requirement for a default constructor. If you have not defined your own default constructor in a base class – that is, a constructor that has no parameters, when the compiler inserts a call to the default constructor you will get a message that the constructor is not there.

Try It Out — Testing a Derived Class

We can try out our class Dog with the following code:

```
public class TestDerived
{
  public static void main(String[] args)
  {
    Dog aDog = new Dog("Fido", "Chihuahua");    // Create a dog
    Dog starDog = new Dog("Lassie");            // Create a Hollywood dog
    System.out.println(aDog);                   // Let's hear about it
    System.out.println(starDog);                // and the star
  }
}
```

Of course, the files containing the Dog and Animal class definition must be in the same directory as TestDerived.java. The example produces the rather uninformative output:

```
This is a Dog
This is a Dog
```

How It Works

Here, we create two Dog objects, and then output information about them using the `println()` method. This will implicitly call the `toString()` method for each. You could try commenting out the call to `super()` in the constructors of the derived class to see the effect of the compiler's efforts to call the default base class constructor.

We have called the inherited method `toString()` successfully, but this only knows about the base class data members. At least we know that the `private` member, `type`, is being set up properly. What we really need though, is a version of `toString()` for the derived class.

Overriding a Base Class Method

You can define a method in a derived class that has the same signature as a method in the base class. The access attribute for the method in the derived class can be the same as that in the base class or less restrictive, but it cannot be more restrictive. This means that if a method is declared as `public`, in the base class for example, any derived class definition of the method must also be declared as `public`. You cannot omit the access attribute in the derived class in this case, or specify it as `private` or `protected`.

When you define a new version of base class method in this way, the derived class method will be called for a derived class object, not the method inherited from the base class. The method in the derived class **overrides** the method in the base class. The base class method is still there though, and it is still possible to call it in a derived class. Let's see an overriding method in a derived class in action.

Try It Out — Overriding a Base Class Method

We can add the definition of a new version of `toString()` to the definition of the derived class, Dog:

```
// Present a dog's details as a string
public String toString()
{
  return "It's " + name + " the " + breed;
}
```

With this change to the example, the output will now be:

```
It's Fido the Chihuahua
It's Lassie the Unknown
```

How It Works

This method **overrides** the base class method because it has the same signature. You will recall from the last chapter that the signature of a method is determined by its name and the parameter list. So, now whenever you use the `toString()` method for a Dog object either explicitly or implicitly, this method will be called – not the base class method.

> Note that you are obliged to declare this method as `public`. **When you override a base class method, you cannot change the access attributes of the new version of the method to be more stringent than that of the base class method that it overrides.**

Of course, ideally we would like to output the member, `type`, of the base class, but we can't reference this in the derived class, because it is not inherited. However, we can still call the base class version of `toString()`. It's another case for the `super` keyword.

Try It Out — Calling a Base Class Method from a Derived Class

We can rewrite the derived class version of `toString()` to call the base method:

```
// Present a dog's details as a string
public String toString()
{
  return super.toString() + "\nIt's " + name + " the " + breed;
}
```

Running the example again will produce the output:

```
This is a Dog
It's Fido the Chihuahua
This is a Dog
It's Lassie the Unknown
```

How It Works

The keyword `super` is used to identify the base class version of `toString()` that is hidden by the derived class version. We used the same notation to refer to superclass data members that were hidden by derived class data members with the same name. Calling the base class version of `toString()` returns the `String` object for the base part of the object. We then append extra information to this about the derived part of the object to produce a `String` object specific to the derived class.

Choosing Base Class Access Attributes

You now know the options available to you in defining the access attributes for classes you expect to use to define subclasses. You know what effect the attributes have on class inheritance, but how do you decide which you should use?

There are no hard and fast rules – what you choose will depend on what you want to do with your classes in the future, but there are some guidelines you should consider. They follow from basic object oriented principles:

❑ The methods that make up the external interface to a class should be declared as `public`. As long as there are no overriding methods defined in a derived class, public base class methods will be inherited and fully available as part of the external interface to the derived class. You should not normally make data members public unless they are constants intended for general use.

❑   If you expect other people will use your classes as base classes, your classes will be more secure if you keep data members `private`, and provide `public` methods for accessing and manipulating them. In this way you control how a derived class object can affect the base class data members.

❑   Making base class members `protected` allows them to be accessed from other classes in the same package, but prevents direct access from a class in another package. Base class members that are `protected` are inherited in a subclass and can, therefore, be used in the implementation of a derived class. You can use the `protected` option when you have a package of classes in which you want uninhibited access to the data members of any class within the same package, because they operate in a closely coupled way, for instance, but you want free access to be limited to subclasses in other packages.

❑   Omitting the access attribute for a class member makes it directly available to other classes in the same package, while preventing it from being inherited in a subclass that is not in the same package – it is effectively `private` when viewed from another package.

Polymorphism

Class inheritance is not just about reusing classes that you have already defined as a basis for defining a new class. It also adds enormous flexibility to the way in which you can program your applications, with a mechanism called **polymorphism**. So what is polymorphism?

The word 'polymorphism' means the ability to assume several different forms or shapes. In programming terms it means the ability of a single variable of a given type to be used to reference objects of different types, and to automatically call the method that is specific to the type of object the variable references. This enables a single method call to behave differently, depending on the type of the object which the call applies.

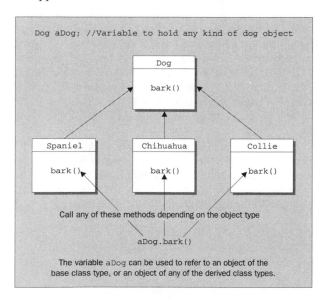

There are a few requirements that need to be fulfilled to get polymorphic behavior, so let's step through them. First of all, polymorphism works with derived class objects. It depends on a new capability that is possible within a class hierarchy. Up to now, we have always been using a variable of a given type to reference objects of the same type. Derived classes introduce some new flexibility in this. Of course, we can store a reference to a derived class object in a variable of the derived class type, but we can also store it in a variable of any direct or indirect base class. For instance, as shown in the previous diagram, a variable of type Dog object can be used to store a reference to an object of any type derived from Dog. If the Dog class was derived from the Animal class here, a variable of type Animal could also be used to reference Spaniel, Chihuahua, or Collie objects.

To get polymorphic operation when calling a method, the method must be a member of the base class as well as any derived classes involved. You cannot call a method for a derived class object using a variable of a base class if the method is not a member of the base class. Any definition of the method in a derived class must have the same signature and the same return type as in the base class, and must have an access specifier that is no more restrictive. Indeed, if you define a method in a derived class with the same signature as a method in a base class, any attempt to specify a different return type, or a more restrictive access specifier, will be flagged as an error by the compiler.

The conditions that need to be met if you want to use polymorphism can be summarized as:

❑ The method call for a derived class object must be through a variable of a base class type.

❑ The method called must also be a member of the base class.

❑ The method signature must be the same in the base and derived classes.

❑ The method return type must be the same in the base and derived classes.

❑ The method access specifier must be no more restrictive in the derived class than in the base

When you call a method using a variable of a base class type, polymorphism results in the method that is called being selected based on the type of the object stored, not the type of the variable. Because a variable of a base type can store a reference to an object of any derived type, the kind of object stored will not be known until the program executes. Thus the choice of which method to execute has to be made dynamically when the program is running – it cannot be determined when the program is compiled. The bark() method that is called through the variable of type Dog in the earlier illustration, may do different things depending on what kind of object the variable references. As we will see, this introduces a whole new level of capability in programming using objects. It implies that your programs can adapt at runtime to accommodate and process different kinds of data quite automatically.

Note that polymorphism only applies to methods. It does not apply to data members. When you access a data member of a class object, the variable type always determines the class to which the data member belongs. This implies that a variable of type Dog can only be used to access data members of the Dog class. Even when it references an object of type Spaniel, for instance, you can only use it to access data members of the Dog part of a Spaniel object.

Using Polymorphism

As we have seen, polymorphism relies on the fact that you can assign an object of a subclass to a variable that you have declared as being of the base class type. Suppose you declare the variable:

```
Animal theAnimal;       // Declare a variable of type Animal
```

You can quite happily make this refer to an object of any of the subclasses of the class Animal. For example, you could use it to reference an object of type Dog:

```
theAnimal = new Dog("Rover");
```

As you might expect, you could also initialize the variable theAnimal when you declare it:

```
Animal theAnimal = new Dog("Rover");
```

This principle applies quite generally. You can use a variable of a base class type to store a reference to an object of any class type that you have derived, directly or indirectly, from the base. We can see what magic can be wrought with this in practice by extending our previous example. We can add a new method to the class Dog which will display the sound a Dog makes. We can add a couple of new subclasses which will represent some other kinds of animals.

Try It Out — Enhancing the Dog Class

First of all we will enhance the class Dog by adding a method to display the sound that a dog makes:

```java
public class Dog extends Animal
{
  // A barking method
  public void sound()
  {
    System.out.println("Woof    Woof");
  }

  // Rest of the class as before...
}
```

We can also derive a class Cat from the class Animal:

```java
public class Cat extends Animal
{
  public Cat(String aName)
  {
    super("Cat");             // Call the base constructor
    name = aName;             // Supplied name
    breed = "Unknown";        // Default breed value
  }

  public Cat(String aName, String aBreed)
  {
```

```
      super("Cat");          // Call the base constructor
      name = aName;          // Supplied name
      breed = aBreed;        // Supplied breed
    }
    // Return a String full of a cat's details
    public String toString()
    {
      return super.toString() + "\nIt's " + name + " the " + breed;
    }

    // A miaowing method
    public void sound()
    {
      System.out.println("Miiaooww");
    }

    private String name;      // Name of a cat
    private String breed;     // Cat breed
}
```

Just to make it a crowd, we can derive another class – of ducks:

```
public class Duck extends Animal
{
  public Duck(String aName)
  {
    super("Duck");          // Call the base constructor
    name = aName;           // Supplied name
    breed = "Unknown";      // Default breed value
  }

  public Duck(String aName, String aBreed)
  {
    super("Duck");          // Call the base constructor
    name = aName;           // Supplied name
    breed = aBreed;         // Supplied breed
  }

  // Return a String full of a duck's details
  public String toString()
  {
    return super.toString() + "\nIt's " + name + " the " + breed;
  }

  // A quacking method
  public void sound()
  {
    System.out.println("Quack quackquack");
  }

  private String name;      // Duck name
  private String breed;     // Duck breed
}
```

You can fill the whole farmyard, if you need the practice, but three kinds of animal are sufficient to show you how polymorphism works.

We need to make one change to the class `Animal`. To select the method `sound()` dynamically for derived class objects, it needs to be a member of the base class. We can add a content-free version of `sound()` to the class `Animal`:

```
class Animal
{
   // Rest of the class as before...

   // Dummy method to be implemented in the derived classes
   public void sound(){}
}
```

We need a program that will use these classes. To give the classes a workout, we can create an array of type `Animal` and populate its elements with different subclass objects. We can then select an object random from the array, so that there is no possibility that the type of the object selected is known ahead of time. Here's the code to do that:

```
import java.util.Random;

public class TryPolymorphism
{
  public static void main(String[] args)
  {
    // Create an array of three different animals
    Animal[] theAnimals = {
                          new Dog("Rover", "Poodle"),
                          new Cat("Max", "Abyssinian"),
                          new Duck("Daffy","Aylesbury")
                        };

    Animal petChoice;                            // Choice of pet

    Random select = new Random();                // Random number generator
    // Make five random choices of pet
    for(int i = 0; i < 5; i++)
    { // Choose a random animal as a pet
      petChoice = theAnimals[select.nextInt(theAnimals.length)];

      System.out.println("\nYour choice:\n" + petChoice);
      petChoice.sound();                         // Get the pet's reaction
    }
  }
}
```

When I ran this I got the output:

```
Your choice:
This is a Duck
It's Daffy the Aylesbury
Quack quackquack
```

```
Your choice:
This is a Cat
It's Max the Abyssinian
Miiaooww

Your choice:
This is a Duck
It's Daffy the Aylesbury
Quack quackquack

Your choice:
This is a Duck
It's Daffy the Aylesbury
Quack quackquack

Your choice:
This is a Cat
It's Max the Abyssinian
Miiaooww
```

The chances are that you will get a different set from this, and a different set again when you re-run the example. The output from the example clearly shows that the methods are being selected at runtime, depending on which object happens to get stored in the variable petChoice.

How It Works

The definition of the method sound() in the Animal class has no statements in the body, so it will do nothing if it is executed. We will see a little later in this chapter how we can avoid including the empty definition for the method, but still get polymorphic behavior in the derived classes.

We need the import statement because we use a Random class object in our example to produce pseudo-random index values in the way we have seen before. The array theAnimals of type Animal contains a Dog object, a Cat object and a Duck object. We select objects randomly from this array in the for loop using the Random object, select, and store the selection in petChoice. We can then call the toString() and sound() methods using the object reference stored. The effect is that the appropriate method is selected automatically to suit the object stored, so our program operates differently depending on what type of object is referenced by petChoice.

Of course, we call the toString() method implicitly in the argument to println(). The compiler will insert a call to this method to produce a String representation of the petChoice object. The particular toString() method will automatically be selected to correspond with the type of object referenced by petChoice.

Polymorphism is a fundamental part of object-oriented programming. We will be making extensive use of polymorphism in many of the examples we will develop later in the book, you will find that you will use it often in your own applications and applets. But this is not all there is to polymorphism in Java, and we will come back to it again later in this chapter.

Multiple Levels of Inheritance

As we indicated at the beginning of the chapter, there is nothing to prevent a derived class being used as a base class. For example, we could derive a class `Spaniel` from the class `Dog` without any problem:

Try It Out — A `Spaniel` Class

Start the `Spaniel` class off with this minimal code:

```
class Spaniel extends Dog
{
  public Spaniel(String aName)
  {
    super(aName, "Spaniel");
  }
}
```

To try this out you can add a `Spaniel` object to the array `theAnimals` in the previous example, by changing the statement to:

```
Animal[] theAnimals = {
                      new Dog("Rover", "Poodle"),
                      new Cat("Max", "Abyssinian"),
                      new Duck("Daffy","Aylesbury"),
                      new Spaniel("Fido")
                  };
```

Don't forget to add in the comma after the `Duck`. Try running the example again.

How It Works

The class `Spaniel` will inherit members from the class `Dog`, including the members of `Dog` that are inherited from the class `Animal`. The class `Dog` is a direct superclass, and the class `Animal` is an indirect superclass of the class `Spaniel`. The only additional member of `Spaniel` is the constructor. This calls the `Dog` class constructor using the keyword `super` and passes the value of `aName` and the `String` object `"Spaniel"` to it.

If you run the `TryPolymorphism` class once more, you should get a choice of the `Spaniel` object from time to time. Thus the class `Spaniel` is also participating in the polymorphic selection of the methods `toString()` and `sound()`, which in this case are inherited from the parent class, `Dog`. The inherited `toString()` method works perfectly well with the `Spaniel` object, but if you wanted to provide a unique version, you could add it to the `Spaniel` class definition. This would then be automatically selected for a `Spaniel` object rather than the method inherited from the `Dog` class.

Abstract Classes

In the class `Animal`, we introduced a version of the method `sound()` that did nothing because we wanted to call the `sound()` method in the subclass objects dynamically. The method `sound()` has no meaning in the context of the generic class `Animal`, so implementing it does not make much sense. This situation often arises in object-oriented programming. You will often find yourself creating a superclass from which you will derive a number of subclasses, just to take advantage of polymorphism.

To cater for this, Java has **abstract classes**. An abstract class is a class in which one or more methods are declared, but not defined. The bodies of these methods are omitted, because, as in the case of the method `sound()` in our class `Animal`, implementing the methods does not make sense. Since they have no definition, they are called **abstract methods**. The declaration for an abstract method ends with a semi-colon and you specify the method with the keyword `abstract` to identify it as such. To define an abstract class you use the keyword `abstract` in front of the class name.

We could have defined the class `Animal` as an abstract class by amending it as follows:

```
public abstract class Animal
{
  public abstract void sound();    // Abstract method

  public Animal(String aType)
  {
    type = new String(aType);
  }

  public String toString()
  {
    return "This is a " + type;
  }

  private String type;
}
```

The previous program will work just as well with these changes. It doesn't matter whether you prefix the class name with `public abstract` or `abstract public`, they are equivalent, but you should be consistent in your usage. The sequence `public abstract` is typically preferred. The same goes for the declaration of an abstract method, but both `public` and `abstract` must precede the return type specification, which is `void` in this case.

An `abstract` method cannot be `private` since a `private` method cannot be inherited, and therefore cannot be redefined in a subclass.

You cannot instantiate an object of an abstract class, but you can declare a variable of an abstract class type. With our new abstract version of the class `Animal`, we can still write:

```
Animal thePet;    // Declare a variable of type Animal
```

just as we did in the `TryPolymorphism` class. We can then use this variable to store objects of the subclasses, `Dog`, `Spaniel`, `Duck` and `Cat`.

When you derive a class from an abstract base class, you don't have to define all the abstract methods in the subclass. In this case the subclass will also be abstract and you won't be able to instantiate any objects of the subclass either. If a class is abstract, you must use the `abstract` keyword when you define it, even if it only inherits an abstract method from its superclass. Sooner or later you must have a subclass that contains no abstract methods. You can then create objects of this class.

The Universal Superclass

I must now reveal something I have been keeping from you. *All* the classes that you define are subclasses by default – whether you like it or not. All your classes have a standard class, `Object`, as a base, so `Object` is a superclass of every class. You never need to specify the class `Object` as a base in the definition of your classes – it happens automatically.

There are some interesting consequences of having `Object` as a universal superclass. For one thing, a variable of type `Object` can hold an object of any class. This is useful when you want to write a method that needs to handle objects of unknown type. You can use a variable of type `Object` as a parameter to a method, to receive an object, and then include code in the method that figures out what kind of object it actually is (we will see something of the tools that will enable you to do this a little later in this chapter).

Of course, your classes will inherit members from the class `Object`. These all happen to be methods, of which seven are `public`, and two are `protected`. The seven `public` methods are:

Method	Purpose
`toString()`	This method returns a `String` object that describes the current object. In the inherited version of the method, this will be the name of the class, followed by '@' and the hexadecimal representation for the object. This method is called automatically when you concatenate objects with `String` variables using +. You can override this method in your classes to return your own `String` object for your class.
`equals()`	This compares the object passed as an argument with the current object, and returns `true` if they are the same object (not just equal – they must be one and the same object). It returns `false` if they are different objects, even if the objects have identical values for their data members.
`getClass()`	This method returns an object of type `Class` that identifies the class of the current object. We will see a little more about this later in this chapter.
`hashCode()`	This method calculates a hash code value for an object and returns it as type `int`. Hash code values are used in classes defined in the package `java.util` for storing objects in hash tables. We will see more about this in Chapter 10.

Method	Purpose
notify()	This is used to wake up a thread associated with the current object. We will discuss in Chapter 11 how threads work.
notifyAll()	This is used to wake up all threads associated with the current object. We will also discuss this in Chapter 11.
wait()	This method causes a thread to wait for a change in the current object. We will discuss this method in Chapter 11.

Note that getClass(), notify(), notifyAll(), and wait() cannot be overridden in your own class definitions – they are 'fixed' with the keyword final in the class definition for Object (see the section on the final modifier later in this chapter).

It should be clear now why we could get polymorphic behavior with toString() in our derived classes when our base class did not define the method. There is always a toString() method in all your classes that is inherited from Object.

The two protected methods your classes inherit from Object are:

Method	Purpose
clone()	This will create an object that is a copy of the current object regardless of type. This can be of any type as an Object variable can refer to an object of any class. Note that this does not work with all class objects and does not always do precisely what you want, as we will see later in this section.
finalize()	This is the method that is called to clean up as an object is destroyed. As you have seen in the last chapter you can override this to add your own clean-up code.

Since all your classes will inherit the methods defined in the Object class we should look at them in a little more detail.

The toString() Method

We have already made extensive use of the toString() method and you know that it is used by the compiler to obtain a String representation of an object when necessary. It is obvious now why we must always declare the toString() method as public in a class. It is declared as such in the Object class and you can't declare it as anything else.

You can see what the toString() method, that is inherited from class Object, will output for an object of one of your classes by commenting out the toString() method in Animal class in the previous example. A typical sample of the output for an object is:

```
Your choice:
Spaniel@b75778b2
It's Fido the Spaniel
Woof    Woof
```

The second line here is generated by the toString() method implemented in the Object class. This will be inherited in the Animal class, and it is called because we no longer override it. The hexadecimal digits following the @ in the output are the hash code of the object.

Determining the Type of an Object

The getClass() method, that all your classes inherit from Object, will return an object of type Class that identifies the class of an object. Suppose you have a variable pet, of type Animal, that might refer to an object of type Dog, Cat, Duck, or even Spaniel. To figure out what sort of thing it really is, you could write the following statements:

```
Class objectType = pet.getClass();            // Get the class type
System.out.println(objectType.getName());     // Output the class name
```

The method getName() is a member of the class Class which returns the fully qualified name of the class as a String object – the second statement will output the name of the class for the pet object. If pet referred to a Duck object this would output:

```
Duck
```

This is the fully qualified name in this case as the class is in the default package which has no name. For a class defined in a named package the class name would be prefixed with the package name. If you just wanted to output the class identity you need not explicitly store the Class object. You can combine both statements into one:

```
System.out.println(pet.getClass().getName());   // Output the class name
```

This will produce the same output as before.

Members of the class Class

When your program is executing there are instances of the class Class representing each of the classes and interfaces in your program. These are generated by the Java Virtual Machine when your program is loaded. Since Class is intended for use by the Java Virtual Machine, it has no public constructors, so you can't create objects of type Class yourself.

Class defines a lot of methods, but most of them are not relevant in normal programs. The primary use you will have for Class is obtaining the class of an object by calling the getClass() method for the object as we have just discussed. However, you also get a number of other useful methods with an object of class Class:

Method	Purpose
forName()	You can get the Class object for a known class type with this method. You pass the name of the class as a String object to this method, and it returns a Class object for the class that has the name you have supplied. If no class of the type you specify exists, a ClassNotFoundException exception will be thrown. You can use this method to test whether an object is of a particular class type.
newInstance()	This method will call the default constructor for the class, represented by the current Class object, and will return the object created as type Object. Unless you want to store the result in a variable of type Object, you must cast the object to the appropriate type. When things don't work as they should, this method can throw two exceptions – InstantiationException or IllegalAccessException.
	If you use this method and don't provide for handling the exceptions, your program will not compile. We'll learn how to deal with this in the next chapter.
getSuperClass()	This method returns a Class object for the superclass of the class for the current Class object. For example, for the Class object objectType for the variable pet we just defined, this would return a Class object for the class Animal. You could output the name of the superclass with the statement: `System.out.println(pet.getClass().getSuperClass().getName());` Where your class is not a derived class, the method will return a Class object for the class Object.
isInterface()	This method returns true if the current Class object represents an interface. We will discuss interfaces a little later in this chapter.
getInterface()	This method will return an array of Class objects that represent the interfaces implemented by the class. We will investigate interfaces later in this chapter.
toString()	This method returns a String object representing the current Class object. For example, the Class object, objectType, corresponding to the pet variable we created would output: `class Duck`

This is not an exhaustive list. There are a number of other methods defined in the class Class that enable you to find out details of the contents of a class – the fields or data members in other words, the public methods defined in the class, even the classes defined in the class. If you need this kind of capability you can find out more by browsing the API documentation that comes with the JDK.

Although you can use the `forName()` method in the table above to get the `Class` object corresponding to a particular class type, there is a more direct way. If you append `.class` to the name of any class, you have a reference to the `Class` object for that class. For example, `String.class` references the `Class` object for the `String` class and `Duck.class` references the `Class` object for our `Duck` class. This may not seem particularly relevant at this point, but keep it in mind. We will need to use this later on when we get to explore the capabilities of the Java Sound API. Because there is only one `Class` object for each class or interface type, you could test for the class of an object programmatically. Given a variable, pet, of type `Animal`, we could check whether the object referenced was of type `Duck` with the statement:

```
if(pet.getClass()==Duck.class)
  System.out.println("By George - it is a duck!");
```

This tests whether the object referenced by `pet` is of type `Duck`. Because each `Class` object is unique, this is a precise test. If `pet` contained a reference to an object that was a subclass of `Duck`, the result of the comparison in the `if` would be `false`. We will see a little later in this chapter that we have an operator in Java, `instanceof`, that does almost the same thing – but not quite.

Copying Objects

As you saw in the summary at the beginning of this section, the `protected` method, `clone()`, that is inherited from the class `Object` will create a new object that is a copy of the current object. It will only do this if the class of the object to be cloned indicates that cloning is acceptable. This is the case if the class implements the `Cloneable` interface. Don't worry about what an interface is at this point – we will look into this a little later in this chapter.

The `clone()` method that is inherited from `Object` clones an object by creating a new object of the same type as the current object, and setting each of the fields in the new object to the same value as the corresponding fields in the current object. When the data members of the original object refer to class objects, the objects referred to are not duplicated when the clone is created – only the references are copied from the fields in the old object to the fields in the cloned object. This is not typically what you want to happen – both the old and the new class objects can now be modifying a single shared object that is referenced through their corresponding data members, and not recognizing that this is occurring.

If objects are to be cloned, the class must implement the `Cloneable` interface. We will discuss interfaces later in this chapter where we will see that implementing an interface typically involves implementing a specific set of methods. All that is required to make a class implement this interface is to declare it in the first line of the class definition. This is done using the `implements` keyword – for example:

```
class Dog implements Cloneable
{
  // Details of the definition of the class...
}
```

This makes `Dog` objects cloneable since we have declared that the class implements the interface.

We can understand the implications of the inherited `clone()` method more clearly if we take a simple specific instance. Let's suppose we define a class `Flea` that has a method that allows the name to be changed:

243

```java
public class Flea extends Animal implements Cloneable
{
  // Constructor
  public Flea(String aName, String aSpecies)
  {
    super("Flea");                      // Pass the type to the base
    name = aName;                       // Supplied name
    species = aSpecies;                 // Supplied species
  }

  // Change the flea's name
  public void setName(String aName)
  {
    name = aName;                       // Change to the new name
  }


  // Return the flea's name
  public String getName()
  {
    return name;
  }

  // Return the species
  public String getSpecies()
  {
    return species;
  }

  public void sound()
  {
    System.out.println("Psst");
  }


  // Present a flea's details as a String
  public String toString()
  {
    return super.toString() + "\nIt's " + name + " the " + species;
  }

  // Override inherited clone() to make it public
  public Object clone() throws CloneNotSupportedException
  {
    return super.clone();
  }

  private String name;                          // Name of flea!
  private String species;                       // Flea species
}
```

We have defined accessor methods for the name and the species. We don't need them now but they will be useful later. By implementing the `Cloneable` interface we are indicating that we are happy to clone objects of this class. Since we have said that `Flea` is cloneable, we must implement the `Cloneable` interface in the base class, so the class `Animal` needs to be changed to:

```
public class Animal implements Cloneable
{
  // Details of the class as before...
}
```

No other changes are necessary to the Animal class here. We can now define a class PetDog that contains a Flea object as a member that is also cloneable:

```
public class PetDog extends Animal implements Cloneable
{
  // Constructor
  public PetDog(String name, String breed)
  {
    super("Dog");
    petFlea = new Flea("Max","circus flea");      // Initialize petFlea
    this.name = name;
    this.breed = breed;
  }


  // Rename the dog
  public void setName(String name)
  {
    this.name = name;
  }

  // Return the dog's name
  public String getName()
  {
    return name;
  }

  // Return the breed
  public String getBreed()
  {
    return breed;
  }

  // Return the flea
  public Flea getFlea()
  {
    return petFlea;
  }

  public void sound()
  {
    System.out.println("Woof");
  }

  // Return a String for the pet dog
  public String toString()
  {
```

```
         return super.toString() + "\nIt's " + name + " the " + breed +
                                              " & \n" + petFlea;
  }


  // Override inherited clone() to make it public
  public Object clone() throws CloneNotSupportedException
  {
    return super.clone();
  }

  private Flea petFlea;                      // The pet flea
  private String name;                       // Dog's name
  private String breed;                      // Dog's breed
}
```

To make it possible to clone a PetDog object, we override the inherited clone() method with a public version that calls the base class version. Note that the inherited method throws the CloneNotSupportedException so we must declare the method as shown – otherwise it won't compile. We will be looking into what exceptions are in the next chapter.

We can now create a PetDog object with the statement:

```
PetDog myPet = new PetDog("Fang", "Chihuahua");
```

After seeing my pet, you want one just like it, so we can clone him:

```
PetDog yourPet = (PetDog)myPet.clone();
```

Now we have individual PetDog objects that regrettably contain references to the same Flea object. The clone() method will create the new PetDog object, yourPet, and copy the reference to the Flea object from the thePet data member in myPet to the member with the same name in yourPet. If you decide that you prefer the name "Gnasher" for yourPet, we can change the name of your pet with the statement:

```
yourPet.setName("Gnasher");
```

Your dog will probably like a personalized flea too, so we can change the name of its flea with the statement:

```
yourPet.getFlea().setName("Atlas");
```

Unfortunately Fang's flea will also be given the name Atlas because, under the covers, Fang and Gnasher both share a common Flea. If you want to demonstrate this, you can put all the classes together in an example, with the following class:

```
// Test cloning
public class TestFlea
{
  public static void main(String[] args)
  {
```

```
      try
      {
        PetDog myPet = new PetDog("Fang", "Chihuahua");
        PetDog yourPet = (PetDog)myPet.clone();
        yourPet.setName("Gnasher");                    // Change your dog's name
        yourPet.getFlea().setName("Atlas");            // Change your dog's flea's name
        System.out.println("\nYour pet details:\n"+yourPet);
        System.out.println("\nMy pet details:\n"+ myPet);
      }
      catch(CloneNotSupportedException e)
      {
        System.out.println(e);
      }
    }
}
```

Don't worry about the `try` and `catch` blocks – these are necessary to deal with the exception that we mentioned earlier. You will learn all about exceptions in Chapter 7. If you run the example it will output the details on `myPet` and `yourPet` after the name for `yourPet` has been changed. Both names will be the same so the output will be:

```
C:\Java\3668\Ch06\TestFlea>java TestFlea
Your pet details:
This is a Dog
It's Gnasher the Chihuahua &
This is a Flea
It's Atlas the circus flea

My pet details:
This is a Dog
It's Fang the Chihuahua &
This is a Flea
It's Atlas the circus flea
```

Choosing a name for your pet's flea has changed the name for my pet's flea too. Unless you really want to share objects between the variables in two separate objects, you should implement the `clone()` method in your class to do the cloning the way you want. As an alternative to cloning (or in addition to) you could add a constructor to your class to create a new class object from an existing object. This creates a duplicate of the original object properly. You saw how you can do this in the previous chapter. If you implement your own `public` version of `clone()` to override the inherited version, you would typically code this method in the same way as you would the constructor to create a copy of an object. You could implement the `clone()` method in the `PetDog` class like this:

```
public Object clone() throws CloneNotSupportedException
{
  PetDog pet = new PetDog(name, breed);
  pet.setName("Gnasher");
  pet.getFlea().setName("Atlas");

  return pet;
}
```

247

Here the method creates a new `PetDog` object using the name and breed of the current object. We then call the two objects' `setName()` methods to set the clones' names. If you compile and run the program, again with this change, altering the name of `myPet` will not affect `yourPet`. Of course, you could use the inherited `clone()` method to duplicate the current object, and then explicitly clone the `Flea` member to refer to an independent object:

```
// Override inherited clone() to make it public
public Object clone() throws CloneNotSupportedException
{
   PetDog pet = (PetDog)super.clone();
   pet.petFlea = (Flea)petFlea.clone();

   return pet;
}
```

The new object created by the inherited `clone()` method is of type `PetDog`, but it is returned as a reference of type `Object`. In order to access the `thePet` member, we need a reference of type `PetDog` so the cast is essential. The same is true of our cloned `Flea` object. The effect of this version of the `clone()` method is the same as the previous version.

Casting Objects

You can cast an object to another class type, but only if the current object type and the new class type are in the same hierarchy of derived classes, and one is a superclass of the other. For example, earlier in this chapter we defined the classes `Animal`, `Dog`, `Spaniel`, `Cat` and `Duck`, and these classes are related in the hierarchy shown below:

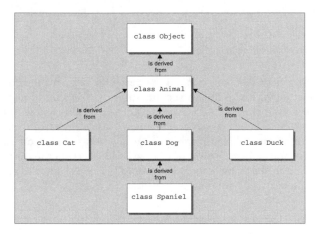

You can cast an object of a class upwards through its direct and indirect superclasses. For example, you could cast an object of type `Spaniel` directly to type `Dog`, type `Animal` or type `Object`. You could write:

```
Spaniel aPet = new Spaniel("Fang");
Animal theAnimal = (Animal)aPet;    // Cast the Spaniel to Animal
```

When you are assigning an object to a variable of a superclass type, you do not have to include the cast. You could write the assignment as:

```
Animal theAnimal = aPet;            // Cast the Spaniel to Animal
```

and it would work just as well. The compiler is always prepared to insert a cast to a superclass type.

When you cast an object to a superclass type, Java retains full knowledge of the actual class to which the object belongs. If this were not the case, polymorphism would not be possible. Since information about the original type of an object is retained, you can cast down a hierarchy as well. However, you must always write the cast explicitly since the compiler is not prepared to insert it, and the object must be a legitimate instance of the class you are casting to – that is, the class you are casting to must be the original class of the object, or must be a superclass of the object. For example, you could cast the variable theAnimal above to type Dog or type Spaniel, since the object was originally a Spaniel, but you could not cast it to Cat or Duck, since an object of type Spaniel does not have Cat or Duck as a superclass. To cast theAnimal to type Dog, you would write:

```
Dog aDog = (Dog)theAnimal;          // Cast from Animal to Dog
```

Now the variable aDog refers to an object of type Spaniel that also happens to be a Dog. Note that you can only use the variable aDog to call the polymorphic methods from the class Spaniel that override methods that exist in Dog. You can't call methods that are not defined in the class Dog. If you want to call a method that is in the class Spaniel and not in the class Dog, you must first cast aDog to type Spaniel.

Although you cannot cast between unrelated objects, from Spaniel to Duck for instance, you can achieve a conversion by writing a suitable constructor but only where it makes sense to do so. You just write a constructor in the class to which you want to convert, and make it accept an object of the class you are converting from as an argument. If you really thought Spaniel to Duck was a reasonable conversion, you could add the constructor to the Duck class:

```
public Duck(Spaniel aSpaniel)
{
    // Back legs off, and staple on a beak of your choice...
    super("Duck");            // Call the base constructor
    name = aSpaniel.getName();
    breed = "Barking Coot";   // Set the duck breed for a converted Spaniel
}
```

This assumes you have added a method, getName(), in the class Dog which will be inherited in the class Spaniel, and which returns the value of name for an object. This constructor accepts a Spaniel and turns out a Duck. This is not the same as a cast though. This creates a completely new object that is separate from the original, whereas a cast presents the same object as a different type.

When to Cast Objects

You will have cause to cast objects in both directions through a class hierarchy. For example, whenever you execute methods polymorphically, you will be storing objects in a variable of a base class type, and calling methods in a derived class. This will generally involve casting the derived class objects to the base class. Another reason you might want to cast up through a hierarchy is to pass an object of several possible subclasses to a method. By specifying a parameter as base class type, you have the flexibility to pass an object of any derived class to it. You could pass a Dog, Duck or Cat to a method as an argument for a parameter of type Animal, for instance.

The reason you might want to cast down through a class hierarchy is to execute a method unique to a particular class. If the Duck class has a method layEgg(), for example, you can't call this using a variable of type Animal, even though it references a Duck object. Casting downwards through a class hierarchy always requires an explicit cast.

Try It Out — Casting Down to Lay an Egg

We'll amend the Duck class and use it along with the Animal class in an example. Add layEgg() to the Duck class as:

```
public class Duck extends Animal
{
  public void layEgg()
  {
    System.out.println("Egg laid");
  }

    // Rest of the class as before...
}
```

If you now try to use this with the code:

```
public class LayEggs
{
  public static void main(String[] args)
  {
    Duck aDuck = new Duck("Donald", "Eider");
    Animal aPet = aDuck;                   // Cast the Duck to Animal
    aPet.layEgg();                         // This won't compile!
  }
}
```

you will get a compiler message to the effect that layEgg() is not found in the class Animal.

Since you know this object is really a Duck, you can make it work by writing the call to layEgg() in the code above as:

```
    ((Duck)aPet).layEgg();                 // This works fine
```

The object pointed to by aPet is first cast to type Duck. The result of the cast is then used to call the method layEgg(). If the object were not of type Duck, the cast would cause an exception to be thrown.

> In general, you should avoid explicitly casting objects as much as possible, since it increases the potential for an invalid cast and can therefore make your programs unreliable. Most of the time you should find that if you design your classes carefully, you can minimize the need for casting.

Identifying Objects

There are circumstances when you may not know what sort of object you are dealing with. This can arise if a derived class object is passed to a method as an argument for a parameter of a base class type, for example, in the way we discussed in the previous section. In some situations you may need to cast it to its actual class type, perhaps to call a class specific method. If you try to make an illegal cast, an exception will be thrown, and your program will end, unless you have made provision for catching it. One way to obviate this situation is to test that the object is the type you expect before you make the cast.

We saw earlier in this chapter how we could use the getClass() method to obtain the Class object corresponding to the class type, and how we could compare it to a Class instance for the class we are looking for. You can also do this using the operator instanceof. For example, suppose you have a variable, pet, of type Animal, and you want to cast it to type Duck. You could code this as:

```
Duck aDuck;                    // Declare a duck

if(pet instanceof Duck)
{
  aDuck = (Duck)pet;           // It is a duck so the cast is OK
  aDuck.layEgg();              // and we can have an egg for tea
}
```

If pet does not refer to a Duck object, an attempt to cast the object referenced by pet to Duck would cause an exception to be thrown. This code fragment will only execute the cast and lay an egg if pet does point to a Duck object. The code fragment above could have been written much more concisely as:

```
if(pet instanceof Duck)
  ((Duck)pet).layEgg();                 // It is a duck so we can have an egg for tea
```

So what is the difference between this and using getClass()? Well, it's quite subtle. The instanceof operator checks whether a cast of the object referenced by the left operand to the type specified by the right operand is legal. The result will be true if the object is the same type as the right operand, *or of any subclass type*. We can illustrate the difference by choosing a slightly different example.

Suppose pet stores a reference to an object of type Spaniel. We want to call a method defined in the Dog class so we need to check that pet does really reference a Dog object. We can check for whether or not we have a Dog object with the statements:

```
if(pet instanceof Dog)
  System.out.println("We have a dog!");
else
  System.out.println("It's definitely not a dog!");
```

We will get confirmation that we have a Dog object here even though it is actually a Spaniel object. This is fine though for casting purposes. As long as the Dog class is in the class hierarchy for the object, the cast will work OK, so the operator is telling us what we need to know. However, suppose we write:

```
if(pet.getClass() == Dog.class)
  System.out.println("We have a dog!");
else
  System.out.println("It's definitely not a dog!");
```

Here the if expression will be false because the class type of the object is Spaniel, so its Class object is different from that of Dog.class – we would have to write Spaniel.class to get true from the if expression.

The conclusion is that for casting purposes you should always use the instanceof operator to check the type of a reference. You only need to resort to checking the Class object corresponding to a reference when you need to confirm the exact type of the reference.

Designing Classes

A basic problem in object-oriented programming is deciding how the classes in your program should relate to one another. One possibility is to create a hierarchy of classes by deriving classes from a base class that you have defined, and adding methods and data members to specialize the subclasses. Our Animal class and the subclasses derived from it are an example of this. Another possibility is to define a set of classes which are not hierarchical, but which have data members that are themselves class objects. A Zoo class might well have objects of types derived from Animal as members, for instance. You can have class hierarchies which contain data members that are class objects – we already have this with our classes derived from Animal since they have members of type String. The examples so far have been relatively clear-cut as to which approach to choose, but it is not always so evident. Quite often you will have a choice between defining your classes as a hierarchy, and defining classes which have members that are class objects. Which is the best approach to take?

Like all questions of this kind, there are no clear-cut answers. If object-oriented programming was a process that we could specify by a fixed set of rules that you could just follow blindly, we could get the computer to do it. There are some guidelines though, and some contexts in which the answer may be more obvious.

Aside from the desirability of reflecting real-world relationships between types of objects, the need to use polymorphism is a primary reason for using subclasses (or interfaces as we shall see shortly). This is the essence of object-oriented programming. Having a range of related objects that can be treated equivalently can greatly simplify your programs. You have seen how having various kinds of animals specified by classes derived from a common base class `Animal` allows us to act on different types of animal as though they are the same, producing different results depending on what kind of animal is being dealt with, and all this automatically.

A Classy Example

Many situations involve making judgments about the design of your classes. The way to go may well boil down to a question of personal preference. Let's try to see how the options look in practice by considering a simple example. Suppose we want to define a class `PolyLine` to represent lines consisting of one or more connected segments, as illustrated in the diagram.

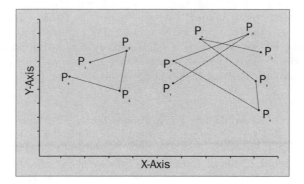

This shows two polylines, one defined by four points, the other defined by seven points.

It seems reasonable to represent points as objects of a class `Point`. Points are well-defined objects that will occur in the context of all kinds of geometric entities. We have seen a class for points earlier that we put in the package `Geometry`. Rather than repeat the whole thing, we will define the bare bones we need in this context:

```
public class Point
{
  // Create a point from its coordinates
  public Point(double xVal, double yVal)
  {
    x = xVal;
    y = yVal;
  }

  // Create a point from another point
  public Point(Point point)
  {
    x = point.x;
    y = point.y;
  }
```

```
    // Convert a point to a string
    public String toString()
    {
       return x+","+y;
    }

    // Coordinates of the point
    protected double x;
    protected double y;
}
```

Both data members will be inherited in any subclass because they are specified as `protected`. They are also insulated from interference from outside the package containing the class. The `toString()` method will allow `Point` objects to be concatenated to a `String` object for automatic conversion – in an argument passed to the `println()` method for example.

The next question you might ask is, "Should I derive the class `PolyLine` from the class `Point`?" This has a fairly obvious answer. A polyline is clearly not a kind of point, so it is not logical to derive the class `PolyLine` from the `Point` class. This is an elementary demonstration of what is often referred to as the '**is a**' test. If you can say that one kind of object 'is a' specialized form of another kind of object, you may have a good case for a derived class (but not always – there may be other reasons not to!). If not, you don't.

The complement to the 'is a' test is the '**has a**' test. If one object 'has a' component that is an object of another class, you have a case for a class member. A `House` object 'has a' door, so a `Door` variable is likely to be a member of the class `House`. Our `PolyLine` class will contain several points, which looks promising, but we should look a little more closely at how we might store them, as there are some options.

Designing the PolyLine Class

With the knowledge we have of Java, an array of `Point` objects looks like a good candidate to be a member of the class. There are disadvantages though. A common requirement with polylines is to be able to add a segment or two to an existing object. With an array storing the points, we will need to create a new array each time we add a segment, then copy all the points from the old array to the new one. This could be time consuming if we have a `PolyLine` object with a lot of segments.

We have another option. We could create a **linked list** of points. In its simplest form, a linked list of objects is an arrangement where each object in the list has a reference to the next object. As long as you have a variable containing the first `Point` object, you can access all the points in the list, as shown in the following diagram:

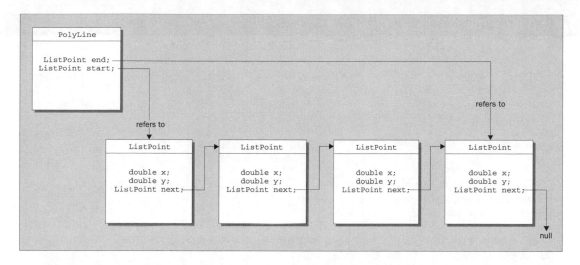

This illustrates the basic structure we might have for a linked list of points stored as a `PolyLine`. The points are stored as `ListPoint` objects. As well as constructors the `PolyLine` class will need a method to add points, but before we look into that, let's consider the `ListPoint` class in more detail.

There are at least three approaches you could take to define the `ListPoint` class, and there are arguments in favor of all three.

❑   You could define the `ListPoint` class with the x and y coordinates stored explicitly. The main argument against this would be that we have already encapsulated the properties of a point in the `Point` class, so why not use it.

❑   You could regard a `ListPoint` object as something that contains a reference to a `Point` object, plus members that refer to previous and following `ListPoint` objects in the list. This is not an unreasonable approach. It is easy to implement and not inconsistent with an intuitive idea of a `ListPoint`.

❑   You could view a `ListPoint` object as a specialized kind of `Point` so you would derive the `ListPoint` class from `Point`. Whether or not this is reasonable depends on whether you see this as valid. To my mind this is stretching the usual notion of a point somewhat – I would not use this.

The best option looks like the second approach. We could implement the `ListPoint` class with a data member of type `Point`, which defines a basic point with its coordinates. A `ListPoint` object would have an extra data member next, which would be of type `ListPoint`, and for each object in the list, except the last, next will contain a reference to the next object in the list. For the last object in the list, the variable next will be `null`.

Try It Out — The ListPoint Class

We can define the ListPoint class using the class Point with the code:

```
public class ListPoint
{
  // Constructor
  public ListPoint(Point point)
  {
    this.point = point;          // Store point reference
    next = null;                 // Set next ListPoint as null
  }

  // Set the pointer to the next ListPoint
  public void setNext(ListPoint next)
  {
    this.next = next;            // Store the next ListPoint
  }

  // Get the next point in the list
  public ListPoint getNext()
  {
    return next;                 // Return the next ListPoint
  }

  // Return String representation
  public String toString()
  {
    return "(" + point + ")";
  }

    private ListPoint next;      // Refers to next ListPoint in the list
    private Point point;         // The point for this list point
}
```

How It Works

A ListPoint object is a means of creating a list of Point objects that originate elsewhere so we don't need to worry about duplicating Point objects stored in the list. We can just store the reference to the Point object passed to the constructor in the data member, point. The data member, next, should contain a reference to the next ListPoint in the list, and since that is not defined here, we set next to null.

The setNext() method will enable the next data member to be set for the existing last point in the list, when a new point is added to the list. A reference to the new ListPoint object will be passed as an argument to the method. The getNext() method enables the next point in the list to be determined, so this method is the means by which we can iterate through the entire list.

By implementing the toString() method for the class, we enable the automatic creation of a String representation for a ListPoint object when required. Here we differentiate the String representation of our ListPoint object by enclosing the String representation of point between parentheses.

We could now have a first stab at implementing the `PolyLine` class.

Try It Out — The `PolyLine` Class

We can define the `PolyLine` class to use the `ListPoint` class as follows:

```java
public class PolyLine
{
  // Construct a polyline from an array of points
  public PolyLine(Point[] points)
  {
    if(points != null)                           // Make sure there is an array
    {
      // Create a one point list
      start = new ListPoint(points[0]);          // 1st point is the start
      end = start;                               // as well as the end

      // Now add the other points
      for(int i = 1; i < points.length; i++)
        addPoint(points[i]);
    }
  }

  // Add a Point object to the list
  public void addPoint(Point point)
  {
    ListPoint newEnd = new ListPoint(point);     // Create a new ListPoint
    if(start == null)
      start = newEnd;                            // Start is same as end
    else
      end.setNext(newEnd);         // Set next variable for old end as new end
    end = newEnd;                                // Store new point as end
  }

  // String representation of a polyline
  public String toString()
  {
    StringBuffer str = new StringBuffer("Polyline:");
    ListPoint nextPoint = start;                 // Set the 1st point as start
    while(nextPoint != null)
    {
      str.append(" "+ nextPoint);                // Output the current point
      nextPoint = nextPoint.getNext();           // Make the next point current
    }
    return str.toString();
  }

  private ListPoint start;                        // First ListPoint in the list
  private ListPoint end;                          // Last ListPoint in the list
}
```

You might want to be able to add a point to the list by specifying a coordinate pair. You could overload the addPoint() method to do this:

```
// Add a point to the list
public void addPoint(double x, double y)
{
  addPoint(new Point(x, y));
}
```

We just create a new Point object in the expression that is the argument to the other version of addPoint().

You might also want to create a PolyLine object from an array of coordinates. The constructor to do this would be:

```
// Construct a polyline from an array of coordinates
 public PolyLine(double[][] coords)
 {
    if(coords != null)
   {
     // Create a one point list
     start = new ListPoint(new Point(coords[0][0], coords[0][1]));
                                            // First is start
     end = start;                           // as well as end

     // Now add the other points
     for(int i = 1; i < coords.length ; i++)
       addPoint(coords[i][0], coords[i][1]);
   }
 }
```

How It Works

The PolyLine class has the data members start and end that we saw in the diagram. These will reference the first and last points of the list, or null if the list is empty. The constructor accepts an array of Point objects and starts the process of assembling the object, by creating a list containing one ListPoint object produced from the first element in the array. It then uses the addPoint() method to add all the remaining points in the array to the list.

Adding a point to the list is deceptively simple. All the addPoint() method does is create a ListPoint object from the Point object passed as an argument, sets the next member of the old end point in the list to refer to the new point and finally stores a reference to the new end point in the member end.

The method toString() will return a string representing the PolyLine object as a list of point coordinates. Note how the next member of the ListPoint objects controls the loop that runs through the list. When the last ListPoint object is reached, the next member will be returned as null, and the while loop will end.

We can now give the `PolyLine` class a whirl.

Try It Out — Using `PolyLine` Objects

We can create a simple example to illustrate how to use the `PolyLine` class:

```java
public class TryPolyLine
{
  public static void main(String[] args)
  {
    // Create an array of coordinate pairs
    double[][] coords = { {1., 1.}, {1., 2.}, { 2., 3.},
                          {-3., 5.}, {-5., 1.}, {0., 0.} };


    // Create a polyline from the coordinates and display it
    PolyLine polygon = new PolyLine(coords);
    System.out.println(polygon);

    // Add a point and display the polyline again
    polygon.addPoint(10., 10.);
    System.out.println(polygon);

    // Create Point objects from the coordinate array
    Point[] points = new Point[coords.length];
    for(int i = 0; i < points.length; i++)
      points[i] = new Point(coords[i][0],coords[1][1]);

    // Use the points to create a new polyline and display it
    PolyLine newPoly = new PolyLine(points);
    System.out.println(newPoly);
  }
}
```

Remember that all three classes, `Point`, `ListPoint`, and `PolyLine` need to be together in the same directory as this class. If you have keyed everything in correctly, the program will output three `PolyLine` objects.

```
Polyline: (1.0,1.0) (1.0,2.0) (2.0,3.0) (-3.0,5.0) (-5.0,1.0) (0.0,0.0)
Polyline: (1.0,1.0) (1.0,2.0) (2.0,3.0) (-3.0,5.0) (-5.0,1.0) (0.0,0.0)
                                                                 (10.0,10.0)
Polyline: (1.0,1.0) (1.0,2.0) (2.0,3.0) (-3.0,5.0) (-5.0,1.0) (0.0,0.0)
```

The first and the third lines of output are the same, with the coordinates from the `coords` array. The second has the extra point (10, 10) at the end.

The `PolyLine` class works well enough but it doesn't seem very satisfactory. Adding all the code to create and manage a list to what is essentially a geometric entity is not very object-oriented is it? Come to think of it, why are we making a list of points? Apart from the type of the data members of the `ListPoint` class, there's very little to do with `Point` objects in its definition, it's all to do with the linking mechanism. We might also have lots of other requirements for lists. If we were implementing an address book for instance, we would want a list of names. A cookery program would need a list of recipes. We might need lists for all kinds of things. Let's see if we can do better.

259

Let's put together a more general purpose linked list, and then use it to store polylines as before. Save this in a new directory as we will implement it as a whole new example.

A General Purpose Linked List

The key to implementing a general purpose linked list is the Object class that we discussed earlier in this chapter. Because the Object class is a superclass of every class, a variable of type Object can be used to store any kind of object. We could re-implement the ListPoint class in the form of a ListItem class. This will represent an element in a linked list that can reference any type of object:

```
class ListItem
{
  // Constructor
  public ListItem(Object item)
  {
    this.item = item;          // Store the item
    next = null;               // Set next as end point
  }

  // Return class name & object
  public String toString()
  {
    return "ListItem " + item ;
  }

  ListItem next;               // Refers to next item in the list
  Object item;                 // The item for this ListItem
}
```

It's basically similar to the ListPoint class except that we have omitted the methods to set and retrieve the next member reference. We will see why we don't need these in a moment. The toString() method assumes that the object referenced by item implements a toString() method. We won't use the toString() method here when we come to exercise the general linked list we are implementing, but it is a good idea to implement the toString() method for your classes anyway. If you do, class objects can always be output using the println() method which is very handy for debugging.

We can now use objects of this class in a definition of a class that will represent a linked list.

Defining a Linked List Class

The mechanics of creating and handling the linked list will be similar to what we had in the PolyLine class, but externally we need to deal in the objects that are stored in the list, not in terms of ListItem objects. In fact, we don't need to have the ListItem class separate from the LinkedList class. We can make it an inner class:

```
public class LinkedList
{
  // Default constructor - creates an empty list
  public LinkedList() {}
```

```
    // Constructor to create a list containing one object
    public LinkedList(Object item)
    {
      if(item != null)
        current=end=start=new ListItem(item);    // item is the start and end
    }

    // Construct a linked list from an array of objects
    public LinkedList(Object[] items)
    {
      if(items != null)
      {
        // Add the items to the list

        for(int i = 0; i < items.length; i++)
          addItem(items[i]);
        current = start;
      }
    }

    // Add an item object to the list
    public void addItem(Object item)
    {
      ListItem newEnd = new ListItem(item);   // Create a new ListItem
      if(start == null)                       // Is the list empty?
        start = end = newEnd;                 // Yes, so new element is start and end
      else
      {                                       // No, so append new element
        end.next = newEnd;                    // Set next variable for old end
        end = newEnd;                         // Store new item as end
      }
    }

    // Get the first object in the list
    public Object getFirst()
    {
      current = start;
      return start == null ? null : start.item;
    }

    // Get the next object in the list
    public Object getNext()
    {
      if(current != null)
        current = current.next;         // Get the reference to the next item
      return current == null ? null : current.item;
    }

    private ListItem start = null;        // First ListItem in the list
    private ListItem end = null;          // Last ListItem in the list
    private ListItem current = null;      // The current item for iterating
```

```
   private class ListItem
   {
     // Class definition as before
   }
}
```

This will create a linked list containing any types of objects. The class has data members to track the first and last items in the list, plus the member `current`, which will be used to iterate through the list. We have three class constructors. The default constructor creates an empty list. There is a constructor to create a list with a single object, and another to create a list from an array of objects. Any list can also be extended by means of the `addItem()` method. Each of the constructors, apart from the default, sets the `current` member to the first item in the list, so if the list is not empty this will refer to a valid first item. You can see that since the `ListItem` class is a member of the `LinkedList` class, we can refer to its data members directly. This obviates the need for any methods in the `ListItem` class to get or set its fields. Since it is `private` it will not be accessible outside the `LinkedList` class so there is no risk associated with this – as long as we code the `LinkedList` class correctly of course.

The `addItem()` method works in much the same way as the `addPoint()` method did in the `PolyLine` class. It creates a new `ListItem` object, and updates the next member of the previous last item to refer to the new one. The complication is the possibility that the list might be empty. The check in the `if` takes care of this. We take special steps if `start` holds a `null` reference.

The `getFirst()` and `getNext()` methods are intended to be used together to access all the objects stored in the list. The `getFirst()` method returns the object stored in the first `ListItem` object in the list, and sets the `current` data member to refer to the first `ListItem` object. After calling the `getFirst()` method, successive calls to the `getNext()` method will return subsequent objects stored in the list. The method updates `current` to refer to the next `ListItem` object, each time it is called. When the end of the list is reached, `getNext()` returns `null`.

Try It Out - Using the General Linked List

We can now define the `PolyLine` class so that it uses a `LinkedList` object. All we need to do is to put a `LinkedList` variable as a class member that we initialize in the class constructors and implement all the other methods we had in the previous version of the class to use the `LinkedList` object:

```
public class PolyLine
{
  // Construct a polyline from an array of coordinate pairs
  public PolyLine(double[][] coords)
  {
    Point[] points = new Point[coords.length];  // Array to hold points

    // Create points from the coordinates
    for(int i = 0; i < coords.length ; i++)
      points[i] = new Point(coords[i][0], coords[i][1]);

    // Create the polyline from the array of points
    polyline = new LinkedList(points);
  }
```

```
  // Construct a polyline from an array of points
  public PolyLine(Point[] points)
  {
    polyline = new LinkedList(points);       // Create the polyline
  }


  // Add a Point object to the list
  public void addPoint(Point point)
  {
    polyline.addItem(point);                 // Add the point to the list
  }

  // Add a point from a coordinate pair to the list
  public void addPoint(double x, double y)
  {
      polyline.addItem(new Point(x, y));     // Add the point to the list
  }


  // String representation of a polyline
  public String toString()
  {
    StringBuffer str = new StringBuffer("Polyline:");
    Point point = (Point) polyline.getFirst();
                                             // Set the 1st point as start
    while(point != null)
    {
      str.append(" ("+ point+ ")");          // Append the current point
      point = (Point)polyline.getNext();     // Make the next point current
    }
    return str.toString();
  }

  private LinkedList polyline;               // The linked list of points
}
```

You can exercise this using the same code as last time – in the TryPolyLine.java file. Copy this file to the directory for this example.

How It Works

The PolyLine class implements all the methods that we had in the class before, so the main() method in the TryPolyLine class works just the same. Under the covers, the methods in the PolyLine class work a little differently. The work of creating the linked list is now in the constructor for the LinkedList class. All the PolyLine class constructors do is assemble a point array if necessary, and call the LinkedList constructor. Similarly, the addPoint() method creates a Point object from the coordinate pair it receives, and passes it to the addItem() method for the LinkedList object, polyline.

Note that the cast from Point to Object when the addItem() method is called is automatic. A cast from any class type to type Object is always automatic because the class is up the class hierarchy – remember that all classes have Object as a base. In the toString() method, we must insert an explicit cast to store the object returned by the getFirst() or the getNext() method. This cast is down the hierarchy so you must specify the cast explicitly.

You could use a variable of type `Object` to store the objects returned from `getFirst()` and `getNext()`, but this would not be a good idea. You would not need to insert the explicit cast, but you would lose a valuable check on the integrity of the program. You put objects of type `Point` into the list, so you would expect objects of type `Point` to be returned. An error in the program somewhere could result in an object of another type being inserted. If the object is not of type `Point` – due to the said program error for example – the cast to type `Point` will fail and you will get an exception. A variable of type `Object` can store anything. If you use this, and something other than a `Point` object is returned, it would not register at all.

Now that we have gone to the trouble of writing our own general linked list class, you may be wondering why someone hasn't done it already. Well, they have! The `java.util` package defines a `LinkedList` class that is much better than ours. Still, putting our own together was good experience which I hope you found interesting. We will look at the `LinkedList` class of `java.util` in Chapter 10.

Using the final Modifier

We have already used the keyword `final` to fix the value of a static data member of a class. You can also apply this keyword to the definition of a method, and to the definition of a class.

It may be that you want to prevent a subclass from overriding a method in your class. When this is the case, simply declare that method as `final`. Any attempt to override a `final` method in a subclass will result in the compiler flagging the new method as an error. For example, you could declare the method `addPoint()` as `final` within the class, `PolyLine`, by writing its definition in the class as:

```
public final void addPoint(Point point)
{
    ListPoint newEnd = new ListPoint(point);   // Create a new ListPoint
    end.setNext(newEnd);      // Set next variable for old end as new end
    end = newEnd;             // Store new point as end
}
```

Any class derived from `PolyLine` would not be able to redefine this method. Obviously an `abstract` method cannot be declared as `final` – as it must be defined in a subclass.

If you declare a class as `final`, you prevent any subclasses from being derived from it. To declare the class `PolyLine` as `final`, you would define it as:

```
public final class PolyLine
{
    // Definition as before...
}
```

If you now attempt to define a class based on `PolyLine` you will get an error message from the compiler. An abstract class cannot be declared as `final` since this would prevent the abstract methods in the class from ever being defined. Declaring a class as `final` is a drastic step that prevents the functionality of the class being extended by derivation, so you should be very sure that you want to do this.

Interfaces

In the classes that we derived from the class Animal, we had a common method, sound(), that was implemented individually in each of the subclasses. The method signature was the same in each class, and the method could be called polymorphically. The main point to defining the class Animal first, and then subsequently the classes Dog, and Cat, and so on from it, was to be able to get polymorphic behavior. When all you want is a set of one or more methods to be implemented in a number of different classes so that you can call them polymorphically, you can dispense with the base class altogether. You can achieve the same end result much more simply by using a Java facility called an **interface**. The name indicates its primary use – specifying a set of methods that represent a particular class interface, that can then be implemented individually in a number of different classes. All of the classes will then share this common interface, and the methods in it can be called polymorphically. This is just one aspect of what you can do using an interface. We should start by examining what an interface is from the ground up, and then look at what we can do with it.

An **interface** is essentially a collection of constants and abstract methods. To make use of an interface, you **implement** the interface in a class – that is, you declare that the class implements the interface and you write the code for each of the methods declared in the interface as part of the class definition. When a class implements an interface, any constants that were defined in the interface definition are available directly in the class, just as though they were inherited from a base class. An interface can contain either constant or abstract methods, or both.

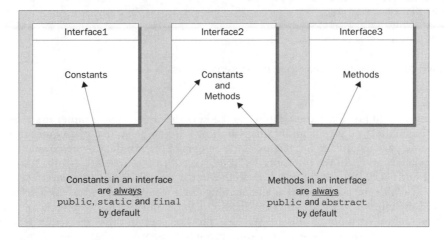

The methods in an interface are always public and abstract, so you do not need to specify them as such – it is considered to be bad programming practice to specify any attributes for them. The constants in an interface are always public, static and final, so you do not need to specify the attributes for these either.

The syntax for defining an interface is very much like that of a class. Let's see how it looks by taking a concrete example.

Try It Out — Defining Interfaces

Here is an interface containing only constants:

```
public interface ConversionFactors
{
  double INCH_TO_MM = 25.4;
  double OUNCE_TO_GRAM = 28.349523125;
  double POUND_TO_GRAM = 453.5924;
  double HP_TO_WATT = 745.7;
  double WATT_TO_HP = 1.0/HP_TO_WATT;
}
```

Here we have five constants for conversions of various kinds – remember that these are `public`, `static`, and `final` by default.

You might also want to define an interface containing methods for conversion:

```
public interface Conversions
{
  double inchToMM(double inches);
  double ounceToGram(double ounces);
  double poundToGram(double pounds);
  double HPToWatt(double hp);
  double wattToHP(double watts);
}
```

This interface declares five methods to perform conversions.

How It Works

An interface is defined just like a class, but using the keyword `interface` rather than the keyword `class`. The name that you give to an interface must be different from that of any other interface or class in the same package. Just as for classes, the members of the interface – the constants and methods – appear between braces. All the constants INCH_TO_MM, OUNCE_TO_GRAM, POUND_TO_GRAM, HP_TO_WATT and WATT_TO_HP are `public`, so they are accessible outside the interface. Incidentally, they are also available outside the package containing the `ConversionFactors` interface because we have declared the interface as `public`. They're also `static` and `final` by default so we must initialize them and they cannot be altered. We have no choice about this – constants defined in an interface always have these attributes. The names given to these use capital letters to indicate that they are `final` and cannot be altered – this is a common convention in Java. You can define the value of one constant in terms of a preceding constant, as in the definition of WATT_TO_HP. If you try to use a constant that is defined later in the interface – if, for example the definition for WATT_TO_HP appeared first – your code will not compile.

The only access attribute you can use with an interface definition is `public`. This makes the interface accessible outside the package containing it. If you omit the keyword `public`, your interface is only accessible from within its containing package.

As you see, the `Conversions` interface only defines the signature for each method. It is up to the class that implements the interface to supply the code for each method.

Extending Interfaces

You can define one interface based on another by using the keyword `extends` to identify the base interface name. This is essentially the same form we use to derive one class from another. For example, the interface `Conversions` would, perhaps be more useful if it contained the constants that the interface `ConversionFactors` contains.

We could do this by defining the interface `Conversions` as:

```
public interface Conversions extends ConversionFactors
{
  double inchToMM(double inches);
  double ounceToGram(double ounces);
  double poundToGram(double pounds);
  double HPToWatt(double hp);
  double wattToHP(double watts);
}
```

Now the interface `Conversions` also contains the members of the interface `ConversionFactors`. Any class implementing the `Conversions` interface will have the constants from `ConversionFactors` available to implement the methods. The interface `ConversionFactors` is referred to as a **super-interface** of the interface `Conversions`.

An interface can use the contents of several other interfaces. To define an interface that includes the members of several other interfaces, you specify the names of the interfaces, separated by commas, following the keyword `extends`. For example,

```
public interface MyInterface extends HisInterface, HerInterface
{
  // Interface members - constants and abstract methods...
}
```

Now `MyInterface` will incorporate all the methods and constants that are members of `HisInterface` and `HerInterface`. Some care is necessary if you do this. If both super-interfaces have a method with the same signature, that is, with identical name and parameters, they must also have the same return type, otherwise the compiler will report an error. This is because it would be impossible for a class to implement both, as they have the same signature.

Implementing an Interface

As we saw earlier, to implement an interface in a class, you just add the keyword, `implements`, followed by the interface name, after the class name in the class definition, plus the implementation for each of the methods declared in the interface definition. Let's look at what sort of effort is involved in implementing interfaces in a class.

Implementing an Interface Defining Constants

To implement the interface `ConversionFactors` in a class `MyClass`, you define the class as:

```
public class MyClass implements ConversionFactors
{
  double poundsWeight;                    // A weight in pounds

  public double getMetricWeight()
  {
    return poundsWeight*POUND_TO_GRAM;
  }

  // Definition of the rest of class...
}
```

All the constants defined in the interface `ConversionFactors` are available in `MyClass` as though they were data members of the class. You can reference them freely in any of the methods in the class. Because they are `public`, they will also be accessible members of objects of type `MyClass`.

Implementing an Interface Defining Methods

When the interface contains methods, the class needs a bit more work. We have to implement the methods that are in the interface. For example, we can implement the `Conversions` interface in the class, `MyClass` as follows:

```
public class MyClass implements Conversions
{
  // Implementation of the methods in the interface
  public double inchToMM(double inches)
  {
    return inches*INCH_TO_MM;
  }

  public double ounceToGram(double ounces)
  {
    return ounces*OUNCE_TO_GRAM;
  }

  public double poundToGram(double pounds)
  {
    return pounds*POUND_TO_GRAM;
  }

  public double HPToWatt(double hp)
  {
    return hp*HP_TO_WATT;
  }

  public double wattToHP(double watts)
  {
    return watts*WATT_TO_HP;
  }
}
```

Every method declared in the interface should have a definition within the class if you are going to create objects of the class. Since the methods in an interface are, by definition, `public`, you must use the `public` keyword when you define them in your class – otherwise your code will not compile. The implementation of an interface method must not have an access specifier that is more restrictive than that implicit in the abstract method declaration, and you can't get less restrictive than `public`.

Since the `Conversions` interface extends the `ConversionFactors` interface, all the constants defined in the `ConversionFactors` interface are available as full members of this version of `MyClass`. We can, therefore, use them in the implementation of the interface methods.

Where several classes are implementing the same interface, they will typically have different ways of implementing the methods. That obviously doesn't apply to the methods we have in the `Conversions` interface. You might, however, have an interface declaring a method `draw()` that is supposed to display an entity. If the interface was implemented in classes defining geometric shapes, the implementation of a `draw()` method for a `Circle` object would be quite different from that for a `Rectangle` object.

Of course, you don't *have to* implement every method in the interface, but there are some consequences.

A Partial Interface Implementation

We could omit the implementation of one or more of the methods from the interface in the class `MyClass`, but in this case we would need to declare the class as `abstract`:

```
public abstract class MyClass implements Conversions
{
  // Implementation of two of the methods in the interface
  public double inchToMM(double inches)
  {
    return inches*INCH_TO_MM;
  }

  public double ounceToGram(double ounces)
  {
    return ounces*OUNCE_TO_GRAM;
  }

  // Definition of the rest of the class...
}
```

With this version of `MyClass`, you cannot create objects of the class. For the class to be useful, you must define a subclass of `MyClass` that implements the remaining methods in the interface. The declaration of the class as `abstract` is mandatory when you don't implement all of the methods that are declared in an interface. The compiler will complain if you forget to do this.

Now we know how to write the code to use an interface, we can tie up something we met earlier in this chapter. We mentioned that you need to implement the interface `Cloneable` to use the inherited method `clone()`. In fact this interface is empty, so all you need to do to implement it in a class is to specify that the class in question implements it in the class declaration. This means that you just need to write something like:

```
public MyClass implements Cloneable
{
   // Detail of the class...
}
```

The sole purpose of the Cloneable interface is to act as a flag signalling that you are prepared to allow objects of your class to be cloned. If you don't specify that your class implements Cloneable, the compiler will not permit the clone() method to be called for objects of your class type.

Using Interfaces

What you have seen up to now has primarily illustrated the mechanics of creating an interface and incorporating it into a class. The really interesting question is – what should you use interfaces for?

We have already illustrated one use for interfaces. An interface is a very handy means of packaging up constants. You can use an interface containing constants in any number of different classes that have access to the interface. All you need to do is make sure the class implements the interface and all the constants it contains are available. The constants are static and so will be shared among all objects of a class.

We hinted at the most important use at the beginning of this discussion. Interfaces enable you to expedite polymorphism without necessarily defining subclasses. This is an extremely useful and powerful facility. Let's have a look at how this works.

Interfaces and Polymorphism

When we first introduced the idea of a class, we referred to the public methods in a class as 'the interface to the class'. Where several classes share a common set of methods with given signatures, but with possibly different implementations, you can separate the set of methods common to the classes into an **interface**. This interface can then be implemented by each of the classes.

Earlier in this chapter we implemented several classes, with a common set of methods, by defining them as subclasses of a base class from which the subclasses inherited the common methods. This enabled us to take advantage of the flexibility provided by polymorphism. We can achieve exactly the same effect by defining an interface and implementing this interface in each class. Our example, using the class Animal called the methods in the subclasses dynamically. We can see how polymorphism works with an interface by implementing the same example with the classes Dog, Spaniel, Cat, and Duck, but using an interface to specify the common sound() method, rather than the base class Animal.

Try It Out — An Animal Interface

We first need to define an interface that includes the methods we want to select dynamically:

```
public interface PetOutput
{
  void sound();
}
```

The interface, PetOutput, includes the method that was previously in the base class Animal. Now all we need to do is make sure each of the classes implements this interface. We won't reproduce all of the detail of each class here, as the code is much the same as before with essentially the same modifications to each of the direct subclasses of Animal. Here is the definition for the class Dog:

```java
public class Dog implements PetOutput
{
  public Dog(String aName)
  {
    name = aName;             // Supplied name
    breed = "Unknown";        // Default breed value
  }

  public Dog(String aName, String aBreed)
  {
    name = aName;             // Supplied name
    breed = aBreed;           // Supplied breed
  }

  // Present a dog's details as a string
  public String toString()
  {
    return "It's " + name + " the " + breed;
  }

  // A barking method
  public void sound()
  {
    System.out.println("Woof    Woof");
  }

  public String getName()
  {
    return name;
  }

  private String name;       // Name of a dog
  private String breed;      // Dog breed
}
```

There is no base class now so we must remove the super() calls in each of the constructors. The toString() has also been changed so that it does not call the base class toString() method. If it did it would be the version from the Object class. The Cat and Duck classes need to be modified in a similar way. The definition of the class, Spaniel, will remain as it was:

```java
class Spaniel extends Dog
{
  public Spaniel(String aName)
  {
    super(aName, "Spaniel");
  }
}
```

Here is the code that tries out the classes:

```java
import java.util.Random;

public class TestInterface
{
  public static void main(String[] args)
  {
    PetOutput[] thePets = {
                            new Dog("Rover", "Poodle"),
                            new Cat("Max", "Abyssinian"),
                            new Duck("Daffy","Aylesbury"),
                            new Spaniel("Fido")
                          };

    PetOutput petChoice;

    Random select = new Random();                 // Random number generator
    for(int i = 0; i < 5; i++)
    {
      petChoice = thePets[select.nextInt(thePets.length)];
      System.out.println("\nYour choice:\n" + petChoice);
      petChoice.sound();
    }
  }
}
```

If you run this it will generate the following sort of output:

```
Your choice:
It's Fido the Spaniel
Woof    Woof

Your choice:
It's Max the Abyssinian
Miiaooww

Your choice:
It's Fido the Spaniel
Woof    Woof

Your choice:
It's Rover the Poodle
Woof    Woof

Your choice:
It's Rover the Poodle
Woof    Woof
```

No ducks this time around – purely by chance!

How It Works

The `Dog`, `Duck` and `Cat` classes are no longer subclasses of `Animal`. They just implement the `PetOutput` interface. We no longer have the variable, `type`, that was originally inherited from the class `Animal`. You can add it in to the class definitions if you want, and then set it in the constructors. The calls to the superclass constructors that we had in the class constructors are now not applicable, so they have been removed.

The interface method `sound()` is defined in each class, but of course, the call to the `toString()` method works polymorphically because the method is defined in `Object`.

The `Spaniel` class is a subclass of `Dog`, and will be implemented in the same way here as it was earlier in the chapter. Of course, the `Spaniel` class will inherit the interface methods from the superclass and they will be quite satisfactory. Even if you need to redefine the methods in this class, you won't need to explicitly specify the interface as being implemented by the class.

The relationship between the classes and the interface is shown in the next illustration.

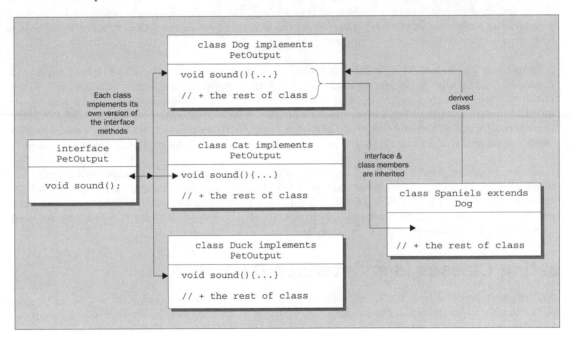

For polymorphism to work, we need one variable that is capable of referring to any of the four different kinds of object, `Dog`, `Spaniel`, `Duck` or `Cat`. We no longer have the base class `Animal`, so we can't use a variable of that type. However, because we are using an interface to specify the methods that are common to the classes, we can use a variable of the interface type, `PetOutput`, to store any of the class objects.

If you declare a variable to be an interface type, such as we have for the variable petChoice in our example, you can use it to reference an object of any class that is declared to implement the interface. This excludes abstract classes of course, since you cannot define an object of an abstract class, but it does include subclasses that inherit the interface methods from a direct or indirect superclass. We can therefore use petOutput to refer to objects of the class Spaniel in our example, which inherits the interface methods from the class Dog.

Other than that the test code works in the same way as before. A random selection from the array, thePets, which is now of type PetOutput, is stored in the variable petChoice, which is also of type PetOutput. The variable petChoice is then used to call the appropriate version of the method sound(). This will be selected from the class corresponding to the object referenced by the variable petChoice. The loop makes five random selections from the array, thePets. We also have the implicit toString() call that is inserted by the compiler in the argument expression to the println() method being selected dynamically too.

Using Multiple Interfaces

A derived class can only have a single base class in Java. However, you are not restricted to the number of interfaces a class can implement. This introduces a further level of flexibility in how you write your programs and make use of polymorphism.

A simple use for implementing multiple interfaces in a class is to use one interface to hold application constants, and another to declare methods that you want to use polymorphically. You can put all the constant values that you need in a program into a single interface definition, and then implement the interface in any class that needs access to the constants. This only involves adding implements and the interface name to the first line of the class definition. You can also implement any other interface in these classes that declares methods that are to be executed polymorphically, as and when necessary.

At a more complex level – which we will just touch on – you can have several classes that each implement multiple interfaces that declare methods. To call the methods declared in a particular interface polymorphically, you will need to use a variable of that interface type. Of course, you cannot use this variable to call methods in any other interface that a class implements. You will always need a variable of a type corresponding to the interface that declares the method.

Nesting Classes in an Interface Definition

You can put the definition of a class inside the definition of an interface. The class will be an inner class to the interface. An inner class to an interface will be static and public by default. The code structure would be like this:

```
interface Port
{
  // Methods & Constants declared in the interface...

  class Info
  {
    // Definition of the class...
  }
}
```

This declares the interface, `Port`, with an inner class, `Info`. Objects of the inner class would be of type `Port.Info`. You might create one with a statement like this:

```
Port.Info info = new Port.Info();
```

The standard class library includes a number of interfaces with inner classes, including one with the name `Port` (in the `javax.sound.sampled` package) that has an inner class with the name `Info`, although the `Info` class does not have the default constructor that we have used in the illustration here. The circumstances where you might define a class as an inner class to an interface would be when objects of the inner class type have a strong logical association with the interface.

A class that implements the interface would have no direct connection with the inner class to the interface – it would just need to implement the methods declared by the interface, but it is highly likely it would make use of objects of the inner class type.

Interfaces and the Real World

An interface type is sometimes used to reference an object that encapsulates something that exists outside of Java, such as a particular physical device. This is done when the external device does not require methods implemented in Java code because all the function is provided externally. The interface method declarations just identify the mechanism for operating on the external object.

The example of the `Port` interface in the library is exactly that. A reference of type `Port` refers to an object that is a physical port on a sound card, such as that for the speaker or the microphone. The inner class, `Port.Info`, defines objects that encapsulate data to define a particular port. You can't create a `Port` object directly since there is no class of type `Port`. Indeed it doesn't necessarily make sense to do so since your system may not have any ports. Assuming your PC has sound ports you obtain a reference of type `Port` to an object that encapsulates a real port such as the microphone, by calling a static method defined in another class. The argument to the method would be a reference to an object of type `Port.Info` specifying the kind of port that you want. All of the methods defined in the `Port` interface would correspond to methods written in native machine code that would operate on the port. To call them you just use the `Port` reference that you have obtained.

Anonymous Classes

There are occasions where you need to define a class for which you will only ever want to define one object in your program, and the only use for the object is to pass it directly as an argument to a method. In this case, as long as your class extends an existing class, or implements an interface, you have the option of defining the class as an **anonymous class.** The definition for an anonymous class appears in the new expression, in the statement where you create and use the object of the class, so that there is no necessity to provide a name for the class.

We will illustrate how this is done using an example. Supposing we want to define an object of a class that implements the interface `ActionListener` for one time use. We could do this as follows:

```
pickButton.addActionListener(new ActionListener()
                 {
                          // Code to define the class
```

```
                                      // that implements the ActionListener interface
                      }
          );
```

The class definition appears in the new expression that creates the argument to the `addActionListener()` method. This method requires a reference of type `ActionListener` – in other words a reference to a class that implements the `ActionListener` interface. The parentheses following the name of the interface indicate we are creating an object reference of this type, and the details of the class definition appear between the parentheses. The anonymous class can include data members as well as methods, but obviously not constructors because the class has no name. Here all the methods declared in the `ActionListener` interface would need to be defined.

If the anonymous class extends an existing class, the syntax is much the same. In this case you are calling a constructor for the base class and, if this is not a default constructor, you can pass arguments to it by specifying them between the parentheses following the base class name. The definition of the anonymous class must appear between braces, just as in the previous example.

An anonymous class can be convenient where the class definition is short and simple. This technique should not be used extensively as it tends to make the code very difficult to understand.

Summary

You should now understand polymorphism, and how to apply it. You will find that this technique can be utilized to considerable advantage in the majority of your Java programs. It will certainly appear in many of the examples in the remaining chapters.

The important points we have covered in this chapter are:

❑ An **abstract method** is a method that has no body defined for it, and is declared using the keyword `abstract`.

❑ An **abstract class** is a class that contains one or more abstract methods. It must be defined with the attribute `abstract`.

❑ You can define one class based on another. This is called class derivation or inheritance. The base class is call a **superclass** and the derived class is called a **subclass**. A superclass can also be a subclass of another superclass.

❑ A subclass inherits certain members of its superclass. An inherited member of a class can be referenced and used as though it was declared as a normal member of the class.

❑ A subclass does not inherit the superclass constructors.

❑ The `private` members of a superclass are not inherited in a subclass. If the subclass is not in the same package as the superclass, then members of the superclass that do not have an access attribute are not inherited.

❑ The first statement in the body of a constructor for a subclass should call a constructor for the superclass. If it does not, the compiler will insert a call for the default constructor for the superclass.

❑ A subclass can re-implement, or overload, the methods inherited from its superclass. If two or more subclasses, with a common base class, re-implement a common set of methods, these methods can be selected for execution at run-time.

❑ A variable of a superclass can point to an object of any of its subclasses. Such a variable can then be used to execute the subclass methods inherited from the superclass.

❑ A subclass of an abstract class must also be declared as abstract if it does not provide definitions for all of the abstract methods inherited from its superclass.

❑ A class defined inside another class is called a nested class or inner class. An inner class may itself contain inner classes.

❑ An interface can contain constants, abstract methods, and inner classes.

❑ A class can implement one or more interfaces by declaring them in the class definition, and including the code to implement each of the interface methods.

❑ A class that does not define all the methods for an interface it implements must be declared as abstract.

❑ If several classes implement a common interface, the methods declared as members of the interface can be executed polymorphically.

Exercises

1. Define an abstract base class Shape that includes protected data members for the (x, y) position of a shape, a public method to move a shape, and a public abstract method show() to output a shape. Derive subclasses for lines, circles and rectangles. Also define the class PolyLine that you saw in this chapter with Shape as its base class. You can represent: a line as two points, a circle as a center and a radius, and a rectangle as two points on diagonally opposite corners. Implement the toString() method for each class. Test the classes by selecting ten random objects of the derived classes, then invoking the show() method for each. Use the toString() methods in the derived classes.

2. Define a class, ShapeList, that can store an arbitrary collection of any objects of subclasses of the Shape class.

3. Implement the classes for shapes using an interface for the common methods, rather than inheritance from the superclass, while still keeping Shape as a base class.

4. Extend the LinkedList class that we defined in this chapter so that it supports traversing the list backwards as well as forwards.

5. Add methods to the class LinkedList to insert and delete elements at thecurrent position.

6. Implement a method in the LinkedList class to insert an object following an object passed as an argument. (Assume the objects stored in the list implement an equals() method that compares the This object with an object passed as an argument, and returns true if they are equal.)

Exceptions

Java uses exceptions as a way of signaling serious problems when you execute a program. They are used extensively by the standard classes. Since they arise in your Java programs when things go wrong, and if something can go wrong in your code, sooner or later it will, they are a very basic consideration when you are designing and writing your programs.

The reason we've been sidestepping the question of exceptions for the past six chapters is that you first needed to understand classes and inheritance before you could understand what an exception is, and appreciate what happens when an exception occurs. Now that you have a good grasp of these topics we can delve into how to use and deal with exceptions in a program.

In this chapter you will learn:

- ❑ What an exception is

- ❑ How you handle exceptions in your programs

- ❑ The standard exceptions in Java

- ❑ How to guarantee that a particular block of code in a method will always be executed

- ❑ How to define and use your own types of exceptions

- ❑ How to throw exceptions in your programs

The Idea Behind Exceptions

An exception usually signals an error, and is so-called because errors in your Java programs are bound to be the exception rather than the rule – by definition! An exception doesn't always indicate an error though – it can also signal some particularly unusual event in your program that deserves special attention.

If, in the midst of the code that deals with the normal operation of the program, you try to deal with the myriad, and often highly unusual, error conditions that might arise, your program structure will soon become very complicated and difficult to understand. One major benefit of having an error signaled by an exception is that it separates the code that deals with errors from the code that is executed when things are moving along smoothly. Another positive aspect of exceptions is that they provide a way of enforcing a response to particular errors – with many kinds of exceptions, you must include code in your program to deal with them, otherwise your code will not compile.

One important idea to grasp is that not all errors in your programs need to be signaled by exceptions. Exceptions should be reserved for the unusual or catastrophic situations that can arise. A user entering incorrect input to your program for instance is a normal event, and should be handled without recourse to exceptions. The reason for this is that dealing with exceptions involves quite a lot of processing overhead, so if your program is handling exceptions a lot of the time it will be a lot slower than it needs to be.

An **exception** in Java is an object that's created when an abnormal situation arises in your program. This exception object has data members that store information about the nature of the problem. The exception is said to be **thrown**, that is, the object identifying the exceptional circumstance is tossed, as an argument, to a specific piece of program code that has been written specifically to deal with that kind of problem. The code receiving the exception object as a parameter is said to **catch** it.

The situations that cause exceptions are quite diverse, but they fall into four broad categories:

Code or Data Errors	For example, you attempt an invalid cast of an object, you try to use an array index that's outside the limits for the array, or an integer arithmetic expression that has a zero divisor.
Standard Method Exceptions	For example, if you use the substring() method in the String class, it can throw a StringIndexOutOfBoundsException exception.
Throwing your own Exceptions	We'll see later in this chapter how you can throw a few of your own when you need to.
Java Errors	These can be due to errors in executing the Java Virtual Machine which runs your compiled program, but usually arise as a consequence of an error in your program.

Before we look at how you make provision in your programs for dealing with exceptions, we should understand what specific classes of exceptions can arise.

Types of Exceptions

An exception is always an object of some subclass of the standard class Throwable. This is true for exceptions that you define and throw yourself, as well as the standard exceptions that arise due to errors in your code. It's also true for exceptions that are thrown by methods in one or other of the standard packages.

All the standard exceptions are covered by two direct subclasses of the class `Throwable` – the class `Error` and the class `Exception`. Both these classes themselves have subclasses which identify specific exception conditions.

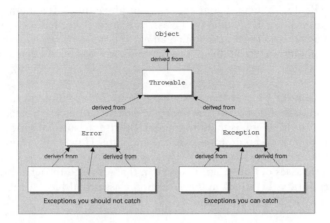

Error Exceptions

The exceptions that are defined by the class `Error`, and its subclasses, are characterized by the fact that they all represent conditions that you aren't expected to do anything about and, therefore, you aren't expected to catch them. There are three direct subclasses of `Error` – `ThreadDeath`, `LinkageError`, and `VirtualMachineError`. The first of these sounds the most serious, but in fact it isn't. A `ThreadDeath` exception is thrown whenever an executing thread is deliberately stopped, and in order for the thread to be destroyed properly you should not catch this exception. There are circumstances where you might want to - for clean-up operations for instance - in which case you must be sure to rethrow the exception to allow the thread to die. When a `ThreadDeath` exception is thrown and not caught, it's the thread that ends, not the program. We will deal with threads in detail in Chapter 11.

The `LinkageError` exception class has subclasses that record serious errors with the classes in your program. Incompatibilities between classes or attempting to create an object of a non-existent class type are the sorts of things that cause these exceptions to be thrown. The `VirtualMachineError` class has four subclasses that specify exceptions that will be thrown when a catastrophic failure of the Java Virtual Machine occurs. You aren't prohibited from trying to deal with these exceptions but, in general, there's little point in attempting to catch them. The exceptions that correspond to objects of classes derived from `LinkageError` and `VirtualMachineError` are all the result of catastrophic events or conditions. There is little or nothing you can do to recover from them during the execution of the program. In these sorts of situations, all you can usually do is read the error message generated by the exception, and then, particularly in the case of a `LinkageError` exception, try to figure out what might be wrong with your code to cause the exception to be thrown.

RuntimeException Exceptions

For almost all the exceptions that are represented by subclasses of the Exception class, you must include code in your programs to deal with them if your code may produce them. If a method in your program has the potential to generate an exception of some such class, you must either handle the exception within the method, or register that your method may throw such an exception. If you don't, your program will not compile. We'll see in a moment how to handle exceptions and how to specify that a method can throw an exception.

One group of subclasses of Exception that are exempted from this are those derived from RuntimeException. The reason that RuntimeException exceptions are treated differently, and that the compiler allows you to ignore them, is that they generally arise because of serious errors in your code. In most situations there is little you can do to recover the situation. However, in some contexts for some of these exceptions, this is not always the case, and you may well want to include code to recognize them. There are quite a lot of subclasses of RuntimeException that are used to signal problems in various packages in the Java class library. Let's look at the exception classes that have RuntimeException as a base that are defined in the java.lang package.

The subclasses of RuntimeException defined in the standard package java.lang are:

Class Name	Exception Condition Represented
ArithmeticException	An invalid arithmetic condition has arisen such as an attempt to divide an integer value by zero.
IndexOutOfBoundsException	You've attempted to use an index that is outside the bounds of the object it is applied to. This may be an array, a String object, or a Vector object. The class Vector is defined in the standard package, java.util. We will be looking into the Vector class in Chapter 10.
NegativeArraySizeException	You tried to define an array with a negative dimension.
NullPointerException	You used an object variable containing null, when it should refer to an object for proper operation – for example, calling a method or accessing a data member.
ArrayStoreException	You've attempted to store an object in an array that isn't permitted for the array type.
ClassCastException	You've tried to cast an object to an invalid type – the object isn't of the class specified, nor is it a subclass or a superclass of the class specified.
IllegalArgumentException	You've passed an argument to a method which doesn't correspond with the parameter type.
SecurityException	Your program has performed an illegal operation that is a security violation. This might be trying to read a file on the local machine from an applet.

Class Name	Exception Condition Represented
IllegalMonitor StateException	A thread has tried to wait on the monitor for an object that the thread doesn't own. (We'll look into threads in Chapter 11).
IllegalStateException	You tried to call a method at a time when it was not legal to do so.
Unsupported OperationException	Thrown if you request an operation to be carried out that is not supported.

In the normal course of events you shouldn't meet up with the last three of these. The ArithmeticException turns up quite easily in your programs, as does the IndexOutOfBoundsException. A mistake in a for loop limit will produce the latter. In fact there are two subclasses of IndexOutOfBoundsException that specify the type of exception thrown more precisely – ArrayIndexOutOfBoundsException and StringIndexOutOfBoundsException. A NullPointerException can also turn up relatively easily, as can ArrayStoreException, ClassCastException, and IllegalArgumentException surprisingly enough. The last three here arise when you are using a base class variable to call methods for derived class objects. Explicit attempts to perform an incorrect cast, or store a reference of an incorrect type or pass an argument of the wrong type to a method will all be picked up by the compiler. These exceptions can, therefore, only arise from using a variable of a base type to hold references to a derived class object

The IllegalArgumentException class is a base class for two further exception classes, IllegalThreadStateException and NumberFormatException. The former arises when you attempt an operation that is illegal in the current thread state. The NumberFormatException exception is thrown by the valueOf(), or decode() method in the classes representing integers – that is, the classes Byte, Short, Integer, and Long. The parseXXX() methods in these classes can also throw this exception. The exception is thrown if the String object passed as an argument to the conversion method is not a valid representation of an integer – if it contains invalid characters for instance. In this case a special return value cannot be used, so throwing an exception is a very convenient way to signal that the argument is invalid.

We will try out some of the RuntimeException exceptions later in the chapter as some of them are so easy to generate, but let's see what other sorts of exception classes have Exception as a base.

Other Subclasses of Exception

For all the other classes derived from the class Exception, the compiler will check that you've either handled the exception in a method where the exception may be thrown, or you've indicated that the method can throw such an exception. If you do neither your code won't compile. We'll look more at how we ensure the code does compile in the next two sections.

Apart from a few that have RuntimeException as a base, all exceptions thrown by methods in the Java class library are of a type that you must deal with. In Chapter 8 we will be looking at input and output where the code will be liberally sprinkled with provisions for exceptions being thrown.

> We'll see later in this chapter that when you want to define your own exceptions, you
> do this by subclassing from the class Exception. Wherever your exception can be
> thrown by a method, the compiler will verify either that it is caught in the method, or
> that the method definition indicates that it can be thrown by the method, just as it
> does for the built-in exceptions.

Dealing with Exceptions

As we discussed in the previous sections, if your code can throw exceptions other than those of type Error
or type RuntimeException, (you can take it that we generally include the subclasses when we talk about
Error and RuntimeException exceptions) you must do something about it. Whenever you write code
that can throw an exception, you have a choice. You can supply code within the method to deal with any
exception that is thrown, or you can essentially ignore it by enabling the method containing the exception
throwing code to pass it on to the code that called the method.

Let's first see how you can pass an exception on.

Specifying the Exceptions a Method Can Throw

Suppose you have a method which can throw an exception which is neither a subclass of
RuntimeException nor Error, an IOException for example, because your method involves some file
input and output operations. If the exception isn't caught and disposed of in the method, you must at least
declare that the exception can be thrown. But how do you do that?

You do it simply by adding a throws clause in the definition of the method. Suppose we write a method
that uses the methods from classes that support input/output that are defined in the package java.io.
You'll see in the next chapter that some of these can throw exceptions represented by objects of classes
EOFException and FileNotFoundException. Neither of these are subclasses of RuntimeException
or Error, and so the possibility of an exception being thrown needs to be declared. Since the method can't
handle any exceptions it might throw, for the simple reason that we don't know how to do it yet, it must be
defined as:

```
double myMethod() throws EOFException, FileNotFoundException
{
  // Detail of the method code...
}
```

As the fragment above illustrates, to declare that your method can throw exceptions you just put the
throws keyword after the parameter list for the method. Then add the list of classes for the exceptions that
might be thrown, separated by commas. This has a knock-on effect – if another method calls this method, it
too must take account of the exceptions this method can throw. After all, calling a method that can throw
an exception is clearly code where an exception may be thrown. The calling method definition must either
deal with the exceptions, or declare that it can throw these exceptions as well. It's a simple choice. You
either pass the buck, or decide that the buck stops here. The compiler checks for this and your code will not
compile if you don't do one or the other. The reasons for this will become obvious when we look at the way
a Java program behaves when it encounters an exception.

Handling Exceptions

If you want to deal with the exceptions where they occur, there are three kinds of code block that you can include in a method to handle them - try, catch and finally:

❑ A try block encloses code that may give rise to one or more exceptions. Code that can throw an exception that you want to catch must be in a try block.

❑ A catch block encloses code that is intended to handle exceptions of a particular type that may be thrown in a try block.

❑ The code in a finally block is always executed before the method ends, regardless of whether any exceptions are thrown in the try block.

Let's dig into the detail of try and catch blocks first, then come back to the application of a finally block a little later.

The try Block

When you want to catch an exception, the code in the method which might cause the exception to arise must be enclosed in a try block. Code that can cause exceptions need not be in a try block but, in this case, the method containing the code won't be able to catch any exceptions that are thrown. In this event the method must declare that it can throw the types of exceptions that are not caught.

A try block is simply the keyword try, followed by braces enclosing the code that can throw the exception:

```
try
{
    // Code that can throw one or more exceptions
}
```

Although we are discussing primarily exceptions that you must deal with here, a try block is also necessary if you want to catch exceptions of type Error or RuntimeException. When we come to a working example in a moment, we will use an exception type that you don't have to catch, simply because exceptions of this type are easy to generate.

The catch Block

You enclose the code to handle an exception of a given type in a catch block. The catch block must immediately follow the try block which contains the code that may throw that particular exception. A catch block consists of the keyword catch followed by a parameter between parentheses that identifies the type of exception that the block is to deal with. This is followed by the code to handle the exception enclosed between braces:

```
try
{
    // Code that can throw one or more exceptions
}
```

285

```
catch(ArithmeticException e)
{
  // Code to handle the exception
}
```

This catch block only handles ArithmeticException exceptions. This implies this is the only kind of exception that can be thrown in the try block. If others can be thrown, this won't compile. We will come back to handling multiple exception types in a moment.

In general, the parameter for a catch block must be of type Throwable or one of the subclasses of the class Throwable. If the class that you specify as the parameter type has subclasses, the catch block will be expected to process exceptions of that class, plus all subclasses of the class. If you specified the parameter to a catch block as type RuntimeException for example, the code in the catch block would be invoked for exceptions defined by the class RuntimeException, or any of its subclasses.

We can see how this works with a simple example. It doesn't matter what the code does – the important thing is that it throws an exception we can catch.

Try It Out – Using a try and a catch Block

The following code is really just an exhaustive log of the program's execution:

```
public class TestTryCatch
{
  public static void main(String[] args)
  {
    int i = 1;
    int j = 0;

    try
    {
      System.out.println("Try block entered " + "i = "+ i + " j = "+j);
      System.out.println(i/j);          // Divide by 0 - exception thrown
      System.out.println("Ending try block");
    }
    // Catch the exception
    catch(ArithmeticException e)
    {
      System.out.println("Arithmetic exception caught");
    }

    System.out.println("After try block");
    return;
  }
}
```

If you run the example, you should get the output:

```
Try block entered i = 1 j = 0
Arithmetic exception caught
After try block
```

How It Works

The variable j is initialized to 0, so that the divide operation in the try block will throw an ArithmeticException exception. We must use the variable j here because the Java compiler will not allow you to explicitly divide by zero – that is, the expression i/0 will not compile. The first line in the try block will enable us to track when the try block is entered, and the second line will throw an exception. The third line can only be executed if the exception isn't thrown – which can't occur in this example.

This shows that when the exception is thrown, control transfers immediately to the first statement in the catch block. It's the evaluation of the expression that is the argument to the println() method that throws the exception so the method never gets called. After the catch block has been executed, execution then continues with the statement following the catch block. The statements in the try block following the point where the exception occurred aren't executed. You could try running the example again after changing the value of j to 1 so that no exception is thrown. The output in this case will be:

```
Try block entered i = 1 j = 1
1
Ending try block
After try block
```

From this you can see that the entire try block is executed, then execution continues with the statement after the catch block. Because no arithmetic exception was thrown, the code in the catch block isn't executed.

> **You need to take care when adding try blocks to existing code. A try block is no different to any other block between braces when it comes to variable scope. Variables declared in a try block are only available until the closing brace for the block. It's easy to enclose the declaration of a variable in a try block, and, in doing so, inadvertently limit the scope of the variable and cause compiler errors.**

The catch block itself is a separate scope from the try block. If you want the catch block to output information about objects or values that are set in the try block, make sure the variables are declared in an outer scope.

Try/Catch Bonding

The try and catch blocks are bonded together. You must not separate them by putting statements between the two blocks, or even by putting braces around the try keyword and the try block itself. If you have a loop block that is also a try block, the catch block that follows is also part of the loop. We can see this with a variation of the previous example.

Try It Out – A Loop Block that is a try Block

We can make j a loop control variable and count down so that eventually we get a zero divisor in the loop:

```
public class TestLoopTryCatch
{
  public static void main(String[] args)
  {
    int i = 12;

    for(int j=3 ;j>=-1 ; j--)
  try
    {
      System.out.println("Try block entered " + "i = "+ i + " j = "+j);
      System.out.println(i/j);          // Divide by 0 - exception thrown
      System.out.println("Ending try block");
    }
    // Catch the exception
    catch(ArithmeticException e)
    {
      System.out.println("Arithmetic exception caught");
    }

    System.out.println("After try block");
    return;
  }
}
```

This will produce the output:

```
Try block entered i = 12 j = 3
4
Ending try block
Try block entered i = 12 j = 2
6
Ending try block
Try block entered i = 12 j = 1
12
Ending try block
Try block entered i = 12 j = 0
Arithmetic exception caught
Try block entered i = 12 j = -1
-12
Ending try block
After try block
```

How It Works

The try and catch blocks are all part of the loop since the catch is inextricably bound to the try. You can see this from the output. On the fourth iteration, we get an exception thrown because j is 0. However, after the catch block is executed, we still get one more iteration with j having the value –1.

Even though both the try and catch blocks are within the for loop, they have separate scopes. Variables declared within the try block cease to exist when an exception is thrown. You can try this by declaring an arbitrary variable, k say, in the try block, and then adding a statement to output k in the catch block. Your code will not compile in this case.

Suppose you wanted the loop to end when an exception was thrown. You can easily arrange for this. Just put the whole loop in a try block, thus:

```
   public static void main(String[] args)
   {
     int i = 12;
     try
     {
       System.out.println("Try block entered.");
       for(int j=3 ;j>=-1 ; j--)
       {
         System.out.println("Loop entered " + "i = "+ i + " j = "+j);
         System.out.println(i/j);          // Divide by 0 - exception thrown
       }
       System.out.println("Ending try block");
     }
     // Catch the exception
     catch(ArithmeticException e)
     {
       System.out.println("Arithmetic exception caught");
     }

     System.out.println("After try block");
     return;
   }
```

With this version of main(), the previous program will produce the output:

```
Try block entered.
Loop entered i = 12 j = 3
4
Loop entered i = 12 j = 2
6
Loop entered i = 12 j = 1
12
Loop entered i = 12 j = 0
Arithmetic exception caught
After try block
```

Now we no longer get the output for the last iteration because, when the exception is thrown, control passes to the catch block, which is now outside the loop.

Multiple catch Blocks

If a try block can throw several different kinds of exception, you can put several catch blocks after the try block to handle them.

```
try
{
  // Code that may throw exceptions
}
catch(ArithmeticException e)
{
  // Code for handling ArithmeticException exceptions
}
catch(IndexOutOfBoundsException e)
{
  // Code for handling IndexOutOfBoundsException exceptions
}
// Execution continues here...
```

Exceptions of type `ArithmeticException` will be caught by the first `catch` block, and exceptions of type `IndexOutOfBounds` exception will be caught by the second. Of course, if an `ArithmeticException` exception is thrown, only the code in that `catch` block will be executed. When it is complete, execution continues with the statement following the last `catch` block.

When you need to catch exceptions of several different types for a `try` block, the order of the `catch` blocks can be important. When an exception is thrown, it will be caught by the first `catch` block that has a parameter type that is the same as that of the exception, *or a type that is a superclass of the type of the exception.* An extreme case would be if you specified the `catch` block parameter as type `Exception`. This will catch any exception that is of type `Exception`, or of a class type that is derived from `Exception`, which is virtually all the exceptions you are likely to meet in the normal course of events.

This has implications for multiple `catch` blocks relating to exception class types in a hierarchy. The `catch` blocks must be in sequence with the most derived type first, and the most basic type last. Otherwise your code will not compile. The simple reason for this is that if a `catch` block for a given class type precedes a `catch` block for a type that is derived from the first, the second `catch` block can never be executed.

Suppose you have a `catch` block for exceptions of type `ArithmeticException`, and exceptions of type `Exception` as a catch-all. If you write them in the following sequence, exceptions of type `ArithmeticException` could never reach the second `catch` block as they will always be caught by the first.

```
// Invalid catch block sequence - won't compile!
try
{
  // try block code
}
catch(Exception e)
{
  // Generic handling of exceptions
}
catch(ArithmeticException e)
{
  // Specialized handling for these exceptions
}
```

Of course, this won't get past the compiler – it would be flagged as an error.

To summarize – if you have `catch` blocks for several exception types in the same class hierarchy, you must put the `catch` blocks in order, starting with the lowest subclass first, and then progressing to the highest superclass.

In principle, if you're only interested in generic exceptions, all the error handling code can be localized in one `catch` block for exceptions of the superclass type. However, in general it is more useful, and better practice, to have a `catch` block for each of the specific types of exceptions that a `try` block can throw.

The finally Block

The immediate nature of an exception being thrown means that execution of the `try` block code breaks off, regardless of the importance of the code that follows the point at which the exception was thrown. This introduces the possibility that the exception leaves things in an unsatisfactory state. You might have opened a file, for instance, and because an exception was thrown the code to close the file is not executed.

The `finally` block provides the means to clean up at the end of executing a `try` block. You use a `finally` block when you need to be sure that some particular code is run before a method returns, no matter what exceptions are thrown within the previous `try` block. A `finally` block is always executed, regardless of what happens during the execution of the method. If a file needs to be closed, or a critical resource released, you can guarantee that it will be done if the code to do it is put in a `finally` block.

The `finally` block has a very simple structure:

```
finally
{
   // Clean-up code to be executed last
}
```

Just like a `catch` block, a `finally` block is associated with a particular `try` block, and it must be located immediately following any `catch` blocks for the `try` block. If there are no `catch` blocks then you position the `finally` block immediately after the `try` block. If you don't do this, your program will not compile.

> **The primary purpose for the `try` block is to identify code that may result in an exception being thrown. However, you can use it to contain code that doesn't throw exceptions for the convenience of using a `finally` block. This can be useful when the code in the `try` block has several possible exit points – `break` or `return` statements for example, but you always want to have a specific set of statements executed after the `try` block has been executed to make sure things are tidied up – such as closing any open files. You can put these in a `finally` block. Note: if a value is returned within a `finally` block, this return overrides any return executed in the `try` block.**

Structuring a Method

We've looked at the blocks you can include in the body of a method, but it may not always be obvious how they are combined. The first thing to get straight is that a `try` block, plus any corresponding `catch` blocks, and the `finally` block all bunch together in that order:

```
try
{
   // Code that may throw exceptions...
}
```

```
catch(ExceptionType1 e)
{
  // Code to handle exceptions of type ExceptionType1 or subclass
}
catch(ExceptionType2 e)
{
  // Code to handle exceptions of type ExceptionType2 or subclass
}

// More catch blocks if necessary...

finally
{
  // Code always to be executed after try block code
}
```

You can't have just a `try` block by itself. Each `try` block must always be followed by at least one block that is either a `catch` block or a `finally` block.

You must not include other code between a `try` block and its `catch` blocks, or between the `catch` blocks and the `finally` block. You can have other code that doesn't throw exceptions after the `finally` block, and you can have multiple `try` blocks in a method. In this case, your method might be structured as shown in the following diagram.

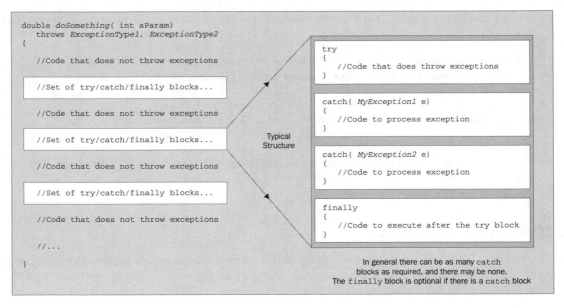

In many cases, a method will only need a single `try` block followed by all the `catch` blocks for the exceptions that need to be processed in the method, perhaps followed by a `finally` block. Java, however, gives you the flexibility to have as many `try` blocks as you want. This makes it possible for you to separate various operations in a method by putting each of them in their own `try` block - an exception thrown as a result of a problem with one operation does not prevent subsequent operations from being executed.

The throws clause that follows the parameter list for the method identifies exceptions that can be thrown in this method, but which aren't caught by any of the catch blocks within the method. We saw this earlier in this chapter. Exceptions that aren't caught can be thrown by code anywhere in the body of the method - in code not enclosed by a try block.

Execution Sequence

We saw how the sequence of execution proceeded with the simple case of a try block and a single catch block. We also need to understand the sequence in which code is executed when we have the try-catch-finally combinations of blocks, when different exceptions are thrown. This is easiest to comprehend by considering an example. We can use the following code to create a range of exceptions and conditions.

Try It Out – Execution Sequence of a `try` Block

It will be convenient, in this example, to use an input statement to pause the program. The method we will use can throw an exception of a type defined in the java.io package. We will start by importing the java.io.IOException class into the source file. We will give the class containing main() the name TryBlockTest, and we will define another method, divide(), in this class that will be called in main(). The overall structure of the TryBlockTest class source file will be:

```java
import java.io.IOException;

public class TryBlockTest
{
  public static void main(String[] args)
  {
    // Code for main()..
  }

  // Divide method
  public static int divide(int[] array, int index)
  {
    // Code for divide()...
  }
}
```

The idea behind the divide() method is to pass it an array and an index as arguments. By choosing the values in the array and the index value judiciously, we can get ArithmeticException and ArrayIndexOutOfBoundsException exceptions thrown. We'll need a try block plus two catch blocks for the exceptions, and we will throw in a finally block for good measure. Here's the code for divide():

```java
public static int divide(int[] array, int index)
{
  try
  {
    System.out.println("\nFirst try block in divide() entered");
    array[index + 2] = array[index]/array[index + 1];
    System.out.println("Code at end of first try block in divide()");
    return array[index + 2];
  }
```

```
      catch(ArithmeticException e)
      {
        System.out.println("Arithmetic exception caught in divide()");
      }
      catch(ArrayIndexOutOfBoundsException e)
      {
        System.out.println(
                "Index-out-of-bounds exception caught in divide()");
      }
      finally
      {
        System.out.println("finally block in divide()");
      }
      System.out.println("Executing code after try block in divide()");
      return array[index + 2];
    }
```

We can define the main() method with the following code:

```
  public static void main(String[] args)
  {
    int[] x = {10, 5, 0};                  // Array of three integers

    // This block only throws an exception if method divide() does
    try
    {
      System.out.println("First try block in main() entered");
      System.out.println("result = " + divide(x,0));  // No error
      x[1] = 0;                            // Will cause a divide by zero
      System.out.println("result = " + divide(x,0));  // Arithmetic error
      x[1] = 1;                            // Reset to prevent divide by zero
      System.out.println("result = " + divide(x,1));  // Index error
    }
    catch(ArithmeticException e)
    {
      System.out.println("Arithmetic exception caught in main()");
    }
    catch(ArrayIndexOutOfBoundsException e)
    {
      System.out.println(
                "Index-out-of-bounds exception caught in main()");
    }

    System.out.println("Outside first try block in main()");
    System.out.println("\nPress Enter to exit");

    // This try block is just to pause the program before returning
    try
    {
      System.out.println("In second try block in main()");
      System.in.read();                    // Pauses waiting for input...
      return;
    }
    catch(IOException e)             // The read() method can throw exceptions
```

```
    {
        System.out.println("I/O exception caught in main()");
    }
    finally                          // This will always be executed
    {
        System.out.println("finally block for second try block in main()");
    }

        System.out.println("Code after second try block in main()");
    }
```

Because the read() method for the object in (this object represents the standard input stream, analogous to out) can throw an I/O exception, it must itself be called in a try block and have an associated catch block, unless we chose to add a throws clause to the header line of main().
If you run the example it will produce the output:

```
First try block in main()entered

First try block in divide() entered
Code at end of first try block in divide()
finally block in divide()
result = 2

First try block in divide() entered
Arithmetic exception caught in divide()
finally block in divide()
Executing code after try block in divide()
result = 2

First try block in divide() entered
Index-out-of-bounds exception caught in divide
finally block in divide()
Executing code after try block in divide()
Index-out-of-bounds exception caught in main()
Outside first try block in main()

Press Enter to exit
In second try block in main()

finally block for second try block in main()
```

How It Works

All the try, catch and finally blocks in the example have output statements so we can trace the sequence of execution.

Within the divide() method the code in the try block can throw an arithmetic exception if the element array[index + 1] of the array passed to it is 0. It can also throw an ArrayIndexOutOfBounds exception in the try block if the index value passed to it is negative, or it results in index + 2 being beyond the array limits. Both these exceptions are caught by one or other of the catch blocks so they will not be apparent in the calling method main().

Note, however, that the last statement in divide() can also throw an index-out-of-bounds exception:

```
return array[index+2];
```

This is outside the `try` block, and will not, therefore, be caught but will be thrown by the method when it is called in `main()`. However, we aren't obliged to declare that the `divide()` method throws this exception because the `ArrayIndexOutOfBoundsException` class is a subclass of `RuntimeException`, and is therefore exempted from the obligation to deal with it.

The method `main()` has two `try` blocks. The first `try` block encloses three calls to the method `divide()`. The first call will execute without error; the second call will cause an arithmetic exception in the method; and the third call will cause an index-out-of-bounds exception. There are two `catch` blocks for the first `try` block in `main()` to deal with these two potential exceptions.

The `read()` method in the second `try` block in `main()` can cause an I/O exception to be thrown. Since this is one of the exceptions that the compiler will check for, we must either put the statement that calls the `read()` method in a `try` block, and have a `catch` block to deal with the exception, or declare that `main()` throws the `IOException` exception. If neither is done, the program will not compile.

Using the `read()` method in this way has the effect of pausing the program until the *Enter* key is pressed. We'll be looking in detail at `read()`, and other I/O methods, in the next chapter. The class `IOException` is in the package `java.io`, so we need the `import` statement for this class because we refer to it in the `catch` block. Remember that only classes defined in `java.lang` are included in your program automatically.

Normal Execution of a Method

The first line of output from the example, `TryBlockTest`, indicates that execution of the `try` block in `main()` has begun. The next block of four lines of output from the example are the result of a straightforward execution of the method `divide()`. No exceptions occur in `divide()`, so no `catch` blocks are executed.

The code at the end of the method `divide()`, following the `catch` blocks, isn't executed because the `return` statement in the `try` block ends the execution of the method. However, the `finally` block in `divide()` is executed before the return to the calling method occurs. If you comment out the `return` statement at the end of the `divide()` method's `try` block and run the example again, the code that follows the `finally` block will be executed.

The sequence of execution when no exceptions occur is shown in the diagram.

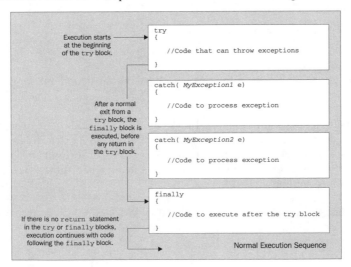

Normal Execution Sequence

The previous diagram illustrates the normal sequence of execution in an arbitrary `try-catch-finally` set of blocks. If there's a `return` statement in the `try` block, this will be executed immediately after the `finally` block completes execution - so this prevents the execution of any code following the `finally` block. A `return` statement in a `finally` block will cause an immediate return to the calling point and the code following the `finally` block wouldn't be executed in this case.

Execution when an Exception is Thrown

The next block of five lines in the output correspond to an `ArithmeticException` being thrown and caught in the method `divide()` as a result of the value of the second element in the array x being zero. When the exception occurs, execution of the code in the `try` block is stopped, and you can see that the code that follows the `catch` block for the exception in the method `divide()` is then executed. The `finally` block executes next, followed by the code after the `finally` block. The value in the last element of the array isn't changed from its previous value, because the exception occurs during the computation of the new value, before the result is stored.

The general sequence of execution in an arbitrary `try-catch-finally` set of blocks when an exception occurs is shown here.

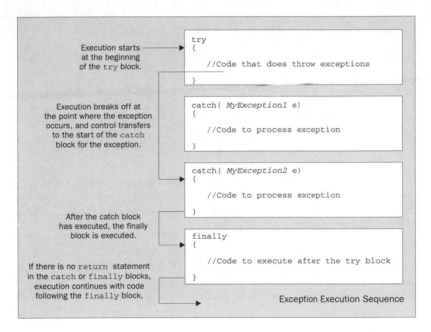

Execution of the `try` block stops at the point where the exception occurs, and the code in the `catch` block for the exception is executed immediately. If there is a `return` statement in the `catch` block, this isn't executed until after the `finally` block has been executed. As discussed earlier, if a `return` statement that returns a value is executed within a `finally` block, that value will be returned, not the value from any previous `return` statement.

Execution when an Exception is not Caught

The next block of six lines in the output are a consequence of the third call to the method `divide()`. This causes an `ArrayIndexOutOfBoundsException` to be thrown in the `try` block, which is then caught. However, the code at the end of the method which is executed after the `finally` block, throws another exception of this type. This can't be caught in the method `divide()` because the statement causing it isn't in a `try` block. Since this exception isn't caught in the method `divide()`, the method terminates immediately and the same exception is thrown in `main()` at the point where the method was called. This causes the code in the relevant `catch` block in `main()` to be executed in consequence.

An exception that isn't caught in a method is always propagated upwards to the calling method. It will continue to propagate up through each level of calling method until either it is caught, or the uppermost-level method is reached. If it isn't caught at the top-level, the program will terminate and a suitable message be displayed. This situation is illustrated here.

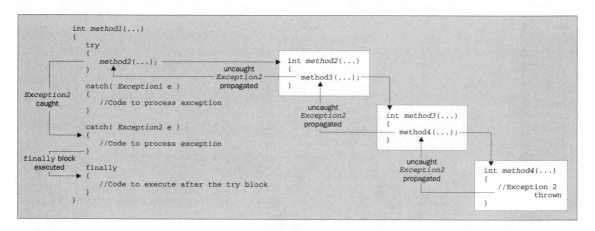

This shows `method1()` calling `method2()` which calls `method3()`, which calls `method4()` in which an exception of type `Exception2` is thrown. This exception isn't caught in `method4()` so execution of `method4()` ceases and the exception is thrown in `method3()`. It isn't caught, and continues to be rethrown until it reaches `method1()` where there's a `catch` block to handle it.

In our *Try It Out*, execution continues in `main()` with the output statements outside the first `try` block. The `read()` method pauses the program until you press the *Enter* key. No exception is thrown, and execution ends after the code in the `finally` block is executed. The `finally` block is tied to the `try` block that immediately precedes it, and is executed even though there's a `return` statement in the `try` block.

Nested try Blocks

We will not be going into these in detail, but you should note that you can have nested `try` blocks, as illustrated in this diagram.

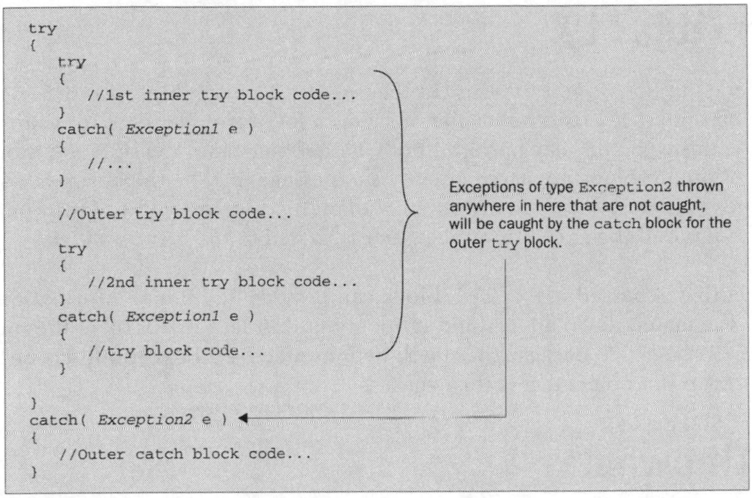

```
try
{
    try
    {
        //1st inner try block code...
    }
    catch( Exception1 e )
    {
        //...
    }

    //Outer try block code...

    try
    {
        //2nd inner try block code...
    }
    catch( Exception1 e )
    {
        //try block code...
    }

}
catch( Exception2 e )
{
    //Outer catch block code...
}
```

Exceptions of type `Exception2` thrown anywhere in here that are not caught, will be caught by the `catch` block for the outer `try` block.

The `catch` blocks for the outer `try` block can catch any exceptions that are thrown, but not caught, by any code within the block, including code within inner `try-catch` blocks. In the example shown, the `catch` block for the outer `try` block will catch any exception of type `Exception2`. Such exceptions could originate anywhere within the outer `try` block. The illustration shows two levels of nesting, but you can specify more if you know what you're doing.

Rethrowing Exceptions

Even though you may need to recognize that an exception has occurred in a method by implementing a `catch` clause for it, this is not necessarily the end of the matter. In many situations, the calling program may need to know about it – perhaps because it will affect the continued operation of the program, or because the calling program may be able to compensate for the problem.

If you need to pass an exception that you have caught on to the calling program, you can rethrow it from within the `catch` block using a `throw` statement. For example:

```
try
{
    // Code that originates an arithmetic exception
}
catch(ArithmeticException e)
{
    // Deal with the exception here
    throw e;                // Rethrow the exception to the calling program
}
```

The `throw` statement is the keyword `throw` followed by the exception object to be thrown. When we look at how to define our own exceptions later in this chapter, we'll be using exactly the same mechanism to throw them.

Exception Objects

Well, you now understand how to put try blocks together with catch blocks and finally blocks in your methods. You may be thinking, at this point, that it seems a lot of trouble to go to, just to display a message when an exception is thrown. You may be right, but whether you can do very much more depends on the nature and context of the problem. In many situations a message may be the best you can do, although you can produce messages that are a bit more informative than those we've used so far in our examples. For one thing we have totally ignored the exception object that is passed to the catch block.

The exception object that is passed to a catch block can provide additional information about the nature of the problem that originated it. To understand more about this, let's first look at the members of the base class for exceptions Throwable, because these will be inherited by all exception classes and are therefore contained in every exception object that is thrown.

The Class Throwable

The class Throwable is the class from which all Java exception classes are derived – that is, every exception object will contain the methods defined in this class. The class Throwable has two constructors, a default constructor, and a constructor that accepts an argument of type String. The String object that is passed to the constructor is used to provide a description of the nature of the problem causing the exception. Both constructors are public.

Objects of type Throwable contain two items of information about an exception:

❑   A message, that we have just referred to as being initialized by a constructor

❑   A record of the **execution stack** at the time the object was created

The execution stack keeps track of all the methods that are in execution at any given instant. It provides the means whereby executing a return gets back to the calling point for a method. The record of the execution stack that is stored in the exception object will consist of the line number in the source code where the exception originated followed by a trace of the method calls that immediately preceded the point at which the exception occurred. This is made up of the fully qualified name for each of the methods called, plus the line number in the source file where each method call occurred. The method calls are in sequence with the most recent method call appearing first. This will help you to understand how this point in the program was reached.

The Throwable class has the following public methods that enable you to access the message and the stack trace:

Method	Description
getMessage()	This returns the contents of the message, describing the current exception. This will typically be the fully qualified name of the exception class (it will be a subclass of Throwable), and a brief description of the exception.

Method	Description
printStackTrace()	This will output the message and the stack trace to the standard error output stream – which is the screen in the case of a console program.
printStackTrace (PrintStream s)	This is the same as the previous method except that you specify the output stream as an argument.

There's another method, fillInStackTrace(), which will update the stack trace to the point at which this method is called. For example, if you put a call to this method in the catch block:

```
e.fillInStackTrace();
```

The line number recorded in the stack record for the method in which the exception occurred will be the line where fillInStackTrace() is called. The main use of this is when you want to rethrow an exception (so it will be caught by the calling method) and record the point at which it is rethrown. For example:

```
e.fillInStackTrace();        // Record the throw point
throw e;                     // Rethrow the exception
```

In practice, it's often more useful to throw an exception of your own. We'll see how to define your own exceptions in the next section, but first, let's exercise some of the methods defined in the Throwable class, and see the results.

Try It Out – Dishing the Dirt on Exceptions

The easiest way to try out some of the methods we've just discussed is to make some judicious additions to the catch blocks in the divide() method we have in the TryBlockTest class example:

```
public static int divide(int[] array, int index)
{
  try
  {
    System.out.println("\nFirst try block in divide() entered");
    array[index + 2] = array[index]/array[index + 1];
    System.out.println("Code at end of first try block in divide()");
    return array[index + 2];
  }
  catch(ArithmeticException e)
  {
    System.out.println("Arithmetic exception caught in divide()\n" +
                       "\nMessage in exception object:\n\t" +
                       e.getMessage());
    System.out.println("\nStack trace output:\n");
    e.printStackTrace();
    System.out.println("\nEnd of stack trace output\n");
  }
  catch(ArrayIndexOutOfBoundsException e)
  {
```

```
        System.out.println(
                        "Index-out-of-bounds exception caught in divide()\n" +
                        "\nMessage in exception object:\n\t" + e.getMessage());
        System.out.println("\nStack trace output:\n");
        e.printStackTrace();
        System.out.println("\nEnd of stack trace output\n");
      }
      finally
      {
        System.out.println("finally clause in divide()");
      }
      System.out.println("Executing code after try block in divide()");
      return array[index + 2];
    }
```

If you recompile the program and run it again, it will produce all the output, as before, but with extra information when exceptions are thrown in the divide() method. The new output generated for the ArithmeticException will be:

```
Message in exception object:
        / by zero

Stack trace output:

java.lang.ArithmeticException: / by zero
        at TryBlockTest.divide(TryBlockTest.java:54)
        at TryBlockTest.main(TryBlockTest.java:15)

End of stack trace output
```

The additional output generated for the ArrayIndexOutOfBoundsException will be:

```
Message in exception object:
        3

Stack trace output:

java.lang.ArrayIndexOutOfBoundsException: 3
        at TryBlockTest.divide(TryBlockTest.java:54)
        at TryBlockTest.main(TryBlockTest.java:17)

End of stack trace output
```

How It Works

The extra lines of code in each of the catch blocks in the divide() method output the message associated with the exception object e, by calling its getMessage() method. We could have just put e here which would invoke the toString() method for e and, in this case, the class name for e would precede the message. These are a couple of extra println() calls around the call to printStackTrace() to make it easier to find the stack trace in the output.

The first stack trace, for the arithmetic exception, indicates that the error originated at line 54 in the source file, `TryBlockText.java`, and the last method call was at line 15 in the same source file. The second stack trace provides similar information about the index-out-of-bounds exception, including the offending index value. As you can see, with the stack trace output, it's very easy to see where the error occurred, and how this point in the program was reached.

Standard Exceptions

The majority of predefined exception classes in Java don't add further information about the conditions that created the exception. The type alone serves to differentiate one exception from another in most cases. This general lack of additional information is because it can only be gleaned, in the majority of cases, by prior knowledge of the computation that is being carried out when the exception occurs, and the only person who is privy to that is you, since you're writing the program.

This should spark the glimmer of an idea. If you need more information about the circumstances surrounding an exception, you're going to have to obtain it, and, equally important, communicate it to the appropriate point in your program. This leads to the notion of defining your own exceptions.

Defining your own Exceptions

There are two basic reasons for defining your own exception classes:

❑   You want to add information when a standard exception occurs, and you can do this by rethrowing an object of your own exception class.

❑   You may have error conditions that arise in your code that warrant the distinction of a special exception class.

However, you should bear in mind that there's a lot of overhead in throwing exceptions, so it is not a valid substitute for 'normal' recovery code that you would expect to be executed frequently. If you have recovery code that will be executed often, then it doesn't belong in a `catch` block, rather in something like an `if-then-else` loop.

Let's see how to create our own exceptions.

Defining an Exception Class

Your exception classes must always have `Throwable` as a superclass, otherwise they will not define an exception. Although you can derive them from any of the standard exceptions, your best policy is to derive them from the `Exception` class. This will allow the compiler to keep track of where such exceptions are thrown in your program, and check that they are either caught or declared as thrown in a method. If you use `RuntimeException` or one of its subclasses, the compiler checking for `catch` blocks of your exception class will be suppressed.

Let's go through an example of how you define an exception class:

```
public class DreadfulProblemException extends Exception
{
  // Constructors
  public DreadfulProblemException(){ }        // Default constructor

  public DreadfulProblemException(String s)
  {
    super(s);                          // Call the base class constructor
  }
}
```

This is the minimum you should supply. By convention, your exception should include a default constructor and a constructor that accepts a String object as an argument. The message stored in the superclass, Exception (in fact in Throwable, which is the superclass of Exception) will automatically be initialized with the name of your class, whichever constructor for your class objects is used. The String passed to the second constructor will be appended to the name of the class to form the message stored in the exception object.

Of course, you can add other constructors. In general, you'll want to do so, particularly when you're rethrowing your own exception after a standard exception has been thrown. In addition, you'll typically want to add instance variables to the class that store additional information about the problem, plus methods that will enable the code in a catch block to get at the data. Since your exception class is ultimately derived from Throwable, the stack trace information will be automatically available for your exceptions.

Throwing your Own Exception

As we saw earlier, we throw an exception with a statement that consists of the keyword throw, followed by an exception object. This means you can throw your own exception with the statements:

```
DreadfulProblemException e = new DreadfulProblemException();
throw e;
```

The method will cease execution at this point – unless the code snippet above is in a try or a catch block with an associated finally clause; the contents of which will be executed before the method ends. The exception will be thrown in the calling program at the point where this method was called. The message in the exception object will only consist of the qualified name of our exception class.

If you wanted to add a specific message to the exception, you could define it as:

```
DreadfulProblemException e = new DreadfulProblemException("Uh-Oh, trouble.");
```

We're using a different constructor here. In this case the message stored in the superclass will be a string which consists of the class name with the string passed to the constructor appended to it. The getMessage() method inherited from Throwable will, therefore, return a String object containing the string:

```
"DreadfulProblemException: Uh-Oh, trouble."
```

You can also create an exception object and throw it in a single statement. For example:

```
throw new DreadfulProblemException("Terrible difficulties");
```

In all the examples, the stack trace record inherited from the superclass, `Throwable`, will be set up automatically.

An Exception Handling Strategy

You should think through what you want to achieve with the exception handling code in your program. There are no hard and fast rules. In some situations you may be able to correct a problem and enable your program to continue as though nothing happened. In other situations an error message and a fast exit will be the best approach – a fast exit being achieved by calling the `exit()` method in the `System` class. Here we'll take a look at some of the things you need to weigh up when deciding how to handle exceptions.

Consider the last example where we handled arithmetic and index-out-of-bounds exceptions in the method, `divide()`. While this was a reasonable demonstration of the way the various blocks worked, it wasn't a satisfactory way of dealing with the exceptions in the program, for at least two reasons. First, it does not make sense to catch the arithmetic exceptions in the `divide()` method without passing them on to the calling method. After all, it was the calling method that set the data up, and only the calling program has the potential to recover the situation. Second, by handling the exceptions completely in the `divide()` method, we allow the calling program to continue execution, without any knowledge of the problem that arose. In a real situation this would undoubtedly create chaos, as further calculations would proceed with erroneous data.

We could have simply ignored the exceptions in the `divide()` method. This might not be a bad approach in this particular situation, but the first problem the calling program would have is determining the source of the exception. After all, such exceptions might also arise in the calling program itself. A second consideration could arise if the `divide()` method was more complicated. There could be several places where such exceptions might be thrown, and the calling method would have a hard time distinguishing them.

An Example of an Exception Class

Another possibility is to catch the exceptions in the method where they originate, then pass them on to the calling program. You can pass them on by throwing new exceptions that provide more **granularity** in identifying the problem (by having more than one exception type, or by providing additional data within the new exception type). For example, you could define more than one exception class of your own that represented an `ArithmeticException`, where each reflected the specifics of a particular situation. This situation is illustrated here.

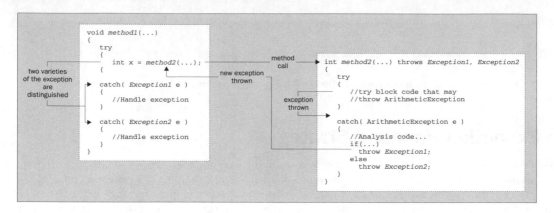

This shows how two different circumstances causing an `ArithmeticException` in `method2()`, are differentiated in the calling method, `method1()`. The method, `method2()`, can throw either an exception of type `Exception1`, or of type `Exception2`, depending on the analysis that is made in the `catch` block for the `ArithmeticException` type. The calling method has a separate `catch` block for each of the exceptions that may be thrown.

You could also define a new exception class that had instance variables to identify the problem more precisely. Let's suppose that in the last example, we wanted to provide more information to the calling program about the error that caused each exception in the `divide()` method. The primary exception can be either an `ArithmeticException` or an `ArrayIndexOutOfBoundsException`, but since we're dealing with a specific context for these errors we could give the calling program more information by throwing our own exceptions.

Let's take the `ArithmeticException` case as a model and define our own exception class to use in the program to help identify the reason for the error more precisely.

Try It Out – Define Your Own Exception Class

We can define the class which will correspond to an `ArithmeticException` in the method `divide()` as:

```
public class ZeroDivideException extends Exception
{
  private int index = -1;        // Index of array element causing error

  // Default Constructor
  public ZeroDivideException(){ }

  // Standard constructor
  public ZeroDivideException(String s)
  {
    super(s);                            // Call the base constructor
  }

  public ZeroDivideException(int index)
  {
    super("/ by zero");                  // Call the base constructor
```

```
    this.index = index;                        // Set the index value
    }

    // Get the array index value for the error
    public int getIndex()
    {
      return index;                            // Return the index value
    }
  }
```

How It Works

As we've derived the class from the class Exception, the compiler will check that the exceptions thrown are either caught, or identified as thrown in a method. Our class will inherit all the members of the class Throwable via the Exception class, so we'll get the stack trace record and the message for the exception maintained for free. It will also inherit the toString() method which is satisfactory in this context, but this could be overridden if desired.

We've added a data member, index, to store the index value of the zero divisor in the array passed to divide(). This will give the calling program a chance to fix this value if appropriate in the catch block for the exception. In this case the catch block would also need to include code that would enable the divide() method to be called again with the corrected array.

Let's now put it to work in our first TryBlockTest code example.

Try It Out – Using the Exception Class

We need to use the class in two contexts – in the method divide() when we catch a standard ArithmeticException, and in the calling method, main(), to catch the new exception. Let's modify divide() first:

```
public static int divide(int[] array, int index)
                                   throws ZeroDivideException
{
  try
  {
    System.out.println("First try block in divide() entered");
    array[index + 2] = array[index]/array[index + 1];
    System.out.println("Code at end of first try block in divide()");
    return array[index + 2];
  }
  catch(ArithmeticException e)
  {
    System.out.println("Arithmetic exception caught in divide()");
    throw new ZeroDivideException(index + 1);   // Throw new exception
  }
  catch(ArrayIndexOutOfBoundsException e)
  {
    System.out.println(
                "Index-out-of-bounds index exception caught in divide()");
  }
  System.out.println("Executing code after try block in divide()");
  return array[index + 2];
}
```

The first change is to add the `throws` clause to the method definition. Without this we'll get an error message from the compiler. The second change adds a statement to the `catch` block for `ArithmeticException` exceptions which throws a new exception.

This new exception needs to be caught in the calling method `main()`:

```
public static void main(String[] args)
{
  int[] x = {10, 5, 0};                    // Array of three integers

  // This block only throws an exception if method divide() does
  try
  {
    System.out.println("First try block in main()entered");
    System.out.println("result = " + divide(x,0));  // No error
    x[1] = 0;                              // Will cause a divide by zero
    System.out.println("result = " + divide(x,0));  // Arithmetic error
    x[1] = 1;                              // Reset to prevent divide by zero
    System.out.println("result = " + divide(x,1));  // Index error
  }
  catch(ZeroDivideException e)
  {
    int index = e.getIndex();              // Get the index for the error
    if(index > 0)                          // Verify it is valid
    {                                      // Now fix up the array...
      x[index] = 1;                        // ...set the divisor to 1...
      x[index + 1] = x[index - 1];         // ...and set the result
      System.out.println("Zero divisor corrected to " + x[index]);
    }
  }
  catch(ArithmeticException e)
  {
    System.out.println("Arithmetic exception caught in main()");
  }
  catch(ArrayIndexOutOfBoundsException e)
  {
    System.out.println
            ("Index-out-of-bounds exception caught in main()");
  }
  System.out.println("Outside first try block in main()");
}
```

How It Works

All we need to add is the `catch` block for the new exception. We need to make sure that the index value for the divisor stored in the exception object is positive so that another exception is not thrown when we fix up the array. As we arbitrarily set the array element that contained the zero divisor to 1, it makes sense to set the array element holding the result to the same as the dividend. We can then let the method `main()` stagger on.

> A point to bear in mind is that the last two statements in the `try` block will not have been executed. After the `catch` block has been executed, the method continues with the code following the `try-catch` block set. In practice you would need to consider whether to ignore this. One possibility is to put the whole of the `try-catch` block code in `main()` in a loop that would normally only run one iteration, but where this could be altered to run additional iterations by setting a flag in the `catch` block.

This is a rather artificial example – so what sort of circumstances could justify this kind of fixing up of the data in a program? If the data originated through some kind of instrumentation measuring physical parameters such as temperatures or pressures, the data may contain spurious zero values from time to time. Rather than abandon the whole calculation you might well want to amend these as they occurred, and press on to process the rest of the data.

Summary

In this chapter you have learned what exceptions are and how to deal with them in your programs. You should make sure that you consider exception handling as an integral part of developing your Java programs. The robustness of your program code depends on how effectively you deal with exceptions that can be thrown within it.

The important concepts we have explored in this chapter are:

❑　Exceptions identify errors that arise in your program.

❑　Exceptions are objects of subclasses of the class `Throwable`.

❑　Java includes a set of standard exceptions that may be thrown automatically, as a result of errors in your code, or may be thrown by methods in the standard classes in Java.

❑　If a method throws exceptions that aren't caught, and aren't represented by subclasses of the class `Error`, or by subclasses of the class `RuntimeException`, then you must identify the exception classes in a `throws` clause in the method definition.

❑　If you want to handle an exception in a method, you must place the code that may generate the exception in a `try` block. A method may have several `try` blocks.

❑　Exception handling code is placed in a `catch` block that immediately follows the `try` block that contains the code that can throw the exception. A `try` block can have multiple `catch` blocks that deal with different types of exception.

❑　A `finally` block is used to contain code that must be executed after the execution of a `try` block, regardless of how the `try` block execution ends. A `finally` block will always be executed before execution of the method ends.

❑　You can throw an exception by using a `throw` statement. You can throw an exception anywhere in a method. You can also rethrow an existing exception in a `catch` block to pass it to the calling method.

❑　You can define your own exception classes which, in general, should be derived from the class `Exception`.

Exercises

1. Write a program that will generate exceptions of type NullPointerException, NegativeArraySizeException and IndexOutOfBoundsException. Record the catching of each exception by displaying the message stored in the exception object, and the stack trace record.

2. Add an exception class to the last example that will differentiate between the index-out-of-bounds error possibilities, rethrow an appropriate object of this exception class in divide(), and handle the exception in main().

3. Write a program that calls a method which throws an exception of type ArithmeticException at a random iteration in a for loop. Catch the exception in the method, and pass the iteration count when the exception occurred to the calling method, by using an object of an exception class you define.

4. Add a finally block to the method in the previous example to output the iteration count when the method exits.

Streams, Files and Stream Output

The package that supports stream input/output is `java.io`, and it is vast. It defines a large number of classes, many of which have many of methods. There are also classes in the package, `java.util.zip`, that are closely related to those in `java.io`. Consequently, we need two chapters to cover this topic adequately. In this chapter, we will discuss stream output and, in the next, stream input.

In this chapter, you will see how to create and write to files. The next chapter deals primarily with stream input including how to read the files created in this chapter. Although we won't be able to cover all of the classes in detail, we will go into enough depth for you to be able to get to grips with anything else you need without too much difficulty. Further details can be found in the JDK documentation.

By the end of this chapter, you will have learned:

❑   What a stream is and what classes Java provides to support stream operations

❑   How to use `File` objects to create and test files and directories

❑   How to write to a stream

❑   How to write a file to a ZIP archive

❑   How to output numeric data to a stream in a fixed width field

Understanding Streams

Java file input and output involves using **streams**. A **stream** is an abstract representation of an input or output device that is a source of, or destination for, data. You can write data to a stream and read data from a stream. You can visualize a stream as a sequence of bytes that flows into or out of your program.

When you write data to a stream, the stream is called an **output stream**. The output stream can go to any device to which a sequence of bytes can be transferred, such as a file on a hard disk, a file on a remote system or a printer. An output stream can also go to your display screen, but only at the expense of limiting it to a fraction of its true capability. When you write to your display screen using a stream, it can only display characters, not graphical output, which requires more specialized support. (See Chapter 12 onwards.)

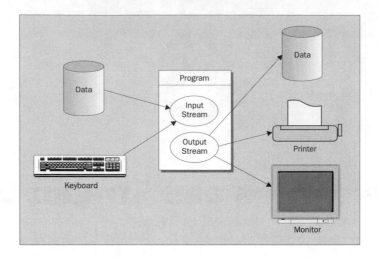

You read data from an **input stream**. In principle this can be any serial source of data but is typically a disk file, the keyboard or a remote computer.

File input and output for the machine on which your program is executing is only available to Java applications under normal circumstances. It is not usually available to Java applets. Otherwise, a Java applet embedded in a Web page could trash your hard disk. An IOException will normally be thrown by any operation on disk files on the local machine in a Java applet. However, the directory containing the applet and its subdirectories are freely accessible to the applet. Also, the security features in Java can be used to control what an applet (and an application running under a Security Manager) can access so that an applet can access files or other resources *for which it has explicit permission*.

The main reason for using a stream as the basis for input and output operations in Java is to make your program code for these operations independent of the device involved. This has two advantages. First, you don't have to worry about the detailed mechanics of each device, which are taken care of behind the scenes. Second, your program will work for a variety of input/output devices without any changes to the source, or even to the object code.

Stream input and output methods generally permit very small amounts of data, such as a single character or byte, to be written or read in a single operation. Sending data transfers like this to a physical device, such as a disk drive, would be extremely inefficient, so a stream is often equipped with a **buffer**, in which case it is called a **buffered stream**. A buffer is simply a block of memory that is used to batch up data transfers to or from an external device.

Buffered streams ensure that the actual data transfers between memory and an external device are in sufficiently large chunks to make the input/output operations reasonably efficient.

When you write to a buffered output stream, the data is sent to the buffer, not to the external device. The amount of data in the buffer is tracked automatically, and the data is usually sent to the device when the buffer is full. However, you will sometimes want the data in the buffer to be sent to the device before the buffer is full, and there are methods provided to do this. This operation is usually termed **flushing** the buffer.

Buffered input streams work in a similar way. Any read operation on a buffered input stream will read data from the buffer, and when the buffer is empty, a complete buffer-full of data will be read automatically from the device, if sufficient data is available.

Stream Input/Output Operations

The `java.io` package supports two types of stream, **binary streams**, which contain binary data, and **character streams**, which contain character data. When you write data to a stream as a series of bytes, that is binary data, it is written to the stream exactly as it appears in memory. No transformation of the data takes place. Numerical values are just written as a series of bytes. As you know, Java stores its characters internally as Unicode characters, so when you write Unicode characters to a stream as binary data, each 16-bit character is written as two bytes, the high byte being written first.

Character streams are used for storing and retrieving text. You also use character streams to read a text file not written by a Java program. All numeric data is converted to a textual representation before being written to the stream. This involves formatting the data to generate a character representation of the data value. Reading numeric data from a stream that contains text involves much more work than reading binary data. Reading from the stream requires that you determine how many characters make up a single numeric value and convert the characters from the stream appropriately. You need to recognize where each numerical value begins and ends, and convert the token – the sequence of characters representing the value – to the binary form of the value. This is illustrated below.

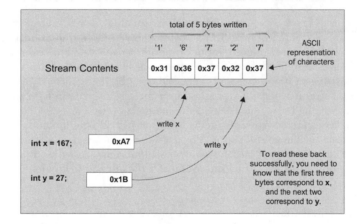

When you write strings to a stream as character data, the Unicode characters are automatically converted to the local representation of the characters, as used by the host machine, and these are then written to the file. When you read a string, the data in the file is automatically converted from the local machine representation to Unicode characters. With character streams, your program reads and writes Unicode characters, but the file will contain characters in the equivalent character encoding used by the local computer. (See also locales in Chapter 10.)

The underlying stream, or what ends up in an external file, is always just a sequence of bytes, whether you write binary or character data.

The Classes for Input and Output

There are quite a number of classes involved in stream input and output, but as you will see, they form a very logical structure. Once you see how they are related, you shouldn't have much trouble using them. We will work through the class hierarchy from the top down, so you will be able to see how the classes hang together, and how you can combine them in different ways to suit different situations.

The package `java.io` contains the classes that provide the foundation for Java's support for stream I/O.

Class	Description
File	An object of this class represents a pathname either to a file that you will access for input or output or to a directory.
OutputStream	The base class for byte stream output operations.
InputStream	The base class for byte stream input operations.
Writer	The base class for character stream output operations.
Reader	The base class for character stream input operations.
RandomAccessFile	This class provides support for random access to a file.

`InputStream`, `OutputStream`, `Reader` and `Writer` are all `abstract` classes. As you are well aware by now, you cannot create instances of an abstract class – these classes only serve as a base from which to derive classes with more concrete input or output capabilities. However, all four of these classes declare methods that define a basic set of operations for the streams that they represent, so the fundamental characteristics of how a stream is accessed is set by these classes. Generally, the `InputStream` and `OutputStream` classes and their subclasses represent byte streams and provide the means of reading and writing binary data within the methods of those classes. The `Reader` and `Writer` classes and their subclasses are not streams themselves, but provide the methods you use for reading and writing byte streams as character streams. Thus, a `Reader` or `Writer` object is often created using an underlying `InputStream` or `OutputStream` object that represents the stream. As we will see, `Reader` and `Writer` objects can also be used to transfer data to and from memory for data conversion or formatting purposes.

We will look at each of these four classes first to get an overview of how operations with streams work. We will then look at the classes that are derived from them and try some of them out in practical examples.

> **First, a note of caution. Before running any of the examples in this chapter, be sure to back up the files that they operate on, and the directory that contains the files. Ideally, you should set up a separate directory for storing the files that you are using when you are testing programs.**
>
> **The old adage, "If anything can go wrong, it will," applies particularly in this context, as does the complementary principle, "If anything can't go wrong, it will". Remember also that the probability of something going wrong increases in proportion to the inconvenience it is likely to cause.**

The file streams that you define using classes derived from `InputStream` and `OutputStream` and operate on using `Reader` and `Writer` are inherently serial in nature. You cannot process them randomly. For storing and retrieving data in a random access file, you must use the `RandomAccessFile` class. There is no fundamental difference between a file created as a serial byte stream and a file created using a `RandomAccessFile` object. The class object that you use to access a file only affects the way in which you deal with the data in the file.

A good place to start is with the `File` class, since you use objects of this class to identify the physical file that you work with whenever you define a stream object.

Defining a File

Keep in mind that a `File` object represents a pathname to a physical file or directory on your hard disk, not a stream. You can create a stream object corresponding to a specific file from a `File` object that represents the pathname for the file, as we will see. As well as enabling you to create objects that represent paths to files or directories, the `File` class also provides several methods for you to test the objects you create. You can determine whether an object represents a path to an existing file or to a directory, for example. You can also modify a `File` object in a number of ways.

When creating `File` objects, you have a choice of three constructors. The simplest accepts a `String` object as an argument, which specifies the path for a file or a directory. For example, you could write the statement:

```
File myDir = new File("F:/jdk1.3/src/java/io");
```

On Windows 95, 98 or NT/2000, you can also use an escaped back slash separator, '\\', instead of '/'.

To specify a pathname to a file, you just need to make sure that the string that you pass as an argument to the constructor does refer to a file. For example, the statement,

```
File myFile = new File("F:/jdk1.3/src/java/io/File.java");
```

sets the object, `myFile`, to correspond to the source file for the definition of the class, `File`.
You can also create a `File` object that represents a pathname for a file by specifying a `File` object that corresponds to the path for the directory and then specifying the file name separately. You just use a version of the `File` constructor that accepts two arguments. The first argument to the constructor is a `File` object that represents the directory, and the second argument is a `String` object referencing the file name. For example, to identify the source file for the definition of the class `File`, we could write:

```
File myDir = new File("F:/jdk1.3/src/java/io");      // Object for directory
File myFile = new File(myDir, "File.java");          // Object for the file
```

The first statement creates a file object that refers to the directory for the package `io`, and the second statement creates a file object that corresponds to the file, `File.java`, in that directory. This approach is handy when you need `File` objects for several files in a given directory.

The third constructor also accepts two arguments, but the first argument is a `String` object identifying the directory, rather than a `File` object. The second argument is still a `String` object referring to the file name. We could use this constructor to achieve the same result as the previous two statements:

```
File myFile = new File("F:/jdk1.3/src/java/io", "File.java");
```

Having a `File` object defining a directory can be useful if you intend to process more than one file in it. With a separate `File` object representing the directory, you can find out what files the directory contains, for example.

The Pathname and Relative Paths

The pathnames we have used in the above code fragments have all been absolute paths, since we included the drive letter in the path for Windows, or a forward slash to identify the Unix root directory. If you omit this, the pathname string will be interpreted as a path relative to the current directory.

An absolute path in a Windows environment can also use the UNC (Universal Naming Convention) representation of a path that provides a machine independent way of identifying paths to shared resources on a network. The UNC representation of a path always begins with two backslashes followed by the machine name followed by the share name. On a computer with the name `myPC`, with a shared directory `"shared"`, you could create a `File` object as follows:

```
File myFile = new File("\\\\myPC\\shared\\jdk1.3\\src\\java\\io",
                       "File.java");
```

Testing and Checking File Objects

The `File` class provides a whole bunch of methods that you can apply to `File` objects, so we will look at them grouped by the sort of thing that they do. For testing and checking `File` objects, you have the following methods.

Method	Description
`exists()`	Returns `true` if the file or directory referred to by the `File` object exists and `false` otherwise.
`isDirectory()`	Returns `true` if the `File` object refers to a directory and `false` otherwise.
`isFile()`	Returns `true` if the `File` object refers to a file and `false` otherwise.
`isHidden()`	Returns `true` if the `File` object refers to a file that is hidden and `false` otherwise.
`isAbsolute()`	Returns `true` if the file object refers to an absolute path name, and `false` otherwise. Under Windows 95, 98 or NT, an absolute path name begins with either a drive letter followed by a colon, and a backslash or a double backslash. Under Unix an absolute path is specified from the root directory down.

Method	Description
canRead()	Returns true if you are permitted to read the file referred to by the File object, and false otherwise. This method can throw a SecurityException if read access to the file is not permitted.
canWrite()	Returns true if you are permitted to write the file referred to by the File object and false otherwise. This method may also throw a SecurityException if you are not allowed to write to the file.
equals()	You use this method for comparing two File objects for equality. If the File object passed as an argument to the method has the same path as the current object, the method returns true. Otherwise, it returns false.

> Note that all operations that involve accessing the files on the local machine can throw a SecurityException **if access is not authorized — in an applet for instance. This is the case with the** canRead() **and** canWrite() **methods here. For a** SecurityException **to be thrown a security manager must exist on the local machine.**

To see how the above methods go together, we can try a simple example.

Try It Out — Testing for a File

Try the following source code. Don't forget the import statement for the java.io package, since the example won't compile without it. If you haven't the Java source code installed, you could try the example with the file that contains the source code for the example itself — TryFile.java.

> **In all the examples in this chapter, you will need to substitute paths to suit your environment.**

```
import java.io.*;                    // For input & output classes

public class TryFile
{
  public static void main(String[] args)
  {
    // Create an object that is a directory
    File myDir = new File("I:/jdk1.3/src/java/io");
    System.out.println(myDir +
                (myDir.isDirectory()?" is":" is not") + " a directory.");

    // Create an object that is a file
    File myFile = new File(myDir, "File.java");
    System.out.println(myFile +
                (myFile.exists()?" does":" does not") + " exist");
    System.out.println("You can" +
                (myFile.canRead()?" ":"not ") + "read " + myFile);
```

```
        System.out.println("You can" +
                          (myFile.canWrite()?" ":"not ") + "write " + myFile);
        return;
    }
}
```

On my machine, the above example produces the output:

```
I:\jdk1.3\src\java\io is a directory.
I:\jdk1.3\src\java\io\File.java does exist
You can read I:\jdk1.3\src\java\io\File.java
You can write I:\jdk1.3\src\java\io\File.java
```

How It Works

This program first creates an object corresponding to the directory containing the `java.io` package. You will need to check the path to this directory on your own system and insert that as the argument to the constructor. The output statement then uses the conditional operator, `?:`, in conjunction with the `isDirectory()` method to display a message. If `isDirectory()` returns `true`, then " is" is selected. Otherwise, " is not" is selected. The program then creates another `File` object corresponding to the file `File.java` and displays another message using the same sort of mechanism. Finally, the program uses the `canRead()` and `canWrite()` methods to determine whether read or write access to the file is prevented.

With the code above, if a `SecurityException` is thrown, it will not be caught. To provide for this, you would need to put the statements involving the calls to `canRead()` and `canWrite()` in a `try` block, followed by a `catch` block for the exception. On Windows, you could also try out the separator, `\\`, with this example and see if it makes a difference.

Accessing File Objects

You can get information about a `File` object by using the following methods:

Method	Description
getName()	Returns a `String` object containing the name of the file without the path – in other words the last name in the path stored in the object. For a `File` object representing a directory, just the directory name is returned.
getPath()	Returns a `String` object containing the path for the `File` object – including the file or directory name.
getAbsolutePath()	Returns the absolute path for the directory or file referenced by the current `File` object.
getParent()	Returns a `String` object containing the name of the parent directory of the file or directory represented by the current `File` object. This will be the original path without the last name.

Method	Description
list()	If the current File object represents a directory, a String array is returned containing the names of the members of the directory. If the directory is empty the array will be empty. If the current file object is a file, null is returned. The method will throw an exception of type, SecurityException, if access to the directory is not authorized.
listFiles()	If the object for which this method is called is a directory, it returns an array of File objects corresponding to the files and directories in that directory. If the directory is empty the array that is returned will be empty. The method will return null if the object is not a directory or if an I/O error occurs. The method will throw an exception of type SecurityException if access to the directory is not authorized.
length()	Returns a value of type long that is the length in bytes of the file represented by the current File object. If the current object represents a directory, zero is returned.
lastModified()	Returns a value of type long that represents the time that the directory or file represented by the current File object was last modified. This time is the number of milliseconds since midnight on 1st January 1970 GMT. Zero is returned if the file does not exist.
toString()	This returns a String representation of the current File object and is called automatically when a File object is concatenated with a String object. We have used this method implicitly in output statements.
hashCode()	Returns a hash code value for the current File object. We will see more about what hash codes are used for in Chapter 10.

There is also a static method, listRoots(), which returns an array of File objects. Each element in the array that is returned corresponds to a root directory in the current file system. The path to every file in the system will begin with one or other of these roots. In the case of a Unix system for instance, the array returned will contain just one element corresponding to the single root on a Unix system, "/". You could list all the root directories on a system with the code:

```
File[] roots = File.listRoots();
for(int i = 0 ; i<roots.length ; i++)
    System.out.println("Root directory "+i+": "+roots[i]);
```

This only lists the elements of the array returned by the listRoots() method.

With a variation on the last example, we can try out some of these methods.

Try It Out — Getting More Information

We can arrange to list all the files in a directory and record when they were last modified with the following program:

```java
import java.io.*;                              // For input & output classes
import java.util.Date;                         // For the Date class

public class TryFile2
{
  public static void main(String[] args)
  {
    // Create an object that is a directory
    File myDir = new File("I:/jdk1.3/src/java/io");
    System.out.println(myDir.getAbsolutePath()
                + (myDir.isDirectory()?" is ":" is not ") + "a directory");
    System.out.println("The parent of " + myDir.getName()
                      + " is " + myDir.getParent());

    // Get the contents of the directory
    File[] contents = myDir.listFiles();

    // List the contents of the directory
    if(contents!=null)
    {
      System.out.println("\nThe " + contents.length
                  + " items in the directory " + myDir.getName() + " are:");
      for(int i = 0; i < contents.length; i++)
        System.out.println(contents[i] + " is a " +
                        (contents[i].isDirectory() ? "directory":"file")
              + " last modified " + new Date(contents[i].lastModified()));
    }
    else
      System.out.println(myDir.getName() + " is not a directory");

    return;
  }
}
```

Again, you need to use a path that is appropriate for your system. You should not have any difficulty seeing how this works. The first part of the program creates a `File` object representing the same directory as in the previous example. The second part itemizes all the files and subdirectories in the directory. The output will look something like this,

```
I:\jdk1.3\src\java\io is a directory
The parent of io is I:\jdk1.3\src\java

The 75 items in the directory io are:
I:\jdk1.3\src\java\io\BufferedInputStream.java is a file last modified Fri Jan 22
16:37:10 GMT 1999
I:\jdk1.3\src\java\io\BufferedOutputStream.java is a file last modified Fri Jan 22
16:37:10 GMT 1999
```

and so on.

How It Works

You can see that the `getName()` method just returns the file name or the directory name, depending on what the `File` object represents.

The `listFiles()` method returns a `File` array, and each element of the array represents a member of the directory, which could be a subdirectory or a file. We store the reference to the array returned by the method in our array variable, `contents`. After outputting a heading, we check that the array is not `null`. We then list the contents of the directory in the `for` loop. We use the `isDirectory()` method to determine whether each item is a file or a directory, and create the output accordingly. We could just as easily have used the `isFile()` method here. The `lastModified()` method returns a `long` value that represents the time when the file was last modified in milliseconds since midnight on January 1st 1970. To get this to a more readable form, we use the value to create a `Date` object, and the `toString()` method for the class returns what you see in the output. The `Date` class is defined in the `java.util` package. (See Chapter 10.) We need to import this into the program file. If the `contents` array is `null`, we just output a message. You could easily add code to output the length of each file here, if you want.

Filtering a File List

The `list()` and `listFiles()` methods are overloaded with versions that accept an argument that is used to filter a file list. This enables you to get a list of those files with a given extension, or with names that start with a particular sequence of characters. The argument that you pass to the `list()` method must be a variable of type `FilenameFilter` whereas the `listFiles()` method is overloaded with versions to accept arguments of type `FilenameFilter` or `FileFilter`. Both `FilenameFilter` and `FileFilter` are interfaces that contain the abstract method `accept()`. The `FilenameFilter` interface is defined as:

```
public interface FilenameFilter
{
  public abstract boolean accept(File directory, String filename);
}
```

The `FileFilter` interface is very similar:

```
public interface FileFilter
{
  public abstract boolean accept(File pathname);
}
```

The only distinction between these two is the argument list for the method in the interfaces. The filtering of the list is achieved by the `list()` or `listFiles()` method calling the method, `accept()`, for every item in the raw list. If the method returns `true`, the item stays in the list, and if it returns `false` the item is not included. Obviously, these interfaces act as a vehicle to allow the mechanism to work, so you need to define your own class that implements the appropriate interface. If you are using the `list()` method, your class must implement the `FilenameFilter` interface. If you are using the `listFiles()` method you can implement either interface. How you actually filter the filenames is entirely up to you. You can arrange to do whatever you like within your class that implements the filter interface. We can see how this works by extending the previous example further.

Try It Out — Using the `FilenameFilter` Interface

We can define a class to specify a file filter as:

```java
import java.io.*;                           // For FilenameFilter
import java.util.Date;                      // For the Date class

public class FileListFilter implements FilenameFilter
{
  private String name;                      // File name filter
  private String extension;                 // File extension filter

  // Constructor
  public FileListFilter(String name, String extension)
  {
    this.name = name;
    this.extension = extension;
  }

  public boolean accept(File directory, String filename)
  {
    boolean fileOK = true;

    // If there is a name filter specified, check the file name
    if(name != null)
      fileOK &= filename.startsWith(name);

    // If there is an extension filter, check the file extension
    if(extension != null)
      fileOK &= filename.endsWith('.' + extension);
    return fileOK;
  }
}
```

This uses the methods, `startsWith()` and `endsWith()`, defined in the `String` class that we
discussed in Chapter 4. Save this source in the same directory as the previous example, as
`FileListFilter.java`.

Now we can use this in the previous example by changing the code in `TryFile`'s `main()` method that
lists the contents of the directory:

```java
    // Create an object that is a directory
    File myDir = new File("I:/jdk1.3/src/java/io");
    System.out.println(myDir.getAbsolutePath()
            + (myDir.isDirectory()?" is ":" is not ") + "a directory");
    System.out.println("The parent of " + myDir.getName()
                    + " is " + myDir.getParent());

    // Define a filter for java source files beginning with F
    FilenameFilter select = new FileListFilter("F", "java");

    // Get the contents of the directory
    File[] contents = myDir.listFiles(select);
```

```
        // List the contents
        if(contents != null)
        {
          System.out.println("\nThe " + contents.length +
                  " matching items in the directory, " + myDir.getName() + ",
      are:");
          for(int i = 0; i < contents.length; i++)
            System.out.println(contents[i] + " is a " +
                    (contents[i].isDirectory() ? "directory":"file") +
                    " last modified " + new Date(contents[i].lastModified()));
        }
        else
          System.out.println(myDir.getName() + " is not a directory");

        return;
    }
```

When you run the code, you should get something like,

```
I:\jdk1.3\src\java\io is a directory
The parent of io is I:\jdk1.3\src\java

The 15 matching items in the directory, io, are:
I:\jdk1.3\src\java\io\File.java is a file last modified Fri Jan 22 16:37:10 GMT
1999
I:\jdk1.3\src\java\io\FileDescriptor.java is a file last modified Fri Jan 22
16:37:10
 GMT 1999
```

and so on.

How It Works

Our `FileListFilter` class has two instance variables - `name` and `extension`: `name` which stores the file name prefix and `extension` which selects files to be included in a list. These variables are set by the constructor, and the value of either can be omitted when the constructor is called by specifying the appropriate argument as `null`. If you want a really fancy filter, you can have just one argument to the constructor and specify the filter as `*.java`, or `A*.java`, or even `A*.j*`. You would just need a bit more code in the constructor or possibly the `accept()` method to analyze the argument. Our implementation of the `accept()` method here only returns `true` if the file name, passed to it by the `list()` method, has initial characters that are identical to `name`, and the file extension is the same as that stored in `extension`.

In the modified example, we construct an object of our filter class using the string, `"F"`, as the file name prefix and the string, `"java"`, as the extension. This version of the example will now only list files with names beginning with `"F"` and with the extension `.java`.

Modifying File Objects and Files

There are several methods defined in the `File` class that you can use to change a `File` object. There are also methods that enable you to create files and directories, and to delete them. The methods providing this capability are:

Method	Description
`renameTo (File path)`	The file represented by the current object will be renamed to the path represented by the `File` object, passed as an argument to the method. Note that this does *not* change the current `File` object in your program; it alters the physical file. Thus the file that the `File` object represents will no longer exist after executing this method, because the file will have a new name and possibly be located in a different directory. If the file's directory in the new path is different from the original, the file will be moved. The method will fail if the directory in the new path for the file does not exist, or if you don't have write access to it. If the operation is successful, `true` will be returned. Otherwise, `false` will be returned.
`setReadOnly()`	Sets the file represented by the current object as read-only and returns `true` if the operation is successful.
`mkdir()`	Creates a directory with the path specified by the current `File` object. The method will fail if the directory in the path (containing the directory to be created) does not exist. The method returns `true` if it is successful and `false` otherwise.
`mkdirs()`	Creates the directory represented by the current `File` object, including any parent directories that are required. It returns `true` if the new directory is created successfully, and `false` otherwise.
`createNewFile()`	Creates a new empty file with the pathname defined by the current `File` object as long as the file does not already exist. The method returns `true` if the file was created successfully.
`createTempFile (String prefix, String suffix, File directory)`	This is a static method that creates a temporary file in the directory, `directory`, with a name created using the first two arguments. The string, `prefix`, represents the start of the file name and must be at least three characters long. The string, `suffix`, specifies the file extension. The file name will be formed from `prefix` followed by five or more generated characters, followed by `suffix`. If `suffix` is `null`, `".tmp"` will be used. If `prefix` or `suffix` are too long for file names on the current system, they will be truncated, but prefix will not be truncated to less than three characters, and suffix will not be truncated to less that `.xxx`. The method returns a `File` object corresponding to the file that is created. If the `directory` argument is `null`, the system temporary directory will be used. If the file cannot be created, an `IOException` will be thrown. If `prefix` has less than three characters, an `IllegalArgumentException` will be thrown.

Method	Description

`createTempFile`
`(String prefix,`
` String suffix)`
	Equivalent to `createTempFile(String prefix,`
	`                            String suffix,`
	`                            null)`.

`delete()`	This will delete the file or directory represented by the current `File` object and return `true` if the delete was successful. It won't delete directories that are not empty. To delete a directory, you must first delete the files it contains.
`deleteOnExit()`	Causes the file or directory represented by the current `File` object to be deleted when the program ends. This method does not return a value. Once you call the method for a `File` object, the delete operation is irrevocable, so you will need to be cautious with this method.

Note that, in spite of the name, the files that you create by using the `createTempFile()` method are not deleted automatically. You must use `delete()` or `deleteOnExit()` to remove files that you no longer require.

You can arrange for a temporary file to be deleted at the end of the program by calling the `deleteOnExit()` method when you create it. For example, you might write:

```
File.createTempFile("list", null).deleteOnExit();
```

This statement will create a temporary file with a name of the form `listxxxxx.tmp` in the default temporary directory, (usually `c:\temp` under Windows and `/tmp` under Unix). The xxxxx part of the name is generated automatically. Because we did not supply a suffix, the file extension will be `.tmp` by default. The `File` object returned by `createTempFile()` is used to call its `deleteOnExit()` method, so we are assured that this file won't be left lying around after the program finishes.

We will be trying out some of these methods in examples later in this chapter. Now we understand how to define physical files in a Java program, we can move on to stream operations. We will look at byte streams first. Then we will cover character streams.

Byte Output Streams

The `OutputStream` class is an `abstract` class designed to act as a base class for all the other classes that represent a byte output stream. Classes derived from the class `OutputStream` will inherit the following five methods, all of which have return type, `void`:

Method	Description
`write(int b)`	This is an `abstract` method that is intended to write the low order byte of the argument, b, to the output stream.
`write(byte[] b)`	This method writes the array of bytes, b, to the output stream.

Table continued on following page

Method	Description
`write(byte[] b, int offset, int length)`	This method writes `length` bytes from the array, b, to the output stream, starting with the element, `b[offset]`.
`flush()`	This method forces any buffered output data to be written to the output stream. If this data is being transferred to another nested stream, the nested stream will also be flushed. We will see how this works a little later in this chapter.
`close()`	This method closes the output stream and any nested output streams.

All of these methods will throw an `IOException` if an error occurs.

Although the first version of the method, `write()`, is the only method that is abstract, the classes derived from `OutputStream` will typically implement their own versions of all of these methods. For example, the `flush()` and `close()` methods as defined in the class, `OutputStream`, don't actually do anything, and the `write()` methods that are implemented in the class simply use the version that writes one byte at a time.

> We will often create a stream object using an existing stream object, incorporating functionality from the first stream object into the second. This object can then be used to create another stream object, and so on. This is the nesting process referred to in the context of the `flush()` and `close()` methods.

Subclasses of OutputStream

There are five direct subclasses of the `abstract` class, `OutputStream`, defined in `java.io`. One of these, `ObjectOutputStream`, is used for writing objects to a file. Since this is a rather different process from writing ordinary data to a file, we will deal with this class separately in Chapter 9.

The other four subclasses of `OutputStream` are shown in the diagram below. You can use three of these to create objects that represent byte output streams of different kinds. The fourth direct subclass is a base class for further classes that you can use to extend the capabilities of the first three classes.

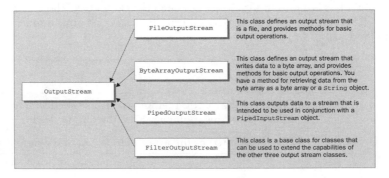

The basic output operations supported by these classes are the `byte` output functions supported by the `write()` methods inherited from the `OutputStream` class. They include no provision for writing other types of data to a file. To handle other types of data, you need to use one of the output filter classes that are derived from the class, `FilterOutputStream`. We will need to look at these in some detail. First, we should examine the basic output streams.

The FileOutputStream Class

You use a `FileOutputStream` object to write to a physical file. There are four constructors for this class.

Constructor	Description
`FileOutputStream (String filename)`	Creates an output stream for the file, `filename`. The existing contents of the file will be overwritten. If the file cannot be opened for writing, an `IOException` will the thrown.
`FileOutputStream (String filename, boolean append)`	Creates an output stream for the file, `filename`. Data written to the file will be appended following the existing contents if append is `true`. If the file cannot be opened for writing, an `IOException` will the thrown.
`FileOutputStream (File file)`	Creates a file output stream for the file represented by the object, `file`. If the file can not be opened for writing, an `IOException` will the thrown.
`FileOutputStream (FileDescriptor desc)`	Creates an output stream corresponding to the argument, `desc`. A `FileDescriptor` object represents an existing connection to a file so, since the file must exist, this constructor does not throw an `IOException`.

All of these constructors can throw a `SecurityException` if writing to the file is not authorized.

To create a stream object of type, `FileOutputStream`, you can pass either a `File` object to a constructor, or a `String` object that defines the path and file name. (We will come back to `FileDescriptor` objects in a moment.) You will usually find it more convenient to use a `File` object, since you can then check the properties of the file before you try to use it. You could create an output stream with the following statement.

```
try
{
   FileOutputStream file1 = new FileOutputStream("myFile.txt");
}
catch(IOException e)
{
   System.out.println(aFile + " not found");
}
```

However, if the file cannot be opened, the constructor will throw a `FileNotFoundException` which won't be very convenient in most circumstances. Since the constructor can throw an exception, we must put it in a `try` block and catch the exception, unless of course we arrange for the method containing the constructor call to bypass the exception with a `throws` clause. We might not want the file to be overwritten if it exists, in which case we can use a `File` object and do some checking.

```
String filename = "myFile.txt";
File aFile = new File(filename);
try
{
  if (!aFile.exists())
  {
    // Open for overwriting
    FileOutputStream file1 = new FileOutputStream(aFile);
    System.out.println("myFile.txt output stream created");
  }
  else
    System.out.println("myFile.txt already exists.");
}
catch(IOException e)
{
  System.out.println(e);
}
```

This creates the same `FileOutputStream` object as before, but in this case we've used the methods provided by the class `File` to check whether or not the file exists before using it.

You might want to append data to the file if it exists and create a new file if it doesn't. Either way, you have a file output stream to work with. You could do this with the following code.

```
String filename = "myFile.txt";
File aFile = new File(filename);
try
{
  aFile.createNewFile();      // Create a new file if aFile does not exist

  // Open to append
  FileOutputStream file1 = new FileOutputStream(aFile, true);
}
catch(IOException e)
{
  System.out.println(e);
}
```

As well as the methods inherited from the base class, a `FileOutputStream` object has a method, `getFD()`, which returns an object of type, `FileDescriptor`, that represents the current connection to the physical file. Once you have finished writing a file, the `FileDescriptor` object can be used to create a byte input stream object. You can therefore read the same file back since the `FileInputStream` class has a constructor that accepts a `FileDescriptor` object. We will discuss this when we look into byte input streams. A benefit of using a file descriptor is that since it represents an existing connection, we don't need to check for the existence of the file. As we saw, the `FileOutputStream` class also has a constructor that accepts a `FileDescriptor` object as an argument.

You cannot create a `FileDescriptor` object yourself. You can only obtain a `FileDescriptor` object by calling the `getFD()` method for a byte stream object that represents a file stream.

The `FileDescriptor` class also defines three public static data members, `in`, `out` and `err`, which are of type, `FileDescriptor`, and which correspond to the standard system input, the standard system output and the standard error stream respectively. You can use these in the creation of byte and character stream objects.

> Don't confuse the data members of the `FileDescriptor` class with the data members of the same name defined by the **System** class in the `java.lang` package. The `in`, `out` and `err` data members of the `System` class are of type `PrintStream`, so they have the `print()` and `println()` methods. The `FileDescriptor` data members do not.

We will see later in this chapter that you can use a `FileDescriptor` object to create character stream objects.

The ByteArrayOutputStream Class

As its name suggests, a `ByteArrayOutputStream` is a stream that you can use to transfer data to a byte array. You would typically use the `ByteArrayOutputStream` class when you want to transform data in some way, perhaps by using a filter output stream. Since data is written to a `byte` array that is a member of the stream object, operations are very fast and you can retrieve the contents of the `byte` array whenever you want by using methods provided by the class. Data is stored in a `ByteArrayOutputStream` object as shown below.

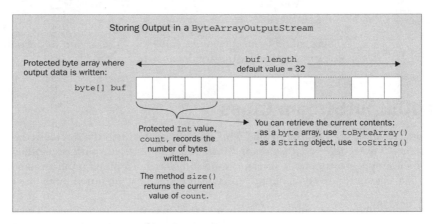

Storing Output in a `ByteArrayOutputStream`

Protected byte array where output data is written:
`byte[] buf`

buf.length
default value = 32

Protected Int value, `count`, records the number of bytes written.

The method `size()` returns the current value of `count`.

You can retrieve the current contents:
- as a byte array, use `toByteArray()`
- as a `String` object, use `toString()`

The `ByteArrayOutputStream` class has two constructors. One takes no arguments and will create an object containing a byte array of a default size of 32 bytes. The other accepts a value of type, `int`, as an argument which specifies the initial size of the byte array. The byte array is automatically increased in size as required. The advantage of being able to specify an initial size is in avoiding the overhead of frequently increasing the size when you write a lot of data to the stream. A small starting size will result in more frequent extensions to the buffer.

The `ByteArrayOutputStream` class implements the following methods.

Method	Description
`size()`	Returns the number of valid bytes in the buffer as an `int` value which is obtained from the instance variable `count`.
`reset()`	Resets the value of `count` to 0. Any bytes previously written to the buffer are lost. You use this to reset the stream object when you want to use it again. The return type is `void`.
`toByteArray()`	Returns the contents of the stream as a `byte` array of length, `count`.
`toString()`	Returns the contents of the stream as a `String` object of length, `count`. The high-order byte in each Unicode character in the return string will be 0.
`toString (String enc)`	Returns an object of type `String` that is produced by converting the contents of the stream according to the character encoding specified by `enc`. The character encoding, `enc`, will typically correspond to the character encoding used to convert between Unicode and the host machine character codes. It can be obtained by using the `getEncoding()` method for an `OutputStreamWriter` object, as we will see later.
`write(int b)`	This method writes the low-order byte of the argument, b, to the stream.
`write (byte b[], int offset, int length)`	This method writes `length` bytes from the array, b, to the stream starting with b[offset].
`writeTo (OutputStream out)`	This method writes the entire contents of the stream to the output stream specified by the argument to the method.

The PipedOutputStream Class

A piped output stream is used in conjunction with a piped input stream that receives the data written to the output stream. Two independent program threads can communicate with each other by using piped streams. A piped output stream in one thread can be connected to a piped input stream in another thread. The data written to the piped output stream can be read by the piped input stream.

There are two constructors you can use to create a `PipedOutputStream` object. The default constructor creates a stream that is not connected to a piped input stream. Before you can use it, you must either call the `connect()` method of the `PipedOutputStream` object specifying a `PipedInputStream` object as an argument, or get the `PipedInputStream` object to connect itself to the `PipedOutputStream` object.

More simply, the second constructor for the `PipedOutputStream` class accepts a `PipedInputStream` object as an argument, to which the output stream object will be connected.

The FilterOutputStream Classes

The `FilterOutputStream` class is a base class for classes that operate on an existing output stream of some kind, usually by modifying the data in some way before it gets written to the underlying stream. There are a total of ten classes that are derived directly or indirectly from the `FilterOutputStream` class. Five of these subclasses are shown in the diagram below.

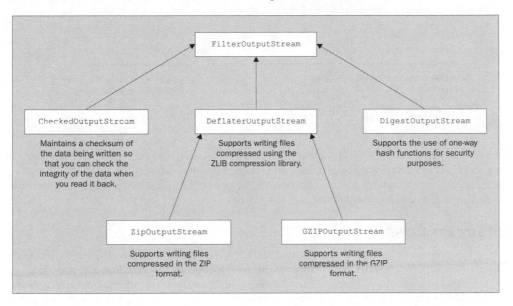

The `DigestOutputStream` class is defined in the `java.security` package. The four other subclasses of `FilterOutputStream` shown here are defined in the `java.util.zip` package.

> *The `DigestOutputStream` involves the computation of one-way hash values for security purposes. Some methods involved in this are not included with Java, but must be supplied by a service provider. Further discussion of the use of this class is outside the scope of this book.*

The `CheckedOutputStream` class maintains a checksum for the data that is written to the file. Creating a checksum when you write the file provides the possibility of using the checksum when you read the same data back to verify that the data is the same as the data that was written. The `CheckedInputStream` class, which we will see later, derives from the `FilterInputStream` class, complements this class for the purpose of checking that the data read is the same as the data that was written.

The remaining three classes shown in the diagram enable you to write compressed files. We won't be going through the detail of all of these, but we will write a ZIP file later in this chapter.

Let's turn now to the three subclasses of `FilterOutputStream` that you will use most often. They are shown in the following diagram.

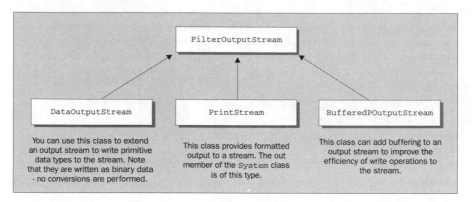

The filter output stream classes are designed to augment an existing output stream class in order to construct an object of either of these filter output classes. You must first create an object of type, `FileOutputStream`, `PipedOutputStream` or `ByteArrayOutputStream`, and then use this object in the constructor for the filter output stream class of your choice.

The PrintStream Class

Up to now, we have made extensive use of the `println()` method from the `PrintStream` class in our examples to output formatted information to the screen. The `out` object in the expression, `System.out.println()`, is of type, `PrintStream`. In previous Java implementations, this was the only class available for outputting data of any of the basic types as a string. For example, an `int` value of `12345` becomes the string, `"12345"`, as generated by the `toString()` method from the class, `Integer`. However, for general formatted output to a stream, `PrintStream` has largely been made obsolete by the `PrintWriter` class introduced in Java 1.1, which is not in itself a stream but implements output to a character stream.

`PrintWriter` is a significant improvement over the `PrintStream` class, because it takes care of conversions between Unicode and the character encoding on the local computer, whatever that happens to be. The old `PrintStream` class did not always work correctly in this respect. You can still use `System.out.println()` for text output to the screen without any problems though. We will look at the `PrintWriter` class later in this chapter.

Note that the `PrintWriter` class has no particular connection with printing – in spite of its name. Of course, you could create a `PrintWriter` object for a file and then arrange for the file to be redirected to your printer. However, you are more likely to write to your system printer using a totally different mechanism. We will look at this in Chapter 16.

The DataOutputStream Class

The DataOutputStream class provides methods that enable you to write any of the basic types of data or a String to a byte stream. If you are writing data to a file that includes binary data, then you should use this class. All data is written as a sequence of bytes corresponding to the original binary data in memory. No conversions are made on any of the data types. The class provides you with methods for writing data of each of the basic types.

Method	Description
writeByte(int value)	Writes the low-order byte of the int argument to the stream.
writeBoolean(boolean value)	Writes a boolean value to the stream as a byte with the value, 1, for true and the value, 0, for false.
writeChar(int value)	Writes the low-order two bytes of the argument to the stream.
writeShort(int value)	Writes the low-order two bytes of the argument to the stream.
writeInt(int value)	Writes all four bytes of the int argument to the stream.
writeLong(long value)	Writes all eight bytes of the long argument to the stream.
writeFloat(float value)	Writes the four bytes of the float argument to the stream.
writeDouble(double value)	Writes the eight bytes of the double argument to the stream.

With all the methods here that write numerical data to the stream, bytes are written in a sequence with the high byte always written first and the low byte last.

> **None of these methods returns a value but any of them can throw an IOException if an error occurs.**

Creating a DataOutputStream Object

The constructor for the `DataOutputStream` class requires an argument of type `OutputStream` that must represent a real destination for the data. The three possibilities that you are most likely to use for this object are:

Constructor argument	Description
`PipedOutputStream`	This object will represent a connection to a `PipedInputStream` for another thread. This will connect two threads in your application and allow data to be transferred from one to the other. All of the data that you write to the `DataOutputStream` will be available to the connected `PipedInputStream`.
`ByteArrayOutputStream`	This object will represent an array in memory. All of the data that you write to the `DataOutputStream` will be written to the array in the `ByteArrayOutputStream` object.
`FileOutputStream`	This object will represent a physical file on your hard disk. Data that you write to the `DataOutputStream` will be written to the physical file.

Since the third option is by far the most used, we will look at that. We need to go through three distinct stages to create a `DataOutputStream` object that will enable us to write a file:

❑ Create a suitable `File` object, for example:
```
File aFile = new File("data.txt");
```

❑ Create a `FileOutputStream` object using the `File` object, for example:
```
FileOutputStream fStream = new FileOutputStream(aFile);
```

❑ Create the `DataOutputStream` object using the `FileOutputStream` object, for example:
```
DataOutputStream myStream = new DataOutputStream(fStream);
```

These steps don't have to be entirely separate though. Let's see how this works out in a practical example.

Try It Out — Using the `DataOutputStream` Class

To write a `String` to a stream you have the method, `writeChars()`, available which accepts an argument of type, `String`. We can try this out here. The example will create a directory, `MyData`, on your `C:` drive, and then create a file, `data.txt`, in that directory. You will need to change this if it conflicts with existing directories on your machine. Here's the code.

```java
import java.io.*;
import java.util.Date;

public class TestDataStream
{
  public static void main(String[] args)
  {
```

```
      String myStr = new String("Garbage in, garbage out");
      String dirName = "C:/MyData";    // Directory name

      try
      {
        File dir = new File(dirName);  // File object for directory
        if(!dir.exists())              // If directory does not exist
          dir.mkdir();                 // ...create it
        else
          if(!dir.isDirectory())
          {
            System.err.println(dirName + " is not a directory");
            return;
          }

        File aFile = new File(dir, "data.txt");
        aFile.createNewFile();            // Now create a new file if necessary

        // Create the byte output stream
        DataOutputStream myStream = new DataOutputStream(
                                    new FileOutputStream(aFile));
        myStream.writeChars(myStr);     // Write the string to the file
      }
      catch(IOException e)
      {
        System.out.println("IO exception thrown: " + e);
      }
    }
  }
```

After you have compiled and run this program, you can inspect the contents of the file, data.txt, using a plain text editor. They will look something like the following.

```
G a r b a g e   i n ,   g a r b a g e   o u t
```

There are spaces between the characters, because we are writing Unicode characters to the file – two bytes are written for each character in the original string. Your text editor may represent these as other than spaces, or possibly not at all, as they are bytes that contain zero.

How It Works

We have defined two String objects, myStr, that we will write to the file, and dirName which is the name of the directory we will create. In the try block we first create a File object to represent the directory. If this directory does not exist, the exists() method will return false and the mkdir() method for dir will be called to create it. If the exists() method returns true, we must make sure that the File object represents a directory, and not a file.

Having established the directory one way or another, we create a file object, aFile, to represent the file, data.txt, in the directory. Calling the createNewFile() method for aFile will create a new file if it does not already exist, so we will use an existing file. We use this object as an argument to the FileOutputStream constructor, and we pass the object produced to the DataOutputStream constructor to create the object, myStream.

Once we have the stream object, we write the string stored in myStr to the file, data.txt. Of course, if you were writing several strings of varying lengths to a file you would need to include some way of knowing where the end of each string is when you come to read it back. After all, whatever you wrote to the file is just stored as bytes. One way would be to write the length of each string to the file before writing the string. Then you can read the length and use that to read the correct number of characters for each string.

In addition to the output methods we have just seen, you also have a method, size(), which will return the total number of bytes written to the stream as a value of type, int. You could try this out by adding the following statement immediately after the statement that writes myStr to the file.

```
System.out.println(myStream.size() + " bytes written to the file");
```

You should see that 46 bytes are written to the file since myStr contains 23 characters.

Buffered Output Streams

You can add a buffer to an output stream to make the output operations more efficient by using the BufferedOutputStream class. As you write data to a buffered stream, the data is accumulated in a buffer in memory and is only written to the ultimate output stream when the buffer is full. Output operations to a file are very slow compared to the time it takes to write data to a buffer in memory. Since using a buffer will reduce the number of actual output operations to the file, this will make the output faster over all. You can always cause the current contents of a buffered output stream to be written by calling the flush() method. Closing the stream by calling the close() method will also cause any residual data in the buffer to be written to the stream.

To create a buffered output stream, you pass the output stream object for the stream that you want buffered to the constructor for BufferedOutputStream. The default buffer size is dependent on the particular implementation of Java. For the JDK 1.3 implementation under Windows, it is 512 bytes. You can specify the size of the buffer yourself by passing the number of bytes in the buffer as a second argument of type, int, to the constructor.

Buffered Stream Operations

The process of writing a disk file using a buffered stream is quite straightforward. If we want to create an output stream to write data of basic types to the file, it will need to be an object of type, DataOutputStream, as that has the methods we need to write the data. The whole process of creating the output stream that connects to the physical file is very similar to the last example.

You first create an object of the class, File, using the name and path for the file to which you want to write. You can then use the File object as an argument to a constructor for a FileOutputStream class to create the stream object that corresponds to the physical file. Since we want the stream to be buffered, we pass this object to the BufferedOutputStream constructor. We finally pass the BufferedOutputStream object to the DataOutputStream object to get the stream object that we will use to write the data.

We can't do it the other way round. If we created a DataOutputStream object first and passed that to the BufferedOutputStream constructor, we would end up with an object that would not contain the methods needed to write the basic data types.

We could create a buffered output stream to store primes as follows.

```
File myPrimes = new File(myPrimeDir, fileName);  // The file object
myPrimes.createNewFile();                        // If it doesn't exist, create it

// Create a buffered data output stream for the file
DataOutputStream myFile = new DataOutputStream(
                          new BufferedOutputStream(
                          new FileOutputStream(myPrimes)));
```

We define a `File` object specifying the new file in the directory we have created. We then use it to create a `DataOutputStream` object which we pass to the `BufferedOutputStream` constructor. We will use the `BufferedOutputStream` object to write to the file. If the file already exists, we will access it (and overwrite it!), and if it doesn't, it will be created as a result of the call to `createNewFile()`. Let's put this into a working example.

Try It Out — Buffered Output to a Disk File

We could add this code to the example in Chapter 4 for creating primes to see how this works. We write the primes to a file instead of the display:

```java
import java.io.*;

public class TryPrimesOutput
{
  public static void main(String[] args)
  {
    long[] primes = new long[200];      // Array to store primes
    primes[0] = 2;                      // Seed the first prime
    primes[1] = 3;                      // and the second
    int count = 2;                      // count of primes found so far

    long number = 5;                    // Next integer to be tested

    outer:
    for( ; count < primes.length; number += 2L)
    {
      // The maximum divisor we need to try is square root of number
      long limit = (long)Math.ceil(Math.sqrt((double)number));

      // Divide by all the primes we have up to limit
      for(int i = 1; i < count && primes[i] <= limit; i++)
        if(number%primes[i] == 0)        // Is it an exact divisor?
          continue outer;                // yes, try the next number

      primes[count++] = number;          // We got one!
    }

    // Write the primes to a file
    try
    {
      String dirName = "c:\\JunkData";   // Directory for the file
      String fileName = "Primes.bin";    // The file name

      File myPrimeDir = new File(dirName);      // Define directory object
```

```
        if(!myPrimeDir.exists())              // If directory does not exist
          myPrimeDir.mkdir();                 // ...create it
        else
          if(!myPrimeDir.isDirectory())       // Verify it is a directory
          { // It is not
            System.err.println(dirName+" is not a directory");
            return;
          }

        // Create the file object
        File primesFile = new File(myPrimeDir, fileName);
        primesFile.createNewFile();           // If it doesn't exist, create it

        // Create a buffered data output stream for the file
        DataOutputStream primesStream = new DataOutputStream(
                                new BufferedOutputStream(
                                new FileOutputStream(primesFile)));

        // Write primes to the file
        for(int i = 0; i < primes.length; i++)
          primesStream.writeLong(primes[i]);

        primesStream.close();                 // Flush and close the file
        System.out.println("File size = " + primesStream.size());
      }
      catch(IOException e)                     // Catch any output errors
      {
        System.out.println("IOException " + e + " occurred");
      }
    }
  }
```

This produces the output:

```
File size = 1600
```

This looks reasonable since we wrote 200 values of type long, and they are 8 bytes each.

How It Works

The size of the array, primes[], has been increased so that we create a more appreciable number of primes to be written to the file. The example uses the statements you have already seen to create the buffered stream object. All we do then is to write the primes to the stream using the writeLong() method. When all the primes have been written, we call flush() to make sure that everything is sent to the stream and then output the number of bytes written to the file that we obtain using the size() method. Lastly, we close the file. As you see, we include a catch block to catch any exceptions that occur in the write operations on the file. If we didn't do this, we would need to declare that the method main() may throw an IOException.

The object, myFile, will therefore be a buffered file stream with the data output stream methods available. The file will only be written each time the buffer is filled, or when the stream is flushed. In between, the write operations will just place data in the buffer – all automatically. Easy, isn't it?

Since this file contains binary data, we will not want to view it except perhaps for debugging purposes. We will see how to read it back in the next chapter.

Writing a Compressed File

To see how to write a compressed file, we will look at writing ZIP files. This is a common compression method. We are not going to explore every nook and cranny of the classes involved in writing ZIP files but just enough to enable you to put it into practice at a basic level. You can take it from there. To be able to write ZIP files, we need to understand the `ZipOutputStream` class.

There is one constructor for `ZipOutputStream` objects, and this accepts an argument of type, `OutputStream`, which will typically be a `FileOutputStream` object. For example, we could define the name of the directory to contain the ZIP file and the ZIP file name with the statements:

```
String dirName = "c:/JunkData";       // Directory for the ZIP file
String zipName = "Primes.zip";        // The ZIP file name
```

Then, after the usual checks that everything is legitimate, we can construct the `ZipOuputStream` object with the statements:

```
File myPrimeZip = new File(myPrimeDir, zipName);  // The file object
ZipOutputStream myZipFile = new ZipOutputStream(
                           new FileOutputStream(myPrimeZip));
```

This creates the file object, as we have seen before, and uses it to create a `FileOutputStream` object which we pass to the `ZipOutputStream` constructor. This creates our object, `myZipFile`, which corresponds to the physical file, `Primes.zip`, in the directory, `C:\JunkData`.

Of course, we won't be writing data directly to this file, although it is possible to do so. A ZIP file contains one or more compressed files, and each file in the ZIP is identified by a **ZIP entry**. A ZIP entry is represented by an object of the class, `ZipEntry`, which has one constructor that accepts a `String` object, which will be the name of the entry. This is usually a file name. We could define a `ZipEntry` object with the statements:

```
String fileName = "Primes.bin";    // The name of the file to be compressed
ZipEntry myZipEntry = new ZipEntry(fileName);   // The ZIP entry
```

The `ZipEntry` object also contains information about how the file should be compressed. You can set this by passing a value of type, `int`, to the `setMethod()` method for the `ZipEntry` object. The argument can be either `ZipEntry.STORED` which will leave the entry uncompressed, or `ZipEntry.DEFLATED` which specifies that the entry should be compressed. The latter is also the default so we don't need to call `setMethod()` when we are compressing a file.

Now that we have a ZIP entry defined, we must pass the information to the `ZipOutputStream` object with the statement:

```
myZipFile.putNextEntry(myZipEntry);      // Start the ZIP entry
```

This defines the next zip entry for the `ZipOutputStream` object. We can write the ZIP entry – the file we want to add to the ZIP, and when we are done we call the `closeEntry()` for the `ZipOutputStream` object:

```
myZipFile.closeEntry();
```

341

This closes the entry, not the stream, so we can then start a new ZIP entry corresponding to the next file we want to add to the ZIP. If you want to close the file stream as well as the entry, call the ZipOutputStream's close() method.

So, how do we write the data for the entry to the ZIP? We will usually want to write a file represented by a DataOutputStream object because that has the methods to write different types of data values to the file, such as integers or floating point values. We can arrange for this to be the case by passing our ZipOutputStream object to the DataOutputStream constructor, then when we call methods for the DataOutputStream object, the data will be written to the ZIP. We construct the DataOutputStream object with the statement:

```
DataOutputStream myFile = new DataOutputStream(myZipFile);
```

This creates the DataOutputStream object from the ZipOutputStream object, but we can actually do better than that. We can buffer the output as well by using a BufferedOutputStream object along the way:

```
DataOutputStream myFile = new DataOutputStream(
                             new BufferedOutputStream(myZipFile));
```

Once you have finished writing an entry in a ZIP, you can find out how many bytes were written to the ZIP by calling the getCompressedSize() method for the ZipEntry object. You can also get the size of the uncompressed file by calling the size() method for the DataOutputStream object.

The last example is a good candidate for illustrating how you can write data to a compressed ZIP file for real, particularly since all the code fragments in this section fit so well, so let's apply what we know about the ZipOutputStream class to write the primes directly to a compressed file.

Try It Out — Writing Primes to a ZIP File

This is going to be very easy. It's just a question of plugging the code fragments we have just been looking at into the previous example. This will write a ZIP file to the same directory as the previous example, JunkData. Here's the code:

```
import java.io.*;
import java.util.zip.*;

public class TryCompressedPrimesOutput
{
  public static void main(String[] args)
  {
    long[] primes = new long[200];    // Array to store primes
    primes[0] = 2;                     // Seed the first prime
    primes[1] = 3;                     // and the second
    int count = 2;                     // count of primes found - up to now
    long number = 5;                   // Next integer to be tested

    outer:
    for( ; count < primes.length; number += 2L)
    {
      // The maximum divisor we need to try is square root of number
      long limit = (long)Math.ceil(Math.sqrt((double)number));
```

```
        // Divide by all the primes we have up to limit
        for(int i = 1; i < count && primes[i] <= limit; i++)
          if(number%primes[i] == 0)              // Is it an exact divisor?
            continue outer;                       // yes, try the next number

        primes[count++] = number;      // We got one!
      }

      // Write the primes to a file
      try
      {
        String dirName = "c:/JunkData";        // Directory for the ZIP file
        String zipName = "NewPrimes.zip";      // The ZIP archive name
        String fileName = "NewPrimes.bin";     // Name of the compressed file
        File myPrimeDir = new File(dirName);   // Define directory object

        if(!myPrimeDir.exists())               // If directory does not exist
          myPrimeDir.mkdir();                  // ...create it
        else
          if(!myPrimeDir.isDirectory())
          {
            System.err.println(dirName + " is not a directory");
            return;
          }

        File myPrimeZip = new File(myPrimeDir, zipName);  // The file object
        myPrimeZip.createNewFile();                       // Make sure we have one

        // Creat the zip output stream
        ZipOutputStream myZipFile = new ZipOutputStream(
                          new FileOutputStream(myPrimeZip));

        // Create the zip entry for the file and write it to the zip output
        // stream
        ZipEntry myZipEntry = new ZipEntry(fileName);
        myZipFile.putNextEntry(myZipEntry);

        // Create the output stream to the zip output stream
        DataOutputStream myFile = new DataOutputStream(
                          new BufferedOutputStream(myZipFile));

        // Write primes to the file
        for(int i = 0; i < primes.length; i++)
          myFile.writeLong(primes[i]);

        myFile.flush();                        // Make sure all is written
        myZipFile.closeEntry();                // End the ZIP entry
        myFile.close();                        // Close the file stream
        System.out.println("File size = " + myFile.size());
        System.out.println("Compressed file size = " +
                                    myZipEntry.getCompressedSize());
      }
      catch(IOException e)                     // Catch any output errors
      {
        System.out.println("IOException " + e + " occurred");
      }
    }
  }
```

If you compile and run this it will produce the output:

```
File size = 1600
Compressed file size = 424
```

Thus the primes file is compressed by almost four to one. You can use WinZip, PKUNZIP or Infozip's unzip to view the contents of the zip that this program creates.

How It Works

This uses almost exactly the code we saw in the text. We have an extra String object to define the name of the ZIP file which is used in the File object constructor, and the original file name is passed to the ZipEntry constructor to identify the file within the ZIP. Once we have created the DataOutputStream object, writing the data proceeds exactly as before.

When we have finished writing the data, we call flush() for the DataOutputStream object to ensure any residual data is written to the file. At this point, we also call closeEntry() for the myZipFile object to indicate the end of the current entry. Finally, we call close() for the DataOutputStream object which will call close() for the BufferedOutputStream object, which in turn will call close() for the ZipOutputStream object. If we had not already called flush() and closeEntry(), the call to close() would have done it anyway.

After we have closed the file, we retrieve the sizes of the uncompressed file and the ZIP.

Character Output Streams

Character output to a stream always involves writing character data. Unicode characters will be automatically converted to the character coding used by the local computer when the data is transferred to the stream. This contrasts with the byte output streams, where no conversion of characters is done. You use the character streams when you want to write text to a file, or when you want to write the string representation of your data values. You can also use a character output stream to obtain the local machine representation for a character string.

All the classes that provide character operations on a stream are derived from the abstract class, Writer. The subclasses of Writer are shown in the diagram.

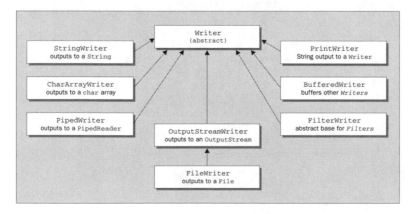

The FilterWriter class is an abstract class intended to be used as a base class for defining character filter streams. Writing filter stream classes is outside the scope of this book, so we won't discuss the FilterWriter class further.

The PipedWriter class defines a character stream that is connected to a PipedReader stream so that two threads in a program can pass data between them. The PipedReader class is a character input stream class derived from the class, Reader. We will look at character input streams in the next chapter.

The BufferedWriter class is used to buffer output for character streams that write to a physical file. This makes the write operations much more efficient by reducing the number of writes to the physical file, as we saw for byte output streams. We will see how to use the BufferedWriter class when we look at how to write to files using character stream classes.

The abstract base class for the character output streams, Writer, defines the following methods that will be inherited by its subclasses:

Method	Description
write(int c)	Writes the character, c, to the stream. The return type is void.
write(char[] cArray)	Writes the array, cArray, to the stream.
write(char[] cArray, int offset, int length)	Writes length characters from the array, cArray, to the stream starting at the element with the index offset. The return type is void.
write(String str)	Writes the string, str, to the stream. The return type is void.
write(String str, int offset, int length)	Writes length characters from the string, str, to the stream starting at position offset. The return type is void.

All of these methods can throw an IOException if an error occurs. In many cases the base class methods shown here will be overridden in the derived classes to provide more efficient implementations.

The Writer class also declares two abstract methods that will be implemented in its subclasses:

Abstract Method	Description
flush()	Flushes the stream. If the output is transferred to another stream, that stream will also be flushed, as will all nested streams.
close()	Flushes and closes the stream. All nested streams will also be flushed and closed.

The return type for both of these methods is void. You generally use flush() when you want to complete a series of output operations on a stream (by transferring any data still lying in a buffer to the stream) but still maintain the connection to the stream for further operations. You call close() to complete all operations and close the connection to the physical medium corresponding to the stream.

Writing Characters to an Array or a String Buffer

The StringWriter and CharArrayWriter classes convert the data written to the stream from Unicode to local character codes and then transfer it to a StringBuffer and an array of type, char[], respectively, which are internal to the class object. Both classes have a default constructor that creates the object with the internal StringBuffer object or char[] array set to a default size. CharArrayWriter also has a constructor that accepts an argument of type, int, that defines the size of the internal buffer. For example, you could create a CharArrayWriter object with a buffer to hold 100 characters with the statement:

```
CharArrayWriter charArrayOut = new CharArrayWriter(100);
```

The StringWriter class defines the following methods:

Method	Description
write(int c)	Writes the character, c, to the buffer in the stream object. The return type is void.
write(char[] cArray, int offset, int length)	Writes length characters from the array, cArray, to the buffer in the stream object starting at the element with the index offset. The return type is void.
write(String str)	Writes the string, str, to the buffer in the stream object. The return type is void.
write(String str, int offset, int length)	Writes length characters from the string, str, to the buffer in the stream object starting at position, offset. The return type is void.
getBuffer()	Returns the buffer in the stream object as type, StringBuffer.
toString()	Returns the current contents of the buffer in the stream object as type, String.

Several of these overridden methods are inherited from the `Writer` class. The `CharArrayWriter` class also defines the methods shown above, excepting the `getBuffer()` method. Nor does it override `write(String str)`. The extra methods for the `CharArrayWriter` class are:

Method	Description
`writeTo(Writer outStream)`	Writes the contents of the buffer in the stream object to the stream, `outStream`.
`toCharArray()`	Returns a copy of the data in the buffer as type, `char[]`.
`reset()`	Resets the current buffer in the stream object so that you can use it again. This saves you having to create a new stream object with a new buffer.
`size()`	Returns the current size of the buffer as type, `int`.

You can use either of the classes as a means of obtaining the local machine equivalent of a Unicode string or array in your program, since both classes include methods to retrieve the contents of the internal buffer.

Connecting a Character Stream to a Byte Stream

The `OutputStreamWriter` class enables you to write character output to an object representing a byte output stream. The automatic conversion of the data will be written from Unicode characters to the local machine representation of the characters. The `OutputStreamWriter` object will convert the characters written to the stream before they are transferred to the byte stream.

The `OutputStreamWriter` class constructor accepts an argument of type `OutputStream`, so the destination for the converted data can be any kind of byte output stream. After you have written the byte output stream, you can read it back as a byte input stream and thus obtain the data in the local machine representation.

The methods defined by the `OutputStreamWriter` class for writing the data override or implement the base class methods. To write to a byte output stream that represents a physical file, you would normally buffer the output using the `BufferedWriter` class. For example, if you wanted to write character data to the screen with automatic conversion to the local character representation, you could define a character output stream object as:

```
Writer out = new BufferedWriter(new OutputStreamWriter(System.out));
```

Using a Character Stream to Write a File

The `FileWriter` class has a constructor that accepts an object of type `File` as an argument, so you can use a `FileWriter` object to write a file. In fact, you can use one of four constructors for `FileWriter` objects.

Constructor	Description
`FileWriter(File aFile)`	Creates an object from the object, `aFile`, that represents a physical file.
`FileWriter(FileDescriptor fileDesc)`	Creates an object from a `FileDescriptor` object. A `FileDescriptor` object represents a standard system file.
`FileWriter(String fileName)`	Creates an object from the string, `fileName`, that is the name of a physical file.
`FileWriter(String fileName, boolean append)`	Creates an object from the string, `fileName`, that is the name of a physical file. If the value of `append` is `true`, data will be appended to the file if it exists. Otherwise, a new file will be created.

As we saw earlier, the `FileDescriptor` class has public static data members of type `FileDescriptor`, `in`, `out` and `err`, that represent the standard input stream, the standard output stream and the standard error stream respectively. You can also use a `FileDescriptor` object that was obtained from a byte stream object to create a `FileWriter` object. You obtain this by calling the `getFD()` method for the stream object in question.

Curiously, in the current implementation of the `java.io` package, the only `FileWriter` class constructor that will create a character output stream to which you can append data is the last in the list above. Thus to append data to a file, you must create the stream object directly from a `String` object containing the file path. However, you can still create a `File` object to check the status of the physical file if necessary.

Let's see how that works with a simple example.

Try It Out — Appending Data to a File

We will just write some proverbs to a file that we will access with the `FileWriter` constructor that allows us to append data. Here's the code.

```
// Appending data to a file
import java.io.*;

class WriteCharacters
{
  public static void main(String[] args)
  {
    try
    {
```

```
        String dirName = "c:/JunkData"; // Directory for the output file
        String fileName = "Proverbs.txt";   // Name of the output file
        File output = new File(dirName, fileName);
        output.createNewFile();                 // Create a new file if necessary

        if(!output.isFile())                    // Verify we have a file
        {
          System.out.println("Creating " + output.getPath() + " failed.");
          return;
        }

        BufferedWriter out = new BufferedWriter(
                            new FileWriter(output.getPath(), true));

        String[] sayings = { "Indecision maximixes flexibility.",
                             "Only the mediocre are always at their best.",
                             "A little knowledge is a dangerous thing.",
                             "Many a mickle makes a muckle.",
                             "Who begins too much achieves little.",
                             "Who knows most says least.",
                             "A wise man sits on the hole in his carpet."};

        // Write the proverbs to the file preceded by the string length
        for(int i = 0; i < sayings.length; i++)
        {
          out.write(sayings[i].length() + sayings[i]);
        }
        out.close();
      }
      catch(IOException e)
      {
        System.out.println("Error writing the file " + e);
      }
    }
  }
```

How It Works

In the `try` block, we create a `BufferedWriter` object from a `FileWriter` object that will append data to the output file. You can see that we can use the `File` object for checking the physical file and use its `getPath()` method to get the string to pass to the `FileWriter` constructor.

We create a `String` array, `sayings[]`, that contains seven proverbs that are written to the stream in the `for` loop. We write the length of each proverb to the stream preceding the string for the proverb. This is done by concatenating the proverb with the value returned from the `length()` method for the string. Of course, the length will be converted to a string before it is written to the stream, so the program that reads this back will need to figure out where the length value begins and ends. Finally, we close the stream. The `catch` block will catch any exceptions that are thrown as a result of errors writing the file.

The program doesn't produce any output, other than the file. However, you can use any program that views text files to check that it is written as required. The first time you run the program, the file doesn't exist, so it will be created. You can then look at the contents. If you run the program again, the same proverbs will be appended to the file, so there will be a second set. Alternatively, you could modify the `sayings[]` array to contain different proverbs the second time around. Each time the program runs, the data will be added at the end of the existing file.

If you change the second argument to the `FileWriter` constructor to `false`, any existing data in the file is overwritten each time you run the program. This is also the case with any of the other `FileWriter` constructors. As we will write a program to read this file back in the next chapter, you should leave it on your disk.

PrintWriter Character Streams

You can output binary numerical data such as type, `int`, or type, `double`, converted to character form to a stream by using the `PrintWriter` class. However, the output format for each data type is fixed so that you can not control the width of the output field or the number of digits presented. In each case, it is determined by the `valueOf()` method that is defined in the `String` class for the data type. If you need to alter the format of the output dynamically, you must derive your own classes to do so. We will look at an elementary approach to this later in this chapter.

You can create a `PrintWriter` object for a byte output stream object, or for an object of type, `OutputStreamWriter`. You have a choice of four constructors.

Constructors	Description
`PrintWriter (OutputStream stream)`	Creates a `PrintWriter` object from the `stream` object passed as an argument. This will construct an `OutputStreamWriter` internally, from the byte stream object passed as an argument.
`PrintWriter (OutputStream stream, boolean flush)`	Creates a `PrintWriter` object from the `stream` object passed as an argument. If the argument `flush` is `true`, the stream will be flushed automatically whenever the `println()` method is called for the stream.
`PrintWriter (Writer writer)`	Creates a `PrintWriter` object from the `writer` object passed as an argument. This should be an `OutputStreamWriter` object.
`PrintWriter (Writer writer, boolean flush)`	Creates a `PrintWriter` object from the `writer` object passed as an argument. If the argument `flush` is `true`, the stream will be flushed each time the `println()` method is called for the stream.

Ultimately, the `PrintWriter` object is always based on a byte stream object, since you need to have a byte output stream in order to create an `OutputStreamWriter` object. Calling either of the constructors with one argument is equivalent to calling it with the second argument as `false`.

The `PrintWriter` class adds a range of methods to an existing output stream that can convert data of any of the basic types to a character representation of the value. The conversion in each case is fixed and is the result of calling the `toString()` method in the class from `java.lang` corresponding to the basic type, `Integer` for `int` values, `Double` for `double` values, and so on as described in Chapter 5. For class objects, the `toString()` method for the class is called by one of two methods, `print()` and `println()`. Both of these are overloaded to accept any of the following argument types:

char	char[]	String	Object	
boolean	int	long	float	double

The difference between the `print()` and `println()` methods is that the latter writes an end of line character to the stream after outputting the characters for the value of its argument, whereas the `print()` method does not. When `println()` has no argument, it just writes an end of line character to the stream.

The methods in the `PrintWriter` class do not throw exceptions. If an output error occurs, an internal flag is set in the object to record the event. You can check whether there have been any output errors by calling the method, `checkError()`. This returns `true` if one or more errors occurred, and `false` otherwise.

We can modify the example in Chapter 4 for calculating primes to use a character output stream.

Try It Out — Displaying Primes on a Character Output Stream

Make the following changes to the source code:

```java
import java.io.*;

public class PrimeCharacters
{
  public static void main(String[] args)
  {
    long[] primes = new long[20];        // Array to store primes
    primes[0] = 2;                        // Seed the first prime
    primes[1] = 3;                        // and the second
    int count = 2;                        // Count of primes found - up to now
                                          // which is also the array index
    long number = 5;                      // Next integer to be tested

    outer:
    for( ; count < primes.length; number += 2)
    {
      // The maximum divisor we need to try is square root of number
      long limit = (long)Math.ceil(Math.sqrt((double)number));

      // Divide by all the primes we have up to limit
      for(int i = 1; i < count && primes[i] <= limit; i++)
        if(number%primes[i] == 0)        // Is it an exact divisor?
          continue outer;                // yes, try the next number

      primes[count++] = number;          // We got one!
    }

    // Output the primes array using a buffered stream
    PrintWriter output = new PrintWriter(
                    new BufferedWriter(
                    new FileWriter(FileDescriptor.out)));

    for(int i=0; i < primes.length; i++)
      // New line after every fifth prime
      output.print((i%5==0 ? "\n" : "   ") + primes[i]);
    output.close();                      // Close the stream
  }
}
```

This produces the output:

```
 2   3   5   7   11
13  17  19  23   29
31  37  41  43   47
53  59  61  67   71
```

How It Works

To output the `primes[]` array, we create the object `output`, which is of type, `PrintWriter`. This is created from a `BufferedWriter` object so that we get buffering for the output. Without this, a physical write would occur for every call to `print()`. With the buffer, a physical write will occur when the buffer is full, or when the stream is flushed, by calling the `flush()` or the `close()` method for the stream. The `BufferedWriter` object is constructed from a `FileWriter` object which is constructed from the `FileDescriptor` object, `out`, which refers to the standard output device, usually the screen.

Writing the array to `output` takes place in the last `for` loop. We call the `print()` method for the `PrintWriter` object, `output`, for each iteration. The expression used as the argument to the `print()` method outputs two spaces before each prime value, except for every fifth value, when it outputs a new line.

Calling `close()` for the `PrintWriter` object will cause the `close()` method to be called for each of the nested character streams. As we saw earlier, the `close()` method flushes the stream before closing it, so any data still in the buffer for the `BufferedWriter` object will be written to the `FileWriter` stream.

The output is a little ragged. It would be nice to have it aligned in columns, so let's see how to do that.

Formatting Printed Output

Output formatting involves a considerable amount of work, particularly for floating point values. It takes quite a bit of code to sort out the decimal places and exponent values and it is a little beyond the scope of this book. However, it is quite easy to line your numeric output up in columns by defining your own subclass of `PrintWriter`.

Try It Out — Formatting Prime Output

We will define the class so that it contains a data member containing the width of the field for a data member. The basic class definition will be:

```java
import java.io.*;

public class FormatWriter extends PrintWriter
{
  private int width = 10;        // Field width required for output

  // Basic constructor for a default field width
  public FormatWriter(Writer output)
  {
    super(output);                    // Call PrintStream constructor
  }
```

```
    // Constructor with a specified field width
    public FormatWriter(Writer output, int width)
    {
      super(output);                // Call PrintStream constructor
      this.width = width;           // Store the field width
    }

    // Constructor with autoflush option
    public FormatWriter(Writer output, boolean autoflush)
    {
      super(output, autoflush);     // Call PrintStream constructor
    }

    // Constructor with a specified field width and autoflush option
    public FormatWriter(Writer output, boolean autoflush, int width)
    {
      super(output, autoflush);     // Call PrintStream constructor
      this.width = width;           // Store the field width
    }
}
```

How It Works

This class is intended to output data in a fixed field width. The only data member in our class FormatWriter, is the variable, width, of type, int, which holds the output field width. Since we derive our class from PrintWriter, we have all the facilities of the PrintWriter class available. Our constructors are essentially the same as the base class constructors, with the addition of the width parameter to specify the number of characters required for the field width. In each of our constructors, after calling the appropriate base class constructor, we just set the width member. However, we have only implemented constructors that accept a Writer object. You can add constructors to accept an OutputStream object if you need them.

At the moment, if you call print() or println() for a FormatWriter object, it will call the base class method, so the behavior will be exactly the same as a PrintWriter object. To change this, we will add our own print() and println() methods that override the base class methods. First, we will add a helper method.

Overriding print() and println()

We know that we want to output width characters for each value that we output. We will assume that the data value is to be right justified in the field, so all we need to do is figure out how many characters there are in each data value, subtract that from the total field width and output that many blanks before we write the data value to the stream.

Since we need a character representation for each data value to do this, we will implement a method, output(), in our FormatWriter class that will accept a String object as an argument, and output this object right justified in the field.

```
    // Helper method for output
    private void output(String str)
    {
      int blanks = width - str.length();    // Number of blanks needed

      // If the length is less than the width, add blanks to the start
      for(int i = 0; i < blanks; i++)
        super.print(' ');                   // Output a space
      super.print(str);                     // Use base method for output
    }
```

We will only use this method inside the class, so we make it `private`. The spaces are output by calling the `print()` method for the base class, `PrintWriter`, that accepts a single character as an argument. The `for` loop outputs the spaces required. The method then outputs the string using the base class method that accepts a `String` object. If the string, `str`, has more characters than the field width, then it will just output the string. This will mess up the nice neat columns, but that's better than truncating the output.

We can now implement the `print()` method for `long` values in our class very easily using the `output()` method:

```
// Output type long formatted in a given width
public void print(long value)
{
   output(String.valueOf(value));            // Pad to width and output
}
```

The `print(long value)` method calls the `static valueOf()` method in the `String` class to convert the value to a character string. The string is then passed to the `output()` method for output within the field width.

The `print()` method for `double` values will be almost identical:

```
// Output type double formatted in a given width
public void print(double value)
{
   output(String.valueOf(value));            // Pad to width and output
}
```

You should be able to implement all the other versions of `print()` if you need them.

The `println()` method is also very simple. Here's the implementation for a `long` value:

```
// Output type long formatted in a given width plus a newline
public void println(long value)
{
   this.print(value);                        // Call current method
   super.println();                          // Call base method
}
```

In the `println()` method, we call the `print()` method for our class to output the value in the field, and then call the base class `println()` method to end the line. It is important to do this, rather than write a newline character to the stream, if you want to mirror the behavior of the `PrintWriter` class. Writing a newline does not necessarily flush the stream, whereas calling the base class version of `println()` does, because the base class constructor that we call in our class constructor flushes by default.

The `println()` method for `double` values is almost identical.

```
// Output type double formatted in a given width plus a newline
public void println(double value)
{
  this.print(value);                     // Call current method
  super.println();                       // Call base method
}
```

The `println()` methods for the other data types will be much the same – only a different parameter type is needed, once you have implemented the corresponding `print()` method.

If you want more flexibility with objects of the `FormatWriter` class, you can add a `setWidth()` member to change the field width and perhaps a `getWidth()` member to find out what it is currently. The `setWidth()` method will be:

```
public void setWidth(int width)
{
  this.width = width>0 ? width : 1;
}
```

With the `setWidth()` method, you can then set an individual field width for each value that you output, if necessary. You could also implement `print()` methods that accept a width value as a second argument.

We can use the `FormatWriter` class to help us output the primes from the previous example in five tidy columns.

Try It Out — Outputting Data in Fixed Fields

We only need to modify the code at the end of the previous example so that it uses our `FormatWriter` class:

```
import java.io.*;

public class NeatPrimesOutput
{
  public static void main(String[] args)
  {

    ...

      // Divide by all the primes we have up to limit
      for(int i = 1; i < count && primes[i] <= limit; i++)
        if(number%primes[i] == 0)        // Is it an exact divisor?
          continue outer;                // yes, try the next number

      primes[count++] = number;          // We got one!
    }

    // Output the primes array using a formatted buffered stream
    FormatWriter out = new FormatWriter(
                  new BufferedWriter(
                  new FileWriter(FileDescriptor.out)), 12);
```

```
      for(int i=0; i < primes.length; i++)
      {
        if(i%5==0)                    // New line before every fifth prime
          out.println();

        out.print(primes[i]);         // Output a prime
      }
      out.close();                    // Close the stream
    }
  }
```

Of course, the file containing this class definition needs to be in the same directory as the definition for the `FormatWriter` class. This example should produce the output:

```
     2          3          5          7         11
    13         17         19         23         29
    31         37         41         43         47
    53         59         61         67         71
```

How It Works

As we want to output the data to the standard output stream, we create a `FileWriter` object from the `out` member of the `FileDescriptor` class. The `FileWriter` object is passed to a `BufferedWriter` constructor to obtain a buffered stream, and this stream is passed as the first argument to a constructor for a `FormatWriter` object. The second argument to the constructor is the field width, 12. If we omit the second argument, we will get an object with the default field width, 10.

After the stream object has been created, we output the primes. Before each line of five prime values, we call the `println()` method that our `FormatWriter` class inherits from `PrintWriter`. This outputs a newline character to the stream and flushes the buffer. Finally, we call `close()` to flush and close the stream.

We will find out how to read the data back in the next chapter.

Summary

In this chapter, we have discussed the facilities for outputting basic types of data to a stream. The important points we have discussed include:

❑ The path to a physical file can be represented by an object of the class `File`

❑ A physical file can also be represented by an object of type `FileDescriptor`

❑ A stream is an abstract representation of a source of serial input, or a destination for serial output

❑ The classes supporting stream operations are contained in the package `java.io`

❑ Two kinds of stream operations are supported, **byte stream operations** will result in streams that contain bytes, and **character stream operations** are for streams that contain characters in the local machine character encoding

- No conversion occurs when characters are written to, or read from, a byte stream. Characters are converted from Unicode to the local machine representation of characters when a characters stream is written

- Byte output streams are represented by sub-classes of the class `OutputStream`

- Character output stream operations are provided by sub-classes of the `Writer` class

- Classes derived from `OutputStream` allow you to write a file

- The filter output stream classes can be used to enhance the functionality of the basic output stream class objects that represent a physical file

- If you want to format the data that you write to a stream ,you must implement the formatting capability yourself

Exercises

1. Write a program that using an integer array of date values containing month, day, year as integers for some number of dates (10 say), write a file with a string representation of each date. For example, the date values 3,2,1990 would be written to the file as "2nd March 1990".

2. Extend the previous example to write a second file at the same time as the first, but containing the month, day, year values as binary data.

3. Write a program that, for a given `String` object defined in the code, will write strings to a file corresponding to all possible permutations of the words in the string. e.g. For the string, "the fat cat", you would write the strings: "the fat cat", "the cat fat", "cat the fat", cat fat the", "fat the cat", "fat cat the", to the file, although not necessarily in that sequence. (Don't use very long strings; with n words in the string, the number of permutations is n!)

Stream Input, and Object Streams

In this chapter, we will see how to read back the sort of data that we wrote to streams in the previous chapter. We will also look into reading and writing random access files, and how you can transfer objects to and from a stream. By the end of this chapter you will have learnt:

❑ How to read from a stream.

❑ How to read a file from a ZIP archive.

❑ How to concatenate several streams so you can read them as a single stream.

❑ How to read or write at any position in a file (random access).

❑ How to read the value of basic Java types from the keyboard.

❑ How to write objects to a file and read them back.

❑ How to obtain formatted input from a character stream.

Byte Input Streams

Byte input streams are defined using sub-classes of the `abstract` class, `InputStream`. Java supports what are known as **markable streams**. A markable stream is a stream in which any position can be marked by calling a special method, so that you can return to that same position later simply by calling another method. This is achieved by keeping track of how many bytes have been read from the stream (within the stream object). This feature makes it very easy to process a block of data repeatedly, from a file or from the keyboard.

The classes derived from the `InputStream` class all inherit the following methods.

Method	Description
`read()`	This version of the `read()` method is `abstract` and therefore always needs to be implemented by a subclass. The method should read a single byte of data from the stream and return it as type, `int`.
`read(` `byte[] buffer)`	This method reads sufficient bytes to fill the array `buffer`, or until the end of the stream is reached. The method returns the number of bytes read as type, `int`.

`read(`
  `byte buffer,`
  `int offset,`
  `int length)`
	This version reads bytes into the array buffer starting at element `buffer[offset]`. The method will read up to `length` bytes into the array, or until the end of the stream is reached, and will return the number of bytes read as type, `int`.

`skip(long n)`	This method will read and discard n bytes from the stream, or until the end of the stream is reached, and return the number of bytes skipped as type `long`. You would use this to skip over parts of a file that you don't want to process.
`mark(` `int readlimit)`	This method marks the current position in the input stream so that you can return to it using the `reset()` method. If you read more than `readlimit` bytes from the stream after the mark has been set, the mark will be invalidated.
`reset()`	This method positions the stream at the point defined by a previous call of the `mark()` method. If the `mark()` method has not been called previously, or if the mark operation is not supported for the stream, then an `IOException` may be thrown.
`markSupported()`	This method returns `true` if the `mark` operation is supported for the stream and `false` otherwise.
`available()`	This method returns an `int` value that is the number of bytes that can be read from the current stream without blocking. If you try to read more bytes than the number returned by this method, the read operation will not return and your program thread will not continue until all the data required becomes available. This is referred to as **blocking**. For example, stream input from the keyboard can be blocked until you press the *Enter* key. The method throws an `IOException` if an error occurs.
`close()`	This method closes the input stream. It throws an `IOException` if an error occurs.

With all these versions of the `read()` method, -1 is returned if the end of the stream has been reached and an exception, of type `IOException`, will be thrown if any other error occurs. Although the basic `read()` method is the only `abstract` method in the class, subclasses will typically implement their own versions of most of these methods. Note that there is no `open()` method complementing the `close()` method. Once an input stream object has been created, you can read from the stream immediately.

Sub-classes of InputStream

There are six classes derived directly from the abstract class, `InputStream`.

> **One of these, the** `ObjectInputStream` **class, is specific to reading from a stream that contains class objects, including objects of classes that you define. Reading and writing objects is a somewhat different process from reading and writing ordinary data, so we will defer discussion of this until later in this chapter when we will look at how you can write objects of your own classes to a stream, and read them back.**

We will concentrate here on the other five subclasses of `InputStream`. You can use four of these for various kinds of stream input operations. The fifth is a base class for further classes that can process data from an input stream in various ways. The direct subclasses of the class, `InputStream`, excluding the `ObjectInputStream` class, are show below.

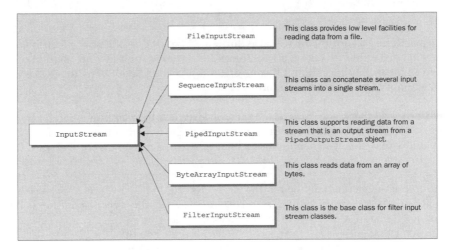

As you can see, three of these subclasses of `InputStream` enable you to define three different kinds of input stream, each with a different data source. The three options you have for a data source are a file, a `byte` array and a piped output stream from another process or thread. The two other subclasses enable you to add capabilities to an input stream. The class `SequenceInputStream` will allow you to concatenate several input streams into a single stream, and the `FilterInputStream` class is designed to be a base for deriving a number of filter stream classes.

The derived classes in the diagram, other than `FilterInputStream`, only provide the ability to read a single byte or an array of bytes from a file. This is not very convenient when you want to read data of one of the other primitive types from a file.

To do this, you can use the subclasses of `FilterInputStream` to create objects that provide more flexibility in the way data input is handled. Of course, all this applies to reading binary data from a stream. To read character data, we will be using an `InputReader` object that operates on an `InputStream` object. The classes `PipedInputStream` and `ByteArrayInputStream` are designed to complement the equivalent classes for output.

The FileInputStream Object

You can create a `FileInputStream` object corresponding to a particular disk file by passing a `File` object to the constructor for the class.

```
File myPrimes = new File("c:/JunkData/Primes.bin");
FileInputStream myStream = new FileInputStream(myPrimes);
```

This defines the stream, `myStream`, which refers to the file that we created in the previous example using an `OutputStream` object. The `FileInputStream` constructor will throw a `FileNotFoundException` if the file is not found.

There is also another constructor for `FileInputStream` objects which will accept a `String` containing the file path. For example, we could create the input stream object `myStream` with the statement:

```
FileInputStream myStream =
                       new FileInputStream("c:/JunkData/Primes.bin");
```

This `FileInputStream` constructor will also throw a `FileNotFoundException` if the file does not exist, so you will need either to write a `catch` block for this exception in your method or to declare that your method can throw this exception. Of course, it is also a good idea to create a `File` object and test it before you attempt to create the stream object.

Once you have created the stream object, the file is available to be read immediately. However, all you have available are the `read()` methods that will read a single byte or a byte array from the stream. To get more capability than this, you need to use a filter input stream class, as we will see a little later.

In addition to the methods defined in the base class, the `FileInputStream` also has the method `getFD()` which returns a `FileDescriptor` object corresponding to the file that the `FileInputStream` object represents. The `FileInputStream` class has a constructor that accepts a `FileDescriptor` object, as do the `FileOutputStream`, `FileReader` and `FileWriter` classes.

Sequence Input Streams

You can combine several streams into a single stream by using the `SequenceInputStream` class. The streams are combined by effectively concatenating them head to tail in the sequence in which you specify them when you construct your `SequenceInputStream` object.

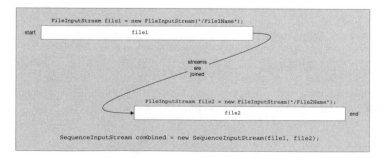

The `SequenceInputStream` class has two constructors – one which combines two stream objects into a single stream and another which combines several. You can see the effect of combining two byte input streams, `file1` and `file2`, into a single stream in the diagram above. The code to create and combine the streams is shown in the diagram.

The constructor that combines several streams accepts a single argument of type, `Enumeration`. Each object in the `Enumeration` must be of a type that has `InputStream` as a base. We will see how an `Enumeration` object is created in Chapter 10, but here's a code fragment that uses an `Enumeration` to create a `SequenceInputStream` object to which you can refer if necessary:

```
Vector streams = new Vector();                          // Vector to hold the streams

// Add the streams to the Vector
streams.addElement(new FileInputStream("/File1Name"));
streams.addElement(new FileInputStream("/File2Name"));
streams.addElement(new FileInputStream("/File3Name"));
streams.addElement(new FileInputStream("/File4Name"));

// Create a stream combining all four file input streams
SequenceInputStream allFour = new SequenceInputStream(streams.elements());
```

As you will see in Chapter 10, a `Vector` object is something like an array that can store objects of any kind, and its `elements()` method returns an `Enumeration` that we can pass to the `SequenceInputStream` contructor.

You don't have to use an enumeration to concatenate multiple streams. In fact, you can easily combine multiple byte input streams using the first constructor just by nesting sequence input streams. Given that we have the `SequenceInputStream` object `combined`, we could construct a stream that concatenates a further two streams to this with the statements:

```
FileInputStream file3 = new FileInputStream("/File3Name");
FileInputStream file4 = new FileInputStream("/File4Name");
SequenceInputStream allFour = new SequenceInputStream(combined,
                             new SequenceInputStream(file3, file4));
```

After constructing the two `FileInputStream` objects, these are combined to create a `SequenceInputStream` object which in turn is passed as the second argument to the constructor for `SequenceInputStream`. This creates the stream, `allFour`, which will be the result of concatenating all four files. While this avoids the need to use an enumeration, it is less efficient when more than two streams are to be concatenated.

When you read from a sequence input stream, the transition from one concatenated stream to the next is automatic. When the end of one stream is reached, its `close()` method will be called, and data will then be read from the next stream. You have no means of detecting when this occurs. So far as you are concerned you are dealing with a single seamless stream. Only when you read past the end of the last stream will an end-of-file condition be registered for the `SequenceInputStream` object. If you call the `close()` method for a `SequenceInputStream` object, any of the streams making up the object that are open will be closed.

The Input Filter Classes

There are quite a few sub-classes of the `FilterInputStream` classes, so we will need to go through them in stages. Four of them complement the byte output stream classes we have seen, and are concerned with normal byte input stream operations, as shown below.

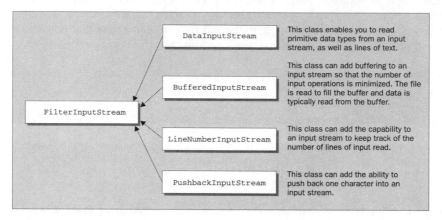

All these subclasses are defined in the `java.io` package. The `DataInputStream` class only supports reading data from a file in binary form. This kind of file will normally have been created by the `DataOutputStream` class methods.

Within the Java classes supporting input from a stream, you have no methods that will convert numerical data from a character stream, such as the keyboard for instance, to binary integer or floating point data values. Neither the `InputStream` classes themselves nor the `Reader` classes for reading characters from a stream provide this capability. If you need to be able to read formatted numerical data from an input stream, you must implement it yourself. However, as we will see later in this chapter, you do get quite a bit of help from another class in the `java.io` package – `StreamTokenizer`, so it's not as difficult as it sounds.

A further five sub-classes of the `FilterInputStream` class are shown in the diagram below.

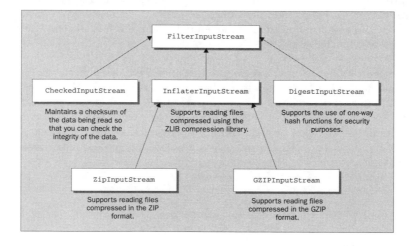

The `DigestInputStream` class is in the package `java.security`. It is the complement of the `DigestOutputStream` we saw in the last chapter. The other four subclasses of the `FilterInputStream` class that appear above are in the package `java.util.zip`. The `CheckedInputStream` class computes a checksum for the bytes that are read from the file and is used with files that were written using a `CheckedOutputStream` class object. The other three classes complement the output stream classes that support compression. We will look at how we can read a ZIP and retrieve the data from the compressed file later in this chapter.

There is one other input stream class not shown in the diagram that is a direct subclass of `FilterInputStream`. The `ProgressMonitorInputStream` class is intended to be used with streams where the input may be slow. An object of this class monitors the operation of reading from the stream and displays a dialog to inform the user of progress. This class is defined in the `javax.swing` package and is used with applications that implement a graphical user interface.

Reading from an Input Stream

To read from an input stream, particularly if the stream is a disk file, you will normally use one of the filter input streams. Without a filter stream, all you can read from a stream is bytes, whereas, in practice, the minimum you will want is to read values of the basic types. First we will look at how to read the basic types of data values from a disk file.

Reading from a Disk File

Reading binary data from a disk file using a filter input stream is analogous to the mechanism we saw for writing binary data to an output stream. You need to create a `DataInputStream` object from a `FileInputStream` object that identifies the file you want to read.

To see how this works in practice, we could create a program to read the file of prime numbers that we created in the last chapter. We will read the primes from the file using a byte input stream and write them to the screen using a character stream.

Try It Out – Reading in the Primes.bin File

Let's start with the code to create the input stream object for the file:

```
import java.io.*;

public class ReadPrimes
{
  public static void main(String[] args)
  {
    try
    {
      // Create a File object and an input stream object for the file
      String directory = "c:/JunkData";      // Directory path
      String fileName = "Primes.bin";          // File name
      File myPrimes = new File(directory, fileName);

      DataInputStream primesIn = new DataInputStream(
                          new FileInputStream(myPrimes));
```

```
      // Code to read the primes from the stream - listed below

      out.close();                      // Flush and close the output stream
      primesIn.close();                 // Close the input stream
    }
    catch(FileNotFoundException e)      // Stream creation exception
    {
      System.err.println(e);
      return;
    }
    catch(IOException e)                // File read exception
    {
      System.err.println("Error reading input file" + e );
      return;
    }
  }
}
```

We can now add the code to read the primes from the stream and to output them to the screen. We will use a `FormatWriter` object to manage the output to the screen, so be sure to copy the `FormatWriter.java` file to the same directory as the current class file is stored, or copy the `FormatWriter.class` file to the "`/JDK1.3/jre/classes`" directory. The code to read the primes from the file and display them is as follows:

```
      // Create a default formatted character output stream
      FormatWriter out = new FormatWriter(
                     new BufferedWriter(
                     new FileWriter(FileDescriptor.out)));

      long[] primes = new long[6];      // Array for one line of primes
      boolean EOF = false;              // End of file flag

      while(!EOF)

      {
        int index = 0;                  // Index for storing primes
        try
        {
          // Fill the array with primes from the file
          for(index = 0; index < primes.length; index++)
            primes[index] = primesIn.readLong();
        }
        catch(EOFException e)
        {
          EOF = true;                   // This will end the while loop
        }

        // Output the number of primes in the array
        for(int j = 0; j < index; j++)
          out.print(primes[j]);
        out.println();                  // Write end of line
      }
```

The output from this example should begin:

```
      2           3           5           7           11          13
      17          19          23          29          31          37
```

Just the first few are shown here. There are 200 primes in the complete output.

How It Works

At the start of the `ReadPrimes` class, a `File` object is created from the `directory` and `fileName` strings, and this object is passed to the `FileInputStream` constructor to create a byte input stream for the file. The directory and the file should be the same as that used to write primes to the file in the example in the last chapter. The `FileInputStream` constructor will throw a `FileNotFoundException` if the file is not found. Since we catch this exception in the `catch` block following the `try` block, we don't need to test explicitly that the directory and file name are valid.

> You can check out how the `FileNotFoundException` is caught by deliberately putting an invalid file path in the call to the **`File`** constructor. This is not difficult because even a leading space in the file name will cause the file not to be found.

The `FileInputStream` object is passed to the `DataInputStream` constructor to create the byte stream object that we will use to read the file. This object will provide us with the methods that we need to read primitive data types from the file. The `FileInputStream` object only has the basic `read()` methods for a single byte or a byte array, that are declared in the base class, `InputStream`.

The file is read in the `while` loop, controlled by the flag, `EOF`, which we set to `false` initially. Because we read the file in groups of six values and then output them to the screen, we have included a mechanism to automatically signal when we reach the end of the file. We use the fact that the read operation will throw an `EOFException` when the end of file is reached.

We read a block of primes to fill the `primes[]` array from the file, in the `try` block inside the `while` loop. As long as no `EOFException` is thrown, the code immediately following the `catch` block is executed. This writes the block of primes to the `out` stream in the `for` loop, and the `while` loop continues. The `for` loop to write the primes is controlled by the value of `index` in order to deal with the situation that can arise when the end of the file is reached. If the number of values in the file is not a multiple of the size of the `primes[]` array, the array will not be full for the last line of output. The number of elements will be the value stored in the variable `index`. We must declare the variable, `index`, outside the `try` block in the `while` loop, otherwise it won't exist when we output the primes.

When the `EOFException` is thrown, the `catch` block following the inner `try` block is executed. This will set the `EOF` flag to `true`. Thus the `while` loop will end after the current iteration, once the last line of primes has been written to `out`. If an error occurs on reading the file, an `IOException` will be thrown, so we need a `catch` block for this at the end of the main `try` block.

Reading a ZIP Archive

You can use an object of the `ZipInputStream` class to read a ZIP archive containing compressed files. The argument to the class constructor must be an `InputStream` object that represents a physical ZIP archive. We can define an object corresponding to the ZIP we obtained from the `primes.bin` file in the last chapter with the statements:

```
String dirName = "c:/JunkData";           // Directory for the ZIP file
String zipName = "NewPrimes.zip";          // The ZIP archive name
File myPrimeZip = new File(dirName, zipName);  // The file object
ZipInputStream myZipFile = new ZipInputStream(
                      new FileInputStream(myPrimeZip));
```

The `ZipInputStream` class defines the following methods.

Method	Description
getNextEntry()	Returns a `ZipEntry` object for the next ZIP entry in the archive and positions the stream at the beginning of the entry.
closeEntry()	Closes the current ZIP entry and positions the stream for reading the next entry.

read(byte[] array,
        int offset,
        int length)
	Reads `length` bytes from the ZIP entry into array, starting at index position `offset` in the array. This method can throw an `IOException` if an I/O error occurs, or a `ZipException` if a ZIP file error occurs.

skip(long byteCount)	Skips over the next `byteCount` bytes in the ZIP entry. This can also throw an `IOException` or a `ZIPEXception`.
close()	Closes the ZIP input stream. This method can throw an `IOException`.

The process for reading from a ZIP entry is to call `getNextEntry()` for the `ZipInputStream` object before starting read operations. You can use the `ZipEntry` object returned to get the name of the file in the ZIP entry by calling the `getName()` method. When you finish reading the ZIP entry, you call `closeEntry()`. Then you can call `getNextEntry()` for the next ZIP entry if there are additional entries. When you are done with the stream, you call its `close()` method to close it.

Of course, the basic `read()` method here is not what we want to use to read our `NewPrimes.zip` file from the archive. We want to read values of type `long`, so we will need to wrap another input stream around the `ZipInputStream`:

```
DataInputStream primesIn = new DataInputStream(
                      new BufferedInputStream(myZipFile));
```

Let's see how this works in practice. We can extract the ZIP file and write the contents to the screen.

Try It Out – A Prime Unzipping Example

If you have tested all the code in the last chapter, you should have a file, `NewPrimes.zip`, containing some prime numbers in a directory, `c:\JunkData`. We will use the fragments of code we have just seen to read all the primes from the archive, `NewPrimes.zip`, and write them to the standard output stream using our `FormatWriter` class. If you have copied `FormatWriter.class` to the `classes` subdirectory of the `jre` directory, it will automatically be accessible for this and any other examples.

Here's the code to read the file:

```java
import java.io.*;
import java.util.zip.*;

class ReadZippedPrimes
{
  public static void main(String[] args)
  {
    try
    {
      // Create a default formatted character output stream
      FormatWriter out = new FormatWriter(
                     new BufferedWriter(
                     new FileWriter(FileDescriptor.out)));

      String dirName = "c:/JunkData";    // Directory for the ZIP file
      String zipName = "NewPrimes.zip";   // The ZIP archive name

      File myPrimeZip = new File(dirName, zipName);  // The file object
      ZipInputStream myZipFile = new ZipInputStream(
                          new FileInputStream(myPrimeZip));
      ZipEntry myZipEntry = myZipFile.getNextEntry();

      out.println("Compressed File is " + myZipEntry.getName());
      DataInputStream primesIn = new DataInputStream(
                          new BufferedInputStream(myZipFile));

      long[] primes = new long[6];        // Array for one line of primes
      boolean EOF = false;                // End of file flag

      while(!EOF)
      {
        int index = 0;                    // Index for storing primes
        try
        {
          // Fill the array with primes from the file
          for(index = 0; index < primes.length; index++)
            primes[index] = primesIn.readLong();
        }
        catch(EOFException e)
        {
          EOF = true;                     // This will end the while loop
        }
        // Output the number of primes in the array
        for(int j = 0; j < index; j++)
          out.print(primes[j]);
        out.println();                    // Write end of line
      }
      out.close();                        // Flush and close the output stream
      primesIn.close();                   // Close the input stream
    }
```

```
    catch(FileNotFoundException e)              // Stream creation exception
    {
      System.err.println(e);
      return;
    }
    catch(IOException e)                         // File read exception
    {
      System.out.println("Error reading input file" + e );
      return;
    }
  }
}
```

This will output the name of the file in the archive, plus the primes,

```
Compressed File is Primes.bin
            2          3          5          7         11         13
           17         19         23         29         31         37
```

and so on.

How It Works

We create the `ZipInputStream` object from a `FileInputStream` object exactly as we saw earlier. We get the `ZipEntry` object by calling the `getNextEntry()` method for the `ZipInputStream` object and use its `getName()` method to output the name of the file. We then create the `primesIn` stream object and read the values in much the same way as we used to read the uncompressed `Primes.bin` file in the earlier example.

> **There is another class, `ZipFile`, supporting the reading of ZIP files that is defined in the package `java.util.zip`. This is intended to ease the processing of ZIP archives that contain multiple compressed files. A `ZipFile` object can return an enumeration of all the entries in a zip so that you can then process all of them quite easily in a loop.**

Character Input Streams

The character input operations that read data from a stream as Unicode characters are provided by classes derived from `Reader`. Where the external source is a file, automatic character code conversion is provided by the `Reader` object. You would use a `Reader` object to read a stream written by a `Writer` object. There are nine classes derived from the `Reader` class as shown in the diagram.

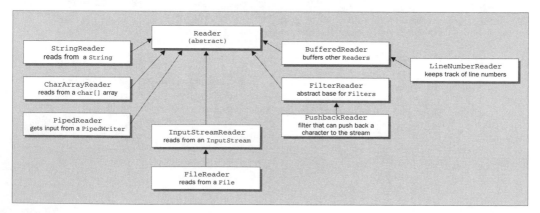

Most of the character input classes complement the corresponding class for character output. A `PipedReader` class object is intended to be used in conjunction with a `PipedWriter` object to link two threads. The `StringReader` and `CharArrayReader` classes read from a `String` or a `char[]` array that you pass to the constructor. You use the `BufferedReader` class to buffer operations for another `Reader` object, usually a `FileReader` or an `InputStreamReader` object that you pass to the `BufferedReader` class constructor.

To read a physical file, you can create an object using either the `FileReader` class or the `InputStreamReader` class. You can create a `FileReader` object from a `File` object, a `FileDescriptor` object or a string defining the file name. You create an `InputStreamReader` object from an `InputStream` object. The `FileReader` class provides automatic conversion from the character coding used by the local computer to Unicode as the data is read.

The `PushbackReader` constructor accepts a `Reader` object as an argument – typically a `FileReader` or an `InputStreamReader` object. The `PushbackReader` stream allows you to read characters from the stream, and then push them back on the stream to allow them to be read again. This gives you a read-ahead mechanism that you can use to check what is in the stream, reset the stream back to its original condition and then select the appropriate method to process the stream.

The methods that all the character input stream classes inherit from the `Reader` class are:

Method	Description
`read()`	Reads a character from the stream and returns it as type, `int`. With each of the `read()` methods, `-1` is returned if the end of the stream has been reached. If an error occurs, an exception of type, `IOException`, will be thrown.
`read(char[] array)`	Reads characters from the stream to fill `array`. The method returns the number of bytes read as type `int`.
`read(char[] array, int offset, int length)`	Reads `length` characters from the stream into `array` starting at the index position, `offset`. The method returns the number of bytes read as type, `int`.
`markSupported()`	Returns `true` if the stream is markable, and `false` otherwise.
`mark(int readAheadLimit)`	Marks the current position in the stream. The argument specifies the maximum number of characters that can be read from the stream without losing track of the current mark position.
`reset()`	Resets the stream to the previous mark position. If the stream was not marked, it may sometimes be reset to the beginning.
`ready()`	Returns `true` if the stream is ready to be read and `false` otherwise.

Table continued on following page

Method	Description
`skip(long charCount)`	Skips over `charCount` characters in the stream. The method returns the number of characters skipped which will be less than `charCount` if the end of the stream is reached or if an input error stops the process.
`close()`	Closes the stream.

All these methods, with the exception of `markSupported()` can throw an `IOException` if an error occurs. All the read methods will block, that is, they will not return to the calling point until some characters can be read from the stream, the end of the stream is reached, or an error occurs.

Reading a File as a Character Stream

We could read the file of proverbs that we wrote as an exercise for the character output streams. Remember that we wrote the string length to the file preceding the text for each proverb. This data is not binary – we had to write the string equivalent of the length to the file. We therefore have some work to do to figure out where the string length characters end and where the proverb begins. We can do this by using a `PushBackReader` object.

We can create a `File` object for the file first:

```
String dirName = "c:/JunkData";           // Directory for the output file
String fileName = "Proverbs.txt";          // Name of the output file
File input = new File(dirName, fileName);  // The file object
```

This creates a `File` object from `String` objects for the directory and file names. We won't need to verify that the file exists as the `FileReader` constructor will throw a `FileNotFoundException` if it doesn't.

We will buffer the `FileReader` stream by passing it to a `BufferedReader` stream constructor. We can then create the `PushBackReader` object from the `BufferedReader` object with the statement:

```
PushbackReader in = new PushbackReader(
                    new BufferedReader(
                    new FileReader(input)));
```

The `PushbackReader` object we create here will allow only one character to be pushed back onto the stream, but this is sufficient for our purposes. If we needed to push more characters back onto the stream, we could use the `PushbackReader` constructor that accepts a second argument of type `int` specifying the maximum number of characters that can be pushed back.

Each proverb is preceded by its length. We can use the special capabilities of the `PushbackReader` stream to help us deal with this. As well as the methods defined in the `Reader` base class, the `PushbackReader` class defines three methods that write characters back to the stream:

`unread()` Methods	Description
`unread(int c)`	Writes the character, c, back to the stream.
`unread(char[] array)`	Writes the entire contents of `array` back to the stream.
`unread(char[] array, int offset, int length)`	Writes `length` elements of `array` back to the stream starting at index position, `offset`.

All of these will throw an `IOException` if an error occurs. We will be able to read the characters that correspond to the length of a proverb from the stream. When we find a character that is not a digit, we know that we have come to the end of the characters for the string length, so we can write it back to the stream. (It is rather unlikely that we have a proverb starting with a digit!) We can assemble the characters that make up the length of the proverb into a string, `number`, as follows.

```
String number = "";              // String length as characters

// Get the characters for the length
while(Character.isDigit((char)(c = in.read())))
  number += (char)c;

// Test for end of file here - c will be -1

in.unread(c);                    // Push back the last character
```

The `read()` method for the `PushbackReader` object, `in`, returns a character from the stream as type, `int`, which we store in the variable, `c`. This will have the value -1 if the end of file is detected. After casting c to type, `char`, we pass it as an argument to the `isDigit()` method in the `Character` class. This returns `true` if the character is a digit so the `while` loop will continue as long as this is the case. On each iteration of the `while` loop, we add the digit character read from the stream to the end of the string, `number`. When the `while` loop ends, we will have all the digits for the length of the next proverb in the `String` object, `number`.

When the `while` loop ends, we must test for an end of file condition – indicated by c having the value, -1. This will occur immediately after the last proverb has been read. We will fill in this detail later. If it is not the end of file, the last character read must be the first character of the proverb, so we write c back to the file by calling the `unread()` method for the stream object, `in`.

We now have enough information to read the next proverb.

```
char[] proverb = new char[Integer.parseInt(number)];
in.read(proverb);                              // Read a proverb
```

This creates an array of type `char[]` that has precisely the number of elements required for the complete proverb. We convert the `String` object, `number`, to an `int` value by passing it to the `parseInt()` method from the `Integer` class.

Let's put all this together in a working example.

Try It Out – Using a PushbackReader on a Character Stream

The example will read the file and output all the proverbs to the screen. Here's the complete program.

```
// Using the push back reader
import java.io.*;

class ReadCharacters
{
  public static void main(String[] args)
  {
    try
    {

      String dirName = "c:/JunkData";          // Directory for the output file
      String fileName = "Proverbs.txt";        // Name of the output file

      File input = new File(dirName, fileName); // The file object

      PushbackReader in = new PushbackReader(
                          new BufferedReader(
                          new FileReader(input)));

      int c;                                   // Character store
      while(true)
      {
        String number ="";                     // String length as characters

        // Get the characters for the length
        while(Character.isDigit((char)(c = in.read())))
          number += (char)c;

        if(c==-1)                              // Check for end of file
          break;                               // End the loop
        else                                   // It is not end of file so
          in.unread(c);                        // push back the last character

        char[] proverb = new char[Integer.parseInt(number)];
        in.read(proverb);                      // Read a proverb
        System.out.println(proverb);
      }
    }
    catch(FileNotFoundException e)             // Stream creation exception
    {
      System.err.println(e);
      return;
    }
    catch(IOException e)                       // File read exception
    {
      System.err.println("Error reading input file" + e );
      return;
    }
  }
}
```

The output will depend on what is in the file which will depend on how many times you ran the program that wrote it. I get the following output.

```
Indecision maximises flexibility.
Only the mediocre are always at their best.
A little knowledge is a dangerous thing.
Many a mickle makes a muckle.
Who begins too much achieves little.
Who knows most says least.
A wise man sits on the hole in his carpet.
Indecision maximixes flexibility.
Only the mediocre are always at their best.
A little knowledge is a dangerous thing.
Many a mickle makes a muckle.
Who begins too much achieves little.
Who knows most says least.
A wise man sits on the hole in his carpet.
```

How It Works

The overall read operation takes place in the indefinite `while` loop. Each iteration of this loop reads one proverb from the file. If an end of file condition is recognized, the `break` will be executed, and this will end the loop. The `try` block inside the `while` loop uses the code we saw earlier to read the length of the proverb and then read the proverb itself into an array, `proverb`, of the correct size. This is written to `System.out`. Note that the `String` variable, `number`, will be re-initialized on each iteration of the while loop controlled by `EOF`. Similarly, for each proverb that we read, we create a new object of type `char[]` with the appropriate number of elements.

Formatted Stream Input

As we said earlier, you can get a lot of help with formatted input from the `StreamTokenizer` class in the `java.io` package. The term **token** refers to a data item, such as a number or a string, that will in general consist of several consecutive characters from the stream. The class has the name `StreamTokenizer` because it can read characters from a stream and make the data available as a series of tokens or data items. By default a token is either a number, which can include a minus sign, digits and a decimal point, or it is a string which is enclosed between single quotes or double quotes. Any sequence of letters, digits, decimal points and minus signs that begins with a letter and is delimited by whitespace is also treated as a string token and is referred to as a **word**. Any other character that is not whitespace, is not enclosed within quotes or double quotes and is not part of a comment is read as `null`. The `StreamTokenizer` class will ignore Java style comments beginning with `//` or between `/*` and `*/`, and whitespace, which by default includes `newline`.

You construct a `StreamTokenizer` object from a character input stream object. For example, you could construct a `StreamTokenizer` object corresponding to the standard input stream with the statement:

```
StreamTokenizer myStream = new StreamTokenizer(
                      new FileReader(FileDescriptor.out));
```

You can cause a token – a data item in other words – to be read from the stream that you used to construct a `StreamTokenizer` object by calling the `nextToken()` method for the `StreamTokenizer` object:

```
int dataType = myStream.nextToken();
```

The integer that is returned by the method indicates what sort of token was read. The token that was read from the stream is itself stored in one of two instance variables of the `StreamTokenizer` object. If the data item is a number, it is stored in a `public` data member, `nval`, which is of type `double`. If the data item is a quoted string or a word, a reference to a `String` object is stored in the `public` data member, `sval`, which of course is of type, `String`. The analysis that segments the stream into tokens is fairly simple, and the way in which an arbitrary stream is broken into tokens is illustrated below.

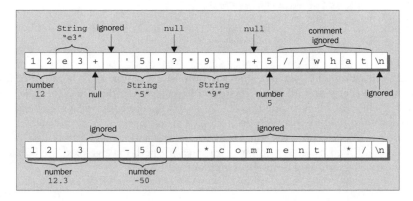

As we have said, the `int` value returned by the `nextToken()` method indicates what kind of data item was read. It can be one of the following standard values, which are defined in the class.

Token Value	Description
TT_NUMBER	The token is a number that has been stored in the member, `nval`.
TT_WORD	The token is a word that has been stored in `sval`, where a word is defined as a series of characters delimited by whitespace characters.
TT_EOF	The end of file has been read from the stream.
TT_EOL	An end of line character has been read. This is only set if the `eolIsSignificant()` method has been called with the argument, `true`. Otherwise end of line characters are ignored.

If a quoted string is read from the stream, the value that will be returned by `nextToken()` will be the quote character – a single or a double quote – as type `int`, so in this case you retrieve the reference to the string that was read from `sval`. The value indicating what kind of token was read last is also available from a public data member, `ttype`, of the `StreamTokenizer` class.

The default tokenizing mode can be modified by calling one or other of the following methods.

Method	Description
resetSyntax()	Resets the state of the tokenizer object so no characters have any special significance. This has the effect that all characters are regarded as ordinary and will be read from the stream as single characters. The value of each character will be stored in the ttype field.
ordinaryChar (int ch)	Sets the character, ch, as an 'ordinary' character. An 'ordinary' character is a character that has no special significance. It will be read as a single character whose value will be stored in the ttype field.
ordinaryChars (int low, int hi)	Causes all characters from low to hi inclusive to be treated as 'ordinary' characters.
whitespaceChars (int low, int hi)	Causes all characters from low to hi inclusive to be treated as whitespace characters. Unless they appear in a string, whitespace characters are treated as delimiters between tokens.
wordChars (int low, int hi)	Specifies that the characters from low to hi inclusive are word characters. A word is at least one of these characters.
commentChar(int ch)	Specifies that ch is a character that indicates the start of a comment. All characters to the end of the line following the character, ch, will be ignored.
quoteChar(int ch)	Specifies that matching pairs of the character, ch, enclose a string.
slashStarComments (boolean flag)	If the argument is false, this switches off recognizing comments between /* and */. A true argument switches it on again.
slashSlashComments (boolean flag)	If the argument is false, this switches off recognizing comments starting will a double slash. A true argument switches it on again.
lowerCaseMode (boolean flag)	An argument of true causes strings to be converted to lower case before being stored in sval. An argument of false switches off lower case mode.
pushback()	Calling this method causes the next call of the nextToken() method to return the ttype value that was set by the previous nextToken() call and to leave sval and nval unchanged.

Let's see how we can use this class to read data items from the keyboard.

Try It Out – Creating a Formatted Input Class

One way of reading formatted input is to define our own class that uses a `StreamTokenizer` object to read from standard input. We can define a class, `FormattedInput`, which defines methods to return particular types of data items retrieved from the standard input stream by the `StreamTokenizer` object.

```java
import java.io.*;

public class FormattedInput
{
  // Method to read an int value...

  // plus methods to read various other data types...

  // Object to tokenize input from the standard input stream
  private StreamTokenizer tokenizer = new StreamTokenizer(
                                 new InputStreamReader(System.in));
}
```

We don't need a constructor, because the instance variables are already initialized. All we need to add are the methods to read the data values that we want. We will start with a method to read values of type, `int`:

```java
  // Method to read an int value
  public int intRead()
  {
    try
    {
      for(int i = 0; i < 5; i++)
      {
        if(tokenizer.nextToken()==tokenizer.TT_NUMBER)
          return (int)tokenizer.nval;    // Value is numeric, so return as int
        else
        {
          System.out.println("Incorrect input: " + tokenizer.sval +
                           " Re-enter an integer");
          continue;                      // Retry the read operation
        }
      }
      System.out.println("Five failures reading an int value" +
                                 " - program terminated");
      System.exit(1);                    // End the program
      return 0;
    }
    catch(IOException e)                  // Error reading in nextToken()
    {
      System.out.println(e);             // Output the error
      System.exit(1);                    // End the program
      return 0;
    }
  }
```

Something you can do if you want, is to throw an exception in the case of failure here. You will need to define your own exception class for this. We can try out our `FormattedInput` class by adding some code to our previous example, `TryPrimesOutput`, which calculates primes, so that it will read the number of primes required from the keyboard:

```
import java.io.*;

public class TryPrimesOutput2
{
  public static void main(String[] args)
  {
    FormattedInput keyboard = new FormattedInput(); // Keyboard stream

    System.out.print("Enter the number of primes required: ");
    int numPrimes = keyboard.intRead();              // Number of primes wanted
    long[] primes = new long[numPrimes];             // Array to store primes

    // Rest of the code as before...
  }
}
```

How It Works

The code for the `intRead()` method is in a `try` block because the `nextToken()` method can throw an `IOException` if a read error occurs. We call `nextToken()` for the `tokenizer` object in the `if` statement to cause the next token to be read. If the value returned is `TT_NUMBER`, we assume it is a valid integer.

If the token read is not a number, we display a message and go to the next iteration of the `for` loop to read another token. The loop will repeat up to five times when the correct value is not present. After five failures, another message is displayed and the program is terminated by calling the static `exit()` method in the class `System`. The argument is a status code of type `int`. A non-zero value is used to indicate an error condition caused the termination.

Based on this model you should be able to add other methods to the class to deal with other data types.

In the test program, `TryPrimesOutput`, aside from the prompt for input, there are only two changes necessary to `main()`. The value for the number of primes required is read into the variable, `numPrimes`, and we use this value to specify the number of elements in the array that stores the primes.

The input conversions supported by the `StreamTokenizer` class are fairly primitive. If you want to be able to enter floating point values with exponents, or to input numbers with a leading plus sign, you have to write your own code to do the analysis of the character string from the keyboard. At the moment, the `intRead()` method will read floating point values and just convert them to `int`. You could prevent this by putting an additional check in the `if` test that verifies the data type.

```
if(tokenizer.nextToken() == tokenizer.TT_NUMBER &&
                      tokenizer.nval==(double)((long)tokenizer.nval))
  return (int)tokenizer.nval;              // Value is integral, so return as int
else
{
  System.out.println("Incorrect input: " + tokenizer.sval +
                                          " Re-enter an integer");
  continue;                               // Retry the read operation
}
```

If `nval` is not an integer, casting it to an integer type will truncate the fractional part, so when it is cast back to `double`, its value will be different from the original.

You don't have to worry about this when implementing a `doubleRead()` method. As long as a number was entered, you can return it.

Random Access Files

If you want to access a file randomly, you must use the `RandomAccessFile` class. There are two available constructors that you can use to create a random access file stream object, and both require two arguments. For one constructor, the first argument is a `File` object that identifies the file path, and the second is a `String` object that specifies the access mode. With the other constructor, the first argument is a `String` object specifying the file path, and the second argument is a `String` defining the access mode (as before). Since a random access file object is not a stream, you cannot buffer it.

The access mode can be `"r"` which indicates that you just want to read the file, or it can be `"rw"` which indicates that you want to be able to read and write the file. If you specify the mode as anything else, the constructor will throw an `IllegalArgumentException`.

To create a `RandomAccessFile` object, you could write:

```
File myPrimes = new File("c:/JunkData/Primes.bin");
RandomAccessFile myFile = new RandomAccessFile(myPrimes, "rw");
```

This will create the random access file object, `myFile`, corresponding to the physical file, `Primes.bin`, and will open it for both reading and writing. If the file does not exist with `"rw"` specified as the mode, it will be created since it is assumed you intend to write it before you try to read it. If you specify the mode as `"r"`, the file must already exist. If it doesn't, an `IOException` will be thrown by the constructor.

You can get a `FileDescriptor` object corresponding to the file that a `RandomAccessFile` object represents by calling the method `getFD()` for the object. You could use the `FileDescriptor` object to create a stream object for this file. You cannot create a `RandomAccessFile` object from a `FileDescriptor` object.

Input and Output Operations

The `RandomAccessFile` class defines methods for all the read operations that are available with `DataInputStream`, and all the write operations that are defined in `DataOutputStream`. It implements the same interfaces as these two classes, so you can read and write data values that are `String` objects, or any of the basic types. You can replace the `DataInputStream` object in the earlier example that displayed the contents of the file, `Primes.bin`, with a `RandomAccessFile` object, and the program will work just the same.

Apart from being able to read and write the same file, the added value you get with the `RandomAccessFile` class is the ability to change the current position in the file, so let's look at the methods we have for doing that.

Changing the File Position

The current position from the beginning of the file is the **offset** for the byte where the next read or write operation will begin. There are three methods that relate to the business of altering the current position in a file.

Method	Description
seek(long pos)	Moves the current position in the file to the offset from the beginning of the file, specified by the argument, pos.
getFilePointer()	Returns a value of type, long, that is the current position in the file – the offset from the beginning of the file.
length()	Returns a value of type, long, that is the length of the file in bytes.

You use the method seek() to move the current file position to the point where you want the next read or write to start. The argument could be a value that you previously obtained using the getFilePointer() method, or it could be a value that you calculated based of the length of the file and the amount of data that you write per record.

Let's see random access file streams in action in a final version of our program to compute prime numbers.

Using Random Access Files

Once we have filled the primes[] array with values, we can write the primes to a file. We can then access them when we want to check for a new prime. Once the file has been created, we can simply retrieve primes from the file if the number of primes requested is less than the total number that we have stored. To do this, we will need to change the program logic quite a bit. Because we are adding quite a bit more code, it will also be better if we implement the program as more than one method. We will therefore recreate the program from scratch.

We will put the code to test whether a number is prime in a separate method, to avoid making main() too long. This will accept the number to be tested as an argument of type long, and return true if the number is prime. We can also break out the code to output the number of primes requested in a separate method. This will be a self-contained piece of code with no return value and will use our FormatWriter class to display the primes in neat columns. We will also use the FormattedInput class that we implemented to handle keyboard input, so we will need to copy the files containing the definitions for these two classes to the directory for this example.

Try It Out – The Skeleton PrimesFile Class

The structure of the basic program class will be very simple. It will have the variables that are to be accessed by all the methods in the class as `static` data members, and it will have three `static` methods – the method `main()` where execution starts, a method to test if a number is prime and a method to output the number of primes requested.

```java
// Using a random access file to store primes
import java.io.*;

public class PrimesFile
{
  static RandomAccessFile myFile = null;    // File stream
  static boolean file = false;              // True if file contains primes
  static long[] primes = new long[10];      // Array to store primes
  static int current = 0;                   // Free element in primes array
  final static int LONGSIZE = 8;            // Number of bytes for type long

  // The main computation
  public static void main(String[] args)
  {
    try
    {
      // Read the number of primes required from the keyboard...
      // Access or create the random access file...
      // Compute any primes needed that are not in the file...
      // Output the primes
    }
    catch(IOException e)
    {
      // deal with error reading the file
    }
  }

  // Test whether a number is prime
  static boolean primeTest(long number)
  {
    // Code to test for primeness...
  }

  // Method to display primes
  static void outputPrimes(long numPrimes) throws IOException
  {
    // Code to output primes...
    // We will not catch IOExceptions from file read here
  }
}
```

How It Works

We have declared four `static` class variables that will be available to any method in the class. All three methods, `main()`, `primeTest()` and `outputPrimes()`, will need to have access to the `RandomAccessFile` object, `myFile`. The other three class variables will be needed in `main()` as well as in the method, `primeTest()`.

We will add code to catch any `IOExceptions` that are thrown in the `primeTest()` method, but in the `outputPrimes()` method we will not catch them, so they will be need to be caught in `main()`.

Try It Out – Testing for a Prime

We want the method `primeTest()` to use the primes stored in the file in the test. However, the file may be empty. This will be so if the program is being run for the first time, or if the file has been deleted. We want the method to be able to recognize this situation and just use the primes that are stored in memory in the array `primes[]`. The code to do this will be:

```
static boolean primeTest(long number)
{
    // The maximum divisor we need to try is the square root of number
    long limit = (long)Math.ceil(Math.sqrt((double)number));
    try
    {
        if(file)                        // Check whether we have primes on file...
        {                               // Yes, we do
            long prime = 0;                             // Stores prime from file
            myFile.seek(0);                             // Go to file start
            long primeCount = myFile.length()/LONGSIZE; // Number of primes on file

            // Check the number using the primes from file
            for(int i = 0; i < primeCount; i++)
            {
                prime = myFile.readLong();          // Read a prime
                if(prime > limit)
                    return true;        // No exact division - prime found
                if(number%prime == 0)
                    return false;       // Exact division - not a prime
            }
        }
    }
    catch(IOException e)                             // Handle read error
    { // Exception thrown - output message
        System.err.println("Error in primeTest():\n" + e);
        System.exit(1);                             // End the program
    }

    // Otherwise check using primes in memory
    for(int i = 0; i < current; i++)
    {
        if(primes[i] > limit)
            return true;                // No exact division - prime found
        if(number%primes[i] == 0)
            return false;               // Exact division - not a prime
    }
    return true;
}
```

How It Works

The method uses the `file` flag to determine whether there are any primes in the file. If there are, we seek from the beginning of the file with offset, `0`, and then read one prime at a time from the file. If we read a prime that is greater than `limit`, `number` is prime and we return `true`. If we find an exact divisor, `number` is not prime so we return `false`. The code reading the file is in a `try` block so we can catch any exceptions that are thrown during input operations.

If the file is empty, we do the same test using primes from the `primes[]` array that we declared as a class variable. The class variable, `current`, is the index of the next free element in `primes`, so the loop variable must be less than this value.

Try It Out – Outputting Primes

Outputting primes is very simple so the method is quite short, particularly since we don't catch
IOExceptions. You need to copy the FormatWriter class that we created earlier to the same
directory as the example.

```
static void outputPrimes(int numPrimes) throws IOException
{
    // Create a buffered formatted output stream
    FormatWriter out = new FormatWriter(
                    new BufferedWriter(
                    new FileWriter(FileDescriptor.out)), true, 12);

    myFile.seek(0);                     // Go to file start
    for(int i = 0; i < numPrimes; i++)  // Output the primes
    {
        long prime = myFile.readLong();   // Read a prime from the file

        if(i%5 == 0)
            out.println();                  // After every 5th, a newline

        out.print(prime);               // Output the prime
    }
    out.close();                        // Close the stream
}
```

How It Works

To pass IOExceptions on up to the calling class, we just add the throws clause to the definition of
the method. Output uses our FormatWriter class, so you will need a copy of the source file for this
class in the directory for the current program. We will output primes five to a line with a field width of
12 characters. To display the primes, we find the beginning of the file and read numPrimes primes
from the file, one at a time. For every fifth prime we call println() for the stream object to start a
new line. The primes should appear right justified in five neat columns on your display. We call the
close() method for the object out, which will flush the stream to display any primes still in the buffer
and then close it.

Try It Out – The main() Method

All we need now is the code for main() to tie it all together:

```
public static void main(String[] args)
{
    try
    {
        // Define the file to store primes
        File myPrimes = new File("c:/JunkData/Primes.bin");
        myFile = new RandomAccessFile(myPrimes, "rw");

        // Read the number of primes required
        FormattedInput in = new FormattedInput();    // Keyboard stream

        // Prompt for keyboard input
        System.out.print("Enter the number of primes required: ");
        int numPrimes = in.intRead();               // Number of primes required
```

```
      long count = myFile.length()/LONGSIZE;       // Number of primes in the file
      long number = 0;                              // Next number to be tested

      // Check for file contents
      if(count == 0)                    // Nothing in the file

      {
        file = false;
        primes[0] = 2;                  // Seed the first prime...
        primes[1] = 3;                  // ...and the second
        current = 2;                    // Index of next element
        count = 2;                      // count of primes found - up to now
        number = 5;                     // Next integer to be tested
      }
      else
      {       // Get the next number to test - the last prime + 2
        file = true;
        myFile.seek(myFile.length() - LONGSIZE);
        number = myFile.readLong() + 2;
      }

      // Find additional primes required for the total primes requested
      for( ; count < numPrimes; number += 2)
      {
        if(primeTest(number))                     // Test for a prime
        {
          primes[current++] = number;             // We got one!
          ++count;                                // Increment prime count

          if(current == primes.length)            // Check for array full
          {// Array is full so write them away
            myFile.seek(myFile.length());         // Go to the end of the file
            for(int i = 0; i < primes.length; i++)
              myFile.writeLong(primes[i]);        // Write the primes
            current = 0;                          // Set free array element index
            file = true;                          // Indicate file has primes
          }
        }
      }

      // Check if there are still primes in the array
      if(current > 0)
      { // There are - so write them to the file
        myFile.seek(myFile.length());             // Go to the end of the file
        for(int i = 0; i < current ; i++)
          myFile.writeLong(primes[i]);            // Write the primes
        current = 0;                              // Set free array element index
        file = true;                              // Indicate file has primes
      }
      outputPrimes(numPrimes);                    // Output the primes
    }
    catch(IOException e)
    {
      System.err.println("Error in main()\n" + e);   // Output the error
    }
  }
}
```

The class `PrimesFile` is now complete.

How It Works

The first step is to define the `RandomAccessFile` object for the file. If the file exists, it will be opened for read and write operations. If it doesn't, a new file will be created. You can use a different file path, if you want. We get input from the keyboard using the class `FormattedInput` class that we defined earlier in this chapter, so you will need to make sure the class file for this is in the same directory as this program. By outputting the prompt using the `print()` method, we can get the input value on the same line.

Before we start looking for primes, we need to see how many primes there are in the file. Since a `long` value always occupies eight bytes, we can get the number of primes in the file by dividing the length by eight. If the file, `Primes.bin`, exists and is not empty, then it should at least contain the numbers, 2 and 3. If there are primes in the file, we get the next number we want to test by adding two to the last prime we recorded in the file. This will ensure that we only look for new primes. We also need to set the `file` flag and the `current` index appropriately. If there are no primes in the file, we must seed the array `primes[]`, with the first two prime numbers to start the process.

Primes are found in the `for` loop. Note that if the number of primes requested is less than the number on file, the program won't calculate any more; it will go straight to the call to the `outputPrimes()` method. If `primeTest()` returns `true`, the current number is stored and the values of `count` and `current` are incremented. Whenever `current` is the same as the length of the array `primes[]`, the contents of the array are written to the end of the file. Note how the seek to the end of the file is achieved. You just call the `seek()` method with the file length as the argument. When the array has been written, the index, `current`, is reset to zero so the next prime will be stored in the first element of the array. At this point we also set the `file` flag to `true`, since we are now sure that there are primes in the file. At the end of the `for` loop, any primes left in the `primes` array are also written to the file and the `outputPrimes()` method is called to display the requested number of primes.

The program always keeps all the primes in the file, so no time is wasted re-computing primes. Any new primes calculated are always added to the end of the file. The only constraints on the number of primes the program can produce is the amount of disk space you have and the capacity of a `long` variable.

Storing Objects in a File

The process of storing and retrieving objects in an external file is called **serialization**. Writing an object to a file is referred to as **serializing** the object, and reading an object from a file is called **deserializing** an object. I think you will be surprised at how easy this is. Perhaps the most impressive aspects of the way serialization is implemented in Java is that you can generally read and write objects of almost any class, including objects of classes that you have defined yourself, without adding any code to the classes involved to support this mechanism. For the most part, everything is taken care of automatically.

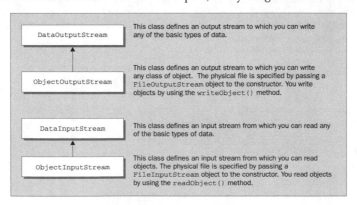

Two classes from the `java.io` package are used for serialization. The output process for objects is managed by an object of the class `ObjectOutputStream`, and input is handled by an object of the class `ObjectInputStream`. These are derived from `DataOutputStream` and `DataInputStream`, respectively, so that they also have the capability to process basic types of data through inherited methods.

Writing an Object to a File

The constructor for the `ObjectOutputStream` class requires a `FileOutputStream` object as an argument that defines the stream for the file where you intend to store your objects. You could create an `ObjectOutputStream` object using the file, `MyFile`, with the following statements.

```
FileOutputStream output = new FileOutputStream("MyFile");
ObjectOutputStream objectOut = new ObjectOutputStream(output);
```

To write an object to the file, `MyFile`, you call the `writeObject()` method for `objectOut` with the object as the argument. Since this method accepts an object of type `Object` as an argument, you can pass an object of any class to the method. There are three basic conditions that have to be met for an object to be written to a stream:

❑   The class must be declared as `public`.

❑   The class must implement the `Serializable` interface.

❑   If the class has a direct or indirect base class that is not serializable, then that base class must have a default constructor   that is, a constructor that requires no arguments. The derived class must take care of transferring the base class data members to the stream.

Implementing the `Serializable` interface is a lot less difficult than it sounds, and we will see how in a moment. Later we will come back to the question of how to deal with a non-serializable base class.

If `myObject` is an instance of a public class that implements `Serializable`, then to write `myObject` to the stream that we defined above, you would use the statement:

```
objectOut.writeObject(myObject);
```

This takes care of writing to the stream everything necessary to reconstitute the object later in a read operation. This includes information about the class and all its superclasses, as well as the contents and types of the data members of the class. Remarkably, this works even when the data members are themselves class objects, as long as they are objects of `Serializable` classes. Our `writeObject()` call will cause the `writeObject()` method for each object that is a data member to be called, and this mechanism continues recursively until everything that makes up our object has been written to the stream. Each independent object that you write to the stream requires a separate call to the `writeObject()` method, but the objects that are members of an object are taken care of automatically. This is not completely foolproof in that the relationships between the class objects can affect the situation, but for the most part this is all you need to do. We will be using serialization to write quite complex objects to files in Chapter 16.

As we said earlier, you can write data of any of the basic types using the methods that are inherited in the `ObjectOutputStream` class from `DataOutputStream`. You can mix writing data of the basic types and class objects to the stream. If you have a mixture of objects and data items of basic types that you want to store in a file, you can write them all to the same `ObjectOutputStream`. We discussed the methods for writing values of the basic data types to a stream earlier in this chapter, and you apply them in exactly the same way in this context.

Exceptions Thrown during Object Serialization

The constructor for an `ObjectOutputStream` object can throw an `IOException` if things go wrong. The `writeObject()` method can throw the following exceptions:

Exception	Description
InvalidClassException	Thrown when there is something wrong with the class definition for object being written. This might be because the class is not `public`, for instance.
NotSerializableException	Thrown if the object's class, or the class of a data member of the class, does not implement the `Serializable` interface.
IOException	Thrown when a file output error occurs.

The first two exception classes here are subclasses of `ObjectStreamException`, which is itself a subclass of `IOException`. If you don't want to catch individual exceptions during object serialization, you can put your code in a `try` block with a `catch` block for `IOException` to take care of all of them, but you will usually want to know if your program fails because a class is not serializable, or because a class is invalid for serialization.

Implementing the Serializable Interface

In most instances, to implement the `Serializable` interface for a class, you need only declare that the class implements the interface. No other code is necessary. For example, the following declares a class that implements the interface.

```
public MyClass implements Serializable
{
  // Definition of the class...
}
```

There is a small fly in the ointment. All the fields in the class must be serializable (or transient – which we will come to) which implies they are either basic types or class types that are themselves serializable and all superclasses of the class must also be serializable. That will most likely be fine for your own classes, but there are one or two classes that come along with Java that do not implement the `Serializable` interface, and what's more, you can't make them serializable. The `Graphics` class in the package `java.awt` is an example of such a class – we will see more of this class when we get into programming using windows. All is not lost however. There is an escape route.

Transient Data Members of a Class

If your class has data members that are not serializable, or that you don't want to have written to the stream, you can declare them as `transient`. For example:

```
public class MyClass implements Serializable
{
  transient protected Graphics g;     // Transient class member

  // Rest of the class definition
}
```

Declaring the data member as `transient` will prevent the `writeObject()` method from attempting to write the data member to the stream. When the class object is read back, it will be created properly, including any members declared as `transient`. They just won't have their values set, because they were not written to the stream.

You may want to declare data members that are objects of some of your own classes as `transient`. You would do this when they have a value that is not meaningful or out of context – objects that represent the current time, or today's date, for instance. These need to be reconstructed explicitly when the object that contains them is read from the stream.

Reading an Object from a File

Reading back objects from a file is just as easy as writing them. First, you need to create an `ObjectInputStream` object. Then you call the `readObject()` method for that object. This will return an object as type `Object`, so you need to cast it to the appropriate type in order to use it. The `readObject()` method can throw the following exceptions.

Exception	Description
ClassNotFoundException	Thrown if the definition of the class for an object read from the stream is not in the current program.
InvalidClassException	Thrown if there is something wrong with the class for an object. This is commonly caused by changing the definition of a class for an object between writing and reading the file.
StreamCorruptedException	Thrown when control information in the stream is inconsistent.
OptionalDataException	Thrown when basic types of data are read rather than an object.
IOException	Thrown if an error occurred reading the stream.

Clearly, if you do not have a full and accurate class definition for each type of object that you want to read from the stream, the read will fail. The last four exception classes are subclasses of `IOException`, so you can use that as a catch-all if you don't want to catch them individually. However, `ClassNotFoundException` is derived from `Exception`, so you must put a separate `catch` block for this exception in your program. Otherwise it will not compile.

For example, if the object in the previous code fragment was of type MyClass, you could read it back from the file with the statements:

```
MyClass theObject;      // Store the object here

try
{
  // Create the object input stream for file MyFile
  FileInputStream input = new FileInputStream("MyFile");
  ObjectInputStream objectIn = new ObjectInputStream(input);

  // Deserialize the object
  theObject = (MyClass)objectIn.readObject();
}
catch(IOException e)
{
  System.out.println(e);
}
catch(ClassNotFoundException e)
{
  System.out.println(e);
}
```

Try it out for yourself with a suitable class.

This time we are creating an ObjectInputStream object using a FileInputStream object corresponding to the file MyFile. To deserialize the object, we call the method readObject() and cast the object returned to the type MyClass. The method readObject() can throw ClassNotFoundException if the class for the object read from the file is not defined in the current application. Since this is not a subclass of IOException, we need a separate catch block for this exception.

For the most part, you will know what the class of the object is when you read it back. It is possible that occasionally you won't, in which case you can test it. Of course, you must have definitions for all of the classes that it might be within your program. We could test the object in the code above before storing it in theObject as follows:

```
MyClass theObject;
Object temp = objectIn.readObject();
if( temp.getClass().getName().equals("MyClass") )
  theObject = (MyClass) temp;
```

This calls the getClass() method for the object (inherited from Object) that returns the Class object representing the class of the object. Calling the getName() method for the Class object returns the fully qualified name of the class. If the class name for the object read from the stream is the same as that of theObject, we can safely cast it to that type. An alternative approach would be to just execute the cast to type MyClass, and catch the ClassCastException that is thrown when the cast is invalid.

Just to make sure that the process of serializing and deserializing objects is clear, we will use it in an example.

Using Object Serialization

Back in Chapter 6, we produced an example that created PolyLine objects containing Point objects in a generalized linked list. This is a good basis for demonstrating how effectively serialization takes care of handling objects that are members of objects. We can just modify the class TryPolyLine to use serialization.

Try It Out – Serializing a Linked List

The classes PolyLine, Point, LinkedList and the inner class ListItem, are exactly the same as in Chapter 6 except that we need to implement the Serializable interface in each of them.

The PolyLine definition needs to be amended to:

```java
import java.io.*;

public final class PolyLine implements Serializable
{
  // Class definition as before...
}
```

The Point definition needs a similar change:

```java
import java.io.*;

public class Point implements Serializable
{
  // Class definition as before...
}
```

The LinkedList class and its inner class likewise:

```java
import java.io.*;

public class LinkedList implements Serializable
{
  // Class definition as before...

  private class ListItem implements Serializable
  {
    // Inner class definition as before...
  }
}
```

Of course, each source file must also have an import statement for the java.io package as in the code above.

The modified version of the TryPolyLine class to write the PolyLine objects to a stream looks like this:

```java
import java.io.*;

public class TryPolyLine
{
```

```
  public static void main(String[] args)
  {
    // Create an array of coordinate pairs
    double[][] coords = { {1., 1.}, {1., 2.}, { 2., 3.},
                          {-3., 5.}, {-5., 1.}, {0., 0.} };

    // Create a polyline from the coordinates and display it
    PolyLine polygon = new PolyLine(coords);
    System.out.println(polygon);

    // Add a point and display the polyline again
    polygon.addPoint(10., 10.);
    System.out.println(polygon);

    // Create Point objects from the coordinate array
    Point[] points = new Point[coords.length];
    for(int i = 0; i < points.length; i++)
      points[i] = new Point(coords[i][0],coords[i][1]);

    // Use the points to create a new polyline and display it
    PolyLine newPoly = new PolyLine(points);
    System.out.println(newPoly);

// Write both polyline objects to the file
    try
    {
      // Create the object output stream
      ObjectOutputStream objectOut =
                  new ObjectOutputStream(
                  new BufferedOutputStream(
                  new FileOutputStream("c:/JunkData/Polygons.bin")));

      objectOut.writeObject(polygon);          // Write first object
      objectOut.writeObject(newPoly);          // Write second object
      objectOut.close();                       // Close the output stream
    }
    catch(NotSerializableException e)
    {
      System.err.println(e);
    }
    catch(InvalidClassException e)
    {
      System.err.println(e);
    }
    catch(IOException e)
    {
      System.err.println(e);
    }

    // Read the objects back from the file

    System.out.println("\nReading objects from the file: ");
    try
    {
      ObjectInputStream objectIn =
                  new ObjectInputStream(
                  new BufferedInputStream(
                  new FileInputStream("c:/JunkData/Polygons.bin")));
```

```
        PolyLine theLine = (PolyLine)objectIn.readObject();
        System.out.println(theLine);                // Display the first object
        theLine = (PolyLine)objectIn.readObject();
        System.out.println(theLine);                // Display the second object
        objectIn.close();                           // Close the input stream
      }
      catch(IOException e)
      {
        System.err.println(e);
      }
      catch(ClassNotFoundException e)
      {
        System.err.println(e);
      }
    }
  }
```

This produces the output:

```
Polyline: (1.0,1.0) (1.0,2.0) (2.0,3.0) (-3.0,5.0) (-5.0,1.0) (0.0,0.0)
Polyline: (1.0,1.0) (1.0,2.0) (2.0,3.0) (-3.0,5.0) (-5.0,1.0) (0.0,0.0) (10.0,10.0)
Polyline: (1.0,1.0) (1.0,2.0) (2.0,3.0) (-3.0,5.0) (-5.0,1.0) (0.0,0.0)

Reading objects from the file:
Polyline: (1.0,1.0) (1.0,2.0) (2.0,3.0) (-3.0,5.0) (-5.0,1.0) (0.0,0.0) (10.0,10.0)
Polyline: (1.0,1.0) (1.0,2.0) (2.0,3.0) (-3.0,5.0) (-5.0,1.0) (0.0,0.0)
```

How It Works

We create two different `PolyLine` objects in the same manner as in the original example and we display them on standard output as before. We then create an `ObjectOutputStream` for the file, `Polygons.bin`, in the `C:\JunkData` directory and write each of the `PolyLine` objects to the file using the `writeObject()` method. You may need to adjust the file name and directory to suit your environment as necessary. We then call the `close()` method to close the output stream. We don't need to explicitly write the `LinkedList` and `Point` objects to the stream. These are part of the `PolyLine` object so they are taken care of automatically. The same goes for when we read the `PolyLine` objects back. All the subsidiary objects are reconstructed automatically.

To read the file, we create an `ObjectInputStream` object for `Polygons.bin`. We then read the first object using the `readObject()` method and store the reference to it in the variable `theObject`. We then output the object, `read`, to the standard output stream. The same process is repeated for the second `PolyLine` object. It couldn't be simpler really, could it?

Serializing Classes Yourself

We mentioned in passing a couple of situations where the default serialization we used in the example won't work. One occurs if your class has a superclass that is not serializable. In this situation, the superclass must have a default constructor, and you must take care of serializing the fields inherited from the superclass yourself. Another situation arises if your class has fields that don't travel well, hash codes for instance, or vast numbers of fields with 0 values for instance that you won't want to have written to the file. These are also cases where do-it-yourself serialization is needed.

To control the serialization of a class, you must implement two private methods in the class, one for input from an `ObjectInputStream` object, and the other for output to an `ObjectOutputStream` object. The `readObject()` and `writeObject()` methods for the stream will call these methods to perform I/O on the stream if you implement them.

Even though it isn't necessary in this class, we will take the `PolyLine` class as a demonstration vehicle for how this works. To do our own serialization, the class would be:

```
class PolyLine implements Serializable
{
  // Class definition as before...

  // Serialized input method
  private void readObject(ObjectInputStream in) throws IOException
  {
    // Code to do the serialized input...
  }

// Serialized input method
  private void writeObject(ObjectOutputStream out)
                                    throws IOException, ClassNotFoundException
  {
    // Code to do the serialized output...
  }
}
```

These two methods must have exactly the same signature in any class where they are required, and they must be declared as `private`.

In a typical situation, you will want to use the default serialization operations provided by the object stream and just add your own code to fix up the data members that you want to take care of – or have to in the case of a non-serialized base class. To get the default serialization done on input, you just call the `defaultReadObject()` method for the stream in your serialization method:

```
private void readObject(ObjectInputStream in) throws IOException
{
  in.defaultReadObject();                    // Default serialized input
  // Your code to do serialized input...
}
```

You can get the default serialized output operation in a similar fashion by calling the `defaultWriteObject()` method for the stream object that is passed to your output method. Obviously, you must read back the data in exactly the same sequence as it was written, so the two methods will have essentially mirror operations on the same sequence of data items.

Serialization Problems

For most classes and applications, serialization will work in a straightforward fashion. There are situations that can cause confusion though. Suppose you write an object to a file – a `PolyLine` object say. A little later in your code, you modify the `PolyLine` object in some way, by moving a point perhaps, and you now write the object to the file again in its modified state. What happens?

All variables of a class type are references, not objects, and you may have several variables referring to the same object in your program. For this reason, the serialization output process keeps track of the objects that are written to the stream. Any attempt to write the same object to the stream will not result in duplicates of the object being written. Only a **handle**, which is a sort of reference, will be written to connect with the first occurrence of the object in the stream. Thus in the hypothetical example we started with, the modified version of the `PolyLine` object will not be written to the stream. Only a reference to the original unmodified object will be created so the changes will be lost.

The appropriate course of action in such situations is obviously going to be application dependent. You can make the `ObjectOutputStream` object forget the objects it has previously written to a stream by calling its `reset()` member:

```
out.reset();        // Reset the stream
```

This clears the record that is kept within the stream object of what has been written and writes a 'reset marker' to the stream. When an `ObjectInputStream` object reads a 'reset marker' it too clears its record of what has been read, so that subsequent object read operations will be as if the stream started at that point. To make effective use of this, your code will clearly need to accommodate the possibility of multiple versions of the same object existing in the stream. It's your code, so you will know what you want to do.

A further complication arises with serialized objects when you change the definition of a class in some way. When an object is written to a file, part of the information identifying the class is a sort of hashcode called a **version ID**, that is intended to ensure that the definition of the class used when you are reading an object from a file is the same as the class definition used when the object was written. Even cosmetic changes between writing and reading a stream, such as changing the name of a field, can alter the version ID, so in this case a read operation will fail. In general, you need to make sure that the class definitions in a program reading a file are the same as those used when the file was written, although you can explicitly set the version number and deal with any changes yourself.

For more complex situations, it is possible to take complete control of the serialization process within your classes by implementing the `Externalizable` interface. A detailed discussion of what is involved in this is outside the scope of this book.

Summary

In the last two chapters we have explored how to use most of the stream input and output capabilities built into Java. These can be used in console programs or in window-based applications, but not in applets unless specifically authorized in a policy file in the system on which the applet is executing. The important points in this chapter are:

❑   Byte input streams are defined by subclasses of the class, `InputStream`, and character input stream operations are provided by subclasses of `Reader`.

❑   The filter input stream classes complement the filter output stream classes that we saw in the previous chapter.

❑ The class System in the package java.lang defines the member in, representing the standard input stream, usually the keyboard; the member, out, representing the standard output stream, usually the screen; and the member err, which represents the standard error stream, usually also the screen.

❑ The RandomAccessFile class allows you to both read and write a file.

❑ You can access a file randomly using objects of the RandomAccessFile class.

❑ You can use the StreamTokenizer class for reading formatted data from a stream.

❑ Object serialization is supported through the ObjectOutputStream and ObjectInputStream classes.

❑ Objects are written to a file by calling the writeObject() method for the ObjectOutputStream object corresponding to the file.

❑ Objects are read from a file by calling the readObject() method for the ObjectInputStream object corresponding to the file.

Exercises

1. Write a program to copy a file that will allow you to enter the paths for both the file to be copied and the new file from the keyboard.

2. Extend the PrimesFile example that we produced in this chapter to optionally display the nth prime, when n is entered from the keyboard.

3. Extend the program further to output a given number of primes, starting at a given number. For example, output 50 primes starting at the 500th. The existing capabilities should be retained.

4. Write a program using a serial stream to store names in a file, entered as surname followed by first name.

5. Extend the previous program to sort the name file in ascending alphabetical order with the surname sorted first.

Utility Classes

In this chapter we'll look at the most useful components of the package java.util, which is something of a general purpose tool kit. Several of the classes that this package contains are often referred to as **container classes**, which you can use to manage data in your programs in various ways. These enable you to deal with situations where you don't know in advance how many items of data you'll need to store, or where you need a bit more flexibility in the mechanism for retrieving an item than the indexing mechanism provided by an array.

In this chapter you will learn:

- ❏ What sets, lists and maps are and how they work
- ❏ What an Iterator object is used for
- ❏ Which container classes are available
- ❏ What a Vector is and how to use Vector objects in your programs
- ❏ How to manage Vector objects so that storing and retrieving elements is type safe
- ❏ What a Stack is and how you use it
- ❏ How you store and retrieve objects in a hash table represented by a HashMap object
- ❏ How you can generate hash codes for your own class objects
- ❏ How to use the Observable class and the Observer interface to communicate between objects
- ❏ What facilities the Random class provides
- ❏ How to create and use Calendar and Date objects

Understanding the Utility Classes

The `java.util` package provides a set of general purpose classes that cover a wide variety of uses. We won't be able to cover all of these in depth, as there are just too many, but we will cover those that you will find most useful at a level that will enable you to apply them yourself. The **container classes** in `java.util` support various ways for you to store and manage objects of any kind in memory, and include a professional implementation of a linked list that we took so much trouble to develop back in Chapter 6. If you want an array that automatically expands to accommodate however many objects you throw into it, or you need to be able to store and retrieve an object based on what it is, rather than using an index or a sequence number, then look no further. You get all this and more in the container classes.

We'll be exploring the following capabilities provided by the package:

Class/Interface	Description
The `Iterator` interface	Declares methods for iterating through elements of a set, one at a time.
The `Vector` class	Supports an array-like structure for storing any kind of class object. The number of objects that you can store in a `Vector` object increases automatically as necessary.
The `Stack` class	Supports the storage of any kind of class object in a push down stack.
The `HashMap` class	Supports the storage of any kind of class object in a hash table, sometimes called a map.
The `Observable` class	Provides a method for signaling other class objects when one class object changes.
The `Observer` interface	Defines a method called by an `Observable` object to signal when an object has changed.
The `Random` class	Defines a more sophisticated random number generator than that provided by the method `Math.random()`.
The `Date` class	Enables you to manipulate date and time information and obtain the current date and time.

We'll start by looking in general terms at various possible types of collections for objects.

Collections of Objects

Back in Chapter 6 we put together a basic class defining a linked list. An object of type `LinkedList` represented an example of a collection of objects that could be of any type. A **collection** is used as a generic term for any object that represents a set of objects grouped together by some means. A linked list is only one of a number of ways of grouping a number of objects together in a collection.

There are three main types of collections: **sets**, **sequences** and **maps**. Let's first get an understanding of how these three types of collections work in principle, and then come back to look at the Java classes that implement versions of these. One point I would like to emphasize about the following discussion is that when we talk about a collection of objects, we mean a collection of references to objects. In Java collection only stores references – the objects themselves are external to the collection.

Sets

A **set** is probably the simplest kind of collection you can have. Here the objects are not usually ordered in any particular way at all and objects are simply added to the set without any control over where they go. It's a bit like putting things in your pocket – you just put things in and they rattle around inside your pocket in no particular order.

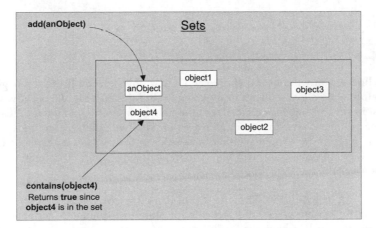

The principal access mechanism that you have for a set is simply to check whether a given object is a member of the set or not. For this reason, you cannot have duplicate objects in a set – each object in the set must be unique. Of course, you can also remove a given object from a set, but only if you know what the object is in the first place – in other words if you have a reference to the object in the set.

There are variations on the basic set that we have described here. For instance, sets can be ordered, so objects added to a set will be inserted into a sequence of objects ordered according to some criterion of comparison. Such sets require that the class that defines the objects to be stored implements suitable methods for comparing objects.

Sequences

A linked list is an example of a more general type of collection called a **sequence** or a **list**. A primary characteristic of a list is that the objects are stored in a linear fashion, not necessarily in any particular order, with a beginning and an end. This contrasts with a set where there is no order at all. An ordinary array is basically another example of a list, but is much more limited than a collection because it is fixed.

Collections generally have the ability to expand to accommodate as many elements as necessary. The Vector class, for example, is a collection class that provides similar functionality to an array, but which also has this ability to accommodate new elements as and when required.

401

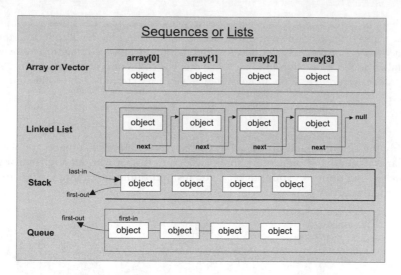

Because a list is linear, you will only be able to add a new object to the list at the beginning, or at the end, or inserted following a given object in sequence – after the fifth say. Generally, you can retrieve an object from a list in several ways. You can select the first or the last; you can get the object at a given position – as in indexing an array; or you can search for an object identical to a given object by checking all the objects in the sequence either backwards or forwards. You can also iterate through the list backwards or forwards accessing each object in sequence. We didn't implement all these capabilities in our linked list class in Chapter 6, but we could have done.

You can delete objects from a list in the same sort of ways that you retrieve an object; that is, you can remove the first or the last, an object at a particular position in sequence or an object that is equal to a given object. Sequences or lists have the facility that they can store several copies of the same object at different places in the sequence. This is not true of all types of collections as we will see.

A **stack**, which is a last-in first-out storage mechanism, is also considered to be a list, as is a **queue**, which is a first-in first-out mechanism. It is easy to see that a linked list can act as a stack, since using the methods to add and remove objects at the end of a list makes the list operate as a stack. Similarly, only adding objects by using the method to add an object to the end of a linked list, and only retrieving objects from the head of the list makes it operate as a queue.

Maps

A map is rather different from a set or a sequence because the entries involve pairs of objects. A map is also referred to sometimes as a **dictionary** because of the way it works. Each object that is stored in a map has an associated **key** object, and both the object and its key are stored as a pair. The key determines where the object is stored in the map, and when you want to retrieve an object you must supply the appropriate key – so it acts as the equivalent of a word that you look up in a regular dictionary.

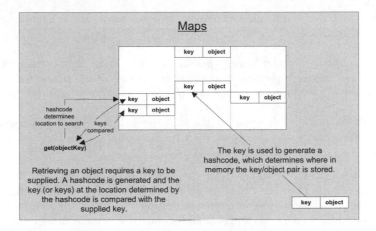

Maps

The key is used to generate a hashcode, which determines where in memory the key/object pair is stored.

hashcode determines location to search

keys compared

get(objectKey)

Retrieving an object requires a key to be supplied. A hashcode is generated and the key (or keys) at the location determined by the hashcode is compared with the supplied key.

A key can be any kind of object that you want to use to reference the object stored. Because the key has to uniquely identify the object, all the keys in a map must be different. To put this in context let's take an example. Suppose you were creating a program to provide an address book. You might store all the details of each person – their name, address, phone number or whatever – in a single object of type Entry perhaps, and store a reference to the object in a map. The key is the mechanism for retrieving objects, so assuming that all names are different, the name of the person would be a natural choice for the key. Thus the entries in the map in this case would be Name/Entry pairs. You would supply a Name object as the key, and get back the Entry object corresponding to the key. You might well have another map in this application where entries were keyed on the phone number. Then you could retrieve an entry corresponding to a given number. Of course, in practice, names are not unique – hence the invention of such delightful attachments to the person as social security numbers.

Hashing

Where a key/object pair is stored in a map is determined from the key by a process known as **hashing**. Hashing processes the key object to produce an integer value called a **hash code**. The hashCode() method that is defined in the Object class produces a hash code of type int for an object. The hash code is typically used as an offset from the start of the memory that has been allocated within the map, to determine the location where the key/object pair is to be stored. Ideally the hashing process should result in values that are uniformly distributed within a given range, and every key should produce a different hash code. In general, this may not be the case, but there are ways around this so it is not a problem. We will look at keys and hash codes in a little more detail when we discuss using maps later in this chapter.

Now let's look at how we can move through a collection.

Iterators

In the LinkedList class that we developed in Chapter 6 you might have thought that the mechanism for getting the objects from the list was a little cumbersome. It was necessary to obtain the first element by using one method, getFirst(), and successive elements by another method, getNext(). This makes the first element in a list a 'special case' so processing the elements has to take account of this and is a little more complicated than perhaps it needs to be.

A much better approach that can be used to process the elements from a collection sequentially involves something called an **iterator**.

It is worth noting at this point that Java also provides something called an enumerator. An enumerator provides essentially the same capability as an iterator, but it is recommended in the Java documentation that you should use an iterator in preference to an enumerator for collections.

In general an iterator is an object that you can use to retrieve all the objects in a collection one by one. Someone dealing cards from a deck one by one is acting as an iterator for the card deck – without the shuffle, of course.

In Java, an iterator is an interface that can be implemented by a collection class. Any collection object can create an object of type `Iterator` that encapsulates references to all the objects in the original collection in some sequence, and that can be accessed using the `Iterator` interface methods. In other words an iterator provides an easy way to get at all the objects in a collection one at a time. The basic mechanism for using an iterator in Java is illustrated below.

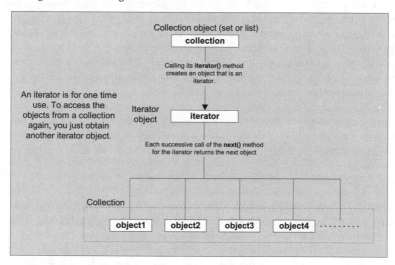

The `Iterator` interface in `java.util` declares just three methods:

Method	Description
next()	Returns an object as type `Object` starting with the first, and sets the `Iterator` object to return the next object on the next call of this method. If there is no object to be returned the method throws a `NoSuchElementException` exception.
hasNext()	Returns `true` if there is a next object to be retrieved by a call to `next()`.
remove()	Removes the last object returned by `next()` from the collection that supplied the `Iterator` object. If `next()` has not been called or if you call `remove()` twice after calling `next()`, an `IllegalStateException` will be thrown. Not all iterators support this method, in which case an `UnsupportedOperation` exception will be thrown if you call it.

Since calling the next() method for an object that implements Iterator returns successive objects from the collection, starting with the first, you can progress through all the objects in a collection very easily with a loop such as:

```
MyClass item;                            // Store an object from the collection
while(iter.hasNext())                    // Check that there's another
{
  item = (MyClass)iter.next();           // Retrieve next object
  // Do something with item...
}
```

This assumes iter is of type Iterator and stores a reference to an object obtained from whatever collection class we were using. As we shall see shortly, objects that are collections have a method, iterator() that returns an iterator for the current contents of the collection. The loop continues as long as the hasNext() method returns true. Since the next() method returns the object as type Object, we will usually need to cast it to its actual type. Each time you need to go through the objects in a collection you obtain another iterator, as an iterator is a 'use once' object.

Only the Java collection classes that are sets or lists make iterators available directly. However, as we will see, a map provides methods to enable the keys or objects, or indeed the key/object pairs, to be viewed as a set, so an iterator can then be obtained to iterate over the objects in the set view of the map.

The iterator we have seen here is a one way street – we can go through the objects in a collection one at a time, and that's it. This is fine for many purposes and is a lot safer than a hand coded loop as there's no possibility of getting the boundary conditions wrong. However, if this is not enough, and there will be times when it isn't, there's another kind of iterator that is more flexible.

List Iterators

The ListIterator interface declares methods that you can use to traverse a collection of objects backwards or forwards. You don't have to elect for a particular direction either. You can change from forwards to backwards and *vice versa*, so an object can be retrieved more than once.

The ListIterator interface extends the Iterator interface so the iterator methods you have seen still apply. The methods defined in the ListIterator interface that you use to traverse the list of objects are:

Method	Description
next()	Retrieves the next object in sequence – the same as for the Iterator interface.
hasNext()	Returns true if there is an object that will be returned by next().
nextIndex()	Returns the index of the object that will be returned by the next call to next(), or returns the number of elements in the list if the ListIterator object is at the end of the list.
previous()	Returns the previous object in sequence in the list. You use this method to run backwards through the list.

Table Continued on Following Page

Method	Description
hasPrevious()	Returns true if the next call to previous() will return an object.
previousIndex()	Returns the index of the object that will be returned by the next call to previous(), or returns -1 if the ListIterator object is at the beginning of the list.

You can alternate between calls to next() and previous() to go backwards and forwards through the list. Calling previous() immediately after calling next() will return the same element – and *vice versa*.

With a ListIterator you can add and replace objects, as well as remove them from the collection. ListIterator declares the following methods for this:

Method	Description
remove()	Removes the last object that was retrieved by next() or previous(). The UnsupportedOperation exception is thrown if the remove operation is not supported for this collection, and IllegalStateException will be thrown if next() or previous() have not yet been called for the iterator.
add(Object obj)	Adds the argument immediately before the object that would be returned by the next call to next(), and after the object that would be returned by the next call to previous(). The call to next() after the add() operation will return the object that was added. The next call to previous() will not be affected. This method throws an UnsupportedOperationException if objects cannot be added, a ClassCastException if the class of the argument prevents it from being added and IllegalOperationException if there is some other reason why the add cannot be done.
set(Object obj)	Replaces the last object retrieved by a call to next() or previous(). If neither next() nor previous() have been called, or add() or remove() have been called most recently, an IllegalStateException will be thrown. If the set() operation is not supported for this collection an UnsupportedOperationException will be thrown. If the class of the reference passed as an argument prevents the object being stored in the collection, a ClassCastException will be thrown. If some other characteristic of the argument prevents it being stored in the collection, an IllegalArgumentException will be thrown.

Now we know about iterators we need to find out a bit about the collection classes themselves in order to make use of them.

Collection Classes

You have a total of nine classes in `java.util` that you can use to manage collections of objects, and they support collections that are sets, lists, or maps, as follows:

	Class	Description
Sets:	HashSet	An implementation of a set that uses `HashMap` under the covers. Although a set is by definition unordered, there has to be *some* way to find an object reasonably efficiently. The use of a `HashMap` object to implement the set enables store and retrieve operations to be done in a constant time.
	TreeSet	An implementation of a set that orders the objects in the set in ascending sequence. This means that an iterator obtained from a `TreeSet` object will provide the objects in ascending sequence. The `TreeSet` classes use a `TreeMap` under the covers.
Lists:	Vector	Implements a list as an array that automatically increases in size to accommodate as many elements as you need. Objects are stored and retrieved using an index as in a normal array. You can also use an iterator to retrieve objects from a `Vector`. The `Vector` is the only container class that is synchronized – that is it is well-behaved when concurrently accessed by two or more threads. We will discuss threads and synchronization in the next chapter.
	Stack	This class is derived from `Vector` and adds methods to implement a stack – a last-in first-out storage mechanism.
	LinkedList	Implements a linked list. The linked list defined by this class can also be used as a stack or a queue.
	ArrayList	Implements an array that can vary in size and can also be accessed as a linked list. This provides similar function to the `Vector` class but is unsynchronized.
Maps:	Hashtable	Implements a map, where all keys must be non-null. The class defining a key must implement the `hashcode()` method and the `equals()` method to work effectively. This class is a legacy of previous Java implementations and it is usually better to use the other classes that implement maps.
	HashMap	Implements a map that allows null objects to be stored and allows a key to be null (only one of course, since keys must be unique).
	WeakHashMap	Implements a map such that if a key to an object is no longer referenced ordinarily, the key/object pair will be discarded. This contrasts with `HashMap` where the presence of the key in the map maintains the life of the key/object pair, even though the program using the map no longer has a reference to the key, and therefore cannot retrieve the object.
	TreeMap	Implements a map such that the objects are arranged in ascending key order.

We can't go into all these classes in detail, but to introduce you to how these can be applied we will explore the three that you are likely to find most useful, `Vector`, `LinkedList` and `HashMap`. Before we get into the specifics of using the container classes we need to look at the interfaces they implement, since these provide the means of applying them.

Collection Interfaces

The `java.util` package defines six collection interfaces that determine the methods that you use to work with each type of collection class. There are three basic collection interfaces, the `Set`, `List` and `Map` interfaces, that relate to the fundamental organization of objects in a collection. These are implemented amongst the classes as follows:

Interface	Implemented by
Set	HashSet, TreeSet
List	Vector, Stack, ArrayList, LinkedList
Map	Hashtable, TreeMap, HashMap, WeakHashMap

The relationships between the interfaces that are implemented by the collection classes are shown in the diagram.

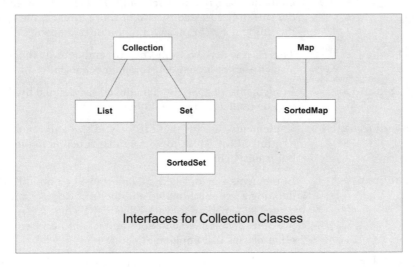

Interfaces for Collection Classes

The `Set` and `List` interface both extend a common interface `Collection`. Note that the `Map` interface does not extend `Collection`. Don't confuse the `Collection` *interface* with the `Collections` *class* (with an 's', that we will see later). The two other interfaces for collections are `SortedSet` that extends the `Set` interface, and `SortedMap` that extends the `Map` interface. The `SortedSet` interface is implemented by the `TreeSet` class, and the `SortedMap` interface is implemented by the `TreeMap` class.

It is important to keep in mind that any collection class object that implements the `Collection` interface can be referenced using a variable of type `Collection`. This means that any of the list or set collections can be referenced in this way, only the map class types are excluded (but not entirely, as you can obtain a list from a map). You will see that using a parameter of type `Collection` is a standard way of passing a list or set to a method.

These interfaces involve quite a number of methods so rather than go through them in the abstract, let's see them at work in the context of specific classes. We will look at the `Vector` class first since it is close to the notion of an array.

Using a Vector Collection

The `Vector` class defines a collection of elements of type `Object` that works rather like an array, but with the additional feature that it can grow itself automatically when you need more capacity. It implements the `List` interface so it can be used as a list. Because it stores elements of type `Object`, and `Object` is a superclass of every object, you can store any type of object in a `Vector`. This also means that potentially you can use a single `Vector` object to store objects that are instances of a variety of different classes. This is another advantage the `Vector` class has over arrays but the circumstances where this is desirable are relatively rare.

This ability to store diverse objects has a downside. It implies that it's very easy for you to store objects in a `Vector` by mistake. You can set up a `Vector` in which you plan to store a particular kind of object, but there's nothing to prevent the storage of some other kind of object in the `Vector`, or signal that this may cause problems. If you need to protect against this kind of error, you must program for it yourself. This isn't terribly difficult. As you'll see later in this chapter, all you need to do is package your `Vector` as a private member of a class that you define, and then supply methods to store objects in the `Vector` that will only accept the type that you want.

> Like arrays, vectors only hold object references, not actual objects. To keep things simple we refer to a `Vector` as holding objects. We'll make the distinction only when it's important, but you should keep in mind that all the collection classes you're about to encounter hold object references.

Creating a Vector

There are four constructors for a `Vector`. The default constructor creates an empty `Vector` object with the capacity to store up to a default number of objects, and the `Vector` object will increase in size each time you add an element when the `Vector` is full. The default capacity of a `Vector` object is ten objects, and the `Vector` object will double in size when you add an object when it is full. For example:

```
Vector transactions = new Vector();       // Create an empty Vector
```

If the default capacity isn't suitable for what you want to do, you can set the initial capacity of a `Vector` explicitly when you create it by using a different constructor. You just specify the capacity you require as an argument of type `int`. For example:

```
Vector transactions = new Vector(100);    // Vector to store 100 objects
```

409

The Vector object we're defining here will store 100 elements initially. It will also double in capacity each time you exceed the current capacity. The process of doubling the capacity of the Vector when more space is required can be quite inefficient. For example, if you end up storing 7000 objects in the Vector we've just defined, it will actually have space for 12,800 objects. If each object reference requires 4 bytes say, you'll be occupying more than 20 kilobytes of memory unnecessarily.

One way of avoiding this is to specify the amount by which the Vector should be incremented as well as the initial capacity when you create the Vector object. Both of these arguments to the constructor are of type int. For example:

```
Vector transactions = new Vector(100,10);
```

This Vector object has an initial capacity of 100, but the capacity will only be increased by 10 elements each time more space is required.

> *Why don't we increment the Vector object by 1 each time then? The reason is that the process of incrementing the capacity takes time. The bigger the vector is, the longer the copy takes and that might impact the program's performance. Besides, in programming Java for desktop computers, you shouldn't overly concern yourself with memory issues. It's a different story, however, when you're concerned with embedded devices.*

The last constructor creates a Vector object containing object references from another collection that is passed to the constructor as an argument of type Collection. Since all the set and list collection classes implement the Collection interface, the constructor argument can be of any set or list class type, including another Vector. The objects are stored in the Vector object that is created in the sequence they are returned from the iterator for the Collection object that is passed as the argument.

Let's see a vector working.

Try It Out – Using a Vector

We'll take a very simple example here, just storing a few strings in a vector:

```java
import java.util.*;

public class TrySimpleVector
{
  public static void main(String[] args)
  {
    Vector names = new Vector();
    String[] firstnames = { "Jack", "Jill", "John", "Joan", "Jeremiah",
"Josephine"};

    for(int i = 0 ; i<firstnames.length ; i++)
      names.add(firstnames[i]);

    for(int i = 0 ; i<names.size() ; i++)
      System.out.println((String)names.get(i));
  }
}
```

If you compile and run this, it will list the names that are defined in the program.

How It Works

We copy the references to the Vector object, names, in the first for loop. The add() method adds the object to the vector at the next available position. The second for loop retrieves the String references from the vector using the get() method. This returns the reference at the index position specified by the argument as type Object, so we have to cast it to the original type, String, in the println() call. The size() method returns the number of elements in the Vector, so this is the upper limit for the second for loop. Note that the Vector object doesn't care what type of objects are added – we could pass any type of reference to the add() method, even type Vector.

The Capacity and Size of a Vector

Although we said at the beginning that a Vector works like an array, this isn't strictly true. One significant difference is in the information you can get about the storage space it provides. An array has a single measure, its length, which is the count of the total number of elements it can reference. A vector has two measures relating to the space it provides – the **capacity**, and the **size**.

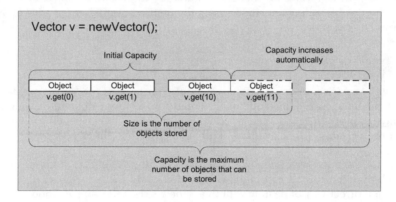

The **capacity** of a Vector is the maximum number of objects that it can hold at any given instant. Of course, the capacity can vary over time because when you store an object in a Vector object that is full, its capacity will automatically increase. For example, the Vector object, transactions, that we defined in the last of the constructor examples earlier, had an initial capacity of 100. After you've stored 101 objects in it, its capacity will be 110 objects. A vector will typically contain fewer objects than its capacity.

You can obtain the capacity of a Vector with the method capacity() which returns it as a value of type int. For example:

```
int transMax = transactions.capacity();   // Get current capacity
```

If this statement follows the current definition we have for transactions, the variable transMax will have the value 100.

You can also ensure that a Vector has a sufficient capacity for your needs by calling its ensureCapacity() method. For example:

```
transactions.ensureCapacity(150);        // Set minimum capacity to 150
```

If the capacity of `transactions` is less than 150, the capacity will be increased to that value. If it's already 150 or greater, it will be unchanged by this statement. The argument you specify for `ensureCapacity()` is of type `int`. There's no return value.

Changing the Size

When you first create a `Vector` object, the elements don't reference anything. An element will be occupied once you've stored an `object` in it. The number of elements that are occupied by objects in a `Vector` is referred to as the **size** of the `Vector`. The size of a `Vector` clearly can't be greater than the capacity. As we have seen, you can obtain the size of a `Vector` object as a value of type `int` by calling the `size()` method for the object. For example, you could calculate the number of free entries in the `Vector` object, `transactions`, with the statement:

```
int freeCount = transactions.capacity() - transactions.size();
```

You usually increase the size value for a `Vector` indirectly by storing an object in it, but you can also change the size directly by calling a method. Using the method, `setSize()`, you can increase and decrease the size. For example:

```
transactions.setSize(50);              // Set size to 50
```

The size of the `Vector` is set to the argument value (of type `int`). If the `Vector`, `transactions`, has less than fifty elements occupied, the additional elements up to fifty will be filled with `null` references. If it already contains more than fifty objects, all object references in excess of fifty will be discarded. The objects themselves may still be available if other references to them exist.

Looking back to the situation we discussed earlier, we saw how the effects of incrementing the capacity by doubling each time the current capacity was exceeded could waste memory. A `Vector` object provides you with a direct way of dealing with this – the `trimToSize()` method. This just changes the capacity to match the current size. For example:

```
transactions.trimToSize();             // Set capacity to size
```

If the size of the `Vector` is 50 when this statement executes, then the capacity will be too. Of course, you can still add more objects to the `Vector` as it will grow to accommodate them.

Storing Objects in a Vector

The simplest way to store an object in a `Vector` is to use the `add()` method as we did in the last example. To store a transaction in the `transactions` vector, you could write:

```
transactions.add(aTransaction);
```

This will add a reference to the object, `aTransaction`, to the `Vector` object called `transactions`, after any other existing object in the vector, and increase the size of the `Vector` by 1. All the objects that were already stored in the `Vector` remain at their previous index.

You can also store an object at a particular index position in a `Vector` using another version of `add()` with two parameters. The first argument is the index position and the second argument is the object to be stored. The index value must be less than or equal to the size of the `Vector`, which implies that this element already contains an object reference or is the next in line to receive one. The index value is the same as for an array – an offset from the first element – so you reference the first element using an index value of zero. For example, to insert the object `aTransaction` as the third entry of `transactions`, you would write:

```
transactions.add(2, aTransaction);
```

The index value is of type `int`, and represents the index value for the position of the new object. Thus the new object, `aTransaction`, is inserted in front of the object that previously corresponded to the index value 2, so objects stored in elements with index values equal to or greater than 2, will be shuffled along, and their index values will increase by 1. If you specify an index value argument that is negative, or greater than or equal to the size of the `Vector`, the method will throw `ArrayIndexOutOfBoundsException`.

To change an element in a vector you use the `set()` method. This accepts two arguments: the first argument is the index position where the object specified by the second argument is to be stored. To change the third element in the `Vector` object `transactions` to `theTransaction`, you would write:

```
transactions.set(2, theTransaction);
```

The method returns a reference of type `Object` to the object that was previously stored at this position. If the first argument is negative, or is greater than or equal to the current size of the `Vector`, the method will throw `ArrayIndexOutOfBoundsException`.

You can add all the objects from another collection to a vector, either appended at the end, or inserted following a given index position. For instance to append the contents of a `LinkedList` object, `myList`, to a `Vector` object `transactions`, you would write:

```
transactions.addAll(myList);
```

The parameter to the method is of type `Collection`, so the objects in any list or set can be added. To insert the collection objects at a particular position, you specify the index position as the first argument. So to insert the objects in `myList` starting at index position i, you would write:

```
transactions.addAll(i, myList);
```

The object originally at position i, and objects originally to the right of position i, will all be shuffled to the right to make room for the new objects. If the index value passed as the first argument is negative, or is not less than the size of `transactions`, an `ArrayIndexOutOfBoundsException` object will be thrown. Adding a collection will increase the size of the vector by the number of objects added.

Retrieving Objects from a Vector

As we saw in the simple example earlier, if you have the index for an element, you can obtain the element at a particular position by using the `get()` method for the `Vector`. For the `transactions` vector you could write:

```
Transaction theTransaction = (Transaction)transactions.get(4);
```

This statement will retrieve the fifth element in the vector. Note that the explicit cast is essential here. If you don't cast the object returned to the type of the variable that you're using to store it you'll get an error.

Of course, this is where an object of an incorrect type in the Vector will cause a problem. If the object returned here isn't of type Transaction, an exception will be thrown. Although you could always store it in a variable of type Object, you should always cast it to the original or most appropriate type. Note that the get() method will throw an exception of type ArrayIndexOutOfBoundsException if the argument is an illegal index value. The index must be non-negative and less than the size of the vector.

You can retrieve the first element in a Vector by using the firstElement() method, which returns the object stored as type Object. For example:

```
Transaction theTransaction = (Transaction)transactions.firstElement();
```

You can also retrieve the last element in a Vector by using the method lastElement() in a similar manner. However, a vector has a flavor of a list about it and if you want to process the objects in your vector like a list, you can obtain an iterator.

Accessing Elements through an Iterator

You can also obtain all the elements in a Vector object by using an Iterator object that you obtain from the Vector object. In most instances this will be the preferred way of accessing the elements in a vector. You obtain a reference to an iterator by calling the iterator() method for the Vector object:

```
Iterator theData = names.iterator();
```

The method iterator() returns an Iterator object that you can use to iterate through all the elements in the Vector object. You can now process them serially using the methods defined for Iterator class that we discussed earlier. For example, you could now output the elements from names in the last example we ran using the iterator:

```
while(theData.hasNext())
   System.out.println((String)theData.next());
```

This loop iterates through all the elements referenced by theData one at a time, and outputs each String object to the display. When we've retrieved the last element from the Iterator, the method hasNext() will return false and the loop will end.

You can also obtain a ListIterator reference from a vector by calling the listIterator() method:

```
ListIterator listIter = names.listIterator();
```

Now you can go backwards or forwards though the objects using the ListIterator methods that we saw earlier.

It is also possible to obtain a `ListIterator` object that encapsulates just a part of the vector, using a version of the `listIterator()` method that accepts an argument specifying the index position of the first vector element in the iterator:

```
ListIterator listIter = names.listIterator(2);
```

This statement will result in a list iterator that encapsulates the elements from transactions from the element at index position 2 to the end. The argument must not be negative and must be less than the size of transactions, otherwise an `IndexOutOfBoundsException` will be thrown. Take care not to mix the interface name with a capital L with the method name with a small l.

To cap that you can retrieve an internal subset of the objects in a vector as a collection of type `List` using the `subList()` method:

```
List list = names.subList(2, 5);    //Extract elements 2 to 4 as a sublist
```

The first argument is the index position of the first element from the vector to be included in the list, and the second index is the element at the upper limit – *not* included in the list. Thus this statement extracts elements 2 to 4 inclusive. Both arguments to `subList()` must be positive, the first argument must be less than the size of the vector, and the second argument must not be greater than the size, otherwise an `IndexOutOfBoundsException` will be thrown.

There are lots of ways of using the `subList()` method in conjunction with other methods, for example:

```
ListIterator listIter = transactions.subList(5, 15).listIterator(2);
```

Here we obtain a list iterator for elements 2 to the end of the list returned by the `subList()` call, which will be elements 7 to 14 inclusive from the `transactions` vector.

Extracting All the Elements from a Vector

A `Vector` provides you with tremendous flexibility in use, particularly with the ability to automatically adjust its capacity. Of course, the flexibility you get through using a `Vector` comes at a price. There is always some overhead involved when you're retrieving elements. For this reason, there may be times when you want to get the elements contained in a `Vector` object back as a regular array. The method `toArray()` will do this for you. You would typically use the method `toArray()` to obtain the elements of a `Vector` object, `transactions`, as follows:

```
Object[] data = transactions.toArray();  // Extract the vector elements
```

The `toArray()` method returns an array of type `Object` containing all the elements from `transactions` in the correct sequence.

It may be inconvenient to have the elements returned as an array of type `Object`. You may need to cast each element to its proper type before using it, for instance. There is another version of `toArray()` that will return an array of the type that you specify as an argument. You might use this with the transactions `Vector` as follows:

```
Transaction[] data = new Transaction(transactions.size());
data = transactions.toArray(data);
```

We allocate sufficient space for the elements using the `size()` member of our `Vector` object. You could supply an array as an argument that has more elements than are necessary to store the contents of the `Vector`. In this case the extra elements will be set to null. You can also supply an array that is too small as the argument to `toArray()`. In this case a new array will be created of the type you specify for the argument, with sufficient space to hold all the objects from the vector.

Of course the type of objects stored in the vector must be the same as, or a supertype of, the type of the array. If not, an exception of type `ArrayStoreException` will be thrown.

Removing Objects from a Vector

You can remove the reference at a particular index position by calling the `remove()` method with the index position of the object as the argument. For example,

```
transactions.remove(3);
```

will remove the fourth reference from `transactions`. The references following this will now be at index positions that are one less than they were before, so that what was previously the fifth object reference will now be at index position 3. Of course, the index value that you specify must be legal for the `Vector` on which you're operating, meaning greater than or equal to 0 and less than its `size()`, otherwise an exception will be thrown. This version of the `remove()` method returns a reference to the object removed, so it provides a means for you to retain a reference to the object after you remove it from the vector:

```
Transaction aTransaction = (Transaction)transactions.remove(3);
```

Here we save a reference to the object that was removed in `aTransaction`. The cast is necessary because the reference is returned as type `Object`.

Sometimes you'll want to remove a particular reference, rather than the reference at a given index. If you know what the object is that you want to remove, you can use another version of the `remove()` method to delete it:

```
boolean deleted = transactions.remove(aTransaction);
```

This will search the vector `transactions`, from the beginning to find the first reference to the object `aTransaction`, and remove it. If the object is found and removed from the vector, the method returns `true`, otherwise it returns `false`.

Another way to remove a single element is to use the `removeElementAt()` method, which requires an argument specifying the index position for the element to be removed. This is clearly similar to the version of `remove()` that accepts an index as an argument, the difference being that here the return type is `void`.

There is also a `removeAll()` that accepts an argument of type `Collection`, and removes elements from the collection passed to the method if they are present in the vector. The method returns `true` if the `Vector` object is changed by the operation, that is, at least one element was removed. You could use this in conjunction with the `subList()` method to remove a specific set of elements:

```
transactions.removeAll(transactions.subList(5,15));
```

This will remove elements 5 to 14 inclusive from the `Vector` object `transactions`, plus any duplicates of those objects that are in the vector.

If you want to discard all the elements in a `Vector`, you can use the `clear()` method to empty the `Vector` in one go:

```
transactions.clear();       // Dump the whole lot
```

With all these ways of removing elements from a `Vector`, there's lots of potential for ending up with an empty `Vector`. It's often handy to know whether a `Vector` contains elements or not, particularly if there's been a lot of adding and deleting of elements. You can check whether or not a `Vector` contains elements by using the `isEmpty()` method. This returns `true` if a `Vector` object has zero `size`, and `false` otherwise.

> Note that a `Vector` may contain only `null` references, but this doesn't mean the `size()` will be zero or that `isEmpty()` will return `true`. To empty a `Vector` object you must actually remove the elements, not just set the elements to `null`.

Searching a Vector

You can get the index position of an object stored in a `Vector` by passing the object as an argument to the method `indexOf()`. For example, the statement,

```
int position = transactions.indexOf(aTransaction);
```

will search the `Vector` from the beginning for the object `aTransaction` using the `equals()` method for the argument, so your class needs to have a proper implementation of `equals()` for this to work. The variable `position` will either contain the index of the first reference to the object in `transactions`, or -1 if the object isn't found.

You have another version of the method `indexOf()` available that accepts a second argument which is an index position where the search for the object should begin. The main use for this arises when an object can be referenced more than once in a `Vector`. You can use the method in this situation to recover all occurrences of any particular object, as follows:

```
int position = 0;                                // Search starting index
while(position<transactions.size() && position >= 0)   // Search with a valid index
{
  position = transactions.indexOf(aTransaction, position); // Find next

  // Code to process the object in some way...

  ++position;                                    // Search from the next element
}
```

The `while` loop will continue as long as the method `indexOf()` returns a valid index value and the index doesn't get incremented beyond the end of the `Vector`.

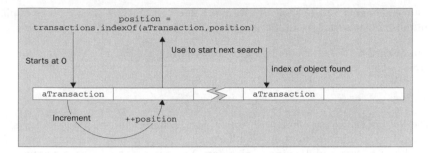

Each iteration will search `transactions` from the element given by the index stored in the variable `position`. When no further references to the object can be found from the position specified by the second argument, the method `indexOf()` will return −1 and the loop will end.

Using Vectors

Let's implement a simple example to see how using a `Vector` works out in practice. We will write a program to model a collection of people where we can add the names of the persons that we want in the crowd, from the keyboard. We'll first define a class to represent a person:

```
public class Person
{
  // Constructor
  public Person(String firstName, String surname)
  {
    this.firstName = firstName;
    this.surname = surname;
  }

  public String toString()
  {
    return firstName + " " + surname;
  }

  private String firstName;     // First name of person
  private String surname;       // Second name of person
}
```

The only data members are the `String` members to store the first and second names for a person. By overriding the default implementation of the `toString()` method, provided by the `Object` class, we allow objects of the `Person` class to be used as arguments to the `println()` method for output, since as you are well aware by now, `toString()` will be automatically invoked in this case.

Now we can define a class that will represent a crowd. We could just create a `Vector` object in `main()` but this would mean any type of object could be stored. By defining our own class we can ensure that only `Person` objects can be stored in the `Vector` and in this way make our program less prone to errors.

The class definition representing a crowd is:

```
import java.util.*;
```

```
class Crowd
{
  // Constructors
  public Crowd()
  {
    // Create default Vector object to hold people
    people = new Vector();
  }

  public Crowd(int numPersons)
  {
    // Create Vector object to hold people with given capacity
    people = new Vector(numPersons);
  }

  // Add a person to the crowd
  public boolean add(Person someone)
  {
    return people.add(someone);      // Use the Vector method to add
  }

  // Get the person at a given index
  Person get(int index)
  { return (Person)people.get(index); }

  // Get number of persons in crowd
  public int size()
  { return people.size(); }

  // Get people store capacity
  public int capacity()
  { return people.capacity(); }

  // Get an iterator for the crowd
  public Iterator iterator()
  { return people.iterator(); }

  // Person store - only accessible through methods of this class
  private Vector people;
}
```

We've defined two constructors for the class for illustration purposes, one to create a Vector with a default capacity, and the other to create a Vector with the capacity given by the argument. Both constructors just call the appropriate Vector constructor. You could easily add the ability to provide the capacity increment with a third constructor, if necessary.

By keeping the Vector member of the class private, we ensure the only way an object can be added to the Vector is by using the add() method in the class. Since this method only accepts an argument of type Person, we can be sure that it's impossible to store elements of any other type. Of course, if you wanted to allow other specific types to be stored, an object of type Child for example, you could arrange to derive the class Child from Person, so the add() method would allow an argument of type Child, since Person would be its superclass.

The remaining methods here are just to show how simple it is to implement the equivalent of the Vector methods for our class. In each case they use the Vector method to produce the required result. Now we are ready to put together a working example.

419

Try It Out – Creating the Crowd

We can now add a class containing a `main()` method to test these classes. We'll call it `TryVector`:

```java
import java.util.*;
import java.io.*;

public class TryVector
{
  public static void main(String[] args)
  {
    Person aPerson;                    // A person object
    Crowd filmCast = new Crowd();

    // Populate the crowd
    for( ; ; )                         // Indefinite loop
    {
      aPerson = readPerson();          // Read in a film star
      if(aPerson == null)              // If null obtained...
        break;                         // We are done...
      filmCast.add(aPerson);           // Otherwise, add to the cast
    }

    int count = filmCast.size();
    System.out.println("You added " + count +
      (count == 1 ? " person": " people") + " to the cast.\n");

    // Show who is in the cast using an iterator
    Iterator thisLot = filmCast.iterator();  // Obtain an iterator

    while(thisLot.hasNext())     // Output all elements
      System.out.println( thisLot.next() );
  }
}
```

Note the two `import` statements at the beginning. The first is needed for the `Iterator` in `main()`. The other is used for the `BufferedReader` and `InputStreamReader` objects in the `readPerson()` method. Let's now add this method to the `TryVector` class:

```java
// Read a person from the keyboard
static public Person readPerson()
{
  FormattedInput in = new FormattedInput();

  // Read in the first name and remove blanks front and back
  System.out.println(
                "\nEnter first name or ! to end:");
  String firstName = in.stringRead().trim();          // Read and trim a string

  if(firstName.charAt(0) == '!')                       // Check for ! entered
    return null;                                       // If so, we are done...
```

```
    // Read in the surname, also trimming blanks
      System.out.println("Enter surname:");
      String surname = in.stringRead().trim();            // Read and trim a string
      return new Person(firstName,surname);
  }
```

Here we read the first name followed by the surname as two separate strings, and then create the `Person` object that is returned. If a ! character was entered instead of a first name, `null` is returned signaling the end of the input. Since this method uses the `FormattedInput` class that we defined in Chapter 9, you need to copy the file containing the definition of this class to the same directory as the `TryVector` class. The `readPerson()` method is also expecting to find a `stringRead()` method available, so add the code for it to the `FormattedInput` class definition:

```
public class FormattedInput
  {
    // Read a  string
    public String stringRead()
    {
      try
      {
        for(int i = 0; i < 5; i++)
        {
          int tokenType = tokenizer.nextToken();        // Read a token
          if(tokenType==tokenizer.TT_WORD || tokenType == '\"')    // Type is a
string
            return tokenizer.sval;                               // so return it
          else if(tokenType == '!')                    // Non-alpha returned as
type
            return "!";                                 // so return end string
          else
          {
            System.out.println(
                    "Incorrect input. Re-enter a string between double quotes");
            continue;            // Retry the read operation
          }
        }
        System.out.println("Five failures reading a string" +
                                    " - program terminated");
        System.exit(1);            // End the program
        return null;
      }
      catch(IOException e)        // Error reading in nextToken()
      {
        System.out.println(e);    // Output the error
        System.exit(1);            // End the program
        return null;
      }
    }
    // Plus the rest of the class as before...
  }
```

You will recall that if you enter a string delimited by quotes, the quote character that you use is returned by the nextToken() method. If a character string is entered without quotes, then TT_WORD is returned. Thus the first if expression will be true if either of these is the case, so we return the string stored in sval. Of course, this will not include the double quote characters if they are present. Programming the method like this provides for quoted and unquoted strings, so we can enter names that contain spaces by putting them between quotes.

When a ! is entered, it is returned by the nextToken() method, so in this case we return a string containing just this character to signal to the calling program that this is the end of the input. You could use any non-alphanumeric character for this.

If you've added this method to the FormattedInput class, and placed the source files for the other classes to the same directory, you should be ready to give it a whirl. With a modest film budget, I got the output:

```
Enter first name or ! to end:
Roy
Enter surname:
Rogers

Enter first name or ! to end:
Marilyn
Enter surname:
Monroe

Enter first name or ! to end:
Robert
Enter surname:
"de Niro"

Enter first name or ! to end:
!
You added 3 people to the cast.

Roy Rogers
Marilyn Monroe
Robert de Niro
```

How It Works

Here we'll be assembling an all-star cast for a new blockbuster. The method main() creates a Person variable which will be used as a temporary store for an actor or actress, and a Crowd object, filmCast, to hold the entire cast.

The for loop uses the readPerson() method to obtain the necessary information from the keyboard and create a Person object. If !, or "!" is entered from the keyboard, readPerson() will return null and this will end the input process for cast members.

We then output the members of the cast by obtaining an Iterator. As you see, this makes the code for listing the members of the cast very simple. Instead of an iterator we could also have used the get() method that we implemented in Crowd to retrieve the actors:

```
for(int i = 0 ; i<filmCast.size() ; i++)
  System.out.println(filmCast.get());
```

Sorting

The output from the last example appears in the sequence in which you enter it. If we want to be socially correct, say, in the creation of a cast list, we should arrange them in alphabetical order. We could write our own method to sort `Person` objects in the `Crowd` object, but it will be a lot less trouble to take advantage of another feature of the `java.util` package, the `Collections` class – not to be confused with the `Collection` interface. The `Collections` class defines a variety of handy static methods that you can apply to collections, and one of them happens to be a `sort()` method.

The `sort()` method will only sort lists, that is, collections that implement the `List` interface. Obviously there also has to be some way for the `sort()` method to determine the order of objects from the list that it is sorting – in our case, `Person` objects. The most suitable way to do this for `Person` objects is to implement the `Comparable` interface for the class. The `Comparable` interface only declares one method, `compareTo()`. We saw this method in the `String` class so you know it returns – 1, 0 or +1 depending on whether the current object is less than, equal to or greater than, the argument passed to the method. If the `Comparable` interface is implemented for the class, we just pass the collection object as an argument to the `sort()` method. The collection is sorted in place so there is no return value.

We can implement the `Comparable` interface very easily for our `Person` class, as follows:

```
public class Person implements Comparable
{
  // Constructor
  public Person(String firstName, String surname)
  {
    this.firstName = firstName;
    this.surname = surname;
  }

  public String toString()
  {
    return firstName + " " + surname;
  }

  // Compare Person objects
  public int compareTo(Object person)
  {
    int result = surname.compareTo(((Person)person).surname);
    return result == 0 ? firstName.compareTo(((Person)person).firstName):result;
  }

  private String firstName;    // First name of person
  private String surname;      // Second name of person
}
```

We use the `compareTo()` method for `String` objects to compare the surnames, and if they are equal the result is determined from the first names. We can't apply the `sort()` method from the `Collections` class to a `Crowd` object though – a `Crowd` is not a list since it doesn't implement the `List` interface. A `Vector` does though, so we can sort the `people` member of the `Crowd` class by adding a `sort()` method to the class:

```
class Crowd
{
  // Sort the people
  public void sort()
  {
    Collections.sort(people);                // Use the static sort method
  }

  // Rest of the class as before...
}
```

We can just pass our `Vector` object to the `sort()` method, and this will use the `compareTo()` method in the `Person` class to compare members of the list.

Let's see if it works for real.

Try It Out—Sorting the Stars

You can now add a statement to the `main()` method in `TryVector`, to sort the cast members:

```
public static void main(String[] args)
{
  Person aPerson;                    // A person object
  Crowd filmCast = new Crowd();

  // Populate the cast
  for( ; ; )                         // Indefinite loop
  {
    aPerson = readPerson();          // Read in a film star
    if(aPerson == null)              // If null obtained...
      break;                         // We are done...
    filmCast.add(aPerson);           // Otherwise, add to the cast
  }


  int count = filmCast.size();
  System.out.println("You added "+count +
    (count == 1 ? " person":  " people")+ " to the cast.\n");


  filmCast.sort();                   // Sort the cast

  // Show who is in the cast using an iterator
  Iterator thisLot = filmCast.iterator();  // Obtain an iterator

  while(thisLot.hasNext())           // Output all elements
    System.out.println( thisLot.next() );
}
```

If you run the example with these changes, the cast will be in alphabetical order in the output. Here's what I got:

```
Enter first name or ! to end:
Roy
Enter surname:
Rogers
```

```
Enter first name or ! to end:
Mae
Enter surname:
West

Enter first name or ! to end:
Charles
Enter surname:
Chaplin

Enter first name or ! to end:
!
You added 3 people to the cast.

Charles Chaplin
Roy Rogers
Mae West
```

How It Works

The sort() method for the Crowd object calls the sort() method defined in the Collections class, and this sorts the objects in the people vector in place. Like shelling peas!

Stack Storage

A stack is a storage mechanism that works on a last-in first-out basis, often abbreviated to LIFO. Don't confuse this with FIFO, which is first-in first-out, or FIFI, which is a name for a poodle. The operation of a stack is analogous to the plate stack you see in some self-service restaurants. The stack of plates is supported by a spring that allows the stack of plates to sink into a hole in the counter-top so that only the top plate is accessible. The plates come out in the reverse order to the way they went in so the cold plates are at the bottom, and the hot plates fresh from the dishwasher are at the top.

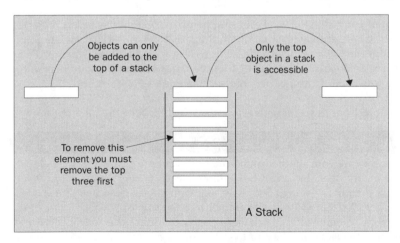

A Stack

A stack in Java doesn't have a spring, but it does have all the facilities of a Vector object because the class Stack is derived from the class Vector. Of course, since we know the Vector class implements the List interface, a Stack object is also a List.

The Stack class adds five methods to those inherited from Vector, two of which provide you with the LIFO mechanism, and the other three give you extra capabilities. These methods are:

Method	Description
push (Object anObject)	Pushes a reference to the object, passed as an argument to the method, onto the top of the stack.
pop()	Pops the object reference off the top of the stack and returns it as type Object. This removes the reference from the stack. If the stack contains no references when you call this method the EmptyStackException will be thrown.
peek()	This method allows you to take a look at the object reference at the top of the stack without popping it off the stack. It returns the reference from the top of the stack as type Object without removing it. Like the previous method, this method can throw an EmptyStackException.
search (Object anObject)	This will return an int value which is the position on the stack of the reference to the object passed as an argument. The reference at the top of the stack is at position 1, the next reference is at position 2 and so on. Note that this is quite different from referencing elements in a Vector or an array, where indexes are an offset, so they start at 0. If the object isn't found on the stack, −1 is returned.
empty()	This method returns true if the stack is empty, and false otherwise.

The only constructor for a Stack object is the default constructor. This will call the default constructor for the base class, Vector, so you'll always get an initial capacity for 10 objects, but since it's basically a Vector, it will grow automatically in the same way.

One possible point of confusion is the relationship between the top of a Stack object, and the elements in the underlying Vector. Intuitively, you might think that the top of the stack is going to correspond to the first element in the Vector, with index 0. If so you would be totally *wrong*! The push() method for a Stack object is analogous to the add() for a Vector which adds an object to the end of the Vector. Thus the top of the Stack corresponds to the end of the Vector.

Let's try a Stack object out in an example so we get a feel for how the methods are used.

Try It Out – Dealing Cards

We can use a Stack along with another useful method from the Collections class to simulate dealing cards from a card deck. Let's start by defining a class to represent a card. Our Card class can use two integer data members – one to define the suit with values from 0 to 3 for clubs, diamonds, hearts and spades, and the other with values from 1 to 13 to specify the face value of the card – 1 being an ace and 11 through 13 being jack, queen and king. It will make the code clearer if we define some constants representing the suits and the court card values. Let's put that as a skeleton class definition:

```
class Card
{
  // Suit values
  public static final int HEARTS = 0;
```

```
  public static final int CLUBS = 1;
  public static final int DIAMONDS = 2;
  public static final int SPADES = 3;

  // Card face values
  public static final int ACE = 1;
  public static final int JACK = 11;
  public static final int KING = 12;
  public static final int QUEEN = 13;
private int suit;
  private int value;
}
```

We need a constructor that ensures that the suit and face value of a card are legal values. We can implement the constructor like this:

```
class Card
{
  public Card(int value, int suit) throws IllegalArgumentException
  {
    if(value >= ACE && value <= KING)
      this.value = value;
    else
      throw new IllegalArgumentException("Invalid card value");
    if(suit >= HEARTS && suit <= SPADES)
      this.suit = suit;
    else
      throw new IllegalArgumentException("Invalid suit");
  }

  // Other members as before...
}
```

To deal with invalid arguments to the constructor, we just throw an exception of the standard type, IllegalArgumentException, that we create with a suitable message.

We will undoubtedly need to display a card so we will need a String representation of a Card object. The toString() method will do this for us:

```
class Card
{
  public String toString()
  {
    String cardStr;
    switch(value)
    {
      case ACE: cardStr = "A";
                break;
      case JACK: cardStr = "J";
                break;
      case QUEEN: cardStr = "Q";
                break;
```

```
            case KING: cardStr = "K";
                   break;
            default: cardStr = Integer.toString(value);
                   break;
      }

      switch(suit)
      {
        case CLUBS: cardStr += "C";
                break;
        case DIAMONDS: cardStr += "D";
                break;
        case HEARTS: cardStr += "H";
                break;
        case SPADES: cardStr += "S";
                break;
      }
      return cardStr;
  }

    // Other members as before...
}
```

Here we just use two `switch` statements to sort out the strings to represent the face value and the suit respectively from the values of the data members. In general, we might need to be able to compare cards, so we could also implement the `Comparable` interface:

```
class Card implements Comparable
{

    // Compare two cards
    public int compareTo(Object card)
    {
      if(suit != ((Card)card).suit)
        return suit < ((Card)card).suit ? -1: 1;
      else
        if(value == ((Card)card).value)
          return 0;
        else
          return value < ((Card)card).value ? -1 : 1;
    }

    // Other members as before...
}
```

We could represent a hand of cards that is dealt from a deck as an object of type Hand. A Hand object will need to be able to accommodate an arbitrary number of cards as this will depend on what game the hand is intended for. We can define the Hand class using a Stack object to store the cards:

```
// Class defining a hand of cards
import java.util.*;

class Hand
```

```
{
  public void add(Card card)
  {
    hand.push(card);
  }
  public String toString()
  {
    Iterator cards = hand.iterator();

    StringBuffer str = new StringBuffer();
    while(cards.hasNext())
      str.append(" "+ (Card)cards.next());
    return str.toString();
  }

  private Stack hand = new Stack();        // Stores the cards in the hand
}
```

The default constructor generated by the compiler will create a Hand object containing an empty Stack member, hand. The add() member will add the Card object passed as an argument by pushing it onto the hand. We also have implemented a toString() method here. We obtain an iterator to traverse the cards in the hand, and construct a string representation of the complete hand. Note that we should not use the pop() method here, because it removes an object from the stack, so using it here would remove all the cards from the hand.

We might well want to compare hands in general, but this is completely dependent on the context. The best approach to accommodate this when required would be to derive a game-specific class from Hand – PokerHand for instance – and make it implement the Comparable interface.

The last class we need will represent a deck of cards, and will also deal a hand:

```
import java.util.*;

class CardDeck
{
  // Create a deck of 52 cards
  public CardDeck()
  {
    for(int theSuit = Card.HEARTS; theSuit<= Card.SPADES; theSuit++)
      for(int theValue = Card.ACE; theValue <= Card.KING; theValue++)
        deck.push(new Card(theValue, theSuit));
  }

  // Deal a hand
  public Hand dealHand(int numCards)
  {
    Hand hand = new Hand();
    for(int i = 0; i<numCards; i++)
      hand.add((Card)deck.pop());
    return hand;
  }

  private Stack deck = new Stack();
}
```

The card deck is stored as a `Stack` object, `deck`. In the constructor, the nested `for` loops create the cards in the deck. For each suit in turn, we generate all the `Card` objects from ace to king and push them onto the `Stack` object, `deck`.

The `dealHand()` method creates a `Hand` object, and then pops `numCards` objects off the deck stack and adds each of them to `hand`. The `Hand` object is then returned. At the moment our deck is completely sequenced. We need a method to shuffle the deck:

```
class CardDeck
{
    // Shuffle the deck
    public void shuffle()
    {
        Collections.shuffle(deck);
    }

    // Rest of the class as before...
}
```

With the aid of another static method from the `Collections` class it couldn't be easier. The `shuffle()` method in `Collections` shuffles any collection that implements the `List` interface in place, so we end up with a shuffled deck of `Card` objects. For those interested in the details of shuffling, this `shuffle()` method randomly permutes the list by running backwards through its elements swapping the current element with some other element at random. The time taken is proportional to the number of elements in the list if the elements are accessible at random, but is likely to be proportional to the square of the number of elements if the list can only be accessed sequentially. An overloaded version of the `shuffle()` method allows you to supply an object of type `Random` as the second argument that is to be used for selecting elements at random.

The final piece is a class that defines `main()`:

```
class TryDeal
{
  public static void main(String[] args)
  {
    CardDeck deck = new CardDeck();
    deck.shuffle();

    Hand myHand = deck.dealHand(5);
    Hand yourHand = deck.dealHand(5);
    System.out.println("\nMy hand is" + myHand);
    System.out.println("\nYour hand is" + yourHand);
  }
}
```

I got the output:

```
My hand is 3D KD 7D 8C 7S

Your hand is 9C 6D 6C 3C AS
```

You will almost certainly get something different.

How It Works

The code for main() first creates a CardDeck object and calls its shuffle() method to randomize the sequence of Card objects. It then creates two Hand objects of 5 cards by calling the dealHand() method. The output statements just display the hands that were dealt.

A Stack object is particularly suited to dealing cards, as we want to remove each card from the deck as it is dealt and this is done automatically by the pop() method that retrieves an object. When we need to go through the objects in a Stack collection without removing them, we can use an iterator as we did in the toString() method in the Hand class. Of course, since the Stack class is derived from Vector, all the Vector class methods are available too, when you need them.

I think you'll agree that using a stack is very simple. Stacks are a powerful tool in lots of applications. They are often applied in applications that involve syntactical analyses, such as compilers and interpreters – including those for Java.

Linked Lists

The LinkedList collection class implements a generalized linked list. We have already seen quite a few of the methods that the class implements as the members of the List interface implemented in the Vector class. Nonetheless, let's quickly go through the methods that the LinkedList class implements. There are two constructors, a default constructor that creates an empty list, and a constructor that accepts a Collection argument that will create a LinkedList object containing the objects from the collection that is passed to it.

To add you have the add() and addAll() methods exactly as we discussed for a Vector object. You can also add an object at the beginning of a list using the addFirst() method, and you can add at the end using addLast(). Both methods accept an argument of type Object and do not return a value. Of course, the addLast() method provides the same function as the add() method.

To retrieve an object at a particular index position in the list you can use the get() method, as in the Vector class. You can also obtain references to the first and last objects in the list by using the getFirst() and getLast() methods, respectively. To remove an object you can use the remove() method with an argument that is either an index value, or a reference to the object that is to be removed. The removeFirst() and removeLast() methods do what you would expect.

Replacing an existing element in the list at a given index position is achieved by using the set() method. The first argument is the index value and the second argument is the new object at that position. The old object is returned and the method will throw an IndexOutOfBoundsException if the index value is not within the limits of the list. The size() method returns the number of elements in the list.

As with a Vector object, you can obtain an Iterator object by calling iterator(), and you can obtain a ListIterator object by calling listIterator(). You will recall that an Iterator object only allows you to go forward through the elements, whereas a ListIterator enables you to iterate backwards or forwards.

We could change the TryPolyLine example from Chapter 6 to use a LinkedList collection object rather than our homemade version.

Try It Out – Using a Genuine Linked List

We will put this example in a new directory, TryNewPolyLine. We can use the TryPolyLine class that contains main() and the Point class exactly as they are, so if you still have them, copy the source files to the new directory. We just need to change the PolyLine class definition:

```java
import java.util.*;

public class PolyLine
{
  // Construct a polyline from an array of points
  public PolyLine(Point[] points)
  {
    // Add the  points
    for(int i = 0; i < points.length; i++)
      polyline.add(points[i]);
  }
  // Construct a polyline from an array of coordinate
  public PolyLine(double[][] coords)
  {
    // Add the points
    for(int i = 0; i < coords.length; i++)
        polyline.add(new Point(coords[i][0], coords[i][1]));
  }

  // Add a Point object to the list
  public void addPoint(Point point)
  {
    polyline.add(point);     // Add the new point
  }

  // Add a point to the list
  public void addPoint(double x, double y)
  {
    polyline.add(new Point(x, y));
  }

  // String representation of a polyline
  public String toString()
  {
    StringBuffer str = new StringBuffer("Polyline:");
    Iterator points = polyline.iterator();            // Get an iterator

    while(points.hasNext())
      str.append(" "+ (Point)points.next());          // Append the current point

    return str.toString();
  }

  private LinkedList polyline = new LinkedList();    // Stores points for polyline
}
```

The class is a lot simpler because all the mechanics of operating a linked list are provided by the `LinkedList` class. Since the interface to the `PolyLine` class is the same as the previous version, the original version of `main()` will run unchanged, and produce exactly the same output.

How It Works

The only interesting bit is the change to the `PolyLine` class. `Point` objects are now stored in the linked list implemented by the `LinkedList` object, `polyline`. We use the `add()` method to add points in the constructors and the `addPoint()` methods. The `toString()` method now uses an iterator to go through the points in the list. Using a collection class makes the `PolyLine` class very straightforward.

Using Maps

As we saw at the beginning of this chapter, a **map** is a way of storing data that minimizes the need for searching when you want to retrieve an object. Each object is associated with a key which is used to determine where to store the reference to the object, and both the key and the object are stored in the map. Given a key, you can always go more or less directly to the object that has been stored in the map based on the key. It's important to understand a bit more about how the storage mechanism works for a map, and in particular what are the implications of using the default hashing process. We will explore the use of maps primarily in the context of the `HashMap` class.

The Hashing Process

A map sets aside an array in which it will store key and object pairs. The index to this array is produced from the key object by using the hash code for the object to compute an offset into the array for storing key/object pairs. By default, this uses the `hashCode()` method for the object that's used as a key. This is inherited in all classes from `Object`.

Note that, while every key must be unique, each key doesn't have to result in a unique hash code. When two or more different keys produce the same hash value, it's called a **collision**. A `HashMap` object deals with collisions by replacing the object already in the map, associated with an existing hash value, with the new object and then returning the old object .

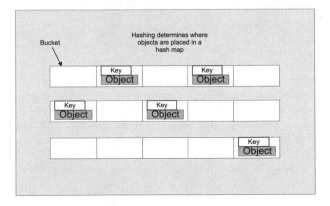

The price of reducing the possibility of collisions in a hash table is having plenty of empty space in the table.

The class `Object` defines the method `hashCode()` so any object can be used as a key and it will hash by default. The method as it is implemented in `Object` in Java, however, isn't a panacea. Since it usually uses the memory address where an object is stored to produce the hash value, distinct objects will always produce different hash values. In one sense this is a plus, because the more likely it is that a unique hash value will be produced for each key, the more efficient the operation of the hash map is going to be. The downside is that different object instances that have identical data will produce different hash values, so you can't compare them.

This becomes a nuisance if you use the default `hashCode()` method in objects that you're using as keys. In this case, an object stored in a hash map can never be retrieved using a different key object instance, even though that key object may be identical in all other respects. Yet this is precisely what you'll want to do in many cases.

Consider an application such as a simple address book. You might store map entries keyed on the names of the people to whom the entries relate, and you would want to search the map based on a name that was entered from the keyboard. However, the object representing the newly entered name is inevitably going to be distinct from that used as a key for the entry. Using the former, you will not be able to find the entry corresponding to the name.

The solution to this problem is somehow to make a hash of the instance variables of the object. Then, by comparing the values of the data members of the new name object with those for the name objects used as keys in the hash map, you'll be able to make a match.

Using Your Own Class Objects as Keys

For objects of one of your own classes to be usable as keys in a hash table, you must override the `equals()` method of the `Object` class. In its default form, `equals()` accepts an object of the same class as an argument, and returns a `boolean` value. The `equals()` method is used by methods in the `HashMap` class to determine when two keys are equal, so, in order to enable the changes discussed in the previous section, your version of this method should return `true` when two different objects contain identical data values.

You can also override the default `hashCode()` method, which returns the hash value for the object as type `int`. The `hashCode()` method is used to generate the `int` value that is the key. Your `hashCode()` method should produce hash codes that are reasonably uniform over the possible range of keys, and generally unique for each key.

Generating Hash Codes

The various techniques for generating hash codes form a big topic, and we can only scratch the surface here. How you write the `hashCode()` method for your class is up to you, but it needs to meet certain requirements if it is to be effective. You should aim to return a number of type `int` for an object that has a strong probability of being unique to that object, and the numbers that you produce for several different objects should be as widely distributed across the range of `int` values as possible.

To achieve the uniqueness you will typically want to combine the values of all the data members in an object to produce the hash code, so the first step is to produce an integer corresponding to each data member. You must then combine these integers to generate the return value that will be the hash code for the object. One technique you can use to do this is to multiply each of the integers corresponding to the data members by a different prime number and then sum the results. This should produce a reasonable distribution of values that have a good probability of being different for different objects. It doesn't matter which prime numbers you use as multipliers, as long as:

❑ They aren't so large as to cause the result to fall outside the range of type int

❑ You use a different one for each data member

So how do you get from a data member of a class to an integer? Generating an integer for data members of type String is easy: you just call the hashCode() method for the member. This has been implemented in the String class to produce good hash code values that will be the same for identical strings (take a look at the source code if you want to see how). You can use integer data members as they are, but floating point data members need a bit of judgment. If they have a small range in integer terms, you need to multiply them by a value that's going to result in a unique integer when they are cast to type int. If they have a very large range in integer terms you may need to scale them down.

Suppose you intended to use a Person object as a key in a hash table, and the class data members were firstName and surname of type String, and age of type int. You could implement the hashCode() method for the class as:

```
public int hashCode()
{
    return 13*firstName.hashCode() + 17*surname.hashCode() + 19*age;
}
```

Wherever a data member is an object of another class rather than a variable of one of the basic types, you need to implement the hashCode() method for that class. You can then use that in the computation of the hash code for the key class.

Creating a HashMap

As we saw, all map classes implement the Map interface, so an object of any map class can be referenced using a variable of type Map. We will look in detail at the HashMap class since it is good for most purposes. There are four constructors you can use to create a HashMap object:

Constructor	Description
HashMap()	Creates a map with the capacity to store a default number of objects. The default capacity is 101 objects and the default load factor (more on the load factor below) is 0.75.
HashMap(int capacity)	Creates a map with the capacity to store the number of objects you specify in the argument, and a default load factor of 0.75.
HashMap(int capacity, float loadFactor)	Creates a hash table with the capacity and load factor that you specify.
HashMap(Map map)	Creates a map with the capacity and load factor of the Map object passed as an argument.

To create a map using the default constructor, you can write something like this:

```
Hashmap theMap = new HashMap();
```

The capacity for a map is simply the number of key/object pairs it can store. The capacity increases automatically as necessary, but this is a relatively time consuming operation. The capacity value of the map is combined with the hash code for the key that you specify to compute the index that determines where an object and its key are to be stored. To make this computation produce a good distribution of index values, you should ideally use prime numbers for the capacity of a hash table when you specify it yourself. For example:

```
HashMap myMap = new HashMap(151);
```

This map has a capacity for 151 objects and their keys, although the number of objects stored can never actually reach the capacity. There must always be spare capacity in a map for efficient operation. With too little spare capacity, there is an increased likelihood that keys will generate the same table index, collisions become more likely and there is a danger that you might inadvertently lose an object in the map as a result.

The **load factor** is used to decide when to increase the size of the hash table. When the size of the table reaches a value which is the product of the load factor and the capacity, the capacity will be increased automatically to twice the old capacity plus 1 – the plus one ensuring it is at least odd, if not prime. The default load factor of 0.75 is a good compromise, but if you want to reduce it you could do so by using the third constructor:

```
HashMap aMap = new HashMap(151, 0.6f);  // 60% load factor
```

This map will work a bit more efficiently than the current default, but at the expense of having more unoccupied space. When ninety objects have been stored, the capacity will be increase to 303, (2*151+1).

Storing, Retrieving and Removing Objects

Storing, retrieving and removing objects in a HashMap is very simple. The four methods involved in this are:

Method	Description
put(Object key, Object value)	Stores the object value in the map using the key specified by the first argument. value will displace any existing object associated with key. The ejected object will be returned as type Object. If no object is stored at that map location or the key was used to store null as an object, null is returned.
putAll(Map map)	Transfers all the key/object pairs from map to the current map, replacing any objects that exist with the same keys.

Method	Description
get(Object key)	Returns the object stored with the same key as the argument. If no object was stored with this key or null was stored as the object, null is returned. Note that the object remains in the table.
remove(Object key)	Removes the entry associated with key if it exists, and returns the object as type Object. A null is returned if the entry does not exist, or if null was stored using key.

Any kind of object can be stored in a map, since all objects are stored as type Object. As with objects stored in a Vector, you can cast an object back to its original type when you retrieve it. The same caveats we saw for Vector objects, relating to the potential for storing objects of different types, apply to hash maps. If you want to limit the type of object that can be stored, you can use a HashMap object as a member of your own class, and implement its interface get(), put() and putAll() methods yourself, to restrict what can be stored.

If you attempt to retrieve an object using get() and a null is returned, it is still possible that a null was stored as the object associated with the key that you supplied to the get() method. You can determine if this is the case by passing your key object to the containsKey() method for the map. This will return true if the key is stored in the map.

You should check that the value returned from the put() method is null. If it isn't, you may unwittingly displace an object that was stored in the table earlier using the same key:

```
String myKey = "Goofy";
Integer theObject = new Integer(12345);

if(aMap.put(myKey, theObject) != null)
  System.out.println("Uh-oh, we bounced an object...");
```

Of course, you could throw your own exception here instead of displaying a message.

Note that the get() operation will return the object associated with the key, but it does not remove it from the table. To retrieve an object and delete it from the table, you must use the remove() method. This accepts a key of type Object as an argument, and returns the object corresponding to the key:

```
theObject = (Integer)aMap.remove(theKey);
```

As was noted in the table, if there's no stored object corresponding to theKey or null was stored as the object, null will be returned. Note how we have to explicitly cast the object returned from the hash map to the correct class.

Processing all the Elements in a Map

The Map interface provides three ways of obtaining a collection view of the contents of a map. You can obtain all the keys or all the key/object pairs from a map object as an object of type Set. You can also get a `Collection` object that references all the objects in the map. Note that the `Set` or `Collection` object is essentially a view of the contents of a map, so changes to a `HashMap` object will be reflected in the associated `Set` or `Collection`, and vice versa. The three methods involved are:

Method	Description
keySet()	Returns a `Set` object referencing the keys from the map.
entrySet()	Returns a `Set` object referencing the key/object pairs – each pair being an object of type `Map.Entry`.
values()	Returns a `Collection` object referencing the objects stored in the map.

The type of the key/object pairs in the set returned by `entrySet()` looks a little unusual. The key/object pairs are of type `Map.Entry` because `Entry` is an interface declared within the `Map` interface.

Let's first see how we can use a set of keys. The method `keySet()` for the `HashMap` class returns a `Set` object referencing the set of keys that you can either use directly to access the keys, or indirectly to get at the objects stored in the map. For a `HashMap` object, `aMap`, you could get the set of all the keys in the map with the statement:

```
Set keys = aMap.keySet();
```

Now you can get an iterator for this set of keys with the statement:

```
Iterator keyIter = keys.iterator();
```

You can use the `iterator()` method for the object, `keys`, to iterate over all the keys in the map. Of course, you can combine these two operations to get the iterator directly. For example:

```
Iterator keyIter = aMap.keySet().iterator();         // Get the iterator

while(keyIter.hasNext())                             // Iterate over the keys
  System.out.println((KeyType)keyIter.next());
```

This iterates over all the keys and outputs their `String` representation – `KeyType` in this fragment represents the class type of the keys.

The method `entrySet()` returns a `Set` object referencing the key/ object pairs. In a similar way to that we used for the set of keys, you can obtain an iterator to make the `Map.Entry` objects available. Each `Map.Entry` object will contain the following methods to operate on it:

Method	Description
getKey()	Returns the key object for the `Map.Entry` object as type `Object`.
getValue()	Returns the object for the `Map.Entry` object as type `Object`.

Method	Description
setValue(Object new)	Sets the object for this Map.Entry object to the argument and returns the original object. Remember that this alters the original map. This method throws:
	UnsupportedOperationException if put() is not supported by the underlying map.
	ClassCastException if the argument cannot be stored because of its type.
	IllegalArgumentException if the argument is otherwise invalid.
	NullPointerException if the map does not allow null objects to be stored. This last exception does not apply to HashMap.

A Map.Entry object will also need an equals() method for comparisons with another Map.Entry object passed as an argument and a hashCode() method to compute a hashCode() for the Map.Entry object.

With a set of Map.Entry objects you can obviously access the keys and the corresponding objects by obtaining an iterator, and modify the object part of each key/object pair if you need to.

Finally the values() method for a HashMap object will return a Collection object that is a collection of all the objects in the map. This enables you to use the iterator() member to obtain an iterator for the collection of objects.

We have waded through a lot of the theory for HashMap objects, let's put together an example that applies it.

We can put together a very simple phone book that uses a map. We won't worry too much about error recovery so that we don't bulk up the code too much. We will reuse the Person class that we saw earlier, and the FormattedInput class, so copy them to a new directory called TryHashMap or something similar. Besides the Person class we will need a PhoneNumber class, plus an Entry class that represents an entry in our phone book combining the name and number. We could add other stuff such as the address, but this is not necessary to show the principles. We will also define a PhoneBook class to represent the phone book.

Try It Out—Using a HashMap Map

We need to improve our old Person class to make Person objects usable as keys in the map that we will use to store the phone book entries. We must add an equals() method and we'll override the default hashCode() method just to show how this can work. The extended version of the class will be as follows:

```
public class Person implements Comparable, Serializable
{
  public boolean equals(Object person)
```

```
  {
    return compareTo(person) == 0;
  }

  public int hashCode()
  {
    return 7*firstName.hashCode()+13*surname.hashCode();
  }

  // The rest of the class as before...
}
```

Since the `String` class defines a good `hashCode()` method, we can easily produce a hash code for a `Person` object from the data members. To implement the `equals()` method we just call the method that we implemented for the `Comparable` interface. As it is likely to be required in this application, we have made the class serializable

There's another thing we could do that will be useful. We could add a `static` method to read data for a `Person` object from the keyboard:

```
import java.io.*;

public class Person implements Comparable, Serializable
{
  // Read a person from the keyboard
  public static Person readPerson()
  {
    FormattedInput in = new FormattedInput();
    // Read in the first name and remove blanks front and back
    System.out.println("\nEnter first name:");
    String firstName = in.stringRead().trim();
    // Read in the surname, also trimming blanks
    System.out.println("Enter surname:");
    String surname = in.stringRead().trim();
    return new Person(firstName,surname);
  }

  // Rest of the class as before...
}
```

You should have no trouble seeing how this works as it's almost identical to the `readPerson()` method we used previously.

We can make the `PhoneNumber` class very simple:

```
class PhoneNumber implements Serializable
{
  public PhoneNumber(String areacode, String number)
  {
    this.areacode = areacode;
    this.number = number;
```

```
      }

      public String toString()
      {   return areacode + ' ' + number;   }

      private String areacode;
      private String number;
}
```

We could do a whole lot of validity checking of the number here, but it's not important for our example.

We could use a `static` method to read a number from the keyboard so let's add that too:

```
import java.io.*;

class PhoneNumber implements Serializable
{
  // Read a phone number from the keyboard
  public static PhoneNumber readNumber()
  {
    FormattedInput in = new FormattedInput();

    // Read in the area code
    System.out.println("\nEnter the area code:");
    String area = Integer.toString(in.intRead());

    // Read in the number
    System.out.println("Enter the local code:");
    String number = Integer.toString(in.intRead());

    System.out.println("Enter the number:");
    number += " " + Integer.toString(in.intRead());

    return new PhoneNumber(area,number);
  }

    // Rest of the class as before...
}
```

This is again similar to the `readPerson()` method except that we read the parts of the telephone number as integers and convert them to `String` objects. If you wanted to read them as `String` objects, then they would need to be entered between quotes if spaces are to be permitted.

An entry in the phone book will combine the name and the number, and would probably include other things such as the address. We can get by with the basics:

```
import java.io.*;

class BookEntry implements Serializable
{
  public BookEntry(Person person, PhoneNumber number)
  {
```

```
    this.person = person;
      this.number = number;
    }

  public Person getPerson()
  {   return person;   }

  public PhoneNumber getNumber()
  {   return number;   }

  public String toString()
  {
    return person.toString() + '\n' + number.toString();
  }

  // Read an entry from the keyboard
  public static BookEntry readEntry()
  {
    return new BookEntry(Person.readPerson(), PhoneNumber.readNumber());
  }

  private Person person;
  private PhoneNumber number;
}
```

This is all pretty standard stuff. In the `static` method, `readEntry()`, we just make use of the methods that read `Person` and `PhoneNumber` objects so this becomes very simple.

Now we come to the class that implements the phone book – called the `PhoneBook` class, of course:

```
import java.io.*;
import java.util.*;

class PhoneBook implements Serializable
{
  public void addEntry(BookEntry entry)
  {
    phonebook.put(entry.getPerson(), entry);
  }

  public BookEntry getEntry(Person key)
  {   return (BookEntry)phonebook.get(key);   }
  public PhoneNumber getNumber(Person key)
  {   return getEntry(key).getNumber();   }

  private HashMap phonebook = new HashMap();
}
```

To store `BookEntry` objects we use a `HashMap` member, `phonebook`. We will use the `Person` object corresponding to an entry as the key, so the `addEntry()` method only has to retrieve the `Person` object from the `BookEntry` object that is passed to it, and use that as the first argument to the `put()` method for `phonebook`. Note that when we retrieve an entry, we must cast the object that is returned by the `get()` method to the `BookEntry` type, as `get()` returns type `Object`.

All we need now is a class containing `main()` to test these classes:

```
class TryPhoneBook
{
  public static void main(String[] args)
  {
    PhoneBook book = new PhoneBook();              // The phone book
    FormattedInput in = new FormattedInput();      // Keyboard input
    Person someone;

    for(;;)
    {
      System.out.println("Enter 1 to enter a new phone book entry\n"+
                         "Enter 2 to find the number for a name\n"+
                         "Enter 9 to quit.");

      int what = in.intRead();
      switch(what)
      {
        case 1:
          book.addEntry(BookEntry.readEntry());
          break;
        case 2:
          someone = Person.readPerson();
          BookEntry entry = book.getEntry(someone);
          if(entry == null)
            System.out.println("The number for " + someone +
                               " was not found. ");
          else
            System.out.println("The number for " + someone +
                               " is " + book.getEntry(someone).getNumber());
          break;
        case 9:
          System.out.println("Ending program.");
          return;
        default:
          System.out.println("Invalid selection, try again.");
          break;
      }
    }
  }
}
```

This is what the example produces with my input:

```
Enter 1 to enter a new phone book entry
Enter 2 to find the number for a name
Enter 9 to quit.
1
Enter first name:
Slim
Enter surname:
Pickens
```

```
Enter the area code:
914
Enter the local code:
238
Enter the number:
6778
Enter 1 to enter a new phone book entry
Enter 2 to find the number for a name
Enter 9 to quit.
2

Enter first name:
Slim
Enter surname:
"Pickens"
The number for Slim Pickens is 914 238 6778
Enter 1 to enter a new phone book entry
Enter 2 to find the number for a name
Enter 9 to quit.
9
Ending program.
```

Of course, you can try it with several entries if you have the stamina.

How It Works

The `main()` method runs an ongoing loop that will continue until a 9 is entered. When a 1 is entered, the `addEntry()` method for the `PhoneBook` object is called with the expression `BookEntry.readEntry()` as the argument. The `static` method `readEntry()` calls the `static` methods in the `Person` class and the `PhoneNumber` class to read from the keyboard and create objects of these classes. The `readEntry()` method then passes these objects to the constructor for the `BookEntry` class, and the object that is created is returned. This object will be added to the `HashMap` member of the `PhoneBook` object.

If a 2 is entered, the `getEntry()` method is called. The argument expression calls the `readPerson()` member of the `Person` class to obtain the `Person` object corresponding to the name entered from the keyboard. This object is then used to retrieve an entry from the map in the `PhoneBook` object. Of course, if there is no such entry `null` will be returned, so we have to check for it and act accordingly.

Storing a Map in a File

This phone book is not particularly useful. The process of echoing what we just keyed in doesn't hold one's interest for long. What we need is a phone book that is held in a file. That's not difficult. We just need to add a constructor and another method to the `PhoneBook` class:

```java
import java.util.*;
import java.io.*;
class PhoneBook implements Serializable
{
  public PhoneBook()
  {
    if(filename.exists())
    try
    {
      ObjectInputStream in = new ObjectInputStream(
```

```
                              new FileInputStream(filename));
      phonebook = (HashMap)in.readObject();
      in.close();
    }
    catch(ClassNotFoundException e)
    {
      System.out.println(e);
    }
    catch(IOException e)
    {
      System.out.println(e);
    }
  }

  public void save()
  {
    try
    {
      System.out.println("Saving phone book");
      ObjectOutputStream out = new ObjectOutputStream(
                              new FileOutputStream(filename));
      out.writeObject(phonebook);
      System.out.println(" Done");
      out.close();
    }
    catch(IOException e)
    {
      System.out.println(e);
    }
  }

  private File filename = new File("Phonebook.bin");

  // Other members of the class as before...
}
```

The new private data member, `filename`, defines the name of the file where the map holding the phone book entries is to be stored. Since we have only specified the file name and extension the file will be assumed to be in the current directory. The `filename` object is used in the constructor that now reads the `HashMap` object from the file if it exists. If it doesn't exist it does nothing and the `PhoneBook` object will use the default empty `HashMap` object.

The `save()` method provides for storing the map away, so we will need to call this method before ending the program. To make it a little more interesting we could add a method to list all the entries in a phonebook:

```
import java.util.*;
import java.io.*;
class PhoneBook implements Serializable
{
  // List all entries in the book
  public void listEntries()
```

```
{
    // Get the keys as a list
    LinkedList persons = new LinkedList(phonebook.keySet());
    Collections.sort(persons);                    // Sort the keys
    Iterator iter = persons.iterator();           // Get iterator for sorted
keys

    while(iter.hasNext())
      System.out.println(phonebook.get((Person)iter.next()));
  }

  // Other members as before...
}
```

If we want to list the entries in name sequence we have to do a little work. The keySet() method in HashMap returns a Set object for the keys, which are Person objects, but these will not be ordered in any way. By creating a LinkedList object from the set, we obtain a collection that we can sort using the sort() method from the Collections class. Finally we get an iterator to go through the HashMap using the keys in alphabetical order in the collection.

We can update main() to take advantage of the new features of the PhoneBook class:

```
class TryPhoneBook
{
  public static void main(String[] args)
  {
    PhoneBook book = new PhoneBook();              // The phone book
    FormattedInput in = new FormattedInput();      // Keyboard input
    Person someone;

    for(;;)
    {
      System.out.println("Enter 1 to enter a new phone book entry\n"+
                         "Enter 2 to find the number for a name\n"+
                         "Enter 3 to list all the entries\n" +
                         "Enter 4 to quit.");

      int what = in.intRead();
      switch(what)
      {
        case 1:
          book.addEntry(BookEntry.readEntry());
          break;
        case 2:
          someone = Person.readPerson();
          BookEntry entry = book.getEntry(someone);
          if(entry == null)
            System.out.println("The number for "+someone +
                         " was not found. ");

          else
            System.out.println("The number for "+someone +
                         " is " + book.getEntry(someone).getNumber());
```

```
        break;

    case 3:
      book.listEntries();
      break;
    case 4:
      book.save();
      System.out.println("Ending program.");
      return;
    default:
      System.out.println("Invalid selection, try again.");
      break;
    }
  }
 }
}
```

The first changes here are a new case in the switch to list the entries in the phone book and an updated prompt to suit. The other change is to call the save() method to write the map that stores the phone book to a file.

> Be aware of the default hashCode() method in the Object class when storing maps. The hash codes are usually generated from the address of the object, and getting a key object back from a file in exactly the same place in memory is about as likely as finding hairs on a frog. The result is that the hashCode() generated from the key when it is read back will be different from when it was originally produced, so you will never find the entry in the map to which it corresponds.
>
> If we override the default hashCode() method then our hash codes are produced from the data members of the key objects, so they are always the same regardless of where the key objects are stored in memory.

Now let's move on to look at some of the other components from the java.util package.

Observable and Observer Objects

The class Observable provides you with an interesting mechanism for communicating a change in one class object to a number of other class objects. One use for this mechanism is in GUI programming where you often have one object representing all the data for the application – a text document for instance, or a geometric model of a physical object, and several other objects that represent views of the data that are displayed in separate windows, where each shows a different representation or perhaps a subset of the data. This is referred to as the **document/view architecture** for an application, or sometimes the **model/view architecture**. This is a contraction of something referred to as the model/view/controller architecture and we will come back to this when we discuss creating graphical user interfaces. The document/view terminology is applied to any collection of application data – geometry, bitmaps or whatever. It isn't restricted to what is normally understood by the term 'document'.

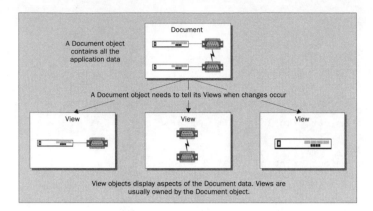

When the document object changes, all the views need to be notified that a change has occurred, since they may well need to update what they display. The document is **observable** and all the views are **observers**. This is exactly what the Observable class is designed to achieve, when used in combination with an interface, Observer. A document can be considered to be an Observable object, and a view can be thought of as an Observer object. This enables the view to respond to changes in the document.

The document/view architecture portrays a many-to-many relationship. A document may have many observers, and a view may observe many documents.

Defining Classes of Observable Objects

You use the Observable class in the definition of a class of objects that may be observed. You simply derive the class for objects to be monitored, Document say, from the class Observable.

Any class that may need to be notified when a Document object has been changed, must implement the interface Observer. This doesn't in itself cause the observer objects to be notified when a change in an observed object occurs, it just establishes the potential for this to happen. You need to do something else to link the observers to the observable, which we'll come to in a moment.

The definition of the class for observed objects could be of the form:

```
public class Document extends Observable
{
  // Details of the class definitions
}
```

The class Document here will inherit methods from the class Observable which operate the communications to the observer objects.

A class for observers could be defined as:

```
public class View implements Observer
{
  // Method for the interface
  public void update(Observable theObservableObject, Object arg)
  {
```

```
   // This method is called when the observed object changes
 }

 // Rest of the class definition...
}
```

To implement the `Observer` interface we need to define just one method, `update()`. This method is called automatically when an associated `Observable` object changes, and the `Observable` object that changed and caused the `update()` method to be called is passed as the first argument to the `update()` method. This enables the `View` object to access public methods in the associated `Observable` object, which would be used to access the data to be displayed for example. The second argument passed to `update()` is used to convey additional information to the observer object.

Observable Class Methods

The `Observable` class maintains an internal record of all the `Observer` objects related to the object to be observed. Your class, derived from `Observable`, will inherit the data members that deal with this. Your class of observable objects will also inherit nine methods from the class `Observable`. These are the following:

Method	Description
addObserver(Observer o)	Adds the object passed as an argument to the internal record of observers. Only observer objects in the internal record will be notified when a change in the observable object occurs.
deleteObserver (Observer o)	Deletes the object passed as an argument, from the internal record of observers.
deleteObservers()	Deletes all observers from the internal record of observers.
notifyObservers (Object arg)	Calls the `update()` method for all of the observer objects in the internal record if the current object has been set as changed. The current object is set as changed by calling the `setChanged()` method below. The current object and the argument passed to the `notifyObservers()` method will be passed to the `update()` method for each `Observer` object.
notifyObservers()	Calling this method is equivalent to the previous method with a `null` argument. (See `setChanged()` method below.)
countObservers()	The count of the number of observer objects for the current object is returned as type `int`.
setChanged()	Sets the current object as changed. You must call this method before calling the `notifyObservers()` method. Note that this method is `protected`.

Table Continued on Following Page

449

Method	Description
hasChanged()	Returns true if the object has been set as 'changed', and false otherwise.
clearChanged()	Resets the changed status of the current object to unchanged. Note that this method is also protected.

It's fairly easy to see how these methods are used to manage the relationship between an observable object and its associated observers. To connect an observer to an observable object, the observer object must be registered with the observable object by calling its addObserver() method. Once this is done the observer will be notified automatically when changes to the observable object occur. An observable object is responsible for adding observer objects to its internal record through the addObserver() method. In practice, the observer objects are typically created as objects that are dependent on the observable object and then added to the record, so there's an implied ownership relationship.

This makes sense if you think about how the mechanism is often used in an application using the document/view architecture. A document has permanence since it represents the data for an application. A view is a transient presentation of some or all of the data in the document, so a Document object should naturally create and own its View objects. A view will be responsible for managing the interface to the application's user, but the update of the underlying data in the Document object would be carried out by methods in the Document object, which would then notify other View objects that a change has occurred.

Of course, you're in no way limited to using the Observable class and the Observer interface in the way in which we've described here. You can use it in any context where you want changes that occur in one class object to be communicated to others. We can exercise the process in a silly example.

Try It Out – Observing the Observable

We'll first define a class for an object that can exhibit change:

```
import java.util.*;

public class JekyllAndHyde extends Observable
{
  String name = "Dr. Jekyll";

  public void drinkPotion()
  {
    name = "Mr.Hyde";
    setChanged();
    notifyObservers();
  }

  public String getName()
  {
    return name;
  }
}
```

Now we can define the class of person who's looking out for this kind of thing:

```
import java.util.*;

public class Person implements Observer
{
  String name;              // Person's identity
  String says;              // What they say when startled

  // Constructor
  public Person(String name, String says)
  {
    this.name = name;
    this.says = says;
  }

  // Called when observing an object that changes
  public void update(Observable thing, Object o)
  {
    System.out.println("It's " + ((JekyllAndHyde)thing).getName() +
                       "\n" + name + ": " + says);
  }
}
```

We can gather a bunch of observers to watch Dr. Jekyll with the following class:

```
// Try out observers
import java.util.*;

public class Horrific
{
  public static void main(String[] args)
  {
    JekyllAndHyde man = new JekyllAndHyde();  // Create Dr. Jekyll

    Observer[] crowd = {
                    new Person("Officer","What's all this then?"),
                    new Person("Eileen Backwards",
                            "Oh, no, it's horrible - those teeth!"),
                    new Person("Phil McCavity",
                         "I'm your local dentist - here's my card."),
                    new Person("Slim Sagebrush",
                            "What in tarnation's goin' on here?"),
                    new Person("Freaky Weirdo",
                       "Real cool, man. Where can I get that stuff?")};

    // Add the observers
    for(int i = 0; i < crowd.length; i++)
      man.addObserver(crowd[i]);

    man.drinkPotion();              // Dr. Jekyll drinks up
  }
}
```

If you compile and run this, you should get the output:

```
It's Mr.Hyde
Freaky Weirdo: Real cool, man. Where can I get that stuff?
It's Mr.Hyde
Slim Sagebrush: What in tarnation's goin' on here?
It's Mr.Hyde
Phil McCavity: I'm your local dentist - here's my card.
It's Mr.Hyde
Eileen Backwards: Oh, no, it's horrible - those teeth!
It's Mr.Hyde
Officer: What's all this then?
```

How It Works

`JekyllAndHyde` is a very simple class with just two methods. The `drinkPotion()` method encourages Dr. Jekyll to do his stuff, and the `getName()` method enables anyone who is interested to find out who he is. The class extends the `Observable` class so we can add observers for an object of this class.

The revamped `Person` class implements the `Observer` interface, so an object of this class can observe an observable object. When notified of a change in the object being observed, the `update()` method will be called. Here, it just outputs who the person is, and what they say.

In the `Horrific` class, after defining Dr. Jekyll in the variable, `man`, we create an array, `crowd`, of type `Observer` to hold the observers – which are of type `Person`, of course. We can use an array of type `Observer` because the class `Person` implements the `Observer` interface. We pass two arguments to the `Person` class constructor, a name, and a string that is what the person will say when they see a change in Dr. Jekyll. We add each of the observers for the object `man` in the `for` loop.

Calling the `drinkPotion()` method for the object `man`, results in the internal name being changed, the `setChanged()` method being called for the `man` object, and the `notifyObservers()` method that is inherited from the `Observable` class being called. This causes the `update()` method for each of the registered observers to be called which generates the output. If you comment out the `setChanged()` call in the `drinkPotion()` method, and compile and run the program again, you'll get no output. Unless `setChanged()` is called, the observers aren't notified.

Now let's move on to look at the `java.util.Random` class.

Generating Random Numbers

We have already used the `Random` class a little, but let's investigate this in more detail. The class `Random` enables you to create multiple random number generators that are independent of one another. Each object of the class is a separate random number generator. Any `Random` object can generate pseudo-random numbers of types `int`, `long`, `float` or `double`. These numbers are created using an algorithm that takes a 'seed' and 'grows' a sequence of numbers from it. Initializing the algorithm twice with the same seed would produce the same sequence because the algorithm is deterministic.

The integer values generated will be uniformly distributed over the complete range for the type, and the floating point values will be uniformly distributed over the range 0.0 to 1.0 for both types. You can also generate numbers of type `double` with a **Gaussian** (or normal) distribution that has a mean of 0.0 and a standard deviation of 1.0. This is the typical bell-shaped curve that represents the probability distribution for many random events.

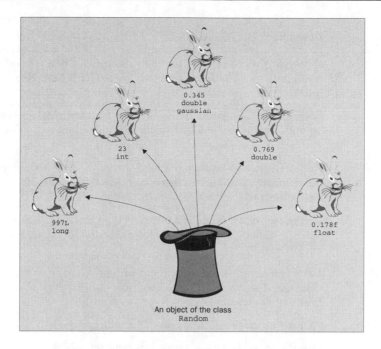

An object of the class
Random

There are two constructors for a Random object. The default constructor will create an object that uses the current time from your computer clock as the seed value for generating pseudo-random numbers. The other constructor accepts an argument of type long which will be used as the seed.

```
Random lottery = new Random();        // Sequence not repeatable
Random repeatable = new Random(997L); // Repeatable sequence
```

If you use the default constructor, the sequence of numbers that is generated will be different each time a program is run, although beware of creating two generators in the same program with the default constructor. The time resolution used is one millisecond, so if you create two objects in successive statements they will usually generate the same sequence because the times used for the starting seed values will be identical. Random objects created using the same seed will always produce the same sequence, which can be very important when you are testing a program. Testing a program where the output is not repeatable can be a challenge! A major feature of random number generators created using a given seed in Java is that not only will they always produce the same sequence of pseudo-random numbers from a given seed, but they will also do so even on totally different computers.

Random Operations

The public methods provided by a Random object are:

Method	Description
nextInt()	Returns a pseudo-random number of type int. Values generated will be uniformly distributed across the complete range of values for a number of type int.

Table Continued on Following Page

Method	Description
NextInt (int limit)	Returns a pseudo-random number of type int that is greater than or equal to 0, and less than limit – very useful for creating random array index values.
nextLong()	Returns a pseudo-random number of type long. Values generated will be uniformly distributed across the complete range of values for a number of type long.
nextFloat()	Returns a pseudo-random number of type float. Values generated will be uniformly distributed across the range 0.0f to 1.0, including 0.0f but excluding 1.0f.
nextDouble()	Returns a pseudo-random number of type double. Values generated will be uniformly distributed across the range 0.0 to 1.0, including 0.0 but excluding 1.0..
nextGaussian()	Returns a pseudo-random number of type double selected from a Gaussian distribution. Values generated will have a mean of 0.0, and a standard deviation of 1.0.
nextBoolean()	Returns true or false as pseudo-random values.
nextBytes (byte[] bytes)	Fills the array, bytes, with pseudorandom values.
setSeed (long seed)	Resets the random number generator to generate values using the value passed as an argument as a starting seed for the algorithm.

To produce a pseudo-random number of a particular type, you just call the appropriate method for a Random object. You can repeat the sequence of numbers generated by a Random object that you created with a seed value, by calling the setSeed() method with the same seed value as an argument.

We can give the Random class an outing with a simple program that simulates throwing a pair of dice. We'll assume you get six throws to try to get a double six.

Try It Out—Using Random Objects

Here's the program:

```
import java.util.Random;
import java.io.IOException;

public class Dice
{
  public static void main(String[] args)
  {
    System.out.println("You have six throws of a pair of dice.\n" +
              "The objective is to get a double six. Here goes...\n");

    Random diceValues = new Random();       // Random number generator
    String[] theThrow = {"First ", "Second ", "Third ",
                    "Fourth ", "Fifth ", "Sixth "};
```

```
   int die1 = 0;                          // First die value
   int die2 = 0;                          // Second die value

   for(int i = 0; i < 6; i++)
   {
     die1 = 1 + Math.abs(diceValues.nextInt())%6;  // Number from 1 to 6
     die2 = 1 + Math.abs(diceValues.nextInt())%6;  // Number from 1 to 6
     System.out.println(theThrow[i] + "throw: " + die1 + ", " + die2);

     if(die1 + die2 == 12)                          // Is it double 6?
     {
       System.out.println("      You win!!");       // Yes !!!
       return;
     }
   }
   System.out.println("Sorry, you lost...");
   return;
 }
}
```

How It Works

We use one random number generator here that we create using the default constructor, so it will be seeded with the current time and will produce a different sequence of values each time the program is run. We simulate throwing the dice in the `for` loop. For each throw we need a random number between 1 and 6 for each die. The easiest way to produce this is to use the remainder from dividing the random integer produced by the `diceValues` object by 6, and adding 1. Remember that the pseudo-random integer values that we get from the `nextInt()` method will be uniformly distributed across the whole range of possible values for type `int`, positive and negative. That's why we need to use the `abs()` method from the `Math` class to make sure we end up with a positive die value.

Remember that the odds against a double six are 36:1, so you'll only succeed once on average out of every six times you run the example.

Now we'll move on to look at dates and times.

Dates and Times

There are quite a few classes in the `java.util` package that are involved with dates and times, including the `Date` class, the `Calendar` class and the `GregorianCalendar` class. In spite of the class name, a `Date` class object actually defines a particular instant in time to the nearest millisecond, measured from January 1, 1970, 00:00:00 GMT. Since it is relative to a particular instant in time, it also corresponds to a date. The `Calendar` class is the base class for `GregorianCalendar` that represents the sort of day/month/year calendar everybody is used to, and also provides methods for obtaining day, month and year information from a `Date` object. A calendar object is always set to a particular date – a particular instant on a particular date to be precise, but you can change it by various means. From this standpoint a `GregorianCalendar` object is more like one of those desk calendars that just show one date, and you can flip over the days, months or years to show another date.

There is also the `TimeZone` class that defines a time zone that can be used in conjunction with a calendar, and that you can use to specify the rules for clock changes due to daylight saving time. The ramifications of handling dates and times are immense so we will only be able to dabble here, but at least you will get the basic ideas. Let's take a look at `Date` objects first.

The Date Class

With the `Date` class you can create an object that represents a given date and time. You have two ways to do this using the following constructors:

Method	Description
`Date()`	Creates an object based on the current time from your computer clock to the nearest millisecond.
`Date(long time)`	Creates an object based on the time value in milliseconds since 00:00:00 GMT on January 1st 1970 that is passed as an argument.

With either constructor you create a `Date` object that represents a specific instant in time to the nearest millisecond. Carrying dates around as the number of milliseconds since the dawn of the year 1970 won't grab you as being incredibly user-friendly – but we'll come back to how we can interpret a `Date` object better in a moment. The `Date` class provides three methods for comparing `Date` objects:

Comparison Methods	Description
`after` `(Date earlier)`	Returns `true` if the current object represents a date that's later than the date represented by the argument, `earlier`, and `false` otherwise.
`before` `(Date later)`	Returns `true` if the current object represents a date that's earlier than the date represented by the argument `later`, and `false` otherwise.
`equals` `(Object aDate)`	Returns `true` if the current object and the argument represents the same date and time, and `false` otherwise. This implies that they would both return the same value from `getTime()`.

The `equals()` method returns `true` if two different `Date` objects represent the same date and time. Since the `hashCode()` method is also implemented for the class, you have all you need to use `Date` objects as keys in a hash table.

Interpreting Date Objects

The `DateFormat` class is an abstract class that you can use to create meaningful `String` representations of `Date` objects. It isn't in the `java.util` package though – it's defined in the package `java.text`. There are four standard representations for the date and the time that are identified by constants defined in the `DateFormat` class. The effects of these will vary in different countries, because the representation for the date and the time will reflect the conventions of those countries. The constants in the `DateFormat` class defining the four formats are:

Date Format	Description
SHORT	A completely numeric representation for a date or a time, such as 2/2/97 or 4:15am.
MEDIUM	A longer representation than SHORT, such as 5-Dec-97.
LONG	A longer representation than MEDIUM, such as December 5, 1997.
FULL	A comprehensive representation of the date or the time such as Friday, December 5, 1997 AD or 4:45:52 PST (Pacific Standard Time).

A country is defined by a Locale object which you can generate from a class constructor that accepts ISO codes for the language and the country. The language codes are defined by ISO-639 and the country codes ISO-3166. You can find the country codes on the Internet at,

http://www.chemie.fu-berlin.de/diverse/doc/ISO_3166.html

and you can find the language codes at,

http://www.ics.uci.edu/pub/ietf/http/related/iso639.txt

For some countries, the easiest way to specify the locale if you don't have the ISO codes on the tip of your tongue, is to use the final Locale objects defined within the Locale class. In Java 2 these are:

UK	US	CANADA	FRANCE	GERMANY	ITALY
JAPAN	KOREA	CHINA	TAIWAN		

Because the DateFormat class is abstract, you can't create objects of the class directly, but you can obtain DateFormat objects by using any of the following static methods, each of which return a value of type DateFormat:

Static Method	Description
getTimeInstance()	Returns a time formatter for the default locale that uses the default style for the time.
getTimeInstance (int timeStyle)	Returns a time formatter for the default locale that uses the style for the time that is specified by the argument.
getTimeInstance (int style, Locale aLocale)	Returns a time formatter for the locale specified by the second argument that uses the style for the time that is specified by the first argument.
getDateInstance()	Returns a date formatter for the default locale that uses the default style for the date.
getDateInstance (int dateStyle)	Returns a date formatter for the default locale that uses the style for the date specified by the argument.

Table Continued on Following Page

457

Static Method	Description

`getDateInstance`
`  (int dateStyle,`
`   Locale aLocale)`
	Returns a date formatter for the locale specified by the second argument that uses the style for the date that is specified by the first argument.

`getInstance()`	Returns a default date and time formatter that uses the SHORT style for both the date and the time.
`getDateTimeInstance()`	Returns a date and time formatter for the default locale that uses the default style for both the date and the time.

`getDateTimeInstance`
`  (int dateStyle,`
`   int timeStyle)`
	Returns a date and time formatter for the current locale that uses the styles for the date and the time specified by the arguments.

`getDateTimeInstance`
`  (int dateStyle,`
`   int timeStyle,`
`   Locale aLocale)`
	Returns a date and time formatter for aLocale with the styles for the date and the time as specified by the first two arguments.

When you've obtained a `DateFormat` object for the country and the style that you want, and the sort of data you want to format – the date or the time or both – you're ready to produce a `String` from the `Date` object.

All you need to do is to pass the `Date` object to the `format()` method for the `DateFormat` object. For example:

```
Date today = new Date();   // Object for now - today's date
DateFormat fmt = getDateTimeInstance(Locale.FULL, Locale.US);
String formatted = fmt.format(today);
```

After executing these statements, the `String` variable, `formatted`, will contain a full representation of the date and the time when the `Date` object, `today`, was created.

We can try out some dates and formats in a simple example.

Try It Out—Producing Dates and Times

This example will show the four different date formats for four countries:

```
// Trying date formatting
import java.util.*;
import java.text.*;

public class TryDateFormats
{
  public static void main(String[] args)
  {
    Date today = new Date();
    Locale[] locales = {Locale.US, Locale.UK,
                        Locale.GERMANY, Locale.FRANCE};
```

```
        int[] styles = {DateFormat.FULL,DateFormat.LONG,
                        DateFormat.MEDIUM,DateFormat.SHORT};
      DateFormat fmt;
      String[] styleText = {"FULL", "LONG", "MEDIUM", "SHORT"};

      // Output the date for each local in four styles
      for(int i = 0; i < locales.length; i++)
      {
        System.out.println("\nThe Date for " +
                           locales[i].getDisplayCountry() + ":");
        for(int j = 0; j < styles.length; j++)
        {
          fmt = DateFormat.getDateInstance(styles[j], locales[i]);
          System.out.println( "\tIn " + styleText[j] +
                              " is " + fmt.format(today));
        }
      }
    }
  }
}
```

When I compiled and ran this it produced the following output:

```
The Date for United States:
        In FULL is Wednesday, April 14, 1999
        In LONG is April 14, 1999
        In MEDIUM is 14-Apr-99
        In SHORT is 4/14/99

The Date for United Kingdom:
        In FULL is Wednesday, 14 April 1999
        In LONG is 14 April, 1999
        In MEDIUM is 14-Apr-99
        In SHORT is 14/04/99

The Date for Germany:
        In FULL is Mittwoch, 14. April 1999
        In LONG is 14. April 1999
        In MEDIUM is 14.4.1999
        In SHORT is 14.4.99

The Date for France:
        In FULL is mercredi, 14 avril 1999
        In LONG is 14 avril 1999
        In MEDIUM is 14 avr 99
        In SHORT is 14/04/99
```

Of course, when you run it the output will be different.

How It Works

The program creates a Date object for the current date and time, and an array of Locale objects for four countries using values defined in the Locale class. It then creates an array of the four possible styles, and another array containing a String representation for each style which will be used in the output.

459

The output is produced in the nested `for` loops. The outer loop iterates over the countries, and the inner loop iterates over the four styles for each country. A `DateFormat` object is created for each combination of style and country, and the `format()` method for the `DateFormat` object is called to produce the formatted date string in the inner call to `println()`.

There are a couple of ways you could change the program. You could initialize the `locales []` array with the expression `DateFormat.getAvailableLocales()`. This will return an array of type `Locale` containing all of the supported locales, but be warned – there are a lot of them. You'll also find that the characters won't display for many countries because your machine doesn't support the country-specific character set. You could also use the method `getTimeInstance()` or `getDateTimeInstance()` instead of `getDateInstance()` to see what sort of output they generate.

Under the covers, a `DateFormat` object contains a `DateFormatSymbols` object that contains all the strings for the names of days of the week, and other fixed information related to time and dates. This class is also in the `java.text` package. Normally you don't use the `DateFormatSymbols` class directly, but it can be useful when all you want are the days of the week.

Obtaining a Date Object from a String

The `parse()` method for a `DateFormat` object interprets a `String` object passed as an argument as a date and time, and returns a `Date` object corresponding to the date and the time. The `parse()` method will throw a `ParseException` if the `String` object can't be converted to a `Date` object, so you must call it within a `try` block.

The `String` argument to the `parse()` method must correspond to the country and style that you used when you obtained the `DateFormat` object. This makes it a bit tricky to use successfully. For example, the following code will parse the string properly:

```
Date aDate;
DateFormat fmt = DateFormat.getDateInstance(DateFormat.FULL, Locale.US);
try
{
   aDate = fmt.parse("Saturday, July 4, 1998 ");
   System.out.println("The Date string is: " + fmt.format(aDate));
}
catch(ParseException e)
{
   System.out.println(e);
}
```

This works because the string is what would be produced by the locale and style. If you omit the day from the string, or you use the `LONG` style or a different locale, a `ParseException` will be thrown.

Gregorian Calendars

The Gregorian calendar is the calendar generally in use today in the western world, and is represented by an object of the `GregorianCalendar` class. There are no less than seven constructors for `GregorianCalendar` objects from the default that creates a calendar with the current date and time in the default locale for your machine through to a constructor where you can specify the year, month, day, hour, minute and second. The default suits most situations.

You can create a calendar with a statement such as:

```
GregorianCalendar calendar = new GregorianCalendar();
```

This will be set to the current instant in time, and you can retrieve this as a `Date` object by calling the `getTime()` method for the calendar:

```
Date now = calendar.getTime();
```

There is also a `setTime()` method that you can pass a `Date` object to set the current time for the `GregorianCalendar` object.

You can get information such as the day, the month and the year from a `GregorianCalendar` object by using the `get()` method and specifying what you want as an argument. Some of the possible arguments to the `get()` method defined as static members of the `Calendar` class and inherited in the `GregorianCalendar` class are:

Field	Possible values returned by `get()`
AM_PM	AM or PM which correspond to values of 0 and 1.
DAY_OF_WEEK	SUNDAY, MONDAY, etc. through to SATURDAY which correspond to values of 1 to 7.
DAY_OF_YEAR	A value from 1 to 366.
MONTH	JANUARY, FEBRUARY, etc. through to DECEMBER corresponding to values of 0 to 11.
DAY_OF_MONTH or DATE	A value from 1 to 31.
WEEK_OF_MONTH	A value from 1 to 6.
WEEK_OF_YEAR	A value from 1 to 54.
HOUR_OF_DAY	A value from 0 to 23
HOUR	A value from 1 to 12 being the current hour in the am or pm.
MINUTE	The current minute in the current hour – a value from 0 to 59.
SECOND	The second in the current minute, 0 to 59.
MILLISECOND	The millisecond in the current second, 0 to 999.
YEAR	The current year, e.g. 1998.

All values returned are of type `int`. For example, you could get the day of the week with the statement:

```
int day = calendar.get(calendar.DAY_OF_WEEK);
```

You could now test this for a particular day using the constant defined in the class:

```
if(day == calendar.SATURDAY)
  // Go to game...
```

Of course, you might want to alter the current instant in the calendar, and for this you have the add() method. The first argument determines what units you are adding in, and you specify this argument using the same field designators as in the previous list. For example, you can add 14 to the year with the statement:

```
calendar.add(calendar.YEAR, 14);  // 14 years into the future
```

To go into the past, you just make the second argument negative:

```
calendar.add(calendar.MONTH, -6);  // Go back 6 months
```

You can increment or decrement a field of a calendar by 1 using the roll() method. This method modifies the field specified by the first argument by +1 or –1, depending on whether the second argument is true or false. For example, to decrement the current month in the object, calendar, you would write:

```
calendar.roll(calendar.MONTH, false);  // Go back a month
```

The change can affect other fields. If the original month was January, rolling it back by one will make the date December of the previous year.

Of course, having modified a GregorianCalendar object, you can get the current instant back as a Date object using the getTime() method that we saw earlier. You can then use a DateFormat object to present this in a readable form.

Comparing Calendars

Checking the relationship between dates is a fairly fundamental requirement and you have three methods available for comparing Calendar objects:

Method	Description
before()	Returns true if the current object corresponds to a time before that of the Calendar object passed as an argument. Note that this implies a true return can occur if the date is the same but the time is different.
after()	Returns true if the current object corresponds to a time after that of the Calendar object passed as an argument.
equals()	Returns true if the current object corresponds to a time that is identical to that of the Calendar object passed as an argument.

These are very simple to use. To determine whether the object `thisDate` defines a time that precedes the time defined by the object `today`, you could write:

```
if(thisDate.before(today))
   // Do something
```

Alternatively you could write the same thing as:

```
if(today.after(thisDate))
   // Do something
```

It's time to look at how we can use calendars.

Try It Out – Using a Calendar

This example will deduce important information about when you were born. It uses the `FormattedInput` class to get input from the keyboard, so copy the class to the directory containing the source file for this example. Here's the code:

```java
import java.util.*;
import java.text.DateFormatSymbols;

class TryCalendar
{
  public static void main(String[] args)
  {
    FormattedInput in = new FormattedInput();

    // Get the date of birth from the keyboard
    System.out.println("Enter your birth date as dd mm yyyy: ");
    int day = in.intRead();
    int month = in.intRead();
    int year = in.intRead();

    // Create birth date calendar - month is 0 to 11
    GregorianCalendar birthdate = new GregorianCalendar(year, month-1,day);
    GregorianCalendar today = new GregorianCalendar();  // Today's date

    // Create this year's birthday
    GregorianCalendar birthday = new GregorianCalendar(
                                  today.get(today.YEAR),
                                  birthdate.get(birthdate.MONTH),
                                  birthdate.get(birthdate.DATE));

    int age = today.get(today.YEAR) - birthdate.get(birthdate.YEAR);

    String[] weekdays = new DateFormatSymbols().getWeekdays(); // Get day names

    System.out.println("You were born on a " +
                      weekdays[birthdate.get(birthdate.DAY_OF_WEEK)]);
    System.out.println("This year you " +
                      (birthday.after(today)   ?"will be " : "are ") +
```

```
                         age + " years old.");
        System.out.println("This year your birthday "+
                           (today.before(birthday)? "will be": "was")+
                           " on a "+ weekdays[birthday.get(birthday.DAY_OF_WEEK)]);
    }
  }
```

I got the output:

```
Enter your birth date as dd mm yyyy:
5 12 1964
You were born on a Saturday
This year you will be 34 years old.
This year your birthday will be on a Saturday
```

How It Works

We start by prompting for the day, month and year for a date of birth to be entered through the keyboard as integers. We then create a calendar object corresponding to this date. Note the adjustment of the month – the constructor expects January to be specified as 0. We need a calendar object for today's date so we use the default constructor for this. To compute the age this year, we just have to subtract the year of birth from this year, both of which we get from the GregorianCalendar objects.

To get at the strings for the days of the week, we create a DateFormatSymbols object and call its getWeekdays() method. This returns an array of eight String objects, the first of which is empty to make it easy to index using day numbers from 1 to 7. The second element in the array contains "Sunday". You can also get the month names using the getMonths() method.

To display the day of the week for the date of birth we call the get() method for the GregorianCalendar object, birthdate, and use the result to index the weekdays[] array. To determine the appropriate text in the next two output statements, we use the after() and before() methods for calendar objects to compare today with the birthday date this year.

Summary

All of the classes in this chapter will be useful sooner or later when you're writing your own Java programs. We'll be applying many of them in examples throughout the remainder of the book.

The important elements we've covered are:

❑   You can use a Vector object as a kind of flexible array which expands automatically to accommodate any number of objects stored

❑   The Stack class is derived from the Vector class and implements a pushdown stack

❑   The HashMap class defines a hash map in which objects are stored based on an associated key

❑   An Iterator is an interface for retrieving objects from a collection sequentially. An Iterator object allows you to access all the objects it contains serially – but only once. There's no way to go back to the beginning

❏ The `ListIterator` interface provides methods for traversing the objects in a collection backwards or forwards.

❏ Objects stored in any type of collection can be accessed using `Iterator` objects.

❏ Objects stored in a `Vector`, a `Stack` or a `LinkedList` can be accessed using `ListIterator` objects.

❏ Objects of type `Random` can generate pseudo-random numbers of type `int`, `long`, `float` and `double`. The integers are uniformly distributed across the range of the type, `int` or `long`. The floating point numbers are between 0.0 and 1.0. You can also generate numbers of type `double` with a Gaussian distribution with a mean of 0.0 and a standard deviation of 1.0, and random `boolean` values.

❏ Classes derived from the `Observable` class can signal changes to classes that implement the `Observer` interface. You define the `Observer` objects that are to be associated with an `Observable` class object by calling the `addObserver()` method. This is primarily intended to be used to implement the document/view architecture for applications in a GUI environment

❏ You can create `Date` objects to represent a date and time that you specify in milliseconds since January 1, 1970, 00:00:00 GMT, or the current date and time from your computer clock

❏ You can use a `DateFormat` object to format the date and time for a `Date` object as a string. The format will be determined by the style and the locale that you specify

❏ A `GregorianCalendar` object represents a calendar set to an instant in time on a given date.

Exercises

1. Implement a version of the program to calculate prime numbers that we saw in Chapter 4 to use a `Vector` object instead of an array to store the primes. (Hint – remember the `Integer` class.)

2. Write a program to store a deck of 52 cards in a linked list in random sequence using a `Random` class object. You can represent a card as a two character string – "1C" for the ace of clubs, "JD" for the jack of diamonds, and so on. Output the cards from the stack as four hands of 13 cards.

3. Extend the program from the chapter that used a map to store names and telephone numbers such that you can enter a number to retrieve the name.

4. Implement a phone book so that just a surname can be used to search and have all the entries corresponding to the name display.

5. For the adventurous gambler – use a stack and a `Random` object in a program to simulate a game of Blackjack for one player using two decks of cards.

6. Write a program to display the sign of the Zodiac corresponding to a birth date entered through the keyboard.

Threads

In this chapter we'll investigate the facilities Java has to enable you to overlap the execution of segments of a single program. As well as ensuring your programs run more efficiently, this capability is particularly useful when your program has, of necessity, to do a number of things at the same time. For example: a server program on a network that needs to communicate with multiple clients.

In this chapter you will learn:

- ❑ What a thread is and how you can create threads in your programs.
- ❑ How to control interactions between threads.
- ❑ What synchronization means and how to apply it in your code.
- ❑ What deadlocks are, and how to avoid them.
- ❑ How to set thread priorities.
- ❑ How to get information about the threads in your programs.

Understanding Threads

Many programs, of any size, contain some code segments that are more or less independent of one another, and that may execute more efficiently if the code segments could be overlapped in time. Threads provide a way to do this. Of course, if like most people your computer only has one processor, you can't execute more than one computation at any instant, but you can overlap input/output operations with processing. Another reason for using threads is to allow processes in a program that need to run continuously, such as a continuously running animation, to be overlapped with other activities in the same program. Java applets in a web page are executed under the control of your browser, and threads make it possible for multiple applets to be executing concurrently. In this case the threads serve to segment the activities running under the control of the browser so that they appear to run concurrently. If you only have one processor, this is an illusion created by your operating system since only one thread can actually be executing instructions at any given instant, but it's a very effective illusion. To produce animation, you typically put some code that draws a succession of still pictures in a loop that runs indefinitely.

The code to draw the picture generally runs under the control of a timer so that it executes at a fixed rate, say 20 times per second. Of course, nothing else can happen in the same thread while the loop is running. If you want to have another animation running, it must be in a separate thread. Then the multitasking capability of your operating system can allow the two threads to share the available processor time, thus allowing both animations to run. We will explore how we can program animations in Chapter 16.

Let's get an idea of the principles behind how threads operate. Consider a very simple program that consists of three activities:

❑   Reads a number of blocks of data from a file

❑   Performs some calculation on each block of data

❑   Writes the results of the calculation to another file

You could organize the program as a single sequence of activities. In this case the activities, read file, process, write file, run in sequence, and the sequence is repeated for each block to be read and processed. You could also organize the program so that reading a block from the file is one activity, performing the calculation is a second activity, and writing the results is a third activity. Both of these situations are illustrated below.

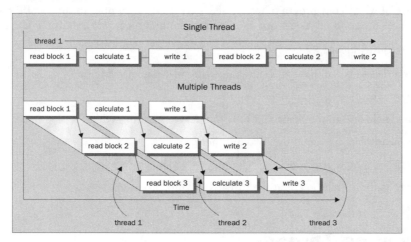

Once a block of data has been read, the computation process can start, and as soon as the computation has been completed, the results can be written out. With the program executing each step in sequence (that is, as a single thread), as shown in the top half of the diagram, the total time for execution will be the sum of the times for each of the individual activities. However, suppose we were able to execute each of the activities independently, as illustrated in the lower half of the diagram. In this case, reading the second block of data can start as soon as the first block has been read, and in theory we can have all three activities executing concurrently. This is possible even though you only have one processor because the input and output operations are likely to require relatively little processor time while they are executing, so the processor can be doing other things while they are in progress. This can have the effect of reducing the total execution time for the program. These three processes that we have identified that run more or less independently of one another – one to read the file, another to process the data and a third to write the results – are called **threads**. Of course, the first example at the top of the diagram has just one thread that does everything in sequence. Every Java program has at least one thread.

However, the three threads in the lower example aren't completely independent of one another. After all, if they were, you might as well make them independent programs. There are practical limitations too – the potential for overlapping these threads will be dependent on the capabilities of your computer, and of your operating system. However, if you can get some overlap in the execution of the threads, the program is going to run faster. There's no magic in using threads though. Your computer has only a finite capacity for executing instructions, and if you have many threads running you may in fact increase the overall execution time because of the overhead implicit in managing the switching of control between threads.

An important consideration when you have a single program running as multiple threads is that the threads are unlikely to have identical execution times, and, if one thread is dependent on another, you can't afford to have one overtaking the other – otherwise you'll have chaos. Before you can start calculating in the example in the diagram, you need to be sure that the data block the calculation uses has been read, and before you can write the output, you need to know that the calculation is complete. This necessitates having some means for the threads to communicate with one another.

The way we have shown the threads executing in the previous diagram isn't the only way of organizing the program. You could have three threads, each of which reads the file, calculates the results and writes the output, as shown here.

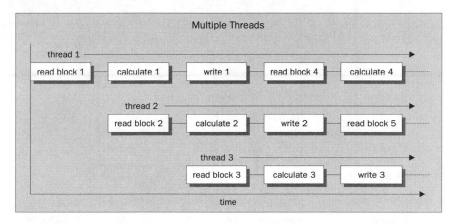

Now there's a different sort of contention between the threads. They are all competing to read the file and write the results, so there needs to be some way of preventing one thread from getting at the input file while another thread is already reading from it. The same goes for the output file. There's another aspect of this arrangement that is different from the previous version. If one thread, *thread1* say, reads a block, *block4* perhaps, that needs a lot of time to compute the results, another thread, *thread2* say, could conceivably read a following block, *block5* maybe, calculate and write the results for *block5*, before *thread1* has written the results for *block4*. If you don't want the results appearing in a different sequence from the input, you should do something about this. Before we delve into the intricacies of making sure our threads don't get knotted, let's first look at how we create a thread.

Creating Threads

Your program always has at least one thread: the one created when the program begins execution. With a program, this thread starts at the beginning of main(). With an applet, the browser is the main thread. When your program creates a thread, it is in addition to the thread of execution that created it. As you might have guessed, creating an additional thread involves using an object of a class, and the class you use is java.lang.Thread. Each additional thread that your program creates is represented by an object of the class Thread, or of a subclass of Thread. If your program is to have three additional threads, you will need to create three such objects.

To start the execution of a thread, you call the start() method for the Thread object. The code that executes in a new thread is always a method called run(),which is public, accepts no arguments and doesn't return a value. Threads other than the main thread in a program always start in the run() method for the object that represents the thread. A program that creates three threads is illustrated diagrammatically here.

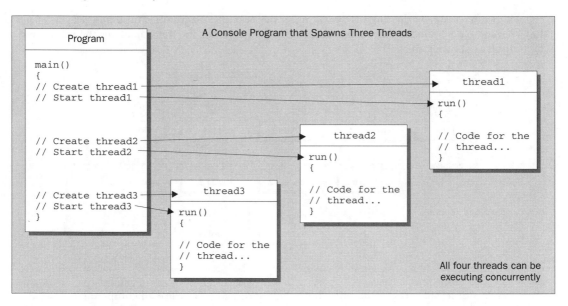

For a class representing a thread in your program to do anything, you must implement the run() method as the version defined in the Thread class does nothing. Your implementation of run() can call any other methods you want. Our illustration shows main() creating all three threads, but that doesn't have to be the case. Any thread can create more threads.

Note that you don't call the run() method to start a thread, you call the start() method for the object representing the thread and that causes the run() method to be called. When you want to stop the execution of a thread that is running, you call the stop() method for the Thread object.

There are two ways in which you can define a class that is to represent a thread. One way is to define your class as a subclass of Thread and provide a definition of the method run() that overrides the inherited method. The other possibility is to define your class as implementing the interface, Runnable, which declares the method run(), and then create a Thread object in your class when you need it. We will look at and explore the advantages of each approach in a little more detail.

Try It Out — Deriving a Subclass of Thread

We can see how this works by using an example. We'll define a single class, TryThread, that we'll derive from Thread. Execution starts in the method main():

```java
import java.io.IOException;

public class TryThread extends Thread
{
  private String firstName;              // Store for first name
  private String secondName;             // Store for second name
  private long aWhile;                   // Delay in milliseconds

  public TryThread(String firstName, String secondName, long delay)
  {
    this.firstName = firstName;          // Store the first name
    this.secondName = secondName;        // Store the second name
    aWhile = delay;                      // Store the delay
    setDaemon(true);                     // Thread is daemon
  }

  public static void main(String[] args)
  {
    // Create three threads
    Thread first = new TryThread("Hopalong ", "Cassidy ", 200L);
    Thread second = new TryThread("Marilyn ", "Monroe ", 300L);
    Thread third = new TryThread("Slim ", "Pickens ", 500L);

    System.out.println("Press Enter when you have had enough...\n");
    first.start();                       // Start the first thread
    second.start();                      // Start the second thread
    third.start();                       // Start the third thread
    try
    {
      System.in.read();                  // Wait until Enter key pressed
      System.out.println("Enter pressed...\n");
    }
    catch (IOException e)                // Handle IO exception
    {
      System.out.println(e);             // Output the exception
    }
    System.out.println("Ending main()");
    return;
  }

  // Method where thread execution will start
  public void run()
  {
    try
    {
      while(true )                                  // Loop indefinitely...
      {
```

```
        System.out.print(firstName);           // Output first name
        sleep(aWhile);                          // Wait aWhile msec.
        System.out.print(secondName + "\n");    // Output second name
    }
}
```

```
    catch(InterruptedException e)            // Handle thread interruption
    {
      System.out.println(firstName + secondName + e);      // Output the exception
    }
  }
}
```

If you compile and run the code, you'll see something like this:

```
Press Enter when you have had enough...

Hopalong Marilyn Slim Cassidy
Hopalong Monroe
Marilyn Cassidy
Hopalong Pickens
Slim Monroe
Marilyn Cassidy
Hopalong Cassidy
Hopalong Monroe
Marilyn Pickens
Slim Cassidy
Hopalong Monroe
Marilyn Cassidy
Hopalong Cassidy
Hopalong Monroe
Marilyn Pickens
Slim Cassidy
Hopalong Cassidy
Hopalong Monroe
Marilyn
Enter pressed...

Ending main()
```

How It Works

There are three instance variables in our class `TryThread` and these are initialized in the constructor. The two `String` variables hold first and second names, and the variable `aWhile` stores a time period in milliseconds. The constructor for our class, `TryThread()`, will automatically call the default constructor, `Thread()`, for the base class.

Our class containing the method `main()` is derived from `Thread`, and implements `run()`, so objects of this class represent threads. The fact that each object of our class will have access to the method `main()` is irrelevant – the objects are perfectly good threads. Our method `main()` creates three such objects: `first`, `second` and `third`.

Daemon and User Threads

The call to `setDaemon()`, with the argument `true` in the `TryThread` constructor, makes the thread that is created a **daemon thread**. A daemon thread is simply a background thread that is subordinate to the thread that creates it, so when the thread that created the daemon thread ends, the daemon thread dies with it. In our case, the method `main()` creates the daemon threads so that when `main()` returns, all the threads it has created will also end. If you run the example a few times pressing *Enter* at random, you should see that the daemon threads die after the `main()` method returns, because, from time to time, you will get some output from one or other thread after the last output from `main()`.

A thread that isn't a daemon thread is called a **user thread**. The diagram below shows two daemon threads and a user thread that are created by the main thread of a program.

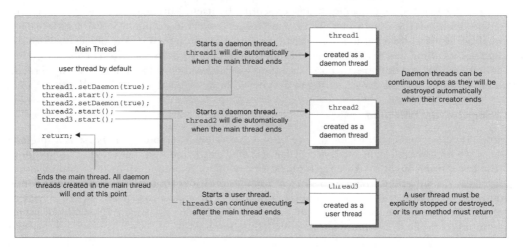

A user thread has a life of its own that is not dependent on the thread that creates it. It can continue execution after the thread that created it has ended. The default thread that contains `main()` is a user thread, as shown in the diagram, but `thread3` shown in the diagram could continue to execute after `main()` has returned. Threads that run for a finite time are typically user threads, but there's no reason why a daemon thread can't be finite. Threads that run indefinitely should usually be defined as daemon threads simply because you need a means of stopping them. A hypothetical example might help you to understand this so let's consider how a network server handling transactions of some kind might work in principle.

A network server might be managed overall by a user thread that starts one or more daemon threads to listen for requests. When the server starts up the operator starts the management thread and this thread creates daemon threads to listen for requests. Each request recognized by one of these daemon threads might be handled by another thread that is created by the listening thread, so that each request will be handled independently. Where processing a transaction takes a finite time, and where it is important that the requests are completed before the system shuts down, the thread handling the request might be created as a user thread to ensure that it runs to completion, even if the listening thread that created it stops. When the time comes to shut the system down, the operator doesn't have to worry about how many listening threads are running. When the main thread is shut down, all the listening threads will also shut down because they are daemon threads. Any outstanding threads dealing with specific transactions will then run to completion.

Note that you can only call `setDaemon()` for a thread before it starts; if you try to do so afterwards, the method will throw an `IllegalThreadStateException` exception. Also, a thread that is itself created by a daemon thread will be daemon by default.

Creating Thread Objects

In the method `main()`, we create three `Thread` variables that store three different objects of our class `TryThread`. As you can see, each object has an individual name pair as the first two arguments to its constructor, and a different delay value passed as the third argument. All objects of the class `TryThread` are daemon threads because we call `setDaemon()` with the argument `true` in the constructor. Since the output can continue indefinitely, we display a message to explain how to stop it.

Once you've created a thread, it doesn't start executing by itself. You need to set it going. As we said earlier, you don't call the `run()` method for the `Thread` object to do this, you call its `start()` method. Thus we start the execution of each of the threads represented by the objects, `first`, `second` and `third`, by calling the `start()` method that is inherited from `Thread` for each object. The `start()` method starts the object's `run()` method executing, then returns to the calling thread. Eventually all three threads are executing in parallel with the original application thread, `main()`.

Implementing the run() Method

The `run()` method contains the code for the thread execution. The code in this case is a single, infinite `while` loop which we put in a `try` block because the `sleep()` method that is called in the loop can throw the exception caught by the `catch` block. The code in the loop outputs the first name, calls the method `sleep()` inherited from `Thread` and then outputs the second name. The `sleep()` method suspends execution of the thread for the number of milliseconds that you specify in the argument. This gives any other threads that have previously been started a chance to execute. This allows the possibility for the output from the three threads to become a little jumbled.

Each time a thread calls the method `sleep()`, one of the other waiting threads jumps in. You can see the sequence in which the threads execute from the output. From the names in the output you can deduce that they execute in the sequence `first`, `second`, `third`, `first`, `first`, `second`, `second`, `first`, `first`, `third` and so on. The actual sequence depends on your operating system scheduler so this is likely to be different on different computers. The execution of the `read()` method that is called in `main()` is blocked until you press *Enter*, but all the while the other threads continue executing. The output stops when you press *Enter* because this allows the main thread to continue, and execute the `return`. Executing `return` ends the thread for `main()` and since the other threads are daemon threads they also die when the thread that created them dies, although as you may have seen, they can run on a little after the last output from `main()`.

Stopping a Thread

If we did not create the threads in the last example as daemon threads, they would continue executing independently of `main()`. If you are prepared to terminate the program yourself (use *Ctrl+C* in a DOS session running Java) you can demonstrate this by commenting out the call to `setDaemon()` in the constructor. Pressing *Enter* will end `main()`, but the other threads will continue indefinitely.

A thread can signal another thread that it should stop executing by calling the interrupt() method for that Thread object. This in itself doesn't necessarily stop the thread. It just sets a flag in the thread that needs to be checked in the run() method to have any effect. As it happens the sleep() method checks whether the thread has been interrupted, and throws an InterruptedException if it has been. You can see that in action by altering the previous example a little.

Try It Out — Interrupting a Thread

Make sure the call to the setDaemon() method is still commented out in the constructor, and modify the main() method as follows:

```java
public static void main(String[] args)
{
  // Create three threads
  Thread first = new TryThread("Hopalong ", "Cassidy ", 200L);
  Thread second = new TryThread("Marilyn ", "Monroe ", 300L);
  Thread third = new TryThread("Slim ", "Pickens ", 500L);

  System.out.println("Press Enter when you have had enough...\n");
  first.start();                         // Start the first thread
  second.start();                        // Start the second thread
  third.start();                         // Start the third thread
  try
  {
    System.in.read();                    // Wait until Enter key pressed
    System.out.println("Enter pressed...\n");

    // Interrupt the threads
    first.interrupt();
    second.interrupt();
    third.interrupt();
  }
  catch (IOException e)                   // Handle IO exception
  {
    System.out.println(e);               // Output the exception
  }
  System.out.println("Ending main()");
  return;
}
```

Now the program will produce output that is something like:

```
Press Enter when you have had enough...

Slim Hopalong Marilyn Cassidy
Hopalong Monroe
Marilyn Cassidy
Hopalong Pickens
Slim Cassidy
Hopalong Monroe
Marilyn
```

```
Enter pressed...

Ending main()
Marilyn Monroe java.lang.InterruptedException: sleep interrupted
Slim Pickens java.lang.InterruptedException: sleep interrupted
Hopalong Cassidy java.lang.InterruptedException: sleep interrupted
```

How It Works

Since the method main() calls the interrupt() method for each of the threads after you press the *Enter* key, the sleep() method called in each thread registers the fact that the thread has been interrupted and throws an InterruptedException. This is caught by the catch block in the run() method and produces the new output you see. Because the catch block is outside the while loop, the run() method for each thread returns and each thread terminates.

You can check whether a thread has been interrupted by calling the isInterrupted() method for the thread. This returns true if interrupt() has been called for the thread in question. Since this is an instance method, you can use this to determine in one thread whether another thread has been interrupted. For example, in main() you could write:

```
if(first.isInterrupted())
    System.out.println("First thread has been interrupted.");
```

Note that this only determines whether the interrupted flag has been set by a call to interrupt() for the thread – it does not determine whether the thread is still running. A thread could have its interrupt flag set and continue executing – it is not obliged to terminate because interrupt() is called. To test whether a thread is still operating you can call its isAlive() method. This returns true if the thread has not terminated.

The instance method isInterrupted() has no effect on the interrupt flag in the thread – if it was set, it remains set. However, the static method interrupted() in the Thread class is different. It tests whether the currently executing thread has been interrupted and, if it has, it clears the interrupted flag in the current Thread object and returns true.

When an InterruptedException is thrown, the flag that registers the interrupt in the thread is cleared, so a subsequent call to isInterrupted() or interrupted() will return false.

Connecting Threads

If you need to wait in one thread until another thread dies, you can call the join() method for the thread which you expect isn't long for this world. Calling the join() method with no arguments, will halt the current thread for as long as it takes the specified thread to die:

```
thread1.join();        // Suspend the current thread until thread1 dies
```

You can also pass a long value to the join() method to specify the number of milliseconds you're prepared to wait for the death of a thread:

```
thread1.join(1000); // Wait up to 1 second for thread1 to die
```

If this is not precise enough, there is a version of join() with two parameters. The first is a time in milliseconds and the second is a time in nanoseconds. The current thread will wait for the duration specified by the sum of the arguments. Of course, whether or not you get nanosecond resolution will depend on the capability of your hardware.

The join() method can throw an InterruptedException if the current thread is interrupted by another thread, so you should put a call to join() in a try block and catch the exception.

Thread Scheduling

The scheduling of threads depends to some extent on your operating system, but each thread will certainly get a chance to execute while the others are 'asleep', that is, when they've called their sleep() methods. If your operating system uses preemptive multitasking, as Windows 98 does, the program will work without the call to sleep() in the run() method (you should also remove the try and catch blocks, if you remove the sleep() call). However, if your operating system doesn't schedule in this way, without the sleep() call in run(), the first thread will hog the processor, and will continue indefinitely.

The diagram below illustrates how four threads might share the processor over time by calling the sleep() method to relinquish control.

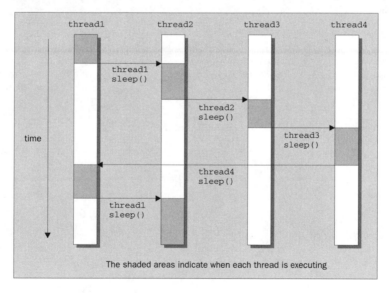

The shaded areas indicate when each thread is executing

Note that there's another method, yield(), defined in the Thread class, that gives other threads a chance to execute. You would use this when you just want to allow other threads a look-in if they are waiting, but you don't want to suspend execution of the current thread for a specific period of time. When you call the sleep() method for a thread, the thread will not continue for at least the time you have specified as an argument, even if no other threads are waiting. Calling yield() on the other hand will cause the current thread to resume immediately if no threads are waiting.

Implementing the Runnable Interface

As an alternative to defining a new subclass of Thread, we can implement the interface Runnable in a class. You'll find that this is generally much more convenient than deriving a class from Thread because you can derive your class from a class other than Thread, and it can still represent a thread. Because Java only allows a single base class, if you derive your class from Thread, it can't inherit functionality from any other class. The interface Runnable only declares one method, run(), and this is the method that will be executed when the thread is started.

Try It Out — Using the Runnable Interface

To see how this works in practice, we can write another version of the previous example. We'll call this version of the program JumbleNames:

```java
import java.io.IOException;

public class JumbleNames implements Runnable
{
  private String firstName;                        // Store for first name
  private String secondName;                       // Store for second name
  private long aWhile;                             // Delay in milliseconds

  // Constructor
  public JumbleNames(String firstName, String secondName, long delay)
  {
    this.firstName = firstName;                    // Store the first name
    this.secondName = secondName;                  // Store the second name
    aWhile = delay;                                // Store the delay
  }

  // Method where thread execution will start
  public void run()
  {
    try
    {
      while(true)                                  // Loop indefinitely...
      {
        System.out.print(firstName);               // Output first name
        Thread.sleep(aWhile);                      // Wait aWhile msec.
        System.out.print(secondName+"\n");         // Output second name
      }
    }
    catch(InterruptedException e)                  // Handle thread interruption
    {
      System.out.println(firstName + secondName + e);    // Output the exception
    }
  }

  public static void main(String[] args)
  {
    // Create three threads
```

```
      Thread first = new Thread(new JumbleNames("Hopalong ", "Cassidy ", 200L));
      Thread second = new Thread(new JumbleNames("Marilyn ", "Monroe ", 300L));
      Thread third = new Thread(new JumbleNames("Slim ", "Pickens ", 500L));

      // Set threads as daemon
      first.setDaemon(true);
      second.setDaemon(true);
      third.setDaemon(true);

      System.out.println("Press Enter when you have had enough...\n");
      first.start();                              // Start the first thread
      second.start();                             // Start the second thread
      third.start();                              // Start the third thread
      try
      {
        System.in.read();                         // Wait until Enter key pressed
        System.out.println("Enter pressed...\n");
      }
      catch (IOException e)                        // Handle IO exception
      {
        System.out.println(e);                     // Output the exception
      }
      System.out.println("Ending main()");
      return;
    }
  }
```

How It Works

We have the same data members in this class as we had in the previous example. The constructor is almost the same as previously. We can't call `setDaemon()` in this class constructor because our class isn't derived from `Thread`. Instead, we need to do that in `main()` after we've created the objects representing the threads. The `run()` method implementation is also very similar. Our class doesn't have `sleep()` as a member, but because it's a `public static` member of the class `Thread`, we can call it in our `run()` method by using the class name.

In the method `main()`, we still create a `Thread` object for each thread of execution, but this time we use a constructor that accepts an object of type `Runnable` as an argument. We pass an object of our class `JumbleNames` to it. This is possible because our class implements `Runnable`.

Thread Names

Threads have a name, which, in the case of the `Thread` constructor we're using in the example, will be a default name composed of the string `"Thread*"` with a sequence number appended. If you want to choose your own name for a thread, you can use a `Thread` constructor that accepts a `String` object specifying the name you want to assign to the thread. For example, we could have created the `Thread` object `first`, with the statement:

```
Thread first = new Thread(new JumbleNames ("Hopalong ", "Cassidy ", 200L),
                            "firstThread");
```

This assigns the name `"firstThread"` to the thread. Note that this name is only used when displaying information about the thread. It has no relation to the identifier for the `Thread` object, and there's nothing, apart from common sense, to prevent several threads being given the same name.

You can obtain the name assigned to a thread by calling the `getName()` method for the `Thread` object. The name of the thread is returned as a `String` object. You can also change the name of a thread by calling the `setName()` method defined in the class `Thread`, and passing a `String` object to it.

Once we've created the three `Thread` objects in the example, we call the `setDaemon()` method for each. The rest of `main()` is the same as in the original version of the previous example, and you should get similar output when you run this version of the program.

Managing Threads

In both the examples we've seen in this chapter, the threads are launched and then left to compete for computer resources. Because all three threads compete in an uncontrolled way for the processor, the output from the threads gets muddled. This isn't normally a desirable feature in a program. In most instances where you use threads, the way in which they execute will need to be managed so that they don't interfere with each other.

Of course, in our examples, the programs are deliberately constructed to release control of the processor part way through outputting a name. While this is very artificial, similar situations can arise in practice, particularly where threads are involved in a repetitive operation. It is important to appreciate that a thread can be interrupted while a source statement is executing. For instance, suppose a thread executes the statement:

```
i = i+1;
```

It is quite possible for the thread execution to be interrupted while the execution of this statement is still in progress, perhaps after the value of i has been fetched to increment it, but before the result has been stored back in i. Without the proper controls, another thread that has access to i could alter it at this point. The effect would be that the increment of i by 1 in this thread would be lost.

Where two or more threads share a common resource, such as a file or a block of memory, you'll need to take steps to ensure that one thread doesn't modify a resource while that resource is still being used by another thread. Having one thread update a record in a file while another thread is part way through retrieving the same record, is a recipe for disaster. One way of managing this sort of situation is to use **synchronization** for the threads involved.

Synchronization

The objective of synchronization is to ensure that, when several threads want access to a single resource, only one thread can access it at any given time. There are two ways in which you can use synchronization to manage your threads of execution:

❑   You can manage code at the method level – this involves synchronizing methods.

❑   You can manage code at the block level – using synchronizing blocks.

We'll look at how we can use synchronized methods first.

Synchronized Methods

You can make a subset (or indeed all) of the methods for any class object mutually exclusive, so that only one of the methods can execute at any given time. You make methods mutually exclusive by declaring them in the class using the keyword `synchronized`. For example:

```
class MyClass
{
   synchronized public void method1()
   {
     // Code for the method...
   }

   synchronized public void method2()
   {
     // Code for the method...
   }

   public void method3()
   {
     // Code for the method...
   }
}
```

Now, only one of the synchronized methods in a class object can execute at any one time. Only when the currently executing synchronized method for an object has ended can another synchronized method start for the same object. The idea here is that each synchronized method has guaranteed exclusive access to the object while it is executing, at least so far as the other synchronized methods for the class object are concerned.

The synchronization process makes use of an internal **lock** that every object has associated with it. The lock is a kind of flag that is set by a process referred to as **locking**, or a **lock action**, when a synchronized method starts execution. Each synchronized method for an object checks to see whether the lock has been set by another method. If it has, it will not start execution until the lock has been reset by an **unlock action**. Thus, only one synchronized method can be executing at one time, because that method will have set the lock that prevents any other synchronized method from starting.

> Note that there's no constraint here on simultaneously executing synchronized methods for two *different* objects of the same class. It's only concurrent access to any one object that is controlled.

Of the three methods in myClass, two are declared as synchronized, so for any object of the class, only one of these methods can execute at one time. The method that isn't declared as synchronized, method3(), can always be executed by a thread, regardless of whether a synchronized method is executing.

It's important to keep clear in your mind the distinction between an object which has instance methods that you declared as synchronized in the class definition, and the threads of execution that might use them. A hypothetical relationship between three threads and two objects of the class myClass is illustrated in the following diagram:

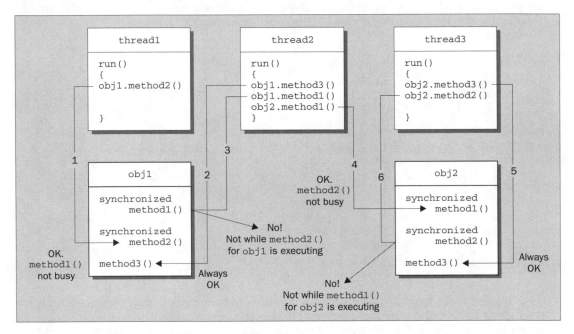

The numbers on the arrows in the diagram indicate the sequence of events. **No!** indicates that the thread waits until the method is unlocked so it can execute it. While method1() in obj2 is executing, method2() for the same object can't be executed. The synchronization of these two instance methods in an object provides a degree of protection for the object, in that only one synchronized method can mess with the data in the object at any given time.

However, each object is independent of any other object when it comes to synchronized instance methods. When a thread executes a synchronized method for an object, it is assured exclusive access to the object insofar as the synchronized methods in that object are concerned. Another thread, though, can still call the same method for a different object. While method1() is being executed for obj1, this doesn't prevent method1() for obj2 being executed by some other thread. Also, if there's a method in an object that has not been declared as synchronized – method3() in obj1 for example – any thread can call that at any time, regardless of the state of any synchronized methods in the object.

If you apply synchronization to static methods in a class, only one of those static methods in the class can be executing at any point in time, and this is per class synchronization and the class lock is independent of any locks for objects of the class.

An important point of principle that you need to understand is that the only method that is necessarily part of a thread in a class object that represents a thread is the run() method. Other methods for the same class object are only part of the thread if they are called directly or indirectly by the run() method. All the methods that are called directly or indirectly from the run() method for an object are all part of the same thread, but they clearly don't have to be methods for the same Thread object. Indeed they can be methods that belong to any other objects, including other Thread objects that have their own run() methods.

Using Synchronized Methods

To see how synchronization can be applied in practice, we'll construct a program that provides a simple model of a bank. Our bank is a very young business with only one customer account initially, but we'll have two clerks each working flat out to process transactions for the account, one handling debits and the other handling credits. The objects in our program are illustrated here:

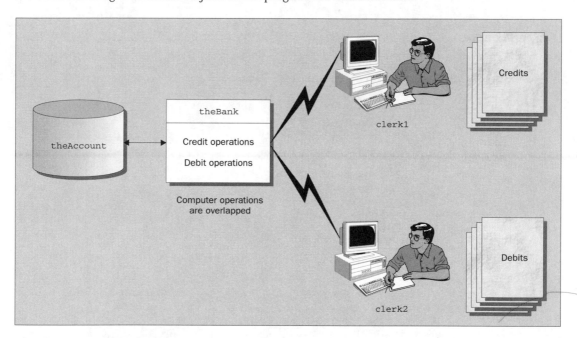

The bank in our model is actually a computer that performs operations on the account, and the account is stored separately. Each clerk can communicate directly with the bank. We'll be defining four classes that we will use in our program to model banking operations:

- ❑ A Bank class to represent the bank computer.

- ❑ An Account class to represent the account at the bank.

- ❑ A Transaction class to represent a transaction on the account – a debit or a credit for instance.

- ❑ A Clerk class to represent a bank clerk.

We will also define a class containing the method main() that will start the process off and determine how it all works.

> As we develop the code, we won't necessarily get it right first time, but we will improve as we find out more about how to program using threads. This will expose some of the sorts of errors and complications that can arise when you're programming using threads.

Try It Out — Defining a Bank Class

The bank computer is the agent that will perform the operations on an account so we will start with that. We can define the Bank class that will represent this as:

```java
// Define the bank
class Bank
{
  // Perform a transaction
  public void doTransaction(Transaction transaction)
  {
    int balance = transaction.getAccount().getBalance();   // Get current balance

    switch(transaction.getTransactionType())
    {
      case Transaction.CREDIT:
        // Credits require a lot of checks...
        try
        {
          Thread.sleep(100);
        }
        catch(InterruptedException e)
        {
          System.out.println(e);
        }
        balance += transaction.getAmount();                // Increment the balance
        break;

      case Transaction.DEBIT:
        // Debits require even more checks...
        try
        {
          Thread.sleep(150);
        }
        catch(InterruptedException e)
        {
          System.out.println(e);
        }
        balance -= transaction.getAmount();                // Decrement the balance
        break;
```

```
      default:                                          // We should never get here
        System.out.println("Invalid transaction");
        System.exit(1);
    }
    transaction.getAccount().setBalance(balance);       // Restore the account
balance
  }
}
```

How It Works

The `Bank` class is very simple. It keeps no records of anything locally as the accounts will be identified separately, and it only has one method that carries out a transaction. The `Transaction` object will provide all the information about what the transaction is, and to which account it applies. We have only provided for debit and credit operations on an account, but the switch could easily be extended to accommodate other types of transactions. Both of the transactions supported involve some delay while the standard nameless checks and verifications, that all banks have, are carried out. The delay is simulated by calling the `sleep()` method belonging to the `Thread` class.

Of course, during this time, other things in other threads may be going on. There are no instance variables to initialize in a `Bank` object so we don't need a constructor. Since our `Bank` object works using a `Transaction` object, let's define the class for that next.

Try It Out — Defining a Transaction on an Account

The `Transaction` class could represent any transaction on an account, but we are limiting ourselves to debits and credits. We can define the class as:

```
class Transaction
{
  // Transaction types
  public static final int DEBIT = 0;
  public static final int CREDIT = 1;
  public static String[] types = {"Debit","Credit"};

  // Constructor
  public Transaction(Account account, int transactionType, int amount)
  {
    this.account = account;
    this.transactionType = transactionType;
    this.amount = amount;
  }

  public Account getAccount()
  {  return account;  }

  public int getTransactionType()
  {  return transactionType;  }

  public int getAmount()
  {  return amount;  }
```

```
  public String toString()
  {
    return types[transactionType] + " A//C: " + ": $" + amount;
  }

  private Account account;
  private int amount;
  private int transactionType;
}
```

How It Works

The identification of a transaction is specified by the transactionType field that must be one of the values defined for transaction types. We should build in checks in the constructor to ensure only valid transactions are created, but we'll forego this to keep the code volume down, and you certainly know how to do this sort of thing by now. A transaction records the amount for the transaction and a reference to the account to which it applies, so a Transaction object specifies a complete transaction. The methods are very straightforward, just accessor methods for the data members that are used by the Bank object, plus the toString() method in case we need it.

Try It Out — Defining a Bank Account

We can define an account as:

```
// Defines a customer account
public class Account
{
  // Constructor
  public Account(int accountNumber, int balance)
  {
    this.accountNumber = accountNumber;                // Set the account number
    this.balance = balance;                            // Set the initial balance
  }

  // Return the current balance
  public int getBalance()
  {  return balance;  }

  // Set the current balance
  public void setBalance(int balance)
  {  this.balance = balance;  }

  public int getAccountNumber()
  {  return accountNumber;  }

  public String toString()
  {
    return "A//C No. "+accountNumber+" : $"+balance;
  }

  private int balance;                                 // The current account balance
  private int accountNumber;                           // Identifies this account
}
```

How It Works

The `Account` class is also very simple. It just maintains a record of the amount in the account as a balance, and provides methods for retrieving and setting the current balance. Operations on the account are performed externally by the `Bank` object. We have a bit more than we need in the `Account` class at the moment, but the methods we don't use in the current example may be useful later.

Try It Out — Defining a Bank Clerk

A clerk is a slightly more complicated animal. He or she retains information about the bank, details of the current transaction and is responsible for initiating debits and credits on an account by communication with the central bank. Each clerk will work independently of the others so they will each be a separate thread:

```java
public class Clerk implements Runnable
{
  private Bank theBank;                    // The employer - an electronic marvel
  private Transaction inTray;              // The in-tray holding a transaction

  // Constructor
  public Clerk(Bank theBank)
  {
    this.theBank = theBank;                // Who the clerk works for
    inTray = null;                         // No transaction initially
  }

  // Receive a transaction
  public void doTransaction(Transaction transaction)
  {  inTray = transaction;    }

  // The working clerk...
  public void run()
  {
    while(true)
    {
      while(inTray == null)                // No transaction waiting?
      {
        try
        {
          Thread.sleep(150);               // Then take a break...
        }
        catch(InterruptedException e)
        {
          System.out.println(e);
        }
      }

      theBank.doTransaction(inTray);
      inTray = null;                       // In-tray is empty
    }
  }
```

```
    // Busy check
    public boolean isBusy()
    {
      return inTray != null;              // A full in-tray means busy!
    }
  }
```

How It Works

A Clerk object is a thread since it implements the Runnable interface. Each clerk has an in-tray, capable of holding one transaction, and while the in-tray is not null, the clerk is clearly busy. A clerk needs to be aware of the Bank object that is employing him or her, so a reference is stored in theBank when a Clerk object is created. A transaction is placed in the in-tray for a clerk by calling his or her doTransaction() method. You can check whether a clerk is busy by calling the isBusy() member which will return true if a transaction is still in progress.

The real work is actually done in the run() method. If the in-tray is empty, indicated by a null value in inTray, then there's nothing to do, so after sleeping a while the loop goes around again for another look at the in-tray. When a transaction has been recorded, the method in theBank object is called to carry it out and the inTray is reset to null.

All we need now is the class to drive our model world which we'll call BankOperation. This class only requires the method main(), but there are quite a lot of things to do in this method so we'll put it together piece by piece.

Try It Out — Defining the Operation of the Bank

Apart from setting everything up, the main() method has to originate transactions on the accounts and pass them on to the clerks to be expedited. We will start with just one account and a couple of clerks. Here's the basic structure:

```java
import java.util.Random;

public class BankOperation
{
  public static void main(String[] args)
  {
    int initialBalance = 500;      // The initial account balance
    int totalCredits = 0;          // Total credits on the account
    int totalDebits =0;            // Total debits on the account
    int transactionCount = 20;     // Number of debits and credits

    // Create the account, the bank and the clerks...

    // Create the threads for the clerks as daemon, and start them off

    // Generate the transactions of each type and pass to the clerks

    // Wait until both clerks are done

    // Now output the results
  }
}
```

The import for the Random class is there because we will need it in a moment. To create the bank object, the clerks, and the account we need to add the following code:

```
// Create the bank, the clerks, and the account...
Bank theBank = new Bank();                       // Create a bank
Clerk clerk1 = new Clerk(theBank);               // Create the first clerk
Clerk clerk2 = new Clerk(theBank);               // Create the second clerk
Account account = new Account(1, initialBalance);// Create an account
```

The next step is to add the code to create the threads for the clerks and start them going:

```
// Create the threads for the clerks as daemon, and start them off
Thread clerk1Thread = new Thread(clerk1);
Thread clerk2Thread = new Thread(clerk2);
clerk1Thread.setDaemon(true);                    // Set first as daemon
clerk2Thread.setDaemon(true);                    // Set second as daemon
clerk1Thread.start();                            // Start the first
clerk2Thread.start();                            // Start the second
```

The code to generate the transactions looks a lot, but is quite repetitive:

```
// Generate transactions of each type and pass to the clerks
Random rand = new Random();                       // Random number generator
Transaction transaction;                          // Stores a transaction
int amount;                                       // stores an amount of money
for(int i = 1; i <= transactionCount; i++)
{
  amount = 50 + rand.nextInt(26);                 // Generate amount of $50 to $75
  transaction = new Transaction(account,          // Account
                                Transaction.CREDIT, // Credit transaction
                                amount);          //  of amount
      totalCredits += amount;                     // Keep total credit tally

  // Wait until the first clerk is free
  while(clerk1.isBusy())
  try
  {
    Thread.sleep(25);                             // Busy so try later
  }
  catch(InterruptedException e)
  {
    System.out.println(e);
  }

  clerk1.doTransaction(transaction);              // Now do the credit

  amount = 30 + rand.nextInt(31);                 // Generate amount of $30 to $60
  transaction = new Transaction(account,          // Account
                                Transaction.DEBIT, // Debit transaction
                                amount);          //  of amount
  totalDebits += amount;                          // Keep total debit tally
```

```
  // Wait until the second clerk is free
  while(clerk2.isBusy())
  try
  {
    Thread.sleep(25);                            // Busy so try later
  }
  catch(InterruptedException e)
  {
    System.out.println(e);
  }

  clerk2.doTransaction(transaction);             // Now do the debit
}
```

Once all the transactions have been processed, we can output the results. However, the clerks could still be busy after we exit from the loop, so we need to wait for both of them to be free before outputting the results. We can do this with a `while` loop:

```
// Wait until both clerks are done
while(clerk1.isBusy() || clerk2.isBusy())
try
{
  Thread.sleep(25);
}
catch(InterruptedException e)
{
  System.out.println(e);
}
```

Lastly, we output the results:

```
// Now output the results
System.out.println(
          "Original balance    : $" + initialBalance+"\n" +
          "Total credits       : $" + totalCredits+"\n" +
          "Total debits        : $" + totalDebits+"\n" +
          "Final balance       : $" + account.getBalance() + "\n" +
          "Should be           : $" + (initialBalance + totalCredits -
                                                      totalDebits));
```

How It Works

The variables in the `main()` method that track the total debits and credits, and record the initial account balance, are to help us figure out what has happened after the transactions have been processed. The number of debits and credits to be generated is stored in `transactionCount`, so the total number of transactions will be twice this value. We have added five further blocks of code to perform the functions indicated by the comments, so let's now go through each of them in turn.

The `Account` object is created with the account number as 1 and with the initial balance stored in `initialBalance`. We pass the bank object, `theBank`, to the constructor for each of the `Clerk` objects, so that they can record it.

The `Thread` constructor requires an object of type `Runnable`, so we can just pass the `Clerk` objects in the argument. There's no problem in doing this because the `Clerk` class implements the interface `Runnable`. You can always implicitly cast an object to a type which is any superclass of the object, or any interface type that the object class implements.

All the transactions are generated in the `for` loop. The handling of debits is essentially the same as the handling of credits, so we'll only go through the code for the latter in detail. A random amount between $50 and $75 is generated for a credit transaction by using the `nextInt()` method for the `rand` object of type `Random` that we create. You'll recall that `nextInt()` returns an `int` value in the range 0 to one less than the value of the argument, so by passing 26 to the method, we get a value between 0 and 25 returned. We add 50 to this and, hey presto, we have a value between 50 and 75. We then use this amount to create a `Transaction` object that represents a credit for the account. To keep a check on the work done by the clerks, we maintain the total of all the credits generated in the variable `totalCredits`. This will allow us to verify whether or not the account has been updated properly.

Before we pass the transaction to `clerk1`, we must make sure that he or she isn't busy. Otherwise we would overwrite the clerk's in-tray. The `while` loop does this. As long as the `isBusy()` method returns `true`, we continue to call the `sleep()` method for a twenty five millisecond delay, before we go round and check again. When `isBusy()` returns `false`, we call the `doTransaction()` method for the clerk with the reference to the `transaction` object as the argument. The `for` loop will run for twenty iterations, so we'll generate twenty random transactions of one or other type.

The third `while` loop works in the same way as the previous check for a busy clerk – the loop continues if either of the clerks is busy.

Lastly, we output the original account balance, the totals of credits and debits, and the final balance plus what it should be for comparison. That's all we need in the method `main()`, so we're ready to give it a whirl. Remember that all four classes need to be in the same directory.

Running the Example

Now, if you run the example the final balance will be wrong. You should get results something like the following:

```
Original balance    : $500
Total credits       : $1252
Total debits        : $921
Final balance       : $89
Should be           : $831
```

Of course, your results won't be the same as this, but they should be just as wrong. The customer will not be happy. His account balance is seriously out – in the bank's favor of course, as always. So how has this come about?

The problem is that both clerks are operating on the same account at the same time. Both clerks call the `doTransaction()` method for the `Bank` object, so this method is executed by both clerk threads. Separate calls on the same method are overlapping.

Try It Out — Synchronizing Methods

One way we can fix this is by simply declaring the method that operates on an account as
`synchronized`. This will prevent one clerk getting at it while it is still in progress with the other clerk.
To implement this you should amend the `Bank` class definition as follows:

```
// Define the bank
class Bank
{
   // Perform a transaction
   synchronized public void doTransaction(Transaction transaction)
   {
      // Code exactly as before...
   }
}
```

How It Works

Declaring this method as `synchronized` will prevent a call to it from being executed while another is
still in operation. If you run the example again with this change, the result will be something like:

```
Original balance    : $500
Total credits       : $1201
Total debits        : $931
Final balance       : $770
Should be           : $770
```

The amounts may be different because the transaction amounts are random, but your final balance
should be the same as adding the credits to the original balance and subtracting the debits.

As we saw earlier, when you declare methods in a class as `synchronized`, it prevents concurrent
execution of those methods within a single object, *including concurrent execution of the same method*. It is
important not to let the fact that there is only one copy of a particular method confuse you. A given
method can be potentially executing in any number of threads – as many threads as there are in the
program in fact. If it was not synchronized, the `doTransaction()` method could be executed
concurrently by any number of clerks.

Although this fixes the problem we had in that the account balance is now correct, the bank is still
amazingly inefficient. Each clerk is kicking their heels while another clerk is carrying out a transaction.
At any given time a maximum of one clerk is working. On this basis the bank could sack them all bar
one and get the same throughput. We can do better, as we shall see.

Synchronizing Statement Blocks

In addition to being able to synchronize methods on a class object, you can also specify a statement or a
block of code in your program as `synchronized`. This is more powerful, since you specify which
particular object is to benefit from the synchronization of the statement or code block, not just the
object that contains the code as in the case of a synchronized method. Here we can set a lock on any
object for a given statement block. When the block that is synchronized on the given object is
executing, no other code block or method that is synchronized on the same object can execute. To
synchronize a statement, you just write:

```
synchronized(theObject)
  statement;              // Synchronized with respect to theObject
```

No other statements or statement blocks in the program that are synchronized on the object, theObject, can execute while this statement is executing. Naturally, this applies even when the statement is a call to a method, which may in turn call other methods. The statement here could equally well be a block of code between braces. This is powerful stuff. Now we can lock a particular object while the code block that is working is running.

To see precisely how you can use this in practice, let's create a modification of the last example. Let's up the sophistication of our banking operation to support multiple accounts. To extend our example to handle more than one account, we just need to make some changes to main(). We'll add one extra account to keep the output modest, but we'll modify the code to handle any number.

Try It Out — Handling Multiple Accounts

We can modify the code in main() that creates the account and sets the initial balance to create multiple accounts as follows:

```
public class BankOperation
{
  public static void main(String[] args)
  {
    int[] initialBalance = {500, 800};  // The initial account balances
    int[] totalCredits = new int[initialBalance.length];  // Total cr's
    int[] totalDebits = new int[initialBalance.length];   // Total db's
    int transactionCount = 20;          // Number of debits and of credits

    // Create the bank and the clerks...
    Bank theBank = new Bank();                      // Create a bank
    Clerk clerk1 = new Clerk(theBank );             // Create the first clerk
    Clerk clerk2 = new Clerk(theBank );             // Create the second clerk
    // Create the accounts, and initialize total credits and debits
    Account[] accounts = new Account[initialBalance.length];
    for(int i = 0; i < initialBalance.length; i++)
    {
      accounts[i] = new Account(i+1, initialBalance[i]); // Create accounts
      totalCredits[i] = totalDebits[i] = 0;
    }

    // Create the threads for the clerks as daemon, and start them off

    // Create transactions randomly distributed between the accounts

    // Wait until both clerks are done

    // Now output the results
  }
}
```

We now create an array of accounts in a loop, the number of accounts being determined by the number of initial balances in the `initialBalance` array. Account numbers are assigned successively starting from 1. The code for creating the bank and the clerks and for creating the threads and starting them, is exactly the same as before. The shaded comments that follow the code indicate the other segments of code in `main()` that we need to modify.

The next piece we need to change is the creation and processing of the transactions:

```
// Generate transactions of each type and pass to the clerks
Random rand = new Random();
Transaction transaction;                         // Stores a transaction
int amount;                                      // Stores an amount of money
int select;                                      // Selects an account
for(int i = 1; i <= transactionCount; i++)
{
  // Generate a random account index for credit operation
  select = rand.nextInt(accounts.length);
  amount = 50 + rand.nextInt(26);                // Generate amount of $50 to $75
  transaction = new Transaction(accounts[select],    // Account
                            Transaction.CREDIT, // Credit transaction
                            amount);            //   of amount
  totalCredits[select] += amount;                // Keep total credit tally

  // Wait until the first clerk is free
  while(clerk1.isBusy())
  try
  {
    Thread.sleep(25);                            // Busy so try later
  }
  catch(InterruptedException e)
  {
    System.out.println(e);
  }

  clerk1.doTransaction(transaction);             // Now do the credit

  // Generate a random account index for debit operation
  select = rand.nextInt(accounts.length);
  amount = 30 + rand.nextInt(31);                // Generate amount of $30 to $60
  transaction = new Transaction(accounts[select],    // Account
                            Transaction.DEBIT,  // Debit transaction
                            amount);            //   of amount
  totalDebits[select] += amount;                 // Keep total debit tally

  // Wait until the second clerk is free
  while(clerk2.isBusy())
  try
  {
    Thread.sleep(25);                            // Busy so try later
  }
  catch(InterruptedException e)
  {
```

```
      System.out.println(e);
   }

   clerk2.doTransaction(transaction);                // Now do the debit
   }
```

The last modification we must make to the method main() is for outputting the results. We now do this in a loop. seeing as we have to process more than one account:

```
for(int i = 0; i < accounts.length; i++)
   System.out.println("Account Number:"+accounts[i].getAccountNumber()+"\n"+
      "Original balance    : $" + initialBalance[i] + "\n" +
      "Total credits       : $" + totalCredits[i] + "\n" +
      "Total debits        : $" + totalDebits[i] + "\n" +
      "Final balance       : $" + accounts[i].getBalance() + "\n" +
      "Should be           : $" + (initialBalance[i] + totalCredits[i] -
                                         totalDebits[i]) + "\n");
```

This is much the same as before except that we now extract values from the arrays we have created. If you run this version it will, of course, work perfectly. A typical set of results are:

```
Account Number:1
Original balance    : $500
Total credits       : $659
Total debits        : $614
Final balance       : $545
Should be           : $545

Account Number:2
Original balance    : $800
Total credits       : $607
Total debits        : $306
Final balance       : $1101
Should be           : $1101
```

How It Works

We now allocate arrays for the initial account balances, the total of credits and debits for each account and the accounts themselves. The number of initializing values in the initialBalance[] array will determine the number of elements in each of the arrays. In the for loop, we create each of the accounts with the appropriate initial balance, and initialize the totalCredits[] and totalDebits[] arrays to zero.

In the modified transactions loop, we select the account from the array for both the debit and the credit transactions by generating a random index value which we store in the variable, select. The index, select, is also used to keep a tally of the total of the transactions of each type.

This is all well and good, but by declaring the methods in the class `Bank` as `synchronized`, we're limiting the program quite significantly. No operation of any kind can be carried out while any other operation is in progress. This is unnecessarily restrictive since there's no reason to prevent a transaction on one account while a transaction for a different account is in progress. What we really want to do is constrain the program to prevent overlapping of operations on the same account, and this is where declaring blocks of code to be synchronized on a particular object can help.

Let's consider the methods in the class `Bank` once more. What we really want is the code in the `doTransaction()` method to be synchronized so that simultaneous processing of the same account is prevented, not that processing of different accounts is inhibited. What we need to do is synchronize the processing code for a transaction on the account object that is involved.

Try It Out — Applying synchronized Statement Blocks

We can do this with the following changes:

```
class Bank
{
  // Perform a transaction
  public void doTransaction(Transaction transaction)
  {
    switch(transaction.getTransactionType())
    {
      case Transaction.CREDIT:
      synchronized(transaction.getAccount())
      {
        // Get current balance
        int balance = transaction.getAccount().getBalance();

        // Credits require require a lot of checks...
        try
        {
          Thread.sleep(100);
        }
        catch(InterruptedException e)
        {
          System.out.println(e);
        }
        balance += transaction.getAmount();              // Increment the balance...
        transaction.getAccount().setBalance(balance);    // Restore account balance
        break;
      }
      case Transaction.DEBIT:
      synchronized(transaction.getAccount())
      {
        // Get current balance
        int balance = transaction.getAccount().getBalance();
```

```
      // Debits require even more checks...
      try
      {
        Thread.sleep(150);
      }
      catch(InterruptedException e)
      {
        System.out.println(e);
      }
      balance -= transaction.getAmount();          // Increment the balance...
      transaction.getAccount().setBalance(balance); // Restore account balance
      break;
    }
  default:                                          // We should never get here
    System.out.println("Invalid transaction");
    System.exit(1);
    }
  }
}
```

How It Works

The expression in parentheses following the keyword `synchronized` specifies the object for which the synchronization applies. Once one synchronized code block is entered with a given account object, no other code block or method can be entered that has been synchronized on the same object. For example, if the block performing credits is executing with a reference to the object `accounts[1]` returned by the `getAccount()` method for the transaction, the execution of the block carrying out debits cannot be executed for the same object, but it could be executed for a different account.

The object in a synchronized code block acts rather like a baton in a relay race that serves to synchronize the runners in the team. Only the runner with the baton is allowed to run. The next runner in the team can only run once they get hold of the baton. Of course, in any race there will be several different batons so you can have several sets of runners. In the same way, you can specify several different sets of `synchronized` code blocks in a class, each controlled by a different object. It is important to realize that code blocks that are synchronized with respect to a particular object don't have to be in the same class. They can be anywhere in your program where the appropriate object can be specified.

Note how we had to move the code to access and restore the account balance inside both synchronized blocks. If we hadn't done this, accessing or restoring the account balance could occur while a synchronized block was executing. This could obviously cause confusion since a balance could be restored by a debit transaction after the balance had been retrieved for a credit transaction. This would cause the effect of the debit to be wiped out.

If you want to verify that we really are overlapping these operations in this example, you can add output statements to the beginning and end of each method in the class `Bank`. Outputting the type of operation, the amount and whether it is the start or end of the transaction will be sufficient to identify them. For example, you could modify the `doTransaction()` method in the `Bank` class to:

```
public void doTransaction(Transaction transaction)
{
  switch(transaction.getTransactionType())
  {
    case Transaction.CREDIT:
    synchronized(transaction.getAccount())
    {
        System.out.println("Start credit of " +
                transaction.getAccount() + " amount: " +
                transaction.getAmount());
        // Code to process credit...
        System.out.println("  End credit of " +
                transaction.getAccount() + " amount: " +
                transaction.getAmount());
      break;
    }
    case Transaction.DEBIT:
    synchronized(transaction.getAccount())
    {
        System.out.println("Start debit of " +
                transaction.getAccount() + " amount: " +
                transaction.getAmount());
        // Code to process debit...
        System.out.println("  End debit of " +
                transaction.getAccount() + " amount: " +
                transaction.getAmount());
      break;
    }
    default:                                 // We should never get here
        System.out.println("Invalid transaction");
        System.exit(1);
  }
}
```

This will produce quite a lot of output, but you can always comment it out when you don't need it. You should be able to see how a transaction for an account that is currently being worked on is always delayed until the previous operation on the account is completed. You will also see from the output that operations on different accounts do overlap. Here's a sample of what I got:

```
Start credit of A//C No. 2 : $800 amount: 74
  End credit of A//C No. 2 : $874 amount: 74
Start debit of A//C No. 2 : $874 amount: 52
Start credit of A//C No. 1 : $500 amount: 51
  End debit of A//C No. 2 : $822 amount: 52
  End credit of A//C No. 1 : $551 amount: 51
Start debit of A//C No. 2 : $822 amount: 38
  End debit of A//C No. 2 : $784 amount: 38
Start credit of A//C No. 2 : $784 amount: 74
  End credit of A//C No. 2 : $858 amount: 74
Start debit of A//C No. 1 : $551 amount: 58
Start credit of A//C No. 2 : $858 amount: 53
  End debit of A//C No. 1 : $493 amount: 58
...
```

You can see from the third and fourth lines here that a credit for account 1 starts before the preceding debit for account 2 is complete, so the operations are overlapped. If you want to force overlapping debits and credits on the same account, you can comment out the calculation of the value for `select` for the debit operation in the `for` loop in `main()`. This modification is shown shaded:

```
// Generate a random account index for debit operation
// select = rand.nextInt(accounts.length);
totalDebits[select] += amount;                    // Keep total debit tally
```

This will make the debit transaction apply to the same account as the previous credit, so the transactions will always be contending for the same account.

Of course, this is not the only way of getting the operations to overlap. Another approach would be to equip accounts with methods to handle their own credit and debit transactions, and declare these as synchronized methods.

While testing that you have synchronization right is relatively easy in our example, in general it is extremely difficult to be sure you have tested a program that uses threads adequately. Getting the design right first is essential, and there is no substitute for careful design in programs that have multiple threads (or indeed any real time program that has interrupt handlers). You can never be sure that a real world program is 100% correct, only show it works correctly most of the time!

Deadlocks

Since you can synchronize code blocks for a particular object virtually anywhere in your program, there's potential for a particularly nasty kind of bug called a **deadlock**. This involves a mutual interdependence between two threads. One way this arises is when one thread executes some code synchronized on a given object, `theObject` say, and then needs to execute another method that contains code synchronized on another object, `theOtherObject` say. Before this occurs though, a second thread executes some code synchronized to `theOtherObject`, and needs to execute a method containing code synchronized to first object, `theObject`. This situation is illustrated here:

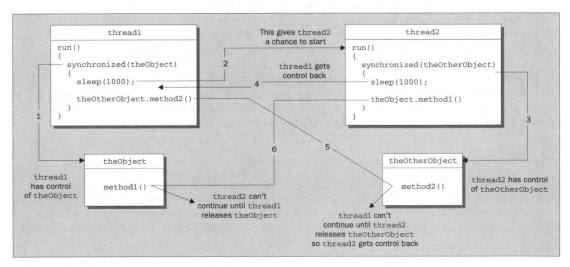

The sequence of events is as follows:

- ❑ thread1 starts first, and synchronizes on theObject. This prevents any methods for theObject being called by any other thread.

- ❑ thread1 then calls sleep() so thread2 can start.

- ❑ thread2 starts and synchronizes on theOtherObject. This prevents any methods for theOtherObject being called by any other thread.

- ❑ thread2 then calls sleep() allowing thread1 another go.

- ❑ thread1 wakes up and tries to call method2() for theOtherObject, but it can't until the code block in thread2 that is synchronized on theOtherObject completes execution.

- ❑ thread2 gets another go because thread1 can't proceed, and tries to call method1() for theObject. This can't proceed until the code block in thread1 that is synchronized on theObject completes execution.

Neither thread has any possibility of continuing – they are deadlocked. Finding and fixing this sort of problem can be very difficult, particularly if your program is complicated and has other threads which will continue to execute.

You can create a trivial deadlock in the last example by making the for loop in main() synchronized on one of the accounts. For example:

```
synchronized(accounts[1]){
    for(int i = 1; i <= transactionCount; i++)
    {
        // code for generating transactions etc...
    }
}
```

A deadlock occurs as soon as a transaction for accounts[1] arises because the doTransaction() method in theBank object that is called by a Clerk object to handle the transaction will be synchronized to the same object and can't execute until the loop ends. Of course, the loop can't continue until the method in theBank object terminates so the program hangs.

In general, ensuring that your program has no potential deadlocks is extremely difficult. If you intend to do a significant amount of programming using threads, you will need to study the subject in much more depth than we can deal with here. A good book on the subject is *Concurrent Programming in Java: Design Principles and Patterns* written by Doug Lea (ISBN 0-201-69581-2).

Communicating between Threads

We've seen how we can lock methods or code blocks using synchronization to avoid the problems that uncontrolled thread execution can cause. While this gives us a degree of control, we're still introducing inefficiencies into the program. In the last example, there were several occasions where we used a loop to wait for a clerk thread to complete an operation before the current thread could sensibly continue. For example, we couldn't pass a transaction to a `Clerk` object while that object was still busy with the previous transaction. Our solution to this was to use a `while` loop to test the busy status of the `Clerk` object from time to time and call the `sleep()` method in between. But there's a much better way.

The `Object` class defines the methods, `wait()`, `notify()` and `notifyAll()`, that you can use to provide a more efficient way of dealing with this kind of situation. Since all classes are derived from `Object`, all classes inherit these methods. You can only call these methods from within a `synchronized` method, or from within a synchronized code block, and an exception of type `IllegalMonitorStateException` will be thrown if you don't. The functions that these methods perform are:

Method	Description
`wait()`	There are three overloaded versions of this method.
	This version suspends the current thread until the `notify()` or `notifyAll()` method is called for the object to which the `wait()` method belongs. Note that when any version of `wait()` is called, the thread releases the synchronization lock it has on the object, so any other method or code block synchronized on the same object can execute. As well as enabling `notify()` or `notifyAll()` to be called by another thread, this also allows another thread to call `wait()` for the same object.
	Since all versions of the `wait()` method can throw an `InterruptedException`, you must call it in a `try` block with a `catch` block for this exception, or at least indicate that the method calling it throws this exception.
`wait(long timeout)`	This version suspends the current thread until the number of milliseconds specified by the argument has expired, or until the `notify()` or `notifyAll()` method for the object to which the `wait()` method belongs, is called, if that occurs sooner.
`wait(long timeout, int nanos)`	This version works in the same way as the previous version, except the time interval is specified by two arguments, the first in milliseconds, and the second in nanoseconds.
`notify()`	This will restart a thread that has called the `wait()` method for the object to which the `notify()` method belongs. If several threads have called `wait()` for the object, you have no control over which thread is notified, in which case it is better to use `notifyAll()`. If no threads are waiting, the method does nothing.

Table continued on following page

Method	Description
notifyAll()	This will restart all threads that have called wait() for the object to which the notifyAll() method belongs.

The basic idea of the wait() and notify() methods is that they provide a way for methods or code blocks that are synchronized on a particular object to communicate. One block can call wait() to suspend its operation until some other method or code block synchronized on the same object changes it in some way, and calls notify() to signal the change is complete. A thread will typically call wait() because some particular property of the object it is synchronized on is not set, or some condition is not fulfilled, and this is dependent on action by another thread. Perhaps the simplest situation is where a resource is busy because it is being modified by another thread, but you are by no means limited to that.

The major difference between calling sleep() and calling wait() is that wait() releases any objects on which the current thread has a lock, whereas sleep() does not. It is essential that wait() should work this way, otherwise there would be no way for another thread to change things so that the condition required by the current thread is met.

Thus the typical use of wait() is:

```
synchronized(anObject)
{
  while(condition-not-met)
    anObject.wait();
  // Condition is met so continue...
}
```

Here the thread will suspend operation when the wait() method is called until some other thread synchronized on the same object calls notify() (or more typically notifyAll()). This latter allows the while loop to continue and check the condition again. Of course, it may still not be met, in which case the wait() method will be called again so another thread can operate on anObject. You can see from this that wait() is not just for getting access to an object. It is intended to allow other threads access until some condition has been met. You could even arrange that a thread would not continue until a given number of other threads had called notify() on the object to ensure that a minimum number of operations had been carried out.

It is generally better to use notifyAll() rather than notify() when you have more than two threads synchronized on an object. If you call notify() when there are two or more other threads suspended having called wait(), only one of the threads will be started but you have no control over which it is. This opens the possibility that the thread that is started calls wait() again because the condition it requires is not fulfilled. This will leave all the threads waiting for each other, with no possibility of continuing.

Although the action of each of these methods is quite simple, applying them can become very complex. You have the potential for multiple threads to be interacting through several objects with synchronized methods and code blocks. We'll just explore the basics by seeing how we can use wait() and notifyAll() to get rid of a couple of the while loops we had in the last example.

Using wait() and notifyAll() in the Bank Program

In the `for` loop in `main()` that generates the transactions and passes them to the `Clerk` objects, we have two `while` loops that call the `isBusy()` method for a `Clerk` object. These were needed so that we didn't pass a transaction to a clerk while the clerk was still busy. By altering the `Clerk` class, so that it can use `wait()` and `notifyAll()`, we can eliminate the need for these.

Try It Out — Slimming Down the Transactions Loop

We want to make the `doTransaction()` method in the `Clerk` class conscious of the state of the `inTray` for the current object. If it is not `null`, we want the method to wait until it becomes so. To use `wait()` the block or method must be synchronized on an object – in this case the `Clerk` object since `inTray` is what we are interested in. We can do this by making the method synchronized:

```
public class Clerk implements Runnable
{
  synchronized public void doTransaction(Transaction transaction)
  {
    while(inTray != null)
      try
      {
        wait();
      }
      catch(InterruptedException e)
      {
        System.out.println(e);
      }
    inTray = transaction;
    notifyAll();
  }

  // Rest of the class as before...
}
```

When `inTray` is `null`, the transaction is stored and the `notifyAll()` method is called to notify other threads waiting on a change to this `Clerk` object. If `inTray` is not `null`, this method waits until some other thread calls `notifyAll()` to signal a change to the `Clerk` object. We now need to consider where the `inTray` field is going to be modified elsewhere. The answer is in the `run()` method for the `Clerk` class of course, so we need to change that too:

```
class Clerk
{
  synchronized public void run()
  {
    while(true)
    {
      while(inTray == null)              // No transaction waiting?
        try
        {
          wait();                        // Then take a break until there is
        }
        catch(InterruptedException e)
        {
          System.out.println(e);
        }
```

```
        theBank.doTransaction(inTray);
        inTray = null;                    // In-tray is empty
        notifyAll();                      // Notify other threads locked on this clerk
    }
  }


  // Rest of the class as before...
}
```

Just to make it clear which methods are in what threads, the situation in our program is illustrated below.

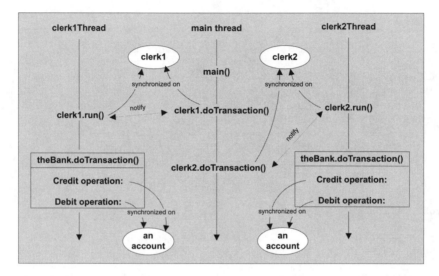

Here the `run()` method is synchronized on the `Clerk` object that contains it, and the method waits if `inTray` is `null`. Eventually the `doTransaction()` method for the current object should store a transaction in `inTray`, and then notify the thread that is waiting on the `Clerk` object – which will be the thread running the `theBank.doTransaction()` method for the object – that it should continue.

It may seem odd having two methods in the same object synchronized on one and the same object that owns them, but remember that the `run()` and `doTransaction()` methods for a particular `Clerk` object are in separate threads.

The transaction processing method for the bank can be in both of the clerk threads, whereas the methods that hand over a transaction to a clerk are in the main thread. The diagram also shows which code is synchronized on what objects.

We can now modify the code in the `for` loop in `main()` to pass the transactions directly to the clerks:

```
        // Generate transactions of each type and pass to the clerks
    for(int i = 1; i <= transactionCount; i++)
        {
        // Generate a random account index for credit operation
```

```
    select = rand.nextInt(accounts.length);
    amount = 50 + rand.nextInt(26);              // Generate amount of $50 to $75
    transaction = new Transaction(accounts[select],    // Account
                                  Transaction.CREDIT, // Credit transaction
                                  amount);             //  of amount
    totalCredits[select] += amount;              // Keep total credit tally

    clerk1.doTransaction(transaction);           // Now do the credit

    // Generate a random account index for debit operation
    select = rand.nextInt(accounts.length);
    amount = 30 + rand.nextInt(31);              // Generate amount of $30 to $60
    transaction = new Transaction(accounts[select],    // Account
                                  Transaction.DEBIT,  // Debit transaction
                                  amount);             //  of amount
    totalDebits[select] += amount;               // Keep total debit tally

    clerk2.doTransaction(transaction);           // Now do the debit
}
```

We have just deleted the loop blocks that were waiting until a clerk became free. This makes our code a lot shorter.

The example will now run without the need for checking whether the Clerk objects are busy in the transaction processing loop in main().

With a small change to the isBusy() method in the Clerk class, we can eliminate the need for the while loop before we output the results in main():

```
synchronized public void isBusy()
{
  while(inTray != null)              // Is this object busy?
    try
    {
      wait();                        // Yes, so wait for notify call
    }
    catch(InterruptedException e)
    {
      System.out.println(e);
    }
  return;                            // It is free now
}
```

Now the isBusy() method will only return when the clerk object has no transaction waiting or in progress, so no return value is necessary. The while loop in main() before the final output statements can be replaced by:

```
// Wait if clerks are busy
clerk1.isBusy();
clerk2.isBusy();
```

How It Works

The doTransaction() method for a Clerk object calls the wait() method if the inTray field contains a reference to a transaction object, as this means the Clerk object is still processing a credit or a debit. This will result in the current thread (which is the main thread) being suspended until the thread corresponding to this Clerk object – which is in the run() method – calls notifyAll() to indicate a change to the clerk.

Because the run() method is also synchronized on the Clerk object, it too can call wait(), in this case, if the inTray contains null, since this indicates that there is no transaction waiting for the clerk to expedite. A call to the doTransaction() method for the Clerk object will result in a transaction being stored in inTray, and the notifyAll() call will wake up the run() method to continue execution.

Because we've declared the isBusy() method as synchronized, we can call the wait() method to suspend the current thread if transactions are still being processed. Since we don't return from the method until the outstanding transaction is complete, we have no need of a boolean return value.

Thread Priorities

All threads have a priority which determines which thread is executed when several threads are waiting for their turn. This makes it possible to give one thread more access to processor resources than another. Let's consider an elementary example of how this could be used. Suppose you have one thread in a program that requires all the processor resources – some solid long running calculation, and some other threads that require relatively little resource. By making the thread that requires all the resources a low priority thread, you ensure that the other threads get executed promptly, while the processor bound thread can make use of the processor cycles that are left over after the others have had their turn.

The possible values for thread priority are defined in static data members of the class Thread. These members are of type int, and declared as final. The maximum thread priority is defined by the member MAX_PRIORITY which has the value 10. The minimum priority is MIN_PRIORITY defined as 1. The value of the default priority that is assigned to the main thread in a program is NORM_PRIORITY which is set to 5. When you create a thread, its priority will be the same as that of the thread that created it.

You can modify the priority of a thread by calling the setPriority() method for the Thread object. This method accepts an argument of type int which defines the new priority for the thread. An IllegalArgumentException will be thrown if you specify a priority that is less than MIN_PRIORITY or greater than MAX_PRIORITY.

If you're going to be messing about with the priorities of the threads in your program, you need to be able to find out the current priority for a thread. You can do this by calling the getPriority() method for the Thread object. This will return the current priority for the thread as a value of type int.

Using Thread Priorities

In the last example, you could set priorities for the threads by adding statements to main():

```
clerk1Thread.setPriority(Thread.MIN_PRIORITY);      // Credits are a low priority
clerk2Thread.setPriority(Thread.MAX_PRIORITY);      // Debits are a high priority
```

You can put these statements following the call to the start() method for each of the Thread objects for the clerks. However, this can't have much effect in our program since one clerk can't get ahead of the other. This is because each clerk only queues one transaction and they are allocated alternately to each clerk.

In the interests of learning more about how thread priorities affect the execution of your program, let's change the example once more to enable a Clerk object to queue transactions. We can do this quite easily using a LinkedList object, which we discussed in the previous chapter. There are a couple of points to be aware of though.

The first point is that only the Vector class out of the collection classes is thread-safe – that is, safe for modification by more than one thread. For the others you must either only access them by methods or code blocks that are synchronized on the collection object, or wrap the collection class in a thread-safe wrapper. Let's change the example to incorporate the latter.

The second point is that whether thread priorities have any effect depends on your operating system. If it doesn't support thread priorities, then setting thread priorities in your Java code will have no effect. Let's run it anyway to see how it works.

Try It Out — Setting Thread Priorities

We can extend the Clerk class to handle a number of Transaction objects by giving the in-tray the capacity to store several transactions in a list, but not too many – we don't want to overwork the clerks. The Collections class provides methods for creating synchronized sets, lists and maps from unsynchronized objects. The static synchronizedList() method in the Collections class accepts an argument that is a list and returns a List object that is synchronized. We can use this to make our inTray a synchronized list for storing transactions.

```java
import java.util.*;

public class Clerk implements Runnable
{
  Bank theBank;
  // The in-tray holding transactions
  private List inTray = Collections.synchronizedList(new LinkedList());

  private int maxTransactions = 8;        // Maximum transactions in the in-tray

  // Constructor
  public Clerk(Bank theBank)
  {
    this.theBank = theBank;                   // Who the clerk works for
    //inTray      = null;                     //Commented out: don't need this now
  }
// Plus the rest of the class...
}
```

Note that we have deleted the statement from the constructor that originally set inTray to null. Now that we are working with a list, we must change the doTransaction() method in the Clerk class to store the transaction in the list as long as there are less than maxTransactions in the list. Here's the revised code to do this:

```
synchronized public void doTransaction(Transaction transaction)
{
  while(inTray.size() >= maxTransactions)
  try
  {
    wait();
  }
  catch(InterruptedException e)
  {
    System.out.println(e);
  }
  inTray.add(transaction);
  notifyAll();
}
```

The size() method for the list returns the number of objects it contains so checking this is trivial. We use the add() method to add a new Transaction object to the end of the list.

The run() method for a clerk retrieves objects from the in-tray so we must update that to deal with a list:

```
synchronized public void run()
{
  while(true)
  {
    while(inTray.size() == 0)        // No transaction waiting?
      try
      {
        wait();                      // Then take a break until there is
      }
      catch(InterruptedException e)
      {
        System.out.println(e);
      }
    theBank.doTransaction((Transaction)inTray.remove(0));
    notifyAll();                     // Notify other threads locked on this clerk
  }
}
```

The remove() method in the List interface that we are using here removes the object at the index position in the list specified by the argument and returns a reference to it. Since we use 0 as the index we retrieve the first object in the list to pass to the doTransaction() method for the Bank object.

Since we now use a list to store transactions, the isBusy() method for a Clerk object needs to be changed:

```
synchronized public void isBusy()
{
  while(inTray.size() != 0)              // Is this object busy?
    try
    {
      wait();                            // Yes, so wait for notify call
    }
    catch(InterruptedException e)
    {
      System.out.println(e);
    }
  return;                                // It is free now
}
```

Now the clerk is not busy if there are no transactions in the inTray list. Hence we test the value returned by size().

That's all we need to buffer transactions in the in-tray of each clerk. If you reactivate the output statements that we added to the method in the Bank class, you'll be able to see how the processing of transactions proceeds.

With the priorities set by the calls to setPriority() we saw earlier, the processing of credits should run ahead of the processing of debits although the fact that the time to process a debit is longer than the time for a credit will also have a significant effect. To make the thread priority the determining factor, set the times in the calls to the sleep() method in the Bank class to the same value. You could then try changing the values for priorities around to see what happens to the sequence in which transactions are processed. Of course, if your operating system does not support priority scheduling, then it won't have any effect anyway.

How It Works

We've made the inTray object a synchronized LinkedList, by passing it to the static synchronizedList() method in the Collections class. This method returns a thread-safe List based on the original LinkedList object. We use the thread-safe List object to store up to maxTransactions transactions – eight in this case. The doTransaction() method for a Clerk object makes sure that a transaction is only added to the list if there are less than eight transactions queued.

The doTransaction() method for the Bank object always obtains the first object in the List, so the transactions will be processed in the sequence in which they were added to the list.

If your operating system supports priority scheduling, altering the thread priority values will change the pattern of servicing of the transactions.

Summary

In this chapter you have learned about threads and how you can create and manage them. We will be using threads from time to time in examples later in this book so be sure you don't move on from here without being comfortable with the basic ideas of how you create and start a thread.

The essential points that we have covered in this chapter are:

- ❑ Threads are subtasks in a program that can be in execution concurrently.

- ❑ A thread is represented by an object of the class `Thread`. Execution of a thread begins with the execution of the `run()` method defined in the class `Thread`.

- ❑ You define the code to be executed in a thread by implementing the `run()` method in a class derived from `Thread`, or in a class that implements the interface `Runnable`.

- ❑ A thread specified as **daemon** will cease execution when the thread that created it ends.

- ❑ A thread that isn't a daemon thread is called a **user thread**. A user thread will not be terminated automatically when the thread that created it ends.

- ❑ You start execution of a thread by calling the `start()` method for its `Thread` object. If you need to halt a thread before normal completion you can stop execution of a thread by calling the `interrupt()` method for its `Thread` object.

- ❑ Methods can be declared as `synchronized`. Only one `synchronized` instance method for an object can execute at any given time. Only one `synchronized static` method for a class can execute at one time.

- ❑ A code block can be declared as `synchronized` on an object. Only one synchronized code block for an object can execute at any given time.

- ❑ In a synchronized method or code block, you can call the `wait()` method inherited from the class `Object` to halt execution of a thread. Execution of the waiting thread will continue when the `notify()` or `notifyAll()` method inherited from `Object` is called by a thread synchronized on the same object.

- ❑ The `notify()` or `notifyAll()` method can only be called from a method or code block that is synchronized to the same object as the method or block that contains the `wait()` method that halted the thread.

- ❑ You can modify the relative priority of a thread by calling its `setPriority()` method. This only has an effect on execution in environments that support priority scheduling.

Exercises

1. Modify the last example in the chapter so that each transaction is a debit or a credit at random.

2. Modify the result of the previous exercise to incorporate an array of clerks, each running in their own thread, and each able to handle both debits and credits.

3. Extend the result of the previous exercise to incorporate two supervisors for two teams of clerks, where the supervisors each run in their own thread. The supervisor threads should originate transactions and pass them to the clerks they supervise.

Creating Windows

In this chapter, we will investigate how to create a window for a Java application and we will take a first look at some of the components we can put together to create a graphical user interface in Java.

You will learn:

- ❑ How to create a resizable window.
- ❑ What components and containers are.
- ❑ How you can add components to a window.
- ❑ How to control the layout of components.
- ❑ How to create a menu bar and menus for a window.
- ❑ What a menu shortcut is and how you can add a shortcut for a menu item.
- ❑ What the restrictions on the capabilities of an applet are.
- ❑ How to convert an application into an applet.

Graphical User Interfaces in Java

There is a vast amount of functionality in the Java class libraries devoted to supporting graphical user interface (GUI) creation and management, far more than it is feasible to cover in a book – even if it is a big one. Just the JFrame class, which we will be exploring in a moment, contains more than 200 methods when one includes those inherited from superclasses! We will therefore have to be selective in what we get into in detail, in terms of both the specific classes we discuss and their methods. We will however cover the basic operations that you need to understand to create your own applications and applets. With a good grasp of the basics, you should be able to explore other areas of the Java class library beyond those discussed without too much difficulty.

The basic elements that you need to create a GUI reside in two packages, `java.awt` and `javax.swing`. The `java.awt` package was the primary repository for classes you would use to create a GUI in Java 1.1 – 'awt' being an abbreviation for **A**bstract **W**indowing **T**oolkit, but many of the classes it defines have been superceded in Java 2 by `javax.swing`. Most of the classes in the `javax.swing` package define GUI elements, referred to as **Swing components**, that provide much-improved alternatives to components defined by classes in `java.awt`. We will be looking into the `JButton` class in the Swing set that defines a button, rather than the `Button` class in `java.awt`. However, the Swing component classes are generally derived from, and depend on, fundamental classes within `java.awt`, so you can't afford to ignore these.

The Swing classes are part of a more general set of GUI programming capabilities that are collectively referred to as the **Java Foundation Classes**, or **JFC** for short. JFC covers not only the Swing component classes, such as those defining buttons and menus, but also classes for 2D drawing from the `java.awt.geom` package, and classes that support drag-and-drop capability in the `java.awt.dnd` package. The JFC also includes an API defined in the `javax.accessibility` package that allows applications to be implemented that provide for users with disabilities.

The Swing component classes are more flexible than the component classes defined in the `java.awt` package because they are implemented entirely in Java. The `java.awt` components depend on native code to a great extent, and are, therefore, restricted to a 'lowest common denominator' set of interface capabilities. Because Swing components are pure Java, they are not restricted by the characteristics of the platform on which they run. Apart from the added function and flexibility of the Swing components, they also provide a feature called **pluggable look-and-feel** that makes it possible to change the appearance of a component. You can programmatically select the look-and-feel of a component from those implemented as standard, or you can create your own look-and-feel for components if you wish. The pluggable look-and-feel of the Swing components has been facilitated by designing the classes in a particular way, called the **MVC architecture**.

Model-View-Controller (MVC) Architecture

The design of the Swing component classes is loosely based on something called the **Model-View-Controller** architecture, or MVC. This is not of particular consequence in the context of applying the Swing classes, but it's important to be aware of it if you want to modify the pluggable look and feel of a component. MVC is not new, and did not originate with Java. In fact the idea of MVC emerged some time ago within the context of the Smalltalk programming language. MVC is an idealized way of modeling a component as three separate parts:

❑ The **model** that stores the data which defines the component.

❑ The **view** that creates the visual representation of the component from the data in the model.

❑ The **controller** that deals with user interaction with the component and modifies the model and/or the view in response to a user action as necessary.

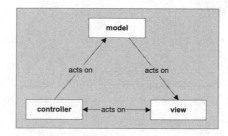

In object-oriented terms, each of the three logical parts for a component – the model, the view and the controller – would ideally be represented by a different class type. In practice this turns out to be difficult because of the dependencies between the view and the controller. Since the user interacts with the physical representation of the component, the controller operation is highly dependent on the implementation of the view. For this reason the view and controller are typically represented by a single composite object that corresponds to a view with an integrated controller. In this case the MVC concept degenerates into the document/view architecture that we introduced when we discussed the `Observable` class and `Observer` interface. Sun call it the **Separable Model architecture**.

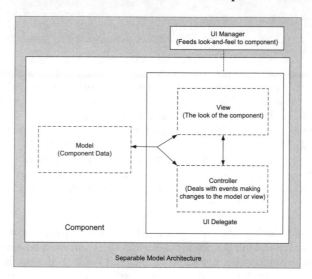

The way the Swing components provide for a pluggable look-and-feel is to make the visual appearance of a component and the interface to the user the responsibility of an independent object called the **UI delegate**. This is the view+controller part of the MVC model. Thus a different UI delegate can provide a component with a new look-and-feel.

The details of how you modify the look-and-feel of a component is beyond the scope of this book. It is, however, as well to be aware of the MVC architecture on which the Swing components are based since it appears quite often in the literature around Java, and you may want to change the look and feel of a component at some time.

Creating a Window

A basic window in Java is represented by an object of the class `Window` in the package `java.awt`. Objects of the class `Window` are hardly ever used directly since borders and a title bar are fairly basic prerequisites for a typical application window, and this class provides neither. The library class `JFrame`, defined in `javax.swing`, is a much more useful class for creating a window, since as well as a title bar and a border, it provides a wealth of other facilities. Its superclasses are shown below.

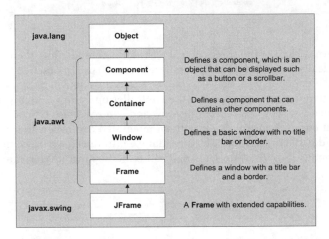

The `Component` class is the grandmother of all component classes – it defines the basic properties and methods shared by all components. We will see later that all the Swing components have the `Component` class as a base. The `Container` class adds the capability for a `Component` object to contain other components, which is a frequent requirement. Since `JFrame` has `Container` as a superclass, a `JFrame` object can contain other components. Beyond the obvious need for a window to be able to contain the components that represent the GUI, a menubar should contain menus, for instance, which in turn will contain menu items: a toolbar will obviously contain toolbar buttons, and there are many other examples. For this reason the `Container` class is also a base for all the classes that define Swing components

The `Window` class adds methods to the `Container` class that are specific to a window, such as the ability to handle events arising from user interaction with the window. The `Frame` class is the original class in `java.awt` that provided a proper window, with a title bar and a border, with which everyone is familiar. The `JFrame` class adds functionality to the `Frame` class to support much more sophisticated facilities for drawing and displaying other components. You can deduce from the hierarchy in the diagram how a `JFrame` object can easily end up with its 200+ methods as it has five superclasses from which it inherits members. We aren't going to trawl through all these classes and methods: we'll just look into the ones we need in context as we go along, and then see how they are applied for real. After a while you will have learnt about the most important ones.

You can display an application window simply by creating an object of type `JFrame`, calling a method for the object to set the size of the window, and then calling a method to display the window. Let's try that right away.

Try It Out – Framing a Window

Here's the code:

```
import javax.swing.*;

public class TryWindow
{
  // The window object
  static JFrame aWindow = new JFrame("This is the Window Title");

  public static void main(String[] args)
  {
    aWindow.setBounds(50, 100, 400, 150);       // Set position and size
    aWindow.setDefaultCloseOperation(JFrame.EXIT_ON_CLOSE);
    aWindow.setVisible(true);                    // Display the window
  }
}
```

Under Microsoft Windows, the program will display the window shown:

Try resizing the window by dragging a border or a corner with the mouse. You can also try minimizing the window by clicking on the icons to the right of the title bar. Everthing should work OK so we are getting quite a lot for so few lines of code. You can close the application by clicking on the ☒ icon.

> This example will terminate OK if you have entered the code correctly, however errors could prevent this. If an application doesn't terminate properly for any reason you will have to get the operating system to end the task. Under MS Windows, switching to the DOS window and pressing *Ctrl+C* will do it.

How It Works

The import statement adds the definitions for all the classes in the package java.swing to our program. This will be virtually standard from now on since most of our programs will be using the components defined in this package. The object of type JFrame is created and stored as the initial value for the static data member of the class TryWindow, so it will be created automatically when the TryWindow class is loaded. The argument to the constructor defines the title to be displayed in the application window.

The `main()` method calls three methods for the `aWindow` object. The method `setBounds()` defines the size and position of the window; the first pair of arguments correspond to the *x* and *y* coordinates of the top-left corner of our application window relative to the top-left corner of the display screen, and the second pair of arguments specify the width and height of the window in pixels. The screen coordinate system has the origin point, (0, 0), at the top-left corner of the screen, with the positive *x*-axis running left to right and the positive *y*-axis from top to bottom. The positive *y*-axis in screen coordinates is therefore in the opposite direction to that of the usual Cartesian coordinate system.

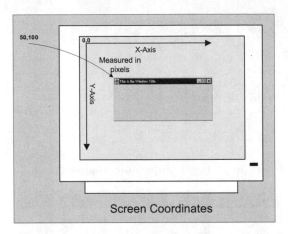

We have specified the top-left corner of our application window at position (50, 100) on the screen, which will be 50 pixels to the right and 100 pixels down. Since the window will be 400 pixels wide and 150 pixels high, the bottom right corner will be at position (450, 250). The actual physical width and height of the window as well as its position relative to the edge of the screen will depend on the size of your screen and the display resolution. For a given screen size, the higher the display resolution, the smaller the window will be and the closer it will be to the top left-hand corner, simply because the pixels on the screen will be closer together. We will see how we can get around this potential problem later in this chapter.

The `setDefaultCloseOperation()` method determines what happens when you close the window by clicking on either the ☒ icon or selecting close from the menu displayed after you click on 🍵. There are four possible argument values you can use here. The constant we have used at the argument to the method, `EXIT_ON_CLOSE`, is defined in the `JFrame` class. The effect of this is to close the window, dispose of the window resources and those of any components it contains, and finally to terminate the application. There are three other argument values you could use with the `setDefaultCloseOperation()` method that are defined in the `WindowConstants` interface. These values are:

Argument	Description
DISPOSE_ON_CLOSE	This causes the frame and any components it contains to be destroyed but doesn't terminate the application.
DO_NOTHING_ON_CLOSE	This makes the close operation for the frame window ineffective.
HIDE_ON_CLOSE	This just hides the window by calling its setVisible() method with an argument of false. This is the default action if you don't call the setDefaultCloseOperation() method with a different argument value. When a window is hidden, you could always display the window again later by calling setVisible() with an argument of true.

Of course, you may want to take some action beyond the options we have discussed here when the user chooses to close the window. If the program involves entering a lot of data for instance, you may want to ensure that the user is prompted to save the data before the program ends. This involves handling an event associated with the close menu item or the close button, and we will be investigating this in Chapter 13.

The method setVisible() with the argument set to true, displays our application window on top of any other windows currently visible on the screen. If you wanted to hide the window somewhere else in the program, you would call setVisible() with the argument set to false.

It's a very *nice* window, but not overly useful. All you can do with it is move, resize and reshape it. You can drag the borders and maximize and minimize it. The close icon works because our program elected to dispose of the window and exit the program when the close operation is selected by setting the appropriate option through the setDefaultCloseOperation() method. If we omitted this method call, the window would close but the program would not terminate.

The setBounds() and setVisible() methods are members of the JFrame class inherited from the Component class, so these are available for any component. However, you don't normally set the size and position of other components as we will see. The setDefaultCloseOperation() method is defined in the JFrame class so this method only applies to JFrame window objects.

Before we expand our JFrame example we need to look a little deeper into the make-up of the component classes.

Components and Containers

A component represents a graphical entity of one kind or another that can be displayed on the screen. A component is any object of a class that is a subclass of Component. As we have seen, a JFrame window is a component, but there are many others. Before getting into specifics, let's first get a feel for the general relationship between the groups of classes that represent components. Part of the class hierarchy with Component as a base is shown below. The arrows in the diagram point towards the superclass.

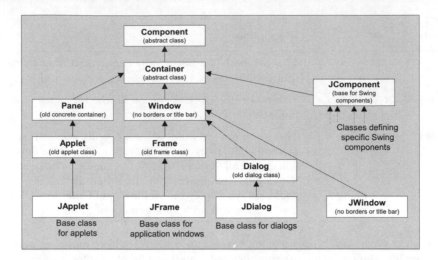

This shows some of the sub-classes of Component – the ones that are important to us at the moment. We discussed the chain through to JFrame earlier, but the other branches are new. The classes that we will be using directly are all the most commonly derived classes. All the classes derived from Container can contain other objects of any of the classes derived from Component, and are referred to generically as **containers**. Since the Container class is a sub-class of the Component class, every container object is a Component too, so a container can contain other containers. The exception is the Window class and its subclasses, as objects of type Window (or of a subclass type) can't be contained in another container. If you try to do this, an exception will be thrown. The JComponent class is the base for all the Swing components used in a window as part of the GUI, so, since this class is derived from Container, all of the Swing components are also containers.

As you can see, the JApplet class, which is a base class for all Swing applets, is derived from Component via the Container class. An applet will, therefore, also inherit the methods from the Container and Component classes. It also inherits methods from the old Applet class, which it extends and improves upon. You should note that the JApplet, JFrame and JDialog classes, and the JComponent class and its subclasses, are all in the package javax.swing. The Applet class is in java.applet, and all the others are in java.awt. The package java.applet is tiny – it only contains the one class plus three related interfaces, but we won't need to use it directly. We will always be using the JApplet class to define an applet, as it's significantly better than Applet.

Window and Frame Components

The basic difference between a JFrame object and a Window object is that a JFrame object represents the main window for an application, whereas a Window object does not – you always need a JFrame object before you can create a Window object.

Since the JDialog class is derived directly from the Window class, you can only create a JDialog object in an application in the context of a JFrame object. Apart from the default constructor, the constructors for the JDialog class generally require a JFrame object to be passed as an argument. This JFrame object is referred to as the **parent** of the JDialog object. A JFrame object has a border, is resizable and has the ability to hold a menu bar built in. Since a JFrame object is the top-level window in an application, its size and location are defined relative to the screen. A JDialog object with a JFrame object as a parent will be located relative to its parent.

Let's summarize how you would typically use the key classes in the hierarchy we've discussed:

Class	Use
JFrame	This is used as the basic Java application window. An object of this class has a title bar and provision for adding a menu. You can also add other components to it. You will usually subclass this class to create a window class specific to your application. It is then possible to add GUI components or draw in this window if required, as we will see.
JDialog	You use this class to define a dialog window that is used for entering data into a program in various ways. You usually code the creation of a dialog in response to some menu item being selected.
JApplet	This is the base class for a Java 2 applet – a program designed to run embedded in a web page. All your Java 2 applets will have this class as a base. You can draw in a JApplet and also add menus and other components.
JComponent	The subclasses of JComponent define a range of standard components such as menus, buttons, checkboxes and so on. You will use these classes to create the GUI for your application or applet.

Note that while we will discuss applets based on the JApplet class in this book, there is still a significant role for applets based on the more restricted capabilities of the Applet class. This is because as yet browsers do not support Java 2 applets by default. Both Netscape Navigator and Microsoft Internet Explorer require the Java Plug-In from Sun to be installed before a Java2 applet can be executed. You can download the Java Plug-In from the Sun Java web site at http://java.sun.com/products.

As we said, the JApplet, JFrame and JDialog classes are all containers because they have Container as a base class and therefore, in principle, can contain any kind of component. They are also all components themselves since they are derived ultimately from the Component class. However, things are not quite as simple as that. You don't add the components for your application or applet GUI *directly* to the JFrame or JApplet object for your program. Let's look at how it actually works in practice.

Window Panes

When you want to add GUI components or draw in a window displayed from a JFrame object, you add the components to, or draw on, a **window pane** that is managed by the JFrame object. The same goes for an applet. Broadly, window panes are objects that are containers which represent an area of a window, and they come in several different types.

You will use a window pane called the **content pane** most of the time, but there are others. The relationship between the contentPane object, other window panes, and the application window itself is shown here.

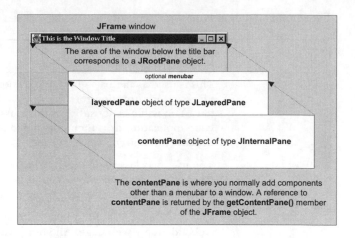

As you see, the area below the title bar in a JFrame window corresponds to a JRootPane object. This contains another pane, the layeredPane object in the illustration, which is of type JLayeredPane. This pane corresponds to the whole of the area occupied by the JRootPane object in the window and manages the menubar if the window has one. The area in the layeredPane below the menubar corresponds to the contentPane object, and it's here that you typically add GUI components. You also display text or do any drawing in the area covered by the content pane.

The layeredPane object has special properties for advanced applications that permit groups of components to be managed in separate layers that overlay one another within the pane. With this capability you can control how components are displayed relative to one another, because the layers are displayed in a particular order from back to front. The components in a layer at the front will appear on the screen in front of those in a layer that is towards the back.

There is also an additional pane not shown in the diagram. This is the glassPane object, and this also corresponds to the complete JRootPane area. The contents of the glassPane object displays on top of all the other panes, so this is used to display components that you always want to display on top of anything else displayed in the window – such as pop-up menus. You can also use the glassPane to display graphics that need to be updated relatively frequently – such as when you create an animation. When part of what is displayed is to be animated, a static background can be displayed independently via the contentPane. Since this doesn't need to be reprocessed each time the animated objects need to be redrawn the whole process can be much more efficient.

The JFrame class defines methods to provide you with a reference to any of the panes:

Method	Description
getRootPane()	Returns the root pane as type JRootPane.
getLayeredPane()	Returns the layered pane as type JLayeredPane.
getContentPane()	Returns the content pane as type Container. This is the method you will use most frequently, since you normally add components to the content pane.
getGlassPane()	Returns the glass pane as type Component.

All the classes discussed here that represent panes are themselves Swing components, defined in the `javax.swing` package. A `JApplet` object has the same arrangement of panes as a `JFrame` object, so adding components to an applet, or drawing on it works in exactly the same way. An applet defined as a `JApplet` object can also have a menubar just like an application window.

All the panes, as well as the menubar, are components, so before we start delving into how to add a menubar or other components to a window, let's unearth a little more about the make-up of components in general.

Basics of Components

There's quite a lot of basic stuff to examine before we can apply components properly that is common to all components, and has application in many different contexts. While this may seem like something of a catalog of classes and methods, without much practical application, please stay with it. To understand the fundamental things we can do with Swing components, we will examine what functionality they inherit from the `Component` and `Container` classes.

When a component is contained within another component, the outer object is referred to as the **parent**. You can find out what the parent of any given component is by calling its `getParent()` method. This method is inherited from the `Component` class and it returns the parent as type `Container`, since only a subclass of `Container` can hold other components. If there is no parent, `null` is returned.

Component Attributes

The `Component` class defines attributes, which record the following information about an object:

- ❏ The **position** is stored as (x, y) coordinates. This fixes where the object is in relation to its container in the coordinate system of the container object.

- ❏ The **name** of the component is stored as a `String` object.

- ❏ The **size** is recorded as values for the width and the height of the object.

- ❏ The **foreground color** and **background color** that apply to the object. These color values are used when the object is displayed.

- ❏ The **font** used by the object when text is displayed.

- ❏ The **cursor** for the object – this defines the appearance of the cursor when it is over the object.

- ❏ Whether the object is **enabled** or not – if the component is enabled it is active and can be accessed by the user.

- ❏ Whether the object is **visible** on the screen or not – if an object is not marked as visible it is not drawn on the screen.

- ❏ Whether the object is **valid** or not – if an object is not valid, layout of the entities that make up the object has not been determined. This is the case before an object is made visible. You can make a `Container` object invalid by changing its contents. It will then need to be validated before it is displayed correctly.

You can only modify the characteristics of a `Component` object by calling its methods or affecting it indirectly in some way, since none of its data members, that store the characteristics, are directly accessible – they are all `private`. For example, you can change the name of a `Component` object `myWindow` with the statement:

```
myWindow.setName("The Name");
```

If you subsequently want to retrieve the name of an object you can use the `getName()` method which returns the name as a `String` object. For example:

```
String theName = myWindow.getName();
```

The `isVisible()`, `isEnabled()` and `isValid()` methods return `true` if the object is visible, enabled or valid respectively. You can set an object as visible or enabled by passing a value `true` as an argument to the methods `setVisible()` or `setEnabled()`.

Let's see how we can change the size and position of a `Component` object.

The Size and Position of a Component

Position is defined by x and y coordinates of type `int`, or by an object of type `Point`. A `Point` object has two public data members, x and y, corresponding to the x and y coordinate values. Size is defined by `width` and `height`, also values of type `int`, or by an object of type `Dimension`. The class `Dimension` has two public members of type `int`, namely `width` and `height`. The size and position of a component are often specified together by an object of type `Rectangle`. A `Rectangle` object has public data members, x and y, defining the top left corner of the rectangle, with `width` and `height` members defining its size. All these data members are of type `int`.

Components have a 'preferred' size, which depends on the particular object. For example, the preferred size of a `JButton` object that defines a button is the size that accommodates the label for the button. Note that you will not normally adjust the size of a component unless you are placing it relative to your display screen, since the size will be managed automatically when it has a parent component. We will see the reason for this later in this chapter. A component also has a minimum size and if the space available to it is less than the minimum size, the component will not be displayed.

The methods to retrieve or alter the size and position are:

Method	Description
void setBounds(int x, int y, int width, int height)	Sets the position of the `Component` object to the coordinates (x, y), and the width and height of the object to the values defined by the third and fourth arguments.
void setBounds(Rectangle rect)	Sets the position and size of the `Component` object to be that of the `Rectangle` argument, rect.
Rectangle getBounds()	Returns the position and size of the object as an object of type `Rectangle`.

Method	Description
void setSize(Dimension d)	Sets the width and height of the Component object to the values stored in the members of the object d.
Dimension getSize()	Returns the current size of the Component object as a Dimension object.
setLocation(int x, int y)	Sets the position of the component to the point defined by (x, y).
setLocation(Point p)	Sets the position of the component to the point p.
Point getLocation()	Returns the position of the Component object as an object of type Point.

Another important method defined in the Component class is getToolkit(). This returns an object of type Toolkit which contains information about the environment in which your application is running, including the screen size in pixels. You can use the getToolkit() method to help set the size and position of a window on the screen. We can modify the previous example to demonstrate this.

Try It Out – Sizing Windows with Toolkit

We'll use the Toolkit object to display the window in the center of the screen with the width and height set as half of the screen width and height:

```java
import javax.swing.*;
import java.awt.*;

public class TryWindow
{
  // The window object
  static JFrame aWindow = new JFrame("This is the Window Title");

  public static void main(String[] args)
  {
    Toolkit theKit = aWindow.getToolkit();        // Get the window toolkit
    Dimension wndSize = theKit.getScreenSize();  // Get screen size

    // Set the position to screen center & size to half screen size
    aWindow.setBounds(wndSize.width/4, wndSize.height/4,    // Position
                  wndSize.width/2, wndSize.height/2);  // Size
    aWindow.setDefaultCloseOperation(JFrame.EXIT_ON_CLOSE);
    aWindow.setVisible(true);                        // Display the window
  }
}
```

If you try this example, you should see the application window centered on your display with a width and height of half that of the screen.

How It Works

The `Toolkit` object, `theKit`, is obtained by calling the `getToolkit()` method for the `JFrame` object, `aWindow`. This object represents the environment on your computer so it encapsulates all the properties and capabilities of that environment as far as Java is concerned, including the screen resolution and size.

> **Note that you can't create a `Toolkit` object directly since `Toolkit` is an abstract class. There is only one `Toolkit` object in an application – the one that you get a reference for when you call `getToolKit()` for a component.**

The `getScreenSize()` method that is a member of the `Toolkit` object returns an object of type `Dimension` containing data members `width` and `height`. These hold the number of pixels for the width and height of your display. We use these values to set the coordinates for the position of the window, and the width and height of the window through the `setBounds()` method.

Points and Rectangles

Let's digress briefly into more detail concerning the `Point` and `Rectangle` classes before continuing with the `Component` class methods, as since they will come up quite often. Both these classes are defined in `java.awt`. You will find many of the methods provided by the `Point` and `Rectangle` classes very useful when drawing in a window. Entities displayed in a window will typically have `Rectangle` objects associated with them that define the areas within the window that they occupy. `Point` objects are used in the definition of other geometric entities such as lines and circles, and to specify their position in a window.

Note that neither `Point` nor `Rectangle` objects have any built in representation on the screen. They aren't components; they are abstract geometric entities. If you want to display a rectangle you have to draw it. We will see how to do this in Chapter 13.

Point Objects

As we said, the `Point` class defines a point by two `public` data members of type `int`, `x` and `y`. Let's look at the methods that the class provides.

Try It Out – Playing with `Point` Objects

Try the following code:

```java
import java.awt.*;

public class PlayingPoints
{
  public static void main(String[] args)
  {
    Point aPoint = new Point();            // Initialize to 0,0
    Point bPoint = new Point(50,25);
    Point cPoint = new Point(bPoint);
    System.out.println("aPoint is located at: " + aPoint);
```

```
        aPoint.move(100,50);                    // Change to position 100,50

        bPoint.x = 110;
        bPoint.y = 70;

        aPoint.translate(10,20);                // Move by 10 in x and 20 in y
        System.out.println("aPoint is now at: " + aPoint);

        if(aPoint.equals(bPoint))
          System.out.println("aPoint and bPoint are at the same location.");
    }
  }
```

If you run the program you should see:

```
    aPoint is located at: java.awt.Point[x=0,y=0]
    aPoint is now at: java.awt.Point[x=110,y=70]
    aPoint and bPoint are at the same location.
```

How It Works

You can see the three constructors that the `Point` class provides in action in the first few lines. We then manipulate the `Point` objects we've instantiated.

You can change a `Point` object to a new position with the `move()` method. Alternatively, you can use the `setLocation()` method to set the values of the x and y members. The `setLocation()` method does exactly the same as the `move()` method. It is included in the `Point` class for compatibility with the `setLocation()` method for a component. For the same reason, there is also a `getLocation()` method in the `Point` class that returns a copy of the current `Point` object. As the example shows, you can also translate a `Point` object by specified distances in the x and y directions using the `translate()` method.

Lastly, you can compare two `Point` objects using the `equals()` method. This compares the x and y coordinates of the two `Point` objects, and returns `true` if both are equal. The final output statement is executed because the `Point` objects are equal.

Note that this is not the only class that represents points. We will see other classes that define points when we discuss how to draw in a window.

Rectangle Objects

As discussed earlier, the `Rectangle` class defines four `public` data members, all of type `int`. The position of a `Rectangle` object is defined by the members x and y, and its size is defined by the members `width` and `height`. As they are all `public` class members, you can retrieve or modify any of these directly, but your code will be a little more readable if you use the methods provided.

There are no less than seven constructors that you can use:

Constructor	Description
`Rectangle()`	Creates a rectangle at (0, 0) with zero width and height.
`Rectangle(int x, int y, int width, int height)`	Creates a rectangle at (x, y) with the specified width and height.
`Rectangle(int width, int height)`	Creates a rectangle at (0, 0) with the specified width and height.
`Rectangle(Point p, Dimension d)`	Creates a rectangle at point p with the width and height specified by d.
`Rectangle(Point p)`	Creates a rectangle at point p with zero width and height.
`Rectangle(Dimension d)`	Creates a rectangle at (0, 0) with the width and height specified by d.
`Rectangle(Rectangle r)`	Creates a rectangle with the same position and dimensions as r.

You can retrieve or modify the position of a `Rectangle` object using the methods `getLocation()` which returns a `Point` object, and `setLocation()` which comes in two versions, one of which requires *x* and *y* coordinates of the new position as arguments and the other, which requires a `Point` object. You can also apply the `translate()` method to a `Rectangle` object, in the same way as the `Point` object.

To retrieve or modify the size of a `Rectangle` object you use the methods `getSize()`, which returns a `Dimension` object, and `setSize()` which requires either a `Dimension` object specifying the new size as an argument, or two arguments corresponding to the new width and height values as type `int`.

There are also several methods that you can use to combine `Rectangle` objects, and also to extend a `Rectangle` object to enclose a point. The effects of each of these methods are shown in the following diagram.

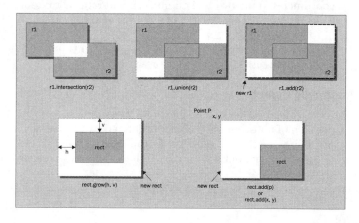

The rectangle that results from each operation is shown dashed. The methods illustrated in the diagram are:

Method	Description
`Rectangle intersection( Rectangle r)`	Returns a `Rectangle` object that is the intersection of the current object and the argument. If the two rectangles do not intersect, the `Rectangle` object returned is at position (0, 0) and the `width` and `height` members are zero so the rectangle is empty.
`Rectangle union( Rectangle r)`	Returns the smallest `Rectangle` object enclosing both the current `Rectangle` object and the `Rectangle` object r, passed as an argument.
`void add(Rectangle r)`	Expands the current `Rectangle` object to enclose the argument `Rectangle`.
`void add(Point p)`	Expands the current `Rectangle` object to enclose the `Point` object p. The result will be the smallest rectangle that encloses the original rectangle and the point.
`void add(int x, int y)`	Expands the current `Rectangle` object to enclose the point at (x, y).
`void grow(int h, int v)`	Enlarges the current `Rectangle` object by moving the boundary out from the center by h horizontally and v vertically.

You can also test and compare `Rectangle` objects in various ways with the following methods:

Method	Description
`boolean isEmpty()`	Returns `true` if the `width` and `height` members of the current `Rectangle` object are zero, and `false` otherwise.
`boolean equals( Object rect)`	Returns `true` if the `Rectangle` object passed as an argument is equal to the current `Rectangle` object, and returns `false` otherwise.
	The two rectangles will be equal if they are at the same position and have the same width and height. If the argument is not a `Rectangle` object, `false` is returned.
`boolean intersects( Rectangle rect)`	Returns `true` if the current `Rectangle` object intersects the `Rectangle` object passed as an argument, and `false` otherwise.
`boolean contains( Point p)`	Returns `true` if the current `Rectangle` object encloses the `Point` argument p, and `false` otherwise.
`boolean contains( int x, int y)`	Returns `true` if the current `Rectangle` object encloses the point (x, y), and `false` otherwise.

All of these will be useful when dealing with the contents of a Java window. You will then be dealing with points and rectangles describing the contents drawn in the window. For example, you might want to enable the user of your program to select some geometric shape from among those displayed on the screen, in order to work with it. You could use the contains() method to check whether the point corresponding to the current cursor position is within any of the Rectangle objects that enclose each of the circles, lines or whatever is displayed in the window. Then you can decide which of the objects displayed on the screen the user wants to choose.

There are other classes defining rectangles that we shall meet when we start drawing in a window.

Visual Characteristics of a Component

The visual appearance of a component is determined by two things: the representation of the component created by the Java code in the component class that is executed when the component is displayed, and whatever you draw on the component. You can draw on a Component object by implementing its paint() method. We used this method in Chapter 1 to output the text for our applet. The paint() method is called automatically when the component needs to be drawn.

The need to draw a component can arise for a variety of reasons – for example, if your program requests that the area that the component occupies should be redrawn, or if the user resizes the window containing the component. Your implementation of this method must include code to generate whatever you want drawn within the Component object. Note that the component itself – the JButton or JFrame or whatever, will be drawn for you. You only need to override the paint() method for anything additional that you want to draw on it. We will be overriding the paint() method in Chapter 13 to draw in a window, so we will leave further discussion of it until then.

You can alter the appearance of the basic component by calling methods for the object. The following methods have an effect on the appearance of a Component object:

Method	Description
void setBackground(Color aColor)	Sets the background color to aColor. The background color is the color used for the basic component, as created by the operating system.
Color getBackground()	Retrieves the current background color.
void setForeground(Color bColor)	Sets the foreground color to bColor. The foreground color is the color used for anything appearing on the basic component, such as the label on a button, for example.
Color getForeground()	Retrieves the current foreground color.
void setCursor(Cursor aCursor)	Sets the cursor for the component to aCursor. This sets the appearance of the cursor within the area occupied by the Component object.
void setFont(Font aFont)	Sets the font for the Component object.
Font getFont()	Returns the Font object used by the component.

To be able to make use of these properly, we need to understand what `Color` objects are, and we also need to know how to create `Cursor` and `Font` objects.

Defining Color

A screen color is represented by an object of class `Color`. You define a color value as a combination of the three primary colors; red, green, and blue. They are usually expressed in that sequence, and are often referred to as **RGB values**. There are other ways of specifying colors in Java, but we will confine ourselves to RGB. You can specify the intensity of each primary color to be a value between 0 and 255. If the intensities of all three are 0, you have the color black, and if all three are set to 255 you have white. If only one intensity is positive and the others are zero, you will have a pure primary color; for example (0, 200, 0) will be a shade of green. We could define variables corresponding to these colors with the statements:

```
Color myBlack = new Color(0,0,0);           // Color black
Color myWhite = new Color(255,255,255);     // Color white
Color myGreen = new Color(0,200,0);         // A shade of green
```

The three arguments to the constructor correspond to the intensities of the red, green, and blue components of the color respectively. The `Color` class defines a number of standard color constants as `public final static` variables, whose RGB values are given in parentheses:

white	(255, 255, 255)	red	(255, 0, 0)	pink	(255, 175, 175)
lightGray	(192, 192, 192)	orange	(255, 200, 0)	magenta	(255, 0, 255)
gray	(128, 128, 128)	yellow	(255, 255, 0)	cyan	(0, 255, 255)
darkGray	(64, 64, 64)	green	(0, 255, 0)	blue	(0, 0, 255)
black	(0, 0, 0,)				

So if we want our window in the previous example to have a pink background, we could add the statement:

```
aWindow.setBackground(Color.pink);
```

When you have created a `Color` object, you can brighten or darken the color it represents by calling its `brighter()` or `darker()` methods which will increase or decrease the intensity of the color components by a predefined factor:

```
thisColor.brighter();       // Brighten the color
thatColor.darker();         // Darken the color
```

The intensities of the component colors will always remain between 0 and 255. When you call `brighter` and a color component is already at 255, it will remain at that value. The other component intensities will be increased if they are less than 255. In a similar way, the `darker()` method will not change a component intensity if it is zero. The factor used for darkening a color component is 0.7. To brighten a color component the intensity is increased by 1/0.7.

A fundamental point to remember here is that you can only obtain the colors available within the computer and the operating system environment on which your Java program is running. If you only have a limited range of colors, the `brighter()` and `darker()` methods may appear to have no effect. If your computer only supports sixteen colors, then although you can create `Color` objects that are supposed to represent all kinds of colors, you will always end up with one of your sixteen. If your machine supports 24-bit color and this is supported in your system environment, then everything should be fine and dandy.

You can obtain any of the component intensities by calling `getRed()`, `getGreen()` or `getBlue()` for a `Color` object. A color can also be obtained as a value of type `int` that is a composite of the red, green and blue components of the color represented by a `Color` object. The `getRGB()` method returns this value. You can also create a `Color` object from a single RGB value of type `int`.

To compare two `Color` objects you can use the `equals()` method. For example to compare two color objects `colorA` and `colorB`, you could write:

```
if(colorA.equals(colorB))
    // Do something...
```

The `equals()` method will return `true` if all three components of the two `Color` objects are equal. You could also use the `getRGB()` method to do the same thing:

```
if(colorA.getRGB() == colorB.getRGB())
    // Do something....
```

This compares the two integer RGB values for equality.

System Colors

The package `java.awt` defines the class `SystemColor` as a sub-class of the `Color` class. The `SystemColor` class encapsulates the standard system colors used for displaying various components. The class contains definitions for 24 `public final static` variables of type `SystemColor` that specify the standard system colors used by the operating system for a range of GUI components. For example, the system colors for a window are referenced by:

`window`	Defines the background color for a window.
`windowText`	Defines the text color for a window.
`windowBorder`	Defines the border color for a window.

You can find the others covering colors used for menus, captions, controls, and so on, if you need them by looking at the documentation for the `SystemColor` class.

If you want to compare a `SystemColor` value with a `Color` object you have created, then you must use the `getRGB()` method in the comparison. This is because the `SystemColor` class stores the colors internally in a way that makes use of the fields it inherits from the `Color` class differently from a normal `Color` object. For example, to see whether `colorA` corresponds to the system background color for a window you would write:

```
if(colorA.getRGB() == SystemColor.window.getRGB())
    // colorA is the window background color...
```

Creating Cursors

An object of the `Cursor` class represents a mouse cursor. The `Cursor` class contains a range of `final static` constants that specify standard cursor types. You use these to select or create a particular cursor. The standard cursor types are:

DEFAULT_CURSOR	N_RESIZE_CURSOR	NE_RESIZE_CURSOR
CROSSHAIR_CURSOR	S_RESIZE_CURSOR	NW_RESIZE_CURSOR
WAIT_CURSOR	E_RESIZE_CURSOR	SE_RESIZE_CURSOR
TEXT_CURSOR	W_RESIZE_CURSOR	SW_RESIZE_CURSOR
HAND_CURSOR	MOVE_CURSOR	

The resize cursors are the ones you see when resizing a window by dragging its boundaries. Note that these are not like the `Color` constants, which are `Color` objects – constants of type `int`, not type `Cursor` and are intended to be used as arguments to a constructor.

To create a `Cursor` object representing a text cursor you could write:

```
Cursor myCursor = new Cursor(Cursor.TEXT_CURSOR);
```

Alternatively you can retrieve a cursor of the predefined type using a `static` class method:

```
Cursor myCursor = Cursor.getPredefinedCursor(Cursor.TEXT_CURSOR);
```

This method is particularly useful when you don't want to store the `Cursor` object, but just want to pass it to a method, such as `setCursor()` for a `Component` object.

If you want to see what the standard cursors look like, you could add a cursor to the previous example, along with the pink background:

Try It Out – Color and Cursors

We will change the background color of the content pane for the application window and try out a different cursor. Make the following changes to `TryWindow.java`:

```java
import javax.swing.*;
import java.awt.*;

public class TryWindow
{
  // The window object
  static JFrame aWindow = new JFrame("This is the Window Title");

  public static void main(String[] args)
  {
    Toolkit theKit = aWindow.getToolkit();        // Get the window toolkit
    Dimension wndSize = theKit.getScreenSize();   // Get screen size

    // Set the position to screen center & size to half screen size
    aWindow.setBounds(wndSize.width/4, wndSize.height/4,    // Position
                      wndSize.width/2, wndSize.height/2);   // Size
    aWindow.setDefaultCloseOperation(JFrame.EXIT_ON_CLOSE);
    aWindow.setCursor(Cursor.getPredefinedCursor(Cursor.CROSSHAIR_CURSOR));
    aWindow.getContentPane().setBackground(Color.pink);
    aWindow.setVisible(true);                              // Display the window
  }
}
```

You can try all the cursors by plugging in each of the standard cursor names in turn. You could also try out a few variations on the background color.

Selecting Fonts

A font is represented by an object of type `Font`, and this is actually quite a complicated class, so we'll only scratch the surface enough for our needs here. The `Font` class differentiates between a **character**, the letter uppercase 'Q' say, and a **glyph** which is the shape defining its appearance when it is displayed or printed. For fonts corresponding to languages that do not use the Latin character set, a character may involve more than one glyph to display it. A `Font` object contains a table that maps the Unicode value for each character to the glyph code or codes that create the visual representation of the character.

To create a `Font` object you must supply the font name, the style of the font and the point size. For example, consider the following statement:

```java
Font myFont = new Font("Serif", Font.ITALIC, 12);
```

This defines a 12-point Times Roman italic font. The other options you could use for the style are `PLAIN` and `BOLD`. The name we have given to the font here, `"Serif"`, is a **logical font name**. Other logical font names we could have used are `"Dialog"`, `"DialogInput"`, `"Monospaced"`, `"SansSerif"` or `"Symbol"`. Instead of a logical font name, we can supply a font face name – the name of a particular font such as `"Times New Roman"` or `"Palatino"`. Of course, you need to know what font face names are available in the system on which your code is running. We will come back to this in a moment.

You can specify combined styles by adding them together. If we want myFont to be BOLD and ITALIC we would have written the statement as:

```
Font myFont = new Font("Serif", Font.ITALIC + Font.BOLD, 12);
```

You retrieve the style and size of an existing Font object by calling its methods getStyle() and getSize(),both of which return a value of type int. You can also check the individual font style for a Font object with the methods isPlain(), isBold() and isItalic(). Each of these methods returns a boolean value indicating whether the Font object has that style.

Before you create a font using a particular font face name, you need to know that the font is available on the system where your code is executing. For this you need to use a method, getAllFonts(), in the GraphicsEnvironment class defined in the java.awt package. We could do this as follows:

```
GraphicsEnvironment e = GraphicsEnvironment.getLocalGraphicsEnvironment();
Font[] fonts = e.getAllFonts();        // Get the fonts
```

You can't create a GraphicsEnvironment object directly, but you can get a reference to the object for the current machine by calling the static method getLocalGraphicsEnvironment() as illustrated. We then use this to call its getAllFonts() method. The getAllFonts() method returns an array of Font objects consisting of those available on the current system. You can then check this list for the font you want to use. Each of the Font instances in the array will be of a 1 point size, and since 1 point is approximately 1/72 of an inch, you will typically want to change this. To change the size and/or style of a font you call its deriveFont() method. This method comes in three versions, all of which return a new Font object with the specified size and/or style:

deriveFont() Method	Description
deriveFont(int Style)	Creates a new Font object with the style specified – one of PLAIN, BOLD, ITALIC or BOLD+ITALIC
deriveFont(float size)	Creates a new Font object with the size specified.
deriveFont(int Style, float size)	Creates a new Font object with the style and size specified.

To use the last font from the array of Font objects to create an equivalent 12 point font you could write:

```
Font newFont = fonts[fonts.length-1].deriveFont(10.0f);
```

If you look in the documentation for the Font class you will see that there is a fourth version of deriveFont() that involves an AffineTransform, but we'll leave AffineTransform objects until Chapter 15.

Getting a `Font` object for every font in the system can be a time consuming process if you have many fonts installed. A much faster alternative is to get the font names, and then use one of these to create the `Font` object that you require. You can get the face names for all the fonts in a system like this:

```
GraphicsEnvironment e = GraphicsEnvironment.getLocalGraphicsEnvironment();
String[] fontnames = e.getAvailableFontFamilyNames();
```

The array `fontnames` will contain the names of all the font faces available, and you can use one or more of these to create the `Font` objects you need.

Try It Out – Getting the List of Fonts

This program will output your screen size and resolution, as well as the list of font family names installed on your machine:

```java
import java.awt.*;

public class SysInfo
{
  public static void main(String[] args)
  {
    Toolkit theKit = Toolkit.getDefaultToolkit();

    System.out.println("\nScreen Resolution: "
                       + theKit.getScreenResolution() + " dots per inch");

    Dimension screenDim = theKit.getScreenSize();
    System.out.println("Screen Size: "
                       + screenDim.width + " by "
                       + screenDim.height + " pixels");

    GraphicsEnvironment e = GraphicsEnvironment.getLocalGraphicsEnvironment();
    String[] fontnames = e.getAvailableFontFamilyNames();
    System.out.println("\nFonts available on this platform: ");
    for (int i = 0; i < fontnames.length; i++)
      System.out.println(fontnames[i]);

    return;
  }
}
```

On my system I get the following output:

Screen Resolution: 96 dots per inch
Screen Size: 1024 by 768 pixels

Fonts available on this platform:
Abadi MT Condensed Light
Albertus
Albertus Extra Bold
Albertus Medium
Algerian
Alien
Allegro BT
AmerType Md BT
Andes
Angerthas
Antique Olive
Antique Olive Compact
Architect
Arial
Arial Alternative
Arial Alternative Symbol
Arial Black
Arial MT Black

...plus many more.

How It Works

We first get a `Toolkit` object by calling the `static` method `getDefaultToolkit()` – this is the key to the other information. The `getScreenResolution()` returns the number of pixels per inch as a value of type `int`. The `getScreenSize()` method returns a `Dimension` object which specifies the width and height of the screen in pixels.

We use the `getAllFonts()` method discussed previously to get a `String` array containing the names of the fonts which we output to the screen.

Font Metrics

Every component has a method `getFontMetrics()` that you can use to retrieve **font metrics** – the wealth of dimensional data about a font. You pass a `Font` object as an argument to the method, and it returns an object of type `FontMetrics` that you can use to obtain data relating to the particular font. For example, if `aWindow` is a `Frame` object and `myFont` is a `Font` object, you could obtain a `FontMetrics` object corresponding to the font with the statement:

```
FontMetrics metrics = aWindow.getFontMetrics(myFont);
```

You could use the `getFont()` method for a component to explore the characteristics of the font that the component contains. For example:

```
FontMetrics metrics = aWindow.getFontMetrics(aWindow.getFont());
```

You can now call any of the following `FontMetrics` methods for the object to get at the basic dimensions of the font:

Method	Description
int getAscent()	Returns the **ascent** of the font, which is the distance from the baseline to the top of the majority of the characters in the font. The **baseline** is the line on which the characters rest. Depending on the font, some characters can extend beyond the ascent.
int getMaxAscent()	Returns the maximum ascent for the font. No character will exceed this ascent.
int getDescent()	Returns the **descent** of the font, which is the distance from the baseline to the bottom of most of the font characters that extend below the base line. Depending on the font, some characters may extend beyond the descent for the font.
int getMaxDescent()	Returns the maximum descent of the characters in the font. No character will exceed this descent.
int getLeading()	Returns the **leading** for the font, which is the line spacing for the font – that is the spacing between the bottom of one line of text and the top of the next. The term originated when type was actually made of lead, and there was a strip of lead between one line of type and the next when a page was typeset.
int getHeight()	Returns the height of the font, which is defined as the sum of the ascent, the descent and the leading.

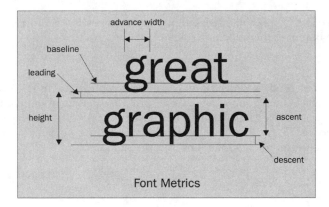

Font Metrics

The diagram shows how the dimensions relate to the font. The **advance width** for a character is the distance from the reference point of the character to the reference point of the next character. The **reference point** for a character is on the base line at the left edge of the character. Each character will have its own advance width which you can obtain by calling a `FontMetrics` method `charWidth()`. For example, to obtain the advance width for the character 'X' the following statement could be used:

```
int widthX = metrics.charWidth('X');
```

You can also obtain the advance widths for all the characters in the font as an array of type int with the method getWidths():

```
int[] widths = metrics.getWidths();
```

The numerical value for the character is used to index the array, so you can get the advance width for the character 'X' with the expression widths['X']. If you just want the maximum advance width for the characters in the font, you can call the method getMaxAdvance(). Lastly, you can get the total advance width for a String object by passing the object to the method stringWidth(). The advance width is returned as a value of type int.

Although you now know a great deal about how to create and manipulate fonts, we haven't actually created and used one. We will remedy this after we have got a feel for what Swing components can do and learnt a little about using containers.

Swing Components

Swing components all have the JComponent class as a base which itself extends the Component class to add the following capability:

❑   Supports pluggable look-and-feel for components, allowing you to change the look and feel programmatically, or implement your own look-and-feel for all components displayed.

❑   Support for tooltips – a **tooltip** being a message describing the purpose of a component when the mouse cursor lingers over it. Tooltips are defined by the JTooltip class.

❑   Support for automatic scrolling in a list, a table or a tree when a component is dragged with the mouse.

❑   Special debugging support for graphics, providing component rendering in slow motion so you can see what is happening.

❑   Component classes can be easily extended to create your own custom components.

All the Swing component classes are defined in the javax.swing package and have class names that begin with J. There are quite a few Swing components, so we'll get an overview of what's available and how the classes relate to one another and then go into the detail of particular components when we use them in examples.

Buttons

The Swing button classes define various kinds of buttons operated by clicking with a mouse. The button classes have AbstractButton as a base, as shown below.

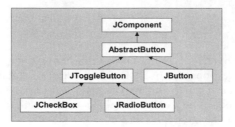

The JButton class defines a regular pushbutton that you would use as a dialog button or in a toolbar.

  This is an example of a JButton object. This component has a border of type BevelBorder added to it.

The JToolBar class is used in conjunction with the JButton class to create a toolbar containing buttons. A toolbar is dockable without any additional programming effort on your part, as we will see.

JToggleButton defines a two state button, pressed or not, and there are two more specialized versions defined by JCheckBox and JRadioButton. Radio buttons defined as JRadioButton objects generally operate in a group so that only one button can be in the pressed state at any one time. This grouping is established by adding the JRadioButton object to a ButtonGroup object that takes care of the state of the buttons in the group.

  This is an example of a JCheckBox object. Clicking on the checkbox changes its state from checked to unchecked or vice versa.

All the buttons can be displayed with a text label, an icon or both.

Menus

The Swing components include support for pop-up or context menus as well as menu bars. The classes defining elements of a menu are shown below.

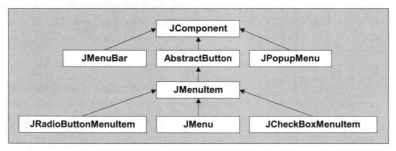

The JMenuBar class defines a **menubar** usually found at the top of an application window. A JMenu object represents a top level menu item on a menubar that pops up a list of menu items when it is clicked. The items in a menu are defined by the JMenuItem class. The JPopupMenu class defines a context menu typically implemented to appear at the current cursor position when the right mouse button is clicked. A JCheckBoxMenuItem component is a menu item with a checkbox that is ticked when the item is selected. The JRadioButtonMenuItem class defines a menu item that is part of a group where only one item can be selected at any time. The group is created by adding JRadioButtonMenuItem objects to a ButtonGroup object. We will be implementing a menu in an application and an applet later in this chapter.

Text Components

The capability of the Swing text components is very wide indeed.

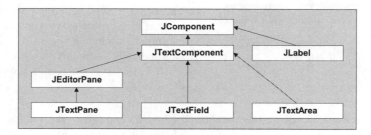

The most elementary text component is a JLabel object:

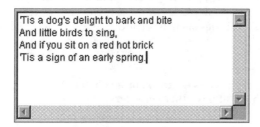

A JLabel component is passive and does not react to input events so you can't edit it.

A JTextField component looks similar in that it displays a single line of text, but in this case it is editable. The JTextArea defines a component that allows editing of multi-line text.

```
Tis a dog's delight to bark and bite
And little birds to sing,
And if you sit on a red hot brick
Tis a sign of an early spring.
```

This is an example of a JTextArea component. The scrollbars are supplied automatically and you can also display multiple rows and columns.

The JEditPane and JTextPane components are a different order of complexity from the others and enable you to implement sophisticated editing facilities relatively easily. The JEditPane supports editing of plain text, text in HTML and RTF (Rich Text Format). The JTextPane class extends JEditPane and allows you to embed images or other components within the text managed by the component.

Other Swing Components

Other Swing components you will use regularly include the `JPanel` component. The `JPanel` class defines something like a physical panel that you can use to group a set of components. For instance, you might use two `JPanel` objects to support two separate groups of `JButton` components in the content pane of an application window.

The `JList` and `JTable` components are also very useful.

Shadrach
Meshach
Abednego

This is a `JList` component that implements a list of items. This component has a border of type `EtchedBorder` added to it. You can select entries from the list.

First Name	Second Name
Marilyn	Monroe
Slim	Pickens
Clint	Eastwood

This is a `JTable` component that implements a table of items from which you can select a row, or a column, or a single element. A `JTable` component automatically takes care of reordering the columns when a column is dragged to a new position using the mouse.

Any component can have a border added, and the `javax.swing.borders` package contains eight classes representing different kinds of borders you can use for a component.

We have not introduced all the Swing component classes by any means, and you will be meeting a few more as you progress through the rest of the book.

Using Containers

A container is any component with the `Container` class as a base, so all the Swing components are containers. The `Container` class is the direct base class for the `Window` class and it provides the ability to contain other components. Since the `Container` class is an `abstract` class, you cannot create instances of `Container`. Instead it is objects of the sub-classes such as `Window`, `JFrame` or `JDialog` that inherit the ability to contain other components.

> **Note that a container cannot contain an object of the class `Window`, or an object of any of the classes derived from `Window`. An object of any other class derived from `Component` can be contained.**

The components within a container are displayed within the area occupied by the container on the display screen. A dialog box, for example, might contain a `JList` object offering some choices: `JCheckbox` objects offering other options and `JButton` objects representing buttons enabling the user to end the dialog or enter the selections – all these components would appear within the boundaries of the dialog box. Of course, for the contained components to be visible the container must itself be displayed, as the container effectively 'owns' its components. The container also controls how its embedded components are laid out by means of a **layout manager**.

Before we look at what a layout manager is, and how the layout of the components is determined, let's look into the basic methods defined in the Container class, and therefore available to all containers.

You can find out about the components in a container object by using the following methods defined in the Container class:

Method	Description
int getComponentCount()	Returns a count of the number of components contained by the current component
Component getComponent (int index)	Returns the component identified by the index value. The index value is an array index so it must be between 0 and one less than the number of components contained, otherwise an ArrayIndexOutOfBoundsException will be thrown.
Component[] getComponents()	Returns an array of all the components in the current container.

If we have a Container object, content, perhaps the content pane of a JFrame window, we could iterate through the components in the Container with the following statements:

```
Component aComponent = null;                          // Stores a Component
int numComponents = content.getComponentCount();    // Get the count

for(int i = 0; i < numComponents; i++)
{
   aComponent = content.getComponent(i);            // Get each component
   // Do something with it...
}
```

This retrieves the components in content one at a time in the for loop. Alternatively we could retrieve them all at once:

```
Component[] theComponents = content.getComponents(); // Get all components

for(int i = 0; i < theComponents.length; i++)
{
   // Do something with theComponents[i]...
}
```

Adding Components to a Container

The components stored in a container are recorded in an array within the `Container` object. The array is increased in size when necessary to accommodate as many components as are present. To add a component to a container you use the method `add()`. The `Container` class defines the following four overloaded versions of the `add()` method:

`add()` Method	Description
`Component add(Component c)`	Add the component c to the end of the list of components stored in the container. The return value is c.
`Component add(Component c, int index)`	Adds the component c to the list of components in the container at the position specified by index. If index is -1, the component is added to the end of the list. If the value of index is not -1 it must be less than the number of components in the container, and greater than or equal to 0. The return value is c.
`void add(Component c, Object constraints)`	Add the component c to the end of the list of components stored in the container. The position of the component relative to the container is subject to the constraints defined by the second parameter. We will see what constraints are in the next section.
`void add(Component c, Object constraints, int index)`	Adds the component c to the list of components in the container at the position specified by index, and position subject to constraints. If index is -1, the component is added to the end of the list. If the value of index is not -1 it must be less than the number of components in the container, and greater than or equal to 0.

Note that adding a component does not displace any components already in the container. When you add a component at a given position, other components are moved in the sequence to make room for the new one. However, a component can only be in one container at a time. Adding a component to a container that is already in another container will remove it from the original container.

In order to try adding components to a container we need to understand what the constraints are that appear in some of the `add()` methods, and look at how the layout of components in a container is controlled.

Container Layout Managers

An object called a **layout manager** determines the way that components are arranged in a container. All containers will have a default layout manager but you can choose a different layout manager when necessary. There are many layout manager classes provided in the `java.awt` and `javax.swing` packages, so we will introduce those that you are most likely to need. It is possible to create your own layout manager classes, but creating layout managers is beyond the scope of this book. The layout manager for a container determines the position and size of all the components in the container: you should not change the size and position of such components yourself. Just let the layout manager take care of it.

Since the classes that define layout managers all implement the `LayoutManager` interface, you can use a variable of type `LayoutManager` to store any of them if necessary. We will look at six layout manager classes in a little more detail. The names of these classes and the basic arrangements that they provide are as follows:

Layout Manager	Description
FlowLayout	Places components in successive rows in a container, fitting as many on each row as possible, and starting on the next row as soon as a row is full. This works in much the same way as your text processor placing words on a line. Its primary use is for arranging buttons although you can use it with other components. It is the default layout manager for `JPanel` objects.
BorderLayout	Places components against any of the four borders of the container and in the center. The component in the center fills the available space. This layout manager is the default for the `contentPane` in a `JFrame`, `JDialog` or `JApplet` object.
CardLayout	Places components in a container one on top of the other – like a deck of cards. Only the 'top' component is visible at any one time.
GridLayout	Places components in the container in a rectangular grid with the number of rows and columns that you specify.
GridBagLayout	This also places the components into an arrangement of rows and columns but where the rows and columns can vary in length. This is a complicated layout manager with a lot of flexibility in how you control where components are placed in a container.
BoxLayout	This arranges components either in a row or in a column. In either case the components are clipped to fit if necessary, rather than wrapping to the next row or column. The `BoxLayout` manager is the default for the `Box` container class.

The `BoxLayout` and `Box` classes are defined in the `javax.swing` package. The other layout manager classes in the list above are defined in `java.awt`.

One question to ask is why do we need layout managers at all? Why don't we just place components at some given position in a container? The basic reason is to ensure that the GUI elements for your Java program are displayed properly in every possible Java environment. Layout managers automatically adjust components to fit the space available. If you fix the size and position of each of the components, they could run into one another and overlap if the screen area available to your program is reduced.

To set the layout manager of a container, you can call the `setLayout()` method for the container. For example, you could change the layout manager for the container object aWindow of type `JFrame` to flow layout with the statements:

```
FlowLayout flow = new FlowLayout();
aWindow.getContentPane().setLayout(flow);
```

Remember that we can't add components directly to a `JFrame` object – we must add them to the content pane for the window. The same goes for `JDialog` and `JApplet` objects.

With some containers you can set the layout manager in the constructor for that container, as we shall see in later examples. Let's look at how the layout managers work, and how to use them in practice.

The Flow Layout Manager

The flow layout manager places components in a row, and when the row is full, it automatically spills components onto the next row. The default positioning of the row of components is centered in the container. There are actually three possible row positioning options specified by constants defined in the class. This can be `FlowLayout.LEFT`, `FlowLayout.RIGHT` or `FlowLayout.CENTER` – this last option being the default.

The flow layout manager is very easy to use, so let's jump straight in and see it working in an example.

Try It Out – Using a Flow Layout Manager

As we said earlier, this layout manager is used primarily to arrange a few components whose relative position is unimportant. Let's implement a `TryFlowLayout` program based on the `TryWindow` example:

```
import javax.swing.*;
import java.awt.*;

public class TryFlowLayout
{
  // The window object
  static JFrame aWindow = new JFrame("This is a Flow Layout");

  public static void main(String[] args)
  {
    Toolkit theKit = aWindow.getToolkit();            // Get the window toolkit
    Dimension wndSize = theKit.getScreenSize();       // Get screen size
```

```
                 // Set the position to screen center & size to half screen size
                 aWindow.setBounds(wndSize.width/4, wndSize.height/4,    // Position
                                 wndSize.width/2, wndSize.height/2);   // Size
                 aWindow.setDefaultCloseOperation(JFrame.EXIT_ON_CLOSE);

                 FlowLayout flow = new FlowLayout();                // Create a layout manager
                 Container content = aWindow.getContentPane();      // Get the content pane
                 content.setLayout(flow);                           // Set the container layout mgr

                 // Now add six button components
                 for(int i = 1; i <= 6; i++)
                   content.add(new JButton("Press " + i));          // Add a Button to content pane

                 aWindow.setVisible(true);                          // Display the window
             }
         }
```

Since it is based on the TryWindow class, only the new code is highlighted. The new code is quite simple. We create a FlowLayout object and make this the layout manager for aWindow by calling setLayout(). We then add six JButton components of a default size to aWindow in the loop.

If you compile and run the program you should get a window similar to the following:

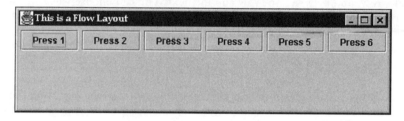

The Button objects are positioned by the layout manager flow. As you can see, they have been added to the first row in the window, and the row is centered. You can confirm that the row is centered and see how the layout manger automatically spills the components on to the next row once a row is full by reducing the size of the window.

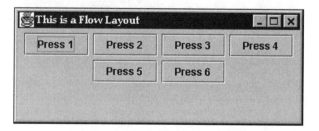

Here the second row is clearly centered. Each button component has been set to its preferred size which comfortably accommodates the text for the label. The centering is determined by the alignment constraint for the layout manager which defaults to CENTER.

It can also be set to RIGHT or LEFT by using a different constructor. For example, you could have created the layout manager with the statement:

```
FlowLayout flow = new FlowLayout(FlowLayout.LEFT);
```

The flow layout manager then left-aligns each row of components in the container. If you run the program with this definition and resize the window, it will look like:

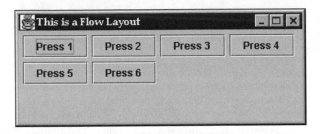

Now the buttons are left-aligned. Two of the buttons have spilled from the first row to the second because there is insufficient space across the width of the window to accommodate them all.

The flow layout manager in the previous examples applies a default gap of 5 pixels between components in a row, and between one row and the next. You can choose values for the horizontal and vertical gaps by using yet another FlowLayout constructor. You can set the horizontal gap to 20 pixels and the vertical gap to 30 pixels with the statement:

```
FlowLayout flow = new FlowLayout(FlowLayout.LEFT, 20, 30);
```

If you run the program with this definition of the layout manager, when you resize the window you will see the components distributed with the spacing specified. The window below has been resized to the same size as the previous window.

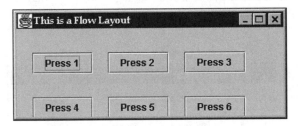

You can also set the gaps between components and rows explicitly by calling the setHgap() or the setVgap() method. To set the horizontal gap to 35 pixels, you would write:

```
flow.setHgap(35);                        // Set the horizontal gap
```

Don't be misled by this. You can't get differential spacing between components by setting the gap before adding each component to a container. The last values for the gaps between components that you set for a layout manager will apply to all the components in a container. The methods getHgap() and getVgap() will return the current setting for the horizontal or vertical gap as a value of type int.

As we've said, you add components to an applet created as a JApplet object in the same way as for a JFrame application window. We can verify this by adding some buttons to an example of an applet. We can try out a Font object and add a border to the buttons to brighten them up a bit at the same time.

Try It Out – Adding Buttons to an Applet

We can define the class for our applet as follows:

```java
import javax.swing.*;
import java.awt.*;
import javax.swing.border.*;                              // For the border classes

public class TryApplet extends JApplet
{
  public void init()
  {
    Container content = getContentPane();                 // Get content pane
    content.setLayout(new FlowLayout(FlowLayout.RIGHT));  // Set layout

    JButton button;                                       // Stores a button
    Font[] fonts = { new Font("Arial", Font.ITALIC, 10),  // Two fonts
                     new Font("Playbill", Font.PLAIN, 14)
                   };

    BevelBorder edge = new BevelBorder(BevelBorder.RAISED);  // Bevelled border

    // Add the buttons using alternate fonts
    for(int i = 1; i <= 6; i++)
    {
      content.add(button = new JButton("Press " + i));  // Add the button
      button.setFont(fonts[i%2]);                       // One of our own fonts
      button.setBorder(edge);                           // Set the button border
    }
  }
}
```

Of course, to run the applet we will need an .html file containing the following:

```
<APPLET CODE="TryApplet.class" WIDTH=300 HEIGHT=200>
</APPLET>
```

This specifies the width and height of the applet – you can use your own values here if you wish. You can save the file as TryApplet.html.

Once you have compiled the applet source code using javac, you can execute it with the appletviewer program by entering the following command under Windows:

```
C:\>appletviewer TryApplet.html
```

You should see the AppletViewer window displaying our applet.

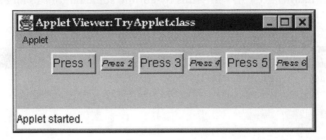

The arrangement of the buttons is now right justified in the flow layout. We have the button labels alternating between the two fonts that we created. The buttons also look more like buttons with a beveled edge.

How It Works

As we saw in Chapter 1, an applet is executed rather differently from a Java program and it is not really an independent program at all. The browser (or appletviewer in this case) initiates and controls the execution of the applet. An applet does not require a main() method. To execute the applet, the browser first creates an instance of our applet class, TryApplet, and then calls the init() method for it. This method is inherited from the Applet class (the base for JApplet) and you typically override this method to provide your own initialization.

We need the import statement for java.awt in addition to that for javax.swing because our code refers to the Font, Container and FlowLayout classes.

Before creating the buttons, we create a BevelBorder object that we will use to specify the border for each button. In the loop that adds the buttons to the content pane for the applet, we select one or other of the Font objects we have created depending on whether the loop index is even or odd, and then set edge as the border by calling the setBorder() member. This would be the same for any component. Note how the size of each button is automatically adjusted to accommodate the button label. Of course, the font selection depends on the two fonts being available on your system, so if you don't have the ones that appear in the code, change it to suit what you have.

The buttons look much better with raised edges. If you wanted them to appear sunken, you would specify BevelBorder.LOWERED as the constructor argument. You might like to try out a SoftBevelBorder too. All you need to do is use the class name, SoftBevelBorder, when creating the border.

Using a Border Layout Manager

The border layout manager is intended to place up to five components in a container. Possible positions for these components are on any of the four borders of the container and in the center. Only one component can be at each position. If you add a component at a position that is already occupied, the previous component will be displaced. A border is .selected by specifying a constraint that can be NORTH, SOUTH, EAST, WEST, or CENTER. These are all final static constants defined in the BorderLayout.class.

You can't specify the constraints in the `BorderLayout` constructor since a different constraint has to be applied to each component. You specify the position of each component in a container when you add it using the `add()` method. We can modify the earlier application example to add five buttons to the content pane of the application window in a border layout:

Try It Out – Testing the `BorderLayout` Manager

Make the following changes to `TryFlowLayout.java` to try out the border layout manager and exercise another border class:

```java
import javax.swing.*;
import java.awt.*;
import javax.swing.border.*;                     // For the border classes

public class TryBorderLayout
{
  // The window object
  static JFrame aWindow = new JFrame("This is a Border Layout");

  public static void main(String[] args)
  {
    Toolkit theKit = aWindow.getToolkit();        // Get the window toolkit
    Dimension wndSize = theKit.getScreenSize();   // Get screen size

    // Set the position to screen center & size to half screen size
    aWindow.setBounds(wndSize.width/4, wndSize.height/4,    // Position
                      wndSize.width/2, wndSize.height/2);   // Size
    aWindow.setDefaultCloseOperation(JFrame.EXIT_ON_CLOSE);

    BorderLayout border = new BorderLayout();          // Create a layout manager
    Container content = aWindow.getContentPane();      // Get the content pane
    content. setLayout(border);                        // Set the container layout mgr
    EtchedBorder edge = new EtchedBorder(EtchedBorder.RAISED);   // Button border

    // Now add five JButton components and set their borders
    JButton button;
    content.add(button = new JButton("EAST"), BorderLayout.EAST);
    button.setBorder(edge);
    content.add(button = new JButton("WEST"), BorderLayout.WEST);
    button.setBorder(edge);
    content.add(button = new JButton("NORTH"), BorderLayout.NORTH);
    button.setBorder(edge);
    content.add(button = new JButton("SOUTH"), BorderLayout.SOUTH);
    button.setBorder(edge);
    content.add(button = new JButton("CENTER"), BorderLayout.CENTER);
    button.setBorder(edge);

    aWindow.setVisible(true);                          // Display the window
  }
}
```

If you compile and execute the example, you will see the window shown below.

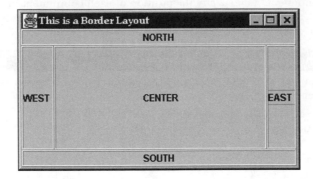

You can see here how a raised EtchedBorder edge to the buttons looks.

How It Works

Components laid out with a border layout manager are extended to fill the space available in the container. The "NORTH" and "SOUTH" buttons are the full width of the window and the "EAST" and "WEST" buttons occupy the height remaining unoccupied once the "NORTH" and "SOUTH" buttons are in place. It always works like this, regardless of the sequence in which you add the buttons – the "NORTH" and "SOUTH" components occupy the full width of the container and the "CENTER" component takes up the remaining space. If there are no "NORTH" and "SOUTH" components, the "EAST" and "WEST" components will extend to the full height of the container.

The width of the "EAST" and "WEST" buttons is determined by the space required to display the button labels. Similarly, the "NORTH" and "SOUTH" buttons are determined by the height of the characters in the labels.

You can alter the spacing between components by passing arguments to the BorderLayout constructor – the default gaps are zero. For example, you could set the horizontal gap to 20 pixels and the vertical gap to 30 pixels with the statement:

```
content.setLayout(new BorderLayout(20, 30));
```

Like the flow layout manager, you can also set the gaps individually by calling the methods setHgap() and setVgap() for the BorderLayout object. For example:

```
BorderLayout border = new BorderLayout();   // Construct the object
content.setLayout(border);                   // Set the layout
border.setHgap(20);                          // Set horizontal gap
```

This sets the horizontal gap between the components to 20 pixels and leaves the vertical gap at the default value of zero. You can also retrieve the current values for the gaps with the getHgap() and getVgap() methods.

Using a Card Layout Manager

The card layout manager generates a stack of components, one on top of the other. The first component that you add to the container will be at the top of the stack, and therefore visible, and the last one will be at the bottom. You can create a `CardLayout` object with the default constructor, `CardLayout()`, or you can specify horizontal and vertical gaps as arguments to the constructor. The gaps in this case are between the edge of the component and the boundary of the container. We can see how this works in an applet:

Try It Out – Dealing Components

Because of the way a card layout works, we need a way to interact with the applet to switch from one component to the next. We will implement this by enabling mouse events to be processed, but we won't explain the code that does this in detail here. We will leave that to the next chapter.

Try the following code:

```java
import javax.swing.*;
import java.awt.*;
import java.awt.event.*;                          // Classes to handle events

public class TryCardLayout extends JApplet
                           implements ActionListener // For event handling
{
  CardLayout card = new CardLayout(50,50);        // Create layout

  public void init()
  {
    Container content = getContentPane();
    content.setLayout(card);                       // Set card as the layout mgr
    JButton button;                                // Stores a button
    for(int i = 1; i <= 6; i++)
    {
      content.add(button = new JButton("Press " + i), "Card" + i);  // Add a
button
      button.addActionListener(this);              // Add listener for button
    }
  }

  // Handle button events
  public void actionPerformed(ActionEvent e)
  {
    card.next(getContentPane());                   // Switch to the next card
  }
}
```

If you run the program the applet should be as shown below. Click on the button—and the next button will be displayed.

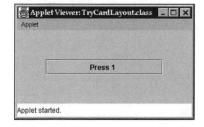

How It Works

The `CardLayout` object, `card`, is created with horizontal and vertical gaps of fifty pixels. In the `init()` method for our applet, we set `card` as the layout manager and add six buttons to the content pane. Note that we have two arguments to the `add()` method. Using card layout requires that you identify each component by some `Object`. In this case we pass a `String` object as the second argument to the `add()` method. We use an arbitrary string for each consisting of the string `"Card"` with the sequence number of the button appended to it.

Within the loop we call the `addActionListener()` method for each button to identify our applet object as the object that will handle events generated for the button (such as clicking on it with the mouse). When you click on a button, the `actionPerformed()` method for the applet object will be called. This just calls the `next()` method for the layout object to move the next component in sequence to the top. We will look at event handling in more detail in the next chapter.

The argument to the `next()` method identifies the container as the `TryCardLayout` object that is created when the applet starts. The `CardLayout` class has other methods that you can use for selecting from the stack of components:

Method	Description
void previous (Container parent)	Selects the previous component in the container, `parent`.
void first (Container parent)	Selects the first component in the container, `parent`.
void last (Container parent)	Selects the last component in the container, `parent`.
void show (Container parent, String name)	Selects the component in the container, `parent`, associated with the `String` object, name. This must be one of the `String` objects specified when you called the `add()` method to add components.

Using the `next()` or `previous()` methods you can cycle through the components repeatedly, since the next component after the last is the first, and the component before the first is the last.

The `String` object that we supplied when adding the buttons identifies each button and can be used to switch to any of them. For instance, you could switch to the button associated with `"Card4"` before the applet is displayed by adding the following statement after the loop that adds the buttons:

```
    card.show(content,"Card4");     // Switch to button "Card4"
```

This calls the `show()` method for the layout manager. The first argument is the container and the second argument is the object identifying the component to be at the top.

Using a Grid Layout Manager

A grid layout manager arranges components in a rectangular grid within the container. There are three constructors for creating `GridLayout` objects:

Constructor	Description
`GridLayout()`	Creates a grid layout manager that will arrange components in a single row (that is, a single column per component) with no gaps between components.
`GridLayout(int rows, int cols)`	Creates a grid layout manager that arranges components in a grid with `rows` number of rows and `cols` number of columns, and with no gaps between components.
`GridLayout(int rows, int cols, int hgap, int vgap)`	Creates a grid layout manager that arranges components in a grid with `rows` number of rows and `cols` number of columns, and with horizontal and vertical gaps between components of `hgap` and `vgap` pixels, respectively.

In the second and third constructors shown above, you can specify either the number of rows, or the number of columns as zero (but not both). If you specify the number of rows as zero, the layout manager will provide as many rows in the grid as are necessary to accommodate the number of components you add to the container. Similarly, setting the number of columns as zero indicates an arbitrary number of columns. If you fix both the rows and the columns, and add more components to the container than the grid will accommodate, the number of columns will be increased appropriately.

We can try a grid layout manager out in a variation of a previous application:

Try It Out – Gridlocking Buttons

Make the highlighted changes to `TryWindow.java`.

```
import javax.swing.*;
import java.awt.*;
import javax.swing.border.*;                 // For the border classes

public class TryGridLayout
{
  // The window object
  static JFrame aWindow = new JFrame("This is a Grid Layout");

  public static void main(String[] args)
  {
    Toolkit theKit = aWindow.getToolkit();            // Get the window toolkit
    Dimension wndSize = theKit.getScreenSize();       // Get screen size

    // Set the position to screen center & size to half screen size
    aWindow.setBounds(wndSize.width/4, wndSize.height/4,    // Position
                      wndSize.width/2, wndSize.height/2);   // Size
    aWindow.setDefaultCloseOperation(JFrame.EXIT_ON_CLOSE);
```

```
        GridLayout grid = new GridLayout(3,4,30,20);      // Create a layout manager
        Container content = aWindow.getContentPane();      // Get the content pane
        content. setLayout(grid);                          // Set the container layout
mgr

        EtchedBorder edge = new EtchedBorder(EtchedBorder.RAISED);   // Button border

        // Now add ten Button components
        JButton button;                                              // Stores a button
        for(int i = 1; i <= 10; i++)
        {
          content.add(button = new JButton("Press " + i));          // Add a Button
          button.setBorder(edge);                                   // Set the border
        }

        aWindow.setVisible(true);                                   // Display the window
    }
  }
```

We create a grid layout manager, `grid`, for three rows and four columns, and with horizontal and vertical gaps between components of 30 and 20 pixels respectively. With ten buttons in the container, the application window will be as shown below.

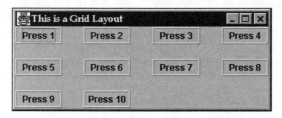

Using a BoxLayout Manager

The `BoxLayout` class defines a layout manager that arranges components in either a single row or a single column. You specify whether you want a row-wise or a columnar arrangement when creating the `BoxLayout` object. The `BoxLayout` constructor requires two arguments. The first is a reference to the container to which the layout manager applies, and the second is a constant value that can be either `BoxLayout.X_AXIS` for a row arrangement, or `BoxLayout.Y_AXIS` for a column.

Components are added from left to right in a row, or from top to bottom in a column. Components in the row or column do not spill onto the next row or column when the row is full. When this occurs, the layout manager will reduce the size of components or even clip them if necessary and keep them all in a single row or column. With a row of components, the box layout manager will try to make all the components the same height, and try to set a column of components to the same width.

The container class, `Box`, is particularly convenient when you need to use a box layout since it has a `BoxLayout` manager built in. It also has some added facilities providing more flexibility in the arrangement of components than other containers, such as `JPanel` objects, provide. The `Box` constructor accepts a single argument that specifies the orientation as either `BoxLayout.X_AXIS` or `BoxLayout.Y_AXIS`. The class also has two static methods, `createHorizontalBox()` and `createVerticalBox()`, that each return a reference to a `Box` container with the orientation implied.

As we said earlier a container can contain another container, so you can easily place a Box container inside another Box container to get any arrangement of rows and columns that you want. Let's try that out.

Try It Out – Boxes Containing Boxes

We will create an application that has a window containing a column of radio buttons on the left, a column of checkboxes on the right, and a row of buttons across the bottom. Here's the code:

```java
import javax.swing.*;
import java.awt.*;
import javax.swing.border.*;


public class TryBoxLayout
{
  // The window object
  static JFrame aWindow = new JFrame("This is a Box Layout");

  public static void main(String[] args)
  {
    Toolkit theKit = aWindow.getToolkit();        // Get the window toolkit
    Dimension wndSize = theKit.getScreenSize();   // Get screen size

    // Set the position to screen center & size to half screen size
    aWindow.setBounds(wndSize.width/4, wndSize.height/4,    // Position
                      wndSize.width/2, wndSize.height/2);   // Size
    aWindow.setDefaultCloseOperation(JFrame.EXIT_ON_CLOSE);


    // Create left column of radio buttons
    Box left = Box.createVerticalBox();
    ButtonGroup radioGroup = new ButtonGroup();              // Create button group
    JRadioButton rbutton;                                    // Stores a button
    radioGroup.add(rbutton = new JRadioButton("Red"));       // Add to group
    left.add(rbutton);                                       // Add to Box
    radioGroup.add(rbutton = new JRadioButton("Green"));
    left.add(rbutton);
    radioGroup.add(rbutton = new JRadioButton("Blue"));
    left.add(rbutton);
    radioGroup.add(rbutton = new JRadioButton("Yellow"));
    left.add(rbutton);


    // Create right columns of checkboxes
    Box right = Box.createVerticalBox();
    right.add(new JCheckBox("Dashed"));
    right.add(new JCheckBox("Thick"));
    right.add(new JCheckBox("Rounded"));


    // Create top row to hold left and right
    Box top = Box.createHorizontalBox();
    top.add(left);
    top.add(right);
```

```
       // Create bottom row of buttons
       JPanel bottomPanel = new JPanel();
       Border edge = BorderFactory.createRaisedBevelBorder();  // Button border
       JButton button;
       Dimension size = new Dimension(80,20);
       bottomPanel.add(button = new JButton("Defaults"));
       button.setBorder(edge);
       button.setPreferredSize(size);
       bottomPanel.add(button = new JButton("OK"));
       button.setBorder(edge);
       button.setPreferredSize(size);
       bottomPanel.add(button = new JButton("Cancel"));
       button.setBorder(edge);
       button.setPreferredSize(size);
```

```
       // Add top and bottom panel to content pane
       Container content = aWindow.getContentPane();        // Get content pane
       content.setLayout(new BorderLayout());               // Set border layout
   manager
       content.add(top, BorderLayout.CENTER);
       content.add(bottomPanel, BorderLayout.SOUTH);
```

```
       aWindow.setVisible(true);                            // Display the window
     }
   }
```

When you run this example and try out the radio buttons and checkboxes, it should produce a window something like that shown below.

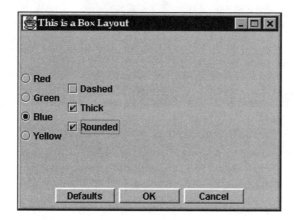

It's not an ideal arrangement, but we will improve on it.

How It Works

The shaded code is of interest – the rest we have seen before. The first block creates the left column of radio buttons providing a color choice. A `Box` object with a vertical orientation is used to contain the radio buttons. If you tried the radio buttons you will have found that only one of them can ever be selected. This is the effect of the `ButtonGroup` object that used – to ensure radio buttons operate properly, you must add them to a `ButtonGroup` object.

The `ButtonGroup` object ensures that only one of the radio buttons it contains can be selected at any one time. Note that a `ButtonGroup` object is not a component – it's just a logical grouping of radio buttons – so you can't add it to a container. We must still independently add the buttons to the `Box` container that manages their physical arrangement. The `Box` object for the right hand group of `JCheckBox` objects works in the same way as that for the radio buttons.

Both the `Box` objects holding the columns are added to another `Box` object that implements a horizontal arrangement to position them side by side. Note how the vertical `Box` objects adjust their width to match that of the largest component in the column. That's why the two columns are bunched towards the left side. We will see how to improve on this in a moment.

We use a `JPanel` object to hold the buttons. This has a flow layout manager by default, which suits us here. Calling the `setPreferredSize()` method for each button sets the preferred width and height to that specified by the `Dimension` object, `size`. This ensures that, space permitting, each button will be 80 pixels wide and 20 pixels high.

We have introduced another way of obtaining a border for a component here. The `BorderFactory` class (defined in the `javax.swing.border` package) contains static methods that return standard borders of various kinds. The `createBevelBorder()` method returns a reference to a `BevelBorder` object as type `Border` – `Border` being an interface that all border objects implement. We use this border for each of the buttons. We will try some more of the methods in the `BorderFactory` class later.

To improve the layout of the application window, we can make use of some additional facilities provided by a `Box` container.

Struts and Glue

The `Box` class contains static methods to create an invisible component called a **strut**. A vertical strut has a given height in pixels and zero width. A horizontal strut has a given width in pixels and zero height. The purpose of these struts is to enable you to insert space between your components, either vertically or horizontally. By placing a horizontal strut between two components in a horizontally arranged `Box` container, you fix the distance between the components. By adding a horizontal strut to a vertically arranged `Box` container, you can force a minimum width on the container. You can use a vertical strut in a horizontal box to force a minimum height.

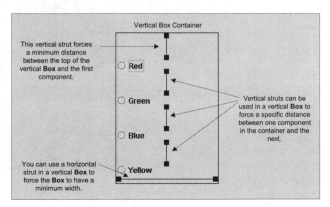

A vertical strut is returned as an object of type Component by the static createVerticalStrut() method in the Box class . The argument specifies the height of the strut in pixels. To create a horizontal strut, you use the createHorizontalStrut() method.

We can space out our radio buttons by inserting struts between them:

```
// Create left column of radio buttons
Box left = Box.createVerticalBox();
left.add(Box.createVerticalStrut(30));                    // Starting space
ButtonGroup radioGroup = new ButtonGroup();              // Create button group
JRadioButton rbutton;                                     // Stores a button
radioGroup.add(rbutton = new JRadioButton("Red"));       // Add to group
left.add(rbutton);                                        // Add to Box
left.add(Box.createVerticalStrut(30));                    // Space between
radioGroup.add(rbutton = new JRadioButton("Green"));
left.add(rbutton);
left.add(Box.createVerticalStrut(30));                    // Space between
radioGroup.add(rbutton = new JRadioButton("Blue"));
left.add(rbutton);
left.add(Box.createVerticalStrut(30));                    // Space between
radioGroup.add(rbutton = new JRadioButton("Yellow"));
left.add(rbutton);
```

The extra statements add a 30 pixel vertical strut at the start of the columns, and a further strut of the same size between each radio button and the next. We can do the same for the checkboxes:

```
// Create right columns of checkboxes
Box right = Box.createVerticalBox();
right.add(Box.createVerticalStrut(30));                   // Starting space
right.add(new JCheckBox("Dashed"));
right.add(Box.createVerticalStrut(30));                   // Space between
right.add(new JCheckBox("Thick"));
right.add(Box.createVerticalStrut(30));                   // Space between
right.add(new JCheckBox("Rounded"));
```

If you run the example with these changes the window will look like this.

It's better, but far from perfect. The distribution of surplus space is different in the two columns because the number of components is different. We can control where surplus space goes in a `Box` object with **glue**. Glue is an invisible component that has the sole function of taking up surplus space in a `Box` container. While the name gives the impression that it binds components together, it, in fact, provides an elastic connector between two components that can expand or contract as necessary, so it acts more like a spring. Glue components can be placed between the actual components in the `Box` and at either or both ends. Any surplus space that arises after the actual components have been accommodated is distributed between the glue components added. If you wanted all the surplus space to be at the beginning of a `Box` container, for instance, you should first add a single glue component in the container.

You create a component that represents glue by calling the `createGlue()` method for a `Box` object. You then add the glue component to the `Box` container in the same way as any other component wherever you want surplus space to be taken up. You can add glue at several positions in a row or column, and spare space will be distributed between the glue components. We can add glue after the last component in each column to make all the spare space appear at the end of each column of buttons. For the radio buttons we can add the statement,

```
            // Statements adding radio buttons to left Box object
            left.add(Box.createGlue());                    // Glue at the end
```

and similarly for the right box. The glue component at the end of each column of buttons will take up all the surplus space in each vertical `Box` container. This will make the buttons line up at the top. Running the program with added glue will result in the following application window.

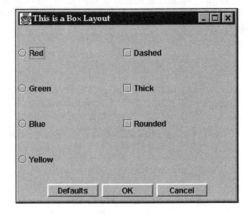

It's better now, but let's put together a final version of the example with some additional embroidery.

Try It Out – Embroidering Boxes

We will use some `JPanel` objects with a new kind of border to contain the vertical `Box` containers.

```
import javax.swing.*;
import java.awt.*;
import javax.swing.border.*;

public class TryBoxLayout
{
  // The window object
  static JFrame aWindow = new JFrame("This is a Box Layout");

  public static void main(String[] args)
  {
    // Set up the window as before...

    // Create left column of radio buttons with struts and glue as above...
    // Create a panel with a titled border to hold the left Box container
    JPanel leftPanel = new JPanel(new BorderLayout());
    leftPanel.setBorder(new TitledBorder(
                          new EtchedBorder(),      // Border to use
                          "Line Color"));          // Border title
    leftPanel.add(left, BorderLayout.CENTER);

    // Create right columns of checkboxes with struts and glue as above...
    // Create a panel with a titled border to hold the right Box container
    JPanel rightPanel = new JPanel(new BorderLayout());
    rightPanel.setBorder(new TitledBorder(
                          new EtchedBorder(),      // Border to use
                          "Line Properties"));     // Border title
    rightPanel.add(right, BorderLayout.CENTER);

    // Create top row to hold left and right
    Box top = Box.createHorizontalBox();
    top.add(leftPanel);
    top.add(Box.createHorizontalStrut(5));          // Space between vertical boxes
    top.add(rightPanel);

    // Create bottom row of buttons
    JPanel bottomPanel = new JPanel();
    bottomPanel.setBorder(new CompoundBorder(
          BorderFactory.createLineBorder(Color.black, 1),          // Outer border
          BorderFactory.createBevelBorder(BevelBorder.RAISED)));   // Inner border

    // Create and add the buttons as before...
```

```
        Container content = aWindow.getContentPane();  // Set the container layout mgr
        BoxLayout box = new BoxLayout(content, BoxLayout.Y_AXIS);
                                                    // Vertical for content pane
        content.setLayout(new BorderLayout());          // Set box layout manager
        content.add(top, BorderLayout.CENTER);
        content.add(bottomPanel, BorderLayout.SOUTH);

        aWindow.setVisible(true);                        // Display the window
    }
}
```

The example will now display the window shown below.

How It Works

Both vertical boxes are now contained in a JPanel container. Since JPanel objects are Swing components, we can add a border, and this time we add a TitledBorder border that we create directly using the constructor. A TitledBorder is a border specified by the first argument to the constructor, plus a title that is a String specified by the second argument to the constructor. We use a border of type EtchedBorder here, but you can use any type of border.

We introduce space between the two vertically aligned Box containers by adding a horizontal strut to the Box container that contains them. If you wanted space at each side of the window, you could add struts to the container before and after the components.

The last improvement is to the panel holding the buttons along the bottom of the window. We now have a border that is composed of two types, one inside the other: a LineBorder and a BevelBorder. A CompoundBorder object defines a border that is a composite of two border objects, the first argument to the constructor being the outer border and the second being the inner border. The LineBorder class defines a border consisting of a single line of the color specified by its first constructor argument and a thickness in pixels specified by the second. There is a static method defined for the class, createBlackLineBorder() that creates a black line border that is one pixel wide, so we could have used that here.

Using a GridBagLayout Manager

The `GridBagLayout` manager is much more flexible than the other layout managers and, consequently, rather more complicated to use. The basic mechanism arranges components in arbitrary rectangular grid, but the rows and columns of the grid are not necessarily the same height or width. A component is placed at a given cell position in the grid specified by the coordinates of the cell, where the cell at the top left corner is at position (0, 0). A component can occupy more than one cell in a row and/or column in the grid, but it always occupies a rectangular group of cells.

Each component in a `GridBagLayout` has its own set of constraints. These are defined by an object of type `GridBagConstraints` that you associate with each component, before adding the component to the container. The location of each component, its relative size and the area it occupies in the grid are all determined by its associated `GridBagConstraints` object.

A `GridBagConstraints` object has no less than eleven public instance variables that may be set to define the constraints for a component. Since they also interact with each other there's more entertainment here than with a Rubik's cube. Let's first get a rough idea of what these instance variables in a `GridBagConstraints` object do:

Instance Variable	Description
`gridx` and `gridy`	Determines the position of the component in the container as coordinate positions of cells in the grid, where (0, 0) is the top left position in the grid.
`gridwidth` and `gridheight`	Determines the size of the area occupied by the component in the container.
`weightx` and `weighty`	Determines how free space is distributed between components in the container.
`anchor`	Determines where a component is positioned within the area allocated to it in the container.
`ipadx` and `ipady`	Determines by how much the component size is to be increased above its minimum size.
`fill`	Determines how the component is to be enlarged to fill the space allocated to it.
`insets`	Specifies the free space that is to be provided around the component within the space allocated to it in the container.

That seems straightforward enough. We can now explore the possible values we can set for these and then try them out.

GridBagConstraints Instance Variables

A component will occupy at least one grid position, or **cell**, in a container that uses a `GridBagLayout` object, but it can occupy any rectangular array of cells. The total number of rows and columns, and thus the cell size, in the grid for a container is variable, and determined by the constraints for all of the components in the container. Each component will have a position in the grid plus an area it is allocated defined by a number of horizontal and vertical grid positions.

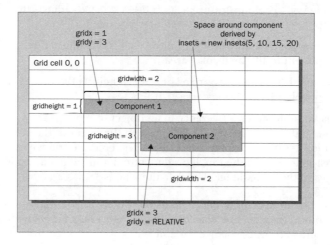

The top-left cell in a layout is at position (0, 0). You specify the position of a component by defining where the top-left cell that it occupies is, relative to either the grid origin, or relative to the previous component that was added to the container. You specify the position of the top-left cell that a component occupies in the grid by setting values of type `int` for the `gridx` and `gridy` members of the `GridBagConstraints` object. The default value for `gridx` is `GridBagConstraints.RELATIVE` – a constant that places the top-left grid position for the component in the column immediately to the right of the previous component. The same value is the default for `gridy`, which places the next component immediately below the previous one.

You specify the number of cells occupied by a component horizontally and vertically by setting values for the `gridwidth` and `gridheight` instance variables for the `GridBagConstraints` object. The default value for both of these is 1. There are two constants you can use as values for these variables. With a value of `GridBagConstraints.REMAINDER`, the component will be the last one in the row or column. If you specify the value as `GridBagConstraints.RELATIVE`, the component will be the penultimate one in the row or column.

If the preferred size of the component is less than the display area, you can control how the size of the component is adjusted to fit the display area by setting the `fill` and `insets` instance variables for the `GridBagConstraints` object.

Variable	Description
fill	The value for this variable is of type int, and it determines how the size of the component is adjusted in relation to the array of cells it occupies. The default value of GridBagConstraints.NONE means that the component is not resized.
	A value of GridBagConstraints.HORIZONTAL adjusts the width of the component to fill the display area.
	A value of GridBagConstraints.VERTICAL adjusts the height of the component to fill the display area.
	A value of GridBagConstraints.BOTH adjusts the height and the width to completely fill the display area.
insets	This variable stores a reference to an object of type Insets. An Insets object defines the space allowed between the edges of the components and boundaries of the display area it occupies. Four parameter values to the class constructor define the top, left side, bottom and right side padding from the edges of the component. The default value is Insets(0, 0, 0, 0).

If you don't intend to expand a component to fill its display area, you may still want to enlarge the component from its minimum size. You can adjust the dimensions of the component by setting the following GridBagConstraints instance variables:

Variable	Description
ipadx	An int value that defines the number of pixels by which the top and bottom edges of the component are to be expanded. The default value is 0.
ipady	An int value that defines the number of pixels by which the left and right edges of the component are to be expanded. The default value is 0.

If the component is still smaller than its display area in the container, you can specify where it should be placed in relation to its display area by setting a value for the anchor instance variable of the GridBagConstraints object. Possible values are NORTH, NORTHEAST, EAST, SOUTHEAST, SOUTH, SOUTHWEST, WEST, NORTHWEST and CENTER, all of which are defined in the GridBagConstraints class.

The last GridBagConstraints instance variables to consider are weightx and weighty which are of type double. These determine how space in the container is distributed between components in the horizontal and vertical directions. You should always set a value for these, otherwise the default of 0 will cause the components to be bunched together adjacent to one another in the center of the container. The absolute values for weightx and weighty are not important. It is the relative values that matter. If you set all the values the same (but not zero), the space for each component will be distributed uniformly. Space is distributed in the proportions defined by the values. For example, if three components in a row have weightx values of 1.0, 2.0, and 3.0, the first will get 1/6 of the total in the x direction, the second will get 1/3, and the third will get half. The proportion of the available space that a component gets in the x direction is the weightx value for the component divided by the sum of the weightx values in the row. This also applies to the weighty values for allocating space in the y direction.

We'll start with a simple example of placing two buttons in a window, and introduce another way of obtaining a standard border for a component.

Try It Out – Applying the `GridBagConstraints` Object

Make the following changes to the previous program and try out the `GridBagLayout` manager.

```java
import javax.swing.*;
import java.awt.*;
import javax.swing.border.*;

public class TryGridBagLayout
{
  // The window object
  static JFrame aWindow = new JFrame("This is a Gridbag Layout");

  public static void main(String[] args)
  {
    Toolkit theKit = aWindow.getToolkit();        // Get the window toolkit
    Dimension wndSize = theKit.getScreenSize();   // Get screen size

    // Set the position to screen center & size to half screen size
    aWindow.setBounds(wndSize.width/4, wndSize.height/4,   // Position
                      wndSize.width/2, wndSize.height/2);  // Size
    aWindow.setDefaultCloseOperation(JFrame.EXIT_ON_CLOSE);
    GridBagLayout gridbag = new GridBagLayout();       // Create a layout manager
    GridBagConstraints constraints = new GridBagConstraints();
    aWindow.getContentPane().setLayout(gridbag);       // Set the container layout mgr

    // Set constraints and add first button
    constraints.weightx = constraints.weighty = 10.0;
    constraints.fill = constraints.BOTH;               // Fill the space
    addButton("Press", constraints, gridbag);          // Add the button

    // Set constraints and add second button
    constraints.gridwidth = constraints.REMAINDER; // Rest of the row
    addButton("GO", constraints, gridbag);          // Create and add button

    aWindow.setVisible(true);                                // Display the window
  }

  static void addButton(String label,
                  GridBagConstraints constraints, GridBagLayout layout)
  {
    // Create a Border object using a BorderFactory method
    Border edge = BorderFactory.createRaisedBevelBorder();

    JButton button = new JButton(label);               // Create a button
    button.setBorder(edge);                            // Add its border
    layout.setConstraints(button, constraints);        // Set the constraints
    aWindow.getContentPane().add(button);              // Add button to content pane
  }
}
```

The program window will look like that shown below.

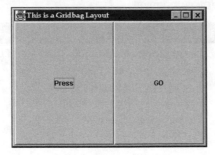

As you see, the left button is slightly wider than the right button. This is because the length of the button label affects the size of the button.

How It Works

Because the process will be the same for every button added, we have implemented the helper function addButton(). This creates a Button object, associates the GridBagConstraints object with it in the GridBagLayout object, and then adds it to the content pane of the frame window.

After creating the layout manager and GridBagConstraints objects we set the values for weightx and weighty to 10.0. A value of 1.0 would have the same effect. We set the fill constraint to BOTH to make the component fill the space it occupies. Note that when the setConstraints() method is called to associate the GridBagConstraints object with the button object, a copy of the constraints object is stored in the layout – not the object we created. This allows us to change the constraints object and use it for the second button without affecting the constraints for the first.

The buttons are more or less equal in size in the *x* direction (they would be exactly the same size if the labels were the same length) because the weightx and weighty values are the same for both. Both buttons fill the space available to them because the fill constraint is set to BOTH. If fill was set to HORIZONTAL, for example, the buttons would be the full width of the grid positions they occupy, but just high enough to accommodate the label, since they would have no preferred size in the *y* direction.

If we alter the constraints for the second button to:

```
// Set constraints and add second button
constraints.weightx = 5.0;                      // Weight half of first
constraints.insets = new Insets(10, 30, 10, 20); // Left 30 & right 20
constraints.gridwidth = constraints.RELATIVE;   // Rest of the row
addButton("GO", constraints, gridbag);          // Add button to content pane
```

the application window will be as shown.

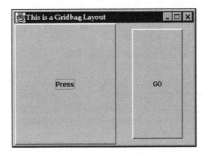

Now the second button occupies one third of the space in the *x* direction – that is a proportion of 5/(5+10) of the total – and the first button occupies two thirds. Note that the buttons still occupy one grid cell each – the default values for `gridwidth` and `gridheight` of 1 apply – but the `weightx` constraint values have altered the relative sizes of the cells for the two buttons in the *x* direction.

The second button is also inset within the space allocated – ten pixels at the top and bottom, thirty pixels on the left and twenty on the right (set with the `insets` constraint). You can see that for a given window size here, the size of a grid position depends on the number of objects. The more components there are, the less space they will each be allocated.

Suppose we wanted to add a third button, the same width as the **Press** button, and immediately below it. We could do that by adding the following code immediately after that for the second button:

```
// Set constraints and add third button
constraints.insets = new Insets(0,0,0,0);      // No insets
constraints.gridx - 0;                         // Begin new row
constraints.gridwidth = 1;                      // Width as "Press"
addButton("Push", constraints, gridbag);        // Add button to content pane
```

We reset the `gridx` constraint to zero to put the button at the start of the next row. It has a default `gridwidth` of 1 cell, like the others . The window would now look like:

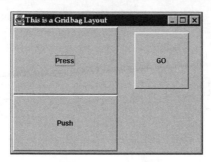

Having seen how it looks now, clearly it would be better if the **GO** button were the height of **Press** and **Push** combined. To arrange them like this, we need to make the height of the **GO** button twice that of the other two buttons. The height of the **Press** button is 1 by default, so by making the height of the **GO** button 2, and resetting the `gridheight` constraint of the **Push** button to 1, we should get the desired result. Modify the code for the second and third buttons to:

```
// Set constraints and add second button
constraints.weightx = 5.0;                         // Weight half of first
constraints.gridwidth = constraints.REMAINDER;     // Rest of the row
constraints.insets = new Insets(10, 30, 10, 20);   // Left 30 & right 20
constraints.gridheight = 2;                        // Height 2x "Press"
addButton("GO", constraints, gridbag);             // Add button to content pane

// Set constraints and add third button
constraints.gridx = 0;                             // Begin new row
constraints.gridwidth = 1;                         // Width as "Press"
constraints.gridheight = 1;                        // Height as "Press"
constraints.insets = new Insets(0, 0, 0, 0);       // No insets
addButton("Push", constraints, gridbag);           // Add button to content pane
```

569

With these code changes, the window will be:

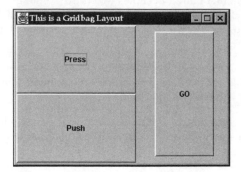

We could also see the effect of padding the components out from their preferred size by altering the button constraints a little:

```
// Create constraints and add first button
constraints.weightx = constraints.weighty = 10.0;
constraints.fill = constraints.NONE;
constraints.ipadx = 30;                           // Pad 30 in x
constraints.ipady = 10;                           // Pad 10 in y
addButton("Press", constraints, gridbag);         // Add button to content pane

// Set constraints and add second button
constraints.weightx = 5.0;                        // Weight half of first
constraints.fill = constraints.BOTH;              // Expand to fill space
constraints.ipadx = constraints.ipady = 0;        // No padding
constraints.gridwidth = constraints.REMAINDER;    // Rest of the row
constraints.gridheight = 2;                        // Height 2x "Press"
constraints.insets = new Insets(10, 30, 10, 20); // Left 30 & right 20
addButton("GO", constraints, gridbag);            // Add button to content pane

// Set constraints and add third button
constraints.gridx = 0;                            // Begin new row
constraints.fill = constraints.NONE;
constraints.ipadx = 30;                           // Pad component in x
constraints.ipady = 10;                           // Pad component in y
constraints.gridwidth = 1;                        // Width as "Press"
constraints.gridheight = 1;                        // Height as "Press"
constraints.insets = new Insets(0, 0, 0, 0);     // No insets
addButton("Push", constraints, gridbag);          // Add button to content pane
```

With the constraints for the buttons as above, the window will look like:

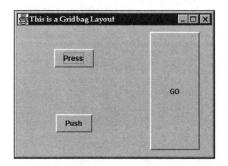

Both the Push and the Press button occupy the same space in the container, but, because fill is set to NONE, they are not expanded to fill the space in either direction. The ipadx and ipady constraints specify by how much the buttons are to be expanded from their preferred size – by thirty pixels on the left and right, and ten pixels on the top and bottom. The overall arrangement remains the same.

You need to experiment with using GridBagLayout and GridBagConstraints to get a good feel for how the layout manager works because you are likely to find yourself using it quite often.

Adding a Menu to a Window

As we have already discussed, a JMenuBar object represents the menu bar that is placed at the top of a window. You can add JMenu or JMenuItem objects to a JMenuBar object and these will be displayed on the menu bar. A JMenu object is a menu item with a label that can display a pull-down menu when clicked. A JMenuItem object represents a simple menu item with a label that results in some program action when clicked – such as opening a dialog. A JMenuItem can have an icon in addition to, or instead of, a String label. Each item on the pull-down menu for an object of either type JMenu, can be an object of either type JMenu, JMenuItem, JCheckBoxMenuItem or JRadioButtonMenuItem.

A JCheckBoxMenuItem is a simple menu item with a checkbox associated with it. The checkbox can be checked and unchecked and typically indicates that that menu item was selected last time the pull-down menu was displayed. You can also add separators in a pull-down menu. These are simply bars to separate one group of menu items from another. A JRadioButtonMenuItem is a menu item much like a radio button in that it is intended to be one of a group of like menu items added to a ButtonGroup object. Both JCheckBoxMenuItem and JRadioButtonMenuItem objects can have icons.

Creating JMenu and JMenuItem

To create a JMenu object you call a JMenu class constructor and pass a String object to it that contains the label for the menu. For example, to create a File menu you would write:

```
JMenu fileMenu = new JMenu("File");
```

Creating a JMenuItem object is much the same:

```
JMenuItem openMenu = new JMenuItem("Open");
```

If you create a JCheckboxMenuItem object by passing just a String argument to the constructor, the object will represent an item that is initially unchecked. For example, you could create an unchecked item with the following statement:

```
JCheckboxMenuItem circleItem = new JCheckboxMenuItem("Circle");
```

Another constructor for this class allows you to set the check mark by specifying a second argument of type `boolean`. For example:

```
JCheckboxMenuItem lineItem = new JCheckboxMenuItem("Line", true);
```

This creates an item with the label, `Line`, that will be checked initially. You can, of course, also use this constructor to explicitly specify that you want an item to be unchecked by setting the second argument to `false`.

A `JRadioButtonMenuItem` object is created in essentially the same way:

```
JRadioButtonMenuItem item =
          new JRadioButtonMenuItem("Curve", true);
```

This creates a radio button menu item that is selected.

If you want to use a menu bar in your application window, you must create your window as a `JFrame` object, since the `JFrame` class incorporates the capability to manage a menu bar. You can also add a menu bar to `JDialog` and `JApplet` objects. Let's see how we can create a menu on a menu bar.

Creating a Menu

To create a window with a menu bar, we will define our own window class as a sub-class of `JFrame`. This will be a much more convenient way to manage all the details of the window compared to using a `JFrame` object directly as we have been doing up to now. By extending the `JFrame` class, we can add our own members that will customize a `JFrame` window to our particular needs. We can also override the methods defined in the `JFrame` class to modify their behavior, if necessary.

We will be adding functionality to this example over several chapters, so create a directory for it with the name `Sketcher`. This program will be a window-based sketching program that will enable you to create sketches using lines, circles, curves and rectangles, and to annotate them with text. By building an example in this way, you will gradually create a much larger Java program than the examples seen so far, and you will also gain experience of combining many of the capabilities of `javax.swing` and other standard packages in a practical situation.

Try It Out – Building a Menu

To start with, we will have two class files in the Sketcher program. The file `Sketcher.java` will contain the method `main()` where execution of the application will start, and the file `SketchFrame.java` will contain the class defining the application window.

We will define a preliminary version of our window class as:

```
// Frame for the Sketcher application
import javax.swing.*;

public class SketchFrame extends JFrame
{
```

```
  // Constructor
  public SketchFrame(String title)
  {
    setTitle(title);                          // Set the window title
    setDefaultCloseOperation(EXIT_ON_CLOSE);

    setJMenuBar(menuBar);                     // Add the menu bar to the window

    JMenu fileMenu = new JMenu("File");       // Create File menu
    JMenu elementMenu = new JMenu("Elements"); // Create Elements menu

    menuBar.add(fileMenu);                    // Add the file menu
    menuBar.add(elementMenu);                 // Add the element menu
  }

  private JMenuBar menuBar = new JMenuBar();  // Window menu bar
}
```

After you have entered this code into a new file, save the file in the Sketcher directory as
SketchFrame.java.

Next, you can enter the code for the Sketcher class in a separate file:

```
// Sketching application
import java.awt.*;

public class Sketcher
{
  static SketchFrame window;                  // The application window

  public static void main(String[] args)
  {
    window = new SketchFrame("Sketcher");     // Create the app window
    Toolkit theKit = window.getToolkit();     // Get the window toolkit
    Dimension wndSize = theKit.getScreenSize(); // Get screen size

    // Set the position to screen center & size to half screen size
    window.setBounds(wndSize.width/4, wndSize.height/4,      // Position
                     wndSize.width/2, wndSize.height/2);     // Size

    window.setVisible(true);
  }
}
```

Save this file as `Sketcher.java` in the `Sketcher` directory. If you compile and run `Sketcher` you should see the window shown.

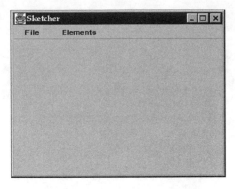

How It Works

The `Sketcher` class has a `SketchFrame` variable as a data member, which we will use to store the application window object. We must declare this variable as `static` as there will be no instances of the `Sketcher` class around. The variable, `window`, is initialized in the method `main()` that is called when program execution begins. Once the `window` object exists, we set the size of the window based on the screen size in pixels, which we obtain using the `Toolkit` object. This is exactly the same process that we saw earlier in this chapter. Finally in the method `main()`, we call the `setVisible()` method for the window object with the argument `true` to display the application window.

In the constructor for the `SketchFrame` class, we could pass the title for the window to the superclass constructor to create the window with the title bar directly. However, later when we have developed the application a bit more we will want to add to the title, so we call the `setTitle()` member to set the window title here. Next we call the `setJMenuBar()` method that is inherited from the `JFrame` class, to specify `menuBar` as the menu bar for the window. To define the two menus that are to appear on the menu bar, we create one `JMenu` object with the label `"File"` and another with the label `"Elements"` – these labels will be displayed on the menu bar. We add the `fileMenu` and `elementMenu` objects to the menu bar by calling the `add()` method for the `menuBar` object.

The instance variable that we have defined in the `SketchFrame` class represents the menu bar. Both the menu items on the menu bar are of type `JMenu`, so we need to add pull-down menus to each of them. The **File** menu will provide the file input, output and print options, and we will eventually use the **Elements** menu to choose the kind of geometric figure we want to draw. Developing the menu further, we can now add the menu items.

Adding Items to a Pull-Down Menu

Both the items on the menu bar need a pull-down menu – they can't do anything by themselves because they are of type `JMenu`. You use a version of the `add()` method defined in the `JMenu` class to add items to a pull-down menu.

The simplest version creates a menu item with the label that you pass as an argument. For example:

```
JMenuItem newMenu = fileMenu.add("New");          // Add the menu item "New"
```

This will create a JMenuItem object with the label "New", add it to the menu for the fileMenu item, and return a reference to it. You will need the reference to react to the user clicking the item.

You can also create the JMenuItem object explicitly and use the second version of the add() method to add it:

```
JMenuItem newMenu = new JMenuItem("New");        // Create the item
fileMenu.add(newMenu);                            // and add it to the menu
```

You can operate on menu items by using the following methods defined in the JMenuItem class:

Method	Description
void setEnabled(boolean b)	If b has the value true the menu item is enabled. If b has the value false the menu item is disabled. The default state is enabled.
void setText(String label)	Sets the menu item label to the string stored in label.
String getText()	Returns the current menu item label.

Since the JMenu class is a sub-class of JMenuItem, these methods also apply to JMenu objects.

To add a separator to a pull-down menu you call the addSeparator() method for the JMenu object.

Let's now create the pull down menus for the **File** and **Element** menus on the menu bar in the Sketcher application, and try out some of the menu items.

Try It Out – Adding Pull-Down Menus

We can change the definition of our SketchFrame class to do this:

```
// Frame for the Sketcher application
import javax.swing.*;

public class SketchFrame extends JFrame
{
  // Constructor
  public SketchFrame(String title)
  {
    setTitle(title);                             // Set the window title
    setDefaultCloseOperation(EXIT_ON_CLOSE);

    setJMenuBar(menuBar);                        // Add the menu bar to the window

    JMenu fileMenu = new JMenu("File");          // Create File menu
    JMenu elementMenu = new JMenu("Elements");   // Create Elements menu
```

```java
      // Construct the file pull down menu
      newItem = fileMenu.add("New");                 // Add New item
      openItem = fileMenu.add("Open");               // Add Open item
      closeItem = fileMenu.add("Close");             // Add Close item
      fileMenu.addSeparator();                       // Add separator
      saveItem = fileMenu.add("Save");               // Add Save item
      saveAsItem = fileMenu.add("Save As...");       // Add Save As item
      fileMenu.addSeparator();                       // Add separator
      printItem = fileMenu.add("Print");             // Add Print item

      // Construct the Element pull down menu
      elementMenu.add(lineItem = new JRadioButtonMenuItem("Line", true));
      elementMenu.add(rectangleItem = new JRadioButtonMenuItem("Rectangle", false));
      elementMenu.add(circleItem = new JRadioButtonMenuItem("Circle", false));
      elementMenu.add(curveItem = new JRadioButtonMenuItem("Curve", false));
      ButtonGroup types = new ButtonGroup();
      types.add(lineItem);
      types.add(rectangleItem);
      types.add(circleItem);
      types.add(curveItem);

      elementMenu.addSeparator();

      elementMenu.add(redItem = new JCheckBoxMenuItem("Red", false));
      elementMenu.add(yellowItem = new JCheckBoxMenuItem("Yellow", false));
      elementMenu.add(greenItem = new JCheckBoxMenuItem("Green", false));
      elementMenu.add(blueItem = new JCheckBoxMenuItem("Blue", true));

      menuBar.add(fileMenu);                         // Add the file menu
      menuBar.add(elementMenu);                      // Add the element menu
   }

   private JMenuBar menuBar = new JMenuBar();        // Window menu bar

   // File menu items
   private JMenuItem newItem,   openItem,    closeItem,
                     saveItem, saveAsItem, printItem;

   // Element menu items
   private JRadioButtonMenuItem lineItem,   rectangleItem, circleItem,  // Types
                                curveItem, textItem;
   private JCheckBoxMenuItem    redItem,    yellowItem,                 // Colors
                                greenItem, blueItem ;
   }
```

If you recompile Sketcher once more, you can run the application again to try out the menus. If you extend the File menu, you will see that it has the menu items that we have added.

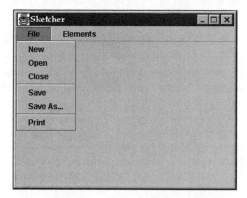

Now if you extend the Elements menu it should appear as shown with the Line and Blue items checked.

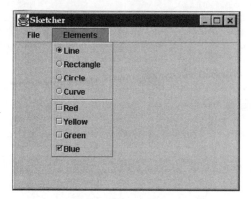

How It Works

We have defined the variables storing references to the menu items for the dropdown menus as private members of the class. For the File menu items they are of type JMenuItem. In the Element menu the items select a type of shape to be drawn, and, as these are clearly mutually exclusive, we are using type JRadioButtonMenuItem for them. We could use the same type for the element color items, but in order to try it out we are using the JCheckBoxMenuItem type.

To create the items in the File menu, we pass the String for the label for each to the add() method and leave it to the JMenu object to create the JMenuItem object.

The first group of Elements menu items are JRadioButtonMenuItem objects and we create each of these in the argument to the add() method. To ensure only one is checked at a time, we also add them to a ButtonGroup object. The color menu items are of type JCheckBoxMenuItem so the current selection is indicated by a check mark on the menu. We will make Line the default element type and Blue the default color, so we set both of these as checked by specifying true as the second argument to the constructor.

The other items will be unchecked initially because we have specified the second argument as `false`. We could have omitted the second argument to leave these items unchecked by default. It then means that you need to remember the default in order to determine what is happening. It is much better to set the checks explicitly.

You can see the effect of the `addSeparator()` method from the `JMenu` class. It produces the horizontal bar separating the items for element type from those for color. If you select any of the unchecked element type items on the **Elements** pull-down menu, they will be checked automatically and only one can appear checked. More than one of the color items can be checked at the moment, but we will add some code in the next chapter to make sure only one of these items is checked at any given time.

We could try putting the color selection item in an additional pull down menu. We could do this by changing the code which follows the statement adding the separator in the **Elements** menu as follows:

```
        elementMenu.addSeparator();
```

```
        JMenu colorMenu = new JMenu("Color");          // Color sub-menu
        elementMenu.add(colorMenu);                    // Add the sub-menu
        colorMenu.add(redItem = new JCheckBoxMenuItem("Red", false));
        colorMenu.add(yellowItem = new JCheckBoxMenuItem("Yellow", false));
        colorMenu.add(greenItem = new JCheckBoxMenuItem("Green", false));
        colorMenu.add(blueItem = new JCheckBoxMenuItem("Blue", true));
```

Now we add a `JMenu` object, `colorMenu`, to the pull-down menu for **Elements**. This has its own pull-down menu consisting of the color menu items. The **Color** item will be displayed on the **Elements** menu with an arrow to show a further pull-down menu is associated with it. If you run the application again and extend the pull-down menus, the window should be as shown.

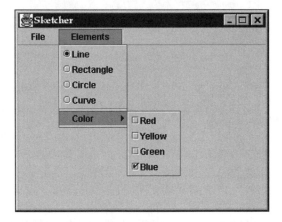

Whether you choose this menu structure or the previous one is a matter of taste. It might even be better to have a separate item on the menubar but we'll leave it at that for now. We will see in the next chapter that the programming necessary to deal with menu selections by the user is the same in either case.

Adding an Shortcut for a Menu Item

A **shortcut** is a unique key combination used to select a menu on the menu bar direct from the keyboard. A typical shortcut under Windows would be the *Alt* key plus a letter from the menu item label, so the shortcut for the File menu item might be *Alt+F*. When you enter this key combination the menu is displayed. We can add shortcuts for the File and Elements menu items by adding the following statements after we add the menu items to the menu bar:

```
fileMenu.setMnemonic('F');                        // Create shortcut
elementMenu.setMnemonic('E');                      // Create shortcut
```

The `setMnemonic()` method is inherited from the `AbstractButton` class, so all subclasses of this class inherit this method. The argument is a character in the `String` that is the label for the item that is to be the shortcut character – under Windows the File menu would then pop-up if you key *Alt+F*. The effect of `setMnemonic()` is to implement the shortcut and underline the shortcut character letter in the menu label.

An **accelerator** is a key combination that you can enter to select an item from a menu. Under Windows, the *Ctrl* key is frequently used in combination with a letter as an accelerator for a menu item, so *Ctrl+L* might be the combination for the Line item in the Elements menu. For menu items you call the `setAccelerator()` method to define an accelerator. For example, for the Line menu item you could write:

```
lineItem.setAccelerator(KeyStroke.getKeyStroke('L',Event.CTRL_MASK ));
```

The `KeyStroke` class defines a keystroke combination. The static method, `getKeyStroke()` returns the `KeyStroke` object corresponding to the arguments. The first argument is the character and the second argument specifies the modifier key. The `Event` class (in `java.awt`) defines `Event.SHIFT_MASK`, `Event.ALT_MASK`, and what we used here, `Event.CTRL_MASK`. If you want to combine the *Alt* and *Ctrl* keys for instance, you can add them – `Event.ALT_MASK + Event.CTRL_MASK`.

Let's see how this works in practice.

Try It Out – Adding Menu Shortcuts

We can add some shortcuts to Sketcher by amending the statements that add the items to the File menu in the `SketchFrame` class constructor:

```
// Frame for the Sketcher application
import javax.swing.*;
import java.awt.*;

public class SketchFrame extends JFrame
{
  // Constructor
  public SketchFrame(String title)
  {
    setTitle(title);                                // Call the base constructor
    setDefaultCloseOperation(EXIT_ON_CLOSE);
```

```
        setJMenuBar(menuBar);                           // Add the menu bar to the window

    JMenu fileMenu = new JMenu("File");                 // Create File menu
    JMenu elementMenu = new JMenu("Elements");          // Create Elements menu
    fileMenu.setMnemonic('F');                          // Create shortcut
    elementMenu.setMnemonic('E');                       // Create shortcut

    // Construct the file pull down menu as before...

    // Add File menu accelerators
    newItem.setAccelerator(KeyStroke.getKeyStroke('N',Event.CTRL_MASK ));
    openItem.setAccelerator(KeyStroke.getKeyStroke('O',Event.CTRL_MASK ));
    saveItem.setAccelerator(KeyStroke.getKeyStroke('S',Event.CTRL_MASK ));
    printItem.setAccelerator(KeyStroke.getKeyStroke('P',Event.CTRL_MASK ));

    // Construct the Element pull down menu as before...

    // Add element type accelerators
    lineItem.setAccelerator(KeyStroke.getKeyStroke('L',Event.CTRL_MASK ));
    rectangleItem.setAccelerator(KeyStroke.getKeyStroke('E',Event.CTRL_MASK ));
    circleItem.setAccelerator(KeyStroke.getKeyStroke('I',Event.CTRL_MASK ));
    curveItem.setAccelerator(KeyStroke.getKeyStroke('V',Event.CTRL_MASK ));

    elementMenu.addSeparator();

    // Create the color submenu as before...

    // Add element color accelerators
    redItem.setAccelerator(KeyStroke.getKeyStroke('R',Event.CTRL_MASK ));
    yellowItem.setAccelerator(KeyStroke.getKeyStroke('Y',Event.CTRL_MASK ));
    greenItem.setAccelerator(KeyStroke.getKeyStroke('G',Event.CTRL_MASK ));
    blueItem.setAccelerator(KeyStroke.getKeyStroke('B',Event.CTRL_MASK ));

    menuBar.add(fileMenu);                              // Add the file menu
    menuBar.add(elementMenu);                           // Add the element menu
  }

  // File menu items and the rest of the class as before...
}
```

If you save SketchFrame.java after you have made the changes, you can recompile Sketcher and run it again. The file menu will now appear as show below.

How It Works

We use the `setMnemonic()` method to set the shortcuts for the menu bar items and the `setAccelerator()` method to add accelerators to the submenu items. You must make sure that you do not use duplicate key combinations, and the more menu items you have accelerators for, the trickier this gets. The File menu here defines the standard Windows accelerators. You can see that the `setAccelerator()` method adds the shortcut key combination to the item label.

The menus don't actually work at the moment but at least they look good! We will start adding the code to implement menu operations in the next chapter.

More on Applets

Applets are a peculiar kind of program as they are only intended to be executed in the context of a web browser. This places some rather severe restrictions on what you can do in an applet, to protect the environment in which they execute. Without these restrictions they would be a very direct means for someone to interfere with your system – in short, a virus delivery vehicle.

System security in Java programs is managed by a **security manager.** This is simply an object that provides methods for setting and checking security controls that determine what is and what is not allowed for a Java program. What an applet can and cannot do is determined by both the security manager that the browser running the applet has installed, and the security policy that is in effect for the system.

Unless permitted explicitly by the security policy in effect, the main default limitations on an applet are:

❑   An applet cannot have any access to files on the local computer.

❑   An applet cannot invoke any other program on the local computer.

❑   An applet cannot communicate with any computer other than the computer from which the HTML page containing the applet was downloaded.

Obviously there will be circumstances where these restrictions are too stringent. In this case you can set up a security policy that allows certain operations for specific trusted programs, applets or sites, by authorizing them explicitly in a **policy file**. A policy file is an ASCII text file that defines what is permitted for a particular code source. We won't be going into details on this, but if you need to set up a policy file for your system, it is easiest to use the `policytool` program supplied with the JDK.

Because they are intended to be shipped over the Internet as part of an HTML page, applets should be compact. This doesn't mean that they are inevitably simple or unsophisticated. Because they can access the host computer from which they originated, they can provide a powerful means of enabling access to files on that host, but they are usually relatively small to allow them to be easily downloaded.

The JApplet class includes the following methods, which are all called automatically by the browser or appletviewer controlling the applet:

Method	Description
void init()	You implement this method to do any initialization that is necessary for the applet. This method is called once by the browser when the applet starts execution.
void start()	You implement this method to start the processing for the applet. For example, if your applet displays an animated image, you would start a thread for the animation in this method.
	This method is called by the browser immediately after init(). It is also called if the user returns to the current .html page after leaving it.
void stop()	This method is called by the browser when the user moves off the page containing the applet. You implement this to stop any operations that you started in the start() method.
void destroy()	This method is called after the stop() method when the browser is shut down. In this method you can release any resources your applet uses that are managed by the local operating system. This includes such things as resources used to display a window.

These are the basic methods you need to implement in the typical applet. We really need some graphics knowledge to go further with implementing an applet, so we will return to the practical application of these methods in Chapter 13.

Converting an Application to an Applet

Subject to the restrictions described in the previous section, you can convert an application to an applet relatively easily. You just need to be clear about how each part of program executes. You know that an application is normally started in the method main(). The method main() is not called for an applet but the method init() is, so one thing you should do is add an init() method to the application class. The other obvious difference is that an applet always extends the JApplet class.

We can demonstrate how to convert an application so that it also works as an applet, by changing the definition of the Sketcher class. This doesn't make a very sensible applet, but you can see the principles at work.

Try It Out – Running Sketcher as an Applet

You need to modify the contents of Sketcher.java so that it contains the following:

```
// Sketching application
import java.awt.*;
import javax.swing.*;
```

```
public class Sketcher extends JApplet
{
  public static void main(String[] args)
  {
    theApp = new Sketcher();              // Create the application object
    theApp.init();                        // ...and initialize it
  }

  public void init()
  {
    window = new SketchFrame("Sketcher");     // Create the app window
    Toolkit theKit = window.getToolkit();     // Get the window toolkit
    Dimension wndSize = theKit.getScreenSize(); // Get screen size

    // Set the position to screen center & size to half screen size
    window.setBounds(wndSize.width/4, wndSize.height/4,      // Position
                     wndSize.width/2, wndSize.height/2);      // Size

    window.setVisible(true);
  }

  private static SketchFrame window;          // The application window
  private static Sketcher theApp;             // The application object
}
```

To run Sketcher as an applet, you should add a .html file to the Sketcher directory with the contents:

```
<APPLET CODE="Sketcher.class" WIDTH=300 HEIGHT=200>
</APPLET>
```

If you recompile the revised version of the Sketcher class, you can run it as before, or using AppletViewer.

How It Works

The class now extends the class JApplet, and an import statement has been added for the javax.swing package.

The init() method now does most of what the method main() did before. The method main() now creates an instance of the Sketcher class and stores it in the static data member theApp. The method main() then calls the init() method for the new Sketcher object. The window variable no longer needs to be declared as static since it is always created in the init() method.

The class member, theApp, must be declared as static for the case when the program is run as an application. When an application starts execution, no Sketcher object exists, so the data member, theApp, does not exist either. If theApp is not declared as static, you can only create the Sketcher object as a local variable in main().

Even if Sketcher is running as an applet, the application window appears as a detached window from the AppletViewer window, and it is still positioned relative to the screen.

Of course, when we come to implement the File menu, it will no longer be legal to derive the Sketcher class from the JApplet class since it will contravene the rule that an applet must not access the files on the local machine. It is also not recommended to create frame windows from within an untrusted applet, so you will get a warning from the appletviewer about this.

All you need to do to revert back to just being an application is to remove the import statement for javax.swing and remove extends JApplet from the Sketcher class header line. Everything else can stay as it is.

Summary

In this chapter you have learnt how to create an application window, and how to use containers in the creation of the GUI for a program. We discussed the following important points:

❑ The package javax.swing provides classes for creating a graphical user interface (GUI).

❑ A component is an object that is used to form part of the GUI for a program. All components have the class Component as a super-class.

❑ A container is a component that can contain other components. A container object is created with a class that is a sub-class of Container. The classes JPanel, JApplet, JWindow, JFrame and JDialog are containers.

❑ The class JApplet is the base class for an applet. The JFrame class is a base class for an application window with a title bar, borders and a menu.

❑ The arrangement of components in a container is controlled by a layout manager.

❑ The default layout manager for the content pane of JFrame, JApplet and JDialog objects is BorderLayout.

❑ The GridBagLayout provides the most flexible control of the positioning of components in a container. The position of a component in a GridBagLayout is controlled by a GridBagConstraints object.

❑ A Box container can be used to arrange components or containers in rows and columns. You can use multiple nested Box containers in combination to create more complex arrangements quite easily, that otherwise might require GridBagLayout to be used.

❑ A menu bar is represented by a JMenuBar object. Menu items can be objects of type JMenu, JMenuItem, JCheckBoxMenuItem or JRadioButtonMenuItem.

❑ You associate a pull-down menu with an item of type JMenu.

❑ You can create a shortcut for a menu by calling its setMnemonic() method, and you can create an accelerator key combination for a menu item by calling its setAccelerator() method.

In the next chapter we will move on to look at events – that is, how we associate program actions with menu items and components within a window, and how to close a window when the close icon is clicked.

Exercises

1. Create an application, with a square window in the center of the screen which is half the height of the screen, by deriving your own window class from JFrame.

2. Add six buttons to the application in the previous example in a vertical column on the left side of the application window.

3. Add a menu bar containing the items File, Edit, Window and Help.

4. Add a pull-down menu for Edit containing the two groups of items of your own choice with a separator between them.

5. Add another item to the Edit pull-down menu which itself has a pull-down menu, and provide accelerators for the items in the menu.

Handling Events

In this chapter you will learn how a window-based Java application is structured, and how to respond to user actions in an application or an applet. This is the fundamental mechanism you will be using in virtually all of your graphical Java programs. Once you understand how user actions are handled in Java, you will be equipped to implement the application-specific code that is necessary to make your program do what you want.

In this chapter you will learn:

- ❏ What an event is.
- ❏ What an event-driven program is and how it is structured.
- ❏ How events are handled in Java.
- ❏ How events are categorized in Java.
- ❏ How components handle events.
- ❏ What an event listener is, and how you create one.
- ❏ What an adapter class is and how you can use it to make programming the handling of events easier.
- ❏ What actions are and how you use them.
- ❏ How to create a toolbar.

Window-based Java Programs

Before we get into the programming specifics of window-based programs, we need to understand a little of how such programs are structured, and how they work. There are fundamental differences between the console programs that we have been producing up to now, and a window-based Java program. With a console program, you start the program, and the program code determines the sequences of events. Generally everything is predetermined. You enter data when required and the program will output data when it wants. At any given time, the specific program code to be executed next is generally known.

A window-based application, or an applet come to that, is quite different. The operation of the program is driven by what you do with the GUI. Selecting menu items or buttons using the mouse, or through the keyboard, causes particular actions within the program. At any given moment you have a whole range of possible interactions available to you, each of which will result in a different program action. Until you do something, the specific program code that is to be executed next is not known.

Event-driven Programs

Your actions when you're using the GUI for a window-based program or an applet – clicking a menu item or a button, moving the mouse and so on – are first identified by the operating system. For each action, the operating system determines which of the programs currently running on your computer should know about it, and passes the action on to that program. When you click a mouse button, it's the operating system that registers this and notes the position of the mouse cursor on the screen. It then decides which application controls the window where the cursor was when you pressed the button, and communicates the mouse button-press to that program. The signals that a program receives from the operating system as a result of your actions are called **events**.

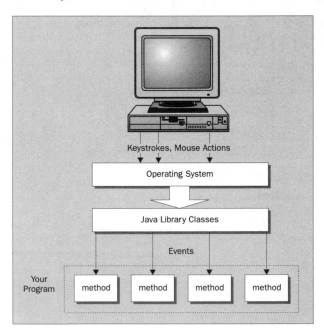

A program is not obliged to respond to any particular event. If you just move the mouse, for instance, the program need not include any code to react to that. If it doesn't, the event is quietly disposed of. Each event that the program does recognize is associated with one or more methods, and when the event occurs – when you click a menu item, for example – the appropriate methods will be called automatically. A window-based program is called an **event-driven program**, because the sequence of events created as a result of your interaction with the GUI drives and determines what happens in the program.

> **Events are not limited to window-based applications — they are a quite general concept. Most programs that control or monitor things are event-driven. Any occurrence external to a program such as a switch closing, or a preset temperature being reached, can be registered as an event. In Java you can even create events within your program to signal some other part of the code that something noteworthy has happened. However, we're going to concentrate of the kinds of events that occur when you interact as a user with a program.**

The Event-handling Process

To manage the user's interaction with the components that make up the GUI for a program, we must understand how events are handled in Java. To get an idea of how this works, let's consider a specific example. Don't worry too much about the class names and other details here. Just try to get a feel for how things connect together.

Suppose the user clicks a button in the GUI for your program. The button is the **source** of this event. The event generated as a result of the mouse click is associated with the JButton object in your program that represents the button on the screen. An event always has a source object – in this case the JButton object. When the button is clicked, it will create a new object that represents and identifies this event – in this case an object of type ActionEvent. This object will contain information about the event and its source. Any event that is passed to a Java program will be represented by a particular event object – and this object will be passed as an argument to the method that is to handle the event.

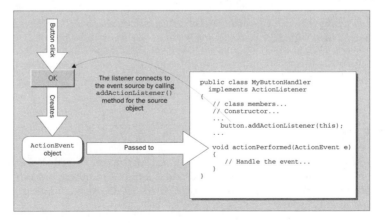

The event object corresponding to the button click will be passed to any **listener** object that has previously registered an interest in this kind of event – a listener object being simply an object that listens for particular events. A listener is also called a **target** for an event. Here, 'passing the event to the listener' just means the event source calling a particular method in the listener object and passing the event object to it as an argument. A listener object can listen for events for a particular object – just a single button for instance, or it can listen for events for several different objects – a group of menu items for example. Which approach you take depends on the context, and which is most convenient from a programming point of view. Your programs will often involve both.

So how do you define a listener? You can make the objects of any class listener objects by making the class implement a **listener interface**. There's quite a variety of listener interfaces, to cater for different kinds of events. In the case of our button click, the `ActionListener` interface needs to be implemented to receive the event from the button. The code that is to receive this event object and respond to the event is implemented in a method declared in the listener interface. In our example, the `actionPerformed()` method in the `ActionListener` interface is called when the event occurs, and the event object is passed as an argument. Each kind of listener interface defines particular methods for receiving the events that that listener has been designed to deal with.

Simply implementing a listener interface isn't sufficient to link the listener object to an event source. You still have to connect the listener to the source, or sources, of the events that you want it to deal with. You register a listener object with a source by calling a particular method in the source object. In this case, we call the `addActionListener()` method for the `JButton` object, and pass the listener object as an argument to the method.

This mechanism for handling events using listeners is very flexible, and very efficient, particularly for GUI events. Any number of listeners can receive a particular event. However, a particular event is only passed to the listeners that have registered to receive it, so only interested parties are involved in responding to each event. Since being a listener just requires a suitable interface to be implemented, you can receive and handle events virtually anywhere you like. The way in which events are handled in Java, using listener objects, is referred to as the **delegation event model**. This is because the responsibility for responding to events that originate with a component, such as a button or a menu item, is not handled by the objects that originated the events themselves – but is delegated to separate listener objects.

> *Not all event handling necessarily requires a separate listener. A component can handle its own events, as we shall see a little later in this chapter.*

Let's now get down to looking at the specifics of what kinds of events we can expect, and the range of listener interfaces that process them.

Event Classes

There are many different kinds of events to which your program may need to respond – from menus, from buttons, from the mouse, from the keyboard and a number of others. In order to have a structured approach to handling events, these are broken down into subsets. At the topmost level, there are two broad categories of events in Java:

❏ **Low-level Events** – these are events that arise from the keyboard or from the mouse, or events associated with operations on a window such as reducing it to an icon or closing it. The meaning of a low-level event is something like 'the mouse was moved', 'this window has been closed' or 'this key was pressed'

❏ **Semantic Events** – these are specific component-related events such as pressing a button by clicking it to cause some program action, or adjusting a scrollbar. They originate, and you interpret them, in the context of the GUI you have created for your program. The meaning of a semantic event is typically something like 'the OK button was pressed' or 'the Save menu item was selected'. Each kind of component, a button or a menu item for example, can generate a particular kind of semantic event.

These two categories can seem to be a bit confusing as they overlap in a way. If you click a button, you create a semantic event as well as a low level event. The click produces a low-level event object in the form of 'the mouse was clicked' as well as a semantic event 'the button was pushed'. In fact it produces more than one mouse event as we shall see. Whether your program handles the low-level events or the semantic event, or possibly both kinds of event, depends on what you want to do.

Most of the events relating to the GUI for a program are represented by classes defined in the package `java.awt.event`. This package also defines the listener interfaces for the various kinds of events that it defines. The package `javax.swing.event` defines classes for events that are specific to Swing components.

Low-level Event Classes

There are four kinds of low-level events that you can elect to handle in your programs. They are represented by the following classes in the `java.awt.event` package:

Event	Description
FocusEvent	Objects of this class represent events that originate when a component gains or loses focus. The focus of an application is the part that's currently active – it will usually be highlighted or have the cursor. Any component can create these events.
MouseEvent	Objects of this class represent events that result from user actions with the mouse such as moving the mouse or pressing a mouse button.
KeyEvent	Objects of this class represent events that arise from pressing keys on the keyboard.
WindowEvent	Objects of this class represent events that relate to a window, such as activating or deactivating a window, reducing a window to its icon or closing a window. These events relate to objects of the `Window` class or any subclass of `Window`.

Just so that you know, this isn't an exhaustive list of all of the low-level event classes. It's a list of the ones you need to know about. For example, there's the **PaintEvent** class which is concerned with the internals of how components get painted on the screen. There's also another low-level event class, **ContainerEvent**, which defines events relating to a container such as adding or removing components. You can ignore this class as these events are handled automatically.

Each of these classes define methods that enable you to analyze the event. For a MouseEvent object, for example, you can get the coordinates of the cursor when the event occurred. These low-level event classes also inherit methods from their superclasses, and are related in the manner shown in the diagram:

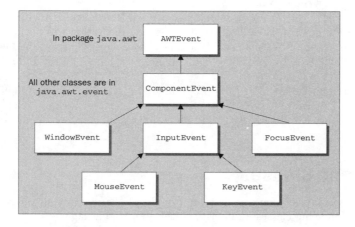

The class AWTEvent is itself a subclass of java.util.EventObject. The EventObject class implements the Serializable interface, so all objects of the event classes in the diagram are serializable. It also defines a method, getSource(), which returns the object that is the source of an event as type Object. This method is inherited by all the event classes shown.

The class AWTEvent defines constants, which are public final values identifying the various kinds of events. These constants are named consistently in the form of the event name in capital letters, followed by _MASK. The constants identifying the low-level events which we're interested in are:

MOUSE_EVENT_MASK	MOUSE_MOTION_EVENT_MASK
KEY_EVENT_MASK	FOCUS_EVENT_MASK
ITEM_EVENT_MASK	TEXT_EVENT_MASK
WINDOW_EVENT_MASK	ADJUSTMENT_EVENT_MASK

Each of these constants is a value of type `long` corresponding to a single bit being 1. They are defined this way so you can combine them when necessary by using a bitwise OR operator. There are two constants covering mouse events – these separate the mouse button events from those for mouse movement. As we'll see there are two listener interfaces for mouse events covering the two categories of events identified by MOUSE_EVENT_MASK and MOUSE_MOTION_EVENT_MASK, plus another listener that combines both.

> The list of event masks above is not exhaustive. There are masks for component events represented by objects of the class **ComponentEvent**, and for container events. These events occur when a component is moved or resized, or a component is added to a container, for example. There is also a mask for events associated with components that receive text input. You won't normally need to get involved in these events so we won't be discussing them further.

You use the identifiers for event masks to enable a particular group of events in a component object. You call the `enableEvents()` method for the component, and pass the variable for the events you want enabled as an argument. However, you *only* do this when you aren't using a listener. Registering a listener automatically enables the events that the listener wants to hear, so you don't need to call the `enableEvents()` method. The circumstance when you might do this is when you want an object to handle some of its own events although you can achieve the same result using a listener.

Making a Window Handle its own Events

Using listeners is the preferred way of handling events since it is easier than enabling events directly for an object and the code is clearer. Nonetheless, we should take a look at how you deal with events after calling `enableEvents()`. An example of where you might want to call `enableEvents()` exists in our `SketchFrame` class in the Sketcher program.

As you may recall from the previous chapter, we used the `setDefaultCloseOperation()` method to determine what happened when you close the window by clicking on the ❌ icon. Although the EXIT_ON_CLOSE argument value that we used disposed of the frame and closed the application, it didn't provide any opportunity to do any checking or clean-up before causing the program to exit. We can respond to the close icon being clicked in the program ourselves, rather than letting the `JFrame` facilities handle the associated event within the window object itself. This will eventually enable us to provide for prompting the user to save any data that has been created, and then shut down the application ourselves when a close event occurs, so let's give it a try.

Try It Out — Closing a Window

We need to modify the `SketchFrame` class definition from the previous chapter as follows:

```
// Frame for the Sketcher application
import javax.swing.*;
import java.awt.*;
import java.awt.event.*;

public class SketchFrame extends JFrame
{
```

```
    // Constructor
    public SketchFrame(String title)

    {
       setTitle(title);                              // Set the window title
       //  setDefaultCloseOperation(EXIT_ON_CLOSE);

       setJMenuBar(menuBar);                         // Add the menu bar to the
window

       JMenu fileMenu = new JMenu("File");          // Create File menu
       JMenu elementMenu = new JMenu("Elements");   // Create Elements menu
       fileMenu.setMnemonic('F');                   // Create shortcut
       elementMenu.setMnemonic('E');                // Create shortcut

       // Construct the file pull down menu
       newItem = fileMenu.add("New");               // Add New item
       openItem = fileMenu.add("Open");             // Add Open item
       closeItem = fileMenu.add("Close");           // Add Close item
       fileMenu.addSeparator();                     // Add separator
       saveItem = fileMenu.add("Save");             // Add Save item
       saveAsItem = fileMenu.add("Save As...");     // Add Save As item
       fileMenu.addSeparator();                     // Add separator
       printItem = fileMenu.add("Print");           // Add Print item

       // Add File menu accelerators
       newItem.setAccelerator(KeyStroke.getKeyStroke('N',Event.CTRL_MASK ));
       openItem.setAccelerator(KeyStroke.getKeyStroke('O',Event.CTRL_MASK ));
       saveItem.setAccelerator(KeyStroke.getKeyStroke('S',Event.CTRL_MASK ));
       printItem.setAccelerator(KeyStroke.getKeyStroke('P',Event.CTRL_MASK ));

       // Construct the Element pull down menu
       elementMenu.add(lineItem = new JRadioButtonMenuItem("Line", true));
       elementMenu.add(rectangleItem = new JRadioButtonMenuItem("Rectangle", false));
       elementMenu.add(circleItem = new JRadioButtonMenuItem("Circle", false));
       elementMenu.add(curveItem = new JRadioButtonMenuItem("Curve", false));
       ButtonGroup types = new ButtonGroup();
       types.add(lineItem);
       types.add(rectangleItem);
       types.add(circleItem);
       types.add(curveItem);

       // Add element type accelerators
       lineItem.setAccelerator(KeyStroke.getKeyStroke('L',Event.CTRL_MASK ));
       rectangleItem.setAccelerator(KeyStroke.getKeyStroke('e',Event.CTRL_MASK ));
       circleItem.setAccelerator(KeyStroke.getKeyStroke('l',Event.CTRL_MASK ));
       curveItem.setAccelerator(KeyStroke.getKeyStroke('v',Event.CTRL_MASK ));

       elementMenu.addSeparator();
```

```
JMenu colorMenu = new JMenu("Color");          // Color sub-menu
elemcntMenu.add(colorMenu);                    // Add the sub-menu
colorMenu.add(redItem = new JCheckBoxMenuItem("Red", false));
colorMenu.add(yellowItem = new JCheckBoxMenuItem("Yellow", false));
colorMenu.add(greenItem = new JCheckBoxMenuItem("Green", false));
colorMenu.add(blueItem = new JCheckBoxMenuItem("Blue", true));

// Add element color accelerators
redItem.setAccelerator(KeyStroke.getKeyStroke('R',Event.CTRL_MASK ));
yellowItem.setAccelerator(KeyStroke.getKeyStroke('Y',Event.CTRL_MASK ));
greenItem.setAccelerator(KeyStroke.getKeyStroke('G',Event.CTRL_MASK ));
blueItem.setAccelerator(KeyStroke.getKeyStroke('B',Event.CTRL_MASK ));


menuBar.add(fileMenu);                          // Add the file menu
menuBar.add(elementMenu);                       // Add the element menu
enableEvents(AWTEvent.WINDOW_EVENT_MASK);       // Enable window events
}

// Handle window events
protected void processWindowEvent(WindowEvent e)
{
  if (e.getID() == WindowEvent.WINDOW_CLOSING)
  {
    dispose();                      // Release resources
    System.exit(0);                 // Exit the program
  }
  super.processWindowEvent(e);      // Pass on the event
}

private JMenuBar menuBar = new JMenuBar();       // Window menu bar

// File menu items
private JMenuItem newItem,  openItem,   closeItem,
                  saveItem, saveAsItem, printItem;

// Element menu items
private JRadioButtonMenuItem lineItem,   rectangleItem, circleItem,  // Types
                            curveItem, textItem;
private JCheckBoxMenuItem    redItem,    yellowItem,                  // Colors
                            greenItem, blueItem ;
}
```

Note that we have commented out the statement that sets EXIT_ON_CLOSE as the close option for the window. You could delete the statement if you want. When you compile SketchFrame and run Sketcher, you'll be able to close the window as before, and the program will shut down gracefully. However, this time its our method that's doing it.

How It Works

The import statement makes the `java.awt.event` package and its various event classes available to the class file. We call `enableEvents()` in the constructor with `WINDOW_EVENT_MASK` as the argument to enable window events. This enables all the window events represented by the `WindowEvent` class. An object of this class can represent one of a number of different window events that are each identified by an **event ID**, which is a constant defined within the class. The event IDs for the `WindowEvent` class are:

Event ID	Description
WINDOW_OPENED	The event that occurs the first time a window is made visible.
WINDOW_CLOSING	The event that occurs as a result of the close icon being selected or **Close** being selected from the window's system menu.
WINDOW_CLOSED	The event that occurs when the window has been closed.
WINDOW_ACTIVATED	The event that occurs when the window is activated – obtains the focus in other words. When another GUI component has the focus, you could make the window obtain the focus by clicking on it for instance.
WINDOW_DEACTIVATED	The event that occurs when the window is deactivated – loses the focus in other words. Clicking on another window would cause this event, for example.
WINDOW_ICONIFIED	The event that occurs when the window is minimized and reduced to an icon.
WINDOW_DEICONIFIED	The event that occurs when the window is restored from an icon.

If any of these events occur, the `processWindowEvent()` method that we have added to the class will be called. Our version of the method overrides the base class method from `java.awt.Window` which is responsible for passing the event to any listeners that have been registered. The argument of type `WindowEvent` that is passed to the method will contain the event ID that identifies the particular event that occurred. To obtain the ID of the event, we call the `getID()` method for the event object e, and compare that with the ID identifying the `WINDOW_CLOSING` event. If the event is `WINDOW_CLOSING`, we call the `dispose()` method for the window to close the window and release the system resources it is using. We then call the `exit()` method defined in the class `System` to close the application.

> The `getID()` method is defined in the class `AWTEvent` which is a superclass of all the low-level event classes we have discussed, so all event objects of these types have this method.

In our `SketchFrame` class, the `dispose()` method is inherited originally from the `Window` class via the base class, `JFrame`. This method releases all the resources for the window object including those for all components owned by the object. Calling the `dispose()` method doesn't affect the window object itself in our program. It just tells the operating system that the resources used to display the window and the components it contains on the screen are no longer required. The window object is still around together with its components, so you could call its methods or even open it again.

> Note that we call the `processWindowEvent()` method in the superclass if it is not the closing event. This is very important as it allows the event to be passed on to any listeners that have been registered for these events. If we don't call `processWindowEvent()` for the superclass, any events that we do not handle will be lost, because the base class method is normally responsible for passing the event to the listeners that have been registered to receive it.

If we had not commented out the call to the `setDefaultCloseOperation()` method, our `processWindowEvent()` method would still have been called when the close icon was clicked. In this case we did not need to call `dispose()` and `exit()` ourselves. It would have been taken care of automatically after our `processWindowEvent()` method had finished executing. This would be preferable as means there would be less code in our program, and the code to handle the default close action is there in the `JFrame` class anyway.

Enabling Other Low-level Events

The `enableEvents()` method is inherited from the `Component` class. This means that any component can elect to handle its own events. You just call the `enableEvents()` method for the component and pass an argument defining the events you want the component to handle. If you want to enable more than one type of event for a component, you just combine the event masks from `AWTEvent` that we saw earlier by linking them with a bitwise OR. To make our window handle mouse events as well as window events, you could write:

```
enableEvents(AWTEvent.WINDOW_EVENT_MASK|AWTEvent.MOUSE_EVENT_MASK);
```

Of course, you must now also implement `processMouseEvent()` for the class. Like the `processWindowEvent()` method, this method is `protected` and has `void` as a return type. It passes the event as an argument of type `MouseEvent`. The set of other event-handling methods that you can override to handle component events are:

Event Handling Methods	Description
`processEvent(AWTEvent e)`	This method is called first for any events that are enabled for the component. If you implement this method, and fail to call the base class method, none of the methods for specific groups of events will be called.
`processFocusEvent( FocusEvent e)`	This method will be called for focus events, if they are enabled for the component.
`processKeyEvent(KeyEvent e)`	This method will be called for key events, if they are enabled for the component.
`processMouseEvent( MouseEvent e)`	This method will be called for mouse button events, if they are enabled for the component.
`processMouseMotionEvent( MouseEvent e)`	This method will be called for mouse move and drag events, if they are enabled for the component.

597

These are all `protected` methods that have a return type of `void`. The method `processWindowEvent()` is only available for objects of type `Window`, or for a `subclass of Window`, so don't try to enable window events on other components.

> Although it was very convenient to handle the window closing event in the **SketchFrame** class by implementing **processWindowEvent()**, as a general rule you should use listeners to handle events. Using listeners is the recommended approach to handling events in the majority of circumstances, since separating the event handling from the object that originated the event results in a simpler code structure that is easier to understand, and is less error prone. We will change this in the Sketcher code a little later in this chapter.

Low-level Event Listeners

To create a class that defines an event listener, your class must implement a listener interface. All event listener interfaces extend the interface `java.util.EventListener`. This interface doesn't declare any methods though – it's just used to identify an interface as being an event listener interface. It also allows a variable of type `EventListener` to be used for storing a reference to any kind of event listener object.

There are five low-level event listener interfaces corresponding to the five event masks that are of interest to us. These declare the following methods:

WindowListener

Defined Methods	Description
windowOpened(WindowEvent e)	Called the first time the window is opened.
windowClosing(WindowEvent e)	Called when the system menu Close item or the window close icon is selected.
windowClosed(WindowEvent e)	Called when the window has been closed.
windowActivated(WindowEvent e)	Called when the window is activated – by clicking on it, for example.
windowDeactivated(WindowEvent e)	Called when a window is deactivated – by clicking on another window, for example.
windowIconified(WindowEvent e)	Called when a window is minimized and reduced to an icon.
windowDeiconified(WindowEvent e)	Called when a window is restored from an icon.

MouseListener

Defined Methods	Description
mouseClicked(MouseEvent e)	Called when a mouse button is clicked on a component – that is, when the button is pressed and released.
mousePressed(MouseEvent e)	Called when a mouse button is pressed on a component.
mouseReleased(MouseEvent e)	Called when a mouse button is released on a component.
mouseEntered(MouseEvent e)	Called when the mouse enters the area occupied by a component.
mouseExited(MouseEvent e)	Called when the mouse exits the area occupied by a component.

MouseMotionListener

Defined Methods	Description
mouseMoved(MouseEvent e)	Called when the mouse is moved within a component.
mouseDragged(MouseEvent e)	Called when the mouse is moved within a component while a mouse button is held down.

KeyListener

Defined Methods	Description
keyTyped(KeyEvent e)	Called when a key on the keyboard is pressed then released.
keyPressed(KeyEvent e)	Called when a key on the keyboard is pressed.
keyReleased(KeyEvent e)	Called when a key on the keyboard is released.

FocusListener

Defined Methods	Description
focusGained(FocusEvent e)	Called when a component gains the keyboard focus.
focusLost(FocusEvent e)	Called when a component loses the keyboard focus.

There is a further listener interface, `MouseInputListener`, that is defined in the `javax.swing.event` package. This listener implements both the `MouseListener` and `MouseMotionListener` interfaces so it declares methods for all possible mouse events in a single interface.

There's a method declared in the `WindowListener` interface corresponding to each of the event IDs defined in the `WindowEvent` class that we saw earlier. If you deduced from this that the methods in the other listener interfaces correspond to event IDs for the other event classes, well, you're right. All the IDs for mouse events are defined in the `MouseEvent` class. These are:

MOUSE_CLICKED	MOUSE_PRESSED	MOUSE_DRAGGED
MOUSE_ENTERED	MOUSE_EXITED	MOUSE_RELEASED
MOUSE_MOVED		

The `MOUSE_MOVED` event corresponds to just moving the mouse. The `MOUSE_DRAGGED` event arises when you move the mouse while keeping a button pressed.

The event IDs defined in the `KeyEvent` class are:

KEY_TYPED	KEY_PRESSED	KEY_RELEASED

Those defined in the `FocusEvent` class are:

FOCUS_GAINED	FOCUS_LOST

To implement a listener for a particular event type you just need to implement the interface methods. We could handle the window events for our `SketchFrame` class by making the application class the listener for window events.

Try It Out — Implementing a Low-level Event Listener

First, delete the call to the `enableEvents()` method in the `SketchFrame()` constructor. Then delete the definition of the `processWindowEvent()` method from the class definition.

Now we can modify the `Sketcher` class so that it is a listener for window events:

```
// Sketching application
import java.awt.*;
import java.awt.event.*;

public class Sketcher implements WindowListener
{
  public static void main(String[] args)
  {
```

```
      theApp = new Sketcher();                 // Create the application object
      theApp.init();                           // ...and initialize it
    }

    // Initialization of the application
    public void init()
    {
      window = new SketchFrame("Sketcher");        // Create the app window
      Toolkit theKit = window.getToolkit();        // Get the window toolkit
      Dimension wndSize = theKit.getScreenSize();  // Get screen size

      // Set the position to screen center & size to 2/3 screen size
      window.setBounds(wndSize.width/6, wndSize.height/6,       // Position
                  2*wndSize.width/3, 2*wndSize.height/3);   // Size

      window.addWindowListener(this);              // theApp as window listener
      window.setVisible(true);                     // Display the window
    }

    // Handler for window closing event
    public void windowClosing(WindowEvent e)
    {
      window.dispose();                            // Release the window resources
      System.exit(0);                              // End the application
    }

    // Listener interface functions we must implement - but don't need
    public void windowOpened(WindowEvent e) {}
    public void windowClosed(WindowEvent e) {}
    public void windowIconified(WindowEvent e) {}
    public void windowDeiconified(WindowEvent e) {}
    public void windowActivated(WindowEvent e) {}
    public void windowDeactivated(WindowEvent e) {}

    private static SketchFrame window;           // The application window
    private static Sketcher theApp;              // The application object
  }
```

If you run the Sketcher program again, you will see it works just as before, but now the close operation is being handled by the Sketcher class object.

How It Works

The import statement for the package java.awt.event that we have added to the source file is essential here because we need access to the WindowListener interface. The Sketcher class implements the WindowListener interface, so an object of type Sketcher can handle window events. The method main() now creates a Sketcher object and calls the init() method that we have added to the class definition to initialize it. The init() method does what main() did in the previous version of Sketcher. It also calls the addWindowListener() method for the window object. The argument to addWindowListener() is the listener object that is to receive window events. Here it is the variable this – which references the application object. If we had other listener objects that we wanted to register to receive this event, we would just need to add more calls to the addWindowListener() method – one call for each listener.

To implement the `WindowListener` interface in the `Sketcher` class, we must implement all seven methods that are declared in the interface. Only the `windowClosing()` method has any code here – all the rest are empty because we don't need to use them. The `windowClosing()` method does the same as the `processWindowEvent()` method that we implemented for the previous version of the `SketchFrame` class, but here we don't need to check the object passed to it as this method is only called for a `WINDOW_CLOSING` event. We don't need to pass the event on either: this is only necessary when you handle events in the manner we discussed earlier. Here, if there were other listeners around for our window events they would automatically receive the event.

We have included the code that calls `dispose()` and `exit()` here, but if we have set the default close operation in `SketchFrame` to `EXIT_ON_CLOSE`, we could omit these too. We really only need to put our application clean-up code in the `windowClosing()` method, and this will just be prompting the user to save any application data. We will get to that eventually.

Having to implement six methods that we don't need is rather tedious. But we have a way to get around this though – by using what is called an **adapter class**, to define a listener.

Using Adapter Classes

An **adapter class** is a term for a class that implements a listener interface with methods that have no content, so they do nothing. The idea of this is to enable you to derive your own listener class from any of the adapter classes that are provided, and then implement just the methods that you are interested in. The other empty methods will be inherited from the adapter class so you don't have to worry about them. There's an adapter class for each of the low-level listener interfaces defined in the `java.awt.event` package, plus an adapter class that is defined in the `javax.swing.event` package that defines the methods for the `MouseInputListener` interface:

FocusAdapter	WindowAdapter	MouseMotionAdapter
MouseAdapter	KeyAdapter	MouseInputAdapter

They each implement all of the methods in the corresponding listener interface.

To handle the window closing event for the Sketcher application, we could derive our own class from the `WindowAdapter` class and just implement the `windowClosing()` method. If we also make it an inner class for the class `Sketcher`, it will automatically have access to the members of the `Sketcher` object regardless of their access specifiers.

Try It Out — Implementing an Adapter Class

The version of the `Sketcher` class to implement this will be as follows, with changes to the previous version highlighted:

```
// Sketching application
import java.awt.*;
import java.awt.event.*;

public class Sketcher
{
  public static void main(String[] args)
  {
```

```
      theApp = new Sketcher();                  // Create the application object
      theApp.init();                            // ...and initialize it
   }

   // Initialization of the application
   public void init()
   {
      window = new SketchFrame("Sketcher");
      Toolkit theKit = window.getToolkit();             // Get the window toolkit
      Dimension wndSize = theKit.getScreenSize();       // Get screen size

      // Set the position to screen center & size to 2/3 screen size
      window.setBounds(wndSize.width/6, wndSize.height/6,        // Position
                    2*wndSize.width/3, 2*wndSize.height/3);      // Size

      window.addWindowListener(new WindowHandler());  // Add window listener
      window.setVisible(true);                        // Display the window
   }

   // Handler class for window events
   class WindowHandler extends WindowAdapter
   {
      // Handler for window closing event
      public void windowClosing(WindowEvent e)
      {
         window.dispose();                      // Release the window resources
         System.exit(0);                        // End the application
      }
   }

   private static SketchFrame window;                  // The application window
   private static Sketcher theApp;                     // The application object
}
```

How It Works

As the `Sketcher` class is no longer the listener for `window`, it doesn't need to implement the `WindowListener` interface. The `WindowHandler` class is the listener class for window events. Because the `WindowHandler` class is an inner class to the `Sketcher` class, it has access to all the members of the class, so calling the `dispose()` method for the `window` object is still quite straightforward – we just access the `window` member of the top-level class. The `WindowAdapter` object that is the listener for the `window` object is created in the argument to the `addWindowListener()` method for `window`. We don't need an explicit variable to contain it. It will be stored in a data member of the `Window` class object. This data member is inherited from the `Window` superclass for our `SketchFrame` class.

> An easy mistake to make when you're using adapter classes is to misspell the name of the method that you are using to implement the event — typically by using the wrong case for a letter. In this case, you won't be overriding the adapter class method at all; you will be adding a new method. Your code will compile perfectly well but your program will not handle any events. They will all be passed to the method in the adapter class with the name your method should have had — which does nothing of course. This can be a bit mystifying until you realize where the problem is.

603

We haven't finished with low-level events yet by any means and we'll return to handling more low-level events in the next chapter when we begin to add drawing code to the Sketcher program. In the meantime, let's start looking at how we can manage semantic events.

Semantic Events

As we saw earlier, semantic events relate to operations on the components in the GUI for your program. If you select a menu item or click on a button for example, a semantic event is generated. There are three classes that represent the basic semantic events you will be dealing with most of the time, and they are derived from the AWTEvent class, as shown in the diagram.

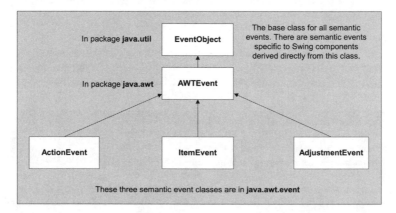

An ActionEvent is generated when you perform an action on a component such as clicking on a menu item or a button. An ItemEvent occurs when a component is selected or deselected and an AdjustmentEvent is produced when an adjustable object, such as a scrollbar, is adjusted.

Different kinds of components can produce different kinds of semantic event. The components that can originate these events are:

Event Type	Produced by Objects of Type
ActionEvent	Buttons: JButton, JToggleButton, JCheckBox
	Menus: JMenuItem, JMenu, JCheckBoxMenuItem, JRadioButtonMenuItem
	Text: JTextField
ItemEvent	Buttons: JButton, JToggleButton, JCheckBox
	Menus: JMenuItem, JMenu, JCheckBoxMenuItem, JRadioButtonMenuItem
AdjustmentEvent	JScrollbar

These three types of event are also generated by the old AWT components but we won't go into these here as we are concentrating on the Swing components. Of course, any class you derive from these component classes to define your own customized components can be the source of the event that the base class generates. If you define your own class for buttons, MyFancyButton say, your class will have JButton as a base class, inherit all of the methods from the JButton class, and objects of your class will originate events of type ActionEvent and ItemEvent.

There are quite a large number of semantic events that are specific to Swing components. Classes that have AbstractButton as a base, which includes menu items and buttons, can generate ChangeEvent events that signal some change in the state of a component. Components corresponding to the JMenuItem class and classes derived from JMenuItem can generate MenuDragMouseEvent and MenuKeyEvent events. An AncestorEvent is an event that is communicated to a child component from a parent component. We will look at the detail of some of these additional events when we need to handle them to apply the components in question.

As with low-level events, the most convenient way to handle semantic events is to use listeners, so we'll delve into the listener interfaces for semantic events next.

Semantic Event Listeners

We have a listener interface defined for each of the three semantic event types that we have introduced so far, and they each declare a single method:

Listener Interface	Method
ActionListener	void actionPerformed(ActionEvent e)
ItemListener	void itemStateChanged(ItemEvent e)
AdjustmentListener	void adjustmentValueChanged(AdjustmentEvent e)

Since each of these semantic event listener interfaces declares only one method, there is no need for corresponding adapter classes. The adapter classes for the low-level events were only there because of the number of methods involved in each listener interface. To define your semantic event listener objects, you just define a class that implements the appropriate listener interface. We can try that out by implementing a simple applet now, and then see how we can deal with semantic events in a more complicated context by adding to the Sketcher program later.

Semantic Event Handling in Applets

Event handling in an applet is exactly the same as in an application, but we ought to see it for ourselves. Let's see how we would handle events for buttons in an applet. We can create an applet that uses some buttons that have listeners. To make this example a bit more gripping, we'll throw in the possibility of monetary gain. That's interesting to almost everybody. Let's suppose we want to have an applet to create random numbers for a lottery. The requirement is to generate six different random numbers between 1 and 49. It would also be nice to be able to change a single number if you don't like it, so we'll add that capability as well. Since your local lottery may not be like this, we will implement the applet to make it easy for you to adapt the applet to fit your requirements.

By displaying the six selected numbers on buttons, we can provide for changing one of the choices by processing the action event for that button. Thus, clicking a button will provide another number. We'll also add a couple of control buttons, one to make a new selection for a complete set of lottery numbers, and another just for fun to change the button color. Here's how the applet will look when running under AppletViewer:

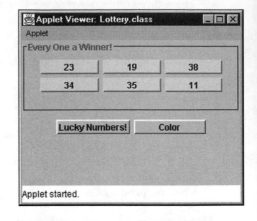

Try It Out — A Lottery Applet

We can outline the broad structure of the applet's code as follows:

```java
// Applet to generate lottery entries
import javax.swing.*;
import javax.swing.border.*;          // For component borders
import java.util.Random;              // For random number generator
import java.awt.*;
import java.awt.event.*;

public class Lottery extends JApplet
{
  // Initialize the applet
  public void init()
  {
    // Set up the lucky numbers buttons...

    // Set up the control buttons...
  }

  // Custom button showing lottery selection
  // Each button listens for its own events
  class Selection extends JButton
                  implements ActionListener
  {
    // Constructor
    public Selection(int value)
    {
      // Create the button showing the value...
    }

    // Handle selection button event
    public void actionPerformed(ActionEvent e)
    {
      // Change the current selection value to a new selection value
    }
```

```
       // Details of the rest of the selection class definition...
     }

     // Class defining a handler for a control button
     class HandleControlButton implements ActionListener
     {
       // Constructor...

       // Handle button click
       public void actionPerformed(ActionEvent e)
       {
          // Handle button click for a particular button...
       }

       // Rest of the inner class definition...
     }

     final static int numberCount = 6;                    // Number of lucky numbers
     final static int minValue = 1;                       // Minimum in range
     final static int maxValue = 49;                      // Maximum in range
     static int[] values = new int[maxValue-minValue+1];  // Array of possible values
     static                                               // Initialize array
     {
       for(int i = 0 ; i<values.length ; i++)
         values[i] = i + minValue;
     }

     // An array of custom buttons for the selected numbers
     private Selection[] luckyNumbers = new Selection[numberCount];

     private static Random choice = new Random();         // Random number generator
   }
```

How It Works

The applet class is called `Lottery` and it contains two inner classes, `Selection` and `HandleControlButton`. The `Selection` class provides a custom button that will show a number as its label, the number being passed to the constructor as an argument. We can make an object of the `Selection` class listen for its own action events. As we said at the outset, an event for a selection button will change the label of the button to a different value so of course we'll need to make sure this doesn't duplicate any of the values for the other buttons.

The two control buttons will use separate listeners to handle their action events and the response to an event will be quite different for each of them. One control button will create a new set of lucky numbers while the other control button will just change the color of the buttons.

The number of values that will be created is set by the `numberCount` member of the `Lottery` class, and the range of possible values is specified by the `minValue` and `maxValue` members. The possible values for selections are stored in the `values` array, and this is set up in the static initialization block. The `Lottery` class has an array of `Selection` objects as a data member – we can have arrays of components just like arrays of any other kind of object. Since the `Selection` buttons will all be the same, it's very convenient to create them as an array, and having an array of components will enable us to set them up in a loop. We also have a `Random` object as a member as we will need to generate some random integers.

We can now set about filling in the sections of the program that we roughed out previously.

Filling in the Details

To generate `maxCount` random values from the elements in the `values` array is quite independent of everything else here, so we'll define a static method in the `Lottery` class to do this.

```
public class Lottery extends JApplet
{
// Generate numberCount random selections from the values array
  static int[] getNumbers()
  {
    int[] numbers = new int[numberCount];     // Store for the numbers to be
returned
    int candidate = 0;                        // Stores a candidate selection
    for(int i = 0; i < numberCount; i++)      // Loop to find the selections
    {
      search:
      for(;;)                                 // Loop to find a new selection
      {                                       // different from any found so far
        candidate = values[choice.nextInt(values.length)];
        for(int j = 0 ; j<i ; j++)            // Check against existing selections
          if(candidate==numbers[j])           // If it is the same
            continue search;                  // get another random selection

        numbers[i] = candidate;               // Store the selection in numbers
array
        break;                                // and go to find the next
      }
    }
    return numbers;                           // Return the selections
  }

    // Plus the rest of the class definition...
}
```

The `getNumbers()` method returns a reference to an `int` array containing the selections – which must all be different, of course. We start the process by creating an array to hold the selections, and a variable, `candidate` to hold a potential selection from the `values` array. We generate a new selection for each iteration of the outer `for` loop. The process is quite simple. In the indefinite `for` loop with the label, `search`, we choose a random value from the `values` array using our random number generator, and then check its value against any selections already stored in the `numbers` array. If it is the same as any of them, the labeled `continue` will go to the next iteration of the indefinite `for` loop. This will continue until a selection if found that is different from the others. In this way we ensure that we end up with a set of selections that are all different.

Let's implement the `init()` method for the `Lottery` class next, as this sets up the `Selection` buttons and the rest of the applet.

Try It Out — Setting Up the Lucky Number Buttons

In the class outline we identified two tasks for the init() method. The first was setting up the lucky number buttons to be contained in the luckyNumbers array.

Here's the code to do that:

```
// Initialize the applet
public void init()
{
  // Set up the selection buttons
  Container content = getContentPane();
  content.setLayout(new GridLayout(0,1));  // Set the layout for the applet

  // Set up the panel to hold the lucky number buttons
  JPanel buttonPane = new JPanel();  // Add the pane containing numbers

  // Let's have a fancy panel border
  buttonPane.setBorder(BorderFactory.createTitledBorder(
                       BorderFactory.createEtchedBorder(Color.cyan,
                                                        Color.blue),
                                                        "Every One a Winner!"));

  int[] choices = getNumbers();            // Get initial set of numbers
  for(int i = 0; i<numberCount; i++)
  {
   luckyNumbers[i] = new Selection(choices[i]);
   buttonPane.add(luckyNumbers[i]);
  }
  content.add(buttonPane);

  // Set up the control buttons...
}
```

How It Works

The first step is to define the layout manager for the applet. To make the layout easier, we will use one panel to hold the selection buttons and another to hold the control buttons. We can position these panels one above the other by specifying the layout manager for the content pane of the applet as a grid layout with one column. The top panel will contain the lucky number buttons and the bottom panel will contain the control buttons.

The buttonPane panel that holds the lucky number buttons is of type JPanel, so it has a FlowLayout object as its layout manager by default. A flow layout manager allows components to assume their 'natural' or 'preferred size', so we will set the preferred size for the buttons in the Selection class constructor. We decorate the panel with a border by calling its setBorder() method. The argument is returned by the static createTitledBorder() method from the BorderFactory class. The first argument passed to createTitledBorder() is the border to be used, and the second is the title. We use an etched border that is returned by another static method in the BorderFactory class. The two arguments to this method are the highlight and shadow colors to be used for the border. A big advantage of using the BorderFactory methods rather than creating border objects from the border class constructors directly is that border objects will be shared where possible, so you can use a particular border in various places in your code and only one object will be created.

The buttons to display the chosen numbers will be of type `Selection`, and we will get to the detail of this inner class in a moment. We call our static method `getNumbers()` to obtain the first set of random values for the buttons. We then create and store each button in the `luckyNumbers` array and add it to the panel in the `for` loop. Since these buttons are going to listen for their own events, we don't need to worry about setting separate action listeners for them. The last step here is to add the `buttonPane` panel to the `content` pane for the applet.

We should now add the code for the control buttons to the `init()` method.

Try It Out — Setting up the Control Buttons

The listeners for each of the control buttons will be of the same class type, so the listener object will need some way to determine which button originated a particular event. One way to do this is to use constants as IDs to identify the control buttons, and pass the appropriate ID to the class constructor for the listener object. We could define the constants `PICK_LUCKY_NUMBERS` and `COLOR` as fields in the `Lottery` class for this purpose. The `COLOR` control button will also reference a couple of `Color` variables, `startColor` and `flipColor`. You can add the following statements to the `Lottery` class after the definition of the `luckyNumbers` array:

```
// An array of custom buttons for the selected numbers
private Selection[] luckyNumbers = new Selection[numberCount];
```

```
final public static int PICK_LUCKY_NUMBERS = 1;          // Select button
ID
final public static int COLOR = 2;                       // Color button ID

Color flipColor = new Color(
                  Color.yellow.getRGB()^Color.red.getRGB());  // swap colors

Color startColor = new Color(Color.yellow.getRGB());     // start color
```

The code to add the other panel and the control buttons is as follows:

```
// Initialize the applet
public void init()
{
    // Setting up the selections buttons as previously...

    // Add the pane containing control buttons
    JPanel controlPane = new JPanel(new FlowLayout(FlowLayout.CENTER, 5, 10));

    // Add the two control buttons
    JButton button;                                   // A button variable
    Dimension buttonSize = new Dimension(100,20);     // Button size

    controlPane.add(button = new JButton("Lucky Numbers!"));
    button.setBorder(BorderFactory.createRaisedBevelBorder());
    button.addActionListener(new HandleControlButton(PICK_LUCKY_NUMBERS));
    button.setPreferredSize(buttonSize);

    controlPane.add(button = new JButton("Color"));
```

```
      button.setBorder(BorderFactory.createRaisedBevelBorder());
      button.addActionListener(new HandleControlButton(COLOR));
      button.setPreferredSize(buttonSize);

      content.add(controlPane);
   }
```

How It Works

We create another `JPanel` object to hold the control buttons and just to show that we can, we pass a layout manager object to the constructor. It's a `FlowLayout` manager again, but this time we explicitly specify that the components are to be centered and the horizontal and vertical gaps are to be 5 and 10 pixels respectively.

We declare the `button` variable for use as a temporary store for the reference to each button while we set it up. We also define a `Dimension` object that we will use to set a common preferred size for the buttons. The buttons are `JButton` components, not custom components, so we must set each of them up here with a listener and a border. We add a raised bevel border to each button to make them look like buttons – again using a `BorderFactory` method. The listener for each button is an object of the inner class `HandleControlButton`, and we pass the appropriate button ID to the constructor for reasons which will be apparent when we define that class. To set the preferred size for each button object, we call its `setPreferredSize()` method. The argument is a `Dimension` object that specifies the width and height. Finally, after adding the two buttons to `controlPane`, we add that to the content pane for the applet.

The listener object for each control button is defined by the inner class `HandleControlButton`, so let's implement that next:

Try It Out — Defining the Control Button Handler Class

We have already determined that the class constructor will accept an argument that identifies the particular button for which it is listening. This is to enable the `actionPerformed()` method in the listener class to choose the course of action appropriate to the button. Here's the inner class definition to do that:

```
class HandleControlButton implements ActionListener
{
  private int buttonID;

  // Constructor
  public HandleControlButton(int buttonID)
  {
    this.buttonID = buttonID;                      // Store the button ID
  }

  // Handle button click
  public void actionPerformed(ActionEvent e)
  {
    switch(buttonID)
    {
      case PICK_LUCKY_NUMBERS:
```

```
            int[] numbers = getNumbers();            // Get maxCount random numbers
            for(int i = 0; i < numberCount; i++)
              luckyNumbers[i].setValue(numbers[i]);   // Set the button values
            break;
          case COLOR:
            Color color = new Color(
                    flipColor.getRGB()^luckyNumbers[0].getBackground().getRGB());
            for(int i = 0; i < numberCount; i++)
              luckyNumbers[i].setBackground(color);   // Set the button colors
            break;
        }
      }
    }
```

How It Works

The constructor stores its argument value in the data member, `buttonID`, so each listener object will have the ID for the button available. This is used in the `actionPerformed()` method to select the appropriate code to execute for a particular button. Each case in the `switch` statement corresponds to a different button. You could extend this to enable the class to handle as many different buttons as you want by adding case statements. Because of the way we have implemented the method, each button must have a unique ID associated with it. Of course, this isn't the only way to do this as we'll see in a moment.

For the `PICK_LUCKY_NUMBERS` button, we just call the `getNumbers()` method to produce a set of numbers, and then call the `setValue()` method for each selection button and pass a number to it. We will implement the `setValue()` method when we define the selection class in detail, in a moment.

For the `COLOR` button, we create a new color by exclusive ORing (i.e. XOR) the `RGB` value of `flipColor` with the current button color. You will recall from our discussion of the ^ operator (in Chapter 2) that you can use it to exchange two values, and that is what we are doing here. `flipColor` was defined as the two colors, `Color.yellow` and `Color.red`, exclusive ORed together. Exclusive ORing this with either color will produce the other so we flip from one color to the other automatically for each button by exclusive ORing the background and `flipColor`. We must get the RGB value for each color and operate on those – you can't apply the ^ operator to the objects. We then turn the resulting RGB value back into a `Color` object.

Let's now add the inner class, `Selection`, that defines the lucky number buttons.

Try It Out — Defining the Selection Buttons

Each button will need to store the value shown on the label, so the class will need a data member for this purpose. The class will also need a constructor, the `setValue()` method to set the value for the button to a new value and a method to compare the current value for a button to a given value. We need to be able to set the value for a button for two reasons – we call it when we set up all six selections in the listener for the control button, and we want to reset the value for a button to change it individually.

The method to compare the value set for a button to a given integer will enable us to exclude a number that was already assigned to a button in the process of generating the button values. We'll also need to implement the `actionPerformed()` method to handle the action events for the button, as the buttons are going to handle their own events. Here's the basic code for the class definition:

```java
class Selection extends JButton
                implements ActionListener
{
  // Constructor
  public Selection(int value)
  {
    super(Integer.toString(value));    // Call base constructor and set the
label
    this.value = value;                // Save the value
    setBackground(startColor);
    setBorder(BorderFactory.createRaisedBevelBorder());    // Add button border
    setPreferredSize(new Dimension(80,20));
    addActionListener(this);           // Button listens for itself
  }


  // Handle selection button event
  public void actionPerformed(ActionEvent e)
  {
    // Change this selection to a new selection
    int candidate = 0;
    for(;;)                                    // Loop to find a different selection
    {
      candidate = values[choice.nextInt(values.length)];
      if(isCurrentSelection(candidate))        // If it is not different
        continue;                              // find another
      setValue(candidate);                     // We have one so set the button
value
      return;
    }
  }
  // Set the value for the selection
  public void setValue(int value)
  {
    setText(Integer.toString(value));    // Set value as the button label
    this.value = value;                  // Save the value
  }


  // Check the value for the selection
  boolean hasValue(int possible)
  {
    return value==possible;              // Return true if equals current value
  }


  // Check the current choices
  boolean isCurrentSelection(int possible)
  {
    for(int i = 0; i < numberCount; i++)       // For each button
      if(luckyNumbers[i].hasValue(possible))   // check against possible
        return true;                           // Return true for any =
    return false;                              // Otherwise return false
  }

  private int value;                           // Value for the selection button
}
```

How It Works

The constructor calls the base class constructor to set the initial label for the button. It also stores the value of type `int` that is passed as an argument. The `setValue()` method just updates the value for a selection button with the value passed as an argument and changes the button label by calling the `setText()` method which is inherited from the base class, `JButton`. The `hasValue()` method returns `true` if the argument value passed to it is equal to the current value stored in the data member `value`, and `false` otherwise.

The `actionPerformed()` method has a little more meat to it but the technique is similar to that in the `getNumbers()` method. To change the selection to a new selection, we must create a new random value for the button from the numbers `values` array, but excluding all the numbers currently assigned to the six buttons. To do this we just check each candidate against the six existing selections by calling the `isCurrentSelection()`, and continue choosing a new candidate until we find one that's different.

In the `isCurrentSelection()` method, we just work through the array of `Selection` objects, `luckyNumbers`, comparing each value with the `possible` argument using the `hasValue()` method. If any button has the same value as `possible`, the method returns `true`, otherwise it returns `false`.

We're ready to start generating lottery entries. If you compile the `Lottery.java` file you can run the applet using `AppletViewer`. You will need an HTML file of course. The following contents for the file will do the job:

```
<APPLET CODE="Lottery.class" WIDTH=300 HEIGHT=200>
</APPLET>
```

You can adjust the width and height values to suit your monitor resolution if necessary.

The applet should produce a selection each time you click the left control button. Clicking on any of the selection buttons will generate an action event that will cause a new value to be created for the button. This enables you to replace any selection that you know to be unlucky with an alternative.

> *Undoubtedly, anyone who profits from using this applet will have immense feelings of gratitude and indebtedness towards the author, who will not be offended in the slightest by any offers of a portion of that success, however large!*

Alternative Event Handling Approaches

As we indicated in the discussion, there are various approaches to implementing listeners. Let's look at a couple of other ways in which we could have dealt with the control button events.

Instead of passing a constant to the listener class constructor to identify which button was selected, we could have used the fact that the event object has a method, `getSource()`, that returns a reference to the object that is the source of the event. To make use of this, a reference to both button objects would need to be available to the `actionPerformed()` method. We could easily arrange for this to be the case by adding a couple of fields to the `Lottery` class:

```
JButton pickButton = new JButton("Lucky Numbers!");
JButton colorButton = new JButton("Color");
```

The inner class could then be defined as:

```
class HandleControlButton implements ActionListener
{
  // Handle button click
  public void actionPerformed(ActionEvent e)
  {
    Object source = e.getSource();                    // Get source object reference

    if(source == pickButton)                          // Is it the pick button?
    {
      int[] numbers = getNumbers();                   // Get maxCount random numbers
      for(int i = 0; i < numberCount; i++)
        luckyNumbers[i].setValue(numbers[i]);         // Set the button values
    }
    else if(source == colorButton)                    // Is it the color button?
    {
      Color color = new Color(
                    flipColor.getRGB()^luckyNumbers[0].getBackground().getRGB());
      for(int i = 0; i < numberCount; i++)
        luckyNumbers[i].setBackground(color);         // Set the button colors
    }
  }
}
```

We no longer need to define a constructor as the default will do. The `actionPerformed()` method now decides what to do by comparing the reference returned by the `getSource()` method for the event object with the two button references. With the previous version of the listener class, we stored the ID as a data member, so a separate listener object was needed for each button. In this case there are no data members in the listener class, so we can use one listener object for both buttons.

The code to add these buttons in the `init()` method would then be:

```
// Add the two control buttons
Dimension buttonSize = new Dimension(100,20);
pickButton.setPreferredSize(buttonSize);
pickButton.setBorder(BorderFactory.createRaisedBevelBorder());

colorButton.setPreferredSize(buttonSize);
colorButton.setBorder(BorderFactory.createRaisedBevelBorder());

HandleControlButton controlHandler = new HandleControlButton();
pickButton.addActionListener(controlHandler);
colorButton.addActionListener(controlHandler);

controlPane.add(pickButton);
controlPane.add(colorButton);
content.add(controlPane);
```

The only fundamental difference here is that we use one listener object for both buttons.

There is another possible way to implement listeners for these buttons. We could define a separate class for each listener – this would not be unreasonable as the actions to be performed in response to the semantic events for each button are quite different. We could use anonymous classes in this case – as we discussed back in Chapter 6. We could do this by adding the listeners for the button objects in the `init()` method like this:

```
// Add the two control buttons
Dimension buttonSize = new Dimension(100,20);
pickButton.setPreferredSize(buttonSize);
pickButton.setBorder(BorderFactory.createRaisedBevelBorder());

colorButton.setPreferredSize(buttonSize);
colorButton.setBorder(BorderFactory.createRaisedBevelBorder());

pickButton.addActionListener(new ActionListener()
                            {
                              public void actionPerformed(ActionEvent e)
                              {
                                int[] numbers = getNumbers();
                                for(int i = 0; i < numberCount; i++)
                                  luckyNumbers[i].setValue(numbers[i]);
                              }
                            });
colorButton.addActionListener(new ActionListener()
                            {
                              public void actionPerformed(ActionEvent e)
                              {
                                Color color = new Color(
flipColor.getRGB()^luckyNumbers[0].getBackground().getRGB());
                                for(int i = 0; i < numberCount; i++)
                                  luckyNumbers[i].setBackground(color);
                              }
                            });

controlPane.add(pickButton);
controlPane.add(colorButton);
content.add(controlPane);
```

Now the two listeners are defined by anonymous classes, and the implementation of the `actionPerformed()` method in each just takes care of the particular button for which it is listening. This is a very common technique when the action to be performed in response to an event is simple.

Handling Low-level and Semantic Events

We said earlier in this chapter that a component generates both low-level and semantic events, and you could handle both if you want. We can demonstrate this quite easily with a small extension to the Lottery applet. Suppose we want to change the cursor to a hand cursor when it is over one of the selection buttons. This would be a good cue that you can select these buttons individually. We can do this by adding a mouse listener for each button.

Try It Out — A Mouse Listener for the Selection Buttons

There are many ways in which you could define the listener class. We'll define it as a separate class, called `MouseHandler`. Here's the class definition:

```
// Mouse event handler for a selection button

class MouseHandler extends MouseAdapter
{
  Cursor handCursor = new Cursor(Cursor.HAND_CURSOR);
  Cursor defaultCursor = new Cursor(Cursor.DEFAULT_CURSOR);

  // Handle mouse entering the selection button
  public void mouseEntered(MouseEvent e)
  {
    e.getComponent().setCursor(handCursor);     // Switch to hand cursor
  }

  // Handle mouse exiting the selection button
  public void mouseExited(MouseEvent e)
  {
    e.getComponent().setCursor(defaultCursor); // Change to default cursor
  }
}
```

All we need to do to expedite this is to add a mouse listener for each of the six selection buttons. We only need one listener object and after creating this we only need to change the loop in the `init()` method for the applet to add the listener:

```
    MouseHandler mouseHandler = new MouseHandler();     // Create the listener
    for(int i = 0 ; i<numberCount ; i++)
    {
      luckyNumbers[i] = new Selection(choices[i]);
      luckyNumbers[i].addMouseListener(mouseHandler);
      buttonPane.add(luckyNumbers[i]);
    }
```

How It Works

The `mouseEntered()` method will be called when the mouse enters the area of the component with which the listener is registered, and we can then change the cursor for the component to a hand cursor. When the cursor is moved out of the area occupied by the component, the `mouseExited()` method is called, and we restore the default cursor.

There are just two extra statements in `init()` which create the listener object and then add it for each selection button within the loop. If you recompile the applet and run it again, a hand cursor should appear whenever the mouse is over the selection buttons. Of course, you are not limited to just changing the cursor in the event handle. You could highlight the button by changing its color for instance. You could apply the same technique for any kind of component where the mouse is the source of actions for it.

Semantic Event Listeners in an Application

An obvious candidate for implementing semantic event listeners is in the Sketcher program, to support the operation of the menu bar in the class SketchFrame. When we click on an item in one of the pull-down menus, a semantic event will be generated which we can listen for and then use to determine the appropriate program action.

Listening to Menu Items

We will start with the Elements menu. This is concerned with identifying the type of graphic element to be drawn next, and the color in which it will be drawn. We won't be drawing them for a while, but we can put in the infrastructure to set the type and color for an element without worrying about how it will actually be created and drawn.

To identify the type of element, we can define constants that will act as IDs for the four types of element we have provided for in the menu so far. This will help us with the operation of the listeners for the menu item as well as provide a way to identify a particular type of element. Since we will accumulate quite a number of application wide constants, it will be convenient to define them in an interface that can be implemented by any class that refers to any of the constants. Here's the initial definition including constants to define line, rectangle, circle and curve elements:

```
// Defines application wide constants

public interface Constants
{
  // Element type definitions
  int LINE      = 101;
  int RECTANGLE = 102;
  int CIRCLE    = 103;
  int CURVE     = 104;

  // Initial conditions
  int DEFAULT_ELEMENT_TYPE = LINE;
}
```

Save this in the same directory as the rest of the Sketcher program as Constants.java. Each element type ID is an integer constant with a unique value and we can obviously extend the variety of element types if necessary. We have defined a constant, DEFAULT_ELEMENT_TYPE, representing the initial element type to apply when the application starts. We should do the same thing for the Color submenu and supply a constant that specifies the initial element color:

```
// Defines application wide constants
import java.awt.*;

public interface Constants
{
  // Element type definitions
  int LINE      = 101;
  int RECTANGLE = 102;
```

```
int CIRCLE    = 103;
int CURVE     = 104;

// Initial conditions
int DEFAULT_ELEMENT_TYPE = LINE;
Color DEFAULT_ELEMENT_COLOR = Color.blue;
}
```

We have defined the DEFAULT_ELEMENT_COLOR as type Color, so we have added an import statement for java.awt to get the definition for the Color class. When we want to change the default start-up color or element type, we just need to change the values of the constants in the Constants interface. This will automatically take care of setting things up – as long as we implement the program code appropriately.

We can add fields to the SketchFrame class to store the current element type and color, since these are application-wide values, and are not specific to a view:

```
private Color elementColor = DEFAULT_ELEMENT_COLOR;      // Current element color
private int elementType = DEFAULT_ELEMENT_TYPE;          // Current element type
```

We can now use these to ensure the menu items are checked appropriately when the application starts. We also want the constants from the Constants interface available, so make the following changes to the SketchFrame class definition:

```
public class SketchFrame extends JFrame
                         implements Constants
{
  // Constructor
  public SketchFrame(String title)
  {
    setTitle(title);                              // Set the window title
    setJMenuBar(menuBar);                         // Add the menu bar to the window
    setDefaultCloseOperation(EXIT_ON_CLOSE);

    // Code to create the File menu...

    // Construct the Element pull down menu
    elementMenu.add(lineItem = new JRadioButtonMenuItem(
                                      "Line", elementType==LINE));
    elementMenu.add(rectangleItem = new JRadioButtonMenuItem(
                                      "Rectangle", elementType==RECTANGLE));
    elementMenu.add(circleItem = new JRadioButtonMenuItem(
                                      "Circle", elementType==CIRCLE));
    elementMenu.add(curveItem = new JRadioButtonMenuItem(
                                      "Curve", elementType==CURVE));

    // ...plus the rest of the code for the element types as before...
```

```
          elementMenu.addSeparator();

      JMenu colorMenu = new JMenu("Color");           // Color sub-menu
      elementMenu.add(colorMenu);                      // Add the sub-menu
      colorMenu.add(redItem = new JCheckBoxMenuItem(
                      "Red", elementColor.equals(Color.red)));
      colorMenu.add(yellowItem = new JCheckBoxMenuItem(
                      "Yellow", lementColor.equals(Color.yellow)));
      colorMenu.add(greenItem = new JCheckBoxMenuItem(
                      "Green", elementColor.equals(Color.green)));
      colorMenu.add(blueItem = new JCheckBoxMenuItem(
                      "Blue", elementColor.equals(Color.blue)));

      // ... plus the rest of the constructor as before...
    }

    // ...plus the rest of the class including the two new data members...
  }
```

When we construct the element objects, we use the `elementType` and `elementColor` members to set the state of each menu item. Only the element type menu item corresponding to the default type set in `elementType` will be checked because that's the only comparison that will produce a true result as an argument to the `JRadioButtonMenuItem` constructor. The mechanism is the same for the color menu items, but note that we use the `equals()` method defined in the `Color` class for a valid comparison. We might just get away with using `==` since we are only using constant `Color` values defined in the class, but as soon as we use a color that is not one of these, this would no longer work. Of course, we have to use `==` for the element type items because the IDs are of type `int`.

Having got that sorted out, we can have a go at implementing the listeners for the Elements menu, starting with the type menu items.

Try It Out — Handling Events for the Element Type Menu

We will add an inner class that will define listeners for the menu items specifying the element type. This class will implement the `ActionListener` interface because we want to respond to actions on these menu items. Add the following definition as an *inner* class to `SketchFrame`:

```
// Handles element type menu items
class TypeListener implements ActionListener
{
  // Constructor
  TypeListener(int type)
  {
    this.type = type;
  }

  // Sets the element type
  public void actionPerformed(ActionEvent e)
  { elementType = type; }
```

```
        private int type;                    // Store the type for the menu
    }
```

Now we can use objects of this class as listeners for the menu items. Add the following code to the `SketchFrame` constructor, after the code that sets up the type menu items for the **Elements** menu:

```
    // Add type menu item listeners
    lineItem.addActionListener(new TypeListener(LINE));
    rectangleItem.addActionListener(new TypeListener(RECTANGLE));
    circleItem.addActionListener(new TypeListener(CIRCLE));
    curveItem.addActionListener(new TypeListener(CURVE));
```

It will also be necessary to add the `import` statement to the `SketcherFrame` class for the package `java.awt.event`. Recompile Sketcher and see how it looks.

How It Works

It won't look any different as the listeners just set the current element type in the `SketchFrame` object. The listener class is remarkably simple. Each listener object stores the type corresponding to the menu item that is passed as the constructor argument. When an event occurs, the `actionPerformed()` method just stores the type in the listener object in the `elementType` member of the `SketchFrame` object.

Now we can do the same for the color menu items.

Try It Out — Implementing Color Menu Item Listeners

We will define another class that is an inner class to `SketchFrame` that defines listeners for the **Color** menu items:

```
    // Handles color menu items
    class ColorListener implements ActionListener
    {
      public ColorListener(Color color)
      {
        this.color = color;
      }

      public void actionPerformed(ActionEvent e)
      {
        elementColor = color;
      }

      private Color color;
    }
```

We just need to create listener objects and add them to the menu items. Add the following code to the `SketchFrame` constructor after the code that sets up the **Color** submenu:

```
    // Add color menu item listeners
```

```
redItem.addActionListener(new ColorListener(Color.red));
yellowItem.addActionListener(new ColorListener(Color.yellow));
greenItem.addActionListener(new ColorListener(Color.green));
blueItem.addActionListener(new ColorListener(Color.blue));
```

This adds a listener object for each menu item in the Color menu.

How It Works

The `ColorListener` class works in the same way as the `TypeListener` class. Each class object stores an identifier for the menu item for which it is listening – in this case a `Color` object corresponding to the color the menu item sets up. The `actionPerformed()` method just stores the `Color` object from the listener object in the `elementColor` member of the `SketchFrame` object.

Of course, the menu doesn't quite work as it should. The menu item check marks are not being set correctly, as you can see below. We want an exclusive check, as with the radio buttons.

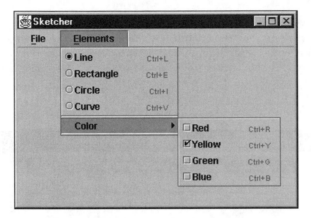

Fixing the Color Menu Checks

One way to deal with the problem is to make the listener object for a color menu item set the checks for all the menu items. You could code this in the `ColorListener` class as:

```
class ColorListener implements ActionListener
{
  public void actionPerformed(ActionEvent e)
  {
    elementColor = color;

    // Set the checks for all menu items
    redItem.setState(color.equals(Color.red));
    greenItem.setState(color.equals(Color.green));
    blueItem.setState(color.equals(Color.blue));
    yellowItem.setState(color.equals(Color.yellow));
  }
```

```
            // Rest of the class as before...
    }
```

This calls the `setState()` method for each menu item. If the argument is `true` the checkmark is set, and if it is `false`, it isn't. Clearly this will only set the checkmark for the item that corresponds to the color referenced by `color`. This is quite straightforward but there is a better way.

A `ButtonGroup` object works with `JCheckBoxMenuItem` objects because they have `AbstractButton` as a base class. Therefore we could add these menu items to their own button group in the `SketchFrame` constructor, and it will all be taken care of. The `ButtonGroup` object tracks the state of all of the buttons in the group. When any button is turned on, all the others are turned off, so only one button in the group can be on at one time. So add the following code – it could go anywhere after the items have been created but place it following the code that adds the items to the Color menu for consistency with the element type code.

```
        ButtonGroup colors = new ButtonGroup();      // Color menu items button group
        colors.add(redItem);
        colors.add(yellowItem);
        colors.add(greenItem);
        colors.add(blueItem);
```

Now our Color menu checks are set automatically so we can forget about them.

Using Actions

One difficulty with the code we have added to support the menus is that it is very menu specific. What I mean by this is that if we are going to do a proper job on the Sketcher application, we will undoubtedly want it to have a toolbar. The toolbar will surely have a whole bunch of buttons that perform exactly the same actions as the menu items we have just implemented, so we will be in the business of doing the same thing over again in the toolbar context. Of course, the only reason I brought it up, as I'm sure you anticipated, is that there is another way of working with menus, and that is to use an **action** object.

An action object is a bit of a strange beast, and it can be quite hard to understand at first so we will take it slowly. First of all let's look at what we mean by an 'action' here, as it is a precise term in this context. An action is an object of any class that implements the `Action` interface. This interface declares methods that operate on an action object, for example storing properties relating to the action, enabling it and disabling it. The `Action` interface happens to extend the `ActionListener` interface so an `action` object is a listener as well as an action. Now that we know an `Action` object can get and set properties, and is also a listener, how does that help us in implementing the Sketcher GUI?

The answer is in the last capability of an `Action` object. Some Swing components, such as those of type `JMenu` and `JToolBar`, have an `add()` method that accepts an argument of type `Action`. When you add an `Action` object to either of these using the `add()` method, the method creates a component from the `Action` object that is *automatically of the right type*. If you add an `Action` object to a `JMenu` object, a `JMenuItem` will be created and returned by the `add()` method. On the other hand, when you add exactly the same `Action` object to a `JToolBar` object, an object of type `JButton` will be created and returned. This means that you can add the very same `Action` object to both a menu and a toolbar, and since the `Action` object is its own listener you automatically get both supporting the same action. Clever, eh?

First, we should look at the `Action` interface.

The Action Interface

In general, properties are items of information that relate to a particular object and are stored as part of the object. Properties are often stored in a map, where a key identifies a particular property, and the value corresponding to that property can be stored in association with the key. The `Properties` class that is defined in the `java.util` package does exactly that. The `Action` interface has provision for storing seven basic standard properties that relate to an `Action` object:

❑ A **name** — a `String` object that is used as the label for a menu item or a toolbar button.

❑ A **small icon** – an `Icon` object to be displayed on a toolbar button.

❑ A **short description** of the action – a `String` object to be used as a tooltip.

❑ An **accelerator key** for the action – defined by a `KeyStroke` object.

❑ A **long description** of the action –a `String` object that is intended to be used as context sensitive help.

❑ A **mnemonic key** for the action – this is a key code of type `int`.

❑ An **action command key** – defined by an entry in a `KeyMap` object associated with a component.

Just so you are aware of them I have included the complete set here, but we will concentrate on just using the first three. We haven't met `Icon` objects before, but we will get to them a little later in this chapter. You are not obliged to provide for all of these properties in your action classes, but the interface provides the framework for it. These properties are intended to be stored internally in a map collection in your action class, so the `Action` interface defines a constant that is intended to be used as a key for each of the standard properties. These constants are all of type `String`, and the ones we are interested in are NAME, SMALL_ICON, and SHORT_DESCRIPTION. The others are ACCELERATOR_KEY, LONG_DESCRIPTION, MNEMONIC_KEY, and ACTION_COMMAND_KEY. There is another constant of type `String` defined in the interface with the name DEFAULT. This is for you to use to store a default property for the action.

The `Action` interface also declares the following methods:

Method	Description
`void putValue(String key, Object value)`	Stores the `value` with the key `key` in the map supported by the action class. To store the name of an action within a class method you might write: `putValue(NAME, theName);` This uses the standard key, NAME to store the object `theName`.

Method	Description

`Object getValue(String key)`	This retrieves the object from the map corresponding to the key `key`. To retrieve a small icon within an action class method you might write:
	
	`Icon lineIcon =`
	`(Icon)getValue(SMALL_ICON);`

`boolean isEnabled()`	Returns `true` if the action object is enabled and `false` otherwise.
`void setEnabled(boolean state)`	Sets the action object as enabled if the argument state is `true` and disabled if it is `false`. This operates on both the toolbar button and the menu item if they have been created using the same object.
`void addPropertyChangeListener (PropertyChangeListener listener)`	This adds the listener passed as an argument that listens for changes to properties such as the enabled state of the object. This is used by a container for an action object to track property changes.
`void removePropertyChangeListener (PropertyChangeListener listener)`	This removes the listener passed as an argument. This is also for use by a `Container` object. Of course, since the `Action` interface extends the `ActionListener` interface, it also incorporates the `ActionPerformed()` method that you are already familiar with.

So far, all we seem to have with this interface is a license to do a lot of work in implementing it but it's not as bad as that. The `javax.swing` package defines a class, `AbstractAction`, that already implements the `Action` interface. If you extend this class to create your own action class, you get a basic infrastructure for free. Let's try it out in the context of Sketcher.

Using Actions as Menu Items

This will involve major surgery on our `SketchFrame` class. Although we'll be throwing away all those fancy varieties of menu items we spent so much time putting together, at least you know how they work now, and we'll end up with much less code after re-engineering the class, as you'll see. As the saying goes, you've got to crack a few eggs to make a soufflé.

We'll go back nearly to square one and reconstruct the class definition. First we will delete a lot of code from the existing class definition. Comments show where we will add code to re-implement the menus using actions. Get your definition of `SketchFrame` to the following state:

```
// Frame for the Sketcher application
import javax.swing.*;
import java.awt.*;
import java.awt.event.*;
```

```java
public class SketchFrame extends JFrame
                          implements Constants
{
  // Constructor
  public SketchFrame(String title)
  {
    setTitle(title);                        // Set the window title
    setJMenuBar(menuBar);                   // Add the menu bar to the window
    setDefaultCloseOperation(EXIT_ON_CLOSE);    // Default is exit the application

    JMenu fileMenu = new JMenu("File");           // Create File menu
    JMenu elementMenu = new JMenu("Elements");    // Create Elements menu
    fileMenu.setMnemonic('F');                    // Create shortcut
    elementMenu.setMnemonic('E');                 // Create shortcut

    // We will construct the file pull down menu here using actions...

    // We will add the types menu items here using actions...

    elementMenu.addSeparator();

    JMenu colorMenu = new JMenu("Color");         // Color sub-menu
    elementMenu.add(colorMenu);                   // Add the sub-menu

    // We will add the color menu items here using actions...

    menuBar.add(fileMenu);                        // Add the file menu
    menuBar.add(elementMenu);                     // Add the element menu
  }

  // We will add inner classes defining action objects here...

  // We will add action objects as members here...

  private JMenuBar menuBar = new JMenuBar();            // Window menu bar
  private Color elementColor = DEFAULT_ELEMENT_COLOR;   // Current element color
  private int elementType = DEFAULT_ELEMENT_TYPE;       // Current element type
}
```

Note that we have put the statement to set the default close operation as EXIT_ON_CLOSE back in so we won't need to call dispose() and exit() in the window event handler. The old inner classes have been deleted, as well as the fields storing references to menu items. All the code to create the menu items has been wiped as well, along with the code that added the listeners. We are ready to begin reconstruction. We can rebuild it, stronger, faster, better!

Defining Action Classes

We will need three inner classes defining actions, one for the File menu items, another for the element type menu items, and the third for element colors. We will derive all these from the AbstractAction class that already implements the Action interface. The AbstractAction class has three constructors:

Method	Description
AbstractAction()	Defines an object with a default name and icon.
AbstractAction(String name)	Defines an object with the name specified by the argument and a default icon.
AbstractAction(String name, Icon icon)	Defines an object with the name and icon specified by the arguments.

The AbstractAction class definition already provides the mechanism for storing action properties. For the last two constructors, the argument values that are passed will be stored using the standard keys that we described earlier. For the moment, we will only take advantage of the second constructor, and leave icons till a little later.

We can define the FileAction inner class as follows:

```
class FileAction extends AbstractAction
{
  // Constructor
  FileAction(String name)
  {
    super(name);
  }

  // Constructor
  FileAction(String name, KeyStroke keystroke)
  {
    this(name);
    if(keystroke != null)
      putValue(ACCELERATOR_KEY, keystroke);
  }

  // Event handler
  public void actionPerformed(ActionEvent e)
  {
    // We will add action code here eventually...
  }
}
```

We have two constructors. The first just stores the name for the action by calling the base class constructor. The second stores the name by calling the first constructor and then stores the accelerator keystroke using the appropriate key if the argument is not null. Calling the other constructor rather than the base class constructor is better here, in case we add code to the other constructor later on (as we shall!).

Since our class is an action listener, we can implement the actionPerformed() method in it. We don't yet know what we are going to do with the File menu item actions, so we will leave it open for now and let the actionPerformed() method do nothing. Add this inner class to SketchFrame where the comment indicates.

The `SketchFrame` class will need a data member of type `FileAction` for each menu item we intend to add, so add the following statement to the `SketchFrame` class definition:

```
// File actions
private FileAction newAction, openAction, closeAction,
                   saveAction, saveAsAction, printAction;
```

We can define an inner class for the element type menus next:

```
class TypeAction extends AbstractAction
{
  TypeAction(String name, int typeID)
  {
    super(name);
    this.typeID = typeID;
  }

  public void actionPerformed(ActionEvent e)
  { elementType = typeID;  }

  private int typeID;
}
```

Add this definition to the `SketchFrame` class following the previous inner class. The only extra code here compared to the previous action class is that we retain the `typeID` concept to identify the element type. This makes the listener operation simple and fast. Because each object corresponds to a particular element type, there is no need for any testing of the event – we just store the current `typeID` as the new element type in the `SketchFrame` class object. We won't be adding accelerator key combinations for type menu items so we don't need to provide for them in the class.

Add the following statement to the `SketchFrame` class for the members that will store references to the `TypeAction` objects:

```
// Element type actions
private TypeAction lineAction, rectangleAction, circleAction, curveAction;
```

The third inner class is just as simple:

```
// Handles color menu items
class ColorAction  extends AbstractAction
{
  public ColorAction(String name, Color color)
  {
    super(name);
    this.color = color;
  }

  public void actionPerformed(ActionEvent e)
  {
    elementColor = color;
```

```
        // This is temporary - just to show it works
        getContentPane().setBackground(color);
      }

    private Color color;
  }
```

We also use the same idea that we used in the listener class for the color menu items in the previous implementation of `SketchFrame`. Here we have a statement in the `actionPerformed()` method that sets the background color of the content pane to the element color. When you click on a color menu item, the background color of the content pane will change so you will be able to see that it works. We'll remove this code later.

Add the following statement to the `SketchFrame` class for the color action members:

```
// Element color actions
  private ColorAction redAction, yellowAction,
                      greenAction, blueAction;
```

We can try these action classes out now.

Try It Out — Actions in Action

All we need to do to create the menu items is use the `add()` method to add a suitable `Action` object to a menu. This all happens in the `SketchFrame` constructor – with the aid of a helper method that will economize on the number of lines of code:

```
public SketchFrame(String title)
{
  setTitle(title);                             // Set the window title
  setJMenuBar(menuBar);                        // Add the menu bar to the window
  setDefaultCloseOperation(EXIT_ON_CLOSE);     // Default is exit the application

  JMenu fileMenu = new JMenu("File");          // Create File menu
  JMenu elementMenu = new JMenu("Elements");   // Create Elements menu
  fileMenu.setMnemonic('F');                   // Create shortcut
  elementMenu.setMnemonic('E');                // Create shortcut

  // Create the action items for the file menu
  newAction = new FileAction("New", KeyStroke.getKeyStroke('N',Event.CTRL_MASK ));
  openAction = new FileAction("Open", KeyStroke.getKeyStroke('O',Event.CTRL_MASK ));
  closeAction = new FileAction("Close");
  saveAction = new FileAction("Save", KeyStroke.getKeyStroke('S',Event.CTRL_MASK ));
  saveAsAction = new FileAction("Save As...");
  printAction = new FileAction("Print",
                          KeyStroke.getKeyStroke('P',Event.CTRL_MASK ));
```

```
    // Construct the file pull down menu
    addMenuItem(fileMenu, newAction);
    addMenuItem(fileMenu, openAction);
    addMenuItem(fileMenu, closeAction);
    fileMenu.addSeparator();                              // Add separator
    addMenuItem(fileMenu, saveAction);
    addMenuItem(fileMenu, saveAsAction);
    fileMenu.addSeparator();                              // Add separator
    addMenuItem(fileMenu, printAction);


    // Construct the Element pull down menu
    addMenuItem(elementMenu, lineAction = new TypeAction("Line", LINE));
    addMenuItem(elementMenu, rectangleAction = new TypeAction("Rectangle",
                                                      RECTANGLE));

    addMenuItem(elementMenu, circleAction = new TypeAction("Circle", CIRCLE));
    addMenuItem(elementMenu, curveAction = new TypeAction("Curve", CURVE));

    elementMenu.addSeparator();

    JMenu colorMenu = new JMenu("Color");           // Color sub-menu
    elementMenu.add(colorMenu);                     // Add the sub-menu

    addMenuItem(colorMenu, redAction = new ColorAction("Red", Color.red));
    addMenuItem(colorMenu, yellowAction = new ColorAction("Yellow", Color.yellow));
    addMenuItem(colorMenu, greenAction = new ColorAction("Green", Color.green));
    addMenuItem(colorMenu, blueAction = new ColorAction("Blue", Color.blue));

    menuBar.add(fileMenu);                           // Add the file menu
    menuBar.add(elementMenu);                        // Add the element menu
  }
```

We have added four blocks of code. The first two are for the file menu, one creating the action object and the other calling a helper method, addMenuItem(), to create the menu items. The other two are for the element type and color menus. We create the action items for these menus in the arguments to the helper method calls. It's convenient to do this, as the constructor calls are relatively simple.

The helper method will add an item specified by its second argument to the menu specified by the first. By declaring the second argument as type Action, we can pass a reference to an object of any class type that implements the Action interface, so this includes any of our action classes. Here's the code:

```
  private JMenuItem addMenuItem(JMenu menu, Action action)
  {
    JMenuItem item = menu.add(action);                      // Add the menu item

    KeyStroke keystroke = (KeyStroke)action.getValue(action.ACCELERATOR_KEY);
    if(keystroke != null)
      item.setAccelerator(keystroke);
    return item;                                            // Return the menu item
  }
```

As you can see, the method takes care of adding the accelerator key for the menu item if one has been defined for the Action object. If there isn't one, the getValue() method will return null, so it's easy to check. We don't need access to the menu item that is created in the method at the moment since it is added to the menu. However, it is no problem to return the reference from the method and it could be useful if we wanted to add code to do something with the menu item at some point.

If you compile and run Sketcher, you will get a window that looks like this:

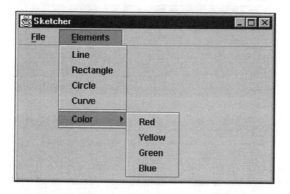

How It Works

We create an Action object for each item in the file menu. We then call our private addMenuItem() method for each item in turn to create the menu items corresponding to the Action objects, and add them to the file menu. The addMenuItem() method automatically adds an accelerator key for a menu item if it exists in the Action object. We declare the addMenuItem() method as private because it has no role outside of the SketchFrame class and therefore should not be accessible.

The items for the other menus are created in the same way using the addMenuItem() method. We create the Action objects in the expressions for the arguments to the method as they are relatively simple expressions. Because we store the references to the Action objects, they will be available later when we want to create toolbar buttons corresponding to the menu items. Note that we have omitted the accelerators for the Elements menu items here on the grounds that they were not exactly standard or convenient.

You may be wondering at this point why we have to set the accelerator key for a menu item explicitly, and why an accelerator key stored within an Action object is not added to the menu item automatically. There's a very good reason for not having the add() method automatically set an accelerator key from an Action object. Pressing an accelerator key combination would the equivalent of clicking any item created from a corresponding Action object. This could be a toolbar button and a menu item. Thus if the accelerator key were automatically set for both components, you would get events from both components when you pressed the accelerator key combination – not exactly what you would want as each action would then be carried out twice!

If you try out the color menus you should see the background color change. If it doesn't there's something wrong somewhere.

Now we have the menus set up using action objects, we are ready to tackle adding a toolbar to our application.

Adding a Toolbar

A toolbar is a bar, usually positioned below the menu bar, which contains a row of buttons that typically provides a more direct route to menu options. We could add a toolbar to the Sketcher program for the menu items that are likely to be most popular. Just so that you know where we are heading, the kind of toolbar we will end up with ultimately is shown below.

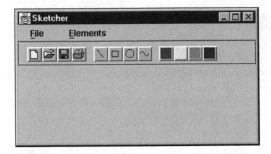

The four buttons in the first group are for the most used functions in the file menu. The other two groups of four buttons select the element type and element color respectively. So how are we going to put this toolbar together?

Adding the toolbar itself couldn't be easier. A toolbar is a Swing component defined by the `JToolBar` class. You can add a member to the `SketchFrame` class for a toolbar by adding the following to the class definition:

```
private JToolBar toolBar = new JToolBar();      // Window toolbar
```

You can position this following the declaration of the `menuBar` member. It simply creates a `JToolBar` object as a member of the class. To add it to the frame window, you need to add the following statement after the existing code in the `SketchFrame` constructor:

```
getContentPane().add(toolBar, BorderLayout.NORTH);
```

This adds the toolbar to the top of the content pane for the frame window. The content pane has the `BorderLayout` manager as the default, which is very convenient. A `JToolBar` object should be added to a `Container` using the `BorderLayout` manager since it is normally positioned at one of the four sides of a component. An empty toolbar is not much use though, so let's see how to add buttons.

Adding Buttons to a Toolbar

The `JToolBar` class inherits the `add()` methods from the `Container` class, so you could create `JButton` objects and add them to the toolbar. However, since a toolbar almost always has buttons corresponding to menu functions, a much better way is to use the `add()` method defined in the `JToolBar` class to add an `Action` object to the toolbar. We can use this to add any of the `Action` objects that we created for our menus, and have the toolbar button events taken care of without any further work.

For example, we could add a button for the openAction object corresponding to the **Open** menu item in the **File** menu with the statement:

```
toolBar.add(openAction);              // Add a toolbar button
```

That's all you need basically. The add() method will create a JButton object based on the Action object passed as the argument. A reference to the JButton object is returned in case you want to store it to manipulate it in some way – adding a border for instance. Let's see how that looks.

Try It Out — Adding a Toolbar Button

Assuming you have added the declaration for the toolBar object to the SketchFrame class, you just need to add a couple of statements preceding the last statement in the constructor to add the toolbar to the content pane:

```
public SketchFrame(String title)
{
  // Constructor code as before...

  JButton button = toolBar.add(openAction);                  // Add toolbar button
  button.setBorder(BorderFactory.createRaisedBevelBorder());// Add button border
  getContentPane().add(toolBar, BorderLayout.NORTH);         // Add the toolbar
}
```

If you recompile Sketcher and run it, the window should look like that shown below.

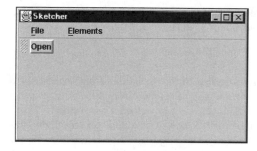

How It Works

There's not much to say about this. The add() method for the toolBar object created a button based on the openAction object that we passed as an argument. We store the reference returned in button so we can add a border to the button.

A feature that comes for free with a JToolBar object is that it is automatically dockable, and can float as an independent window. You can drag the toolbar using the mouse by clicking the cursor in the gray area to the left of the button, and it will turn into a free-floating window.

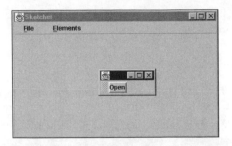

You can also drag the toolbar to any of the four sides of the content pane to dock it again. You must drag with the cursor in the gray area of the toolbar to dock it. Dragging with the cursor in the toolbar title area just moves the window. It's not always convenient to have the toolbar floating or docked against borders other than its normal position. You can inhibit the ability to drag the toolbar around by calling the setFloatable() method for the JToolBar object. Let's do this for Sketcher, so add the following statement to the SketchFrame constructor before the statement that adds the toolbar to the content pane:

```
toolBar.setFloatable(false);    // Inhibit toolbar floating
```

A true argument to the method will allow the toolbar to float, so you can switch this on and off in your program as you wish. You can also test whether the toolbar can float by calling the isFloatable() method for the JToolBar object. This will return true if the toolbar is floatable, and false otherwise.

The button that has been created uses the name from the Action object as its label by default. We really want toolbar buttons with icons, so that's got to be the next step.

Adding Icons

A reference to an icon is generally stored in a variable of type Icon. Icon is an interface that declares methods to obtain the height and width of an icon in pixels – the getHeight() and getWidth() methods respectively, and to paint the icon image on a component – the paint() method. One class that implements the Icon interface is ImageIcon and it is this class that you use to create an icon object in your program from a file containing the icon image. The class provides several constructors that create an ImageIcon object and the one we will use accepts a String argument that specifies the file where the icon image is to be found. The String object can be just a file name, in which case the file should be in the current directory – the one that contains the .class files for the application or applet. You can also supply a string that specifies the path and file name where the file containing the image is to be found. The ImageIcon constructors accept icon files in **PNG** (**P**ortable **N**etwork **G**raphics format, which are .png files), **GIF** (**G**raphics **I**nterchange **F**ormat, which are .gif files), or **JPEG** (**J**oint **P**hotographic **E**xperts **G**roup format, which are .jpg files) formats, but we will assume GIF files in our code.

We will put the icons for Sketcher in a subdirectory of the Sketcher directory called Images, so create a subdirectory to your Sketcher application directory with this name. To create an icon for the openAction object from an image in a file open.gif in the Images directory, we could write:

```
openAction.putValue(Action.SMALL_ICON, new ImageIcon ("Images/open.gif"));
```

This stores the ImageIcon object in our Action object associated with the SMALL_ICON key. The add() method for the toolbar object will then look for the icon for the toolbar button it creates using this key. Let's see if it works.

> *You will need to create the GIF files containing the icons. Any graphics editor that can save files in the GIF format will do, Paint Shop Pro for instance. I created my icons as 16x16 pixels since it is a fairly standard size for toolbar buttons. Make sure the file for the openAction object is called open.gif, and stored in the Images subdirectory. We will need GIF files for other buttons too, and they will each have a file name that is the same as the label on the corresponding menu item, so if you want to put them together in one go, for the file menu toolbar button you will need save.gif, new.gif and print.gif, for the element types you will need line.gif, rectangle.gif, circle.gif and curve.gif, and for the colors you will need red.gif, yellow.gif, green.gif and blue.gif. GIF files for all these icons are available along with the Sketcher source code at the Wrox website:*
> http://www.wrox.com/Consumer/Store/Download.asp .

Try It Out — A Button with an Icon

You can add the statement to create the icon for the Action object just before we create the toolbar button:

```
public SketchFrame(String title)
{
  // Constructor code as before...

  openAction.putValue(Action.SMALL_ICON, new ImageIcon ("Images/open.gif"));
  JButton button = toolBar.add(openAction);                    // Add toolbar button
  button.setBorder(BorderFactory.createRaisedBevelBorder());// Add button border

  toolBar.setFloatable(false);                              // Inhibit toolbar floating
  getContentPane().add(toolBar, BorderLayout.NORTH);        // Add the toolbar
}
```

In fact you could put the statement anywhere after the openAction object is created, but here will be convenient. If you recompile Sketcher and run it again, you should see the window below.

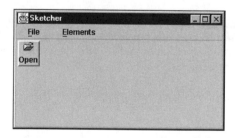

How It Works

The `ImageIcon` object that we store in our `openAction` object is automatically used by the `add()` method for the `toolBar` object to add the icon to the button. Unfortunately we get the label as well which looks a bit untidy. Let's consider what we can do about it.

We could remove the label by storing null in the `openAction` object associated with the `NAME` key with a statement such as:

```
openAction.putValue(Action.NAME, null);
```

This has a serious drawback though. The `String` object stored using the `NAME` key is used as the menu item text, so if we remove it the corresponding menu item will lose its text. What we need to do is to alter the `JButton` object that is created by the `add()` method for the `toolBar` object. We can do this by calling the `setText()` method for the `JButton` object:

```
button.setText(null);
```

If you insert this statement after the `button` object is created, when you recompile and run the program again you should get the window shown below.

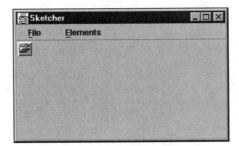

Of course, we are going to have to fix the text for all the toolbar buttons, and create a border for each. This will involve a lot of repetitive code that we can reduce by adding another helper method that will create any toolbar button. We might as well alter the inner classes for the `Action` objects to add icons, too. Let's try that now.

Try It Out — Adding All the Toolbar Buttons

We can modify the constructor for each inner class to add the corresponding icon. Here's how we can implement this in the `FileAction` class:

```
FileAction(String name)
{
  super(name);
  String iconFileName = "Images/" + name + ".gif";
  if(new File(iconFileName).exists())
    putValue(SMALL_ICON, new ImageIcon(iconFileName));
}
```

Because we refer to the File class here, we need to add an import statement for the java.io package to the beginning of the SketchFrame.java source file. This code assumes all icon files follow the convention that their name is the same as the String associated with the NAME key. If you want to have any file name, you could pass the String defining the file name to the constructor. If the icon file is not available then nothing happens, so the code will work whether or not an icon is defined. We only need to add the code to this constructor since the other constructors in the FileAction class call this one.

The code that you add to the constructors for the TypeAction and ColorAction inner classes is exactly the same as here, so go ahead and copy it across.

We can define a helper method in the SketchFrame class to create toolbar buttons as follows:

```
private JButton addToolBarButton(Action action)
{
    JButton button = toolBar.add(action);                   // Add toolbar button
    button.setBorder(BorderFactory.createRaisedBevelBorder());// Add button border
    button.setText(null);                                   // No button text
    return button;
}
```

The argument is the Action object for the toolbar button that is to be added, and the code is essentially the same as the specific code we had in the SketchFrame constructor to create the button for the openAction object. We can remove that from the SketchFrame constructor and replace it by the following code to create all the buttons that we need:

```
public SketchFrame(String title)
{
    // Constructor code as before...

    // Add file buttons
    toolBar.addSeparator();                                 // Space at the start
    addToolBarButton(newAction);
    addToolBarButton(openAction);
    addToolBarButton(saveAction);
    addToolBarButton(printAction);

    // Add element type buttons
    toolBar.addSeparator();
    addToolBarButton(lineAction);
    addToolBarButton(rectangleAction);
    addToolBarButton(circleAction);
    addToolBarButton(curveAction);

    // Add element color buttons
    toolBar.addSeparator();
    addToolBarButton(redAction);
    addToolBarButton(yellowAction);
    addToolBarButton(greenAction);
    addToolBarButton(blueAction);
    toolBar.addSeparator();                                 // Space at the end
```

637

```
        toolBar.setBorder(BorderFactory.createCompoundBorder(        // Toolbar border
                   BorderFactory.createLineBorder(Color.darkGray),
                   BorderFactory.createEmptyBorder(2,2,4,2)));

      toolBar.setFloatable(false);                          // Inhibit toolbar floating
      getContentPane().add(toolBar, BorderLayout.NORTH); // Add the toolbar
   }
```

Now you should get the window with the toolbar that we showed at the beginning, with a nice neat toolbar. You can see the color buttons in action since they will change the background color.

How It Works

The extra code in the inner class constructors stores an icon in each object if there is a GIF file with the appropriate name in the `Images` subdirectory. We create each of the toolbar buttons by calling our `addToolBarButton()` helper method with an `Action` item corresponding to a menu item. The helper method passes the `Action` object to the `add()` method for the `JToolBar` object to create a `JButton` object. It also sets the text for the button to `null` and adds a border. The `addToolBarButton()` method also returns a reference to the button object in case we need it.

We have added a further statement to add a border to the toolbar. We use the `createCompoundBorder()` method to create a border with an outer border that is a single line, and an inner border that is empty but inserts space around the inside of the outer border as specified by the arguments. The arguments to `createEmptyBorder()` are the width in pixels of the border in the sequence top, left, bottom and right.

Fixing the Menus

Things are still not quite as we would have them. If you take a look at the menus you will see what I mean.

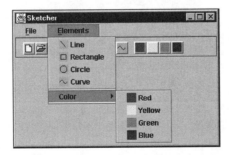

All of the menu items now have icons too, which is a bit excessive. Of course, if you like it you could always leave them in, but it makes the menus look a little ragged so I prefer them without. We could get rid of the icons in a similar way to that which we used for the toolbar buttons. We can modify the menu items that are created by the `add()` method for the `JMenu` objects in the `addMenuItem()` method. The `JMenuItem` class has a `setIcon()` method that accepts a reference of type `Icon` to set an icon for a menu item. If we want to remove the icon, we just pass `null` to it.

We just need to add a statement to addMenuItem() method in the SketchFrame class to remove the icon, like this:

```
private JMenuItem addMenuItem(JMenu menu, Action action)
{
  JMenuItem item = menu.add(action);                    // Add the menu item

  KeyStroke keystroke = (KeyStroke)action.getValue(action.ACCELERATOR_KEY);
  if(keystroke != null)
    item.setAccelerator(keystroke);
  item.setIcon(null);                                   // Remove the icon
  return item;                                          // Return the menu item
}
```

When you run Sketcher with this modification to SketchFrame, you should see the menu items without icons.

How It Works

When we construct each of the menu items using our helper method addMenuItem() we remove the icon from the JMenuItem that is created by passing null to its setIcon() method. Thus none of the menu item objects has an icon associated with it. Of course, the toolbar buttons are unaffected and retain the icons defined by the Action objects they are created from.

Adding Tooltips

I'm sure you have seen tooltips in operation. These are the little text prompts that appear automatically when you let the mouse cursor linger over certain GUI elements on the screen for a second or two. They disappear automatically when you move the cursor. I think you will be surprised at how easy it is to implement support for tooltips in Java.

The secret is in the Action objects that we are using. Action objects have a built-in capability to store tooltip text because it is already provided for with the SHORT_DESCRIPTION key that is defined in the interface. All we have to do is store the tooltip text in our inner classes that are derived from AbstractAction. The tooltip will then be automatically available on the toolbar buttons that we create. Let's work through our Action classes and provide for tooltip text.

We can provide for tooltip text in each of our inner classes by adding constructors with an extra parameter for it. We need two additional constructors in the FileAction class, one for when the Action item has an accelerator key, and the other for when it doesn't. The definition of the first new FileAction class constructor will be:

```
FileAction(String name, KeyStroke keystroke, String tooltip)
{
  this(name, keystroke);                          // Call the other constructor
```

```
      if(tooltip != null)                          // If there is tooltip text
        putValue(SHORT_DESCRIPTION, tooltip);      // ...squirrel it away
    }
```

This just calls the constructor that accepts arguments defining the name and the keystroke. It then stores the tooltip string using the SHORT_DESCRIPTION key, as long as it isn't null. Although you wouldn't expect a null to be passed for the tooltip text reference, it's best not to assume it as this could crash the program. If it is null we do nothing.

The other constructor will take care of a tooltip for an Action item without an accelerator keystroke:

```
    FileAction(String name, String tooltip)
    {
      this(name);                                  // Call the other constructor
      if(tooltip != null)                          // If there is tooltip text
        putValue(SHORT_DESCRIPTION, tooltip);      // ...squirrel it away
    }
```

Of course, we must now change the code in the SketchFrame constructor that creates FileAction items so that we incorporate the tooltip argument:

```
    // Construct the file pull down menu
    newAction = new FileAction("New", KeyStroke.getKeyStroke
('N',Event.CTRL_MASK ), "Create new sketch");
    openAction = new FileAction("Open", KeyStroke.getKeyStroke('O',Event.CTRL_MASK),
    "Open existing sketch");
    closeAction = new FileAction("Close", "Close sketch");
    saveAction = new FileAction("Save", KeyStroke.getKeyStroke('S',Event.CTRL_MASK),
    "Save sketch");
    saveAsAction = new FileAction("Save As...", "Save as new file");
    printAction = new FileAction("Print", KeyStroke.getKeyStroke('P',Event.CTRL_MASK
), "Print sketch");
```

We can do exactly the same with the TypeAction class – just add the following constructor definition:

```
    TypeAction(String name, int typeID, String tooltip)
    {
      this(name, typeID);
      if(tooltip != null)                          // If there is a tooltip
        putValue(SHORT_DESCRIPTION, tooltip);      // ...squirrel it away
    }
```

We must then modify the code in the `SketchFrame` constructor to pass a tooltip string when we create a `TypeAction` object:

```
// Construct the Element pull down menu
addMenuItem(elementMenu, lineAction = new TypeAction
                          ("Line", LINE, "Draw lines"));
addMenuItem(elementMenu, rectangleAction = new TypeAction
                          ("Rectangle",RECTANGLE, "Draw rectangles"));
addMenuItem(elementMenu, circleAction = new TypeAction
                          ("Circle", CIRCLE, "Draw circles"));
addMenuItem(elementMenu, curveAction = new TypeAction
                          ("Curve", CURVE, "Draw curves"));
```

And a constructor that does exactly the same needs to be added to the `ColorAction` class:

```
public ColorAction(String name, Color color, String tooltip)
{
  this(name, color);
  if(tooltip != null)                         // If there is a tooltip
    putValue(SHORT_DESCRIPTION, tooltip);     // ...squirrel it away
}
```

The corresponding changes in the `SketchFrame` constructor are:

```
JMenu colorMenu = new JMenu("Color");               // Color sub-menu
elementMenu.add(colorMenu);                         // Add the sub-menu
addMenuItem(colorMenu, redAction = new ColorAction
                          ("Red", Color.red, "Draw in red"));
addMenuItem(colorMenu, yellowAction = new ColorAction
                          ("Yellow", Color.yellow, "Draw in yellow"));
addMenuItem(colorMenu, greenAction = new ColorAction
                          ("Green", Color.green, "Draw in green"));
addMenuItem(colorMenu, blueAction = new ColorAction
                          ("Blue", Color.blue, "Draw in blue"));
```

Of course, if you want to put your own tooltip text for any of these, you can. You should keep it short since it is displayed on the fly. We can try our tooltips out now we have the last piece in place. Just recompile the `SketchFrame` class and run Sketcher again. You should be able to see the tooltip when you let the cursor linger over a button.

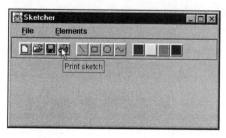

How It Works

An `Action` objects act as a repository for the tooltip text for a toolbar button. If an `Action` object contains a tooltip property, a toolbar button that you create from it will automatically have the tooltip operational.

Disabling Actions

You won't want to have all of the menu items and toolbar buttons enabled all of the time. For instance, while there is no sketch active, the **Save** and **Print** menu items should not be operational, and neither should the corresponding buttons. The `Action` objects provide a single point of control for enabling or disabling menu items and the corresponding toolbar buttons. To disable an action, you call the `setEnabled()` method for the `Action` object with an argument of `false`. You can restore the enabled state by calling the method with a `true` argument. The `isEnabled()` method for an `Action` object returns `true` if the action is enabled, and `false` otherwise.

Let's see toolbar button inaction in action in Sketcher.

Try It Out — Disabling Actions

We will disable the actions corresponding to the **Save**, **Close** and **Print** actions. Add the following statements to the end of the `SketchFrame` constructor:

```
// Disable actions
saveAction.setEnabled(false);
closeAction.setEnabled(false);
printAction.setEnabled(false);
```

That's all that's necessary. If you run the modified version of Sketcher, menu items and toolbar buttons corresponding to the `Action` objects we have disabled will be grayed out and non-operational.

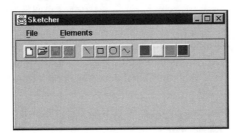

If you extend the **File** menu, you will see that the corresponding menu items are grayed out, too.

How It Works

The state of both the `JMenuItem` and `JButton` objects created from an `Action` object is determined by the state of the `Action` object. Disabling the `Action` object disables any menus or toolbar buttons created from it. If you want a demonstration that they really are disabled, try disabling a couple of the color actions.

Summary

In this chapter you have learnt how to handle events in your applications and in your applets. Events are fundamental to all window-based applications, as well as most applets, so you will be applying the techniques from this chapter throughout the rest of the book.

The most important points we have discussed in this chapter are:

❑ A user interaction generates an event in the context of a component.

❑ There are two categories of events associated with a component: **low-level events** from the mouse, keyboard or window system events such as opening or closing a window, and **semantic events** which represent component actions such as pressing a button or selecting a menu item.

❑ Both low-level and semantic events can arise simultaneously.

❑ An event for a component can be handled by the component object itself, or by a separate object that implements a listener interface corresponding to the event type.

❑ A component that is to handle its own events does so by calling its `enableEvents()` method and implementing the class method to process the kind of event that has been enabled.

❑ A listener object that is registered with a component will receive notification of the events originating with the component that correspond to the type(s) of events the listener can handle.

❑ A listener interface for low-level events requires several event handling methods to be implemented.

❑ A listener interface for semantic events declares a single event handling method.

❑ An adapter class defines a set of empty methods for a low-level event interface. You can derive your own class defining a low-level event listener by deriving your class from an adapter class, and then implementing the event handling methods in which you are interested.

❑ Events in applications and in applets are handled in exactly the same way.

❑ An `Action` object is an object of a class that implements the `Action` interface. `Action` objects can be used to create menu items and associated toolbar buttons.

❑ An `Action` object is automatically the listener for the menu item and toolbar button that are created from it.

Exercises

1. Modify Sketcher to add an Exit action for the File menu and the toolbar.

2. Modify the lottery applet to present the six numbers selected in ascending sequence.

3. Replace the action listener for the selection buttons in the Lottery applet with a mouse listener, and use the `mousePressed()` method to update the selection with a new value.

4. Modify the Lottery applet to implement the mouse listener for a selection button as an inner class to the `Lottery` class.

5. Modify the Lottery applet to implement the control buttons on a toolbar based on `Action` objects.

6. Change the Lottery applet to handle the MOUSE_ENTERED and MOUSE_EXITED events within the toolbar buttons you added in the previous exercise.

7. Add tooltips to the lucky number buttons and the toolbar buttons in the Lottery applet. (You can make the tooltip the same for each of the lucky number buttons.)

Drawing in a Window

In this chapter we will look at how you can draw using the Java 2D facilities that are part of JFC. We will see how to draw in an applet and in an application. We will investigate how we can combine the event-handling capability we learned about in the previous chapter with the drawing facilities we'll explore in this chapter, so that we can implement an interactive graphical user interface for creating a sketch.

By the end of this chapter you will have learned:

- ❏ What components are available to make use of.
- ❏ How coordinates are defined for drawing on a component.
- ❏ How you implement drawing on a component.
- ❏ How to structure the components in a window for drawing.
- ❏ What kinds of shapes you can draw on a component.
- ❏ How you implement mouse listener methods to enable interactive drawing operations.

Using the Model/View Architecture

We need to develop an idea of how we're going to manage the data for a sketch in the Sketcher program before we start drawing a sketch, because this will affect where and how we handle events. We already have a class that defines an application window, SketchFrame, but this class would not be a very sensible place to store the underlying data that defines a sketch. For one thing, we'll want to save a sketch in a file, and serialization is the easiest way to do that. If we're going to use serialization to store a sketch, we won't want all the stuff in the implementation of the SketchFrame class muddled up with the data relating to the sketch we have created. For another, it will make the program easier to implement if we separate out the basic data defining a sketch from the definition of the GUI. This will be along the lines of the MVC architecture that we first mentioned in Chapter 11, a variant of which is used in the definition of Swing components.

Ideally, we should manage the sketch data in a class designed specifically for that purpose – this class will be the **model** for a sketch.

A class representing a **view** of the data in the model class will display the sketch and handle user interactions – so this class will combine viewing functions and a sketch controller. The general GUI creation and operations not specific to a view we will deal with in the SketchFrame class. This is not the only way of implementing the things we want in the Sketcher program, but it's quite a good way.

Our model object will contain a mixture of text and graphics that will go to make up a sketch. We'll call our model class SketchModel and we'll call the class representing a view of the model SketchView, although we won't be adding the view to the program until the next chapter. The following diagram illustrates the relationships between the classes we will have in Sketcher.

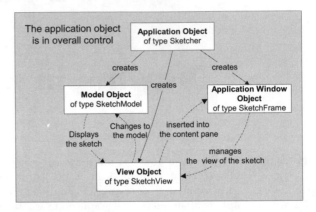

The application object will have overall responsibility for managing links between the other objects involved in the program. Any object that has access to the application object will be able to communicate with any other object as long as the application class has methods to make each of the objects available. Thus the application object will act as the communication channel between objects.

Note that SketchFrame is not the view class – it just defines the application window and the GUI components associated with that. When we create a SketchView object in the next chapter, we'll arrange to insert the SketchView object into the content pane of the SketchFrame object, and manage it using the layout manager for the content pane. By defining the view class separately from the application class, we separate the view of a sketch from the menus and other components we use to interact with the program. One benefit of this is that the area in which we display the document has its own coordinate system, independent of that of the application window.

To implement the foundations for the model/view design in Sketcher we need to define classes for the model and the view, at least in outline. The class to contain the data defining a sketch we can define in skeleton form as:

```
import java.util.*;

class SketchModel extends Observable
{
   // Detail of the rest of class to be filled in later...
}
```

We obviously have a bit more work to do on this class, so we will add to this as we go along. Since it extends the Observable class, we will be able to register the view class with it as an observer, and automatically notify the view of any changes. This facility will come into its own when we have multiple views.

We can define the view class as a component by deriving it from JComponent. This will build in all the methods for operating as a component and we can override any of these as necessary. The view class also needs to implement the Observer interface so that we can register it with the model. Here's the outline:

```
import javax.swing.*;
import java.util.*;                      // For Observer

class SketchView extends JComponent
                 implements Observer
{
  public SketchView(Sketcher theApp)
  {
    this.theApp = theApp;
  }

  // Method called by Observable object when it changes
  public void update(Observable o, Object rectangle)
  {
    // Code to respond to changes in the model...
  }

  private Sketcher theApp;              // The application object
}
```

The view is definitely going to need access to the model in order to display it, so the constructor has a parameter to enable the application object to be passed to it. By storing the application object in the view, rather than a reference to the model, and adding a method to the application object to return a reference to the model, we make the view object independent of the model object. If a completely different object represents the model because, for example, a new file is loaded, we don't need to change the view object. As long as the view object is registered as an observer for the new model, the view will automatically redraw the new sketch when it is notified by the model that it has changed.

To integrate a model and its view into the Sketcher application, we just need to add some code to the Sketcher class:

```
import java.awt.*;
import java.awt.event.*;
import java.util.*;

public class Sketcher
{
  public static void main(String[] args)
  {
    theApp = new Sketcher();               // Create the application object
    theApp.init();                         // ... and initialize it
  }
```

```
    public void init()
    {
       window = new SketchFrame("Sketcher", this);      // Create the app window
       Toolkit theKit = window.getToolkit();             // Get the window toolkit
       Dimension wndSize = theKit.getScreenSize();       // Get screen size

       // Set the position to screen center & size to 2/3 screen size
       window.setBounds(wndSize.width/6, wndSize.height/6,        // Position
                        2*wndSize.width/3, 2*wndSize.height/3);   // Size

       window.addWindowListener(new WindowHandler()); // Add window listener

       sketch = new SketchModel();                       // Create the model
       view = new SketchView(this);                      // Create the view
       sketch.addObserver((Observer)view);               // Register the view with the model
       window.getContentPane().add(view, BorderLayout.CENTER);
       window.setVisible(true);
    }

    // Return a reference to the application window
    public SketchFrame getWindow()
    {
       return window;
    }

    // Return a reference to the model
    public SketchModel getModel()
    {
       return sketch;
    }

    // Return a reference to the view
    public SketchView getView()
    {
       return view;
    }


    // Handler class for window events
    class WindowHandler extends WindowAdapter
    {
       // Handler for window closing event
       public void windowClosing(WindowEvent e)
       {
         // Code to be added here later...
       }
    }

    private SketchModel sketch;              // The data model for the sketch
    private SketchView view;                 // The view of the sketch
    private static SketchFrame window;       // The application window
    private static Sketcher theApp;          // The application object
}
```

There is no code in the windowClosing() method at present, so this assumes we have restored EXIT_ON_CLOSE as the default closing action in the SketchFrame class. We will be adding code to the windowClosing() method when we get to save sketches on disk. The SketchFrame constructor needs to be modified as follows:

```
public SketchFrame(String title, Sketcher theApp)
{
    setTitle(title);                            // Set the window title
    this.thcApp = theApp;
    setJMenuBar(menuBar);                       // Add the menu bar to the window
    setDefaultCloseOperation(EXIT_ON_CLOSE);    // Default is exit the application

    // Rest of the constructor as before...
}
```

You need to add the theApp variable to the SketchFrame class

```
    private Sketcher theApp;
```

There are new methods in the Sketcher class that return a reference to the application window, the model and the view, so any of these are accessible from anywhere that a reference to the application object is available.

After creating the model and view objects, we register the view as an observer for the model to enable the model to notify the view when it changes. We then add the view to the content pane of the window object, which is the main application window. Since it is added in the center using the BorderLayout manager for the content pane, it will occupy all the remaining space in the pane.

Now that we know roughly the direction in which we are heading, let's move on down the road.

Coordinate Systems in Components

In Chapter 11, we saw how your computer screen has a coordinate system that is used to define the position and size of a window. We also saw how we can add components to a container with their position established by a layout manager. This coordinate system is analogous to the screen coordinate system. The origin is at the top-left corner of the container, with the positive x-axis running horizontally from left to right, and the positive y-axis running from top to bottom. The positions of buttons in a JWindow or a JFrame object are specified as a pair of (x, y) pixel coordinates, relative to the origin at the top-left corner of the container object on the screen. Below you can see the coordinate system for the Sketcher application window.

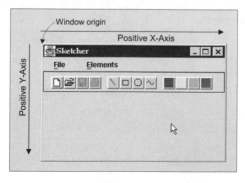

Of course, the layered pane for the window object will have its own coordinate system with the origin in the top-left corner of the pane, and this is used to position the menu and the content pane. The content pane will have its own coordinate system too that will be used to position the components it contains.

It's not just containers and windows that have their own coordinate system: each JButton object also has its own system, as do JToolBar objects. In fact, *every* component has its own coordinate system.

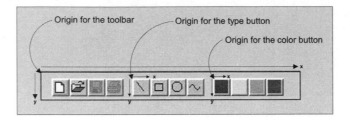

It's clear that a container needs a coordinate system for specifying the positions of the components it contains. You also need a coordinate system to draw on a component – to draw a line for instance you need to be able to specify where it begins and ends in relation to the component – and while the coordinate system here is similar to that used for positioning components in a container, it's not exactly the same. It's more complicated when you are drawing – but for very good reasons. Let's see how the coordinate system for drawing works.

Drawing on a Component

Before we get into the specifics of how you draw on a component, let's understand the principle ideas behind it. When you draw on a component using the Java 2D capabilities, there are two coordinate systems involved. When you draw something – a line or a curve for instance – you specify the line or the curve in a device-independent logical coordinate system called the **user coordinate system** for the component, or **user space**. By default this coordinate system has the same orientation as the system that we discussed for positioning components in containers. The origin is at the top-left corner; the positive *x*-axis runs from left to right, and the positive *y*-axis from top to bottom. Coordinates are usually specified as floating point values, although integers can also be used.

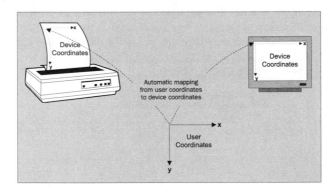

A particular graphical output device will have its own **device coordinate system, or device space.** This has the same orientation as the default user coordinate system, but the coordinate units depend on the characteristics of the device. Your display, for instance, will have a different device coordinate system for each configuration of the screen resolution, so the coordinate system when your display is set to 1024x768 resolution will be different from the coordinate system for 800x600 pixels.

> *Incidentally, the drawing process is often referred to as **rendering**, since graphical output devices are generally raster devices and the drawing elements such as lines, rectangles, text and so on need to be rendered into a rasterized representation before they can be output to the device.*

Having a device-independent coordinate system for drawing means that you can use essentially the same code for outputting graphics to a variety of different devices – to your display screen, for example, or to your printer – even though these devices themselves have quite different coordinate systems with different resolutions. The fact that your screen might have 90 pixels per inch while your printer may have 600 dots per inch is automatically taken care of Java 2D will deal with converting your user coordinates to the device coordinate system that is specific to the output device you are using.

With the default mapping from user coordinates to device coordinates, the units for user coordinates are assumed to be 1/72 of an inch. Since for most screen devices the pixels are approximately 1/72 inch apart, the conversion amounts to an identity transformation. If you want to use user coordinates that are in some other units, you have to provide for this yourself. We will look into the mechanism that you would use to do this when we discuss transformations in the next chapter.

Graphics Contexts

The user coordinate system for drawing on a component using Java 2D is encapsulated in an object of type `Graphics2D`, which is usually referred to as a **graphics context**. It provides all the tools you need to draw whatever you want on the surface of the component. A graphics context enables you to draw lines, curves, shapes, filled shapes, as well as images, and gives you a great deal of control over the drawing process.

The `Graphics2D` class is derived from the `Graphics` class that defined device contexts in earlier versions of Java, so if you feel the need to use the old drawing methods, they are all inherited in the `Graphics2D` class. We will be concentrating on the new more powerful and flexible facilities provided by `Graphics2D` but, as you will see, references to graphics contexts are usually passed around as type `Graphics` so you need to be aware of it. Note that both the `Graphics` and `Graphics2D` classes are abstract classes, so you can't create objects of either type directly. An object representing a graphics context is entirely dependent on the component to which it relates, so a graphics context is always obtained for use with a particular component.

The `Graphics2D` object for a component takes care of mapping user coordinates to device coordinates, so it contains information about the device that is the destination for output as well as the user coordinates for the component. The information required for converting user coordinates to device coordinates is encapsulated in three different kinds of object:

❑ A `GraphicsEnvironment` object encapsulates all the graphics devices (as `GraphicsDevice` objects) and fonts (as `Font` objects) that are available on your computer.

❑ A `GraphicsDevice` object encapsulates information about a particular device such as a screen or a printer, and stores it in one or more `GraphicsConfiguration` objects.

653

❑ A GraphicsConfiguration object defines the characteristics of a particular device such as a screen or a printer. Your display screen will typically have several GraphicsConfiguration objects associated with it, each corresponding to a particular combination of screen resolution and number of displayable colors.

The graphics context also maintains other information necessary for drawing operations such as the drawing color, the line style and the specification of the fill color and pattern for filled shapes. We will see how to work with these attributes in examples later in this chapter.

Since a graphics context defines the drawing context for a specific component, before you can draw on a component you must have a reference to its graphics context object. For the most part, you will draw on a component by implementing the paint() method that is called whenever the component needs to be reconstructed. An object representing the graphics context for the component is passed as an argument to the paint() method, and you use this to do the drawing. The graphics context includes all the methods that you use to draw on a component and we will be looking into many of these in this chapter.

The paint() method is not the only way of drawing on a component. You can obtain a graphics context for a component at any time just by calling its getGraphics() method.

There are occasions when you want to get a component redrawn while avoiding a direct call of the paint() method. In such cases you should call repaint() for the component. There are five versions of this method that you can use; we'll look at four:

repaint() Method	Description
repaint()	Causes the entire component to be repainted by calling its paint() method after all of the currently outstanding events have been processed.
repaint(long msec)	Requests that the entire component is repainted within msec milliseconds.
repaint(int msec, int x, int y, int width, int height)	Adds the region specified by the arguments to the **dirty region** list if the component is visible. The dirty region list is simply a list of areas of the component that need to be repainted. The component will be repainted by calling its paint() method when all currently outstanding events have been processed or within msec milliseconds. The region is the rectangle at position (x, y) with the width and height as specified by the last two arguments.
repaint(Rectangle rect)	Adds the rectangle specified by rect to the dirty region list if the component is visible.

You will find that the first and the last methods are the ones you use most of the time.

That's enough theory for now. Time to get a bit of practice.

Let's get an idea of how we can draw on a component by drawing on the SketchView object that we added to Sketcher. All we need to do is implement the paint() method in the SketchView class.

Try It Out — Drawing in a View

Add the following implementation of the method to the `SketchView` class:

```java
import javax.swing.*;
import java.util.*;                                    // For Observer
import java.awt.*;                                     // For Graphics

class SketchView extends JComponent
                 implements Observer
{
  public void paint(Graphics g)
  {
    // Temporary code
    Graphics2D g2D = (Graphics2D)g;                    // Get a Java 2D device context

    g2D.setPaint(Color.red);                           // Draw in red
    g2D.draw3DRect(50, 50, 150, 100, true);            // Draw a raised 3D rectangle
    g2D.drawString("A nice 3D rectangle", 60, 100);    // Draw some text
  }

  // Rest of the class as before...
}
```

If you recompile the file `SketchFrame.java` and run Sketcher, you can see what the `paint()` method produces. You should see the window shown here.

How It Works

The graphics context is passed as the argument to the `paint()` method as type `Graphics` (the base class for `Graphics2D`) so to use the methods defined in the `Graphics2D` class we must first cast it to that type. The `paint()` method has a parameter type of `Graphics` for compatibility reasons.

Once we have cast the graphics context, we then set the color in which we will draw by calling the `setPaint()` method for the `Graphics2D` object and passing the drawing color as an argument. All subsequent drawing operations will now be in `Color.red`. We can change this again later with another call to `setPaint()` when we want to draw in a different color.

Next we call the `draw3DRect()` method defined in the `Graphics2D` class that draws a 3D rectangle. The first two arguments are integers specifying the *x* and *y* coordinates of the top-left corner of the rectangle to be drawn, relative to the user space origin of the component – in this case the top-left corner of the view object in the content pane. The third and fourth arguments are the width and height of the rectangle respectively, also in user coordinates.

The `drawString()` method draws the string specified as the first argument at the position determined by the second and third argument – these are the *x* and *y* coordinates in user coordinates of the bottom-left corner of the first letter of the string. The string will be drawn by obtaining the glyphs for the current `Font` object in the device context corresponding to the characters in the string. As we said when we discussed `Font` objects, the glyphs for a font define the physical appearance of the characters.

However, there's more to drawing than is apparent from this example. The graphics context has information about the line style to be drawn, as well as the color, the font to be used for text and more besides. Let's dig a little deeper into what is going on.

The Drawing Process

A `Graphics2D` object maintains a whole heap of information that determines how things are drawn. Most of this information is contained in six attributes within a `Graphics2D` object:

- ❑ The **paint** attribute determines the drawing color for lines. It also defines the color and pattern to be used for filling shapes. The paint attribute is set by calling the `setPaint(Paint paint)` method for the graphics context. The default paint attribute is the color of the component.

- ❑ The **stroke** attribute defines a **pen** that determines the line style, such as solid, dashed or dotted lines, and the line thickness. It also determines the shape of the ends of lines. The stroke attribute is set by calling the `setStroke(Stroke s)` method for a graphics context. The default stroke attribute defines a square pen that draws a solid line with a thickness of 1 user coordinate unit. The ends of the line are square and joins are mitered.

- ❑ The **font** attribute determines the font to be used when drawing text. The font attribute is set by calling the `setFont(Font font)` method for the graphics context. The default font is the font set for the component.

- ❑ The **transform** attribute defines the transformations to be applied during the rendering process. What you draw can be translated, rotated and scaled as determined by the transforms currently in effect. There are several methods for applying transforms to what is drawn as we will see. The default transform is the identity transform, which leaves things unchanged.

- ❑ The **clip** attribute defines the boundary of an area on a component. Rendering operations are restricted so that drawing only takes place within the area enclosed by the clip boundary. The clip attribute is set by calling one of the two `setClip()` methods for a graphics context. The default clip attribute is the whole component area.

- ❑ The **composite** attribute determines how overlapping shapes are drawn on a component. You can alter the transparency of the fill color of a shape so an underlying shape shows through. You set the composite attribute by calling the `setComposite(Composite comp)` method for the graphics context. The default composite attribute causes a new shape to be drawn over whatever is already there, taking account of the transparency of any of the colors used.

All of the objects representing attributes are stored as references within a `Graphics2D` object. Therefore, you must always call a `setXXX()` method to alter an attribute in a graphics context, not try to modify an external object directly. If you alter an object externally that has been used to set an attribute, the results are unpredictable.

> *You can also affect how the rendering process deals with 'jaggies' when drawing lines. The process to eliminate 'jaggies' on sloping lines is called **antialiasing**, and you can change the antialiasing that is applied by calling one of the two `setRenderingHints()` methods for a graphics context. We will not be going into this aspect of drawing further though.*

There's a huge amount of detail on attributes under the covers. Rather than going into all that here, we'll explore how to apply new attributes to a graphics context piecemeal where it is relevant to the various examples we will create.

Rendering Operations

There are the following basic methods available to a `Graphics2D` object for rendering various kinds of entity:

Method	Description
draw(Shape shape)	Renders a shape using the current attributes for the graphics context. We will be discussing what a shape is next.
fill(Shape shape)	Fills a shape using the current attributes for the graphics context. We will see how to do this later in this chapter.
drawString(String text)	Renders a text string using the current attributes for the graphics context. We will be applying this further in the next chapter.
drawImage()	Renders an image using the current attributes for the graphics context. This is quite a complicated operation so we won't be getting very far into this.

Let's see what shapes are available. They'll help make Sketcher a lot more useful.

Shapes

Classes that define geometric shapes are contained in the `java.awt.geom` package, so to use them in a class we will need an `import` statement for this package at the beginning of the class file. You can add one to `SketchView.java` right now if you like. While the classes that define shapes are in `java.awt.geom`, the `Shape` interface is defined in `java.awt`, so you will usually need to import both packages into your source file.

A shape is defined by any class that implements the `Shape` interface – visually it will be some composite of straight lines and curves. Straight lines, rectangles, ellipses and curves are all shapes.

A graphic context knows how to draw Shape objects. To draw a shape on a component, you just need to pass the object defining the shape to the draw() method for the Graphics2D object for the component. To look at this in detail, we'll split the shapes into three groups, straight lines and rectangles, arcs and ellipses, and freeform curves. First though, we must take a look at how points are defined.

Classes Defining Points

There are two classes in the java.awt.geom package that define points, Point2D.Float and Point2D.Double. From the class names you can see that these are both inner classes to the class Point2D, which also happens to be an abstract base class for both too. The Point2D.Float class defines a point from a pair of (x,y) coordinates of type float, whereas the Point2D.Double class defines a point as a coordinate pair of type double. The Point class in the java.awt package also defines a point, but in terms of a coordinate pair of type int. This class also has Point2D as a base.

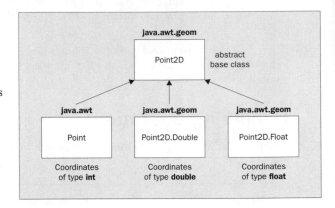

The Point class actually predates the Point2D class, but the class was redefined to make it a subclass of Point2D when Point2D was introduced, hence the somewhat unusual class hierarchy with only two of the subclasses as inner classes. The merit of this arrangement is that all of the subclasses inherit the methods defined in the Point2D class, so operations on each of the three kinds of point are the same.

The three subclasses of Point2D define a default constructor that defines the point 0,0, and a constructor that accept a pair of coordinates of the type appropriate to the class type.

The operations that each of the three concrete point classes inherit are:

1. Accessing coordinate values:

The getX() and getY() methods return the x and y coordinates of a point as type double, regardless of how the coordinates are stored. These are abstract methods in the Point2D class so they are defined in each of the subclasses. Although you get coordinates as double values from all three concrete classes via these methods you can always access the coordinates with their original type directly since the coordinates are stored in public fields with the same names, x and y, in each case.

2. Calculating the distance between two points:

You have no less that three overloaded versions of the `distance()` method for calculating the distance between two points, and returning it as type double:

```
distance(double x1, double y1, double x2, double y2)
```

This is a static version of the method that calculates the distance between the points x1,y1 and x2,y2.

```
distance(double xNext, double yNext)
```

Calculates the distance from the current point (the object for which the method is called) and the point xNext,yNext.

```
distance(Point2D nextPoint)
```

Calculates the distance from the current point to the point, nextPoint. The argument can be any of the subclass types, Point, Point2D.Float or Point2D.Double.

Here's how you might calculate the distance between two points:

```
Point2D.Double p1 = new Point2D.Double(2.5, 3.5);
Point p2 = new Point(20, 30);
double lineLength = p1.distance(p2);
```

You could also have calculated this distance without creating the points by using the static method:

```
double lineLength = Point2D.distance(2.5, 3.5, 20, 30);
```

Corresponding to each of the three `distance()` methods there is a convenience method, `distanceSq()`, with the same parameter list that returns the square of the distance as type `double`.

3. Comparing points:

The `equals()` method compares the current point with the point object referenced by the argument and returns true if they are `equal` and `false` otherwise.

4. Setting a new location for a point:

The inherited `setLocation()` method comes in two versions. One accepts an argument that is a reference of type `Point2D`, and sets the coordinate values of the current point to those of the point passed as an argument. The other accepts two arguments of type double that are the x and y coordinates of the new location. The `Point` class also defines a version of `setLocation()` that accepts two arguments of type int to define the new coordinates.

Lines and Rectangles

The `java.awt.geom` package contains the following classes for shapes that are straight lines and rectangles:

Class	Description
Line2D	This is an abstract base class defining a line between two points. There are two concrete subclasses – `Line2D.Float` and `Line2D.Double` that define lines in terms of user coordinates of type `float` and `double` respectively. You can see from their names that the subclasses are nested classes to the abstract base class, `Line2D`.
Rectangle2D	This is the abstract base class for the `Rectangle2D.Double` and `Rectangle2D.Float` classes that define rectangles. A rectangle is defined by the coordinates of the position of its top-left corner plus its width and height. The `Rectangle2D` class is also the abstract base class for the `Rectangle` class in the `java.awt` package, which stores the position coordinates and the height and width as values of type `int`.
RoundRectangle2D	This is the abstract base class for `RoundRectangle2D.Double` and `RoundRectangle2D.Float` classes that define rectangles with rounded corners. The rounded corners are specified by a width and height.

As with the classes defining points, the `Rectangle` class that is defined in the `java.awt` package predates the `Rectangle2D` class, but the definition of the `Rectangle` class was changed to make `Rectangle2D` a base for compatibility reasons. Note that there is no equivalent to the `Rectangle` class for lines defines by integer coordinates. If you are browsing the documentation, you may notice there is a `Line` interface, but this is nothing to do with geometry, as we will see when we dip into the sound capabilities of Java.

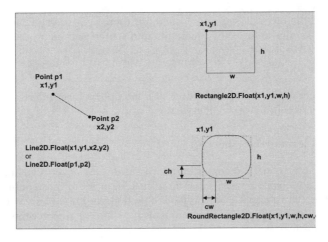

You can define a line by supplying two `Point2D` objects to a constructor, or two pairs of (*x*, *y*) coordinates. For example, here's how you define a line by two coordinate pairs:

```
Line2D.float line = new Line2D.Float(5.0f, 100.0f, 50.0f, 150.0f);
```

This draws a line from the point (5.0, 100.0) to the point (50.0, 150.0). You could also create the same line using `Point2D.Float` objects:

```
Point2D.Float p1 = new Point2D.Float(5.0f, 100.0f);
Point2D.Float p2 = new Point2D.Float(50.0f, 150.0f);
Line2D.float line = new Line2D.Float(p1, p2);
```

You draw a line using the `draw()` method for a `Graphics2D` object, for example:

```
g2D.draw(line);          // Draw the line
```

To create a rectangle, you specify the coordinates of its top-left corner, and the width and height:

```
float width = 120.0f;
float height = 90.0f;
Rectangle2D.Float rectangle = new Rectangle2D.Float(50.0f, 150.0f, width, height);
```

The default constructor creates a rectangle at the origin with a zero width and height. You can set the position, width, and height of a rectangle by calling the `setRect()` method. There are three versions of this method. One of them accepts arguments for the coordinates of the top-left corner and the width and height as `float` values, exactly as in the constructor. Another accepts the same arguments but of type `double`. The third accepts an argument of type `Rectangle2D` so you can pass either type of `Rectangle2D` to it.

A `Rectangle2D` object has `getX()` and `getY()` methods for retrieving the coordinates of the top-left corner, and `getWidth()` and `getHeight()` methods that return the width and height.

A round rectangle is a rectangle with rounded corners. The corners are defined by a width and a height and are essentially a quarter segment of an ellipse (we will get to ellipses later). Of course, if the corner width and height are equal then the corner will be a quarter of a circle.

You can define a round rectangle using coordinates of type `double` with the statements:

```
Point2D.Double position = new Point2D.Double(10, 10);
double width = 200.0;
double height = 100;
double cornerWidth = 15.0;
double cornerHeight = 10.0;
RoundRectangle2D.Double roundRect = new RoundRectangle2D.Double(
                  position.x, position.y,      // Position of top-left
                  width, height,               // Rectangle width & height
                  cornerWidth, cornerHeight);  // Corner width & height
```

The only difference between this and defining an ordinary rectangle is the addition of the width and height to be applied for the corner rounding.

Combining Rectangles

You can combine two rectangles to produce a new rectangle that is either the **union** of the two original rectangles or the **intersection**. Let's take a couple of specifics to see how this works. We can create two rectangles with the statements:

```
float width = 120.0f;
float height = 90.0f;
Rectangle2D.Float rect1 = new Rectangle2D.Float(50.0f, 150.0f, width, height);
Rectangle2D.Float rect2 = new Rectangle2D.Float(80.0f, 180.0f, width, height);
```

We can obtain the intersection of the two rectangles with the statement:

```
Rectangle2D.Float rect3 = rect1.createIntersection(rect2);
```

The effect is illustrated in the diagram below by the shaded rectangle. Of course, the result is the same if we call the method for `rect2` with `rect1` as the argument. If the rectangles don't overlap the rectangle that is returned will be the rectangle from the bottom right of one rectangle to the top right of the other that does not overlap either.

The following statement produces the union of the two rectangles:

```
Rectangle2D.Float rect3 = rect1.createUnion(rect2);
```

The result is shown in the diagram by the rectangle with the heavy boundary that encloses the other two.

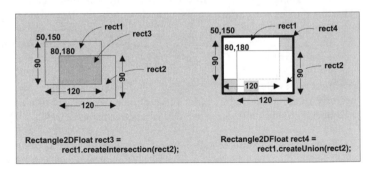

Testing Rectangles

Perhaps the simplest test you can apply is for an empty rectangle. The `isEmpty()` method that is implemented in all the rectangle classes returns `true` if the `Rectangle2D` object is empty – which is when either the width or the height (or both) are zero.

You can also test whether a point lies inside any type of rectangle object by calling its `contains()` method. There are `contains()` methods for all the rectangle classes that accept a `Point2D` argument or a pair of (x, y) coordinates of a type matching that of the rectangle class: they return `true` if the point lies within the rectangle. Each shape class defines a `getBounds2D()` method that returns a `Rectangle2D` object that encloses the shape.

This method is frequently used in association with the `contains()` method to test efficiently whether the cursor lies within a particular shape. Testing whether the cursor is within the enclosing rectangle will be a lot faster in general than testing whether it is within the precise boundary of the shape, and is good enough for many purposes – when selecting a particular shape on the screen to manipulate it in some way for instance.

There are also versions of the `contains()` method to test whether a given rectangle lies within the area occupied by a rectangle object – this obviously enables you to test whether a shape lies within another shape. The given rectangle can be passed to the `contains()` method as the coordinates of its top-left corner and its height and width as type `double`, or as a `Rectangle2D` reference. The method returns `true` if the rectangle object completely contains the given rectangle.

Let's try drawing a few simple lines and rectangles by inserting some code in the `paint()` method for the view in Sketcher.

Try It Out — Drawing Lines and Rectangles

If you haven't already done so, add an `import` statement to `SketchView.java` for the `java.awt.geom` package:

```
import java.awt.geom.*;
```

Now replace the previous code in the `paint()` method in the `SketchView` class with the following:

```
public void paint(Graphics g)
{
  // Temporary code
  Graphics2D g2D = (Graphics2D)g;               // Get a Java 2D device context

  g2D.setPaint(Color.red);                      // Draw in red

  // Position width and height of first rectangle
  Point2D.Float p1 = new Point2D.Float(50.0f, 10.0f);
  float width1 = 60;
  float height1 = 80;

  // Create and draw the first rectangle
  Rectangle2D.Float rect = new Rectangle2D.Float(p1.x, p1.y, width1, height1);
  g2D.draw(rect);

  // Position width and height of second rectangle
  Point2D.Float p2 = new Point2D.Float(150.0f, 100.0f);
  float width2 = width1 + 30;
  float height2 = height1 + 40;

  // Create and draw the second rectangle
  g2D.draw(new Rectangle2D.Float(
                    (float)(p2.getX()), (float)(p2.getY()), width2, height2));
```

```
        g2D.setPaint(Color.blue);                              // Draw in blue

        // Draw lines to join corresponding corners of the rectangles
        Line2D.Float line = new Line2D.Float(p1,p2);
        g2D.draw(line);

        p1.setLocation(p1.x + width1, p1.y);
        p2.setLocation(p2.x + width2, p2.y);
        g2D.draw(new Line2D.Float(p1,p2));

        p1.setLocation(p1.x, p1.y + height1);
        p2.setLocation(p2.x, p2.y + height2);
        g2D.draw(new Line2D.Float(p1,p2));

        p1.setLocation(p1.x - width1, p1.y);
        p2.setLocation(p2.x - width2, p2.y);
        g2D.draw(new Line2D.Float(p1, p2));

        p1.setLocation(p1.x, p1.y - height1);
        p2.setLocation(p2.x, p2.y - height2);
        g2D.draw(new Line2D.Float(p1, p2));

        g2D.drawString("Lines and rectangles", 60, 250); // Draw some text
    }
```

If you type this in correctly and recompile `SketchView` class, the Sketcher window will look like:

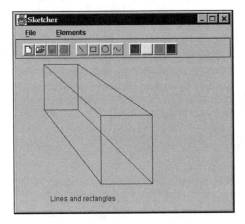

How It Works

After casting the graphics context object that is passed to the `paint()` method to type `Graphics2D` we set the drawing color to red. All subsequent drawing that we do will be in red until we change the color with another call to `setPaint()`. We define a `Point2D.Float` object to represent the position of the first rectangle, and we define variables to hold the width and height of the rectangle. We use these to create the rectangle by passing them as arguments to the constructor that we have seen before, and display the rectangle by passing the `rect` object to the `draw()` method for the graphics context, `g2D`. The second rectangle is defined by essentially the same process, except that this time we create the `Rectangle2D.Float` object in the argument expression for the `draw()` method.

Note that we have to cast the values returned by the getX() and getY() members of the Point2D object as they are returned as type double. It is generally more convenient to reference the x and y fields directly as we do in the rest of the code.

We change the drawing color to blue so that you can see quite clearly the lines we are drawing. We use the setLocation() method for the point objects to move the point on each rectangle to successive corners, and draw a line at each position. The caption also appears in blue since that is the color in effect when we call the drawString() method to output the text string.

Arcs and Ellipses

The abstract class representing a generic ellipse is:

Class	Description
Ellipse2D	This is the abstract base class for the Ellipse2D.Double and Ellipse2D.Float classes that define ellipses. An ellipse is defined by the top-left corner, width and height of the rectangle that encloses it.

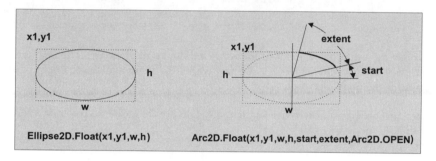

The class representing an elliptic arc is:

Class	Description
Arc2D	This is the abstract base class for the Arc2D.Double and Arc2D.Float classes that define arcs as a portion of an ellipse. The full ellipse is defined by the position of the top-left corner and the width and height of the rectangle that encloses it. The arc length is defined by a start angle measured in degrees anti-clockwise relative to the horizontal axis of the full ellipse, plus an angular extent measured anti-clockwise from the start angle in degrees. An arc can be OPEN, which means the ends are not connected; CHORD, which means the ends are connected by a straight line, or PIE which means the ends are connected by straight lines to the center of the whole ellipse. These constants are defined in Arc2D.

Arcs and ellipses are closely related since an arc is just a segment of an ellipse. To define an ellipse you supply the data necessary to define the enclosing rectangle – the coordinates of the top-left corner, the width and the height. To define an arc you supply the data to define the ellipse, plus additional data that defines the segment that you want. The seventh argument to the arc constructor determines the type, whether OPEN, CHORD or PIE.

You could define an ellipse with the statements:

```
Point2D.Double position = new Point2D.Double(10,10);
double width = 200.0;
double height = 100;
Ellipse2D.Double ellipse = new Ellipse2D.Double(
                       position.x, position.y, // Top-left corner
                       width, height);         // width & height of rectangle
```

You could define an arc that is a segment of the previous ellipse with the statement:

```
Arc2D.Double arc = new Arc2D.Double(
                       position.x, position.y, // Top-left corner
                       width, height,          // width & height of rectangle
                       0.0, 90.0,              // Start and extent angles
                       Arc2D.OPEN);            // Arc is open
```

This defines the upper-right quarter segment of the whole ellipse as an open arc. The angles are measured anticlockwise from the horizontal in degrees. As we saw earlier the first angular argument is where the arc starts, and the second is the angular extent of the arc.

Of course, a circle is just an ellipse where the width and height are the same, so the following statement defines a circle with a diameter of 150:

```
double diameter = 150.0;
Ellipse2D.Double circle = new Ellipse2D.Double(
                       position.x, position.y,  // Top-left corner
                       diameter, diameter);     // width & height of rectangle
```

This presumes the point position is defined somewhere. You will often want to define a circle by its center and radius – this is easily done by adjusting the arguments to the constructor a little:

```
Point2D.Double center = new Point2D.Double(200, 200);
double radius = 150;
Ellipse2D.Double newCircle = new Ellipse2D.Double(
               center.x-radius, center.y-radius,   // Top-left corner
               2*radius, 2*radius);                // width & height of rectangle
```

The fields storing the coordinates of the top-left corner of the enclosing rectangle and the width and height are public members of Ellipse2D and Arc2D objects – x, y, width and height respectively. An Arc2D object also has public members, start and extent that store the angles.

Try It Out — Drawing Arcs and Ellipses

Let's modify the paint() method in SketchView.java once again to draw some arcs and ellipses.

```java
public void paint(Graphics g)
{
  // Temporary code
  Graphics2D g2D = (Graphics2D)g;                    // Get a Java 2D device context

  Point2D.Double position = new Point2D.Double(50,10);  // Initial position
  double width = 150;                                // Width of ellipse
  double height = 100;                               // Height of ellipse
  double start = 30;                                 // Start angle for arc
  double extent = 120;                               // Extent of arc
  double diameter = 40;                              // Diameter of circle

  // Define open arc as an upper segment of an ellipse
  Arc2D.Double top = new Arc2D.Double(position.x, position.y,
                                width, height,
                                start, extent,
                                Arc2D.OPEN);

  // Define open arc as lower segment of ellipse shifted up relative to 1st
  Arc2D.Double bottom = new Arc2D.Double(
                                position.x, position.y - height + diameter,
                                width, height,
                                start + 180, extent,
                                Arc2D.OPEN);

  // Create a circle centered between the two arcs
  Ellipse2D.Double circle1 = new Ellipse2D.Double(
                                position.x + width/2 - diameter/2,position.y,
                                diameter, diameter);

  // Create a second circle concentric with the first and half the diameter
  Ellipse2D.Double circle2 = new Ellipse2D.Double(
                    position.x + width/2 - diameter/4, position.y + diameter/4,
                    diameter/2, diameter/2);

  // Draw all the shapes
  g2D.setPaint(Color.black);                         // Draw in black
  g2D.draw(top);
  g2D.draw(bottom);

  g2D.setPaint(Color.blue);                          // Draw in blue
  g2D.draw(circle1);
  g2D.draw(circle2);
  g2D.drawString("Arcs and ellipses", 80, 100);      // Draw some text
}
```

667

Running Sketcher with this version of the paint() method in SketchView will produce the window shown here.

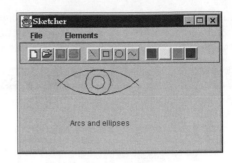

How It Works

This time we create all the shapes first and then draw them. The two arcs are segments of ellipses of the same height and width. The lower segment is shifted up with respect to the first so that they intersect, and the distance between the top of the rectangle for the first and the bottom of the rectangle for the second is diameter, which is the diameter of the first circle we create.

Both circles are created centered between the two arcs and are concentric. Finally we draw all the shapes – the arcs in black and the circles in blue.

Curves

There are two classes that define arbitrary curves, one defining a quadratic or second order curve and the other defining a cubic curve. The cubic curve just happens to be a Bézier curve (so called because it was developed by a Frenchman, Monsieur P. Bézier, and first applied in the context of defining contours for programming numerically-controlled machine tools.) The classes defining these curves are:

Class	Description
QuadCurve2D	This is the abstract base class for the QuadCurve2D.Double and QuadCurve2D.Float classes that define a quadratic curve segment. The curve is defined by its end points plus a control point that defines the tangent at each end. The tangents are the lines from the end points to the control point.
CubicCurve2D	This is the abstract base class for the CubicCurve2D.Double and CubicCurve2D.Float classes that define a cubic curve segment. The curve is defined by its end points plus two control points that define the tangent at each end. The tangents are the lines from the end points to the corresponding control point.

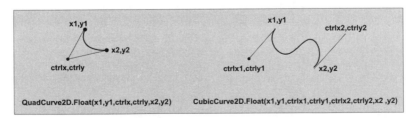

In general, there are many other methods for modeling arbitrary curves, but the two defined in Java have the merit that they are both easy to understand, and the effect on the curve segment when the control point is moved is quite intuitive.

An object of each curve type defines a curve segment between two points. The control points – one for a QuadCurve2D curve and two for a CubicCurve2D curve control the direction and magnitude of the tangents at the end points. A QuadCurve2D curve constructor has six parameters corresponding to the coordinates of the starting point for the segment, the coordinates of the control point and the coordinates of the end point. We can define a QuadCurve2D curve from a point start to a point end, plus a control point, control, with the statements:

```
Point2D.Double startQ = new Point2D.Double(50, 150);
Point2D.Double endQ = new Point2D.Double(150, 150);
Point2D.Double control = new Point2D.Double(80,100);

QuadCurve2D.Double quadCurve = new QuadCurve2D.Double(
                         startQ.x, startQ.y,          // Segment start
point
                         control.x, control.y,        // Control point
                         endQ.x, endQ.y);             // Segment end point
```

The QuadCurve2D subclasses have public members storing the end points and the control point so you can access them directly. The coordinates of the start and end points are stored in the fields, x1, y1, x2 and y2. The coordinates of the control point are stored in ctrlx and ctrly.

Defining a cubic curve segment is very similar – you just have two control points, one for each end of the segment. The arguments are the (x, y) coordinates of the start point, the control point for the start of the segment, the control point for the end of the segment and finally the end point. We could define a cubic curve with the statements:

```
Point2D.Double startC = new Point2D.Double(50, 300);
Point2D.Double endC = new Point2D.Double(150, 300);
Point2D.Double controlStart = new Point2D.Double(80, 250);
Point2D.Double controlEnd = new Point2D.Double(160, 250);

CubicCurve2D.Double cubicCurve = new CubicCurve2D.Double(
              startC.x, startC.y,              // Segment start point
              controlStart.x, controlStart.y,  // Control point for
start
              controlEnd.x, controlEnd.y,      // Control point for end
              endC.x, endC.y);                 // Segment end point
```

The cubic curve classes also have public members for all the points: x1, y1, x2 and y2 for the end points, and ctrlx1, ctrly1, ctrlx2 and ctrly2 for the corresponding control points.

We can understand these better if we try them out. This time let's do it with an applet.

Try It Out — Drawing Curves

We can define an applet to display the curves we used as examples above:

```java
import javax.swing.*;
import java.awt.*;
import java.awt.geom.*;

public class CurveApplet extends JApplet
{
  // Initialize the applet
  public void init()
  {
    pane = new CurvePane();                    // Create pane containing curves
    Container content = getContentPane();      // Get the content pane

    // Add the pane displaying the curves to the content pane for the applet
    content.add(pane);                         // BorderLayout.CENTER is default position
  }

  // Class defining a pane on which to draw
  class CurvePane extends JComponent
  {
    // Constructor
    public CurvePane()
    {
      quadCurve = new QuadCurve2D.Double(            // Create quadratic curve
                      startQ.x, startQ.y,            // Segment start point
                      control.x, control.y,          // Control point
                      endQ.x, endQ.y);               // Segment end point

      cubicCurve = new CubicCurve2D.Double(          // Create cubic curve
                      startC.x, startC.y,            // Segment start point
                      controlStart.x, controlStart.y,  // Control point for
start
                      controlEnd.x, controlEnd.y,    // Control point for end
                        endC.x, endC.y);             // Segment end point
    }
```

```java
    public void paint(Graphics g)
    {
      Graphics2D g2D = (Graphics2D)g;               // Get a 2D device
context

      // Draw the curves
      g2D.setPaint(Color.blue);
      g2D.draw(quadCurve);
      g2D.draw(cubicCurve);
    }
  }
```

```
    // Points for quadratic curve
    Point2D.Double startQ = new Point2D.Double(50, 150);        // Start point
    Point2D.Double endQ = new Point2D.Double(150, 150);         // End point
    Point2D.Double control = new Point2D.Double(80, 100);       // Control point

    // Points for cubic curve
    Point2D.Double startC = new Point2D.Double(50, 300);        // Start point
    Point2D.Double endC = new Point2D.Double(150, 300);         // End point
    Point2D.Double controlStart = new Point2D.Double(80, 250);  // 1st control
point
    Point2D.Double controlEnd = new Point2D.Double(160, 250);   // 2nd control
point

    QuadCurve2D.Double quadCurve;                               // Quadratic curve
    CubicCurve2D.Double cubicCurve;                             // Cubic curve
    CurvePane pane = new CurvePane();                           // Pane to contain curves
}
```

You will need an HTML file to run the applet. The contents can be something like:

```
<APPLET CODE="CurveApplet.class" WIDTH=300 HEIGHT=400></APPLET>
```

If you run the applet using `appletviewer`, you will get a window
looking like that here.

How It Works

We need an object of our own class type so that we can implement the `paint()` method for it. We define
the inner class `CurvePane` for this purpose with `JComponent` as the base class so it is a Swing component.
We create an object of this class (which is a member of the `CurveApplet` class) and add it to the content
pane for the applet using its inherited `add()` method. The layout manager for the content pane is
`BorderLayout`, and the default positioning is `BorderLayout.CENTER` so the `CurvePane` object fills the
content pane.

The points defining the quadratic and cubic curves are defined as fields in the `CurveApplet` class and these
are referenced in the `paint()` method for the `CurvePane` class to create the objects representing curves.
These points are used in the `CurvePane` class constructor to create the curves. We draw the curves by
calling the `draw()` method for the `Graphics2D` object and passing a reference to a curve object as the
argument.

671

It's hard to see how the control points affect the shape of the curve, so let's add some code to draw the control points.

Try It Out — Displaying the Control Points

We will mark the position of each control point by drawing a small circle around it. We can define a marker using an inner class of `CurveApplet` that we can define as:

```
// Inner class defining a control point marker
class Marker
{
  public Marker(Point2D.Double control)
  {
    center = control;                    // Save control point as circle center

    // Create circle around control point
    circle = new Ellipse2D.Double(control.x-radius, control.y-radius,
                               2.0*radius, 2.0*radius);
  }

  // Draw the marker
  public void draw(Graphics2D g2D)
  {
    g2D.draw(circle);
  }

  // Get center of marker - the control point position
  Point2D.Double getCenter()
  {
    return center;
  }

  Ellipse2D.Double circle;               // Circle around control point
  Point2D.Double center;                 // Circle center - the control point
  static final double radius = 3;        // Radius of circle
}
```

The argument to the constructor is the control point that is to be marked. The constructor stores this control point in the member, `center`, and creates an `Ellipse2D.Double` object that is the circle to mark the control point. The class also has a method, `draw()`, to draw the marker using the `Graphics2D` object reference that is passed to it. The `getCenter()` method returns the center of the marker as a `Point2D.Double` reference. We will use this method when we draw tangent lines from the end points of a curve to the corresponding control points.

We will add fields to the `CurveApplet` class to define the markers for the control points. These definitions should follow the member that define the points:

```
// Markers for control points
Marker ctrlQuad = new Marker(control);
Marker ctrlCubic1 = new Marker(controlStart);
Marker ctrlCubic2 = new Marker(controlEnd);
```

We can now add code to the paint() method for the CurvePane class to draw the markers and the tangents from the endpoints of the curve segments:

```
public void paint(Graphics g)
{
  // Code to draw curves as before...

  // Create and draw the markers showing the control points
  g2D.setPaint(Color.red);                      // Set the color
  ctrlQuad.draw(g2D);
  ctrlCubic1.draw(g2D);
  ctrlCubic2.draw(g2D);

  // Draw tangents from the curve end points to the control marker centers
  Line2D.Double tangent = new Line2D.Double(startQ, ctrlQuad.getCenter());
  g2D.draw(tangent);
  tangent = new Line2D.Double(endQ, ctrlQuad.getCenter());
  g2D.draw(tangent);

  tangent = new Line2D.Double(startC, ctrlCubic1.getCenter());
  g2D.draw(tangent);
  tangent = new Line2D.Double(endC, ctrlCubic2.getCenter());
  g2D.draw(tangent);
}
```

If you recompile the applet with these changes, when you execute it again you should see the window shown here.

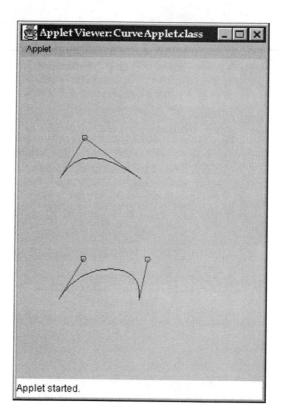

673

How It Works

In the `Marker` class constructor, the top-left corner of the rectangle enclosing the circle for a control point is obtained by subtracting the radius from the *x* and *y* coordinates of the control point. We then create an `Ellipse2D.Double` object with the width and height as twice the value of `radius` – which is the diameter of the circle.

In the `paint()` method we call the `draw()` method for each of the `Marker` objects to draw a red circle around each control point. The tangents are just lines from the endpoints of each curve segment to the centers of the corresponding `Marker` objects.

It would be good to see what happens to a curve segment when you move the control points around. Then we could really see how the control points affect the shape of the curve. That's not as difficult to implement as it might sound, so let's give it a try.

Try It Out — Moving the Control Points

We will arrange to allow a control point to be moved by positioning the cursor on it, pressing a mouse button and dragging it around. Releasing the mouse button will stop the process for that control point, so you will then be free to manipulate another one. To do this we will add another inner class to `CurveApplet` that will handle mouse events:

```java
class MouseHandler extends MouseInputAdapter
{
  public void mousePressed(MouseEvent e)
  {
    // Check if the cursor is inside any marker
    if(ctrlQuad.contains(e.getX(), e.getY()))
      selected = ctrlQuad;
    else if(ctrlCubic1.contains(e.getX(), e.getY()))
      selected = ctrlCubic1;
    else if(ctrlCubic2.contains(e.getX(), e.getY()))
      selected = ctrlCubic2;
  }

  public void mouseReleased(MouseEvent e)
  {
    selected = null;                             // Deselect any selected
marker
  }

  public void mouseDragged(MouseEvent e)
  {
    if(selected != null)                         // If a marker is selected
    {
      // Set the marker to current cursor position
      selected.setLocation(e.getX(), e.getY());
      pane.repaint();                            // Redraw pane contents
    }
  }

  Marker selected = null;                        // Stores reference to selected marker
}
```

We need to add two `import` statements to the beginning of the source file, one because we reference the `MouseInputAdapter` class, and the other because we refer to the `MouseEvent` class:

```
import javax.swing.event.*;
import java.awt.event.*;
```

The `mousePressed()` method calls a method `contains()` that should test whether the point defined by the arguments is inside the marker. We can implement this in the `Marker` class like this:

```
// Test if a point x,y is inside the marker
public boolean contains(double x, double y)
{
  return circle.contains(x,y);
}
```

This just calls the `contains()` method for the `circle` object that is the marker. This will return `true` if the point (x, y) is inside.

The `mouseDragged()` method calls a method `setLocation()` for the selected `Marker` object, so we need to implement this in the `Marker` class, too:

```
// Sets a new control point location
public void setLocation(double x, double y)
{
  center.x = x;              // Update control point
  center.y = y;              // coordinates
  circle.x = x-radius;       // Change circle position
  circle.y = y-radius;       // correspondingly
}
```

After updating the coordinates of the point, `center`, we also update the position of `circle` by setting its data member directly. We can do this because x and y are public members of the `Ellipse2D.Double` class.

We can create a `MouseHandler` object in the `init()` method for the applet and set it as the listener for mouse events for the pane object:

```
public void init()
{
  pane = new CurvePane();                    // Create pane containing curves
  Container content = getContentPane();      // Get the content pane

  // Add the pane displaying the curves to the content pane for the applet
  content.add(pane);                 // BorderLayout.CENTER is default position

  MouseHandler handler = new MouseHandler();  // Create the listener
  pane.addMouseListener(handler);             // Monitor mouse button presses
  pane.addMouseMotionListener(handler);       // as well as movement
}
```

Of course, to make the effect of moving the control points apparent, we must update the curve objects before we draw them. We can add the following code to the paint() method to do this:

```
public void paint(Graphics g)
{
    Graphics2D g2D = (Graphics2D)g;                    // Get a 2D device
context

    // Update the curves with the current control point positions
    quadCurve.ctrlx = ctrlQuad.getCenter().x;
    quadCurve.ctrly = ctrlQuad.getCenter().y;
    cubicCurve.ctrlx1 = ctrlCubic1.getCenter().x;
    cubicCurve.ctrly1 = ctrlCubic1.getCenter().y;
    cubicCurve.ctrlx2 = ctrlCubic2.getCenter().x;
    cubicCurve.ctrly2 = ctrlCubic2.getCenter().y;

    // Rest of the method as before...
}
```

We can update the data members that store the control point coordinates for the curves directly because they are public members of each curve class. We get the coordinates of the new positions for the control points from their markers by calling the getCenter() method for each, and then accessing the appropriate data member of the Point2D.Double object that is returned.

If you recompile the applet with these changes and run it again you should get something like the window here.

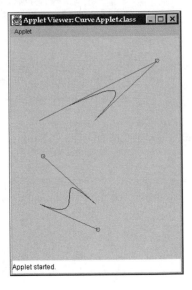

You should be able to drag the control points around with the mouse. If it is a bit difficult to select the control points, just make the value of radius a bit larger. Note how the angle of the tangent as well as its length affects the shape of the curve.

How It Works

In the `MouseHandler` class, the `mousePressed()` method will be called when you press a mouse button. In this method we check whether the current cursor position is within any of the markers enclosing the control points. We do this by calling the `contains()` method for each marker object and passing the coordinates of the cursor position to it. The `getX()` and `getY()` methods for the `MouseEvent` object supply the coordinates of the current cursor position. If one of the markers does enclose the cursor, we store a reference to the `Marker` object in the `selected` member of the `MouseHandler` class for use by the `mouseDragged()` method.

In the `mouseDragged()` method, we set the location for the `Marker` object referenced by `selected` to the current cursor position and call `repaint()` for the `pane` object. The `repaint()` method causes the `paint()` method to be called for the component, so everything will be redrawn, taking account of the modified control point position.

Releasing the mouse button will cause the `mouseReleased()` method to be called. In here we just set the `selected` field back to `null` so no `Marker` object is selected. Remarkably easy, wasn't it?

Complex Paths

You can define a more complex shape as an object of type `GeneralPath`. A `GeneralPath` object can be a composite of lines, `Quad2D` curves, and `Cubic2D` curves, or even other `GeneralPath` objects.

The process for determining whether a point is inside or outside a `GeneralPath` object is specified by the **winding rule** for the object. There are two winding rules that you can specify by constants defined in the class:

Winding Rule	Description
WIND_EVEN_ODD	In this case, a point is interior to a `GeneralPath` object if the boundary is crossed an odd number of times by a line from a point exterior to the `GeneralPath` to the point in question. You can use this winding rule for any kind of shape, including shapes with holes.
WIND_NON_ZERO	In this case, whether a point is inside or outside a path is determined by considering how the path crosses a line drawn from the point in question to infinity taking account of the direction in which the path is drawn. Looking along the line from the point, the point is interior to the `GeneralPath` object if the difference between the number of times the line is crossed by a boundary from left to right, and the number of times from right to left is non-zero. You can use this rule for general paths without holes – in other words shapes that are bounded by a single contiguous path. This rule does not work for shapes bounded by more than one contiguous path – with holes in other words – since the result will vary depending on the direction in which each path is drawn. However, it does work for a closed re-entrant path – a path that intersects itself.

These winding rules are illustrated below:

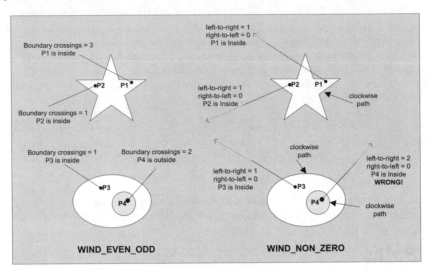

The safe option is WIND_EVEN_ODD.

There are four constructors for GeneralPath objects:

Constructor	Description
GeneralPath()	Defines a general path with a default winding rule of WIND_NON_ZERO.
GeneralPath(int rule)	Creates an object with the winding rule specified by the argument. This can be WIND_NON_ZERO or WIND_EVEN_ODD.
GeneralPath(int rule, int capacity)	Creates an object with the winding rule specified by the first argument and the number of path segments specified by the second argument. In any event, the capacity is increased when necessary.
GeneralPath(Shape shape)	Creates an object from the object passed as an argument.

We can create a GeneralPath object with the statement:

```
GeneralPath p = new GeneralPath(GeneralPath.WIND_EVEN_ODD);
```

A GeneralPath object embodies the notion of a current point of type Point2D from which the next path segment will be drawn. You set the initial current point by passing a pair of (x, y) coordinates as values of type float to the moveTo() method for the object. For example:

```
p.moveTo(10.0f,10.0f);            // Set the current point to 10,10
```

A segment is added to the general path, starting at the current point, and the end of each segment that you add becomes the new current point that is used to start the next segment. Of course, if you want disconnected segments in a path, you can call `moveTo()` to move the current point to wherever you want before you add a new segment. If you need to get the current position at any time, you can call the `getCurrentPoint()` method for a `GeneralPath` object and get the current point as type `Point2D`.

You can use the following methods to add segments to a `GeneralPath` object:

Methods to Add Segments	Description
`lineTo(float x, float y)`	Draws a line from the current point to the point (x, y).
`quadTo(float ctrlx, float ctrly, float x2, float y2)`	Draws a quadratic curve segment from the current point to the point $(x2, y2)$ with $(ctrlx, ctrly)$ as the control point.
`curveTo(float ctrlx1, float ctrly1, float ctrlx2, float ctrly2, float x2, float y2)`	Draws a Bezier curve segment from the current point with control point $(ctrlx1, ctrly1)$ to $(x2, y2)$ with $(ctrlx2, ctrly2)$ as the control point.

Each of these methods updates the current point to be the end of the segment that is added. A path can consist of several subpaths since a new subpath is started by a `moveTo()` call. The `closePath()` method closes the current subpath by connecting the current point after the last segment to the point defined by the previous `moveTo()` call.

Let's illustrate how this works with a simple example. We could create a triangle with the following statements:

```
GeneralPath p = new GeneralPath(GeneralPath.WIND_EVEN_ODD);
p.moveTo(50.0f, 50.0f);         // Start point for path
p.lineTo(150.0f, 50.0f);        // Line from 50,50 to 150,50
p.lineTo(150.0f, 250.0f);       // Line from 150,50 to 150,250
p.closePath();                  // Line from 150,250 back to
start
```

The first line segment starts at the current position set by the `moveTo()` call. Each subsequent segment begins at the endpoint of the previous segment. The `closePath()` call joins the latest endpoint to the point set by the previous `moveTo()` – which in this case is the beginning of the path. The process is much the same using `quadTo()` or `curveTo()` calls and of course you can intermix them in any sequence you like.

Once you have created a path for a `GeneralPath` object by calling its methods to add segments to the path, you can remove them all by calling its `reset()` method. This empties the path.

The `GeneralPath` class implements the `Shape` interface, so a `Graphics2D` object knows how to draw a path. You just pass a reference to the `draw()` method for the graphics context. To draw the path, p, that we defined above in the graphics context g2D, you would write:

```
g2D.draw(p);    // Draw path p
```

Let's try an example.

Try It Out — Reaching for the Stars

You won't usually want to construct a `GeneralPath` object as we did above. You will probably want to create a particular shape, a triangle or a star say, and then draw it at various points on a component. You might think you can do this by subclassing `GeneralPath`, but unfortunately `GeneralPath` is declared as `final` so subclassing is not allowed. However, you can always add a `GeneralPath` object as a member of your class. Let's draw some stars using our own `Star` class. We will use a `GeneralPath` object to create the star shown in the diagram.

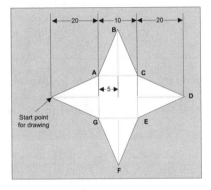

Here's the code for a class defining the star:

```
import java.awt.geom.*;
import java.awt.*;

class Star
{
  public Star(float x, float y)
  {
    start = new Point2D.Float(x, y);                        // store start point
    createStar();
  }

  // Create the path from start
  void createStar()
  {
    Point2D.Float point = start;
    p = new GeneralPath(GeneralPath.WIND_NON_ZERO);
    p.moveTo(point.x, point.y);
    p.lineTo(point.x + 20.0f, point.y - 5.0f);              // Line from start to A
    point = (Point2D.Float)p.getCurrentPoint();
```

```
      p.lineTo(point.x + 5.0f, point.y - 20.0f);        // Line from A to B
      point = (Point2D.Float)p.getCurrentPoint();
      p.lineTo(point.x + 5.0f, point.y + 20.0f);        // Line from B to C
      point = (Point2D.Float)p.getCurrentPoint();


      p.lineTo(point.x + 20.0f, point.y + 5.0f);        // Line from C to D
      point = (Point2D.Float)p.getCurrentPoint();
      p.lineTo(point.x - 20.0f, point.y + 5.0f);        // Line from D to E
      point = (Point2D.Float)p.getCurrentPoint();
      p.lineTo(point.x - 5.0f, point.y + 20.0f);        // Line from E to F
      point = (Point2D.Float)p.getCurrentPoint();
      p.lineTo(point.x - 5.0f, point.y - 20.0f);        // Line from F to g
      p.closePath();                                    // Line from G to start
    }

  Shape atLocation(float x, float y)
  {
    start.setLocation(x, y);                            // Store new start
    p.reset();                                          // Erase current path
    createStar();                                       // create new path
    return p;                                           // Return the path
  }

  // Make the path available
  Shape getShape()
  {
    return p;
  }

  private Point2D.Float start;                          // Start point for star
  private GeneralPath p;                                // Star path
}
```

We can draw stars on an applet:

```
import javax.swing.*;
import java.awt.*;
import java.awt.geom.*;

public class StarApplet extends JApplet
{
  // Initialize the applet
  public void init()
  {
    Container content = getContentPane();

    // Add the panel to the content pane for the applet
    content.add(pane);                    // BorderLayout.CENTER is default position
  }
```

```
    // Class defining a pane on which to draw
    class StarPane extends JComponent
    {
      public void paint(Graphics g)
      {
        Graphics2D g2D = (Graphics2D)g;
        Star star = new Star(0,0);              // Create a star
        float delta = 60f;                       // Increment between stars
        float starty = 0f;                       // Starting y position


        // Draw 3 rows of 4 stars
        for(int yCount = 0; yCount < 3; yCount++)
        {
          starty += delta;                       // Increment row position
          float startx = 0f;                     // Start x position in a row

          // Draw a row of 4 stars
          for(int xCount = 0; xCount<4; xCount++)
            g2D.draw(star.atLocation(startx += delta, starty));
        }
      }
    }

    StarPane pane = new StarPane();              // Pane containing stars
}
```

The HTML file for this applet could contain:

```
<APPLET CODE="StarApplet.class" WIDTH=360 HEIGHT=240> </APPLET>
```

This is large enough to accommodate our stars. If you compile and run the applet, you should see the **AppletViewer** window shown here.

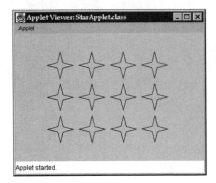

How It Works

The `Star` class has a `GeneralPath` object, p, as a member. The constructor sets the coordinates of the `start` point from the arguments, and calls the `createStar()` method that creates the path for the star. The first line is drawn relative to the `start` point that is set by the call to `moveTo()` for p. For each subsequent line, we retrieve the current position by calling `getCurrentPoint()` for p and drawing the line relative to that. The last line to complete the star is drawn by calling `closePath()`.

We always need a `Shape` reference to draw a `Star` object, so we have included a `getShape()` method in the class that simply returns a reference to the current `GeneralPath` object as type `Shape`. The `atLocation()` method recreates the path at the new position specified by the arguments and returns a reference to it.

The `StarApplet` class draws stars on a component defined by the inner class `StarPane`. We draw the stars using the `paint()` method for the `StarPane` object, which is a member of the `StarApplet` class. Each star is drawn in the nested loop with the position specified by (x, y). The y coordinate defines the vertical position of a row, so this is incremented by `delta` on each iteration of the outer loop. The coordinate x is the position of a star within a row so this is incremented by `delta` on each iteration of the inner loop.

Filling Shapes

Once you know how to create and draw a shape, filling it is easy. You just call the `fill()` method for the `Graphics2D` object and pass a reference of type `Shape` to it. This works for any shape but for sensible results the boundary should be closed.

Let's try it out by modifying the previous example.

Try It Out — Filling Stars

To fill the stars we just need to call the `fill()` method for each star in the `paint()` method of the `StarPane` object. Modify the `paint()` method as follows:

```
public void paint(Graphics g)
{
  Graphics2D g2D = (Graphics2D)g;
  Star star = new Star(0,0);              // Create a star
  float delta = 60;                       // Increment between stars
  float starty = 0;                       // Starting y position

  // Draw 3 rows of 4 stars
  for(int yCount = 0 ; yCount<3; yCount++)
  {
    starty += delta;                      // Increment row position
    float startx = 0;                     // Start x position in a row

    // Draw a row of 4 stars
    for(int xCount = 0 ; xCount<4; xCount++)
    {
      g2D.setPaint(Color.blue);           // Drawing color blue
      g2D.draw(star.atLocation(startx += delta, starty));
      g2D.setPaint(Color.green);          // Color for fill is green
      g2D.fill(star.getShape());          // Fill the star
    }
  }
}
```

Now the applet window will look something like that shown here – but in color of course.

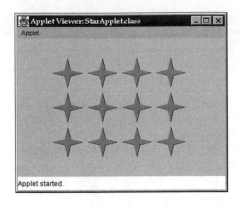

How It Works

We set the color for drawing and filling the stars separately, simply to show that we get both. You can fill a shape without drawing it – just call the `fill()` method. You could amend the example to do this by modifying the inner loop to:

```
for(int xCount = 0 ; xCount<4; xCount++)
{
  g2D.setPaint(Color.green);                        // Color for fill is green
  g2D.fill(star.atLocation(startx += delta, starty)); // Fill the star
}
```

Now all we will get is the green fill for each shape – no outline.

Gradient Fill

You are not limited to filling a shape with a uniform color. You can create a `GradientPaint` object that represents a graduation in shade from one color to another and pass that to the `setPaint()` method for the graphics context. There are four `GradientPaint` class constructors:

Constructor	Description

`GradientPaint`
`(Point2D p1, Color c1,`
` Point2D p2, Color c2)`
	Defines a gradient from point p1 with the color c1 to the point p2 with the color c2. The color varies linearly from color c1 at point p1 to color c2 at point p2.

	By default the gradient is **acyclic**, which means the color variation only applies between the two points. Beyond either end of the line the color is the same as the nearest end point.

`GradientPaint`
`(float x1, float y1, Color c1,`
` float x2, float y2, Color c2)`
	The same as the previous constructor but with the points specified by their coordinates.

Constructor	Description
GradientPaint (Point2D p1, Color c1, Point2D p2, Color c2, boolean cyclic)	With the last argument specified as false, this is identical to the first constructor. If you specify cyclic as true, the color gradation repeats cyclically off either end of the line – i.e. you get repetitions of the color gradient in both directions.
GradientPaint (float x1, float y1, Color c1, float x2, float y2, Color c2, boolean cyclic)	This is the same as the previous constructor except for the explicit point coordinates.

Points off the line defining the color gradient will have the same color as the normal (that is, right-angle) projection of the point onto the line.

This stuff is easier to demonstrate than to describe, so here's the output from the example we're about to code:

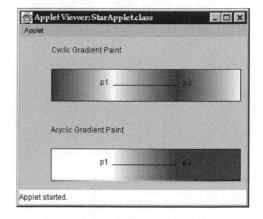

Try It Out — Color Gradients

We will modify the previous applet to draw rectangles with GradientPaint fills. Here's the complete code but only the lines that have changed substantially from the previous applet are shaded:

```java
import javax.swing.*;
import java.awt.*;
import java.awt.geom.*;

public class GradientApplet extends JApplet
{
  // Initialize the applet
  public void init()
  {
    Container content = getContentPane();

    // Add the panel to the content pane for the applet
    content.add(pane);               // BorderLayout.CENTER is default position
  }
```

```
      // Class defining a pane on which to draw
      class GradientPane extends JComponent
      {
        public void paint(Graphics g)
        {
          Graphics2D g2D = (Graphics2D)g;

          Point2D.Float p1 = new Point2D.Float(150.f, 75.f);      // Gradient line
start
          Point2D.Float p2 = new Point2D.Float(250.f, 75.f);      // Gradient line end
          float width = 300;
          float height = 50;
          GradientPaint g1 = new GradientPaint(p1, Color.white,
                                               p2, Color.darkGray,
                                               true);             // Cyclic gradient
          Rectangle2D.Float rect1 = new Rectangle2D.Float(
                                     p1.x-100, p1.y-25, width,height);
          g2D.setPaint(g1);                                       // Gradient color
fill
          g2D.fill(rect1);                                        // Fill the rectangle
          g2D.setPaint(Color.black);                             // Outline in black
          g2D.draw(rect1);                                        // Fill the rectangle
          g2D.draw(new Line2D.Float(p1, p2));
          g2D.drawString("Cyclic Gradient Paint", p1.x-100, p1.y-50);
          g2D.drawString("p1", p1.x-20, p1.y);
          g2D.drawString("p2", p2.x+10, p2.y);

          p1.setLocation(150, 200);
          p2.setLocation(250, 200);
          GradientPaint g2 = new GradientPaint(p1, Color.white,
                                               p2, Color.darkGray,
                                               false);            // Acyclic gradient
          rect1.setRect(p1.x-100, p1.y-25, width, height);
          g2D.setPaint(g2);                                       // Gradient color
fill
          g2D.fill(rect1);                                        // Fill the rectangle
          g2D.setPaint(Color.black);                             // Outline in black
          g2D.draw(rect1);                                        // Fill the rectangle
          g2D.draw(new Line2D.Float(p1, p2));
          g2D.drawString("Acyclic Gradient Paint", p1.x-100, p1.y-50);
          g2D.drawString("p1", p1.x-20, p1.y);
          g2D.drawString("p2", p2.x+10, p2.y);
        }
      }

      GradientPane pane = new GradientPane();   // Pane containing filled rectangles
    }
```

If you run this version of the applet you should get the window shown above. Note that to get a uniform color gradation, your monitor needs to be set up for at least 16 bit (65536 colors) colors, preferably 24 bits (1.7 million colors).

How It Works

The applet displays two rectangles, and they are annotated to indicate which is which. The applet also displays the gradient lines, which lie in the middle of the rectangles. You can see the cyclic and acyclic gradients quite clearly. You can also see how points off the gradient line have the same color as the normal projection onto the line.

The first block of shaded code in the `paint()` method creates the upper rectangle where the `GradientPaint` object that is used is `g1`. This is created as a cyclic gradient between the points `p1` and `p2` varying from white to dark gray. These shades have been chosen because the book is in black and white, but you can try any color combination you like. To set the color gradient for the fill, we call `setPaint()` for the `Graphics2D` object and pass `g1` to it. Any shapes drawn and/or filled subsequent to this call will use the gradient color, but here we just fill the rectangle, `rect1`.

To make the outline and the annotation clearer, we set the current color back to black before calling the `draw()` method to draw the outline of the rectangle, and the `drawString()` method to annotate it.

The code for the lower rectangle is essentially the same as that for the first. The only important difference is that we specify the last argument to the constructor as `false` to get an acyclic gradient. This causes the colors of the ends of the gradient line to be the same as the end points. We could have omitted the Boolean parameter here, and got an acyclic gradient by default.

The applet shows how points off the gradient line have the same color as the normal projection onto the line. This is always the case regardless of the orientation of the gradient line. Try changing the definition of `g1` for the upper rectangle to:

```
GradientPaint g1 = new GradientPaint(p1.x, p1.y - 20, Color.white,
                                     p2.x, p2.y + 20, Color.darkGray,
                                     true);              // Cyclic
  gradient
```

You will also need to draw the gradient line in its new orientation:

```
g2D.draw(new Line2D.Float(p1.x, p1.y - 20, p2.x, p2.y + 20));
```

The annotation for the end points will also have to be moved:

```
g2D.drawString("p1",p1.x - 20,p1.y - 20);
g2D.drawString("p2",p2.x + 10,p2.y + 20);
```

If you run the applet with these changes, you can see how the gradient is tilted, and how the colors of a point off the gradient line matches that of the point that is the orthogonal projection onto it.

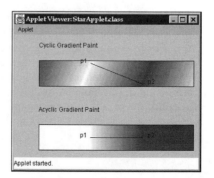

Managing Shapes

When shapes are created in Sketcher, we'll have no idea of the sequence of shape types that will occur. This is determined totally by the person using the program to produce a sketch. We'll therefore need to be able to draw shapes and perform other operations on them without knowing what they are – and polymorphism can help here.

We don't want to use the shape classes defined in java.awt.geom directly as we will want to add our own attributes such as color or line style, and store them as part of the object. We could consider using the shape classes as base classes for our shapes, but we couldn't use the GeneralPath class in this scheme of things because, as we have already seen, it's final and we might not want this restriction.

Taking all of this into account, the easiest approach might be to define a common base class for our shape classes, and include a member in each class to store a shape object of one kind or another. We'll then be able to include a polymorphic method to return a reference to a shape as type Shape for use with the draw() method of a Graphics2D object.

We can start by defining a base class, Element, from which we'll derive the classes defining specific types of shapes. The Element class will have data members that are common to all types of shapes, and we can put the methods that we want to execute polymorphically in this class too. All we need to do is make sure that each shape class that is derived from the Element class has its own implementation of these methods.

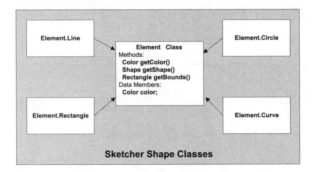

The diagram shows the initial members that we will declare in the Element base class. The only data member for now is the color member to store the color of a shape. The getShape() and getBounds() methods will be abstract here since the Element class is not intended to define a shape, but we will be able to implement the getColor() method in this class. The other methods will be implemented by the subclasses of Element.

Initially, we'll define the five classes shown in the diagram that represent shapes, with the Element class as a base. They provide objects that represent straight lines, rectangles, circles, freehand curves and blocks of text. These classes will all inherit the data members that we define for the Element class. As you can see from the names of our shape classes, they are all nested classes to the class Element. The Element class will serve as the base class, as well as house our shape classes. This will avoid any possible confusion with other classes that might have names such as Line or Circle for instance. Since there will be no Element objects around, we will declare our shape classes as static members of the Element class.

We can now define the base class, `Element`. Note that this won't be the final version, as we'll be adding more functionality in later chapters. Here's the code that needs to go in `Element.java` in the Sketcher directory:

```java
import java.awt.*;

public abstract class Element
{
  public Element(Color color)
  { this.color = color;   }

  public Color getColor()
  { return color;   }

  public abstract Shape getShape();
  public abstract java.awt.Rectangle getBounds();

  protected Color color;                                    // Color of a shape
}
```

We have defined a constructor to initialize the data member, and the `getColor()` method. The other methods are `abstract`, so they must be implemented by the subclasses.

Note that the return type for the abstract `getBounds()` method is fully qualified using the package name. This is to prevent confusion with our own `Rectangle` class that we will add later on in this chapter.

Storing Shapes in the Document

Even though we haven't defined the classes for the shapes that Sketcher will create, we can implement the mechanism for storing them in the `SketchModel` class. We'll be storing all of them as objects of type `Element`. We can use a `LinkedList` collection class object to hold an arbitrary number of `Element` objects, since a `LinkedList` can store any kind of object. It also has the advantage that deleting a shape from the list is fast.

We can add a member to the `SketchModel` class that we added earlier to the Sketcher program to store elements:

```java
import java.util.*;

class SketchModel extends Observable
{
  protected LinkedList elementList = new LinkedList();
}
```

We will want methods to add and delete `Element` objects from the linked list, and a method to return an iterator for the list, so we should add those to the class too:

```
import java.util.*;
import java.awt.*;

class SketchModel extends Observable
{
  public boolean remove(Element element)
  {
    boolean removed = elementList.remove(element);
    if(removed)
    {
      setChanged();
      notifyObservers(element.getBounds());
    }

    return removed;
  }

  public void add(Element element)
  {
    elementList.add(element);
    setChanged();
    notifyObservers(element.getBounds());
  }

  public Iterator getIterator()
  {  return elementList.listIterator();  }

  protected LinkedList elementList = new LinkedList();
}
```

All three methods make use of methods defined in the `LinkedList` class so they are very simple. The `add()` and `remove()` functions have a parameter type of `Element` so only our shapes can be added to the linked list or removed from it. When we add or remove an element, the model is changed and therefore we call the `setChanged()` method inherited from `Observable` to record the change, and the `notifyObservers()` method to communicate this to any observers that have been registered with the model. We pass the `Rectangle` object returned by `getBounds()` for the shape to `notifyObservers()`. Each of the shape classes defined in `java.awt.geom` implements the `getBounds()` method to return the rectangle that bounds the shape. We will be able to use this in the view to specify the area that needs to be redrawn.

In the `remove()` method, it is possible that the element was not removed – because it was not there for instance – so we test the `boolean` value returned by the `remove()` method for the `LinkedList` object. We also return this value as the caller may want to know if an element was removed or not.

Next, even though we haven't defined any of our specific shape classes, we can still make provision for displaying them in the view class.

Drawing Shapes

We will draw the shapes in the `paint()` method for the `SketchView` class, so remove the old code from the `paint()` method now. We can replace it for drawing our own shapes like this:

```
import javax.swing.*;
import java.util.*;                    // For Observer
import java.awt.*;

class SketchView extends JComponent
                 implements Observer
{
  public SketchView(Sketcher theApp)
  {
    this.theApp = theApp;
  }

  // Method called by Observable object when it changes
  public void update(Observable o, Object rectangle)
  {
    // Code to respond to changes in the model...
  }

  public void paint(Graphics g)
  {
    Graphics2D g2D = (Graphics2D)g;                       // Get a 2D device context
    Iterator elements = theApp.getModel().getIterator();
    Element element;                                      // Stores an element

    while(elements.hasNext())                             // Go through the list
    {
      element = (Element)elements.next();                 // Get the next element
      g2D.setPaint(element.getColor());                   // Set the element color
      g2D.draw(element.getShape());                       // Draw its shape
    }
  }

  private Sketcher theApp;              // The application object
}
```

The `getModel()` method that we implemented in the `Sketcher` class returns a reference to the `SketchModel` object, and this is used to call the `getIterator()` method which will return an iterator for the list of elements. Using a standard `while` loop, we iterate through all the elements in the list. For each element, we obtain its color and pass that to the `setPaint()` method for the graphics context. We then pass the `Shape` reference returned by the `getShape()` method to the `draw()` method for `g2D`. This will draw the shape in the color passed previously to the `setPaint()` method. In this way we can draw all the elements stored in the model.

It's time we put in place the mechanism for creating Sketcher shapes.

Drawing Using the Mouse

We've drawn shapes so far using data internal to the program. In our Sketcher program we want to be able to draw a shape using the mouse in the view, and then store the finished shape in the model. We want the process to be as natural as possible, so we'll implement a mechanism that allows you to draw by pressing the left mouse button (more accurately, button 1) and dragging the cursor to draw the selected type of shape. So for a line, the point where you depress the mouse button will be the start point for the line, and the point where you release the button will be the end point.

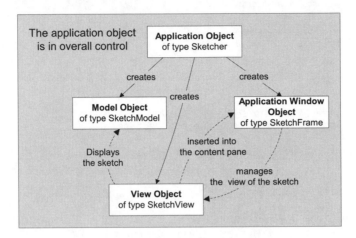

As you drag the mouse with the button down, we'll display the line as it looks at that point. Thus the line will be displayed dynamically all the time the mouse cursor is being dragged and the left button remains pressed. This process is called **rubber-banding**.

We can use essentially the same process of pressing the mouse button and dragging the cursor for all four of our shapes. Each shape will thus be defined by two points – the cursor position where the mouse button is pressed, and the cursor position where the mouse button is released, (plus the color for the shape, of course). This implies that our shape constructors will all have three parameters, the two points and the color. Let's look at how we handle mouse events to make this work.

Handling Mouse Events

Because all the drawing operations for a sketch will be accomplished using the mouse, we must implement the process for creating elements within the methods that will handle the mouse events. The mouse events we're interested in will originate in the SketchView object because that's where we'll be drawing shapes. We will make the view responsible for handling all its own events, which will include events that occur in the drawing process as well as interactions with existing shapes.

Drawing a shape, such as a line, interactively will involve us in handling three different kinds of mouse event. Let's summarize what they are, and what we need to do when they occur:

Event	Action
Left Button (Button 1) pressed	Save the cursor position somewhere as the starting point for the line. We'll store this in a data member of the inner class to SketchView that we'll create to define listeners for mouse events.
Mouse dragged	Save the current cursor position somewhere as the end point for the line. Erase any previously drawn temporary line, and create a new temporary line from the starting point that was saved initially. Draw the new temporary line.
Left Button (Button 1) released	If there's a reference to a temporary line stored, add it to the model, and redraw it.

You'll remember from the previous chapter that there are two mouse listener interfaces: MouseListener which has methods for handling events that occur when the mouse buttons are pressed or released and MouseMotionListener which has methods for handling events that arise when the mouse is moved. You will also recall that the MouseInputAdapter class implements both, and since we need to implement methods from both interfaces, we'll add an inner class to the SketchView class that extends the MouseInputAdapter class.

Since there's quite a lot of code involved in this, we will first define the bare bones of the class to handle mouse events, and then build in the detail until it does what we want.

Try It Out — Implementing a Mouse Listener

Add the following class outline as an inner class to SketchView:

```
import javax.swing.*;
import java.util.*;                  // For Observer
import java.awt.*;
import java.awt.geom.*;
import java.awt.event.*;             // For events
import javax.swing.event.*;          // For mouse input adapter

class SketchView extends JComponent
                 implements Observer

{
  // Rest of the class as before

  class MouseHandler extends MouseInputAdapter
  {
    public void mousePressed(MouseEvent e)
    {
      // Code to handle mouse button press...
    }
```

```
      public void mouseDragged(MouseEvent e)
      {
        // Code to handle the mouse being dragged...
      }

      public void mouseReleased(MouseEvent e)
      {
        // Code to handle the mouse button being release...
      }

      private Point start;              // Stores cursor position on press
      private Point last;               // Stores cursor position on drag
      private Element tempElement;      // Stores a temporary element
    }
  }
```

We have implemented the three methods that we will need to create an element. The mousePressed() method will store the position of the cursor in the start member of the MouseHandler class, so it will be available to the mouseDragged() method that will be called repeatedly when you drag the mouse cursor with the button pressed. The mouseDragged() method will create an element using the current cursor position and the position saved in start, and store a reference to it in the tempElement member of the class. The last member will be used to store the cursor position when mouseDragged() is called. Both start and last are of type Point since this is the type that we will get for the cursor position, but remember that Point is a subclass of Point2D, so you can always cast a Point reference to Point2D when necessary. The process ends when you release the mouse button, causing the mouseReleased() method to be called.

An object of type MouseHandler will be the listener for mouse events for the view object, so we should put this in place in the SketchView constructor. Add the following code at the end of the existing code:

```
      public SketchView(Sketcher theApp)
      {
        this.theApp = theApp;
        MouseHandler handler = new MouseHandler();    // create the mouse
    listener
        addMouseListener(handler);                    // Listen for button events
        addMouseMotionListener(handler);              // Listen for motion events
      }
```

We call the addMouseListener() and addMotionListener() methods and pass the same listener object because our listener class deals with both.

Let's go for the detail of the MouseHandler class now, starting with the mousePressed() method.

Handling Mouse Button Press Events

The first thing we will need to do is find out which button is pressed. It is generally a good idea to make mouse button operations specific to a particular button. That way you avoid potential confusion when you extend the code to support more functionality. Mouse buttons have a few complications that we need to understand first, though.

The `getModifiers()` method for the `MouseEvent` object that is passed to a listener method returns a value of type `int` containing one or more flags to indicate which button was pressed. A `MouseEvent` in Java supports a mouse with up to three buttons, so, when you operate a mouse, the modifier for the event will contain one of the flags `BUTTON1_MASK`, `BUTTON2_MASK` or `BUTTON3_MASK`, depending on which mouse button you press. Because some systems don't support multiple mouse buttons, there are other flags that are used in combination with the three flags for the buttons. These are `ALT_MASK`, `CTRL_MASK`, `SHIFT_MASK`, and `META_MASK`, corresponding to the *Alt*, *Ctrl*, *Shift* and *Meta* keys, the *Meta* key being available on a Mac. For a mouse with a single button – on the Mac for instance, holding down the *Alt* key when pressing the button simulates button 2, and pressing the *Meta* key with the mouse button simulates button 3. To circumvent these complications, it is best to bitwise AND the flag for the button that you want with the value returned by `getModifiers()`. This filters out any other flags that might be set. We can test for button 1 being pressed with statements such as:

```
int modifier = e.getModifiers();
if((modifier & e.BUTTON1_MASK) != 0)
   // Handle button 1 press
```

Here, `e` is the `MouseEvent` object.

A `MouseEvent` object records the current cursor position, and you can get a `Point` reference to it by calling the `getPoint()` method. For example:

```
start = e.getPoint();     // Save the cursor position in start
```

As well as saving the cursor position, our implementation of `mousePressed()` must set things up to enable the `mouseDragged()` method to create an element and display it. The `mouseDragged()` method is going to be called very frequently, and to implement rubber-banding each time, the redrawing of the element needs to be very fast. We don't want to have the whole view redrawn each time as this will carry a lot of overhead.

Using XOR Mode

One way to do this is to draw in **XOR mode**. You set XOR mode by calling the `setXORMode()` method for a graphics context, and passing a color to it – usually the background color. In this mode the pixels are not written directly to the screen. The color in which you are drawing is combined with the color of the pixel currently displayed together with a third color that you specify, by exclusive ORing them together, and the resultant pixel color is written to the screen. The third color is usually set to be the background color, so the color of the pixel that is written is the result of the following operation:

```
resultant_Color = foreground_color^background_color^current_color
```

The effect of this is to flip between the drawing color and the background color. The first time you draw a shape, the result will be in the color you are drawing with, except for overlaps with other shapes, since they won't be in the background color. When you draw the same shape a second time the result will be the background color so the shape will disappear. Drawing a third time will make it reappear. We saw how this works back in Chapter 2 when we were discussing the bitwise exclusive OR operation.

Based on what we have said, we can implement the `mousePressed()` method like this:

```java
public void mousePressed(MouseEvent e)
{
  start = e.getPoint();                                   // Save cursor position
  int modifier = e.getModifiers();                        // Get modifiers

  if((modifier & e.BUTTON1_MASK) != 0)
  {
    g2D = (Graphics2D)getGraphics();                      // Get graphics context
    g2D.setXORMode(getBackground());                      // Set XOR mode
    g2D.setPaint(theApp.getWindow().getElementColor());   // Set color
  }
}
```

If button 1 was pressed, we obtain a graphics context for the view, so we must add a member to the `MouseHandler` class to store this:

```java
private Graphics2D g2D;                           // Temporary graphics context
```

We use the object, g2D, to set XOR mode, as we will use this mode in the `mouseDragged()` method to erase a previously drawn shape without reconstructing the whole sketch. The last thing that is done here is to retrieve the current drawing color that is recorded in the `SketchFrame` object. You will remember that this is set when you select a menu item or a toolbar button. We use `theApp` object stored in the view to get the `SketchFrame` object, and then call its `getElementColor()` member to retrieve the color. This method doesn't exist in `SketchFrame`, but it's not difficult. Add the following method to the `SketchFrame` class definition:

```java
public Color getElementColor()
{
  return elementColor;
}
```

With the button press code in place, we can have a go at implementing `mouseDragged()`.

Handling Mouse Dragging Events

We can obtain the cursor position in the `mouseDragged()` method in the same way as for the `mousePressed()` method, which is by calling `getPoint()` for the event object, so we could write:

```java
last = e.getPoint();                     // Get cursor position
```

But then we only want to handle drag events for button 1, so we will have to check the modifiers here too. When `mouseDragged()` is called for the first time, we won't have created an element, so we can just create one from the points stored in `start` and `last`, and then draw it using the graphics context saved by the `mousePressed()` method. The `mouseDragged()` method will be called lots of times while you drag the mouse though, and for every occasion other than the first, we must take care to redraw the old element before creating the new one. Since we are in XOR mode, drawing the element a second time will draw it in the background color, so it will disappear. Here's how we can do all that:

```
public void mouseDragged(MouseEvent e)
{
  last = e.getPoint();                              // Save cursor position
  int modifier = e.getModifiers();                  // Get modifiers

  if((modifier & e.BUTTON1_MASK) != 0)
  {
    if(tempElement == null)                          // Is there an element?
      tempElement = createElement(start, last);      // No, so create one
    else
    {
      g2D.draw(tempElement.getShape());              // Yes - draw to erase it
      tempElement.modify(start, last);               // Now modify it
    }
    g2D.draw(tempElement.getShape());                // and draw it
  }
}
```

If button 1 is pressed we are interested, so we check for an existing element by comparing the reference in `tempElement` with `null`. If there isn't one we create an element of the current type by calling a method, `createElement()`, that we will add to `SketchView` class in a moment. We save a reference to the element that is created in the `tempElement` member of the listener object.

If `tempElement` is not `null` then an element already exists so we modify the existing element to incorporate the latest cursor position by calling a method `modify()` for the element object that we will add for each element type. Finally we draw the latest version of the element referenced by `tempElement`. Since we expect to call the `modify()` method for an element polymorphically, we should add it to the base class, `Element`. It will be abstract in the `Element` class so add the following declaration to the class definition:

```
public abstract void modify(Point start, Point last);
```

We can implement `createElement()` as a `private` member of the `MouseHandler` class, since it's not needed anywhere else. The parameters for the method are just two points that will be used to define each element. Here's the code:

```
private Element createElement(Point start, Point end)
{
  switch(theApp.getWindow().getElementType())
  {
    case LINE:
      return new Element.Line(start, end,
                              theApp.getWindow().getElementColor());
```

697

```
        case RECTANGLE:
            return new Element.Rectangle(start, end,
                                       theApp.getWindow().getElementColor());

        case CIRCLE:
            return new Element.Circle(start, end,
                                     theApp.getWindow().getElementColor());

        case CURVE:
          return new Element.Curve(start, end,
                                  theApp.getWindow().getElementColor());
      }
    return null;
  }
```

Since we refer to the constants identifying element types here, we must make the `SketchView` class implement the `Constants` interface, so modify the class to do that now. The first line of the definition will be:

```
class SketchView extends JComponent
                 implements Observer, Constants
```

The `createElement()` method returns a reference to a shape as type `Elements`. We determine the type of shape to create by retrieving the element type ID stored in the `SketchFrame` class by the menu item listeners that we put together in the previous chapter. The `getElementType()` method isn't there in the `SketchFrame` class yet, but you can add it now as:

```
public int getElementType()
{
  return elementType;
}
```

The `switch` statement in `createElement()` selects the constructor to be called, and as you see, they are all essentially of the same form. If we fall through the switch with an ID that we haven't provided for, we return `null`. Of course, none of these shape class constructors exists in Sketcher yet. So if you want to try compiling the code we have so far, you will need to comment out each of the return statements.

Let's add the next piece we need – handling button release events.

Handling Button Release Events

When the mouse button is released, we will have created an element. In this case all we need to do is to add the element referred to by the `tempElement` member of the `MouseHandler` class to the `SketchModel` object that represents the sketch. One thing we need to consider though. Someone might click the mouse button without dragging it. In this case there won't be an element to store, so we just clean up the data members of the `MouseHandler` object.

```java
public void mouseReleased(MouseEvent e)
{
  int modifier = e.getModifiers();               // Get modifiers

  if((modifier & e.BUTTON1_MASK) != 0)
  {
    if(tempElement != null)
    {
      theApp.getModel().add(tempElement);        // Add element to the model
      tempElement = null;                        // No temporary stored
    }
    if(g2D != null)
    {
      g2D.dispose();                             // Release graphic context resource
      g2D = null;                                // Set it to null
    }
    start = last = null;                         // Remove the points
  }
}
```

If there is a reference stored in `tempElement` we add it to the model by calling the `add()` method that we defined for it and set `tempElement` back to `null`. It is important to set `tempElement` back to `null` here. Failing to do that would result in the old element reference being added to the model when you click the mouse button.

When we add the new element to the model, the view will be notified as an observer, so the `update()` method in the view will be called. We can implement the `update()` method in the `SketchView` class like this:

```java
public void update(Observable o, Object rectangle)
{
  if(rectangle == null)
    repaint();
  else
    repaint((Rectangle)rectangle);
}
```

If `rectangle` is not `null`, then we have a reference to a `Rectangle` object that was provided by the `notifyObservers()` method call in the `add()` method for the `SketchModel` object. This rectangle is the area occupied by the new element, so we pass this to the `repaint()` method for the view to add just this area to the area to be redrawn on the next call of the `paint()` method. If `rectangle` is `null`, we call the version of `repaint()` that has no parameter to redraw the whole view.

Another important operation here is calling the dispose() method for the g2D object. Every graphics context makes use of finite system resources. If you use a lot of graphics context objects and you don't release the resources they use, your program will consume more and more resources. Under Windows for instance you may eventually run out, your computer will stop working and you'll have to reboot. When you call dispose() for a graphics context object it can merely no longer be used, so we set g2D back to null to be on the safe side.

> A reminder about a potential error in using adapter classes – be sure to spell the method names correctly. If you don't, your method won't get called, the base class member will. The base class method does nothing so your code won't work as you expect. There will be no warning or error messages about this because your code will be perfectly legal – though quite wrong. You will simply have added an additional and quite useless method to those defined in the adapter class.

We have implemented all three methods that we need to draw shapes. We could try it out if only we had a shape to draw.

Defining Our Own Shape Classes

All the classes that define shapes in Sketcher will be static nested classes of the Element class. As we already said, as well as being a convenient way to keep our shape class definitions together, this will also avoid possible conflict with classes such as the Rectangle class in the Java class library.

We can start with the simplest – a class representing a line.

Defining Lines

A line will be defined by two points and its color. We can define the Line class as a nested class in the base class Element, as follows:

```java
import java.awt.*;                    // For the Shape class
import java.awt.geom.*;              // For classes defining shapes

public abstract class Element
{
  // Code defining the base class...

  // Nested class defining a line
  public static class Line extends Element
  {
    public Line(Point start, Point end, Color color)
    {
      super(color);
      line = new Line2D.Double(start, end);
    }
```

```
    public Shape getShape()
    {
      return line;
    }


    public java.awt.Rectangle getBounds()
    {
      return line.getBounds();
    }


    public void modify(Point start, Point last)
    {
      line.x2 = last.x
      line.y2 = last.y
    }

    private Line2D.Double line;
  }
}
```

The Line class is static so there is no dependency on an Element object being available. The constructor has three parameters, the two end points of the line as type Point and the color. Point arguments to the constructor can be of type Point2D or type Point as Point2D is a superclass of Point. After passing the color to the base class constructor, we create the line as a Line2D.Double object. Since this implements the Shape interface, we can return it as type Shape from the getShape() method.

The getBounds() method couldn't be simpler. We just return the Rectangle object produced by the getBounds() method for the object, line. However, note how we have fully qualified the return type. This is because we will be adding a Rectangle class as a nested class to the Element class. When we do, the compiler will interpret the type Rectangle here as our rectangle class, and not the one defined in the java.awt package. You can always supply the fully qualified class name when conflicts like this arise.

Try It Out — Drawing Lines

If you have saved the Element class definition as Element.java in the same directory as the rest of the Sketcher classes, all you need to do is make sure all the constructor calls other than Element.Line are commented out in the createElement() member of the MouseHandler class, that is an inner class to SketchView. The code for the method should look like this:

```
    private Element createElement(Point start, Point end)
    {
      switch(theApp.getWindow().getElementType())
      {
        case LINE:
          return new Element.Line(start, end,
                                  theApp.getWindow().getElementColor());
```

```
        case RECTANGLE:
//            return new Element.Rectangle(start, end,
//                                    theApp.getWindow().getElementColor());

        case CIRCLE:
//            return new Element.Circle(start, end,
//
theApp.getWindow().getElementColor());

        case CURVE:
//            return new Element.Curve(start, end,
//
theApp.getWindow().getElementColor());
        }
        return null;
    }
```

If you compile and run Sketcher you should be able to draw a figure like that shown below.

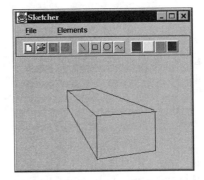

You can only draw lines at this point though. Trying to draw anything else will result in a `NullPointerException` being thrown because the `createElement()` method will return `null` rather than a reference to a shape.

How It Works

As you drag the mouse `Element.Line` objects are being repeatedly created and drawn to produce the rubber banding effect. Each line is from the point where you pressed the mouse button to the current cursor position. Try drawing different colors. It should all work. If it doesn't, maybe you forgot to remove the `getContentPane().setBackground(color)` call that we put temporarily in `ColorActions` `actionPerformed()` method in `SketchFrame`.

If you are typing in the code as you go (and I hope that you are!), you may have made a few mistakes as there's been such a lot of code added to Sketcher. In this case don't look back at the code in the book first to find out why. Before you do that, try using the Java debugger that comes with the JDK, or even just instrumenting the methods that might be the problem with `println()` calls so you can trace what's going on. It's good practice for when you are writing your own code.

Defining Rectangles

The interactive mechanism for drawing a rectangle is similar to that for a line. When you are drawing a rectangle, the point where the mouse is pressed will define one corner of the rectangle, and as you drag the mouse the cursor position will define an opposite corner, as illustrated below.

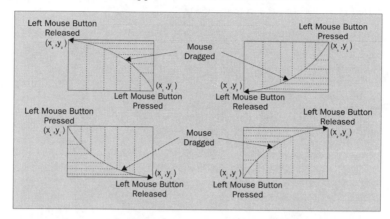

Releasing the mouse button will establish the final rectangle shape to be stored in the model. As you can see, the cursor position when you press the mouse button can be any corner of the rectangle. This is fine from a usability standpoint, but our code needs to take account of the fact that a Rectangle2D object is always defined by the top-left corner, plus a width and a height.

The diagram shows the four possible orientations of the mouse path as it is dragged in relation to the rectangle drawn. The top-left corner will have coordinates that are the minimum x and the minimum y from the points at the ends of the diagonal. The width will be the absolute value of the difference between the x coordinates for the two ends, and the height will be the absolute value of the difference between the y coordinates. From that we can define our class.

Try It Out — The Element.Rectangle Class

Here's the definition of the class for a rectangle object:

```
class Element
{
  // Code for the base class definition...

  // Nested class defining a line...

  // Nested class defining a rectangle
  public static class Rectangle extends Element
  {
    public Rectangle(Point start, Point end, Color color)
    {
      super(color);
      rectangle = new Rectangle2D.Double(
        Math.min(start.x, end.x), Math.min(start.y, end.y),     // Top-left corner
        Math.abs(start.x - end.x), Math.abs(start.y - end.y)); // Width & height
    }
```

```
    public Shape getShape()
    {
      return rectangle;
    }
```

```
    public java.awt.Rectangle getBounds()
    {
      return rectangle.getBounds();
    }

    public void modify(Point start, Point last)
    {
      rectangle.x = Math.min(start.x, last.x);
      rectangle.y = Math.min(start.y, last.y);
      rectangle.width = Math.abs(start.x - last.x);
      rectangle.height = Math.abs(start.y - last.y);
    }

    private Rectangle2D.Double rectangle;
  }
}
```

If you uncomment the line in the `createElement()` method that creates rectangles and recompile, you will be ready to draw rectangles as well as lines.

You only need to recompile `Element.java` and `SketchView.java`. The rest of Sketcher is still the same. If you run it again, you should be able to draw rectangles and lines – in various colors, too.

How It Works

The code works in essentially the same way as for lines. You can drag the mouse in any direction to create a rectangle. The constructor sorts out the correct coordinates for the top-left corner. This is because the rectangle is being defined from its diagonal, so the rectangle is always defined from the point where the mouse button was pressed to the current cursor position. Because the position of a `Rectangle2D` object is always defined by its top left corner, we can no longer tell from this object which diagonal was used to define it.

Defining Circles

The most natural mechanism for drawing a circle is to make the point where the mouse button is pressed the center, and the point where the mouse button is released the end of the radius – that is, on the circumference. We'll need to do a little calculation for this.

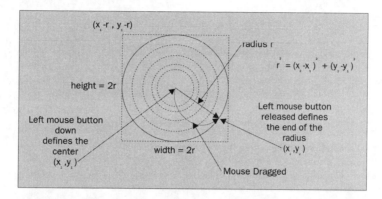

The diagram illustrates the drawing mechanism. Circles will be drawn dynamically as the mouse is dragged, with the cursor position being on the circumference of the circle. Pythagoras' theorem, as shown in the diagram, provides the formula that you might use to calculate the radius from the point at the center and the point on the circumference. However, Java makes this easy. Remember the distance() method defined in Point2D class? That does exactly what is shown here so we will be able to use that to obtain the radius directly. When we have that we can then calculate the top-left point by subtracting the radius from the coordinates of the center. We will create a circle shape as a particular case of an Ellipse2D object and so the height and width of the enclosing rectangle will be just twice the radius.

Try It Out — Adding Circles

Here's how this is applied in the definition of the Element.Circle class:

```
class Element
{
  // Code defining the base class...

  // Nested class defining a line...

  // Nested class defining a rectangle...

  // Nested class defining a circle
  public static class Circle extends Element
  {
    public Circle(Point center, Point circum, Color color)
    {
      super(color);

      // Radius is distance from center to circumference
      double radius = center.distance(circum);
```

```
            circle = new Ellipse2D.Double(center.x - radius, center.y - radius,
                                    2.*radius, 2.*radius );
        }

        public Shape getShape()
        {
          return circle;
        }

        public java.awt.Rectangle getBounds()
        {
          return circle.getBounds();
        }

        public void modify(Point center, Point circum)
        {
          double radius = center.distance(circum);
          circle.x = center.x - (int)radius;
          circle.y = center.y - (int)radius;
          circle.width = circle.height = 2*radius;
        }

        private Ellipse2D.Double circle;
    }
}
```

If we amend the createElement() method in the MouseHandler class by uncommenting the line that creates Element.Circle objects, we will be ready to draw circles. You are now equipped to produce artwork such as that shown here.

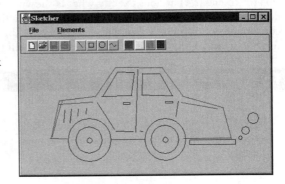

How It Works

The circle is generated with the button down point as the center and the cursor position while dragging is on the circumference. The distance() method defined in the Point2D class is used to calculate the radius, and then this value is used to calculate the coordinates of the top-left corner of the enclosing rectangle. The circle is stored as an Ellipse2D.Double object with a width and height as twice the radius.

Drawing Curves

Curves are a bit trickier to deal with than the other shapes. We want to be able to create a freehand curve by dragging the mouse, so that as the cursor moves the curve extends. This will need to be reflected in how we define the `Element.Curve` class. Let's first consider how the process of drawing a curve is going to work, and define the `Element.Curve` class based on that.

The `QuadCurve2D` and `CubicCurve2D` classes don't really suit our purpose here. A curve is going to be represented by a series of connected line segments, but we don't know ahead of time how many there are going to be – as long as the mouse is being dragged we'll collect more points. This gives us a hint as to the approach we could adopt for creating a curve.

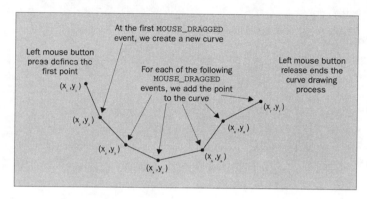

This looks like a job for a `GeneralPath` object. It can handle any number of segments and we can add to it. If we construct an initial curve as soon as we have two points – which is when we receive the first `MOUSE_DRAGGED` event – we can extend the curve by calling the `modify()` method to add another segment for each of the subsequent `MOUSE_DRAGGED` events.

Try It Out — The `Element.Curve` Class

This means that the outline of the `Curve` class is going to be:

```
class Element
{
  // Code defining the base class...

  // Nested class defining a line...

  // Nested class defining a rectangle...

  // Nested class defining a circle...

  // Nested class defining a curve
  public static class Curve extends Element
  {
    public Curve(Point start, Point next, Color color)
    {
      super(color);
```

```
            curve = new GeneralPath();
            curve.moveTo(start.x, start.y);


            curve.lineTo(next.x, next.y);
        }
        // Add another segment
        public void modify(Point start, Point next)
        {
            curve.lineTo(next.x,
                          next.y);
        }

        public Shape getShape()
        {
            return curve;
        }

        public java.awt.Rectangle getBounds()
        {
            return curve.getBounds();
        }

        private GeneralPath curve;
    }
}
```

The `Curve` class constructor creates a `GeneralPath` object and adds a single line segment to it by moving the current point to `start` by calling `moveTo()`, and then calling its `lineTo()` method with `next` as the argument. Additional segments are added by the `modify()` method. This calls `lineTo()` for the `GeneralPath` member of the class with the new point as the argument. This will add a line from the end of the last segment that was added to the new point.

Try It Out — Drawing Curves

Of course, we need to uncomment the line creating an `Element.Curve` object in the `createElement()` method. Then we are ready to roll again. If we recompile Sketcher we will be able to give freehand curves a whirl, and produce elegant sketches such as that here.

How It Works

Drawing curves works in essentially the same way as drawing the other elements. The use of XOR mode is superfluous with drawing a curve since we only extend it, but it would be quite a bit of work to treat it as a special case. This would only be justified if drawing curves was too slow and produced excessive flicker.

You may be wondering if you can change from XOR mode back to the normal mode of drawing in a graphics context. Certainly you can: just call the setPaintMode() method for the graphics context object to get back to the normal drawing mode.

There's some fabricated text in the last screenshot. In the next chapter we'll add a rather more sophisticated facility for adding text to a sketch. Don't draw too many masterpieces yet. We won't be able to preserve them for the nation and posterity by saving them in a file until the chapter after the next.

Summary

In this chapter you have learned how to draw on components and how you can use mouse listeners to implement a drawing interface. The important points we have covered in this chapter are:

❑ A Graphics2D component represents the drawing surface of the component.

❑ You draw on a component by calling methods for its Graphics2D object.

❑ The user coordinate system for drawing on a component has the origin in the top-left corner of the component by default with the positive x-axis from left to right, and the positive y-axis from top to bottom. This is automatically mapped to the device coordinate system, which is in the same orientation.

❑ You normally draw on a component by implementing its paint() method. The paint() method is passed a Graphics2D object that is the graphics context for the component but as type Graphics. You must cast the Graphics object to type Graphics2D to be able to access the Graphics2D class methods. The paint() method is called whenever the component needs to be redrawn.

❑ You can't create a Graphics2D object. If you want to draw on a component outside of the paint() method, you can obtain a Graphics2D object for the component by calling its getGraphics() method.

❑ There is more than one drawing mode that you can use. The default mode is **paint mode**, where drawing overwrites the background pixels with pixels of the current color. Another mode is **XOR mode** where the current color is combined with the background color. This is typically used to alternate between the current color and a color passed to the setXORMode() method.

❑ The Graphics2D class defines methods for drawing outline shapes as well as filled shapes.

❑ The java.awt.geom package defines classes that represent 2D shapes.

Exercises

1. Add the code to the Sketcher program to support drawing an ellipse.

2. Modify the Sketcher program to include a button for switching fill mode on and off.

3. Extend the classes defining rectangles, circles and ellipses to support filled shapes.

4. Extend the curve class to support filled shapes.

5. (Harder – for curve enthusiasts!) Implement an applet to display a curve as multiple CubicCurve2D objects from points on the curve entered by clicking the mouse. The applet should have two buttons – one to clear the window and allow points on the curve to be entered, and the other to display the curve. Devise your own scheme for default control points.

6. (Also harder!) Modify the previous example to ensure that the curve is continuous – this implies that the control points either side of an interior point, and the interior point itself, should be on a straight line. Allow control points to be dragged with the mouse, but still maintaining the continuity of the curve.

Extending the GUI

In this chapter we will investigate how we can improve the GUI for Sketcher. After adding a status bar, we will investigate how to create dialogs, and how we can use them to communicate with the user and to manage input. Another GUI capability we will be exploring is pop-up menus and we will be using these to enhance the Sketcher application. All of this will give you a lot more practice in implementing event listeners and more besides.

In this chapter you will learn:

❑   How to create a status bar

❑   How to create a dialog

❑   What a modal dialog is and how it differs from a non-modal dialog

❑   How to create a message box dialog

❑   How you can use components in a dialog to receive input

❑   What a pop-up menu is

❑   What context menus are and how you can implement them

Creating a Status Bar

One limitation of the Sketcher program as it stands is that you have no direct feedback on what current element type and color have been selected. As a gentle start to this chapter, let's fix that now. A window status bar is a common and very convenient way of displaying the status of various application parameters, each in its own pane.

We can make up our own class, StatusBar for instance, that will define a status bar. Ideally we would design a class for a generic status bar and customize it for Sketcher, but we will take the simple approach of designing a class that is specific to Sketcher. The JPanel class would be a good base for our StatusBar class since it represents a panel, and we can add objects representing status bar panes to it. We can use the JLabel class as a base for defining status bar panes and add sunken borders to them for a distinct appearance.

Let's start with a status bar at the bottom of Sketcher with two panes to show the current element type and color. Then we will know exactly what we are about to draw. We can start by defining the `StatusBar` class that will represent the status bar in the application window, and we'll define the `StatusPane` class as an inner class to `StatusBar`.

Try It Out – Defining a Status Bar Class

Here's an initial stab at the definition for the `StatusBar` class:

```java
// Class defining a status bar
import javax.swing.*;
import javax.swing.border.*;
import java.awt.*;

class StatusBar extends JPanel
                implements Constants
{
  // Constructor
  public StatusBar()
  {
    setLayout(new FlowLayout(FlowLayout.LEFT, 10, 3));
    setBackground(Color.lightGray);
    setBorder(BorderFactory.createLineBorder(Color.darkGray));
    setColorPane(DEFAULT_ELEMENT_COLOR);
    setTypePane(DEFAULT_ELEMENT_TYPE);
    add(colorPane);                       // Add color pane to status bar
    add(typePane);                        // Add type pane to status bar
  }

  // Set color pane label
  public void setColorPane(Color color)
  {
    // Code to set the color pane text...
  }

  // Set type pane label
  public void setTypePane (int elementType)
  {
    // Code to set the type pane text....
  }

  // Panes in the status bar
  private StatusPane colorPane = new StatusPane("BLUE");
  private StatusPane typePane = new StatusPane("LINE");

  // Class defining a status bar pane
  class StatusPane extends JLabel
  {
    public StatusPane(String text)
    {
      setBackground(Color.lightGray);          // Set background color
      setForeground(Color.black);
```

```
        setFont(paneFont);                    // Set the fixed font
        setHorizontalAlignment(CENTER);       // Center the pane text
        setBorder(BorderFactory.createBevelBorder(BevelBorder.LOWERED));
        setPreferredSize(new Dimension(100,20));
        setText(text);                        // Set the text in the pane
    }

  // Font for pane text
    private Font paneFont = new Font("Serif", Font.PLAIN, 10);
  }
}
```

How It Works

Since the StatusBar class implements our Constants interface, all the variables that represent possible element types and colors are available. This outline version of StatusBar has two data members of type StatusPane, which will be the panes showing the current color and element type. The initial information to be displayed by a StatusPane object is passed to the constructor as a String object.

In the StatusBar constructor, we update the information to be displayed in each pane by calling the setColorPane() and setTypePane() methods. These ensure that initially the StatusPane objects display the default color and type that we've defined for the application. One or other of these methods will be called whenever it is necessary to update the status bar. We'll complete the definitions for setColorPane() and setTypePane() when we've been through the detail of the StatusPane class.

The StatusBar panel has a FlowLayout manager which is set in the constructor. The panes in the status bar need only display a small amount of text, so we've derived the StatusPane class from the JLabel class – so a pane for the status bar will be a specialized kind of JLabel. This means that we can call the setText() method that is inherited from JLabel to set the text for our StatusPane objects. The StatusPane objects will be left-justified when they are added to the status bar, as a result of the first argument to the setLayout() method call in the StatusBar constructor. The layout manager will leave a ten-pixel horizontal gap between successive panes in the status bar, and a three-pixel vertical gap between rows of components. The border for the status bar is a single dark gray line that we add using the BorderFactory method.

The only data member in the StatusPane class is the Font object, font. We've defined the font to be used for pane text as a standard 10-point Serif. In the constructor we set the background color to light gray, the foreground color to dark gray, and we set the standard font. We also set the alignment of the text as centered by calling the inherited method setHorizontalAlignment(), and passing the value CENTER to it – this is defined in the base class, JLabel.

If we can maintain a fixed width for each pane, it will prevent the size of the pane jumping around when we change the text. So we've set the setPreferredSize() at the minimum necessary for accommodating our longest text field. Lastly, in the StatusPane constructor we set the text for the pane by calling the inherited setText() method.

Try It Out – Updating the Panes

We can code the `setColorPane()` method as:

```java
// Set color pane label
public void setColorPane(Color color)
{
  String text;                          // Text for the color pane
  if(color.equals(Color.red))
    text = "RED";

  else if(color.equals(Color.yellow))
    text = "YELLOW";
  else if(color.equals(Color.green))
    text = "GREEN";
  else if(color.equals(Color.blue))
    text = "BLUE";
  else
    text = "CUSTOM COLOR";
  colorPane.setForeground(color);
  colorPane.setText(text);              // Set the pane text
}
```

In the code for the `setTypePane()` method we can use `switch` rather than `if` statements to test the parameter value because it is of type `int`:

```java
// Set type pane label
public void setTypePane(int elementType)
{
  String text;        // Text for the type pane
  switch(elementType)
  {
    case LINE:
      text = "LINE";
      break;
    case RECTANGLE:
      text = "RECTANGLE";
      break;
    case CIRCLE:
      text = "CIRCLE";
      break;
    case CURVE:
      text = "CURVE";
      break;
    default:
      text = "ERROR";
      break;
  }
  typePane.setText(text);   // Set the pane text
}
```

How It Works

This code is quite simple. The text to be displayed in the color pane is selected in the series of `if-else` statements. They each compare the color passed as an argument with the standard colors we use in Sketcher and set the `text` variable accordingly. The last `else` should never be reached at the moment, but it will be obvious if it is. This provides the possibility of adding more flexibility in the drawing color later on. Note that we also set the foreground color to the currently selected element color, so the text will be drawn in the color to which it refers.

The type pane uses a `switch` as it is more convenient but the basic process is the same as for the color pane.

All we need now is to implement the status bar in the `SketchFrame` class. For this we must add a data member to the class that defines the status bar, add the status bar to the content pane of the window in the class constructor and extend the `actionPerformed()` methods in the `TypeAction` and `ColorAction` classes to update the status bar when the element type or color is altered.

Try It Out – The Status Bar in Action

You can add the following statement to the `SketchFrame` class to define the status bar as a data member, following the members defining the menu bar and toolbar:

```
StatusBar statusBar = new StatusBar();     // Window status bar
```

We create `statusBar` as a data member so that it can be accessed throughout the class definition, including from within the `Action` classes. You need to add one statement to the end of the `SketchFrame` class constructor:

```
public SketchFrame(String title, Sketcher theApp)
{
  // Constructor code as before...

   getContentPane().add(statusBar, BorderLayout.SOUTH);        // Add the
statusbar
}
```

This adds the status bar to the bottom of the application window. To update the status bar when the element type changes, you can add one statement to the `actionPerformed()` method in the inner class, `TypeAction`:

```
public void actionPerformed(ActionEvent e)
{
   elementType = typeID;
   statusBar.setTypePane(typeID);
}
```

The type pane is updated by calling the `setTypePane()` method for the status bar and passing the current element type to it as an argument.

We can add a similar statement to the `actionPerformed()` method to update the color pane:

```
public void actionPerformed(ActionEvent e)
{
  elementColor = color;
  statusBar.setColorPane(color);
}
```

If you now recompile and run Sketcher again, you'll see the status bar in the application.

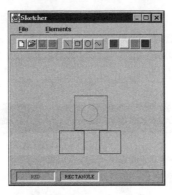

As you change the element type and color, the status bar will be updated automatically.

Using Dialogs

A dialog is a window that is displayed within the context of another window – its parent. You use dialogs to manage input that can't be handled conveniently through interaction with the view: selecting from a range of options for instance, or enabling data to be entered from the keyboard. You can also use dialogs for information messages or warnings. Dialogs are defined by the `JDialog` class in the `javax.swing` package, and a `JDialog` object is a specialized sort of `Window`. A `JDialog` object will typically contain one or more components for displaying information or allowing data to be entered, plus buttons for selection of dialog options (including closing the dialog), so there's quite a bit of work involved in putting one together. However, for many of the typical dialogs you will want to use, the `JOptionPane` class provides an easy shortcut to creating dialogs. Below is a dialog that we'll create later in this chapter using just one statement.

We'll use this dialog to provide a response to clicking on a **Help/About** menu item that we will add to Sketcher in a moment. First though, we need to understand a little more about how dialogs work.

Modal and Non-modal Dialogs

There are two different kinds of dialog that you can create, and they have distinct operating characteristics. You have a choice of creating either a **modal dialog** or a **non-modal dialog**. When you display a modal dialog – by selecting a menu item or clicking a button, it inhibits the operation of any other windows in the application until you close the dialog. The dialog above that displays a message in a modal dialog. Operation of the application cannot continue until you click the OK button. Modal dialogs that manage input will normally have at least two buttons, an OK button that you use to accept whatever input has been entered and then close the dialog, and a Cancel button to just close the dialog and abort the entry of the data. Dialogs that manage input are almost always modal dialogs, simply because you won't generally want to allow other interactions to be triggered until your user's input is complete.

A non-modal dialog can be left on the screen for as long as you want, since it doesn't block interaction with other windows in the application. You can also switch back and forth between using a non-modal dialog and using any other application windows that are on the screen.

Whether you create a modal or a non-modal dialog is determined either by an argument to a dialog class constructor, or by which constructor you choose, since three of them create non-modal dialogs by default. There's a choice of five constructors for a JDialog object:

Constructor	Description		
	titlebar	parent window	mode
JDialog()	(empty)	(shared hidden frame)	non-modal
JDialog(Frame parent)	(empty)	parent	non-modal
JDialog(Frame parent, String title)	title	parent	non-modal
JDialog(Frame parent, boolean modal)	(empty)	parent	modal (when modal arg is true)
			non-modal (when modal arg is false)
JDialog(Frame parent, String title, boolean modal)	title	parent	modal (when modal arg is true)
			non-modal (when modal arg is false)

After you've created a JDialog object using any of the constructors, you can change the kind of dialog window it will produce from modal to non-modal, or vice versa, by calling the setModal() method for the object. If you specify the argument to the method as true, the dialog will be modal, and a false argument will make it non-modal. You can also check whether a JDialog object is modal or not. The isModal() method for the object will return true if it represents a modal dialog, and false otherwise.

All JDialog objects are initially invisible so to display them you must call the setVisible() method for the JDialog object with the argument true. This method is inherited from the Component class via the Container and Window classes. If you call setVisible() with the argument false, the dialog window is removed from the screen. Once you've displayed a modal dialog window, the user can't interact with any of the other application windows until you call setVisible() for the dialog object with the argument false, so you typically do this in the event handler which is called to close the dialog. Note that the setVisible() method only affects the visibility of the dialog. You still have a perfectly good JDialog object so that when you want to display the dialog again, you just call its setVisible() method with an argument set to true. Of course, if you call dispose() for the JDialog object, or set the default close operation to DISPOSE_ON_CLOSE, then you won't be able to use the JDialog object again.

To set or change the title bar for a dialog, you just pass a String object to the setTitle() method for the JDialog object. If you want to know what the current title for a dialog is, you can call the getTitle() method which will return a String object containing the title bar string.

Dialog windows are resizable by default, so you can normally change the size of a dialog window by dragging its boundaries. If you don't want to allow a dialog window to be resized, you can inhibit this by calling the setResizable() for the JDialog object with the argument as false. An argument value of true re-enables the resizing capability.

A Simple Modal Dialog

The simplest kind of dialog is one which just displays some information. We could see how this works by adding a Help menu with an About menu item, and then displaying an About dialog to provide information about the application.

Let's derive our own dialog class from JDialog so we can create an About dialog.

Try It Out – Defining the AboutDialog Class

The constructor for our AboutDialog class will need to accept three arguments – the parent Frame object, which will be the application window in Sketcher, a String object defining what should appear on the title bar and a String object for the message we want to display. We'll only need one button in the dialog window, an OK button to close the dialog. We can make the whole thing self-contained by making the AboutDialog class the action listener for the button, and since it's only relevant in the context of the SketchFrame class, we can define it as an inner class.

```
public class SketchFrame extends JFrame
                         implements Constants
{
  // SketchFrame class as before...

  // Class defining a general purpose message box
  class AboutDialog extends JDialog implements ActionListener
  {
    public AboutDialog(Frame parent, String title, String message)
    {
      super(parent, title, true);
```

```
      // If there was a parent, set dialog position inside
      if(parent != null)
      {
        Dimension parentSize = parent.getSize();       // Parent size
        Point p = parent.getLocation();                // Parent position
        setLocation(p.x+parentSize.width/4,p.y+parentSize.height/4);
      }

      // Create the message pane
      JPanel messagePane = new JPanel();
      messagePane.add(new JLabel(message));
      getContentPane().add(messagePane);

      // Create the button pane
      JPanel buttonPane = new JPanel();
      JButton button = new JButton("OK");            // Create OK button
      buttonPane.add(button);                        // add to content pane
      button.addActionListener(this);
      getContentPane().add(buttonPane, BorderLayout.SOUTH);
      setDefaultCloseOperation(DISPOSE_ON_CLOSE);
      pack();                                        // Size window for components
      setVisible(true);
    }

    // OK button action
    public void actionPerformed(ActionEvent e)
    {
      setVisible(false);                             // Set dialog invisible
      dispose();                                     // Release the dialog resources
    }
  }
}
```

How It Works

The constructor first calls the base `JDialog` class constructor to create a modal dialog with the title bar given by the `title` argument. It then defines the position of the dialog relative to the position of the frame.

> When we create an instance of the `AboutDialog` class in the Sketcher program a little later in this chapter, we'll specify the `SketchFrame` object as the parent for the dialog. The parent relationship between the application window and the dialog implies a lifetime dependency. When the `SketchFrame` object is destroyed, the `AboutDialog` object will be too, because it is a child of the `SketchFrame` object. This doesn't just apply to `JDialog` objects – any `Window` object can have another `Window` object as a parent.

By default the `AboutDialog` window will be positioned relative to the top-left corner of the screen. To position the dialog appropriately, we set the coordinates of the top-left corner of the dialog as one quarter of the distance across the width of the application window, and one quarter of the distance down from the top-left corner of the application window.

You add the components you want to display in a dialog to the content pane for the JDialog object. The content pane has a BorderLayout manager by default, just like the content pane for the application window, and this is quite convenient for our dialog layout. The dialog contains two JPanel objects that are created in the constructor, one to hold a JLabel object for the message that is passed to the constructor, and the other to hold the OK button that will close the dialog. The messagePane object is added so that it fills the center of the dialog window. The buttonPane position is specified as BorderLayout.SOUTH, so it will be at the bottom of the dialog window. Both JPanel objects have a FlowLayout manager by default.

We want the AboutDialog object to be the listener for the OK button so we pass the this variable as the argument to the addActionListener() method call for the button.

The pack() method is inherited from the Window class. This method packs the components in the window, setting the window to an optimal size for the components it contains. Note that if you don't call pack() here, the size for your dialog will not be set and you won't be able to see it.

The actionPerformed() method will be called when the OK button is selected. This just disposes of the dialog by calling the dispose() method for the AboutDialog object so the dialog window will disappear from the screen and the resources it was using will be released.

To add a Help menu with an About item to our Sketcher application, we need to insert some code into the SketchFrame class constructor.

Try It Out – Creating an About Menu Item

You shouldn't have any trouble with this. We can make the SketchFrame object the listener for the About menu item so add ActionListener to the list of interfaces implemented by SketchFrame:

```
public class SketchFrame extends JFrame
                    implements Constants, ActionListener
```

The changes to the constructor to add the Help menu will be:

```
  public SketchFrame(String title , Sketcher theApp)
  {
    setTitle(title);                         // Set the window title
    this.theApp = theApp;

    setJMenuBar(menuBar);                    // Add the menu bar to the
window

    JMenu fileMenu = new JMenu("File");      // Create File menu
    JMenu elementMenu = new JMenu("Elements"); // Create Elements menu
    JMenu helpMenu = new JMenu("Help");      // Create Help menu

    fileMenu.setMnemonic('F');               // Create shortcut
    elementMenu.setMnemonic('E');            // Create shortcut
    helpMenu.setMnemonic('H');               // Create shortcut

    // All the stuff for the previous menus and the toolbar, as before...
```

```
      // Add the About item to the Help menu
      aboutItem = new JMenuItem("About");          // Create the item
      aboutItem.addActionListener(this);           // Listener is the frame
      helpMenu.add(aboutItem);                     // Add item to menu
      menuBar.add(helpMenu);                       // Add the Help menu
    }
```

Add `aboutMenu` as a private member of the `SketchFrame` class:

```
      // Sundry menu items
      private JMenuItem aboutItem;
```

Lastly, we need to implement the method in the `SketchFrame` class to handle the **About** menu item's events:

```
      // Handle About menu action events
      public void actionPerformed(ActionEvent e)
      {
        if(e.getSource() == aboutItem)
        {
          // Create about dialog with the app window as parent
          AboutDialog aboutDlg = new AboutDialog(this, "About Sketcher",
                                    "Sketcher Copyright Ivor Horton
    2000");
        }
      }
```

You can now recompile `SketchFrame.java` to try out our smart new dialog.

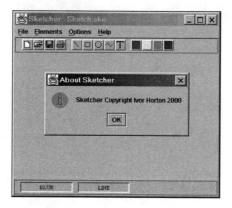

The dialog pops up when you select the **About** item in the **Help** menu. Until you select the **OK** button in the **About Sketcher** dialog, you can't interact with the application window at all since we created this as a modal dialog. By changing the last argument in the call to the superclass constructor in the `AboutDialog` constructor, you can make it non-modal and see how that works. This kind of dialog is usually modal though.

If you resize the application window before you display the **About** dialog, you'll see that its position of the dialog relative to the application window is adjusted accordingly.

How It Works

This is stuff that should be very familiar by now. We create a JMenu object for the **Help** item on the menu bar, and add a shortcut for it by calling its setMnemonic() member. We create a JMenuItem object which is the **About** menu item and call its addActionListener() method to make the SketchFrame object the listener for the item. After adding the menu item to the **Help** menu, we add the helpMenu object to the menubar object.

We create an AboutDialog object in the actionPerformed() method for the SketchFrame object, as this will be called when the **About** menu item is clicked. Before we display the dialog, we verify that the source of the event is the menu item, aboutItem. This is not important now, but we will add other menu items later, and we will want to handle their events using the same actionPerformed() method. The dialog object is self-contained and disposes of itself when the **OK** button is clicked. The dialog that we want to display here will always display the same message, so there's no real point in creating and destroying it each time we want to display it. You could arrange for the dialog box object to be created once, and the reference stored as a member of the SketchFrame class. Then you make it visible in the actionPerformed() method for the menu item and make it invisible in the actionPerformed() method responding to the dialog **OK** button event.

This is all very well, but it was a lot of work just to get a dialog with a message displayed. Deriving a class from JDialog gives you complete flexibility as to how the dialog works, but we didn't really need it in this case. Didn't we say there was an easier way?

Instant Dialogs

The JOptionPane class defines a number of static methods that will create and display standard modal dialogs for you. The simplest dialog you can create this way is a message dialog rather like our **About** message dialog. The following methods produce message dialogs:

Dial-a-Dialog Methods	Description

showMessageDialog(
  Component parent,
  Object message)
	This method displays a modal dialog with the default title `"Message"`. The first argument is the parent for the dialog. The `Frame` object containing the component will be used to position the dialog. If the first argument is `null`, a default `Frame` object will be created and that will be used to position the dialog centrally on the screen.
	
	The second argument specifies what is to be displayed in addition to the default **OK** button. This can be a `String` object specifying the message or an `Icon` object defining an icon to be displayed. It can also be a `Component`, in which case the component will be displayed. If some other type of object is passed as the second argument, its `toString()` method will be called, and the `String` object that is returned will be displayed. You will usually get a default icon for an information message along with your message.
	
	You can pass multiple items to be displayed by passing an array of type `Object[]` for the second argument. Each array element will be processed as above according to its type and they will be arranged in vertical stack. Clever, eh?

showMessageDialog(
  Component parent,
  Object message,
  String title,
  int messageType)
	This displays a dialog as above, but with the title specified by the third argument. The fourth argument, `messageType`, can be:
	
	ERROR_MESSAGE
	INFORMATION_MESSAGE
	WARNING_MESSAGE
	QUESTION_MESSAGE
	PLAIN_MESSAGE
	
	These determine the style of the message constrained by the current look and feel. This will usually include a default icon, such as a question mark for `QUESTION_MESSAGE`.

showMessageDialog(
  Component parent,
  Object message,
  String title,
  int messageType,
  Icon icon)
	This displays a dialog as above except that the icon will be what you pass as the fifth argument. Specifying a null argument for the icon will produce a dialog the same as the previous version of the method.

We could have used one of these for the About dialog instead of all that messing about with inner classes. Let's see how.

Try It Out – An Easy About Dialog

Delete the inner class, `AboutDialog`, from `SketchFrame` – we won't need that any longer. Change the implementation of the `actionPerformed()` method in the `SketchFrame` class to:

```
public void actionPerformed(ActionEvent e)
{
  if(e.getSource() == aboutItem)
  {
    // Create about dialog with the menu item as parent
    JOptionPane.showMessageDialog(this,                     // Parent
                         "Sketcher Copyright Ivor Horton 2000", // Message
                         "About Sketcher",                  // Title
                            JOptionPane.INFORMATION_MESSAGE); // Message
type
  }
}
```

Compile SketchFrame again and run Sketcher. When you click on the Help/About menu item, you should get something like the following:

The pretty little icon comes for free.

How It Works

All the work is done by the static showMessageDialog() method in the JOptionPane class. What you get is controlled by the arguments that you supply, and the Swing look-and-feel in use. By default this will correspond to what is usual for your system. On a PC running Windows, we get the icon you see because we specified the message type as INFORMATION_MESSAGE. You can try plugging in the other message types to see what you get.

Input Dialogs

JOptionPane also has four static methods that you can use to create standard modal input dialogs:

```
showInputDialog(Object message)
```

This method displays a default modal input dialog with a text field for input. The message you pass as the argument is set as the caption for the input field and the default also supplies an OK button, a Cancel button and Input as a title. For example, if you pass the message "Enter Input:" as the argument in the following statement,

```
String input = JOptionPane.showInputDialog("Enter Input:");
```

the dialog shown will be displayed.

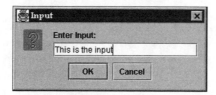

When you click on the **OK** button, whatever you entered in the text field will be returned and stored in input – `"This is the input"` in this case. If you click on the **Cancel** button, `null` will be returned. Note that this is not the same as no input. If you click on **OK** without entering anything in the text field a reference to an empty `String` object will be returned.

```
showInputDialog(Component parent, Object message)
```

This produces the same dialog as the previous method, but with the component you specify as the first argument as the parent of the dialog.

```
showInputDialog(Component parent, Object message,
                String title, int messageType)
```

In this case the title of the dialog is supplied by the third argument, and the style of the message is determined by the fourth argument. The values for the fourth argument can be any of those discussed earlier in the context of message dialogs. For instance, you could display the dialog shown with the following statement:

```
String input = JOptionPane.showInputDialog(null, "Enter Input:",
                          "Dialog for Input", JOptionPane.WARNING_MESSAGE);
```

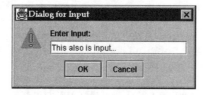

The data that you enter in the text field is returned by the `showInputDialog()` method when the **OK** button is pressed as before.

```
showInputDialog(Component parent, Object message,
                String title, int messageType,
                Icon icon, Object[] selections,
                object initialSelection)
```

This version of the method provides a list of choices in a dropdown list box. The items from which to choose are passed as the sixth argument as an array and they can be of any class type. The initial selection to be displayed when the dialog is first displayed is specified by the seventh argument. Whatever is chosen when the **OK** button is clicked will be returned as type `Object`, and, if the **Cancel** button is clicked, `null` will be returned. You can specify your own icon to replace the default icon by passing a reference of type `Icon` as the fifth argument. The following statements display the dialog shown:

```
String[] choices = {"Money", "Health", "Happiness", "This", "That", "The Other"};
String input = (String)JOptionPane.showInputDialog(null, "Choose now...",
                               "The Choice of a Lifetime",
                               JOptionPane.QUESTION_MESSAGE,
                               null,           // Use default icon
                               choices,        // Array of choices
                               choices[1]);    // Initial choice
```

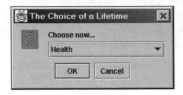

Note that you have to cast the reference returned by this version of the showInputDialog() method to the type of choice value you have used. Here we are using type String, but the selections could be type Icon, or whatever you want.

Using a Dialog to Create Text Elements

It would be good if our Sketcher program also provided a means of adding text to a picture – after all, you might want to put your name to a sketch. A dialog is the obvious way to provide the mechanism for entering the text when we create text elements. We can use one of the showInputDialog() methods for this, but first we need to add a Text menu item to the Elements menu, and we will need a class to represent text elements, the Element.Text class of course, with Element as a base class. Let's start with the Element.Text class.

Text is a little tricky. For one thing we can't treat it just like another element. There is no object that implements the Shape interface that represents a text string so, unless we want to define one, we can't use the draw() method for a graphics context to display text. We have to use the drawString() method. We'll also have to figure out the bounding rectangle for the text on screen for ourselves. With Shape objects you could rely on the getBounds() method supplied by the 2D shape classes in java.awt.geom, but with text you're on your own.

Ideally we want to avoid treating text elements as a special case. Having many tests for types while we're drawing a sketch in the paint() method for the view generates considerable processing overhead that we would be better off without. One way round this is to make every element draw itself. We could implement a polymorphic method in each element class, draw() say, and pass a Graphics2D object to it. Each shape or text element could then figure out how to draw itself. The paint() method in the view class would not need to worry about what type of element was being drawn at all.

Try It Out – Defining the Element.Text Class

Let's see how that works out. We can start by adding an abstract method, draw() to the Element class definition:

```
public abstract class Element
{
  public Element(Color color)
  {  this.color = color;  }

  public   Color getColor()
  {  return color;  }

  public abstract java.awt.Rectangle getBounds();
  public abstract void modify(Point start, Point last);
  public abstract void draw(Graphics2D g2D);

  protected Color color;                  // Color of a shape

  // Plus definitions for our shape classes...
}
```

Note that we have deleted the getShape() method as we won't be needing it further. You can remove it from all the nested classes of the Element class. The draw() method now needs to be implemented in each of the nested classes to the Element class, but because each of the current classes has a Shape member, it will be essentially the same in each. The version for the Element.Line class will be:

```
public void draw(Graphics2D g2D)
{
  g2D.setPaint(color);                     // Set the line color
  g2D.draw(line);                          // Draw the line
}
```

This just sets the color and passes the Shape object that is a member of the class to the draw() method for the Graphics2D object. For the other classes, just replace the argument to the g2D.draw() method call with the name of the Shape member of the class, and update the comments. You can now change the implementation of the paint() method in the SketchView class to:

```
public void paint(Graphics g)
{
  Graphics2D g2D = (Graphics2D)g;                        // Get a 2D device context
  Iterator elements = theApp.getModel().getIterator();
  Element element;                                       // Stores an element
  while(elements.hasNext())                              // Go through the list
  {
    element = (Element)elements.next();                  // Get the next element
    element.draw(g2D);                                   // Draw its shape
  }
}
```

It's now one statement shorter as the element sets its own color in the graphics context. We are ready to get back to the Element.Text class.

We can define the `Element.Text` class quite easily now. We will need five arguments for the constructor though – the font to be used for the string, the string to be displayed, the position where it is to be displayed, its color and its bounding rectangle. To get a bounding rectangle for a string, we need access to a graphics context, so it will be easier to create the bounding rectangle before we create a text element.

Here's the class definition:

```java
class Element
{
  // Code that defines the base class...

  // Definitions for the other shape classes...

  // Class defining text element
  public static class Text extends Element
  {
    public Text(Font font, String text, Point position, Color color,
                                     java.awt.Rectangle bounds)
    {
      super(color);
      this.font = font;
      this.position = position;
      this.text = text;
      this.bounds = bounds;
      this.bounds.setLocation(position.x, position.y - (int)bounds.getHeight());
    }

    public java.awt.Rectangle getBounds()
    {
      return getBounds(bounds);
    }

    public void draw(Graphics2D g2D)
    {
      g2D.setPaint(color);
      Font oldFont = g2D.getFont();                    // Save the old font
      g2D.setFont(font);                               // Set the new font
      g2D.drawString(text, position.x, position.y);
      g2D.setFont(oldFont);                            // Restore the old font
    }

    public void modify(Point start, Point last)
    {
      // No code is required here, but we must supply a definition
    }

    private Font font;                       // The font to be used
    private String text;                     // Text to be displayed
    Point position;                          // The start of the text string
    java.awt.Rectangle bounds = null;        // The bounding rectangle
  }
}
```

How It Works

In the constructor we pass the color to the superclass constructor, and store the other argument values in data members of the `Element.Text` class. When we create the bounding rectangle to pass to the constructor, the default reference point for the top-left corner of the rectangle will be (0, 0). This is not what we want for our text object so we have to modify it.

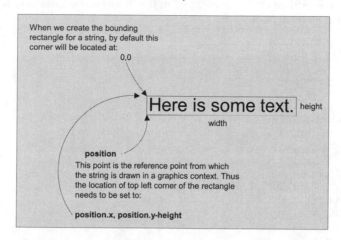

In the constructor, we adjust the coordinates of the top-left corner of the bounding rectangle relative to the point, `position`, where the string will be drawn. Remember that the point coordinates passed to the `drawString()` method correspond to the bottom-left corner of the first character in the string.

The code to draw text is not difficult – it's just different from drawing shapes. It amounts to calling `setPaint()` to set the text color, setting the font in the graphics context by calling its `setFont()` method and finally calling `drawString()` to display the text.

To work with text, we could do with a menu item and a toolbar button to set the element type to text, so let's deal with that next.

Try It Out – Adding the Text Menu Item

We'll add a `textAction` member to the `SketchFrame` class, so amend the declaration for the `TypeAction` members to:

```
private TypeAction lineAction, rectangleAction, circleAction,
                   curveAction, textAction;
```

You will need an icon in the `Images` directory that is a subdirectory to the Sketcher directory if you want to create a toolbar button for text. I just created an icon with 'T' on it, ![T icon], but you can create something fancier if you have a mind to. The file containing the icon should have the name `Text.gif`, because that's what the `TypeAction` object will assume.

To add the menu item, you need to add a statement to the `SketchFrame` constructor following the statements that create the other items in the element menu:

```
      // Construct the Element pull down menu
      // Code to add the other Element menu items as before...
      addMenuItem(elementMenu, textAction = new TypeAction("Text", TEXT,
                                                "Draw text"), null);
```

This assumes we have defined the value of TEXT in the `Constants` interface, so add that and a default font for use with text elements now:

```
public interface Constants
{
   // Element type definitions
   int LINE      = 101;
   int RECTANGLE = 102;
   int CIRCLE    = 103;
   int CURVE     = 104;
   int TEXT      = 105;

   // Initial conditions
   int DEFAULT_ELEMENT_TYPE = LINE;
   Color DEFAULT_ELEMENT_COLOR = Color.blue;
   Font DEFAULT_FONT = new Font("Times New Roman",Font.PLAIN, 12);
}
```

If you don't have the Times New Roman font on your machine, choose a font that you do have. We will need a data member in the application window object to hold a reference to the current font. It will start out as the default font, but we will be adding the means to alter this later. Add the following data member after the others in `SketchFrame`:

```
   private Color elementColor = DEFAULT_ELEMENT_COLOR;     // Current element
color
   private int elementType = DEFAULT_ELEMENT_TYPE;         // Current element type
   private Font font = DEFAULT_FONT;                        // Current font
```

Of course, we also need a method to retrieve it from the application window object:

```
public Font getCurrentFont()
{  return font;  }
```

Now the view will be able to get the current font when necessary, via the application object.

If you want the toolbar button as well, you will need to add one statement to the `SketchFrame` constructor following the others that add element type selection buttons:

```
      // Add element type buttons
      toolBar.addSeparator();
      // Code to add other buttons as before...
      addToolBarButton(textAction);
```

The action events for the menu item and toolbar button for text are taken care of and the final piece is dealing with mouse events when we create a text element.

Text elements are going to be different to shapes in how they are created. To create a text element we need to know what the text is, its color, its font and where it is to be placed. We will also have to construct its bounding rectangle. This sounds as though it might be easier than geometric elements, but there are complications.

Try It Out – Creating Text Elements

We start the process of creating geometric elements in SketchView's `MouseHandler` class, but we can't simply start with the `mousePressed()` method, as would at first seem logical. The problem is the sequence of events. We want to display a dialog to manage the text entry, but if we display a dialog in the `mousePressed()` method, the `mouseReleased()` event will get lost, unless you're happy to hold down the mouse button while typing into the text field with the other hand! A simple solution is to separate the creation of text elements altogether, and create them in the `mouseClicked()` method. This method is called after the mouse button is released, so all the other events will have occurred and been dealt with.

We can implement this method in the inner class, `MouseHandler`, to create a text element as follows:

```
public void mouseClicked(MouseEvent e)
{
  int modifier = e.getModifiers();                    // Get modifiers
  if((modifier & e.BUTTON1_MASK) != 0 &&
     (theApp.getWindow().getElementType() == TEXT))
  {

    start = e.getPoint();                // Save cursor position - start of text
    String text = JOptionPane.showInputDialog(
              (Component)e.getSource(),             // Used to get the frame
              "Enter Text:",                        // The message
              "Dialog for Text Element",            // Dialog title
              JOptionPane.PLAIN_MESSAGE);           // No icon

    if(text != null)                                // If we have text
    {                                               // create the element
      g2D = (Graphics2D)getGraphics();
      Font font = theApp.getWindow().getCurrentFont();

      // Create the text element
      tempElement = new Element.Text(
          font,
          text,
          start,
          theApp.getWindow().getElementColor(),
          font.getStringBounds(text, g2D.getFontRenderContext()).getBounds());

      if(tempElement != null)                       // If we created one
          theApp.getModel().add(tempElement);       // add it to the model
      tempElement = null;
```

```
          g2D.dispose();
          g2D = null;
          start = null;
        }
      }
    }
```

We only want to do something here if it was mouse button 1 that was clicked and the current element type is TEXT. In this case we save the cursor position and pop a dialog to permit the text string to be entered. If there was one, we go ahead and create a text element.

We need the `Graphics2D` object in order to determine the bounding rectangle for the text element. This is done in the rather fearsome looking expression for the last argument to the constructor. It's much easier than it looks so let's take it apart.

The `getStringBounds()` method for the `Font` object returns a reference of type `Rectangle2D` to the bounding rectangle for the string that you supply as the first argument. The second argument to this method is a reference to a `FontRenderContext` object. This happens to be a container class for the information that is necessary to render text in a particular graphics context, and it provides the mapping from point sizes to pixels for instance. The `getStringBounds()` method needs a `FontRenderContext` object to produce the bounding rectangle for the string, and we can supply one by calling the `getFontRenderContext()` method for the g2D object. We need an object of type `Rectangle` rather than type `Rectangle2D` to store bounds because our `Element.Text` constructor argument is of this type. We get this by calling the `getBounds()` method for the `Rectangle2D` object that is returned by `getStringBounds()`.

Once the element has been created, we just add it to the model, and clean up the variables that we were using.

We must now make sure that the other mouse event handlers do nothing when the current element is TEXT.

We can update the `mouseDragged()` method with a similar approach. The `if` expression will only be true if button 1 was pressed and the current element type is not TEXT.

```
public void mouseDragged(MouseEvent e)
{
  last = e.getPoint();                         // Save cursor position
  int modifier = e.getModifiers();             // Get modifiers

  if((modifier & e.BUTTON1_MASK) != 0 &&
     (theApp.getWindow().getElementType()  != TEXT))
  {
    if(tempElement == null)                    // Is there an element?
      tempElement = createElement(start, last); // No so create one
    else
    {
      tempElement.draw(g2D);                   // Yes - draw to erase it
      tempElement.modify(start, last);         // Modify it
    }
```

```
                    tempElement.draw(g2D);                          // and draw it
               }
          }
```

The `mouseReleased()` method just cleans up `tempElement` and `g2D`, so we don't need to change that. The only other change we need to make is to make the status bar respond to the `TEXT` element type being set. To do this we just need to make a small addition to the definition of the `setTypePane()` method in the `StatusBar` class:

```
     public void setTypePane(int elementType)
     {
       String text;          // Text for the type pane
       switch(elementType)
       {
         // case label as before...

         case TEXT:
           text = "TEXT";
           break;
       }
       typePane.setText(text);   // Set the pane text
     }
```

How It Works

The `mouseClicked()` handler responds to mouse button 1 being clicked when the element type is `TEXT`. This method will be called after the `mouseReleased()` method. Within the `if` statement that determines this, we create a dialog to receive the text input by calling the static `showInputDialog()` in the `JOptionPane` class. If you selected the **Cancel** button in the dialog, text will be `null` so in this case we do nothing. If text is not `null`, we create an `Element.Text` object at the current cursor position containing the text string that was entered in the dialog. We then add this to the model, as long as it's not `null`. It is important to remember to reset the `start` and `tempElement` members back to `null`, so as not to confuse subsequent event handling operations. Incidentally, although there isn't a method to detect double clicks on the mouse button, it's easy to implement. The `getClickCount()` method for the `MouseEvent` object that is passed to `mouseClicked()` returns the click count. To respond to a double click you would write:

```
     if(e.getClickCount() == 2)
     {
       //Response to double click...
     }
```

The other event handling methods behave as before so far as the geometric elements are concerned, and do nothing if the element type is `TEXT`. We can try it out.

Testing the TextDialog Class

All you need to do now is recompile Sketcher and run it again. To open the text dialog, select the new toolbar button or the menu item and click in the view where you want the text to appear.

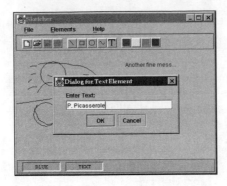

You just type the text that you want and click on the OK button. The text will be displayed starting at the point in the view where you clicked the mouse button. You can draw text in any of the colors – just like the geometric elements.

A Font Selection Dialog

We don't really want to be stuck with 12 point Times New Roman. We need to be free to be creative! A font dialog that pops up in response to a click on a suitable menu item should enable us to change the font for text elements to any of those available on the system. It should also give us a chance to see how we can get at and process the fonts that are available. We can also learn more about how to add components in a dialog. But first let's establish what our font dialog will do.

We want to be able to choose the font name from those available on the system, the style of the font, whether plain, bold or italic, as well as the point size. It would also be nice to see what a font looks like before we decide to use it. The dialog will therefore need to obtain a list of the fonts available and display them in a component. It will also need a component to allow the point size to be selected, and some means for choosing the style.

This is not going to be a wimpy dialog like those we have seen so far. This is going to be a real Java programmer's dialog. We can drag in a diversity of components here, just for the experience. We will build it step by step as it will be quite a lot of code. Just so you know where we're headed, the finished dialog is shown below.

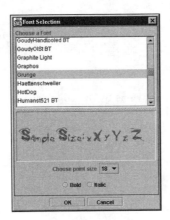

The component for choosing the font is a Swing component of type JList that can display a list of any type of component. Below that is a panel holding a JLabel object that displays a sample of the current font. The list of font names and the panel below are displayed in a split pane defined by the JSplitPane class. Here the pane is split vertically but it can also hold two panels side by side. The point size is displayed in another Swing component called a combobox, which is an object of type JComboBox. The font style options are radio buttons so only one can be selected at any time. Finally we have two buttons to close the dialog.

We can start by defining the FontDialog class with its data members and its constructor, and then build on that.

Try It Out – A FontDialog Class

The major work will be in the dialog class constructor. That will set up all the GUI elements as well as the necessary listeners to respond to operations with the dialog. The dialog object will need access to the SketchFrame object that represents the Sketcher application window to store the font that is selected, so we will pass a SketchFrame reference to the constructor.

Here's the code for the outline of the class:

```
// Class to define a dialog to choose a font
import java.awt.*;
import javax.swing.*;
import javax.swing.event.*;
import javax.swing.border.*;
import java.awt.event.*;

class FontDialog extends JDialog
                 implements Constants

{
  // Constructor
  public FontDialog(SketchFrame window)
  {
    // Code to initialize the data members...

    // Code to create buttons and the button panel...

    // Code to create the data input panel...

    // Code to create the font choice and add it to the input panel...

    // Code to create the font size choice
    //   and add it to the input panel...

    // Code to create the font style check boxes
    //   and add them to the input panel...

    // ...and then some!
  }
```

```
        private SketchFrame window;        // The application window
        private Font font;                 // Currently selected font
        private int fontStyle;             // Font style - Plain,Bold,Italic
        private int fontSize;              // Font point size
    }
```

We will be adding a few more data members shortly, but at least we know we will need these. The code to initialize the data members within the `FontDialog` constructor of the font dialog is easy. We will initialize the `font` member and the associated `fontStyle` and `fontSize` members from the current font in the application window:

```
public FontDialog(SketchFrame window)
{
    // Call the base constructor to create a modal dialog
    super(window, "Font Selection", true);

    this.window = window;                // Save the window reference
    font = window.getCurrentFont();      // Get the current font
    fontStyle = font.getStyle();         // ...style
    fontSize = font.getSize();           // ...and size

    // Plus the code for the rest of the constructor...
}
```

We call the base class constructor and pass the window object to it as parent. The second argument is the title for the dialog and the third argument determines that it is modal. The `getCurrentFont()` method returns the font stored in the window object, and we use this to initialize the `fontStyle` and `fontSize` members, so the first time we open the dialog this will be the default setting.

Creating the Buttons

Next we can add the code to the constructor that will create the button panel with the OK and Cancel buttons. We will place this at the bottom of the content pane for the dialog using the default `BorderLayout` manager:

```
public FontDialog(SketchFrame window)
{
    // Initialization as before...

    // Create the dialog button panel
    JPanel buttonPane = new JPanel();               // Create the panel to hold
buttons

    // Create and add the buttons to the buttonPane
    buttonPane.add(ok = createButton("OK"));        // Add the OK button
    buttonPane.add(cancel = createButton("Cancel")); // Add the Cancel button
    getContentPane().add(buttonPane, BorderLayout.SOUTH); // Add pane to content
pane

    // Plus the code for the rest of the constructor...
}
```

The `buttonPane` object will have a `FlowLayout` manager by default, so this will take care of positioning the buttons. We add the button pane to the dialog content pane using `BorderLayout.SOUTH` to place it at the bottom of the window. Because creating each button involves several steps, we are using a helper method `createButton()` that only requires the button label as an argument. Note that we store each button reference in a variable, so we will need to add these as members of the `FontDialog` class:

```
private JButton ok;                              // OK button
private JButton cancel;                          // Cancel button
```

We will use these references in the listeners for the button as we will see in a moment.

We can code the `createButton()` method as a member of the `FontDialog` class as follows:

```
JButton createButton(String label)
{
  JButton button = new JButton(label);           // Create the button
  button.setPreferredSize(new Dimension(80,20)); // Set the size
  button.addActionListener(this);                // Listener is the
dialog
  return button;                                 // Return the button
}
```

We set the preferred size of the button here to ensure the buttons are all the same size. Without this call, each button would be sized to fit its label, so it would look a bit untidy. The listener is the `FontDialog` class, so the `FontDialog` must implement the `ActionListener` interface, which implies an `actionPerformed()` method:

```
class FontDialog extends JDialog
               implements Constants,
                          ActionListener        // For buttons etc
{
  // Constructor definition...

  // createButton() definition...

  public void actionPerformed(ActionEvent e)
  {
    Object source = e.getSource();              // Get the source of the event
    if(source == ok)                            // Is it the OK button?

    {
      window.setCurrentFont(font);              // Set the selected font
      setVisible(false);                        // Hide the dialog
    }
    else if(source == cancel)                   // If it is the Cancel button
      setVisible(false);                        // just hide the dialog
  }

  // Plus the rest of the class definition...
}
```

The getSource() member of the ActionEvent object, e, returns a reference to the object that originated the event, so we can use this to determine which button the method is being called for. We just compare the source object (which is holding the reference to the object to which the event applies) to each button object in turn. If it is the OK button, we call the setCurrentFont() method in the SketchFrame object to set the font. If it is the Cancel button we just hide the dialog so Sketcher can continue. Of course we must add the definition of setCurrentFont() to the SketchFrame class. The code for this will be:

```
public void setCurrentFont(Font font)
{  this.font = font;  }
```

Let's now get back to the FontDialog constructor.

Adding the Data Pane

We can now add a panel to contain the components that will receive input. We will have a JList object for the font names, a JComboBox object for the point size of the font and three JRadioButton objects for selecting the font style. We will add the code to create the panel first:

```
public FontDialog(SketchFrame window)
{
  // Initialization as before...

  // Button panel code as before...

  // Code to create the data input panel
  JPanel dataPane = new JPanel();                          // Create the data entry
panel
  dataPane.setBorder(BorderFactory.createCompoundBorder(    // Create pane border
                  BorderFactory.createLineBorder(Color.black),
                  BorderFactory.createEmptyBorder(5, 5, 5, 5)));
  GridBagLayout gbLayout = new GridBagLayout();             // Create the layout
  dataPane.setLayout(gbLayout);                             // Set the pane layout
  GridBagConstraints constraints = new GridBagConstraints();

  // Plus the code for the rest of the constructor...
}
```

Here we use a GridBagLayout manager so we can set constraints for each component that we add to the dataPane container. We also set a black line border for dataPane with an inset empty border five pixels wide. This uses the BorderFactory static methods that you have seen before.

The first component we will add to dataPane is a label prompting for the font selection:

```
public FontDialog(SketchFrame window)
{
  // Initialization as before...

  // Button panel code as before...

  // Set up the data input panel to hold all input components as before...
```

```
    // Code to create the font choice and add it to the input panel
    JLabel label = new JLabel("Choose a Font");
    constraints.fill = GridBagConstraints.HORIZONTAL;
    constraints.gridwidth = GridBagConstraints.REMAINDER;
    gbLayout.setConstraints(label, constraints);
    dataPane.add(label);

    // Plus the code for the rest of the constructor...
    }
```

With the `fill` constraint set as HORIZONTAL, the components in a row will fill the width of the dataPane container, but without affecting the height. With the width constraint set to REMAINDER, the label component will fill the width of the row.

Implementing the Font List

The next component we will add is the `JList` object that displays the list of fonts, but we won't add this directly to the `dataPane`. The list of fonts will have to be obtained using the `GraphicsEnvironment` object that encapsulates information about the system in which the application is running. You will remember that we must call a `static` method in the `GraphicsEnvironment` class to get the object. Here's the code to create the list of font names:

```
    public FontDialog(SketchFrame window)
    {
      // Initialization as before...

      // Button panel code as before...

      // Set up the data input panel to hold all input components as before...

      // Add the font choice prompt label as before...

      // Code to set up font list choice component
      GraphicsEnvironment e = GraphicsEnvironment.getLocalGraphicsEnvironment();
      String[] fontNames = e.getAvailableFontFamilyNames();   // Get the font names

      fontList = new JList(fontNames);                        // Create list of font names
      fontList.setValueIsAdjusting(true);                     // single event selection
      fontList.setSelectionMode(ListSelectionModel.SINGLE_SELECTION); // Choose 1 font
      fontList.setSelectedValue(font.getFamily(),true);
      fontList.addListSelectionListener(this);
      JScrollPane chooseFont = new JScrollPane(fontList);     // Scrollable list
      chooseFont.setMinimumSize(new Dimension(300,100));

      // Plus the code for the rest of the constructor...
    }
```

We obtain the list of font family names for the system on which Sketcher is running by calling the `getAvailableFontFamilyNames()` method for the `GraphicsEnvironment` object. The `fontList` variable will need to be accessible in the method handling events for the list, so this will be another data member of the class:

```
        private JList fontList;                    // Font list
```

The `JList` object, `fontList`, is created by passing the `fontNames` array to the constructor. The `fontNames` array holds `String` objects, but you can create a `JList` object for any kind of object, images for example. You can also create a `JList` object by passing a `Vector` that contains the objects you want in the list to the constructor. It is possible to allow multiple entries from a list to be selected, in which case the selection process may cause multiple events – when you drag the cursor over several list items for example. You can ensure that there is only one event for a selection, even though multiple items are selected, by calling the `setValueIsAdjusting()` method with the argument `true`. Calling `setSelectionMode()` with the argument `SINGLE_SELECTION` ensures that only one font name can be selected. You have two possible multiple selections you can enable. Passing the value `SINGLE_INTERVAL_SELECTION` to the method allows a series of consecutive items to be selected. Passing `MULTIPLE_SELECTION_INTERVAL` provides you with total flexibility and allows any number of items anywhere to be selected. The initial selection in the list is set by the `setSelectedValue()` call. We pass the family name for the current font as the argument specifying the initial selection. There is a complementary method, `getSelectedValue()`, that we will be using in the event handler.

There's a special kind of listener for `JList` selection events that implements the `ListSelectionListener` interface. Since we set the `FontDialog` object as the listener for the list in the call to the `addListSelectionListener()` method, we had better make sure the `FontDialog` class implements the interface:

```
class FontDialog extends JDialog
                  implements Constants,
                             ActionListener,        // For buttons etc
                             ListSelectionListener  // For list box
```

There's only one method in the `ListSelectionListener` interface, and we can implement it like this:

```
// List selection listener method
public void valueChanged(ListSelectionEvent e)
{
  if(!e.getValueIsAdjusting())
  {
    font = new Font((String)fontList.getSelectedValue(), fontStyle, fontSize);
    fontDisplay.setFont(font);
    fontDisplay.repaint();
  }
}
```

This method is called when you select an item in the list. We have only one list so we don't need to check which object was the source of the event. If we needed to, we could call the `getSource()` method for the event object that is passed to `valueChanged()`, and compare it with the references to the `JList` objects.

The `ListSelectionEvent` object that is passed to the `valueChanged()` method contains records of the index positions of the list items that changed. You can obtain these as a range by calling `getFirstIndex()` for the event object for the first in the range, and `getLastIndex()` for the last. We don't need to worry about this because we have disallowed multiple selections and we just want the newly selected item in the list.

We have to be careful though. Since we start out with an item already selected, selecting another font name from the list will cause two events – one for deselecting the original font name, and the other for selecting the new name. We make sure we only deal with the last event by calling the `getValueIsAdjusting()` method for the event object in the `if` expression. This returns `false` when all changes due to a selection are complete, and `true` if things are still changing. Once we are sure nothing further is changing, we retrieve the selected font name from the list by calling its `getSelectedValue()` method. The item is returned as type `Object` so we have to cast it to type `String` before using it. We create a new `Font` object using the selected family name and the current values for `fontStyle` and `fontSize`. We store the new font in the data member `font`, and also call the `setFont()` member of a data member `fontDisplay` that we haven't added yet. This will be a `JLabel` object displaying a sample of the current font. After we've set the new font, we call `repaint()` for the label, `fontDisplay`, to get it redrawn.

> *If we allowed multiple selections on the list with the* `SINGLE_SELECTION_INTERVAL` *method, we could use the* `getFirstIndex()` *and* `getLastIndex()` *methods to get the range of index values for the item that may have changed. If on the other hand you employ the* `MULTIPLE_SELECTION_INTERVAL` *option, you would need to figure out which items in the range were actually selected. You could do this by calling the* `getSelectedIndices()` *method or the* `getSelectedValues()` *method for the list object. The first of these returns an* `int` *array of index values for selected items, and the second returns an array of type* `Object` *containing references to the selected items.*

A `JList` object doesn't support scrolling directly, but it is scrolling 'aware'. To get a scrollable list, one with scrollbars, you just need to pass the `JList` object to the `JScrollPane` constructor, as we do in the `FontDialog` constructor. This creates a pane with scrollbars – either vertical, horizontal or both, as necessary. We set a minimum size for the `JScrollPane` object to limit how small it can be made in the split pane into which we will insert it in a moment.

Displaying the Selected Font

We will display the selected font in a `JLabel` object that we place in another `JPanel` pane. Adding the following code to the constructor will do this:

```
public FontDialog(SketchFrame window)
{
  // Initialization as before...

  // Button panel code as before...

  // Set up the data input panel to hold all input components as before...

  // Add the font choice prompt label as before...

  // Set up font list choice component as before...
```

```
      // Panel to display font sample
      JPanel display = new JPanel();
      fontDisplay = new JLabel("Sample Size: x X y Y z Z");
      fontDisplay.setPreferredSize(new Dimension(300,100));
      display.add(fontDisplay);

      // Plus the code for the rest of the constructor...
   }
```

We create the JPanel object, display, and add the JLabel object, fontDisplay, to it. Remember, we update this object in the valueChanged() handler for selections from the list of font names. We will also be updating it when the font size or style is changed. The fontDisplay object just represents some sample text. You can choose something different if you like.

Just for the experience, let's use a split pane to hold the scroll pane containing the list, chooseFont, and the display panel.

Using a Split Pane

A JSplitPane object represents a pane with a movable horizontal or vertical split, so that it can hold two components. The split pane divider can be adjusted by dragging it with the mouse. Here's the code to do that:

```
   public FontDialog(SketchFrame window)
   {
     // Initialization as before...

     // Button panel code as before...

     // Set up the data input panel to hold all input components as before...

     // Add the font choice prompt label as before...

     // Set up font list choice component as before...

     // Panel to display font sample as before...

     //Create a split pane with font choice at the top
     // and font display at the bottom
     JSplitPane splitPane = new JSplitPane(JSplitPane.VERTICAL_SPLIT,
                                           true,
                                           chooseFont,
                                           display);
     gbLayout.setConstraints(splitPane, constraints);    // Split pane constraints
     dataPane.add(splitPane);                            // Add to the data pane

     // Plus the code for the rest of the constructor...
   }
```

The constructor does it all. The first argument specifies that the pane supports two components, one above the other. You can probably guess that for side by side components you would specify JSplitPane.HORIZONTAL_SPLIT. If the second constructor argument is true, the components are redrawn continuously as the divider is dragged. If it is false the components are not redrawn until you stop dragging the divider.

The third argument is the component to go at the top, or to the left for HORIZONTAL_SPLIT, and the fourth argument is the component to go at the bottom, or to the right, as the case may be.

We don't need to do it here, but you can change the components in a split pane. You have methods setLeftComponent(), setRightComponent(), setTopComponent() and setBottomComponent() to do this. You just pass a reference to a component to whichever method you want to use. There are also corresponding get methods to retrieve the components in a split pane. You can even change the orientation by calling the setOrientation() method and passing JSplitPane.HORIZONTAL_SPLIT or JSplitPane.VERTICAL_SPLIT to it.

There is a facility to provide a widget on the divider to collapse and restore either pane. We don't need it, but if you want to try this here, you can add a statement after the JSplitPane constructor call:

```
splitPane.setOneTouchExpandable(true);
```

Passing false to this method will remove the widget.

Once we have created the splitPane object we add it to the dataPane panel with constraints that make it fill the full width of the container.

Next we can add the font size selection mechanism.

Using a Combobox

We could use another list for this, but to broaden our horizons we will use another Swing component, a JComboBox object.

```
public FontDialog(SketchFrame window)
{
  // Initialization as before...

  // Button panel code as before...

  // Set up the data input panel to hold all input components as before...

  // Add the font choice prompt label as before...

  // Set up font list choice component as before...

  // Panel to display font sample as before...

  // Create a split pane with font choice at the top as before...
```

```
    // Set up the size choice using a combobox
    JPanel sizePane = new JPanel();                    // Pane for size choices
    label = new JLabel("Choose point size");           // Prompt for point size
    sizePane.add(label);                               // Add the prompt
    String[] sizeList = { "8", "10", "12", "14", "16",        // Array of sizes
                          "18", "20", "22", "24"};
    chooseSize = new JComboBox(sizeList);              // Size choice
combobox
    chooseSize.setSelectedItem(Integer.toString(fontSize));  // Default selection

    chooseSize.addActionListener(this);               // Add size listener
    sizePane.add(chooseSize);                         // Add combobox to
pane
    gbLayout.setConstraints(sizePane, constraints);   // Set pane
constraints
    dataPane.add(sizePane);                           // Add the pane

    // Plus the code for the rest of the constructor...
  }
```

We again create a panel to contain the combobox and its associated prompt as it makes the layout easier. The default `FlowLayout` in the panel is fine for what we want. We had better add a couple more members to the `FontDialog` class to store the references to the `chooseSize` and `fontDisplay` objects:

```
    private JComboBox chooseSize;                     // Font size options
    private JLabel fontDisplay;                       // Font sample
```

We create a `JComboBox` object by passing an array of `String` objects to the constructor that specifies a range of point sizes. You can put other types of objects in a combobox if you need to. A combobox provides a list from which you can select, or potentially allows you to enter, a value from the keyboard. We won't enable keyed-in values here but if you wanted it, you would call the `setEditable()` method with the argument `true`. By default, a combobox is not editable. The `setSelectedItem()` method determines which item is selected when the combobox is displayed initially. We set it to the size of the font that we obtained from the `window` object. You can also set an item at a given index position as the selected item by calling the `setSelectedIndex()` method.

A combobox generates `ActionEvent` events when an item is selected and the listener for our combobox is the `FontDialog` object so we need to extend the `actionPerformed()` method to deal with this:

```
    public void actionPerformed(ActionEvent e)
    {
      Object source = e.getSource();
      if(source == ok)
      {
       window.setCurrentFont(font);
        setVisible(false);
      }
```

```
      else if(source == cancel)
        setVisible(false);

      else if(source == chooseSize)
      {
        fontSize = Integer.parseInt((String)chooseSize.getSelectedItem());
        font = font.deriveFont((float)fontSize);
        fontDisplay.setFont(font);
        fontDisplay.repaint();
      }
    }
```

We just add an extra `else if` clause to handle the combobox. We get the item that was selected in the combobox by calling the `getSelectedItem()` method for the event object. The return type is `Object`, so we need to cast it to the type of our entries, `String`.

We store point sizes as integers and we get the integer value corresponding to the string by calling the static `parseInt()` method in the `Integer` class. To produce a `Font` object (like the current `Font` object in `font`) but with the new font size, we call the `deriveFont()` method. Note that we have to cast the value `fontSize` to `float` for this method because the argument is of this type, even though you normally expect font sizes to be integers. The version of `deriveFont()` with an integer parameter derives a font from the current font with a new style. Finally we set the font in the `fontDisplay` label object and repaint it as before.

The last piece we need in our font dialog will handle font styles.

Using Radio Buttons to Select the Font Style

We will create two `JRadioButton` objects for selecting the font style. One will select bold or not, and the other will select italic or not. A plain font is simply not bold or italic. You could use `JCheckBox` objects here if you prefer – they would work just as well. Here's the code:

```
public FontDialog(SketchFrame window)
{
  // Initialization as before...

  // Button panel code as before...

  // Set up the data input panel to hold all input components as before...

  // Add the font choice prompt label as before...

  // Set up font list choice component as before...

  // Panel to display font sample as before...

  // Create a split pane with font choice at the top as before...

  // Set up the size choice using a combobox as before...
```

```
      // Set up style options using radio buttons
      JRadioButton bold = new JRadioButton("Bold", (fontStyle & Font.BOLD) > 0);
      JRadioButton italic = new JRadioButton("Italic", (fontStyle & Font.ITALIC) > 0);
      bold.addItemListener(new StyleListener(Font.BOLD));        // Add button
   listeners
      italic.addItemListener(new StyleListener(Font.ITALIC));
      JPanel stylePane = new JPanel();                           // Create style pane
      stylePane.add(bold);                                       // Add buttons
      stylePane.add(italic);                                     // to style pane...
      gbLayout.setConstraints(stylePane, constraints);          // Set pane
   constraints
      dataPane.add(stylePane);                                   // Add the pane

      getContentPane().add(dataPane, BorderLayout.CENTER);
      pack();
      setVisible(false);
   }
```

It looks like a lot of code but it's repetitive as we have two radio buttons. The second argument to the JRadioButton constructor sets the state of the button. If the existing style of the current font is BOLD and/or ITALIC, the initial states of the buttons will be set accordingly. We add a listener of type StyleListener for each button and we will add this as an inner class to FontDialog in a moment. Note that we pass the style constant corresponding to the set state of the button to the constructor for the listener.

The stylePane object presents the buttons using the default FlowLayout manager, and this pane is added as the last row to dataPane. The final step is to add the dataPane object as the central pane in the content pane for the dialog. The call to pack() lays out the dialog components with their preferred sizes if possible, and the setVisible() call with the argument false means that the dialog is initially hidden. Since this is a complex dialog we won't want to create a new object each time we want to display the font dialog. We will just call the setVisible() method for the dialog object with the argument true.

Listening for Radio Buttons

The inner class, StyleListener, in the FontDialog class will work on principles that you have seen before. A radio button (or a check box) generates ItemEvent events and the listener class must implement the ItemListener interface:

```
   class StyleListener implements ItemListener
   {
     public StyleListener(int style)
     {
       this.style = style;
     }

     public void itemStateChanged(ItemEvent e)
     {
       if(e.getStateChange()==ItemEvent.SELECTED)    // If style was selected
         fontStyle |= style;                          // turn it on in the font style
       else
```

```
        fontStyle &= ~style;                          // otherwise turn it off

      font = font.deriveFont(fontStyle);              // Get a new font
      fontDisplay.setFont(font);                      // Change the label font
      fontDisplay.repaint();                          // repaint
    }

    private int style;                                // Style for this listener
  }
```

The constructor accepts an argument that is the style for the button, so the value of the member, `style`, will be the value we want to set in the `fontStyle` member that we use to create a new `Font` object, – either `Font.BOLD` or `Font.ITALIC`. Since the listener for a particular button already contains the corresponding style, the `itemStateChanged()` method that is called when an item event occurs just switches the value of `style` in the `fontStyle` member of `FontDialog` either on or off, dependent on whether the radio button was selected or deselected. It then derives a font with the new style, sets it in the `fontDisplay` label and repaints it.

We have completed the `FontDialog` class. If you have been creating the code yourself, now would be a good time to try compiling the class. All we need now is some code in the `SketchFrame` class to make use of it.

Try It Out – Using the Font Dialog

To get the font dialog operational in Sketcher, we need to add a new menu, **Options**, to the menubar with a **Choose font...** menu item, and we need to install a listener for it. To keeps things ship-shape it would be best to add the fragments of code in the `SketchFrame` constructor in the places where we do similar things.

Create the **Options** menu with the following constructor code:

```
      JMenu fileMenu = new JMenu("File");             // Create File menu
      JMenu elementMenu = new JMenu("Elements");      // Create Elements
menu
      JMenu optionsMenu = new JMenu("Options");       // Create options menu
      JMenu helpMenu = new JMenu("Help");             // Create Help menu

      fileMenu.setMnemonic('F');                       // Create shortcut
      elementMenu.setMnemonic('E');                    // Create shortcut
      optionsMenu.setMnemonic('O');                    // Create shortcut
      helpMenu.setMnemonic('H');                       // Create shortcut
```

You can add the menu item like this:

```
      // Add the font choice item to the options menu
      fontItem = new JMenuItem("Choose font...");
      fontItem.addActionListener(this);
      optionsMenu.add(fontItem);
```

We can add a declaration for the `fontItem` member of the class by adding it to the existing declaration for the `aboutItem`:

```
private JMenuItem aboutItem, fontItem;
```

You need to add the <u>O</u>ptions menu to the menubar before the <u>H</u>elp menu to be consistent with convention:

```
menuBar.add(fileMenu);                     // Add the file menu
menuBar.add(elementMenu);                  // Add the element menu
menuBar.add(optionsMenu);                  // Add the options menu
menuBar.add(helpMenu);                     // Add the file menu
```

You can create a `FontDialog` object by adding a statement to the end of the `SketchFrame` constructor:

```
fontDlg = new FontDialog(this);
```

Of course, we will need to declare `fontDlg` as a member of the `SketchFrame` class:

```
private FontDialog fontDlg;                         // The font dialog
```

To support the new menu item, you need to modify the `actionPerformed()` method in the `SketchFrame` class to handle its events:

```
public void actionPerformed(ActionEvent e)
{
  if(e.getSource() == aboutItem)
  {

    // Create about dialog with the menu item as parent
    JOptionPane.showMessageDialog(this,                     // Parent
                    "Sketcher Copyright Ivor Horton 2000", // Message
                    "About Sketcher",                      // Title
                    JOptionPane.INFORMATION_MESSAGE);      // Message
type
  }

    else if(e.getSource() == fontItem)
    { // Set the dialog window position
      Rectangle bounds = getBounds();
      fontDlg.setLocation(bounds.x + bounds.width/3, bounds.y + bounds.height/3);

      fontDlg.setVisible(true);               // Show the dialog
    }
  }
```

All the new `else if` block does is make the dialog visible after setting its location in relation to the application window. If you recompile Sketcher you will be able to play with fonts to your hearts content.

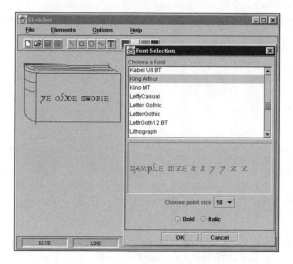

How It Works

This last piece is relatively trivial. The additional menu is added to the menubar just like the other menus. The menu item is a `JMenuItem` object rather than an `Action` object and the `actionPerformed()` method is called when the **Choose font...** menu item is clicked. This sets the top-left corner of the dialog window one third of the way in from the top and left sides of the application window. It then calls `setVisible()` for the dialog object to display it. Note that in the screenshot above, I moved the dialog to make the screenshot more compact.

Pop-up Menus

The `javax.swing` package defines a class, `JPopupMenu`, that represents a menu that you can pop up at any position within a component, but conventionally, you display it at the current mouse cursor position when a particular mouse button is pressed. There are two constructors in the `PopupMenu` class: one to which you pass a `String` object that defines a name for the menu, and a default constructor that defines a menu without a name. If you specify a name for a pop-up menu with a statement such as,

```
generalPopup = new PopupMenu("General");
```

the name is primarily for identification purposes and is not always displayed when the menu is popped up: it depends on your environment. Under Windows for instance it doesn't appear. This is different from a menu on a menu bar where the string you pass to the constructor is what appears on the menu bar.

Let's add a pop-up menu to the `SketchFrame` class by adding a data member of type `JPopupMenu`:

```
private JPopupMenu popup = new JPopupMenu("General");        // Window pop-up
```

To populate a pop-up menu with menu items, you add `JMenuItem` objects or `Action` objects by passing each of them to the `add()` method for the `JPopupMenu` object. You can also pass a `String` object to `add()`, which will create a `JMenuItem` object and add it to the pop-up. A reference to the menu item object is always returned by the various overloaded `add()` methods. Handling the events for the menu items is an identical process to that for regular menu items, and `Action` objects handle their own events as we have seen.

We could add menu items to the pop-up we created above by adding the following code to the class constructor:

```
// Create pop-up menu
popup.add(lineAction);
popup.add(rectangleAction);
popup.add(circleAction);
popup.add(curveAction);
popup.add(textAction);

popup.addSeparator();
popup.add(redAction);
popup.add(yellowAction);
popup.add(greenAction);
popup.add(blueAction);
```

This adds the element menu items to the pop-up. We could also add the font choice menu item but you can't add a `JMenuItem` object to two different menus. You could either create an `Action` object that would pop up the font dialog, or you could add a different menu item to the pop-up that did the same thing when it was clicked.

Displaying a Pop-up Menu

You can display a pop-up within the coordinate system of any component, by calling the `show()` method for the `JPopupMenu` object. The method requires three arguments to be specified, a reference to the component that is the context for the pop-up, and the *x* and *y* coordinates where the menu is to be displayed, relative to the origin of the parent. For example:

```
generalPopup.show(view, xCoord, yCoord);
```

This displays the pop-up at position (xCoord, yCoord) in the coordinate system for the component, `view`.

A pop-up menu is usually implemented as a **context menu**. The principle idea of a context menu is that it's not just a single menu: it displays a different set of menu items depending on the context – that is, what is under the mouse cursor when the button is pressed. The mouse button that you press to display a context menu is sometimes called a **pop-up trigger**, simply because pressing it triggers the display of the pop-up. On systems that support the notion of a pop-up trigger, the pop-up trigger is fixed, but it can be different between systems. It is usually the right mouse button on a two- or three-button mouse, and on systems with a one-button mouse, you typically have to hold down a modifier key while pressing the mouse button.

The `MouseEvent` class has a special method, `isPopupTrigger()`, that returns `true` when the event should display a pop-up menu. This method will only return `true` in the `mousePressed()` or `mouseReleased()` methods. It will always return `false` in methods corresponding to other mouse events. This method helps to get over the problem of different mouse buttons being used on different systems to display a popup. If you use this method to decide when to display a popup, you've got them covered – well, almost. You would typically use this with the following code to display a pop-up.

```
public void mouseReleased(MouseEvent e)
{
  if(e.isPopupTrigger())
    // Code to display the pop-up menu...
}
```

We have shown conceptual code for the mouseReleased() method here. This would be fine for Windows but unfortunately may not work on some other systems – Solaris for instance. This is because in some operating system environments the isPopupTrigger() only returns true when the button is pressed, not when it is released. The popup trigger is not just a particular button – it is a mouse pressed or mouse released event with a particular button. This implies that if you want your code to work on a variety of systems using the 'standard' mouse button to trigger the pop-up in every case, you must implement the code to call isPopupTrigger() and pop the menu in both the mousePressed() and mouseReleased() methods. The method will only return true in one or the other. Of course, you could always circumvent this by ignoring convention and pop the menu for a specific button press with code like this:

```
if((e.getModifiers() & e.BUTTON3_MASK) != 0)
  // Code to display the pop-up menu...
```

Now the pop-up operates with button 3, regardless of the convention for the underlying operating system, but the user may not be particularly happy about having to use a different popup trigger for your Java program compared to other applications on the same system.

We will try a pop-up menu in Sketcher assuming Windows is the applicable environment. You should be able to change it to suit your environment if it is different, or even add the same code for both MOUSE_PRESSED and MOUSE_RELEASED events if you wish.

Try It Out – Displaying a Pop-up Menu

In Sketcher, the pop-up menu would sensibly operate in the area where the sketch is displayed – in other words triggering the pop-up menu has to happen in the view. Assuming you have already added the code that we discussed in the previous section to SketchFrame, we just need to add a method to SketchFrame to make the pop-up available to the view:

```
// Retrieve the pop-up menu
public JPopupMenu getPopup()
{  return popup;  }
```

Now a SketchView object can get a reference to the pop-up in the SketchFrame object by using the application object to get to this method.

We will implement the pop-up triggering in the mouseReleased() method consistent with Windows, but remember, all you need to do to make your code general is to put it in the mousePressed() method too. Here's how mouseReleased() should be in the MouseHandler inner class to SketchView:

```
        public void mouseReleased(MouseEvent e)
        {
          int modifier = e.getModifiers();                    // Get modifiers

          if(e.isPopupTrigger())
          {
            start = e.getPoint();
            theApp.getWindow().getPopup().show((Component)e.getSource(),
                                                     start.x, start.y);

            start = null;
          }

          else if((modifier & e.BUTTON1_MASK) != 0 &&
            (theApp.getWindow().getElementType() != TEXT))
          {
            if(tempElement != null)
            {
              theApp.getModel().add(tempElement);            // Add element to the
    model
              tempElement = null;                            // No temporary stored
            }
            if(g2D != null)
            {
              g2D.dispose();                                 // Release graphic context resource
              g2D = null;                                    // Set it to null
            }
            start = last = null;                             // Remove the points
          }
        }
```

We get hold of a reference to the pop-up menu object by calling getPopup() for the object reference returned by the application object's getWindow() method. The component where the pop-up is to appear is identified in the first argument to the show() method for the pop-up by calling getSource() for the MouseEvent object, e. This will return a reference to the view, as type Object, so we need to cast this to the Component type since that is what the show() method for the pop-up expects. The position, which we store temporarily in start, is just the current cursor position when the mouse button is released. We could use the position stored in start by the mousePressed() method, but if the user drags the cursor before releasing the button, the menu will appear at a different position from where the button is released.

If you recompile Sketcher and run it again, you should get the pop-up menu appearing in response to a right button click, or whatever button triggers a context menu on your system.

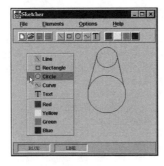

Note how we get the Icons and the label for each of the menu items. This is because we have defined both in the Action objects that we used to generate the menu.

How It Works

The isPopupTrigger() method for the MouseEvent object returns true when the button corresponding to a context menu is pressed or released. In this case we call the show() method for the pop-up menu object that we created in the SketchFrame object. When you click on a menu item in the pop-up, or click elsewhere, the pop-up menu is automatically hidden. Now any element type or color is a couple of clicks away.

This is just a pop-up menu, not a context menu. A context menu should be different depending on what's under the cursor. We will now look more closely at how we could implement a proper context menu capability in Sketcher.

Implementing a Context Menu

As a context menu displays a different menu depending on the context, it follows that the program needs to know what is under the cursor at the time the right mouse button is pressed. Let's take the specific instance of the view in Sketcher where we are listening for mouse events. We could define two contexts for the cursor in the view – one when an already-drawn element is under the cursor, and another when there is no element under the cursor. In the first context, we could display a special pop-up menu that is particularly applicable to an element – with menu items to delete the element, or move it, for example. In the second context we could display the pop-up menu that we created in the previous example. Our context menu when a drawn element is under the cursor is going to look like that shown below.

For the context menu to be really useful, the user will need to know which element is under the cursor before they pop-up the context menu, otherwise they can't be sure to which element the pop-up menu operations will apply. Deleting the wrong element could be irritating.

What we need is some visual feedback to show when an element is under the cursor – highlighting the element under the cursor by changing its color, for instance.

Try It Out – Highlighting an Element

To highlight an element, we will draw it in magenta rather than its normal color. Every element will need a `boolean` variable to indicate whether it is highlighted or not. This variable will be used to determine which color should be used in the `draw()` method. We can add this variable as a data member of the `Element` class:

```
protected boolean highlighted = false;          // Highlight flag
```

You can add this line immediately following the statement for the other data members in the `Element` class definition. The variable `highlighted` will be inherited by all of the sub-classes of `Element`.

We can also add the method to set the `highlighted` flag to the `Element` class:

```
// Set or reset highlight color
public void setHighlighted(boolean highlighted)
{
   this.highlighted = highlighted;
}
```

This method will also be inherited by all of the sub-classes of `Element`, so all of our shapes can be highlighted by calling this method.

To implement the basis for getting highlighting to work, you need to change one line in the `draw()` method for each of the sub-classes of `Element` – that is, `Element.Line`, `Element.Circle`, `Element.Curve`, `Element.Rectangle` and `Element.Text`. The line to change is the one that sets the drawing color – it's the first line in each of the `draw()` methods. You should change it to:

```
g2D.setPaint(highlighted ? Color.magenta : color);
```

Now each element can potentially be highlighted.

How It Works

The `setHighlighted()` method accepts a `boolean` value as an argument and stores it in the data member, `highlighted`. When you want an element to be highlighted, you just call this method with the argument as `true`. To switch highlighting off for an element, you call this method with the argument `false`.

Previously, the `setPaint()` statement just set the color stored in the data member, `color`, as the drawing color. Now, if `highlighted` is `true`, the color will be set to magenta, and if `highlighted` is `false`, the color stored in the data member, `color`, will be used.

To make use of highlighting to provide the visual feedback necessary for a user-friendly implementation of the context menu, we need to determine at all times what is under the cursor. This means we must track and analyze all mouse moves *all the time*!

Tracking Mouse Moves

Whenever the mouse is moved, the `mouseMoved()` method in the `MouseMotionListener` interface is called. We can therefore track mouse moves by implementing this method in the `MouseHandler` class that is an inner class to the `SketchView` class. Before we get into that, we need to decide what we mean by an element being under the cursor, and more crucially, how we are going to find out to which element, if any, this applies.

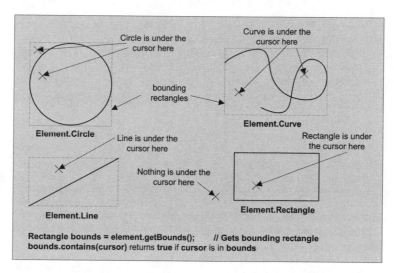

It's not going to be too difficult. We can arbitrarily decide that an element is under the cursor when the cursor position is inside the bounding rectangle for an element. This is not too precise a method, but it has the great attraction that it is extremely simple. Precise hit-testing on an element would carry considerably more processing overhead. Electing to add any greater complexity will not help us to understand the principles here, so we will stick with the simple approach.

So what is going to be the methodology for finding the element under the cursor? Brute force basically: whenever the mouse is moved, we can just search through the bounding rectangles for each of the elements in the document until we find one that encloses the current cursor position. We will then arrange for the first element that we find to be highlighted. If we get right through all the elements in the document without finding a bounding rectangle that encloses the cursor, then there isn't an element under the cursor.

To record a reference to the element that is under the cursor, we will add a data member of type `Element` to the `SketchView` class. If there isn't an element under the cursor, we will make sure that this data member is `null`.

Try It Out – Referring to Elements

Add the following statement after the statement declaring the `theApp` data member in the `SketchView` class definition:

```
    private Element highlightElement;              // Highlighted element
```

The `mouseMoved()` method is going to be called very frequently, so we need to make sure it executes as quickly as possible. This means that for any given set of conditions, we execute the minimum amount of code. Here's the implementation of the `mouseMoved()` method in the `MouseHandler` class in `SketchView`:

```
// Handle mouse moves
public void mouseMoved(MouseEvent e)
{
  Point currentCursor = e.getPoint();  // Get current cursor position
  Iterator elements = theApp.getModel().getIterator();
  Element element;                                      // Stores an element

  while(elements.hasNext())                             // Go through the list
  {
    element = (Element)elements.next();                 // Get the next element
    if(element.getBounds().contains(currentCursor))     // Under the cursor?
    {
      if(element==highlightElement)                     // If its already highlighted
        return;                                         // we are done
      g2D = (Graphics2D)getGraphics();                  // Get graphics context
      if(highlightElement!=null)                        // If an element is highlighted
      {
        highlightElement.setHighlighted(false);// un-highlight it and
        highlightElement.draw(g2D);                     // draw it normal color
      }
      element.setHighlighted(true);                     // Set highlight for new element
      highlightElement = element;                       // Store new highlighted element
      element.draw(g2D);                                // Draw it highlighted
      g2D.dispose();                          // Release graphic context resources
      g2D = null;

      return;
    }
  }

  // Here there is no element under the cursor so...
  if(highlightElement!=null)                            // If an element is highlighted
  {
    g2D = (Graphics2D)getGraphics();                    // Get graphics context
    highlightElement.setHighlighted(false); // ...turn off highlighting
    highlightElement.draw(g2D);                         // Redraw the element
    highlightElement = null;                            // No element highlighted
    g2D.dispose();                          // Release graphic context resources
    g2D = null;
  }
}
```

To check that highlighting works, recompile Sketcher and run it again. If you draw a few elements, you should see them change color as the cursor moves over them.

How It Works

This method is a fair amount of code, so let's work through it step by step. The first statement saves the current cursor position in the local variable, `currentCursor`. The next two statements obtain a `Graphics2D` object and declare a variable, `element`, that we will use to store each element that we retrieve from the model. The variable, `g2D` will be passed to the `draw()` method for any element that we need to redraw highlighted or un-highlighted as the case may be.

We use an iterator we get from the model to go through the elements – you have seen how this works previously. In the loop, we obtain the bounding rectangle for each element by calling its `getBounds()` method, and then call the `contains()` method for the rectangle that is returned. This will return `true` if the rectangle encloses the point, `currentCursor`, that is passed as an argument. When we find an element under the cursor, it is quite possible that the element is already highlighted because the element was found last time the `mouseMoved()` method was called. This will occur when you move the cursor within the rectangle bounding an element. In this case we don't need to do anything, so we return from the method.

If the element found is not the same as last time, we obtain a graphics context for the view since we definitely need it to draw the new element we have found under the cursor in the highlight color. We then check that the variable `highlightElement` is not `null` – it will be `null` if the cursor just entered the rectangle for an element and previously none was highlighted. If `highlightElement` is not `null` we must un-highlight the old element before we highlight the new one. To do this we call its `setHighlighted()` method with the argument `false`, and call its `draw()` method. We don't need to involve the `paint()` method for the view here since we are not adding or removing elements – we are simply redrawing an element that is already displayed. To highlight the new element, we call its `setHighlighted()` method with the argument `true`, store a reference to the element in `highlightElement` and call its `draw()` method to get it drawn in the highlight color. We then release the graphics context resources by calling the `dispose()` method for `g2D`, set the variable back to `null` and return.

The next block of code in the method is executed if we exit the `while` loop because no element is under the cursor. In this case we must check if there was an element highlighted last time around. If there was, we un-highlight it, redraw it in its normal color and reset `highlightElement` to `null`.

Defining the Other Context Menu

The context menu when the cursor is over an element should be implemented in the view. We already have the menu defined in `SketchFrame` for when the cursor is not over an element. All we need is the context menu for when it is – plus the code to decide which to display when `isPopupTrigger()` returns `true` for a mouse event.

You already know that we will have four menu items in the element context menu:

❑   **Move** – to move the element under the cursor to a new position. This will work by dragging it with the left mouse button down (button 1).

❑   **Delete** – this will delete the element under the cursor.

❑   Rotate – this will allow you to rotate the element under the cursor about the top-left corner of its bounding rectangle by dragging it with the left mouse button down.

❑   Send-to-back – this is to overcome the problem of an element not being accessible, never highlighted that is, because it is masked by the bounding rectangle of another element.

Since we highlight an element by searching the list from the beginning, an element towards the end may never be highlighted if the rectangle for an earlier element completely encloses it. Moving the earlier element that is hogging the highlighting to the end of the list will allow the formerly masked element to be highlighted.

Try It Out – Creating Context Menus

We will add the necessary data members to the SketchView class to store the element pop-up reference, and the JMenuItem objects that will be the pop-up menu items:

```
private JPopupMenu elementPopup = new JPopupMenu("Element");
private JMenuItem moveItem, deleteItem,rotateItem, sendToBackItem;
```

We will create the elementPopup context menu in the SketchView constructor:

```
public SketchView(Sketcher theApp)
  {
    this.theApp = theApp;
    MouseHandler handler = new MouseHandler();      // create the mouse listener
    addMouseListener(handler);                       // Listen for button events
    addMouseMotionListener(handler);                 // Listen for motion events

    // Add the pop-up menu items
    moveItem = elementPopup.add("Move");
    deleteItem = elementPopup.add("Delete");
    rotateItem = elementPopup.add("Rotate");

    sendToBackItem = elementPopup.add("Send-to-back");

    // Add the menu item listeners
    moveItem.addActionListener(this);
    deleteItem.addActionListener(this);
    rotateItem.addActionListener(this);
    sendToBackItem.addActionListener(this);
  }
```

We add the menu items using the add() method that accepts a String argument, and returns a reference to the JMenuItem object that it creates. We then use these references to add the view object as the listener for all the menu items in the pop-up.

We must make sure the SketchView class declares that it implements the ActionListener interface:

```
class SketchView extends   JComponent
                 implements Observer,
                            Constants,
                            ActionListener
```

We can add the `actionPerformed()` method to `SketchView` that will handle action events from the menu items.

> As with the new data members above, be careful to add this to the `SketchView` class and not inside the inner `MouseHandler` class by mistake!

```
public void actionPerformed(ActionEvent e )
{
  Object source - e.getSource();
  if(source == moveItem)
  {
    // Process a move...
  }
  else if(source == deleteItem)
  {
    // Process a delete...
  }
  else if(source == rotateItem)
  {
    // Process a rotate
  }
  else if(source == sendToBackItem)
  {
    // Process a send-to-back...
  }
}
```

To pop the menu we need to modify the code in the `mouseReleased()` method a little:

```
public void mouseReleased(MouseEvent e)
{
  int modifier = e.getModifiers();                    // Get modifiers

  if(e.isPopupTrigger())
  {
    start = e.getPoint();

    if(highlightElement == null)
      theApp.getWindow().getPopup().show((Component)e.getSource(),
                                         start.x, start.y);
    else
      elementPopup.show((Component)e.getSource(), start.x, start.y);

    start = null;
  }
```

```
      // Plus the rest of the code as before...
    }
```

This just adds an if-else to display the element dialog when there is an element highlighted. If you recompile Sketcher you should get a different context menu depending on whether an element is under the cursor or not.

How It Works

The mouseReleased() method in the MouseHandler inner class now pops one or other of the two pop-ups we have, depending on whether the reference in highlightElement is null or not. You can select items from the general pop-up to set the color or the element type, but the element pop-up menu does nothing at present. It just needs a few lines of code somewhere to do moves and rotations and stuff. Don't worry – it'll be like falling off a log – but not so painful.

Deleting Elements

Let's take the easiest one first – deleting an element. All that's involved here is calling remove() for the model object from the actionPerformed() method in SketchView. Let's give it a try.

Try It Out – Deleting Elements

The code we need to add to actionPerformed() in the SketchView class looks like this:

```
public void actionPerformed(ActionEvent e)
{
  Object source = e.getSource();
  if(source == moveItem)
  {
    // Process a move...
  }
  else if(source == deleteItem)
  {
    if(highlightElement != null)                    // If there's an element
    {
      theApp.getModel().remove(highlightElement);   // then remove it
      highlightElement = null;                       // Remove the reference
    }
  }
  else if(source == rotateItem)
  {
    // Process a rotate
  }
  else if(source == sendToBackItem)

  {
    // Process a send-to-back...
  }
}
```

This is a cheap operation requiring only six lines. Recompile, create a few elements and then watch them disappear with a right button click.

How It Works

After verifying that `highlightElement` is not `null`, we call the `remove()` method that we added in the `SketchModel` class way back. This will delete the element from the list, so when the view is repainted it will no longer be displayed. The repaint occurs automatically because the `update()` method for the view – the method we implemented for the `Observer` interface - will be called because the model has changed. Of course, we must remember to set `highlightElement` to `null` too, otherwise it could get drawn by a mouse handler even though it is no longer in the model.

Let's do another easy one – Send-to-Back.

Implementing the Send-to-Back Operation

The send-to-back operation is really an extension of the delete operation. We can move an element from wherever it is in the list by deleting it, then adding it again at the end of the list.

Try It Out – The Send-to-Back Operation

The `actionPerformed()` method in the `SketchView` class has the job of removing the highlighted element from wherever it is in the model, and then adding it back at the end:

```
public void actionPerformed(ActionEvent e)
{
  Object source = e.getSource();
  if(source == moveItem)
  {
    // (Process a move...)
  }
  else if(source == deleteItem)
  {
    // Code as inserted here earlier
  }
  else if(source == rotateItem)
  {
    // (Process a rotate)
  }
  else if(source == sendToBackItem)
  {
    if(highlightElement != null)
    {
      theApp.getModel().remove(highlightElement);
      theApp.getModel().add(highlightElement);
      highlightElement.setHighlighted(false);
      highlightElement = null;
      repaint();
    }
  }
}
```

A little harder this time – eight lines of code. You can try this by drawing a few concentric circles, with the outermost drawn first. An outer circle will prevent an inner circle from being highlighted, but applying Send-to-back to the outer circle will make the inner circle accessible.

How It Works

This uses the `remove()` method in `SketchModel` to remove the highlighted element, and then calls the `add()` method to put it back – it will automatically be added to the end of the elements in the list. We switch off the highlighting of the element to indicate that it's gone to the back of the queue, and reset `highlightElement` back to `null`.

We have run out of easy ones. We must now deal with a not quite so easy one – the move operation. To handle this we must look into a new topic – transforming the user coordinate system. If you are not of a mathematical bent, some of what we will discuss here can sound complicated. Even if your math may be very rusty, you should not have too many problems. Like a lot of things it's the unfamiliarity of the jargon that makes it seem more difficult than it is.

Transforming the User Coordinate System

We said when we started learning how to draw on a component that the drawing operations are specified in a user-coordinate system, and the user coordinates are converted to a device coordinate system. The conversion of coordinates from user system to device system is taken care of by the methods in the graphics context object that we use to do the drawing, and they do this by applying a **transformation** to the user coordinates. The term 'transformation' refers to the computational operations that result in the conversion.

By default, the origin, the (0, 0) point, in the user coordinate system corresponds to the (0, 0) point in the device coordinates system. The axes are also coincident too, with positive *x* heading from left to right, and positive *y* from top to bottom. However you can move the origin of the user coordinate system relative to its default position. Such a move is called a **translation**.

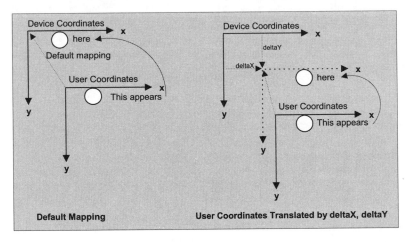

A fixed value, `deltaX` say, is added to each *x* coordinate, and another value, `deltaY` say, is added to every y coordinate and the effect of this is to move the origin of the user coordinate system relative to the device coordinate system: everything will be shifted to the right and down compared to where it would have been without the translation. Of course, the `deltaX` and `deltaY` values can be negative, in which case it would shift things to the left and up.

A translation is one kind of **affine transformation**. Affine is a funny word. Some say it goes back to Laurel and Hardy where Ollie says, "This is affine mess you've got us into", but I don't subscribe to that. An affine transformation is actually a linear transformation that leaves straight lines still straight and parallel lines still parallel. As well as translations, there are other kinds of affine transformation that you can define:

❑ **Rotation** – the user coordinates system is rotated through a given angle about its origin.

❑ **Scale** – the x and y coordinates are each multiplied by a scaling factor, and the multipliers for x and y can be different. This enables you to enlarge or reduce something in size. If the scale factor for one coordinate axis is negative, then objects will be reflected in the other axis. Setting the scale factor for x coordinates to –1, for example, will make all positive coordinates negative and vice versa so everything is reflected in the y axis.

❑ **Shear** – this is perhaps a less familiar operation. It adds a value to each x coordinate that depends on the y coordinate, and adds a value to each y coordinate that depends on the x coordinate. You supply two values to specify a shear, sX and sY say, and they change the coordinates in the following way:

Each x coordinate becomes $(x + $ sX $ * $ $y)$
Each y coordinate becomes$(y + $ sY $ * $ $x)$

The effect of this can be visualized most easily if you first imagine a rectangle that is drawn normally. A shearing transform can squash it by tilting the sides – rather like when you flatten a carton – but keep opposite sides straight and parallel.

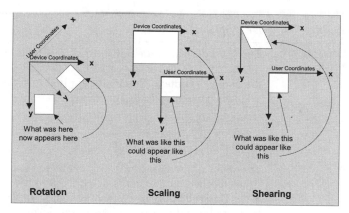

The illustration shows:

❑ A rotation of -π/4 radians, which is –45 degrees. Rotation angles are expressed in radians and a positive angle rotates everything from the positive x axis towards the positive y axis – therefore clockwise. The rotation in the illustration is negative and therefore counterclockwise.

❑ A scaling transformation corresponding to an x scale of 2.5 and a y scale of 1.5.

❑ A shearing operation where only the x coordinates have a shear factor. The factor for the y coordinates is 0 so they are unaffected and the transformed shape is the same height as the original.

765

The AffineTransform Class

In Java, the `AffineTransform` class represents an affine transformation. Every `Graphics2D` graphics context has one. The default `AffineTransform` object in a graphics context is the identity transform which leaves user coordinates unchanged. It is applied to the user coordinate system anyway for everything you draw, but all the coordinates are unaltered by default. You can retrieve a copy of the current transform for a graphics context object by calling its `getTransform()` method. For example:

```
AffineTransform at = g2D.getTransform();      // Get current transform
```

While this retrieves a copy of the current transform for a graphics context, you can also set it with another transform object:

```
g2D.setTransform(at);
```

You can retrieve the transform currently in effect with `getTransform()`, set it to some other operation, and then restore the original transform later with `setTransform()` when you're finished. The fact that `getTransform()` returns a reference to a copy rather than a reference to the original transform object is important. It means you can alter the existing transform and then restore the copy later.

Although the default transform object for a graphics context leaves everything unchanged, you could set it to do something by calling one of its member functions. All of these have a return type of `void` so none of them return anything:

Transform Default	Description

`setToTranslation`
`(double deltaX,`
`  double deltaY)`
	This method makes the transform a translation of `deltaX` in *x* and `deltaY` in *y*. This replaces whatever the previous transform was for the graphics context. You could apply this to the transform for a graphics context with the statements:
	
	```// Save current transform and set a new one\nAffineTransform at = g2D.getTransform();\nat.setToTranslation(5.0, 10.0);```
	
	The effect of the new transform will be to shift everything that is drawn in the graphics context, `g2D`, 5.0 to the right, and down by 10.0. This will apply to everything that is drawn in `g2D` subsequent to the statement that sets the new transform.

`setToRotation` `(double angle)`	You call this method for a transform object to make it a rotation of `angle` radians about the origin. This replaces the previous transform. To rotate the axes 30 degrees clockwise, you could write: `g2D.getTransform().setToRotation(30*Math.PI/180);` This statement gets the current transform object for `g2D` and sets it to be the rotation specified by the expression `30*Math.PI/180`. Since π radians is 180 degrees, this expression produces the equivalent to 30 degrees in radians.

Transform Default	Description

setToRotation
(double angle,
  double deltaX,
  double deltaY)
	This method defines a rotation of angle radians about the point deltaX,deltaY. It is equivalent to three successive transform operations – a translation by deltaX, deltaY, then a rotation through angle radians about the new position of the origin and then a translation back by -deltaX,-deltaY to restore the previous origin point.
	
	You could use this to draw a shape rotated about the shape's reference point. For example, if the reference point for a shape was at shapeX,shapeY, you could draw the shape rotated through $\pi/3$ radians with the following:
	
	``
	g2D.getTransform().setToRotation(Math.PI/3,
	                                 shapeX, shapeY);
	// Draw the shape...
	``
	
	The coordinate system has been rotated about the point shapeX,shapeY and will remain so until you change the transformation in effect. You would probably want to restore the original transform after drawing the shape rotated.

setToScale
(double scaleX,
  double scaleY)
	This method sets the transform object to scale the *x* coordinates by scaleX, and the y coordinates by scaleY. To draw everything half scale you could set the transformation with the statement:
	
	``
	g2D.getTransform().setToScale(0.5, 0.5);
	``

setToShear (double shearX, double shearY)	The *x* coordinates are converted to x+shearX*y, and the *y* coordinates are converted to y+shearY*x.

All of these methods that we have discussed here replace the transform in an AffineTransform object. We can modify the existing transform object in a graphics context, too.

Modifying the Transformation for a Graphics Context

Modifying the current transform for a Graphics2D object involves calling a method for the Graphics2D object. The effect in each case is to *add* whatever transform you are applying to whatever the transform did before. You can add each of the four kinds of transforms that we discussed above using the following methods defined in the Graphics2D class:

```
translate(double deltaX, double deltaY)
translate(int deltaX, int deltaY)
rotate(double angle)
rotate(double angle, double deltaX, double deltaY)
scale(double scaleX, double scaleY)
shear(double shearX, double shearY)
```

Each of these adds or **concatenates** the transform specified to the existing transform object for a `Graphics2D` object. Therefore you can cause a translation of the coordinate system followed by a rotation about the new origin position with the statements:

```
g2D.translate(5, 10);          // Translate the origin
g2D.rotate(Math.PI/3);         // Clockwise rotation 60 degrees.
g2D.draw(line);                // Draw in translate and rotated
space
```

Of course, you can apply more than two transforms to the user coordinate system – as many as you like. However, it is important to note that the order in which you apply the transforms matters. To see why, look at the example below.

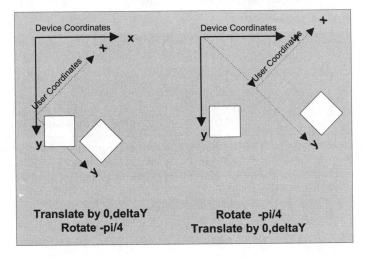

This shows just two transforms in effect, but it should be clear that the sequence they are applied makes a big difference. This is because the second transform is always applied relative to the new position of the coordinate system after the first transform has been applied.

Next on our affine tour – how we can create completely new `AffineTransform` objects.

Creating AffineTransform Objects

Of course, there are constructors for `AffineTransform` objects: the default 'identity' constructor and a number of other constructors but we don't have space here to go into them here. The easiest way to create transform objects is to call a `static` member of the `AffineTransform` class. There are four static methods corresponding to the four kinds of transform that we discussed earlier:

```
getTranslateInstance(double deltaX, double deltaY)
getRotateInstance(double angle)
getScaleInstance(double scaleX, double scaleY)
getShearInstance(double shearX, double shearY)
```

Each of these returns an `AffineTransform` object containing the transform that you specify by the arguments. To create a transform to rotate the user space by 90 degrees, you could write:

```
AffineTransform at = AffineTransform.getRotateInstance(Math.PI/2);
```

Once you have an `AffineTransform` object, you can apply it to a graphics context by passing it as an argument to the `setTransform()` method. It has another use too: you can use it to transform a `Shape` object. The `createTransformedShape()` method for the `AffineTransform` object does this. Suppose we define a `Rectangle` object with the statement:

```
Rectangle rect = new Rectangle(10, 10, 100, 50);
```

We now have a rectangle that is 100 wide by 50 high, at position 10,10. We can create a transform object with the statement:

```
AffineTransform at = getTranslateInstance(25, 30);
```

This is a translation in *x* of 25, and a translation in *y* of 30. We can create a new `Shape` from our rectangle with the statement:

```
Shape transRect = at.createTransformedShape(rect);
```

Our new `transRect` object will look the same as the original rectangle but translated by 25 in *x* and 30 in *y*, so its top-left corner will now be at (35, 40).

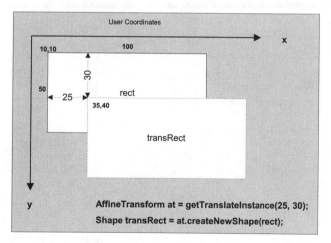

However, even though it will still look like a rectangle it will not be a `Rectangle` object. The `createTransformedShape()` method always returns a `GeneralPath` object since it has to work with any transform. This is because some transformations will deform a shape – applying a shear to a rectangle results in a shape that is no longer a rectangle. The method also has to apply any transform to any `Shape` object, and returning a `GeneralPath` shape makes this possible.

Let's try some of this out. A good place to do this is with our shape classes. At the moment we draw each shape or text element in the place where the cursor happens to be. Let's use a translation to change how this works. We will redefine each nested class to `Element` so that it translates the user coordinate system to where the shape should be, and then draws itself at the origin (0, 0). You could try to do this yourself before reading on. You just need to apply some of the transform methods we have been discussing.

Try It Out – Translation

To make this work we will need to save the position for each element that is passed to the constructor – this is the start point recorded in the `mousePressed()` method – and use this to create a translate transform in the `draw()` method for the element. Since we are going to store the position of every class object that has `Element` as a base, we might as well store the location in a data member of the base class. We can redefine the base class, `Element`, to do this:

```
public abstract class Element
{
  public Element(Color color)
  {  this.color = color;   }

  public Color getColor()
  {  return color;   }

  // Set or reset highlight color
  public void setHighlighted(boolean highlighted)
  {
     this.highlighted = highlighted;
  }

  public Point getPosition()
  {  return position;   }

  public abstract java.awt.Rectangle getBounds();
  public abstract void modify(Point start, Point last);
  public abstract void draw(Graphics2D g2D);

  protected Color color;                          // Color of a shape
  protected boolean highlighted = false;          // Highlight flag
  final static Point origin = new Point();         // Point 0,0
  protected Point position;                        // Element position

  // Definitions for our shape classes...
}
```

You might consider passing the start point to the `Element` constructor, but this wouldn't always work. This is because we need to figure out what the reference point is in some cases – for rectangles, for example. The position of a rectangle will be the top left corner, which is not necessarily the start point. We have included a method to retrieve the position of an element, as we are sure to need it. We also have added another member, `origin`, which is the point (0, 0). This will be useful in all the derived classes, as we will now draw every element at that point. Since we only need one, it is `static`, and since we won't want to change it, it is `final`.

Let's start with the nested class, `Line`.

Translating Lines

We need to update the constructor first of all:

```
public Line(Point start, Point end, Color color)
{
   super(color);
   position = start;
   line = new Line2D.Double(origin, new Point(end.x - position.x,
                                              end.y - position.y));
}
```

We've saved the point start in `position`, and created the `Line2D.Double` shape as the origin. Of course, we have to adjust the coordinates of the end point so that it is relative to (0, 0).

We can now implement the `draw()` method to use a transform to move the coordinate system to where the line should be drawn. We can economize on the code in the element classes a little by thinking about this because a lot of the code is essentially the same. Here's how we would implement the method for the `Element.Line` class directly:

```
public void draw(Graphics2D g2D)
{
   g2D.setPaint(highlighted ? Color.magenta : color);   // Set the line color
   AffineTransform old = g2D.getTransform();             // Save the current
transform
   g2D.translate(position.x, position.y);                // Translate to position
   g2D.draw(line);                                       // Draw the line
   g2D.setTransform(old);                                // Restore original
transform
}
```

To draw the line in the right place, we just have to apply a translation to the coordinate system before the `draw()` operation. Saving a copy of the old transform is most important, as that enables us to restore the original scheme after we've drawn the line. If we don't do this, subsequent draw operations in the same graphics context will have more and more translations applied cumulatively, so objects get further and further away from where they should be. Only one line of code here involves the element itself:

```
g2D.draw(line);                                          // Draw the line
```

All the rest will be common to most of the types of shapes – text being the exception. We could add an overloaded `draw()` method to the base class, `Element`, that we can define like this:

```
protected void draw(Graphics2D g2D, Shape element)
{
   g2D.setPaint(highlighted ? Color.magenta : color);   // Set the element color
   AffineTransform old = g2D.getTransform();             // Save the current
transform
```

```
        g2D.translate(position.x, position.y);           // Translate to position
        g2D.draw(element);                                // Draw the element
        g2D.setTransform(old);                            // Restore original transform
    }
```

This will draw any `Shape` object after applying a translation to the point, `position`. We can now call this method from the `draw()` method in the `Element.Line` class:

```
    public void draw(Graphics2D g2D)
    {
        draw(g2D,line);                                   // Call base draw method
    }
```

You can now go ahead and implement the `draw()` method in exactly the same way for all the nested classes to `Element`, with the exception of the `Element.Text` class. Just pass the underlying `Shape` reference for each class as the second argument to the overloaded `draw()` method. We can't use the base class helper method in the `Element.Text` because text is not a `Shape` object. We will come back to the class defining text as a special case.

We must think about the bounding rectangle for a line now. We don't want the bounding rectangle for a line to be at (0, 0). We want it to be defined in terms of the coordinate system before it is translated. This is because when we use it for highlighting, no transforms are in effect. For that to work the bounding rectangle must be in the same reference frame.

This means that we must apply the translation to the bounding rectangle that corresponds to the `Line2D.Double` shape. A base class helper method will come in handy here too:

```
    protected java.awt.Rectangle getBounds(java.awt.Rectangle bounds)
    {
        AffineTransform at = AffineTransform.getTranslateInstance(
                                                 position.x, position.y);
        return at.createTransformedShape(bounds).getBounds();
    }
```

Just add this method to the code for the `Element` class. We first create an `AffineTransform` object that applies a translation to the point, `position`. Then we apply the `createTransformedShape()` method to the rectangle that is passed as the argument – which will be the bounding rectangle for a shape at (0, 0) – to get a corresponding shape translated to its proper position. Even though we get a `GeneralPath` object back, we can get a rectangle from that quite easily by calling its `getBounds()` method. Thus our helper method accepts a reference to an object of type `java.awt.Rectangle`, and returns a reference to the rectangle that results from translating this to the point, `position`. This is precisely what we want to do with the bounding rectangles we get with our shapes defined at the origin. We can now use this to implement the `getBounds()` method for the `Element.Line` class:

```
public java.awt.Rectangle getBounds()
{
    return getBounds(line.getBounds());
}
```

We just pass the reference to the `line` member of the class as the argument to the base class version of `getBounds()`, and return the rectangle that is returned by that method. The `getBounds()` methods for the nested classes `Rectangle`, `Circle` and `Curve` will be essentially the same – just change the argument to the base class `getBounds()` call to the `Shape` reference corresponding to each class. To implement the `getBounds()` method for the `Text` class, just pass the `bounds` member of that class as the argument to the base class `getBounds()` method.

We must also update the `modify()` method for the `Element.Line` class, and this is going to be specific to the class. To adjust the end point of a line so that it is relative to the start point at the origin, we must change the method in the `Element.Line` class as follows:

```
public void modify(Point start, Point last)
{
    line.x2 = last.x - position.x;
    line.y2 = last.y - position.y;
}
```

That's the `Element.Line` class complete. We can apply the same thing to all the other classes in the `Element` class.

Translating Rectangles

Here's the changes to `Element.Rectangle` constructor:

```
public Rectangle(Point start, Point end, Color color)

{
    super(color);
    this.start = start;
    position = new Point(Math.min(start.x, end.x),
                         Math.min(start.y, end.y));
    rectangle = new Rectangle2D.Double(
                            origin.x,
                            origin.y,
                            Math.abs(start.x - end.x),    // Width
                            Math.abs(start.y - end.y));   // & height
}
```

We still have to keep track of the start point in the `start` member of the class since we will need to take account of the possibility that the initial point was not at the top-left corner in the implementation of the `modify()` method. The expressions for the coordinates for the point, `position`, ensure that we do set it as the location of the top left corner. The rectangle object is defined with its top-left corner at the origin, and its width and height as before. We have to adjust the `modify()` method to adjust the location stored in position, and leave the rectangle defined at the origin:

```
public void modify(Point start, Point last)
{
  position.x = Math.min(start.x, last.x);
  position.y = Math.min(start.y, last.y);
  rectangle.width = Math.abs(start.x - last.x);
  rectangle.height = Math.abs(start.y - last.y);
}
```

You should already have added the revised version of the draw() and getBounds() methods for an Element.Rectangle object essentially the same as that for lines.

Translating Circles

The Element.Circle class constructor is also very easy:

```
public Circle(Point center, Point circum, Color color)
{
  super(color);
  this.center = center;                    // Save the center point

  // Radius is distance from center to circumference
  double radius = center.distance(circum);
  position = new Point(center.x - (int)radius,
                       center.y - (int)radius);

  circle = new Ellipse2D.Double(origin.x, origin.y,      // Position - top-left
                                2.*radius, 2.*radius );  // Width & height

}
```

The radius is calculated as before, and we make the top-left corner of the Ellipse2D.Double object the origin point. Thus position is calculated as for the top-left corner in the previous version of the constructor. We can adjust the modify() method to record the new coordinates of position:

```
public void modify(Point center, Point circum)
{
  double radius = center.distance(circum);
  position.x = center.x - (int)radius;
  position.y = center.y - (int)radius;
  circle.width = circle.height = 2*radius;
}
```

The draw() and getBounds() methods are already done, so it's curves next.

Translating Curves

The Element.Curve class is just as simple:

```
public Curve(Point start, Point next, Color color)
{
  super(color);
```

```
    curve = new GeneralPath();
    position = start;
    curve.moveTo(origin.x, origin.y);
    curve.lineTo(next.x - position.x,
               next.y - position.y);
}
```

We store the start point in `position`, and create the curve starting at (0, 0). The end point has to be adjusted so that it is defined relative to (0, 0). Adding a new segment in the `modify()` method also has to be changed to take account of the new origin for the curve relative to the start point:

```
public void modify(Point start, Point next)
{
    curve.lineTo(next.x - start.x,
               next.y - start.y);
}
```

We just subtract the coordinates of the original start point that we saved in `position` from the point, `next`. The methods for drawing the curve and getting the bounding rectangle have already been updated, so the last piece is the `Element.Text` class.

Translating Text

The first step is to remove the declaration for the member, `position`, from this class, as we will now be using the member of the same name that is inherited from the base class. The only changes we need to make to the constructor are as follows:

```
public Text(Font font, String text, Point position,
                                  Color color, java.awt.Rectangle bounds)
{
    super(color);
    this.font = font;
    this.position = position;
    this.position.y -= (int)bounds.getHeight();
    this.text = text;
    this.bounds = new java.awt.Rectangle(origin.x, origin.y,
                                  bounds.width, bounds.height);
}
```

The bounding rectangle for the text object now has its top left corner at the origin. The point `position` that defines where the text is to be drawn is set to correspond to the top left corner of the rectangle bounding the text, to be consistent with the way it is defined for the other elements. We will need to take account of this in our implementation of the `draw()` method because the `drawString()` method expects the position for the text to be the bottom left corner:

```
public void draw(Graphics2D g2D)
{
    g2D.setPaint(highlighted ? Color.magenta : color);
    Font oldFont = g2D.getFont();                    // Save the old font
    g2D.setFont(font);                               // Set the new font
```

```
        AffineTransform old = g2D.getTransform();        // Save the current
transform
        g2D.translate(position.x, position.y);           // Translate to position
        g2D.drawString(text, origin.x, origin.y+(int)bounds.getHeight());
        g2D.setTransform(old);                           // Restore original
transform

        g2D.setFont(oldFont);                            // Restore the old font
    }
```

The transformation applied in the `draw()` method here is essentially the same as for the other classes. We now add the height of the bounding rectangle to the *y* coordinate of position in the argument to `drawString()`. This specifies the bottom left corner of the first text character.

You can now recompile Sketcher for another trial. If you have done everything right it should still work as before.

How It Works

All the classes defining elements create the elements at the origin, and store their location in a member, `position`, that is inherited from the base class, `Element`. The draw methods all apply a transform to move the coordinate system to the point stored in `position` before drawing the element. The `draw()` methods then restore the original transform to leave the graphics context unchanged. Each of the `getBounds()` methods returns a bounding rectangle in the original un-transformed coordinate system, because that is the context in which we shall be using it. We are now ready to try moving elements around.

Moving an Element

Now we can implement the **Move** operation that we provided for in the context menu. Taking the trouble to define all the elements relative to the origin and using a transform to position them correctly really pays off when you want to apply other transformations to the elements. We can add a `move()` method to the base class, `Element`, that will move any element, and it is just two lines of code:

```
    public void move(int deltax, int deltay)
    {
      position.x += deltax;
      position.y += deltay;
    }
```

Let's review the process that we will implement to make a move. From a user point of view, to move an element you just click on the **Move** menu item, then drag the highlighted element to where you want it to be with button 1 held down.

In programming terms a move will be initiated in the `actionPerformed()` method in `SketchView` that responds to a menu selection. When the **Move** menu item is clicked, we will set the operating mode to what we will define as MOVE mode, so that we can detect this in the mouse handler methods that will expedite a move. The **Rotate** menu will work in exactly the same way, setting a ROTATE mode. To accommodate this we will add a member, `mode`, of type `int`, to store the current operating mode. By default, it will be NORMAL. Add the following declaration to `SketchView`:

```
private int mode = NORMAL;
```

We will add the definitions of these operating modes to the `Constants` interface by adding the following statements:

```
// Operating modes
int NORMAL = 0;
int MOVE   = 1;
int ROTATE = 2;
```

When we set the operating mode to other than `NORMAL`, the methods dealing with mouse events will need to know to which element the mode applies, so we will add another member to `SketchView` to record this:

```
private Element selectedElement;
```

Now we can implement `actionPerformed()` in the `SketchView` class as:

```
public void actionPerformed(ActionEvent e)
{
  Object source = e.getSource();
  if(source == moveItem)
  {
    mode = MOVE;
    selectedElement = highlightElement;
  }
  else if(source == deleteItem)
  {
    if(highlightElement != null)                           // If there's an element
    {
      theApp.getModel().remove(highlightElement);          // then remove it
      highlightElement = null;                             // Remove the reference
    }
  }
  else if(source == rotateItem)
  {
    mode = ROTATE;
    selectedElement = highlightElement;
  }
  else if(source == sendToBackItem)
  {
    if(highlightElement != null)
    {
      theApp.getModel().remove(highlightElement);
      theApp.getModel().add(highlightElement);
      highlightElement.setHighlighted(false);
      highlightElement = null;
    ...
```

All the moving of the highlighted element will be managed in the `mouseDragged()` method in the `MouseHandler` inner class to `SketchView`.

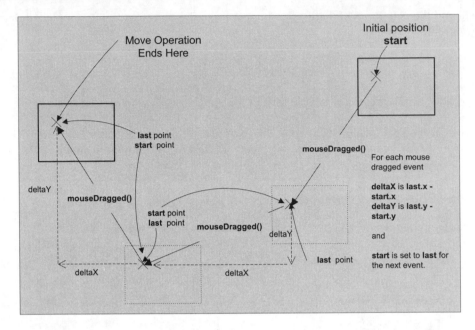

Each move will be from the previous cursor position stored in `start`, to the current cursor position when the `MOUSE_DRAGGED` event occurred. The current cursor position will be obtained by calling the `getPoint()` method for the event object passed to the `mouseDragged()` method. Once each mouse move has been processed, the current cursor position will then be stored in the variable `start`, ready for the next event. For each `MOUSE_DRAGGED` event, we will move the element the distance between successive cursor positions.

Try It Out – Moving Elements

Since the element classes are equipped to move, and we have kitted out `SketchView` to handle the menu item action, we just need to add the code to the methods in `MouseHandler`. The `mousePressed()` method records the start point for a move, and it also sets up the XOR mode for drawing. That's precisely what we will need to move or rotate elements, so we do not need to alter it at all.

We have to test for the setting of `mode` in the `mouseDragged()` method though, and, in principle, execute different code depending on what it is. We have three possibilities, `NORMAL`, where we do as we did before, `MOVE`, where we will execute a move operation, and `ROTATE`, which we will come to later. Here's the new version of `mouseDragged()` to accommodate moving elements:

```
public void mouseDragged(MouseEvent e)
{
    last = e.getPoint();                    // Save cursor position
    int modifier = e.getModifiers();        // Get modifiers
```

```
        if((modifier & e.BUTTON1_MASK) != 0 &&
           (theApp.getWindow().getElementType() != TEXT) &&
           (mode == NORMAL))
      {
        if(tempElement == null)                    // Is there an element?
          tempElement = createElement(start, last);   // No so create one
        else
        {
          tempElement.draw(g2D);                   // Yes - draw to erase it
          tempElement.modify(start, last);         // Modify it
        }
        tempElement.draw(g2D);                     // and draw it
      }
      else if(mode == MOVE && selectedElement != null)
      {
        selectedElement.draw(g2D);                 // Draw to erase the
  element
        selectedElement.move(last.x-start.x, last.y-start.y);  // Move it
        selectedElement.draw(g2D);                 // Draw in its new position
        start = last;                              // Make start current point
      }
    }
```

Now we only execute the previous code in NORMAL mode. For MOVE mode, if there is an element selected to move, we move it by erasing it at the current position, moving the element by calling its move() method, and drawing it at the new position. The current last will be start for the next MOUSE_DRAGGED event.

The final alterations to our code occur in the mouseReleased() method:

```
      public void mouseReleased(MouseEvent e)
      {
        int modifier = e.getModifiers();                   // Get modifiers

        if(e.isPopupTrigger())
        {
          start = e.getPoint();

          if(highlightElement==null)
            theApp.getWindow().getPopup().show((Component)e.getSource(),
                                                    start.x, start.y);
          else
            elementPopup.show((Component)e.getSource(), start.x, start.y);

          start = null;
        }

        else if((modifier & e.BUTTON1_MASK) != 0 &&
             (theApp.getWindow().getElementType() != TEXT) &&
             mode == NORMAL)
```

```
      {
        if(tempElement != null)
        {
          theApp.getModel().add(tempElement);  // Add element to the model
          tempElement = null;
        }
      }
      else if(mode == MOVE || mode == ROTATE)
      {
        if(selectedElement != null)
          repaint();
        mode = NORMAL;
      }

      if(g2D != null)
      {
        g2D.dispose();                         // Release graphic context resource
        g2D = null;                            // Set it to null
      }
      start = last = null;                     // Remove the points
      selectedElement = tempElement = null;    // Reset elements
    }
```

The last block of shaded code is not entirely new – some of it has been relocated from earlier in the code for the previous version. We have an extra condition in the original `if` expression to check for NORMAL mode. The next `if` tests for MOVE mode or ROTATE mode because in either case we will have changed an element by dragging it around, and will therefore want to redraw the view. This is the one place where we must do this explicitly because the model is not aware of these changes. If `selectedElement` is not `null`, we call `repaint()` for the view to get it redrawn and we restore NORMAL mode. Outside of all the `if`s we reset everything back to `null`.

If you recompile Sketcher and rerun it, you can now produce sketches like that below.

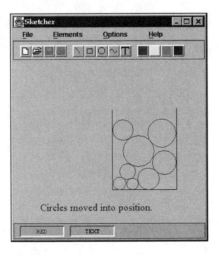

Circles moved into position.

How It Works

Using a transform to position each element means that a move consists of just altering the `position` member of an element. The move operation depends on setting a `MOVE` mode for the mouse event handling methods to respond to. A move for each element is the same: drawing the element in XOR mode in its original position to erase it, moving it and then drawing it again in the new position. You may see pixels left behind as you move elements, particularly text.

This is due to rounding in the floating point operations mapping user coordinates to device coordinates. They all disappear when the move is complete and the whole picture is redrawn.

Now we have made Move work, Rotate will be a piece of cake.

Rotating Elements

Clearly we are going to make use of another transform to implement this. We know how to create a rotate transform, so all we need to figure out is the mechanics of how the user accomplishes the rotation of an element.

The first step is already in place – the `actionPerformed()` method in `SketchView` already sets `ROTATE` mode in response to the Rotate menu action. The user will then drag the element to the angle required with the mouse, while holding button 1 down. We need to work out the rotation angle for each `MOUSE_DRAGGED` event. The diagram below shows what happens when the mouse is dragged for a rotation.

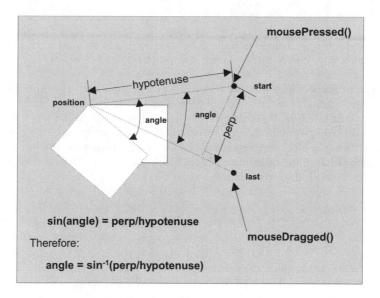

The angle in the diagram is exaggerated so we can see what is going on. The `mousePressed()` method is called when the button is first pressed at some arbitrary position and the cursor position is recorded in `start`. When the `mouseDragged()` method is called, we record the cursor position in `last`, and we now need to calculate `angle`. We must apply a little high school math to get this, which you can ignore if you are rusty with trigonometry.

We can get the length of the perpendicular from the point `start` to the line extending from `position` to `last` with a static method in the `Line2D` class:

```
double perp = Line2D.ptLineDist(position.x, position.y,
                                last.x, last.y,
                                start.x, start.y);
```

The `ptLineDist()` method calculates the perpendicular distance of the point specified by the last two arguments, to the line specified by the first four arguments – the first pair of arguments being the coordinates of the beginning of the line, and the second pair being the coordinates of the end point.

We know how to get the distance from `position` to `start`. We just apply the `distance()` method that is defined in the `Point` class:

```
double hypotenuse = position.distance(start);
```

From the diagram you can see that we can calculate `angle` as

sin-1(perp/hypotenuse)

This comes from the definition of what the sine of an angle is. The `Math` class provides a method to calculate arcsine values, so we can calculate `angle` as:

```
double angle = Math.asin(perp/hypotenuse);
```

The `asin()` method returns an angle in radians between $-\pi/2$ and $\pi/2$, which is fine for us. We are unlikely to create an angle outside this range for a `mouseDragged()` event.

Of course, we need to know which way the rotation is going, clockwise or counterclockwise. Another static method in the `Line2D` class can help out here. The `relativeCCW()` method determines where a point lies with respect to a line. If you have to rotate the line clockwise to reach the point, the method returns –1, and if you have to rotate the line counterclockwise it returns +1. We can use this to test whether the point, `last`, is clockwise or counterclockwise with respect to the line from `position` to `start`. Since angles rotating the coordinate system clockwise are positive, we can calculate a suitably signed value for `angle` with the statement:

```
double angle = -Line2D.relativeCCW(position.x, position.y,
                                   start.x, start.y,
                                   last.x, last.y)*Math.asin(perp/hypotenuse);
```

The minus sign is necessary because the method returns –1 when `last` is clockwise with respect to the line from `position` to `start`. That's all the math we need. Let's do it.

Try It Out – Rotating Elements

To deal with `ROTATE` mode in the `mouseDragged()` method, we can add an extra `else if` clause after the one we added for `MOVE`:

```
        else if(mode == ROTATE && selectedElement != null)
        {
          selectedElement.draw(g2D);                    // Draw to erase the element
          selectedElement.rotate(getAngle(selectedElement.getPosition(),
                                          start, last));
          selectedElement.draw(g2D);                    // Draw in its new position
          start = last;                                 // Make start current point
        }
```

After drawing the element to erase it, we call its `rotate()` method to rotate it and then redraw it in the new position. We will add the definition for the `rotate()` method to the `Element` class in a moment. The argument to the `rotate()` method is the angle in radians through which the element is to be rotated, and that is returned by a helper method, `getAngle()`. We can add that to the `MouseHandler` class as:

```
      // Helper method for calculating getAngle()
      double getAngle(Point position, Point start, Point last)
      {
        // Get perpendicular distance from last to the line from position to start
        double perp = Line2D.ptLineDist(position.x, position.y,
                                        last.x, last.y, start.x, start.y);
        // Get the distance from position to start
        double hypotenuse = position.distance(start);
        if(hypotenuse == 0.0)                         // Make sure its
          hypotenuse = 1.0;                           // non-zero

        // Angle is the arc sine of perp/hypotenuse. Clockwise is positive angle
        return -Line2D.relativeCCW(position.x, position.y,
                                   start.x, start.y,
                                   last.x, last.y)*Math.asin(perp/hypotenuse);
      }
```

This is basically just an assembly of the code fragments calculating the angle in the last section.

We completed the `mouseReleased()` method when we dealt with MOVE mode so there's nothing further to add there.

Now we must empower our element classes to rotate themselves. We will add a data member to the base class to store the rotation angle, and a method to rotate the element:

```
    public abstract class Element
    {
      public Element(Color color)
      { this.color = color; }

      public   Color getColor()
      {  return color;  }

      // Set or reset highlight color
      public void setHighlighted(boolean highlighted)
      {
```

```
      this.highlighted = highlighted;
   }

   public Point getPosition()
   {  return position;  }

   protected void draw(Graphics2D g2D, Shape element)
   {
      g2D.setPaint(highlighted ? Color.magenta : color);   // Set the element color
      AffineTransform old = g2D.getTransform();             // Save the current transform
      g2D.translate(position.x, position.y);                // Translate to position
      g2D.rotate(angle);                                    // Rotate about position
      g2D.draw(element);                                    // Draw the element
      g2D.setTransform(old);                                // Restore original transform
   }

   protected java.awt.Rectangle getBounds(java.awt.Rectangle bounds)
   {
      AffineTransform at = AffineTransform.getTranslateInstance(
                                                    position.x,
position.y);
      at.rotate(angle);
      return  at.createTransformedShape(bounds).getBounds();
   }

   public void move(int deltax, int deltay)
   {
      position.x += deltax;
      position.y += deltay;
   }

   public void rotate(double angle)
   {  this.angle += angle;  }

   public abstract void draw(Graphics2D g2D);

   public abstract Rectangle getBounds();

   protected Color color;                       // Color of a shape
   protected boolean highlighted = false;       // Highlight flag
   final static Point origin = new Point();      // Point 0,0
   protected Point position;                     // Element position
   protected double angle = 0.0;                 // Rotation angle
   }
```

All the rotate() method does is add the angle passed to it to the current value of angle. The value of angle is assumed to be in radians. Naturally, when we create an element the angle will be zero. We have modified the draw() method in the base class to apply a rotation through angle radians about the point position. It is important that we apply the rotation after the translation, otherwise the translation would be applied in the rotated coordinate system, which would give quite a different result from what we require. Since we now have the possibility of rotated shapes, the getBounds() method also has to take account of this, so we apply a rotation here, too. We mustn't forget that the draw() method in the Element.Text class is a special case. We need to add a line to this method to apply the rotation:

```
public void draw(Graphics2D g2D)
{
  g2D.setPaint(highlighted ? Color.magenta : color);
  Font oldFont = g2D.getFont();                  // Save the old font
  g2D.setFont(font);                             // Set the new font

  AffineTransform old = g2D.getTransform();      // Save the current
transform
  g2D.translate(position.x, position.y);         // Translate to position
  g2D.rotate(angle);                             // Rotate about position
  g2D.drawString(text, origin.x, origin.y+(int)bounds.getHeight());
  g2D.setTransform(old);                         // Restore original
transform

  g2D.setFont(oldFont);                          // Restore the old font
}
```

Recompile all the stuff we have changed and try out the new context menus. Having a rotate capability adds flexibility and with the move operation giving you much more precision in positioning elements relative to one another, this should enable a massive leap forward in the quality of your artwork.

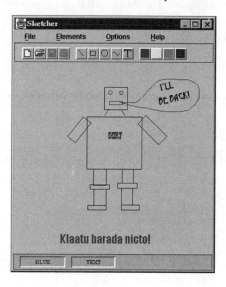

How It Works

Rotating elements just involves adding an extra transform before each element is drawn. Because we draw each element at the origin, rotating an element becomes relatively simple.

Choosing Custom Colors

We made provision in the status bar for showing a custom color. It would be a shame not to make use of this, so let's add a dialog to enable any color to be chosen. This is going to be a lot easier than you imagine.

To keep it simple, we will implement this as a facility on the general pop-up menu, although in practice you would probably want it accessible from the main menu and the toolbar. We will add a member to the SketchFrame class for the menu item:

```
private JMenuItem customColorItem;
```

We just need to add this to the pop-up and to add an action listener for it. This requires two statements in the SketchFrame constructor:

```
customColorItem = popup.add("Custom Color...");    // Add the item
customColorItem.addActionListener(this);            // and add its listener
```

You can add these statements following the others that set up the pop-up menu. Selecting this menu item will now cause the actionPerformed() method in the SketchFrame class to be called so we will implement the custom color choice in there. Let's try it out.

Try It Out – Choosing a Custom Color

We will use the facilities provided by the JColorChooser class that does precisely what we want. Here's how we will use it in the actionPerformed() method:

```
public void actionPerformed(ActionEvent e)
{
  if(e.getSource() == aboutItem)
  {

    // Create about dialog with the menu item as parent as before...
  }
  else if(e.getSource() == fontItem)
  {
    // Display font dialog as before...
  }
  else if(e.getSource() == customColorItem)
  {
    Color color = JColorChooser.showDialog(this, "Select Custom Color",
                                                  elementColor);
    if(color != null)
    {
      elementColor = color;
      statusBar.setColorPane(color);
    }
  }
}
```

If you recompile and rerun Sketcher and select the Custom Color... menu item from the general pop-up, you will see the dialog below.

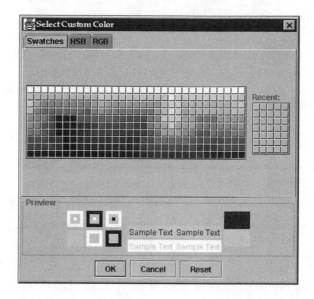

How It Works

The JColorChooser class defines a complete color choosing facility that you can use in your own dialog, or create a complete modal dialog by calling the static method showDialog() as we have done here. The arguments to showDialog() are a reference to the parent component for the dialog, the title for the dialog and the initial color selection. You can choose a color using any of the three tabs that provide different mechanisms for defining the color that you want. When you click on OK the color that you chose is returned as type Color. Exiting the dialog by any other means than selecting the OK button returns null. We just store the color returned in elementColor, and set it in the status bar pane.

Summary

In this chapter you have learnt how to use dialogs to manage data input. You have also learned how to implement context menus which can bring a professional feel to the GUI in your applications. You have applied scrollbars to varying data values as well as scrolling a window, so you should be in a position to use them in whatever context you need.

The important points we have covered in this chapter are:

❑ A modal dialog blocks input from other windows in the same application as long as it is displayed

❑ A non-modal dialog does not block input to other windows. You can switch the focus between a non-modal dialog and other windows in the application whenever necessary

❑ The JOptionPane class provides static methods for creating simple dialogs.

❑   A pop-up menu is a menu that can be displayed at any point within the coordinate system of a component

❑   A context menu is a pop-up menu that is specific to what lies at the point where the menu is displayed – so the contents of the menu depend on the context

❑   A context menu is displayed as a result of a pop-up trigger, which is usually a right mouse button click

❑   The `AffineTransform` class defines an affine transformation that can be applied to a graphics context and to a `Shape` object.

❑   A `Graphic2D` object always contains an `AffineTransform` object, and the default transform leaves coordinates unchanged.

❑   The transform for a graphics context is applied immediately before user coordinates for a shape are converted to device coordinates.

❑   There are four kinds of transform you can create: translations, rotations, scaling and shearing.

❑   You can combine any number of transformations in a single `AffineTransform` object.

Exercises

1.   Implement a dialog initiated from a toolbar button to select the current element color.

2.   Add a menu item to the `Element` context menu that will display information about the element at the cursor in a dialog – what it is and its basic defining data.

3.   Display a special context menu when the cursor is over a `TEXT` object that provides a menu option to edit the text through a dialog.

4.   Change the implementation of the element classes to make use of the combined translate and rotate operation.

5.   Add a toolbar button to switch highlighting on and off. The same button should turn it on when it is off and vice versa, so you need to change the button label appropriately.

6.   Add a Scale menu item to the element context menu that will allow an element to be scaled by dragging the mouse cursor.

7.   Implement a main menu item and a toolbar button for choosing a custom color.

Filing and Printing Documents

In this chapter we will explore serializing and printing documents in an application, and adding these as the finishing touches to our Sketcher program. These capabilities are not available in an untrusted applet for security reasons, so everything we will cover here only applies to applications and trusted applets. Although we have already covered serialization in Chapter 9, you will find that there is quite a difference between understanding how the basic methods for object input and output work, and applying them in a practical context.

In this chapter you will learn:

- ❑ How to use the JFileChooser class.
- ❑ How to save a sketch in a file.
- ❑ How to implement the **Save As** menu mechanism.
- ❑ How to open a sketch stored in a file and integrate it into the application.
- ❑ How to create a new sketch and integrate it into the application.
- ❑ How to ensure that the current sketch is saved before the application is closed or a new sketch is loaded.
- ❑ How printing in Java works.
- ❑ How to print in landscape orientation rather than portrait orientation.
- ❑ How to implement multipage printing.
- ❑ How to output components to your printer.

Serializing the Sketch

Our Sketcher program can only be considered to be a practical application if we can save sketches in a file, and retrieve them later – in other words we need to implement serialization for a `SketchModel` object and use that to make the File menu work. Ideally, we want to be able to write the model for a sketch to a file and be able to read it back at a later date and reconstruct exactly the same model object. This naturally leads us to choose serialization as the way to do this, because the primary purpose of serialization is the accurate storage and retrieval of objects.

We've seen how to serialize objects, way back in Chapter 9. All we need to do to serialize a sketch document in our Sketcher program is to apply what we learned then. Of course, there are a few more classes lying around that are involved in a document but it will be remarkably easy, considering the potential complexity of a sketch – I promise!

Of course, saving a sketch on disk and reading it back from a file implies supporting the File menu, and that will be significantly more work than implementing serialization for the document. The logic of opening and saving files so as not to lose anything accidentally can get rather convoluted. Before we get into that, there is a more fundamental point we should address – our sketch doesn't have a name. We should at least make provision for assigning a file name to a sketch, and maybe display the name in the title bar of the application window.

Try It Out – Assigning a Document Name

Since the sketch is going to have a name, because we intend to store it somewhere, let's define a default directory to hold sketches. Add the following lines to the end of the `Constants` interface:

```
File DEFAULT_DIRECTORY = new File("C:/Sketches");
String DEFAULT_FILENAME = "Sketch.ske";
```

If you want to store your sketches in a different directory you can set the definition of `DEFAULT_DIRECTORY` to suit your needs. The extension, `.ske`, to identify sketches is also arbitrary. You can change this if you would prefer to use something different. Since we reference the `File` class here, we must add an `import` statement to the `Constants` source file to get at it:

```
import java.io.File;
```

We can now add the following data members to the `SketchFrame` class definition:

```
private String frameTitle;                              // Frame title
private String filename = DEFAULT_FILENAME;             // Current model file name
private File modelFile;                                 // File for the current
sketch
```

The `frameTitle` member specifies the basic title for the Sketcher application window. We will append the file name for the sketch to this. The `modelFile` member will eventually hold a reference to the `File` object identifying the file containing the current sketch, once the sketch has been saved.

We can arrange for the `frameTitle` to be initialized and the default file name to be appended to the basic window title in the `SketchFrame` constructor. We can also make sure that `DEFAULT_DIRECTORY` exists and is valid. The following code will do this:

```
public SketchFrame(String title, Sketcher theApp)
{
    // Remove call to setTitle() at the beginning...
    // Code as before...

    frameTitle = title + ": ";
    setTitle(frameTitle + filename);

    if(!DEFAULT_DIRECTORY.exists())
      if(!DEFAULT_DIRECTORY.mkdirs())
        JOptionPane.showMessageDialog(this,
                                      "Error creating default directory",
                                      "Directory Creation Error",
                                      JOptionPane.ERROR_MESSAGE);
}
```

Since we will be implementing the event handling for the File menu, you can remove or comment out the statements from the constructor that disable the actions for this. Just to remind you, they are:

```
// Disable actions
saveAction.setEnabled(false);
closeAction.setEnabled(false);
printAction.setEnabled(false);
```

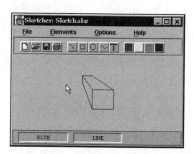

If you recompile Sketcher and run it, you should now see the default file name for a sketch displayed in the title bar.

We now have a name assigned to the document, but there's another point to consider if we're preparing to store a sketch. When we close the application, we should have a means of checking whether the document needs to be saved. Otherwise it will be all too easy to close Sketcher and lose the brilliant sketch that you have just spent three hours crafting. Checking whether the sketch needs to be saved isn't difficult. We just need to record the fact that the document has changed.

Try It Out – Recording Changes to a Sketch

To provide the means of recording whether a sketch has been changed or not we can add a `boolean` data member to the `SketchFrame` class that we will set to `true` when the `SketchModel` object changes, and to `false` when it is unchanged – as is the case when it has just been loaded or saved in a file. Add the following data member definition to the class:

```
private boolean sketchChanged = false;            // Model changed flag
```

This is sometimes referred to as the 'dirty' flag for the model, because it records when something has been done to sully the pristine state of the model data. The flag is `false` initially because the sketch is empty and therefore unchanged by definition. Any change that the user makes to the model should result in the flag being set to `true`, and when the model is written to a file, the flag should be reset to `false`.

We already have in place the means to signal changes to a sketch, since the `SketchModel` class has `Observable` as a base class. An `Observable` object can automatically notify any registered `Observer` objects when a change takes place. All we need to do is to make the `SketchFrame` class implement the `Observer` interface, and register the application window as an observer of the sketch object.

```
public class SketchFrame extends JFrame
                         implements Constants, ActionListener, Observer
{
  // Method called by SketchModel object when it changes
  public void update(Observable o, Object obj)
  {
    sketchChanged = true;
  }

  // Rest of the class as before...
}
```

The `Observer` interface and the `Observable` class are defined in the `java.util` package, so we must import them into the `SketchFrame.java` file with the statement:

```
import java.util.*;
```

We can register the application window as an observer for the `SketchModel` object by adding one statement to the `init()` method in the `Sketcher` class:

```
sketch.addObserver((Observer)window);            // Register window as observer
```

Whenever an element is added to the sketch, or deleted from it, the application window object will be notified. That's just about all the odds and ends we need. We can now press ahead with serializing the document.

Implementing the Serializable Interface

As I hope you still remember, the fundamental step in making objects serializable is to implement the `Serializable` interface in every class that defines objects we want written to a file. We need a methodical approach here, so how about top-down – starting with the `SketchModel` class.

This is where we get a great deal from astonishingly little effort. To implement serialization for the `SketchModel` class you must first modify the class definition header to:

```
class SketchModel extends Observable
                  implements Serializable
```

The `Serializable` interface is defined in the package `java.io` so we need to add an `import` statement to the beginning of the `SketchModel.java` file:

```
import java.io.*;
```

The `Serializable` interface declares no methods – so that's it!

Is that enough to serialize a sketch? Not quite. For a class to be serializable, all its data members must be serializable or declared as `transient`. If this is not the case then an exception of type `NotSerializableException` will be thrown when an attempt is made to serialize an object that is not serializable. To avoid this we must trawl through the data elements of the `SketchModel` class, and if any of these are our own classes we must make sure they either implement the `Serializable` interface, or are declared as `transient`. We also must not assume that objects of a standard class type are serializable, because some most definitely are not. It's a fairly quick fishing trip though, because our `SketchModel` class only has one data member – the linked list of elements that make up the sketch. If the `SketchModel` object is to be serializable we simply need to make sure the `elementList` member is serializable.

Serializing the List of Elements

The `LinkedList` class is serializable, so all we need to worry about are the list elements themselves. We can make the base class for our shape classes, `Element`, serializable by declaring that it implements the interface:

```
public abstract class Element
                      implements Serializable
```

Don't forget that we now need an import statement for the `java.io` package in `Element.java`. The data members of the `Element` class that are object references are of type `Color` or of type `Point`, and since both of these classes are serializable as you can verify from the JDK documentation, our `Element` class is serializable. Now we need to look at the inner classes to `Element`.

Subclasses of `Element` will inherit the implementation of the `Serializable` interface but there is a snag. At the time of writing, *none* of the `Shape` classes in the `java.awt.geom` package are serializable, and we have been using them all over the place. We are not done for though. Remember that you can always implement the `readObject()` and `writeObject()` methods in a class and then implement your own serialization. We can take the data that we need to recreate the required `Shape` object and serialize that in our implementation of the `writeObject()` method., We will then be able to reconstruct the object from the data in the `readObject()` method. Let's start with our `Element.Line` class.

Serializing Lines

The `writeObject()` method that serializes objects will need to have the form:

```
private void writeObject(ObjectOutputStream out)
                                        throws IOException
{
  // Code to serialize the object...
}
```

Our `Element.Line` objects are always drawn from (0, 0) so there's no sense in saving the start point in a line – it's always the same. We just need to serialize the end point so add the following to the `Element.Line` class:

```
private void writeObject(ObjectOutputStream out)
                                        throws IOException
{
    out.writeDouble(line.x2);
    out.writeDouble(line.y2);
}
```

That wasn't too hard, was it? We don't need to worry about exceptions that might be thrown by the `writeDouble()` method at this point. These will be passed on to the method that calls `writeObject()`. The coordinates are public members of the `Line2D.Double` object so we can reference them directly to write them to the stream. The rest of the data relating to a line is stored in the base class, `Element`, and as we said earlier they are all taken care of. The base class members will be serialized automatically when an `Element.Line` object is written to a file. We just need the means to read it back.

To recap what you already know, the `readObject()` method to deserialize an object is also of a standard form:

```
private void readObject(java.io.ObjectInputStream in)
                throws IOException, ClassNotFoundException
{
    // Code to deserialize an object...
}
```

For the line class, the implementation will read the coordinates of the end point of the line and reconstitute `line` – the `Line2D.Double` member of the class. Adding the following method to the `Element.Line` class will do it:

```
private void readObject(java.io.ObjectInputStream in)
                throws IOException, ClassNotFoundException
{
    double x2 = in.readDouble();
    double y2 = in.readDouble();
    line = new Line2D.Double(0,0,x2,y2);
}
```

That's lines serialized. Looks as though it's going to be easy. We can do rectangles next.

Serializing Rectangles

A rectangle is always drawn with its top left corner at the origin, so we only need to write the width and height to the file:

```
private void writeObject(ObjectOutputStream out)
                                            throws IOException
{
    out.writeDouble(rectangle.width);
    out.writeDouble(rectangle.height);
}
```

The `width` and `height` members of the `Rectangle2D.Double` object are `public`, so we can access them directly to write them to the stream.

Deserializing an `Element.Rectangle` object is almost identical to that of a line:

```
private void readObject(ObjectInputStream in)
                throws IOException, ClassNotFoundException
{
    double width = in.readDouble();
    double height = in.readDouble();
    rectangle = new Rectangle2D.Double(0,0,width,height);
}
```

An `Element.Circle` object is actually going to be easier.

Serializing Circles

A circle is drawn as an ellipse with the top left corner of the bounding rectangle at the origin. The only item of data we will need to reconstruct a circle is the diameter:

```
private void writeObject(ObjectOutputStream out)
                                            throws IOException
{
    out.writeDouble(circle.width);
}
```

The diameter is recorded in the `width` member (and also in the `height` member) of the `Ellipse2D.Double` object. We just write it to the file.

We can read a circle back with the following code:

```
        private void readObject(ObjectInputStream in)
                        throws IOException, ClassNotFoundException
        {
          double width = in.readDouble();
          circle = new Ellipse2D.Double(0,0,width,width);
        }
```

This reconstitutes the circle using the diameter that was written to the file.

We can do curves next.

Serializing Curves

Curves are a little trickier. One complication is that we create a curve as a `GeneralPath` object, and we have no idea how many segments make up the curve. We can obtain a special iterator object of type `PathIterator` for a `GeneralPath` object that will make available to us all the information necessary to create the `GeneralPath` object. `PathIterator` is an interface that declares methods for retrieving details of the segments that make up a `GeneralPath` object, so a reference to an object of type `PathIterator` encapsulates all the data defining that path.

The `getPathIterator()` method in the `GeneralPath` class returns a reference of type `PathIterator`. The argument to `getPathIterator()` is an `AffineTransform` object that is applied to the path. This is based on the assumption that a single `GeneralPath` object may be used to create a number of different appearances on the screen. You might have a `GeneralPath` object that defines a complicated object, a boat say. You could draw several boats on the screen simply by applying a transform before you draw each boat to set its position and orientation and use the same `GeneralPath` object for all. This avoids the overhead of creating multiple instances of what are essentially identical objects. That's why the `getIterator()` method enables you to obtain an iterator for a particular transformed instance of a `GeneralPath` object. However, we want an iterator for the unmodified path to get the basic data that we need, so we pass a default `AffineTranform` object, which does nothing.

The `PathIterator` interface declares four methods:

Method	Description
`currentSegment( double[] coords)`	See below for description.
`currentSegment( float[] coords)`	
`getWindingRule()`	Returns a value of type int defining the winding rule. The value can be `WIND_EVEN_ODD` or `WIND_NON_ZERO`.
`next()`	Moves the iterator to the next segment as long as there is another segment.
`isDone()`	Returns `true` if the iteration is complete, and `false` otherwise.

```
currentSegment(double[] coords)
currentSegment(float[] coords)
```

The array argument, `coords`, that you pass to either version of the `currentSegment()` method is used to store data relating to the current segment, and should have six elements to record the coordinates of one, two, or three points, depending on the current segment type. The method returns an `int` value that indicates the type of the segment, and can be one of the following values:

Segment Type	Description
SEG_MOVETO	The segment corresponds to a `moveTo()` operation. The coordinates of the point moved to are returned as the first two elements of the array, `coords`.
SEG_LINETO	The segment corresponds to a `lineTo()` operation. The coordinates of the end point of the line are returned as the first two elements of the array, `coords`.
SEG_QUADTO	The segment corresponds to a `quadTo()` operation. The coordinates of the control point for the quadratic segment are returned as the first two elements of the array, `coords`, and the end point is returned as the third and fourth elements.
SEG_CUBICTO	The segment corresponds to a `curveTo()` operation. The array `coords` will contain coordinates of the first control point, the second control point, and the end point of the cubic curve segment.
SEG_CLOSE	The segment corresponds to a `closePath()` operation. The segment closes the path by connecting the current point to the first point in the path. No values are returned in the `coords` array.

We have all the tools we need to get the data on every segment in the path. We just need to get a `PathIterator` reference and use the `next()` method to go through it. Our case is simple: we only have a single `moveTo()` segment – always to (0, 0) – followed by one or more `lineTo()` segments. We will still test the return type though, to show how it's done, and in case there are errors. We're going to end up with an array of coordinates with an unpredictable number of elements: it sounds like a case for a `Vector`, particularly since `Vector` objects are serializable.

A `Vector` object only stores object references, not `float` values, so we'll have to convert our coordinate values to objects of type `Float` before storing them. The first segment is a special case. It is always a move to (0, 0), whereas all the others will be lines. Thus the procedure will be to get the first segment and discard it after verifying it is a move, and then get the remaining segments in a loop. Here's the code:

```
private void writeObject(ObjectOutputStream out)
                                           throws IOException
{
  PathIterator iterator = curve.getPathIterator(new AffineTransform());
  Vector coords = new Vector();          // Stores coordinate objects
```

```
    int maxCoordCount = 6;                          // Maximum coordinates for a segment
    float[] temp = new float[maxCoordCount];              // Stores segment data

    int result = iterator.currentSegment(temp);          // Get first segment
    if(!(result == iterator.SEG_MOVETO))                 // ... should be moveTo
      throw new IOException("No starting moveTo for curve");
    iterator.next();                                      // Next segment
    while(!iterator.isDone())                             // While we have segments
    {
      result = iterator.currentSegment(temp);     // Get the segment data
      if(!(result == iterator.SEG_LINETO))        // Should all be lines
        throw new IOException("Invalid segment type in curve");
      coords.add(new Float(temp[0]));             // Add x coordinate to Vector
      coords.add(new Float(temp[1]));             // Add y coordinate
      iterator.next();                            // Go to next segment
    }

    out.writeObject(coords);                  // Save the Vector
  }
```

All six elements are used when the segment is a cubic Bezier curve. In our case fewer are used but we must still supply an array with six elements as an argument to the currentSegment() method because that's what the method expects to receive. We use the Float class constructor to create Float objects to store in the Vector object, coords. We will need an import statement for java.util.Vector to make the class accessible in the Element.java source file.

It's worth considering how we might handle a GeneralPath object that consisted of a variety of different segments in arbitrary sequence. For the case where the path consisted of a set of line, quad, or cubic segments, you could get away with using a Vector object to store the coordinates for each segment, and then store these objects in another Vector. You could deduce the type of segment from the number of coordinates. In the general case you would need to define classes to represent the segments of various types, plus moves of course. If these had a common base class, then you could store all the objects for a path in a Vector as base class references. Of course, you would need to make sure your segment classes were serializable too.

To deserialize a curve, we just have to read the Vector object from the file, and recreate the GeneralPath object for the Element.Curve class:

```
    private void readObject(ObjectInputStream in)
                    throws IOException, ClassNotFoundException
    {
      Vector coords = (Vector)in.readObject();    // Read the coordinates Vector
      curve = new GeneralPath();                  // Create a path

      curve.moveTo(0,0);                          // Move to the origin

      float x, y;                                 // Stores coordinates
      for(int i = 0 ; i<coords.size() ; i += 2 )  // For each pair of elements
      {
        x = ((Float)coords.get(i)).floatValue();   // Get x value
        y = ((Float)coords.get(i+1)).floatValue(); // Get y value
```

```
            curve.lineTo(x,y);                        // Create a line segment
        }
    }
```

This should be very easy to follow now. We read the data we wrote to the stream – the Vector of Float objects. The first segment is always a move to the origin. All the succeeding segments are lines specified by pairs of elements from the Vector. The floatValue() method for the Float objects that are stored in the Vector object return the numerical coordinate values. We use these to create the line segments.

Serializing Text

Element.Text is the last element type we have to deal with. Fortunately, Font, String, and java.awt.Rectangle objects are all serializable already, which means that Element.Text is serializable by default and we have nothing further to do. We can now start implementing the listener operations for the File menu.

Supporting the File Menu

To support the menu items in the File menu, we must add some code to the actionPerformed() method in the FileAction class. We can try to put a skeleton together but a problem presents itself immediately: the source of an event will be either a toolbar button (a JButton object) or a menu item (a JMenuItem object) but all the while the actionPerformed() method is a member of the FileAction class – which is neither of these. We only have one definition of the actionPerformed() method shared amongst all FileAction class objects so we need a way to associate the event with a particular FileAction object. That way we can decide what we should do in response to the event.

Each FileAction object stores a String that was passed to the constructor as the name argument, and was then passed on to the base class constructor. If only we had thought of saving it, we could compare the name for the current object with the name for each of the FileAction objects in the SketchFrame class. Then we could tell which object the actionPerformed() method was called for. All is not lost though. We can call the getValue() method to retrieve the name, and then compare that with the name for each of the FileAction objects in the SketchFrame class. We can therefore implement the actionPerformed() member of the FileAction class like this:

```
    public void actionPerformed(ActionEvent e)
    {
        String name = (String)getValue(NAME);
        if(name.equals(saveAction.getValue(NAME)))
        {
            // Code to handle file Save operation...
        }
        else if(name.equals(saveAsAction.getValue(NAME)))
        {
            // Code to handle file Save As operation...
        }
        else if(name.equals(openAction.getValue(NAME)))
        {
```

```
      // Code to handle file Open operation...
    }
    else if(name.equals(newAction.getValue(NAME)))
    {
      // File to handle file New operation...
    }
    if(name.equals(printAction.getValue(NAME)))
    {
      // Code to handle Print operation..
    }
  }
```

Calling getValue() with the key, NAME, returns the String object that was stored for the FileAction object. If the name for the current object matches that of a particular FileAction object, then that must be the action to which the event applies, so we know what to do. We have one if or else-if block for each action, and we will code these one by one.

Many of these operations will involve dialogs. We need to get at the file system and display the list of directories and files to choose from, for an **Open** operation for instance. It sounds like a lot of work, and it certainly would be, if it weren't for a neat facility provided by the JFileChooser class.

Using a File Chooser

The JFileChooser class in the javax.swing package provides an easy to use mechanism for creating file dialogs for opening and saving files. You can use a single object of this class to create all the file dialogs you need, so add a member to the SketchFrame class to store a reference to a JFileChooser object that we will create in the constructor:

```
    private JFileChooser files;                        // File dialog
```

There are several JFileChooser constructors but we will discuss just a couple of them here. The default constructor creates an object with the current directory as the default directory but that won't quite do for our purposes. What we want is for the current directory to be the DEFAULT_DIRECTORY, which we defined in the Constants interface, so we'll use the constructor that accepts a File object specifying a default directory to create a JFileChooser object in the SketchFrame constructor. Add the following statement to the constructor following the statements that we added earlier that ensured DEFAULT_DIRECTORY actually existed on the hard drive:

```
    files = new JFileChooser(DEFAULT_DIRECTORY);
```

Any dialogs created by the files object will have DEFAULT_DIRECTORY as the default directory that is displayed. We can now use the files object to implement the event handling for the **File** menu. There are a considerable number of methods in the JFileChooser class, so rather than trying to summarize them all, which would take many pages of text and be incredibly boring, let's try out the ones that we can apply to Sketcher to support the **File** menu.

File Save Operations

In most cases we will want to display a modal **File Save** dialog when the **Save** menu item or toolbar button is selected. As luck would have it, the `JFileChooser` class has a method `showSaveDialog()` that does precisely what we want. All we have to do is pass it a reference to the `Component` object that will be the parent for the dialog to be displayed. The method returns a value indicating how the dialog was closed. We could display a save dialog in a `FileAction` method with the statement:

```
int result = files.showSaveDialog(SketchFrame.this);
```

This will automatically create a file-save dialog with the `SketchFrame` object as parent, and with a **Save** button and a **Cancel** button in the bargain. The `SketchFrame.this` notation is used to refer to the `this` pointer for the `SketchFrame` object from within a method of an inner class object of type `FileAction`. The file chooser dialog will be displayed centered in the parent component – our `SketchFrame` object here. If you specify the parent component as null, the dialog will be centered on the screen. This also applies to all the other methods we will discuss that display file chooser dialogs.

When you need a file open dialog, you can call the `showOpenDialog()` member of a `JFileChooser` object. Don't be fooled here though. A save dialog and an open dialog are essentially the same. They only differ in minor details – the title bar and one of the button labels. The sole purpose of both dialogs is simply to select a file – for whatever purpose. If you wanted to be perverse, you could pop a save dialog to open a file and vice versa!

You also have the possibility to display a customized dialog from a `JFileChooser` object. Although it's not strictly necessary for us here – we could make do with the standard file dialogs – we will adopt a custom approach, as it will give us some experience of using a few more `JFileChooser` methods.

You can display a dialog by calling the `showDialog()` method for the `JFileChooser` object: you supply two arguments. The first is the parent component for the dialog window, and the second is the approve button text – the approve button being the button that you click on to expedite the operation rather than cancel it. You could display a dialog with a **Save** button with the statement:

```
int result = files.showDialog(SketchFrame.this, "Save");
```

If you pass `null` as the second argument here, the button text will be whatever was set previously – possibly the default.

Before you display a custom dialog though, you would normally do a bit more customizing of what is to be displayed. We will be using the following `JFileChooser` methods to customize our dialogs:

Method	Description
`setDialogTitle()`	The `String` object passed as an argument is set as the dialog title bar text.
`setApproveButtonText()`	The `String` object passed as an argument is set as the approve button label.

Method	Description
setApproveButtonToolTipText()	The String object passed as an argument is set as the approve button tooltip.
setApproveButtonMnemonic()	The character passed as an argument is set as the approve button mnemonic defining a shortcut. The shortcut will appear as part of the tooltip.

A file chooser can be used to select files, directories, either, or both. You can determine which of these is allowed by calling the setFileSelectionMode() method. The argument must be one of the constants FILES_ONLY, DIRECTORIES_ONLY, and FILES_AND_DIRECTORIES that are defined in the JFileChooser class. You also have the getFileSelectionMode() method to enable you to determine what selection mode is set. To allow multiple selections to be made from the list in the file dialog, you call the setMultiSelectionEnabled() method for your JFileChooser object with the argument true.

If you want the dialog to have a particular file selected when it opens, you can pass a File object specifying that file to the setSelectedFile() method for the JFileChooser object. This will pre-select the file in the file list for the dialog if the file already exists, and insert the name in the file name field if it doesn't. The file list is created when the JFileChooser object is created but naturally files may be added or deleted over time and when this occurs you will need to reconstruct the file list. Calling the rescanCurrentDirectory() method before you display the dialog will do this for you. You can change the current directory at any time by passing a File object specifying the directory to the setCurrentDirectory() method.

That's enough detail for now. Let's put our customizing code together.

Try It Out – Creating a Customized File Dialog

We will first add a method to the SketchFrame class to create our customized file dialog and return the File object corresponding to the file selected, or null if a file was not selected:

```
    // Display a custom file save dialog
    private File showDialog (String dialogTitle,
                             String approveButtonText,
                             String approveButtonTooltip,
                             char approveButtonMnemonic,
                             File file)                  // Current file - if any
    {
      files.setDialogTitle(dialogTitle);
      files.setApproveButtonText(approveButtonText);
      files.setApproveButtonToolTipText(approveButtonTooltip);
      files.setApproveButtonMnemonic(approveButtonMnemonic);
      files.setFileSelectionMode(files.FILES_ONLY);
      files.rescanCurrentDirectory();
      files.setSelectedFile(file);
      int result = files.showDialog(SketchFrame.this, null);  // Show the dialog
      return (result == files.APPROVE_OPTION) ? files.getSelectedFile() : null;
    }
```

This method accepts five arguments that are used to customize the dialog – the dialog title, the button label, the button tooltip, the shortcut character for the button, and the `File` object representing the file for the current sketch. Each of the options is set using one of the methods for the `JFileChooser` object that we discussed earlier. The last argument is used to select a file in the file list initially. If it is `null`, no file will be selected from the file list.

Note that we reconstruct the file list for the dialog by calling the `rescanCurrentDirectory()` method. This is to ensure that we always display an up to date list of files. If we didn't do this, the dialog would always display the list of files that were there when we created the `JFileChooser` object. Any changes to the contents of the directory since then would not be taken account of.

The return value from the `showDialog()` member of the `JFileChooser` object, `files`, determines whether the approve button was selected or not. If it was, we return the `File` object from the file chooser that represents the selected file, otherwise we return `null`. A method calling our `showDialog()` method can determine whether or not a file was chosen by testing the return value for `null`.

We can now use this method when we implement handling of a **Save** menu item action event. A **Save** operation is a little more complicated than you might imagine at first sight, so let's consider it in a little more detail.

Implementing the Save Operation

First of all, what happens in a save operation should depend on whether the current file has been saved before. If it has, the user won't want to see a dialog every time. Once it has been saved the first time, the user will want it written away without displaying the dialog. We can use the `modelFile` member of the `SketchFrame` class to determine whether we need to display a dialog or not. We added this earlier to hold a reference to the `File` object for the sketch. Before a sketch has been saved this will be `null`, and if it is not `null` we don't want to show the dialog. When the sketch has been saved we will store a reference to the `File` object in `modelFile` so this will generally hold a reference to the file holding the last version of the sketch that was saved.

Secondly, if the sketch is unchanged – indicated by the `sketchChanged` member being `false`, either because it is new and therefore empty or because it hasn't been altered since it was last saved, we really don't need to save it at all.

We can package up these checks for when we need to save and when we display the dialog, in another method in the `SketchFrame` class. We'll call it `saveOperation()`, and make it a `private` member of the `SketchFrame` class:

```
// Save the sketch if it is necessary
private void saveOperation()
{
  if(!sketchChanged)
    return;
  if(modelFile != null)
    saveSketch(modelFile);
  else
  {
```

```
                File file = showDialog("Save Sketch",
                                       "Save",
                                       "Save the sketch",
                                       's',
                                       new File(files.getCurrentDirectory(), filename));
        if(file == null)
          return;
        else
          if(file.exists())                         // Check for existence
            if(JOptionPane.NO_OPTION ==             // Overwrite warning
               JOptionPane.showConfirmDialog(SketchFrame.this,
                                     file.getName() + " exists. Overwrite?",
                                     "Confirm Save As",
                                     JOptionPane.YES_NO_OPTION,
                                     JOptionPane.WARNING_MESSAGE))
              return;                                // No selected file
        saveSketch(file);
      }
    }
```

We first check the sketchChanged flag. If the flag is true, the sketch is either empty, or it hasn't been changed since the last save. Either way there's no point in writing it to disk, so we return immediately. If modelFile is not null, then we just call the saveSketch() method to write the file to modelFile – we will get to the detail of the saveSketch() method in a moment. If modelFile is null then this is the first time we are saving the current sketch: we must display a save dialog so the user can choose or enter the file name. We do this by calling our showDialog() method. Since modelFile is null, we have to create a File object corresponding to a file with the default name in filename, which is itself in the JFileChooser object's current directory.

If the value returned by our showDialog() method in the SketchFrame class is not null then the user has selected a file, so we check whether the selected file already exists on the disk. We need to do this to prevent existing files from being overwritten accidentally. If saving the file will overwrite a file that does exist, we display a confirmation dialog using a static method from our old friend the JOptionPane class. This just warns of the overwrite potential. If the response is positive, we save the sketch by passing the File object for the selected file to our helper method saveSketch().

Writing a Sketch to a File

Writing a sketch to a file just means making use of what we learned about writing objects to a file. We have already ensured that a SketchModel object is serializable, so we can write the sketch to an ObjectOutputStream with the following method in SketchFrame:

```
// Write a sketch to outFile
private void saveSketch(File outFile)
{
  try
  {
    ObjectOutputStream out =  new ObjectOutputStream(
                      new BufferedOutputStream(
                      new FileOutputStream(outFile)));
    out.writeObject(theApp.getModel());        // Write the sketch to the stream
    out.close();                               // Flush & close it
  }
```

```
      catch(IOException e)
      {
        System.err.println(e);
        JOptionPane.showMessageDialog(SketchFrame.this,
                              "Error writing a sketch file.",
                              "File Output Error",
                              JOptionPane.ERROR_MESSAGE);
        return;                                   // Serious error - return
      }
    if(outFile != modelFile)                      // If we are saving to a new
  file
      {                                           // we must update the window
        modelFile = outFile;                      // Save file reference
        filename = modelFile.getName();           // Update the file name
        setTitle(frameTitle + modelFile.getPath()); // Change the window title
      }
    sketchChanged = false;                        // Set as unchanged
  }
```

The saveSketch() method writes the current SketchModel object to the object output stream that we create from the File object that is passed to it. If an error occurs, an exception of type IOException will be thrown, in which case we write the exception to the standard error output stream, and pop a dialog indicating that an error has occurred. We assume the user might want to retry the operation so we just return rather than terminate the application.

If the write operation succeeds, then we need to consider whether the data members in the window object relating to the file need to be updated. This will be the case when the File object passed to the saveSketch() method is not the same as the reference in modelFile. If this is so, we update the modelFile and filename members of the window object, and set the window title to reflect the new file name and path. In any event, the sketchChanged flag is reset to false, as the sketch is now safely stored away in the file.

We can now put together the code to handle the **Save** menu item event.

Try It Out – Saving a Sketch

The code to handle the **Save** menu item event will go in the actionPerformed() method of the inner class, FileAction. We have done all the work, so it amounts to just one statement:

```
public void actionPerformed(ActionEvent e)
  {
    String name = (String)getValue(NAME);
    if(name.equals(saveAction.getValue(NAME)))
    {
      saveOperation();
    }
    // Plus the rest of the code for the method...
  }
```

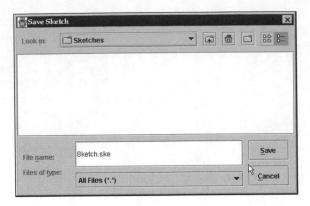

You can recompile Sketcher and run it again. The <u>S</u>ave menu item and toolbar button should now be working. When you select either of them, you should get the dialog displayed above. This version has the look-and-feel of Windows of course. If you are using a different operating system it won't be exactly the same.

Of course, there are no files in the directory, as we haven't saved anything yet. All the buttons in the dialog are fully operational. Go ahead and try them out, and then save the sketch using the default name. Next time you save the sketch the dialog won't appear. Be sure to check out the button tooltips. You should see the shortcut key combination as well as our tooltip text.

If you create a few sketch files, you should also get a warning if you intend to overwrite an existing sketch file with a new one.

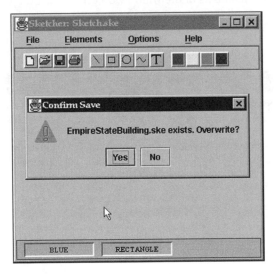

You can now save any sketch in a file – regardless of its complexity – with protection against accidentally overwriting existing files. I hope you agree that the save operation was remarkably easy to implement.

How It Works

This just calls our `saveOperation()` method in the `SketchFrame` object associated with the `FileAction` object containing the `actionPerformed()` method. This carries out the save as we have discussed.

Creating a File Filter

One customizing option we haven't used but you might like to try, is to supply a file filter for our sketch files. The default filter in a `JFileChooser` object accepts any file or directory but you can add filters of your own. A file filter for use with a `JFileChooser` object is represented by a class that has the `FileFilter` class as a base, and that implements two abstract methods declared in the `FileFilter` class:

Method	Description
`accept(File file)`	Returns `true` if the file represented by the object file is accepted by the file filter, and `false` otherwise.
`getDescription()`	Returns a `String` object describing the filter – for example, `"Sketch files"`.

The `FileFilter` class is defined in the `javax.swing.filechooser` package. Note that there is a `FileFilter` *interface* defined in the `java.io` package that declares just one method, `accept()` which is the same as the method in the `FileFilter` class. This interface is for use with the `listFiles()` method that is defined in the `File` class, not for `JFileChooser` objects, so make sure you don't confuse them. The filter object that you use with a file chooser must have the `FileFilter` *class* as a superclass, and your filter class must define the `getDescription()` method as well as the `accept()` method.

We can define our own file filter class for Sketcher as:

```
import javax.swing.filechooser.FileFilter;
import java.io.File;

public class ExtensionFilter extends FileFilter
{
  public ExtensionFilter(String ext, String descr)
  {
    extension = ext.toLowerCase();                // Store the extension as lower
case
    description = descr;                          // Store the description
  }

  public boolean accept(File file)
  {
    return (file.isDirectory() ||
file.getName().toLowerCase().endsWith(extension));
  }
```

```
      public String getDescription()
      {   return description;   }

      private String description;              // Filter description
      private String extension;                // File extension, including .
    }
```

To create a filter for files with the extension .ske we could write:

```
ExtensionFilter sketchFilter = new ExtensionFilter(".ske", "Sketch files
(*.ske)");
```

If you add the ExtensionFilter.java source file to the Sketcher program directory, we could try this out by adding a little code to the showSaveDialog() member of the SketchFrame class.

Try It Out – Using a File Filter

We only need to add three lines of code:

```
      private File showDialog(String dialogTitle,
                              String approveButtonText,
                              String approveButtonTooltip,
                              char approveButtonMnemonic,
                              File file)                    // Current file - if any
  {
    files.setDialogTitle(dialogTitle);
    files.setApproveButtonText(approveButtonText);
    files.setApproveButtonToolTipText(approveButtonTooltip);
    files.setApproveButtonMnemonic(approveButtonMnemonic);
    files.setFileSelectionMode(files.FILES_ONLY);
    files.rescanCurrentDirectory();
    files.setSelectedFile(file);

      ExtensionFilter sketchFilter = new ExtensionFilter(".ske",
                                        "Sketch files (*.ske)");
      files.addChoosableFileFilter(sketchFilter);            // Add the filter
      files.setFileFilter(sketchFilter);                     // and select it

      int result = files.showDialog(SketchFrame.this, null);  // Show the dialog
      return (result == files.APPROVE_OPTION) ? files.getSelectedFile() : null;
  }
```

Now when you display a file save dialog, it will use the sketcher file filter by default, and will only display directories or files with the extension .ske.

How It Works

The file filter, filter, that we create, is added to the list of available filters in the JFileChooser object by passing a reference to the addChoosableFileFilter() method. We then set this filter as the one in effect by calling the setFileFilter() method. The JFileChooser object will check each file in the file list by passing a File object to the accept() method for our file filter object. This will only return true for directories or files with the extension .ske. The description of the filter is obtained by the JFileChooser object calling the getDescription() method in the SketcherFileFilter class and displaying it in the dialog.

Of course, the available list of file filters will include the 'accept all' filter that is there by default. You might want to suppress this in some situations and there is a method defined in the `JFileChooser` class to do this:

```
files.setAcceptAllFileFilter(false);     // Remove 'all files' filter
```

Of course, passing an argument of `true` to this method will restore the filter to the list. You can also discover whether the all files filter is used by calling the `isAcceptAllFileFilterUsed()` method, which will return `true` if it is and `false` otherwise.

You can also remove specific `FileFilter` object from the list maintained by the `JFileChooser` object. Just pass a `FileFilter` reference to the `removeChoosableFileFilter()` method for your file chooser – for example:

```
files.removeChoosableFileFilter(sketchFilter);     // removes our filter
```

This would remove our filter we have defined for Sketcher files.

File Save As Operations

For Save As... operations, we will always display a save dialog, regardless of whether the file has been saved before. Apart from that and some cosmetic differences in the dialog itself, the operation is identical to the Save menu item event handling. With the `showDialog()` method available in the `SketchFrame` class, the implementation becomes almost trivial.

Try It Out – File Save-As Operations

The code in the `else-if` block in `actionPerformed()` for this operation will be:

```
else if(name.equals(saveAsAction.getValue(NAME)))
{
    File file = showDialog("Save Sketch As",
                           "Save",
                           "Save the sketch",
                           's',
                           modelFile == null ? new File(
                               files.getCurrentDirectory(), filename):modelFile);
    if(file != null)
    {
        if(file.exists() && !file.equals(modelFile))
          if(JOptionPane.NO_OPTION ==                    // Overwrite warning
             JOptionPane.showConfirmDialog(SketchFrame.this,
                           file.getName()+" exists. Overwrite?",
                           "Confirm Save As",
                           JOptionPane.YES_NO_OPTION,
                           JOptionPane.WARNING_MESSAGE))
             return;                                      // No file selected
        saveSketch(file);
    }
    return;
}
```

Recompile with these additions and you will have a working **Save As...** option on the <u>F</u>ile menu, with a file filter in action too!

How It Works

Most of this is under the **Save** menu operation. We have a fancy expression as the last argument to the `showDialog()` method. This is because the **Save As...** operation could be with a sketch that has been saved previously, or with a sketch that has never been saved. The expression passes `fileModel` as the argument if it is not `null`, and creates a new `File` object as the argument from the current directory and file name if it is. If we get a non-null `File` object back from the `showDialog()` method, then we check for a potential overwrite of an existing file. This will be the case if the selected file exists and is also different from `modelFile`. In this instance we display the dialog warning of this. If the dialog is closed by selecting the **No** button, we just return, otherwise we save the current sketch in the file.

Since we have sketches written to disk, let's now look at how we can implement the operation for the **Open** menu item so we can try reading them back.

File Open Operations

Supporting the **File/Open** operation is in some ways a little more complicated than **Save**. We have to consider the currently displayed sketch first of all. Opening a new sketch will replace it, so does it need to be saved before the file open operation? If it does, we must deal with that before we can read a new sketch from the file. Fortunately, most of this is already done by our `saveOperation()` method. We just need to add a prompt for the save operation when necessary. We could put this in a `checkForSave()` method that we can implement in the `SketchFrame` class as:

```
// Prompt for save operation when necessary
public void checkForSave()
{
  if(sketchChanged)
    if(JOptionPane.YES_OPTION ==
          JOptionPane.showConfirmDialog(SketchFrame.this,
                          "Current file has changed. Save current file?",
                          "Confirm Save Current File",
                          JOptionPane.YES_NO_OPTION,
                          JOptionPane.WARNING_MESSAGE))
      saveOperation();
}
```

This will be useful outside the `SketchFrame` class a little later on, so we have declared it as a public class member. If the `sketchChanged` flag is `true`, we pop a confirm dialog to verify that the sketch needs to be saved. If it does, we call the `saveOperation()` method to do just that.

When we get to the point of reading a sketch from the file, some further slight complications arise. We must replace the existing `SketchModel` object and its view in the application with a new `SketchModel` object and its view.

With those few thoughts, I think we are ready to make it happen.

Try It Out – Implementing the Open Menu Item Operation

The file open process will be similar to a save operation but instead of writing the file, it will read it. We'll add a helper method `openSketch()` to `SketchFrame` that, given a `File` object, will do the reading. Using this method, the code to handle the **Open** menu item event will be:

```
else if(name.equals(openAction.getValue(NAME)))
{
  checkForSave();

  // Now open a sketch file
  File file = showDialog("Open Sketch File",         // Dialog window title
                         "Open",                      // button lable
                         "Read a sketch from file",   // Button tooltip text
                         'o',                          // Shortcut character
                         null);                        // No file selected
  if(file != null)                                    // If a file was
selected
     openSketch(file);                                // then read it
}
```

We can implement the `openSketch()` method in the `SketchFrame` class as:

```
// Method for opening file
public void openSketch(File inFile)
{
  try
  {
    ObjectInputStream in = new ObjectInputStream(new BufferedInputStream(
                                  new FileInputStream(inFile)));
    theApp.insertModel((SketchModel)in.readObject());
    in.close();
    modelFile = inFile;
    filename = modelFile.getName();               // Update the file name
    setTitle(frameTitle+modelFile.getPath());     // Change the window title
    sketchChanged = false;                        // Status is unchanged
  }
  catch(Exception e)
  {
    System.out.println(e);
    JOptionPane.showMessageDialog(SketchFrame.this,
                              "Error reading a sketch file.",
                                "File Input Error",
                                JOptionPane.ERROR_MESSAGE);
  }
}
```

The `SketchModel` object that is read from the file is passed to a new method in the `Sketcher` class, `insertModel()`. This method has to replace the current sketch with the new one that is passed as the argument. We can implement the method like this:

```
    public void insertModel(SketchModel newSketch)
    {
      sketch = newSketch;                         // Store the new sketch
      sketch.addObserver((Observer)view);         // Add the view as observer
      sketch.addObserver((Observer)window);       // Add the app window as
  observer
      view.repaint();                             // Repaint the view
    }
```

After we have loaded the new model, we update the window title bar and record the status as unchanged in the SketchFrame object. If you compile Sketcher once more, you can give the file open operation a workout.

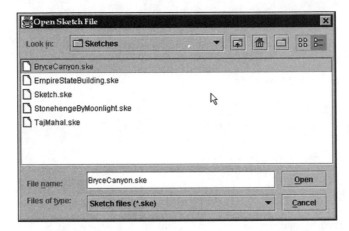

Don't forget to try out the tooltip for the Open button. You should see the shortcut key combination, *Alt+O*, appended to the tooltip text.

How It Works

After dealing with saving the current sketch in the actionPerformed() member of the FileAction class, we use our showDialog() method that we defined in the SketchFrame class to display a file open dialog. Our showDialog() method is all-purpose – we can put any kind of label on the button or title in the dialog title bar so we can use it to display any of the dialog we need for file operations.

If a File object was selected in the dialog, we pass this to the openSketch() member of SketchFrame to read a new sketch from the file. The openSketch() method creates an ObjectInputStream object from the File object passed as an argument, and reads a SketchModel object from the stream by calling the readObject() method. The object returned by the readObject() method has to be cast to the appropriate type – SketchModel in our case. We pass this SketchModel object to the insertModel() method for the application object. This replaces the current sketch reference in the sketch member of the application object with a reference to the new sketch, and then sets the view and the application window as observers. Calling repaint() for the view object displays the new sketch since the paint() method for the view object obtains a reference to the current model by calling the getModel() member of the application object, which will return the reference to the new model.

Starting a New Sketch

The File/New menu item simply starts a new sketch. This is quite similar to the **Open** operation except that we must create an empty sketch rather than read a new one from disk. The process of checking for the need to save the current sketch, and inserting the new `SketchModel` object into the application will be the same.

So let's do it.

Try It Out – Implementing the New Operation

We need to place the code to do this in the `else-if` block corresponding to the `newAction` object event:

```
else if(name.equals(newAction.getValue(NAME)))
{
  checkForSave();
  theApp.insertModel(new SketchModel());          // Insert new empty sketch
  modelFile = null;                               // No file for it
  filename = DEFAULT_FILENAME;                     // Default name
  setTitle(frameTitle + files.getCurrentDirectory() + "\\" + filename);
  sketchChanged = false;                          // Not changed yet
}
```

Now you can create a new sketch.

How It Works

All the saving of the existing sketch is dealt with by our `checkForSave()` method. The new part is the last five lines of code. We call the `SketchModel` constructor to create a new empty sketch, and pass it to the `insertModel()` method for the application object. This will insert the new sketch into the application and get the view object to display it. We then update the data members of the window that record information about the file for the current sketch and its status. We also set the `sketchChanged` flag to `false` as it's an empty sketch.

Preventing Data Loss on Close

At the moment we're still not calling `checkForSave()` when we close the application with the window icon. This means we could lose hours of work in an instant. But it's very simple. We just need to get the event handler for the window closing event to call the `checkForSave()` method for the window object.

Try It Out – Prompting for Save on Close

To implement this we can use the `WindowListener` for the application window that we have already added in the `init()` method in the `Sketcher` class. This listener receives notification of events associated with opening and closing the window as well as minimizing, maximizing and iconifying it. We just need to add some code to the body of the `windowClosing()` method for the listener. We require two extra lines in the `Sketcher` class definition:

```
public void init()
{
    window = new SketchFrame("Sketcher", this);       // Create the app window
    Toolkit theKit = window.getToolkit();             // Get the window toolkit
    Dimension wndSize = theKit.getScreenSize();  // Get screen size

    // Set the position to screen center & size to 2/3 screen size
    window.setBounds(wndSize.width/6, wndSize.height/6,        // Position
                    2*wndSize.width/3, 2*wndSize.height/3);    // Size

    window.addWindowListener(new WindowAdapter()       // Add window listener
            {
                // Handler for window closing event
                public void windowClosing(WindowEvent e)
                {      window.checkForSave();       }
            } );

    // Rest of the code as before...
}
```

The anonymous class is a subclass of the WindowAdapter class, as we discussed in Chapter 13. In the subclass you just define the methods you are interested in to override the empty versions in the adapter class. The WindowListener interface declares the following seven methods corresponding to various window events:

windowActivated(WindowEvent e)	Called when the window receives the focus and becomes the currently active window.
windowDeactivated(WindowEvent e)	Called when the window ceases to be the currently active window.
windowIconified(WindowEvent e)	Called when the window is minimized.
windowDeiconified(WindowEvent e)	Called when the window returns to its normal state from a minimized state.
windowOpened(WindowEvent e)	Called the first time a window is made visible.
windowClosed(WindowEvent e)	Called when a window has been closed by calling its dispose() method.
windowClosing(WindowEvent e)	Called when the user selects the close icon or the Close item from the system menu for the window.

Clearly using the WindowAdapter class as a base saves a lot of time and effort. Without it we would have to define all seven of the methods declared in the interface in our class. Because our anonymous class is an inner class its methods can access the fields of the Sketcher class so the windowClosing() method we have defined can call our checkForSave() method for the window member of the Sketcher class object.

Now if you close the application window without having saved your sketch, you will be prompted to save it.

How It Works

This makes use of the code that we implemented for the Save operation, packaged in the `checkForSave()` method. This does everything necessary to enable the sketch to be saved before the application window is closed. Defining methods judiciously makes for economical coding.

This still leaves us with the now redundant File/Close button to tidy up. As it's not really any different from the File/New function, let's change it to an application Exit button and reposition it at the bottom of the File menu. First we'll insert a couple of statements in the `else-if` block corresponding to the `closeAction` object event in `SketchFrame`:

```
else if(name.equals(closeAction.getValue(NAME)))
{
  checkForSave();
  System.exit(0);
}
```

and then redo the menu layout in the File menu constructor and add the mnemonic key `Ctrl-X` for Exit:

```
fileMenu.addSeparator();                                    // Add separator
addMenuItem(fileMenu, printAction = new FileAction("Print", "Print Sketch"),
                      KeyStroke.getKeyStroke('P',Event.CTRL_MASK ));

fileMenu.addSeparator();                                    // Add separator
addMenuItem(fileMenu, closeAction = new FileAction("Exit", "Exit Sketcher"),
                      KeyStroke.getKeyStroke('X',Event.CTRL_MASK ));

// We will add the types menu items here using actions...
```

All but one of our File actions are now operable. To complete the set we just need to get Print up and running.

Printing in Java

Printing is always a messy business – inevitably so, because you have to worry about tedious details such as the size of a page, the margin sizes and how many pages you're going to need for your output. The way through this is to take it one step at a time. Let's understand the general principles first.

All the classes and interfaces supporting the printing operations that we will use are defined in the `java.awt.print` package so you will need to add an `import` for this when you are using these classes in your code. The classes in the package that we will be using are:

`PrinterJob`	`PageFormat`
`Book`	`Paper`

There are also `PageAttributes` and `JobAttributes` classes within the package and they together with their inner classes define the characteristics of a page and a printing job respectively, but they don't work with the new printing mechanism introduced with Java 2 yet so we won't discuss them further. Currently they can only be applied with the old printing mechanism that uses the `PrintJob` class in the `java.awt` package. The `PageAttributes` and `JobAttributes` classes will be supported within the new printing mechanism eventually, so keep a look out for them in any new releases.

The `PrinterJob` class in the `java.awt.print` package drives the printing process. Don't confuse this with the `PrintJob` class in the `java.awt` package – this is now superseded by the `PrinterJob` class. A `PrinterJob` class object provides the interface to the printing system in your environment, and you use `PrinterJob` class methods to set up and initiate the printing process. You start printing off one or more pages by calling the `print()` method for the `PrinterJob` object.

A `PageFormat` object encapsulates information about its page, such as its dimensions, margin sizes and orientation. An object of type `Paper` describes the characterisics of a physical sheet of paper that will be part of a `PageFormat` object. A `Book` is a document consisting of a collection of pages that are typically processed in an individual way. We will be getting into the detail of how you work with these a little later in this chapter

There are three interfaces in the package:

When you print a page, what is actually printed is determined by an object of a class that you define so that it implements the `Printable` interface. Such an object is referred to as a **page painter**.

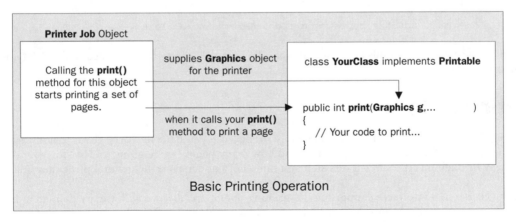

Basic Printing Operation

The `Printable` interface only defines one method, `print()`, that is called by a `PrinterJob` object when a page should be printed. Thus the `print()` method does the printing of a page. Note that we have mentioned two `print()` methods, one defined in the `PrinterJob` class, and another declared in the `Printable` interface that you implement in your class that is to do the printing legwork.

The printing operation itself that you must code works through a graphics context object that provides the means for writing to your printer. The first argument that is passed to the print() method when it is called by a PrinterJob object is a reference of type Graphics that represents the graphics context for the printer. The object that it references is actually of type Graphics2D. This parallels the process you are already familiar with for drawing to a component that is displayed on the screen by implementing the paint() method. Just as with writing to the display, you use the methods that are defined in the Graphics and Graphics2D classes to print what you want, and the basic mechanism for printing on a page is identical to drawing on a component. The Graphics object for a printer also happens to implement the PrinterGraphics interface (not to be confused with the PrintGraphics interface in the java.awt package!) that declares just one method, getPrinterJob(). You call this to obtain a reference to the object that is managing the print process. You would do this if you need to call PrinterJob methods to extract information about the print job, such as the job name or the user name.

A class that implements the Pageable interface defines an object that represents a set of pages to be printed. This is used for more complicated printing situations where each page may be printed by a different page painter using an individual PageFormat object. It's the job of the Pageable object to supply information to the PrinterJob object about which page painter and PageFormat object should be used to print each page. The interface declares three methods: getNumberOfPages(), getPageFormat(), and getPrintable(), these return the values indicated by their names.

A Book object also encapsulates a document that consists of a number of pages, each of which may be processed individually for printing. The difference between this and an object of a class that implements Pageable is that you can add individual pages to a Book object programmatically, whereas a class implementing Pageable encapsulates the pages. We will look at how both of these options work later in this chapter.

Creating and Using PrinterJob Objects

Because the PrinterJob class encapsulates your specific physical printing system, you can't create an object of type PrinterJob directly. One will already exist if you have printing capability on your system, so you just call a static method, getPrinterJob(), that is defined in the PrinterJob class to obtain a reference to it:

```
PrinterJob printJob = PrinterJob.getPrinterJob();    // Get a printing object
```

The object, printJob, provides the interface to the printing system, and controls each print job. When you want to provide the user with control over the printing process, you can display a print dialog by calling the printDialog() method. This displays the modal dialog that applies to your particular print facility. If the dialog is closed using the button that indicates printing should proceed, the printDialog() method will return true. Then you should initiate printing by calling the print() method for the PrinterJob object. This method will throw an exception of type PrinterException if an error in the print system causes printing to be aborted.

Of course, the `PrinterJob` object can have no prior knowledge of what you want to print so you have to call a method to tell the `PrinterJob` object where the printed pages are coming from. The simplest way to do this is to call the `setPrintable()` method, and pass a reference to a class that implements the `Printable` interface as the argument. In Sketcher, the obvious candidate to print a sketch is the `SketchView` object (a reference to which is stored in the `view` member of the application object) so to allow sketches to be printed, we could make the `SketchView` class implement the `Printable` interface. That done, we could then set the source of the printed output just by passing a reference to the view to the `setPrintable()` method for a `PrinterJob` object. You might consider the `SketchModel` object to be a candidate to do the printing, but printing is not really related to a sketch, any more than plotting or displaying on the screen is. The model is the input to the printing process, not the owner of it. It is generally better to keep the model dedicated to encapsulating the data that represents the sketch.

Starting the Printing Process

We could use what we now know about printing to add some code to the `actionPerformed()` method in the `FileAction` class. This will handle the event for the `printAction` object in the `SketchFrame` class:

```
if(name.equals(printAction.getValue(NAME)))
{
    PrinterJob printJob = PrinterJob.getPrinterJob(); // Get a printing object
    printJob.setPrintable(theApp.getView());        // The view is the page
source

    if(printJob.printDialog())                      // Display print dialog
    {                                               // If true is
returned...
        try
        {
            printJob.print();                       // then print
        }
        catch(PrinterException pe)
        {
            System.out.println(pe);
            JOptionPane.showMessageDialog(SketchFrame.this,
                              "Error printing a sketch.",
                                  "Printer Error",
                                  JOptionPane.ERROR_MESSAGE);

        }
    }
}
```

The code here obtains a `PrinterJob` object, and sets the view as the printable source. The `if` expression will display a print dialog, and if the return value from the `printDialog()` method call is true, we call the `print()` method for the `printJob` object to start the printing process. You will need to add an `import` statement for the `java.awt.print` package to the `SketchFrame.java` file to make the `PrinterJob` class accessible. The `SketchFrame` class won't compile at the moment, as we haven't made the `SketchView` class implement the `Printable` interface yet.

Printing Pages

The class object that you pass to the setPrintable() method is responsible for all the detail of the printing process. This class must implement the Printable interface, which implies defining the print() method in the same class. We can make the SketchView class implement the Printable interface like this:

```
import javax.swing.*;
import java.awt.*;
import java.util.*;               // For Observer
import java.awt.event.*;          // For events
import javax.swing.event.*;       // For mouse input adapter
import java.awt.geom.*;
import java.awt.print.*;

class SketchView extends      JComponent
                  implements Observer,
                             Constants,
                             ActionListener,
                             Printable
{
  public int print(Graphics g,               // Graphics context for
printing

                   PageFormat pageFormat,     // The page format
                   int pageIndex)             // Index number of current page
                   throws PrinterException
  {
    // Code to do the printing
  }

    // Rest of the class definition as before...
}
```

The PrinterJob object will call the print() method here for each page to be printed. This process starts when you call the print() method for the PrinterJob object that has overall control of the printing process. You can see that our print() method can throw an exception of type PrinterException. If you identify a problem within your print() method code, the way to signal the problem to the PrinterJob object is to throw an exception of this type.

One point to keep in mind – you should not assume that the PrinterJob object will call the print() method for your Printable object just once per page. In general the print() method is likely to be called several times for each page as the output destined for the printer is buffered within the Java printing system and the buffer will not necessarily be large enough to hold a complete page. You don't need to worry about this unduly. Just don't build any assumptions into your code about how often print() is called for a given page.

Of course, our `PrinterJob` object in the `actionPerformed()` method code has no way of knowing how many pages need to be printed. When we call the `PrinterJob` object's `print()` method, it will continue calling the `SketchView` object's `print()` method until the value returned indicates there are no more pages to be printed. You can return one of two values from the `print()` method in the `Printable` interface – PAGE_EXISTS to indicate you have rendered a page, or NO_SUCH_PAGE if there are no more pages to be printed. Both of these constants are defined in the `Printable` interface. The `PrinterJob` object will continue calling `print()` until the NO_SUCH_PAGE value is returned.

You can see that there are three arguments passed to the `print()` method in the `Printable` interface. The first is the graphics context that you must use to write to the printer. The reference passed to the method is actually of type `Graphics2D`, so you will typically cast it to this type before using it – just as we did within the `paint()` method for a component to draw on the screen. In the `print()` method in our view class, we could draw the sketch on the printer with the statements:

```
public int print(Graphics g,            // Graphics context for printing
                 PageFormat pageFormat,  // The page format
                 int pageIndex)          // Index number of current page
                 throws PrinterException
{
    Graphics2D g2D = (Graphics2D) g;
    paint(g2D);
    return PAGE_EXISTS;
}
```

This will work after a fashion, but we have more work to do before we can try this out. At the moment, it will print the same page over and over, indefinitely, so let's take care of that as a matter of urgency!

It's the third argument that carries an index value for the page. The first page in a print job will have index value 0, the second will have index value 1, and so on for as long as there are more pages to be printed. If we intend to print our sketch on a single page, we can stop the printing process by checking the page index:

```
public int print(Graphics g,            // Graphics context for printing
                 PageFormat pageFormat,  // The page format
                 int pageIndex)          // Index number of current page
                 throws PrinterException
{
    if(pageIndex>0)
      return NO_SUCH_PAGE;
    Graphics2D g2D = (Graphics2D) g;
    paint(g2D);                          // Draw the sketch
    return PAGE_EXISTS;
}
```

We only want to print one page, so if the value passed as the third parameter is greater than 0, we return NO_SUCH_PAGE to stop the printing process.

While at least we won't now print endlessly, we still won't get an output formatted the way we want it. We must look into how we can use the information provided by the second argument that is passed to the `print()` method, the `PageFormat` object, to position the output properly.

The PageFormat Class

The `PageFormat` reference that is passed to the `print()` method for a page provides details of the page size, the position and size of the printable area on the page, and the orientation – portrait or landscape.

Perhaps the most important pieces of information you can get are where the top left corner of the **printable area** (or **imageable area** to use the terminology of the method names) is on the page, and its width and height, since this is the area you have available for printing your output. The printable area on a page is simply the area within the current margins defined for your printer. The position of the printable area is returned by the methods `getImageableX()` and `getImageableY()`. These return the *x* and *y* coordinates of the upper left corner of the printable area in user coordinates of type `double` for the printing context, which happen to be in units of 1/72 of an inch which corresponds to a point – as in point size for a font. The width and height of the printable area are returned in the same units by the `getImageableWidth()` and `getImageableHeight()` methods.

The origin of the page coordinate system, the point (0,0), corresponds initially to the top left corner of the paper. If you want the output to be placed in the printable area on the page, the first step will be to move the origin of the graphics context that you will use for writing to the printer to the position of the top left corner of the printable area.

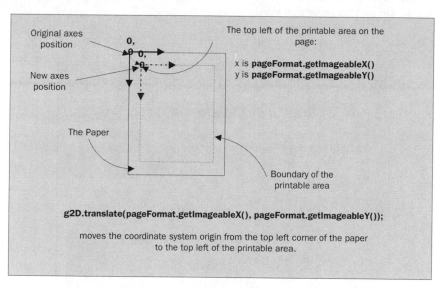

We know how to do this – its exactly what we have been doing in the `draw()` method for each of our element classes. We call the `translate()` method for the graphics context. Here's how this would work for the `print()` method in the `SketchView` class:

```
    public int print(Graphics g,                    // Graphics context for
printing
                     PageFormat pageFormat,          // The page format
                     int pageIndex)                  // Index number of current page
                     throws PrinterException
    {
```

```
    if(pageIndex>0)
       return NO_SUCH_PAGE;
    Graphics2D g2D = (Graphics2D) g;

    // Move origin to page printing area corner
    g2D.translate(pageFormat.getImageableX(), pageFormat.getImageableY());

    paint(g2D);                                    // Draw the sketch
    return PAGE_EXISTS;
  }
```

The `translate()` method call moves the user coordinate system so that the (0, 0) point is positioned at the top left corner on the printable area on the page.

Let's see if that works in practice.

Try It Out – Printing a Sketch

You should have added the code we saw earlier to the `actionPerformed()` method to handle the Print menu item event, and the code to `SketchView` to implement the `Printable` interface that we have evolved. Don't forget the import statement for `java.awt.print`. If you compile and run Sketcher, you should be able to print a sketch.

On my system, when I select the toolbar button to print, I get the dialog shown below.

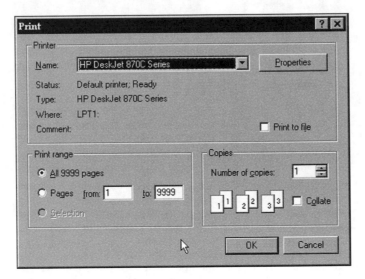

This is the standard dialog for my printer under Windows. In your environment you will get a dialog for your printer. The reason the dialog indicates that there are 9999 pages to be printed is that we haven't said how many, so the maximum is being assumed.

How It Works

The code in the `actionPerformed()` method displays the print dialog by calling the `printDialog()` method for the `PrinterJob` object that we obtain. Clicking on the **OK** button causes the `print()` method for the `PrinterJob` object to be called. This in turn causes the `print()` method in the `SketchView` class to be called once for each page to be printed, and one more time to end the process.

In the `print()` method in `SketchView`, we adjust the origin of the user coordinate system for the graphics context so that its position is at the top left corner of the printable area on the page. Only one page is printed because we return `NO_SUCH_PAGE` when the page index value that is passed to the `print()` method is greater than 0. Incidentally, if you want to see how many times the `print()` method gets called for a page, just add a statement at the beginning of the method to output some trace information to the console.

I used the print facility to print the sketch shown here, and frankly, I was disappointed.

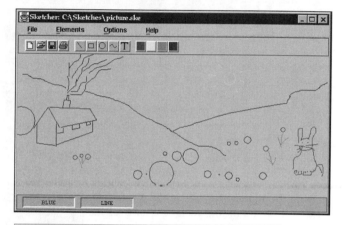

The picture that I get printed on the paper is shown here. There's only one flower in view, and that exceptionally interesting cross between a rabbit and a cat is completely missing.

The boulder on the left only appears in part. I know it's not all on the screen, but it's all in the model, so I was hoping to see the picture in its full glory. If you think about it, it's very optimistic to believe that we could automatically get the whole sketch printed. First of all, neither the `PrinterJob` object or the view object have any idea how big the sketch is. That's a fairly fundamental piece of data if you want a complete sketch printed. Another consideration is that the left extremity of the boulder on the left of the sketch is to the left of the *y* axis, but I'd rather like to see it in the picture. It would be nice if we could take account of that too. Let's see how we might do it.

Printing the Whole Sketch

A starting point is to figure out the extent of the sketch. Ideally we need a rectangle that encloses all the elements in the sketch. It's really surprisingly easy to get that. Every element has a getBounds() method that returns a Rectangle object enclosing the element. As we saw in Chapter 14, the Rectangle class also defines a member add() method. It combines a Rectangle object passed as an argument with the Rectangle object for which it is called, and returns the smallest Rectangle object that will enclose both: this is referred to as the **union** of the two rectangles. With these two bits of information and an iterator from the SketchModel object, we can get the rectangle enclosing the entire sketch by implementing the following method in the SketchView class:

```
// Get the rectangle enclosing an entire sketch
Rectangle getModelExtent()
{
  Iterator elements = theApp.getModel().getIterator();
  Rectangle rect = new Rectangle();            // An empty rectangle
  Element element;                             // Stores an element
  while(elements.hasNext())                    // Go through the list
  {
    element = (Element)elements.next();        // Get the next element
    rect.add(element.getBounds());             // Expand union
  }
  if(rect.width == 0)                          // Make sure width
    rect.width = 1;                            // is non-zero
  if(rect.height == 0)                         // and the height
    rect. height = 1;
  return rect;
}
```

Using the iterator for the model, we expand the bounding rectangle for every element so we end up with a rectangle that bounds everything in the sketch. A zero width or height for the rectangle is unlikely, but we want to be sure it can't happen because we will use these values as divisors later.

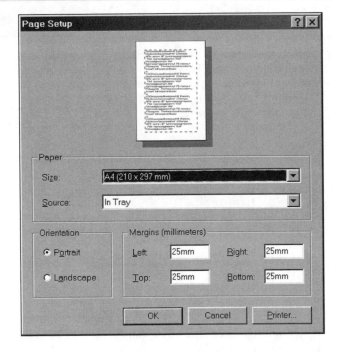

You can see from the illustration how the rectangle returned by the getModelExtent() method is simply the rectangle that encloses all the bounding rectangles for the individual elements. If you visualize the origin of the user coordinate system being placed at the top left corner of the printable area on the page, you can appreciate that a section of the sketch in the illustration will be hanging out to the left outside the printable area. This can arise quite easily in Sketcher, when you are drawing a circle with the center close to either of the axes for instance, or if you move a shape so this is the case. We can avoid missing part of the sketch from the printed output by first translating the origin of the coordinate system to the top left corner of rect, and then translating the origin at this position to the top left corner of the printable area on the page.

The following code in the print() method will do this:

```
    public int print(Graphics g,                  // Graphics context for
printing
                  PageFormat pageFormat,           // The page format
                  int pageIndex)                   // Index number of current page
                  throws PrinterException
  {
    if(pageIndex>0)
      return NO_SUCH_PAGE;
    Graphics2D g2D = (Graphics2D) g;
    Rectangle rect = getModelExtent();             // Get sketch bounds

    // Move origin to page printing area corner
    g2D.translate(pageFormat.getImageableX(), pageFormat.getImageableY());
    g2D.translate(-rect.x, -rect.y);               // Move origin to rect top left

    paint(g2D);                                    // Draw the sketch
    return PAGE_EXISTS;
  }
```

We get the rectangle bounding the sketch by calling the getModelExtent() method that we put together just now. We then use rect in the second statement that calls translate() for the Graphics2D object to position the top left corner of rect at the origin. We could have combined these two translations into one, but we will keep them separate, first to make it easier to see what is going on, and second because we will be adding some other transformations later in between these translations. There is a potentially puzzling aspect to the second translation – why are the arguments to the translate() method negative?

To understand this, it is important to be clear about what we are doing. It's easy to get confused by this so we'll take it step by step. First of all, remember that the paper is a physical entity with given dimensions and its coordinate system just defines where each point will end up on the paper when you print something. Of course, we can move the coordinate system about in relation to the paper, and we can scale or even rotate it to get something printed where we want.

Now consider our sketch. The point (rect.x, rect.y) is the top left corner of the rectangle bounding our sketch, the area we want to transfer to the page, and this point is fixed – we can't change it to make it the origin for instance. With the current paper coordinates at the top left of the printable area, it might print somewthing like that shown overleaf.

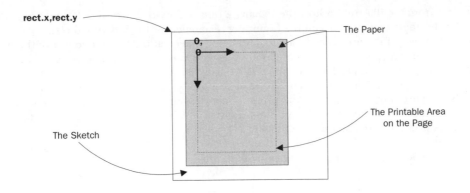

Initial Position of Paper Coordinates

When we print our sketch we really want the point (rect.x, rect.y) to end up at the top left corner of the printable area on the page. In other words, we have to move the origin of the coordinate system for the paper so that the point (rect.x, rect.y) in the new coordinate system is the top left corner of the printable area. To do this we must move the origin to the new position shown.

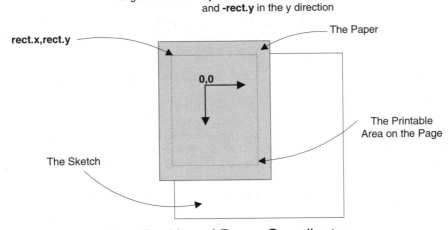

New Position of Paper Coordinates

Thus a translation of the origin to the point (-rect.x, -rect.y) does the trick.

We have the sketch in the right place on the page, but it won't necessarily fit into the space available on the paper. We must scale the sketch so that it doesn't hang out beyond the right side or below the bottom of the printable page area.

Scaling the Sketch to Fit

We saw earlier that we can get the width and height of the printable area on a page area by calling the `getImageableWidth()` and `getImageableHeight()` methods for the `PageFormat` object that is passed to the `print()` method. We also have the width and height of the rectangle that encloses the entire sketch. This gives the information that we need to scale the sketch to fit on the page. There are a couple of tricky aspects that we need to think about though.

Firstly, note that when you scale a coordinate system, a unit of length along each of the axes changes in size, so things move relative to the origin as well as relative to one another. When you scale up with a factor greater than 1, everything moves away from the origin. The reverse happens with scale factors less than 1. We want to make sure that we scale the sketch to fit the page while keeping its top left corner at the top left of the printable area. This means that we can't just apply the scaling factor necessary to make the sketch fit the page in the new coordinate system we showed in the previous illustration. If we were to scale with this coordinate system, the sketch will move in relation to the origin, away from it if we are scaling up, or towards it if we are scaling down, as is the case in the illustration. As a consequence, the top left corner of the sketch would no longer be at the top left of the printable area. Thus we must apply the scaling operation to make the sketch fit on the page *after* we have translated the paper origin to the top left corner of the printable area, but *before* we translate this origin point to make the top left corner of the sketch appear at the top left corner of the printable area. This will ensure that the sketch is scaled to fit the page and the top left of the sketch will stay at the top left corner of the printable area on the page and not move to some other point.

Secondly, we want to make sure that we scale *x* and *y* by the same factor. If we apply different scales to the *x* and *y* axes in the user coordinate system, the relative proportions of a sketch will not be maintained and our circles will become ellipses.

We can calculate the scale factors we need to apply to get the sketch to fit within the printable area of the page with the following statements:

```
// Calculate the x and y scales to fit the sketch to the page
double scaleX = pageFormat.getImageableWidth()/rect.width;
double scaleY = pageFormat.getImageableHeight()/rect.height;
```

We are using variables of type `double` for the scale factors here because the `getImageableWidth()` and `getImageableHeight()` methods return values of type `double`. The scale factor for the *x* axis needs to be such that when we multiply the width of the sketch, `rect.width`, by the scale factor, the result is the width of the printable area on the page returned by `getImageableWidth()`, and similarly for scaling the *y* axis. Since we want to apply the same scale to both axes, we should calculate the minimum of the scale factors `scaleX` and `scaleY`. If we then apply this minimum to both axes, the sketch will fit within the width and height of the page and still be in proportion.

Let's try that out.

Try It Out – Printing the Whole Sketch

We just need to add some code to the `print()` method in `SketchView` to calculate the required scale factor, and then use the `scale()` method for the `Graphics2D` object to apply the scaling transformation:

```
public int print(Graphics g,              // Graphics context for printing
                 PageFormat pageFormat,   // The page format
                 int pageIndex)           // Index number of current page
                 throws PrinterException
{
  if(pageIndex>0)
    return NO_SUCH_PAGE;
  Graphics2D g2D = (Graphics2D) g;
  Rectangle rect = getModelExtent();       // Get sketch bounds

  // Calculate the scale to fit sketch to page
  double scaleX = pageFormat.getImageableWidth()/rect.width;
  double scaleY = pageFormat.getImageableHeight()/rect.height;
  double scale = Math.min(scaleX, scaleY);         // Get minimum scale factor

  // Move origin to page printing area corner
  g2D.translate(pageFormat.getImageableX(), pageFormat.getImageableY());

  g2D.scale(scale, scale);                 // Apply scale factor

  g2D.translate(-rect.x, -rect.y);         // Move origin to rect top left

  paint(g2D);                              // Draw the sketch
  return PAGE_EXISTS;
}
```

If you compile and run Sketcher with these changes, you should now be able to print each sketch within a page.

How It Works

We calculate the scaling factors for each axis as the ratio of the dimension of the printable area on the page to the corresponding dimension of the rectangle enclosing the sketch. We then take the minimum of these two scale factors as the scale to be applied to both axes. As long as the scale transformation is applied after the translation of the coordinate system to the top left corner of the printable page area, one or other dimension of the sketch will fit exactly within the printable area of the page.

The output is now fine, but if the width of the sketch is greater than the height, we waste a lot of space on the page. Ideally in this situation we would want to print with a landscape orientation rather than the default portrait orientation. Let's see what possibilities we have for that.

Printing in Landscape Orientation

We can easily determine when a landscape orientation would be preferable by comparing the width of a sketch with its height. If the width is larger than the height, a landscape orientation will make better use of the space on the paper and we will get a larger scale picture.

You can set the orientation in a `PageFormat` object by calling its `setOrientation()` method. You can pass one of three possible argument values, which are defined within the `PageFormat` class:

Argument Value	Description
PORTRAIT	The origin is at the top left corner of the page with the positive *x* axis running from left to right and the positive *y* axis from top to bottom. This is the Windows and Postscript portrait definition.
LANDSCAPE	The origin is at the bottom left corner of the page with the positive *x* axis running from bottom to top and the positive *y* axis from left to right.
REVERSE_LANDSCAPE	The origin is at the top right corner of the page with the positive *x* axis running from top to bottom and the positive *y* axis running from right to left. This is the Macintosh landscape definition.

In each case the long side of the paper is in the same orientation as the *y* axis, but note that a Macintosh landscape specification has the origin at the top right corner of the page.

Let's incorporate `LANDSCAPE` into the `print()` method in `SketchView`:

```
public int print(Graphics g,            // Graphics context for printing
                 PageFormat pageFormat,  // The page format
                 int pageIndex)          // Index number of current page
                 throws PrinterException
{
  if(pageIndex>0)
    return NO_SUCH_PAGE;
  Graphics2D g2D = (Graphics2D) g;
  Rectangle rect = getModelExtent();     // Get sketch bounds

  // If the width is more than the height, set landscape
  if(rect.width>rect.height)
    pageFormat.setOrientation(pageFormat.LANDSCAPE);

  // Rest of the code as before...
}
```

Having set the orientation for the `PageFormat` object, the methods returning the coordinates for the position of the printable area and the width and height all return values consistent with the orientation. Thus the width of the printable area will be greater than the height if the orientation has been set to `LANDSCAPE`. Everything looks hunky-dory until we try it out. If you recompile with this modification to `SketchView`, the sketch is printed landscape, but the output is clipped so that a portion of the sketch to the right of the page in landscape orientation is missing. Indeed it looks very much as though the width of the printable area in landscape orientation is the same as that for portrait orientation.

That's exactly true, and this is a clue to what's wrong. We have modified the `PageFormat` object to landscape orientation, but the `Graphics2D` object that was passed to our `print()` method was produced based on the `PageFormat` object in its original state – portrait orientation. If we had known ahead of time back in the `actionPerformed()` method in the `FileAction` inner class to `SketchFrame`, we could have set up the `PageFormat` object for the print job before our `print()` method ever gets called. This could be done by modifying the code that initiates printing in the `actionPerformed()` method like this:

```
PrinterJob printJob = PrinterJob.getPrinterJob();  // Get a printing object
PageFormat pageFormat = printJob.defaultPage();
SketchView theView = theApp.getView();
Rectangle rect = theView.getModelExtent();           // Get sketch bounds

// If the sketch width is greater than the height, print landscape
if(rect.width>rect.height)
  pageFormat.setOrientation(pageFormat.LANDSCAPE);

printJob.setPrintable(theView, pageFormat);
```

Calling the `defaultPage()` method for a `PrinterJob` object returns a reference to the default page for the current printer. You can then change that to suit the conditions that you want to apply in the printing operation and then pass the reference to an overloaded version of the `setPrintable()` method. The call to `setPrintable()` here makes the `printJob` object print using `theView` object as the `Printable` using the `PageFormat` object specified by the second argument. With this code we would need to worry about the orientation in the `print()` method for the `Printable` object. It is taken care before `print()` ever gets called.

However, we have made our bed and must lie on it so let's see how we make our `print()` method accommodate landscape orientation. To make the printing work properly we need to reset the clip rectangle in the `Graphics2D` object to reflect the landscape orientation of the paper. It actually isn't that difficult. We can amend print like this:

```
  public int print(Graphics g,                    // Graphics context for
printing
                   PageFormat pageFormat,         // The page format
                   int pageIndex)                 // Index number of current page
                   throws PrinterException
  {
    if(pageIndex>0)
      return NO_SUCH_PAGE;
    Graphics2D g2D = (Graphics2D) g;
    Rectangle rect = getModelExtent();             // Get sketch bounds
```

```
        // If the width is more than the height, set landscape
        if(rect.width>rect.height)
        {
            pageFormat.setOrientation(pageFormat.LANDSCAPE);
    // Now set the clip rectangle to the printable page area
            g2D.setClip((int)pageFormat.getImageableX(),        // x coordinate
                        (int)pageFormat.getImageableY(),        // x coordinate
                        (int)pageFormat.getImageableWidth(),       // width
                        (int)pageFormat.getImageableHeight());     // height
        }

        // Rest of the code as before...
    }
```

The new rectangle defining the boundaries for clipping the output is exactly the printable area on the page. We have to cast the coordinates and the width and height from double to int because that type is required for the arguments to the setClip() method. If you recompile and try printing a sketch that is wider than it is long, it should come out perfectly in landscape orientation.

User Page Setup

Of course, there are many situations where the best orientation from a paper usage point of view may not be what the user wants. Instead of automatically setting landscape or portrait based on the dimensions of a sketch, you could just provide the user with a dialog to select the page setup parameters. The PrinterJob class makes this very easy since it provides a method to display the dialog and set the user selections in a PageFormat object. To make use of this we could change the printing code in the SketchFrame class like this:

```
    PrinterJob printJob = PrinterJob.getPrinterJob(); // Get a printing object
    PageFormat pageFormat = printJob.defaultPage();   // Get the page format
    pageFormat = printJob.pageDialog(pageFormat);     // Show page setup dialog

    // Print using the user page format settings
    printJob.setPrintable(theApp.getView(),pageFormat);
```

The defaultPage() method returns a reference to a PageFormat object that is initialized to the default size and orientation for the current printer. We pass this reference to the pageDialog() method, and this displays the dialog shown using the values from the PageFormat object.

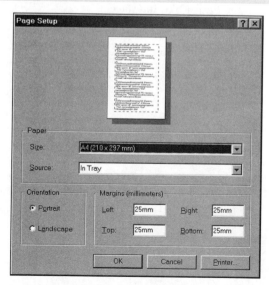

As you can see, with my printer I can select the paper size and the source tray. I can also set the margin sizes as well as select portrait or landscape orientation. When the dialog is closed normally with the OK button, the method returns a new PageFormat object that incorporates the values set by the user in the dialog. If the Cancel button is used to close the dialog, the original reference that was passed as an argument is returned. The overloaded setPrintable() method with two parameters will use the PageFormat object passed as the second argument when the print() method for the object referenced by the first argument is called.

Of course, the print() method in SketchView should just use whatever PageFormat object is handed to it. This will be set with the options that the user chose in the dialog and the Graphics object will be created consistent with that. This corresponds with the version of the print() method that we used in the example 'Printing the Whole Sketch'.

Multi-Page Printing

If you need to print multiple pages in a print job, you can do it in the implementation of the print() method declared in the Printable interface. The PrinterJob object will continue to call this method until the value NO_SUCH_PAGE is returned. However, this won't be convenient in every case. In a more complicated application than Sketcher, you may want to have different class objects printing different kinds of pages – rendering the same data as graphical or textual output for instance. You can't do this conveniently with just one class implementing the Printable interface. You also need something more flexible than just passing a class object that does printing to the PrinterJob object by calling its setPrintable() method.

The solution is to implement the Pageable interface in a class, and call the setPageable() method for the PrinterJob object instead of setPrintable().

Implementing the Pageable Interface

A class implementing the Pageable interface defines a set of pages to be printed. A Pageable object must be able to supply the PrinterJob object a count of the number of pages for a job, a reference of type Printable for the object that is to print each page, plus a PageFormat object defining the format of each page. The PrinterJob acquires this information by calling the three methods declared in the Pageable interface:

Method	Description
getNumberOfPages()	Must return an int value specifying the number of pages to be printed. If the number of pages cannot be determined then the value UNKNOWN_NUMBER_OF_PAGES can be returned. This value is defined in the Pageable interface.
getPageFormat(int pageIndex)	This method must return a PageFormat object for the page specified by the page index that is passed to it.
getPrintable(int pageIndex)	This method must return a reference of type Printable to the object responsible for printing the page specified by the page index that is passed to it.

At the start of a print job the `PrinterJob` object will call the `getNumberOfPages()` method to determine how many pages are to be printed. If you return the value UNKNOWN_NUMBER_OF_PAGES then the process relies on a `Printable` object returning NO_SUCH_PAGE at some point to stop printing. It is therefore a good idea to supply the number of pages when it can be determined.

For each page index, the `PrinterJob` object will call the `getPageFormat()` method to obtain the `PageFormat` object to be used, and call the `getPrintable()` method to obtain a reference to the object that will do the printing. Of course, just because you can supply a different `Printable` object for each page doesn't mean that you have to. You could use as many or as few as you need for your application. Note that the `print()` method for a `Printable` object may be called more than once by the `PrinterJob` object to print a particular page and the page should be rendered each time, so you must not code the method in a way that presumes otherwise.

Creating PageFormat Objects

As we saw earlier, you can get the default `PageFormat` object for your printer by calling the `defaultPage()` method for a `PrinterJob` object. The default `PageFormat` class constructor can also be used to create an object that is portrait oriented but in this case you have no guarantee that it is compatible with the current printer. A `PageFormat` object encapsulates information about the size of the paper and the margins in effect, so the object produced by the default constructor is unlikely to correspond with your printer setup. If you want to go this route, you can pass a reference to a `PageFormat` object to the `validatePage()` method for a `PrinterJob()` object. For example:

```
PrinterJob printJob = PrinterJob.getPrinterJob();      // Object for current printer
PageFormat pageFormat = printJob.validatePage(new PageFormat());  // Validated
page
```

Note that the `validatePage()` method does not return the same reference that is passed as an argument. The method clones the object that was passed to it and returns a reference to the clone, which will have been modified if necessary to suit the current printer. Since it does not modifiy the object in place, you always need to store the reference that is returned.

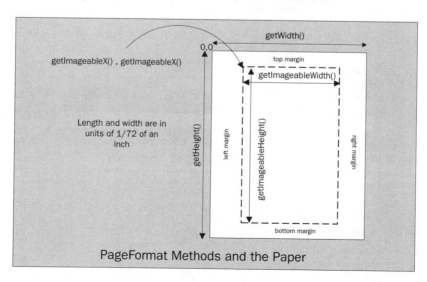

PageFormat Methods and the Paper

Once you have a `PageFormat` object, you can modify the orientation of the page by calling its `setOrientation()` method as we have seen. The `PageFormat` class defines several methods to retrieve information about the paper – we have seen that we can get the position and size of the printable area on the page for instance by calling the `getImageableX()`, `getImageableY()`, `getImageableWidth()` and `getImageableHeight()` methods. You also have `getWidth()` and `getHeight()` methods in the `PageFormat` class that return the overall width and height of the page. These are all actually properties of the paper itself that is represented by an object of the `Paper` class. You can also work with the `Paper` object for a `PageFormat` object directly.

Dealing with Paper

The `Paper` class encapsulates the size of the paper and the size and position of the printable area on the page. The default constructor for the `Paper` class creates an American letter sized sheet with one inch margins – the printable area being the area inside the margins. You can change the size of the paper by calling the `setSize()` method for the `Paper` object as we'll see in a moment.

Rather than creating an independent `Paper` object, you will normally retrieve a reference to the `Paper` object for a `PageFormat` object by calling its `getPaper()` method. If you then want to change the size of the paper or the printable area – the page margins in other words – you call the `setSize()` or the `setImageableArea()` method for the `Paper` object. You can restore the paper details by passing an object of type `Paper` back to the `PageFormat` object by calling its `setPaper()` method with a reference to a `Paper` object as the argument.

The `setSize()` method for a `Paper` object has two parameters of type `double` that are the width and height of the paper in units of 1/72 of an inch. If you use A4 paper, you could specify the size of the paper for a `PageFormat` object with the following statements:

```
Paper paper = pageFormat.getPaper();
final double MM_TO_PAPER_UNITS = 1.0/25.4*72;    // 25.4 mm to an inch
double widthA4 = 210*MM_TO_PAPER_UNITS;
double heightA4 = 297*MM_TO_PAPER_UNITS;
paper.setSize(widthA4, heightA4);
```

If you use letter size paper that is 8.5 by 11 inches, it's somewhat simpler:

```
Paper paper = pageFormat.getPaper();
double widthLetterSize = 72*8.5;
double heightLetterSize = 72*11.0;
paper.setSize(widthLetterSize, heightLetterSize);
```

The `setImageableArea()` method expects four arguments of type `double` to be supplied. The first two are the coordinates of the top left corner of the printable area and the next two are the width and the height. All these values are in units of 1/72 of an inch. To set 20mm margins on your A4 sheet you could write:

```
double marginSize = 20* MM_TO_PAPER_UNITS;                   // 20 mm wide
paper.setImageableArea(marginSize, marginSize,              // Top left
                               widthA4-2*marginSize,        // Width
                               heightA4-2*marginSize);      // Height
```

If you are printing on letter size paper, a one inch margin might be more appropriate so you would write:

```
double marginSize = 72.0;                                   // 1 inch
wide
paper.setImageableArea(marginSize, marginSize,              // Top left
                       widthLetterSize-2*marginSize,        // Width
                       heightLetterSize-2*marginSize);      // Height
```

Of course, there's no reason why a class that implements Pageable cannot also implement Printable, so we could do this in Sketcher, just to get a feel for the Pageable interface in action.

Try It Out – Using the Pageable Interface

We will just print two pages in a print job in Sketcher, a cover page with a title for the sketch, plus the sketch itself, which may be portrait or landscape of course. We could produce both pages in SketchView, but to make it more interesting, let's define a separate class to represent a Printable object for the cover page:

```
import java.awt.*;
import java.awt.geom.*;
import java.awt.print.*;
class SketchCoverPage implements Printable
{
  public SketchCoverPage(Sketcher theApp)
  {
    this.theApp = theApp;
  }

  // Print the cover page
  public int print(Graphics g,
              PageFormat pageFormat,
              int pageIndex)
              throws PrinterException
  {
    // If it's page 0 print the cover page...
  }

  private Sketcher theApp;
}
```

The sole reason for having the Sketcher field in the class is so we can get at the name of the sketch to print on the cover page. Since the need has come up we should add a method, getSketchName() to the SketchFrame class that will supply a reference to the String object containing the file name:

```
public String getSketchName()
{ return filename; }
```

We can use this in the implementation of the print() method in the SketchCoverPage class. The method needs to recognize when it is being called to print the first page – that is when the page index is zero, and then print the cover page. You could do whatever you like here to produce a fancy cover page, but we'll just put the code to draw a line border inset from the page, and put the sketch file name in the middle in a box. Here's how we would do that:

```java
public int print(Graphics g,
                 PageFormat pageFormat,
                 int pageIndex)
                 throws PrinterException
{
  if(pageIndex>0)
    return NO_SUCH_PAGE;

  Graphics2D g2D = (Graphics2D) g;
  float x = (float)pageFormat.getImageableX();
  float y = (float)pageFormat.getImageableY();

  GeneralPath path = new GeneralPath();
  path.moveTo(x+1, y+1);
  path.lineTo(x+(float)pageFormat.getImageableWidth()-1, y+1);
  path.lineTo(x+(float)pageFormat.getImageableWidth()-1,
                              y+(float)pageFormat.getImageableHeight()-1);
  path.lineTo(x+1, y+(float)pageFormat.getImageableHeight()-1);
  path.closePath();

  g2D.setPaint(Color.red);
  g2D.draw(path);

  // Get a 12 pt bold version of the default font
  Font font = g2D.getFont().deriveFont(12.f).deriveFont(Font.BOLD);

  g2D.setFont(font);                            // Set the new font
  String sketchName = theApp.getWindow().getSketchName();
  Rectangle2D.Float textRect = (Rectangle2D.Float)font.getStringBounds(
                                  sketchName, g2D.getFontRenderContext());
  double centerX = pageFormat.getWidth()/2;
  double centerY = pageFormat.getHeight()/2;
  Rectangle2D.Double surround = new Rectangle2D.Double(
                                   centerX-textRect.width,
                                   centerY-textRect.height,
                                   2*textRect.width,
                                   2*textRect.height);
  g2D.draw(surround);

  // draw text in the middle of the printable area
  g2D.setPaint(Color.blue);
  g2D.drawString(sketchName, (float)(centerX-textRect.width/2),
                             (float)(centerY+textRect.height/2));
  return PAGE_EXISTS;
}
```

To center the file name on the page we need to know the width and height of the text string when it is printed. The getStringBounds() method in the Font class returns the rectangle bounding the string. The second argument is a reference to an object of type FontRenderContext that is returned by the method we have called here for g2D. A FontRenderContext object contains all the information the getStringBounds() method needs to figure out the rectangle bounding the text when it is printed. This includes information about the size of the font as well as the resolution of the output device – the printer in our case.

Let's now implement the Pageable interface in the SketchView class. We must add three methods to the class, getNumberOfPages() that returns the number of pages to be printed, getPrintable() that returns a reference to the Printable object that will print a page with a given index, and getPageFormat() that returns a reference to a PageFormat object corresponding to a particular page.

```java
import javax.swing.*;
import java.awt.*;
import java.util.*;                    // For Observer
import java.awt.event.*;               // For events
import javax.swing.event.*;            // For mouse input adapter
import java.awt.geom.*;
import java.awt.print.*;

class SketchView extends      JComponent
                 implements Observer,
                            Constants,
                            ActionListener,
                            Printable,
                            Pageable
{
  // Always two pages
  public int getNumberOfPages()
  { return 2; }

  // Return the Printable object that will render the page
  public Printable getPrintable(int pageIndex)
  {
    if(pageIndex == 0)
      return new SketchCoverPage(theApp);
    else
      return this;
  }

  public PageFormat getPageFormat(int pageIndex)
  {
    // Code to define the PageFormat object for the page...
  }

  public int print(Graphics g,
                   PageFormat pageFormat,
                   int pageIndex)
                   throws PrinterException
  {
    // Revised printing code...
  }
// Plus the rest of the class as before...
}
```

The first two methods are already implemented here. We will always print two pages, the first page being printed by a `SketchCoverPage` object and the second page by the view object. Since we are providing custom `PageFormat` objects for each page, we will need to amend the `print()` method in `SketchView` to just use the `PageFormat` object it gets. First, let's see how we can produce the `PageFormat` object for a page. To make use of some of the methods we have discussed, we will double the size of the margins for the cover page but leave the margins for the other page at their default sizes. We will also sort out whether the second page should be printed in portrait or landscape orientation. Here's the code to do that:

```java
public PageFormat getPageFormat(int pageIndex)
{
    // Get the default page format and its Paper object.
    PageFormat pageFormat = PrinterJob.getPrinterJob().defaultPage();
    Paper paper = pageFormat.getPaper();

    if(pageIndex==0)                    // If it's the cover page...
    {                                   // ...make the margins twice the size
        double leftMargin = paper.getImageableX();   // Top left corner is indented
        double topMargin = paper.getImageableY();    // by the left and top margins

        // Get right and bottom margins
        double rightMargin = paper.getWidth()-paper.getImageableWidth()-leftMargin;
        double bottomMargin = paper.getHeight()-paper.getImageableHeight()
                                                           -topMargin;

        // Double the margin sizes
        leftMargin *= 2;
        rightMargin *= 2;
        topMargin *= 2;
        bottomMargin *= 2;

        paper.setImageableArea(leftMargin, topMargin,        // Set new printable area
                        paper.getWidth()-leftMargin-rightMargin,
                        paper.getHeight()-topMargin-bottomMargin);
        pageFormat.setPaper(paper);                          // Restore the paper
    }
    else
    { // We are printing a sketch so decide on portrait or landscape
        Rectangle rect = getModelExtent();                   // Get sketch bounds

        // If the width is more than the height, set landscape
        if(rect.width>rect.height)
            pageFormat.setOrientation(pageFormat.LANDSCAPE);
    }
    return pageFormat;                                        // Return the page format
}
```

Since we are going to deal with the cover page as a special page, we don't really have to adjust the paper margins here – we could just adjust the position of the text when we print the cover page. However, this way the page format is determined independently of the print operation, which is a more sensible approach, and you get to see how margins can be set.

We now want to change the `print()` method implementation in `SketchView` just to draw the page with the `PageFormat` object it is given. Here's the modified `print()` method:

```
public int print(Graphics g,
                 PageFormat pageFormat,
                 int pageIndex)
                 throws PrinterException
{
  if(pageIndex != 1)
    return NO_SUCH_PAGE;

  Graphics2D g2D = (Graphics2D) g;
  Rectangle rect = getModelExtent();                   // Get sketch bounds

  // Calculate the scale to fit sketch to page
  double scaleX = pageFormat.getImageableWidth()/rect.width;
  double scaleY = pageFormat.getImageableHeight()/rect.height;

  double scale = Math.min(scaleX,scaleY);  // Get minimum scale factor

  // Move origin to page printing area corner
  g2D.translate(pageFormat.getImageableX(), pageFormat.getImageableY());
  g2D.scale(scale,scale);                    // Apply scale factor
  g2D.translate(-rect.x, -rect.y);           // Move top left to the origin

  paint(g2D);                                // Draw the sketch
  return PAGE_EXISTS;
}
```

It works much as before – the code dealing with the page orientation has been removed, and we only print when the page index is 1. The orientation of the page is taken care of automatically because the `PageFormat` object is set up before this method is called. The `Graphics` object that is passed to `print()` will reflect the orientation specified in the `PageFormat` object.

The last thing we need to do is alter the code in the `actionPerformed()` method for the inner class, `FileAction`, in `SketchFrame`. We must replace the `setPrintable()` method call with a `setPageable()` call:

```
if(name.equals(printAction.getValue(NAME)))
{
  PrinterJob printJob = PrinterJob.getPrinterJob(); // Get a printing object
  printJob.setPageable(theApp.getView());         // The view is the page source
  if(printJob.printDialog())                       // Display print dialog
  {                                                // If true is returned
```

```
        try
        {
            printJob.print();                // then print
        }
        catch(PrinterException pe)
        {
            System.out.println(pe);
            JOptionPane.showMessageDialog(SketchFrame.this,
                                    "Error printing a sketch.",
                                      "Printer Error",
                                      JOptionPane.ERROR_MESSAGE);
        }
    }
}
```

On my system, the print dialog now shows the correct number of pages to be printed, courtesy of the `Pageable` interface implementation that we added to Sketcher

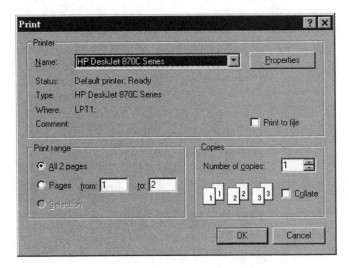

How It Works

The `PrinterJob` object now calls methods in the `Pageable` interface that we have implemented for the view. The number of pages is now determined by our `getNumberOfPages()` method, and the `PageFormat` and `Printable` objects are now obtained individually for each page.

Printing Using a Book

A `Book` object is a repository for a collection of pages where the pages may be printed using different formats. The page painter for a page in a book is represented by a `Printable` object, and each `Printable` object within a book can print one or possibly several pages with a given format.

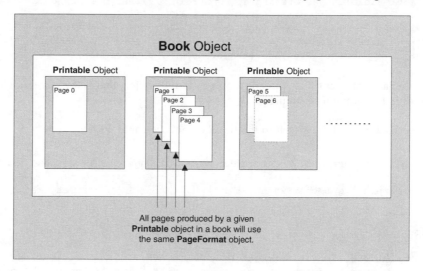

Because the `Book` class implements the `Pageable` interface, you print a book in the same way as you print a `Pageable` object. Once you have assembled all the pages you want in a `Book` object, you just pass a reference to it to the `setPageable()` method for your `PrinterJob` object. Let's take it from the top.

The `Book` class only has a default constructor, and that creates an empty book. Thus, we create a book like this:

```
Book sketchBook = new Book();
```

You add a page to a book by calling the `append()` method for the `Book` object. There are two overloaded versions of `append()`, one to add a `Printable` object that represents a single page, and the other to add a `Printable` object that represents several pages. In the latter case, all the pages are printed using the same `PageFormat` object.

The first version of `append()` accepts two arguments, a reference to the `Printable` object and a reference to an associated `PageFormat` object. We could add the cover page of a sketch just as in the previous example to the `sketchBook` object like this:

```
PageFormat pageFormat = PrinterJob.getPrinterJob().defaultPage();
Paper paper = pageFormat.getPaper();

double leftMargin = paper.getImageableX();   // Top left corner is indented
double topMargin = paper.getImageableY();       // by the left and top margins
double rightMargin = paper.getWidth()-paper.getImageableWidth()-leftMargin;
double bottomMargin = paper.getHeight()-paper.getImageableHeight()-topMargin;
```

```
leftMargin *= 2;                                // Double the left margin...
rightMargin *= 2;                               // ...and the right...
topMargin *= 2;                                 // ...and the top...
bottomMargin *= 2;                              // ...and the bottom

paper.setImageableArea(leftMargin, topMargin,   // Set new printable area
                  paper.getWidth()-leftMargin-rightMargin,
                  paper.getHeight()-topMargin-bottomMargin);
pageFormat.setPaper(paper);                      // Restore the paper
sketchBook.append(new SketchCoverPage(theApp), pageFormat);
```

Apart from the last statement that appends the `Printable` object that is the page painter, all this code is the same as in the previous example.

To add the second page of the sketch to the `Book` object, we could write:

```
pageFormat = PrinterJob.getPrinterJob().defaultPage();  // Get another default
page
Rectangle rect = getModelExtent();                      // Get sketch bounds


if(rect.width>rect.height)                              // If width is more
                                                        // than the height
  pageFormat.setOrientation(pageFormat.LANDSCAPE);      // ... set landscape
sketchBook.append(theApp.getView(), pageFormat);        // Append the page
```

Now we have assembled the book we can tell the `PrinterJob` object that we want to print the book:

```
printJob.setPageable(sketchBook);                       // The book is the
                                                        source of pages
```

Now all we need to do is call the `print()` method for the `PrinterJob` object to start printing. To expedite printing, the `PrinterJob` will communicate with the `Book` object to get the number of pages to be printed and to get the page painter and page format appropriate to print each page. The total number of pages is returned by the `getNumberOfPages()` method for the `Book` object. A reference to the `Printable` object for a given page index is returned by the `getPrintable()` method for the `Book` object and the `PageFormat` object for a given page index is returned by the `getPageFormat()` method. Obviously in the case of Sketcher, using a `Book` object doesn't offer much advantage over the `Pageable` object that we used in the previous example. In situations where you have more complex documents with a lot of pages with diverse formats it can make things much easier.

You use the other version of `append()` for a `Book` object to add a given number of pages to a book that will be produced by a single `Printable` object, and where all the pages have the same format. Here's an example:

```
Book book = new Book();
book.append(painter, pageFormat, pageCount);
```

Here the `painter` argument is a reference of type `Printable` that will print `pageCount` pages all with the same format, `pageFormat`. A typical instance where you might use this might be a long text document. The document could consist of many pages but they all are printed with the same page format. The view object for the document would typically provide a method to figure out the number of pages that are necessary to output the document.

Printing Components

Printing components is easier than you might think. Swing components are particularly easy to print because they already know how to draw themselves. You should not call a Swing components's `paint()` method when you want to print it though. Rendering of Swing components is buffered by default so printing one by calling its `paint()` method adds a lot of unnecessary overhead to the printing operation. Instead you should call the `print()` method that is defined in the `JComponent` class. This will render the component directly to the graphics context that is passed as an argument, so there is no buffering of the output. The method automatically prints any child components that the component contains, so you only need to call `print()` directly for a top-level component.

The `print()` method for a Swing component that has `JComponent` as a base calls three protected methods to actually carry out the printing:

`printComponent(Graphics g)`	Prints the component.
`printBorder(Graphics g)`	Prints the component border.
`printChildren(Graphics g)`	Prints components that are children of the component.

If you want to customize how a Swing component is printed you can subclass the component and override any or all of these. This doesn't apply to a `JFrame` component though. The `JFrame` class is a subclass of `Frame` and does not have `JComponent` as a super class. However, you can still call the `print()` method for a `JFrame` component to print it. In this case it's inherited from the `Container` class.

Let's implement a capability to print the Sketcher application window to see how this can be done.

Printing the Sketcher Window

First we will add a menu item to the <u>File</u> menu in Sketcher to print the window. We will define this using an instance the `FileAction` class:

```
public SketchFrame(String title, Sketcher theApp)
{
  super(title);                              // Call the base constructor
  setDefaultCloseOperation(EXIT_ON_CLOSE);
  this.theApp = theApp;
  setJMenuBar(menuBar);                      // Add the menu bar to the window

  JMenu fileMenu = new JMenu("File");        // Create File menu
  JMenu elementMenu = new JMenu("Elements"); // Create Elements menu
  JMenu helpMenu = new JMenu("Help");        // Create Help menu
  JMenu optionsMenu = new JMenu("Options");  // Create options menu
```

```
        fileMenu.setMnemonic('F');                    // Create shortcut
        elementMenu.setMnemonic('E');                 // Create shortcut
        helpMenu.setMnemonic('H');                    // Create shortcut
        optionsMenu.setMnemonic('O');                 // Create shortcut

        // Construct the file pull down menu
        addMenuItem(fileMenu, newAction = new FileAction("New", "Create new sketch"),
                                    KeyStroke.getKeyStroke('N',Event.CTRL_MASK ));
        addMenuItem(fileMenu, openAction = new FileAction("Open", "Open existing sketch"),
                                    KeyStroke.getKeyStroke('O',Event.CTRL_MASK ));
        addMenuItem(fileMenu, closeAction = new FileAction("Close", "Close sketch"),null);

        fileMenu.addSeparator();                        // Add separator
        addMenuItem(fileMenu, saveAction = new FileAction("Save", "Save sketch"),
                                    KeyStroke.getKeyStroke('S',Event.CTRL_MASK ));
        addMenuItem(fileMenu, saveAsAction = new FileAction("Save As...",
                                               "Save as new file"),null);

        fileMenu.addSeparator();                        // Add separator
        addMenuItem(fileMenu, printAction = new FileAction("Print", "Print sketch"),
                                    KeyStroke.getKeyStroke('P',Event.CTRL_MASK ));
        addMenuItem(fileMenu, printWindowAction = new FileAction("Print window",
                "Print current window"), KeyStroke.getKeyStroke('W',Event.CTRL_MASK ));

    // Rest of the code as before...
  }
```

Our new menu item is a `FileAction` object, so events originating from it will invoke the handler that we defined in the `FileAction` inner class. We need to add some code to the `actionPerformed()` method in the inner class to deal with them. Add the following code after the `if` that deals with the `printAction` events:

```
        else if(name.equals(printWindowAction.getValue(NAME)))
        {
          PrinterJob printJob = PrinterJob.getPrinterJob(); // Get a
                                                            //    printing object
          PageFormat pageFormat = printJob.defaultPage();    // and default format
          pageFormat = printJob.pageDialog(pageFormat);      // Pop the dialog

          // The app window is the page source
          printJob.setPrintable(theApp.getWindow(),pageFormat);

          if(printJob.printDialog())                // Display print dialog
          {                                         // If true is returned...
            try
            {
              printJob.print();                     // ...then print
            }
```

```
            catch(PrinterException pe)
            {
              System.err.println(pe);
              JOptionPane.showMessageDialog(SketchFrame.this,
                                    "Error printing the window.",
                                    "Printer Error",
                                    JOptionPane.ERROR_MESSAGE);

            }
          }
```

The application window, which is the SketchFrame object, window, is responsible for printing the window because it is obviously best placed to do this, so we must make the SketchFrame class implement the Printable interface. After adding an import statement for the java.awt.print package, change the first line of the class definition to:

```
public class SketchFrame extends JFrame
                  implements Constants, ActionListener, Observer, Printable
```

Now we can add the definition of the print() method to the class:

```
  // Print the window
  public int print(Graphics g,
               PageFormat pageFormat,
               int pageIndex)
               throws PrinterException
{
  if(pageIndex>0)
    return NO_SUCH_PAGE;

  // Scale the component to fit
  Graphics2D g2D = (Graphics2D) g;

  // Calculate the scale factor to fit the window to the page
  double scaleX = pageFormat.getImageableWidth()/getWidth();
  double scaleY = pageFormat.getImageableHeight()/getHeight();

  double scale = Math.min(scaleX,scaleY);   // Get minimum scale factor

  // Move paper origin to page printing area corner
  g2D.translate(pageFormat.getImageableX(), pageFormat.getImageableY());
  g2D.scale(scale,scale);                        // Apply the scale factor

  print(g2D);                                // Draw the component
  return PAGE_EXISTS;
}
```

If you recompile and run Sketcher once more, the File/Print Window menu item should be operational.

How It Works

The menu operation and the printing mechanism is as we have already discussed. The SketchFrame object is the page painter for the window so the print() method is where it all happens. After checking the page index value and casting the Graphics reference passed to the method to Graphics2D, we calculate the scaling factor to fit the window to the page. The getWidth() and getHeight() methods inherited in our SketchFrame class return the width and height of the window respectively. We then apply the scale just as we did for printing a sketch. The coordinates of the top left corner of the window are at 0,0 so we can just print it once we have applied the scaling factor. Calling the inherited print() method with g2D as the argument does this.

I'm sure you will have noticed that the output has deficiencies. The title bar and window boundary are missing. Of course, a JFrame object is a top-level window, and since it is derived from the Frame class it is a heavyweight component with its appearance determined by its peer, which is outside the Java code. The print() method does not include the peer created elements of the window. Calling the printAll() method that is inherited in the JFrame class from the Component class should result in everything being printed including the bits implemented by the peer, but at the time of writing it results in an exception of type ClassCastException being thrown in the Microsoft Windows environment. I believe it works OK in other environments such as Solaris. You might like to try replacing print() by printAll() if your JDK is later than 1.3.0. This printing problem is specific to JFrame. The other Swing components do not depend on a peer so they will each be printed in their entirety by the print() method that they inherit from the JComponent class.

Summary

In this chapter you have added full support for the File menu to the Sketcher application, for both sketch storage and retrieval, and for printing. You should find that the techniques that you have used here are readily applicable in other Java applications. The approach to saving and restoring a model object is not usually dependent on the kind of data it contains. Of course, if your application is a word processor, you will have a little more work to do taking care that the number of lines on each page is a whole number of lines. In other words you avoid having the top half of a line of text on one page, and the bottom half on the next. There are other Java classes to help with that, however, and we don't really have the space to discuss them here – but look them up – the javax.swing.text package is a veritable gold mine for text handling!

If you have been following all the way with Sketcher, you now have an application that consists of well over a thousand lines of code, so you should be pretty pleased with yourself.

The important points we have covered in this chapter are:

❑ You can implement writing your model object to a file and reading it back by making it serializable

❑ The JFileChooser class provides a generalized way for displaying a dialog to enable a file to be chosen

❑ A printing operation is initiated by creating a PrinterJob object. This object encapsulates the interface to your printer and is used to manage the printing process

❑ The format for a page is defined by a `PageFormat` object, and methods for this object can provide information on the paper size and orientation and the printable area on the page.

❑ The page is defined by an object of type `Paper`

❑ Printing a page is always done by an object of a class that implements the `Printable` interface

❑ You print a page by calling methods for the `Graphics` object passed to the `print()` method in the `Printable` interface by the `PrinterJob` object

❑ You can manage multi-page print jobs by implementing the `Pageable` interface in a class. This will enable different types of class object to be used to print different pages

❑ A `Book` object can encapsulate a series of pages to be printed. Each `Printable` object that is appended to a book prints one or more pages in a given format.

Exercises

1. At the moment in Sketcher, you can close a file selection dialog with the approve button but without a file being selected. Modify Sketcher so that the dialog will continue to be displayed until you select a file or close the dialog with the **Cancel** button.

2. Modify the Sketcher program to print the title at the top of the page on which the sketch is printed.

3. Modify the printing of a sketch so that a solid black boundary line is drawn around the sketch on the page.

4. Modify Sketcher to print a single sketch laid out on four pages. The sketch should be enlarged to provide the best fit on the four pages without distorting circles – that is, the same scale should be applied to the x and y axes.

5. Use a `Book` object to print a cover page plus the sketch spread over four pages as in the previous exercise.

Images and Animation

In this chapter we will introduce some of the basic techniques for reading images from a file and displaying them, and creating animation effects in your applications and applets. In this chapter you will learn:

- ❏ How to read an image into an application or an applet.
- ❏ How to display an image.
- ❏ How to create animation effects.
- ❏ How to draw on an image.
- ❏ How to create an image internally to your program.
- ❏ What alpha compositing is.
- ❏ How to set the transparency of an image and create fading effects.

We will use applets as the primary vehicle for working examples in this chapter, but don't forget that everything you will learn here can also be applied to your applications.

Applet Operations

We have already seen a few simple examples of applets, but we haven't really gone into how they are structured in any detail. Since we will be writing several rather more complicated applets in this chapter, we will remedy this right now.

To recap, an applet is defined by a class that has the `Applet` class as a base. We will use the Swing class `JApplet` which is derived from `Applet` to define our applets because it provides more capabilities. As you know, an applet is a program that is embedded in a web page, so it executes under the control of a web browser, or the **appletviewer** program that comes with the Java Development Kit. As we discussed in Chapter 1, you are likely to need to have the Java plug-in installed if Java 2 applets are to run with your browser. If you want to be sure that your applet will run with Netscape or Microsoft browsers without the plug-in being installed, then you must forgo the added capabilities of the `JApplet` class and limit yourself to using the `Applet` class as the base for your applet.

Whether an applet runs or not, and when it starts execution and when it stops, are all controlled by the browser, not by code in the applet. Of course, whether things work as they should still depends on the applet being implemented properly. When a browser loads a web page containing an applet, it will create an object of the class defining the applet. It will then use four methods for the applet class object to control the operation of the applet. All four methods are `public`, have a `void` return type and require no arguments. These methods are:

Method	Description
init()	To start your applet, the browser always calls the default constructor for your applet class to create the object, and then calls its `init()` method to do any initialization that is necessary. When `init()` is called, the applet is loaded and any parameters specified for the applet are available. You typically create any objects that are needed within the applet in this method and initialize any data members of the applet class. You will also implement the `init()` method to create any threads that the applet requires. Of course, your applet class can still have data members that you supply initial values for just like any other class. You can also implement the default constructor and do the initialization of data members there, too.
start()	This method is called by the browser to start or restart the operation of the applet. When the applet is started initially, the `start()` method will be called after the `init()` method has executed. The `start()` method is typically used to start any additional threads required in the applet. You don't always have to implement this method, but we will be using it a lot in this chapter to start animations.
stop()	This method is called when an applet should stop what it is doing temporarily – when the applet is 'hidden', for instance – because the user has scrolled the web page so the applet region is no longer visible. You would typically stop any continuously running operations that are in separate threads in this method – ones that might display an animation, for instance. This avoids wasting processor time on preparing images that can't be seen. To restart the applet the browser will call the `start()` method.
destroy()	This is called when the applet is being terminated so you should use it to free up any system resources that your applet uses. The `stop()` method is always called prior to this method being called.

The default implementations of these methods are inherited in your applet class, but they all do nothing. It is up to you to implement your versions of these methods so that they do what is necessary in the context of your applet. One other method that your applets should implement is `getAppletInfo()`. This method is expected to return a `String` object that contains information about the author, the version and copyright for the applet suitable for displaying in an "About" dialog.

The browser finds out about your applet through the HTML code that appears in the web page, so let's take a quick look at the bits that are likely to be involved.

HTML for Applets

In this section we will show HTML tags and attributes in upper case to highlight them, although they are not case sensitive. The basic HTML tags you need for embedding an applet in a web page are as follows:

```
<APPLET     CODE = "AppletName.class"
            WIDTH = "Applet_width_in_pixels"
            HEIGHT = "Applet_height_in_pixels" >
Optional alternate text displayed if the APPLET tag is not supported
</APPLET>
```

The optional default text after the APPLET tag is useful to signal when a browser does not support the APPLET tag – when the applet will not be executed. Other than that, the HTML tags above are the minimum required to include an applet in a page. The value for the CODE attribute in the APPLET tag identifies the .class file for the applet. This presumes the applet is in the same directory as the page containing the applet. If this is not the case you must not put the path as part of the CODE value. Instead, you should add a CODEBASE attribute that has a URL as a value that identifies the source for the applet – the URL can be absolute (which would start with "http://") or it can be relative to the directory containing the web page. While the WIDTH and HEIGHT attributes are mandatory, they only determine the initial space allocated to the applet. The applet can adjust these itself, as we shall see in this chapter. The double quotes around the parameter values can be omitted if the parameter value does not contain spaces or other characters that might cause confusion.

You can also specify parameter values to be read by your applet by placing <PARAM> tags between the <APPLET> and </APPLET> entries, one for each parameter. For example:

```
<APPLET     CODE=MyApplet.class  WIDTH=200  HEIGHT=100>
<PARAM  NAME="frameRate"  VALUE="10">
<PARAM  NAME="description"  VALUE="Some text">

</APPLET>
```

These tags will execute the MyApplet applet from the directory containing the HTML file, and make a parameter with the name frameRate available with the value "10", plus a second parameter, description, with the value "Some text". These values can be retrieved programmatically from within the applet – usually from within the init() method – by calling the getParameter() method with a String defining the parameter name for which the value is requested as the argument. If it is available, the parameter value is returned as a String, which you can then convert to numeric form where necessary. For example, to retrieve the value of the parameter with the name, frameRate, we could write:

```
int frameRate = 5;                             // Default frame rate
String value = getParameter("frameRate");  // Get the value of the parameter
frameRate
if(value != null)
  frameRate = Integer.parseInt(value);
```

It is important to verify that the String returned by the getParameter() method is not null. It will be if there is no PARAM tag specifying the value. Note that the parameter name is not case sensitive, so "FRAMERATE" would specify the same parameter as "framerate".

When your applet expects to read parameter values, it is a good idea to override the default `getParameterInfo()` method in your applet class to identify their names, their types, and their description in an array of strings. The version of the method that your applet class will inherit from the `Applet` class returns `null`. This method can be used by the applet context (the web page) to find out about your applet. For the applet `MyApplet`, that expects values for the parameters `frameRate` and description, you would implement the `getParamterInfo()` method as:

```
public String[][] getParameterInfo()
{
  String[][] pInfo = {
                       { "frameRate",    "integer", "The frames per second"       },
                       { "description", "String",   "Description of the animation"}
                     };
    return pInfo;
}
```

There must be three elements in each row of the array providing information about a particular parameter. The three elements in a row describe the parameter name, the type of value and the purpose of the parameter respectively.

> *Remember to use the OBJECT and EMBED tags as shown in Chapter 1 to add Java 2 support to browsers other than* `appletviewer`.

> *If you are using this book in non-linear fashion you will find more on deploying applets at the end of Chapter 12 where I also briefly discuss the security issues relating to applets. This is an extensive topic and a thorough discussion of it is beyond the scope of this book. For the most up-to-date documentation regarding the security architecture in Java 2, refer to the web pages at:* http://java.sun.com/security/

Let's now turn to the fundamentals of dealing with images, and then look at how we can implement an applet from the ground up – this time to handle an image.

Obtaining an Image

We have already seen one way to obtain an image from a file using the `ImageIcon` class back in Chapter 13. The `ImageIcon` class doesn't really care about the size of the image, that is, it is not constrained to be a typical icon size, so an image represented by an object of this class can be anything. We only considered one `ImageIcon` constructor when we read icons for our toolbars buttons from a file. That constructor happened to accept a `String` argument that specified the file name. There are a number of other `ImageIcon` constructors, so here's the complete set:

Constructor	Description
`ImageIcon()`	Creates an uninitialized object that you must initialize with an `Image` object before use.
	You would do this by passing a reference to an `Image` object to the `setImage()` method for the `ImageIcon` object.
`ImageIcon(String filename)`	Creates an object from the file specified by `filename`, which represents either an absolute path for the file, or a path relative to the current directory.
`ImageIcon(String filename, String description)`	As the constructor above, but stores a description of the image specified by the second argument, and which can be retrieved by calling the `getDescription()` method for the `ImageIcon` object.
`ImageIcon(URL location)`	Creates an object specified by the file that is located at the source specified by the argument. The `URL` class represents a uniform resource locator specification that identifies a source on the World Wide Web. We will come back to this class a little later in the chapter.
`ImageIcon(URL location, String description)`	Same as the previous constructor but adds a description of the image that can be retrieved by calling the `getDescription()` method for the `ImageIcon` object.
`ImageIcon(Image image)`	Creates an `ImageIcon` object from the `Image` object supplied as the argument. We will discuss the `Image` class later in this section.
`ImageIcon(Image image, String description)`	Creates an `ImageIcon` object from the `Image` object supplied as the first argument. The second argument provides a description of the image.
`ImageIcon(byte[] imageData)`	Creates an object from the `byte` array that must contain data containing an image in a supported format – which can be GIF, PNG, or JPEG at the present time. The data can be read from a file or created programmatically.
`ImageIcon(byte[] imageData, String description)`	As the previous constructor but also stores a description of the image.

An `ImageIcon` object contains a reference to an object of type `Image` as a member. The `Image` class is an abstract class that is a superclass of all classes that represent images in Java, so a reference of type `Image` can refer to any instance of a graphical image being used. You can obtain a reference to the `Image` member of an `ImageIcon` object by calling its `getImage()` method. An object of type `Image` can be created from data in GIF (Graphics Interchange Format), PNG (Portable Network Graphics), or JPEG (Joint Photographic Experts Group) format. So, whether the image data is passed to the constructor as an array – as is the case for two of the `ImageIcon` constructors, or is obtained from an external source such as a file or a `URL` object, it must be a GIF, PNG, or JPEG representation of an image.

While the GIF format for images is very common, it has some limitations. A GIF image can contain a maximum of 256 different colors, albeit selected from a palette of 16 million colors. The JPEG image format has been designed to store photographs, and is a much more sophisticated way of representing a color image. The sophistication comes at a price though. The complexity of the format and the data compression technique used means that it takes much longer to process than a GIF image, but it does make it feasible to transmit good quality photographic images over the net. The JPEG compression technique is also 'lossy', so the quality is not as good as the original image. The PNG image format is also much more flexible than GIF images and it stores images in a lossless form. It is designed to be a portable image storage form for computer-originated images. You can represent grayscale, indexed-color and true color images in PNG format, and you can also include an alpha channel that determines the transparency of the image when it is combined with others.

The constructors that create the `ImageIcon` object by referencing a `String` object specifying a file name, or by referencing a `URL` object defining an Internet source, always construct the internal `Image` object before returning. When you specify a `URL` as the source of the image data, there can be a considerable delay before the `ImageIcon` object creation is completed, depending on how long it takes to retrieve the image data from the source. Being able to create an `ImageIcon` object from a `URL` object is particularly relevant to applets. You can retrieve any images, or indeed any other external data that you use in your applet from an Internet source. Since URLs are so important, let's take a brief detour into how URLs and the `URL` class work.

Identifying Sources on a Network

Data sources on a network are identified by a **Uniform Resource Locator**, or **URL**. A source identified by a URL can be a file, or can be some other facility that makes data available, such as a search engine for instance. A URL is a relatively straightforward extension of the normal way of identifying a data source file by the path. It just has some extra bits to identify the computer that contains the source, and how you should communicate with the computer to get at the file. A URL is made up of four pieces of information, some of which may be omitted entirely or take default values:

Protocol	Domain Name	Port Number	Path and File Name
`http://`	`www.wrox.com`	`:80`	`/index.html`
`ftp://`	`java.sun.com`	`:21`	

The protocol identifies the particular communications method that is to be used to get at the file. **HTTP** is the **H**yper**T**ext **T**ransfer **P**rotocol used on the World Wide Web, **FTP** is the **F**ile **T**ransfer **P**rotocol, and there are others (we'll see one in the next chapter).

The domain name identifies the data source uniquely. The last part of the name identifies the kind of organization that owns the computer. For instance, a domain name ending in .com is usually a commercial organization in the USA such as Wrox Press or Sun, .co.uk is a UK company, .edu is an educational establishment in the USA, .ac.uk is an academic or research organization in the UK and .gov is a government or other public body. These are just a few examples. There are lots of others.

A port is just a number identifying a particular service on a computer. A computer can have many ports – each providing a different service. You don't usually need to specify the port number in a URL because a standard port number, which is typically associated with a particular protocol, will be assigned by default. The port number for the http protocol is 80 for example, and the port number for ftp is 21.

Because the domain name is part of the reference to a data source, every data source in a network has a unique URL. As long as you know the URL for the source of the data you want on the Internet, and the machine containing it is connected and active, you can go straight to it. Assuming, of course, you have permission!

The URL Class

As you saw when we discussed ImageIcon constructors, the URL class encapsulates URLs. This class is defined in the java.net package, so you will need an import statement for the package or for the class when you refer to the URL class in your code. A URL object identifies a particular URL and provides you with the tools to access it and read it, wherever it is on the network. You can create a URL object from a string specifying the URL, for example:

```
URL sourceURL = new URL("http://www.wrox.com/");
```

This defines a URL object corresponding to the home (or default) page on the Wrox web site.

Perhaps the most commonly used URL constructor accepts two arguments – a URL object identifying an Internet source, plus a String argument which is a specification for a source within the context of the URL specified by the first argument. The popularity of this form is due to the definition within the Applet class of a method, getCodeBase(), which returns the URL for the source where the .class file for the applet is stored. This enables you to create the URL for a file, picture.gif say, which is stored in the same directory as the applet code, wherever it is, with a statement such as:

```
URL getThePicture = new URL(getCodeBase(), "picture.gif");
```

There is another method in the Applet class (and therefore inherited in the JApplet class) that provides a useful URL object. This is the getDocumentBase() method that returns a URL object corresponding to the URL for the document (the .html file in other words) that contains the applets. This may well be different from the location of the applet itself. You could call this method to obtain the URL like this:

```
URL doc = getDocumentBase();            // Get the document containing the applet
```

You can also define a URL object by supplying a constructor with separate values for the protocol, the host name, the port number and the source name. You specify the port number as type int, and the other arguments as type String. The web site defined by the domain name "www.ncsa.uiuc.edu" contains a page that explains what a URL is. The file path and name for the page is "/demoweb/url-primer.html". You could define a URL object for this page with the statement:

```
URL sourceURL = new URL("http",                    // Protocol
                        "www.ncsa.uiuc.edu",       // Host name
                        "/demoweb/url-primer.html");  // File
```

This uses the default port number for the protocol. You just need to supply the protocol, the domain name and the file path as `String` objects. Note that URL paths are always specified using forward slashes as separators, regardless of the type of server hosting the data source.

There is an alternative constructor defined in the `URL` class:

```
URL sourceURL = new URL("http",                    // Protocol
                        "www.ncsa.uiuc.edu",       // Host name
                        80,                        // Port number
                        "/demoweb/url-primer.html");  // File
```

The value of 80 for the port number is the standard port number for `http`. The value of -1 for the port name selects the default port number for the protocol. If you specify a protocol that cannot be identified, a `MalformedURLException` will be thrown.

Once you have a `URL` object, you can get the components of the URL by calling the `getProtocol()`, `getHost()`, `getPort()` and `getFile()` methods for the object. The `getPort()` method returns the port number as type `int`, and the other methods return objects of type `String`.

The `URL` class also implements an `equals()` method that you can use to compare two `URL` objects. The expression `URL1.equals(URL2)` will return `true` if `URL1` and `URL2` specify the same file on the same host via the same port number and using the same protocol.

Perhaps the most useful method in the `URL` class is the `openStream()` method. This returns an object of type `InputStream`, which you can use to read the file represented by the `URL`. We can try this out by reading the file referenced by the `sourceURL` object we created in the code fragment above.

Try It Out – Reading a URL

This example assumes you have a live connection to the Internet. So when the program closes, the connection may still be open, in which case you will need to close it manually. Here's the program to read a URL:

> **The program assumes that the directory** `JunkData` **that we used in Chapter 8 is still on your** `C:` **drive. If it isn't, you can add it, or better still, add the code to check that the directory is there, and if it isn't, create it.**

```
import java.net.*;
import java.io.*;

class ReadURL
{
```

```
public static void main(String[] args)
{
  try
  {
    // Define a URL
    URL sourceURL = new URL(
                "http://www.ncsa.uiuc.edu/demoweb/url-primer.html");

    // Get a character input stream for the URL
    BufferedReader in = new BufferedReader(
                    new InputStreamReader(
                        sourceURL.openStream()));

    // Create the stream for the output file
    PrintWriter out = new PrintWriter(
                    new BufferedWriter(
                    new FileWriter(
                    new File("C:/JunkData/netdata.html")))));

    System.out.println("Reading the file " + sourceURL.getFile() +
                " on the host " + sourceURL.getHost() +
                " using " + sourceURL.getProtocol());

    // Read  the URL and write it to a file
    String buffer;                          // Buffer to store lines
    while(!(null==(buffer=in.readLine())))
      out.println(buffer);

    in.close();                             // Close the input stream
    out.close();                            // Close the output file
  }
  catch(MalformedURLException e)
  {
    System.out.println("Failed to create URL:\n" + e);
  }
  catch(IOException e)
  {
    System.out.println("File error:\n" + e);
  }
}
}
```

While we have used a URL that references a source on the Internet, you could also use a URL to specify a file on your local machine. Executing this as written produces the output:

```
Reading the file /demoweb/url-primer.html on the host www.ncsa.uiuc.edu using http
```

It will also write the text contents of the URL to the file `netdata.html`. Have a look at what you've captured. It's a good read.

How It Works

The object `sourceURL` is created directly from the URL string. Because the constructor can throw a `MalformedURLException` – if you type the URL string incorrectly, for example – we have a `catch` block for this exception following the `try` block. Note that this exception is derived from `IOException` so the `catch` block for this must precede the `catch` block for `IOException`. Depending on whether your dial-up-networking is working properly, another typical exception can be `java.net.UnknownHostException`.

By calling the `openStream()` method for the URL object, we obtain a stream that we can pass to the `InputStreamReader` constructor. A character reader will automatically take care of converting characters from the stream to Unicode. From the `InputStreamReader` we create a `BufferedReader` object so input from the stream will be buffered in memory.

The file is a sizable `.html` file, so rather than writing it to the screen, we write it to a file in the `JunkData` directory that we used in Chapter 8. You will then be able to view the file using your web browser. Once we have the `BufferedReader` object for the URL, the reading of the URL and writing the local file follows the sort of process you have already seen in Chapter 8. We just use the `readLine()` method to read a line at a time from the URL into the string buffer, and we use the `println()` method to transfer the buffer contents to the local file. You can now read more about URLs by reading the file contents at your leisure. In the meantime, let's get back to images.

Displaying an Image

You display an image in essentially the same way as you display anything else – by calling a method for a `Graphics` or `Graphics2D` object. The `drawImage()` method will draw an image in a graphics context, so from this you can immediately deduce that you can draw images on any components you like. Let's go straight away to trying this out in a working example using an `ImageIcon` object in the first instance.

Try It Out – Displaying an Image

We will implement an applet that creates an `ImageIcon` from a file in the same directory as the applet's `.class` file. The code here will refer to an image file `wrox_logo.gif`. If you want to use this file, you can download it from the Wrox web site. Alternatively you can use your own `.gif` or `.jpg` file. Here's the code for the applet:

```java
import java.awt.*;
import javax.swing.*;
import java.net.*;

public class DisplayImage extends JApplet
{
  public void init()
  {
    ImageIcon icon = null;
    try
    {
      icon = new ImageIcon(new URL(getCodeBase(),"Images/wrox_logo.gif"));
    }
    catch(MalformedURLException e)
```

```
    {
      System.out.println("Failed to create URL:\n" + e);
      return;
    }

    int imageWidth = icon.getIconWidth();       // Get icon width
    int imageHeight = icon.getIconHeight();      // and its height
    resize(imageWidth,imageHeight);              // Set applet size to fit the image

    // Create panel a showing the image
    ImagePanel imagePanel = new ImagePanel(icon.getImage());

    getContentPane().add(imagePanel);            // Add the panel to the content pane
  }

  // Class representing a panel displaying an image
  class ImagePanel extends JPanel
  {
    public ImagePanel(Image image)
    {
      this.image = image;
    }

    public void paint(Graphics g)
    {
      g.drawImage(image, 0, 0, this);            // Display the image
    }

    Image image;                                 // The image
  }
}
```

You will need an HTML file to run the applet. You could call it `DisplayImage.html`, and make the contents:

```
<applet code="DisplayImage.class" width=50 height=50></applet>
```

This just sets the width and height parameters for the applet to arbitrary values. The applet will resize itself to accommodate the image. When I ran this with `appletviewer`, it displayed the window shown: (You may prefer to refer back to Chapter 1, which explains how to run the applet in a browser using the plug-in.)

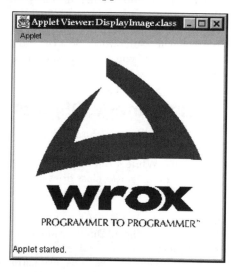

861

How It Works

We retrieve the icon from the file `wrox_logo.gif` in the `Images` directory relative to the URL that holds the code for the applet. The `URL` class constructor can throw an exception, so we must arrange to catch exceptions of type `MalformedURLException` here in order to get the code to compile. The `ImageIcon` class constructor does everything necessary to obtain the data from the file, and uses it to create the image. The constructor will only return when this has been completed.

The `getIconWidth()` and `getIconHeight()` methods for the `ImageIcon` object return the width and height of the image respectively, and we use these as arguments to the `resize()` method for the `JApplet` object, to adjust the size of the applet to accommodate the image.

We have to remember that an applet based on the `JApplet` class is similar to a window based on the `JFrame` class in that anything we want to display in an applet must be added to the content pane for the applet object. For this reason we define an inner class, `ImagePanel`, that will draw the image for the `ImageIcon` object, and we can add an object of this class to the content pane for the applet. The `ImagePanel` class is quite simple. The constructor saves the reference to the `Image` object that is passed to it in a data member of the class, and the `paint()` method calls `drawImage()` to display the image.

Note that no cast to `Graphics2D` is necessary in the `paint()` method since the `drawImage()` method that we are using is defined in the `Graphics` class. There are several other overloaded versions of this method, including two that are defined in the `Graphics2D` class, so when you want to use these, a cast will be necessary. The arguments to the version of `drawImage()` that we use here are:

- ❑ A reference to the `Image` object to be drawn
- ❑ The coordinates of the position where the image is to be drawn
- ❑ A reference to an `ImageObserver` object

An image is defined by its top-left corner point, so in our applet we place the top-left corner of the image at the origin of the user coordinate system for our panel. An `ImageObserver` object is an object of a class that implements the `ImageObserver` interface, and since the `Component` class implements this interface, any component, including objects of our inner class `ImagePanel`, are `ImageObserver` objects. The `ImageObserver` interface handles the process of accessing image data from Internet sources where there may be a considerable time delay in loading the image. This interface provides the means to allow you to determine whether an image has been loaded or not, and we will come back to this on the next page.

Creating Image Objects

The `Image` class is at the heart of all images in Java. An image will always be an object of a class that has `Image` as a base. You can't directly create an `Image` object that contains an image because the class is abstract. While a reference of type `Image` is used to refer to an object that encapsulates the data for an image, the `Image` class does not provide you with the means of obtaining the image data. There has to be some other mechanism for creating an `Image` object corresponding to a particular image.

The `Applet` class defines two overloaded versions of a method, `getImage()`, that return a reference to an `Image` object. One version accepts an object of type `URL` as an argument that specifies the source of the image data. The other accepts two arguments, a `URL` object plus a `String` object, where the `String` object defines the specification of the source of the image data in the context of the `URL` object. In the previous example, we could have created an `Image` object directly with the following statement:

```
Image image = getImage(new URL(getCodeBase(),"Images/wrox_logo.gif"));
```

We still need to put this in a `try` block because of the possibility of a `MalformedURLException` (or others) being thrown by the `URL` class constructor. There is a significant difference between this statement obtaining a reference to an `Image` object for an image from a given source, and the statement in the example that created an `ImageIcon` object. When the `ImageIcon` class constructor returned to the `init()` method, the object was fully constructed and the image was available. In the statement above we get a reference to an `Image` object returned that *may* at some time in the future contain the data for the image. This gets over the problem implicit in using an `ImageIcon` object – it hangs up your applet until all the image data for the icon has been retrieved from the source. When you call `getImage()`, your applet code can continue to execute and get on with other things while the image data is being downloaded. This still leaves the question of determining when the image is actually here which is where the `ImageObserver` interface comes in.

Image Observers

The `Component` class implements the `ImageObserver` interface so all components will inherit this implementation. The `ImageObserver` interface declares one method, `imageUpdate()`, that is called automatically when information about an image that was previously requested becomes available. The `imageUpdate()` method will draw the image on the component. So how do you request information about an image?

One way is to call the `drawImage()` method for a `Graphics` object. By calling this method you implicitly request all the information necessary to draw the image in the graphics context – the width, the height, the pixel data and so on. As you saw, the last argument to the `drawImage()` method was a reference to an `ImageObserver` object that in our case was the panel on which the image was to be drawn. If any of the image data was not available at the time of the call, the `imageUpdate()` method for the `ImageObserver` object would be called as more information became available.

Another way you can request information about an image is to call methods for the `Image` object itself. The `Image` class defines methods `getWidth()` and `getHeight()` to access the width and height of the image. Both of these methods require a reference of type `ImageObserver` to be passed – normally a reference to the component on which the image is to be drawn – and that object's `imageUpdate()` method is called when the information becomes available.

The last part we need to understand in all this is exactly what the `imageUpdate()` method does when it is called. It simply draws the image incrementally with the information available. This has the effect on a slow Internet link or with a large image of making the image appear piecemeal, as and when the data becomes available. This usually gives the user a visual cue that, even though the entire image has not been retrieved yet, something is still happening.

Implementing imageUpdate()

Most of the time, the default implementation of `imageUpdate()` is sufficient – it just repaints the component. If we use the `getImage()` method in the previous example to load the image, we have two objects that are interested in the image data, the applet object and the `ImagePanel` object. For the `ImagePanel` object, the default `imageUpdate()` method is fine. The applet object is different. It wants to know the height and the width of the image so it can resize itself to fit the image. Calling `getWidth()` and `getHeight()` for the `Image` object provide these values if they are available, but these may not be available during the execution of the `init()` method even when the image file is local, in which case these methods will return –1. In this case therefore, we can usefully implement our own version of the `imageUpdate()` method to do what we want.

There are six parameters to the imageUpdate() method and it returns a boolean value so its outline implementation is like this:

```
public boolean imageUpdate(Image img,     // Reference to the image
                           int flags,     // Flags identifying what is availiable

                           int x,         // x coordinate
                           int y,         // y coordinate
                           int width,     // Image width
                           int height)    // Image height
{
  // Code to respond to data that is available...
}
```

The imageUpdate() method will be called when any new item of image data becomes available, so the data will typically be incomplete. You might have the width of the image available for instance but not the height. A return value of false indicates that you have received all the image data that you need, otherwise the method should return true so it will be called again later when more information is available.

The reference passed as the first parameter identifies the image that the call relates to, so if your class object is observing more than one image, you can use this to tell to which Image object the call of the method relates. The second parameter provides the key to determining what image data is available. The flags value is a combination of one or more of the following single bit flags:

Parameter	Description
WIDTH	The width of the image is available.
HEIGHT	The height of the image is available.
SOMEBITS	Some more pixels required for a scaled version of the image are available, and the bounding rectangle for these is given by the x, y, width and height values.
ALLBITS	This flag indicates that all the bits of an image that has been drawn previously are now available. This enables the updateImage() method to decide when to return false when an image is being drawn incrementally.
FRAMEBITS	This indicates that another complete frame of a multi-frame image that has been previously drawn is now available to be drawn again. This can be used to determine when to call the repaint() method to display more of an image.
PROPERTIES	This flag indicates that the properties of the image are now available. These are obtained by calling the getProperties() method for the Image object.
ABORT	This flag indicates that the process of retrieving the image was aborted and no further image data will be available.
ERROR	This flag indicates that an error has occurred retrieving the image and no further image data will be available.

We aren't going to go into the detail of how all these flags are used, but the complete set is here for reference. We are only interested in the height and the width of the image in our applet, so we can implement the `imageUpdate()` method as:

```
public boolean imageUpdate(Image img,        // Reference to the image
                           int flags,        // Flags identifying what is available
                           int x,            // x coordinate
                           int y,            // y coordinate
                           int width,        // Image width
                           int height)       // Image height
{
  if((flags & WIDTH) > 0 && (flags & HEIGHT) > 0)
  {
    resize(width,height);               // Set applet size to fit the image
    repaint();                          // Repaint the applet in its new size
    return false;
  }
  else
    return true;                        // More info required
}
```

We only want to resize the applet when we have both the width and height of the image, so we test for each of these flags by bitwise ANDing the `flags` value with the `WIDTH` and `HEIGHT` values that are defined in the `ImageObserver` interface. If the results of both operations are positive, both flags were set so we can resize the applet and repaint it. While either or both of the `WIDTH` and `HEIGHT` flags are not set, we return `true` so the method will be called again. Of course, the HTML rendering in a browser will work much better if the correct size for the applet is specified at the outset.

Try It Out – Implementing the `imageUpdate()` Method

Let's try out the whole applet in its revised guise:

```
import java.awt.*;
import javax.swing.*;
import java.net.*;

public class DisplayImage extends JApplet
{
  public void init()
  {
    Image image = null;
    try
    {
      // Image from a file specified by a URL
      image = getImage(new URL(getCodeBase(),"Images/wrox_logo.gif"));
    }
    catch (MalformedURLException e)
    {
      System.out.println("Failed to create URL:\n" + e);
      return;
    }
```

```
        int imageWidth = image.getWidth(this);      // Get its width
        int imageHeight = image.getHeight(this);     // and its height
        if(imageWidth != -1 && imageHeight != -1)    // If they are available
           resize(imageWidth,imageHeight);           // set applet size to fit

      ImagePanel imagePanel = new ImagePanel(image);// Create panel showing the image
        getContentPane().add(imagePanel);            // Add the panel to the
content pane
    }

    public boolean imageUpdate(Image img,      // Reference to the image
                               int flags,      // Flags identifying what is available
                               int x,          // x coordinate
                               int y,          // y coordinate
                               int width,      // Image width
                               int height)     // Image height
    {
      if((flags & WIDTH) > 0 && (flags & HEIGHT) > 0)
      {
        resize(width,height);                  // Set applet size to fit the image
        repaint();                             // Repaint the applet in its new size
        return false;
      }
      else
        return true;                           // More info required
    }

    // Class representing a panel displaying an image
    class ImagePanel extends JPanel
    {
      public ImagePanel(Image image)
      {
        this.image = image;
      }

      public void paint(Graphics g)
      {
        g.drawImage(image, 0, 0, this);        // Display the image
      }

      Image image;                             // The image
    }
  }
```

How It Works

The effect of the applet will appear much the same as before because the image file is local so everything will happen quite quickly. You can verify that the image data is not available in the `init()` method for the applet by commenting out the `if` that checks for a value of –1 for the `width` or the `height` before calling `resize()`. Without this check, the `resize()` method will be called with either or both arguments as –1 so the size of the applet will briefly become miniscule and the applet viewer window along with it.

A further experiment will show that our `imageUpdate()` method in the `DisplayImage` class is only called if we have previously requested image data that is not available. Modify the code in the `init()` method that calls the methods to obtain the image size like this:

```
int imageWidth = 30, imageHeight = 30;              // Added...

//   imageWidth = image.getWidth(this);            // Get its width
//   imageHeight = image.getHeight(this);          // and its height
//   if(imageWidth != -1 && imageHeight != -1)
//      resize(imageWidth,imageHeight);            // Set applet size to fit the image
```

Now the applet will not be resized at all and the image will not be displayed. If you uncomment either or both of the statements calling `imageWidth` and `imageHeight` and recompile, everything will work as it should. To see when `imageUpdate()` is called, you could add a call to `System.out.println()` at the beginning of the method.

The default `imageUpdate()` method is called automatically for the `ImagePanel` object because the `paint()` method calls `drawImage()` and identifies the object as the image observer. The default version calls `repaint()` as new data becomes available, so over a slow link our image will be drawn incrementally.

Animation

You can create animated effects in Java on any component. You can create animation in a window or a panel, your buttons can have animated labels, and you can even animate your menu items if you wish. The general principles for producing animated images on your screen are the same as for a film. You display, or draw, a series of static images on the screen with a fixed interval of time between one image and the next. Each image differs slightly from its predecessor so that an object that is in a different position on successive images will appear to move. Since you know how to display one image you are part way there, and since you also know how to create a loop it is clearly not going to be too difficult to implement animated images.

There are two basic ways in which animation can be generated. You can create or obtain a set of images that are snapshots of the position of everything at fixed intervals, and then display them in sequence. Alternatively you can create or obtain an image of whatever you want to have moving, and display it at different positions at fixed intervals of time. Of course, before you display the moving entity at any given position, you must erase it at whatever position it was previously. Come to think of it, you already know one way to do this. Drawing a line or a circle in `Sketcher` produces an animated effect while you drag the mouse cursor.

Animation is often used in applets to make web pages more interesting and eye catching and there can be multiple, independent animated images in a page. The code producing an animated effect generally runs continuously, so you usually have to make this independent of any other code that may be running to allow the apparent concurrent operations. For this reason, you always implement code that generates an animated effect as a separate thread. If you don't implement your animation in a separate thread, it is unlikely to work properly, and other code that you expect to be executable while the animation is running will not work either. This goes for animations in applications as well as applets. We have already discussed threads in some detail so we just need to dredge the stuff up again and apply it for drawing images.

An Animated Applet

Just so that you know where we are heading, our first program illustrating animation will be an applet that drops the Wrox logo from a great height to see what happens. Since Wrox Press is an immensely resilient company, the logo will bounce.

To implement this we just need to draw the logo at its new position at fixed intervals of time – the new position being determined by how far the logo has fallen during the time interval. We can store the coordinates of the current location of the image in data members of the applet class, `imageX` and `imageY` and the `paint()` method of the inner class `ImagePanel` will draw the image at that position. The animation code in the `run()` method will need access to the height of the image so it can work out when the image hits the ground, so we should store the image dimensions, `imageWidth` and `imageHeight`, as data members too.

We will call the applet class `LogoBounce`, so the outline contents of the source file will be:

```
import java.awt.*;
import java.awt.image.*;
import javax.swing.*;
import java.net.*;

public class LogoBounce extends JApplet
                        implements Runnable
{
  // This method is called when the applet is loaded
  public void init()
  {
    // Code to initialize the applet...
  }

  // This method is called when the browser starts the applet
  public void start()
  {
    bouncer = new Thread(this);                    // Create animation thread
    bouncing = true;
    bouncer.start();                               // and start it
  }

  // This method is called when the browser wants to stop the applet
  //   - when is it not visible for example
  public void stop()
  {
    bouncing = false;                              // Stop the animation loop
    bouncer = null;                                // Discard the thread
  }

  // This method is called when the animation thread is started
  public void run()
  {
    // Code for the animation thread...
    while(bouncing)
    {
      // Code for the animation loop
    }
```

```
  }
class ImagePanel extends JPanel
{
  public ImagePanel(Image image)
  {
    this.image = image;
  }

  public void paint(Graphics g)
  {
    // Initialize the animation...

  }

  Image image;                        // The image
}

Thread bouncer;                       // The animation thread
boolean bouncing = false;             // Controls animation thread
ImagePanel imagePanel;                // Panel for the image
int imageWidth, imageHeight;          // Image dimensions
int imageX, imageY;                   // Current image position
}
```

All the basic things we need are here. In the `init()` method we will set up a component on which we can draw an image and add this to the content pane for the applet, just as we did in the previous example. The `start()` method creates the animation thread, `bouncer`; sets the variable, `bouncing`, that will control the animation loop to `true`; and starts the thread. The `run()` method will contain the animation loop that will continue to run as long as `bouncing` is `true`. In the `stop()` method we just set `bouncing` to false to stop the animation loop in the `run()` method, then discard the animation thread object by setting `bouncer` to `null`. The `start()` method will create a new thread if the animation needs to be restarted.

We will fetch the image from the file in the `init()` method using the `getImage()` method as we did in the previous example. There's a complication here though. The browser will call `start()` as soon as the `init()` method returns to start the applet, and this will start the thread to do the animation. Since this will involve calculations involving the height of the image, we don't want this to go ahead until we are sure the height is available. One way of determining when an image has been loaded is to make use of something called a **media tracker**.

Using a Media Tracker

A media tracker is an object of type `MediaTracker` that is used specifically for tracking the loading of images. This class is defined in the `java.awt` package, and while it only manages the loading of images at present, it may be extended in the future to track the loading of other kinds of media. There is just one `MediaTracker` constructor that expects to be passed a reference to a component as the argument – the component object being the one that is loading the images.

Using a media tracker is quite simple. After calling the `getImage()` method to obtain a reference to the `Image` object, you then pass the `Image` reference to the tracker by calling its `addImage()` method. This makes the `MediaTracker` object responsible for loading the image. There are two arguments to the `addImage()` method: the reference to the image to be tracked and an identifier of type `int` that is used to track the image. We can create and track our image in the `init()` method with the code:

```
public void init()
{
    tracker = new MediaTracker(this);
    Image image = null;
    try
    {
      // Image from a file specified by a URL
      image = getImage(new URL(getCodeBase(),"Images/wrox_logo.gif"));
    }
    catch(MalformedURLException e)
    {
      System.out.println("Failed to create URL:\n" + e);
    }
    tracker.addImage(image,1);

    // Plus the rest of the code for the method...
}
```

We have specified the identifier for our image as 1. You can use a single `MediaTracker` object to track multiple images and several images can have the same identifier. The value of the identifier determines the priority for loading images; images associated with an identifier of a lower value will be loaded first. You start loading all the images associated with a particular identifier and wait for them to be loaded by calling the `waitForID()` method for the tracker object, and passing the identifier to it. This method will only return when all the images associated with the identifier have been loaded. This method can throw an exception of type `InterruptedException` if this thread gets interrupted by another thread, so you must put calls in a `try` block and catch the exception. In our implementation of `init()` we could write:

```
try
{
    tracker.waitForID(1);               // Load and wait for images with ID of 1
}
catch(InterruptedException e)
{
    System.out.println(e);              // Thread was interrupted
}
```

Clearly, if you want to wait for individual images to be loaded, you should give each of them a unique identifier. A common technique when loading multiple images is to store the references in an array, and use the array index for each image as its identifier.

You can also initiate loading and wait for all the images being tracked to be loaded by calling the `waitForAll()` method for the tracker. We could equally well write in our `init()` method:

```
try
{
   tracker.waitForAll();                    // Load and wait for all images
}
catch(InterruptedException e)
{
   System.out.println(e);                   // Thread was interrupted
}
```

This will initiate loading of our single image and return when it has been loaded.

While the two wait methods we have discussed will wait indefinitely, there are overloaded versions of both methods that accept an extra argument specifying the maximum number of milliseconds that the method should wait for the image to be loaded. In this case you won't know when the method returns whether the image or images have actually been loaded, or whether the time ran out. You can call the checkAll() method for the MediaTracker object with an ID as the argument to test this. A true return value indicates that the images for the ID have been loaded. You can also use a version of checkAll() with no argument to check whether all the images associated with the tracker have been loaded.

Even though checkAll() may indicate that all images have been loaded, you can't assume that no errors occurred while the images were loading. You must test for errors explicitly. You can call the isErrorAny() method to determine if any errors occurred with any of the images – a false return value indicating that there were no errors. If you want to test for errors more specifically, you can pass an ID to the isErrorID() method. A return value of true indicates that an error occurred in loading at least one of the images associated with the ID. If you want to know which image or images caused an error, you can call the getErrorsID() method with the ID as the argument. This method will return an array of references (as type Object[]) to the images for which a loading error occurs. Of course, if you use a unique ID for each image, you won't need to do this.

We can implement the init() for our applet as:

```
public void init()
{
   tracker = new MediaTracker(this);
   Image image = null;
   try
   {
     // Image from a file specified by a URL
     image = getImage(new URL(getCodeBase(),"Images/wrox_logo.gif"));
   }
   catch(MalformedURLException e)
   {
     System.out.println("Failed to create URL:\n" + e);
   }

   tracker.addImage(image,0);

   try
   {
     tracker.waitForAll();                   // Wait for image to load
     if(tracker.isErrorAny())                // If there is an error
       return;                               // give up
```

```
        imageWidth = image.getWidth(this);      // Get image width
        imageHeight = image.getHeight(this);    // and its height
        resize(imageWidth,imageHeight);         // set applet size to fit
        imageY = -imageHeight;                  // for image
        imagePanel = new ImagePanel(image);     // Create panel showing the image
        getContentPane().add(imagePanel);       // Add the panel to the content pane
    }
    catch(InterruptedException e)
    {
        System.out.println(e);
    }
}
```

We use a media tracker to manage loading of the image, and we only get the height and width of the image once we are sure that the image has been loaded with no errors. We set the applet size to accommodate the image and set the y coordinate of the starting position so that the image will be just out of sight above the x axis – which is the top of the applet. We create an `ImagePanel` object to display the image and add it to the content pane of the applet object.

The `init()` code assumes that `tracker` is a data member of our applet class, so add the following line to your class:

```
    MediaTracker tracker;           // Tracks image loading
```

Of course, if there was an error loading the image, we don't want to start the animation thread, so we modify the `start()` method:

```
    public void start()
    {
        if(tracker.isErrorAny())            // If any image errors
            return;                         // don't create the thread
        bouncer = new Thread(this);
        bouncing = true;
        bouncer.start();
    }
```

That's sufficient information about media trackers for our purposes, so let's get back to our animation. The main purpose of the code in the animation thread, the `run()` method in our applet, will be to determine when the next image has to be drawn. It will therefore boil down to calling a method that draws an image at fixed intervals. If you want your animation to display 10 frames per second, then every 100 milliseconds you want it to display another frame. Let's look at how we can implement the `run()` method to determine when the required time interval is up, to cue the drawing of another image.

Measuring Time Intervals

We will want to display an image at fixed intervals, of `interval` milliseconds say, from some arbitrary start time. We can record a starting time by calling the static `currentTimeMillis()` method in the `System` class. This returns the current time from the system clock in milliseconds as a value of type `long`. We could save this as our starting time with the statement:

```
   long time = System.currentTimeMillis();
```

At this point we will immediately draw the image, so the next instance of drawing the image should be at the time `time+interval`. Of course, we have to take account of the time spent processing subsequent to the instance when the image was last displayed, so the time we need to wait before displaying the next image is going to be less than `interval`. However, this is not too difficult to organize. All we need to do is wait until the value returned by `currentTimeMillis()` is equal to or greater than this value, and the `sleep()` method for a thread will do this very nicely. After each interval, we just add the `interval` value to `time` to get the time when the next repaint of the image should occur. We also need to figure out where the image is at the end of each interval.

The basic code for the `run()` method is going to be:

```
public void run()
{
  long time = System.currentTimeMillis(); // Starting time
  long interval = 20;                      // Time interval msec

  // Move image while bouncing is true
  while(bouncing)
  {
    imagePanel.repaint();                  // Repaint the image

    // Wait until the end of the next interval
    try
    {
      time += interval;
      Thread.sleep(Math.max(0, time - System.currentTimeMillis()));
    }
    catch (InterruptedException e)
    {
      break;
    }

    // Calculate distance moved in interval msecs and update position of
    // image...
  }
}
```

After initializing `time` with the current time, and setting up the value of `interval`, we have a loop that runs as long as the `bouncer` thread is running. Within the loop we call `repaint()` for the `imagePanel` object to draw the image, and then update the value of `time` to the end of the next interval. The variable `time` will therefore define points in time that are exactly `interval` milliseconds apart. We then call `sleep()` for the animation thread and pass the number of milliseconds remaining between now – determined by calling `currentTimeMillis()` – and the end of the interval, which is the instant specified by the value of `time`. This automatically takes account of the time we spend executing code in the loop to repaint the image and doing other housekeeping. Using the static `max()` method from the `Math` class just ensures that if the repaint and housekeeping took longer than the interval, we pass a zero value to the `sleep()` method so the thread won't sleep at all.

All that's left is for us to work out how far the image moves in `interval` milliseconds.

Dropping the Logo

We will need to know the velocity of the image as it drops and at the end of each time interval. The velocity will increase gradually as it drops due to the force of gravity. We won't worry about the precise physics of this – we are interested in the image handling aspects so we just want to get a nice easy motion for the logo. We will calculate the change in velocity of the image at the end of each time interval as the acceleration multiplied by the time interval in seconds, and the distance traveled as the average velocity times the time interval in seconds. If we assume our units of distance are feet, then the acceleration due to gravity while the logo is dropping is 32 feet per second per second – that is, the velocity increases by 32 feet per second for every second the image drops. We'll also assume the image is stationary to start with so the initial velocity is zero.

The only other thing we need to consider is what happens when the logo hits the ground. The logo image will deform as it is very flexible, and as a consequence will experience a force upwards that increases as it is compressed. We will arbitrarily make this proportional to the degree by which the logo is compressed.

Eventually the downward velocity will be zero and the upward acceleration will then accelerate the image back up again – in other words it will bounce. We can implement this with the following code in the `run()` method:

```
public void run()
{
  long time = System.currentTimeMillis(); // Starting time
  long interval = 20;                      // Time interval msec
  float t = interval/1000.0f;              // and in seconds
  final float g = 32;                      // Acceleration due to gravity
  float a = g;                             // Initial acceleration
  float v = 0.0f;                          // Initial velocity

  // Move image while the bouncer thread is running
  while(Thread.currentThread() == bouncer)
  {
    imagePanel.repaint();                  // Repaint the image

    // Wait until the end of the next interval
    try
    {
      time += interval;
      Thread.sleep(Math.max(0, time - System.currentTimeMillis()));
    }
    catch (InterruptedException e)
    {
      break;
    }

    imageY += (long)(t*(v+a*t/2));         // New image position
    v += a*t;                              // New velocity

    // Calculate distance moved in interval
    if(imageY>0)                           // Image compressed?
      a = g - 10.000f*g*imageY/imageHeight;// acceleration in opposite direction

    if(imageY<=0)                          // Image not compressed?
      a = g;                               // -then falling under gravity
  }
}
```

Outside the loop we initialize a variable t that stores the time interval in seconds as a value of type float. We will use this in our calculations for the image position and velocity. We also define a constant g, and initialize the acceleration, a, and the velocity v, of the image. Within the loop we just apply the calculations that we discussed earlier.

The image is compressed when the y coordinate, imageY, is positive. This is because the top of the applet is where *y* is 0, and the bottom of the applet is where *y* is imageHeight, so when the top-left corner of the image is below the top of the applet, it is being squashed. In this case, if the image is still heading downwards, we apply an acceleration in the opposite direction that is the value of the expression -10.000f*g*imageY/imageHeight. This expression is arbitrary, but it has the effect of slowing the image down more and more as it is compressed. When imageY is negative, the image is off the ground so we set the acceleration back to g.

Displaying the Image

The image is displayed by the ImagePanel object, so we need to implement the paint() method for this class to display the image normally when imageY is zero or negative, and deal with squashing the image when imageY is positive. This is going to be easy since we can use the drawImage() method we used in the previous example to draw the image normally, and use an overloaded version that is specifically intended for scaling an image on the fly to fit a particular area. The overloaded method has the following arguments:

```
drawImage(Image image,            // The image
          int destinationX,       // x coordinate of the display area
                                  //   top left
          int destinationY,       // y coordinate of the display area
                                  //   top left
          int destinationWidth,   // Width of the display area
          int destinationHeight,  // Height of the display area
          int imageX,             // x coordinate of the image top left
          int imageY,             // y coordinate of the image top left
          int imageWidth,         // Width of the image
          int imageHeight,        // Height of the image
          ImageObserver observer  // The image observer
)
```

When you call this method, the image is scaled on the fly to fit the destination area specified by the arguments. Since you specify the coordinates of the top-left of the image, as well as its width and height, it is possible to use this method to display part of an image, and fit it to the destination space that you specify. Like all the drawImage() methods, this method can draw part of an image when loading of the image is not complete. In this case the method returns false. The ImageObserver that is passed as the last argument – usually the applet itself – is notified when more of the image becomes available, with the result that the image is repainted. When the entire image has been drawn, the drawImage() method returns true.

It would also be useful to color the background with a color that contrasts with the image. With this in mind we can implement the paint() method for the ImagePanel class as:

```
public void paint(Graphics g)
{
    Graphics2D g2D = (Graphics2D)g;
```

```
        g2D.setPaint(Color.lightGray);                              // Set a background color
        g2D.fillRect(0, 0, imageWidth, imageHeight);                // paint background
        if(imageY<=0)
          g2D.drawImage(image, imageX, imageY, this);                   // Draw normally
        else                                                            // or scaled...
          g2D.drawImage(image,                                          // The image
                        imageX, imageY, imageWidth, imageHeight,//      Destination
                        0, 0, imageWidth, imageHeight,           //     Image area
                        this);                                   //     Image observer
      }
```

The `fillRect()` method fills the entire area of the applet with the color that we set in the
`setPaint()` call, `Color.lightGray`. When `imageY` is greater than 0, we use the version of
`drawImage()` that scales the image on the fly to fit the area available, from the `imageY` position to the
bottom of the applet at the y coordinate, `imageHeight`.

It is worth noting that a `JPanel` object is double-buffered by default. This means that all rendering for
a new image that is to be displayed is done in a buffer in memory, and only when image is complete are
the pixels for the entire picture written to the screen. Since the existing image that is displayed is not
altered while the new image is being created, this eliminates the flicker and flashing that can occur if
your display buffer is updated incrementally while it is displayed.

If you have put together all the bits of code we have discussed, you should have a working applet.

Transforming Images

We have already seen back in Chapter 15 that we can apply a transformation to a graphics context to
modify the user coordinate system relative to the device coordinate system. The transformation can be a
translation, a rotation, a scaling operation, a shearing operation or a combination of all four. Of course,
such a transformation applies to images that you draw as well as anything else.

In our previous example we adjusted the size of the applet to accommodate the image. In many
situations you would not want to do this. Typically, there are likely to be all kinds of things on the web
page so you would want your applet to keep within the space allotted to it. We could have done this by
scaling the image to fit the space available. Rather than go over the old ground let's create a new applet
to try this out, and to add a bit of spice this time we will spin the image about its center, rather than
dropping it. That way we will get to use a more complicated transform.

Try It Out – Spinning an Image

This applet will create an animation that spins the image about its center point. We will therefore need
to make the diagonal of the image fit within both the height and width of the applet if we want to see all
of it as it rotates. We also want the scaled image to fit in the center of the applet, so we will translate the
user space after we have applied the scale transform.

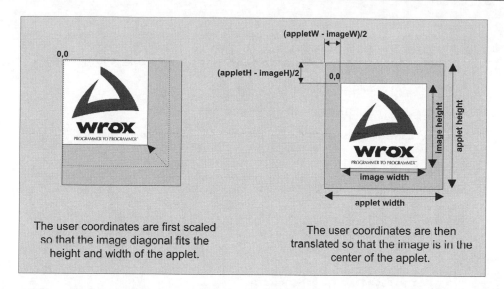

The user coordinates are first scaled so that the image diagonal fits the height and width of the applet.

The user coordinates are then translated so that the image is in the center of the applet.

Once the image is loaded, we can calculate the length of the diagonal of the image as the square root of the sum of the squares of the width and height. We can then calculate the scale factor that we require by dividing the width and height of the applet by the diagonal of the image, and taking the minimum of these two values. We can create an `AffineTransform` object in the `init()` method that combines both the scaling and the translation, and then just apply it in the `paint()` method for the `ImagePanel` class.

This applet class will contain the same methods as the previous example but with different implementations. The rotation will be accomplished by an additional transformation. We will also have an inner `ImagePanel` class to define the panel that will display the image. This will only differ in the implementation of the `paint()` method.

Let's start with the `init()` method and the data members in the `Applet` class. The loading of the image will be identical to the previous example, so we need the `image` and `tracker` members too. After the image has been loaded, we will calculate the scaling and translation that is necessary.

Here's the applet class with its data members and the `init()` method:

```java
import java.awt.*;
import java.awt.image.*;
import javax.swing.*;
import java.net.*;
import java.awt.geom.*;                           // For AffineTransform

public class WhirlingLogo extends JApplet
                          implements Runnable
{
  // This method is called when the applet is loaded
  public void init()
  {
    tracker = new MediaTracker(this);
    Image image = null;
```

```
    try
    {
      // Image from a file specified by a URL
      image = getImage(new URL(getCodeBase(),"Images/wrox_logo.gif"));
    }
    catch(MalformedURLException e)
    {
      System.out.println("Failed to create URL:\n" + e);
    }
    tracker.addImage(image,0);                      // Load image
    try
    {
      tracker.waitForAll();                         // Wait for image to load
      if(tracker.isErrorAny())                      // If there is an error
        return;                                     // give up

      Dimension size = getSize();                   // Get applet size
      imageWidth = image.getWidth(this);            // Get image width
      imageHeight = image.getHeight(this);          // and its height

      // Calculate scale factor so diagonal of image fits width and height
      double diagonal = Math.sqrt(
                     imageWidth*imageWidth + imageHeight*imageHeight);
      double scaleFactor = Math.min(size.width/diagonal, size.height/diagonal);

      // Create a transform to translate and scale the image
      at.setToTranslation((size.width-imageWidth*scaleFactor)/2,
                          (size.height-imageHeight*scaleFactor)/2);
      at.scale(scaleFactor,scaleFactor);

      imagePanel = new ImagePanel(image);         // Create panel showing the image
      getContentPane().add(imagePanel);           // Add the panel to the content pane
    }
    catch(InterruptedException e)
    {
      System.out.println(e);
    }
  }

  // Plus the rest of the applet

  Thread whirler;                                 // Animation thread
  boolean whirling = false;                       // Animation control
  MediaTracker tracker;                           // Tracks image loading
  ImagePanel imagePanel;
  AffineTransform at = new AffineTransform();
  int imageWidth, imageHeight;                    // Image dimensions
  double angle;                                   // Rotation angle
  final int INTERVAL = 50;                         // Time interval msec
  final int ROTATION_TIME = 2000;                 // Complete rotation time msec
  final int STEPS_PER_ROTATION = ROTATION_TIME/INTERVAL;
  int stepCount;                                  // Total number of steps
}
```

The unshaded code is exactly the same as in the previous method. The `AffineTransform` member, `at`, stores a transform that scales and translates the image. The `angle` member will store the rotation angle in radians that will be calculated in the `run()` method for the `whirler` thread, and applied in the `paint()` method for the `imagePanel` object. We have made this is a member of the class rather than declare it as a local variable in the `run()` method so we can pick up the value when the applet is stopped and restarted. The other fields that follow `angle` are all concerned with orienting and drawing the image.

The constant, `INTERVAL`, stores the time interval between one instance of drawing the image and the next. We store the time for a complete rotation of the image through 360 degrees, which is 2π radians, in `ROTATIONTIME`. The variable `STEPS_PER_ROTATION` holds the number of steps for a complete rotation, so with the values we have set for the previous two variables, this will be 40. Finally, the variable, `stepCount`, will accumulate the total number of steps modulo `STEPS_PER_ROTATION`. The methods to start and stop the animation thread are the same as in the previous example, apart from the new names for the thread and the control variable:

```java
// This method is called when the browser starts the applet
public void start()
{
  if(tracker.isErrorAny())                    // If any image errors
    return;                                   // don't create the thread
  whirler = new Thread(this);                 // Create the animation thread
  whirling = true;
  whirler.start();                            // and start it
}

// This method is called when the browser want to stop the applet
// when is it not visible for example
public void stop()
{
  whirling = false;                           // Stop the animation loop
  whirler = null;                             // Discard the thread
}
```

The thread code itself will be very similar to the previous example – the timing mechanism is exactly the same. We now need to increment the rotation angle in each time interval so it will be much simpler:

```java
// This method is called when the animation thread is started
public void run()
{
  long time = System.currentTimeMillis();              // Starting time

  // Move image while whirling is true
  while(whirling)
  {
    imagePanel.repaint();                      // Repaint the image

    // Wait until the end of the interval
    try
    {
      time += INTERVAL;                        // Increment the time
      angle = 2.0*Math.PI*stepCount++/ STEPS_PER_ROTATION;
      stepCount %= STEPS_PER_ROTATION;
      Thread.sleep(Math.max(0, time - System.currentTimeMillis()));
    }
```

```
         catch (InterruptedException e)
         {
          break;
         }
      }
   }
```

The stepCount variable starts at 0 and is incremented by 1 on each iteration of the loop. Since a complete rotation through 2 radians should occur after STEPS_PER_ROTATION steps, after stepCount steps the rotation angle is the result of the expression 2.0*Math.PI*stepCount/STEPS_PER_ROTATION. In the statement calculating the rotation angle we also increment stepCount using the postfix increment operator. The image returns to its original position after STEPS_PER_ROTATION steps, so we maintain the value of stepCount modulo STEPS_PER_ROTATION.

The last bit we need to complete the applet is the ImagePanel class, and this only differs from the previous example in the implementation of the paint() method:

```
class ImagePanel extends JPanel
{
  public ImagePanel(Image image)
  {
    this.image = image;
  }

  public void paint(Graphics g)
  {
    Graphics2D g2D = (Graphics2D)g;
    g2D.transform(at);                                    // Apply scale & translate

    g2D.setPaint(Color.lightGray);
    g2D.fillRect(0, 0, imageWidth, imageHeight);

    g2D.rotate(angle, imageWidth/2.0, imageHeight/2.0);   // Rotate about center

    // draw scaled imaged with background
    g2D.drawImage(image, 0, 0, this);
  }

  Image image;                                            // The image
}
```

That's the complete applet so give it a whirl. It would be a good idea to make the applet dimension larger in the html file – 200x200 say – then you can see the image more clearly. The downside to a larger applet is that it will take more processor time since there are more pixels to process.

How It Works

The basic principles are the same as in the previous example. The thread code in the run() method repaints the imagePanel object every interval milliseconds. The while loop that expedites this increments angle each time, and angle defines the rotation transformation that is applied in the paint() method for the imagePanel object.

We define the rotation with the statement:

```
g2D.rotate(angle, imageWidth/2.0, imageHeight/2.0);     // Rotate about center
```

The transformation specified by this version of the `rotate()` method is concatenated with the existing transform for the graphics context, which is the `AffineTransform` object that we create in the `init()` method for the applet. The transform created by this `rotate()` call is a composite of a translation to the center of the image, the coordinates of which are defined by the last two arguments, a rotation through `angle` radians – supplied as the first argument, then a translation back to the original origin point. Thus the rotation is about the center of the image.

Using Timers

We have adopted a do-it-yourself approach to timing when we need to redraw in animation. This provides a good insight into how animations operate but we can accomplish the same result rather more simply by making use of an object of the `Timer` class and objects of its associated `TimerTask` class. Both classes are defined in the `java.util` package. The `Timer` class we are discussing here schedules an operation that you define with a `TimerTask` object, either once after a given delay, or repeatedly with a given time interval between successive executions of the task. The task that is executed by the `TimerTask` object runs in a separate thread.

Be aware that there is another `Timer` class defined in `javax.swing` that provides a capability that appears somewhat similar at first sight but that has significant differences in the way that it works. The `Timer` class defined in the `javax.swing` package notifies its listeners (of type `ActionListener`) when a given time interval has passed, and it is up to the listener objects to carry out or initiate the task to be executed. As with the other `Timer` class, you can use a `Timer` object do something just once after a given interval, or repeatedly after successive intervals of time. A major difference is that the listener object methods will execute on the same thread unless you provide code to ensure that is not the case.

The `Timer` and `TimerTask` combination of classes provide a way of executing repeated tasks that is easy to apply to animations so we will concentrate on those. While we will be applying them to animations here, keep in mind that you can use these methods for executing any kind of task repeatedly or after a fixed delay. We will start by looking at how you use a `Timer` object to schedule a task.

Timer Objects

You can use a single `Timer` object to schedule several different tasks, where each task will be defined by its own `TimerTask` object. Each `TimerTask` object defines a separate thread, so when you schedule multiple tasks they will each execute in a separate thread. The `Timer` class has been designed to allow large numbers of tasks to be executed concurrently – thousands, according to the documentation – without creating undue task scheduling overhead.

There are two constructors for `Timer` objects. The default constructor simply defines a `Timer` object that has an associated thread that is not run as a daemon thread. You will recall that a daemon thread is subordinate to the thread that created it and dies when its creator dies, whereas a non-daemon thread runs completely independently. You can make the `Timer` thread daemon by creating the `Timer` object using the constructor that accepts an argument of type `boolean`, and specifying the argument as `true`. For instance, the following statement creates a `Timer` object with a daemon thread:

```
Timer clock = new Timer(true);  // Create a daemon Timer
```

When you have no further need of a `Timer` object, you can terminate it by calling its `cancel()` method. Calling the `cancel()` method for a `Timer` object terminates all tasks scheduled by the timer, and terminates the timer's thread, so you cannot use the object again for scheduling tasks.

A `Timer` object provides you with two methods for scheduling tasks, the `schedule()` method and the `scheduleAtFixedRate()` method. Both of these methods come in overloaded flavors, so let's look at the `schedule()` method first.

The `schedule()` method is for executing a task either once at a given instant in time, or repeatedly with each subsequent execution starting after a fixed delay relative to the previous task. If any particular execution is delayed, subsequent executions will be delayed. This mode of repeated task execution is referred to as **fixed-delay execution** because priority is given to maintaining the time interval between task executions, rather than scheduling each execution at a precise time. This is suitable for applications where the priority is for repeated executions of a task to be evenly distributed rather than being at fixed points in time. Animations fall into this category since you will generally want to have the animation as smooth as possible. You have four versions of the `schedule()` method available:

Method	Description
`schedule(TimerTask task, Date time)`	This schedules the task determined by the first argument, `task`, to be executed once at the time instant specified by the second argument, `time`. If the current time is later than the time specified by `time`, then the task executes immediately.
`schedule(TimerTask task, Date firstTime, long period)`	This schedules the task determined by the first argument, `task`, to be executed repeatedly starting at the time specified by the second argument, `firstTime`. The third argument, `period`, specifies the period in milliseconds between the start time of one execution of the task and the start time of the next. If the current time is later than the time specified for the first execution of the task, then the task executes immediately.
`schedule(TimerTask task, long delay)`	This schedules the task determined by the first argument, `task`, to be executed once after a delay relative to the current time of `delay` milliseconds.
`schedule(TimerTask task, long delay, long period)`	This schedules the task determined by the first argument, `task`, to be executed repeatedly with the first execution starting after a delay relative to the current time of `delay` milliseconds. The third argument, `period`, specified the period in milliseconds between the start time of one execution of the task and the start time of the next.

You use the `scheduleAtFixedRate()` method for repeated executions of a task where the precise timing is more important than maintaining the interval between successive executions. This is referred to as **fixed-rate execution**. Each execution is scheduled relative to the first execution of the task, not the preceding one. If you wanted to simulate a clock for instance using `Timer` and `TimerTask` objects you would use the `scheduleAtFixedRate()` method to schedule updating the position of the hands on the clock rather than the `schedule()` method because you want the hand positions to be set as close as possible to absolute time. If any execution of the update to the hand position is delayed for any reason, succeeding executions will 'bunch-up' in time in order to try to maintain their schedule in real time.

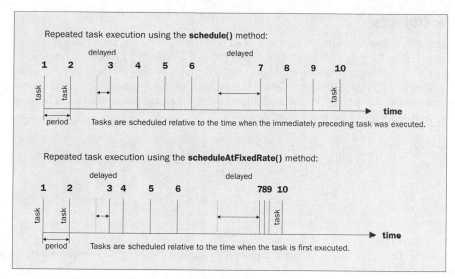

This is shown graphically in the diagram, which contrasts the two types of scheduling operations you can use.

You have two versions of the `scheduleAtFixedRate()` method available to you, both of which are for scheduling a task repeatedly:

Method	Description
`scheduleAtFixedRate` `(TimerTask task,` `Date firstTime,` `long period)`	This schedules the task determined by the first argument, task, to be executed repeatedly starting at the time specified by the second argument, firstTime. The third argument, period, specifies the period in milliseconds between the start time of one execution of the task and the start time of the next. If the current time is later than the time specified for the first execution of the task, then the task executes immediately.
`scheduleAtFixedRate` `(TimerTask task,` `long delay,` `long period)`	This schedules the task determined by the first argument, `task`, to be executed repeatedly with the first execution starting after a delay relative to the current time of `delay` milliseconds. The third argument, `period`, specifies the period in milliseconds between the start time of one execution of the task and the start time of the next.

Both the `schedule()` and `scheduleAtFixedRate()` methods can throw exceptions. An exception of type `IllegalArgumentException` will be thrown if a delay argument is negative or if an argument of type `Date` represents a negative time value (as returned by its `getTime()` method). An exception of type `IllegalStateException` will be thrown if the task was already scheduled or if the task or the timer was cancelled.

Let's turn to how we use the `TimerTask` class to define a task to be scheduled by a `Timer` object.

TimerTask Objects

TimerTask is an abstract class, so you will need to derive your own class from it. The class implements the Runnable interface so a TimerTask object defines a thread. The run() method in the TimerTask class is abstract because it is this method that specifies the task to be executed and it's your job to decide this. Of course, you can define your class with TimerTask as a base in its own source file, but more often than not you will want to define it using an anonymous class. The form of the code for scheduling such a task will be something like this:

```
TimerTask task = new TimerTask()
                {
                    public void run()
                    {
                        // Code defining the task to be executed.
                    }
                }
```

To schedule the task that this creates for repeated execution at one second intervals starting five seconds from now we could write:

```
Timer timer = new Timer(true);              // Create a timer with a daemon thread
timer.scheduleAtFixedRate(task, new Date(System.currentTimeMillis()+5000), 1000);
```

The currentTimeMillis() method returns the current time from the system clock in milliseconds. We add 5000 milliseconds to this to specify the instant five seconds from now. Since we call the scheduleAtFixedRate() method here to schedule the task, the fixed-delay execution method will apply.

The TimerTask class contains just one other method besides the run() method – the cancel() method, which you call to cancel the execution of a task. Calling the cancel() method for a given TimerTask object permanently stops execution of that task, whether it has been scheduled for one-time execution or repeated execution. For example:

```
task.cancel();                          // Terminate the task
```

The task will be terminated and cannot be run again. If you want to run the task again you need to create a new TimerTask object and schedule that for execution. If a task has been canceled previously, calling cancel() again will have no effect. The cancel() method for a TimerTask object provides you with control at a task level. As we said earlier, you can use a Timer object to schedule several different tasks, each of which will be defined by an object that has TimerTask as a superclass. Calling the cancel() method for an individual task will terminate the execution of that task without affecting any others.

When you want to terminate all the tasks currently managed by a Timer object you just call the cancel() method for the Timer object. For instance:

```
timer.cancel();                         // Terminate the timer
```

This terminates all tasks scheduled by timer, and also terminates the Timer object's thread so it cannot be used again.

Let's rewrite the previous WhirlingLogo example to use a Timer object.

Try It Out – Using a Timer

Much of the code will be the same so we will only repeat the essentials here. The class no longer needs to implement the Runnable interface so the run() method is no longer required in the applet class.

```java
import java.awt.*;
import java.awt.image.*;
import javax.swing.*;
import java.net.*;
import java.awt.geom.*;                        // For AffineTransform

public class TimedWhirlingLogo extends JApplet
{
  // This method is called when the applet is loaded
  public void init()
  {
    // Code exactly as before...
  }

  // This method is called when the browser starts the applet
  public void start()
  {
    if(tracker.isErrorAny())                   // If any image errors
      return;                                  // don't create the thread

    timer = new java.util.Timer(true);
    timer.schedule(new java.util.TimerTask()
                  {
                    public void run()
                    {
                      imagePanel.repaint();         // Repaint the image
                      angle = 2.0*Math.PI*stepCount++/ STEPS_PER_ROTATION;
                      stepCount = ++stepCount%STEPS_PER_ROTATION;
                    }
                  },
                  0, INTERVAL);
  }

  // This method is called when the browser wants to stop the applet
  //   - when is it not visible for example
  public void stop()
  {
    timer.cancel();
  }

  // Class representing a panel displaying an image
```

```
class ImagePanel extends JPanel
{
  // Code exactly as before...
)
```

```
java.util.Timer timer;                              // Animation timer
MediaTracker tracker;                               // Tracks image loading
ImagePanel imagePanel;
AffineTransform at = new AffineTransform();
int imageWidth, imageHeight;                        // Image dimensions
double angle;                                       // Rotation angle
final int INTERVAL = 50;                            // Time interval msec
final int ROTATION_TIME = 2000;                     // Complete rotation time msec
final int STEPS_PER_ROTATION = ROTATION_TIME/ INTERVAL;
int stepCount;                                      // Total number of steps
}
```

If you compile and run this applet, it should run just as well as the previous version.

How It Works

The code is a lot shorter because the `Timer` object does all the scheduling work. The `start()` method in our applet class creates the `Timer` object we will use to schedule the animation with the statement:

```
timer = new java.util.Timer(true);
```

The variable, `timer`, is a member of the `TimedWhirlingLogo` class rather than a variable local to the `start()` method because we also need to reference it in the `stop()` method. Note how we have used the fully qualified name for the `Timer` class here, and in the declaration of timer as a member of the applet class. This is essential in this case. Importing the package, `java.util`, containing the `Timer` class would not be sufficient. As we said earlier, the `javax.swing` package also defines a class with the name, `Timer`, so without qualification of the name, the compiler would be unable to decide which class we wanted to use.

We then use the `Timer` object to schedule the animation with the statement:

```
timer.schedule(new java.util.TimerTask()
              {
                public void run()
                {
                  imagePanel.repaint();          // Repaint the image
                  angle = 2.0*Math.PI*stepCount++/ STEPS_PER_ROTATION;
                  stepCount = ++stepCount%STEPS_PER_ROTATION;
                }
              },
              0, INTERVAL);
```

We use the `schedule()` method here because we need the task to be executed at evenly distributed intervals to get a smooth animation. The first argument to the `schedule()` method is defined by an anonymous class derived from `TimerTask`. We again use a fully qualified class name here – not because there is a duplicate use of the name, but because we have not imported the `java.util` package into our source file. The `run()` method in our anonymous class specifies the task to be executed. This consists of two steps: redrawing `imagePanel` containing the logo, and updating `angle` that determines the orientation of the logo next time around. The second argument to `schedule()` specifies a delay of zero milliseconds before the first execution of the task, so the animation will begin immediately. The third argument specifies the interval between successive frames of the animation. Defining the constant, `INTERVAL`, as a member of the applet class enables it to be referenced as an argument to the `schedule()` method and within the `run()` method of the anonymous class.

That's it. Using `Timer` objects makes scheduling animations a lot simpler. Let's try one more example to get a feel for using the `scheduleAtFixedRate()` method.

Try It Out – Fixed-Rate Task Execution

To make use of fixed-rate execution scheduling we'll create an applet that is a clock. The graphics will be much more complicated than the scheduling, but we will have an opportunity to explore yet another way of handling animation. It's quite a lot of code so we'll put it together piece by piece, starting with the applet class.

The basic code for the applet class will be like this:

```
import java.awt.*;
import javax.swing.*;
import java.awt.geom.*;
import java.util.*;

public class NewClock extends JApplet
{
  // This method is called when the applet is loaded
  public void init()
  {
    // Initialize the applet and set up the clock
  }

  // This method is called when the browser starts the applet
  public void start()
  {
    // Start the clock
  }

  // This method is called when the browser wants to stop the applet
  public void stop()
  {
    // Stop the clock
  }
}
```

The class has the name `NewClock` to differentiate from the myriad of other clock programs that are around. This class just contains the three basic methods that we will need to implement for our applet. We won't need to implement the `paint()` method as we will be adding the representation of the clock to the applet object and the clock will take care of drawing itself.

The clock when it is running will look as shown in the illustration.

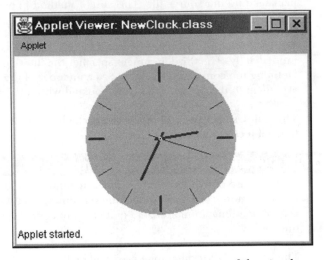

We can consider the clock to be made up of two parts. One part is the face, consisting of the circular dial plus the hour marks, and which is static. The other part is the hands, consisting of the hour, minute, and second hands, plus the central boss holding them in place. This is the bit that is dynamic and has to be updated. By separating the hands from the face of the clock, we can write our applet so that we only need to update the hands as time passes, and avoid having to redraw the face each time we update the time shown on the clock. We can define the two parts of the clock by inner classes to the `NewClock` class. We shall bring all our creativity to bear and name these classes `ClockFace` and `Hands`. Let's define the first one first.

Defining the Clock Face

We can base our `ClockFace` class on `JPanel`. The clock face will need to be sized to fit within the applet so we will construct a `ClockFace` object with a given diameter. The basic geometry of the clock face is shown in the diagram.

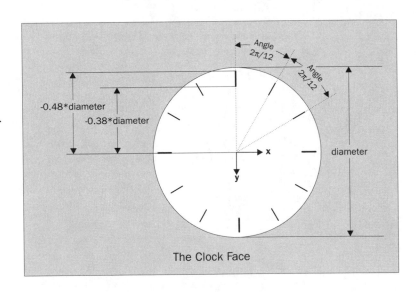

The Clock Face

We can create the circular face as a filled circle, which will be an ellipse object of type `Ellipse2D.Double` with the major and minor axes the same dimension, `diameter`. We want the hour marks to fit just inside the face and the dimensions shown as a proportion of the diameter will suit. We can create all the hour marks around the face very easily from a single vertical line of the appropriate length at the 12 o'clock position. We just need to repeatedly rotate the axes by one twelfth of 2π and redraw the line at a further eleven positions around the dial. We will define the line for the hour mark as an object of type `Line2D.Double`. Based on those ideas, here's the definition of the inner class:

```java
// Class defining the static face of the clock
class ClockFace extends JPanel
{
  // Creates a clock face with the given diameter
  public ClockFace(int diameter)
  {
    this.diameter = diameter;
    face = new Ellipse2D.Double();
    hourMark = new Line2D.Double(0, -diameter*0.38,
                                 0, -diameter*0.48);
    setOpaque(false);                         // Set panel transparent
  }

  public void paint(Graphics g)
  {
    Dimension size = getSize();
    face.setFrame((size.width-diameter)/2,     // Set the size
                  (size.height-diameter)/2,    // of the face centered
                  diameter, diameter);         // and of the given diameter

    Graphics2D g2D = (Graphics2D)g;

    // Clear the panel
    g2D.setPaint(CLEAR);                       // Transparent color
    g2D.fillRect(0,0,size.width,size.height);  // Fill the background

    g2D.setPaint(Color.lightGray);             // Face color
    g2D.fill(face);                            // Fill the clock face
    g2D.setPaint(Color.darkGray);              // Face outline color
    g2D.setStroke(widePen);                    // Use wide pen
    g2D.draw(face);                            // Draw face outline

    // Move origin to center of face
    g2D.translate(size.width/2, size.height/2);

    // Paint hour marks
    for(int i = 0 ; i<12 ; i++)
    {
      if(i%3 == 0)
        g2D.setStroke(widePen);                // Wide pen each quarter position
      else
        g2D.setStroke(narrowPen);              // otherwise narrow pen

      g2D.draw(hourMark);                      // Draw the hour mark
      g2D.rotate(TWO_PI/12.0);                 // Rotate to next mark
    }
  }

  int diameter;                                // Face diameter
  Ellipse2D.Double face;                       // The face
  Line2D.Double hourMark;                       // Mark for hours
}
```

Note that the various shades of gray used here reflect the needs of printing in the book, rather than any somber character trait on my part. You may like to jazz the example up a bit with your own choice of colors.

The face of the clock will be a filled ellipse with major and minor axes equal. We create a default `Ellipse2D.Double` object for this in the constructor, because we will set up the dimensions of the ellipse based on the size of the panel in the `paint()` method. We do this by calling the `setFrame()` method for the ellipse where the first two arguments are the coordinates of the top-left of the enclosing rectangle, and the last two are the dimensions' major and minor axes.

In the constructor, we make the hour mark object a vertical line of type `Line2D.Double` with start and end points such that it fits just within the diameter of the face, and leaves enough room centrally for the hands. We draw the hour marks in the `paint()` method by applying a transform that rotates the axes by $2\pi/12$ between drawing one mark and the next. The marks on quarters need to be a different thickness to the others and for this we use a couple of `BasicStroke` objects that defines lines with specific characteristics. Whenever you draw a shape – a line, an ellipse or whatever, the characteristics of the line that is produced are determined by a `Stroke` object that is stored within the `Graphics2D` object. So far we have just been using the default setup, but you can define your own line types. We haven't met this before, so let's take a brief detour into how strokes work.

Different Strokes for Different Folks

The type of line that applies by default when you draw any shape in a `Graphics2D` context is a solid line with square ends and a line width of 1. By calling the `setStroke()` method for the `Graphics2D` object, you can change the type of line produced to whatever you want. The `setStroke()` method expects an argument of type `Stroke`, but `Stroke` is actually an interface and the class that defines line types and implements the `Stroke` interface is `BasicStroke`. A `BasicStroke` object defines a line in terms of four attributes:

Attribute	Description
Pen Width	This is the width of the line expressed as a value of type `float`.
End Caps	This determines what the end of a line looks like, and you specify it by one of the following three constants, which are of type `int`: `CAP_BUTT` – the end of the line is flat with nothing added. `CAP_ROUND` – a semi-circular end is added with a radius half the width of the line. `CAP_SQUARE` – a square end is added that extends the line by half the width. A default line has this end cap.
Joins	This specifies how connected line segments in a path join, using one of three `int` values: `JOIN_BEVEL` – The outer corners of the two line segments are connected by a straight edge. `JOIN_MITER` – The outer edges of both segments are extended at the join until they meet. There is a limit to the distance over which mitered joins will be made (the default is 10.0). `JOIN_ROUND` – The outer edges of the segments are connected by a circular arc with a radius of half the width of the line.

Attribute	Description
Dash pattern	You specify this by an array of values of type float that define a dashing pattern. The values alternate between the length of a dash in user coordinates and the length of space before the next dash. Clearly a minimum of two elements are necessary to define a typical dashed line, one for the line and one for the space, but there can be more. Another float value defines the distance from the start of a line where the dashing pattern starts. If this value is non-zero, then your line starts with a space rather than a dash. A default line is solid.

The diagram shows the effects of some of these parameters for a Stroke object.

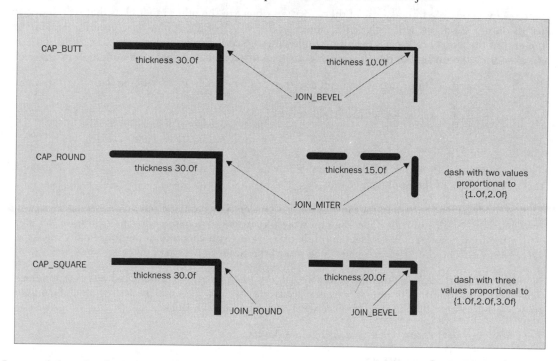

I created these by drawing a path six times in various positions. The lengths of the lines and the dash lengths were defined relative to the width of the area in which they were drawn, so the dash lengths are described in terms of relative proportions.

There are five constructors to define a BasicStroke object. The default constructor defines a default type of line. This corresponds to a line width of 1, CAP_SQUARE as the end and JOIN_MITER for joins with a miter distance limit of 10. The other four constructors have more arguments supplying values to replace the defaults, as follows:

```
BasicStroke(float width)
BasicStroke(float width, int cap, int join)
BasicStroke(float width, int cap, int join, float miterLimit)
BasicStroke(float width, int cap, int join, float miterLimit,
           float[] dashPattern, float offset)
```

Whatever `Stroke` you set in a graphics context applies to all subsequent shapes that you draw – until you set it to a different line type. Of course, there's a lot of potential for applying this in Sketcher. That said, we can return to drawing our clock.

The Stroke of Midnight

We want a `BasicStroke` object that we can use to draw a thicker line at the 12 o'clock position, as well as at 3, 6 and 9. We can define this with the following statement:

```
BasicStroke widePen = new BasicStroke(3.0f,                // Line width
                                   BasicStroke.CAP_ROUND,   // End cap
                                   BasicStroke.JOIN_MITER); // Line join
```

Since we will be able to make use of the `widePen` object in the other inner class that will define the hands on our clock, we will include this object as a member of the applet class. Add this statement to the end of the `NewClock` class definition, following the code for the inner class, `ClockFace`. Note that we also draw the outline of the ellipse using this pen after we have created the filled ellipse.

For the intermediate hour marks we need a narrower line, which we can define with the statement:

```
BasicStroke narrowPen = new BasicStroke(1.0f,
                                   BasicStroke.CAP_ROUND,
                                   BasicStroke.JOIN_MITER);
```

This has a line width of `1.0f`, and the same end cap and join specification as `widePen`. We can add this as a member of the applet class, too.

Back in the `paint()` method for the `ClockFace` inner class, you can see that we set one or other of these `BasicStroke` objects depending on which hour mark we happen to be drawing in the loop. When the loop counter `i` is an exact multiple of 3, we are drawing one of the four heavy marks so we set `widePen` to be the `Stroke` object. The rest of the time we use `narrowPen`.

Note that in the `ClockFace` constructor, we call the `setOpaque()` method with the argument `false`. This method is inherited in our class from `JComponent` class. This call makes the clock face panel transparent, so only the face will obscure whatever is behind the clock.

Let's now turn to the inner class that will define the hands.

Defining the Hands on the Clock

Our clock will have three hands, a second hand, a minute hand, and an hour hand. To ensure the hands always fit within the face, the length of each hand will be defined in terms of the diameter of the clock face, and this dimension will be passed as an argument to the `Hands` constructor. To distinguish the hands, we will draw the second hand using `narrowPen` and the other two hands using `widePen`. To make the clock look more realistic, we will also add a central boss holding the hands on their spindle.

The class will need to know the angular position of each hand. We can store these three values in data members, `secondAngle`, `minuteAngle`, and `hourAngle`, which will be of type `double`, and we will assume the angles are measured in radians from the 12 o'clock position – clockwise of course. We could set these values by passing them to the constructor, but because we are likely to want to reset the positions of the hands whenever the `start()` method for the applet is called, it will be more convenient to add a method, `setPosition()` to the `Hands` class to provide for this.

There are various approaches that we could use to maintain the correct time and perhaps the best and most accurate would be to make the Hands object fetch the current time from the system clock each time the hands are redrawn. However, this would make the accuracy of the clock independent of our Timer object and we really want to try that out. Our clock will operate with our Timer object maintaining the time. In order to maintain the correct position of the hands over time, a Hands object will need to be able to increment the position of each hand when required. We could implement a method that provided a completely general increment capability, but for the sake of simplicity we will code the method to increment all three hands assuming one second has passed.

Here's the code for the Hands inner class to the NewClock class:

```
// Class defining the hands on the clock
class Hands extends JPanel
{
  public Hands(int clockDiameter)
  {
    center = new Ellipse2D.Double(-3,-3,6,6);                   // Central boss
    hourHand = new Line2D.Double(0,6,0,-clockDiameter*0.25);
    minuteHand = new Line2D.Double(0,8,0,-clockDiameter*0.3);
    secondHand = new Line2D.Double(0,14,0,-clockDiameter*0.35);
    setOpaque(false);                                          // Set transparent
  }

  // Paint the hands
  public void paint(Graphics g)
  {
    // Get hand angles for the current time
    double secondAngle = seconds*TWO_PI/60;
    double minuteAngle = (secondAngle+minutes*TWO_PI)/60;
    double hourAngle   = (minuteAngle+hours*TWO_PI)/12;

    Dimension size = getSize();
    Graphics2D g2D = (Graphics2D)g;
    g2D.setPaint(CLEAR);                                // Transparent color
    g2D.fillRect(0,0,size.width,size.height);   // Fill to erase

    g2D.setPaint(Color.darkGray);                       // Hands color
    g2D.translate(size.width/2, size.height/2);// Origin to center
    AffineTransform transform = g2D.getTransform();  // Save this xform

    // Draw hour hand
    g2D.setStroke(widePen);                             // Use wide pen
    g2D.rotate(hourAngle);                              // Rotate to hour position
    g2D.draw(hourHand);                                 // and draw hand

    // Draw minute hand
    g2D.setTransform(transform);                        // Reset transform
    g2D.rotate(minuteAngle);                            // Rotate to minute position
    g2D.draw(minuteHand);                               // and draw hand

    // Draw second hand
    g2D.setStroke(narrowPen);                           // Use narrow pen
    g2D.setTransform(transform);                        // Reset transform
    g2D.rotate(secondAngle);                            // Rotate to second position
    g2D.draw(secondHand);                               // and draw hand
```

```
      g2D.setPaint(Color.white);                    // Center color
      g2D.draw(center);                             // Draw center
   }

   Line2D.Double hourHand;
   Line2D.Double minuteHand;
   Line2D.Double secondHand;
   Ellipse2D.Double center;
   final Color CLEAR = new Color(0,0,0,0);
}
```

The constructor is quite straightforward. The central boss holding the hands on is the `Ellipse2D.Double` object, `center`. This is a circle with a diameter of 6. After defining the lines representing the hands, we call `setOpaque()` for the panel to make the panel transparent.

The `paint()` method looks like a lot of code, but after calculating the angular position for each hand, it is just a series of separate drawing operations. The position of each hand is basically a proportion of 2π. Each second or minute contributes one sixtieth of 2π to the position of the corresponding hand and each hour is one twelfth. To the angular position of the minute hand we add the contribution that the angle of the second hand represents as a fraction of a minute, and for the hour hand we add the contribution of the minute hand. After getting the size of the panel, we fill the entire panel with the color CLEAR. This is to erase the previous instance of the hands drawn on the panel. This `Color` object is defined as a constant member of the class. The first three arguments to the `Color` constructor define the red, green and blue color components of the color to be zero. The fourth argument defines something called the **alpha component** for the color as zero, which defines this color as completely transparent. We will go into the significance of the alpha component in more detail later in this chapter. We'll just use it for now. We want the color to be transparent because the `Hands` panel will be displayed on top of the `ClockFace` panel in the applet, and we want the face to be visible.

After moving the origin to the center of the panel we save the current transform. This will enable us to restore this position after rotating the axes to position each hand. Each hand is drawn in essentially the same way. The `Stroke` for the hand is set, then the axes are rotated to the required angle, and finally we draw the line representing the hand. The last step after drawing the three hands is to draw the central boss in white.

Now we have the inner classes for the face and hands defined, we are ready to complete the applet.

Initializing the Applet

In the `init()` method we will need to create the `ClockFace` object and the `Hands` object that will make up the clock. We just have to decide how the hands are going to overlay the clock face.

Back in Chapter 12 we saw how a `JFrame` object had several window panes, including a **content pane**, to which you typically add the components you want to display, plus a **glass pane** that overlays the content pane. An object of type `JApplet` has exactly the same pane structure. We can add an object of type `ClockFace` to the content pane for the applet, and make the `Hands` object the glass pane. As long as it's transparent, the content pane with its `ClockFace` component will be visible underneath the glass pane – which will be our `Hands` object. In fact, in general, a glass pane can be any object of a class that has `Component` as a superclass. To replace the default glass pane with your component, you just call the `setGlassPane()` method for the applet object with a reference to your component as the argument. Here's the code for the `init()` method that will set our clock up like that:

```
public void init()
{
  Dimension size = getSize();                 // Get the applet size

  // Create the clockface to fit within the applet
  int clockDiameter = Math.min(size.width, size.height)*9/10;
  clock = new ClockFace(clockDiameter);
  getContentPane().add(clock);                // Add clockface to content pane

  hands = new Hands(clockDiameter);           // Create the hands panel
  setGlassPane(hands);                        // Make the hands the glass pane
  hands.setVisible(true);                     // Set glass pane visible
}
```

We get the size of the applet by calling getSize(), and use that to decide the diameter of the clock. Ninety percent of the smaller of the width and height of the applet is a suitable choice to make it fit comfortably. Once we have created the ClockFace object, we just add it to the content pane for the applet. We then create the Hands object and pass it to setGlassPane() to make it the glass pane for the applet. Note that we must call setVisible() for the glass pane because it will be set as invisible by default.

That's all that's necessary to create the visual appearance of the clock. We just need to set it going somewhere, and that's the job of the start() method for the applet object.

Starting the Clock

The operation of the clock will be controlled by a Timer object, but before it starts the hands should be set to correspond to the current time. The static getInstance() method in the Calendar class that we discussed back in Chapter 10 returns a reference to a Calendar object that corresponds to the current time recorded in the system clock. We can then use the get() method to get the second, minute and hour values for the current time as integers. We can use these to figure out the angles for the hand positions and then call the setPosition() method for the Hands object. Here's how that can be coded:

```
public void start()
{
  Calendar now = Calendar.getInstance();      // Calendar for this instant

  // Get current seconds, minutes, and hours
  seconds = now.get(now.SECOND);
  minutes = now.get(now.MINUTE);
  hours = now.get(now.HOUR);

  timer = new java.util.Timer(true);                  // Timer to run clock

  // Use fixed-rate execution to maintain time
  timer.scheduleAtFixedRate(new TimerTask()
                 {
                   public void run()
                   {
                     increment();               // Increment the time
                     hands.repaint();           // and repaint the hands
                   }
                 },
```

```
                        0,                              // ...starting now
                        ONE_SECOND);                    // and at one second intervals

    }
```

The constants TWO_PI and ONE_SECOND need to be added as members of the applet class along with the timer field. We must also add the fields to store the time. The following statements will do that:

```
    final double TWO_PI = 2.0*Math.PI;
    final int ONE_SECOND = 1000;          // One second in milliseconds
    java.util.Timer timer;                // Timer to control the clock
    int seconds, minutes, hours;          // The current time
```

After saving the current time as seconds, minutes and hours, we create a Timer object to control the clock. We use the scheduleAtFixedRate() method to run the clock because we want the clock to be updated at intervals of one second, and if an update is delayed for any reason, we don't want subsequent updates to be delayed. The TimerTask object that is defined by an anonymous class calls the repaint() method for the Hands object, then the increment() method to update the time to the next second.

We can implement the increment() method in the NewClock class like this:

```
    // Increment the time by one second
    public void increment()
    {
        if(++seconds>= 60)                 // If seconds reach 60
          ++minutes;                       // ...increment minutes

        if(minutes>=60)                    // If minutes reach 60
          ++hours;                         // ...increment hours

        seconds %= 60;                     // Seconds 0 to 59
        minutes %= 60;                     // Minutes 0 to 59
        hours %= 12;                       // Hours 0 to 11
    }
```

When we have accumulated 60 seconds after incrementing the time, we must increment the count of the number of minutes by one. Similarly, when minutes reaches 60, we must increment the hour count.

Stopping the Clock

Stopping the clock is just a question of canceling the timer:

```
    public void stop()
    {
        timer.cancel();                    // Cancel the clock timer
    }
```

How It Works

While this example provides an illustration of using the fixed-rate execution mode with a timer, the more interesting aspect is the use of the glass pane to hold the animated portion of an image. You can apply this technique to any animation with any component that has a content pane and a glass pane. This includes components defined by the `JWindow`, `JDialog`, `JFrame` and `JInternalFrame` classes, as well as the `JApplet` class as we have just seen.

Alpha Compositing

Alpha compositing is all about the transparency of an image, and we are just going to look at the basic ideas here. The subject of color representation is itself a major topic with a range of different ways of representing color, but we will assume we are dealing with the RGB model throughout and ignore other color models. Note that Java does provide much more extensive support for color modeling than we have the space to discuss in this book, so if you want to know more, look in the classes of the `java.awt.color` package.

When you want to define an image to be transparent to some degree, so that when it is displayed on top of a background image the underlying image shows through, you can specify the degree of transparency by something called an **alpha component** for each pixel. An image format that has an alpha component for each pixel is said to have an **alpha channel**. Note that not all image formats support an alpha channel, but PNG files do, and GIF images can have a single transparent color. The alpha component value is used when an image is being overlaid by another image. The alpha value is multiplied by each of the color components to modify the contribution of each color component to the visual appearance of the pixel. The alpha value for a pixel in an image can vary from a minimum of 0.0, meaning completely transparent and therefore invisible since all the color components will be 0, to a maximum of 1.0, meaning completely opaque. In an RGB image with an alpha channel, each pixel is defined by four components, the three color components, red, green and blue, plus the alpha component. This allows the transparency to vary over the image, so some parts of the image could be opaque – with an alpha component of 1.0, and other parts may be more or less transparent, with alpha components for the pixels less than 1.0. It's worth noting that both the source image, the image that you are drawing, and the destination image, the background in other words, can have an alpha channel. If an image has no alpha channel, then the alpha component is assumed to be 1.0.

When you draw a source image over a destination image, there are basically two steps to the process. The color components for each pixel in the source image and the corresponding pixels in the destination image will be multiplied by their alpha component – often this will be done once and for all ahead of time for an image to avoid all those multiplications each time you draw an image. The source image is then rendered over the destination image according to the **alpha compositing rule** that is in effect. There are several alpha compositing rules as we shall see, but they each determine the fraction of the source image components and the fraction of the destination image components that contribute to the components of the result. In general, the components of the source and destination pixels are combined as follows:

```
ColorR = ColorS*AlphaS*FractionS + ColorD*AlphaD*FractionD
AlphaR = AlphaS*FractionS + AlphaD*FractionD
```

The first equation applies to each of the three color components. The subscripts R, S and D refer to the resultant pixel, the source pixel and the destination pixel, respectively. Thus, ColorR refers to the color of the resultant pixel produced by combining the source and the destination, AlphaS refers to the alpha component for the source pixel and FractionS represents the fraction of the source pixel determined by the compositing rule in effect.

This sounds a lot more complicated than it really is, so don't be put off by these equations. The alpha compositing rules that you can use in Java are implemented by the AlphaComposite class that is defined in the java.awt package. The Graphics2D class defines the method setComposite() that takes an AlphaComposite argument in order to set the alpha compositing rule to be used when you draw in the graphics context. Let's take a look at the AlphaComposite class in more detail.

The AlphaComposite Class

There is no constructor for the AlphaComposite class, so you cannot create objects directly. There is a static class member, getInstance(), that will return a reference to an AlphaComposite object with the compositing rule specified by the argument, which is a value of type int. There is also an overloaded version of this method where you can specify an alpha value as a second argument of type float, which is multiplied by the alpha for the source image. This is particularly useful when the source image has no alpha channel. Since an image with no alpha channel has an alpha component that is assumed to be 1.0, the alpha value that you specify in the call to getInstance() becomes the alpha value for all the pixels in the source. Most of the time, your images will not have an alpha channel so this is a way for you to specify the transparency of the source image directly in the graphics context.

There are eight possible alpha compositing rules, determined by constants of type int that are defined in the AlphaComposite class. In reviewing these, we will assume that, if the source or destination image has an alpha channel, the color components, ColorS and ColorD, for each pixel have already been pre-multiplied by the alpha component, AlphaS or AlphaD respectively. In the illustration of the effect of each rule described below, the source image is the light gray circle, and this is rendered over the darker gray rectangle (the destination image). The source image has its alpha component set to 0.5f.

SRC_OVER
This is the default rule that applies in a graphics context and is the rule that you are most likely to be using. The fraction of the source that contributes to the result is 1, and the fraction of the destination contributing to the result is 1-AlphaS. Therefore from our general equations, the source pixels are combined with the corresponding destination pixels using the following operations:

```
ColorR = ColorS + (1-AlphaS)*ColorD
AlphaR = AlphaS + (1-AlphaS)*AlphaD
```

The calculation of the resultant color is applied to each of the red, green and blue components of each pixel. You can see from the equations above that if the alpha component for the source, AlphaS, is 1, then the fraction of the destination will be zero so the result is just the original source pixel – in other words the source is opaque. If the alpha component for the source is 0, then the result is just the destination pixel so the source is completely transparent and would be invisible. The illustration shows the source with an alpha of 0.5f so the destination shows through.

SRC

With this rule, the source pixels replace the destination pixels, so the operations determining the resultant color and alpha components for each pixel are:

```
ColorR = ColorS
AlphaR = AlphaS
```

SRC_IN

With this rule, the fraction of the source in the result is the alpha for the destination, `AlphaD`, and the fraction of the destination in the result is zero. Thus only the source pixels that fall within the area destination image are rendered. All other pixels rendered from the source will have zero color components. As you can see, the outline of the destination image acts like a pastry cutter on the source image. The operations for the rule are:

```
ColorR = ColorS*AlphaD
AlphaR = AlphaS*AlphaD
```

SRC_OUT

With this rule, only the source pixels outside the area of the destination will be rendered. The outline of the destination image also acts like a pastry cutter here, but the source image inside the outline is discarded, and only the source image lying outside of the destination image is kept. The area of the source that lies inside the boundary of the destination results in pixels with color components that are zero. The calculation of the components of the result is defined as:

```
ColorR = ColorS*(1 - AlphaD)
AlphaR = AlphaS*(1 - AlphaD)
```

DST_OVER

With this rule, the fraction of each source pixel in the result is 1 - `AlphaD`, and the fraction of the corresponding destination pixel is 1. Where the source overlaps the destination, the destination is effectively rendered over the source. The operation of this rule is defined by:

```
ColorR = ColorS*(1 - AlphaD) + ColorD
AlphaR = AlphaS*(1 - AlphaD) + AlphaD
```

899

Since in our illustration the destination has an alpha of 1.0f, the fraction of the source pixel is 0.0 so the destination completely hides the part of the source that is underneath.

DST_IN
With this rule, the fraction of the source in the result is 0 and the fraction of the destination is AlphaS. The operations are:

```
ColorR = ColorD*AlphaS
AlphaR = AlphaD*AlphaS
```

Thus the destination is rendered inside the boundary of the source, but with the alpha from the source, so it looks lighter than the rest of the destination.

DST_OUT
The source fraction in the result is zero, and the destination fraction is 1 - AlphaS. Thus the rule operation is:

```
ColorR = ColorD*(1 - AlphaS)
AlphaR = AlphaD*(1 - AlphaS)
```

CLEAR
The fractions of the source and destination pixels involved in the operation of this rule are both zero. The effect is that pixels corresponding to the source pixels are cleared, so they will have all color components at zero.

The AlphaComposite class also defines static members that are AlphaComposite objects. Each object corresponds to one of the rules we have just discussed and they all have an alpha of 1.0f. These members are:

SrcOver	SrcIn	SrcOut	Src
DstOver	DstIn	DstOut	Clear

As the `Clear` object has an alpha of 1.0f, using this for alpha compositing will result in an opaque black result.

Since the alpha for an image determines the transparency, we can fade an image into the background by repainting the image with a shrinking value for the alpha. Let's see how that works with an example.

Try It Out – Fading an Image

We will fade the Wrox Press logo into the background until it disappears, and then fade it in again cyclically. We can write an applet to do this and while we are about it, we can try using parameters for the applet that we can set in the web page. Here's the code for the applet:

```java
import java.awt.*;
import java.awt.image.*;
import javax.swing.*;

public class FaderApplet extends JApplet
{
  public void init()
  {
    // Get parameters - if any
    String fade = getParameter("fadeTime");
    if(fade != null)
      fadeTime = Integer.parseInt(fade);
    String fps = getParameter("frameRate");
    if(fps != null)
      frameRate = Integer.parseInt(fps);

    maxCount = frameRate*fadeTime;              // Count of steps to complete fade
    imagePanel = new ImagePanel(getSize());
    getContentPane().add(imagePanel);

    composite = AlphaComposite.SrcOver;
  }
```

```java
  // Parameter information for anyone that needs it
  public String[][] getParameterInfo()
  {
    String[][] info = {
            {"fadeTime" , "integer", "time to complete fade in seconds"},
            {"frameRate", "integer", "frames per second"              }
                    };
    return info;
  }
```

```java
  public void start()
  {
    timer = new java.util.Timer(true);         // Timer to run clock
    count = maxCount;                          // Set repaint counter
    alphaStep = 1.0f/count;
    long frameInterval = ONE_SECOND/frameRate;
```

```java
                // Use fixed-delay execution to get smooth fade
            timer.schedule(new java.util.TimerTask()
                            {
                               public void run()
                               {
                                 imagePanel.repaint();                    // Repaint the image

                                 // Update alpha composite for next frame
                                 if(count ==maxCount)
                                   countDelta = -1;
                                 else if(count == 0)
                                   countDelta = 1;
                                 count += countDelta;
                                 composite = AlphaComposite.getInstance(
                                           AlphaComposite.SRC_OVER,count*alphaStep);
                               }

                               int countDelta = -1; // Anonymous class member - count incr.
                            },
                            0,                                          // ...starting now
                           frameInterval);                              // Repaint interval
        }
```

```java
    public void stop()
    {
      timer.cancel();
    }
```

```java
    class ImagePanel extends JPanel
    {
      // Panel creates its own image from an image icon
      public ImagePanel(Dimension size)
      {
        ImageIcon icon = new ImageIcon("Images/wrox_logo.gif");
        image = icon.getImage();

        // Create a scaled image to fit within the size
        image = image.getScaledInstance(4*size.width/5, 4*size.height/5,
                                                        Image.SCALE_SMOOTH);
        // Wait for scaled image to load
        MediaTracker tracker = new MediaTracker(this);
        tracker.addImage(image,0);                       // Image to track
        try
         {
          tracker.waitForID(0);
         }
         catch(InterruptedException e)
         {
           System.out.println(e);                        // Exception...
```

```
            System.exit(1);                          // ...so abandon ship!
        }
    }

    public void paint(Graphics g)
    {
        Graphics2D g2D = (Graphics2D)g;
        Dimension size = getSize();                  // Get panel size
        g2D.setPaint(Color.lightGray);               // Background color
        g2D.fillRect(0,0,size.width,size.height);    // fill the panel
        g2D.setComposite(composite);                 // Set current alpha

        // Scale and draw image
        g2D.drawImage(image,                         // Image to be drawn
                      size.width/10,size.height/10,  // Image position inset
                      null);
    }

    // ImagePanel data members
    Image image;                     // The image
    int imageWidth;                  // and its width
    int imageHeight;                 // and height
}
```

```
    // Applet data members
    final int ONE_SECOND = 1000;     // One second in milliseconds
    int frameRate = 20;              // Default fade change frequency frames per sec
    int fadeTime = 3;                // Default time to fade completely in seconds
    int count;                       // Repaint cycle counter
    int maxCount;

    ImagePanel imagePanel;           // Panel displaying the image
    AlphaComposite composite;        // Alpha value for the image
    float alphaStep;                 // Alpha increment for fade step
    java.util.Timer timer;           // Timer to control fading
}
```

We can optionally supply parameters for the applet, so you can use the following html:

```
<applet code="FaderApplet.class" width="300" height="330">
<param name="frameRate" value="20">
<param name="fadeTime" value="3">
</applet>
```

You can use `appletviewer` to run the applet with an HTML file with the contents above. You should see the image fade out then back in again.

How It Works

In the `init()` method we try to read the two parameter values. If the `<PARAM>` tags are not specified, then the `String` object returned by the `getParameter()` calls will be `null`. In this case the data members `fadeTime` and `frameRate` will be left at their default values. We use the values in these members to calculate `maxCount`, the count of the number of steps needed to completely fade the image.

Since the `ImagePanel` class loads its own icon image, all we have to do in the `init()` method is create the `ImagePanel` object and add it to the content pane for the applet. We pass the size of the applet to the `ImagePanel` constructor, which will scale the image to fit. We also initialize the composite member that is the `AlphaComposite` object used in the `paint()` method for the `imagePanel` object to `SrcOver`, which implements the `SRC_OVER` rule with the alpha set to 1.

The `Timer` object that we create in the `start()` method manages the animation. After initializing count to the number of steps to a complete fade, we calculate the increment for the alpha value between steps, and the time interval in milliseconds between one step and the next. We use the timer's `schedule()` method to fade the image. In the `run()` method for the `TimerTask` object, the alpha is set to a new value – greater than the previous value if we are fading in, and less than the previous value if we are fading out – after each repaint of the panel. An `AlphaComposite` object with the rule `SRC_OVER` and the current alpha value is stored in the `composite` member of the applet class. In this way we cycle the alpha for the `AlphaComposite` object from 0.0f to 1.0f and back again.

The `ImagePanel` constructor loads the image as an `ImageIcon` object – you will recall that the constructor takes care of loading the image, and will not return until loading is complete. The constructor then extracts the `Image` object from the `ImageIcon` object. Since we want to be sure the image fits comfortably in the space available to the applet, we call the `getScaledInstance()` method for the `Image` object to creates a new object that is scaled to the x and y dimensions supplied as the first two arguments. The third argument to the `getScaledInstance()` method is an integer that must be one of five constant values that are defined in the `Image` class, and that select a particular scaling algorithm:

Scale Algorithm	Description
SCALE_DEFAULT	The default scaling algorithm.
SCALE_FAST	A fast scaling algorithm.
SCALE_SMOOTH	An algorithm designed for a smooth resultant image rather than speed.
SCALE_REPLICATE	Use the algorithm defined by the `ReplicateScaleFilter` class. This algorithm duplicates pixels to scale up, or deletes pixels to scale down.
SCALE_AREA_AVERAGING	Use the algorithm defined by the `AreaAveragingScaleFilter` class.

Scaling an image is achieved by applying an algorithm that calculates the pixel values for the new image from those of the old. Some algorithms such as that defined by the `ReplicateScaleFilter` are very simple, and hence very fast to execute. Others such as the `SCALE_SMOOTH` algorithm are more complex, and hence slower, but produce a much better result.

The `getScaledInstance()` method returns immediately, even if the scaled image has not yet been constructed, so we use a tracker to wait for the image to complete.

The image is drawn in the `paint()` method for the `imagePanel` object. The `paint()` method starts by filling the panel in light gray to provide the background to the image. The current `composite` object is then set in the graphics context and the alpha for this determines the transparency of the image when we draw it. The image is then drawn using the `drawImage()` method. The second and third arguments are the coordinates of the top-left corner of the image. The last argument can be a reference to an `ImageObserver`, but we just supply `null` as we have ensured that the image is completely loaded in the `ImagePanel` constructor.

Synthesizing Images

You don't have to read all your images in from files – you can create your own. The most flexible way of doing this involves using a `BufferedImage` object. This is a subclass of the `Image` class that has the image data stored in a buffer that you can access. It also supports a variety of ways of storing the pixel data: with or without an alpha channel, different types of color model and with various precisions for color components. The `ColorModel` class provides a flexible way to define various kinds of color models for use with a `BufferedImage` object but to understand the basics of how this works we will only use one color model, the default where color components are RGB values, and one buffer type – storing 8 bit RGB color values plus an alpha channel. This type is specified in the `BufferedImage` class by the constant `TYPE_INT_ARGB`, which implies an `int` value is used for each pixel. The value for each pixel stores an alpha component plus the RGB color components as 8 bit bytes. We can create a `BufferedImage` object of this type with a given width and height with statements such as:

```
int width = 200;
int height = 300;
BufferedImage image = new BufferedImage(width, height,
                                BufferedImage.TYPE_INT_ARGB);
```

This creates a `BufferedImage` object that represents an image 200 pixels wide and 300 pixels high. To draw on the image, we need a graphics context, and the `createGraphics()` method for the `BufferedImage` object returns a `Graphics2D` object that relates to the image:

```
Graphics2D g2D = image.createGraphics();
```

Operations using the `g2D` object modify pixels in the `BufferedImage` object, `image`. With this object available you now have the full capability to draw on the `BufferedImage` object – you can draw shapes, images, `GeneralPath` objects or whatever, and you can set the alpha compositing object for the graphics context as we discussed in the previous section. And you also have all the affine transform capability that comes with a `Graphics2D` object.

You can retrieve an individual pixel from a `BufferedImage` object by calling its `getRGB()` method and supplying the x,y coordinates of the pixel as arguments of type `int`. The pixel is returned as type `int` in the `TYPE_INT_ARGB` format, which consists of four 8-bit values for the alpha and RGB color components packed into the 32-bit word. There is also an overloaded version of `getRGB()` that returns an array of pixels from a portion of the image data. You can set an individual pixel value by calling the `setRGB()` method. The first two arguments are the coordinates of the pixel, and the third argument is the value that is to be set, of type `int`. There is also a version of this method that will set the values of an array of pixels. We won't be going into pixel operations further, but we will venture drawing on a `BufferedImage` object with a working example.

We will put together an applet that uses a `BufferedImage` object. The applet will create an animation of the buffered image object that is created against a background of the Wrox logo. This will also demonstrate how you can make part of an image transparent. The applet will be broadly similar to applets we have produced earlier in this chapter; the basic contents of the source file will look like this:

```
import java.awt.*;
import java.awt.image.*;
import java.awt.geom.*;
import javax.swing.*;
```

```
public class ImageDrawDemo extends JApplet
{
   // The init() method to initialize everything...

   // The start() method to start the animation...
   // The stop() method to stop the animation...
   // The ImagePanel class defining the panel displaying the animation...

   // Data members for the applet...
}
```

Creating an Image

A **sprite** is a small graphical image that you can draw over a static image to create an animation. To create the animation effect, you just draw the sprite in different positions and orientations over time, and of course transformations of the coordinate system can be a great help in making this easier. Games often use sprites – they can make the animation take much less processor time because you only need to draw the sprite against a static background. Our interest in using `BufferedImage` objects means we won't get into the best techniques for minimizing processor time. We will instead concentrate on understanding how we can create and use images internally in a program.

Our `BufferedImage` object is going to look as shown below.

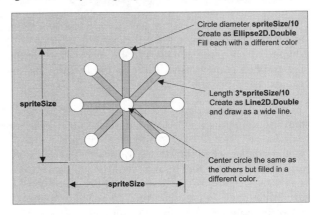

Circle diameter **spriteSize/10**
Create as **Ellipse2D.Double**
Fill each with a different color

Length **3*spriteSize/10**
Create as **Line2D.Double**
and draw as a wide line.

Center circle the same as the others but filled in a different color.

The image is a square with sides of length `spriteSize`. Dimensions of other parts of the image are relative to this. There are really only two geometric entities here, a line and a circle, each repeated in different positions and orientations, so if we create a `Line2D.Double` object for the line, and an `Ellipse2D.Double` object for the circle, we should be able to draw the whole thing by moving the user coordinate system around and drawing one or other of these two objects.

A true object-oriented approach would define a class representing a sprite, possibly as a subclass of `BufferedImage`, but since we are exploring the mechanics of using a `BufferedImage` object, it will suit our purpose better to develop a method, `createSprite()`, that draws the sprite on a `BufferedImage` object. The method will just be a member of our applet class so we will add data members to the applet to store any data required. You can plug the data members we will be using into the applet class outline now:

```
    double totalAngle;              // Current angular position of sprite
    double spriteAngle;             // Rotation angle of sprite about its center
    ImagePanel imagePanel;          // Panel to display animation

    BufferedImage sprite;           // Stores reference to the sprite
    int spriteSize = 100;           // Diameter of the sprite
    Ellipse2D.Double circle;        // A circle - part of the sprite
    Line2D.Double line;             // A line - part of the sprite

    // Colors used in sprite
    Color[] colors = {Color.red , Color.yellow, Color.green   , Color.blue,
    Color.cyan, Color.pink  , Color.magenta, Color.orange};

    java.util.Timer timer;          // Timer for the animation
    long interval = 50;             // Time interval msec between repaints
```

The general use of these members should be clear from the comments. We will see how they are used as we develop the code.

The first thing the `createSprite()` method needs to do is to create the `BufferedImage` object, `sprite`, and we will need a `Graphics2D` object to use to draw on the `sprite` image. The code to do this is as follows:

```
    BufferedImage createSprite(int spriteSize)
    {
        // Create image with RGB and alpha channel
        BufferedImage sprite = new BufferedImage(spriteSize, spriteSize,
                                           BufferedImage.TYPE_INT_ARGB);

        Graphics2D g2D = sprite.createGraphics();         // Context for buffered image
        // plus the rest of the method...
    }
```

The sprite object has a width and height of `spriteSize`, and the image is of the type `TYPE_INT_ARGB`, so the alpha and color components for each pixel will be stored as a single `int` value, and the color will be stored as 8 bit red, green and blue components. This means that our sprite image will occupy 40,000 bytes, which is a small indication of how browsing a web page can gobble up memory. This doesn't affect the download time for the page – this memory is allocated in the local machine when the applet is executed. Apart from the contents of the HTML file that is the page, the download time is affected by the size of the `.class` file for the applet, plus any image or other files that it downloads when it executes.

Creating a Transparent Background

The alpha channel is important in our sprite image because we want the background to be completely transparent – only the sprite object itself should be seen when we draw it, not the whole 100x100 rectangle of the image. We can achieve this quite easily by making the whole sprite image area transparent to start with – that is with an alpha of 0.0f – and then drawing what we want on top of this as opaque with an alpha of 1.0f. Here's the code to make the entire image transparent:

```
    // Clear image with transparent alpha by drawing a rectangle
    g2D.setComposite(AlphaComposite.getInstance(AlphaComposite.CLEAR, 0.0f));
    Rectangle2D.Double rect = new Rectangle2D.Double(0,0,spriteSize,spriteSize);
    g2D.fill(rect);
```

We first set the alpha composite using an `AlphaComposite` object with the `CLEAR` rule – this will set the color components to zero, and with an alpha of 0.0f, which will make it transparent. We then fill a rectangle that covers the whole area of the image. We don't need to set a color since with the `CLEAR` rule the fraction of the foreground and background for each pixel is zero, so neither participates in the resulting pixel. We still have to fill the rectangle though, since this determines the image pixels that are operated on.

At this point we can take a short detour into how you can affect the quality of your images.

Rendering Hints

With many aspects of rendering operations, there is a choice between quality and speed. Rendering operations are like most things – quality comes at a cost and the cost here is processing time. There are defaults set for all of the rendering operations where a choice exists and the default is platform specific, but you can make you own choices by calling the `setRenderingHint()` method for the `Graphics2D` object that is doing the rendering. These are only hints though, and if your computer does not support the option for a rendering operation corresponding to the hint that you specify, the hint will have no effect.

We can ensure that we get the best possible result from our alpha compositing operations by adding the following call to the `createSprite()` method:

```
BufferedImage createSprite(int spriteSize)
{
  // Create image with RGB and alpha channel
  BufferedImage sprite = new BufferedImage(spriteSize, spriteSize,
                                          BufferedImage.TYPE_INT_ARGB);

  Graphics2D g2D = sprite.createGraphics();          // Context for buffered image

  // Set best alpha interpolation quality
  g2D.setRenderingHint(RenderingHints.KEY_ALPHA_INTERPOLATION,
                       RenderingHints.VALUE_ALPHA_INTERPOLATION_QUALITY);

  // Clear image with transparent alpha by drawing a rectangle
  g2D.setComposite(AlphaComposite.getInstance(AlphaComposite.CLEAR, 0.0f));
  Rectangle2D.Double rect = new Rectangle2D.Double(0,0,spriteSize,spriteSize);
  g2D.fill(rect);

  // plus the rest of the method...
}
```

The `RenderingHints` class defines rendering hints of various kinds, and these are stored in a `Graphics2D` object in a map collection, so the arguments to the `setRenderingHint()` method are a key and a value corresponding to the key. The key for the alpha compositing hint is the first argument in our code, and the second argument is the value of the hint. Other possible values for this hint are `VALUE_ALPHA_INTERPOLATION_DEFAULT` for the platform default, and `VALUE_ALPHA_INTERPOLATION_SPEED` for speed rather than quality.

You can also supply a hint for the following keys:

Key	Description
KEY_ANTIALIASING	When you render angled lines, you will get a step-wise arrangement of pixels a lot of the time, making the line look less than smooth, often referred to as 'jaggies'. **Antialiasing** is a technique to set the brightness of pixels for an angled line to make the line appear smoother. Thus this hint determines whether time is spent reducing 'jaggies' when rendering angled lines. Possible values are VALUE_ANTIALIAS_ON, _OFF or _DEFAULT.
KEY_COLOR_RENDERING	Affects how color rendering is done. Possible values are VALUE_COLOR_RENDER_SPEED, _QUALITY or _DEFAULT.
KEY_DITHERING	**Dithering** is a process whereby a broader range of colors can be synthesized with a limited set of colors by coloring adjacent pixels to produce the illusion of a color that is not in the set. Possible values are VALUE_DITHER_ENABLE, _DISABLE or _DEFAULT.
KEY_FRACTIONALMETRICS	Affects the quality of displaying text. Possible values are VALUE_FRACTIONALMETRICS_ON, _OFF or _DEFAULT.
KEY_INTERPOLATION	When you transform a source image, the transformed pixels will rarely correspond exactly with the pixel positions in the destination. In this case the color values for each transformed pixel have to be determined from the surrounding pixels.
	Interpolation is the process by which this is done and there are various techniques that can be used. Possible values from most to least expensive in time are VALUE_INTERPOLATION_BICUBIC, _BILINEAR and _NEAREST_NEIGHBOR.
KEY_RENDERING	This determines the rendering technique trading speed and quality. Possible values are VALUE_RENDERING_SPEED, _QUALITY and _DEFAULT.
KEY_TEXT_ANTIALIASING	This determines whether antialiasing is done when rendering text. Possible values are VALUE_TEXT_ANTIALIASING_ON, _OFF and _DEFAULT.

That's enough of a detour. Let's get back to drawing our sprite.

Drawing on an Image

We have the transparent background so we need to fill in the image. The first step is to change the alpha compositing operation to the SRC_OVER rule with the alpha set so the result is opaque. Adding the following statement at the end of those we have in the createSprite() method will do this:

```
g2D.setComposite(AlphaComposite.SrcOver);
```

This uses the SrcOver member of the AlphaComposite class, which does exactly what we want.

We can create the two geometric entities, the circle and the line with the statements:

```
line = new Line2D.Double(spriteSize/20.0,0,0.3*spriteSize,0);
circle = new Ellipse2D.Double(0,0,spriteSize/10.0, spriteSize/10.0);
```

The line is a horizontal line from an x position of spriteSize/20 (half the diameter of the circle) so this is from the right edge of the center circle of the sprite, to 0.3*spriteSize, which is the length we specified in the design. The circle has its top-left corner at the origin and a diameter of spriteSize/10, 10% of the width of the image.

If you take another look at the diagram, you will see that the sprite has eight arms, all identical apart from their orientation, with each arm rotated $\pi/4$ radians relative to its predecessor. If we had a method to draw one arm in a given orientation, horizontal say, we could draw all eight by rotating the coordinate system by $\pi/4$ radians and calling the method to draw the arm eight times. Good idea!

Drawing an Arm

The drawArm() method will need the Graphics2D object for the image as an argument, plus an index value to select the color of the circle at the end of the arm. In the diagram we noted that we would fill the circles with different colors and we will do this by selecting an element from the colors array. The process is very simple. We will draw the arm aligned horizontally along the x axis. We will then translate the coordinate system so the origin is where the top-left corner of the colored, outer circle should be.

Here's the code for the drawArm() method:

```
    void drawArm(Graphics2D g2D, int i)
  {
    AffineTransform at = g2D.getTransform();        // Save current transform
    g2D.setPaint(Color.darkGray);
    Stroke stroke = g2D.getStroke();                // Save current stroke
    g2D.setStroke(new BasicStroke(3.0f));           // Set stroke as wide line
    g2D.draw(line);                                 // Draw the line
    g2D.setStroke(stroke);                          // Restore old stroke

    g2D.translate(line.getX2(), -spriteSize/20);    // Translate to circle position
    g2D.setPaint(colors[i%colors.length]);          // Set the fill color
    g2D.fill(circle);
    g2D.setTransform(at);                           // Restore original transform()
  }
```

We first save the current transform so we can restore it later, after we have finished messing about with it in the graphics context object, g2D. We will draw all the arms in dark gray, so we set that color in the graphics context first. We then have a couple of statements that save the current line type by calling getStroke() for g2D, and set a new line type with a greater width by calling the setStroke() method with stroke as the argument, which as you see is a line of width 3. The next step is to draw the line by calling the draw() method with line as the Shape argument. This will be drawn in the current color, Color.darkGray.

Before drawing the circle at the end of the arm, we must move the origin to where the top-left corner point of the circle will be. This is at the x coordinate of the end point of the line that we obtain by calling the getX2() method for the line object, and a y coordinate that is up by the radius of the circle, spriteSize/20. With the origin in the right place, we then just need to select the color from the colors array, and fill the circle object.

Completing the Sprite Image

We can use the drawArm() method to draw most of the sprite. By default the method draws the line with the circle at the end horizontally – along the x axis from the origin. We want to apply this eight times at angles that are $\pi/4$ radians apart rotating about the center of the image. If we translate the user coordinate system so that the origin is at the center of the image, we can draw the arms in a loop like this:

```
BufferedImage createSprite(int spriteSize)
{
  // Create image with RGB and alpha channel
  BufferedImage sprite = new BufferedImage(spriteSize, spriteSize,
                              BufferedImage.TYPE_INT_ARGB);

  Graphics2D g2D = sprite.createGraphics();        // Context for buffered image

  // Set best alpha interpolation quality
  g2D.setRenderingHint(RenderingHints.KEY_ALPHA_INTERPOLATION,
                  RenderingHints.VALUE_ALPHA_INTERPOLATION_QUALITY);

  // Clear image with transparent alpha by drawing a rectangle
  g2D.setComposite(AlphaComposite.getInstance(AlphaComposite.CLEAR, 0.0f));
  Rectangle2D.Double rect = new Rectangle2D.Double(0, 0, spriteSize,
                                          spriteSize);
  g2D.fill(rect);

  g2D.setComposite(AlphaComposite.SrcOver);
  line = new Line2D.Double(spriteSize/20.0,0,0.3*spriteSize,0);
  circle = new Ellipse2D.Double(0, 0, spriteSize/10.0, spriteSize/10.0);

  // Since sprite is symmetric, move origin to the center
  g2D.translate(spriteSize/2, spriteSize/2);

  int armCount = 8;                                // Number of arms in the sprite
  for(int i = 0; i < armCount; i++)
  {
    g2D.rotate(2*Math.PI/armCount);               // Rotate by pi/4
    drawArm(g2D, i);                              // Draw the arm
  }

  // plus the rest of the code...
}
```

With the origin at the center of the image, we rotate the coordinate system about the origin by $\pi/4$ radians and draw the arm on each iteration of the loop. The `drawArm()` method also transforms the coordinates, but it always resets the transform back to what it was when the method was called. The rotations in the loop are cumulative, so we draw the arm at successive orientations around the origin.

The last thing we need to do is to fill the circle at the center with the color dark gray. Adding the following statements to the `createSprite()` method will complete it:

```
      g2D.setPaint(Color.lightGray);              // Set the fill color
      g2D.translate(-spriteSize/20,-spriteSize/20);// Move origin to circle top left
      g2D.fill(circle);                           // Fill the circle
      g2D.dispose();                              // Dispose of the context
      return sprite;                             // Return the finished image
```

Now we can create a `BufferedImage` object containing the sprite by calling `createSprite()` in the `init()` method for the applet:

```
      public void init()
      {
        sprite = createSprite(spriteSize);

        imagePanel = new ImagePanel();
        getContentPane().add(imagePanel);
      }
```

The `imagePanel` object's `paint()` method will draw the sprite, but before we get to that, let's look at how the animation thread is going to work.

Animating the Sprite

The `start()` and `stop()` methods for the applet that control the animation will use a `Timer` object, exactly as you have seen before:

```
      public void start()
      {
        timer = new java.util.Timer(true);

        // Do necessary initialization...

        // Use fixed-delay execution to get smooth animation
        timer.schedule(new java.util.TimerTask()
                        {
                          public void run()
                          {
                            // Painting for animation + necessary updating
                          }
                        },
                        0,                          // ...starting now
                        interval);                  // Repaint interval
      }

      public void stop()
      {
        timer.cancel();                             // Stop the timer
      }
```

All the hard work is still to do, in the initialization in the `start()` method and in the `run()` method for the `TimerTask` object, so let's consider first what our animation is going to be. We can draw our sprite anywhere at any orientation just by transforming the coordinate system, so let's choose an animation to show this off. A simple illustration would be to have the sprite roll round the inside of an invisible circle that is four times the diameter of the sprite, as illustrated below.

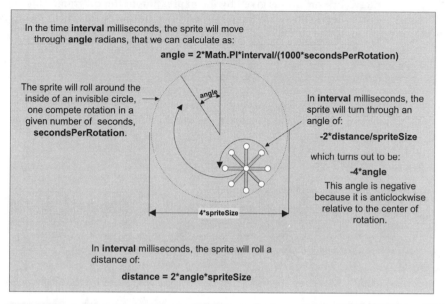

In the time **interval** milliseconds, the sprite will move through **angle** radians, that we can calculate as:

angle = 2*Math.PI*interval/(1000*secondsPerRotation)

The sprite will roll around the inside of an invisible circle, one compete rotation in a given number of seconds, **secondsPerRotation**.

In **interval** milliseconds, the sprite will turn through an angle of:

-2*distance/spriteSize

which turns out to be:

-4*angle

This angle is negative because it is anticlockwise relative to the center of rotation.

4*spriteSize

In **interval** milliseconds, the sprite will roll a distance of:

distance = 2*angle*spriteSize

This will give us plenty of opportunity to use transforms. It may also give those who didn't pay attention to trigonometry in high school some cause for regret. We will set the speed of rotation around the circle by specifying the number of seconds, `secondsPerRotation`, it takes to complete a revolution. We don't want to have this happening too fast – 15 seconds is good. We can add a member to the applet class to define this:

```
double secondsPerRotation = 15;          // Time for one complete revolution
```

We can position the sprite at the end of each time interval for updating the image if we know two angles – the rotation of the position of the sprite about the center of the circle in the given time interval, and the rotation of the sprite about its own center due to rolling. We can then position the sprite at any time by going through a series of transforms. First we will apply a rotation about the center of the circle to establish the angular position of the sprite about the circle. From that position we can apply a translation of the axes to position the center of the sprite. We will then apply a rotation about the new origin to get the sprite to its correct orientation. Finally we will apply another translation of the axes to the position where the top left of the sprite image should be.

Given that we update the image every `interval` milliseconds, we can work out the angle that the sprite moves through, relative to the center of the circle in this time period. We'll call this `angle`. The time, `interval`, divided by the time for a complete rotation, `secondsPerRotation`, will be the fraction of 2π that the sprite will rotate through, since 2π is a complete revolution. These times have to be in the same units of course, either both seconds or both milliseconds. This angle will be positive because the rotation is clockwise with respect to the center of rotation – the center of the circle in this case.

Since we know the circumference of the outer circle is 2π times the radius, which is $2*\text{spriteSize}$, we can easily get the distance traveled around that circle in `interval` milliseconds with the expression shown in the diagram. As the sprite rolls this distance, it is also the distance moved around the circumference of the sprite – which in terms of the sprite's rotation about its center is the angle turned through times the radius, `spriteSize/2`. Thus the angle through which the sprite itself rotates, which we'll call `spriteAngleIncrement`, is given by the expression in the diagram. This angle has to be negative because it is counterclockwise. We can now add two further members to the applet class that we will need for positioning the sprite, `angle` and `spriteAngleIncrement`:

```
double angle = 2.*interval*Math.PI/(1000.0*secondsPerRotation);
double spriteAngleIncrement = -4*angle;
```

We can now use these to complete the `start()` method:

```
public void start()
{
  timer = new java.util.Timer(true);

  // Do necessary initialization...
  totalAngle = 0;                            // Position around the circle
  spriteAngle = 0;                           // Sprite orientation

  // Use fixed-delay execution to get smooth animation
  timer.schedule(new java.util.TimerTask()
                 {
                     public void run()
                     {
                     // Painting for animation + necessary updating
                     imagePanel.repaint();          // Repaint the image
                     totalAngle += angle;           // Increment the total angle
                     spriteAngle += spriteAngleIncrement;// and the sprite angle
                     }

                 },
                 0,                                 // ...starting now
                 interval);                         // Repaint interval
}
```

The calculation of the angles is precisely as we have discussed. The expressions from the diagram are plugged into the code here. You may notice that we continue to increment the values of `totalAngle` and `spriteAngle` indefinitely here. However, since these are both of type `double`, it will be a while before we exceed the number of digits available. All we have to do now is to implement how the sprite is painted.

Painting the Sprite

We do this in the `paint()` method for the `ImagePanel` class. To make it a bit more interesting we will use the Wrox Press logo as the background to our sprite animation. This will show up the fact that the sprite background is transparent, and our alpha compositing is really working. To shorten the code we will get the logo using an `ImageIcon` object, so the constructor for the inner class will be implemented as:

```
class ImagePanel extends JPanel
{
  public ImagePanel()
  {
    ImageIcon icon = new ImageIcon("Images\\wrox_logo.gif");
    image = icon.getImage();
  }

  Image image;                                    // The logo image
}
```

The Wrox logo will be drawn in the center of the space available to the `ImagePanel` object, and the invisible circle will have its center here too, so the first transformation we can apply in the `paint()` method is to move the origin of the user coordinate system to the center of the panel.

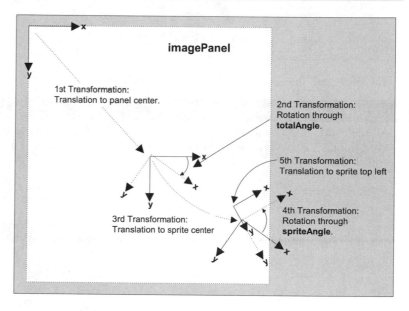

With the coordinate system at the center of the panel, we can then draw the logo image by specifying its top left corner x, y coordinates as minus half its width and minus half its height.

Positioning the sprite using the `totalAngle` and `spriteAngle` angles will involve four further transformations as shown in the diagram, but we will make use of the version of `rotate()` that does a translation followed by a rotation, and then a translation back again, just to try it out. Here's how the `paint()` method looks:

```
public void paint(Graphics g)
{
  Dimension size = getSize();                      // Get panel dimensions
  Graphics2D g2D = (Graphics2D)g;

  // Now fill the panel background
  g2D.setPaint(Color.gray);
  Rectangle2D.Double rect = new Rectangle2D.Double(0, 0, size.width, size.height);
  g2D.fill(rect);
```

```
        g2D.translate(size.width/2, size.height/2);  // Move origin to panel center

        g2D.drawImage(image,                                // Draw the logo
                    -image.getWidth(ImageDrawDemo.this)/2,  // Top left x
                    -image.getWidth(ImageDrawDemo.this)/2,  // Top left y
                    ImageDrawDemo.this);

        g2D.rotate(totalAngle);        // Rotate to the angle for the sprite position

        // Translate and rotate to sprite position - then translate back
        g2D.rotate(spriteAngle, 3*spriteSize/2, 0);

        g2D.translate(spriteSize, -spriteSize/2);   // Translate to sprite top left

        g2D.drawImage(sprite ,null, 0, 0);                  // Draw the sprite
    }
```

The sprite and the applet should be ready to roll, barring typos, so try it out.

Try It Out – Rolling the Sprite

All the code should be there. You need to set the size of the applet so it is sufficient to accommodate everything, so it needs to be at least four times the sprite diameter. I used the following HTML for the applet:

```
<applet code="ImageDrawDemo.class"  width=400 height=400>
</applet>
```

Of course if you want to do a bit more work, you could always either adapt the applet size to fit the size of the sprite – or vice versa. Here is a screenshot of the applet in operation.

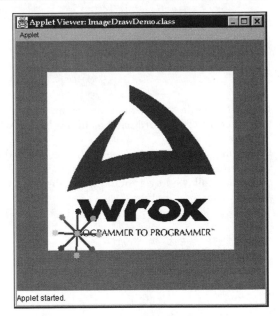

You can see here that the background to the sprite is transparent – the text and the background to the logo under the sprite show quite clearly.

Summary

This chapter has been a basic introduction to handling images and producing animations. Java provides much greater capabilities in this area than we have looked at, but with what you now know, you should not find it too difficult to explore those additional facilities yourself.

The important points that we covered in this chapter were:

- ❏ Implementing an applet generally involves implementing four methods that are called by the browser or the context in which the applet is running – the `init()` method that initializes the applet, the `start()` method that is called to start the applet, the `stop()` method that is called to stop whatever the applet is doing and the `destroy()` method that is called when the applet ends. You should also implement the `getAppletInfo()` and `getParameterInfo()` methods for your applet.

- ❏ Objects of the URL class represent uniform resource locators on the Internet. You can define a URL in an applet either as an absolute URL, or relative to the original URL.

- ❏ An `Image` object represents an image, and you can create images from files in GIF, PNG or JPEG format.

- ❏ The control of the timing interval for an animation generally runs in a separate thread, and in an applet the thread is usually started in the `start()` method and stopped in the `stop()` method.

- ❏ You can use an object of the `java.util.Timer` class to control an animation that you expedite through a `TimerTask` object. You can apply `Timer` and `TimerTask` object to scheduling any operation that recurs at a fixed time interval.

- ❏ The alpha component for a pixel specifies its transparency, where an alpha value of zero is transparent and a value of one is opaque.

- ❏ Alpha compositing determines how the components of the pixels for a source image are combined with the components of the destination image over which it is rendered.

- ❏ Rendering hints provide a way for you to trade between speed and quality in rendering operations.

- ❏ The type of line produced by drawing operations in a graphics context is determined by the current stroke set in the context. A line type is specified by a `BasicStroke` object.

- ❏ The glass pane for a `JApplet` or `JFrame` object overlays the content pane, so you can draw animated elements of an image in the glass pane and reserve the content pane for the fixed elements. You must ensure the background to the glass pane is transparent to enable the content pane to be seen.

- ❏ You can synthesize images by creating a `BufferedImage` object and drawing on it using the `Graphics2D` object that represents the image.

Exercises

1. Create an applet that will create an image from a GIF file and display four copies of it in two rows of two.

2. Modify the result of the previous exercise so that the applet obtains the URL for the image file from a PARAM.

3. Modify the last example to use the glass pane to display the sprite, and arrange that the logo is only visible inside the circle that the sprite rolls around. (Hint: draw an image on top of the logo with a transparent circle.)

4. Adapt the last example of the chapter to simultaneously display a fading logo and the rotating sprite in two threads.

5. The animation in the last example in the chapter could be generated by a fixed sequence of images that repeats cyclically. Generate the animation by creating all the images you need beforehand and making the paint() method in the ImagePanel class display the appropriate image.

6. Modify Sketcher to support lines of various types and widths – at least dashed and dotted lines in addition to solid lines.

7. Create an applet to create a sequence of images from an arbitrary number of GIF files, and replay them as an animation at an interval specified by a <PARAM> tag. (Hint: you can give your GIF files names such as image0.gif, image1.gif, image3.gif and so on. The getImage() method that your applet class inherits returns null if the URL cannot be found.)

Adding Sound to your Programs

In this chapter we will take a brief look into the Java Sound API. This supports sampled sound data processing as well as MIDI. There's far more to this API than we can possibly cover in a single chapter, so the objective is to get a good enough understanding of how it works through some elementary examples to equip you to explore further.

In this chapter you will learn:

❑ What sampled sound data is

❑ What standard sound file types are supported in Java

❑ What the common audio formats are

❑ How to play back sound clips

❑ How to play back sounds of an unlimited duration

❑ How to record sound

❑ What MIDI is

❑ What types of MIDI sequences are supported

❑ How to write a program to play MIDI files

❑ How to synthesize playing MIDI instruments

Some Sound Concepts

Digital sound recording and playback involves a plethora of jargon and abbreviations with which you can amuse your family and baffle your friends. Some of the ideas and terms used in this area can be confusing if you are not familiar with them, so before we get into the specifics of programming for sound in Java, we'll get ourselves equipped with the most common phrases and expressions, and take a quick look at the concepts associated with these. If you already have a reasonable working knowledge of digital sound concepts you can skip this section.

First of all, to make sure we are all on the same wavelength, let's review the basics of what sound is. Sound is produced by a rapidly varying pressure wave, generally in the air, but it can be in water or any medium capable of transmitting such a signal. The range of the variations in pressure determines the loudness of the sound, and the frequency with which the variations in pressure occur in a given time period determines the pitch – the nature of the sound in other words. A low note on a piano corresponds to a low frequency sound and a high note to a higher frequency.

Of course, sounds in general are not single tones of a given frequency. They are composed of a number of different frequencies mixed up together. The component with the highest frequency is of significance because your hearing is limited in the frequencies of sound it can detect. People can hear sounds with frequencies up to around 20,000 cycles per second (20kHz), at least they can when they are young. Many animals, such as dogs for instance, can hear sounds of a much higher frequency than this. Hence the so-called 'silent' dog whistle, which is only silent so far as we are concerned because it emits a sound with a frequency above that detectable by human hearing.

Any measurement that varies continuously, such as the outside temperature, or the pressure in a sound wave, is referred to as an **analog signal**. Sound is recorded in analog form in a cassette recorder as a continuously variable magnetization of the tape. It was also recorded in analog form on the old vinyl records that preceded CDs, and these are interesting because you can see the form of the sound recording. If you look closely at a vinyl record, you will see that the groove for the stylus that reproduces the sound is actually wavy. The waves in the groove are more frequent for high-pitched sounds and spread out over a greater distance along the groove for low-pitched sounds. Your computer can't handle analog signals directly. It can only handle data in a digital form. Digital sound data is a series of discrete numbers that measure the sound pressure at fixed intervals of time. Thus to enable your PC to handle sound, the original analog sound signal has to be converted to a series of binary values.

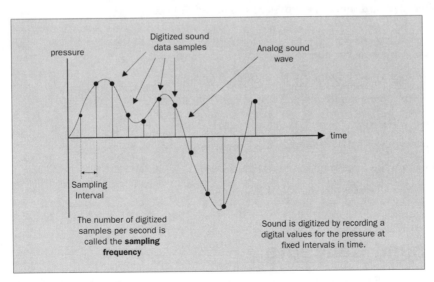

A digital representation of a sound signal is obtained by **sampling** the analog sound signal at fixed intervals of time as illustrated in the diagram, and the set of values produced by sampling an analog signal is called **sampled data**. Each sample is a digital value with a given number of bits representing the sound signal at a given instant, and how often samples are taken is called the **sampling frequency**. The sampling frequency is very important as it determines how well the original analog signal is represented by the series of digital values. If you join up the dots corresponding to the samples, you should get a reasonable approximation to the original sound wave. If you don't, you haven't got a high enough sampling frequency.

The conversion of the analog measure of the sound – typically an electrical signal from a microphone – is achieved using a device called an **analog to digital converter** (often abbreviated to **ADC**). This device converts the level of an analog signal at a given instant to a digital value with a given number of bits, and does this at a given sampling frequency. The reverse process – converting a digital signal back to analog form – is performed by a circuit called a **digital to analog converter** (or **DAC**). This device is used convert the digital sound data back to analog form (a voltage) when you replay a digital sound recording through your PC's speakers.

A sound recording can be **monophonic** – which corresponds to a single sound channel, **stereophonic** with two sound channels, or even several channels, when it is referred to as **polyphonic**. A digital sound recording with two or more channels will have a digital data value for each channel recorded at each instant in time. Thus, for a given number of bits per sample, twice as much data is necessary to record sound in stereo as compared to mono, assuming the data is not compressed.

The medium used to record sound in analog form – tape for instance – is subject to deterioration, which adversely affects the quality of reproduction. Digital sound recording doesn't have this problem. Although the recording medium will deteriorate to some degree, as long as the data is readable, the original recording quality will be maintained. However, the quality of reproduction is highly dependent on how the digital sound data was created.

Digital Sound Quality

Two things affect the quality of a digital sound recording, the number of bits in a sample, and the sampling frequency. Obviously, if more bits are used to record each sample, the value can be represented more accurately. As you know, 8 bits can be used to represent 256 different values, so if a sound sample only has eight bits, only 256 different sound pressure levels (or loudness levels) can be differentiated. Although the more bits in a sample the better, there is a trade-off between quality and the size of the sound file, and the size of the file can be critical, particularly if it is to be transmitted over the Internet – for playing by an applet for instance. An 8 bit sound recording will be of relatively low quality but is likely to be adequate for speech. Sound samples with at least 16 bits are necessary for high quality reproduction of music.

The sampling frequency is at least as importance to the quality of reproduction as the number of bits used in a sample. The higher the frequency of the sound being recorded, the higher the sampling frequency needs to be in order to represent the sound adequately. In fact the sampling frequency must be at least twice the frequency of the highest frequency component in the sound, and preferably more for reasonable reproduction. It's easy to see intuitively why this needs to be so by considering a sound wave of a given frequency, as shown in the diagram overleaf.

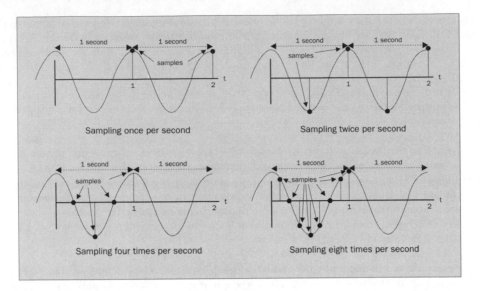

This shows a sound signal that happens to be a single tone of 1 cycle per second. You wouldn't be able to hear this as the frequency is too low, but it will illustrate the point. If we sample this at a frequency of 1 sample per second, you can see from the diagram that all the samples will have the same value, so we have no information about the signal at all. It doesn't matter where the samples are taken in relation to the analog signal illustrated in the diagram. If the sampling frequency is the same as the sound frequency, we get no information about how the signal varies.

If we increase the sampling rate to twice the frequency of the signal – to 2 samples per second, we get two sample values during each cycle, so we now record some idea of how the signal varies. Of course, it is barely adequate, and it should be easy to see that you won't necessarily record the peak values at all. As we increase the sampling rate further, you can see we get a better and better digital representation of the original analog signal. If you join up the dots you get a fair representation of the continuous wave. The minimum sampling rate of twice the maximum frequency in an analog signal is sometimes referred to as the **Nyquist frequency** for the signal, after Henry Nyquist who was a famous pioneer in the field of communications theory. He developed the Nyquist theorem that states that the sampling rate for a signal must be twice that of the highest frequency in the signal. If you sample below the Nyquist frequency, the data that you get will not be an adequate representation of the original signal, and this misrepresentation of the original signal is referred to as **aliasing**.

The minimum sampling rate for a signal has some major practical implications for processing sound data in your PC. Recording an orchestra that might have sound components with frequencies up to 20,000 cycles per second, you need to be sampling the sound at least at 40,000 samples per second (per channel!) to record the sound adequately. If you are recording samples with 16 bits of precision, a stereo recording involves saving 160,000 bytes for each second of sound. The raw data for ten minutes of music will thus be over 90 megabytes. To reduce the volume of digital sound data to more manageable levels, **data compression techniques** are employed. During the recording of a digital sound file, the raw data can be compressed on the fly, given a sufficiently fast processor. On playback, the compressed data needs to be decompressed before it is transferred to the device that will reproduce the sound. The algorithm that does this **co**mpression and **de**compression is called a **codec**.

No single audio codec is suitable for all purposes, and there are a number of different codecs to suit different circumstances. For example, if you are dealing with speech the requirements will be very different from that of music because the range of frequencies necessary for the latter is very much greater than that of the former. If you want to transmit digital sound over the Internet, you need a form that is very different from that used for recording on a music CD because of the bandwidth limitations. You have probably heard of **MP3**, which is an example of an audio codec for the delivery of high quality music over the Internet. MP3 is an abbreviation for **MPEG layer 3** and MPEG is an acronym for the **M**oving **P**ictures **E**xperts **G**roup that defined this standard.

Of course, since codecs are just compression/decompression algorithms, they can be implemented in hardware or in software. As well as sound codecs there are also codecs that apply to other media, such as digital photographs and video, where the volumes of data are even greater. Uncompressed digital video for instance involves very high data rates, up to 27 megabytes for every second of recording. Compression techniques can reduce this by a factor that can be from 8, to more than 30, depending on the particular method applied and the charactersitics of the source material. In these cases the codecs often trade off quality in terms of the accuracy with which the original signal can be reproduced for a greater reduction in the volume of data.

Digital Sound Data

Sound data values can be stored in a variety of **audio formats** to accommodate different requirements for the type of sound and its use. Sound samples are commonly either 8-bit or 16-bit values, although 24-bit samples are used in some high quality sound recording processes. 8-bit samples are typically used for speech, whereas 16-bit samples are used for music where a greater range is essential for accurate reproduction. Java can handle both 8-bit and 16-bit sound data.

The maximum value of a sound signal will depend on the loudness of the sound – the louder the sound the higher the value is going to be. Sound sampling usually uses a technique called **quantization** to accommodate the range of sound values that actually occurs in practice within a given number of bits. This involves mapping the digital value produced by the ADC corresponding to the maximum sound level, to the maximum value that can be represented by the number of bits in the sample. For example, if the maximum value produced by the ADC happened to require ten bits, and 8-bit samples are being stored, you could accommodate this by discarding the low-order two bits in each sample. Thus the quantization of the samples is 4, since a difference of 1 between two sample values will represent a difference of 4 in the original signal.

Generally, 16-bit sound values are **linear**, by which I mean that sound values can vary linearly over the range represented by a 16-bit integer – from -32768 to +32767 for signed sample values and 0 to 65535 for unsigned sample values. 8-bit sound values may also be linear – and may be signed or unsigned values. Linear sound samples are also referred to as **PCM** (**P**ulse **C**ode **M**odulation) samples. With 16-bit sound samples, the byte order can vary – the most significant byte of the two can be first or last in sequence, and it obviously matters. If the first byte (the leftmost) stores the most significant bits, the value is referred to as **big-endian**. If the rightmost byte stores the most significant bits it is described as **little-endian**. This is not specific to sound data particularly. The byte order for numerical data generally can vary between one kind of computer and another.

The **dynamic range**, which is the variation in loudness of the sound, provided by a linear representation of sound values in 8 bits can be a constraint, even for speech. This is because the different levels of loudness are not distributed linearly. With normal speech, by which I mean not shouting or whispering, the variation in loudness is fairly limited, and background noise is usually much softer than the sound that you want to hear. Consequently, the overall quality may suffer recording the sound linearly with just 8 bits. We have only 256 possible different samples and only a small proportion of these will apply to the loudness levels applicable to the speech sounds. We may be devoting almost as many of the available sample values to recording the noise. To get over this, an alternative method for representing sound values in 8 bits is sometimes used that encodes sample values logarithmically. This has the effect of weighting the range of samples in favor of the louder sounds. The diagram shows how sample values are distributed across the range of possible loudness levels with a linear approach, on the left, and with a logarithmic approach on the right.

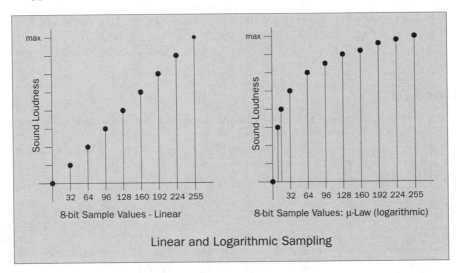

Linear and Logarithmic Sampling

The sample values on the right include intermediate values of 8 and 16 to give you an idea of the loudness corresponding to the lower sample values. Relatively few of the possible sample values in the logarithmic method apply to lower sound levels, as you can see. The loudness values that are less than half the maximum are covered by sample values from 0 to 16 so they are not represented very accurately at all. However, this is the region where the noise in the signal will be, so you don't really care that this is not represented too well. On the other hand the loudness levels above half the maximum loudness, are covered by the sample values from 17 to 255, which is 94% of the number of possible samples. Thus most of the possible 8-bit sample values are devoted to recording precisely the loudness levels where the important bit of the sound signal is – the speech.

If we had included the loudness level for a sample value of 1 for logarithmic samples in the diagram, it would correspond to a value of approximately one eighth of the maximum. Thus for non-zero loudness values less than this, there are no intermediate sample values. We just don't bother with values less than one eighth of the range of sound values. Based on this you can look at logarithmic sampling in another way. Since we devote all of the non-zero sample values to the upper seven eighths of the range, we effectively accommodate a range of values that would require more than 8 bits when encoded linearly. There are two sampling methods that do this. One is called **μ–law** (pronounced mu-law to rhyme with mew, the sound a cat makes), and is used primarily in the USA, and the other is called **A-law** and is used in Europe.

While the principles behind μ–law and A-law are similar, they differ in the details. μ–law compresses 14-bit values into 8 bits whereas A-law compresses 13-bit values into 8 bits. Thus within 8 bits you get the dynamic range provided by 13 or 14 bit linear values. The compression of the dynamic range of individual sound values is called **companding** – an abbreviation of **comp**ressing and exp**anding**. Don't confuse this with the compression of a series of sound values performed by a codec, which results in a reduction in the overall size of the sound file.

The current Java implementation supports processing of sound files containing data encoded linearly, or as μ–law or A-law sample values.

Sound Sampling Rates

Sound can be sampled at any rate to suit the use of the digital sound data, but some sampling rates are more popular than others. Speech is often recorded digitally at 8kHz – 8000 samples per second. Although it is not mandatory, this sampling rate typically applies to μ–law and A-law encoded samples.

Sampling at 8kHz is fine for speech and it is the rate used for digital telephony, but is quite inadequate for music. Digital Audio Tapes (DAT) are recorded at a rate of 48 kHz with 16-bit samples. The sampling rate on a music CD is 44.1 kHz also with 16-bit sample values, and this rate is commonly used for high quality sound recordings on a PC. Half this rate, 22.05 kHz is used to produce economy class recordings and you may come across recordings at a quarter of this rate, 11.025 kHz. Java supports all these sampling rates from 8 kHz to 48 kHz.

Keep in mind that a sound file must be replayed at the same rate that it was sampled if you want it to sound like the original. Unless you have a musician's ear, some small variation – under 2% say – between the original sampling rate and the replay rate, is likely to go undetected. Maintaining the correct data rate is not going to be difficult within your PC, but receiving music as sampled sound data over the Internet may be more problematical. Not only must the average data transfer be at a minimum of the replay rate, but the data buffering must also be sufficient to avoid breaks in the sound.

Audio File Formats

There's potential confusion when we talk about audio file formats. Don't confuse **audio file formats** – which describe the structure of various files that contain sampled sound data, with **audio formats** – which describe the format of the sound data itself. A given audio file format can usually accommodate a variety of different audio formats, although a given file will store the sound data in a given audio format.

There are many different audio file formats, most of which will be characterized by a file header that provides the specifications for the nature of the information in the file. This may include such data as the number of channels, the sampling rate, the encoding technique for the samples and so on. Many of these are tied to specific software products that process sound data in various ways, but there are a number of recognized standard audio file formats. The implementation of the sound API in the present release of Java 2 (JDK 1.3) supports three different sampled sound file formats:

Extension	Description
.au or .snd	This is commonly used for sound files on the Internet and especially on Sun workstations. A file of this type usually stores 8-bit μ–law encoded samples (which are really only suitable for speech), but it can store 8-bit or 16-bit linear samples.
.aif	Audio Interchange File Format (**AIFF**) files are primarily associated with Mac computers. They store sampled sound data as 8-bit or 16-bit samples. Standard .aif files store linear samples, but there is a special version of the AIFF file format (**AIFF-C** for Compression) that supports compressed sound data such as μ–law.
.wav	This is a Windows PC file type (also supported on the Mac) that stores 8-bit or 16-bit samples and can support linear, μ–law, and A-law encoded samples.

Note that the audio data format is not determined by the audio file format. The audio format for the sound samples that an audio file contains will be indicated in the file header.

A glaring omission from the set of supported formats within the Sound API is **MPEG Layer-3**, better known as **MP3**. This is the standard format for commercially distributed music over the Internet. If you need to handle MP3 in your Java programs, it is still possible. The Java Media Framework (JMF) is a set of classes and interfaces that provide support for the recording and playback of all media – video as well as audio, and its audio capability includes support for MP3. JMF makes use of the Sound API, but JMF is not part of core Java. JMF is also well outside the scope of this book. If you can wait a while, undoubtedly we shall see support for MP3 appearing in the Sound API in a future release.

Frames and Frame Rates

For linear sample data a **sample frame** stores all the samples for the sound at a given instant in time. The number of bytes in a frame will therefore be the number of bytes in a sample multiplied by the number of channels. For a linear stereo recording with 16-bit samples for instance, the sample frame will be four bytes – two bytes for each channel. The **frame rate** is the number of frames per second of sound, and in most cases the frame rate will be the same as the sample rate. If you have a sample rate of 44.1kHz from a CD, then the frame rate will also be 44.1 kHz. You need to take particular care when defining memory buffers for sound data. They generally need to accommodate a whole number of frames so the size of a sound buffer should always be an integral multiple of the frame size.

This terminology, frame rate and sample rate, sounds like an unnecessary complication, but it isn't because with compressed sound data things are not quite so straightforward. With compressed sound data, the frame rate will be less than the sample rate – because the data is compressed, and may not be constant. The frame size will not be a simple product of the number of bytes per sample and the number of channels because the data representing the sound is stored in a radically different way.

Simple Sound Output

Before we get to the Sound API proper, let's look at the sound capability in Java that predates it. It is very simple, but it may be adequate in many instances. The simplest mechanism for outputting sound in a Java program doesn't make use of the Sound API at all. If you want to play sounds in an applet, an `Applet` object, and hence a `JApplet` object, has methods built in to do just that.

The sound clip to be played can be created from a file by calling the `getAudioClip()` method for the applet. There are two overloaded versions of this method, One version accepts a single argument that is a reference of type `URL` that identifies the file. The other accepts two arguments, a reference of type `URL` defining the location of the sound file, and a `String` object specifying its name. The method returns a reference of type `AudioClip`. Typically the file containing the clip will be in the same location as the code for the applet so you might create the `AudioClip` object in the `init()` method for the applet like this:

```
class PlayIt extends JApplet
{
  public void init()
  {
    // Get the sound clip
    String fileName - getParameter("clip");               // Get the file name
    clip = getAudioClip(getDocumentBase(), fileName); // Create the clip

    // Rest of the applet initialization...
  }

  AudioClip clip;                                         // The sound clip
}
```

`AudioClip` is actually an interface that defines three methods:

`play()`	Starts playing the audio clip from the beginning. The clip will play once unless `stop()` is called for the `AudioClip` reference before the end of the clip.
`loop()`	Starts the clip playing in a loop that will continue until `stop()` is called.
`stop()`	Stops playing the clip.

To play the clip we just call the `play()` or `loop()` method for the `AudioClip` object. For example, when we want to play the clip once, we would write:

```
clip.play();
```

The call to `getAudioClip()` doesn't actually retrieve the file containing the clip. This only occurs when you call `loop()` or `play()` to play the clip. If the file doesn't happen to be there – as will be the case if you have specified the file name incorrectly for instance, or the sound data is in a format that is not supported, then nothing happens.

Let's put together a complete applet to play a sound clip.

```java
import java.applet.*;
import javax.swing.*;
import java.awt.event.*;

public class PlayIt extends JApplet
{
  public void init()
  {
    // Get the sound clip
    String fileName = getParameter("clip");           // Get the file name
    clip = getAudioClip(getDocumentBase(), fileName);// Create the clip

    // Rest of the applet initialization...
    button = new JButton(play);
    button.addActionListener(new ActionListener()
    {
      public void actionPerformed(ActionEvent e)
      {
        if(e.getActionCommand().equals(play))
        {
          clip.loop();
          button.setText(stop);
        }
        else
        {
          clip.stop();
          button.setText(play);
        }
      }
    }
    );

    getContentPane().add(button);
  }

  AudioClip clip;                                      // The sound clip
  JButton button;
  final String play = "PLAY";                          // Play button label
  final String stop = "STOP";                          // Stop button label
}
```

To run this applet you will have to create an .html file to load the applet, supply its dimensions and to specify the clip attribute as the name of the sound file. For example, the contents of this file might be:

```
<APPLET  CODE = "PlayIt.class" CODEBASE = "." WIDTH = 300 HEIGHT = 50
         clip = "myClip.wav" >

</APPLET>
```

I have shown the clip attribute set to the name of my file that happens to be a .wav file. You need to set it to your own file name. The file containing the sound clip can be an .au, a .wav, or an .aif file. If you are short of a sound file and running Microsoft Windows, you should find some in the Media subdirectory to your Windows directory. Alternatively, a quick search on the Internet should turn up plenty of examples.

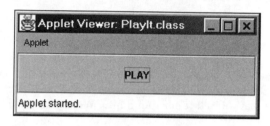

When you run the applet, just click on the button to play the sound clip. Click on it again to stop it.

How It Works

We create the AudioClip object exactly as we described in the text. The only component in the applet is the JButton object, button, which starts out with the label "PLAY". We add an action listener for the button that is defined by an anonymous class. The actionPerformed() method calls play() for the AudioClip object, clip, if the current button command is "PLAY", and we change the button label to "STOP". Otherwise, the button command must be "STOP" so we call the stop() method for clip and set the button label back to "PLAY".

The Applet class also defines a method, play(), that will play an audio clip at a given URL directly. Like the getAudioClip() method, it comes it two flavors, one with a URL argument for the clip file, and the other with a URL argument for the file location plus a String argument for the file name.

Simple Sounds in an Application

The Applet class also defines a static method, newAudioClip() that retrieves an audio clip from a URL specified by the argument(of type URL), and returns a reference of type AudioClip that encapsulates the audio clip. Because this method is static, you don't have to have an Applet object to call it, and the code does not need to be for an applet. You can use it in an application to retrieve a sound clip from a file.

Let's see how this works in practice.

Try It Out – Playing Sound Clips in an Application

We will put together an application that can play any sound file that exists in the current directory. We won't worry too much here about making the GUI fancy – you can do that on your own by now.

First we will need to figure out what sounds files of the acceptable types to Java (`.au`, `.wav`, or `.aif`) exist in the current directory. Of course, the first step in doing that is to find out what the current directory is, and the `getProperty()` method in the `System` class can help with that. To use this method, you need to pass the name of the property that you are interested in and in our case it's `"user.dir"` for the current user directory. The `getProperty()` method will return a reference to a `String` object containing the current directory path, so we can create a `File` object that corresponds to that with the statement:

```
File currentDir = new File(System.getProperty("user.dir"));
```

Now we can use the `list()` method with this `File` object to obtain the names of the files we are interested in. We want a filtered list so we can use the version of the `list()` method that accepts a `FilenameFilter` object that will select our sound files. We can create the filter by using an anonymous class like this:

```
FilenameFilter filter = new FilenameFilter()
{
  public boolean accept(File directory, String filename)
  {
      String name = filename.toLowerCase();
      return name.endsWith(".au")||name.endsWith(".aif")||name.endsWith(".wav");
  }
};
```

The `accept()` method will return `true` for any file that ends with the extensions shown. We just have to use the filter object as an argument to the `list()` method like this:

```
String soundFiles[] = currentDir.list(filter);
```

The list method returns an array of type `String` containing the names of the files from the directory defined by `currentDir` that conform to the filter.

We saw earlier that we can create an `AudioClip` object from a `URL` object that identifies the file containing the sound clip by passing it to the static `newAudioClip()` method in the `Applet` class. We are therefore going to need a `URL` object corresponding to a particular sound file. The `File` class defines a method `toURL()` that will be a great help, and that we can use something like this:

```
URL currentDirURL = currentDir.toURL();
```

The `toURL()` method can throw an exception of type `MalformedURLException` so we will have to put it in a try block when we come to apply it in our application.

We can use this URL object corresponding to the current directory in a call to a URL class constructor that accepts two arguments. The first argument is a reference to a URL object defining a context, and the second is a reference to a String object defining the file in that context. Thus we can construct an AudioClip object for the file name in the first element of the soundFiles array with the statement:

```
AudioClip clip = Applet.newAudioClip(new URL(currentDirURL,soundFiles[0]));
```

Note that the URL class constructors can also throw an exception of type MalformedURLException, so this statement will need to appear in a try block too. We can put all these ideas together in the program. Here's the code:

```
import javax.swing.*;
import java.applet.*;
import java.io.*;
import java.awt.*;
import java.awt.event.*;
import java.net.*;

public class PlaySounds extends JFrame
{
  public PlaySounds()
  {
    // Set up the window
    setDefaultCloseOperation(EXIT_ON_CLOSE);
    setTitle("Sound File Player");
    setSize(250,100);                   // Big enough to show the title bar & components

    // Get the sounds file names from current directory
    File currentDir = new File(System.getProperty("user.dir"));
    try
    {
      currentDirURL = currentDir.toURL();            // Get the directory URL
    }
    catch(MalformedURLException ex)
    {
      System.err.println("Bad URL - terminating...\n"+ex);
      System.exit(1);
    }

    FilenameFilter filter = new FilenameFilter()  // Filter for sound file types
    {
      public boolean accept(File directory, String filename)
      {
        String name = filename.toLowerCase();
        Return name.endsWith(".au")||name.endsWith(".aif")||name.endsWith(".wav");
      }
    };
    String soundFiles[] = currentDir.list(filter);      // Get all the file names
    if(soundFiles == null||soundFiles.length == 0)      // and check we got some
    {
      System.err.println("No sound files - terminating...");
      System.exit(1);
    }
```

```
    soundChoice = new JComboBox(soundFiles);              // Dropdown list box of files
    try
    {                                 // Make a clip from the first file in the list
      clip = Applet.newAudioClip(new URL(currentDirURL,soundFiles[0]));
    }
    catch(MalformedURLException ex)
    {
      System.err.println("Bad URL - terminating...\n"+ex);
      System.exit(1);
    }

    // Add a listener for new sound file chosen
    soundChoice.addActionListener(new ActionListener()
    {
      public void actionPerformed(ActionEvent e)
      {
        try
        {                                 // create the clip from the file chosen
          clip = Applet.newAudioClip(new URL(currentDirURL,
                                (String)soundChoice.getSelectedItem()));
        }
        catch(MalformedURLException ex)
        {
          System.err.println("Bad URL - terminating...\n"+ex);
          System.exit(1);
        }
      }
    }
    );

    // Set up the PLAY button to play the current clip
    JButton play = new JButton("PLAY");
    play.addActionListener(new ActionListener()    // Listen for button selection
    {
      public void actionPerformed(ActionEvent e)
      {
        clip.play();
      }
    }
    );

    // Add the combobox and the button to the application window
    Container content = getContentPane();
    content.add(soundChoice);
    content.add(play,BorderLayout.SOUTH);
  }

  public static void main(String args[])
  {
    PlaySounds player = new PlaySounds();    // Create the application object
    player.setVisible(true);                 // and show the window
  }
```

```
        private URL currentDirURL;              // URL for the current directory
        private JComboBox soundChoice;          // Combobox for choosing the file to play
        private AudioClip clip;                 // The current sound clip
    }
```

How It Works

The main() method just creates an application object, and the class constructor sets up the application window with a combobox displaying the list of sound files in the current directory, and a PLAY button to play the currently selected clip. The current directory and the list of files it contains are obtained as described earlier.

The ActionListener object that listens for events relating to the JComboBox object is created directly from an anonymous class. We could have created an inner class instead, but the class is very simple with just the actionPerformed() method, and that requires minimal code, so an anonymous class is a good approach here. The same goes for the FilenameFilter object that we use to select the file names in the current directory, and the listener for action events associated with the button.

Sound API Basics

The complete set of sound API classes is contained within four packages, but you only need to concern yourself with two of them. The javax.sound.sampled package contains the classes that support the recording and playing of sampled sound, and the javax.sound.midi package contains class that support operations with MIDI data. The other two packages, javax.sound.sampled.spi and javax.sound.midi.spi, are for use when you want to support new audio or MIDI devices, which is a little beyond the scope of this book.

Let's start by looking at how physical sound resources are represented in Java.

Sound System Resources

Most of the time you will want to access a number of physical or simulated sound resources in your system that you will use to record, play, or process sampled sound date. An **audio line** is any resource that is a source or destination for sampled sound data. Remember that, in general, the sound can be mono, stereo, or polyphonic, so a line may encapsulate several channels. You can send audio data to an audio line that is an input line, and you can receive audio data from an output line.

As we will see a little later, there are several different kinds of audio lines. Particular examples of lines are the jacks on the back of your sound card into which you plug the speakers or a microphone. These kinds of physical input and output connections for sound data are called **ports**. In general, lines may have controls such as a **gain** control, which controls the loudness of the sound, a **pan** control, which controls the left to right balance of stereo sound channels, and a reverb control, which determines the amount of echo added to the signal. A reverb control can be used to produce the effect of playing the sound in a particular environment, such as a concert hall for instance.

Audio lines are generally associated with a device called a **mixer**. A **mixer** receives input from one or more audio lines called **source data lines**, and outputs the result of combining the input to an output line called a **target data line**. A mixer is not limited to having one target data line – it can have several. As we shall see, we can gain access to an audio line belonging to a mixer via the mixer itself, or directly, without reference to the mixer with which it is associated.

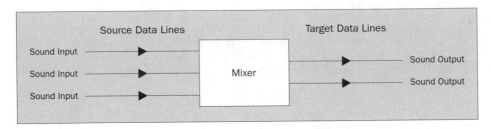

Keep in mind that lines are abstract concepts so one kind of line can correspond to different physical sound resources at different times. The terminology used for lines can be a little confusing here. The names for lines refer to what the line does in the context of a mixer. A source data line is a *source* for a *mixer* – not a source for you. For you, a source data line is a destination for sound data. You write data to a source data line to supply input to the mixer. A target data line on the other hand is the output from the mixer, so for you, a target data line is a source of sound data – you can read from it. Thus a target data line in one instance might simply be the microphone input from your sound card. In another instance it might be a stream from which you can read the sampled sound data that results from mixing two other sound streams.

You can't use a class constructor to create an object encapsulating a particular physical resource such as a line or a mixer. This is because sound resources are physical entities that may or may not exist in a particular system. Instead you use static methods from the `AudioSystem` class that is defined in the `javax.sound.sampled` package. You will typically call one method to establish that the resource you want is available, and then call another static method to obtain a reference to an object that encapsulates a particular physical resource. Sound system resources in Java are encapsulated by objects that are of an interface type, rather than of a class type. An interface relating to a sound resource will declare the methods that provide the operations for that kind of resource.

Of course, another important source of sound data is a sound file on your system, or more generally, a sampled sound source defined by a URL. With the basic sound capability provided by the `Applet` class, all we could do with such a sound source was to create an `AudioClip` object from it. The Sound API is much more general in that it provides the `AudioInputStream` class to represent a stream that is a source of sampled sound data with a specific format. You can create an `AudioInputStream` object from a local sound file on your PC, from another input stream, or from a URL. Again, it is the `AudioSystem` class that provides the methods to do this. Once you have an `AudioInputStream` object, you have a great deal of flexibility as to what you do with it. You might simply want to read the data from it. You could also write its contents to an output stream. The `AudioSystem` class also provides a static method that you can use to convert an audio input stream from one sound format to another.

Sampled Sound Interfaces

There are eight interfaces in the sampled sound package, `javax.sound.sampled`. The `LineListener` interface defines a method, `update()`, that handles audio line events and is passed a reference of type `LineEvent` as an argument. There are line events generated when you start and stop a line, and when you open and close it. We'll see how to apply this a little later in this chapter. The other seven interfaces define the operations that are possible with lines, which represent sound resources. These interfaces are interrelated as shown in the diagram.

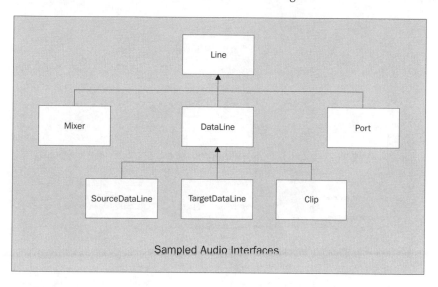

Sampled Audio Interfaces

The `Port` interface defines the operations that are specific to an external input or output port for audio data, a microphone or speaker connection for instance. External input and output ports can also be accessed as `SourceDataLine` or `TargetDataLine` objects. The `Mixer` interface declares the methods for operations you can perform on a mixer, which, as we discussed, incorporates one or more lines that can be input to, or output from the mixer. Thus a `Mixer` object can have `SourceDataLine` objects providing sound input to the mixer, and it will output sound data to one or more `TargetDataLine` objects. Thus your program can *read* sound data from a `TargetDataLine`, and *write* to a `SourceDataLine`.

A `Clip` object is rather different from the other types of lines. A `Clip` encapsulates the sound data for an audio clip in memory, whereas the others act as a conduit for the data. Once a `TargetDataLine` starts for example, if you don't read the data from it, the data will be lost. Once it starts operating, it is essentially a pipe through which sampled sound data is flowing, whether you read it or not. With a `Clip` object, all the sampled sound data is stored within the object so you can retrieve the data or play the clip as often as you want. You obtain the sound data to be stored in a `Clip` object from an audio input stream encapsulated in an `AudioInputStream` object.

We won't elaborate on the methods defined in these interfaces at this point. There are too many to include in a single chapter like this, so we will just look at the most interesting ones. It will be easier to see how they work when we come to use them in context.

Resource Descriptor Classes

The `Line`, `DataLine`, `Mixer` and `Port` interface definitions each include an inner class with the name `Info`, so we have classes `Line.Info`, `DataLine.Info`, `Mixer.Info`, and `Port.Info`. Objects of these inner class types encapsulate data specifying an object of the corresponding interface type – so an object of type `Port.Info` specifies the characteristic of a particular kind of `Port`. The `DataLine.Info` and `Port.Info` classes are derived from `Line.Info` because they both describe kinds of line. A mixer is a somewhat different kind of animal and the `Mixer.Info` class derives from `Object` directly.

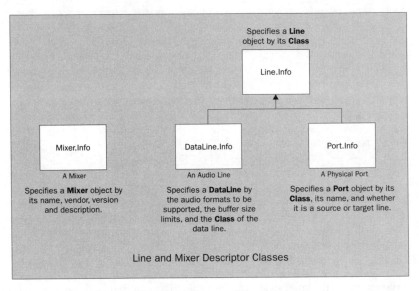

Line and Mixer Descriptor Classes

Note that a `Line.Info` object (as well as objects of the subclasses) defines a line by its class. An object of type `Class` specifies the class of a line here. As we saw back in Chapter 6, you can refer to the `Class` object for any class just by appending `.class` to the class name, so when we need a reference to the `Class` object for `SourceDataLine` class, we just use the expression `SourceDataLine.class`. Thus in the unlikely event that you wanted to create a `Line.Info` object corresponding to this class, you could write:

```
Line.Info info = new Line.Info(SourceDataLine.class);
```

`Line.Info` only has the one constructor that we have used here. The class defines three other methods that will be inherited by its subclasses:

`getLineClass()`	Returns a reference to the `Class` object for the line. You would use this if you have a reference of type Line that could refer to an object of any of the subclasses, and you want to check the specific class type, whether it refers to a `SourceDataLine` or a `TargetDataLine` for instance.
`matches(Line.Info info)`	Returns `true` if the argument is an instance of the same class as the current object, or is an instance of a subclass of the current object type. Otherwise it returns `false`.
`toString()`	Returns a `String` representation of the object.

You won't normally have a need to construct `Line.Info` objects because `DataLine.Info` and `Port.Info` objects are much more useful. However, you will be using the methods inherited from `Line.Info`.

Although you can create a `Port.Info` object using the class constructor, in most instances you will find it more convenient to use the `static` constants of type `Port.Info` that are defined within the class. These are:

LINE_IN	SPEAKER	HEADPHONE
LINE_OUT	MICROPHONE	COMPACT_DISC

The ports these define are obvious from the names, and usually correspond to the jacks on your sound card.

You use a `DataLine.Info` object to describe a source or target data line, or a clip. The `DataLine.Info` class has three constructors, but only two of them are likely to be useful to you, as the third is intended for use by mixer implementations. The two you might want to use are:

`DataLine.Info(`
`    Class        class,`
`    AudioFormat format)`
	Specifies a line of a given class – you can specify the class as we have described – so it could be `SourceDataLine.class`, `TargetDataLine.class`, or `Clip.class`. The second argument indicates the audio format for the line.

`DataLine.Info(`
`    Class        class,`
`    AudioFormat format,`
`    int bufferSize)`
	Specifies a line as above, but with a given buffer size.

You use an object of the `AudioFormat` class to define a particular audio format. In principle the samples can be linear, µ-law or A-law in the current Java Sound API, but you need to verify that what you want to use is actually supported on your system. While the API provides the potential for supporting all three, what is actually supported is implementation dependent.

The `AudioFormat` class has two constructors. The most general constructor requires seven arguments, as follows:

```
AudioFormat(AudioFormat.Encoding  encoding,
            float                 sampleRate,
            int                   sampleSizeInBits,
            int                   channels,
            int                   frameSize,
            float                 frameRate,
            boolean               bigEndian)
```

The first argument can be one of the four constants that are defined in the inner class, `AudioFormat.Encoding`:

ULAW	μ-law encoding.
ALAW	A-law encoding.
PCM_SIGNED	Linear encoding with signed sample values.
PCM_UNSIGNED	Linear encoding with unsigned sample values.

The `sampleRate` argument is the sampling rate, so 44100.0f would be the CD sample rate for instance. The `sampleSizeInBits` argument will be 8 or 16. The `channels` argument will be 1 for mono and 2 for stereo. The `frameSize` argument will be the product of the number of bytes in a sample and the number of channels. The `frameRate` argument will be the same as the sampling rate for the three supported encoding schemes. The last argument will be `true` if the samples are big-endian, as is usually the case, and `false` otherwise. Thus a typical `AudioFormat` object might be created as:

```
AudioFormat format = new AudioFormat(
            AudioFormat.Encoding.PCM_SIGNED,    // Linear
            44100.0f,                           // sample rate
            16,                                 // 16-bit
            2,                                  // stereo
            4,                                  // frame size
            44100.0f,                           // frame rate
            true);                              // big-endian
```

The other `AudioFormat` class constructor creates a signed or unsigned linear encoding, so it only requires five arguments:

```
AudioFormat(float            sampleRate,
            int              sampleSizeInBits,
            int              channels,
            boolean          signed,           // true for signed
            boolean          bigEndian)
```

We could therefore have written the previous statement as:

```
AudioFormat format = new AudioFormat(44100.0f, 16, 2, true, true);
```

Remember that an `AudioFormat` object just defines a format for the audio data. You have no guarantee that a line is available to support audio data with a given format.

Now that we have defined an audio format, we can now create an object encapsulating the specification of a particular line that we want to use. For example, with a statement such as:

```
DataLine.Info clipInfo = new DataLine.Info(Clip.class, format);// Info for a
stereo clip
```

We can now use the `clipInfo` object to ask the system for access to a `Clip` object – but we'll only get it if it's supported and available. We can create a `DataLine.Info` object to describe any kind of line, but whether it is supported in our system is a separate question. Let's see how we can access mixers, lines, and ports on a system.

Accessing Sound Devices

You use the `AudioSystem` class in the `javax.sound.sampled` package to gain access to the physical sound resources on your system. It defines `static` methods that return references to objects that encapsulate the various kinds of resources you have available. For instance, here are methods you can use to obtain a reference to an object encapsulating a line or a mixer:

`getLine(Line.Info info)`	Returns a reference of type `Line` that encapsulates an audio line that corresponds to the description contained in `info`. This can return a reference to a `DataLine` of some kind, or a `Port`, but not a `Mixer`. If the line with the required characteristics is not available, the method will throw an exception of type `LineUnavailableException` and if the type of line is not supported an exception of type `IllegalArgumentException` will be thrown.
`getMixer(Mixer.Info info)`	Returns a reference of type `Mixer` that encapsulates a mixer available in the system that corresponds to the description contained in info. If the mixer with the required characteristics is not available, the method will throw an exception of type `IllegalArgumentException`.

You could use the `getLine()` method like this:

```
AudioFormat format = new AudioFormat(44100.0f, 16, 2, true, true);
DataLine.Info clipInfo = new DataLine.Info(Clip.class, format);// Info for a
stereo clip
Clip clip = null;
try
{
  clip = (Clip)AudioSystem.getLine(clipInfo);
}
```

```
catch(LineUnavailableException e)
{
  System.err.println(e);
}
```

This creates a `Clip` reference if there is a device available that conforms to the `clipInfo` specification. If there's no clip that conforms, an exception will be thrown that we will report in the `catch` block.

There is a significant difference between *availability* and *support* for a line. If the line is not available – there is one but it's busy – the exception of type `LineUnavailableException` will be thrown. If the line we are specifying in the argument to `getLine()` is not supported by any mixer in the system, then an exception of type `IllegalArgumentException` will be thrown. With the code as written, this will pass on the exception of type `IllegalArgumentException`, which may terminate the program.

Fortunately, the `AudioSystem` class also defines some methods that enable you to do a bit of checking whether a line is supported before you dive in to get it:

`isLineSupported(Line.Info info)`	Returns `true` if the line specified by the argument is supported, and `false` other wise. You can use this to check if what you want is actually there.
`getSourceLineInfo(Line.Info info)`	Returns an array of type `Line.Info[]` containing reference to objects describing all the source lines that correspond to the argument and are supported by mixers in the system. This gives you a `Line.Info` reference for every source line, so you can pick one from the array to avoid being caught out.
`getTargetLineInfo(Line.Info info)`	Returns an array of type `Line.Info[]` containing reference to objects describing all the target lines that correspond to the argument and are supported by mixers in the system.

If you check to see whether the line you want is supported before you call the `getLine()` method, you will avoid the possibility of `IllegalArgumentException` being thrown. Since the parameter to the `isLineSupported()` method is of type `Line.Info` you can supply an argument of this type, or any of the types that have `Line.Info` as a base. Thus you can use this method to check whether any of the possible types of line is supported. Thus our previous fragment would be better written as:

```
AudioFormat format = new AudioFormat(44100.0f, 16, 2, true, true);
DataLine.Info clipInfo = new DataLine.Info(Clip.class, format);// Info for a
stereo clip
Clip clip = null;
if(AudioSystem.isLineSupported(clipInfo))
{
  try
  {
    clip = (Clip)AudioSystem.getLine(clipInfo);
  }
```

```
    catch(LineUnavailableException e)
    {
      System.err.println(e);
    }
  }
else
  System.err.printn("Line not supported: " + clipInfo);
```

Here we just explain the problem to the user, but in some situations we could try for another type of line if that was appropriate.

A `Mixer.Info` object is defined by descriptive data relating to a particular mixer, but you would not typically create such an object directly. Generally it will be more flexible to use an `AudioSystem` class method to retrieve `Mixer.Info` references for all the mixers that are available, and then select one of these.

`getMixerInfo()`	Returns an array of type `Mixer.Info[]` containing references to objects describing each of the available mixers in the system.

A `Mixer.Info` object has four methods that provide information about the mixer type, and a String reference is returned in each case. The methods are `getName()`, `getDescription()`, `getVendor()`, and `getVersion()`. In many instances, these methods will not return useful information, as we shall see with the next example.

Let's try some of this out by putting together an example to extract information about the sound system available.

Try It Out – Plumbing the Sound System

We will put together an example that will use what we have learned so far to find out what mixers and lines we have available. We will also discover what audio formats each line is prepared to deal with. Here's the code:

```
import javax.sound.sampled.*;
public class PlumbSoundSystem
{
  public static void main(String args[])
  {
    Mixer.Info[] mixers = AudioSystem.getMixerInfo();  // Info on all mixers
    Mixer mixer = null;
    Line.Info[] lines = null;
    AudioFormat[] formats = null;

    for(int i=0 ; i<mixers.length ; i++)                // For each mixer...
    {                                                   // show the details...
      System.out.println("\nMixer " + (i+1) + ":");
      System.out.println("\tName: "+mixers[i].getName()+
                      " Vendor: "+mixers[i].getVendor()+
                      " Version: " + mixers[i].getVersion() +
                      "\n\t\tDescription: " + mixers[i].getDescription());
```

```
      mixer = AudioSystem.getMixer(mixers[i]);          // Get the mixer...
        lines = mixer.getSourceLineInfo();              // ...and its source lines
 info
        for(int j=0 ; j<lines.length ; j++)             // For each source line...
        {                                               // show the details...
          System.out.println("\tSource Line " + (j+1) + ":" + lines[j]);

          formats = ((DataLine.Info)lines[j]).getFormats();
          for(int k = 0 ; k<formats.length ; k++)       // Show details of the formats
            System.out.println("\t\t" + formats[k]);    // supported
        }

        lines = mixer.getTargetLineInfo();              // Now get the lowdown
        for(int j=0 ; j<lines.length ; j++)             // on the target lines
        {
          System.out.println("\tTarget Line " + (j+1) + ":" + lines[j]);
          formats = ((DataLine.Info)lines[j]).getFormats();
          for(int k = 0 ; k<formats.length ; k++)
            System.out.println("\t\t" + formats[k]);
        }
      }
    }
  }
}
```

You will get quite a lot of output from this. On my system I get output on three mixers. Here are the more interesting bits:

```
Mixer 1:
    Name: Java Sound Audio Engine Vendor: Sun Microsystems Version: 1.0
            Description: Software mixer and synthesizer
    Source Line 1:interface SourceDataLine supporting 8 audio formats
            PCM_SIGNED, -1.0 Hz, 8 bit, mono, audio data
            PCM_UNSIGNED, -1.0 Hz, 8 bit, mono, audio data
            PCM_SIGNED, -1.0 Hz, 8 bit, stereo, audio data
            PCM_UNSIGNED, -1.0 Hz, 8 bit, stereo, audio data
            PCM_SIGNED, -1.0 Hz, 16 bit, mono, big-endian, audio data
            PCM_SIGNED, -1.0 Hz, 16 bit, mono, little-endian, audio data
            PCM_SIGNED, -1.0 Hz, 16 bit, stereo, big-endian, audio data
            PCM_SIGNED, -1.0 Hz, 16 bit, stereo, little-endian, audio data
    Source Line 2:interface Clip supporting 8 audio formats, and buffers of 0 to 4194304 bytes
            PCM_SIGNED, -1.0 Hz, 8 bit, mono, audio data
            PCM_UNSIGNED, -1.0 Hz, 8 bit, mono, audio data
            PCM_SIGNED, -1.0 Hz, 8 bit, stereo, audio data
            PCM_UNSIGNED, -1.0 Hz, 8 bit, stereo, audio data
            PCM_SIGNED, -1.0 Hz, 16 bit, mono, big-endian, audio data
            PCM_SIGNED, -1.0 Hz, 16 bit, mono, little-endian, audio data
            PCM_SIGNED, -1.0 Hz, 16 bit, stereo, big-endian, audio data
            PCM_SIGNED, -1.0 Hz, 16 bit, stereo, little-endian, audio data
    Target Line 1:interface DataLine supporting 24 audio formats
            PCM_UNSIGNED, 11025.0 Hz, 8 bit, mono, audio data
            PCM_UNSIGNED, 11025.0 Hz, 8 bit, stereo, audio data
```

PCM_SIGNED, 11025.0 Hz, 16 bit, mono, little-endian, audio data
PCM_SIGNED, 11025.0 Hz, 16 bit, stereo, little-endian, audio data
PCM_UNSIGNED, 11025.0 Hz, 8 bit, mono, audio data
PCM_UNSIGNED, 11025.0 Hz, 8 bit, stereo, audio data
PCM_SIGNED, 11025.0 Hz, 16 bit, mono, big-endian, audio data
PCM_SIGNED, 11025.0 Hz, 16 bit, stereo, big-endian, audio data
PCM_UNSIGNED, 22050.0 Hz, 8 bit, mono, audio data
PCM_UNSIGNED, 22050.0 Hz, 8 bit, stereo, audio data
PCM_SIGNED, 22050.0 Hz, 16 bit, mono, little-endian, audio data
PCM_SIGNED, 22050.0 Hz, 16 bit, stereo, little-endian, audio data
PCM_UNSIGNED, 22050.0 Hz, 8 bit, mono, audio data
PCM_UNSIGNED, 22050.0 Hz, 8 bit, stereo, audio data
PCM_SIGNED, 22050.0 Hz, 16 bit, mono, big-endian, audio data
PCM_SIGNED, 22050.0 Hz, 16 bit, stereo, big-endian, audio data
PCM_UNSIGNED, 44100.0 Hz, 8 bit, mono, audio data
PCM_UNSIGNED, 44100.0 Hz, 8 bit, stereo, audio data
PCM_SIGNED, 44100.0 Hz, 16 bit, mono, little-endian, audio data
PCM_SIGNED, 44100.0 Hz, 16 bit, stereo, little-endian, audio data
PCM_UNSIGNED, 44100.0 Hz, 8 bit, mono, audio data
PCM_UNSIGNED, 44100.0 Hz, 8 bit, stereo, audio data
PCM_SIGNED, 44100.0 Hz, 16 bit, mono, big-endian, audio data
PCM_SIGNED, 44100.0 Hz, 16 bit, stereo, big-endian, audio data

Mixer 2:
    Name: Microsoft Sound Mapper Vendor: Unknown Vendor Version: Unknown Version
        Description: No details available
    Target Line 1:interface TargetDataLine supporting 48 audio formats
        PCM_SIGNED, 8000.0 Hz, 8 bit, mono, audio data
        PCM_UNSIGNED, 8000.0 Hz, 8 bit, mono, audio data

Plus many more formats for mixer 2....

PCM_SIGNED, 44100.0 Hz, 8 bit, stereo, audio data
PCM_UNSIGNED, 44100.0 Hz, 8 bit, stereo, audio data
PCM_SIGNED, 44100.0 Hz, 16 bit, stereo, big-endian, audio data
PCM_SIGNED, 44100.0 Hz, 16 bit, stereo, little-endian, audio data

Mixer 3:
    Name: WinOS,waveOut,multi threaded Vendor: Unknown Vendor Version: Unknown Version
        Description: No details available
    Source Line 1:interface SourceDataLine supporting 32 audio formats
        PCM_SIGNED, 8000.0 Hz, 8 bit, mono, audio data
        PCM_UNSIGNED, 8000.0 Hz, 8 bit, mono, audio data

Plus many more formats for mixer 3...

PCM_SIGNED, 44100.0 Hz, 16 bit, stereo, little-endian, audio data
PCM_SIGNED, 44100.0 Hz, 16 bit, stereo, big-endian, audio data

The first mixer is the software mixer that comes with the Sound API. Only this mixer supports the Clip interface and none of them support ports at the present time. However, we shall see that this does not prevent playback through the speakers, or recording from the microphone. The software mixer that comes with the Sound API is also the only mixer of the three that returned any details beyond the name.

How It Works

The first statement obtains an array of Mixer.Info references. For every mixer in the system there will be an array element that we can use to obtain information about the mixer. In the outer for loop, we iterate over each element in the mixer array, and each loop iteration will extract detailed information about a particular mixer.

Within the loop we first use the current Mixer.Info reference from the mixers array to output the name, vendor, and description of the mixer. Not all mixers will necessarily make this information available, as may be evident from the output on your machine. We then get a reference to the mixer corresponding to the current Mixer.Info object with the statement:

```
mixer = AudioSystem.getMixer(mixers[i]);          // Get the mixer...
```

We are interested in the details of the lines associated with the mixer so we use the reference to the Mixer object to obtain a reference to the Line.Info object for each source line that the mixer has:

```
lines = mixer.getSourceLineInfo();               // ...and its source lines info
```

We store the reference to the Line.Info[] array that is returned by the getSourceLineInfo() method in our variable lines. We can now use each on the Line.Info references to obtain detailed information about each source line. We get the formats supported by a given line with the statement:

```
formats = ((DataLine.Info)lines[j]).getFormats();
```

Our lines array is of type Line.Info[] – the type corresponding to the reference returned by getSourceLineInfo(). The getFormats() method is defined in the DataLine.Info class so we have to cast each element of the lines array to type DataLine.Info in order to call the method. Once we have the array of formats, we display them in a loop. Using essentially the same process we output the information on the target lines for the mixer.

Playing Sounds

Let's see how we can play a sound file using the API. We will write a program with similar function to the PlaySounds application that we wrote using the sound capability in the Applet class. We'll be able to pick the sound file we want to play from any of those available in the current directory – subject to two caveats. The file must be of a type that is supported, and the format for the audio data that is in the file must be supported by an available line in the system.

Creating an Audio Stream

To access the data in the sound file, we will create an `AudioInputStream` object that encapsulates it. An `AudioInputStream` object contains information about the audio format as well as the source of the sound data. It also may know the number of sample frames that make up the sound. An `AudioInputStream` object can encapsulate sound data from a URL, and from another stream, as well as from a file. The class defines two constructors:

`AudioInputStream` `(TargetDataLine line);`	Creates an object that obtains the sampled sound data from a target data line of a mixer. Data read from the `AudioInputStream` will have the same format as the target data line, and the length is unknown, retrieving the length will return `AudioStream.UNSPECIFIED`. We will be using this a little later to record sound.

`AudioInputStream`
  `(InputStream input,`
 	
   `AudioFormat format,`
 	
   `long length);`
	Creates an object that obtains data from the input stream specified by the first argument. Data from the `AudioInputStream` will be in the format specified by the second argument, and will have the length (in sample frames) as specified by the third argument, `length`.

The `AudioInputStream` class has `InputStream` as a base, however, it overrides all the methods inherited from `InputStream` with its own versions. Just to remind you these methods are:

`int read()`	`void mark()`	`long skip(long n)`
`int read(byte[] b)`	`boolean markSupported()`	`int available()`

`int read(byte[] b,`
     `int off,`
     `int len)`
	`void reset()`	`void close()`

These methods do exactly the same as they did in the `InputStream` class. Beyond these methods, the `AudioInputStream` class defines two additional methods:

`getFormat()`	Returns a reference to an `AudioFormat` object that encapsulates the format of the stream.
`getFrameLength()`	Returns the length of the stream in sample frames. If the length is not known, the value `AudioStream.UNSPECIFIED` is returned.

Clearly the two constructors don't provide a direct way to obtain an `AudioInputStream` object from a file, but the `AudioSystem` class does. The static `getAudioInputStream()` method comes in several overloaded varieties, one of which does precisely what we want. Here's the complete set:

`getAudioInputStream(File file);`	Obtains an `AudioInputStream` that encapsulates the sound file identified by the argument. The format will be that of the sound file. If the file does not contain a header that corresponds to one of the supported sound files (`.au` or `.snd`, `.aif`, or `.wav`), an exception of type `UnSupportedAudioFileException` will be thrown. A `IOException` will be thrown in the event of an I/O error.
`getAudioInputStream(URL source);`	Obtains an audio stream from a URL. The format of the audio stream will be that of the source Exceptions may be thrown as above.
`getAudioInputStream` `    (InputStream source);`	Obtains an audio stream from the stream specified by the first argument. The format of the audio stream will be that of the source. Exceptions may be thrown as above.

`getAudioInputStream`
 	
`      (AudioFormat newFormat,`
 	
`     AudioInputStream source);`
	Obtains an audio stream by converting the stream specified by the second argument to the format specified by the first argument. An exception of type `IllegalArgumentException` will be thrown if the conversion is not supported.

`getAudioInputStream`
` (AudioFormat.Encoding newEncoding,`
 	
`AudioInputStream source);`
	Creates an `AudioInputStream` with the encoding specified by the first argument by converting the stream specified by the second argument. If the conversion is not supported then an exception of type `IllegalArgumentException` will be thrown.

Note that it is the file header information that determines the type of a sound file, not the file extension. You could rename `sound.wav` to `sound.xxx` and it would still be possible to create an `AudioInputStream` object from it. This is *not* recommended however! It is important to maintain the correct file extension consistent with the contents of the file.

We just need a `File` object encapsulating a file and we're there. Thus if we have a file name stored as a `String` object, `filename`, we can create an `AudioInputStream` from it like this:

```
File currentDir = new File(System.getProperty("user.dir"));
File soundFile = new File(currentDir, filename);
try
{
  AudioInputStream source = AudioSystem.getAudioInputStream(soundFile);
}
catch(UnsupportedAudioFileException e)
{
```

```
      System.err.println(" File "+filename+" not supported.\n"+e);
   }
   catch(IOException e)
   {
      System.err.println(e);
   }
```

The getProperty() method in the System class returns the value for a property corresponding to a key. The key here is "user.dir", which retrieves the current directory path as a String reference. We then use that along with the file name to create the File object. We must put the call to getAudioInputStream() in a try block and catch the exceptions, otherwise the code won't compile.

Of course, for an audio file to be supported it's not simply a question of the file extension. Both the format of the file and the format of the sound data it contains need to be supported. An instance of the AudioFileFormat class defines a standard sound file format (for example an **AIFF** or **WAVE** file) and we'll come back to this a little later. The format of the sound data in a file is defined by an object of type AudioFormat. You can obtain a reference to the AudioFormat object that encapsulates the data format for the file by passing the File object as an argument to the static getAudioFileFormat() method that is defined in the AudioSystem class. Overloaded versions of this method will do the same for a URL reference, or a reference to an AudioInputStream object.

Accessing a Clip

We have an audio input stream but we can't play it yet. One way to play it is to create a Clip object from it, but to do that we first need a DataLine.Info object defining the characteristics of the clip. We can get this in the way we saw a little while back:

```
DataLine.Info clipInfo = new DataLine.Info(Clip.class, source.getFormat());
```

This assumes that we have created source as shown in the previous code fragment. We use this to obtain a reference to the AudioFormat object for the data from the stream. Now, with a bit of luck, we can obtain a reference to a Clip object:

```
Clip clip = null;
if(AudioSystem.isLineSupported(clipInfo);
   clip = (Clip)AudioSystem.getLine(clipInfo);
else
   System.err.println("Line not available for " + clipInfo);
```

Note that although we have obtained the Clip reference directly, the Clip will still belong to one or other of the mixers in the system. The Clip object is not tied to the audio stream at this point. We also have no guarantee that a line of type Clip is actually available – only that it is supported. Another program might be using the line for instance. To make our program get control of this specific line that is a clip and load the data from the audio input stream into it, we must call the open() method for the Clip object:

```
try
{
  clip.open(source);
}
catch(LineUnavailableException e)
{
  System.err.println(e);
}
catch(IOException e)
{
  System.err.println(e);
}
```

Assuming an exception is not thrown by the open() method, our program will have control of a line that is a Clip, and the Clip object will contain the sound sample data from the audio input stream. Thus we can now play it from the beginning or from any point in the clip, and stop and restart play whenever we want. We can also play it repeatedly until we choose stop it. This is a whole lot more than we could achieve with an AudioClip object that create using the methods defined in the Applet class.

Playing a Clip

Perhaps the simplest way to play a clip is to call the start() method for the Clip object. This method is inherited from the DataLine interface. You play the clip like this:

```
clip.start();
```

When you call start(), the clip begins playing and continues until the end of the clip is reached or the stop() method is called for the Clip object. Calling start() doesn't necessarily play the clip from the beginning. It plays the clip starting at whatever is the **current position** in the clip. The current position is a given sample frame within the clip, and of course, before you start playing the clip the current position is at the first frame (assuming you haven't done anything else to change it). The frame numbers start from zero. The current position is recorded within the Clip object when you call the stop() method to stop playing a clip. You can set the current position by calling the setFramePosition() method for the clip. The argument is the sample frame number that is to be the new current position so to set the current position to the beginning of the clip you could write:

```
clip.setSampleFrame(0);
```

If you want to find out the frame number that is the current position, the getSampleFrame() method will return it as a value of type int. Of course, if you are going to be setting the current position, you are likely to want to know how any frames there are in the clip. The getFrameLength() method will do this:

```
int frameCount = clip.getFrameLength();
```

Note that this only works properly if the clip is open – in other words the open() method has been called for the clip. If the clip is not open the method will return the value AudioSystem.NOT_SPECIFIED.

You can also set the current position in terms of time rather than sample frames. This is often more useful, especially when you know how long the sound clip lasts. The unit of measure in this case is a microsecond. To set the current position to half a second after the beginning of the clip, you would write:

```
clip.setMicrosecondPosition(500000L);
```

The argument is in microseconds and is a value of type `long`. Obviously the result is not necessarily precise to a microsecond since a current position will always correspond to a frame. The precision of positioning will be to the number of microseconds in a frame, so if the sound was recorded at 8 kHz, the positioning will be to the nearest multiple of 125 microseconds, which is the time for one frame in this case. The `getMicrosecondLength()` method is similar to the `getFrameLength()` method but returns the length of the clip in microseconds as a value of type `long`. If the clip is not open the value `AudioSystem.NOT_SPECIFIED` will be returned.

To play a clip repeatedly you call the `loop()` method for the `Clip` object. This method requires an argument of type `int` that specifies the number of times the clip is to be played. If you just want to play it once, you can pass the value 1 as the argument. To make the clip play indefinitely you just specify the argument value as `Clip.LOOP_CONTINUOUSLY`. Here's how we could play our clip ten times:

```
clip.loop(10);                               // Play the clip ten times
```

To repeat the clip indefinitely we would write:

```
clip.loop(Clip.LOOP_CONTINUOUSLY);           // Play the clip indefinitely
```

If a clip is playing as a result of calling `loop()`, you can cause playing to cease at the end of the current loop – which is the end of the sound samples stored in the clip, by calling `loop()` with an argument value of zero. Note that the effect of calling `loop()` with a non-zero argument is undefined when the clip is already executing a loop operation, so it's a good idea to call to the `isActive()` method that `Clip` inherits from the `DataLine` interface before you call `loop()` to start playing. This method will return `true` if the `Clip` is playing.

You can also arrange that only part of a clip is repeated when you call `loop()`. The `setLoopPoints()` method requires two arguments of type `int` that correspond to the starting frame and the ending frame of the clip that is to be played on each loop. To play a segment of a clip from frame 2001 to frame 8000, and repeat it 5 times you would write:

```
clip.setLoopPoints(2001, 8000);
clip.loop(5);
```

Let's see how playing a clip works in practice.

Try It Out – Playing a Clip

Our program will play any sound file from the current directory that is a supported file type containing in a supported audio data format. The GUI will be the same as our earlier `PlaySounds` example – a combobox displaying a dropdown list of sound file names, and a PLAY button. We'll call this program `SoundPlayer`. It's quite a lot of code so we'll put it together piecemeal. Here's the basics of the class that creates the GUI:

```java
import javax.swing.*;
import java.io.*;
import java.awt.*;
import java.awt.event.*;
import javax.sound.sampled.*;

public class SoundPlayer extends JFrame
{
  public SoundPlayer()
  {
    setDefaultCloseOperation(EXIT_ON_CLOSE);
    setTitle("Sound File Player");
    setSize(250,100);

    // Get the sounds file names from current directory
    currentDir = new File(System.getProperty("user.dir"));
    FilenameFilter filter = new FilenameFilter()
                            {
                              public boolean accept(File directory, String filename)
                                {
                                  String name = filename.toLowerCase();
                                  return name.endsWith(".au")||
                                         name.endsWith(".aif")||
                                         name.endsWith(".wav");
                                }
                            };
    String soundFiles[] = currentDir.list(filter);
    if(soundFiles == null||soundFiles.length == 0)
    {
      JOptionPane.showMessageDialog(this, "No sound files - terminating...",
                              "Sound Files Error", JOptionPane.ERROR_MESSAGE);
      System.exit(1);
    }

    // Create the combobox displaying the list of sound files
    soundChoice = new JComboBox(soundFiles);
    soundChoice.setSelectedIndex(0);            // Select the 1st file
    oldFilename = soundFiles[0];                 // save the selected file name

    player = new ClipPlayer(soundFiles[0]);   // Create a clip player

    // Process selections from the list of files in the combobox
    soundChoice.addActionListener(new ActionListener()
                            {
                              public void actionPerformed(ActionEvent e)
                              {
                                // Set up a new clip from the file selected...
                              }
                            }
                            );
```

```
      // Set up the PLAY button to play the current clip
      play = new JButton("PLAY");
      play.addActionListener(new ActionListener()
                               {
                                 public void actionPerformed(ActionEvent e)
                                 {
                                   if(e.getActionCommand().equals("PLAY"))
                                   {
                                     // Play the selected clip...
                                   }
                                   else
                                   {
                                     // Stop playing the selected clip...
                                   }
                                 }
                               });

    Container content = getContentPane();
    content.add(soundChoice);
    content.add(play,BorderLayout.SOUTH);
    setVisible(true);
  }

  public static void main(String[] args)
  {
    SoundPlayer soundPlayer = new SoundPlayer();
  }

  // Inner class defining a clip player
  public class ClipPlayer
  {

    public ClipPlayer(String filename)
    {
      //Code to create a ClipPlayer object...
    }

    // Other methods for a clip player...

    private Clip clip;                        // The sound clip
  }

  private File currentDir;                    // Current directory
  private JComboBox soundChoice;              // Dropdown list of files
  private JButton play;                       // PLAY button
  private String oldFilename;                 // Last selected file nmae

  private ClipPlayer player;                  // The clip player
}
```

The GUI is defined as we saw in the `PlaySounds` example and the code we have yet to add is indicated by comments. The work will be done in the inner `ClipPlayer` class. The constructor for this class will create a `ClipPlayer` object that will encapsulate a `Clip` object. The `Clip` object will encapsulate the data from the file that is passed as the argument to the constructor. We can code the `ClipPlayer` constructor like this:

```
public ClipPlayer(String filename)
{
    newSound(filename);
}
```

The `newSound()` method will create an `AudioStream` object from the file, then a `Clip` object to support the audio format of the data in the file. The reason for diverting all of this off into a separate method is that when a clip is playing, we want to be able to create a new clip in response to a selection from the combobox. The code to do this will be exactly the same as the code we need in the constructor. Here's the code for the `newSound()` method in the `ClipPlayer` class:

```
public void newSound(String filename)
{
    File soundFile = new File(currentDir, filename);   // File object for filename

    try
    {
        AudioInputStream source = AudioSystem.getAudioInputStream(soundFile);
        DataLine.Info clipInfo = new DataLine.Info(Clip.class, source.getFormat());
        if(AudioSystem.isLineSupported(clipInfo))
        {
            // Create a local clip to avoid discarding the old clip
            Clip newClip = (Clip)AudioSystem.getLine(clipInfo);    // Create the clip
            newClip.open(source);

            // Deal with previous clip
            if(clip != null)
            {
                if(clip.isActive())                        // If it's active
                {
                    clip.stop();                           // ...stop it
                    play.setText("PLAY");                  // ..and reset the button label
                }
                if(clip.isOpen())                          // If it's open...
                    clip.close();                          // ...close it.
            }
            clip = newClip;                                // We have a clip, so discard old
            oldFilename = filename;                        // Save the filename
        }
        else
        {
            JOptionPane.showMessageDialog(null, "Clip not supported",
                              "Clip NotSupported", JOptionPane.WARNING_MESSAGE);
            soundChoice.setSelectedItem(oldFilename);
        }
    }
```

```
      catch(UnsupportedAudioFileException e)
      {
        JOptionPane.showMessageDialog(null, "File not supported",
                        "Unsupported File Type", JOptionPane.WARNING_MESSAGE);
      }
      catch(LineUnavailableException e)
      {
        JOptionPane.showMessageDialog(null, "Clip not available", "Clip Error",
                          JOptionPane.WARNING_MESSAGE);
      }
      catch(IOException e)
      {
        JOptionPane.showMessageDialog(null, "I/O error creating clip", "Clip Error",
                          JOptionPane.WARNING_MESSAGE);
      }
    }
```

Nearly half of this is catching the various exceptions that we have discussed, so it's simpler than it looks. Note how we are using dialog boxes to display warning and error messages, rather than the error output stream. This is just to remind you of the capabilities of the JOptionPane class.

The only complication here, beyond the code fragments we have seen earlier, is that we have to consider the possibility of a file being selected that contains data in a format that is not supported. If this is the case we want to avoid discarding the old clip. In this way we can continue playing the current clip if it happens to be playing when an unsupported or invalid file is selected. We handle this by storing the reference to the Clip object we create in a local variable, newClip. Only when we have managed to open the clip with the new AudioStream do we discard the old Clip object by storing the reference to the new clip in the variable clip.

When a new file name is selected in the combobox, the action listener will call the newSound() method for the ClipPlayer object. We must add the code for this to the SoundPlayer constructor:

```
soundChoice.addActionListener(new ActionListener()
                {
                  public void actionPerformed(ActionEvent e)
                  {
                    player.newSound((String)soundChoice.getSelectedItem());
                  }
                }
              );
```

We will also need to add methods to the ClipPlayer class to start and stop playing the clip. Here's the method to play the clip:

```
// Play the clip
public void play()
{
  if(clip == null)
  {
    JOptionPane.showMessageDialog(null, "No Clip available",
                          "Play Problem",JOptionPane.WARNING_MESSAGE);
    return;
  }
```

```
            clip.loop(clip.LOOP_CONTINUOUSLY);
        }
```

To be on the safe side we check that clip is not null before we call loop() to play it. This plays the clip continuously until the stop() method for the ClipPlayer object is called. Here's the code for that:

```
    // Stop playing the clip
    public void stop()
    {
      if(clip != null)
        clip.loop(0);
    }
```

We will start and stop playing the clip in response to button presses, so we must add this to the code in the SoundPlayer constructor for the button action listener:

```
play.addActionListener(new ActionListener()
                        {
                          public void actionPerformed(ActionEvent e)
                          {
                            if(e.getActionCommand().equals("PLAY"))
                            {
                              player.play();
                              play.setText("STOP");
                            }
                            else
                            {
                              player.stop();
                              play.setText("PLAY");
                            }
                          }
                        });
```

That's the program complete. If you compile and run it you should get a window as shown.

How It Works

The SoundPlayer constructor sets up the combobox with the names of all the sound files in the current directory. It also creates a ClipPlayer object from the first file in the list. Clicking the PLAY button will play the current clip in the ClipPlayer object and reset the button text to "STOP". Clicking the STOP button will stop playing of the clip. You can select a new file from the combobox at any time. If a valid and supported file is selected, a new clip corresponding to the selected file will replace the current clip. If the file is not supported, the current clip will be unaffected.

Note that because we play a clip in a continuous loop, it is important to make sure that we always stop the sound playing properly. For instance, if we were just to discard the old clip reference in the newSound() method by storing the reference to the new clip in the variable, clip, we could find that the old clip is still playing. You can demonstrate this quite easily by commenting out the code:

```
//            if(clip != null)
//            {
//              if(clip.isActive())
//              {
//                clip.stop();
                play.setText("PLAY");
//              }
//              if(clip.isOpen())
//                clip.close();
//            }
```

Now if you select a new clip from the list while a clip is playing, the old clip will continue even when you play the new clip. Since you can no longer access the reference to the old clip, you have no means within the program to stop it.

You might want to always start a new clip from the beginning when you stop it and restart it, rather than playing from where it left off. You could do this by modifiying the stop() method in the ClipPlayer class:

```
public void stop()
{
  clip.stop();                   // Stop the clip
  clip.setFramePosition(0);      // Reset to the start
}
```

The stop() method for the Clip object is inherited in the Clip interface from the DataLine interface. This stops the output activity for the line. After calling stop() for the clip object, we call its setFramePosition() method. This resets the position in the clip to the frame number specified by the argument. When the clip is restarted, the clip will be played from the frame number we have set – the first one in this case.

Another Approach to Playing a Sound File

One limitation of the code in the previous example is that the sound data is stored in the clip in memory. If the sound file is a hundred megabytes it could be an embarrassment, particularly if your PC has only 64 megabytes of memory. There's also the possibility that we have sound that is streamed – from a radio station on the Internet for instance – so the length of the sound data is indefinite. To deal with this we need a different approach. Ideally, we want to grab a block of sound data from the source – the file or wherever the sound is coming from, then play that bunch of sound samples. When that's done, we want to grab another block and play that – and so on. In this way we can play an unlimited amount of sound data.

Reading a block of sound samples is easy. In the previous example we used the `AudioInputStream` object that we created from the contents of the sound file to create a `Clip` object. However, an `AudioInputStream` object is a perfectly good input stream so we can just as well read a block of sound samples from it using its `read()` method – like this:

```
byte[] soundData = new byte[bufferSize];
source.read(soundData, 0, soundData.length);
```

The variable `source`, is the `AudioInputStream` object encapsulating the sound source. Of course, the `read()` method can throw exceptions so we need to put it in a `try` block. We also must ensure that the array, `soundData`, accommodates a whole number of frames. Apart from that all we need now is to decide what to do with the data in the array, `soundData`. If we can figure out how to write the data to the speaker output on the system, we have a way to play a sound recording of unlimited length.

Using a Source Data Line

A source data line is an input to a mixer – you write data to it. If you create a reference to a `SourceDataLine` object, the data that you write to it will be transferred to the speaker output by the mixer. It's that simple – well almost. You have to create a data line that has the same audio format as the data you intend to write to it, but we saw earlier that we can get the format of the data encapsulated in an `AudioInputStream` object by calling its `getFormat()` method.

The process for accessing a `SourceDataLine` is the same as that for a `Clip` object. We must create a `DataLine.Info` object specifying the type of line we are interested in, then call the static `getLine()` method in the `AudioSystem` class with the `DataLine.Info` reference as the argument. Here's the code to do this for the `AudioInputStream` reference, `source`:

```
DataLine.Info sourceInfo = new DataLine.Info(SourceDataLine.class,
source.getFormat());
SourceDataLine sourceLine = null;
try
{
  if(AudioSystem.isLineSupported(sourceInfo))
  {
    sourceLine = (SourceDataLine)AudioSystem.getLine(sourceInfo);
  }
  else
    System.err.println("Line not supported "+sourceInfo);
}
catch(LineUnavailableException e)
{
    System.err.println("Line unavailable "+e);
}
```

Now that we have a `SourceDataLine` reference we can perform two basic operations on it. We can open it by calling its `open()` method, and once we have opened it we can write to it using its `write()` method.

Opening a line causes the line to reserve the system resources it needs and makes the line available to your program. If the resources are unavailable or the line cannot be opened for any other reason, an exception of type `LineUnavailableException` will be thrown. There are two versions of the `open()` method. One accepts a single argument of type `AudioFormat` that specifies the format for the line and the line will be opened with a default size for the buffer that receives the sound data when you write to it. The default size is implementation dependent, but will always be an integral multiple of the frame size. The other version of `open()` accepts an additional argument of type `int` specifying the size of the buffer in bytes. If you use this option the buffer size must be an integral multiple of the frame size defined in the format, otherwise an exception of type `IllegalArgumentException` exception will be thrown.

You can calculate a suitable buffer size using information from the format of the input stream. There are no hard and fast rules for choosing a buffer size. It depends on circumstances. If you want to minimize the delay between writing data to the line, and the sound actually being played, you need to keep the buffer small. If you make the buffer too small, you may not be able to write data to the line fast enough to prevent gaps in the sound from occurring. This is a major consideration of the source of the data is remote – over the Internet for example. Suppose we judge that a buffer that accommodates half a second's worth of samples is appropriate. We can get the format from the `AudioInputStream` object with the statement:

```
AudioFormat format = source.getFormat();
```

The `AudioFormat` class provides methods `getFrameSize()` and `getFrameRate()` to supply the frame size in bytes as type `int`, and the frame rate per second as a value of type `float`. We can therefore calculate the buffer size to accommodate half a second's worth of samples as:

```
int bufferSize = (int)(format.getFrameSize()*format.getFrameRate()/2.0f);
```

You can now use this to open the line, `sourceLine`, with the required buffer size:

```
try
{
   sourceLine.open(format, bufferSize);
}
catch(LineUnavailableException e)
{
   System.err.println(e);
}
```

Note that if you call `open()` for a line that is already open, an exception of type `IllegalStateException` will be thrown.

Opening a line gives you control of it, but before you can write to it you must call its `start()` method:

```
sourceLine.start();
```

The start() method in the SourceDataLine interface is inherited from the DataLine interface and its effect is to make the line operational so you can write to it. If the line was previously started then stopped by calling its stop() method, any data left in the buffer will be output to the speaker. We can avoid this by calling the flush() method for the line after we have stopped it. We'll come back to this method in a moment.

The write() method for a SourceDataLine object accepts three arguments – an array of type byte[] containing the data to be written, an int value specifying the location in the array for the first byte to be written, and a value of type int specifying the number of bytes to be written. If the last value is not an integral multiple of the frame size, then an exception of type IllegalArgumentException will be thrown.

With the line open and started we can write the data read from the AudioInputStream, source, to the SourceDataLine, sourceLine, like this:

```
byte[] soundData = new byte[bufferSize];
int byteCount = 0;                                    // Bytes read
try
{
  while(playing)
  {
    byteCount = source.read(soundData, 0, soundData.length);
    if(byteCount == -1)                               // If it's the end of input
      break;                                          // then stop playing
    sourceLine.write(soundData,0, byteCount);
  }
}
catch(IOException e)                                  // For the stream read operation
{
  System.err.println(e);
}
```

This code must be in a separate thread from the main thread as it will run continuously. The loop is controlled by a boolean variable, playing, so the loop continues as long as playing has the value true. In order to stop playback, the main thread just needs to set playing to false. The write() method for a SourceDataLine object transfers the data from the soundData array to the line buffer. The method blocks (does not return in other words) until the data can be written, so if the data line buffer is still being played, the write will not occur until the buffer is free.

The SourceDataLine interface inherits several useful methods from the DataLine interface, in addition to the start() and stop() methods we have seen. The available() method returns the number of bytes that can be written to the line without blocking, so you could use this if you want to be sure the write() method won't block. There are two methods that you use when you are at the end of a play operation:

`drain()`	Continues playing data from the line buffer until the buffer is empty. You use this to ensure you play what's left in the line buffer when you come to the end of an audio input stream. You should call this method *before* you call `stop()` for the line, otherwise the method will block until the line is restarted.
`flush()`	Discards any residual data from the buffer. You would normally use this method after you have called `stop()` for a line to discard the residual data without playing it.

When we want to end the play operation for our `sourceLine`, to ensure that we play all the data we have written to the line we would call `drain()` before we stop the line, thus:

```
sourceLine.drain();
sourceLine.stop();
```

You can check the status of the line with these two methods:

`isActive()`	Returns `true` if the line is active. A line becomes active when you call its `start()` method. It becomes inactive when you call its `stop()` method.
`isRunning()`	Returns `true` if the line is running. A line is running when data is being transferred by the line and ceases to be in this state when data transfer stops – because either the end of the data is reached, or the `stop()` method is called.

There are five methods that return information about the characteristics of the line:

`getFormat()`	Returns an `AudioFormat` reference defining the audio format for the line.
`getBufferSize()`	Returns the size of the line's buffer in bytes as a value of type `int`. This is useful for checking what you are getting if you open a line with the default buffer size.
`getFramePosition()`	Returns the number of frames that have been played since the line was opened as a value of type `int`.
`getLevel()`	Obtains the current volume level for the line as a value of type float. Silence corresponds to 0.0f and the maximum volume is `1.0f`. The scale is linear.
`getMicrosecondPosition()`	Returns the duration in microseconds of the audio data that has been played since the line was opened. The return value is type long. This value will be the time corresponding to the number of frames that have been played.

We have enough to put together another version of `SoundPlayer` that will play a sound file of any length.

Try It Out – Playing using a SourceDataLine

We will implement the new player with the same GUI as before – a combobox to choose a file to play from those available in the current directory, and a button to start and stop playing of the currently selected file. We will make the operation a little more flexible though.

We should be able to arrange that when you stop the play by selecting the STOP button, you can restart the sound from where it left off by selecting PLAY. When the player reaches the end of the data in a file, playing will stop, but you will be able to play it again from the beginning just by selecting PLAY once more. Selecting a new file from the combobox will stop the current file playing if it is active and select the new file as the next to be played when PLAY is selected. Here's the outline of the class:

```java
import javax.swing.*;
import java.io.*;
import java.awt.*;
import java.awt.event.*;
import javax.sound.sampled.*;

public class NewSoundPlayer extends JFrame
                              implements Runnable
{
  public NewSoundPlayer()
  {
    setDefaultCloseOperation(EXIT_ON_CLOSE);
    setTitle("Sound File Player");
    setSize(250,100);

    // Get the sounds file names from current directory
    currentDir = new File(System.getProperty("user.dir"));
    FilenameFilter filter = new FilenameFilter()
                       {
                         public boolean accept(File directory, String filename)
                         {
                           String name = filename.toLowerCase();
                           return name.endsWith(".au")||
                                  name.endsWith(".aif")||
                                  name.endsWith(".wav");
                         }
                       };
    String soundFiles[] = currentDir.list(filter);
    if(soundFiles == null||soundFiles.length == 0)
    {
      JOptionPane.showMessageDialog(this, "No sound files - terminating...",
                            "Sound Files Error", JOptionPane.ERROR_MESSAGE);
      System.exit(1);
    }
    soundChoice = new JComboBox(soundFiles);
    soundChoice.setSelectedIndex(0);
    newSound(soundFiles[0]);
    oldFilename = soundFiles[0];
```

```
                soundChoice.addActionListener(new ActionListener()
                                    {
                                        public void actionPerformed(ActionEvent e)
                                        {
newSound((String)soundChoice.getSelectedItem());
                                        }
                                    }
                                    );

        // Set up the PLAY button to play the current sound file
        play = new JButton("PLAY");
        play.addActionListener(new ActionListener()
                                {
                                    public void actionPerformed(ActionEvent e)
                                    {
                                        if(e.getActionCommand().cquals("PLAY"))
                                        {
                                            startPlay();
                                            play.setText("STOP");
                                        }
                                        else
                                        {
                                            stopPlay();
                                            play.setText("PLAY");
                                        }
                                    }
                                });
        Container content = getContentPane();
        content.add(soundChoice);
        content.add(play,BorderLayout.SOUTH);
        setVisible(true);
    }

    public static void main(String[] args)
    {
        NewSoundPlayer soundPlayer = new NewSoundPlayer();
    }

    public void newSound(String filename)
    {
        // Set up the current file to be played...
    }

    // Start playing the current file
    public void startPlay()
    {
        // Start playing in a separate thread...
    }

    // Stop playing the current file
    public void stopPlay()
    {
```

```
      playing = false;
  }

  // The playing thread
  public void run()
  {
    // Play the sound file...
  }

  private File currentDir;                      // Current directory
  private String oldFilename;                   // Last selected file name
  private JComboBox soundChoice;                // Dropdown list of files
  private JButton play;                         // PLAY button
  private AudioInputStream source;              // Stream for the sound file
  private SourceDataLine sourceLine;            // The speaker output line
  private byte[] soundData;                     // Buffer to hold samples
  private int bufferSize;                       // Buffer size in bytes
  private Thread thread;                        // Playing thread
  private boolean playing = false;              // Thread control
}
```

The unshaded code is exactly the same as in the previous example. By making the application class implement the Runnable interface, we can use it to create another thread in which to write data to the source data line. All the methods called by the listeners for the combobox and the button are in the application class.

The newSound() method sets up the file to be played, so let's see the code for that:

```
public void newSound(String filename)
{
  File soundFile = new File(currentDir, filename);

  // We may have played a file already
  if(sourceLine != null)                     // If we have a line
  {
    if(sourceLine.isActive())                // ... and it is still active...
      sourceLine.stop();                     // ...stop it
    play.setText("PLAY");                    // Ensure button is PLAY
  }

  // Now try for a stream and a line
  try
  {
    AudioInputStream newSource = AudioSystem.getAudioInputStream(soundFile);

    if(newSource.markSupported())            // If we can mark the stream...
      newSource.mark(Integer.MAX_VALUE);     // mark the start for later reset

    AudioFormat format = newSource.getFormat(); // Get the audio format
    DataLine.Info sourceInfo = new DataLine.Info(SourceDataLine.class, format);
    if(AudioSystem.isLineSupported(sourceInfo)) // If the line type is supported
    {                                           // Get a new line
```

```
          sourceLine = (SourceDataLine)AudioSystem.getLine(sourceInfo);
          bufferSize = (int)(format.getFrameSize()*format.getFrameRate()/2.0f);
          sourceLine.open(format, bufferSize);        // Open the line
          source = newSource;                          // New line is OK so save it
          soundData = new byte[bufferSize];            // Create the buffer for read
          oldFilename = filename;                      // Save the current file name
        }
        else
        {
          JOptionPane.showMessageDialog(null, "Line not supported",
                          "Line NotSupported",JOptionPane.WARNING_MESSAGE);
           soundChoice.setSelectedItem(oldFilename); // Restore the old selection
        }
      }
      catch(UnsupportedAudioFileException e)
      {
        JOptionPane.showMessageDialog(null, "File not supported",
                          "Unsupported File Type",JOptionPane.WARNING_MESSAGE);
        soundChoice.setSelectedItem(oldFilename);
      }
      catch(LineUnavailableException e)
      {
        JOptionPane.showMessageDialog(null, "Line not available", "Line Error",
                          JOptionPane.WARNING_MESSAGE);
        soundChoice.setSelectedItem(oldFilename);
      }
      catch(IOException e)
      {
        JOptionPane.showMessageDialog(null, "I/O Error creating stream",
                          "I/O Error",JOptionPane.WARNING_MESSAGE);
        soundChoice.setSelectedItem(oldFilename);
      }
    }
```

This uses code we have seen in the previous discussion but there are some practical complications. In general, when this method is called we will have a file selected, and each time after the first, we will already have a stream and a line in existence. We don't want to discard these until we set up the new stream and line properly, so we must create the new stream in a local variable and only replace the previous one when we have managed to open the new line. That way, if the selected file is unsupported we can still play the old file because it will still be in place.

Playing a sound file starts when the PLAY button is clicked. The action listener calls the startPlay() method to set things in motion. We can implement that method like this:

```
public void startPlay()
{
  if(sourceLine == null)                              // Verify we have a line
  {
    JOptionPane.showMessageDialog(null, "No line available", "Play Problem",
                          JOptionPane.WARNING_MESSAGE);
    return;
  }
```

```
        thread = new Thread(this);          // Create the playing thread
        playing = true;                     // Set the control to true
        thread.start();                     // Start the thread
    }
```

Starting the new thread will result in the `run()` method being executed. We can implement this to read the sound data from the stream and write it to the source data line – like this:

```
    public void run()
    {
      sourceLine.start();                   // Start the line
      int byteCount = 0;                    // Bytes read
      try
      {
        while(playing)                      // Continue while true
        {
          byteCount = source.read(soundData, 0, soundData.length); // Read the stream

          if(byteCount == -1)               // If it's the end of input
          {
            if(source.markSupported())      // ...and we can reset the stream...
              source.reset();               // ...put it back to the start
            sourceLine.drain();             // Play what is left in the buffer
            playing = false;                // Reset the thread control
            break;                          // then stop playing
          }
          sourceLine.write(soundData,0, byteCount);   // Write the array to the line
        }
      }
      catch(IOException e)                  // For the stream read operation
      {
        System.err.println(e);
      }
      sourceLine.stop();                    // Stop the line
      play.setText("PLAY");                 // Reset the button text
    }
```

Playing the sound occurs in the `while` loop, once we have started the line. We read data from the stream into the buffer, `soundData`, then write it to the line. Although most of the time we will read the number of bytes requested, as specified by the `soundData.length` expression, when we get to the end of the line there may not be that many left. Thus the number of bytes that we write to the line is determined by the value returned by the `read()` method that we store in `byteCount`.

When the STOP button is clicked, the action listener calls the `stopPlay()` method. We can implement this very simply – like this:

```
    public void stopPlay()
    {
      playing = false;
    }
```

Setting the variable, `playing`, to `false` will end the loop in the `run()` method – which of course is running in a separate thread. The code in the `run()` method takes care of stopping the line. The line is then in a state where it will restart playing from where we left off when the PLAY button is clicked.

How It Works

The class constructor sets up the GUI and creates an audio input stream and line ready to play the first file of those available. Clicking the PLAY button will initiate playing of the file, and this is carried out by the `run()` method executing in a separate thread. Selecting a different file in the combobox will terminate the current play operation and assuming it is in a supported format, the new file will be available to be played when the PLAY button is clicked. Clicking the STOP button stops playing of the sound, but allows it to be restarted by clicking PLAY once again.

It would be nice to be able to record our own sound files for playback, converting the PC into a handy dictating machine, so let's try that next.

Sound Recording

To record sampled sound data you need access to a microphone input connected to your sound card, and naturally you must have a microphone plugged into it to run the examples in this section. The current release of the Sound API is not a fully rounded product so some of the functionality is there in skeletal form and not fully operational. Perhaps the obvious way to record from the microphone would be to use a line created from a `Port.Info.MICROPHONE` object, but at the time of writing, ports are not operational in the Sound API so we will take a different route.

Establishing the Recording Input

You can record sound by obtaining a target data line from a mixer. Remember that a target data line is the output from a mixer, so from your point of view it is a source of sound data. Thus once you have hold of a target data line, you can read sampled sound data from it. The process for accessing a target data line is:

❑ Define an `AudioFormat` object for the audio format that you want for the line

❑ Use the audio format object to define a `Line.Info` object specifying the characteristics of the line

❑ Obtain a reference to the line from the `Line.Info` object using `getLine()` method in the `AudioSystem` class.

Put like that it's easy. Here's the code to do that:

```
AudioFormat format = new AudioFormat(AudioFormat.Encoding.PCM_SIGNED, 44100,
                                              16, 1, 2, 44100, true);

DataLine.Info info = new DataLine.Info(TargetDataLine.class, format);
if(!AudioSystem.isLineSupported(info))                     // Verify line is supported
{
```

```
      System.out.println("Line not supported" + info);
      System.exit();
  }
  try
  {
    mike = (TargetDataLine)AudioSystem.getLine(info);     // Get a suitable line
    mike.open(format);                                    // Open the line
  }
  catch(LineUnavailableException e)
  {
    System.out.println("Line not available" + e);
    System.exit();
  }
```

I have chosen the audio format so that it corresponds to one of the supported target lines on my system. The output from the `PlumbSoundSystem` example gives you a list so I was able to check it. Even though the line is supported, there is still the possibility it could be busy, in which case the `getLine()` will throw a `LineUnavailableException`.

The `open()` method for the `TargetDataLine` object opens the line with the specified format and buffer size. If this executes successfully, the line will have acquired any necessary system resources and be ready to go. This method can still throw exceptions – of type `LineUnavailableException` if the resources it needs are not available. If you call `open()` when the line is already open an exception of type `IllegalStateException` will be thrown.

A given line will typically support a number of different formats – not just the one specified by the `Line.Info` object, so we can open a line with a different format from that used to access it. We have requested the buffer size to be that assigned by default, but we could change it by calling the overloaded version of `open()` that accepts a second argument for the buffer size. The argument value is in bytes but you must specify it as an integral number of sample frames, so you need to take care with 16-bit and or stereo formats. If the number of bytes you specify does not represent an integral multiple of the number of bytes in a sample frame, an exception of type `IllegalArgumentException` will be thrown.

Recording the Data

There's more than one way of recording from the target data line. The most direct way is to call the `start()` method for the line to galvanize it into action, like this:

```
  mike.start();
```

This will start the sound samples flowing into the line's buffer. You can then read data from the line's buffer using the `read()` method defined in the `TargetDataLine` interface. This requires three arguments. The first is a reference to an array of type `byte[]` that you have created in which the data will be stored. The second and third arguments are the buffer offset and the number of bytes you want to read respectively, both of type `int`. The second argument will typically be 0 with the third argument as the length of the buffer. Obviously the number of bytes read must be a multiple of the sample frame size, and the array needs to be large enough to accommodate the amount of data that you want to read. You could read from the line in a loop, like this:

```
byte[] soundData = new byte[mike.getBufferSize()];        // Input array
int byteCount = 0;                                         // Count of bytes read
while(recording)
{
  mike.read(soundData, 0, soundData.length);

  // Write soundData away somewhere...
}
```

This fragment would be in the `run()` method of a thread, and `recording` here is a `boolean` variable that is used to control whether we continue reading from the line or not. Within the loop we read a buffer-full of data and then write it away somewhere – a `ByteArrayOutputStream` is a popular choice. The read method for the line will block until the amount of data required is available so the write will not be executed until the read is complete and the data is available in `soundData`. If you wanted to avoid blocking, you can find out how many bytes are available by calling the `available()` method for the line and then just reading that amount of data.

We would stop the process of reading from the line by making the main thread set the value of `recording` to `false`. We would then need to stop the line by calling its `stop()` method and if we had no further use for the line we could call its `close()` method to close it and release its resources. We then have the problem of dealing with the sound data we have stowed away in a `ByteArrayOutputStream`. This is not difficult, but it could be an embarrassment if it is a lot of data because the `ByteArrayOuputStream` object will be in memory. This is quite likely to be the case since even a minute or two of recording can produce a considerable volume of data. We will look at an alternative approach that is simpler, and allows us to write direct to a file, but first we need to take a brief excursion into audio file formats.

Defining Audio File Formats

The format of an audio file is encapsulated in an instance of the `AudioFileFormat` class. The instance stores three characteristics: the type of the file, the format of the audio data, and the length of the data in the file in sample frames. Thus the `AudioFileFormat` class constructor accepts three arguments: a reference to an object of type `AudioFileFormat.Type`, an `AudioFormat` reference, and a value of type `int` that specifies the length of the audio data in sample frames. Where this last value is unknown, the value `AudioSystem.NOT_SPECIFIED` can be used.

The `AudioFileFormat.Type` class is an inner class to the `AudioFileFormat` class. It defines five constants of type `AudioFileFormat.Type` corresponding to the standard types of sound file that we discussed in the introduction to this chapter:

AIFF	AIFC	AU	SND	WAVE

You cannot assume that all these file types are supported for any particular operation. You should always verify that any operation you wish to carry out is supported for the file type in question. The class also defines the `getExtension()` method that returns the extension for the type of file as type `String`. This does not include the period separating the extension from the file name.

The `AudioFileFormat` class defines the following methods:

`getType()`	Returns the audio file type as one of the constants above defined in the inner class `AudioFileFormat.Type`.
`getFormat()`	Returns the reference to an `AudioFormat` object that defines the format of the audio data within the file.
`getByteLength()`	Returns the entire length of the file in bytes as type `int`. This includes the header as well as the audio data. If the length of the audio data is not known, the value `AudioSystem.NOT_SPECIFIED` will be returned.
`getFrameLength()`	Returns the number of sample frames in the file as type `int`. If this is not known, the value `AudioSystem.NOT_SPECIFIED` will be returned.

Now we know about file types, we can get back to transferring our sound recording to a file.

Writing Recorded Data to a File

We could encapsulate the `TargetDataLine` object in an `AudioInputStream` object using the constructor that we saw a while back:

```
AudioInputStream sound = new AudioInputStream(mike);   // Microphone stream
```

We can then `start()` the line by calling its `start()` method as before:

```
mike.start();                                          // Start input
```

Also, as before, you should do this in a separate thread from the main thread in the program. Once you have called `start()`, the buffer for the line will start to fill so we must immediately arrange for it to go somewhere. Since the data is available via the audio input stream, we can use the static `write()` method defined in the `AudioSystem` class to write the contents of a stream to a file. The three arguments to this method are:

❑   A reference of type `AudioInputStream` that encapsulates the data to be written to a file.

❑   A reference of type `AudioFileFormat.Type` that specifies the type of the file to be written.

❑   A reference to a `File` object that encapsulates the physical file.

The `write()` method can throw an `IOException`, so we must call it in a `try` block, like this:

```
try
{
  AudioSystem.write(sound, fileType, fileOut);         // Write input to file
}
catch(IOException e)
{
```

```
        System.out.println(e);
    }
```

That's it! The `write()` method will block as long as data is still available from the stream. The sound samples will continue to flow out of the line until we call `stop()` for the line, so to terminate the recording session we just call `stop()` from the main thread, like this:

```
    mike.stop();     // Stop recording
```

Let's put everything together in an example to record from the microphone. We'll be able to use the `SoundPlayer` program to play the recordings back.

Tr It Out – Recording Sound

Let's consider the mechanics of how our application is going to work. We will record the sound samples for a recording in a file in the current directory. This means that we must be able to create a unique file name and then create a physical file from it. We can display the name of the current sound file in a panel in the GUI for the application. The only other thing we'll need is a RECORD button to start recording. We can make it dual purpose by flipping it to a STOP button once recording has started. We will make the application class extend `JFrame` so it will be a window. We can also make it implement the `Runnable` interface and put the recording operation in the `run()` method.

Here's the basic skeleton for the code:

```
    import javax.swing.*;
    import javax.swing.border.*;
    import java.io.*;
    import java.awt.*;
    import java.awt.event.*;
    import javax.sound.sampled.*;

    public class Recorder extends JFrame
                            implements Runnable
    {
      public static void main(String[] args)
      {
        Recorder recorder = new Recorder();
      }

      public Recorder()
      {
        setDefaultCloseOperation(EXIT_ON_CLOSE);
        setTitle("Sound Recorder");
        setSize(250,200);

        currentDir = new File(System.getProperty("user.dir")); // Get current directory

        // Create a panel for the file name
        JPanel filenamePane = new JPanel(new GridLayout(0,1));
        CompoundBorder border = BorderFactory.createCompoundBorder(
```

```
                              BorderFactory.createEmptyBorder(5,5,5,5),
                              BorderFactory.createRaisedBevelBorder());
    filenamePane.setBorder(BorderFactory.createCompoundBorder(border,
                          BorderFactory.createEmptyBorder(5,5,5,5)));

    if((fileOut = getNewFile())==null)                        // Get a new file
    {
      System.err.println("Cannot create file");
      System.exit(1);
    }

    filenameLabel = new JLabel(fileOut.getName(), SwingConstants.CENTER);
    stopColor = filenameLabel.getForeground();
    filenamePane.add(filenameLabel);
    Container content = getContentPane();
    content.add(filenamePane);

    // Add the Record/Stop button
    record = new JButton("RECORD");
    record.setBorder(border);
    record.addActionListener(new ActionListener()
                            {
                              public void actionPerformed(ActionEvent e)
                              {
                                if(e.getActionCommand().equals("RECORD"))
                                {
                                  record.setText("STOP");
                                  startRecording();
                                }
                                else
                                {
                                  stopRecording();
                                  record.setText("RECORD");
                                }
                              }
                            }
                            );
    content.add(record,BorderLayout.SOUTH);

    setVisible(true);
  }

  // Create a new file
  File getNewFile()
  {
    // Create a new file in the current directory...
  }

  public void startRecording()
  {
    // Start recording....
  }
```

```
    public void stopRecording()
    {
       //Stop recording...
    }

    public void run()
    {
       // Do the recording...
    }


    private JLabel filenameLabel;                 // Displays the current file name
    private JButton record;                       // Record/Stop button


    private File currentDir;                       // Current directory
    private File fileOut;                          // Current sound file

    final Color recordColor = Color.red;          // Recording state color
    Color stopColor;                              // Stop state color
}
```

The method `main()` creates a `Recorder` object and the class constructor create the GUI. There are two GUI elements – a panel containing a label showing the current sound file name, and a button. We add a fancy triple border to the panel to make it look nice and add the outer compound border to the button as well. The `getNewFile()` method returns a `File` object encapsulating the new file, or null if it can't create one. The label in the panel uses the `getName()` method for the `File` object as the source of the file name to display.

We will construct the name of the file by appending an integer to a name string, and then appending the file extension to that. We can add some more data members to the class to store these bits:

```
    private String filename = "samples";          // Basic file name
    private int filenameSuffix = 0;               // Name differentiator
    private String soundFileName;                 // The complete file name
```

To keep it simple, we will fix the file type as a .wav file, and to record this we will add another member to the class defining the file type:

```
    // Sound file type
    private AudioFileFormat.Type fileType = AudioFileFormat.Type.WAVE;
```

While we are about it, let's specify the audio data format we are going to use:

```
    // Our chosen audio format - we could use a different format
    // as long as there is a line to support it
    final int MONO = 1;
    private  AudioFormat format = new AudioFormat(AudioFormat.Encoding.PCM_SIGNED,
                                           44100, 16, MONO, 2, 44100, true);
```

We can implement the `getNewFile()` method like this:

```
File getNewFile()
{
  File file = null;
  try
  {
    do
    {
      soundFileName = filename + (filenameSuffix++) +
                                 '.' + fileType.getExtension();
      file = new File(currentDir, soundFileName);
    }while(!file.createNewFile());
    if(!file.isFile())
    {
        System.out.println("File not created: " + file.getName());
        return null;
    }
  }
  catch(IOException e)
  {
    System.out.println(e);
    return null;
  }
  return file;
}
```

We assemble the file name from the bits we have defined, with the extension being obtained from the `AudioFormat` object specifying the data format. Note how we increment the value, `filenameSuffix`, so we add a different suffix next time. We do this in a `do-while` loop because the file may already exist from a previous execution of `Recorder` for instance. After creating a `File` object in the current directory from the file name, we call the `createNewFile()` method for it in the loop condition. If the file already exists, this method returns `false` so we go round again with a different suffix value. The loop will try as many as 2,147,483,647 different file names, so we have a reasonable chance of creating one that is unique.

The action listener for the RECORD button is defined by an anonymous class in the contructor. The `actionPerformed()` method here starts and stops recording by calling the `startRecording()` and `stopRecording()` methods in the `Recorder` class. Here's how we will implement the `startRecording()` method:

```
public void startRecording()
{
  DataLine.Info info = new DataLine.Info(TargetDataLine.class, format);
  if(!AudioSystem.isLineSupported(info))
  {
    System.out.println("Line not supported" + info);
    record.setEnabled(false);
    return;
  }
```

```
    try
    {
      mike = (TargetDataLine)AudioSystem.getLine(info);
      mike.open(format, mike.getBufferSize());
    }
    catch(LineUnavailableException e)
    {
      System.out.println("Line not available" + e);
      record.setEnabled(false);
      return;
    }
    if(fileOut.length()>0)
    {
      fileOut = getNewFile();
      filenameLabel.setText(fileOut.getName());
    }
    filenameLabel.setForeground(recordColor);
    filenameLabel.repaint();
    thread = new Thread(this);
    thread.start();
}
```

We create the `DataLine.Info` object and verify the line is supported. If it isn't, we won't be able to record so we disable the RECORD button. Next we create the `TargetDataLine` object, `mike`. We must add this as a member of the `Recorder` class along with a `Thread` variable, `thread`, which will store the reference to the thread doing the recording:

```
private TargetDataLine mike;                    // The microphone input
private Thread thread;                          // The recording thread
```

Once `mike` has been created we call its `open()` method to open the line. For the first recording, we will have already created a `fileOut` reference that will relate to an empty file because we haven't made a recording yet. On the second and subsequent occasions we execute this method, `fileOut` will reference the previous file that contains the data for the last recording. In this case the length will be greater than zero so we shall create a new file for this recording. Finally we set the label text color to red as a recording indicator, create the recording thread and start it. This will cause the `run()` method to be called within the new thread, and the code for this will be:

```
public void run()
{
  AudioInputStream sound = new AudioInputStream(mike);   // Microphone stream
  mike.start();                                          // Start input
  try
  {
    AudioSystem.write(sound, fileType, fileOut);         // Write input to file
  }
  catch(IOException e)
  {
    System.out.println(e);
  }
}
```

This does exactly what we described in the last section. We create the audio input stream, start the line, and use the `AudioSystem.write()` method to write the file. The only other piece we need is the `stopRecording()` method:

```
public void stopRecording()
{
  filenameLabel.setForeground(stopColor);
  filenameLabel.repaint();
  mike.stop();
  mike.close();
}
```

Here, we just reset the label text color, stop the line and close it. Couldn't be simpler really, could it?

Sound Events

We haven't had occasion to use sound events in our examples, so let's get an idea of what they are. Any of the lines we have discussed can generate events of type `LineEvent`. The type of a line event is defined by an object of type `LineEvent.Type` – an inner class to the `LineEvent` class. There are four kinds of line events that can be generated, and each of these are constants of type `LineEvent.Type` defined in the `LineEvent.Type` class:

START	The event type that results when you call the `start()` method for a line.
STOP	The event type that results when you call the `stop()` method for a line.
OPEN	The event type that results when you call the `open()` method for a line.
CLOSE	The event type that results when you call the `close()` method for a line.

You can react to a line event by registering a listener of type `LineListener` for a line. The `Line` interface declares the `addLineListener()` method for this purpose, so you can register a line listener with any kind of line. The `LineListener` interface only defines one method `update()`, and this method will receive a reference to a `LineEvent` object as the argument.

The `LineEvent` object has three methods that you can use to analyze the event:

getLine()	Returns a reference to the line originating the event as type `Line`.
getType()	Returns the type of the event as type `LineEvent.Type`. The value will be one of the four constants we have just discussed.
getFramePosition()	Returns the number of frames that have been processed by the line since the line was opened. This will be the current position in the audio data stream. This value is only valid for START and STOP events. For other events the value will be `AudioSystem.NOT_SPECIFIED`.

Registering a listener for these events is not always necessary, as you have seen from our examples. However, when you do need to handle these events they are quite simple. If you always wanted to restart playing a sound from the beginning after it was stopped, you could implement this quite easily using a line listener. You would just need to mark the beginning of the input stream – as we did in the last example, and when a STOP event was registered for the line, call `reset()` for the stream.

Understanding MIDI

MIDI is an acronym for **M**usical **I**nstrument **D**igital **I**nterface, and a MIDI data file defines a piece of music. MIDI music files are not sound files in the strict sense in that they do not contain a digitized sound wave, but they do specify music in terms of notes produced by a set of musical instruments defined by the MIDI standard. This implies that a MIDI file can *only* define music – it can't include speech or singing for instance.

The data in a MIDI file is essentially a series of commands that defines a piece of music in terms of combinations of sounds from a standard range of musical instruments and up to sixteen of the available instruments can be playing concurrently, each playing on a separate MIDI channel. For instance, one command will select a particular instrument for a particular channel – a piano say on channel 1, and subsequent commands – **Note-On** and **Note-Off** will start and stop the current instrument on channel 1 playing a given note. Separate sequences of MIDI commands for various instruments are synchronized to play simultaneously using data defining the tempo and start time for the separate tracks. The time signatures that are stored in a MIDI file can also be used to synchronize the music with an external device such as a video player to obtain synchronized sound and pictures.

The sounds that each of the instruments can produce are not defined within the MIDI file itself. They have to be generated by an external device. Such a device can be a real musical instrument – typically a keyboard instrument, which incorporates electronic circuits to process MIDI commands and recreate the music that the MIDI data describes, and of course the instrument can be played in the normal way using the keyboard. Such instruments are also capable of generating MIDI commands when they are played, and these commands can be fed via a cable to another MIDI instrument so you can play two (or more) MIDI instruments simultaneously. The sounds can also be produced through a device that synthesizes the sounds for a wide variety of instruments. This can be a purpose built device, or simply a PC with a MIDI driver for its sound card. The jargon that is used in the context of MIDI can be a bit confusing if you haven't come across it before (and sometimes even if you have!), so we will look at the principal terms that are used before we get into the Java programming specifics.

MIDI Synthesizers

The electronics that can reproduce the sound from a variety of different musical instruments in response to MIDI commands is called a **MIDI synthesizer**. A MIDI synthesizer can reproduce any of the sounds from the standard instruments defined by MIDI, and it can process a sequence of MIDI commands to recreate a piece of music. As I'm sure you know, a MIDI synthesizer can be a hardware device independent of any musical instrument, just for recreating music from MIDI data. Some PC sound cards incorporate a MIDI synthesizer for instance. A MIDI synthesizer can also be implemented in software, and the Java Sound API incorporates just such a capability.

Note that an instrument – a piano, a guitar, a trombone or whatever – is also called a **timbre** in MIDI-speak. Because real MIDI synthesizers can be connected together by cables routed through a patch panel, an instrument may also be referred to as a **patch**. In Java a patch is a memory location where a particular instrument is stored in a software synthesizer. In fact there are two components to a patch – a **bank number** and a **program number**. A bank can have up to 128 instruments, and there can be up to 128 banks for a synthesizer. Thus, a patch consists of a bank number that can be from 0 to 127, and a program number that identifies the instrument within a bank, and that also can vary from 0 to 127.

As we said, synthesizers can typically reproduce sounds from several different instruments concurrently – to simulate a band or an orchestra for instance. If they have this capability they are described as **multi-timbral**.

A MIDI synthesizer may also be **polyphonic**. This means that the synthesizer can play several notes (also called **voices**) from a given instrument concurrently, so it can play a chord on a piano or a guitar for instance. Don't confuse the multi-timbral capability with polyphony. These are quite separate and a synthesizer may have either, neither or both. The synthesizer supplied as part of JDK 1.3 is both polyphonic and multi-timbral.

MIDI Sequencers

A series of MIDI commands – in a MIDI file for instance – is called a **MIDI sequence**. A **sequencer** is a device that processes a MIDI sequence in order to play it on a synthesizer, or possibly to edit it. The sounds are produced by MIDI instruments within the synthesizer, but it is the sequencer that analyzes the sequence and farms out commands to the appropriate instrument. A sequencer can be a hardware device that is used with physical MIDI instruments of various kinds. It can also be simulated in software – and the Java Sound API includes a software MIDI sequencer.

Standard MIDI

One major advantage of using MIDI files to store pieces of music is that they are very much smaller than the equivalent audio files. A major disadvantage is that the quality of the reproduction is totally dependent on the capability of the MIDI synthesizer(s) that you use to play the music, and these do vary widely. The **General MIDI** specification defines a standard for the minimum level of performance of MIDI devices in terms of their function (note that this is function, <u>not</u> sound quality). This can apply to any kind of MIDI synthesizer including MIDI instruments, PC sound cards, or software implementations that simulate a MIDI synthesizer in your PC. A device conforming to the General MIDI specification must provide:

❑   Availability of a minimum of 128 preset melodic instruments, plus 47 percussive sounds.

❑   Allow a minimum of 16 simultaneous **timbres** to be played where each timbre is one of the available instruments.

❑   A minimum of 24 simultaneous **voices**, where a voice is a note of given velocity (loudness) for any of the available instruments and percussive sounds (or 8 percussive plus 16 melodic instruments).

❑   16 MIDI **channels**, referred to as channels one to sixteen (but identified by a 4 bit code so code values run from 0 to 15), where each channel is **polyphonic** (can play multiple concurrent voices) and can play a different timbre. Percussive sounds are always on channel ten.

MIDI channels are just a way to route MIDI data to particular MIDI devices. A MIDI device can be set to accept input from one or more of the available sixteen channels, in which case it will process the commands associated with those channels. Clearly, to reproduce the sound defined by a MIDI file on your PC, you must have a MIDI synthesis capability available in your system that can reproduce the sounds of each of the various musical instruments. We don't have to worry about this in Java as the Java Sound API implementation includes MIDI synthesis capability in software that provides 16-bit 32-channel sound. In addition, it includes a sound mixer that can combine up to 64 channels of audio and/or synthesized MIDI. It also can use hardware MIDI synthesis when it is available.

MIDI File Types

MIDI files usually have the extension, `.mid`, and there are presently three types of standard MIDI file:

MIDI Type 0	Data is stored in a single track with a single tempo and time signature.
MIDI Type 1	Data is stored in multiple tracks, but the tempo and time signature data that is stored in the first track applies to all tracks.
MIDI Type 2	Data is stored in multiple tracks with separate tempo and time signatures for each track.

The present version of the Sound API (with JDK 1.3) only supports MIDI types 0 and 1. The Java Sound API implementation also supports RMF (Rich Music Format) music files, which is a file format that is proprietary to Beatnik. RMF is for specifying high quality music that is intended for streaming over the Internet. RMF files can contain MIDI data as well as sampled sound data in the form of `.wav` file data or MP3 compressed samples.

That's the MIDI basics out of the way, so let's make some noise.

Working with Midi

The classes and interfaces that support MIDI in the Java Sound API reside in the `javax.sound.midi` package. The design is quite similar to what we have seen for sampled sound processing, with interface types referencing external MIDI resources such as sequencers and synthesizers, and the `MidiSystem` class providing static methods that you use to obtain references to objects encapsulating the resources available.

There's a great deal in the support for MIDI, far more than we can possibly cover in this chapter. The intention is to give you an overview of the capabilities, and then illustrate some aspects of what is available with a couple of examples.

MIDI Resources

The `MidiDevice` interface specifies general operations on a MIDI device. There are two interfaces defining the operations for specific MIDI devices, `Sequencer` and `Synthesizer`.

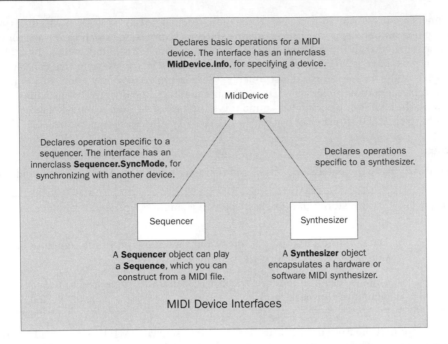

The MidiDevice.Info class that is defined within the MidiDevice interface encapsulates descriptive information in the form of String objects that describe a particular device. To find out what MIDI devices are available on your system you can call the static getMidiDeviceInfo() method that is defined in the MidiSystem class. This returns an array of MidiDevice.Info objects so you could use it like this:

```
MidiDevice.Info[] devices = MidiSystem.getMidiDeviceInfo();
for(int i = 0 ; i<devices.length ; i++)
{
   System.out.println("\nMIDI Device " + (i+1) + ":" + devices[i].getName());
   System.out.println("\tDescription: " + devices[i].getDescription());
   System.out.println("\tVendor      : " + devices[i].getVendor());
   System.out.println("\tVersion      : " + devices[i].getVersion());
}
```

This will itemize each of the sequencers and synthesizers that are accessible in your system. If you want to plug this into main() somewhere and run it, don't forget the import statement for the javax.sound.midi package. On my system I got a total of seven devices listed:

MIDI Device 1:Java Sound Synthesizer
    Description: Software wavetable synthesizer and receiver
    Vendor   : Sun Microsystems
    Version   : Version 1.0

MIDI Device 2:Java Sound Sequencer
    Description: Software sequencer / synthesizer module
    Vendor   : Sun Microsystems
    Version   : Version 1.0

MIDI Device 3:SB16 MIDI In [330]
  Description: No details available
  Vendor : Unknown Vendor
  Version : Unknown Version

MIDI Device 4:MIDI Mapper
  Description: Windows MIDI_MAPPER driver
  Vendor : Unknown Vendor
  Version : Unknown Version

MIDI Device 5:SB AWE32 MIDI Synth [620]
  Description: Internal synthesizer (generic)
  Vendor : Unknown Vendor
  Version : Unknown Version

MIDI Device 6:SB16 MIDI Out [330]
  Description: External MIDI Port
  Vendor : Unknown Vendor
  Version : Unknown Version

MIDI Device 7:Creative Music Synth [220]
  Description: Internal FM synthesizer
  Vendor : Unknown Vendor
  Version : Unknown Version

Accessing MIDI devices works in much the same way as for sampled sound devices. You use static methods defined in the `MidiSystem` class to access objects of type `Sequencer` or `Synthesizer`. For example, we can obtain a reference to a default sequencer with the statement:

```
Sequencer sequencer = MidiSystem.getSequencer();
```

This statement must be in a `try` block because it can throw an exception of type `MidiUnavailableException` if a sequencer cannot be accessed for any reason.

Accessing the default synthesizer is almost exactly the same:

```
Synthesizer synthesizer = MidiSystem.getSynthesizer();
```

This can also throw an exception of type `MidiUnavailableException` so you should put it in a `try` block and catch the exception.

The basic methods declared in the `MidiDevice` interface apply to both sequencers and synthesizers. To access a device and make it operational, you must call its `open()` method. Until you have opened the device, you can't do much with it. If the device cannot be opened – because it is already in use by another program for instance, the method will throw an exception of type `MidiUnavailableException`. When you are finished with a device, you call its `close()` method to release the resources it has acquired.

To play a MIDI file, you don't need to access a synthesizer directly. All you need is a `Sequencer` reference and an object encapsulating the sequence that you want to play. Let's see how we can do that.

Playing a MIDI File

From what we have discussed so far, we know that we can access a sequencer with the statements:

```
Sequencer sequencer = null;
try
{
  sequencer = MidiSystem.getSequencer();
  sequencer.open();
}
catch(MidiUnavailableException e)
{
  System.err.println("No sequencer available");
}
```

If these execute successfully, we will have acquired a reference to a sequencer and opened it ready for action. We now need a MIDI sequence to play.

A MIDI sequence is encapsulated by an object of the Sequence class. You can construct a Sequence object directly from a MIDI file by using a static method from the MidiSystem class, like this:

```
File midiFile = new File("music.mid");
Sequence sequence = null;
try
{
    sequence = MidiSystem.getSequence(midiFile);
}
catch(InvalidMidiDataException e)
{
  System.err.println("MIDI file contains invalid data");
}
catch(IOException e)
{
  System.err.println("I/O error accessing MIDI file");
}
```

The getSequence() method returns a reference to a Sequence object encapsulating the file passed as the argument. There are overloaded versions of the getSequence method to create a Sequence object from a URL object or an InputStream object. The try block is necessary in the fragment above because the getSequence() method can throw the two types of exceptions we are catching here.

Once we have a sequence, we need to hand it over to the Sequencer before we can play it. We can do this by passing it to the setSequence() method for the Sequencer object:

```
sequencer.setSequence(sequence);
```

This method can also throw an exception of type InvalidMidiDataException, so this needs to be in a try block too.

All that is now necessary to play the sequence is to call the start() method for the Sequencer object:

```
sequencer.start();
```

This will start playing the MIDI data from the sequence. To stop the sequencer you just call its stop() method. I think we have enough to construct a MIDI player.

Try It Out – Playing MIDI

We will construct a MIDI player that has the same GUI as the SoundPlayer example that plays sampled sound files. It will operate in the same way – displaying a dropdown list of MIDI files from the current directory with the current selection being played when the PLAY button is clicked. Here's the code:

```java
import javax.swing.*;
import java.io.*;
import java.awt.*;
import java.awt.event.*;
import javax.sound.midi.*;

public class MidiPlayer extends JFrame
{
  public MidiPlayer()
  {
    setDefaultCloseOperation(EXIT_ON_CLOSE);
    setTitle("Midi File Player");
    setSize(250,100);

    // Set up the PLAY button to play the current midi file
    play = new JButton("PLAY");
    play.addActionListener(new ActionListener()
                {
                    public void actionPerformed(ActionEvent e)
                    {
                      if(e.getActionCommand().equals("PLAY"))
                      {
                        startPlay();
                        play.setText("STOP");
                      }
                      else
                      {
                        stopPlay();
                        play.setText("PLAY");
                      }
                    }
                });

    // Get the MIDI file names from current directory
    currentDir = new File(System.getProperty("user.dir"));
    FilenameFilter filter = new FilenameFilter()
        {
```

```
                       public boolean accept(File directory, String filename)
                       {
                         String name = filename.toLowerCase();
                         return name.endsWith(".mid");
                       }
                    };
    String midiFiles[] = currentDir.list(filter);
    if(midiFiles == null || midiFiles.length == 0)
    {
      JOptionPane.showMessageDialog(null, "No midi files - terminating...",
                             "No Playable Files",JOptionPane.ERROR_MESSAGE);

      System.exit(1);
    }
    try
    {
      sequencer = MidiSystem.getSequencer();        // Get a sequencer...
      sequencer.open();                             // ...and open it.
    }
    catch(MidiUnavailableException e)
    {
JOptionPane.showMessageDialog(null, "No sequencer available - terminating.",
                           "Midi System Error", JOptionPane.ERROR_MESSAGE);
        System.exit(1);
    }

    midiChoice = new JComboBox(midiFiles);
    midiChoice.setSelectedIndex(0);
    newSequence(midiFiles[0]);
    oldFilename = midiFiles[0];

    midiChoice.addActionListener(new ActionListener()
                       {
                          public void actionPerformed(ActionEvent e)
                       {newSequence((String)midiChoice.getSelectedItem());
                          }
                       }
                    );

    Container content = getContentPane();
    content.add(midiChoice);
    content.add(play,BorderLayout.SOUTH);
    setVisible(true);
  }

  public static void main(String[] args)
  {
    MidiPlayer midiPlayer = new MidiPlayer();
  }

  void newSequence(String filename)
  {
    File midiFile = new File(currentDir, filename);
```

```
      try
      {
        sequence = MidiSystem.getSequence(midiFile);
        sequencer.setSequence(sequence);
        play.setText("PLAY");
        oldFilename = filename;
      }
      catch(InvalidMidiDataException e)
      {
        JOptionPane.showMessageDialog(null, "File "+filename+
                " contains invalid data","File Error", JOptionPane.ERROR_MESSAGE);
        midiChoice.setSelectedItem(oldFilename);
      }
      catch(IOException e)
      {
        JOptionPane.showMessageDialog(null, "I/O Error "+filename,
                        "Sequence Creation Error", JOptionPane.ERROR_MESSAGE);
        midiChoice.setSelectedItem(oldFilename);
      }
    }

    void startPlay()
    {
      sequencer.start();
    }

    void stopPlay()
    {
      sequencer.stop();
    }

    private File currentDir;               // Current directory
    private String oldFilename;            // Last selected file nmae
    private JComboBox midiChoice;          // Dropdown list of files
    private JButton play;                  // PLAY button
    private Sequencer sequencer;           // Plays a Midi sequence
    private Sequence sequence;             // The Midi sequence
  }
```

If you compile and run this, you should be able to play any MIDI files in the current directory. Note that loading large MIDI files into the sequencer is quite slow, so if the application appears to lock up when you select a new file, wait (possibly more than a minute) for the file to load. Small files – 10 to 20K bytes should load almost instantaneously.

How It Works

The class constructor obtains a sequencer and opens it with the statements:

```
      sequencer = MidiSystem.getSequencer();          // Get a sequencer...
      sequencer.open();                               // ...and open it.
```

The PLAY button and combobox are set up in exactly the same way as the SoundPlayer example. We create the button first here because the newSequence() method resets the button text, and we call this method from the constructor to set up the first sequence. The MIDI file that is selected is loaded into the sequencer by the newSequence() method in the MidiPlayer class. This creates a Sequence object from the file and loads it using the setSequence() method for the sequencer. Clicking the PLAY button invokes the startPlay() method that calls start() for the sequencer. You stop the sequencer playing by clicking the STOP button. This results in the stopPlay() method being called, which calls stop() for the Sequencer object.

The Sequencer interface declares a considerable number of methods for operating the sequencer that we don't have the space to go into. You might like to play with this example by trying out just one of them, the setTempoFactor() method. The tempo for a MIDI sequence is measured in beats per minute, and the given tempo is multiplied by the **tempo factor** stored in the sequencer, which has a default value of 1.0f so the default tempo is that recorded in the MIDI sequence. If you want to play a piece 20% faster, you could pass the float value 1.2f to the setTempoFactor() method for the sequencer before you start it playing.

Using a Synthesizer

Even a brief introduction to programming MIDI would not be complete without synthesizing a few different instruments, so let's work our way towards achieving that. We know how to access the default synthesizer so we will proceed from there.

A software synthesizer often uses a **soundbank** to reproduce the sounds that various instruments make. A soundbank is essentially a collection of sampled sound data for various instruments and the notes they are capable of producing. The soundbank incorporates all the instruments the synthesizer is capable of playing so it is the key to accessing the instruments. Generally, the better the soundbank the more memory it requires, as better sound implies more sound samples. You can get a reference to the default soundbank that is used by a Synthesizer object by calling its getDefaultSoundbank() method:

```
Soundbank soundbank = synthesizer.getDefaultSoundbank();
```

Of course, you must have called open() for the Synthesizer object at this point, otherwise the synthesizer will not have acquired any resources and this method will return null. Once you have the Soundbank reference for the synthesizer, you can obtain an array of available instruments supported by the soundbank:

```
Instrument[] instruments = soundbank.getInstruments();
```

This will return a reference to an array of instances of the Instrument class, each of which will represent a different instrument that the soundbank can synthesize. To get the name of a particular instrument, you call its getName() method, which can come in very useful when you want to display a choice of available instruments in an application.

The instruments supported by a soundbank are arranged in **banks** of instruments, where each bank can contain up to 128 instruments. A soundbank can contain up to 128 banks, so you have the potential for up to 16,384 different instruments in a soundbank. Both banks and instruments are numbered starting with zero, and to reference a particular instrument you need the bank number and the instrument number within the bank. The instrument number is also called the **program number**. The bank and program numbers for a given instrument are encapsulated in an instance of the class `Patch`. You can obtain a reference to the `Patch` object for a given instrument by calling its `getPatch()` method. For example:

```
Patch patch = instruments[0].getPatch();
```

This retrieves a reference to the `Patch` object for the first instrument in the array. You can then use the methods `getBank()` and `getProgram()` for the `Patch` object to obtain the bank and program numbers for the instrument. Note that even though a soundbank may support multiple instrument banks, a synthesizer may not, in which case only the bank 0 instruments will be available.

You don't necessarily have to go through the soundbank for a synthesizer to get at its instruments. The `Synthesizer` interface declares a method `getAvailableInstruments()` that returns an array of type `Instrument[]` containing references to all the instruments that are available. We could get the array of instruments the synthesizer can play with the statement:

```
Instrument[] instruments = synthesizer.getAvailableInstruments();
```

You can also find how polyphonic a synthesizer is by calling its `getMaxPolyphony()` method. This will return a value of type `int` that is the maximum number of concurrent voices for the synthesizer.

Synthesizer Channels

A synthesizer plays one of the instruments that it has available through one of its MIDI channels – we saw in the introduction that a MIDI synthesizer has at least sixteen channels. To access the channels for a synthesizer, you call its `getChannels()` method like this:

```
MidiChannel[] channels = synthesizer.getChannels();
```

This returns an array of references of type `MidiChannel`, each of which encapsulates a MIDI channel capable of playing a given instrument. To associate a given instrument with a particular channel, you can pass the bank and program numbers for the instrument to the `programChange()` method for the `Channel` object. For example, to associate the third instrument from those available with the second synthesizer channel, you could write:

```
Patch patch = instruments[2].getPatch();
channels[1].programChange(patch.getBank(),patch.getProgram());
```

You also have an overloaded version of the `programChange()` method that accepts just the program number to select a different instrument from the current bank, so if we want to assign the third instrument from the current bank to channel 2, we could write:

```
channel[1].programChange(2);
```

Bank 0 is typically the default current bank for a synthesizer.

Playing Notes

Musical notes for any instrument are identified by a **note number** between 0 to 127. Of course, not all instruments can play 128 different notes. A note number of 60 corresponds to middle C. To play a particular note on the current instrument for a given channel, you call the noteOn() method for the MidiChannel object. The noteOn() method requires two arguments of type int, the note number and the velocity. The velocity is a measure of the speed at which the key was depressed – as on a piano for instance. Thus the velocity reflects the volume, or brightness of the note to be played. For example, to play middle C on the instrument currently assigned to channel 0, we could write:

```
channels[0].noteOn(60, 64);
```

The note is played until you call the noteOff() method for the same note number. To stop the note abruptly, you can call the noteOff() method with a single argument specifying the note number:

```
channels[0].noteOff(60);
```

You can also add a second argument specifying the key-up velocity, which can affect how quickly the note decays:

```
channels[0].noteOff(60, 32);
```

We know enough about how MIDI works in the Sound API to put together a simple instrument synthesizer.

Try It Out – Playing a Synthesizer Keyboard

We can implement our synthesizer to display a keyboard that we can play with the mouse. We'll call our synthesizer application MiniMidiSynth, and we will implement it so that we can play any one of up to 128 instruments.

```java
import javax.swing.*;
import javax.swing.event.*;
import javax.swing.table.*;
import java.io.*;
import java.awt.*;
import java.util.*;
import java.awt.event.*;
import javax.sound.midi.*;

public class MiniMidiSynth extends JFrame
{
  public MiniMidiSynth()
  {
    setDefaultCloseOperation(EXIT_ON_CLOSE);
    setTitle("Mini Midi Synthesizer");

    Box box = Box.createVerticalBox();                    // Holds combobox and keyboard
    getContentPane().add(box);
```

```
   // Access the synthesizer
   try
   {
     synthesizer = MidiSystem.getSynthesizer();        // Get the synthesizer...
     synthesizer.open();                               // ...and open it
   }
   catch(MidiUnavailableException e)
   {
JOptionPane.showMessageDialog(null, "No synthesizer available - terminating...",
                          "MIDI Error", JOptionPane.ERROR_MESSAGE);
     System.exit(1);
   }

   MidiChannel[] channels = synthesizer.getChannels();     // Get the channels
   for(int i = 0 ; i< channels.length ; i++)          // Get first non-null channel
     if(channels[i] != null)
     {
       channel = channels[i];
       break;
     }

   instruments = synthesizer.getAvailableInstruments();   // Get the instruments
   if(instruments.length == 0)                            // ...and check we have some
   {
JOptionPane.showMessageDialog(null, "No instruments available - terminating...",
                          "MIDI Error", JOptionPane.ERROR_MESSAGE);
     System.exit(1);
   }


   // Create instrument list in combobox
   instrumentChoice = new JComboBox();
   for(int i = 0 ; i<Math.min(128,instruments.length);i++)
     instrumentChoice.addItem(instruments[i]);

 // Select the first instrument for the channel
   channel.programChange(instruments[0].getPatch().getProgram());
   instrumentChoice.setSelectedIndex(0);                    // Select the chosen one

   // Add listener for new instrument selected
   instrumentChoice.addActionListener(new ActionListener()
       {
         public void actionPerformed(ActionEvent e)
         {
           Patch patch =
                   ((Instrument)instrumentChoice.getSelectedItem()).getPatch();
                   channel.programChange(patch.getBank(),patch.getProgram());
         }
       });

 JPanel instrumentPane = new JPanel(new FlowLayout());  // Panel for instrument
                                                        //   choice
```

```
      instrumentPane.add(instrumentChoice);        // Add combobox
      box.add(Box.createVerticalStrut(10));        // Space above....
      box.add(instrumentPane);                     // ...instrument panel...
      box.add(Box.createVerticalStrut(10));        // ...and below


      // Create keyboard
      JPanel kbPane = new JPanel(new BorderLayout());       // Panel for keyboard
      kbPane.setBorder(BorderFactory.createEmptyBorder(10,5,10,5)); // with space
around
      kbPane.add(new Keyboard());                  // Add the keyboard
      box.add(kbPane);                             // Add the panel to the box


      pack();
      setVisible(true);
    }


    public static void main(String[] args)
    {
      MiniMidiSynth synth = new MiniMidiSynth();
    }


    // Inner class defining a keyboard
    class Keyboard extends JPanel
    {
      // Code for class to define a keyboard....
    }


    private Synthesizer synthesizer;          // The synthesizer
    private MidiChannel channel;              // The channel we will use
    private Instrument instruments[];         // Available instruments
    private JComboBox instrumentChoice;       // Choice of instruments
    private static int velocity = 70;         // Note velocity
  }
```

You should have no trouble seeing how the code in the constructor works. It is essentially using the elements we have just discussed directly. The keyboard is defined by the inner class, and putting this together will be more work than synthesizing the instruments.

We will construct the keyboard based on the JPanel class and we will define a key by the Key class that will be an inner class to the Keyboard class. Since a key has a rectangular shape, it will be helpful to use the java.awt.Rectangle class as the base for our Key class.

We need to think about how best to manage and draw the keys. Because the black keys sit on top of the white keys, to detect which key is being pressed when a mouse click event is received we will need to search the black keys before the white keys. It will therefore be convenient to store the black keys and white keys in separate arrays. Since each key will be a Rectangle, we can check whether the point where the mouse was pressed is inside the boundary of a key by calling its contains() method. As long as we check the black keys before the white keys, we automatically take care of the regions where the keys overlap.

There are twelve keys for each major scale (octave) on a keyboard, seven white keys starting with C and five black keys. This will be a fundamental unit in drawing our keyboard. Our keyboard will consist of an even number of these sequences of twelve keys, and we will position with middle C in the center. If we number the keys in sequence from zero, the white keys will correspond to numbers 0,2,4,5,7,9,and 11, and the black keys will be numbered 1, 3, 6, 8, and 10, as illustrated in the diagram.

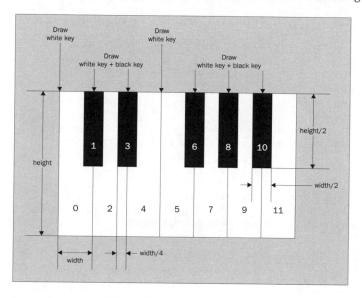

The diagram also shows that the width and height of a black key are half the corresponding dimensions of a white key. The arrows along the top show the sequence in which we can draw all twelve keys. The reference point for each key will be its top left corner and we can draw the keys at one or other of the seven points shown. At each point indicated we either draw just a white key, or a white key followed by a black key. At the first and third points we just draw a white key. At the other points we draw both. The position of each black key that is drawn is shifted a distance of width/4 to the left of the point. If we draw the keys in this way we will ensure that the black keys all lie over the white keys. If we want to create keys for additional octaves, we just repeat the whole process.

Based on that, here's the code for the inner class:

```
class Keyboard extends JPanel
  {
    public Keyboard()
    {
      setLayout(new BorderLayout());
      setPreferredSize(new Dimension(7* OCTAVES*Key.width, Key.height+1));
      int firstKeyNum = 60 - 6* OCTAVES;
      int whiteIDs[] = { 0, 2, 4, 5, 7, 9, 11 };        // White key positions
                                                        // in an octave
      int blackIDs[] = { 0, 1, 3, 0, 6, 8, 10 };        // Black key positions
                                                        // in an octave

      int position = 0;
```

```
      int whiteKeyIndex = 0;                           // Current white key
      int blackKeyIndex = 0;                           // Current black key
      for (int i = 0; i <  OCTAVES; i++)
      {
        int keyNum = i * 12 + firstKeyNum;

        for(int j = 0; j < 7; j++, position += Key.width)
        {
          whiteKeys[whiteKeyIndex++] =
          new Key(position, 0, keyNum + whiteIDs[j], Color.white);

          if(j==0||j==3)
            continue;
          else
            blackKeys[blackKeyIndex++] =
            new Key(position-Key.width/4, 0, keyNum+blackIDs[j],Color.black);
        }
      }

      addMouseListener(new MouseAdapter()
        {
          public void mousePressed(MouseEvent e)
          {
            pressedKey = getKey(e.getPoint());    // Find the key under the cursor
            if(pressedKey == null)                // If there isn't one...
              return;                             // We are done
            pressedKey.press();                   // Press the key...
            repaint();                            // ...and redraw the keyboard
          }

          public void mouseReleased(MouseEvent e)
          {
            if(pressedKey != null)                // If a key is pressed...
            {
              pressedKey.release();               // ...release it...
              repaint();                          //... and redraw the keyboard
            }
          }
        });
    }

    // Find the key at a point
    public Key getKey(Point point)
    {
      for(int i = 0; i < blackKeys.length; i++)
        if(blackKeys[i].contains(point))
          return blackKeys[i];
      for(int i = 0; i < whiteKeys.length; i++)
        if(whiteKeys[i].contains(point))
          return whiteKeys[i];
      return null;
    }
```

```java
public void paint(Graphics g)
{
  Graphics2D g2d = (Graphics2D) g;

  for(int i = 0; i < whiteKeys.length; i++)
    whiteKeys[i].draw(g2d);

  for(int i = 0; i < blackKeys.length; i++)
    blackKeys[i].draw(g2d);
}

final int OCTAVES = 4;                          // Number of octaves on keyboard
Key[] whiteKeys = new Key[7* OCTAVES];          // The white keys
Key[] blackKeys = new Key[5* OCTAVES];          // The black keys
Key pressedKey;                                 // Key that is currently pressed

// Inner class defining a key
class Key extends Rectangle
{
  public Key(int x, int y, int num, Color color)
  {
    super(x, y,
          color.equals(Color.white)? width:width/2,      // Black keys are half
          color.equals(Color.white)?height:height/2);    // width & height
    this.color = color;
    noteNumber = num;
  }

  // Press the key
  public void press()
  {
    keydown = true;                             // Set indicator
    channel.noteOn(noteNumber, velocity);       // and play the note
  }

  // Release the key
  public void release()
  {
    keydown = false;                            // Reset the indicator
    channel.noteOff(noteNumber, velocity/2);    // Stop playing note
  }

  // Draw the key
  public void draw(Graphics2D g2d)
  {
    g2d.setColor(keydown ? Color.blue : color); // Blue when pressed
    g2d.fill(this);                             // Fill key
    g2d.setColor(Color.black);                  // Set outline color
    g2d.draw(this);                             // Draw outline
  }

  final static int width = 20;                  // White key width
```

```
        final static int height = 100;          // White key length
        private boolean keydown = false;         // Key pressed indicator
        private Color color;                     // Key color
        int noteNumber;                          // Note number for the key
    }
}
```

If you compile and run this you should be able to play any of the instruments in the combobox selection.

How It Works

The application uses a single channel to play any instrument with a given default velocity. The `MiniMidiSynthesizer` class constructor accesses the synthesizer, its channels, and its instruments and adds the available instruments to the combobox. It also saves a reference to the first available channel for use in the program. Note that the combobox automatically displays the `String` description of each `Instrument` object in the list, and that we automatically get a scroller for the list.

The keyboard that is displayed below the combobox is an instance of the `Keyboard` class, and consists of a `JPanel` object on which we draw keys. Each key is an instance of the `Key` class, which is a specialization of the `Rectangle` class. Because each `Key` object is also a `Rectangle`, we can draw a key using the `fill()` and `draw()` methods for the `Graphics2D` object that is passed to the `paint()` method for the keyboard.

When a mouse key is pressed in the keyboard panel, the `getKey()` method in the `Keyboard` class searches the `Key` objects in the keyboard to find which one encloses the current mouse cursor position. The `press()` method for that `Key` object is called, which sets an indicator in the key to record that it is pressed and calls `noteOn()` for the key number corresponding to the key to play the note.

When the mouse button is released, the `MouseListener` registered with the `Keyboard` object calls the `release()` method for the key that is currently pressed. This resets the indicator and stops playing the note by calling the `noteOff()` method for the channel.

Summary

In this chapter we have covered the basic mechanisms involved in handling sample sound and MIDI data in Java. The important points that we have covered include:

❑   The `AudioSystem` class provides the facilities for accessing the sampled sound data resources available in your system.

❑   A `Line` provides the capability for input or output of sampled sound data.

- ❑ A `Clip` object encapsulates all the sampled data for a complete sound clip.

- ❑ An `AudioInputStream` object is an input stream for sampled sound data.

- ❑ Each line is associated with a mixer, although you can access available lines directly through methods defined in the `AudioSystem` class.

- ❑ A `SourceDataLine` provides input to a mixer and a `TargetDataLine` produces output from a mixer.

- ❑ You can output sampled sound data to the speaker port using a `SourceDataLine` reference.

- ❑ You can record sampled sound data from the microphone input using a `TargetDataLine` reference.

- ❑ The format for storing sampled sound data is defined by an `AudioFormat` object.

- ❑ The type of an audio file is specified by an object of type `AudioFileFormat`.

- ❑ The Sound API can handle `.au`, `.snd`, `.aif`, and `.wav` files.

- ❑ A MIDI data file describes a piece of music in a manner that enables the music to be played by a MIDI instrument or synthesizer.

- ❑ The `MidiSystem` class provides you with the means of accessing MIDI resources that are available in your system.

- ❑ A synthesizer is encapsulated by a `Synthesizer` object, and may use a `Soundbank` object to generate the sounds for different instruments.

- ❑ A `Sequencer` object is used to play MIDI data.

Exercises

1. Make the `MidiMiniSynthesizer` application play a sound clip (a beep maybe – but your choice) whenever a new instrument is selected.

2. Add a component to the GUI for the `MidiMiniSynthesizer` application to allow the note velocity to be changed.

3. Record your own voice message saying "The program is closing down". You can use the recorder from this chapter to do this. Modify any one of the examples in this chapter to play this message when you close the application.

Talking to Databases

In the next two chapters, we're going to look at how Java programs can interface with relational databases, or any database that can be accessed using Structured Query Language (SQL), using classes that come with the JDK.

First of all we will look at the basic ideas behind databases and how they store data. This leads naturally onto a discussion of SQL, the language that is used with many relational databases to both define and query data, and which is a prerequisite for database access in Java. Then we will look into the Java Database Connectivity (JDBC) class library, which provides a standard way for establishing and maintaining a Java program's connection to a database. Once you have a connection to a database, you can use SQL to access and process the contents.

In this first chapter, we'll take a brief tour of database concepts, SQL and JDBC. In the next chapter we will go into more depth on the capabilities provided by JDBC, and develop a database browsing application. In this chapter you will learn:

- ❑ What databases are
- ❑ What the basic SQL statements are and how you apply them
- ❑ What the rationale behind JDBC is
- ❑ How to write a simple JDBC program
- ❑ What the key elements of the JDBC API are

JDBC Concepts and Terminology

To make sure we have a common understanding of the jargon, we will first take a look at database terminology. Firstly, in general, **data access** is the process of retrieving or manipulating data that is taken from a remote or local **data source**. Data sources don't have to be relational – they can come in a variety of different forms. Some common examples of data sources that you might access are:

❑   A remote relational database on a server, for example, SQL Server

❑   A local relational database on your computer, for example, Personal Oracle or Microsoft Access

❑   A text file on your computer

❑   A spreadsheet

❑   A remote mainframe/midrange host providing data access

❑   An on-line information service (Dow Jones, etc.)

JDBC is, by definition, an interface to **relational** data sources. While it is conceivable that non-relational sources may be accessible through JDBC, we will be concentrating on relational databases throughout this chapter and the next. If you haven't met relational databases before, you should still be able to follow the discussion. The structure of relational databases is logical and fairly easy to learn, and while we can't provide a comprehensive tutorial on it here, we will cover enough of the basics to make what we are doing understandable.

The Java Database Connectivity (JDBC) library provides the means for executing SQL statements to access and operate on a relational database. JDBC was designed as an object-oriented, Java-based application programming interface (API) for database access, and is intended to be a standard to which Java developers and database vendors could adhere.

> *JDBC is based on other standard program-database interfaces – largely the X/Open SQL CLI (Call Level Interface) specification, but knowledge of these standards isn't necessary to use JDBC. However, if you've programmed database access before, you should be able to draw on that experience when using JDBC.*

The library is implemented in the `java.sql` package. It is a set of classes and interfaces that provide a uniform API for access to a broad range of databases.

The following figure shows the basic contents of the `technical_library` database (available from the Wrox Web site) that we will be using both to illustrate some key concepts, and as a base for the examples.

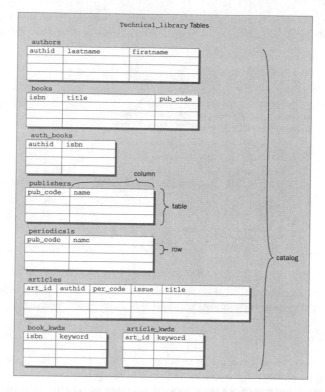

This shows the tables that make up the sample database. In case you are unfamiliar with relational databases, we will be going into what tables are in a moment.

The operations that you want to carry out on a relational database are expressed in a language that was designed specifically for this purpose, the **Structured Query Language** – more commonly referred to as SQL. SQL is not like a conventional programming language, such as Java. SQL is a **declarative** language, which means that SQL statements tell the database server *what* you want to do, but not *how* it should be done – the *how* is up to the server. Each SQL command is analyzed by the database server and the operation it describes is carried out by a separate piece of software that is usually referred to as the **database engine**. A database engine will be associated with a particular implementation of a relational database, although not necessarily uniquely. Different commercial database implementations may use a common database engine.

Tables

A relational database is made of tables. A **table**, such as the `authors` table in our example above, is the primary database construct that you'll be dealing with. Any time that you define, create, update or delete data, you will do so within the context of a table.

When you create a table within a database, you are creating a 'template' for a rectangular grid that will contain the data. In relational parlance, a table is a collection of rows conforming to the specifications of the corresponding columns, and the table is called a **relation**. Each row implies that the set of data items that it contains are related in some way – it expresses a relationship between the data items, and a table can contain as many rows as you want.

The technical term for a row in a table is a **tuple**. The columns define the constituent parts of a row and are referred to as **fields**, and these column-defined items of data in a row are called **attributes**. Thus the number of columns for a given table is fixed.

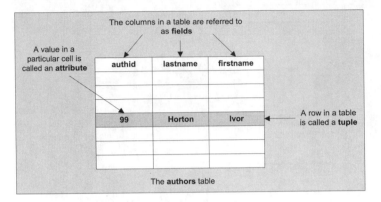

Although a table is logically a set of rows with a fixed number of columns, the physical organization doesn't have to be like that. The physical organization can be anything at all as long as the logical organization – the way it appears when you access it – is as we have described.

Table Columns

As we said, a table behaves as if it is a rectangular grid of cells. The grid has a given number of columns and an arbitrary number of rows. Each column of cells in the grid stores data of a particular kind. Not only is it of a particular data type, it is also a specific category of information specified by the field name. For example, in the previous figure, the field with the name `lastname` is one of three fields defined for the `authors` table. It stores the last name of the authors that appear in the table, and the type of the data will be a text string. SQL has data types that correspond to the basic Java data types – we'll list them later.

It's fundamental to a relational database that the data items in each column in a table have consistent data types *and* semantics. For example, in the `authors` table, the `lastname` column, which is defined as a text field, will only be used to store text – not numbers, so the data type is preserved. The column's semantics must also be preserved, and since the column represents the last name of an author, you would not use this column to store an author's hobbies or favorite movie, even though such data items may be of the same type. If you wanted to record that information, you would need to create new columns in the table.

Table Rows

Each **row** in a table is the collection of data elements that make up an entity referred to as a **tuple**. Some data sources refer to a row as a **record**, and you will often see the term record used in a general purpose programming context when accessing a relational database. The term **recordset** is used to describe a collection of rows that is produced by executing an SQL command.

A row from the `authors` table in the database example that we showed earlier would look like:

20	Celko	Joe

This row contains data items for the `authid`, `lastname` and `firstname` columns. Although in this case there is a data item corresponding to each column, this does not have to be the case. A data item can be empty but it still appears in the row. Note that empty is not the same as zero, and `NULL` is used in SQL to denote the absence of a value. A rough analogy might be a variable in Java of type `Integer` that could contain a reference to an object that represents zero (or some other integer value of course), or could contain `null`. We will come back to the notion of `NULL` when we look at SQL data types.

Database Catalog

In general, the **catalog** refers to the database **system tables**. System tables are similar to the tables used by your application, except that they are used to store information about the databases, the tables, and the composition of those tables, rather than storing application data. The catalog can be queried to find out what tables are available from a data source, what columns are defined for a given table, and so forth. The data describing the contents of a database is also referred to as **metadata** – data about data – or collectively as the **data dictionary**.

In the figure on page 999, 'catalog' refers to the entire `Technical_library` database.

Depending on the particular database to which you're connected, the catalog may contain other information related to accessing the database, such as security details, foreign keys and stored procedures.

> The column values that together uniquely identify a particular row, make up what is referred to as the primary key. Such columns are also called primary key fields or primary key values. Rows may also contain values that refer to key values in different tables. For example, the `auth_books` table contains a column `author_id` whose value is the primary key for a row in the `authors` table. When a table contains columns that are key columns for another table, values in those columns are referred to as foreign keys.

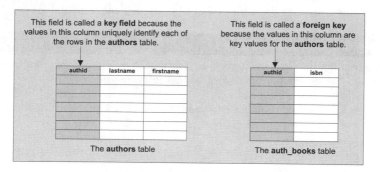

This field is called a **key field** because the values in this column uniquely identify each of the rows in the **authors** table.

This field is called a **foreign key** because the values in this column are key values for the **authors** table.

authid	lastname	firstname

The **authors** table

authid	isbn

The **auth_books** table

Many database servers are capable of executing pre-built scripts, as well as SQL statements. These server-based scripts are called by the application, and are executed by the database server. They are frequently referred to as **stored procedures**, or just **procedures.** They are used to package up commonly used operations on the database, particularly those that enforce specific business rules.

Introducing SQL

Structured Query Language (SQL) is accepted internationally as the official standard for relational database access. A major reason for the acceptance of SQL as *the* relational query language was the move towards client/server architectures that began in the late 1980's.

Not all versions and dialects of SQL are created equal, however. As vendors have incorporated SQL into their products, extensions to the grammar have often been added. That was convenient for the database vendors but tough for anyone else trying to work with more than one database vendor. In order to ensure SQL's place as a standard for database access, organizations like ISO and ANSI have worked with the industry to develop standards for SQL. The current ISO operating standard is SQL-92, to which JDBC adheres. Conformance to the standard does not guarantee that your SQL will work in every case though. A database system that is in conformance with the standard for SQL is not obliged to implement all the capabilities that the standard defines. Indeed most database systems do not do so.

SQL is different from other programming languages that you may be familiar with, in that it is declarative, not procedural. In other words, you don't use SQL to define complex processes, but rather use SQL to issue commands that define and manipulate data.

If you need more information about using SQL, you may want to check out *Instant SQL* by Joe Celko (ISBN 1-874416-50-8), published by Wrox Press.

The first thing that strikes you about SQL is that it is very readable. The way that each query is structured reads like a sentence in English. The syntax is easy to learn, and the constructs and concepts are very easy to grasp. Secondly, with SQL you always issue commands. You send the command to the database and the database either returns the required data, or performs the required action.

Let's look at the example that we saw earlier in the illustration – the `technical_library` database. How would we go about defining the tables we need to implement this database?

Try It Out — Designing Database Tables

The first step in designing the tables you need in your database is to decide what information you want to capture. Then you can design the tables around that information.

With our `technical_library` database, we want to keep track of the following kinds of things:

- ❑ Books
- ❑ Articles
- ❑ Authors
- ❑ Publishers

For each of these information categories, called **entities** in database jargon, we will want to record a specific set of data items, as follows:

Entity	Attribute
Books	ISBN
	Book title
	Author(s)
	Publisher
Articles	Author(s)
	Title
	Periodical it was published in
	Issue of publication
Authors	Last name
	First name
	Books published
	Articles published
Publishers	Publisher code
	Name

Let's start out with a table to keep track of the authors. We'll call this table `authors`, and describe the columns that we want for this table:

Column Heading	Description
authid	Unique identifier, since several authors could have the same name
lastname	Family name
firstname	First name
address1	Address line one
address2	Address line two
city	City
state_prov	State or province
postcode	Zip or postal code
country	Country
phone	Contact phone number
fax	Fax number
email	Email address

We need to assign a data type to each column heading that prescribes the form of the data in the column as it is stored in the table. Of course, these need to be data types meaningful to SQL, not necessarily Java data types. The data types for data in a relational database are those recognized by the SQL implementation supported by the database engine, and these types will have to be mapped to Java data types. Let's look at some examples of SQL data types:

SQL Data Type	Description
CHAR	Fixed length string of characters
VARCHAR	Variable length string of characters
BOOLEAN	Logical value – true or false
SMALLINT	Small integer value, from -127 to +127
INTEGER	Larger integer value, from -32767 to +32767
NUMERIC	A numeric value with a given **precision** – which is the number of decimal digits in the number, and a given **scale** – which is the number of digits after the decimal point. For instance, the value 234567.89 has a precision of 8 and a scale of 2.
FLOAT	Floating point value
CURRENCY	Stores monetary values
DOUBLE	Higher precision floating point value
DATE	Date
TIME	Time
DATETIME	Date and time
RAW	Raw binary data (can be used to store objects in a streamed binary format)

As we said earlier, NULL represents the absence of a value for any SQL type of data, but it is not the same as the null we have been using in Java. For one thing, you can't compare NULL with another NULL in SQL, you can only determine whether a particular attribute is or is not NULL. One effect of this is to introduce four potential values of type BOOLEAN – TRUE and FALSE which you would expect, NULL meaning the absence of a BOOLEAN value, and UNKNOWN which arises when the result cannot be determined – when you compare two NULL values for instance. Note that not all database systems allow BOOLEAN values to be NULL however.

From the data types in the `authors` table above, we can assign a data type for each column in the table that is appropriate for the kind of information in the column:

Column Name	Data Type
authid	INTEGER
lastname	VARCHAR
firstname	VARCHAR
address1	VARCHAR
address2	VARCHAR
city	VARCHAR
state_prov	VARCHAR
pzipcode	VARCHAR
country	VARCHAR
phone	VARCHAR
fax	VARCHAR
email	VARCHAR

How It Works

The column names tell us something about the information that will be stored in that field, but they don't tell the computer what type of information has been stored, or how to store it. While we are interested in the information stored in the columns, all the database engine wants to know is the *type* of information, and that's where the Data Type is invaluable.

You probably noticed that a column labeled `authid` has been placed at the top of the list of columns in the `authors` table. This is to give each record a unique identifier so that an individual record can easily be retrieved. Think of the nightmare you'd have if you were managing books and journals for a large library and you had several authors named John Smith. You wouldn't have any way of distinguishing one John Smith from the another. It's essential to give each row, or record, a unique identifier, and the author's ID serves this purpose here. Of course, it is not always necessary to introduce a column or columns specifically for this purpose. If your table already contains a column or combination of columns that will uniquely identify each row, then you can just use that.

Most of the data in the `authors` table is string information, so the VARCHAR data type was chosen as most convenient, since it allows as much or as little text information to be stored in that field as necessary. However, in practice it is likely to be more efficient to choose fixed length character fields.

> Not all databases support VARCHAR. In such cases, you will have to define these fields as CHAR type anyway, and estimate the maximum number of characters these fields will require. We will be doing this a little later when we get to a final definition of our database tables to allow the same table definitions to work with Access and other databases.

The next requirement is to be able to store information about books. One possibility is to store the data in the authors table using extra columns. If we wanted to store books in the authors table, we might consider adding two columns – title and publisher. However, this would seriously restrict the amount of information about books written by a particular author – to one book in fact. Since each record in the authors table has a unique author ID, each author can have only one record in the table, and thus only one book could be recorded for each author. In practice, authors will frequently write more than one book or article so we must have a way to cope with this. A much more realistic approach is to store books in a separate table.

Try It Out — Defining the Books Table

We can easily store information about individual books by creating a table that will store the following information:

Column Heading	Description
isbn	ISBN is a globally unique identifier for a book
title	Title of the book
pub_code	Code identifying the publisher of the book

We also need an SQL data type assignment for each column in our books table.

Column Heading	Data Type
isbn	VARCHAR
title	VARCHAR
pub_code	CHAR(8)

Here the publisher's code is a fixed length character field. The other two fields vary in length so we have assigned VARCHAR as the most convenient type. Where this is not supported, we would have to use the CHAR type with a length sufficient to accommodate whatever data might turn up – something that is not always easy to decide.

How It Works

The books table allows us to record the ISBN for each book, which uniquely identifies the book, its title, and the publisher of the book. Notice, however, that we haven't included any information about the author. This isn't an oversight. Since more than one author can be involved in the writing of a book and an author can be involved in the writing of more than one book, we need to add some more information linking an author with a book, that will be independent of the books table. Let's see how we might do that.

Designing an Intersection Table

It is not difficult to see that we could create the link between an author and a book by using the `isbn` (the book identifier) and the `authid`. If we create a table with these two pieces of information, we can make a record of each combination of authors and the books they authored or co-authored. This table is simple enough — it merely contains a column for the author identifier and the ISBN. The data types must match the corresponding columns in the `authors` and `books` tables:

Column heading	Data Type
authid	INTEGER
isbn	VARCHAR

This table effectively provides links between the `authors` table and the `books` table. A table like this that links two or more tables is called an **intersection table**, and is illustrated below.

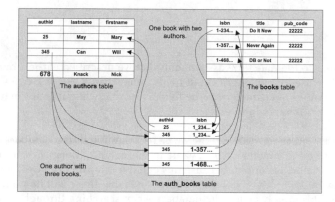

Now that we've decided on the design of the tables, let's see how we use SQL to create and add information to them. Rather than use the `VARCHAR` type for text fields, which is less widely supported, we will use fixed length `CHAR` types so that the database can be created in more environments. It may also be a bit more efficient.

SQL Statements

Most SQL statements, and certainly the ones we will be using, fall neatly into two groups:

❑ **Data Definition Language** (DDL) statements that are used to describe the tables and the data they contain

❑ **Data Manipulation Language** (DML) statements that are used to operate on data in the database. DML can be further divided into two groups:

  a. **SELECT statements** — statements that return a set of results

  b. Everything else — statements that don't return a set of results

In order to create the tables in our example, we would use DDL, which defines a syntax for commands such as CREATE TABLE and ALTER TABLE. We would use DDL statements to define the structure of the database. To carry out operations on the database, adding rows to a table or searching the data for instance, we would use DML statements.

Here's an example of a typical DDL statement:

```
CREATE TABLE authors (
    authid INT NOT NULL PRIMARY KEY,
    lastname CHAR(25) NOT NULL,
    firstname CHAR(15),
    address1 CHAR(25),
    address2 CHAR(25),
    city CHAR(25),
    state_prov CHAR(25),
    zipcode CHAR(10),
    country CHAR(15),
    phone CHAR(20),
    fax CHAR(20),
    email CHAR(25));
```

This is not so dissimilar to the data type assignments that we described earlier, but as you can see, in this SQL statement I've used fixed length CHAR fields rather than VARCHAR types. The values between parentheses are the number of characters in the field. Note that while it is not mandatory, by convention keywords in SQL are written in uppercase.

The clause NOT NULL PRIMARY KEY for the authid column tells the database two things. Firstly, no row of the table is allowed to contain a NULL value in this column. Every row in this column must always contain a valid value. Secondly, because this column is a primary key field, the database should create a unique index in the authid column. This ensures that there will be no more than one row with any given author ID. This greatly assists the database when searching through and ordering records. Think how difficult it would be to search for an entry in an encyclopedia without an index of unique values in one of the volumes.

This is the same principle on which database indexes work. Just to make sure we have some concrete information identifying an author, the lastname field is also not allowed to be NULL. Of course, all the tables in a database have to have unique names, otherwise it would not be possible to determine to which table you were referring. The names for the columns within a table must all be different for the same reason, and it is also helpful if you give all the non-key columns in all the tables in the database unique names, but this is not mandatory.

Now that we have a table created, we need to put data into the table. The SQL INSERT statement does exactly that.

INSERT Statements

There are three basic parts to an **insert statement**:

❑   Define the target table for inserting data

❑   Define the columns that will have values assigned

❑   Define the values for those columns

An insert statement begins with the keywords INSERT INTO, followed by the name of the target table:

```
INSERT INTO authors
```

You then supply a list of the names of the columns that will receive values. The columns are enclosed between parentheses:

```
(authid, lastname, firstname, email)
```

Lastly, you put the keyword VALUES followed by the values between parentheses for the columns you have identified:

```
VALUES (99, 'Phillips', 'Ron', 'ronp@happykitty.com')
```

Thus the complete INSERT statement is:

```
INSERT INTO authors (authid, lastname, firstname, email)
        VALUES (99, 'Phillips', 'Ron', 'ronp@happykitty.com')
```

The result of executing this statement is a new row inserted into the authors table. This statement does not fill in values for every column in the table, however. The SQL database will supply a NULL value where no values were supplied by the INSERT statement. If we had attempted to insert a row without a value for authid, the database would have reported an error, since the table was created with the authid column specified as NOT NULL.

A variation on the INSERT statement can be used when all column values are being filled by the statement: when no columns are specified, SQL assumes that the values following the VALUES keyword correspond to each column in the order that they were specified when the table was created. For example, you could add a row to the books table with the following statement:

```
INSERT INTO books (isbn, title, pub_code)
   VALUES ('1874416680', 'Beginning Linux Programming', 'WROX')
```

Since the books table contains only the three columns, the following statement has exactly the same results:

```
INSERT INTO books
   VALUES ('1874416680', 'Beginning Linux Programming', 'WROX')
```

Note how we have been spreading our SQL statements over two lines, just for readability. Whitespace is ignored generally in SQL, except in the middle of a string of course, so you can add whitespace wherever it helps to make your SQL code more readable.

Now, let us look at a basic SELECT statement, as this will give a starting point for getting some data back from the database we prepared earlier.

Select Statements

You use the SELECT statement to retrieve information from a database. There are four parts to an SQL SELECT statement:

- ❑ Defining what you want to retrieve
- ❑ Defining where you want to get it from
- ❑ Defining the conditions for retrieval – joining tables, and record filtering
- ❑ Defining the order in which you want to see the data.

So, how do you define what you want to retrieve? The first keyword in the SELECT statement, unsurprisingly, is SELECT. This tells the database that we intend to get some data back in the form of a **resultset**, sometimes referred to as a **recordset**. A **resultset** is just a table of data – with fixed numbers of columns and rows – that is some subset of data from a database table generated as a result of the SELECT statement.

The next identifier allows us to define what we want to see – it allows us to specify which columns we want to retrieve and to have as our resultset table headers. We specify each column name as part of a comma-separated list.

So our sample statement so far looks like:

```
SELECT firstname, lastname, authid
```

We now have to specify which table we want to retrieve the data from. When creating a table, there is nothing to stop the developer giving similar column names to each table, so we must ensure that there are no ambiguities when selecting similar column names from two or more tables.

We specify the table or tables that we wish to retrieve data from, in a **FROM clause**. This clause immediately follows the SELECT clause. A FROM clause consists of the keyword FROM, followed by a comma-separated list of tables that you wish to access:

```
FROM authors
```

Giving:

```
SELECT firstname, lastname, authid FROM authors
```

This is a complete statement that will retrieve the name, surname and author ID from each row in the `authors` table.

When a resultset is retrieved from the database, each resultset column has a label that, by default, is derived from the column names in the `SELECT` statement. It is also possible to provide **aliases** for the table column names that are to be used for the resultset column names. Aliases are also referred to as **correlation names**, and are often used so that column names can be abbreviated. Column aliases appear after the column names in the `SELECT` statement following the keyword `AS`. For example:

```
SELECT firstname, lastname, authid AS author_identifier
       FROM authors
```

would alias the `authid` as `author_identifier`. If you require an alias for a column name that includes whitespace, just put the alias between double quotes in the `SELECT` statement.

If you want to select all columns in a `SELECT` statement, there is a wildcard notation you can use. You just specify the columns as `*` to indicate that you want to select all the columns in a table. For example, to select all the columns from the `authors` table you would write:

```
SELECT * FROM authors
```

Suppose I wanted to limit the rows returned by a `SELECT` operation to only include authors that reside within the UK. In order to accomplish that, I would add a `WHERE` clause. `WHERE` clauses are used to filter the set of rows produced as the result of a `SELECT` operation. For example, to get a list of authors in the UK:

```
SELECT lastname, firstname FROM authors
   WHERE country = 'UK'
```

You can also specify multiple criteria for row selection in a `WHERE` clause. For example, I might want to get a list of authors in the UK for whom an email address is also on record:

```
SELECT lastname, firstname, phone FROM authors
   WHERE country = 'UK'
     AND email IS NOT NULL
```

Note the construction of the `WHERE` clause – there are two conditions that a row is required to satisfy before it will be returned. Firstly, the `country` field must contain a value that is equal to the string value UK, and the `email` field must not be `NULL`. If we wanted to find rows where the field is `NULL`, we would omit the `NOT`.

Let's look at one final example of a SELECT statement – a table join. Suppose we want to see a list of all authors and the books they have written. We can write a statement that will return this information like this:

```
SELECT a.lastname, a.firstname, b.title
  FROM authors a, books b, auth_books ab
 WHERE a.authid = ab.authid
   AND b.isbn = ab.isbn
```

The table join appears in the first line of the WHERE clause; we specify the condition for each row that the authid columns of the authors table and the auth_books table must be equal. We also specify that the isbn column of books and auth_books must be equal.

Notice also one small addition to the statement. As you saw earlier, we can alias column names by specifying an alternative name after each table identifier, or expression using the AS keyword. In this statement we are aliasing the table names in the FROM clause by simply putting the alias following the table name. The authors table is aliased as a, the books table is aliased as b and the auth_books table is aliased as ab. Back in the first part of the SELECT statement, the column names are 'qualified' by the aliases for each table. This is the way that column name ambiguities are removed. Since the authid column name appears in more than one table, if we did not have a qualifier in front of each usage of the authid column name, the database engine would have no way of knowing from which table the column was required. Note that if you specify an alias in the FROM clause, column names in the WHERE clause must be qualified with the appropriate table alias.

Update Statements

Update statements provide a way of modifying existing data in a table. Update statements are constructed in a similar way to SELECT statements. You first start with the UPDATE keyword, followed by the name of the table you wish to modify:

```
UPDATE authors
```

You then specify the SET keyword, and the data members you wish to modify, with their new values:

```
SET lastname = 'Burk'
```

Finally, the WHERE clause is used to filter the records that we wish to update. An update statement cannot be performed across a table join, so the WHERE clause is not used to specify a join of this type.

```
WHERE authid = 27
```

The full statement:

```
UPDATE authors SET lastname = 'Burk' WHERE authid = 27
```

will update the author record to reflect a change in last name for the author with the ID of 27.

Update statements do not return a resultset, they merely modify data in the database.

Delete Statements

Delete statements provide a way of deleting particular rows from tables in a database. Delete statements consist of the DELETE keyword, a FROM clause and a WHERE clause. For example:

```
DELETE FROM books WHERE isbn = '0131259075'
```

deletes the record in the books table with the ISBN value '0131259075'. In the case of the books table, there can only be one row with this value, since its primary key is the ISBN. If a similar DELETE statement were executed against the auth_books table, however, it would delete all rows with the matching ISBN value.

By now you should have a reasonably clear idea of:

❑   The way SQL is constructed

❑   How to read SQL statements

❑   How to construct basic SQL statements

> You can expect SQL statements to work with relational databases that adhere to ANSI standards, although each database typically implements a subset of the full standard. For this reason you need to understand the functionality of the SQL that is used by the underlying database you are using, as this will affect the way you use JDBC to write your Java applications.

The JDBC Package

The JDBC library was designed as an interface for executing SQL statements, and not as a high-level abstraction layer for data access. So, although it wasn't designed to automatically map Java classes to rows in a database, it allows large scale applications to be written to the JDBC interface without worrying too much about which database will be deployed with the application. A JDBC application is well insulated from the particular characteristics of the database system being used, and therefore doesn't have to be re-engineered for specific databases.

From the user's point of view, the Java application looks something like this:

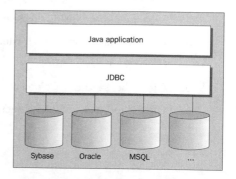

JDBC manages this by having an implementation of the JDBC interface for each specific database – a **driver**. This handles the mapping of Java method calls in the JDBC classes to the database API. We'll learn more about this later on.

Relating JDBC to ODBC

One of the fundamental principles of JDBC's design was to make it practical to build JDBC drivers based on other database APIs. There is a very close mapping between the JDBC architecture and API, and their ODBC counterparts, fundamentally because they are all based on the same standard, the SQL X/Open CLI; but JDBC is a lot easier to use. Because of their common ancestry, they share some important conceptual components:

Driver Manager	Loads database drivers, and manages the connections between the application and the driver.
Driver	Translates API calls into operations for a specific data source.
Connection	A session between an application and a database.
Statement	A SQL statement to perform a query or update operation.
Metadata	Information about returned data, the database and the driver.
Result Set	Logical set of columns and rows of data returned by executing a statement.

JDBC Basics

Assuming you have followed the instructions given at the start of the chapter, and have the requisite sample database and database driver installed on your machine, we are ready to look at a basic JDBC program that involves the following steps:

- ❏ Import the necessary classes
- ❏ Load the JDBC driver
- ❏ Identify the data source
- ❏ Allocate a `Connection` object
- ❏ Allocate a `Statement` object
- ❏ Execute a query using the `Statement` object
- ❏ Retrieve data from the returned `ResultSet` object
- ❏ Close the `ResultSet`
- ❏ Close the `Statement` object
- ❏ Close the `Connection` object

Throughout this chapter we will work towards accumulating a sufficient understanding of JDBC to implement the essential elements of such a program.

The JDBC architecture is based on a collection of Java interfaces and classes that together enable you to connect to data sources, to create and execute SQL statements, and to retrieve and modify data in a database. These operations are illustrated in the figure below:

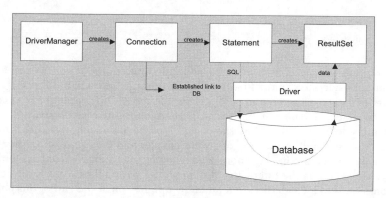

Each of the boxes in the illustration represents a JDBC class or interface that has a fundamental role in accessing a relational database. All your work with JDBC will begin with the `DriverManager` class, but before we look at that let's set up our `technical_library` database so that we will be ready to use it as we progress.

Setting up a Database

Before we get started on learning about the `DriverManager` class, it's worth while setting up a sample database and a suitable JDBC driver for our code to use. The database is called `technical_library`, and it stores information on technical books. This is implemented as an MS Access database and you can download it together with the sample code from the Wrox Web site.

In MS Windows, to use this database with the application that we are going to construct in this chapter, you can set up an Access database driver for the database in the **ODBC Data Source Administrator** dialog box which can be found via **Start -> Settings -> Control Panel**, and then double-clicking on the **ODBC Data Sources** icon. Select the **System DSN** tab at the top of the dialog box, and click on the **Add...** button at the right. In the list box that comes up, select **Microsoft Access Driver (*.mdb)**, and then click on **Finish**. A further dialog box will then come up with the title **ODBC Microsoft Access Setup**. In the **Data Source Name** text box at the top of the dialog, type in technical_library. Type in a suitable description in the **Description** text field if you wish. In the **Database** section of the dialog, click on the **Select** button, and in the file browsing dialog box that comes up, find and select your saved version of technical_library.mdb, then click **OK**. Now click on **OK** in the **ODBC Microsoft Access Setup** dialog. The **System DSN** section of the initial **ODBC Data Source Administrator** dialog should now have technical_library in the list of system data sources available. Click on the **OK** button at the bottom of the dialog to exit. Barring unforeseen problems you should now be able to use this database with the programs in this chapter.

If you're working with a database program other than Access you will need to obtain an appropriate driver for it if you do not already have one. An up-to-date list of suitable drivers for various databases can be found at http://www.javasoft.com/products/jdbc/jdbc.drivers.html.

If you have a database other than Access and the correct driver already set up, you can use a small Java class, build_tables, also included with the book's code, to create the sample database's tables. Simply run:

```
java build_tables buildlibrary_access.sql
```

Note that the program to set up the database takes a little time to run. If you are using something other than Access, you may need to edit the first few lines of the text file buildlibrary_access.sql to use the appropriate database driver, and possibly edit the rest of the instructions to accommodate the data types used by your database system. It is quite common for database systems not to support all of the SQL capabilities defined by the ANSI standard. If you have no luck getting the sample database up and running first time around, try reading on in this chapter and then re-reading your driver and database documentation before having another go. Having got a suitable database and JDBC driver installed, you can try running the InteractiveSQL program that we'll be using in this chapter to show how to send commands to a database. We'll build the application at the end of this chapter, by which time its workings should be plain to you.

> **In all the examples we will write in this chapter we'll be using the JDBC-ODBC Bridge driver — sun.jdbc.odbc.JdbcOdbcDriver — to access the MS Access database, technical_library.mdb, that we've assumed has been set up with a Microsoft Access ODBC driver as described in the section earlier.**

DriverManager

JDBC database drivers are defined by classes that implement the Driver interface. The DriverManager class is responsible for establishing connections to the data sources, accessed through the JDBC drivers. If any JDBC driver has been identified in the "jdbc.drivers" system property (see below) on your computer, then the DriverManager class will attempt to load that when it is loaded.

The system properties are actually stored in a Properties object. The Properties class, defined in the java.util package, associates values with keys in a map, and the contents of the map defines a set of system properties. In general, each key is supplied as a String and the value corresponding to a key can be any valid object. Thus you can use a Properties object to supply as much information as is required by your driver – or anything else that interacts with the system properties for that matter. You just set the key/value pairs for the Properties object that are needed.

You can set the "jdbc.drivers" system property by calling the setProperty() method for the System class, for example:

```
System.setProperty("jdbc.drivers","sun.jdbc.odbc.JdbcOdbcDriver");
```

The first argument is the key for the property to be set and the second argument is the value. This statement identifies the JDBC-ODBC Bridge driver in the system property. This driver supports connections to any ODBC supported database. If you want to specify multiple drivers in the system property value, you should separate the driver names within the string by colons.

If the security manager permits it, you can obtain a reference to the `Properties` object for your system by calling the static `getProperties()` method for the `System` class. If there is no `Properties` object defined containing the system properties, one will be created with a default set of properties. The `Properties` class defines a `list()` method that you can use to list all your system properties as follows:

```
System.getProperties().list(System.out);    // List all properties
```

You could try this out in a simple program of your own if you want to see what your system properties are. The `Properties` class also defines a `setProperty()` method, so once you have a `Properties` object, you can set properties directly by calling this method for the object.

If a security manager is in effect and a security policy has been set up on your system, it may be that you will not be allowed to set the system property, in which case the `setProperty()` call with throw an exception of type `SecurityException`. In this situation, to include the driver that you want to use, you can load the driver explicitly by calling the static `forName()` method in the `Class` class, and passing a `String` object as an argument containing the driver class name. For example:

```
Class.forName("sun.jdbc.odbc.JdbcOdbcDriver");    // Load the ODBC driver
```

The `forName()` method can throw an exception of type `ClassNotFoundException` if the driver class cannot be found, and this must be caught, so a call to the function has to appear in a `try` block with an appropriate `catch` block.

Each driver class will typically create an instance of itself when it is loaded, and register that instance by calling the `DriverManager` class method automatically. You don't need – indeed you can't – create `DriverManager` objects, and all the methods in the `DriverManager` class are `static`. There are `DriverManager` class methods that can be used to determine which drivers have been loaded, as well as methods that register or unregister drivers 'on the fly'. However, for the most part you will only need to call the method that establishes a connection to a data source.

When you need a connection to a JDBC driver, you don't create a new object encapsulating the connection yourself – you ask the `DriverManager` to do it for you. The `DriverManager` class provides several `static` methods for creating objects that implement the `Connection` interface, which we will get to in a moment, and that encapsulate a connection to a database. These are all overloaded versions of the `getConnection()` method.

Creating a Connection to a Data Source

A connection to a specific data source is represented by an object of a class that implements the `Connection` interface. Before you can execute any SQL statements, you must first have a `Connection` object. A `Connection` object represents an established connection to a particular data source, and you use it to create a `Statement` object that enables you to define and execute specific SQL statements. A `Connection` object can also be used to query the data source for information about the data in the database (the metadata), including the names of the available tables, information about the columns for a particular table, and so on.

There are three overloaded `getConnection()` methods in the `DriverManager` class that return a `Connection` object. In the simplest case you can obtain a `Connection` object that represents a session for your database with the following statement:

```
Connection databaseConnection = DriverManager.getConnection(source);
```

The argument, `source`, is a `String` object defining the URL that identifies where the database is located. Note that this is a `String` object specifying the URL, not an object of the `URL` class that we have seen earlier.

URLs and JDBC

As you saw when we discussed the `URL` class, a URL describes an electronic resource, such as a World Wide Web page, or a file on an FTP server, in a manner that uniquely identifies that resource. URLs play a central role in networked application development in Java. JDBC uses URLs to identify the locations of both drivers and data sources. JDBC URLs have the format:

```
jdbc:<subprotocol>://<data source identifier>
```

The scheme `jdbc` indicates that the URL refers to a JDBC data source. The sub-protocol identifies which JDBC driver to use. For example, the JDBC-ODBC Bridge uses the driver identifier `odbc`.

The JDBC driver dictates the format of the data source identifier. In our example above, the JDBC-ODBC Bridge simply uses the ODBC data source name. In order to use the ODBC driver with the `technical_library` ODBC data source, you would create a URL with the format:

```
jdbc:odbc:technical_library
```

The next step to getting data to or from a database is to create a `Connection` object. The `Connection` object essentially establishes a context in which you can create and execute SQL commands. Since the data source that we will use in this chapter's examples doesn't require a user name or password, the simplest form of the `getConnection()` method can be used.

We could exercise the `getConnection()` method in a working example.

Try It Out — Making a Connection

The following source code is a minimal JDBC program that creates a `Connection` object. In this instance the connection will be established using only the URL for the data source. In the next section we will look at how you can also supply a user ID and a password when this is necessary.

```java
import java.sql.*;

public class MakingTheConnection
{
  public static void main(String[] args)
  {
    // Load the driver
    try
    {
      // Load the driver class
      Class.forName("sun.jdbc.odbc.JdbcOdbcDriver");

      // Define the data source for the driver
      String sourceURL = "jdbc:odbc:technical_library";

      // Create a connection through the DriverManager
      Connection databaseConnection =
                        DriverManager.getConnection(sourceURL);
    }
    catch(ClassNotFoundException cnfe)
    {
      System.err.println(cnfe);
    }
    catch(SQLException sqle)
    {
      System.err.println(sqle);
    }
  }
}
```

How It Works

Naturally we need to import the classes and interfaces for the JDBC library. These classes are defined in the `java.sql` package. The `forName()` method call at the beginning of `main()` ensures that the JDBC driver class required by our program is loaded. This will guarantee that any initialization that the JDBC driver must do will be completed before our code actually uses the driver. As we said earlier, the `forName()` method will throw a `ClassNotFoundException` if the driver class cannot be found, and this exception must be caught.

The `forName()` method call causes the Java interpreter's class loader to load the class for the driver specified by the argument. When the driver class is loaded, the class loader will determine if the driver class has any `static` initialization code. If it does, it will execute the `static` initialization code immediately after the class has been loaded. That is how the driver class is able to instantiate itself, and register the instance that is created with the `DriverManager` object. It can also execute other initialization code that may be required, such as loading a dynamic link library if the driver uses native methods for instance, and since this all happens when the class is loaded it is guaranteed to happen before any other driver methods get called.

Most JDBC methods handle errors by throwing an exception of the type SQLException, and the getConnection() method of the DriverManager class does exactly that, so we also have a catch block that handles the SQLException exception. In this example, a simple message will be displayed in the event of a problem loading the JDBC driver or creating a Connection to the data source. In the next chapter, you will learn more sophisticated error handling techniques.

More Complex Connections

If the database requires a user name and password in order to gain access to it, you can use the second form of the getConnection() method:

```
databaseConnection = DriverManager.getConnection(sourceURL,
                                                  myUserName,
                                                  myPassword);
```

All three arguments here are of type String. In some cases, however, the user name and password may not be enough to establish a connection. In order to accommodate those situations, the DriverManager class provides another getConnection() method that accepts a Properties object as an argument.

To supply the properties required by your JDBC driver, you can create a Properties object using the default class constructor, and then set the properties that you need by calling its setProperty() method. In general, at least the user name and password need to be set.

The code fragment below illustrates creation of a connection for the JBDC driver for ODBC.

```
import java.util.Properties;

// ...
```

```
String driverName = "sun.jdbc.odbc.JdbcOdbcDriver";
String sourceURL = "jdbc.odbc:technical_library";

try
{
  Class.forName (driverName);
  Properties prop = new Properties();
  prop.setProperty("user", "ItIsMe");
  prop.setProperty("password", "abracadabra");
  Connection databaseConnection = DriverManager.getConnection(sourceURL, prop);
}
catch(ClassNotFoundException cnfe)
{
  System.err.println("Error loading " + driverName);
}
catch(SQLException sqle)
{
  System.err.println(sqle);
}
```

Note that the `Properties` class is imported from the `java.util` package.

While this pretty much covers everything that most developers will ever do with the `DriverManager` class, there are other methods that may be useful. We will take a look at these next.

Logging JDBC Driver Operations

The `DriverManager` class provides a pair of access methods for the `PrintWriter` object, that is used by the `DriverManager` class and all JDBC drivers, to record logging and trace information. These allow you to set, or reroute, the `PrintWriter` that the driver uses to log information. The two access methods are:

```
public static void setLogWriter(PrintWriter out)
public static PrintWriter getLogWriter()
```

You can disable logging by passing a `null` argument to the `setLogWriter()` method.

Examining the log can be pretty interesting. If you want to find out what's going on behind the scenes, take a look at the information generated by the JDBC-ODBC driver. You'll get a very good idea of how that driver works.

Your application can print to the `PrintWriter` stream using the static `println()` method defined in the `DriverManager` class. Just pass a `String` object as an argument containing the message you want to record in the log. This method is typically used by JDBC drivers, but it may prove useful for debugging or logging database-related errors or events.

Setting the Login Timeout

The `DriverManager` class provides a pair of access methods for the login timeout period. These allow you to specify a timeout period (in seconds) that limits the time that a driver is prepared to wait for logging in to the database. The two access methods are:

```
public static void setLoginTimeout(int seconds)
public static int getLoginTimeout()
```

Specifying a non-default timeout period can be useful for troubleshooting applications that are having difficulty connecting to a remote database server. For example, if your application is trying to connect to a very busy server, the applications might appear to have hung. You can tell the `DriverManager` to fail the connection attempt by specifying a timeout period. The code fragment below tells the `DriverManager` to fail the login attempt after 60 seconds:

```
String driverName = "sun.jdbc.odbc.JdbcOdbcDriver";
String sourceURL =  "jdbc:odbc:technical_library";

try
{
  Class.forName(driverName);
```

```
  // fail after 60 seconds
  DriverManager.setLoginTimeout(60);

  Connection databaseConnection = DriverManager.getConnection(sourceURL);
}
catch(ClassNotFoundException cnfe)
{
  System.err.println("Error loading " + driverName);
}
catch(SQLException sqle)
{
  System.err.println(sqle);
}
```

More on Drivers

When the `DriverManager` class has been loaded, it is then possible to connect to a data source using a particular driver. A driver is represented by an object of type `Driver`. Driver implementations come in four flavors:

❏   JDBC-ODBC Bridge driver

❏   Native API partly-Java

❏   Net protocol all-Java client

❏   Native protocol all-Java

Understanding a little of how drivers are built, and their limitations, will help you to decide which driver is most appropriate for your application.

JDBC-ODBC Bridge Driver

The JDBC-ODBC Bridge – `"sun.jdbc.odbc.JdbcOdbcDriver"` – included with the JDK, enables Java applications to access data through drivers written to the ODBC standard. The driver bridge is very useful for accessing data in data sources for which no pure JDBC drivers exist.

The bridge works by translating the JDBC methods into ODBC function calls. It has the advantage of working with a huge number of ODBC drivers, but it only works under the Microsoft Windows and Sun Solaris operating systems.

Native API/Partly Java Driver

This class of driver is quite similar to the bridge driver. It consists of Java code that accesses data through native methods – typically calls to a particular vendor library. Like the bridge driver, this class of driver is convenient when a C data access library already exists, but it isn't usually very portable across platforms.

Net Protocol All Java Client

This class of driver is implemented as 'middleware', with the client driver completely implemented in Java. This client driver communicates with a separate middleware component (usually through TCP/IP) which translates JDBC requests into database access calls. This form of driver is an extension of the previous class, with the Java and native API separated into separate client and proxy processes.

Native Protocol All Java

This class of driver communicates directly to the database server using the server's native protocol. Unlike the previous driver type, there is no translation step that converts the Java-initiated request into some other form. The client talks directly to the server. If this class of driver is available for your database, then this is the one you should use.

> **There are a number of JDBC drivers available. As we mentioned earlier, the best source of up-to-date information about JDBC drivers is from the JavaSoft JDBC drivers page on their Web site:**
> http://www.javasoft.com/products/jdbc/jdbc.drivers.html.

The only time that you are likely to come into contact with the Driver object is when you install it. Your applications need not ever interact directly with the Driver object itself since the DriverManager class takes care of communicating with it. When you call the getConnection() method of the DriverManager class, it iterates through the drivers that are registered with the DriverManager, and asks each one in turn if it can handle the URL that you have passed to it. The first driver that can satisfy the connection defined by the URL creates a Connection object, which is passed back to the application by way of the DriverManager.

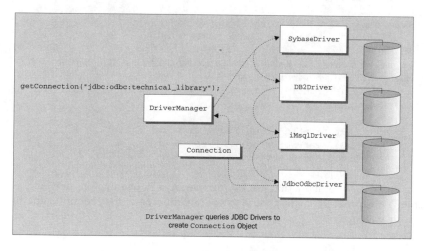

DriverManager queries JDBC Drivers to create Connection Object

There are occasions, however, when you may want to query a specific driver for information, such as its version number. For example, you may know that a particular feature that your program makes use of wasn't incorporated into a driver until version 2.1. You can query the driver to get the version number so your program can handle an earlier version intelligently.

In order to get the `Driver` object, you call the static `getDriver()` method of the `DriverManager` class, passing the URL of the data source to it as the argument. If the `DriverManager` finds a driver that can accommodate the data source, a reference to a `Driver` object encapsulating it is returned. The code fragment below illustrates testing the version of a JDBC driver, looking for versions that are 1.1 or greater.

```
// Load the driver class
Class.forName("sun.jdbc.odbc.JdbcOdbcDriver");

// Define the data source for the driver
String sourceURL = "jdbc:odbc:technical_library";

// Test for driver version
int verMajor;
float verComplete;
float verPreferred;

// Set the minimum preferred version
verPreferred = 1.1f;

// Set the driver
Driver theDriver = DriverManager.getDriver(sourceURL);

// Get the version number to the left of the decimal point, e.g. 1 out of 1.0
verMajor = theDriver.getMajorVersion();

/* Make a float of the complete version number by adding the minor number
    (to the right of the decimal point, e.g. 1108 out of 1.1108)
    on to verMajor */

    verComplete = Float.parseFloat(verMajor + "." +
                theDriver.getMinorVersion());

// Test to see if we have a suitable version of the driver
if(verComplete >= verPreferred)
    System.out.println("Version " + verComplete + " found");
    //Make the connection...
else
    System.out.println("Required version of driver (" +
                verPreferred + ") not found");
    // Otherwise drop out...
```

In practice you could do a lot more that just output messages depending on the version of the driver that is available. Your program might choose to operate differently to account for the limitations of an earlier version for instance.

Statement Objects

A `Statement` object is an object of a class that implements the `Statement` interface. When a `Statement` object is created, it provides a workspace for you to create an SQL query, execute it, and retrieve any results that are returned. You can also assemble multiple SQL statements into a batch, and submit them for processing as a batch to the database.

`Statement` objects are created by calling the `createStatement()` method of a valid `Connection` object. Once you have created a `Statement` object, you can use it to execute an SQL query by calling the `executeQuery()` method for your `Statement` object. You pass a `String` object containing the text of your SQL query as the argument to the method.

The resultset from the query is returned as an object of type `ResultSet`. For instance, if you have a `Statement` object, `statement`, you could write:

```
ResultSet results = statement.executeQuery
                      ("SELECT lastname, firstname FROM authors");
```

This will execute the `SELECT` statement that appears in the argument.

When you want to batch up several SQL statements, you call the `addBatch()` method in the `Statement` object for each of them, passing the `String` object containing the SQL as the argument. When you finally want to execute the batch of SQL that you have created, you call the `executeBatch()` method for the statement object. To clear the batch of statements in readiness for a new set, you call the `clearBatch()` method for the `Statement` object. Because a batch of SQL statements can generate multiple resultsets, accessing them is a little complicated. It involves calling the `getResultSet()` method for the `Statement` object to retrieve the first resultset, and then using `getXXX()` methods for the object reference that is returned to access the contents. To move to the next resultset you call `getMoreResults()` for the `Statement` object. This returns true if the next result is another resultset, and false if the next result is not a resultset or there are no more results. You can then call `getResultSet()` again to obtain a reference to the next resultset if there is one. This is a relatively rare requirement so we won't go into further detail on this.

JDBC provides two other kinds of objects that you can use to execute SQL statements. These objects implement interfaces that are sub-interfaces of the `Statement` interface; the interface `PreparedStatement` that extends the `Statement` interface, and the interface `CallableStatement` that extends the `PreparedStatement` interface.

A `PreparedStatement` reference is returned by the `prepareStatement()` method in the `Connection` interface. In the simplest case, you just pass a `String` object specifying the text of an SQL statement to the method as the argument, but there is a more complex version of the method that provides you with more control over the resultset that is produced. `PreparedStatement` objects differ from `Statement` objects in that the SQL statement is pre-compiled, and can have placeholders for runtime parameter values. `PreparedStatement` objects are particularly useful when a statement will be executed many times (for example, adding new rows to a table), since substantial performance gains can be achieved in many cases.

This is due to the fact that a prepared statement is parsed once and reused, whereas the SQL for a `Statement` object has to be parsed by the server each time it is executed. `PreparedStatement` objects are also helpful when it is not convenient to create a single string containing the entire SQL statement. We'll see an example later in this chapter that will show the same SQL statement executed via both `Statement` and `PreparedStatement` objects.

A `CallableStatement` reference is returned by the `prepareCall()` method for a `Connection` object. There are two overloaded versions of this method, one requiring a single `String` JDBC-ODBC Bridge argument that defines the SQL for the stored procedure, and the other with additional parameters providing more control over the resultset that is produced. You use a `CallableStatement` object for calling procedures on the database. As we said earlier, many database engines have the ability to execute procedures. This allows business logic and rules to be defined at the server level, rather than relying on applications to replicate and enforce those rules.

Whichever type of `Statement` reference you are using, the results of an SQL query are always returned in the same way, so let's look at that.

ResultSet Objects

The results of executing an SQL query are returned in the form of an object that implements the `ResultSet` interface, and that contains the table produced by the SQL query. The `ResultSet` object contains something called a '**cursor**' that you can manipulate to refer to any particular row in the resultset. This initially points to a position immediately preceding the first row. Calling the `next()` method for the `ResultSet` object will move the cursor to the next position. You can reset the cursor to the first or last row at any time by calling the `first()` or `last()` method for the `ResultSet` object. You also have methods `beforeFirst()` and `afterLast()` to set the cursor position before the first row or after the last. The `previous()` method for the `ResultSet` object moves the cursor from its current position to the previous row. This ability to scroll backwards through a resultset is a recent innovation in JDBC (with JDBC 2) and is dependent on your database and your driver supporting this capability.

Usually you will want to process rows from a resultset in a loop, and you have a couple of ways to do this. Both the `next()` and `previous()` methods return `true` if the move is to a valid row, and `false` if you fall off the end, so you can use this to control a `while` loop. You could process all the rows in a resultset with the following loop:

```
while(resultset.next())
{
   // Process the row...
}
```

This assumes `resultset` is the object returned as a result of executing a query and the `resultset` object starts out in its default state with the cursor set to one before the first row. You can also use the `isLast()` or `isFirst()` methods to test whether you have reached the end or the beginning of the resultset.

Now we know how to get at the rows in a resultset, let's look into how we access the fields in a row.

Accessing Data in a Resultset

Using the `ResultSet` reference, you can retrieve the value of any column for the current row (as specified by the cursor) by name or by position. You can also determine information about the columns such as the number of columns returned, or the data types of columns. The `ResultSet` interface declares the following basic methods for retrieving column data for the current row as Java types:

`getAsciiStream()`	`getTimestamp()`	`getTime()`
`getBoolean()`	`getBinaryStream()`	`getString()`
`getDate()`	`getBytes()`	`getByte()`
`getInt()`	`getFloat()`	`getDouble()`
`getShort()`	`getObject()`	`getLong()`

Note that this is not a comprehensive list, but it is not likely you will need to know about the others. For a full list of the methods available take a look at the documentation for the `ResultSet` interface. There are overloaded versions of each of the methods shown above that provide two ways of identifying the column containing the data. The column can be selected by passing the SQL column name as a `String` argument, or by passing an index value for the column of type `int`, where the first column has the index value 1. Note that column names are not case sensitive so `"FirstName"` is the same as `"firstname"`.

The `getDate()`, `getTime()` and `getTimestamp()` methods return objects of type `Date`, `Time`, and `TimeStamp` respectively. The `getAsciiStream()` method returns an object of type `InputStream` that you can use to read the data as a stream of ASCII characters. This is primarily for use with values of the SQL type `LONGVARCHAR` which can be very long strings that you would want to read piecemeal. Most of the basic data access methods are very flexible in converting from SQL data types to Java data types. For instance if you use `getInt()` on a field of type `CHAR`, the method will attempt to parse the characters assuming they specify an integer. Equally, you can read numeric SQL types using the `getString()` method.

With all these methods, an absence of a value – an SQL `NULL` – is returned as the equivalent of zero, or `null` if an object reference is returned. Thus a `NULL` boolean field will return false and a `NULL` numeric field will return 0. If a database access error occurs when executing a `getXXX()` method for a resultset, an exception of type `SQLException` will be thrown.

The JDBC API provides access to metadata, not only for the `Connection` object, but also for the `ResultSet` object. The JDBC API provides a `ResultSetMetaData` object that lets you peek into the data behind the `ResultSet` object. If you plan on providing interactive browsing facilities in your JDBC applications, you'll find this particularly useful and we'll see how to do this later.

Together, these classes and interfaces make up the bulk of the JDBC components that you will be working with. Let's now put them into action with a simple code example.

Try It Out — Using a Connection

We'll do something useful with the `Connection` object created by changing our
`MakingTheConnection` class into a new class for accessing the `technical_library` database. You
can alter the code from the earlier example to that shown below:

```java
import java.sql.*;

public class MakingAStatement
{
  public static void main(String[] args)
  {
    // Load the driver
    try
    {
      // Load the driver class
      Class.forName("sun.jdbc.odbc.JdbcOdbcDriver");

      // This defines the data source for the driver
      String sourceURL = new String("jdbc:odbc:technical_library");

      // Create connection through the DriverManager
      Connection databaseConnection =
                          DriverManager.getConnection(sourceURL);

      Statement statement = databaseConnection.createStatement();

      ResultSet authorNames = statement.executeQuery
                              ("SELECT lastname, firstname FROM authors");

      // Output the resultset data
      while(authorNames.next())
        System.out.println(authorNames.getString("lastname")+" "+
        authorNames.getString("firstname"));
    }
    catch(ClassNotFoundException cnfe)
    {
      System.err.println(cnfe);
    }
    catch(SQLException sqle)
    {
      System.err.println(sqle);
    }
  }
}
```

You can save this as `MakingAStatement.java`. This program will list all the author names, one
author to a line, with the last name first on each line.

How It Works

Once the connection has been established by the getConnection() method call, the next step is to create a Statement object that enables you to execute an SQL statement and retrieve the results. To create a Statement object we simply call the createStatement() method for the Connection object.

Once we have created the statement object, we execute an SQL query against the connected database by passing a String object as the argument to the executeQuery() method for the statement object. The executeQuery() method returns an object that implements the ResultSet interface. As the name implies, the ResultSet interface enables you to get at information that was retrieved by the query. You can think of the ResultSet interface as providing row-at-a-time access to a virtual table of results. The ResultSet object provides an internal **cursor** or logical pointer to keep track of its current row. When the ResultSet is first returned, the cursor is positioned just before the first row of data.

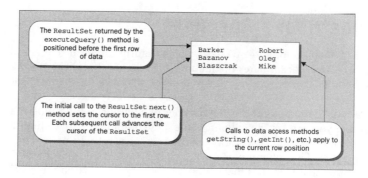

After executing the query and before any column data can be accessed, the row position needs to be advanced by calling the next() method, and we do this in the while loop condition. The next() method advances the row position and returns a boolean value that indicates if the ResultSet is positioned at a valid row (true), or that there are no more rows (false). Thus our while loop continues until we have output the data from all the rows that are in the resultset, authorNames.

Within the while loop, we access the data in the columns using the getString() method for the ResultSet object. In both cases we use the column names to reference the column. Accessing the columns by name has the advantage that you don't need to know the order of the columns. On the other hand you do need to know the column names. If you wanted to process the columns by their index position, you would just use the index values 1 and 2 to refer to data in the first and second columns respectively. Using the column position is slightly faster than using the column name since there is no additional overhead in matching a column name to determine a particular column position. It can also be more convenient to refer to columns using their position when you want to identify the column by means of an expression.

Note that in spite of the illustration above, the rows in the resultset are not ordered. If you want to output the rows in lastname order, you need to change the SQL statement to sort the rows, as follows:

```
ResultSet authorNames = statement.executeQuery(
            "SELECT lastname, firstname FROM authors ORDER BY lastname");
```

The rows in the resultset will be sorted in `lastname` order – in ascending sequence by default. To sort in descending sequence you should add the keyword `DESC` to the end of the SQL statement. You can sort on multiple columns by separating the column names by commas. The sorting applies to the columns successively from left to right, so if you specify the sort columns as `lastname, firstname` in the `SELECT` statement then the rows in the resultset will be ordered by `lastname`, and where two last names are the same, by first name. For instance, if we want the rows in the resultset `authorNames` to be sorted in descending sequence, we could write:

```
ResultSet authorNames = statement.executeQuery(
        "SELECT lastname, firstname FROM authors
            ORDER BY lastname DESC, firstname DESC");
```

Note that we must supply the `DESC` keyword for each column name that we want it to apply to. If you omit it for a column the default ascending sequence will apply.

Getting Metadata for a Resultset

The `getMetaData()` method for a `ResultSet` object returns a reference to an object of type `ResultSetMetaData` that encapsulates the metadata for the resultset. The `ResultSetMetaData` interface declares methods that enable you to get items of metadata for the resultset.

The `getColumnCount()` method returns the number of columns in the resultset as a value of type `int`. For each column, you can get the column name and column type by calling the `getColumnName()` and `getColumnType()` methods respectively. In both cases you specify the column by its index value. The column name is returned as a `String` object and the column type is returned as an `int` value that identifies the SQL type. The `Types` class in the `java.sql` package defines public fields of type `int` that identify the SQL types, and the names of these class data members are the same as the SQL types they represent – such as `CHAR`, `VARCHAR`, `DOUBLE`, `INT`, `TIME`, and so on. Thus you could list the names of the columns in a resultset that were of type `CHAR` with the following code:

```
ResultSetMetaData metadata = results.getMetaData();
int columns = metadata.getColumnCount();                  // Get number of columns

for(int i = 1 ; i<= columns ; i++)                        // For each column
  if(metadata.getColumnType(i) == Types.CHAR)             // if it is CHAR
     System.out.println(metadata.getColumnName(i));       // display the name
```

You could output the data value of each row of a `ResultSet` object, `results`, that were of SQL type `CHAR` with the following code:

```
ResultSetMetaData metadata = results.getMetaData();
int columns = metadata.getColumnCount();                  // Get number of columns

int row = 0;                                              // Row number
while(results.next())                                     // For each row
```

```
{
    System.out.print("\nRow "+(++row)+":");              // increment row count
    for(int i = 1 ; i<= columns ; i++)                   // For each column
        if(metadata.getColumnType(i) == Types.CHAR)      // if it is CHAR display
    it
            System.out.print(" "+results.getString(i));
}
```

You can also get the type name for a column as a `String` by calling the `getColumnTypeName()` method with the column number as the argument. Another very useful method is `getColumnDisplaySize()`, which returns the normal maximum number of characters required to display the data stored in the column. You pass the index number of the column that you are interested in as the argument. The return value is type `int`. You can use this to help format the output of column data.

There are a whole range of other methods that supply other metadata for a resultset that you will find in the documentation for the `ResultSetMetaData` interface. Here's a list of a few more that you may find useful – they all require an argument that is the column number as type `int`:

`getTableName()`	Returns the table name for the column as type `String`.
`getColumnLabel()`	Returns a `String` object that is the suggested label for a column for use in print-outs.
`getPrecision()`	Returns the number of decimal digits for a column as type `int`.
`getScale()`	Returns the number of decimal digits to the right of the decimal point for a column as type `int`.

`isSigned()`	Returns `true` if the column contains signed numbers.
`isCurrency()`	Returns `true` if the column contains currency values.
`isNullable()`	Returns an int value that can be:
	`columnNoNulls` indicating `NULL` is not allowed,
	`columnNullable` indicating `NULL` is allowed,
	`columnNullableUnknown` indicating it is not known if `NULL` is allowed.
`isWritable()`	Returns `true` if a write on the column is likely to succeed.

The Essential JDBC Program

We now have all the pieces to make up the essential JDBC program, which will initialize the environment, create `Connection` and `Statement` objects, and retrieve data by both position and column name.

Try It Out — Putting It All Together

Our application will execute two queries, one that selects specific columns by name, and another that selects all columns. First we will define the application class in outline, with the data members and the `main()` function and the other methods in the class:

```java
import java.sql.*;

public class EssentialJDBC
{

  public static void main (String[] args)
  {
    EssentialJDBC SQLExample = new EssentialJDBC();    // Create application object

    SQLExample.getResultsByColumnName();
    SQLExample.getResultsByColumnPosition();
    SQLExample.getAllColumns();
    SQLExample.closeConnection();
  }

  public EssentialJDBC()
  {
    // Constructor to establish the connection and create a Statement object...
  }

  void getResultsByColumnName()
  {
    // Execute wildcard query and output selected columns...
  }

  void getResultsByColumnPosition()
  {
    // Execute ID and name query and output results...
  }

  void getAllColumns()
  {
    // Execute wildcard query and output all columns...
  }
```

```
   // Close the connection
   void closeConnection()
   {
     if(connection != null)
     try
     {
       connection.close();
       connection = null;
     }
     catch (SQLException ex)
     {
       System.out.println("\nSQLException------------------\n");
       System.out.println("SQLState: " + ex.getSQLState());
       System.out.println("Message : " + ex.getMessage());
     }
   }

   Connection connection;
   Statement statement;
   String sourceURL = "jdbc:odbc:technical_library";
   String queryIDAndName = "SELECT authid, lastname, firstname FROM authors";
   String queryWildcard = "SELECT * FROM authors";          // Select all columns
 }
```

The data source is identified by a URL in the form, `jdbc:driver_name:datasource`. The data source identifier format is defined by the driver. In the case of the JDBC-ODBC Bridge, the data source is the ODBC source name. We have defined a `closeConnection()` method here that closes the connection when we are done. Notice that this method tests the value of the connection to ensure that we don't try to close a `null` connection.

Next we can fill in the details of the constructor for the class. This will establish a connection with the database and create a `Statement` object that will be used for executing queries.

```
   public EssentialJDBC()
   {
     try
     {
       Class.forName("sun.jdbc.odbc.JdbcOdbcDriver");
       connection = DriverManager.getConnection(sourceURL);
       statement = connection.createStatement();
     }
     catch(SQLException sqle)
     {
       System.err.println("Error creating connection");
     }
     catch(ClassNotFoundException cnfe)
     {
       System.err.println(cnfe.toString());
     }
   }
```

Next we can code the getResultsByColumnName() method. We will be using the statement object created from the connection object in the constructor to execute the SQL query to get a resultset back. A while loop with a call to next() as the condition will iterate through all the rows starting at the first:

```
void getResultsByColumnName()
{
  try
  {
    ResultSet authorResults = statement.executeQuery(queryWildcard);
    int row = 0;

    while(authorResults.next())
      System.out.println("Row " + (++row) + ") "+
                         authorResults.getString("authid")+ " " +
                         authorResults.getString("lastname")+ " , "+
                         authorResults.getString("firstname"));

    authorResults.close();
  }
  catch (SQLException sqle)
  {
    System.err.println ("\nSQLException------------------\n");
    System.err.println ("SQLState: " + sqle.getSQLState());
    System.err.println ("Message : " + sqle.getMessage());
  }
}
```

The SQLException handling code here doesn't provide very elegant error handling for this program, but we are obliged to catch this exception.

We can now define the getResultsByColumnPosition() method. This will use the query for the ID and names columns where the order of the columns is determined by the order of the column names in the query:

```
void getResultsByColumnPosition()
{
  try
  {
    ResultSet authorResults = statement.executeQuery(queryIDAndName);

    int row = 0;
    while (authorResults.next())
    {
      System.out.print("\nRow " + (++row) + ") ");
      for(int i = 1 ; i<=3 ; i++)
        System.out.print((i>1?", ":" ")+authorResults.getString(i));
    }
    authorResults.close();                              // Close the result set
  }
```

```
      catch (SQLException ex)
      {
        System.err.println("\nSQLException-------------------\n");
        System.err.println("SQLState: " + ex.getSQLState());
        System.err.println("Message : " + ex.getMessage());
      }
  }
```

Next we can define the `getAllColumns()` method. This uses the wildcard form of `SELECT` statement where the `*` for the columns to be selected will retrieve all columns in the authors table. In general we won't necessarily know how many columns are returned in the resultset, but we can implement the method so that it will deal with any number of columns as well as any number of rows:

```
void getAllColumns()
{
  try
  {
    ResultSet authorResults = statement.executeQuery(queryWildcard);

    ResultSetMetaData metadata = authorResults.getMetaData();
    int columns = metadata.getColumnCount();          // Column count
    int row = 0;
    while (authorResults.next())
    {
      System.out.print("\nRow " + (++row) + ") ");
      for(int i = 1 ; i<=columns ; i++)
        System.out.print((i>1?", ":" ")+authorResults.getString(i));
    }

    authorResults.close();                            // Close the result set
  }
  catch (SQLException ex)
  {
    System.err.println("\nSQLException-------------------\n");
    System.err.println("SQLState: " + ex.getSQLState());
    System.err.println("Message : " + ex.getMessage());
  }
}
```

Running the `EssentialJDBC` program produces three sets of results. The first two sets are the same and consist of the ID and the name columns from the authors table. The third set lists all columns. Although the additional columns are null, you can see that we get them all in this case.

How It Works

The `EssentialJDBC` class provides a `main()` method to declare and allocate an `EssentialJDBC` object by calling the class constructor. It then calls the `getResultsByColumnName()`, the `getResultsByColumnPosition()`, and the `getAllColumns()` methods of the new object.

The constructor initializes member variables, and loads the `JdbcOdbc` driver class. It then creates a `Connection` object by calling the static `getConnection()` method of the `DriverManager` class. It then uses the `Connection` object to create a `Statement` object.

The bulk of the work is done in the three `getXXX()` methods. All three use the same `Statement` object to execute an SQL query. The difference between the three methods is how they retrieve the returned data.

The `getResultsByColumnName()` method executes the wildcard form of an SQL `SELECT` statement where the column names are specified by an * and the column ordering, of the returned results, is determined by the database engine. This query is executed by calling the `executeQuery()` method of the `Statement` object and this method returns the data in a `ResultSet` object. Since the column ordering is unknown ahead of time, we retrieve data by explicitly specifying the column names. The column data is retrieved as strings and written to the standard output stream. Finally, the `ResultSet` is closed. Note that the garbage collection of Java will handle this automatically anyway, but calling `close()` explicitly ensures that the resources, used by the `ResultSet` object, will be cleaned up sooner.

The `getResultsByColumnPosition()` method executes a `SELECT` that explicitly specifies the columns required by name so the column ordering in the resultset is the same as the sequence of column names in the `SELECT` statement. We can therefore use the column position index values to retrieve the data from the `ResultSet`. Like the previous method, the column data is retrieved as strings and printed to the console for each row returned. Finally, the `ResultSet` object is closed as before.

The `getAllColumns()` method uses the wildcard form of `SELECT` statement to retrieve a resultset containing all columns from the `authors` table – the entire table in other words. The method gets the count of the number of columns by means of the `ResultSetMetaData` object for the `ResultSet` object created as a result of the query. This is used to output however many columns there are in the resultset.

Using a PreparedStatement Object

Let's put a prepared statement into action now, to go through the mechanics in a practical context. This won't really show the capabilities of this – we will get to that in the next chapter. We will code an example that will execute the same SQL `SELECT` statement using both `Statement` and `PreparedStatement` objects. For each of these, the results will be displayed along with the metadata.

First `import` the necessary classes from the `java.sql` package. Then define the `StatementTest` class and its member data. Define the class entry point `main()`, which will instantiate a `StatementTest` object, and then call the methods `doStatement()` and `doPreparedStatement()` for that object.

```
import java.sql.*;

public class StatementTest
{
  public static void main(String[] args)
  {
    StatementTest SQLExample;
    try
    {
      SQLExample = new StatementTest();
      SQLExample.doStatement();
      SQLExample.doPreparedStatement();
    }
    catch(SQLException sqle)
    {
      System.err.println("SQL Exception: " + sqle);
    }
    catch(ClassNotFoundException cnfe)
    {
      System.err.println(cnfe.toString());
    }
  }

  Connection databaseConnection;       // Connection to the database
  String driverName;                   // Database driver name
  String sourceURL;                    // Database location
}
```

Next we will define the `StatementTest` class constructor. This constructor assigns the driver name and the source URL that defines where the data will come from. It then loads the driver and calls the static `getConnection()` method of the `DriverManager` class to establish the database connection.

```
public StatementTest() throws SQLException, ClassNotFoundException
{
  driverName = "sun.jdbc.odbc.JdbcOdbcDriver";
  sourceURL = "jdbc:odbc:technical_library";

  Class.forName(driverName);
  databaseConnection = DriverManager.getConnection(sourceURL);
}
```

Next we will define the doStatement() method that is called in main(). This method shows once again how we create a Statement object, and use it to execute a query. The ResultSet object that is returned by the executeQuery() method of the Statement object is passed to the showResults() method of the StatementTest class to display the results.

```
public void doStatement() throws SQLException
{
   Statement myStatement = databaseConnection.createStatement();
   ResultSet myResults = myStatement.executeQuery
                      ("SELECT authid, lastname, firstname FROM authors");

   showResults(myResults);
}
```

Now we will define the doPreparedStatement() method. This method demonstrates how a PreparedStatement is created and executed. For the time being we will define it so that it operates in the same fashion as the doStatement() method.

```
public void doPreparedStatement() throws SQLException
{
   PreparedStatement myStatement = databaseConnection.prepareStatement
                  ("SELECT authid, lastname, firstname FROM authors");
   ResultSet myResults = myStatement.executeQuery();
   showResults(myResults);
}
```

Firstly, define the showResults() method. This method is passed a ResultSet object, from which it extracts both data and metadata. Notice that the first thing this method does is retrieve the ResultSetMetaData object, from which it determines the number of columns returned. It then loops through and retrieves each column value as a string and prints it out.

After the data is displayed, the method extracts information about each column and displays that too.

```
public void showResults(ResultSet myResults) throws SQLException
{
   // Retrieve ResultSetMetaData object from ResultSet
   ResultSetMetaData myResultMetadata = myResults.getMetaData();

   // How many columns were returned?
   int numColumns = myResultMetadata.getColumnCount();

   System.out.println("-------------Query Results----------------");
   // Loop through the ResultSet and get data
   while(myResults.next())
   {
      for(int column = 1; column <= numColumns; column++)
         System.out.print(myResults.getString(column) + "\t");
      System.out.print("\n");
   }
```

```
        System.out.println("\n\n-----------Query Metadata----------------");
        System.out.println("ResultSet contains " + numColumns + " columns");
        for (int column = 1; column <= numColumns; column++)
        {
          System.out.println("Column " + column);
          // Print the column name
          System.out.println("\tcolumn\t\t:" +
                                    myResultMetadata.getColumnName(column));
          // Print the label name
          System.out.println("\tlabel\t\t:" +
                                    myResultMetadata.getColumnLabel(column));
          // Print the column's display size
          System.out.println("\tdisplay width\t:" +
                                myResultMetadata.getColumnDisplaySize(column) +
                                " characters");
          // Print the column's type
          System.out.println("\tdata type:\t:" +
                                myResultMetadata.getColumnTypeName(column));
        }
    }
```

When you run the `StatementTest` program, you should get the following results twice:

```
-------------Query Results----------------
1       Gross                   Christian
2       Roche                   Kevin
3       Tracy                   Michael
4       Horton                  Ivor
...
52      Pompeii                 John
53      Brown                   Marc
54      Woelk                   Darrel


-----------Query Metadata----------------
ResultSet contains 3 columns
Column 1
        name            :authid
        label           :authid
        display width   :11 characters
        data type:      :LONG
Column 2
        name            :lastname
        label           :lastname
        display width   :25 characters
        data type:      :CHAR
Column 3
        name            :firstname
        label           :firstname
        display width   :15 characters
        data type:      :CHAR
```

How It Works

All we've done in this example is to take the concepts that you've seen in this chapter and put them all together into a working program.

The program creates and executes both a `Statement` and a `PreparedStatement` object, which should produce identical results. In this case, there were no parameters for the `PreparedStatement` (not to worry – you'll have more than enough `PreparedStatement` objects in the next chapter!). Since the results were identical, the `ResultSetMetaData` is identical for the two executed SQL statements as well.

Notice that all of the exception handling for this example is handled within `main()`. Each of the other methods that might generate exceptions declare those exceptions in their `throws` clause. If an exception occurs within any of those methods, the method will simply throw that exception back to the calling routine – `main()`.

The InteractiveSQL Tool

So far our examples have been console applications. In practice you will want to implement your database programs as interactive windowed applications, so let's apply what we know to creating an example. We will build an interactive SQL tool that will execute SQL statements to retrieve a resultset.

The InteractiveSQL tool will be a simple front end to the JDBC API. It will provide a means of entering and executing SQL statements, and have a display area for viewing results. This tool will be pretty basic in terms of functionality, but may come in handy for experimenting with SQL statements. You can always add extensions to this utility as you become more familiar with JDBC.

We will set our requirements for the InteractiveSQL tool to be fairly simple:

❑   Enable the user to enter and execute a SQL command

❑   Display the result set from a SQL query

❑   Display error information where appropriate

We will implement this as an application with a window based on the Swing class `JFrame`. We will also use a Swing component that is particularly useful for database applications – a table defined by the `JTable` class. The `JTable` class is defined in the `javax.swing.table` package along with some other classes and interfaces that support tables of data. The resultset that is generated when you execute an SQL `SELECT` statement is a rectangular table of data values, so a `JTable` component is ideal for displaying resultsets. Let's explore the basics of the `JTable` component so we can apply it to our InteractiveSQL program.

Using Tables

You use a JTable component to display a rectangular array of data on the screen. The items of data in the table do not have to be of all the same type, in fact each column of data in the table can be of a different type, either a basic type or class type. This is precisely the situation we have with a resultset. There are several ways to create a JTable component but we will just consider the most convenient in the database context, which is to use an object that encapsulates the data that is to be displayed in the table and implements the TableModel interface. You can create a JTable object directly from such an object by passing a reference of type TableModel to a JTable constructor. For example:

```
JTable table = new JTable(model);
```

Here, model is a variable of type TableModel that stores a reference to your object encapsulating the data to be displayed – the resultset in other words. All we need is a class to define this object, so next we need to know how to implement the TableModel interface.

Understanding the TableModel Interface

The TableModel interface declares methods that are used by a JTable object to access the data item to be displayed at each position in the table. This interface is defined in the javax.swing.table package, along with the JTable class. Our class encapsulating a resultset will need to implement this interface, and therefore define all the methods that the interface declares. The bad news is that there are nine of them. The good news is that there is an abstract class, AbstractTableModel, that implements six of them so that if we extend this class we have a minimum of three methods to define. The full set of methods declared in the TableModel interface is as follows:

getColumnCount()	Returns the number of columns in the table model as type int.
getRowCount()	Returns the number of rows in the table model as type int.
getValueAt(int row, int column)	Returns the value of the data item in the table model at the position specified by the argument as type Object.
getColumnClass(int column)	Returns the class type of the data in the columns specified by the argument as type Class.
getColumnName(int column)	Returns the name of the columns specified by the argument as type String.
setValueAt(Object value, int row, int column)	Sets the value, value, for the data item in the table model at the position specified by the last two arguments. There is no return value.
isCellEditable(int row, int column)	Returns true if the data item at the position specified by the arguments is editable, and false otherwise.
addTableModelListener (TableModelListener tml)	Adds a listener that is notified each time the table model is altered.
removeTableModelListener (TableModelListener tml)	Removes a listener that was listening for table model changes.

Remember, all these methods are called by the `JTable` object, so these provide the means whereby the `JTable` object accesses and manipulates data in the table model. The `AbstractTableModel` class provides default implementations for the last six methods in the list above, so the minimum you have to supply when you extend this class is the first three.

Defining a Table Model

We want to define a class that encapsulates a resultset, and it will be convenient to make the object of our class have the capability to accept a new resultset at any time. This will enable a single `JTable` object to display a series of different resultsets, just by setting a new resultset in the underlying `TableModel` object. We can do this by providing a method that will accept a `ResultSet` object as an argument, and making the contents available through the `TableModel` interface. With this in mind, the basic outline of the class will be:

```java
import java.sql.*;
import javax.swing.table.*;

class ResultsModel extends AbstractTableModel
{
  public void setResultSet(ResultSet results)
  {
    // Make the data in the resultset available through the TableModel
interface...
  }
  public int getColumnCount()
  {
    // Return number of columns...
  }

  public int getRowCount()
  {
    // Return number of rows...
  }

  public Object getValueAt(int row, int column)
  {
    // Return the value at position row,column...
  }

  public String getColumnName(int column)
  {
    // Return the name for the column...
  }
}
```

We could access the data to be returned by the `TableModel` interface methods by going back to the original `ResultSet` object as necessary. This may involve going back to the database each time, and it will be generally more convenient and probably more efficient to cache the data from the resultset in the `ResultsModel` object. This means that the `setResultSet()` method will need to set this up. We will need to store two sets of information in the `ResultsModel` object – the column names, which are `String` objects, and the data in the table, which could be any of the types matching the SQL data types. To keep it simple we will access the data using the `getString()` method for the `ResultSet` object. Any of the SQL data types we will be using can be extracted as type `String`, and it means that we will only have to deal with strings at this point.

We can store the column names in a `String` array, so we can add a data member to the `ResultsModel` class to provide for this:

```
String[] columnNames = new String[0];           // Empty array of names
```

Defining `columnNames` as an array with zero elements ensures that we start out with a non-null array, even though there is no resultset initially. We won't know in advance how many rows or columns of data there are, so we won't want to use an array. A `Vector` object will provide sufficient flexibility to accommodate whatever we need – indeed, although we won't need it here, it can store data items that differ in type, as long as they are objects. We can store the contents of a row as an array of `String` objects that we can then store as an element in the `Vector`. We can define the data member that stores the rows of data values as:

```
Vector dataRows = new Vector();                 // Empty vector of rows
```

Of course, we have set the type for all the data items in a row to `String` here, but if we wanted to accommodate different types within a row a `Vector` object could be used to store each row. These objects could then be stored in the `Vector` object, `dataRows`. We mustn't forget the `import` statement for the `Vector` class – it's defined in `java.util`.

We can now implement the `setResultSet()` method in our `ResultsModel` class as:

```
public void setResultSet(ResultSet results)
{
  try
  {
    ResultSetMetaData metadata = results.getMetaData();

    int columns =  metadata.getColumnCount();       // Get number of columns
    columnNames = new String[columns];              // Array to hold names

    // Get the column names
    for(int i = 0; i < columns; i++)
      columnNames[i] = metadata.getColumnLabel(i+1);


    // Get all rows.
    dataRows = new Vector();                         // New Vector to store the data
    String[] rowData;                               // Stores one row
    while(results.next())                           // For each row...
    {
      rowData = new String[columns];                // create array to hold the
data
      for(int i = 0; i < columns; i++)              // For each column
        rowData[i] = results.getString(i+1);        // retrieve the data item

      dataRows.addElement(rowData);                 // Store the row in the vector
    }
```

```
            fireTableChanged(null);              // Signal the table there is new model
  data
       }
     catch (SQLException sqle)
     {
        System.err.println(sqle);
     }
   }
```

To get the column names and the number of columns, we need access to the `ResultSetMetaData` object corresponding to the `ResultSet` object. The `getColumnLabel()` method for the `metadata` object returns the label to be used to name the column. This will either be the name of the column as known to the database, or the alias if you specify one in the `SELECT` statement used to create the resultset. The column names are stored in the array, `columnNames`.

We create a new `Vector` object to hold the rows from the resultset and store the reference in `dataRows`. This will replace any existing `Vector` object, which will be discarded. Each element in the vector will be an array of `String` objects, `rowData`, that we create in the `while` loop and set the values of its elements in the nested `for` loop, and once it's done we store it in `dataRows`. After all the rows from the resultset have been stored, we call the `fireTableChanged()` method that our class inherits from the base class. This method notifies all listeners for the `JTable` object for this model that the model has changed, so the `JTable` object should redraw itself from scratch. The argument is a reference to an object of type `TableModelEvent` that can be used to specify the parts of the model that have changed. This is passed to the listeners. We can pass a `null` here as we want to invalidate the whole thing.

The method to return the number of columns is now very easy to implement:

```
    public int getColumnCount()
    { return columnNames.length; }
```

The column count is the number of elements in the `columnNames` array.

Supplying the row count is just as easy:

```
    public int getRowCount()
    {
      if(dataRows == null)
        return 0;
      else
        return dataRows.size();
    }
```

The number of rows corresponds to the size of the `Vector` object, `dataRows`. We check to make sure that the value of the `dataRows` vector is not `null` to ensure that the initialization of the InteractiveSQL GUI can take place even when the vector has not been initialized.

The last method that completes the class definition as we have it provides access to the data values. We can implement this as follows:

```
public Object getValueAt(int row, int column)
{ return ((String[])(dataRows.elementAt(row)))[column]; }
```

The `elementAt()` method returns the element in the `Vector` at the position specified by the argument. This is returned as type `Object`, so we must cast it to type `String[]` before we can index it to access the value of the data item.

There is one other method we should add to the class – an implementation of `getColumnName()` that will return the column name given a column index. We can implement this as:

```
public String getColumnName(int column)
{
    return columnNames[column] == null ? "No Name" : columnNames[column];
}
```

We take the precaution here of dealing with a null column name by supplying a default column name in this case.

The Application GUI

The figure seen here shows the user interface for the InteractiveSQL tool. The text field at the top provides an entry area for typing in the SQL statement, and will be implemented using a `JTextField` component. The results display provides a scrollable area for the results of the executed SQL command. This will be implemented using a `JScrollPane` component. A status line, implemented as a `JTextArea` component provides the user with the number of rows returned from the query, or the text of any `SQLException` object generated by the query.

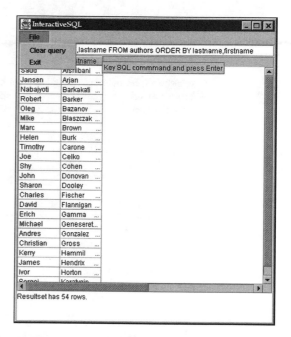

The illustration above also shows the menu items in the File menu, and the tooltip prompt for the SQL input area. The Clear query menu item will just clear the input area where you enter an SQL query.

Try It Out — Defining the GUI

We will derive the `InteractiveSQL` class from the `JFrame` class, and make this the foundation for the application. Its constructor will be responsible for loading the JDBC driver class, creating a connection to the database, and creating the user interface. The code is as follows:

```java
import java.awt.*;
import java.awt.event.*;              // For event classes
import javax.swing.*;                 // For Swing components
import javax.swing.table.*;           // For the table classes
import java.sql.*;                    // For JDBC classes

public class InteractiveSQL extends JFrame
{
  public static void main(String[] args)
  { // Create the application object
    InteractiveSQL theApp = new InteractiveSQL("sun.jdbc.odbc.JdbcOdbcDriver",
                                    "jdbc:odbc:technical_library",
                                    "guest",
                                    "guest");

  }

  public InteractiveSQL(String driver, String url,
                        String user , String password)
  {
    super("InteractiveSQL");                         // Call base constructor
    setBounds(0, 0, 400, 300);                       // Set window bounds
    setDefaultCloseOperation(DISPOSE_ON_CLOSE);      // Close window operation
    addWindowListener(new WindowHandler());          // Listener for window close

    // Add the input for SQL statements at the top
    command.setToolTipText("Key SQL commmand and press Enter");
    getContentPane().add(command, BorderLayout.NORTH);

    // Add the status reporting area at the bottom
    status.setLineWrap(true);
    status.setWrapStyleWord(true);
    getContentPane().add(status, BorderLayout.SOUTH);

    // Create the menubar from the menu items
    JMenu fileMenu = new JMenu("File");              // Create File menu
    fileMenu.setMnemonic('F');                       // Create shortcut
    fileMenu.add(clearQueryItem);                    // Add clear query item
    fileMenu.add(exitItem);                          // Add exit item
    menuBar.add(fileMenu);                           // Add menu to the menubar
    setJMenuBar(menuBar);                            // Add menubar to the window
```

```
      // Establish a database connection and set up the table
      try
      {
        Class.forName(driver);                          // Load the driver
        connection = DriverManager.getConnection(url, user, password);
        statement = connection.createStatement();

        model = new ResultsModel();              // Create a table model
        JTable table = new JTable(model);        // Create a table from the model
        table.setAutoResizeMode(JTable.AUTO_RESIZE_OFF);  // Use scrollbars
        resultsPane = new JScrollPane(table);       // Create scrollpane for table
        getContentPane().add(resultsPane, BorderLayout.CENTER);

      }
      catch(ClassNotFoundException cnfe)
      {
        System.err.println(cnfe);                  // Driver not found
      }
      catch(SQLException sqle)
      {
        System.err.println(sqle);                  // error connection to database
      }
      pack();
      setVisible(true);
    }
    class WindowHandler extends WindowAdapter

    {
      // Handler for window closing event
      public void windowClosing(WindowEvent e)
      {
        dispose();                                // Release the window resources
        System.exit(0);                           // End the application
      }
    }

    JTextField command = new JTextField();        // Input area for SQL
    JTextArea status = new JTextArea(3,1);        // Output area for status and errors
    JScrollPane resultsPane;

    JMenuBar menuBar = new JMenuBar();                      // The menu bar
    JMenuItem clearQueryItem = new JMenuItem("Clear query");  // Clear SQL item
    JMenuItem exitItem = new JMenuItem("Exit");             // Exit item

    Connection connection;                        // Connection to the database
    Statement statement;                          // Statement object for queries
    ResultsModel model;                           // Table model for resultset
}
```

You can try running the application as it is and you should see the basic application interface displayed in the window with a working close operation.

How It Works

The constructor is passed the arguments required to load the appropriate driver and create a Connection to a database. The first executable statement in this constructor calls the constructor for the JFrame class, passing a default window title to it. The constructor then creates and arranges the user interface components. Most of this should be familiar to you but let's pick out a few things that are new, or worthy of a second look.

You can see how we add a tooltip for the JTextField component, command, – the input area for an SQL statement. Don't forget that you can add a tooltip for any Swing component in the same way.

We define the JTextArea object status so that it can display three lines of text. The first argument to the constructor is the number of lines of text, and the second argument is the number of columns. Some of the error messages can be quite long, so we call both the setLineWrap() method to make lines wrap automatically, and the setWrapStyleWord() method to wrap a line at the end of a word – that is on whitespace – rather than in the middle of a word. In both cases the true argument switches the facility on.

We create the JTable object using the default ResultsModel object which will contain no data initially. Since the number of columns in a resultset will vary depending on the SQL query that is executed, we wrap our JTable object in a JScrollPane object to provide automatic scrolling as necessary. The scrollbars will appear whenever the size of the JTable object is larger than the size of the scroll pane. By default, a JTable object will resize the width of its columns to fit within the width of the JTable component. To inhibit this and allow the scroll pane scrollbars to be used, we call the setAutoResizeMode() method with the argument as JTable.AUTO_RESIZE_OFF.

This not only inhibits the default resizing action when the table is displayed, but also allows you to change the size of a column when the table is displayed without affecting the size of the other columns. You change the size of a column by dragging the side of the column name using the mouse. There are other values you can pass to this method that affect how resizing is handled:

AUTO_RESIZE_ALL_COLUMNS	Adjusts the sizes of all columns to take up the change in width of the column being resized. This maintains the overall width of the table.
AUTO_RESIZE_NEXT_COLUMN	Adjusts the size of the next column to provide for the change in the column being altered in order to maintain the total width of the table.
AUTO_RESIZE_LAST_COLUMN	Adjusts the size of the last column to provide for the change in the column being altered in order to maintain the total width of the table.
AUTO_RESIZE_SUBSEQUENT_COLUMNS	Adjusts the size of the columns to the right to provide for the change in the column being altered in order to maintain the total width of the table.

The program only works with the database and driver hard-coded in the program. We can make it a lot more flexible by allowing command line argument to be supplied that specify the database and driver, as well as the user ID and password.

Handling Command Line Arguments

All we need to do is to alter `main()` to accept up to four command line arguments: these will be the values for the user name, password, database URL and JDBC driver

Try It Out — Using Command Line Parameters

We need to modify the code in `main()` to:

```
public static void main(String[] args)
{
    // Set default values for the command line args
    String user     = "guest";
    String password = "guest";
    String url      = "jdbc:odbc:technical_library";
    String driver   = "sun.jdbc.odbc.JdbcOdbcDriver";

    // Up to 4 arguments in the sequence database url,driver url, user ID, password
    switch(args.length)
    {
      case 4:                              // Start here for four arguments
        password = args[3];
        // Fall through to the next case
      case 3:                              // Start here for three arguments
        user = args[2];
        // Fall through to the next case
      case 2:                              // Start here for two arguments
        driver = args[1];
        // Fall through to the next case
      case 1:                              // Start here for one argument
        url = args[0];
    }
      InteractiveSQL theApp = new InteractiveSQL(driver, url, user, password);
}
```

How It Works

This enables you to optionally specify the JDBC URL, the JDBC driver, the user name and the password, on the command line. The mechanism that handles the optional parameters is pretty simple. The `switch` statement tests the number of parameters that were specified on the command line. If one parameter was passed, it is interpreted as the JDBC URL. If two parameters were passed, the second parameter is assumed to be the driver URL, and so on. There are no `break` statements, so control always drops through from the starting case to include each of the following cases.

Handling Events

To make the program operational, we need an event to add the handling logic for the menu items and the input field for the SQL statement. We can handle the menu items in the usual way by making the `InteractiveSQL` class implement the `ActionListener` interface. For the `JTextField` object we can add an action listener to respond to the *Enter* key being pressed at the end of entering an SQL statement.

Try It Out — Events in `InteractiveSQL`

First, we need to add the interface declaration to the class definition. The `InteractiveSQL` class will implement the `ActionListener` interface to handle menu events so you should change the first line of the definition to:

```
public class InteractiveSQL extends JFrame
                            implements ActionListener
```

We can now add code to the class constructor to add listeners for the menu item action events, and the `JTextField` action event.

```
public InteractiveSQL(String driver, String url,
                      String user , String password)
  {
    super("InteractiveSQL");                            // Call base constructor
    setBounds(0, 0, 400, 300);                          // Set window bounds
    setDefaultCloseOperation(DISPOSE_ON_CLOSE);         // Close window operation
    addWindowListener(new WindowHandler());             // Listener for window close

    // Add the input for for SQL statements at the top
    command.setToolTipText("Key SQL commmand and press Enter");
    command.addActionListener(this);
    getContentPane().add(command, BorderLayout.NORTH);
    // Add the status reporting area at the bottom
    status.setLineWrap(true);
    status.setWrapStyleWord(true);
    getContentPane().add(status, BorderLayout.SOUTH);

    // Create the menubar from the menu items
    JMenu fileMenu = new JMenu("File");                 // Create File menu
    fileMenu.setMnemonic('F');                          // Create shortcut
    clearQueryItem.addActionListener(this);
    exitItem.addActionListener(this);
    fileMenu.add(clearQueryItem);                       // Add clear query item
    fileMenu.add(exitItem);                             // Add exit item
    menuBar.add(fileMenu);                              // Add menu to the menubar
    setJMenuBar(menuBar);                               // Add menubar to the window
```

```
  // Establish a database connection and set up the table
  try
  {
    Class.forName(driver);                              // Load the driver
    connection = DriverManager.getConnection(url, user, password);
    statement = connection.createStatement();

    model = new ResultsModel();                 // Create a table model
    JTable table = new JTable(model);           // Create a table from the model
    table.setAutoResizeMode(JTable.AUTO_RESIZE_OFF);    // Use scrollbars
    resultsPane = new JScrollPane(table);       // Create scrollpane for table
    getContentPane().add(resultsPane, BorderLayout.CENTER);

  }
  catch(ClassNotFoundException cnfe)
  {
    System.err.println(cnfe);                   // Driver not found
  }
  catch(SQLException sqle)
  {
    System.err.println(sqle);                   // error connection to database
  }
  pack();
  setVisible(true);
}
```

That's all we need to do to add the listeners. We can now add the actionPerformed() method. This method will get the reference to the component that originated the event from the event object, and use that to determine what action is necessary:

```
public void actionPerformed(ActionEvent e)
{
  Object source = e.getSource();
  if(source == command)                         // Enter key for text field input
    executeSQL();

  else if(source == clearQueryItem)             // Clear query menu item
    command.setText("");                        // Clear SQL entry
  else if(source == exitItem)                   // Exit menu item
  {
    dispose();                                  // Release the window resources
    System.exit(0);                             // End the application
  }
}
```

The final piece is the `executeSQL()` method that will execute the statements that was entered in the text field command, and pass the resultset generated to the table model object, `model`, that supplies the data for the `JTable` object:

```
public void executeSQL()
{
  String query = command.getText();        // Get the SQL statement
  if(query == null)                        // If there's nothing we are done
    return;
  try
  {
    model.setResultSet(statement.executeQuery(query));
    status.setText("Resultset has " + model.getRowCount() + " rows.");
  }
  catch (SQLException sqle)
  {
    status.setText(sqle.getMessage());     // Display error message
  }
}
```

Compile and run the application, and remember the command line parameters: `<URL>` `<driver>` `<user id>` `<password>`. For example, try:

```
java InteractiveSQL jdbc:odbc:technical_library
```

and then execute the SQL query:

```
SELECT firstname AS "First Name", lastname AS Surname FROM authors
                    ORDER BY lastname,firstname
```

You should get the resultset displayed here:

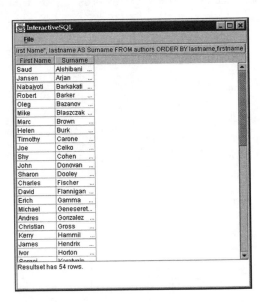

How It Works

Pressing the *Enter* key after typing in the SQL query to be executed causes an action event to be generated for the JTextField object, command, that receives the input. The actionPerformed() method identifies the event by comparing the reference to the originating object with each of the objects in the GUI that have the application object as the action listener. When the event originates with the command object, the executeSQL() method is called. This retrieves the query from the text field and executes it using the Statement object. The ResultSet object that is returned is passed to the setResultSet() method for the model object. The model object extracts the data from the resultset and alerts the JTable object. This causes the data in the resultset to be displayed.

If an error occurs when the query is executed, a SQLException will be thrown. The catch block handling this exception passes the message text from the exception object to the JTextArea object, status.

You now have a simple but useful tool for executing SQL statements through JDBC.

Summary

In this chapter you've been introduced to JDBC programming, and seen it in action. The important points covered in this chapter are:

- ❏ The fundamental classes in JDBC are:
- ❏ DriverManager – manages loading of JDBC drivers and connections to client applications
- ❏ Connection – provides a connection to a specific data source
- ❏ Statement – provides a context for executing SQL statements
- ❏ ResultSet – provides a means for accessing data returned from an executed Statement
- ❏ The essential JDBC program has the following basic structure when writing:
    - ❏ Import the necessary classes
    - ❏ Load the JDBC driver
    - ❏ Identify the data source
    - ❏ Allocate a Connection object
    - ❏ Allocate a Statement object
    - ❏ Execute a query using the Statement object
    - ❏ Retrieve data from the returned ResultSet object
    - ❏ Close the ResultSet
    - ❏ Close the Statement object
    - ❏ Close the Connection object
- ❏ The JTable component provides an easy and convenient way to display the results of database queries.
- ❏ A table model can provide the data to be displayed by a JTable component. A table model is an object of a class that implements the TableModel interface.

Exercises

1. Write a program that outputs all authors in the `technical_library` database with last names starting with the letters A through H.

2. Write a program that lists all books and the authors for that book. (Hint: you will need an SQL join and the `author_books` table.)

3. Modify the `InteractiveSQL` program to allow the user to specify which database to use.

4. Modify the `InteractiveSQL` program to provide separate input areas for each part of a `SELECT` statement – one for the table columns, one for the table, one for a possible `WHERE` clause, and so on.

The JDBC in Action

In this chapter we will expand on the topics that we introduced in the previous chapter, and go into more detail on the JDBC API. In this chapter we're going to learn more about:

- ❑ How you can map relational data onto Java objects.
- ❑ The mapping between SQL and Java data types.
- ❑ How you can limit the data created in a resultset.
- ❑ How to constrain the time spent executing a query.
- ❑ How you use a `PreparedStatement` object to create a parameterized SQL statement.
- ❑ How you can execute database update and delete operations in your Java programs.
- ❑ How you can get more information from `SQLException` objects.
- ❑ What an `SQLWarning` object is and what you can do with it.

Data Types and JDBC

In all of the examples so far, all of the data extracted from a resultset was retrieved as a `String`. You'll certainly need to get other types of data, and as you saw in the previous chapter, the `ResultSet` provides a number of methods for retrieving different data types. In order to use these effectively, we need to look at the SQL data types and understand how they map to the Java data types in your program.

Mapping between Java and SQL Data Types

The SQL-92 standard defines a set of data types that don't map one-for-one with those in Java. As you write applications that move data from SQL to Java and back, you'll have to take account of how JDBC performs that mapping. That is, you need to know the Java data type you need to represent a given SQL data type, and vice versa.

The `Types` class in the `java.sql` package defines constants of type `int` that represent each of the SQL types that are supported. The name given to the data member storing each constant is the same as that of the corresponding SQL type. When you retrieve the SQL type of a table column, by calling the `getColumnType()` method, for a `ResultSet` object for instance, the SQL type is returned as one of the constants defined in the `Types` class.

When you're retrieving data from a JDBC data source, the `ResultSet` implementation will map the SQL data onto Java data types. The table below shows the SQL-to-Java mappings:

SQL Data Type	Java Data Type
CHAR	String
VARCHAR	String
LONGVARCHAR	String
NUMERIC	java.math.BigDecimal
DECIMAL	java.math.BigDecimal
BIT	boolean
TINYINT	byte
SMALLINT	short
INTEGER	int
BIGINT	long
REAL	float
FLOAT	double
DOUBLE	double
BINARY	byte[]
VARBINARY	byte[]
LONGVARBINARY	byte[]
DATE	java.sql.Date
TIME	java.sql.Time
TIMESTAMP	java.sql.Timestamp

Note that the last three are Java class types defined in the `java.sql` package. The `Date`, `Time`, and `Timestamp` classes here that accommodate the requirements of the SQL types are derived from the `Date` class that is defined in the `java.util` package.

Conversely, when you are relating Java-to-SQL data types, the following mappings apply:

Java Data Type	SQL Data Type
String	VARCHAR, LONGVARCHAR
java.math.BigDecimal	NUMERIC
boolean	BIT
byte	TINYINT
short	SMALLINT
int	INTEGER
long	BIGINT
float	REAL
double	DOUBLE
byte[]	VARBINARY, LONGVARBINARY
java.sql.Date	DATE
java.sql.Time	TIME
java.sql.Timestamp	TIMESTAMP

> Note that some databases implement INTEGER data types as NUMERIC. When accessing INTEGER elements through the JDBC, it is important to associate the JDBC data type with the internal data type actually stored in the database.

Most likely you will know ahead of time what the SQL type is for the data you are accessing in a database. When this is not the case, you can easily determine the SQL type for each column in a resultset by calling the getColumnType() method for the ResultSetMetaData object. You can then compare the return value with the constants defined in the Types class to select the getXXX() method for the ResultSet object that is appropriate for retrieving the data.

Mapping Relational Data onto Java Objects

In the previous chapter, you saw how you could get the basic attribute data from a JDBC ResultSet object. Since Java is object oriented, in many cases you won't want to deal with individual data items such as the authors' names and IDs – you will want to work with Author objects that represent the authors. That's what we'll focus on now, and in the process, you'll get some more experience with the Statement and ResultSet interfaces.

The way that information is handled at the object level is usually different from the way that data is stored in a relational database. In the world of objects, the underlying principle is to make those objects exhibit the same characteristics (information and behavior) as their real-world counterparts – in other words, objects function at the level of the conceptual model. Relational databases, on the other hand, work at the data model level. As you saw in the previous chapter, relational databases store information using normalized forms, where conceptual objects like invoices and customers can be decomposed into a number of tables. So how do you deal with the problem of mapping objects to relational data models?

Sometimes there is a straightforward relationship between the columns in a table and the member variables in an object. In that case, the mapping task consists simply of matching the data types of the database with those of Java. The following figure shows this simple application-level SQL-to-object mapping:

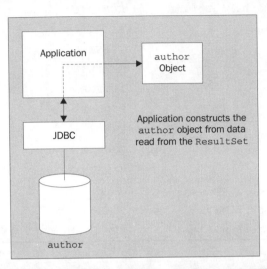

Try It Out — A Simple Mapping from SQL Rows to Java Objects

1. The authors table in the sample database is a good example of a simple mapping. To recap, this table has the following definition:

Column	Datatype	Description
authid	int	Unique identifier for each author
lastname	char(25)	Last name of author
firstname	char(15)	First name of author
address1	char(25)	First line of address
address2	char(25)	Second line of address
city	char(25)	City
state_prov	char(25)	State or province
postcode	char(10)	Postal code
country	char(15)	Country
phone	char(20)	Daytime phone number
fax	char(20)	Fax number
email	char(25)	Email address

2. Let's define a Java class for the authors. Take a look back at the table, which shows you how to map SQL to Java data types. Based on those mappings, we can define the member variables for an `Author` class, and add a constructor, member access methods and a `toString()` method.

```java
public class Author
{
  public Author(int authid, String lastname, String firstname,
                String address[], String city, String state,
                String postcode, String country,
                String phone, String fax, String email)
  {
    this.authid = authid;
    this.lastname = lastname;
    this.firstname = firstname;
    this.address = address;
    this.city = city;
    this.state = state;
    this.postcode = postcode;
    this.country = country;
    this.phone = phone;
    this.fax = fax;
    this.email = email;
  }

  public int getId()
  {  return authid;  }

  public String getLastName()
  {  return lastname;  }

  public String getFirstName()
  {  return firstname;  }

  public String[] getAddress()
  {  return address;  }

  public String getCity()
  {  return city;  }

  public String getState()
  {  return state;  }
  public String getCountry()
  {  return country;  }

  public String getPostCode()
  {  return postcode;  }

  public String getPhone()
  {  return phone;  }
```

```
    public String getFax()
    {   return fax;   }

    public String getEmail()
    {   return email;   }

    public String toString()
    {
      return new String
              ("author ID: " + Integer.toString(authid) +
               "\nname      : " + lastname + "," + firstname +
               "\naddress   : " + address[0] +
               "\n          : " + address[1] +
               "\n          : " + city + " " + state +
               "\n          : " + postcode + " " + country +
               "\nphone     : " + phone +
               "\nfax       : " + fax +
               "\nemail     : " + email);
    }

    int authid;
    String lastname;
    String firstname;
    String address[];
    String city;
    String state;
    String postcode;
    String country;
    String phone;
    String fax;
    String email;
}
```

3. Next, we need to get the data from the database into the `Author` object. Our first strategy for doing this is pretty basic – the application class will create the `Connection`, `Statement` and `ResultSet`, and read the data from the database. The `Author` class constructor will be called using each row of data read. For this example, we will use an SQL statement that is a literal string in the code, rather than creating a `PreparedStatement`.

```
import java.sql.*;

public class TrySimpleMapping
{
  public static void main (String[] args)
  {
    TrySimpleMapping SQLtoJavaExample;
    try
    {
      SQLtoJavaExample = new TrySimpleMapping();
      SQLtoJavaExample.listAuthors();
    }
```

```
      catch(SQLException sqle)
      {  System.err.println(sqle);   }
      catch(ClassNotFoundException cnfe)
      {  System.err.println(cnfe);   }
   }

   public TrySimpleMapping() throws SQLException, ClassNotFoundException
   {
      Class.forName (driverName);
      connection = DriverManager.getConnection(sourceURL, user, password);
   }

   public void listAuthors() throws SQLException
   {
      Author author;

      String query = "SELECT authid, lastname, firstname, address1,"+
                     "address2, city, state_prov, postcode, country,"+
                     "phone, fax, email FROM authors";

      Statement statement = connection.createStatement();
      ResultSet authors = statement.executeQuery(query);

      while(authors.next())
      {
         int id             = authors.getInt(1);
         String lastname    = authors.getString(2);
         String firstname   = authors.getString(3);

         String[] address   = { authors.getString(4), authors.getString(5)};
         String city        = authors.getString(6);
         String state       = authors.getString(7);
         String postcode    = authors.getString(8);
         String country     = authors.getString(9);
         String phone       = authors.getString(10);
         String fax         = authors.getString(11);
         String email       = authors.getString(12);

         author = new Author(id, lastname, firstname,
                             address, city, state, postcode,
                             country, phone, fax, email);

         System.out.println("\n" + author);
      }
      authors.close();
      connection.close();
   }

   Connection connection;
   String driverName = "sun.jdbc.odbc.JdbcOdbcDriver";
   String sourceURL = "jdbc:odbc:technical_library";
   String user = "guest";
   String password = "guest";
}
```

You should get the following output:

```
author ID: 1
name     : Gross                 ,Christian
address  : 1234 Corporate Drive
         : Suite 374
         : Anytown AnyProvince
         : VVV 888 Canada
phone    : null
fax      : null
email    : cgross@anynet.net
```

How It Works

Everything in this example should look pretty familiar, but there are just a couple of new things we need to cover.

Note first that there's an extra step after the data is read, which creates the Author object by calling its constructor with that data. Also in the while loop, as each row is read from the ResultSet, the application uses the appropriate getXXX() method of the ResultSet object to perform the mapping from SQL to Java data types. In each of these method calls, the argument is the index value to select the column. Since the query selects the columns by name, the columns in the resultset will be in the same sequence as the column names in the SQL query. In order to display the data for each Author object, we simply call System.out.println() and pass it the Author object reference. This will automatically invoke the toString() method for the object. Notice that in the output, the literal null appears where there are null values in the database.

> This example uses the JDBC-ODBC Bridge driver with a data source that does not require a user name or password. If you need a user name and password to access that data source, simply modify the code in the TrySimpleMapping constructor to use the appropriate driver, URL and getConnection() method of the DriverManager.

A Better Mapping Strategy

As you saw, the simple strategy described above does in fact transfer the data between the relational database and the Java objects successfully (and this approach can be used in reverse to get data back to the database, as we'll see shortly). It does, however, leave quite a lot to be desired because the movement of data between the database and the Java object is left completely to the application code.

A better, more object-oriented strategy would be to make the Author class handle its own data extraction from a ResultSet object. To do this we could add a static factory method (a method that manufactures Author objects) to the Author class that will synthesize Author objects from data in the database. The code calling the factory method must still do the work of creating the Connection and Statement objects, and use the Statement object to execute the query that retrieves the data. It will also need to ensure that the ResultSet contains the columns required for populating the Author object.

This figure shows this encapsulated SQL-to-object mapping.

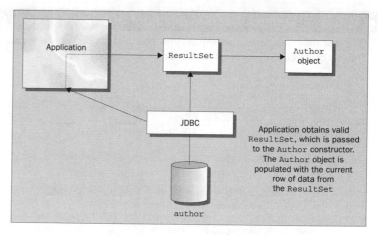

We need to establish an implied 'contract' between this factory method and any code that calls it:

❑ The current row of the ResultSet object that is passed to the factory method must be positioned at a valid row

❑ The ResultSet must contain all the columns from the authors table

We can implement the factory method in the Author class as:

```
public static Author fromResults(ResultSet authors) throws SQLException
{
  String[]address = {
                  authors.getString("address1"),
                  authors.getString("address2")
                  };

  return new Author(
                  authors.getInt("authid"),
                  authors.getString("lastname"),
                  authors.getString("firstname"),
                  address,
                  authors.getString("city"),
                  authors.getString("state_prov"),
                  authors.getString("postcode"),
                  authors.getString("country"),
                  authors.getString("phone"),
                  authors.getString("fax"),
                  authors.getString("email"));
}
```

Here we access the columns by name, so there is no dependency on the order in which they are retrieved in the query. This gives a little added flexibility to the application – to use the wildcard notation for instance. The only requirement is that all the columns should be present in the ResultSet object. If any are not, an exception of type SQLException will be thrown, and this will need to be caught by the calling method. Of course, the Author.java file must now have an import statement added for the java.sql package.

We can see this in action with another example.

Try It Out — Encapsulated Mapping of SQL Rows to Java Objects

We just need to create the application class. This class is nearly identical to `TrySimpleMapping`, except that there's less code in the `listAuthors()` method.

```java
import java.sql.*;

public class TryEncapsulatedMapping
{
  public static void main (String[] args)
  {
    TryEncapsulatedMapping SQLtoJavaExample;
    try
    {
      SQLtoJavaExample = new TryEncapsulatedMapping();
      SQLtoJavaExample.listAuthors();
    }
    catch(SQLException sqle)
    {
      System.err.println(sqle);
    }
    catch(ClassNotFoundException cnfe)
    {
      System.err.println(cnfe);
    }
  }

  public TryEncapsulatedMapping() throws SQLException,
                                         ClassNotFoundException
  {
    Class.forName (driverName);
    databaseConnection = DriverManager.getConnection(sourceURL, user, password);
  }

  public void listAuthors() throws SQLException
  {
    Author author;
    String query = "SELECT authid, lastname, firstname, address1,"+
                   "address2, city, state_prov, postcode, country,"+
                   "phone, fax, email FROM authors";

    Statement statement = connection.createStatement();
    ResultSet authors = statement.executeQuery(query);

    while(authors.next())
      System.out.println("\n" + Author.fromResults(authors));
    authors.close();
    connection.close();
  }

  Connection databaseConnection;
  String driverName = "sun.jdbc.odbc.JdbcOdbcDriver";
  String sourceURL = "jdbc:odbc:technical_library";
  String user = "guest";
  String password = "guest";
}
```

When you run the example, you should get results exactly as those from the previous example.

How It Works

All we've really done in this example is pushed the work of extracting Java types from the `ResultSet` to the class that is using the data. Instead of reading from the `ResultSet` and instantiating a new `Author` object for each row in the `listAuthors()` method, we just call the static `fromResults()` method of the `Author` class, which will create a new `Author` object from the data in the current row of the `ResultSet`.

This approach is better than the previous example because the class itself is responsible for ensuring that the correct mapping is performed between the database and the Java object. That way, applications don't have to duplicate that logic, and don't have the opportunity to attempt bad mappings (such as converting an SQL `REAL` type to an `int`). The mapping is also independent of the sequence of columns in the resultset. Encapsulation of the mapping from the database data to the class object is important for ensuring that classes can be reused easily within and between applications; so, although it's a little more work than the simple mapping method, it's well worth it.

The Statement and PreparedStatement Interfaces

In this section we're going to look in more detail at the `Statement` and `PreparedStatement` interfaces.

We will start with the `Statement` interface, where we learn about the methods that allow you to constrain the query, and how to handle data definition and data manipulation. Next, we'll look at the `PreparedStatement`, discuss the differences between static and dynamic statements, and work with the `PreparedStatement` interface.

The Statement Interface

You were introduced to `Statement` in the last chapter. The `Statement` interface defines a set of methods implemented by an object that is returned to your program by the `Connection` object. The `Statement` is always obtained by calling the `createStatement()` method of the `Connection` with no parameters:

```
try
{
  Statement queryStatement = connection.createStatement();
  // ...
}
catch(SQLException sqle)
{
  System.err.println(sqle);
}
```

Like pretty much every other method defined by JDBC, this code must be within a `try` clause, and include a `catch` statement for `SQLException`.

Once the `Statement` has been created, defining the query is as simple as building a `String` containing a valid SQL statement, and passing that statement as the argument to the `executeQuery()` method of the `Statement` object. The SQL query can be a literal, or it can be a `String` value that you build at runtime, as was the case in our `InteractiveSQL` application in the previous chapter, where the application obtains the SQL string from the text field just before the statement is executed.

Constraining the Resultset

In general, you will not normally know how much data will be returned from executing a query. In our `technical_library` example there isn't any possibility of getting into difficulties because of the volume of data, but with production databases you may need some controls. Getting a million rows back from a `SELECT` operation could be an embarrassment, particularly since a substantial amount of time will be involved, as well as memory. The `Statement` interface allows you to set constraints on the consequences of executing a query. You can limit the number of rows in the resultset that are returned, as well as specifying the maximum field size. You can also limit the amount of time for executing a query.

Maximum Number of Rows

The JDBC driver may impose a limitation on how many rows may be returned by a query, and you may wish to impose your limit on how many rows are returned in a resultset. The `Statement` interface defines the methods `getMaxRows()` and `setMaxRows()` that allow you to query and set the maximum rows returned in the `ResultSet` object, respectively. The value 0 is defined as no limit.

A particular JDBC driver may default to a practical limit on the number of rows in a resultset, or may even have implementation restrictions that limit the returned rows. To determine the row limit in effect, you can call the `getMaxRows()` method for your `Statement` object

```
Statement statement = connection.createStatement();
int maxRows = statement.getMaxRows();
```

When you wish to limit the number of rows returned from a query in an application, to prevent an extremely lengthy query process for example, you can call `setMaxRows()` to limit the number of returned rows:

```
SQLStatement.setMaxRows(30);
```

> It's important to note that, when the maximum row count is set to a non-zero value (zero being unlimited), you will not get any indication when the data that would have been returned is truncated. If the total number of rows exceed the maximum value, the maximum number of rows are returned in the resultset and any remaining rows that meet the query criteria will be silently left behind.

Maximum Field Size

The `Statement` interface also enables you to query and set the maximum field size that applies to all column values returned in a `ResultSet`. Querying this value will tell you if the JDBC driver imposes a practical or absolute limit on the size of the columns returned. The value 0 is defined as no limit.

To determine the maximum field size for statement results, simply call the `getMaxFieldSize()` method of the `Statement`:

```
Statement statement = connection.createStatement();
int maxFieldSize = statement.getMaxFieldSize();
```

The value returned is the maximum number of bytes permitted for any field returned in a resultset. Like the maximum row method pair, there is a corresponding `setMaxFieldSize()` method to set the maximum field size:

```
SQLStatement.setMaxFieldSize(4096);
```

Note that the `setMaxFieldSize()` only applies to columns with the following SQL data types:

BINARY	VARBINARY	LONGVARBINARY
CHAR	VARCHAR	LONGVARCHAR

Any bytes in a field in excess of the maximum will be silently discarded.

Query Time-out

Depending on your JDBC driver and the database to which it is attached, there may be an execution time-out period after which a query will fail and the `executeQuery()` method will throw an exception. You can check the value for the time-out period with the `getQueryTimeout()` method for a `Statement` object, or set the time-out period (for instance, if you want a query to fail after a fixed time period) using the `setQueryTimeout()` method. The time-out period is defined in seconds and time-out value of 0 indicates that there is no limit on the time that a query can take.

Here's a simple program that will test the default query constraints for your JDBC driver. You can substitute an appropriate URL and driver name if you have other JDBC drivers available.

Try It Out — Query Constraints

Since this program is tiny, we'll incorporate everything into the `main()` method:

```java
import java.sql.*;

public class TestQueryTimeOut
{
  public static void main(String[] args)
  {
    Statement statement = null;
    try
    {
      String url = "jdbc:odbc:technical_library";
      String driver = "sun.jdbc.odbc.JdbcOdbcDriver";
      String username = "guest";
      String password = "guest";
```

```
      Class.forName(driver);
      Connection connection =
              DriverManager.getConnection(url, username, password);
      statement = connection.createStatement();
      System.out.println("Driver         :  " + driver);
    }
    catch (ClassNotFoundException cnfe)
    {
      System.out.println(cnfe);
    }
    catch (SQLException sqle)
    {
      System.out.println(sqle);
    }
    // Put each method call in a separate try block to execute them all
    try
    {
      System.out.print("\nMaximum rows     :");
      int maxRows = statement.getMaxRows();
      System.out.print(maxRows == 0 ? " No limit" : " " + maxRows);
    }
    catch (SQLException sqle)
    {
      System.err.print(sqle);
    }
    try
    {
      System.out.print("\nMax field size   :");
      int maxFieldSize = statement.getMaxFieldSize();
      System.out.print(maxFieldSize == 0 ? " No limit" : " " + maxFieldSize);
    }
    catch (SQLException sqle)
    {
      System.err.print(sqle);
    }
    try
    {
      System.out.print("\nTimeout          :" );
      int queryTimeout = statement.getQueryTimeout();
      System.out.print(queryTimeout == 0 ? " No limit" : " " + queryTimeout);
    }
    catch (SQLException sqle)
    {
      System.err.print(sqle);
    }
  }
}
```

Running this with Access should result in the following output:

```
Driver           :  sun.jdbc.odbc.JdbcOdbcDriver

Maximum rows     : No limit
Max field size   :java.sql.SQLException: [Microsoft][ODBC Microsoft Access
Driver]Driver not capable
Timeout          :java.sql.SQLException: [Microsoft][ODBC Microsoft Access
Driver]Driver not capable
```

This is due to the fact that the underlying ODBC driver doesn't support time-out or field size constraints – more sophisticated drivers are likely to support these methods.

How It Works

This code is pretty simple. It creates a `Connection` using a URL defining an Access database called `technical_library`. Once the connection is established, a `Statement` object is created, and using that the values for the query timeout period, the maximum column size, and maximum number of rows can be executed. All three methods providing this information will throw an exception of type `SQLException` if the information is not available – as is the case with the Microsoft Access driver. To make sure that we do call all three methods, even when an exception is thrown, each method call is in a separate `try` block.

Executing DDL and DML

The `executeQuery()` method is used to execute a SQL query statement – a statement that is expected to return some results in a resultset. As we indicated in the previous chapter, there are other types of SQL statements that do not return results.

These statements fall into two primary categories: data definition language (DDL) statements, and data manipulation language (DML) statements. DDL statements are those that change the structure of a database, such as `CREATE TABLE`, and `DROP TABLE`. DML statements are those that change the contents of the database, such as `INSERT`, `UPDATE` and `DELETE` statements.

So far, all of the examples, including the InteractiveSQL application, have used the `executeQuery()` method. If, in the last chapter, you tried to execute an SQL statement that didn't produce a resultset, such as any DDL or DML, you would have seen an exception message reported on the status line:

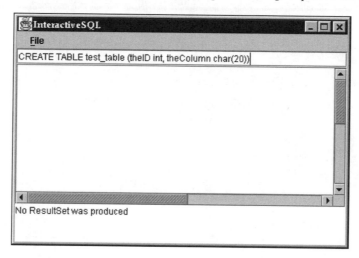

The exception containing the message "No ResultSet was produced" is thrown because the `executeQuery()` method only expects an SQL statement that generates results (note that, even though an exception is thrown in this case, the SQL statement is still executed).

The `Statement` interface provides the `executeUpdate()` method to execute statements that change the contents of the database rather than return results. Like `executeQuery()`, the `executeUpdate()` method accepts a single argument of type `String` specifying the SQL statement that is to be executed. You can use the `executeUpdate()` method to execute UPDATE, INSERT or DELETE SQL statements. You can also use it to execute DDL statements. The method returns a value of type `int` that indicates the number of rows affected by the operation when the database contents are changed, or 0 for statements that do not alter the database.

The code fragment below illustrates use of the `executeUpdate()` method to add a row to the `authors` table.

```
int rowsAdded;

Statement statement = connection.createStatement();
rowsAdded = statement.executeUpdate(
      "INSERT INTO authors (authid, lastname, firstname)
        VALUES(65,'Poe','Edgar')");
```

Using the `executeUpdate()` method, it is pretty easy to write a utility to create and populate a table. The next example does exactly that. In fact, this example is similar in principle to the `build_tables` utility that is included with the book's source code. Rather than reading SQL statements from a file, however, this example keeps them as string literals in the code.

Try It Out — Executing DDL and DML

Again, this is a small example, so the code will all be contained in the `main()` method. The URL and the driver are identified by the `url` and `driver` strings.

```
import java.sql.*;

public class BuildTables
{
  public static void main(String[] args)
  {
    try
    {
      String username = "guest";
      String password = "guest";
      String url = "jdbc:odbc:technical_library";
      String driver = "sun.jdbc.odbc.JdbcOdbcDriver";

      String[]SQLStatements = {
      "CREATE TABLE online_resources (pub_id int, name char(48), url char(80))",
      "INSERT INTO online_resources " +
                          "VALUES(1, 'Wrox Home Page', 'http://www.wrox.com')",
      "INSERT INTO online_resources " +
                    "VALUES(2, 'JavaSoft Home Page', 'http://www.javasoft.com')",
      "INSERT INTO online_resources " +
                      "VALUES(3, 'Imaginary Home Page','http://www.imaginary.com')"
                          };
```

```
        Class.forName(driver);
        Connection connection = DriverManager.getConnection(url, username,
password);
        Statement statement = connection.createStatement();

        for (int i = 0; i < SQLStatements.length; i++)
        {
          statement.executeUpdate(SQLStatements[i]);
          System.out.println(SQLStatements[i]);
        }
      }
      catch (ClassNotFoundException cnfe)
      {
        System.err.println(cnfe);
      }
      catch (SQLException sqle)
      {
        System.err.println(sqle);
      }
    }
  }
}
```

The SQLStatements String array contains the DDL and DML that will be executed by this program. The for loop simply iterates through each statement in the array, and executes it using the executeUpdate() method of the Statement.

You can check the results by running the InteractiveSQL application on the table you created and observing that the rows were inserted. To do this, start that application and execute the SQL statement:

  SELECT * FROM online_resources

After you're satisfied with your results, feel free to delete the table. Using a new instance of the InteractiveSQL application, execute the statement:

  DROP TABLE online_resources

InteractiveSQL will complain that no ResultSet is produced, but will dispose of the table nevertheless.

How It Works

The BuildTables program is very simple. The String array SQLStatements contains all of the SQL statements that we want to execute with executeUpdate() — one statement in each element of thearray. Note that we concatenate two String literals for three of the array element values just to make the presentation clearer on the page here. The for loop iterates through that array, and executes and prints each statement in turn. As usual, the code is inside a try block to catch any exceptions that might be thrown.

The only differences between this example and the other examples you've seen are that the SQL statements are executed with the executeUpdate() method instead of the executeQuery() method, and instead of a ResultSet being returned, the method returns the number of rows affected by the operation.

1073

The PreparedStatement Interface

Earlier in this chapter, ,you saw that you can build SQL strings on the fly and execute them with the executeQuery() method of a Statement. That is one way to introduce parameters into an SQL statement, but it is not the only way, nor is it necessarily the most convenient.

The PreparedStatement interface enables you to define an SQL statement with **placeholders** for arguments. Placeholders are tokens that appear in the SQL statement, and are replaced with actual values before the SQL statement is executed. This is usually much easier than building an SQL statement with specific values by concatenating strings.

A PreparedStatement object, like a Statement object, is created by a Connection object. Instead of calling the createStatement() method of the Connection object however, the PreparedStatement object is created by calling the prepareStatement() method. However, while a Statement object can be used to execute any number of different SQL statements, a PreparedStatement object only executes one predefined SQL statement that has placeholders for the variable parts of the statement. You specify the SQL statement that a PreparedStatement object represents by an argument of type String to the prepareStatement() method. The argument specifies the SQL statement with each placeholder for a value represented by a ? character. For example:

```
String newLastName = "UPDATE authors SET lastname = ? WHERE authid = ?";
PreparedStatement updateLastName = connection.prepareStatement(newLastName);
```

This defines a String object specifying an UPDATE statement with placeholders for the last name and the author ID. This is passed as the argument to the prepareStatement() method call that creates the PreparedStatement object, updateLastName. This will allow any value for lastname to be set for any author.

Setting Query Parameters

The question marks that appear in the changeLastName variable in the code fragment above are the placeholders in the statement for values that have to be supplied before the statement can be executed. You supply the value for a placeholder by calling one of the setXXX() methods of the PreparedStatement interface:

setAsciiStream()	setBigDecimal()	setBinaryStream()
setBoolean()	setByte()	setBytes()
setDate()	setDouble()	setFloat()
setInt()	setLong()	setNull()
setObject()	setShort()	setString()
setTime()	setTimestamp()	setUnicodeStream()

These methods accept, minimally, a position argument that identifies which placeholder you are referring to, and a value argument that is the value to be substituted for the placeholder. Placeholders are indexed in sequence from left to right with the leftmost placeholder being referenced with a position index of 1.

The method that you call for a particular placeholder for an input value depends of the SQL type of the destination column. You must select the method that corresponds to the field type, setInt() for type INTEGER for instance.

You must call an appropriate setXXX() method for each placeholder in the PreparedStatement object before it is executed. To execute the SQL statement that a PreparedStatement object represents, you call either its executeQuery() method if the statement generates a resultset or its executeUpdate() method to update or otherwise alter the database. Neither of these methods require an argument since the PreparedStatement object already has its SQL statement defined.

Once all the placeholders have values set and you have executed the statement, you can update any or all of them (or even none) before re-executing the statement. The following code fragment shows the PreparedStatement placeholder value replacement in action:

```
// Create a PreparedStatement to update the lastname field for an author

String changeLastName = "UPDATE authors SET lastname = ? WHERE authid = ?";
PreparedStatement updateLastName = connection.prepareStatement(changeLastName);

updateLastName.setString(1,"Burk");           // Set lastname placeholder value
updateLastName.setInt(2,27);                   // Set author ID placeholder
value

int rowsUpdated = updateLastName.executeUpdate();       // execute the update
```

Note that placeholders for string arguments are not quoted – they are just a ? character and the PreparedStatement automatically sets up the empty placeholder. Also, it's perfectly OK to set parameters in whatever order you choose – you don't have to set the first placeholder first, the second one next and so forth, just so long as they are all set before the statement is executed.

Let's try the code fragment above in an example that will change the last name of the author whose authid is 27.

Try It Out — Using a PreparedStatement Object

Try out the following code – only the bits that are of particular interest are shaded here:

```
import java.sql.*;

public class TryPlaceHolders
{
  public static void main(String[] args)
  {
    try
    {
      String url = "jdbc:odbc:technical_library";
      String driver = "sun.jdbc.odbc.JdbcOdbcDriver";
      String user = "guest";
      String password = "guest";
```

```
          Class.forName(driver);
          Connection connection = DriverManager.getConnection(url);
          String changeLastName = "UPDATE authors SET lastname = ? WHERE authid = ?";
          PreparedStatement updateLastName =

connection.prepareStatement(changeLastName);

          updateLastName.setString(1,"Burk");        // Set lastname placeholder value
          updateLastName.setInt(2,27);               // Set author ID placeholder value

          int rowsUpdated = updateLastName.executeUpdate();       // execute the update
          System.out.println("Rows affected: " + rowsUpdated);

          connection.close();
       }
       catch (ClassNotFoundException cnfe)
       {
          System.err.println(cnfe);
       }
       catch (SQLException sqle)
       {
          System.err.println(sqle);
       }
    }
 }
```

How It Works

The PreparedStatement object is created from the Connection object by calling the prepareStatement() method. The statement is also defined with the placeholders marked as question marks. Those placeholders, for the last name and author ID columns respectively, are then filled with values at runtime by calling the setString() and setInt() methods of the PreparedStatement interface.

The statement is executed by calling the executeUpdate() method which returns the number of rows affected by the update operation. No arguments are passed to the method since the SQL statement was defined when the PreparedStatement object was created.

Statement versus PreparedStatement

There will be times where the choice between using a Statement object or a PreparedStatement object may not be entirely clear. PreparedStatement objects are great when:

❏   You need to execute the same statement several times, and only need to change specific values

❏   You are working with large chunks of data that make concatenation unwieldy

❏   You are working with a large number of parameters in the SQL statement that make string concatenation unwieldy

Conversely, Statement objects work well when you have simple statements; and of course you have no option if your JDBC driver doesn't support the PreparedStatement interface.

Working with Input Streams

One of the most intriguing features of the `PreparedStatement` interface is the ability to use a stream as the source of data to be inserted in a statement in place of a placeholder. It's very often more convenient to deal with streams when you're working with data types like `LONGVARCHAR` and `LONGVARBINARY`. For example, an application storing binary images can very efficiently populate a `LONGVARBINARY` column by creating a `FileInputStream` object representing the source file.

The `PreparedStatement` interface provides three methods for extracting data from input streams:

Method	Description
setAsciiStream()	Use for columns with the SQL type LONGVARCHAR
setUnicodeStream()	Use for columns with the SQL type LONGVARCHAR
setBinaryStream()	Use for columns with the SQL type LONGVARBINARY

These methods require argument values that indicate the placeholder position, the `InputStream` object that is the source of the data, and the number of bytes to read from the stream. If an end-of-file is encountered before the designated number of bytes have been read, the methods throw an exception of type `SQLException`.

The next example is a simple illustration of using the `setAsciiStream()` method of the `PreparedStatement` to store Java source code in a database. It opens a Java source code file as an `InputStream` object, and uses that `InputStream` to populate a column in the database. Access does not support the `LONGVARCHAR` type, and we have to use `LONGTEXT` as the type for the field that will store the source code in the `CREATE TABLE` command.

Try It Out — PreparedStatement and Input Streams

The program starts out with the usual code. Then a `FileInputStream` object is created from the source code file for this program. The number of bytes contained by the file is obtained by calling the `available()` method:

```java
import java.sql.*;
import java.io.*;

public class TryInputStream
{
  public static void main(String[] args)
  {
    try
    {
      String url = "jdbc:odbc:technical_library";
      String driver = "sun.jdbc.odbc.JdbcOdbcDriver";
      String user = "guest";
      String password = "guest";
      FileInputStream fis = new FileInputStream("TryInputStream.java");
```

```
        Class.forName(driver);
        Connection connection = DriverManager.getConnection(url, user, password);
        Statement createTable = connection.createStatement();

        // Execute the SQL to create the table
        createTable.executeUpdate(
                "CREATE TABLE source_code (name CHAR(20), source LONGTEXT)");

        // Create a PreparedStatement to INSERT a row in the table
        String ins = "INSERT INTO source_code VALUES(?,?)";
        PreparedStatement statement = connection.prepareStatement(ins);

        // Set values for the placeholders
        statement.setString(1, "TryInputStream");        // Set first field
        statement.setAsciiStream(2, fis, fis.available());  // Stream is source

        int rowsUpdated = statement.executeUpdate();
        System.out.println("Rows affected: " + rowsUpdated);
        connection.close();
    }
    catch (Exception e)
    {
      System.err.println(e);
    }
  }
}
```

The code can throw exceptions of types `IOException`, `ClassNotFoundException`, and `SQLException` and they all need to be caught. The `FileInputStream` constructor and the `setAsciiStream()` method of the `PreparedStatement` interface can throw `IOException` exceptions. Since all we will do in each case is output the exception to the error stream, we can economize on the code by catching them all in the same `catch` block that uses `Exception` as the type. This works because all exception objects have the `Exception` class as a base.

You might want to check your results, by running the `InteractiveSQL` application, to verify that the table was created and the rows were inserted. Start that application and execute the SQL statement

    SELECT * FROM source_code

After you're satisfied with your results, feel free to delete the table. Having restarted the `InteractiveSQL` application, execute the statement:

    DROP TABLE source_code

Note that once the table exists, executing the `CREATE TABLE` command will fail, so if you want to run the example more than once be sure to delete the table each time.

How It Works

This program is very similar to the previous example. A `FileInputStream` object is created from the file `TryInputStream.java`. Since the `setXXXStream()` methods need to know how many bytes to read from the stream, we have to get the file size of the `TryInputStream.java` file by calling the `available()` method of the `FileInputStream`.

We first create the table by executing the `CREATE TABLE` SQL command using the `Statement` object, `createTable`. Then the `PreparedStatement` object, `statement`, is created, and the placeholder value for the first column is set by calling the `setString()` method for the `statement` object. The real magic happens in the `setAsciiStream()` method – all you have to do is supply the method with the placeholder position, the `InputStream`, and the number of bytes to be read – returned by the `available()` method for the `FileInputStream` object. When the SQL `INSERT` statement is executed, the bytes are read from the stream and stored in the second column of the row inserted in the database table, source_code.

When your JDBC applications will be dealing with large chunks of data, the `Stream` methods of the `PreparedStatement` interface are a real help.

The ResultSet

Now that we have a good understanding of the capabilities of the `Statement` and `PreparedStatement` interfaces, it's time to dig a little deeper into the details of getting the data back from the query. In this section, we'll add to what you learned about the `ResultSet` object in the last chapter. We will explore the `getXXX()` methods in more depth and look at some of the special SQL data types and how they are handled. We will also look at how to use streams with a `ResultSet` object.

Retrieving Column Data for Specified Data Types

So far we've retrieved data from a resultset as type `String` because data of any SQL type can be retrieved in this way. As we saw briefly in the previous chapter, like the `Statement` and `PreparedStatement` interfaces, the `ResultSet` interface provides methods for working with a variety of data types and retrieving data as a Java type that is more consistent with the original SQL type.

Most of these methods work alike, and come in two overloaded forms. One form specifies the column by the column name:

```
xxxvalue ResultSet.getXXX(String columnName)
```

The other specifies the column name by its index position, the first position index being 1:

```
xxxvalue ResultSet.getXXX(int columnPosition)
```

The mechanics of calling these methods is quite straightforward. But to use these methods effectively, you need to understand the possible mappings between Java data types and SQL data types in both directions.

The following table illustrates the mappings between SQL data types and the appropriate `ResultSet` `getXXX()` methods. To decide which `getXXX()` method you should use, look in the table for the method that maps the column data type to the Java type you will use. The 'preferred' method for a type is indicated with the ✓ symbol. That means that it is the closest mapping to the SQL type. Other methods may also work, however. Those methods are indicated by the ± symbol.

ResultSet method to SQL Data Type Mapping

	TINYINT	SMALLINT	INTEGER	BIGINT	REAL	FLOAT	DOUBLE	DECIMAL	NUMERIC	BIT	CHAR	VARCHAR	LONGVARCHAR	BINARY	VARBINARY	LONGVARBINARY	DATE	TIME	TIMESTAMP
getByte()	✓	±	±	±	±	±	±	±	±	±	±	±							
getShort()	±	✓	±	±	±	±	±	±	±	±	±	±							
getInt()	±	±	✓	±	±	±	±	±	±	±	±	±							
getLong()	±	±	±	✓	±	±	±	±	±	±	±	±							
getFloat()	±	±	±	±	✓	±	±	±	±	±	±	±							
getDouble()	±	±	±	±	±	✓	✓	±	±	±	±	±							
getBigDecimal()	±	±	±	±	±	±	±	✓	✓	±	±	±							
getBoolean()	±	±	±	±	±	±	±	±	±	✓	±	±							
getString()	±	±	±	±	±	±	±	±	±	±	✓	✓	±				±	±	±
getBytes()														✓	✓	±			
getDate()											±	±	±				✓		
getTime()											±	±	±					✓	±
getTimeStamp()											±	±	±				±		✓
getAsciiStream()											±	±	✓	±	±	±			
getUnicodeStream()											±	±	✓	±	±	±			
getBinaryStream()														±	✓	✓			
getObject()	±	±	±	±	±	±	±	±	±	±	±	±	±	±	±	±	±	±	±

Working with Null Values

As we have already said, NULL is a special value in the world of SQL. NULL is not the same thing as an empty string for text columns, nor is it the same thing as zero for a numeric field. NULL means that no data is defined for a column value within a relation. For example, recall the `authors` table, which has several values that may or may not have values assigned, including the `email` column. In order to determine which authors do not have an email address recorded, you could use the query:

```
SELECT authid FROM authors WHERE email = NULL
```

This query will return the ID for each author without an email address.

The `ResultSet` interface provides a method for testing a column value within a result set to determine if it is null. The `wasNull()` method returns a `boolean` value that is `true` if the last column read from the `ResultSet` object was a null, and `false` if it was some other value.

You will need to use the ability to detect a null value for a field in your code unless you created your tables with every column defined as NOT NULL, which would tell the database that it must never allow a null value in any column. However, that's not always a practical or desirable way to design tables.

Let's consider a simple example that selects and displays the author id, last name, first name, and email address for each row in the `authors` table. If any of these values are not assigned a value, the code could throw a `NullPointerException` when the program attempts to display the value. In order to avoid that sort of bad program behavior, this example will use the `wasNull()` method of the `ResultSet` to check for empty fields. Notice that the `wasNull()` method is called after the value is retrieved from the `ResultSet`.

Try It Out — Testing for Null Values in the ResultSet

Here's the code for the example:

```java
import java.sql.*;

public class TestNullValues
{
  public static void main(String[] args)
  {
    String url = "jdbc:odbc:technical_library";
    String driver = "sun.jdbc.odbc.JdbcOdbcDriver";

    String theStatement =
          "SELECT authid, lastname, firstname, email FROM authors";

    try
    {
      Class.forName(driver);
      Connection connection = DriverManager.getConnection(url, "guest", "guest");
      Statement queryAuthors = connection.createStatement();
      ResultSet results = queryAuthors.executeQuery(theStatement);

      String lastname, firstname, email;
      int id;
      while(results.next())
      {
        id = results.getInt(1);
        lastname = results.getString(2);
        firstname = results.getString(3);
        email = results.getString(4);

        if(results.wasNull())
          email = "no email";

        System.out.println(Integer.toString(id) + ", " +
                      lastname.trim() + ", " +
                      firstname.trim() +", " +
                      email.trim());
      }
      queryAuthors.close();
    }
    catch (Exception e)
    {
      System.err.println(e);
    }
  }
}
```

Running this code produces the following results:

```
1, Gross, Christian, no email
2, Roche, Kevin, no email
3, Tracy, Michael, no email
4, Horton, Ivor, no email
...
```

How It Works

In `TestNullValues`, the SQL statement is executed, and the values for the author id, last name, first name and email address are extracted into local variables. Since the value for `email` can be null in the table, we call the `wasNull()` method immediately after retrieving that column from `results` to test if the value read was a null value. If so, we replace the literal string referenced by `email` so outputting the report will work without throwing an exception. Since the `authid`, `lastname` and `firstname` columns are required, we didn't need to test those column values for null values.

Working with Special Data Types

In addition to providing access methods for standard Java data types, the JDBC `java.sql` package also defines some special data types to accommodate the characteristics of particular SQL types.

Date

The `java.sql.Date` class defines the object that is returned by the `ResultSet.getDate()` method. This class subclasses the `Date` class defined in the `java.util` package, so all of the methods for that class can be applied against this class. The `java.sql.Date` class overrides many of these methods, and provides a static `valueOf()` method that converts a string representation (*yyyy-mm-dd* form) of a date into a `Date` object.

Time

Like `java.sql.Date`, the `java.sql.Time` class wraps the `java.util.Date` class as a subclass, and provides a static `valueOf()` method that returns a `Time` object from a string representation (*hh:mm:ss* form) of time into a `Time` object.

Timestamp

The `java.sql.Timestamp` class also subclasses `java.util.Date`, but provides additional support for SQL timestamps with support for nanoseconds (`java.util.Date` only supports time to the nearest millisecond). The static `valueOf()` method creates a `Timestamp` object from a string representation (*yyyy-mm-dd hh:mm:ss.fffffffff* form). It also overloads accessor methods and comparison methods (`before()`, `after()`) to support nanoseconds.

Big Numbers

The SQL NUMERIC and DECIMAL types are mapped to the Java `BigDecimal` class type. This class is defined in the `java.math` package along with the `BigInteger` class. A `BigInteger` object defines an integer of arbitrary precision, with negative values in 2's complement form. A `BigDecimal` object defines a decimal value of arbitrary precision that can be positive or negative. A `BigDecimal` object is implemented as an arbitrary precision signed integer – a `BigInteger` object, plus a scale value that specifies the number of digits to the right of the decimal point. Thus the value of a `BigDecimal` object is the integer value divided by 10^{scale}.

To read a column value of either NUMERIC or DECIMAL SQL type as a Java BigDecimal object, you use the getBigDecimal() method for the ResultSet object.

The BigInteger and BigDecimal classes are worth taking the time to look into. The classes are very useful for applications that require a large number of digits of precision, such as security keys, very large monetary values, and so forth. The BigInteger and BigDecimal classes provide mathematical methods for addition, subtraction, multiplication and division, as well as comparison methods, and methods for returning their value as standard Java types. Additionally, BigInteger objects support bitwise and shift operations. The BigDecimal class provides methods for tailoring the rounding behavior in arithmetic operations.

Like Java String objects, the value of a BigInteger or BigDecimal object is immutable. That is, once an object has been created, you can't change its value. When you apply arithmetic operations to BigInteger and BigDecimal objects using their methods, such as multiply() and divide(), you always get a new object as a result, in much the same way as you get a new String object when you use the concat() or substring() methods of String.

Consider the difficulties you might have if you had to compute very large sums and needed a great deal of accuracy. Suppose you had to accurately calculate the product of the following two floating point numbers:

9876542346257623562356234623462.35632456234567890

and

9898234523235624664376437634674373436547.34586558

You might be tempted to write the following code:

```
class BigMultiplication
{
  public static void main(String[] args)
  {
    Double d1 = Double.valueOf(
        "9876542346257623562356234623462.35632456234567890");
    Double d2 = Double.valueOf(
        "9898234523235624664376437634674373436547.34586558");
    Double d3 = d1.doubleValue() * d2.doubleValue();
    System.out.println(Double.toString(d3));
  }
}
```

And then be very disappointed when your code produced the result:

9.776033242192577E74

Considering the number of digits of precision you entered originally for the factors, you would probably find this unacceptable. Of course, the problem is that the precision for values type double is fixed, and limited to the number of digits that you see above. Enter the BigDecimal class. Let's see how it would work with that.

We can do the calculation using `BigDecimal` objects as follows:

```java
import java.math.*;

public class TestBigDecimal
{
  public static void main(String[] args)
  {
    BigDecimal bn1 = new BigDecimal(
        "98765423462576235623562346234623462.35632456234567890");
    BigDecimal bn2 = new BigDecimal(
        "98982345232356246643764376346747373436547.34586558");
    BigDecimal bn3 = bn1.multiply(bn2);
    System.out.println(bn3);
  }
}
```

When you run the code the program prints the results:

```
977603324219257863723893512231480785031019252779047208595196675768219339448.773313
5102106926932422620
```

How It Works

The `BigDecimal` class has remarkable capabilities. It can support numbers of virtually limitless precision. The precision and scale are both 32-bit signed integer values, so they can be as large as 2,147,483,647 digits—and that's a huge number of decimal digits! In our example we create two `BigDecimal` objects, bn1 and bn2, representing the original values that we want to multiply. We multiply them using the `multiply()` method for bn1, and store the reference to the `BigDecimal` object that is returned containing the result in bn3. We can use this in a `println()` method call since the `BigDecimal` class implements the `toString()` method.

The `BigInteger` class is just as impressive — it provides the same arbitrary precision characteristics for integer values. Of course, there is a price to pay for that precision. Computations using the `BigInteger` and `BigDecimal` classes are notably slower than their counterparts using native Java types.

The `BigInteger` and `BigDecimal` classes manage digits as objects in a vector, so to get the flexibility of unlimited precision, you have to tradeoff computing time for operations on the numbers. Nonetheless, this class is invaluable for many applications.

Working with Streams

Earlier, we looked at using streams to populate LONGVARCHAR and LONGVARBINARY columns, because it's frequently much easier to use streams when you're working with large objects.

The `ResultSet` interface provides three methods for retrieving data from a database as a stream. These methods are:

Method	Description
getAsciiStream()	Use for LONGVARCHAR columns
getUnicodeStream()	Use for LONGVARCHAR columns
getBinaryStream()	Use for LONGVARBINARY columns

Each of these methods require an argument to be supplied that indicates the column either by name or by index position, and returns an `InputStream` object from which you can read the data.

The next example shows a simple example of using the `getAsciiStream()` method of the `ResultSet`. This code extends `TryInputStream.java` in the previous chapter, so please refer back to that section if you need some clarification on anything in this code prior to reading the comments below.

Try It Out — ResultSet Columns as Streams

We can revise our `TryInputStream.java` program file to use a stream by making the following changes:

```java
import java.sql.*;
import java.io.*;

public class TryInputStream2
{
  public static void main(String[] args)
  {
    try
    {
      String url = "jdbc:odbc:technical_library";
      String driver = "sun.jdbc.odbc.JdbcOdbcDriver";
      String user = "guest";
      String password = "guest";

      FileInputStream fis = new FileInputStream("TryInputStream2.java");

      Class.forName(driver);
      Connection connection = DriverManager.getConnection(url, user, password);
      Statement createTable = connection.createStatement();
      createTable.executeUpdate(
      "CREATE TABLE source_code (name char(20), source LONGTEXT)");
      String ins = "INSERT INTO source_code VALUES(?,?)";
      PreparedStatement statement = connection.prepareStatement(ins);

      statement.setString(1, "TryInputStream2");
      statement.setAsciiStream(2, fis, fis.available());

      int rowsUpdated = statement.executeUpdate();
      System.out.println("Rows affected: " + rowsUpdated);
```

```
          // Create a statement object and execute a SELECT
          Statement getCode = connection.createStatement();
          ResultSet theCode = getCode.executeQuery(
                                "SELECT name,source FROM source_code");
          BufferedReader reader;                     // Reader for a column
          String input;                              // Stores an input line

          while(theCode.next())                      // For each row
          {
            // Create a buffered reader from the stream for a column
            reader = new BufferedReader(
                            new InputStreamReader(theCode.getAsciiStream(2)));

            // Read the column data from the buffered reader
            while((input = reader.readLine()) != null)   // While there is a line
              System.out.println(input);                 // display it
          }
        connection.close();
      }
      catch (Exception e)
      {
        System.err.println(e);
      }
    }
}
```

Make sure that the `source_code` table doesn't exist before you run the program. You should see the text of the source code above printed out. After you're satisfied with your results, you can delete the table as before using the `InteractiveSQL` application.

How It Works

Most of this code sets up and populates the `source_code` table. Once that is done we get a `Statement` object from the connection that we will use to retrieve the data from the table. The `while` loop iterates through all the rows in the resultset in the way that we are now very familiar with. Using the `ResultSet` object that is returned from `executeQuery()`, we get an `InputStream` object corresponding to the second column in the current row by calling its `getAsciiStream()` method with the position index argument as 2. The `InputStream` object that is returned is used to create an `InputStreamReader` object, which in turn, is used to create a `BufferedReader` object that provides buffered stream input for the column data. The `readLine()` method for the `BufferedReader` object returns a `String` object containing a line of input. When the end of the stream is reached it returns `null`, so the inner `while` loop will terminate.

Calling Procedures

Many database systems support stored procedures, which are predefined sequences of SQL commands that you can call when you want the function defined by the stored procedure to be carried out. This is a very powerful facility with a lot of ramifications so we will only touch on the basics of how to use this here, just so that you are aware of it. JDBC provides support for this sort of capability through the `CallableStatement` interface that is derived from the `PreparedStatement` interface. You can obtain a `CallableStatement` reference corresponding to a stored procedure call by calling the `prepareCall()` method for a `Connection` object.

The argument to the `prepareCall()` method is a `String` object that defines a string in a format described as **SQL escape syntax**. The purpose of SQL escape syntax is to enable the driver to determine that this is not an ordinary SQL statement, and it needs to be transformed into a form that will be understood by the database system. This enables the idiosyncrasies of how stored procedures are called in different database systems to be accommodated, since it is up to the driver to recognize that the string is SQL escape syntax, and transform it to the format required by the underlying database. Let's first consider the simplest possible form for a string to call a stored procedure:

```
"{call procedureName}"
```

The braces are always present. The procedure that is to be called is `procedureName`. Given that you have a `Connection` object, `connection`, you could call the procedure with the following code:

```
CallableStatement call = connection..prepareCall("{call procedureName}");
ResultSet result = call.executeQuery();              // Execute the procedure call
```

Now you can obtain the data from the `ResultSet` object that is returned by the procedure using `getXXX()` methods in the usual way. This code assumes that the stored procedure produces a single resultset. Of course, it is possible that a procedure may produce multiple resultsets, in which case you would use the `execute()` method to execute the procedure and `getResultSet()` to retrieve the resultset. If the procedure updated the database you would call the `executeUpdate()` method to execute it.

Stored procedures can have arguments that specify input values (called `IN` parameters) to the operation. In this case you specify the parameter list between parentheses following the procedure name. Each parameter is denoted by ?, as for a `PreparedStatement` command, and you set the values for the parameters using the `setXXX()` methods in the way we have seen for `PreparedStatement` objects. For example:

```
CallableStatement call = connection..prepareCall("{call getMonthData(?, ?)}");
call.setInt(1, 6);                                   // Set first argument value
call.setInt(2,1999);                                 // Set second argument value
ResultSet result = call.executeQuery();              // Execute the procedure call
```

As we have seen, each parameter is identified by an index value, the first parameter having the index value 1.

Procedures can also have parameters for returning a result – referred to as `OUT` parameters, and you can set these too. The placeholder for an `OUT` parameter is ? – no different from an `IN` parameter, but obviously the process for setting the parameter is significantly different. For each `OUT` parameter you must identify the type of the output value as one of the types defined in the `java.sql.Types` class, by calling the `registerOutParameter()` method for the `CallableStatement` object. The first argument is the index position of the `OUT` parameter, and the second argument is the type. For instance:

```
call.registerOutParameter(2, Types.INTEGER);     // Second parameter OUT and
INTEGER
```

Once the `OUT` parameters have been registered, you then execute the procedure call in the way we have seen. If a resultset is returned, you can access the data from that in the usual way. To get the value for each `OUT` parameter, you must call the `getXXX()` method for the `CallableStatement` object that corresponds to the parameter type, so for the example above you would write:

```
int value = call.getInt(2);                      // Read second parameter value
```

Procedures can also have parameter that serve as input and output, so-called INOUT parameters. In this case you just combine what we have discussed for IN and OUT parameters, using setXXX() for the input value, registerOutParameter() to set the type for the output, and getXXX() to retrieve the output value.

Finally, a stored procedure may return a value – not as part of the parameter list but as a return value as for a method. In this case you specify it as follows:

```
CallableStatement call = connection.prepareCall("{? = call getData(?, ?)}");
```

This has two parameters plus a return value specified by the first ? – preceding the = in the string. This placeholder is at index position 1, and the two other parameters will be at index position 2 and 3. You now need to register the type of the value that is returned by the procedure before you execute the procedure call. You do this in the in the same way as for any other OUT parameter:

```
call.registerOutParameter(1,Types.DECIMAL);
```

When the procedure has been executed, you can retrieve the return value using the getDouble() method for the call object.

Handling Errors

So far, in all of the examples that we've used, we've glossed over the issue of errors, warnings and exceptions. The examples up until this point have all been predicated on the hope that everything will work OK.

Unfortunately, life is a bit less predictable than that, and you need to take some extra steps in your JDBC applications to handle conditions that generate warnings or errors. In this section, you'll see how to build mechanisms to trap errors, how to use the extra facilities built into JDBC to get detailed warning and error information from the data source, and how to gracefully recover from JDBC exceptions. The first place where we get some extra help is from the SQLException class.

SQLException

Most of the examples that you've seen so far have just output the basic exception that is thrown when an error occurred:

```
try
{
  //do JDBC stuff
}
catch(SQLException sqle)
{
  System.err.println(sqle);
}
```

This invokes the toString() method for the exception object and displays the result. Every method of every JDBC class and interface can throw a SQLException. Using the SQLException exception in this way is a pretty broad-brush approach to handling errors in JDBC, and it is possible to do a little better.

In order to do useful things with the SQLException, you need to know that there are three important pieces of information available from the exception object that is thrown. How you use these pieces of information depends on what is possible in the context of your application.

The Exception Message

The boiler plate information that you get with just about any exception is a string that describes the exception, and as you have seen, is returned by the getMessage() method of the exception object. For the examples that we've presented so far, this is the most useful piece of information. This string, however, varies, depending on the JDBC driver that you're using, so while this information is useful for humans as an indication of why things are not working out as they should, it's difficult for programs to make decisions based on this information. For that you need to use something a little different.

SQL State

There is another piece of information that is available when an error occurs – the SQL state – which can be used within a program to make decisions about how best to proceed. The SQL state is a string that contains a state as defined by the X/Open SQL standard. The SQL state value can be obtained from the SQLException by calling the getSQLState() method.

The X/Open standard defines the SQL state as a five-character string that consists of two parts. The first two characters of the string define the **class** of the state – for example, the characters 01 represent the SQL state "success with warning". Class here is merely a classification – it's nothing to do with class types.

The next three characters define the subclass of the state. The X/Open standard defines specific subclasses, and also provides the value 000 as a general subclass. Specific implementations may define state subclasses of their own using the values 900 through ZZZ where the standard does not provide a specific subclass.

The following table shows the SQL state strings defined in the X/Open standard. When these state codes are set, they may not be directly attributable to your JDBC code, but may reflect an error occurring in the underlying driver. For example, if you're using the JDBC-ODBC Bridge, a SQL state can reflect an error occurring at the ODBC driver level.

Class	Subclass	Description
01		Success with warning
	002	Disconnect error
	004	String data, right truncation
	006	Privilege not revoked
02	000	No data
07		Dynamic SQL error

Class	Subclass	Description
	001	Using-clause does not match dynamic parameters
	006	Restricted data type attribute violation
	008	Invalid descriptor count
08		Connection exception
	001	Server rejected the connection
	002	Connection name in use
	003	Connection does not exist
	004	Client unable to establish connection
	007	Transaction state unknown
	S01	Communication failure
21		Cardinality violation
	S01	Insert value list does not match column list
	S02	Degree of derived table does not match column list
22		Data exception
	001	String data, right truncation
	003	Numeric value out of range
	005	Error in assignment
	012	Divide by zero
23	000	Integrity constraint violation
24	000	Invalid cursor state
25	000	Invalid transaction state
	S02	Transaction still active
	S03	Transaction is rolled back
2D	000	Invalid transaction termination
34	000	Invalid cursor name
37	000	Syntax error or access violation
40	000	Transaction rollback
	001	Statement completion unknown
42	000	Syntax error or access violation

Class	Subclass	Description
HZ	000–ZZZ	RDA(Remote Data Access) errors
S0		Invalid name
	001	Base table or view already exists
	002	Base table not found
	011	Index already exists
	012	Index not found
	021	Column already exists
S1		Call Level Interface specific
	001	Memory allocation error
	002	Invalid column number
	003	Program type out of range
	004	SQL data type out of range
	008	Operation canceled
	009	Invalid argument value
	010	Function sequence error
	012	Invalid transaction operation code
	013	Memory management error
	015	No cursor name available
	900–ZZZ	Implementation defined

The SQL state string is a very useful piece of information if you want to programmatically handle exceptions. As you can see from the table, the subclasses indicate specific problems that in many cases may be recoverable. Using the SQL state value, you can make decisions in your program as to whether it is possible to recover from an exception or not.

For example, if your application creates tables, an exception indicating SQL state S0001 means that the table already exists. Depending on your application, this may not represent a fatal error, and your program can continue. This was the case in the example that generated to the source_code table for instance, and then output the source code from the table to the screen. As written, the example terminated when the exception was thrown, but it would obviously be possible to code the example to use the SQL state information and allow the program to continue with the output operation if the table was already there.

Vendor Error Code

The third piece of information that you can get from the SQLException is a vendor-specific error code. This value is returned as an integer, and its meaning is completely defined by the driver vendor. This value can be obtained by calling the getErrorCode() method of the SQLException.

Let's use an example to take a look at the additional information we can get when an exception is thrown.

Try It Out — Extracting information from SQLException

In this example, we will intentionally create errors in the executed SQL statements to generate exceptions, and then extract the message, vendor code and SQL state from the exception. In order to generate the exception, I've misspelled the name of the table in the variable, theStatement.

```java
import java.sql.*;

public class ExtractSQLExceptionInfo
{
  public static void main(String[] args)
  {
    String url = "jdbc:odbc:technical_library";
    String driver = "sun.jdbc.odbc.JdbcOdbcDriver";

    String user = "guest";
    String password = "guest";

    String theStatement = "SELECT lastname, firstname FROM autors";

    try
    {
      Class.forName(driver);
      Connection connection = DriverManager.getConnection(url, user, password);
      Statement queryAuthors = connection.createStatement();
      ResultSet theResults =  queryAuthors.executeQuery(theStatement);

      queryAuthors.close();
    }
    catch (ClassNotFoundException cnfe)
    {
      System.err.println(cnfe);
    }
    catch (SQLException sqle)
    {
      String sqlMessage = sqle.getMessage();
      String sqlState  = sqle.getSQLState();
      int vendorCode = sqle.getErrorCode();
      System.err.println("Exception occurred:");
      System.err.println("Message: " + sqlMessage);
      System.err.println("SQL state: " + sqlState);
      System.err.println("Vendor code: " + vendorCode +
                         "\n----------------");
    }
  }
}
```

When I ran this example, it produced the following:

```
Exception occurred:
Message: [Microsoft][ODBC Microsoft Access 97 Driver] The Microsoft Jet database
engine cannot find the input table or query 'autors'.  Make sure it exists and
that its name is spelled correctly.
SQL state: S0002
Vendor code: -1305
----------------
```

How It Works

In the `SQLException` exception handler, instead of simply displaying the string representation of the exception, we extract the message, the SQL state, and the vendor-specific error code. In this simple example, this information is formatted and displayed on the screen. In a more sophisticated application, you might want to decide how the program proceeds based on the information, and log this information to a file to help you troubleshoot your application.

The message returned is quite self-explanatory. The text will vary, of course, from driver to driver – hence the importance of the SQL state value. If you look back to the previous table, you will see that the SQL state reported in this exception corresponds to the SQL state 'Base table not found' which correctly identifies the problem. Lastly, the vendor code that was returned indicates the driver vendor's numeric code for the exception.

Chaining SQLExceptions

When an SQL exception is thrown, there may be more than one exception object associated with the error that caused the exception to be thrown. In order to handle this situation, the `SQLException` may be linked to another in a chain of exceptions.

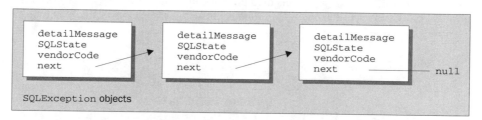

An `SQLException` object is essentially a node in a linked list. The `SQLException` class defines the `setNextException()` method for JDBC drivers and applications – the code throwing the exception in other words – to link a new exception to the chain. When a `catch` block in your program catches an exception of type `SQLException`, it is always the first node in a chain of one or more exception objects. You can call the `getNextException()` method for the `SQLException` that is passed to a `catch` block to obtain the next exception object in the chain if one exists. This method returns either a reference to the next `SQLException` object in the chain, or `null` if there are no more exceptions.

Thus, when your program catches an `SQLException`, you should always use the `getNextException()` method in a loop to get all of the exceptions. The code fragment below illustrates a simple technique for looping.

```
try
{
  // call a method that can throw SQLException
  theProgram.doSQLQuery();
}
catch(SQLException sqle)
{
  do                                  // loop through each exception
  {
    // do something with each exception
    System.err.println("Exception occurred:\nMessage: " + sqle.getMessage());
    System.err.println("SQL state: " + sqle.getSQLState());
    System.err.println("Vendor code: " + sqle.getErrorCode());
  }while((sqle = sqle.getNextException()) != null);
}
```

In the do-while loop, we output information from the exception object, sqle, which is passed to the catch block on the first iteration. The loop condition stores the references returned by the getNextException() for the sqle object back in sqle, and if it is not null, the loop continues. In this way we iterate through all the exceptions in the chain, outputting the information from each.

The next example shows the mechanics of how an application can add a new exception to a chain of SQLException objects in its exception handling. This technique is useful if you are defining a class that wraps one of the JDBC classes, and you want to provide additional information when an exception is thrown.

Try It Out — Chaining SQLExceptions

We will contrive to add an SQLException object to a chain of exceptions by executing the database operations in a method, doQuery(). This method will catch the SQLException when it is thrown, add a new exception object to the chain, and then rethrow the exception so that it can be caught in main(). Here's the code:

```
import java.sql.*;

public class ChainSQLExceptions
{
  public static void main(String[] args)
  {
    ChainSQLExceptions theApp = new ChainSQLExceptions();
    try
    {
      theApp.doQuery();                // Call the method that deals with the DB
    }
    catch(SQLException sqle)           // Catch the exception thrown by the method
    {
      do                              // loop through each exception
      {
        // do something with each exception
        System.err.println("Exception occurred:\nMessage: " + sqle.getMessage());
        System.err.println("SQL state: " + sqle.getSQLState());
```

```
            System.err.println("Vendor code: " + sqle.getErrorCode() +
                            "\n----------------");
        }while((sqle = sqle.getNextException()) != null);
    }
}

// Method to add an exception to a chain of SQLExceptions
public void doQuery() throws SQLException
{
    String url = "jdbc:odbc:technical_library";
    String driver = "sun.jdbc.odbc.JdbcOdbcDriver";
    String user = "guest";
    String password = "guest";
    String theStatement = "SELECT lastname, firstname FROM autors";

    try
    {
        Class.forName(driver);
        Connection connection = DriverManager.getConnection(url, user, password);
        Statement queryAuthors = connection.createStatement();
        ResultSet theResults = queryAuthors.executeQuery(theStatement);

        queryAuthors.close();
    }
    catch(ClassNotFoundException cnfe)
    {
        System.out.println(cnfe);
    }
    catch(SQLException sqle)
    {
        SQLException generatedException = new SQLException(          // New exception
                            "SQL operation cancelled", // Message
                            "S1008",                    // SQL state
                            0);                         // Vendor code
        generatedException.setNextException(sqle);      // Append the old exception
        throw generatedException;       }              // and throw the chain
    }
}
```

When I ran the program with the JDBC-ODBC driver I got:

```
Exception occurred:
Message: SQL operation cancelled
SQL state: S1008
Vendor code: 0
----------------
Exception occurred:
Message: [Microsoft][ODBC Microsoft Access 97 Driver] The Microsoft Jet database
engine cannot find the input table or query 'autors'.  Make sure it exists and
that its name is spelled correctly.
SQL state: S0002
Vendor code: -1305
----------------
```

How It Works

This example demonstrates the code we saw earlier to handle chains of SQLException objects, and how you can add exceptions to the chain.

The main() method calls the doQuery() method, which can throw a SQLException. The exception handler in main() starts with the exception object that is passed to the exception handler, and follows the chain of exceptions outputting the information for each one. For each exception, the message, SQLState and vendor code are displayed.

The doQuery() method contains an exception handler that appends a new SQLException to the chain when an exception is thrown because of an error in the database access code. We just append the old exception to our generatedException, and throw it again.

SQLWarnings

JDBC provides a means of obtaining warning information from JDBC objects. Sometimes conditions may arise that may not be serious enough to throw an exception, but do merit the program being signaled that all is not completely well. Warnings are represented by objects of type SQLWarning, and an SQLWarning object is silently appended to a JDBC object when an operation using the object causes something odd to occur.

The SQLWarning class is derived from SQLException, therefore it inherits the ability of the SQLException objects to define a message, an SQLState code, and a vendor code. An SQLWarning object can also be chained to one or more other SQLWarning objects. The techniques described in the previous section for traversing SQLException object chains apply just as well to SQLWarning object chains. In most respects, the SQLWarning looks a lot like SQLException, except for one very important distinction: you have to ask for an SQLWarning object explicitly. If you don't ask, you won't get.

The ResultSet, Connection and Statement interfaces all declare the getWarnings() method, which returns an SQLWarning object if warnings are present, and null otherwise.

To better understand how SQLWarning objects arise, consider one special class of warnings – data truncation. There is nothing preventing an application from retrieving data from a column as a Java type that is not particularly suitable for the SQL type – for example, accessing a floating point column as an integer type. Of course, this can and probably will result in data loss. This sort of thing will cause an SQLWarning object to be chained to the ResultSet object that requested the inappropriate data conversion. In order to detect this the application can call the getWarnings() method of the ResultSet object.

Since data truncation is a particularly common type of warning, JDBC provides a DataTruncation class that is itself derived from SQLWarning. Let's give it a go.

Try It Out — Using SQLWarning

This example is basically the same code as the previous example, except that here we intentionally retrieve floating point values from the PRODUCTS table integers in order to force a warning. Any warnings arising from data access operations are detected by the checkForWarning() method that we have added to the class. Here's the code:

```java
import java.sql.*;

public class TestSQLWarning
{
  public static void main(String[] args)
  {
    TestSQLWarning theApp = new TestSQLWarning();
    // Rest of the code as before...
  }

  public void doQuery() throws SQLException
  {

    // Connection string as before....
    String theStatement =
             "SELECT title, price FROM books WHERE price <> NULL";
    try
    {
      Class.forName(driver);
      Connection connection = DriverManager.getConnection(url, user, password);
      Statement queryBooks = connection.createStatement();
      ResultSet results = queryBooks.executeQuery(theStatement);
      int price;
      String title;
      while(results.next())
      {
        title = results.getString("title");
        checkForWarning(results.getWarnings());

        price = results.getInt("price");
        checkForWarning(results.getWarnings());

        System.out.println(title + " " + price);
      }
      queryBooks.close();
    }
    catch (ClassNotFoundException cnfe)
    {
      System.out.println(cnfe);
    }
    catch (SQLException sqle)
    {
      SQLException generatedException =
             new SQLException("SQL operation canceled","S1008", 0);
      SQLException lastException = sqle;
      while(lastException.getNextException() != null)
        lastException = lastException.getNextException();
      lastException.setNextException(generatedException);
      throw sqle;
    }
  }

  boolean checkForWarning(SQLWarning w)
  {
    if(w == null)
      return false;
    do
    {
      System.err.println("Warning:\nMessage: " + w.getMessage());
        System.err.println("SQL state: " + w.getSQLState());
```

```
            System.err.println("Vendor code: " + w.getErrorCode() +
                               "\n----------------");
      }while((w = w.getNextWarning())!=null);
      return true;
   }
}
```

When you run the program you should see the output:

```
Professional Java Fundamentals                                    35
Warning:
Message: Data truncation

SQL state: 01004
Vendor code: 0
----------------
Design Patterns                                                   45
```

How It Works

Since SQLWarning objects are just attached to the ResultSet object when unusual conditions arise, the code needs to check the ResultSet object after extracting each value to find out if any warnings were produced. The ResultSet.getWarnings() method returns an SQLWarning object if any warnings were generated, and null otherwise. The value returned by the method call is passed to our checkForWarning() method, which checks for a non-null value, and iterates through the chain of SQLWarning objects in the way we have seen applied to a chain of SQLException objects. For each warning the method outputs the message, the SQL state, and the vendor code. The method also returns a boolean value that is true if there was a warning, just in case the calling method needs to know about it. As you can see, we don't make use of this in our code.

The results displayed by running the program reflect the fact that the book "Professional Java Fundamentals" has a price of $35.00. Retrieving the price as an integer doesn't result in any data truncation. "Design Patterns", however, has a price of $45.25, and the SQLWarning is generated.

Browsing a Database

It's time we put together another 'proper' application with a decent GUI. As a final example on JDBC operations we will put together an application that will enable you to browse any relational database for which you have a JDBC driver available – plus the necessary authority to get at the data of course. Along the way, we will learn a bit more about how we can get hold of metadata for a database – we will need that to start the browsing process off. We will also explore some new components that will be useful in this context, as well as discover a few wrinkles about some that we are already familiar with.

Let's start by deciding the basic appearance of the application window. We will need to provide for an input area where the database URL, user ID and password can be entered. These will basically be single line text input fields, so JTextField objects will do nicely. We can use JLabel objects to annotate the entry areas. The password entry ought to have some protection from prying eyes though, and we can provide this by using the JPasswordField class, which happens to be a subclass of JTextField. The main feature of a JPasswordField object is that the input data is displayed as asterisks, so you can't read what was typed.

We need a regular application window so we can derive the application class from `JFrame`. It will be convenient to locate all the input at the top of the window, and we can arrange the fields and their labels quite easily using `Box` containers, as shown on the next page.

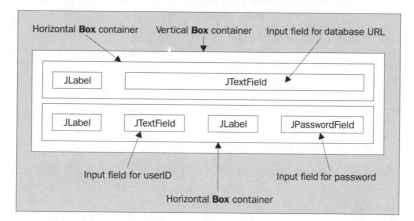

You will recall that the `Box` container uses the `BoxLayout` layout manager, and this arranges everything in a single row or column, depending on the orientation of the `Box` object. Here we have a vertical `Box` container with two horizontal `Box` containers inside it. The horizontal `Box` containers are used to align the input fields and their labels. We could start our application off by putting the code for this together, along with a `JTextArea` component at the bottom of the window to display messages to the user.

Try It Out – Building the Basic GUI

We will call our application class `DatabaseBrowse`, so the initial code will be as follows:

```
import javax.swing.*;
import java.awt.*;
import java.awt.event.*;
import javax.swing.border.*;

class DatabaseBrowse extends JFrame
{
  public static void main(String[] args)
  {
    DatabaseBrowse theApp = new DatabaseBrowse();      // Create application object
  }
  public DatabaseBrowse()
  {
    super("Database Browser");

    setBounds(0, 0, 400, 300);
    setDefaultCloseOperation(DISPOSE_ON_CLOSE);
    addWindowListener(new WindowHandler());
```

```java
      // Create labels for input fields
      JLabel dbURLLabel  = new JLabel( "Database URL: ");
      JLabel userIDLabel = new JLabel( "User ID:", JLabel.RIGHT);
      userIDLabel.setPreferredSize(dbURLLabel.getPreferredSize()); // Set same size
      JLabel passwordLabel = new JLabel("Password: ");
      // Box for database URL input
      Box dbPane = Box.createHorizontalBox();
      dbPane.add(dbURLLabel);
      dbPane.add(database);

      // Box for user ID and password input fields
      Box loginPane = Box.createHorizontalBox();
      loginPane.add(userIDLabel);
      loginPane.add(userIDInput);
      loginPane.add(passwordLabel);
      loginPane.add(passwordInput);

      Box inputPane = Box.createVerticalBox();
      inputPane.add(dbPane);
      inputPane.add(loginPane);
      getContentPane().add(inputPane, BorderLayout.NORTH);

      // Add message area
      status.setText("Enter a database URL and/or press Enter");
      status.setEditable(false);                        // No user input
      status.setLineWrap(true);                         // Lines wrap
      status.setWrapStyleWord(true);                    // on word boundaries
      status.setBorder(BorderFactory.createBevelBorder(BevelBorder.LOWERED));
      getContentPane().add(status, BorderLayout.SOUTH);

      setVisible(true);                                 // Set window visible
      show();                                           // Display the window
      database.requestFocus();                          // Focus to the url input field
   }

   private String userID = "guest";
   private String password = "guest";
   private String url = "jdbc:odbc:technical_library";

   private JTextField database = new JTextField(url);
   private JTextField userIDInput = new JTextField(userID);
   private JPasswordField passwordInput = new JPasswordField(password);
   private JTextArea status = new JTextArea(3,30);


   // Inner class defining handler for window events
   class WindowHandler extends WindowAdapter
   {
     // Handler for window closing event
     public void windowClosing(WindowEvent e)
     {
       dispose();                                       // Release the window resources
       System.exit(0);                                  // End the application
     }
   }
}
```

You can compile and run this as it is. You should see this window when it executes.

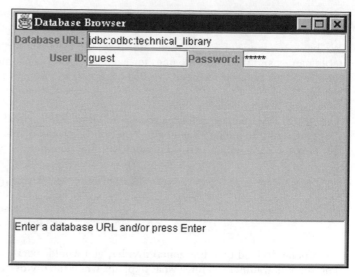

The cursor is on the database URL input field and the default password value appears as asterisks, just as it should.

How It Works

You should have no trouble seeing how this works as it's all standard stuff. The first bit sets up the window and creates a window listener to deal with closing the window using the inner class that we have included for this purpose.

The JTextField and JPasswordField objects and the String objects they display are all members of the DatabaseBrowse class because we will need to refer to these elsewhere. We set the preferred size of the label for the user ID field to be the same as that for the database URL label just to get them to line up nicely. Note how we specify the userIDLabel text as right justified; the second argument to the constructor can have values of RIGHT, LEFT, or CENTER. These values are actually defined in an interface, SwingConstants, that is implemented by the JLabel class. To arrange the input fields and their labels, we just add them all to their respective horizontal Box containers in the appropriate sequence, and then add these Box containers to the vertical Box container. This last Box container serves to arrange the other two one above the other. We then add the vertical Box container to the top of the content pane for the application window.

The message display area at the bottom of the screen is a JTextArea object displaying three lines. We don't want anyone entering data here and since input is allowed by default, we set it as not editable by calling its setEditable() method with the argument false. We also ensure we get line wrapping on word boundaries by calling the setLineWrap() and setWrapStyleWord() methods, both with the argument true.

Once the components are set up, we set the window as visible by calling its setVisible() method, and display it by calling its show() method. We finally call requestFocus() for the URL input field so that it will have the focus initially. Note that calling this method only works when the component is visible on the screen.

Displaying Database Data

We have two kinds of information to display, the metadata for a database, which in our case will be the table names and the column names for each table, and the contents of a particular table, as selected by the user. This suggests we need two display areas, and a `JSplitPane` component will provide just what we need.

The `JSplitPane` class defines a pane with either a horizontal or vertical divider that can be moved by dragging with the mouse. Each half of the split pane can display a separate component. For instance, we can create a pane with a vertical divider with the statement:

```
JSplitPane splitpane = new JSplitPane(JSplitPane.HORIZONTAL_SPLIT,
                             true,              // Continuous relayout
                             leftComponent,     // Left pane content
                             rightComponent);   // Right pane content
```

For a pane divided by a horizontal divider, you would specify the first argument as `VERTICAL_SPLIT`. The second argument defines what happens when the divider is dragged with the mouse. With a `true` argument the two panes are redrawn continuously as the divider is dragged. On a slow machine or with very complicated content for the two halves, you might want to set this to `false` which will only update the two halves when the divider drag operation ends. The last two arguments specify the components to appear in the left or right panes – or the top and bottom panes in the case of a horizontal divider. Any component can appear in either half, including a `JSplitPane` component. In this way you can create a pane that is split into however many panes you need.

In our case we will use a `JSplitPane` object that is split into two panes side by side. We will display the metadata in the left pane, and the contents of a table in the right pane. When it is complete, the application window will look as shown here.

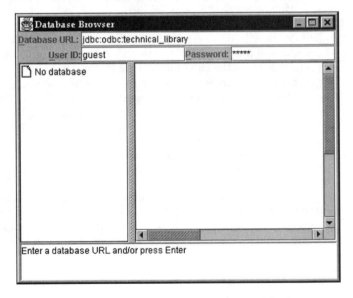

To display the table data in the right pane, we will use the same mechanism that we used in the `InteractiveSQL` example from the previous chapter – a `JTable` object with an underlying `ResultsModel` object displayed in a `JScrollPane` to allow scrolling of the data. For the metadata we will use something new – a `JTree` component – also within a scroll pane. Let's look at the basics of using a `JTree` component.

Using a JTree Component

The `JTree` class defines a component that displays data that is organized in a tree-like structure. There's a bit of jargon used with trees that you need to appreciate. Each element in a tree is referred to as a **node**, and the base node of the tree is referred to as the **root node**. A **parent node** is a node that has other nodes attached to it, and nodes that have a **parent node**, which will be all nodes other than the root node, are called **child nodes**. Nodes that have no children are called **leaf nodes**.

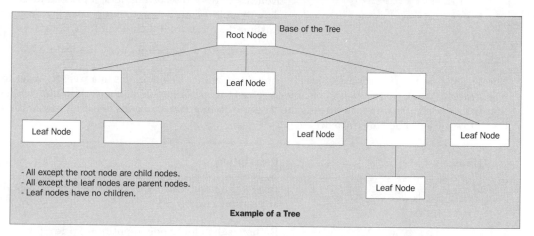

Example of a Tree

The data in a relational database can be visualized as a very simple tree that actually has a fixed number of levels – always three. The root node at the top level is the database itself, and that has child nodes on the next level that are tables. Each table node has child nodes on the next level that are the columns in the table, and since these are the lowest level these will be leaf nodes. The `JTree` class has vastly more capability than we will be using to display database metadata, both in terms of the complexity of the structures it can handle and in terms of the nature of the nodes in the structure. You can use a `JTree` component to display virtually any tree structure where the nodes in the tree can be any kind of object – and they can all be different if you want. You could use it to display people in the management structure of a company for instance, complete with photos of everyone, and different visual cues denoting the level of each person in the hierarchy. We won't be going into this level of detail, but if you have an idea of the potential you may want to explore it further for yourself.

Defining Tree Nodes

A node in a tree can be any object of a class that implements the `TreeNode` interface. The methods declared by the `TreeNode` interface provide the means of navigating a tree:

Method	Description
`getParent()`	Returns the parent node as a `TreeNode` reference and `null` if there isn't one, i.e. it's a root node.
`getChildCount()`	Returns the number of child nodes as type `int`.
`getChildAt(int index)`	Returns the child node at position `index` – child nodes being indexed from 0.

Method	Description
children()	Returns a reference to an Enumeration object that can be used to iterate through the child nodes.
getIndex(TreeNode node)	Returns the index value for the child node, node.
getAllowsChildren()	Returns true if the current node allows children. By default children are allowed, but classes that implement this interface can inhibit children for a node.
isLeaf()	Returns true if the current node is a leaf node.

The TreeNode interface doesn't provide enough capability to link nodes in a tree. In order to create a tree structure, each node needs to be able to refer to its parent node, and any child nodes it has. The MutableTreeNode interface extends the TreeNode interface and adds declarations for the methods that allow a tree to be constructed:

Method	Description
insert (MutableTreeNode child, int index)	Inserts the node, child, as a child of the current node at position index.
remove(int index)	Removes the child node at position index for the current node.
remove (MutableTreeNode node)	Removes node from the set of children of the current node.
removeFromParent()	Removes the current node from the list of children for its parent node.
setParent (MutableTreeNode parent)	Sets parent as the parent of the current node.
setUserObject(Object o)	Sets the object, o, as the object to be displayed for the node in a tree. This is where you set your node information – the table name for a node representing a database table for instance.

While you can create your own class to define nodes if you want, the DefaultMutableTreeNode class in the javax.swing.tree package is adequate for most purposes. This class implements the MutableTreeNode interface and adds a few more methods of its own. The default constructor creates an object with no parent and no children. You can also construct a DefaultMutableTreeNode object containing an object of your own – again with no parent and no children using the constructor that accepts a single argument of type Object – any class type in other words. For instance:

```
DefaultMutableTreeNode tableNode = new DefaultMutableTreeNode("authors");
```

A third constructor accepts a second argument of type boolean, and a value of false prevents the node from having children – forcing it to be a leaf node in other words. We won't need to go into the methods that the DefaultMutableTreeNode class has beyond those we have already discussed, but we do need to know more about how the JTree class works before we can use it.

Tree Models

Like the `JTable` component, the `JTree` component works with an underlying model object that supplies the data that is to be displayed in the tree. A class that defines a model for a tree implements the `TreeModel` interface, which appears in the `javax.swing.tree` package. This is quite an extensive interface with eight methods declared in it, so to save you the work of creating a class from scratch, the `javax.swing.tree` package includes a `DefaultTreeModel` class that implements `TreeModel`, and that you can use 'as is' in many situations. You create a `DefaultTreeModel` object using a single node that is the root node for your tree. For example:

```
DefaultMutableTreeNode dbNode = new DefaultMutableTreeNode("No Database");
DefaultTreeModel dbTreeModel = new DefaultTreeModel(dbNode);
```

Here, we first construct a node object with the `String` argument as the object it stores. We then use this as the root node to create a tree model object, `model`. Now we have a `DefaultTreeModel` object, we can create a `JTree` object from it using the `JTree` class constructor that accepts a `TreeModel` reference as the argument:

```
Tree dbTree = new JTree(dbTreeModel);
```

Our `dbTree` object doesn't do too much. When we want to actually store a database in the tree, we can call `setRoot()` for the `DefaultTreeModel` object to set a new root node that we will add table nodes to using the methods from the `MutableTreeNode` interface. Before we get to that, we need to put the component together in the GUI that will display the metadata. Let's try adding the code for that to our example.

Try It Out – Creating and Displaying a Tree

We will first add the data members to the `DatabaseBrowse` class that we will need to access in various class methods:

```
private DefaultMutableTreeNode dbNode;      // Root node for the database tree
private DefaultTreeModel dbTreeModel;       // Model for the database metadata
private JTree dbTree;                        // Tree to display the metadata
private JScrollPane treePane;               // Scroll pane holding the tree
```

We will also need to add an `import` statement to the `DatabaseBrowse.java` file for the package supporting trees:

```
import javax.swing.tree.*;
```

Now we can add code to the `DatabaseBrowse` class constructor to create the tree and place it in a scroll pane:

```
// Create tree to go in left split pane
dbNode = new DefaultMutableTreeNode("No database");
dbTreeModel = new DefaultTreeModel(dbNode);
dbTree = new JTree(dbTreeModel);
treePane = new JScrollPane(dbTree);
treePane.setBorder(BorderFactory.createLineBorder(Color.darkGray));
```

This code will go just before the call to `setVisible()` in the constructor. As you can see, we are just applying the code we saw earlier to first create a root node, then we create a model from the root node, then a tree object is created from the model, and finally we place the tree in a scroll pane.

We will want to put the scroll pane containing the tree in the left half of a split pane, but first we need to put together the component that goes in the other half that will eventually display the table data. As we discussed, this will be another `JScrollPane` object containing a `JTable` object – just as we had in the `InteractiveSQL` example. We will use the `ResultsModel` class here too, so copy the source file for the class from the directory containing the `InteractiveSQL` files to the directory for our current example. We will need the classes from the `javax.swing.table` package, so add an import statement for that:

```
import javax.swing.table.*;
```

We will need three data members in the `DatabaseBrowse` class to store the model, the table, and the scroll pane object that will contain the table:

```
ResultsModel tableModel;          // Model for table
private JTable table;             // Table holding table data
JScrollPane tablePane;            // Scroll pane holding the table
```

The code to add the table can go immediately following the previous block of code that created the tree:

```
// Create table to go in right split pane
tableModel = new ResultsModel();
JTable table = new JTable(tableModel);
table.setAutoCreateColumnsFromModel(true);
table.setAutoResizeMode(JTable.AUTO_RESIZE_OFF);
tablePane = new JScrollPane(table);
tablePane.setBorder(BorderFactory.createLineBorder(Color.darkGray));
```

We have no idea at this point how many rows and columns there will be in a table. This will vary depending on the table currently selected. By putting the table in a scrollpane we can deal with a table with any number of rows. If there are too many to fit within the available space, the scrollpane will automatically insert a scrollbar to manage the rows. Calling `setAutoCreateColumnsFromModel()` with the argument `true` ensures the table will create columns based on information from the model, rather than using defaults. We also call `setAutoResizeMode()` with the argument `JTable.AUTO_RESIZE_OFF` to prevent the columns being squashed up to fit within the available space for the table. This way we will get a horizontal scrollbar if the column headings exceed the width of the scrollpane.

Now we can create the split pane containing the tree and the table, and add it to the content pane of the application window. This code can follow the code above in the constructor:

```
JSplitPane splitpane = new JSplitPane(JSplitPane.HORIZONTAL_SPLIT,
                                      true,           // Continuous relayout
                                      treePane,       // Left pane content
                                      tablePane);     // Right pane content
getContentPane().add(splitpane, BorderLayout.CENTER);
splitpane.setDividerLocation(150);                    // Left pane 150 pixels
wide
```

We should also call `pack()` for the window to lay out the components at their appropriate sizes:

```
pack();
```

This can go just before the `setVisible()` method call in the constructor.

If you compile the application again and run it, the window should be similar to the screenshot that you saw earlier.

How It Works

The `JTree` and the `JTable` objects have been set up to display data in the left and right panes of the `JSplitPane` object. They each have their respective model objects that will supply the data that is to be displayed. They each have their own scroll pane that will provide scrolling capability when the data is outside the area that is displayed. Each `JScrollPane` object has its own line border, and when we have data to display, we will replace this with a titled border that will show the name of the data that is displayed — the database URL for the left pane, and the table name for the right pane.

Try the split pane divider. The `JSplitPane` object manages this quite automatically, and will arrange for the contents of the panes to be redrawn as necessary.

Getting Database Metadata

We need to obtain the database metadata that will be displayed by the `JTree` object in the left scroll pane. We can do this when a connection has been established, for which we need the database URL plus the user ID and password. Before we can establish a connection we want to be sure the driver is loaded, so add the following data member to the `DatabaseBrowse` class to store the driver names:

```
private String[] drivers = {
                            "sun.jdbc.odbc.JdbcOdbcDriver",        // ODBC bridge
                            "com.imaginary.sql.msql.MsqlDriver"    // mSQL driver
                           };
```

We have added the driver for mSQL – which is a mini SQL implementation that is available as shareware – just to show how easy it is to have multiple drivers. You can also put the names of your own drivers between the braces. We will put code in the constructor that will try to load all the drivers in the drivers array, and failing to load a driver won't matter, as long as you don't need it of course. Add the following code to the end of the code for the constructor:

```
// Attempt to load all drivers
for (int i = 0 ; i < drivers.length ; i++)
  try
  {
    Class.forName(drivers[i]);
  }
  catch(ClassNotFoundException cnfe)
  {
    System.err.println(cnfe);
    status.setText("Driver load failed: " + cnfe.getMessage());
  }
```

The `try` and `catch` blocks are both within the scope of the `for` loop, so failing to load one driver will not prevent the others from being loaded.

The trigger to open a connection with a database will be pressing the *Enter* key for any of the input fields. By default, this will create an action event, so we can respond to this by making the `DatabaseBrowse` class implement the `ActionListener` interface, defining the `actionPerformed()` method in the class, and adding the class object as the action listener for all three input fields. The first line of the class definition will be:

```
class DatabaseBrowse extends JFrame
                        implements ActionListener
```

The `actionPerformed()` method definition will be:

```
public void actionPerformed(ActionEvent e)
{
  Object source = e.getSource();                // Get source of the event
  if(source == database     ||                  // If its URL input,
     source == userIDInput ||                    // or userID input,
     source == passwordInput)                     // or password input,
  {                                              // we will try for a connection
    url = database.getText();                     // Get database URL
    userID = userIDInput.getText();                  // Get user ID

    char[] pw = passwordInput.getPassword();        // Get password
    if(pw != null)
      password = new String(pw);

    if(url == null || url.length()==0)
      {
        status.setText("Please specify a database URL ");
        return;
      }
    openConnection();
    password = null;                                // For security
  }
}
```

Here we get all the input we need, and then call a method `openConnection()` that we will need to add to the `DatabaseBrowse` class before we try compiling the code again. We also need to register the application object as the listener for the events, so add the following code to the constructor preceding the call to `pack()`;

```
// Add event listeners
database.addActionListener(this);
userIDInput.addActionListener(this);
passwordInput.addActionListener(this);
```

Since the `this` pointer references the current object, the application object will be registered as the action listener for all three input fields.

If we add the `openConnection()` method to the `DatabaseBrowse` class, we could take the application for another run.

Try It Out — Opening a Connection

Our application class will need data members to store a `Connection` reference, and to store a
`Statement` reference that we will use to execute an SQL query when we want to display table data.
You can do this by adding the following declarations to the class:

```
Connection connection;
Statement statement;
```

You can add an `import` statement for the `java.sql` package too, at this point, since we need it for the
definition of the `Connection` and `Statement` interfaces.

```
import java.sql.*;
```

Because it will be called each time the user enters a new URL and presses *Enter*, the
`openConnection()` method will need to close any existing connection before opening a new
connection. It will also need to reset the contents of the split pane – both the metadata and any table
data that is displayed. To facilitate resetting the contents of the `JTable` displayed in the right split pane,
we can amend the `ResultsModel` class method, `setResultSet()`, to reset the data when a null
argument is passed to it. We can do this as follows:

```
public void setResultSet(ResultSet results)
{
  if(results == null)
  {
    columnNames = new String[0];        // Reset the columns names
    dataRows.clear();                   // Remove all entries in the Vector
    fireTableChanged(null);             // Tell the table there is new model
data
    return;
  }
  // Rest of the code as before...
}
```

So by passing `null` to this method, we will reset the `JTable` object it supports to display nothing.

We can now implement the first part of the `openConnection()` method in our `DatabaseBrowse`
class as follows:

```
public void openConnection()
{
  try
  {
    if(connection != null)                    // If there is a connection
    {                                         // close it
      connection.close();

      // Reset the table data
      tableModel.setResultSet(null);
      tablePane.setBorder(BorderFactory.createLineBorder(Color.darkGray));
```

```
      // Reset the tree displaying metadata
      dbNode = new DefaultMutableTreeNode("No database");
      dbTreeModel.setRoot(dbNode);
      dbTree.setRootVisible(true);
      treePane.setBorder(BorderFactory.createLineBorder(Color.darkGray));
      dbTreeModel.reload();
    }

    // Code to open the new connection...
  }
  catch(SQLException sqle)
  {
    status.setText(sqle.getMessage());                   // Display first message
    do                                                   // loop through exceptions
    {
      System.err.println("Exception occurred:\nMessage: " + sqle.getMessage());
      System.err.println("SQL state: " + sqle.getSQLState());
      System.err.println("Vendor code: " + sqle.getErrorCode() +
                         "\n----------------");
    }
    while((sqle = sqle.getNextException()) != null);
  }
}
```

If connection is not null, we call close() for the connection object to close it, and reset any table data that is displayed by calling the setResultSet() member of the model object supporting the table. We also have to reset the border for the scroll pane that contains the table, because we will put a title border in place showing the table name when we display data from a table.

To reset the JTree object, we first set a new root node for the underlying TreeModel object by calling its setRoot() method and passing a new node object as the argument. When we display the metadata for a database, what we want to see are the table names, and optionally the columns in each table, and since the root node takes up unnecessary real estate within the application window, we will set it as invisible to provide maximum space for what we want to see. However, we restore the visibility of the "No database" root node when there are no tables in the tree, as we reset the model, and this is done by calling the setRootVisible() method for the JTree object, dbTree, with the argument true. Lastly we have to reset the border for the scroll pane to a line border, because we will use a title border to display the database name when the metadata is displayed.

To open the new connection we can add the following code:

```
public void openConnection()
{
  try
  {

    // Code to close the old connection as before....

    // Now open the new connection
    connection = DriverManager.getConnection(url, userID, password);
    status.setText("Database connection established");
    statement = connection.createStatement();          // Create statement for
query
```

```
        dbNode = new DefaultMutableTreeNode(url);          // Root node is URL
        dbTreeModel.setRoot(dbNode);                       // Set root in model
        setupTree(connection.getMetaData());               // Set up tree with metadata

        treePane.setBorder(BorderFactory.createTitledBorder(
                        BorderFactory.createLineBorder(Color.darkGray),
                        url,
                        TitledBorder.CENTER,
                        TitledBorder.DEFAULT_POSITION));
        dbTree.setRootVisible(false);                      // Now show the root node
        dbTreeModel.reload();                              // Get the tree redisplayed
    }
    catch(SQLException sqle)
    {
      status.setText(sqle.getMessage());                   // Display first message
      do                                                   // loop through exceptions
      {
        System.err.println("Exception occurred:\nMessage: " + sqle.getMessage());
        System.err.println("SQL state: " + sqle.getSQLState());
        System.err.println("Vendor code: " + sqle.getErrorCode() +
                        "\n----------------");
      }
      while((sqle = sqle.getNextException()) != null);
    }
}
```

We open the connection and create a `Statement` object in the way you have seen previously. We create a new root node for the tree model and store the `String` object containing the URL as the user object in the node. To populate the tree with the metadata, we call the method `setupTree()` in our application class — we will come to the implementation of this in a moment. The argument is a `DatabaseMetaData` reference that is returned by the `getMetaData()` method that we call for the `connection` object. To show the database name in the left split pane, we reset the border for the scroll pane containing the tree to a title border showing the database URL. As we discussed above, we won't want to see the root node while the table names are displayed, so we set the root node as invisible by calling the `setRootVisible()` method for the tree with the argument `false`. Calling the `reload()` method for the `DefaultTreeModel` object causes the data to be reloaded into the tree, so the tree display will be updated.

Any exceptions thrown in all this will be caught by the `catch` block. To let the user know directly when an error occurs, we display the message for the exception in the status area at the bottom of the application window. We then iterate through the potential chain of exceptions using the technique that you saw earlier.

If you want to try compiling and running the application again, you can add an empty definition for the `setupTree()` method to the `DatabaseBrowse` class:

```
private void setupTree(DatabaseMetaData metadata)
{
}
```

When you press *Enter*, the connection will be established and the application window will look something like that shown here.

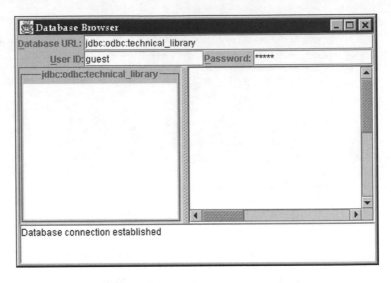

How It Works

Pressing the *Enter* key with the focus in any of the input fields will cause the `openConnection()` method to be called if there is a database URL available. This opens the connection and displays the URL in the border of the left scroll pane. There are no scrollbars yet because there is no data in the scroll pane. The scrollbars are displayed in the right scroll pane because we set the size of the `JTable` object to be larger than the scroll pane. As you can see, the status is displayed at the bottom of the screen. Try entering an invalid database URL and see the effect.

Loading the Database Metadata

The `setupTree()` method will be responsible for retrieving the metadata using the `DatabaseMetaData` reference that is passed as an argument. This interface declares well in excess of 100 methods, so we are not going to be going through them – we will just pick a few that are relevant in the present context, and you can explore the rest in the JDK documentation. One word of caution – all of these methods depend on the underlying driver and database engine supporting access to the metadata that is required, and in many cases this will not be available, in which case the requesting method will throw an exception. For instance, although it would be nice to be able to display the key fields in a table in our example, by using the `getPrimaryKeys()` method in the `DatabaseMetaData` interface, unfortunately this capability is not supported by the ODBC driver for Access.

There are different kinds of metadata you can potentially get at. One broad classification is information related to the capability of the database engine in general. You can request the SQL types supported by calling the `getTypesInfo()` method for instance, or the maximum length of an SQL statement by calling the `getMaxStatementLength()` method. There are a whole series of methods providing data on the limits on table sizes, row length, and other constraints implicit in the database system. You would use this kind of data to condition your application code to work within the prescribed limits. This provides the possibility of your code being able to adapt itself to accommodate the constraints that are peculiar to the current database, and thus avoid exceptions being thrown when attempting operations outside the limits of the database. Of course, if the database and/or driver does not make the data available, it won't be particularly effective, but the architects of JDBC have at least had the foresight to provide for the possibility.

Retrieving Table Names

Most of the time the metadata you will be interested in relates to the particular database that you want to access. You can get information about the tables within the database with the `getTables()` method that is of the form:

```
getTables(String catalog,
          String schemaPattern,
          String tableNamePattern,
          String[] types)
```

The arguments form the basis for deciding which tables in the database are to be identified, and each argument provides a separate way of filtering out the tables that you are interested in. The first argument is a database catalog name, and data will be returned on the tables within the catalog that you specify. If you supply an empty string, `" "`, you will get information on tables without a catalog. If you supply `null` as the argument you will get tables with and without a catalog.

The second argument is a pattern for a schema name. A database schema is a set of declarations for the tables and other entities such as views that make up the database. Only tables for schemas conforming to the pattern will be selected. A pattern is a string of characters where '`%`' means any substring, and '`_`' means any character. For instance the pattern `"%data"` specifies any string ending `"data"`, so `"Mydata"` or `"Yourdata"` would be in, and `"Mydata1"` would be out. The pattern `"data_"` would select `"data1"` or `"dataA"`, but not `"Adata"` or `"Mydata"`. If you supply an empty string, `" "`, you will get information on tables without a schema. If you supply `null`, you will get tables with and without a schema.

The third argument is a pattern for selecting the table names, with the pattern defined as described above. Only data on tables with names corresponding to the pattern will be returned. If you specify the argument as `null`, information on all tables consistent with the other arguments will be returned.

The fourth argument is an array of table type names. Examples of table types are `"TABLE"`, `"SYSTEM TABLE"`, or `"VIEW"` – which is a virtual table constructed from actual tables. A `null` argument selects all table types.

The information on the tables is returned in a `ResultSet` object with each row supplying information about a particular table. The resultset will have five columns:

Column Name	Column Data
TABLE_CAT	A `String` object specifying the table catalog, which can be `null`.
TABLE_SCHEM	A `String` object specifying the table schema, which can be `null`.
TABLE_NAME	A `String` object specifying the table name.
TABLE_TYPE	A `String` object specifying the table type.
REMARKS	A `String` object describing the table.

If an error of any kind occurs when accessing the database, the `getTables()` method will throw an exception of type `SQLException`.

Given a `DatabaseMetaData` reference, `metadata`, we could retrieve all the tables for a database with the statements:

```
String[] tableTypes = { "TABLE"};
ResultSet tables = metadata.getTables(
                                null,
                                null,
                                null,
                                tableTypes);
```

This will return information on tables that are real data tables in the database, not views or system tables. This is because we have only included type `"TABLE"` in the `tableTypes` array. Of course, we would need to take care of handling the exception that could be thrown here.

Retrieving Column Names

To get the column names for particular tables, you can call the `getColumns()` method for a `DatabaseMetaData` object. The first three arguments are the catalog, `schemaPattern`, and `tableNamePattern`, as described for the `getTables()` method. The fourth argument is a `String` object specifying a pattern for selecting column names. This method returns a `ResultSet` object containing no less than 18 columns, where each row provides information about a particular column. The ones you are most likely to be interested in are:

Column Name	Column Data
TABLE_CAT	A `String` object specifying the catalog for the table containing the column, which can be `null`.
TABLE_SCHEM	A `String` object specifying the schema for the table containing the column, which can be `null`.
TABLE_NAME	A `String` object specifying the name of the table containing the column.
COLUMN_NAME	A `String` object specifying the name of the column.
DATA_TYPE	A `String` object specifying the SQL type for the data in the column.
COLUMN_SIZE	The maximum number of characters in the case of character or date types, or the precision for `NUMERIC` or `DECIMAL` types.

Of course, using the third argument that specifies the table name pattern, you can get data on the columns for a specific table, just by supplying the table name here. The `getColumns()` method can also throw an exception of type `SQLException` if an error occurs.

We have enough knowledge to implement our `setupTree()` method, so let's try it.

Try It Out — Displaying Metadata

We just need to apply the `DatabaseMetaData` methods that we just discussed. We won't catch the exceptions in the method. We can let the calling method, `openConnection()` catch them instead. Here's the code for the `setupTree()` method:

```
      private void setupTree(DatabaseMetaData metadata) throws SQLException
      {
        String[] tableTypes = { "TABLE"};                   // We want only tables
        ResultSet tables = metadata.getTables(              // Get the tables info
                                        null,
                                        null,
                                        null,
                                        tableTypes);

          String tableName;                                 // Stores a table name
          DefaultMutableTreeNode tableNode;                 // Stores a tree node for a table
          while(tables.next())                              // For each table
          {
            tableName = tables.getString("TABLE_NAME");     // get the table name
            tableNode = new DefaultMutableTreeNode(tableName);
            dbNode.add(tableNode);                          // Add the node to the tree

            // Get all the columns for the current table
            ResultSet columnNames = metadata.getColumns(null, null, tableName, null);

            // Add nodes for the columns as children of the table node
            while(columnNames.next())
              tableNode.add(new
                        DefaultMutableTreeNode(columnNames.getString("COLUMN_NAME")));
          }
      }
```

You can try the application again.
Pressing *Enter* should display the tables.

Single clicking a table name will select it. Double clicking it will expand the tree to show the column names. Double clicking the node for an expanded table will contract it again. All this function comes for free with the JTree component. If you expand the tree so that its extent is outside the pane, the scrollbars will appear automatically.

Note that holding the *Ctrl* key down enables you to select several individual nodes one after another. When you have selected one node, you can select a block of nodes from the currently selected node to any other node by holding the *Shift* key down.

How It Works

We have a simple application of the getTables() and getColumns() methods from the DatabaseMetaData interface. Our call to getTables() returns a ResultSet object that provides access to information on the tables of type "TABLE". We iterate through the rows in the resultset in the outer while loop. For each row, we retrieve and save the table name, and we add a new node as a child to the root node in the tree model, dbTreeModel. We use the table name that we have saved in tableName to retrieve information on the columns in that table by calling the getColumns() method for metadata. In the inner while loop, we iterate through all the rows in the resultset relating to the columns, and add a child node to the table node corresponding to each column name. This process will add a table node to the root node in dbTreeModel for each table, and add a column node to a table node for every column in the table. Simple really, isn't it.

The last thing we need to figure out, is how to display the contents of a table. There are various ways we could do this but we will choose to do it by listening to our tree.

Using Tree Listeners

There are three different kinds of listeners you can add to a JTree object, each of which has an interface defining the methods involved. The TreeExpansionListener interface declares two methods that are called when a node in a tree is expanded or contracted. The treeExpanded() method is called when a tree node is expanded, and unsurprisingly, the treeCollapsed() method is called when a tree node is collapsed. Each method is passed an event object of type TreeExpansionEvent.

Knowing that the tree was expanded may be too late in some circumstances. There may be things you need to do immediately before the expansion or contraction takes place. In this case you can use a TreeWillExpandListener. The TreeWillExpandListener declares treeWillExpand() and treeWillCollapse() methods with the obvious applications.

We will want to use the third kind of listener for a tree, of type TreeSelectionListener. This declares a single method, valueChanged(), and this method is called when a selection within the tree changes – that is, when a node is selected or deselected. When the method is called, it is passed an object of type TreeSelectionEvent as the argument. This provides methods that you can use to discover which nodes changed their selection state. Since you can make individual, multiple selections, or select a block of nodes, a single event can signal that several nodes have changed their selection state.

The methods in the JTree class that you use to add the listeners we have been talking about are addTreeExpansionListener(), addTreeWillExpandListener(), and addTreeSelectionListener(). Note that the tree event classes and listener interfaces are defined in the javax.swing.event package so you need an import statement for this when you use tree listeners.

1116

Tree Paths

A node that has changed state is identified by a `TreePath` object. A `TreePath` object defines a path to a node from the root node, in other words it contains the sequence of nodes from the root to a particular node. To get a reference to the node identified by a `TreePath` object, you can call its `getLastPathComponent()` method. To provide maximum flexibility, the node is returned as type `Object`, but for a `DefaultTreeNodeModel` the node will actually be of type `TreeNode`.

You have lots of ways to iterate through the nodes in a path. You can use the `getParentPath()` method in conjunction with the `getLastPathComponent()` method. The `getParentPath()` method returns a `TreePath` object that is the parent of the current path – in other words a path that is like the current path, but without the last node in the path. You can also get all the nodes in a path as an array of elements of type `Object` by calling the `getPath()` method for a `TreePath` object. You could use an object, `treepath`, of type `TreePath` like this:

```
MutableTreeNode[] nodes = (MutableTreeNodes[])treepath.getPath();
for(int i = 0 ; i < nodes.length ; i++)
  System.out.println("Node " + (i+1) + " is " + nodes[i]);
```

This just outputs each node on a separate line.

You can also get a count of the number of nodes in a path by calling the `getPathCount()` method. You could then use the `getPathComponent()` method that accepts a zero-based index to a node as an argument to select each node, and return the node as type `Object`. For example, you could get the same effect as the previous code fragment like this:

```
for(int i = 0 ; i < treepath.getPathCount() ; i++)
  System.out.println("Node " + (i+1) + " is " +
                                  ((MutableTreeNode)getPathComponent (i)));
```

A `TreeSelectionEvent` object provides methods to obtain all the paths for nodes that have changed their selection state. The `getPath()` method will return the first path and you can test whether the first path was selected or deselected by calling `isAddedPath()` for the event object. This returns `true` if the path is for a node that was selected – added in other words, and `false` otherwise – it was deselected. The `getPaths()` method for the event object will return all paths to nodes that have changed. To tell whether a particular path is to a node that was selected or deselected, you can call an overloaded version of the `isAddedPath()` method in the `TreeSelectionEvent` class that expects an argument of type `TreeNode`.

Dealing with the paths from a `TreeSelectionEvent` that are a combination of paths to selected and deselected nodes can be quite complicated. If you are only interested in the paths that are selected, you can avoid all this by going direct to the horse's mouth – the `JTree` object. You can use this to get at just the selected nodes. If you have several `JTree` objects you are listening for, you can get a reference to the object originating the event by calling the `getSource()` method for the event object. This method is inherited in the `TreeSelectionEvent` class from the `EventObject` class. If you only have one tree, as we do in our example, you can use your `JTree` reference directly to call the `getSelectionPaths()` method. This returns an array of `TreePath` objects that represent paths to nodes that are selected in the tree. I think we know enough about tree paths to complete our example now, so let's do that.

Try It Out — Displaying Table Data

We should first add the import statement for the package defining tree event class:

```
import javax.swing.event.*;
```

We will make our application class a tree selection listener, so we should declare that it implements the interface:

```
class DatabaseBrowse2 extends JFrame
                      implements ActionListener, TreeSelectionListener
```

We mustn't forget to add the application object as the tree selection listener. Add the following statement after the other three statements in the class constructor that add listeners:

```
dbTree.addTreeSelectionListener(this);
```

The valueChanged() method will display some or all of the columns from a table in the right hand split pane, depending on what is selected. Because we have allowed complete flexibility to select any number of nodes (you can restrict the possibilities though), we need to give a little thought to the problem of what we do under various selection states that can arise. For instance, several table nodes may be selected, possibly with column names selected too. We can deal with this by defining the following rules:

❑ If any table name is selected, we display the entire table for the first table name that we find.

❑ If only columns are selected, we display the selected columns for the first table that we find with selected columns. ·

We now can add the definition for the valueChanged() method to handle selection events:

```
public void valueChanged(TreeSelectionEvent e)
{
  TreePath[] paths = dbTree.getSelectionPaths();
  if(paths == null)
    return;

  boolean tableSelected = false;        // Set true if a table is selected
  String column;                        // Stores a column name from a path
  String table;                         // Stores a table name from a path
  String columnsParam = null;           // Column names in SQL SELECT
  String tableParam = null;             // Table name in SQL SELECT
  String message = null;                // Message for status area
  for(int  j = 0; j < paths.length ; j++)
  {
    switch(paths[j].getPathCount())
    {
      case 2:                           // We have a table selected
        tableParam = (String)
                    (((DefaultMutableTreeNode)
```

```
                                     (paths[j].getPathComponent(1))).getUserObject());
        columnsParam = "*";                  // Select all columns
        tableSelected = true;                // Set flag for a table selected
        message = "Complete " + tableParam + " table displayed";
        break;

      case 3:                                // Column selected
        table = (String)
                  (((DefaultMutableTreeNode)

(paths[j].getPathComponent(1))).getUserObject());
        if(tableParam == null)
          tableParam = table;

        else if(tableParam != table)
          break;
        column = (String)
                  (((DefaultMutableTreeNode)

(paths[j].getPathComponent(2))).getUserObject());
        if(columnsParam == null)            // If no previous columns
          columnsParam = column;            // add the column
        else                                // otherwise
          columnsParam += "," + column;     // we need a comma too
        message = columnsParam + " displayed from " + tableParam + " table.";
        break;
    }
    if(tableSelected)                        // If a table was selected
      break;                                 // we are done
  }
  try
  {
    // Display the columns and change the scroll pane border
    tableModel.setResultSet(
        statement.executeQuery("SELECT " + columnsParam+" FROM " +
tableParam));
    tablePane.setBorder(BorderFactory.createTitledBorder(
                    BorderFactory.createLineBorder(Color.darkGray),
                    tableParam,
                    TitledBorder.CENTER,
                    TitledBorder.DEFAULT_POSITION));
  }
  catch(SQLException sqle)
  {
    message = "Selection event Error\n" + sqle.getMessage();
    System.err.println(message);
  }
  if(message != null)
  status.setText(message);
}
```

If you recompile with these additions, and you have managed this without typos, the whole program should now be working, and you can select table data as illustrated here.

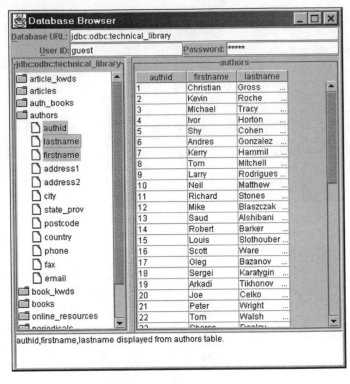

The table data that is displayed is updated as you select or deselect tables or columns. Don't forget you can use the *Shift* and *Ctrl* keys when selecting nodes. If you have one, you can also enter a different database URL.

How It Works

This method is a little tricky with some fearsome looking statements, but they are not as tough as they look. The objective of the `valueChanged()` method is to assemble an SQL SELECT statement for a table, and then execute it. The set of columns in the statement will be assembled in the variable `columnsParam`, and the table name will be stored in the `tableParam` variable.

First of all, we are only interested in paths to selected nodes here, so we get this information direct from the `dbTree` object. Since a database tree has a fixed structure with three levels – as we discussed way back – a `TreePath` will always have either two or three nodes in the path; two when a table is selected, and three when a column is selected. This guides our approach to processing the paths for selected nodes.

We iterate through the paths in the `for` loop. For each path, there will be either two or three elements in the path, and this is returned by the `getPathCount()` method for the path. We use this value to select one or other of the cases in the `switch`. When the value is 2, we have found a table name that is selected, so we retrieve the name with the expression:

```
(String)(((DefaultMutableTreeNode)(paths[j].getPathComponent(1))).getUserObject())
```

This expression is easy to understand if you take it from the inside out. The expression `paths[j].getPathComponent(1)` returns the second node object from the current path, `paths[j]`, as type `Object` – which will be the node storing the table name. We want to call the `getUserObject()` method for the node, but before we can do that, we must cast it to type `DefaultMutableTreeNode`, and we need parentheses around that because of operator precedence. The reference returned by `getUserObject()` is type `Object`, so we have to cast that to type `String` before storing it as the table name in `tableParam`. To select all the columns in the table, we set `columnsParam` to `"*"`, and set the `tableSelected` flag to `true` so we will exit the loop because of the `if` statement that tests this value at the end, and thus we won't look at any other paths.

If the value returned by `getPathCount()` is 3, we have found a column that is selected. We get the column name using essentially the same expression as we used to get the table name. If `columnsParam` is `null`, then this is the first column name we have found, so we just store the name. If `columnsParam` is not `null`, we have an additional column name, so we append it following a comma to the existing string in `columnsParam`. In this way we accumulate all the names of the selected columns. If a table name turns up, we abandon the column names we have recorded and display the whole table.

The last bit after we exit the `for` loop is easy. We pass a `SELECT` statement formed from the `columnsParam` and `tableParam` strings to the `executeQuery()` method for statement. This produces a `ResultSet` object containing the table data that we pass to the `setResultSet()` method for our `ResultsModel` object that supplies data to the table. Finally we update the border for the scroll pane containing the table to display the table name.

Summary

In this chapter, we have applied the basic JDBC skills we learned about in the previous chapter in some new ways and extended our detailed knowledge of some of the topics we covered there, as well as getting into some new ones. The important elements we introduced in this chapter include:

❑ You can create Java objects directly from JDBC data sources by adding a factory method to a class to extract data from a `ResultSet` object and build a class object.

❑ The `Statement` interface provides methods that enable you to limit the field size and number of rows that can be generated in a resultset. You can also set a maximum duration for an SQL query.

❑ A `PreparedStatement` object encapsulates a parameterized SQL statement, and provides methods for you to set values for the parameters. Placeholders for the parameters in the SQL statement are represented by a question mark.

❑ JDBC provides a set of preferred mappings between SQL types and Java types. The methods provided for transferring data between your program and a database also support conversions to other than the preferred types.

❑ The SQL `NUMERIC` and `DECIMAL` data types are mapped to the `BigDecimal` class type that is defined in the `java.math` package. You can use this class and the `BigInteger` class for applications that need numeric precision beyond the capabilities of the base numeric types.

❑ When exceptions are thrown by JDBC methods, there can be a chain of `SQLException` objects linked together. You can access successive objects in the chain by calling the `getNextException()` method for each `SQLException` object in the chain.

❑ If problems are detected by JDBC that do not warrant throwing an exception, an object of type `SQLWarning` is attached to the object originating the problem. `SQLWarning` objects can be attached to `Connection`, `Statement`, and `ResultSet` objects. You can check for a warning by calling the `getWarnings()` method for the JDBC object you are using to access the database.

❑ You can use a `JTree` component to display data structured as a tree.

❑ The `getMetaData()` method for a `Connection` object returns a `DatabaseMetaData` object that has methods that make database metadata available. These only work if the driver and database engine support the capability implied by the methods you are using.

Remember, we have only skimmed the facilities offered by many of the classes we have discussed in this chapter. You will find much more capability under the covers, and time spent browsing the class methods will be very rewarding in most cases.

Exercises

With some additional features, you will find the `InteractiveSQL` utility very useful. Add the following features to `InteractiveSQL`:

1 Keep the last ten queries that were executed, and allow the user to select from that list of previously run queries.

2 Provide a menu option that lets the user close the current connection and open a new one. Prompt the user for the URL, driver name, user name and password.

3 Modify the program to provide full, detailed information about any `SQLException` exceptions that are thrown. You may want to use a separate window that provides more space and keeps a running list of exceptions until these are cleared by the user.

There are also lots of potential extensions to the `DatabaseBrowse` application. Try the following:

4 It would be more efficient to separate the execution of the select statement from the selection events from the tree. Add a toolbar providing button to make a selection and execute a `SELECT` statement. The `SELECT` should apply with whatever table or columns are selected in the tree.

5 Extend the application to allow a `WHERE` condition to be applied. (This is quite hard. You will need to provide an additional mechanism for specifying the `WHERE` conditions – which means you will need to track the columns selected. You could keep a list that you record in the `TreeSelectionEvent` handler, and supply a dialog to allow the condition to be specified.)

6 Extend the application to allow an `ORDER BY` condition to be applied to the `SELECT` statement. (If you have done the previous exercise – this will be a piece of cake.)

Java Archives – JAR files

Once upon a time, distributing a completed program was as easy as slapping a label on a floppy disk and mailing it off. The recipient would then throw the cracked or broken disk in the bin, and ask for another. Alas, this is all in the past, and these days code is more likely to be distributed electronically in a compressed form of one kind or another.

Platform-dependent executables are often distributed using one of a variety of commercial compression algorithms such as ZIP, TAR, LHA, or ARJ. Not only do they make more efficient use of space and make electronic distribution faster and more economical, they can be used to combine multiple files of a related type into a single file called **an archive**, thus providing a more convenient packaging for the files that is easier to manage. Java has its own equivalent to these compression methods – referred to as the **Java Archive**, or **JAR**, specification that is intended primarily for packaging Java classes. This can be applied to packaging applets, applications, and libraries of classes that you have created yourself. All the standard classes that come with the JDK are packaged in a JAR archive, `rt.jar`. Java archive files usually have the extension `.jar`.

The JAR archive can offer substantial advantages when you are distributing Java programs electronically. For instance, where an applet involves several class files that might be transmitted separately, packaging the applet into a single Java archive will allow them to be downloaded as a single file that will require significantly less time to transmit. A JAR archive also has provision for signing the contents – adding digital signatures in other words. This enables a recipient of an archive to verify that the contents originated from a trusted source.

The JAR File Format

The JAR specification corresponds to the well-known ZIP format, as defined by PKWARE. In fact, WinZip version 7.0, or later, that is available as a general archiving tool in the Windows environment can read the contents of a JAR, report relative paths and file sizes; and extract the contents when necessary.

To create, process and manage JAR files, you will normally use the command-line tool that is provided with each release of the JDK, named, appropriately enough, `jar`. This provides all the operations you are likely to need when working with JAR files. While it does provide a very wide range of capabilities that can involve quite a few parameters, a few simple commands are enough to take care of everyday tasks such as creating archives or adding to and extracting files from existing archives.

Using the jar Utility

The basic syntax of `jar` is:

```
jar <option string> [JAR] [manifest file] [input files]
```

The **option string** is used to specify the action to be performed by the `jar` utility and therefore is always required.

The optional JAR argument is the name of the archive file that is the destination for the input files when an existing archive is to be updated, or the name of a new archive that is to be created. It can also be the name of an existing archive from which the contents are to be listed, or from which files are to be extracted.

The **manifest file** is an optional argument to the `jar` utility that identifies a file that describes the contents of an archive with its authentication information. If you don't supply a manifest file, the `jar` utility will create one automatically from other command line information and include it in the archive.

The **input files** option identifies the files that are input to create a new archive, or extend an existing archive.

Jar Options

There are four actions that the jar utility can perform, each specified by a single letter:

Action	Description
c	Creates a new JAR file. The input files from the input files argument are used to create the new archive specified by the JAR argument.
u	Update an existing archive by adding or replacing files.
x	Extracts files from an existing JAR
t	Lists the contents of the specified JAR

You can qualify the action that you specify to the jar utility by one or more optional letters following the action specifier. These are all described on the following page, starting with the one you are most likely to use:

Option	Description
f	Indicates that the JAR file to be processed is specified as the second command line argument. If you omit this option, any input that is required for the operation will be assumed to come from the standard input stream – usually the keyboard, and any output will be sent to the standard output – usually the screen. You will normally specify this option.
v	Selects verbose output from the utility. Normally, the jar utility's output is limited to directory and file names only. This option tells it to include a little more information, such as file sizes and timestamps, so it is helpful to specify this option generally.
0 (zero)	This option is used to bypass compression when creating an archive or adding files to an existing archive. The utility places the files in the archive but without applying ZIP compression to them. You won't normally want to specify this option. One use would be to add signature files to an existing archive.
m	Indicates that the name of a manifest file for the JAR is the next parameter after the JAR file. A manifest file describes the contents of a JAR and its authentication information, and if you don't supply one, the jar utility will create one automatically and include it in an archive. You won't normally need to use this option.
M	Tells jar not to include a manifest file in the archive. You won't normally need to use this option.

Most of the time, you will find that you only need the first two qualifiers to the jar action.

What we need to do now is get some practical experience with the jar utility. We need a simple program that we can operate on to get the feel for how jar works. Here's the code for a program that displays a line of text on the screen:

```
public class Jardemo
{
  public static void main(String[] args)
  {
    System.out.println("I'm ready to be zipped up!");
  }
}
```

Store the file Jardemo.java in a convenient directory, JarTest perhaps, then compile it so the .class file ends up in the same directory. Unless stated otherwise, in the examples we will look at next the commands are assumed to be executed with the JarTest directory as the current directory.

Creating a JAR

Creating a JAR is as easy as specifying the `jar` utility's `c` action. If no other options or files are specified, `jar` will create an empty archive and output it to the standard output (usually the screen). You could use the `c` tag by itself as a way of getting to see inside a JAR archive. A command such as:

```
jar c Jardemo.java
```

will create an archive containing the file, `Jardemo.java`, and output it to the screen. But be warned, it's not a pretty sight.

A more practical application of the `c` action would be the following command:

```
jar cvf jardemo.jar *
added manifest
adding: Jardemo.class (in=539) (out=344) (deflated 36%)
adding: Jardemo.java (in=137) (out=119) (deflated 13%)
```

This creates the archive, `jardemo.jar`, and adds all the files that are in the current directory to it. Any kind of file will be added – including `.jar` files.

> *Note that we could alternatively list the individual files by name in the command, but using wildcards is more efficient. As a rule of thumb, any use of wildcards that works with directory listings will also work with `jar`. Notice too that verbose output gives you all sorts of information about the compression ratio and file sizes. With these you can verify that every file you wanted in the archive did end up there.*

Of course, you might want to create an archive just containing `.class` files for instance. In this case you would use a wildcard specification just for the file name:

```
jar cvf jardemo.jar *.class
```

Note that the `jar` utility automatically recurses through subdirectories, adding their contents to the archive as well. If you want to store just the contents of a particular subdirectory to the current directory, you just supply the subdirectory name. For example, if the current directory contained a subdirectory with the name `Geometry`, you could create an archive of all the `.class` files in that directory with the command:

```
jar cvf geometry.jar Geometry *.class
```

This command is particularly useful for putting the classes in a package into an archive. These files could be classes belonging to a package, `Geometry`. All that is now necessary to make the package available generally to `javac` and `java` is to copy the archive, `geometry.jar`, to the `jre/lib/ext` directory.

Updating an Archive

If you change one of the files that have been stored in an archive, you can update the old archive rather than create a new one. For instance, if the current directory is the `JarTest` directory, you could update the `javademo.jar` archive with the latest versions of the files with the command:

```
jar uvf jardemo.jar *.class
```

This would also add any new files that are in the current directory to the archive.

Listing the Contents of an Archive

To view the contents of the `jardemo.jar` archive that we just created, we could try the following command:

```
jar tf jardemo.jar
META-INF/MANIFEST.MF
Jardemo.class
Jardemo.java
```

This only provides basic information about the files that were added, but you can see that the manifest file, `MANIFEST.MF` was included first in a subdirectory, `META-INF`. The manifest file in an archive always has the same name and is always in the subdirectory with the name as here. When you want to know a little more about the contents of an archive, you can use the verbose option:

```
jar tvf jardemo.jar
    0 Fri Feb 05 10:47:20 GMT 1999 META-INF/
   66 Fri Feb 05 10:47:22 GMT 1999 META-INF/MANIFEST.MF
  539 Fri Feb 05 10:46:06 GMT 1999 Jardemo.class
  137 Fri Feb 05 10:45:46 GMT 1999 Jardemo.java
```

As you see, the precise time and date is displayed when each file or directory was added to the archive. The integer values at the start of each line is the size of the file in bytes.

Extracting the Contents of an Archive

Now, let's extract all of the files from the `jardemo.jar` archive, to verify that they come out the same way they went in.

```
jar xvf jardemo.jar
   created: META-INF/
 extracted: META-INF/MANIFEST.MF
 extracted: Jardemo.class
 extracted: Jardemo.java
```

The `jar` utility automatically created a subdirectory called `META-INF` to preserve the file structure of the archive. If you change to this directory, you can view the manifest file that it generated for your classes using virtually any editor – it's just a text file.

```
Manifest-Version: 1.0
Created-By: 1.2 (Sun Microsystems Inc.)
```

As you see, there's not a lot in there. This is because we are not using signing for any of the files in the archive. Digital signatures can be added to an archive using the `jarsigner` tool that is distributed with the JDK. This will add files to the `META-MF` subdirectory in the archive containing the digital signatures, and update the manifest file. Discussion of JAR signatures is outside the scope of this book.

JARs and Applets

While JAR archives are very useful for physical-medium distribution, and for storing packages, they are invaluable for transmitting applications and applets over the Net. If your applet involves a lot of files – and it may well do because we include image files and other media files in this – then you can reduce download time substantially by storing the file in a JAR archive.

The basic `APPLET` start tag contained four parameters:

```
<APPLET code=AnyClass.class
codebase=MyPrograms/
width=100
height=100>
```

All but the `codebase` parameter are mandatory here. If the class specified in the code parameter, or any resource accessed by it, resides in a JAR archive, you indicate this using the new `archives` parameter – for example:

```
<APPLET code=AnyClass.class
codebase=MyPrograms/
archives="class1.jar, extras/class2.jar"
width=100
height=100>
```

As you can see, archive names are enclosed in quotes, specified by their paths relative to the `codebase` and separated by commas. This example specifies two archives to be downloaded, the first in the `codebase` directory, and the second in the `extras` subdirectory. Each of the archives must be in the `codebase` directory or one of its subdirectories. The archives can contain all the files required by the applet, including its `.class` files and any image or other media files that it uses.

Creating Java Documentation

Documenting your program code is important whatever language you are using. In just about every language there is the possibility of adding comments to the source code to explain its logic, purpose, and usage, and of course, this applies to Java too. However, Java goes one better than most other programming languages by providing a mechanism for generating documentation that is separate from the program code, and that can be viewed independently of it. If you insert special comments in your source files preceding the code for each field, method, class and interface, you can use the javadoc utility that is supplied as part of the Java Development Kit to create separate, self-contained documentation for potential users of your code. The documentation is highly structured with a uniform presentation style, and can provide comprehensive guidance to users on how your classes are intended to be applied, as well as detailed descriptions of how to access and use the class members. The documentation is produced in the form of linked HTML pages with the same appearance and structure as the documentation that is provided for the JDK.

Here you will learn:

❑   How to write javadoc comments

❑   How you can use HTML tags in javadoc comments

❑   What special tags are recognized by javadoc

❑   What options you have when generating documentation

Documenting Your Java Code

The special comments recognized by the javadoc utility are referred to as **javadoc comments**, **documentation comments**, or simply **doc comments**. Since the comments processed by javadoc are aimed at generating independent documentation for users of your code, rather than programmers involved in maintaining or extending it, they are not really an alternative to the normal // and /*...*/ comments that you use to document the code. Ideally you should provide javadoc comments as an addition to the conventional source code comments. You need to bear in mind that documentation comments are somewhat verbose and they tend to clutter the source file making it harder to read. There are often far more lines of documentation comments than there are lines of code. Of course you can add documentation comments right at the outset, since javadoc will even process empty classes and interfaces. However, I have found it easiest to include regular comments in the code as I develop it, but only add the documentation comments at the end, when I have fully tested the code.

The documentation that `javadoc` generates from your source files is primarily oriented towards describing an API that is implemented as a number of classes and interfaces within one or more packages. This involves documenting the intended application of the classes and interfaces themselves, together with the `public` methods and fields of each class. You would not necessarily want to expose information about the `private` and `protected` members of the classes to users, but you can still include `javadoc` comments for them and limit what appears in the documentation that is created by `javadoc`. You can control whether or not documentation on `private` or `protected` class members is generated by means of `javadoc` command line options, as we shall see. This enables you to produce one set of documentation for users of your classes, and another set suited to developers or maintainers of the code. Of course, the documentation that comes with the JDK provides a vast number of good illustrations of how you should approach documenting an API.

You are not constrained to applying `javadoc` to just APIs. You can, and often should, add documentation comments in your code for applications, particularly if they involve a significant number of classes. As an example, on the Wrox Press web site you will find a version of the source code for the Sketcher program we built in this book, which includes documentation comments, together with the documentation produced by `javadoc` for it. The first page of the `javadoc` documentation for Sketcher is shown below.

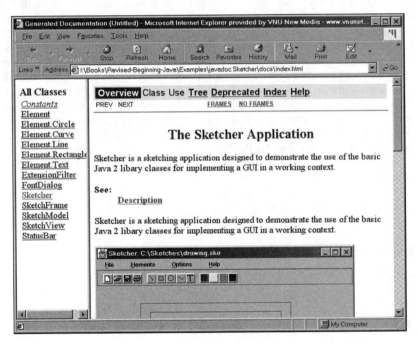

Sketcher is a vehicle for demonstrating how various Java capabilities can be applied, so the documentation comments describe what the various program elements are for, and how they are used. It also serves to illustrate some aspects of how you can add documentation comments to a program. If you download the `javadoc`'d version of Sketcher from the Wrox Press web site, you can use it to experiment with the various possibilities you have in adding documentation comments as well as the options for the `javadoc` utility itself. The examples of documentation comments included here are based on those in the Sketcher program.

Output from `javadoc`

The `javadoc` utility generates a standard set of linked HTML files, explained by the documentation that you can get for the JDK. The precise form of the output that is produced by `javadoc` is determined by **doclets**, which are files containing Java programs that control the output. These are implemented using the **doclet API** that has been defined by Sun and is contained in the `com.sun.javadoc` package. The standard `javadoc` output is produced as a result of a standard doclet that is supplied with the utility. It is possible to modify the standard doclet that produces the output you have seen with the JDK documentation, or even to write your own doclets from scratch, but both of these are beyond the scope of this discussion, so we will concentrate on using the standard doclet.

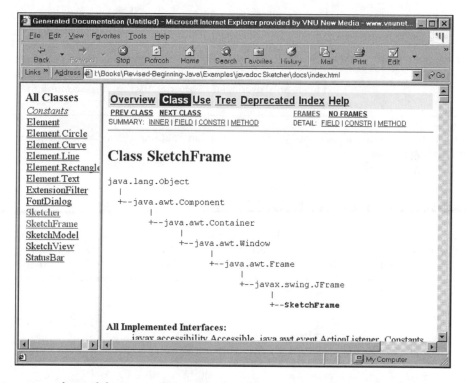

You can see a subset of the types of pages produced by `javadoc` if you look at the documentation files generated for Sketcher. The example above is the page that is displayed when you click on the SketchFrame class in the list of classes. Sketcher does not include any packages, so some types of pages do not appear. The JDK documentation includes examples of the full range of pages that are possible.

The primary documentation generated for Sketcher consists of one page for each class or interface, `className.html`, and one overview page for the program, `overview-summary.html`. The entry point to view the documentation is a file with the name `index.html`. The screenshot in the previous section is the index.html page for Sketcher. By default this page uses frames to display the `allclasses-frame.html` page alongside the `overview-summary.html` page that contains the general description of the application. If there were packages included, the overview page would also include links to package pages, `package-summary.html`, and `javadoc` would generate one page for each package. There are pages generated that cross-reference the primary pages:

`Overview-tree.html`	This contains a tree representation of all classes and interfaces in the Sketcher program. This will include the contents of multiple packages when they are present. You access it by selecting the **Tree** option on the navigation bar.
`Serialized-form.html`	This contains information about the serialized form of all serializable classes in the program code. It is accessed from the **Serialized Form** link below each class description on a `className.html` page.
`Index-all.html`	This provides an index to all classes, interfaces and their members. In general this page would also contain entries for all packages too.
`deprecated-list.html`	Lists all deprecated names – in the Sketcher case there are none.
`ClassName.html`	This file – one per class or interface - is generated in the `Class-use` subdirectory to the directory containing the primary files. It lists where the class or interface is used elsewhere in the program. This is only produced if you specify the `–use` command line option when running `javadoc`.

The `javadoc` also generates a page, `help-doc.html`, that contains a generalized help facility for how the documentation is used.

Documentation Comments

You can add documentation comments to describe packages, classes, interfaces, and methods defined in a class or declared in a class or interface, as well as the data members of a class. You supply one documentation comment for each each of these that you want to have documented, and you place it immediately preceding the first line of source code for the entity. These comments are always of the same form:

```
/**
 * Comment text that will appear in the generated documentation goes here
 * on one or more lines starting with an asterisk.
 * You can include HTML tags in this text.
 * You can also include special documentation tags following
 * this descriptive text.
 * These should be separated from the descriptive text by a blank line that can
 * begin with *, as the next line here:
 *
 * Special documentation tags with their comment text go here,
 * each on a separate line.
 */
```

A documentation comment begins with `/**` and ends with `*/`. The other `*` characters at the beginning of each line are not part of the comments so you can omit them if you want, but this does have an effect beyond making the `javadoc` comments less clear. The leading `*` on each line will be automatically discarded by `javadoc`, but any whitespace characters following the `*` will be retained. If you omit the `*`, then all whitespace characters preceding the first non-whitespace character on a line will be discarded.

The first sentence of each comment should be a summary of whatever the comment applies to. This will be used wherever a summary of the entity being described is required. For instance, every documented entity will appear in the index to the documentation, and the summary sentence will appear as the description for the entity. Thee first sentence ends with a period followed by a blank or a tab or a line terminator. The first tag will end the first sentence if it is not terminated by a period. The full description, including the first sentence, will be used in the full documentation of the entity to which the comment applies.

The text in a doc comment is HTML, so you can include HTML tags to improve the appearance of the descriptive text. You can include <B> or <I> tags to produce bold or italic text for instance. There is a restriction though. You can only include heading tags such as <H1> in class and package comments. If you use them elsewhere, they are likely to upset the document formatting that is created by the javadoc utility. If you want the HTML tag delimiter characters, < and >, to appear in your text, you must write them as < and > and wherever you want an ampersand character to appear, you must write it as &.

You can also embed other files, such as HTML files or image files in a documentation comment. Such files must appear in a directory with the name doc-files, and it must be a subdirectory of the directory containing the package being documented. The Sketcher program files include examples of this. For instance, the following comment for a member of the SketchFrame class includes a .gif file into the text:

```
/**
 * Stores a reference to the action object used to create
 * the <i>File/New</i> menu item.
 * <p>
 * This object is also used to create a toolbar button, so the same object
 *  handles action events from either the menu item or the toolbar button.
 * The effect of this action object is to create a new sketch.
 * <P>
 * The image on the toolbar button created from this object looks like this:
 * <img src="doc-files/New.gif">
 */
```

The special documentation tags that you can place at the end of a documentation comment all begin with @, and they must each appear on a separate line. The complete list of special javadoc tags available with Java 2 is as follows:

@author	Used to create an author entry for a class or interface.
@version	Used to specify version information for the code.
@see	Provides a link to another named entity in the program, such as another class, method, or field. You can also use this tag to link to external pages.
@param	Used to describe a parameter to a method. You need to include one of these for each parameter for a method.
@return	Used to describe the return value for a method when the method returns a value other than void.

Table Continued on Following Page

1137

@exception	Defines an exception that a method may throw. You would use one of these for each exception that can be thrown by a method.
@throws	The same as @exception – an alternative introduced in Java 2.
@deprecated	Specifies a method as deprecated. You would use this to document obsolete methods in the second or subsequent versions of an API.
@serialData	Used to describe the data items that are written or read by writeObject(), readObject(), or writeExternal(), readExternal() methods that are not serializable by default.
@serialField	Used to describe an ObjectStreamField object.
@serial	Used to describe a data member of a class that is serializable by default.
@since	Used to indicate when a feature was introduced into the code. It has the effect of adding a 'Since' heading followed by the text associated with the tag.
{@link #entity label}	Used to add an inline link to the documentation for another entity in your source code – a cross-reference to another method or field for instance. The difference between this and the @see tag is that you use this to generaste a link embedded within the documentation text, whereas the @see tag generates a link on a separate line. Note that the braces around the tag are mandatory
{@doc-root}	Specifies the relative path to the root directory for the documentation from any subdirectory of this directory. The root directory is the directory that contains the index.html file. You use this tag to create a direct link to a specific html file contained in the root directory. The braces are also mandatory here.

Note that the tag names are case sensitive, so @SEE or @serialdata will not be recognized. The @version, @see, @deprecated and @since tags can be used in any documentation comment regardless of the type of entity to which they apply. The others are more restricted, and we will identify the tags that you can use in each context as we discuss them in detail.

Let's look at how we can use these tags in more detail in the context of some practical javadoc comments.

Documenting Classes and Interfaces

Documentation comments for classes and interfaces are essentially of the same form, and can include any of the following documentation tags:

@author	@version	@since
@deprecated	@see	

The @author tag can only be used in a comment for a class or an interface, but as we said in the previous section, the others here can be used in documentation comments for any kind of entity. You can also include {@link } tags in the text that describes a class or an interface.

You will typically want to include one or more @author tags to identify the author or authors of the class or interface. You can also supply a @version tag to specify the version of the code, although you are not obliged to do so. In fact neither of these tags have any effect on the documentation by default – they only produce output if you explicitly request it by specifying the –author and –version command line options when you run javadoc. To use the @author tag, you specify the name of an author separated from the tag name by one or more spaces – for example:

```
 *  @author      Ivor Horton
```

A single @author tag can specify more than one author, in which case the tag text will appear in the documentation as you have written it. If you include several @author tags, the tag text from each of these will appear in the documentation separated by commas.

The @version can specify any text that you want, as there is no check on its contents, but generally you should include the version number of the code and the date. For example:

```
 *  @version      2.14 February 2000
```

The @since tag is intended to specify when the feature – the class or interface in this case – was introduced, and how you specify this is up to you. For instance:

```
 *  @since    version 2.3
```

This shows a version number but you could put any other text you like in this tag, such as a date.

You may also want to include @see tags to cross-reference other related elements in the documentation, but before we get into the detail of specifying links, let's look at an example of a complete documentation comment for a class. The documentation for the Sketcher class is as follows:

```
/**
 * The <code>Sketcher</code> class defines the application object and
 * initializes the application.
 * The <code>Sketcher</code> object creates a <code>SketchFrame</code> object
 * representing the application window, a {@link SketchModel SketchModel
 * object} that encapsulates the data for a sketch, and a
 * <code>SketchView</code> object that displays the sketch.
 * The application object provides communications links, via <code>getXXX()</code>
 * methods between the model, the view, and the frame window.
 *
 * @author    Ivor Horton
 * @version   2.0  February 2000
 * @see <a href="doc-files/Sketcher.html">Source Code</a>
 */
public class Sketcher
{
  // The detailed class definition, including other doc comments
}
```

Each reference to an item in the source code is highlighted using the HTML tag, <CODE>. It's a good idea to identify code elements that appear in the text in this way – unless they are to be links, in which case they will be highlighted automatically as a result of the @link tag.

The example in the text defines a link to the SketchModel class specified following @link, and the link will appear in the text as SketchModel object, which is the text following the SketchModel reference. The comment includes examples of the @author and @version tags that were discussed above. It also includes an example of using the @see tag to link to another HTML page, containing a listing of the source code in this case. This file just contains the original source code with a few HTML tags added to display it appropriately. We'll discuss the ways in which you can define links in more detail in a moment. This documentation comment results in the following output:

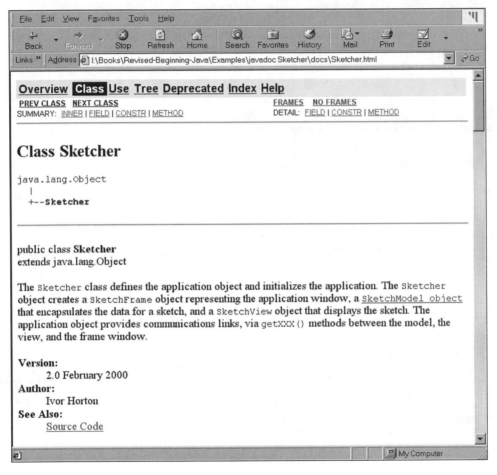

This only shows the text that is produced at the top of the page as a direct result of the comment. The remainder of the page includes further documentation of the members of the Sketcher class. There will also be an entry in the index to the documentation for the Sketcher class, using the first sentence as the definition. The author and version output appear here because the documentation was generated running javadoc with the -author and -version options specified – amongst others.

The complete command line entry looked like this:

```
javadoc -private -use -author -version -overview overview.html -J-Xmx80m
doctitle "The Sketcher Application"  -d .\docs  @jdocfiles
```

We'll come back to the command line options a little later. The highlighted <u>SketchModel object</u> and <u>Source Code</u> elements in the output were produced as a result of the @link and @see tags respectively, so let's look at how links in these tags are specified in a bit more detail.

Defining Links

You can link to a document specified by a URL by using an HTML anchor tag with @link or @see tags. A @see tag in a documentation comment showing the general form of the anchor tag would look like this:

```
 * @see    <a HREF="URL#identifier">Link text</a>
```

URL#identifier defines the link, and this can be a relative or an absolute reference. The @see tag in the documentation comment for the Sketcher class illustrates a relative URL. The link will appear in the comment as <u>Link text</u>, so for our example the link appears as <u>Source Code</u>.

To include unprocessed files – that is, files that are simply included in the documentation by javadoc, but not processed in any other way – you need to put them in the subdirectory of the package directory called doc-files that we introduced back at the beginning. You then reference them relatively – for instance, in the previous example we have:

```
 * @see <a href="doc-files/Sketcher.html">Source Code</a>
```

In this case we are linking to a file containing a listing of the source code, and the source code appears in the file between <pre> tags.

We have already seen that you can define a link to another class, field, or method in the documentation that is being generated. The @link tag in the text of the Sketcher comment was one example of this. Let's look at the general form of this kind of reference using the @see tag:

```
 * @see    reference   label
```

Here, reference is a qualified or unqualified name for the entity that is the target for the link, and label is the text that is to appear for the reference in the generated documentation. If you omit label, the name of the entity will be used to identify the reference. This form is exactly the same with the @link tag, and in the previous example of a documentation comment reference was *SketchModel* and label was *SketchModel object*.

There are many possible variations in how you can specify `reference`, each depending upon the context in which it is used, but the rules are quite simple. There are five kinds of entity you may be referencing from within a given documentation comment: a package, a class or an interface, an inner class, a method, or a field. The entity referenced may or may not be within the same package or class as the entity being documented, and whether it is or not affects what options you have for how you specify the link reference. You can always use fully qualified references, though, so you can use the following for links to the five possible kinds of target:

Link To:	Reference
Package	`PackageName`
Class or Interface	`PackageName.ClassName`
	or
	`PackageName.InterfaceName`
Inner class	`PackageName.ClassName.InnerClassName`
Method	`PackageName.ClassName#MethodName(type1, type2,…)`
	or
	`PackageName.InterfaceName#MethodName(type1, type2,…)`
	or
	`PackageName.ClassName.InnerClassName#MethodName(type1, type2,…)`
Field	`PackageName.ClassName#MemberName`
	or
	`PackageName.ClassName.InnerClassName#MemberName`

For a method, the type of each parameter must appear between parentheses following the method name, as shown in the table. For entities that are not within a named package, the package name and the succeeding period don't apply. You can see that a period separates each qualifier from the next and a # character always precedes a class or interface member name. If there are more levels – referencing members of an inner class to an inner class for instance – you just need additional qualifiers.

Fortunately, you don't have to use fully qualified names as references all the time so let's look at some of the alternatives. We will start with the most common situation:

Referencing Members of the Same Class

If the current documentation comment applies to a class, an interface, or a member of a class or interface, you can reference fields in the same class or interface just by prefixing a # symbol to the field name. For instance, if you wanted to define a link to the `theApp` member of the `Sketcher` class, you could add a `@see` tag to the previous documentation comment:

```
 * @see  #theApp
```

The output produced by the @see tag appears on a separate 'See Also:' line, as illustrated by the Sketcher documentation that appeared earlier.

You reference a method in basically the same way as a field, but you must specify the parameter types between parentheses following the method name. For example, to provide a link from the Sketcher documentation to the insertModel() method in that class, you could add the line:

```
 * @see  #insertModel(SketchModel)
```

Neither this nor the previous example has a label for the link, so the entity name (underlined and in a highlight color), will appear in the documentation that is generated to identify the link. Of course, if you want to supply the class name as a qualifier, you can do so, by writing the previous tag as:

```
 * @see  Sketcher#insertModel(SketchModel)
```

If the class is in a named package, you can always add the package name as a qualifier too. The Sketcher program is not in a named package, so it doesn't apply here.

When referencing an inner class, or a member of an inner class, the inner class name must always be qualified by the outer class name. Here's an example of a complete documentation comment for the selectedElement field in the SketchView class:

```
/**
 * Defines the element selected for a MOVE or ROTATE operation.
 * <p>
 * This will be the element that is highlighted when the corresponding
 * context menu item is selected.
 * This data member is set by the {@link #actionPerformed(ActionEvent)}
 * and it is used by the {@link SketchView.MouseHandler#mouseDragged(MouseEvent)}
 * method that carries out the operation.
 */
    private Element selectedElement;
```

Here you can see a link to the actionPerformed() method in the current class, SketchView, and a link to the mouseDragged() method in the MouseHandler class that is an inner class to SketchView.

Referencing Members of a Different Class

To reference a member of a different class that is in the same package as the current class, the member name must always be at least qualified by the class name followed by #. In all other respects the reference is the same as we have discussed for members of the same class

Thus to reference the selectedElement member of the SketchView class in the documentation comment for the Sketcher class, you could add:

```
 * @see  SketchView#selectedElement
```

We have omitted the label here, so the name of the entity will be used as the reference. To use some alternative text as the reference, you could write the tag as:

```
* @see  SketchView#selectedElement  the currently selected element in SketchView
```

Now the reference will appear as <u>the currently selected element in SketchView</u>.

If the class containing the member is in another package, then the reference must be qualified with the name of the package containing the class.

Documenting Methods

A documentation comment for a method can contain the following special tags, in addition to the four universal tags:

@throws	@exception	
@param	@return	@serialData

As we saw earlier, @throws and @exception are the same – whichever you use is a matter of taste. The general form for these tags is:

```
* @throws  exceptionType  description
```

The @serialData tag only applies to methods that are involved in object serialization, and we shall come back to this tag a little later.

A documentation comment for a method will typically contain one @param tag for each method parameter, and a @return tag if the method returns a value other than void. Of course, constructors never return a value, so the @return tag is never used for a constructor. In all other respects, documentation comments for constructors are the same as for other methods. Note that while you should document each parameter and the return value where appropriate, the javadoc utility does not check that you do so, so any that you leave out will just not be documented. The @param tag requires the parameter name and a description to be supplied:

```
* @param  parameterName  description
```

The @return tag just requires a description:

```
* @return  description
```

Here's an example of a comment applied to the `createElement()` method that is a member of the `MouseHandler` inner class in the `SketchView` class:

```
/**
 * Creates new geometric elements.
 * <p>
 * This method creates a new geometric object determined
 * by the current element type.
 * All elements are created from two points in the first instance,
 * the two end points for a line, the end points of the diagonal for a rectangle,
 * the center plus a circumference point for a circle,
 * and the first two points for a curve.
 * This is a helper method used in the {@link #mouseDragged(MouseEvent)} handler.
 *
 * @param   start    a reference to the first defining point for the element.
 * @param   end      a reference to the second defining point for the element.
 * @return           a reference to the element that was created, or
 * <code>NULL</code>
 *                   if no element was created.
 */
private Element createElement(Point start, Point end)
{
    // Code for the method...
}
```

We have `@param` tags for each of the parameters, and a `@return` tag for the value that is returned. The descriptive text can appear over as many lines as you wish, as illustrated by the case of the `@return` tag in the example.

This comment results in the documentation output shown below.

createElement

```
private Element createElement(java.awt.Point start,
                              java.awt.Point end)
```

Creates new geometric elements.

This method creates a new geometric object determined by the current element type. All elements are created from two points in the first instance, the two end points for a line, the end points of the diagonal for a rectangle, the center plus a circumference point for a circle, and the first two points for a curve. This is a helper method used in the mouseDragged (MouseEvent) handler.

Parameters:
> start - a reference to the first defining point for the element.
> end - a reference to the second defining point for the element.

Returns:
> a reference to the element that was created, or NULL if no element was created.

Methods for Serialization

If a class implements methods involved in serializing and deserializing objects of the class, then you should use the @serialData tag to describe the data that is written or read. You only use this tag for documentation comments that apply to the writeObject() and readObject() methods, or the writeExternal() and readExternal() methods.

Here's an example of a documentation comment for the writeObject() method in the Curve inner class to the Element class in Sketcher:

```
/**
 * Writes the data defining this <code>Element.Curve</code> object to a file.
 * This method supports serialization of <code>Element.Curve</code> objects.
 * <p>
 * The <code>GeneralPath</code> class does not support serialization so we must
 * implement this method to allow our <code>Element.Curve</code> objects to be
 * serialized.
 * @param     out             The output stream to which this curve is written.
 * @exception  java.io.IOException        If an output stream error occurs
 * @serialData             The coordinates of the end points of each line
 *                         segment from the <code>GeneralPath</code> defining
 *                         the curve are stored in a <code>Vector</code>, and
 *                         the <code>Vector</code> object is written to the
 *                         stream. The starting point for the first segment is
 *                         always the origin so that does not need to be stored,
 *                         and the position and orientation of the
 *                         <code>GeneralPath</code> are stored in inherited
 *                         members that are serialized by default.
 */
private void writeObject(ObjectOutputStream out) throws IOException
{
    // Code for the method...
}
```

If you don't qualify the exception class in the @exception or @throws tag, javadoc will search for it. It will search in a predefined sequence, as follows:

1. The current class or interface.

2. Any direct or indirect enclosing class or interface, starting with the direct one.

3. Any base class or interface, starting with the immediate base.

4. The current package

5. Any imported classes interfaces or packages, in the sequence of the import statements starting with the first.

The `javadoc` comment for a serializing method results in two sets of output being produced. The first is the normal documentation that is produced for a method. In this case it includes the documentation of the exception that this method can throw, as you can see below:

writeObject

```
private void writeObject(java.io.ObjectOutputStream out)
                  throws java.io.IOException
```

Writes the data defining this `Element.Curve` object to a file. This method supports serialization of `Element.Curve` objects.

The `GeneralPath` class does not support serialization so we must implement this method to allow our `Element.Curve` objects to be serialized.

Parameters:
> `out` - The output stream to which this curve is written.

Throws:
> java.io.IOException - If an output stream error occurs

You can see the second form of documentation by clicking on the <u>Serialized Form</u> link at the beginning of the page that documents the `Element.Curve` class. This links to documentation of the serialized form for objects of the class. Here, the documentation for the `writeObject()` method includes the description of the data that is written to the stream. This is from the `@serialData` tag:

writeObject

```
private void writeObject(java.io.ObjectOutputStream out)
                  throws java.io.IOException
```

Writes the data defining this `Element.Curve` object to a file. This method supports serialization of `Element.Curve` objects.

The `GeneralPath` class does not support serialization so we must implement this method to allow our `Element.Curve` objects to be serialized.

Serial Data:
> The coordinates of the end points of each line segment from the `GeneralPath` defining the curve are stored in a `Vector`, and the `Vector` object is written to the stream. The starting point for the first segment is always the origin so that does not need to be stored, and the position and orientation of the `GeneralPath` are stored in inherited members that are serialized by default.

Documenting Fields

Documentation comments for fields in a class or interface can include two special tags in addition to the four that you can use generally:

```
@serial                @serialField
```

You should always include the `@serial` tag for fields that are serializable by default. Its general form is:

```
 * @serial  description
```

The `description` is optional. You use the `@serialField` tag to document each `ObjectStreamField` element in a `serialPersistentFields` array. The general form for this tag is:

```
 * @serialField  fieldName  fieldType  description
```

We haven't discussed `ObjectStreamField` objects. These encapsulate descriptions for serializable fields in a serializable class. Unless you are working with more advanced applications of the object serialization mechanism, you will not need to use this tag.

Here's an example of a documentation comment for a field that is serializable by default – the color member of the `Element` class in Sketcher:

```
/**
 * The color in which the shape is to be drawn.
 *
 * @serial
 */
protected Color color;                              // Color of a shape
```

As you can see, no description has been included, as no further information is necessary here. This field will now appear in the standard documentation for the class, as well as the documentation for the serialized form of the class.

If you don't supply a `@serial` tag for a serializable field, the `javadoc` utility will generate a warning message.

Documenting a Package

If your classes are in a named package, you can provide general documentation for the package in a separate source file. The file should have the name `package.html`, and you must put it in the package directory along with the `.java` source files. The contents of the `package.html` file take the following form:

```
<body>
First sentence is a summary description of the package.
The rest of the text can be whatever you want formatted using regular HTML tags
and can include @link tags.

Optional special javadoc tags must appear at the end and can be @see, @since, or
@deprecated
</body>
```

The first sentence is used to describe the package at the top of the package summary page that is generated, and it will also appear on the overview page. Note that most of the `/**` and `*/` delimiters for documentation comments don't apply here. The only ones that are permitted are `@see`, `@since`, `@deprecated`, and `{@link}`. You can include a `package.html` file in each package directory that is being documented.

Overview Documentation

You can optionally supply overview documentation for your code in a separate file. This file is identified in the command to execute `javadoc`, so you can name it anything you like The file should be same in the form as the package document file, and can include `@link`, `@since` and `@see` tags, the last two appearing at the end of the file of course. If you use the `@see` tag, the reference must be a fully qualified name. The Sketcher program includes an example of an overview document file.

Running javadoc

You can apply `javadoc` to a number of specific source files, one or more packages, or a combination of the two. Each successful execution of the utility will generate a set of linked HTML pages documenting all the classes and packages that you specify on the command line. The general form of the command to execute `javadoc` is:

javadoc   [options]   [packages]   [sourcefiles]   [@files]

There are four groups of optional fields in the command, shown here between the square brackets. The square brackets here are not part of the command. They just indicate that the group they enclose is optional. Each field on the command line is separated from the next by one or more spaces.

The purpose of each of the groups of fields on the command line is as follows:

options	This specifies the options that apply when javadoc executes. The ones we shall discuss are those defined as standard. It is possible to extend this set yourself by defining your own doclets, but this is outside the scope of this discussion. You will find further information on this in the JDK documentation. If you want to display the standard options, you can execute the command: javadoc -help
packages	A sequence of package names for the packages that are to be processed. Each name is separated from the next by one or more spaces. Of course, if you are documenting classes in the default unnamed package, then you specify the classes using the sourcefiles and/or @files fields described below.
sourcefiles	A sequence of source file names separated by spaces. You can include wildcards here, so to specify all the sources files in the current directory for instance, you could simply use *.java.
@files	The names of one or more files containing lists of packages and/or source files to be processed separated by spaces. Each file name must be prefixed with @. A file must contain one file or package name per line, and wildcards do not apply here. This option provides a convenient way of handling a large number of packages and/or source files.

With the Java 2 version of javadoc, there are 40 options you can use, many of which can be quite long, so you may find it more convenient to set up the command in a file to suit your operating system, such as a batch file under Windows or shell script under Unix. Putting the source file and package names in a file, rather than putting them on the command line explicitly, makes things much easier to handle too, even for relatively few files.

Let's take a look at some of the more commonly used options for javadoc.

Execution Options

Each option is of the form -optionName, where the option name is case sensitive. Some options are followed by a parameter such as a file name. There are a lot of them so we'll start with those you are most likely to need:

Option	Effect
-author	Causes output for @author tags to be produced
-version	Causes output for @version tags to be produced.
-public	Limits documentation output to public classes and members. The default is to limit output to protected and public classes and members. If you want to explicitly specify the default on the command line, you can use the -protected option.

Option	Effect
`-protected`	Limits documentation output to public classes and protected and public class members. This option applies by default.
`-private`	Results in all classes and members being documented.
`-package`	Limits documentation output to package, protected and public classes and members.
`-use`	Causes a use page to be generated as part of the documentation for each class and interface, listing where the particular class or interface is referenced.
`-overview path\fileName`	Specifies the path and name of the file containing the text that is to appear on the overview page. If the file is in the current directory, then you need not specify the path. Note that for Unix environments the separator is a forward slash.
`-d directoryName`	Causes the `.html` files that `javadoc` generates to be stored in the specified directory. By default they will be stored in the current directory.
`-sourcepath pathList`	Specifies the paths that `javadoc` is to search to find packages that are to be processed (but not `.java` files that you have identified explicitly in the command). The path list must be in the form that you use for `CLASSPATH` – with the paths separated by semi-colons. Each path should not include the package directory itself, but should end at the directory that contains the package directory. If this option is not specified the current class path, as defined by the `CLASSPATH` environment variable or the `-classpath` option, will be searched to find packages.
`-classpath pathList`	Specifies the paths that `javadoc` is to search for classes referenced in the documentation comments. This refers to the source files for your classes or other classes that are not part of the Java platform.
`-extdirs dirList`	Specifies a list of directories containing classes that use the Java extension mechanism. Directories in the list must be separated by semi-colons.
`-bootclasspath pathlist`	This specifies the paths where the Java platform classes are to be found. Most of the time you don't need to specify this option.
`-serialwarn`	Causes `javadoc` to produce warning messages when `@serial` tags are missing. By default no warnings of this kind are produced.
`-verbose`	Causes `javadoc` to produce more comprehensive messages while it is executing.

You could process all classes and members in the source files in the current directory with the command:

```
javadoc -author -version -private *.java
```

This will produce documentation for all classes and all their members and will output author and version information. The documentation will be generated in the current directory. If this is not convenient, you could add the -d option to specify an alternative directory for the output:

```
javadoc -author -version -private -d .\docs *.java
```

This command creates output in the docs subdirectory of the Java file in the current directory. This is an example of Windows command.

To process packages, package1 and package2, as well as the source files in the current directory, you could use the command:

```
javadoc -author -version -private -d .\docs package1 package2 *.java
```

This will only work if the paths for both packages are defined in the class path.

To use the @files option, you need to list the names of all the files and packages that are to be processed in a separate file. For instance, to create the Sketcher documentation, I created a text file with the name jdocfiles that contained the following text:

```
Sketcher.java
SketchModel.java
SketchFrame.java
SketchView.java
FontDialog.java
Constants.java
StatusBar.java
ExtensionFilter.java
Element.java
```

This is just a list of all the source files for Sketcher, one per line. I then referenced this file on the command line as @jdocfiles. In fact the command was also in a separate batch file, jdoc.bat, so I could edit the command line and the list of files to be processed independently of one another. To execute javadoc for Sketcher, I just needed to enter the batch file name to the Windows command line. The command that I used in jdoc.bat is:

```
javadoc -private -use -author -version -overview overview.html -J-Xmx80m
-doctitle "The Sketcher Application"  -d .\docs  @jdocfiles
```

Customizing the Documentation Pages

You have several options that can add information to the pages produced by `javadoc`:

`-windowtitle text`	Uses the specified `text` as the window title. You should not include any HTML tags in text. If this option is omitted, `javadoc` will use the title specified by the `-doctitle` option as the window title.
`-doctitle text`	Uses the specified `text` as the title for the overview page. If `text` contains HTML tags or whitespace, you must enclose it between quotes.
`-header text`	Specifies the header text to be added to each `.html` file that is generated. The header text will be displayed at the right of the upper navigation bar. If `text` includes HTML tags or whitespace characters, you must put it between quotes.
`-footer text`	Specifies the footer text to be added to each `.html` file that is generated. The footer text will be displayed at the right of the lower navigation bar. If `text` includes HTML tags or whitespace characters, you must put it between quotes.
`-bottom text`	Specifies text that is to be displayed below the lower navigation bar on each page that is generated. If text contains HTML tags or whitespace, it must be placed between quotes.

I used the `-doctitle` option to customize the pages produced for the Sketcher program.

Processing Large Programs

Several options only become important when you are generating documentation for a large number of packages and/or classes. A major consideration is memory available to `javadoc`. Since all classes have to be loaded into memory before processing starts, `javadoc` can require a lot of memory to allow it to work. You can set the memory that the Java virtual machine makes available to `javadoc` using the `-J` option. You can specify the initial memory that is allocated, and the maximum that may be used during execution:

-J-ms*n*m	Specifies the initial memory as n megabytes. For example, to specify 64 megabytes as the initial memory, you would specify the option as: `-J-ms64m` Note that there must be no space after the J.
-J-mx*n*m	Specifies the maximum memory that may be used as n megabytes. For example, to specify 128 megabytes as the maximum memory, you would specify the option as: `-J-mx128m`

A second consideration is the documentation that is generated for large programs. You can control some aspects of this using the following options:

`-splitindex`	Causes a separate index file to be produced per starting letter for the index entries, rather than indexing everything in a single index file.
`-group heading patterns`	Lists the packages specified by `patterns` in a single group identified by `heading` on the overview page. Thus you use one instance of the `-group` option for each grouping of packages. The `patterns` can be multiple patterns for package names separated by colons. Each pattern can include * at the end of the pattern as a wildcard. If any pattern includes * then patterns must be between quotes. For example: `-group Basic "Num*:Dig*"` This would group all packages with names beginning with `Num` or `Dig`, such as `Number`, `Digit`, and `Digital`, into a group on the overview page with the heading `Basic`.

Constraining Output

You have the following options for limiting the output that is generated by `javadoc`:

`-nodeprecatedlist`	Prevents the file containing the list of deprecated methods from being generated, as well as the **Deprecated** entry on the navigation bar. Deprecated methods are still identified in the rest of the documentation.
`-nodeprecated`	Prevents any information on deprecated methods from being generated, including the **Deprecated** entry on the navigation bar.
`-notree`	Prevents the tree specifying the class and interface hierarchy from being generated.
`-noindex`	Prevents the index from being generated.
`-nonavbar`	Omits the navigation bar, the header and the footer, from all pages.
`-nohelp`	Prevents the help page from being generated as well as the **Help** entry on the navigation bar.

Other Options

The remaining command line options for the `javadoc` utility are:

`-1.1`	Causes javadoc to behave like the Java 1.1 version of the utility. To get a list of the options that apply in this case you can enter the command: `javadoc -1.1 -help`
`-charset`	Used to specify the HTML character set used for the document.
`-doclet className`	This is used to execute your own doclet. It specifies the name of the class that starts your doclet.
`-docletpath pathList`	Specifies the path or paths to your doclet files.
`-docencoding name`	Specifies the encoding to be used for the `.html` files.
`-encoding`	Specifies the encoding that applies for the source files.
`-help`	Causes `javadoc` to list the command options.
`-helpfile path\file`	Specifies an alternative help file to be used in place of the file that is generated by default.
`-link  URL`	Specifies the URL for existing documentation that is to be linked to/from the generated documentation. You could use this to link to the JDK documentation, for instance, so that documentation for your code will include links to classes and interfaces in the standard documentation.
`-linkoffline URL packageURL`	URL specifies the location of the external documentation, and `packageURL` specifies the location for the package list for the external documentation. This is similar to `-link`, but is typically used when the package list for the external documentation does not exist yet.
`-locale language`	Specifies an alternative country/language to be used in generating the documentation.
`-stylesheetfile path\file`	Specifies a style sheet file that is to be used in place of the default `stylesheet.css` that is generated.

Keywords

The following keywords are reserved in Java, so you must not use them as names in your programs:

abstract	int
boolean	interface
break	long
byte	native
case	new
catch	package
char	private
class	protected
const	public
continue	return
default	short
do	static
double	super
else	switch

extends   synchronized

final   this

finally   throw

float   throws

for   transient

goto   try

if   void

implements   volatile

import   while

instanceof

You should also not attempt to use the boolean values true and false, or null as names in your programs.

ASCII Codes

The first 32 ASCII (American Standard Code for Information Interchange) characters provide control functions. Many of these have not been referenced in this book but are included here for completeness. In the following table, only the first 128 characters have been included. The remaining 128 characters include further special symbols and letters for national character sets.

Decimal	Hexadecimal	Character	Control
000	00	null	NUL
001	01	☺	SOH
002	02	●	STX
003	03	♥	ETX
004	04	♦	EOT
005	05	♣	ENQ
006	06	♠	ACK
007	07	•	BEL(Audible bell)
008	08		BS(Backspace)
009	09		TAB
010	0A		LF(Line feed)
011	0B		VT(Vertical tab)
012	0C		FF(Form feed)
013	0D		CR(Carriage return)
014	0E		SO
015	0F	¤	SI
016	10		DLE

Table Continued on Following Page

Decimal	Hexadecimal	Character	Control
017	11		DC1
018	12		DC2
019	13		DC3
020	14		DC4
021	15		NAK
022	16		SYN
023	17		ETB
024	18		CAN
025	19		EM
026	1A	→	SUB
027	1B	←	ESC(Escape)
028	1C	∟	FS
029	1D		GS
030	1E		RS
031	1F		US

Decimal	Hexadecimal	Character
032	20	
033	21	!
034	22	"
035	23	#
036	24	$
037	25	%
038	26	&
039	27	'
040	28	(
041	29	)
042	2A	*
043	2B	+

Decimal	Hexadecimal	Character
044	2C	,
045	2D	-
046	2E	.
047	2F	/
048	30	0
049	31	1
050	32	2
051	33	3
052	34	4
053	35	5
054	36	6
055	37	7
056	38	8
057	39	9
058	3A	:
059	3B	;
060	3C	<
061	3D	=
062	3E	>
063	3F	?
064	40	@
065	41	A
066	42	B
067	43	C
068	44	D
069	45	E
070	46	F

Table Continued on Following Page

Decimal	Hexadecimal	Character
071	47	G
072	48	H
073	49	I
074	4A	J
075	4B	K
076	4C	L
077	4D	M
078	4E	N
079	4F	O
080	50	P
081	51	Q
082	52	R
083	53	S
084	54	T
085	55	U
086	56	V
087	57	W
088	58	X
089	59	Y
090	5A	Z
091	5B	[
092	5C	\
093	5D	]
094	5E	^
095	5F	_
096	60	`
097	61	a
098	62	b
099	63	c

Decimal	Hexadecimal	Character
100	64	d
101	65	e
102	66	f
103	67	g
104	68	h
105	69	i
106	6A	j
107	6B	k
108	6C	l
109	6D	m
110	6E	n
111	6F	o
112	70	p
113	71	q
114	72	r
115	73	s
116	74	t
117	75	u
118	76	v
119	77	w
120	78	x
121	79	y
122	7A	z
123	7B	{
124	7C	|
125	7D	}
126	7E	~
127	7F	DEL(Delete)

Computer Arithmetic

In the chapters of this book, we have deliberately kept discussion of arithmetic to a minimum. However, it is important overall and fundamental to understanding how some operators work, so I have included a summary of the subject in this appendix. If you feel confident about your math knowledge, this will all be old hat to you and you need read no further. If you find the math parts tough, then this section should show you how easy it really is.

Binary Numbers

First let's consider what we mean when we write a common everyday number such as 321 or 747. Put more precisely we mean:

321 is:
3 x 10 x 10 + 2 x 10 + 1

and 747 is:
7 x 10 x 10 + 4 x 10 + 7

Because it is built around powers of ten, we call this the decimal system (derived from the Latin *decimalis* meaning *of tithes*, which was a tax of 10% – ah, those were the days...).

Representing numbers in this way is very handy for people with ten fingers and ten toes, or creatures with ten of any kind of appendage for that matter. However, your PC is quite unhandy in this context, being built mainly of switches that are either on or off. This is OK for counting up to two, but not spectacular at counting to ten. For this reason your computer represents numbers to base 2 rather than base 10. This is called the **binary** system of counting, analogous to the **bi**cycle (two wheels). With the decimal system, to base 10, the digits used can be from 0 to 9. In the binary system, to base 2, the digits can only be 0 or 1, ideal when you only have on/off switches to represent them. Each digit in the binary system is called a **bit**, being an abbreviation for **b**inary dig**it**. In an exact analogy to our usual base 10 counting, the binary number 1101 is therefore:

1 x 2 x 2 x 2 + 1 x 2 x 2 + 0 x 2 + 1

which amounts to 13 in the decimal system. In the following figure you can see the decimal equivalents of 8-bit binary numbers illustrated.

Binary	Decimal	Binary	Decimal
0000 0000	0	1000 0000	128
0000 0001	1	1000 0001	129
0000 0010	2	1000 0010	130
...	...	...	...
0001 0000	16	1001 0000	144
0001 0001	17	1001 0001	145
...	...	...	...
0111 1100	124	1111 1100	252
0111 1101	125	1111 1101	253
0111 1110	126	1111 1110	254
0111 1111	127	1111 1111	255

Note that using just 7 bits we can represent all the decimal numbers from 0 to 127 which is a total of 2^7, or128 numbers, and using all 8 bits we get 256, or 2^8 numbers. In general, if we have n bits we can represent 2^n integers from 0 to 2^n-1.

Hexadecimal Numbers

When we get to larger binary numbers, for example:

1111 0101 1011 1001 1110 0001

the notation starts to be a little cumbersome, particularly when you consider that if you apply the same method to work out what this in decimal, it's only 16,103,905, a miserable 8 decimal digits. You can sit more angels on a pinhead than that. Well, as it happens, we have an excellent alternative.

Arithmetic to base 16 is a very convenient option. Each digit can have values from 0 to 15 (the digits from 10 to 15 being represented by the letters A to F as shown in the next figure) and values from 0 to 15 correspond quite nicely with the range of values that four binary digits can represent.

Hexadecimal	Decimal	Binary
0	0	0000
1	1	0001
2	2	0010
...	...	...

Hexadecimal	Decimal	Binary
9	9	1001
A	10	1010
B	11	1011
C	12	1100
D	13	1101
E	14	1110
F	15	1111

Since a hexadecimal digit corresponds exactly to 4 binary bits, we can represent the binary number above as a hexadecimal number just by taking successive groups of four binary digits starting from the right, and writing the equivalent base 16 digit for each group. The binary number:

1111 0101 1011 1001 1110 0001

will therefore come out as:

F5B9E1

We have six hexadecimal digits corresponding to the six groups of four binary digits. Just to show it all works out with no cheating, we can convert this number directly from hexadecimal to decimal, by again using the analogy with the meaning of a decimal number, as follows:

F5B9E1 is:
15 x 16 x 16 x 16 x 16 x 16 + 5 x 16 x 16 x 16 x 16 + 11 x 16 x 16 x 16 + 9 x 16 x 16 + 14 x16 + 1

This in turn turns out to be:

15,728,640 + 327,680+ 45,056 + 2304 + 224 + 1

which fortunately totals to the same number we got when we converted the equivalent binary number to a decimal value.

Negative Binary Numbers

There is another aspect to binary arithmetic that you need to understand – negative numbers. So far we have assumed everything is positive – the optimist's view if you will – our glass is still half full. But we can't avoid the negative side of life forever – the pessimist's perspective that our glass is already half empty. How do we indicate a negative number? Well, we only have binary digits at our disposal and indeed they contain the solution.

For numbers that we want to have the possibility of negative values (referred to as **signed** numbers) we must first decide on a fixed length (in other words, the number of binary digits) and then designate the leftmost binary digit as a sign bit. We have to fix the length in order to avoid any confusion about which bit is the sign bit as opposed to bits that are digits. A single bit is quite capable of representing the sign of a number because a number can be either positive – corresponding to a sign bit being 0, or negative – indicated by the sign bit being 1.

Of course, we can have some numbers with 8 bits, and some with 16 bits, or whatever, as long as we know what the length is in each case. If the sign bit is 0 the number is positive, and if it is 1 it is negative. This would seem to solve our problem, but not quite. If we add -8 in binary to +12 we would really like to get the answer +4. If we do that simplistically, just putting the sign bit of the positive value to 1 to make it negative, and then doing the arithmetic with conventional carries, it doesn't quite work:

12 in binary is	0000 1100
-8 in binary we suppose is	1000 1000

since +8 is 0000 1000. If we now add these together we get:

1001 0100

This seems to be -20, which is not what we wanted at all. It's definitely not +4, which we know is 0000 0100. Ah, I hear you say, you can't treat a sign just like another digit. But that is just what we do have to do when dealing with computers because, dumb things that they are, they have trouble coping with anything else. So we really need a different representation for negative numbers. Well, we could try subtracting +12 from +4 since the result should be -8:

+4 is	0000 0100
Take away +12	0000 1100
and we get	1111 1000

For each digit from the fourth from the right onwards we had to borrow 1 to do the sum, analogously to our usual decimal method for subtraction. This supposedly is -8, and even though it doesn't look like it, it is. Just try adding it to +12 or +15 in binary and you will see that it works. So what is it? It turns out that the answer is what is called the **two's complement** representation of negative binary numbers.

Now here we are going to demand a little faith on your part and avoid getting into explanations of why it works. We will just show you how the 2's complement form of a negative number can be constructed from a positive value, and that it does work so you can prove it to yourself. Let's return to our previous example where we need the 2's complement representation of -8. We start with +8 in binary:

0000 1000

We now flip each digit – if it is one make it zero, and vice versa:

1111 0111

This is called the 1's complement form, and if we now add 1 to this we will get the 2's complement form:

	1111 0111
Add one to this	0000 0001
and we get:	1111 1000

Now this looks pretty similar to our representation of -8 we got from subtracting +12 from +4. So just to be sure, let's try the original sum of adding -8 to +12:

+12 is	**0000 1100**
Our version of -8 is	1111 1000
and we get:	0000 0100

So the answer is 4 – magic! It works! The carry propagates through all the leftmost 1's, setting them back to zero. One fell off the end, but we shouldn't worry about that. It's probably the one we borrowed from off the end in the subtraction sum we did to get -8. In fact what is happening is that we are making the assumption that the sign bit, 1 or 0, repeats forever to the left. Try a few examples of your own, you will find it always works quite automatically. The really great thing is, it makes arithmetic very easy (and fast) for your computer.

Floating Point Numbers

We often have to deal with very large numbers: the number of protons in the universe, for example, which needs around 79 decimal digits. Clearly there are lots of situations where we need more than the 10 decimal digits we get from a 4 byte binary number. Equally, there are lots of very small numbers. The amount of time in minutes it takes the typical car salesman to accept your offer on his 1982 Ford LTD (and only covered 380,000 miles...). A mechanism for handling both these kinds of numbers is – as you will have guessed from the title of this section – **floating point** numbers.

A floating point representation of a number is a decimal point followed by a fixed number of digits, multiplied by a power of 10 to get the number you want. It's easier to demonstrate than explain, so let's take some examples. The number 365 in normal decimal notation would be written in floating point form as:

0.365E03

where the E stands for "**e**xponent" and is the power of ten that the 0.365 (the mantissa) is multiplied by, to get the required value. That is:

0.365 x 10 x 10 x 10

which is clearly 365.

Now let's look at a smallish number:

.365E-04

This is evaluated as .365 x 10^{-4} which is .0000365 – exactly the time in minutes required by the car salesman to accept your cash.

The number of digits in the mantissa of a floating point number depends on the type of the floating point number that you are using. The Java type `float` provides the equivalent of approximately 7 decimal digits, and the type `double` provides around 17 decimal digits. The number of digits is approximate because the mantissa is binary, not decimal, and there's not an exact mapping between binary and decimal digits.

Suppose we have a large number such as 2,134,311,179. How does this look as a floating point number? Well, it looks like:

0.2134311E10

It's not quite the same. We have lost three low order digits so we have approximated our original value as 2,134,311,000. This is a small price to pay for being able to handle such a vast range of numbers, typically from 10^{-38} to 10^{+38} either positive or negative, as well having an extended representation that goes from a minute 10^{-308} to a mighty 10^{+308}. As you can see, they are called floating point numbers for the fairly obvious reason that the decimal point "floats" depending on the exponent value.

Aside from the fixed precision limitation in terms of accuracy, there is another aspect you may need to be conscious of. You need to take great care when adding or subtracting numbers of significantly different magnitudes. A simple example will demonstrate the kind of problem that can arise. We can first consider adding .365E-3 to .365E+7. We can write this as a decimal sum:

.000365 + 3,650,000

This produces the result:

3,650,000.000365

Which when converted back to floating point becomes:

.3650000E+7

So we might as well not have bothered. The problem lies directly with the fact that we only carry 7 digits precision. The 7 digits of the larger number are not affected by any of the digits of the smaller number because they are all further to the left. Funnily enough, you must also take care when the numbers are very nearly equal. If you compute the difference between such numbers you may end up with a result that only has one or two digits precision. It is quite easy in such circumstances to end up computing with numbers that are total garbage.

P2P.WROX.COM

Join the Beginning Java 2 mailing list for author and peer support. Our unique system provides **programmer to programmer™** support on mailing lists, forums and newsgroups all in addition to our one-to-one email system. Be confident that your query is not just being examined by a support professional, but by the many Wrox authors and other industry experts present on our mailing lists.

We've extended our commitment to support beyond just while you read the book, to when you start developing applications as well. We'll be there on this crucial second step of your learning. You have the choice of how to receive this information, you can either enroll onto our mailing list, or you can just browse the online forums and newsgroups for an answer. Go to p2p.wrox.com. You'll find several different lists dedicated to our books, each tailored to a specific support issue:

How to Enroll for Support

Just follow this four-step system:

- ❑ Go to p2p.wrox.com
- ❑ Click on the Beginning Java 2 cover graphic
- ❑ Click on the beginning_java mailing list.
- ❑ Fill in your email address and password (of at least 4 digits) and email it to us

Why this System Offers the Best Support

You can choose to join the mailing list or you can receive it as a weekly digest. If you don't have the time or facility to receive the mailing list, then you can search our online archives. You'll find the ability to search on specific subject areas or keywords. As these lists are moderated, you can be confident of finding good, accurate information quickly. Mails can be edited or moved by the moderator into the correct place, making this a most efficient resource. Junk and spam mail are deleted, and your own email address is protected by the unique Lyris system from web-bots that can automatically hoover up newsgroup mailing list addresses. Any queries about joining, leaving lists or any query about the list should be sent to: moderatorbegjava@wrox.com.

Index A - Methods

A

abs(), 54, 455
AbstractAction(), 627
accept(), 323, 325, 809, 810, 932
acos(), 53
actionPerformed(), 554, 590, 605, 611, 612, 614, 616, 621, 622, 627, 629, 717, 718, 722, 724, 739, 746, 750, 751, 761, 762, 763, 776, 781, 786, 801, 807, 809, 811, 814, 820, 822, 824, 825, 832, 841, 846, 931, 935, 974, 1108
add(), 406, 411, 412, 419, 429, 431, 433, 462, 508, 529, 544, 551, 554, 574, 577, 623, 629, 630, 631, 632, 633, 635, 636, 638, 671, 690, 699, 751, 760, 764, 826
addActionListener(), 276, 554, 590, 722, 724
addAll(), 413, 431
addBatch(), 1025
addChoosableFileFilter(), 810
addFirst(), 431
addImage(), 870
addItem(), 262, 263
addLast(), 431
addLineListener(), 976
addListSelectionListener(), 742
addMotionListener(), 694
addMouseListener(), 694
addObserver(), 449
addPoint(), 258, 433
addPropertyChange
Listener(), 625
addSeparator(), 575, 578
addTableModelListener(), 1041
addTreeExpansionListener(), 1116
addTreeSelectionListener(), 1116

addTreeWillExpand
Listener(), 1116
addWindowListener(), 601, 603
adjustmentValueChanged(), 605
after(), 456, 462, 464, 1082
afterLast(), 1026
append(), 150, 151, 152, 843, 844
asin(), 53, 782
atan(), 53
atan2(), 53
AudioInputStream(), 947
available(), 360, 947, 960, 969, 1077, 1079

B

before(), 456, 462, 464, 1082
beforeFirst(), 1026
brighter(), 531

C

cancel(), 882, 884
canRead(), 319, 320
canWrite(), 319, 320
capacity(), 149, 411
CardLayout(), 553
ceil(), 54, 117
charAt(), 136, 137, 153
charWidth(), 538
checkAll(), 871
checkError(), 351
children(), 1104
clear(), 417
clearBatch(), 1025
clearChanged(), 450
clone(), 240, 243, 246, 247, 248, 269
close(), 328, 338, 344, 345, 352, 356, 360, 363, 368, 372, 384, 393, 947, 969, 981, 1036, 1110
closeEntry(), 341, 344, 368

closePath(), 679, 682
commentChar(), 377
compareTo(), 134, 136, 423, 424, 428
connect(), 332
contains(), 529, 662, 675, 677, 759, 990
containsKey(), 437
copyValueOf(), 146
cos(), 53
countComponents(), 543
countObservers(), 449
createBevelBorder(), 559
createBlackLineBorder(), 563
createCompoundBorder(), 638
createGlue(), 561
createGraphics(), 905
createHorizontalBox(), 556
createHorizontalStrut(), 560
createNewFile(), 326, 337, 339, 974
createStatement(), 1025, 1029, 1067
createTempFile(), 326
createTitledBorder(), 609
createTransformedShape(), 769, 772
createVerticalBox(), 556
createVerticalStrut(), 560
currentSegment(), 799, 800
currentTimeMillis(), 872, 873, 884
curveTo(), 679

D

darker(), 531
DataLine.Info(), 939
Date(), 456
decode(), 283
defaultPage(), 832, 833, 835
defaultReadObject(), 394
defaultWriteObject(), 394
delete(), 327
deleteObserver(), 449

H

I

IEEEremainder(), 54
ImageIcon(), 854
imageUpdate(), 863, 864, 867
indexOf(), 138, 139, 140, 141, 143, 144, 417
init(), 550, 554, 582, 583, 601, 609, 615, 616, 617, 675, 794, 852, 853, 866, 869, 870, 871, 877, 881, 894, 903, 912, 929
insert(), 152, 153, 1104
interrupt(), 475, 476
interrupted(), 476
intersection(), 529
intersects(), 188, 190, 206, 529
isAbsolute(), 318
isAcceptAllFileFilterUsed(), 811
isActive(), 961
isAddedPath(), 1117
isAlive(), 476
isBold(), 535
isCellEditable(), 1041
isCurrency(), 1031
isDigit(), 83, 373
isDirectory(), 318, 320, 323
isDone(), 798
isEmpty(), 417, 529, 662
isEnabled(), 524, 625
isErrorAny(), 871
isErrorID(), 871
isFile(), 318, 323
isFirst(), 1026
isFloatable(), 634
isHidden(), 318
isInfinite(), 199
isInterface(), 242
isInterrupted(), 476
isItalic(), 535
isLast(), 1026
isLeaf(), 1104
isLetter(), 83, 138
isLetterOrDigit(), 83
isLineSupported(), 942
isLowerCase(), 83
isModal(), 719
isNaN(), 199
isNullable(), 1031
isPlain(), 535
isPopupTrigger(), 752, 755, 759
isRunning(), 961
isSigned(), 1031
isUpperCase(), 83
isValid(), 524

isVisible(), 524
isWhitespace(), 83, 138
isWritable(), 1031
itemStateChanged(), 605, 749
iterator(), 405, 414, 431, 433, 438, 439

J

join(), 476

K

keyPressed(), 599
keyReleased(), 599
keySet(), 438, 446
keyTyped(), 599

L

last(), 554, 1026
lastElement(), 414
lastIndexOf(), 138, 139, 140, 142
lastModified(), 321, 323
length(), 136, 137, 148, 321, 349, 381
lineTo(), 679, 708, 799
list(), 321, 323, 325, 932, 1017
listFiles(), 321, 323
listIterator(), 414, 431
listRoots(), 321
log(), 55
loop(), 929, 951, 956
lowerCaseMode(), 377

M

mark(), 360, 371, 947
markSupported(), 360, 371, 947
matches(), 939
max(), 54, 873
min(), 54
mkdir(), 326, 337
mkdirs(), 326
mouseClicked(), 599, 733, 735
mouseDragged(), 599, 675, 677, 694, 695, 696, 734, 778, 781, 782
mouseEntered(), 599, 617
mouseExited(), 599, 617

mouseMoved(), 599, 757, 758, 759
mousePressed(), 599, 675, 677, 694, 695, 696, 697, 733, 752, 754, 770, 778, 781
mouseReleased(), 599, 677, 694, 699, 733, 735, 752, 753, 761, 762, 779, 783
move(), 184, 190, 527, 776, 779
moveTo(), 678, 682, 708, 799
multiply(), 1084

N

newAudioClip(), 931, 932
newInstance(), 242
next(), 404, 405, 554, 798, 1026, 1029, 1034
nextBoolean, 454
nextBytes(), 454
nextDouble(), 454
nextFloat(), 454
nextGaussian(), 454
nextIndex(), 405
nextInt(), 212, 213, 453, 455, 491
nextLong(), 454
nextToken(), 376, 379, 422
noteOff(), 988, 994
noteOn(), 988, 994
notify(), 240, 501, 502
notifyAll(), 240, 502, 503, 506
notifyObservers(), 449, 452, 690, 699

O

open(), 949, 958, 959, 968, 975, 981, 986
openStream(), 858, 860
ordinaryChar(), 377
ordinaryChars(), 377

P

pack(), 722, 748, 1107
pageDialog(), 833
paint(), 530, 634, 654, 655, 663, 664, 667, 668, 671, 673, 674, 676, 677, 683, 691, 699, 728, 729, 814, 862, 867, 868, 875, 877, 879, 880, 890, 892, 894, 904, 912, 914, 915, 994
parse(), 460

Index B - General

Symbols

.class appending
  Class object, referencing, 243
2's complement
  negative binary numbers,
  1171

A

AboutDialog class, 720
  JDialog class, 720
  SketchFrame class, 720
abs() method
  Math class, 54, 455
abstract classes, 238
abstract keyword, 238
abstract methods, 238
AbstractAction class, 625
  AbstractAction() method,
  627
  actionPerformed() method,
  627, 629, 717, 718, 801, 807,
  809, 811, 814, 820, 822, 824,
  825, 832, 841, 846
  ColorAction class, 628
  FileAction class, 627
  getValue() method, 801
  TypeAction class, 628
AbstractButton class
  setMnemonic() method, 579
**AbstractTableModel class,
1041**
  fireTableChanged() method,
  1044
  ResultsModel class, 1042
accelerators
  menus, 579
accept() method
  FileFilter class, 809, 810
  FileFilter interface, 323
  FilenameFilter interface, 323,
  325, 932
access attributes
  base class, 230
  choosing, 203

class members, accessing,
199
  Point class, 201
  private, 200, 224
  protected, 200, 224
  public, 200, 224
  specifying, 201
  using, 200
  using with packages, 203
accessing methods, 163
accessing variables, 163
accessor methods, 202
Account class
  defining, 486
acos() method
  Math class, 53
action classes, 626
Action interface, 623
  ActionListener interface, 623
  addPropertyChange
  Listener() method, 625
  getValue() method, 625, 631
  isEnabled() method, 625
  properties, 624
  putValue() method, 624
  removePropertyChangeListe
  ner() method, 625
  setEnabled() method, 625,
  642
  SketchFrame class, 625
ActionEvent class
  AWTEvent class, 604
  getSource() method, 740
ActionListener interface
  Action interface, 623
  actionPerformed() method,
  554, 590, 605, 611, 612, 614,
  616, 621, 622, 722, 724, 739,
  746, 750, 751, 761, 762, 763,
  776, 781, 786, 931, 935, 974,
  1051, 1108
  ColorListener class, 621
  FontDialog class, 739
  implementing in anonymous
  class, 275
  InteractiveSQL class, 1050
  SketchFrame class, 722

SketchView class, 760
  TypeListener class, 620
actionPerformed() method
  AbstractAction class, 627,
  629, 717, 718, 801, 807, 809,
  811, 814, 820, 822, 824, 825,
  832, 841, 846
  ActionListener interface, 554,
  590, 605, 611, 612, 614, 616,
  621, 622, 722, 724, 739, 746,
  750, 751, 761, 762, 763, 776,
  781, 786, 931, 935, 974, 1051,
  1108
  InteractiveSQL class, 1051,
  1053
Actions
  disabling, 642
  menu items, 625
  using, 623, 629
adapter classes, 602
  care in using, 700
ADC
  Sound, basic concepts, 923
add() method
  addToolBarButton() method,
  638
  Component class, 671
  Container class, 544, 551, 554
  GregorianCalendar class, 462
  JMenu class, 574, 577, 630,
  638
  JMenuBar class, 574
  JPopupMenu class, 751, 760
  JToolBar class, 632, 633, 635,
  636, 638
  LinkedList class, 431, 433,
  508, 690, 699, 764
  ListIterator interface, 406
  Rectangle class, 529, 826
  Vector class, 411, 412, 419
addActionListener() method
  JButton class, 276, 554, 590,
  722
  JMenuItem class, 724
addAll() method
  LinkedList class, 431
  Vector class, 413